Lecture Notes in Computer Science   3440

Commenced Publication in 1973
Founding and Former Series Editors:
Gerhard Goos, Juris Hartmanis, and Jan van Leeuwen

T0134755

Nicolas Halbwachs   Lenore D. Zuck (Eds.)

Tools and Algorithms for the Construction and Analysis of Systems

11th International Conference, TACAS 2005
Held as Part of the Joint European Conferences
on Theory and Practice of Software, ETAPS 2005
Edinburgh, UK, April 4-8, 2005
Proceedings

 Springer

Volume Editors

Nicolas Halbwachs
Verimag/CNRS
2, avenue de Vignate, 38610 Gieres, France
E-mail: Nicolas.Halbwachs@imag.fr

Lenore D. Zuck
University of Illinois at Chicago
Department of Computer Science
851 S. Morgan Street, Chicago, Illinois 60607, USA
E-mail: lenore@cs.uic.edu

Library of Congress Control Number: 2005922497

CR Subject Classification (1998): F.3, D.2.4, D.2.2, C.2.4, F.2.2

ISSN 0302-9743
ISBN-10   3-540-25333-5 Springer Berlin Heidelberg New York
ISBN-13   978-3-540-25333-4 Springer Berlin Heidelberg New York

Springer is a part of Springer Science+Business Media

springeronline.com

© Springer-Verlag Berlin Heidelberg 2005
Printed in Germany

Typesetting: Camera-ready by author, data conversion by Scientific Publishing Services, Chennai, India
Printed on acid-free paper   SPIN: 11408130   06/3142   5 4 3 2 1 0

Foreword

ETAPS 2005 was the eighth instance of the European Joint Conferences on Theory and Practice of Software. ETAPS is an annual federated conference that was established in 1998 by combining a number of existing and new conferences. This year it comprised five conferences (CC, ESOP, FASE, FOSSACS, TACAS), 17 satellite workshops (AVIS, BYTECODE, CEES, CLASE, CMSB, COCV, FAC, FESCA, FINCO, GCW-DSE, GLPL, LDTA, QAPL, SC, SLAP, TGC, UITP), seven invited lectures (not including those that were specific to the satellite events), and several tutorials. We received over 550 submissions to the five conferences this year, giving acceptance rates below 30% for each one. Congratulations to all the authors who made it to the final program! I hope that most of the other authors still found a way of participating in this exciting event and I hope you will continue submitting.

The events that comprise ETAPS address various aspects of the system development process, including specification, design, implementation, analysis and improvement. The languages, methodologies and tools which support these activities are all well within its scope. Different blends of theory and practice are represented, with an inclination towards theory with a practical motivation on the one hand and soundly based practice on the other. Many of the issues involved in software design apply to systems in general, including hardware systems, and the emphasis on software is not intended to be exclusive.

ETAPS is a loose confederation in which each event retains its own identity, with a separate program committee and proceedings. Its format is open-ended, allowing it to grow and evolve as time goes by. Contributed talks and system demonstrations are in synchronized parallel sessions, with invited lectures in plenary sessions. Two of the invited lectures are reserved for "unifying" talks on topics of interest to the whole range of ETAPS attendees. The aim of cramming all this activity into a single one-week meeting is to create a strong magnet for academic and industrial researchers working on topics within its scope, giving them the opportunity to learn about research in related areas, and thereby to foster new and existing links between work in areas that were formerly addressed in separate meetings.

ETAPS 2005 was organized by the School of Informatics of the University of Edinburgh, in cooperation with
- European Association for Theoretical Computer Science (EATCS);
- European Association for Programming Languages and Systems (EAPLS);
- European Association of Software Science and Technology (EASST).

The organizing team comprised:
- Chair: Don Sannella
- Publicity: David Aspinall
- Satellite Events: Massimo Felici

- Secretariat: Dyane Goodchild
- Local Arrangements: Monika-Jeannette Lekuse
- Tutorials: Alberto Momigliano
- Finances: Ian Stark
- Website: Jennifer Tenzer, Daniel Winterstein
- Fundraising: Phil Wadler

ETAPS 2005 received support from the University of Edinburgh.

Overall planning for ETAPS conferences is the responsibility of its Steering Committee, whose current membership is:

Perdita Stevens (Edinburgh, Chair), Luca Aceto (Aalborg and Reykjavík), Rastislav Bodik (Berkeley), Maura Cerioli (Genoa), Evelyn Duesterwald (IBM, USA), Hartmut Ehrig (Berlin), José Fiadeiro (Leicester), Marie-Claude Gaudel (Paris), Roberto Gorrieri (Bologna), Reiko Heckel (Paderborn), Holger Hermanns (Saarbrücken), Joost-Pieter Katoen (Aachen), Paul Klint (Amsterdam), Jens Knoop (Vienna), Kim Larsen (Aalborg), Tiziana Margaria (Dortmund), Ugo Montanari (Pisa), Hanne Riis Nielson (Copenhagen), Fernando Orejas (Barcelona), Mooly Sagiv (Tel Aviv), Don Sannella (Edinburgh), Vladimiro Sassone (Sussex), Peter Sestoft (Copenhagen), Michel Wermelinger (Lisbon), Igor Walukiewicz (Bordeaux), Andreas Zeller (Saarbrücken), Lenore Zuck (Chicago).

I would like to express my sincere gratitude to all of these people and organizations, the program committee chairs and PC members of the ETAPS conferences, the organizers of the satellite events, the speakers themselves, the many reviewers, and Springer for agreeing to publish the ETAPS proceedings. Finally, I would like to thank the organizer of ETAPS 2005, Don Sannella. He has been instrumental in the development of ETAPS since its beginning; it is quite beyond the limits of what might be expected that, in addition to all the work he has done as the original ETAPS Steering Committee Chairman and current ETAPS Treasurer, he has been prepared to take on the task of organizing this instance of ETAPS. It gives me particular pleasure to thank him for organizing ETAPS in this wonderful city of Edinburgh in this my first year as ETAPS Steering Committee Chair.

Edinburgh, January 2005   Perdita Stevens
                                          ETAPS Steering Committee Chair

Preface

This volume contains the proceedings of the 11th TACAS, International Conference on *Tools and Algorithms for the Construction and Analysis of Systems*. TACAS 2005 took place in Edinburgh, UK, April 4–8, 2005. TACAS is a forum for researchers, developers, and users interested in rigorously based tools for the construction and analysis of systems. The conference serves to bridge the gaps among communities that are devoted to formal methods, software and hardware verification, static analysis, programming languages, software engineering, real-time systems, and communication protocols. By providing a venue for the discussion of common problems, heuristics, algorithms, data structures, and methodologies, TACAS aims to support researchers in their quest to improve the utility, reliability, flexibility, and efficiency of tools for building systems.

Topics covered by TACAS include specification and verification techniques for finite and infinite state systems, software and hardware verification, theorem-proving and model-checking, system construction and transformation techniques, static and run-time analysis, abstract interpretation, compositional and refinement-based methodologies, testing and test-case generation, analytical techniques for security protocols, real-time, hybrid, and safety-critical systems, integration of formal methods and static analysis in high-level hardware design, tool environments and tool architectures, and applications and case studies.

Two types of papers are traditionally considered: full-length research papers, including those describing tools, and short tool-demonstration papers that give an overview of a particular tool and its applications. TACAS 2005 received 141 research and 20 tool demonstration submissions, and accepted 33 research papers and 8 tool demonstration papers. We'd like to thank the authors of all submitted papers.

To carry out the difficult task of selecting a program from the large number of submissions in a fair and competent manner, we were fortunate to have highly qualified Program Committee members from diverse geographic and research areas. Each submission was evaluated by at least three reviewers. After a four-week reviewing process, the program selection was carried out in a two-week electronic Program Committee meeting. We believe that the result of the committee deliberations is a very strong scientific program. As this year's invited speaker, the Program Committee selected Ken McMillan, who presented work on applications of Craig interpolation.

Special thanks are due to the Program Committee members and all the referees for their assistance in selecting the papers, and to Andreas Kuehlmann for his diligent work as a tool chair. The help of the TACAS Steering Committee, especially of Bernhard Steffen, was invaluable. Martin Karusseit gave us prompt support in dealing with the online conference management service.

TACAS 2005 was part of the 8th European Joint Conference on Theory and Practice of Software (ETAPS), whose aims, organization, and history are detailed in the separate foreword by the ETAPS Steering Committee Chair, Perdita Stevens. In the years since it joined the ETAPS conference federation, TACAS has been the largest of the ETAPS member conferences in terms of number of submissions and papers accepted.

We would like to express our appreciation to the ETAPS Steering Committee and especially to Don Sannella and the wonderful Organizing Committee, for their efforts in making ETAPS 2005 such a successful event.

We hope to see you all in Vienna in 2006!

April 2005   Nicolas Halbwachs and Lenore Zuck

Organization

Steering Committee

Ed Brinksma	University of Twente (The Netherlands)
Rance Cleaveland	SUNY at Stony Brook (USA)
Kim Larsen	Aalborg University (Denmark)
Bernhard Steffen	University of Dortmund (Germany)

Program Committee

Rajeev Alur	University of Pennsylvania, Philadelphia (USA)
Patricia Bouyer	LSV/CNRS, Cachan (France)
Ed Brinksma	University of Twente (The Netherlands)
Randy Bryant	Carnegie Mellon University, Pittsburgh (USA)
Muffy Calder	University of Glasgow (UK)
Rance Cleaveland	University of New York at Stony Brook (USA)
Radhia Cousot	CNRS/Ecole Polytechnique, Palaiseau (France)
Cindy Eisner	IBM, Haifa (Israel)
Javier Esparza	University of Stuttgart (Germany)
Alessandro Fantechi	University of Firenze (Italy)
Patrice Godefroid	Bell Laboratories, Lisle (USA)
Andrew Gordon	Microsoft Research, Cambridge (UK)
Nicolas Halbwachs	Vérimag/CNRS, Grenoble (France)
John Hatcliff	Kansas State University (USA)
Holger Hermanns	Saarland University, Saarbruecken (Germany)
Michael Huth	Imperial College, London (UK)
Kurt Jensen	University of Aarhus, Aarhus (Denmark)
Thierry Jeron	IRISA/INRIA, Rennes (France)
Jens Knoop	Technische Universität Wien, Vienna (Austria)
Andreas Kuehlmann	Cadence Berkeley Labs, Berkeley (USA)
Marta Kwiatkowska	University of Birmingham, Birmingham (UK)
Kim Larsen	Aalborg University, Aalborg (Denmark)
Radu Mateescu	INRIA, Montbonnot (France)
Jens Palsberg	UCLA, Los Angeles (USA)
Andreas Podelski	Max-Planck-Institut für Informatik, Saarbrücken (Germany)
Sriram Rajamani	Microsoft Research, Redmond (USA)
Eli Singerman	Intel, Haifa (Israel)
Bernhard Steffen	Universität Dortmund, Dortmund (Germany)
Lenore Zuck	University of Illinois, Chicago (USA)

Referees

Erika Abraham-Mumm
Tamarah Arons
Gadiel Auerbach
Christel Baier
Ittai Balaban
Michele Banci
Clark Barrett
Gerd Behrmann
Axel Belinfante
Shoham Ben-David
Armin Biere
Henrik Bohnenkamp
Lucas Bordeaux
Laura Brandan Briones
Benoit Caillaud
Sagar Chaki
Trishul Chilimbi
Søren Christensen
Byron Cook
Pedro R. D'Argenio
Dennis Dams
Alexandre David
William Deng
Klaus Dräger
Marie Duflot
Stefan Edelkamp
Erik Ernst
Anton Ertl
Yi Fang
Sebastian Fischmeister
Dana Fisman
Cormac Flanagan
Emmanuel Fleury
Jeff Foster
Pierre Ganty
Michael Gelfond
Dan Ghica
Leonid Gluhovsky
Stefania Gnesi
Mike Gordon
Arnaud Gotlieb
Hervé Grall
Claudia Gsottberger
Peter Habermehl

Tobias Heindel
Keijo Heljanko
Jens Peter Holmegaard
Hardi Hungar
Shahid Jabbar
Lalita J. Jagadeesan
David N. Jansen
Claude Jard
Bertrand Jeannet
Ranjit Jhala
Sven Johr
Jens Bæk Jørgensen
Georg Jung
Joost-Pieter Katoen
Sagi Katz
Sharon Keidar-Barner
Barbara Koenig
Vitali Kozioura
Tomas Krilavicius
Lars M. Kristensen
Antonin Kucera
Eva Kühn
Marcos E. Kurban
Sabine Kuske
Shuvendu Lahiri
Frederic Lang
Rom Langerak
Diego Latella
Axel Legay
Jerome Leroux
Didier Lime
Yoad Lustig
Michael Luttenberger
P. Madhusudan
Thomas Mailund
Herve Marchand
Fabio Martinelli
Mieke Massink
Richard Mayr
Franco Mazzanti
Eduard Mehofer
Robert Meolic
Stephan Merz
Marius Mikucionis

David Monniaux
Laurent Mounier
Markus Mueller-Olm
Madan Musuvathi
Ralf Nagel
Mayur Naik
Elie Najm
Kedar Namjoshi
Ulrich Neumerkel
Ziv Nevo
Mogens Nielsen
Robert Nieuwenhuis
Gethin Norman
Dirk Nowotka
Robert O'Callahan
Robert Palmer
David Parker
Larry Paulson
Sophie Pinchinat
Cory Plock
Pascal Poizat
Virgile Prevosto
Reza Pulungan
Franz Puntigam
Shaz Qadeer
Ishai Rabinovitz
Harald Raffelt
Stefan Ratschan
Pascal Raymond
Jakob Rehof
Iris Reuveni
Robby
Edwin Rodriguez
Sabina Rossi
Bill Roscoe
Oliver Ruething
Vlad Rusu
Theo C. Ruys
Mooly Sagiv
Gwen Salaun
Sven Schewe
Norbert Schirmer
Markus Schordan
Stephan Schulz

Stefan Schwoon
Wendelin Serwe
Jonathan Shalev
Joseph Sifakis
Nishant Sinha
A. Prasad Sistla
Oleg Sokolsky
Emilio Spinicci
Jeremy Sproston
Jiri Srba
Mark Staples
Graham Steel
Alin Stefanescu
Marielle Stoelinga

Ofer Strichman
Andreas Tiemeyer
Cesare Tinelli
P.S. Thiagarajan
Oksana Tkachuk
Stavros Tripakis
Rachel Tzoref
Shmuel Ur
Machiel van der Bijl
Wim Vanderbauwhede
Moshe Vardi
Enrico Vicario
Farn Wang
Todd Wallentine

Andrzej Wasowski
Lisa Wells
Michael Westergaard
Wang Xu
Zijiang Yang
Wang Yi
HaiSeung Yoo
Greta Yorsh
Sergio Yovine
Håkan Younes
Lijun Zhang
Wolf Zimmermann

Table of Contents

Invited Paper

Regular Model-Checking

Infinite State Systems

Abstract Interpretation

Automata and Logics

Probabilistic Systems, Probabilistic Model-Checking

Satisfiability

Testing

Abstraction and Reduction

Specification, Program Synthesis

Model-Checking

Tool Presentations

Applications of Craig Interpolants in
Model Checking

K.L. McMillan

Cadence Berkeley Labs

Abstract. A Craig interpolant for a mutually inconsistent pair of formulas (A, B) is a formula that is (1) implied by A, (2) inconsistent with B, and (3) expressed over the common variables of A and B. An interpolant can be efficiently derived from a refutation of $A \wedge B$, for certain theories and proof systems. We will discuss a number of applications of this concept in finite- and infinite-state model checking.

1 Introduction

A Craig interpolant for a mutually inconsistent pair of formulas (A, B) is a formula that is (1) implied by A, (2) inconsistent with B, and (3) expressed over the common variables of A and B. An interpolant can be efficiently derived from a refutation of $A \wedge B$, for certain theories and proof systems. For example, interpolants can be derived from resolution proofs in propositional logic, and for systems of linear inequalities over the reals [8, 14]. These methods have been recently been extended [10] to combine linear inequalities with uninterpreted function symbols, and to deal with integer models. One key aspect of these procedures is that they yield quantifier-free interpolants when the premises A and B are quantifier-free.

This paper will survey some recent applications of Craig interpolants in model checking. We will see that, in various contexts, interpolation can be used as a substitute for image computation, which involves quantifier elimination and is thus computationally expensive. The idea is to replace the image with a weaker approximation that is still strong enough to prove some property.

For example, interpolation can be used as an alternative to image computation in model checking, to construct an inductive invariant. This invariant contains only information actually deduced by a prover in refuting counterexamples to the property of a fixed number of steps. Thus, in a certain sense, this method abstracts the invariant relative to a given property. This avoids the complexity of computing the strongest inductive invariant (i.e., the reachable states) as is typically done in model checking, and works well in the the case where a relatively localized invariant suffices to prove a property of a large system.

This approach gives us a complete procedure for model checking temporal properties of finite-state systems that allows us to exploit recent advances in SAT solvers for the proof generation phase. Experimentally, the method is found to be quite robust for industrial hardware verification problems, relative to other

N. Halbwachs and L. Zuck (Eds.): TACAS 2005, LNCS 3440, pp. 1–12, 2005.

model checking approaches. The same approach can be applied to infinite-state systems, such as programs and parameterized protocols (although there is no completeness guarantee in this case). For example, it is possible to verify systems of timed automata in this way, or simple infinite-state protocols, such as the N-process "bakery" mutual exclusion protocol.

In addition, interpolants derived from proofs can be mined to obtain predicates that are useful for predicate abstraction, as is done in the Blast software model checker [7]. This approach has been used to verify properties of C programs with in excess of 100K lines of code. Finally, interpolation can be used to approximate the transition relation of a system relative to a given property. This approach can be applied to finite-state model checking and can also be useful in predicate abstraction, where constructing the exact abstract transition relation can be prohibitively costly.

1.1   Outline of the Paper

The next section of the paper introduces the technique of deriving Craig interpolants from proofs. Section 3 then describes the method of interpolation-based model checking, section 4 covers the extraction of predicates for predicate abstraction from interpolants, and section 5 deals with transition relation abstraction.

2   Interpolants from Proofs

Given a pair of formulas (A, B), such that $A \wedge B$ is inconsistent, an *interpolant* for (A, B) is a formula $\hat{A}$ with the following properties:

- A implies $\hat{A}$,
- $\hat{A} \wedge B$ is unsatisfiable, and
- $\hat{A}$ refers only to the common symbols of A and B.

Here, "symbols" excludes symbols such as $\wedge$ and $=$ that are part of the logic itself. Craig showed that for first-order formulas, an interpolant always exists for inconsistent formulas [5]. Of more practical interest is that, for certain proof systems, an interpolant can be derived from a refutation of $A \wedge B$ in linear time. For example, a purely propositional refutation of $A \wedge B$ using the resolution rule can be translated to an interpolant in the form of a Boolean circuit having the same structure as the proof [8, 14].

In [10] it is shown that linear-size interpolants can be derived from refutations in a first-order theory with with uninterpreted function symbols and linear arithmetic. This translation has the property that whenever A and B are quantifier-free, the derived interpolant $\hat{A}$ is also quantifier-free.[1] This property will be exploited in the applications of Craig interpolation that we describe below.

---

[1] Note that the Craig theorem does not guarantee the existence of quantifier-free interpolants. In general this depends on the choice of interpreted symbols in the logic.

Heuristically, the chief advantage of interpolants derived from refutations is that they capture the facts that the prover derived about A in showing that A is inconsistent with B. Thus, if the prover tends to ignore irrelevant facts and focus on relevant ones, we can think of interpolation as a way of filtering out irrelevant information from A.

3   Model Checking Based on Craig Interpolation

We now consider an application of Craig interpolation as a replacement for the costly image operator in symbolic model checking. In effect, interpolation allows us to filter information out of the image that is not relevant to proving the desired property.

3.1   Representing Systems Symbolically

In symbolic model checking, we represent the transition relation of a system with a formula. Here, we assume we are given a first-order signature S, consisting of individual variables and uninterpreted n-ary functional and propositional constants. A *state formula* is a first-order formula over S, (which may include various interpreted symbols, such as $=$ and $+$). We can think of a state formula ϕ as representing a set of states, namely, the set of first-order models of ϕ. We will express the proposition that an interpretation σ over S models ϕ by $\phi[\sigma]$. We also assume a first-order signature S', disjoint from S, and containing for every symbol $s \in S$, a unique symbol s' of the same type. For any formula or term ϕ over S, we will use ϕ' to represent the result of replacing every occurrence of a symbol s in ϕ with s'. Similarly, for any interpretation σ over S, we will denote by σ' the interpretation over S' such that $\sigma's' = \sigma s$. A *transition formula* is a first-order formula over $S \cup S'$. We think of a transition formula T as representing a set of state pairs, namely the set of pairs (σ_1, σ_2), such that $\sigma_1 \cup \sigma_2'$ models T. Will will express the proposition that $\sigma_1 \cup \sigma_2'$ models T by $T[\sigma_1, \sigma_2]$.

Given two state formulas ϕ and ψ, we will say that ψ is *T-reachable* from ϕ (in k steps) when there exists a sequence of states $\sigma_0, \ldots, \sigma_k$, such that $\phi[\sigma_0]$ and for all $0 \le i < k$, $T[\sigma_i, \sigma_{i+1}]$, and $\psi[\sigma_k]$.

3.2   Bounded Model Checking

The fact that ψ is reachable from ϕ for bounded k can be expressed symbolically. For all integers i, let S_i be a first-order signature (representing the state of the system at time i) such that for every $s \in S$, there is a corresponding symbol s_i in S_i of the same type. If f is a formula, we will write f_i to denote the result of substituting s_i for every occurrence of a symbol s, and s_{i+1} for every occurrence of a symbol s', in f. Thus, assuming T is total, ψ is *T-reachable* within k steps from ϕ when this formula is consistent:

$$\phi_0 \wedge T_0 \wedge \cdots T_{k-1} \wedge (\psi_0 \vee \cdots \vee \psi_k)$$

We will refer to this as a *bounded model checking* formula [2], since by testing satisfiability of such formulas, we can determine the reachability of one condition from another within a bounded number of steps.

3.3 Symbolic Model Checking

Let us define the *strongest postcondition* of a state formula ϕ with respect to transition formula T, denoted $\mathrm{sp}_T(\phi)$, as the strongest proposition ψ such that $\phi \wedge T$ implies ψ'. We will also refer to this as the *image* of ϕ with respect to T.

A *transition system* is a pair (I, T), where the initial condition I is a state formula and T is a transition formula. We will say that a state formula ψ is *reachable* in (I, T) when it is T-reachable from I, and it is an *invariant* of (I, T) when $\neg\psi$ is not reachable in (I, T). A state formula ϕ is an *inductive invariant* of (I, T) when I implies ϕ and $\mathrm{sp}_T(\phi)$ implies ϕ (note that an inductive invariant is trivially an invariant).

The strongest invariant of (I, T) can be expressed as a fixed point of sp_T, as follows:

$$R(I, T) = \mu Q.\ I \vee \mathrm{sp}_T(Q)$$

We note that the fixed points with respect to Q are exactly the inductive invariants. To prove the existence of the least fixed point, *i.e.*, the strongest inductive invariant, we have only to show that the transformer sp_T is monotonic.

Now, suppose that we have a method of symbolically computing the strongest postcondition. For example, in the case of propositional logic, the strongest postcondition is given by

$$\mathrm{sp}_T(\phi)' = \exists S.(\phi \wedge T)$$

Thus, we can compute it using well-developed methods for Boolean quantifier elimination [3, 11]. This means that we can compute the strongest inductive invariant (also known as the reachable state set) by simply iterating this operator to a semantic fixed point, a procedure known as symbolic reachability analysis.[2] To verify that some formula ψ is unreachable in (I, T), we have only to show that it is inconsistent with the strongest inductive invariant.

3.4 Approximate Image Based on Interpolation

The disadvantage of the above approach is that it can be quite costly to compute the strongest inductive invariant, yet this invariant may be much stronger than what is needed to prove unreachability of ψ. By carefully over-approximating the image (strongest postcondition), we may simplify the problem while still proving ψ unreachable. An over-approximate image operator is an operator $\bar{\mathrm{sp}}$, such that, for all predicates ϕ, $\mathrm{sp}_T(\phi)$ implies $\bar{\mathrm{sp}}_T(\phi)$. Using $\bar{\mathrm{sp}}$, we can compute an over-approximation $R'(I, T)$ of the reachable states. We will say that an over-approximate image operator $\bar{\mathrm{sp}}$ is *adequate* with respect to ψ when, for any ϕ that cannot reach ψ, $\bar{\mathrm{sp}}_T(\phi)$ also cannot reach ψ. In other words, an adequate

---

[2] Note, convergence of this iteration is guaranteed for finite- but not infinite-state systems.

over-approximation does not add any states to the strongest postcondition that can reach a bad state. If $\bar{\text{sp}}$ is adequate, then ψ is reachable exactly when it is consistent with $R'(I,T)$, the over-approximated reachable states. The question, of course, is how to compute an adequate $\bar{\text{sp}}$. After all, if we knew which states could reach a bad state, we would not require a model checker.

One answer is to bound our notion of adequacy. Let's say that a k-adequate image operator is an $\bar{\text{sp}}$ such that, for any ϕ that cannot reach ψ, $\bar{\text{sp}}_T(\phi)$ cannot reach ψ within k steps. We note that if k is greater than the diameter of the state space, then k-adequate is equivalent to adequate, since by definition any state that can be reached can be reached within the diameter.

The advantage of this notion is that we can use bounded model checking and interpolation to compute a k-adequate image operator. We set up a bounded model checking formula to determine whether a given state formula ϕ can reach ψ in from 1 to $k+1$ steps. However, we break this formula into two parts:

$$A \doteq \phi_0 \wedge T_0$$
$$B \doteq T_1 \wedge \cdots \wedge T_k \wedge (\psi_1 \vee \cdots \vee \psi_{k+1})$$

Now suppose $A \wedge B$ is unsatisfiable and let $\hat{A}$ be some interpolant for (A, B) (which we can derive from the refutation of $A \wedge B$). Note that the symbols common to A and B are in S_1 (the symbols representing the state at time 1) thus $\hat{A}$ is over S_1. Dropping the time subscripts in $\hat{A}$, we obtain a state formula, which we will take as the over-approximate image of ϕ. That is, let

$$\bar{\text{sp}}_T(\phi) \doteq \hat{A}\langle S/S_1 \rangle$$

The properties of interpolants guarantee that $\bar{\text{sp}}$ defined in this way is a k-adequate image over-approximation. Note that, since $\phi_0 \wedge T_0$ implies $\hat{A}$, it follows that every state in $\bar{\text{sp}}_T(\phi)$ is reachable from ϕ in one step, hence $\bar{\text{sp}}$ is an over-approximation. Further, since $\hat{A}$ is inconsistent with B, it follows that no state in $\bar{\text{sp}}_T(\phi)$ can reach ψ within k steps. Hence $\bar{\text{sp}}$ is k-adequate. [3] One way to think about this is that the interpolant is an abstraction of A containing just the information from A that the prover used to prove that ϕ cannot reach ψ in 1 to $k+1$ steps. Thus, it is in a sense an abstraction of the image relative to a (bounded time) property.

Now suppose we use this k-adequate image operator to compute an over-approximation $R'(I,T)$ of the reachable states. If we find that $R'(I,T) \wedge \psi$ is inconsistent, we know that ψ is unreachable. If not, it may be that we have over-approximated too much. In this case, however, we can simply try again with a larger value of k. Note that if the bounded model checking formula $A \wedge B$ turns out to be satisfiable in the first iteration (when $\phi = I$) then ψ is in fact reachable and we terminate with a counterexample.

It is easy to show that, for finite-state systems, if we keep increasing k, this procedure must terminate with either a proof or a counterexample. That is, if

---

[3] Note that if $A \wedge B$ is satisfiable, then ϕ can reach ψ, so our image operator can yield any over-approximation, the simplest being the predicate TRUE.

we keep increasing k, either we will obtain a counterexample, or k will become greater than the diameter of the state space. In the latter case, our k-adequate image operator is in fact an adequate image operator, so our reachability answer must be correct. In practice, we find that the k values at which we terminate are generally smaller than the diameter. This diameter-based termination bound contrasts with the termination bound for the k-induction method [16] which is length of the shortest simple path in the state space (also called the recurrence diameter). The shortest simple path can be exponentially longer than the diameter.

3.5 Practical Experience

In the case of hardware verification, a system is made up of Boolean gates, hence we can model it with a transition formula T which is purely propositional. We can therefore use an efficient Boolean satisfiability (SAT) solver [13, 17] to solve the bounded model checking formulas. Modern SAT solvers use heuristics designed to focus the proof on relevant facts, and are quite robust against the addition of irrelevant constraints. The solvers are also easily modified to produce refutations by resolution in the unsatisfiable case [12].

As an example, the performance of the interpolation-based model checking procedure using a SAT solver was tested on a set of benchmark problems [12] derived from the PicoJava II microprocessor from Sun Microsystems. The properties in this benchmark suite are localizable, meaning that only a relatively small subset of the components of a large design are needed to prove the properties. Thus, the ability to filter out irrelevant information is crucial to verifying these properties. In fact, the SMV model checker based on Binary Decision Diagrams is unable to verify any of the properties, since it performs exact reachability analysis.

On the other hand, the interpolation-based method using a SAT solver can verify 19 out of the 20 problems. It is also interesting to compare the method with another abstraction technique that uses refutations from bounded model checking formulas to identify a subset of system components that are relevant to the property, and then uses standard BDD-based methods to verify this subset [12]. This method is called *proof-based abstraction.*

Figure 1 shows a run-time comparison of the interpolation-based method against the proof-based abstraction method for the PicoJava-II benchmark set. In the figure, each point represents one benchmark problem, with the value on the X axis representing the time in seconds required for the earlier proof-based abstraction method, and the time on the Y axis representing the time in seconds taken by the interpolation-based method. A time value of 1000 indicates a timeout after 1000 seconds. Points below the diagonal therefore indicate an advantage for the interpolation method. We observe 16 wins for interpolation and 3 for proof-based abstraction, with one problem solved by neither method. In five or six cases, the interpolation method wins by two orders of magnitude. As it turns out, the performance bottleneck in both methods is bounded model checking. The interpolation method, however, tends to terminate at smaller values of k, and thus runs faster on average. This trend has been verified on a large set (about 1000 problems) of benchmark problems from industrial applications.

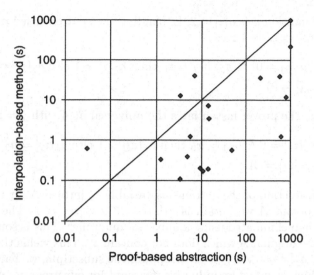

Fig. 1. Run times on PicoJava II benchmarks

3.6   Infinite-State Systems

It is also possible to apply the interpolation method to infinite-state systems whose transition formulas are first-order formulas. In this case, we can use a first-order decision procedure to check satisfiability of the bounded model checking formulas (provided the procedure can produce refutations in a suitable proof system). In this case, the procedure is not guaranteed to terminate.[4] However, using this approach it is possible to verify safety of some simple infinite-state protocols, such as Fischer's timed mutual exclusion protocol, or a simple version of Lamport's "bakery" mutual exclusion algorithm. The method has also been applied to software model checking, though it is not yet clear whether the approach is more efficient than methods based on predicate abstraction [1, 18].

One interesting point to note here is that, using the interpolation procedure of [10], quantifiers occurring in the transition relation T can result in quantifiers in the interpolants (the quantifiers are used to eliminate variables that are introduced into the interpolants by quantifier instantiation). Thus, the method provides a way to synthesize invariants that contain quantifiers.

As an example, suppose we have a simple program whose state consists of an array a, with all elements initialized to 0. At each step, the program inputs a number x and sets $a[x]$ to 1. We would like to prove that, at all times, $a[z] \neq 2$. Thus, our initial condition I is $\forall j.\ a[j] = 0$, our transition condition T is

$$\forall j.\ \text{if } j = x \text{ then } a'[j] = 1 \text{ else } a'[j] = a[j]$$

---

[4] However, it seems likely that convergence could be guaranteed given a suitably restricted prover, if the system has a quantifier-free inductive invariant that proves the property. Convergence can also be guaranteed if the system has a finite bisimulation quotient, as in timed automata.

and our final condition ψ is $a[z] = 2$. Expanding the split bounded model checking formula for $k = 1$, we have:

$$A \doteq (\forall j.\ a_0[j] = 0) \wedge (\forall j.\ \text{if } j = x_0 \text{ then } a_1[j] = 1 \text{ else } a_1[j] = a_0[j])$$
$$B \doteq (a_1[z_1] = 2)$$

In refuting this, the prover instantiates the universal in A with $j = z_1$, yielding:

$$A \doteq a_0[z_1] = 0 \wedge \text{if } z_1 = x_0 \text{ then } a_1[z_1] = 1 \text{ else } a_1[z_1] = a_0[z_1]$$
$$B \doteq (a_1[z_1] = 2)$$

Notice the introduction of the extraneous variable z_1 into A. After refuting this pair, the interpolant $\hat{A}$ we obtain is $a_1[z_1] = 0 \vee a_1[z_1] = 1$. The extraneous variable z_1 is then eliminated using a universal quantifier. This is sound, since $\hat{A}$ is implied by the original A which does not contain z_1. This yields the quantified interpolant $\forall j.\ a_1[j] = 0 \vee a_1[j] = 1$. Dropping the subscripts, we have $\forall j.\ a[j] = 0 \vee a[j] = 1$, which is in fact an inductive invariant for our program, proving that $a[z] = 2$ is not reachable.

This approach makes it possible to verify some parameterized protocols, such as the "bakery" with an arbitrary number of processes, which requires a quantified invariant. It should be noted, however, that the technique is not well suited to protocol verification, since it is based on bounded model checking. Empirically, bounded model checking of protocols is observed to be fairly inefficient. This can be explained by the fact that protocols tend not to be localizable (*i.e.*, there is little state information that can be thrown away without breaking the protocol) and they tend to have interleaving concurrency, which limits the prover's ability to propagate implications across time frames. For such applications, it may be more effective to combine the approach with predicate abstraction, as described in the next section.

4   Predicates from Interpolants

Predicate abstraction [15] is a technique commonly used in software model checking in which the state of an infinite-state system is represented abstractly by the truth values of a chosen set of predicates. In effect, the method computes the strongest inductive invariant of the program expressible as a Boolean combination of the predicates. Typically, if this invariant is insufficient to prove the property in question, the abstraction is refined by adding predicates. For this purpose, the BLAST software model checker uses interpolation in a technique due to Ranjit Jhala [7].

The basic idea of the technique is as follows. A counterexample is a sequence of program locations (a path) that leads from the program entry point to an error location. When the model checker finds a counterexample in the abstraction, it builds a bounded model checking formula that is satisfiable exactly when the path is a counterexample in the concrete model. This formula consists of a set of

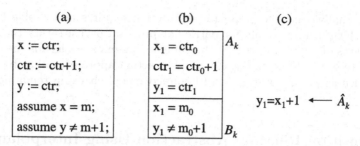

Fig. 2. Predicates from interpolants. Figure shows (a) an infeasible program path, (b) transition constraints, divided into prefix A_k and suffix B_k and (c) an interpolant $\hat{A}_k$ for (A_k, B_k)

constraints: equations that define the values of program variables in each location in the path, and predicates that must be true for execution to continue along the path from each location (these correspond to program branch conditions). As an example, Figure 2 shows a program path, and the corresponding transition constraints.

Now let us divide the path into two parts, at location k. Let A_k be the set of constraints on transitions preceding location k and let B_k be the set of constraints on transitions subsequent to location k. Note that the common variables of A and B represent the values of the program variables at location k. An interpolant for (A_k, B_k) is a fact about location k that must hold if we take the given path to location k, but is inconsistent with the remainder of the path. An example of such a division, and the resulting interpolant, is also shown in 2.

If we derive such interpolants for every location of the path from the same refutation of the constraint set, we can show that the interpolant for location k is sufficient to prove the interpolant for location $k + 1$. As a result, if we add the atomic predicates occurring in the interpolants to the set of predicates defining the abstraction, we are guaranteed to rule out the given path as a counterexample in the abstract model. Note that it is important here that interpolants be quantifier-free, since the predicate abstraction method can synthesize any Boolean combination of atomic predicates, but cannot synthesize quantifiers. We can guarantee that the interpolants are quantifier-free if the transition constraints are quantifier-free.

This interpolation approach to predicate selection has the advantage that it tells us which predicates are relevant to each program location in the path. By using at each program location only predicates that are relevant to that location, a substantial reduction in the number of abstract states can be achieved, resulting in greatly increased performance of the model checker [7]. The fact that the interpolation method can handle both linear inequalities and uninterpreted functions is useful, since linear arithmetic can represent operations on index variables, while uninterpreted functions can be used to represent array lookups or pointer dereferences, or to abstract unsupported operations (such as multiplication).

Notice, finally, that the predicate abstraction requires us to solve bounded model checking instances only for particular program paths, rather than for all possible paths of a given length. Such problems are much easier for the decision procedure to solve. Thus, the predicate abstraction approach might be feasible in cases such as protocols where full bounded model checking tends not to be practical.

5   Transition Relation Abstraction Using Interpolants

Because of the expense of image computation in symbolic model checking, it is often beneficial to abstract the transition relation before model checking, removing information that is not relevant to the property to be proved. Some examples of techniques for this purpose are [4, 12].

Here, we will consider a method of abstracting the transition relation using bounded model checking and interpolation. The technique is based on the notion of a *symmetric interpolant*. That is, given an inconsistent set of formulas $A = \{a_1, \ldots, a_n\}$ a symmetric interpolant for A is a set of formulas $\hat{A} = \{\hat{a}_1, \ldots, \hat{a}_n\}$ such that each a_i implies $\hat{a}_i$, and $\hat{A}$ is inconsistent, and each $\hat{a}_i$ is over the symbols common to a_i and $A \setminus a_i$. We can construct a symmetric interpolant for A from a refutation of $\bigwedge A$ by simply letting $\hat{a}_i$ be the interpolant derived from the given refutation for the pair $(a_i, \bigwedge A \setminus a_i)$. As long as all the individual interpolants are derived from the same proof, we are guaranteed that their conjunction is inconsistent.

Now, given a transition system (I, T), and a formula ψ, let us consider the set of formulas:

$$A = \{I_0, T_0, \ldots, T_{k-1}, (\psi_0 \vee \cdots \psi_k)\}$$

Note that $\bigwedge A$ is exactly the bounded model checking formula for k steps. Suppose we refute this formula, and from the refutation, construct a symmetric interpolant $\hat{A}$. Notice that each $\hat{T}_i$ is a formula implied by the transition relation at time i. If we take the conjunction of these formulas, we have a transition formula that admits no path up to k steps from I to ψ. That is, let the abstract transition relation be

$$\hat{T} = \bigwedge \hat{T}_i \langle S/S_i \rangle \langle S'/S_{i+1} \rangle$$

If we model check unreachability of ψ in the abstract transition system $(I, \hat{T})$, we are guaranteed that there is no counterexample of up to k steps. If ϕ is in fact unreachable in $(I, \hat{T})$, we know it is unreachable in the stronger (I, T). Otherwise, we can refine $\hat{T}$ using a larger value of k. In the finite-state case, this method is guaranteed to converge, since we cannot refine $\hat{T}$ infinitely.

The advantages of $\hat{T}$ as a transition relation are that (1) it contains only facts about the transition relation used in resolving the bounded model checking problem, and (2) it contains only state-holding symbols (those that occur in I or occur primed in T). Thus, for example, free variables introduced to represent inputs of the system are eliminated. This can substantially simplify the image computation.

One potential application of this idea is in predicate abstraction. Since the image computation in predicate abstraction requires in the worst case an exponential number of calls to a decision procedure, software model checkers tend to avoid an exact computation by using approximate methods that lose correlations between predicates [1]. This approximation can lead to false counterexamples. On the other hand, if we derive the transition relation approximation from symmetric interpolants (another idea due to Ranjit Jhala) we can guarantee convergence without using an exact image computation, and at the same time focus the transition relation approximation on relevant facts. We can improve the performance by considering only bad program paths found by the model checker, as opposed to all possible paths of length k. Preliminary experiments show that this approach converges more rapidly than the approach of [6], which uses analysis of the predicate state transitions in the abstract counterexamples to refine the transition relation.

6   Conclusion

We have seen that Craig interpolants derived from proofs have a variety of applications in model checking, primarily in replacing exact image computations with approximate ones. Interpolation allows us to exploit the ability of modern SAT solvers, and decision procedures based on them, to narrow down a proof to relevant facts. We can extract as an interpolant just the information about an image or a transition relation that was actually used by the prover to refute a bounded model checking instance. This allows us in turn to weaken our computation of the strongest invariant, while still proving a given property, or to extract the building blocks from which a suitable invariant might be constructed.

A number of the potential applications of interpolation have yet to be explored. For example, interpolation-based model checking for software seems a promising approach, as does interpolation-based transition relation abstraction for hardware verification. Recently, predicate abstraction methods have been extended to the synthesis of quantified invariants in a method called *indexed predicate abstraction* [9]. It seems plausible that quantified interpolants could be used in the selection of indexed predicates in this method. It also seems plausible that interpolation could be used to good effect for transition relation abstraction in parallel program verification.

Finally, it would be useful to extend the extraction of interpolants from proofs to other theories, for example, first-order arrays and bit vectors. This would extend the utility of interpolant extraction as a tool in the verifier's toolkit.

References

1. T. Ball, A. Podelski, and S. K. Rajamani. Boolean and Cartesian abstraction for model checking C programs. *STTT*, 5(1):49–58, 2003.

2. Armin Biere, Alessandro Cimatti, Edmund Clarke, and Yunshan Zhu. Symbolic model checking without BDDs. In *TACAS'99*, volume 1579 of *LNCS*, pages 193–207, 1999.
3. J. R. Burch, E. M. Clarke, and D. E. Long. Symbolic model checking with partitioned transition relations. In *VLSI '91*, Edinburgh, Scotland, 1991.
4. E. M. Clarke, O. Grumberg, S. Jha, Y. Lu, and H. Veith. Counterexample-guided abstraction refinement. In *Computer Aided Verification*, pages 154–169, 2000.
5. W. Craig. Three uses of the herbrand-gentzen theorem in relating model theory and proof theory. *J. Symbolic Logic*, 22(3):269–285, 1957.
6. Satyaki Das and David L. Dill. Successive approximation of abstract transition relations. In *LICS 2001*, pages 51–60, 2001.
7. T. A. Henzinger, R. Jhala, Rupak Majumdar, and K. L. McMillan. Abstractions from proofs. In *Principles of Prog. Lang. (POPL 2004)*, pages 232–244, 2004.
8. J. Krajíček. Interpolation theorems, lower bounds for proof systems, and independence results for bounded arithmetic. *J. Symbolic Logic*, 62(2):457–486, June 1997.
9. S. K. Lahiri and R. E. Bryant. Constructing quantified invariants via predicate abstraction. In *Verification, Model Checking, and Abstract Interpretation (VMCAI 2004)*, volume 2937 of *LNCS*, pages 267–281. Springer, 2004.
10. K. L. McMillan. An interpolating prover. *Theoretical Computer Science*. To appear.
11. K. L. McMillan. Applying sat methods in unbounded symbolic model checking. In *Computer-Aided Verification (CAV 2002)*, pages 250–264, 2002.
12. K. L. McMillan and N. Amla. Automatic abstraction without counterexamples. In *Int. Conf. on Tools and Algorithms for the Construction and Analysis of Systems (TACAS 2003)*, pages 2–17, 2003.
13. M. W. Moskewicz, C. F. Madigan, Y. Zhao, L. Zhang, and S. Malik. Chaff: Engineering an efficient SAT solver. In *Design Automation Conference*, pages 530–535, 2001.
14. P. Pudlák. Lower bounds for resolution and cutting plane proofs and monotone computations. *J. Symbolic Logic*, 62(2):981–998, June 1997.
15. Hassen Saïdi and Susanne Graf. Construction of abstract state graphs with PVS. In Orna Grumberg, editor, *Computer-Aided Verification, CAV '97*, volume 1254, pages 72–83, Haifa, Israel, 1997. Springer-Verlag.
16. M. Sheeran, S. Singh, and G. Stalmarck. Checking safety properties using induction and a SAT-solver. In *Formal Methods in Computer Aided Design*, 2000.
17. J. P. M. Silva and K. A. Sakallah. GRASP–a new search algorithm for satisfiability. In *Proceedings of the International Conference on Computer-Aided Design, November 1996*, 1996.
18. R. Majumdar T. A. Henzinger, R. Jhala and G. Sutre. Lazy abstraction. In *Principles of Programming Languages (POPL 2002)*, 2002.

Verifying Programs with Dynamic 1-Selector-Linked Structures in Regular Model Checking*

Ahmed Bouajjani[1], Peter Habermehl[1], Pierre Moro[1], and Tomáš Vojnar[2]

[1] LIAFA, University of Paris 7, Case 7014, 2 place Jussieu, F-75251 Paris 5, France
{abou, haberm, moro}@liafa.jussieu.fr
[2] FIT, Brno University of Technology, Božetěchova 2, CZ-61266, Brno, Czech Republic
vojnar@fit.vutbr.cz

Abstract. We address the problem of automatic verification of programs with dynamic data structures. We consider the case of sequential, non-recursive programs manipulating 1-selector-linked structures such as traditional linked lists (possibly sharing their tails) and circular lists. We propose an automata-based approach for a symbolic verification of such programs using the regular model checking framework. Given a program, the configurations of the memory are systematically encoded as words over a suitable finite alphabet, potentially infinite sets of configurations are represented by finite-state automata, and statements of the program are automatically translated into finite-state transducers defining regular relations between configurations. Then, abstract regular model checking techniques are applied in order to automatically check safety properties concerning the shape of the computed configurations or relating the input and output configurations. For this particular purpose, we introduce new techniques for the computation of abstractions of the set of reachable configurations and to refine these abstractions if spurious counterexamples are detected. Finally, we present experimental results showing the applicability of the approach and its efficiency.

1 Introduction

In this paper, we address the problem of automatic verification of programs with *dynamic linked data structures*. Such programs are in general difficult to write and understand, and so the possibility of their *formal verification* is highly desirable. Formal verification of such programs is, however, a very difficult task too. Dynamic allocation leads to a necessity of dealing with infinite state spaces. The objects to be dealt with are in general graphs whose shape is difficult to be restricted in advance. The problem is that the linked data structures may fulfil some shape invariants at certain program points, but these invariants may be temporarily broken in various ways while performing some operations over the data structures.

We consider in this work the case of sequential non-recursive programs manipulating structures with one next pointer such as traditional singly-linked lists and circular

---

* This work was supported in part by the French Ministry of Research (ACI project Securité Informatique) and the Czech Grant Agency (projects GA CR 102/04/0780 and 102/03/D211).

N. Halbwachs and L. Zuck (Eds.): TACAS 2005, LNCS 3440, pp. 13–29, 2005.

lists (possibly sharing their parts) that belong among the most commonly used structures in practice. We propose an automata-based approach for symbolic verification of such programs using the *regular model checking framework* [11, 19, 3]. To the best of our knowledge, this is the first time regular model checking is systematically used in this area—so far, there has only been an isolated ad-hoc attempt to do so in [2].

As our first contribution, we provide a *systematic encoding* of the configurations of considered programs as words over a suitable finite alphabet. Potentially infinite sets of configurations can then be represented by finite-state automata. Moreover, we propose an *automatic translation* of non-recursive sequential C-like programs (without pointer arithmetics and with suitably abstracted non-pointer data values) into finite-state transducers applicable to the sets of program configurations represented by automata and defining regular relations between these configurations. The translation is done statement-by-statement, and one can then either take a union of all statement transducers or use them separately.

By repeatedly applying the transducer (or transducers) representing a program to the automaton encoding a set of possible initial configurations, one can obtain the sets of configurations reachable in any finite number of steps. It is, however, usually impossible to obtain the set of all reachable configurations in this way—the computation will not stop for most programs with loops. One thus has to consider techniques that will accelerate the computation achieving termination as often as possible—a general termination result cannot be obtained as the verification problem considered is clearly undecidable.

In the literature, several different general-purpose techniques have been proposed to *accelerate the computation* of reachable states in regular model checking. They include, e.g., widening [3, 17], collapsing of automata states based on the history of their creation by composing transducers [10, 1], abstraction of automata [2], or inference of languages [6]. In this work, however, as our further contribution, we propose a new set of acceleration techniques that are more tailored for the given domain and thus promise much better performance results. These techniques are based on new language abstractions, which contrary to those introduced in [2], are not defined on the representation structures (i.e. the automata representing sets of configurations), but defined on words (corresponding to configurations). Such abstractions are defined by means of finite-state transducers following different generic schemas. The definitions of these abstractions are guided by the observation that in the configurations of the programs we consider there are some repeated patterns for which it is sufficient to remember their number of repetitions precisely up to some fixed bound. If the number of repetitions is higher, we abstract it to an arbitrary value. The abstraction schemas we define are refinable in the sense that they define infinite sequences of abstraction mappings with increasing precision. Therefore, our verification approach is based on computing abstractions of the sets of reachable configurations, and on refining the abstractions when spurious counterexamples are detected.

These techniques allow us to *fully automatically compute* safe overapproximations of the state space of programs with 1-selector-linked dynamic data structures from whose elements the non-pointer fields are abstracted away. In this way, we can automatically check many important safety properties related to a correct use of dynamically allocated memory—absence of null pointer dereferences, working with uninitialized pointers, memory leakage (i.e. checking that there does not arise any unfreed and un-accessible garbage), etc. Furthermore, we can automatically handle the cases where a finite number of elements of the considered dynamic data structures are allowed to carry other than pointer fields. Using this fact and a simple technique which we pro-pose for describing the desired input/output configurations, we can then automatically verify various properties relating the input and output of the considered programs (e.g., that the output of a list reversing procedure is really exactly the reverse of the input list, etc.). Finally, we show how the techniques can be applied to dealing with linked dynamic data structures whose elements contain any data fields of finite type too.

We have implemented the proposed techniques in a prototype tool and tried it out on a number of procedures manipulating classical singly-linked lists as well as cyclic lists. The results are very encouraging and show the applicability of our approach.

Related Work. Out of the work on verification of programs with dynamic linked data structures published in the literature, the two approaches that are probably the closest to our approach are the ones related to the tools Pale [15] and TVLA [16].

Pale (or more precisely its version for singly-linked structures) based on [8] uses a similar encoding of configurations as the one we propose in the following. The pos-sibility of sharing parts of the lists is, however, not considered there. Moreover, there is no translation of the programs to transducers for manipulating sets of configurations in the Pale approach. The effect of the program is expressed by manipulating a logical description of the configurations, and automata come into play only when deciding the resulting WS1S formulae in Mona [12]. The approach of Pale is not as automatic as ours—only loop-free code can be handled automatically; if there are loops in the code to be checked, the user has to manually provide their invariants. We adopt a different methodology based on abstract symbolic reachability analysis which can also be used to automatically generate invariants.

TVLA is based on abstractions of the arising pointer structures described in a 3-valued logic [16]. The approach is more automatic than the one of Pale, but still the user may be required to provide some instrumentation predicates (or simulation invari-ants in the later approach of [7]) to make the abstraction sufficiently precise. The recent work [13] presents the first steps towards automatically obtaining the necessary instru-mentation predicates by an analysis of spurious counterexamples. Moreover, up to very recently, TVLA had difficulties with cyclic structures that were resolved in a way [14] which like our approach exploits the observation that singly-linked structures exhibit some internal repeated structural patterns.

Both Pale and TVLA are extended to handle structures with more than a single next pointer. We are preparing such an extension of our approach based on tree (or more general) automata too.

Finally, representations of linked memory structures based on automata were used in [9, 5, 18, 4] too. In [5, 18], the special problem of may-alias analysis is primarily considered and a different symbolic representations of memory structures is used—it is based on tuples of automata (one for each pointer variable) and alias relations (using linear constraints). In [4], an alias logic with a Hoare-like proof system is introduced. In this work, one memory structure is represented as a collection of automata whereas our representation is based on representing a set of memory structures with one automaton.

Outline. The rest of the paper is organised as follows. In Section 2 we introduce basic concepts about automata and transducers. In Section 3 we describe our encoding of pointer programs with automata and transducer. Then, we give our verification method in Section 4. Finally, we describe our experimental results in Section 5 and conclude.

2   Automata and Transducers

A *finite-state automaton* is a 5-tuple $A = (Q, \Sigma, \delta, q_{init}, F)$ where Q is a finite set of states, Σ a finite alphabet, $\delta \subseteq Q \times \Sigma \times Q$ a set of labelled transitions, $q_{init} \in Q$ the initial state and $F \subseteq Q$ a set of final states.

The transition relation $\rightarrow \subseteq Q \times \Sigma^* \times Q$ of A is defined as the smallest relation satisfying: (1) $\forall q \in Q : q \xrightarrow{\varepsilon} q$, (2) if $(q, a, q') \in \delta$, then $q \xrightarrow{a} q'$, and (3) if $q \xrightarrow{w} q'$ and $q' \xrightarrow{a} q''$, then $q \xrightarrow{wa} q''$. The (regular) language recognised by A from a state $q \in Q$ is $L(A, q) = \{w : \exists q' \in F. q \xrightarrow{w} q'\}$. The language of A is $L(A) = L(A, q_{init})$. We suppose here that automata are manipulated in their canonical (i.e. minimal deterministic) form.

A *finite-state transducer* over Σ is a 5-tuple $\tau = (Q, \Sigma_\varepsilon \times \Sigma_\varepsilon, \delta, q_{init}, F)$ where Q is a finite set of states, $\Sigma_\varepsilon = \Sigma \cup \{\varepsilon\}$, $\delta \subseteq Q \times \Sigma_\varepsilon \times \Sigma_\varepsilon \times Q$ is a set of transitions, $q_{init} \in Q$ is the initial state, and $F \subseteq Q$ a set of final states. The transition relation $\rightarrow \subseteq Q \times \Sigma^* \times \Sigma^* \times Q$ is defined as the smallest relation satisfying: (1) $q \xrightarrow{\varepsilon, \varepsilon} q$ for every $q \in Q$, (2) if $(q, a, b, q') \in \delta$, then $q \xrightarrow{a, b} q'$ and (3) if $q \xrightarrow{u, v} q'$ and $q' \xrightarrow{a, b} q''$, then $q \xrightarrow{ua, vb} q''$. A transducer τ defines a (regular) relation $R_\tau = \{(u, v) : \exists q' \in F. q_{init} \xrightarrow{u, v} q'\}$.

Given a language $L \subseteq \Sigma^*$ and a relation $R \subseteq \Sigma^* \times \Sigma^*$, let $R(L)$ be the set $\{v \in \Sigma^* : \exists u \in L. (u, v) \in R\}$. Sometimes, we abuse the notation by identifying a transducer τ (resp. an automaton A) with the relation R_τ (resp. the language $L(A)$). For instance, we write $\tau(A)$ to denote $R_\tau(L(A))$.

Let $id \subseteq \Sigma^* \times \Sigma^*$ be the identity relation and $\circ$ the composition of relations. Given a transducer τ, let $\tau^0 = id$, $\tau^{i+1} = \tau \circ \tau^i$, and let $\tau^* = \cup_{i=0}^{\infty} \tau^i$ be the reflexive-transitive closure of τ.

3   From Programs to Transducers

In this section, we describe the translation we propose for automatic verification of sequential, non-recursive programs with 1-selector-linked dynamic data structures in the framework of regular model checking. Our translation is general enough to cover *any* program of this kind (not containing pointer arithmetics and not explicitly covering the possibly necessary abstraction of non-pointer data).

We first describe how to encode as words the so-called program *stores*, i.e. the dynamic memory part of program configurations containing dynamically allocated memory cells linked by pointers. This encoding is similar to the one used in [8], but extended with the possibility of lists sharing their parts. Then, we propose an encoding of the standard C pointer operations (apart from pointer arithmetics) in the form of transducers.

This is different from [8] where operations are encoded by changing a logical description of the configurations. Some of the pointer operations cannot be translated directly to a single transducer, therefore we propose to simulate their effect by computing a limit of a repeated application of certain simple auxiliary transducers.

In the following, we will use as a running example the following procedure reversing a list l. We suppose the data fields normally present in the elements of the data type List to be abstracted away and just the next-pointer fields to be preserved.

```
List x,y,l;
l1: y = null;
l2: while (l != null) {  // i.e. if (l!=null) goto l3; else goto l7;
l3:      y = l->next;
l4:      l->next = x;
l5:      x = l;
l6:      l = y; }          // i.e. l = y; goto l2;
l7: l = x;
l8: // end of program
```

3.1 Encoding Stores as Words

Basically, a store is encoded as the concatenation of several words (separated by a special symbol), each of them representing a list of elements. Successive elements of these lists are given from the left to the right, with positions of pointer variables marked by special symbols. We suppose for the moment that list elements contain no data—later we show that adding data of a finite type is not a problem. We also suppose for the beginning that the store does not contain cycles nor shared parts (i.e. no two different next-pointers point to the same list element). To encode such stores as words, we use the following alphabet Σ: For every pointer variable x used in the program at hand, we have $x \in \Sigma$, and Σ further contains the letters | to separate lists (and some special parts of the configurations), / to separate list elements (i.e. / represents a next-pointer), # to express that a next-pointer points to null, and ! to denote that the next-pointer value is undefined.

Then, we can encode a store without sharing and cycles as a sequence of three parts separated by the symbol | as follows:

- The first part contains a sequence of pointer variables whose values are undefined. In order not to have to consider all their possible orderings, we fix in advance a certain ordering on Σ that is respected here as well as in similar situations below.
- The second part contains pointer variables pointing to null.
- Finally, the third part contains the list sequences separated again by the symbol |. Each list sequence is encoded as follows: Every list element is represented by a (possibly empty) sequence of pointer variables pointing to it, lists elements are separated by the symbol /, and lists end either with the symbol # (null) or ! (undefined).

For example, the word $x\,y\,|\,|\,l\,/\,/\,\#\,|$ encodes a possible initial configuration of the list reversion example: x and y are undefined, no variable points to null, and l points to a list with two elements.

Now, regular expressions (or alternatively finite-state automata) can be used to describe sets of stores. For instance, the regular expression $(x\,y\,|\,|\,l\,/^+\,\#\,|) + (x\,y\,|\,l\,|)$ encodes all possible initial stores for our list reversion example.

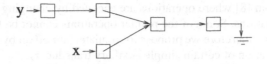

Fig. 1. A store with sharing

Notice that in our encoding, we do not allow garbage (parts of the memory not accessible from pointer variables). As soon as an operation creates garbage, an error is reported. In fact, such a situation corresponds to a memory leak in C (in Java, on the other hand, we can always perform "garbage collection" and remove the garbage).

Remark: Clearly, pointer variables appear exactly once in every word. The separator | and the symbols # and ! appear a bounded number of times since we do not consider stores with garbage. Finally, the symbol / can appear an unbounded number of times.

Lists with Sharing and/or Loops. To encode sharing of parts of lists as, for example, in Figure 1, we extend the alphabet Σ by a finite set of pairs of markers (m_f, m_t, n_f, n_t, etc.). A "from" marker X_f may be used after a next-pointer sign / to indicate that the given next-pointer points to an element marked by X_t (the corresponding "to" marker). Then, e.g., the word $|\,|\,x\,/\,m_f\,|\,y\,/\,/\,n_f\,|\,n_t\,m_t\,/\,/\,\#\,|$ encodes the store of Figure 1.

As one can easily see, the above store could be encoded in several other ways too (for instance, as $|\,|\,x\,/\,n_t\,/\,/\,\#\,|\,y\,/\,/\,n_f\,|$). Although we partially normalize the encoding by imposing a certain ordering on the symbols that are attached to the same memory location, we do not define a canonical representative of the store. However, our experimental results (see Section 5) show that this is not an obstacle to a practical applicability of our method. Furthermore, using a canonical form would complicate the encoding of program statements.

Notice also that markers allow us to encode circular lists (as, e.g., $|\,|\,x\,n_t\,/\,/\,n_f\,|$ corresponding to a circular list of two elements pointed to by x).

It is not difficult to see that given a store with k pointer variables encoded with more than k pairs of markers, one can encode the same store with at most k markers provided that no garbage is allowed: If a "to" marker is at the beginning of a sequence of cells that is not accessible without using markers, we can put these sequence directly in place of the corresponding "from" marker and save one pair of markers. For example, the store $|\,|\,x\,/\,m_f\,|\,y\,/\,/\,n_f\,|\,n_t\,m_t\,/\,/\,\#\,|$ of Figure 1 can be described with one pair of markers as $|\,|\,x\,/\,n_t\,/\,/\,\#\,|\,y\,/\,/\,n_f\,|$ or also as $|\,|\,x\,/\,m_f\,|\,y\,/\,/\,m_t\,/\,/\,\#|$.

Typically, the number of markers that is really needed is even smaller than k as we will demonstrate in our experiments.

3.2   Encoding Program Statements as Transducers

We now describe our encoding of program statements as transducers. We consider non-recursive C programs without pointer arithmetics. Initially, we also suppose all non-pointer data manipulations to be abstracted away—we briefly return to handling them later. Such programs may easily be pre-processed to contain only statements of the form pointer_assignment; goto l; or if (pointer_test) goto l1; else

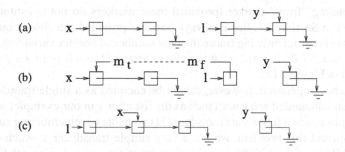

Fig. 2. An example store, the store after the statement 1->next=x, and after a rearrangement

goto 12;. Moreover, by introducing auxiliary variables, we can eliminate multiple pointer dereferences of the form x->next->next and consider single dereferences only.

To encode full configurations of the considered programs, we extend the encoding of stores by adding a letter for the line of the program the control is currently at (followed by a separator |). Moreover, for the needs of our verification procedure, we add a single letter indicating the so-called computation mode. The mode is either n (normal), e (error—a null pointer dereference or working with an undefined pointer has been detected), s (shifting, used later for implementing the pointer manipulation statements that cannot be implemented as a single transducer), and u (unknown result that arises when an insufficient number of markers is used). For instance, the initial configurations of the list reversal example are then $(n\ l_1\ |\ x\ y\ |\ |\ l\ /^+\ \#\ |) + (n\ l_1\ |\ x\ y\ |\ l\ |)$.

Conditional jumps based on tests like x==null or x==y are now quite easy to encode. The transducer just checks whether x is in the null section or in the same section as y (taking / and | as section separators), and according to this changes the letter encoding the current line. If x or y is in the undefined section, we go to the error mode. Similarly, assignments of the form x=null or x=y are easy to handle—x is deleted from its current position (using an x, ε transition) and put to the section of y (using an ε, x transition).

A slightly more involved case is the one of tests based on the x->next construct and the one of the y=x->next assignment. Apart from generating an error when x is undefined or null, one has to consider the successor of x, which may involve going from a "from" marker to the appropriate "to" marker. However, as the number of markers is finite, the transducer can easily remember from which marker to which it is going and skip the part of the configuration between these markers.

Adding/Removing Markers. The most difficult case is then the one of the 1->next=x assignment. The transducer first tries to commit the operation by using a pair of unused markers (say m_f/m_t) out of the in advance chosen set of marker pairs (an unused marker pair is one that does not appear in the current configuration word). Then, behind the section of 1, the transducer puts m_f, and marks the section of x by m_t. For instance, in the list reversal procedure, $n\ l_4\ |\ |\ |\ x\ /\ /\ \#\ |\ l\ /\ y\ /\ \#\ |$ is transformed via 1->next=x into $n\ l_5\ |\ |\ |\ m_t\ x\ /\ /\ \#\ |\ l\ /\ m_f\ |\ y\ /\ \#\ |$ as shown in Figure 2 (a), (b).

However, there may not be any unused markers left. In such a case, the transducer tries to reclaim some by re-arranging the configuration. This can be done by moving some sequence of cells that starts with a "to" marker directly into the place of the corresponding "from" marker (provided these markers do not constitute a loop). As explained in Section 3.1, this is always possible provided the chosen number of pairs of markers is sufficiently big (more than the number of pointer variables). For example, $n\, l_5 \mid \mid \mid m_t\, x\, /\, /\, \# \mid l\, /\, m_f \mid y\, /\, \# \mid$ can be re-arranged to $n\, l_5 \mid \mid \mid l\, /\, x\, /\, /\, \# \mid y\, /\, \# \mid$ as sketched in Figure 2 (c).

The above operation, however, cannot be encoded as a single transducer as it may require an unbounded sequence (such as the list after x in our example) to be shifted to another place, and a finite-state transducer is incapable of remembering such sequences. To circumvent this problem, we use a very simple transducer τ which does one step of the shifting—i.e. it shifts a single element of the sequence by deleting it from its current location and re-producing it at its required location. The desired result is then the limit $\tau^*(Conf)$ where $Conf$ is a regular set of configurations on which the operation is applied. The limit (or an upper approximation of it) is computed using our abstract reachability analysis techniques. In order not to mix half-shifted sequences with the ready-to-use ones, the shifting is done in a special computation mode when no other operations are possible. [3]

If some marker has to be eliminated but this cannot be done, we go to the u mode and stop the computation. Such a situation cannot happen when we use as many markers as pointer variables. Nevertheless, it may happen when the user tries to use a smaller number of them with the aim of reducing the verification time (which is often, but not always possible). If one does not want to use markers at all, the two operations of introducing and eliminating a pair of markers (including shifting) are done at once.

Finally, the remaining malloc(x) and free(x) operations are again easy to encode. The malloc(x) operation introduces a sequence of elements with a single element, pointed to by x, and with an undefined successor. The free(x) operation removes an element, makes x and all its aliases undefined, and possibly makes undefined the next-pointer originally leading to x.

Adding Data Values to List Elements. The encoding can easily be extended to handle list elements containing data of a finite type. Their values are added into Σ and then every memory cell encoded as a sequence surrounded by / and/or | contains not only the pointers (markers) pointing to it, but also the appropriate data value. The tests and assignments on *x may then easily be added by testing whether the appropriate data letter is in the section of x or changing the data letter in this section.

4 Automatic Verification Techniques

We introduce in this section infinite-state verification techniques based on the regular model checking framework. These techniques combine automata-based reachability analysis with abstraction techniques. We concentrate in this work on the verification of safety properties. In the context of regular model checking, given a transducer τ modelling some infinite-state system, an initial set of configurations $Init$, and

---

[3] Let us note that shifting could be implemented as an atomic, special purpose (and rather complex) operation directly on the automata too.

a set of bad configurations *Bad*, the safety verification problem consists in deciding whether

$$\tau^*(Init) \cap Bad = \emptyset \tag{1}$$

Since the problem is undecidable in general (the transitions of any Turing machine can be straightforwardly encoded by a finite-state transducer), we adopt an approach based on computing abstractions of the set $\tau^*(Init)$ and refining these abstractions when spurious counterexamples are detected.

4.1 Abstract Regular Model Checking

A *language abstraction* is a mapping $\alpha : 2^{\Sigma^*} \to 2^{\Sigma^*}$ such that $\forall L \in 2^{\Sigma^*}. L \subseteq \alpha(L)$. An abstraction α' *refines* (or is a *refinement* of) an abstraction α if $\forall L \in 2^{\Sigma^*}. \alpha'(L) \subseteq \alpha(L)$. An abstraction α is *finite-range* if the set $\{L \in 2^{\Sigma^*} : \exists L' \in 2^{\Sigma^*}. \alpha(L') = L\}$ is finite. We say that an abstraction mapping is *regular* if it can be defined by a finite-state transducer.

Given a transducer τ and a language abstraction α, let τ_α be the mapping such that $\forall L \in 2^{\Sigma^*}. \tau_\alpha(L) = \alpha(\tau(L))$.

The first step of our approach is to define a language abstraction α and compute the set $\tau_\alpha^*(Init)$. Clearly, if α is a finite-range abstraction, the iterative computation of $\tau_\alpha^*(Init)$ as $\tau_\alpha(Init) \cup \tau_\alpha^2(Init) \cup \ldots$ eventually terminates. By definition of α, the obtained set $\tau_\alpha^*(Init)$ is an overapproximation of $\tau^*(Init)$, and therefore, if $\tau_\alpha^*(Init) \cap Bad = \emptyset$, the problem (1) has a *positive answer*. Otherwise, the answer to the problem (1) is not necessarily negative since during the computation of $\tau_\alpha^*(Init)$, the abstraction α may introduce extra behaviours leading to *Bad*.

Let us examine this case. Assume that $\tau_\alpha^*(Init) \cap Bad \neq \emptyset$, which means that there is a symbolic path:

$$Init, \tau_\alpha(Init), \tau_\alpha^2(Init), \cdots \tau_\alpha^{n-1}(Init), \tau_\alpha^n(Init) \tag{2}$$

such that $\tau_\alpha^n(Init) \cap Bad \neq \emptyset$. We analyze this path by computing the sets $X_n = \tau_\alpha^n(Init) \cap Bad$, and for every $k \geq 0$, $X_k = \tau_\alpha^k(Init) \cap \tau^{-1}(X_{k+1})$. Two cases may occur: (*i*) either $X_0 = Init \cap (\tau^{-1})^n(X_n) \neq \emptyset$, which means that the problem (1) has a *negative answer*, or (*ii*) there is a $k \geq 0$ such that $X_k = \emptyset$, and this means that the symbolic path (2) is actually a *spurious counterexample* due to the fact that α is too coarse. In this last situation, we need to refine α and iterate the procedure. Therefore, our approach is based on the definition of abstraction schemas allowing to compute families of (automatically) refinable abstractions.

In a previous work [2], we have proposed *representation-oriented* abstractions which consist in defining finite-range abstractions on automata (used as symbolic representation structures for sets of configurations). The general principle of these abstractions is to collapse automata according to some given equivalence relation on their states, regardless of the kind of the represented configurations or the analyzed system.

In this work, we adopt an alternative approach by considering *configuration-oriented* abstractions which are defined on configurations. This approach allows us to define abstraction techniques which are more adapted to the application domain we are considering here. In the next subsections, we propose generic schemas for defining families of refinable configuration-oriented abstractions. Instances of these schemas have been implemented in a prototype tool and used in several experiments (see Section 5).

4.2   Piecewise 0-k Counter Abstractions

The idea behind the first abstraction schema we introduce is to abstract each word by considering some finite decomposition of it, and by applying 0-k counter abstraction (which looses the information about the ordering between symbols and only keeps track of their numbers of occurrences up to k) to each piece of the word in this decomposition. Formally, for $w \in \Sigma^*$, let $dec(w) = (a_1, w_1, a_2, w_2, \cdots, a_n, w_n)$ such that $w = a_1 w_1 a_2 w_2 \cdots a_n w_n$, $\forall i, j \in \{1, \ldots, n\}$. $a_i \in \Sigma$ and $a_i \neq a_j$, and $\forall i \in \{1, \ldots, n\}$. $w_i \in \{a_1, \ldots, a_i\}^*$. Intuitively, $dec(w)$ corresponds to the unique decomposition of w according to the first occurrences in w of each of the symbols in Σ.

Given a word w and a symbol a, let $|w|_a$ denote the number of occurrences of a in w. Given $k \in \mathbb{N}^{>0}$, we define a mapping α_k from words to languages such that for every $w \in \Sigma^*$, if $dec(w) = (a_1, w_1, a_2, w_2, \cdots, a_n, w_n)$, then $\alpha_k(w) = a_1 L_1 a_2 L_2 \cdots a_n L_n$ where $\forall i \in \{1, \ldots, n\}$. $L_i = \{u \in \{a_1, \ldots, a_i\}^* : \forall j \in \{1, \ldots, i\}. |w_i|_{a_j} < k$ and $|u|_{a_j} = |w_i|_{a_j}$, or $|w_i|_{a_j} \geq k$ and $|u|_{a_j} \geq k\}$. We generalize α_k from words to languages in the straightforward way in order to obtain a language abstraction. We can easily prove that:

Proposition 1. *For every $k \geq 0$, α_k is regular and effectively representable by a finite-state transducer.*

Clearly, for every given alphabet Σ, the set of possible 0-k abstractions is finite, and therefore, the number of piecewise 0-k abstractions is also finite since they consist in concatenations of a bounded number of symbols and 0-k abstractions.

Proposition 2. *For every $k \in \mathbb{N}$, the abstraction α_k is finite-range.*

In fact, below, we consider a generalization of the above schema obtained as follows. We allow that decompositions may be computed according to the first occurrences of *only a subset* of the alphabet, called *decomposition symbols*. Furthermore, we allow that the abstraction does not concern some symbols, called *strong symbols*, i.e. all their occurrences are preserved at their original positions. Typically, strong symbols are those which are known to have a bounded number of occurrences in all considered words. For instance, in words corresponding to encodings of program configurations, strong symbols correspond to markers, separators, and pointer variables which are known to have either a fixed or a bounded number of occurrences in all configurations.

Formally, let $\Sigma_1, \Sigma_2 \subseteq \Sigma$ be two sets of symbols such that $\Sigma_1 \cap \Sigma_2 = \emptyset$, where Σ_1 is the set of decomposition symbols and Σ_2 is the set of strong symbols. (Notice that there may be symbols which are neither in Σ_1 nor in Σ_2.) Then, given $w \in \Sigma^*$, we define $dec(w)$ to be the decomposition $(a_1, w_1, a_2, w_2, \cdots, a_n, w_n)$ such that (1) $w = a_1 w_1 a_2 w_2 \cdots a_n w_n$, (2) $\forall i \in \{1, \ldots, n\}$. $a_i \in \Sigma_1 \cup \Sigma_2$ and, $a_i \in \Sigma_1 \Rightarrow |a_1 a_2 \cdots a_n|_{a_i} = 1$, and (3) $\forall i \in \{1, \ldots, n\}$. $w_i \in (\{a_1, \ldots, a_i\} \setminus \Sigma_2)^*$. Then, for each given k, the abstraction α_k is defined precisely as before.

The previous proposition still holds if the number of occurrences of each strong symbol is bounded. Let us call p-Σ_2-bounded language any set of words L such that $\forall w \in L. \forall a \in \Sigma_2. |w|_a \leq p$.

Proposition 3. *For every bound $p \geq 0$, and for every $k \in \mathbb{N}$, the abstraction α_k is finite-range when it is applied to p-Σ_2-bounded languages.*

As for the abstraction refinement issue, it is easy to see that the abstraction schema introduced above defines a family of refinable abstractions.

Proposition 4. *For every p-Σ_2-bounded language L, and for every $k \geq 0$, we have $\alpha_{k+1}(L) \subseteq \alpha_k(L)$. Moreover, if L is infinite, then $\alpha_{k+1}(L) \subsetneq \alpha_k(L)$.*

4.3   Closure Abstractions

We introduce hereafter another family of regular abstractions. Now, the idea is to apply iteratively extrapolation rules which may be seen as rewriting rules replacing words of the form u^k, for some given word u and positive integer k, by the language $u^k u^*$.

Let $u \in \Sigma^*$ and let $k \in \mathbb{N}^{>0}$ be a strictly positive integer. A relation $R \subseteq \Sigma^* \times \Sigma^*$ is an *extrapolation rule* wrt. the pair (u, k) if $R = \{(w, w') \in \Sigma^* \times \Sigma^* : w = u_1 u^k u_2 \text{ and } w' \in u_1 u^k u^* u_2\}$. An *extrapolation system* is a finite union of extrapolation rules.

Clearly, for every language L, we have $L \subseteq R(L)$ (i.e. R defines a language abstraction). In fact, we are interested in abstractions which are the result of *iterating extrapolation systems*. Therefore, let us define a *closure abstraction* as the reflexive-transitive closure R^* of some extrapolation system R.

It is easy to see that every extrapolation system corresponds to a regular relation (i.e. definable by a finite-state transducer). The question is whether closure abstractions of regular languages are still regular and effectively computable. In the general case, the answer is not known. However, we provide a reasonable condition on extrapolation systems which guarantees the effective regularity of closure abstractions.

First of all, we can prove that if we consider a single extrapolation rule, the corresponding closure abstraction if effectively computable.

Lemma 1. *For every extrapolation rule R, and for every regular language L, the set $R^*(L)$ is regular and effectively constructible.*

Proof. Let A be an automaton recognizing L. Let B be an automaton recognizing $u^k u^*$, and let q_i (resp. q_f) be its initial (resp. final) state. Then, for every pair of states (q, q') of A that are related by u^k, we extend A by a unique copy of B and two ε transitions $q \xrightarrow{\varepsilon} q_i$ and $q_f \xrightarrow{\varepsilon} q'$ (which can then be removed by the classical algorithms). $\square$

Now, let $R = R_1 \cup \cdots \cup R_n$ be an extrapolation system where each of the R_i's is an extrapolation rule wrt. a pair $(u_i, k_i) \in \Sigma^* \times \mathbb{N}^{>0}$. Our idea is to define a condition on R such that the computation of $R^*(L)$ can be done for every language L by computing sequentially closures wrt. each of the extrapolation rules R_i in some ordering. Let $\prec \subseteq \Sigma^* \times \Sigma^*$ be the smallest relation such that for every $u, v \in \Sigma^*$, $u \prec v$ if (1) u is not a factor of v (i.e. u does not appear as a subword of v), and (2) u cannot be written as $w_1 v^p w_2$ for any $p \in \mathbb{N}$ and two words w_1, w_2 such that w_1 is a suffix of v and w_2 is a prefix of v. We can prove the following lemma which says that if $u \prec v$, then u can never appear in any power of v.

Lemma 2. *$\forall u, v \in \Sigma^*$, if $u \prec v$ then $\forall p \geq 0. \forall w_1, w_2 \in \Sigma^*. v^p \neq w_1 u w_2$*

Proof. Immediate from the definition of $\prec$: The fact that u can appear in some power of v implies that one of the two conditions defining $u \prec v$ is false. $\square$

We say that the extrapolation system R is *serialisable* if the reflexive closure of the relation $\prec$ (i.e. $\prec \cup id$) defines a partial ordering on the set $\{u_1^{k_1}, \ldots, u_n^{k_n}\}$ (i.e. $\prec$ is antisymmetric and transitive on this set).

Lemma 3. *Let R be a serialisable extrapolation system and let $R_{i_1} R_{i_2} \ldots R_{i_n}$ be a total ordering of the rules of R which is compatible with $\prec$. Then, $R^* = R_{i_n}^* \circ R_{i_{n-1}}^* \cdots \circ R_{i_1}^*$.*

Proof. Follows from Lemma 2: closing by some R_{i_j} never creates new rewriting contexts for any of the R_{i_ℓ} with $\ell < j$. $\qquad\square$

From the two lemmas 1 and 3 we deduce the following fact:

Theorem 1. *For every serialisable extrapolation system R and for every regular language L, the set $R^*(L)$ is regular and effectively constructible.*

Closure abstractions (even serialisable ones) are not finite-range in general. To see this, consider the infinite family of (finite) languages $L_n = (ab)^n$ for $n \geq 0$ and the extrapolation rule R with $U = \{a\}$ and $k = 1$. Then, the images of the languages above form an infinite family of languages defined by $R^*(L_n) = (a^+b)^n$ for every $n \geq 0$.

Therefore, in the verification framework described in Section 4.1, the use of a closure abstraction α does not guarantee the termination of the computation $\tau_\alpha^*(Init)$. However, as our experiments show (see Section 5) the extrapolation principle used in these abstractions is powerful enough to force termination in many practical cases while preserving the necessary accuracy of the analysis of complex properties.

Let us finally mention that the abstraction schema introduced above defines a family of refinable abstractions.

Proposition 5. *Let R be an extrapolation system wrt. a set of pairs $\{(u_1, k_1), \ldots, (u_n, k_n)\}$, let $k_1', \ldots, k_n'$ be integers such that $\forall i.\ k_i' \geq k_i$, and let S be the extrapolation system wrt. $\{(u_1, k_1'), \ldots, (u_n, k_n')\}$. Then, for every language L, we have $S^*(L) \subseteq R^*(L)$. Moreover, if L is infinite, then $S^*(L) \subsetneq R^*(L)$.*

5   Applications and Experimental Results

We have experimented with a prototype implementation of our techniques on several procedures manipulating linked lists. We have implemented a prototype compiler translating programs into transducers as explained in Section 3. As shown in Table 1, we have considered procedures for reversing a list, inserting an element into a list at a given position, deleting an element of a list at a given position, merging two lists element-by-element, and the procedure of Bubblesort over a list. Let us note that although these procedures primarily work with simple linear lists, temporarily they may yield several lists sharing their tails or create circular links. Moreover, we have considered working directly with circular lists too, namely a procedure for reversing such lists and a procedure for removing a segment of a circular list (the motivating example of [14]).

As remarked in Section 3, a store can have several encodings. Therefore, to perform correctly the check $\tau_\alpha^*(Init) \cap Bad = \emptyset$, we require the set Bad to contain *all* possible encodings of bad stores. In all properties we consider below, this can be easily achieved.

5.1   Checking Consistency of Working with the Dynamic Memory

For all the examples, we have firstly checked a basic consistency property that consisted in checking that there is no null pointer dereference, no work with undefined pointers, no memory leak (i.e. there does not arise any undeleted and inaccessible garbage), and that the result is a single list pointed to by the appropriate variable. The specification of such a property for a given procedure is easy and can be derived automatically. For the list reversion example, the set of bad states can be specified using the below extended regular expression[4] where $V = x?\, y?$:

$$(((e+u)\, \Sigma^*) + (\Sigma\, l_8\, \Sigma^*))\ \&\ \neg(n\, l_8\mid V\mid ((l\, V\mid) + (V\mid l\, V\, (/\, V)^*\, /\, \#\mid)))$$

The expression says that it is bad when we try to do a null pointer dereference or work with an undefined pointer value—this is recognized automatically in the transducers and signalized by the first letter of the resulting configuration set to e. If the first letter becomes u (for unknown), the program cannot be verified using the given number of markers and we have to add some. Finally, it is bad when we reach the final line l_8, and the result is not an empty list (represented by l behind #) nor a single list pointed to by l. We do not care about the values of x and y.

The above property of course holds for the correct versions of all the considered procedures. In such a case, our tool provides the user with a safe overapproximation of all the configurations reachable at every line. In this way, we, e.g., automatically obtain the following invariant of the loop of the list reversion procedure:

$$(nl_2\mid y\mid lx\mid) + (nl_2\mid y\mid x\mid l(/)^+\#\mid) + (nl_2\mid\ \mid ly\mid x(/)^+\#\mid) + (nl_2\mid\ \mid\ \mid x(/)^+\#\mid ly(/)^+\#\mid)$$

Roughly, this invariant says that the list is either empty, is pointed to from l, from x, or partially from x and partially from l.

To try out the ability of our techniques to generate counterexamples, we have also tried to examine a faulty version of the list reversion procedure where lines 4 and 5 were swapped. In this case, an error is reported and we are told that from a list with one element (i.e. from a configuration $n\, l_1\mid x\, y\mid\mid l\, /\, \#\mid$), we can obtain a circular list (a configuration $n\, l_8\mid y\mid m_t\, l\, x\, /\, m_f\mid$ where m_f and m_t represent the "from" and "to" versions of a marker m). The user can then also trace the program forwards from the initial configuration or backwards from the erroneous one.

5.2   Checking More Complex Properties

Further, we have tried to verify some more complex properties of the considered programs. Let us start, e.g., with the Bubblesort procedure. When checking just its basic consistency property, we have completely abstracted away the data values stored in the list and made all the conditional jumps fully nondeterministic. To check that the procedure really sorts, we used a technique inspired by [15]. We considered the values of the list elements to be abstracted to being either greater or less than or equal than their successors. The abstracted data values were represented by two special letters (gt and lte) associated with every list item. We supposed lte and gt to be distributed arbitrarily in the initial configurations. We then checked that the basic consistency property holds

---

[4] We use "?" to denote zero or one occurrences and "&" to denote intersection.

and, moreover, the result is a sorted list (i.e. a sequence of elements labelled—up to the last element—by *lte*).

In the case of the merge procedure, we let all elements of the first list be labelled as *a* elements in the initial configuration and all elements of the other list as *b* elements. Then we checked that the output list contains a regular mixture of *a* and *b* elements.

Finally, for the list reversion and insertion and circular list reversion procedures, we did a fully precise verification of their effect. In the case of list reversion, this means that the output contains exactly the same elements as before, but in a reversed order. For the insertion procedure, the required property is that the output list is precisely the input list up to one new element added into the appropriate place.

To check the above rather strong property, we have proposed a simple, yet efficient technique. Let us explain it on the case of list reversion. In the initial configurations, we let the first and last element be labelled by special labels *bgn* and *end*. Next, we consider as initial all the configurations that can arise from the original initial configurations by attaching two further labels—namely *fst* and *snd*—to an arbitrary pair of successive elements. The labels are invisible for the unmodified program—they stay attached to their initial elements. Then, to check the desired property, it suffices that every reachable final configuration starts with *end*, ends with *bgn*, and contains a sequence *snd/fst*. This guarantees that no element can be dropped (then, there would be a way to obtain a configuration without some of the labels), no element can be added (either *end* would not be the first, *bgn* the last, or some *snd/fst* pair would get separated by another element), and the elements must be re-arranged in the given way (otherwise the required resulting ordering of the labels could be broken).

5.3   The Results of the Experiments

For each verification example, we applied one instance of the abstractions presented in Section 4. For checking the basic consistency properties, we used the piecewise 0-2 counter abstraction with no decomposition symbols ($\Sigma_1 = \emptyset$) and with strong symbols Σ_2 containing the pointer variables, the separator |, and the symbol #. Therefore, just the parts of words containing exclusively the / symbols are abstracted. As noticed in Section 3.1, / is the only symbol which can appear an unbounded number of times in lists without data. Therefore, our abstraction is finite range by Proposition 3. For the more complex properties, we used closure abstractions. The extrapolation rules we applied correspond to the loops one naturally expects to possibly arise in the considered structures (e.g., $(/a, 2)$, $(/b, 2)$, $(/a/b, 2)$ for the list merge procedure)—providing such information seems to be easy in many practical situations. In all the cases, the abstractions we used are defined by serialisable extrapolation systems. Therefore, by Theorem 1, they are regular and effectively computable.

We tried out both verification over programs described by a single transducer as well as over programs described by a set of transducers (one per arc of the program control flow graph). Column T of Table 1 shows the running times obtained in the latter case. They were about 1.6 to 6 times better than in the former case. The computation times are presented for the minimum number of markers necessary not to run into the "do not known" result. In the case of inserting into a list, we, however, indicate that sometimes it may be advantageous to use more than a necessary number of markers, which is

Table 1. Some results of experimenting with classical and circular linked lists (obtained at 2.4GHz Intel Pentium 4 from an early prototype tool based on Yap Prolog and the FSA library)

Program	Markers	$|M|_{st.+tr.}^{max}$	T_{sec}	Program	Markers	$|M|_{st.+tr.}^{max}$	T_{sec}
Reverse, bas.cons.	0	51+105	0.3	Merge, bas.cons.	0	209+279	2.7
Reverse, full	0	281+369	4.2	Merge, corr.mix.	0	1080+1415	40.4
Faulty reverse	1	61+138	0.2	Bubblesort, bas.cons.	2	2095+2872	305
Insert, bas.cons.	0	81+102	0.5	Bubblesort, full	2	2339+2887	279
Insert, bas.cons.	2	165+577	0.15	Circ.list rev., bas.cons.	3	655+764	5.4
Insert, full	0	755+936	10.8	Circ.list reverse, full	3	2349+2822	50.6
Delete, bas.cons.	0	55+113	0.3	Circ.l. rem.seg., bas.c.	2	116+291	1.0

especially the case of loop-free procedures where it may completely eliminate the need for the complex operation of shifting. For every experiment, we also indicate the number of states and transitions of the biggest encountered automaton (or transducer).

We further made a comparison with the abstract regular model checking techniques based on automata abstraction introduced in [2]. We observed an equal performance on the faulty reverse example, but on the other examples, the new techniques were about 2.9 to 88 times better (not taking into account the Bubblesort example and checking of the correct mixture property for the list merge example where we stopped the tool based on [2] after 2000 seconds).

We believe that the verification times obtained from our prototype are very encouraging. Some of the verification times that can be found in the literature for similar verification experiments (especially the ones obtained from Pale) are lower but that is partly due to an incomparable degree of automation (especially in Pale where a significant amount of user intervention is needed) and partly due to the fact that our tool is just an early Prolog-based prototype. We expect much better times from a more solid implementation of our tool, which we are now working on.

6   Conclusion

We have proposed a new approach to automatic verification of programs with dynamic linked structures based on a combination of automata-based symbolic reachability analysis with abstraction techniques.

Our approach applies to C-like sequential programs with 1-selector linked structures, for which it allows to verify automatically (safety) properties concerning their data structures. The same techniques can also be used for automatic invariant generation for these programs. Notice that our approach is not restricted to C programs but can be adapted to other languages with similar operations on linked structures too.

The techniques we define are based on simple abstractions of regular sets of configurations which, on one hand, are abstract enough to force termination in many practical cases and, on the other hand, are accurate enough to handle complex properties of the considered data structures. The experimental results are quite encouraging and show the applicability of our approach at least to particular pointer-intensive library routines.

The techniques we propose in this paper are defined in a general way which makes them not restricted to the application domain we consider here. In fact, they can be used as efficient acceleration techniques in the generic framework of regular model checking for the verification of various classes of infinite-state systems as well.

A certain deficiency of the closure abstraction technique as presented above is the need to manually provide the extrapolation rules when non-pointer data fields are not abstracted away. However, very recently, we have proposed a heuristic for automatically deriving such rules based on on-the-fly monitoring of non-looping sequences of states in the encountered automata and on trying to divide them to a given number of equal subsequences, which can then be used as a basis for extrapolation. This heuristic was successful in all the considered examples with a similar time and space efficiency as presented above (the verification times being sometimes worse but sometimes even better). A proper theoretical as well practical investigation of this technique is a part of our future work.

For the future, we plan an extension of our framework to the case of more general linked data structures using representations based on more general classes of automata.

References

1. P.A. Abdulla, J. d'Orso, B. Jonsson, and M. Nilsson. Algorithmic Improvements in Regular Model Checking. In *Proc. of CAV'03*, volume 2725 of *LNCS*. Springer, 2003.
2. A. Bouajjani, P. Habermehl, and T. Vojnar. Abstract Regular Model Checking. In *Proc. of CAV'04*, volume 3114 of *LNCS*. Springer, 2004.
3. A. Bouajjani, B. Jonsson, M. Nilsson, and T. Touili. Regular Model Checking. In *Proc. of CAV'00*, volume 1855 of *LNCS*. Springer, 2000.
4. M. Bozga, R. Iosif, and Y. Lakhnech. Storeless Semantics and Alias Logic. In *Proc. of PEPM'03*. ACM Press, 2003.
5. A. Deutsch. Interprocedural May-Alias Analysis for Pointers: Beyond k-Limiting. In *Proc. of PLDI'94*. ACM Press, 1994.
6. P. Habermehl and T. Vojnar. Regular Model Checking Using Inference of Regular Languages. In *Proc. of the 6th Infinity Workshop*, 2004.
7. N. Immerman, A. Rabinovich, T. Reps, M. Sagiv, and G. Yorsh. Verification via Structure Simulation. In *Proc. of CAV'04*, volume 3114 of *LNCS*. Springer, 2004.
8. J.L. Jensen, M.E. Jørgensen, N. Klarlund, and M.I. Schwartzbach. Automatic Verification of Pointer Programs Using Monadic Second-order Logic. In *Proc. of PLDI '97*, 1997.
9. H.B.M. Jonkers. Abstract Storage Structures. In *Algorithmic Languages*. IFIP, 1981.
10. B. Jonsson and M. Nilsson. Transitive Closures of Regular Relations for Verifying Infinite-State Systems. In *Proc. of TACAS'00*, volume 1785 of *LNCS*. Springer, 2000.
11. Y. Kesten, O. Maler, M. Marcus, A. Pnueli, and E. Shahar. Symbolic Model Checking with Rich Assertional Languages. *Theoretical Computer Science*, 256(1–2), 2001.
12. N. Klarlund and A. Møller. *MONA Version 1.4 User Manual*. BRICS, Department of Computer Science, University of Aarhus, Denmark, 2001.
13. A. Loginov, T. Reps, and M. Sagiv. Abstraction Refinement for 3-Valued-Logic Analysis. Technical Report 1504, Computer Science Dept., University of Wisconsin, USA, 2004.
14. R. Manevich, E. Yahav, G. Ramalingam, and M. Sagiv. Predicate Abstraction and Canonical Abstraction for Singly-Linked Lists. In *Proc. of VMCAI'05*. Springer, 2005.
15. A. Møller and M.I. Schwartzbach. The Pointer Assertion Logic Engine. In *Proc. of PLDI '01*, 2001. Also in SIGPLAN Notices 36(5) (May 2001).

16. S. Sagiv, T.W. Reps, and R. Wilhelm. Parametric Shape Analysis via 3-Valued Logic. *TOPLAS*, 24(3), 2002.
17. T. Touili. Widening Techniques for Regular Model Checking. *ENTCS*, 50, 2001.
18. A. Venet. Automatic Analysis of Pointer Aliasing for Untyped Programs. *Science of Computer Programming*, 35(2), 1999.
19. P. Wolper and B. Boigelot. Verifying Systems with Infinite but Regular State Spaces. In *Proc. of CAV'98*, volume 1427, 1998.

Simulation-Based Iteration of Tree Transducers

Parosh Aziz Abdulla[1], Axel Legay[2,*], Julien d'Orso[3], and Ahmed Rezine[1]

[1] Dept. of Information Technology, Uppsala University,
P.O. Box 337, SE-751 05 Uppsala, Sweden
{parosh, rahmed}@it.uu.se

[2] Université de Liège, Institut Montefiore, B28,
4000 Liège, Belgium
legay@montefiore.ulg.ac.be

[3] IRCCyN - UMR CNRS 6597, BP 92 101,
44321 Nantes CEDEX 03, France
julien.dorso@irccyn.ec-nantes.fr

Abstract. *Regular model checking* is the name of a family of techniques for analyzing infinite-state systems in which states are represented by words, sets of states by finite automata, and transitions by finite-state transducers. The central problem is to compute the transitive closure of a transducer. A main obstacle is that the set of reachable states is in general not regular. Recently, regular model checking has been extended to systems with tree-like architectures. In this paper, we provide a procedure, based on a new implementable acceleration technique, for computing the transitive closure of a tree transducer. The procedure consists of incrementally adding new transitions while merging states which are related according to a pre-defined equivalence relation. The equivalence is induced by a *downward* and an *upward* simulation relation which can be efficiently computed. Our technique can also be used to compute the set of reachable states without computing the transitive closure. We have implemented and applied our technique to several protocols.

1 Introduction

Regular model checking is the name of a family of techniques for analyzing infinite-state systems in which states are represented by words, sets of states by finite automata, and transitions by finite automata operating on pairs of states, i.e. finite-state transducers. The central problem in regular model checking is to compute the transitive closure of a finite-state transducer. Such a representation allows to compute the set of reachable states of the system (which is useful to verify safety properties) and to detect loops between states (which is useful to verify liveness properties). However, computing the transitive closure is in general undecidable; consequently any method for solving the problem is necessarily incomplete. One of the goals of regular model checking is to provide semi-algorithms

---

* This author is supported by a F.R.I.A grant.

N. Halbwachs and L. Zuck (Eds.): TACAS 2005, LNCS 3440, pp. 30–44, 2005.

that terminate on many practical applications. Such semi-algorithms have already been successfully applied to parameterized systems with linear topologies, and to systems that operate on linear unbounded data structures such as queues, integers, reals, and hybrid systems [BJNT00, DLS01, BLW03, BHV04, BLW04].

This work aims at extending the paradigm of regular model checking to verify systems which operate on tree-like architectures. This includes several interesting protocols such as the Percolate Protocol ([KMM+01]) or the Tree-arbiter Protocol ([ABH+97]).

To verify such systems, we use the extension of regular model checking called *tree regular model checking*, which was introduced in [KMM+01, AJMd02, BT02]. In tree regular model checking, states of the systems are represented by trees, sets of states by tree automata, and transitions by tree automata operating on pairs of trees, i.e. tree transducers. As in the case of regular model checking, the central problem is to provide semi-algorithms for computing the transitive closure of a tree transducer. This problem was considered in [AJMd02, BT02]; however the proposed algorithms are most of the time inefficient or non-implementable.

In this work, we provide an efficient and implementable semi-algorithm for computing the transitive closure of a tree transducer. Starting from a tree transducer D, describing the set of transitions of the system, we derive a transducer, called the *history transducer* whose states are *columns* (words) of states of D. The history transducer characterizes the transitive closure of the rewriting relation corresponding to D. The set of states of the history transducer is infinite which makes it inappropriate for computational purposes. Therefore, we present a method for computing a finite-state transducer which is an abstraction of the history transducer. The abstract transducer is generated on-the-fly by a procedure which starts from the original transducer D, and then incrementally adds new transitions and merges equivalent states. To compute the abstract transducer, we define an equivalence relation on columns (states of the history transducer). We identify *good* equivalence relations, i.e., equivalence relations which can be used by our on-the-fly algorithm. An equivalence relation is considered to be *good* if it satisfies the following two conditions:

- *Soundness and completeness:* merging two equivalent columns must not add any traces which are not present in the history transducer. Consequently, the abstract transducer accepts the same language as the history transducer (and therefore characterizes exactly the transitive closure of D).
- *Computability of the equivalence relation:* This allows on-the-fly merging of equivalent states during the generation of the abstract transducer.

We present a methodology for deriving good equivalence relations. More precisely, an equivalence relation is induced by two simulation relations; namely a *downward* and an *upward* simulation relation, both of which are defined on tree automata. We provide sufficient conditions on the simulation relations which guarantee that the induced equivalence is good. Furthermore, we give examples of concrete simulations which satisfy the sufficient conditions. These simulations can be computed by efficient algorithms derived from those of Henzinger *et al.* ([HHK95]) for finite words.

We also show that our technique can be directly adapted in order to compute the set of reachable states of a system without computing its entire transitive closure. When checking for safety properties, such an approach is often (but not always) more efficient.

We have implemented our algorithms in a tool which we have applied to a number of protocols including a Two-Way Token protocol, the Percolate Protocol ([KMM+01]), a parametrized version of the Tree-arbiter Protocol ([ABH+97]), and a tree-parametrized version of a Leader Election Protocol.

Related Work: There are several works on efficient computation of transitive closures for *word* transducers [DLS01, AJNd03, BLW03, BHV04, BLW04]. However, all current algorithms devoted to the computation of the transitive closure of a *tree* transducer are not efficient or not implementable. In [AJMd02], we presented a method for computing transitive closures of tree transducers. The method presented in [AJMd02] is very heavy and relies on several layers of expensive automata-theoretic constructions. The method of this paper is much more light-weight and efficient, and can therefore be applied to a larger class of protocols. The work in [BT02] also considers tree transducers, but it is based on *widening* rather than acceleration. The idea is to compute successive powers of the transducer relation, and detect *increments* in the produced transducers. Based on the detected increments, the method makes a guess of the transitive closure. One of the main disadvantages of this work is that the widening procedure in [BT02] is not implemented. Furthermore, no efficient method is provided to detect the increments. This indicates that any potential implementation of the widening technique would be inefficient. In [AJNd03], a technique for computing the transitive closure of a word transducer is given. This technique is also based on computing simulations. However, as explained in Section 6, those simulations cannot be extended to trees, and therefore the technique of [AJNd03] cannot be applied to tree transducers. In [DLS01], Dams, Lakhnech, and Steffen present an extension of the word case to trees. However, this is done for top-down tree automata which are not closed under determinization (and thus many other operations). In [DLS01], the authors consider several definitions of simulations and bisimulations between top-down tree automata without providing methods for computing them. Hence, it is not clear how to implement their algorithms.

Outline: In the next Section, we introduce basic concepts related to trees and tree automata. In Section 3, we describe tree relations and transducers. In Section 4, we introduce tree regular model checking. Section 5 introduces *history transducers* which characterize the transitive closure of a given transducer. In Section 6, we introduce *downward* and *upward* simulations on tree automata, and give sufficient conditions which guarantee that the induced equivalence relation is exact and computable. Section 7 gives an example of simulations which satisfy the sufficient conditions. In section 8, we describe how to compute the reachable states. In Section 9 we report on the results of running a prototype on a number of examples. Finally, in Section 10 we give conclusions and directions for future work.

Some proofs had to be omitted due to space constraints. A self-contained long version of this paper can be obtained from the authors.

2 Tree Automata

In this section, we introduce some preliminaries on trees and tree automata (more details can be found in [CDG+99]).

A *ranked alphabet* is a pair (Σ, ρ), where Σ is a finite set of symbols and ρ is a mapping from Σ to $\mathbb{N}$. For a symbol $f \in \Sigma$, we call $\rho(f)$ the *arity* of f. We let Σ_p denote the set of symbols in Σ with arity p. Intuitively, each node in a tree is labeled with a symbol in Σ with the same arity as the out-degree of the node. Sometimes, we abuse notation and use Σ to denote the ranked alphabet (Σ, ρ).

Following [CDG+99], the nodes in a tree are represented by words over $\mathbb{N}$. More precisely, the empty word ϵ represents the root of the tree, while a node $b_1 b_2 ... b_k$ is a child of the node $b_1 b_2 ... b_{k-1}$. Also, nodes are labeled by symbols from Σ.

Definition 1. [Trees]
A tree T over a ranked alphabet Σ is a pair (S, λ), where

- *S, called the tree structure, is a finite set of sequences over $\mathbb{N}$ (i.e, a finite subset of $\mathbb{N}^*$). Each sequence n in S is called a node of T. If S contains a node $n = b_1 b_2 ... b_k$, then S will also contain the node $n' = b_1 b_2 ... b_{k-1}$, and the nodes $n_r = b_1 b_2 ... b_{k-1} r$, for $r : 0 \leq r < b_k$. We say that n' is the parent of n, and that n is a child of n'. A leaf of T is a node n which does not have any child, i.e., there is no $b \in \mathbb{N}$ with $nb \in S$.*
- *λ is a mapping from S to Σ. The number of children of n is equal to $\rho(\lambda(n))$. Observe that if n is a leaf then $\lambda(n) \in \Sigma_0$.*

We use $T(\Sigma)$ to denote the set of all trees over Σ.

Sets of trees are recognized using tree automata. There exist various kinds of tree automata. In this paper, we use bottom-up tree automata since they are closed under all operations needed by the classical model checking procedure: intersection, union, minimization, determinization, inclusion test, complementation, etc. In the sequel, we will omit the term bottom-up.

Definition 2. [Tree Automata and Languages]
A tree language is a set of trees.
A tree automaton [CDG+99, Tho90] over a ranked alphabet Σ is a tuple $A = (Q, F, \delta)$, where Q is a set of states, $F \subseteq Q$ is a set of final states, and δ is the transition relation, represented by a set of rules each of the form

$$(q_1, \ldots, q_p) \xrightarrow{f} q$$

where $f \in \Sigma_p$ and $q_1, \ldots, q_p, q \in Q$. Unless stated otherwise, we assume Q and δ to be finite.

We say that A is *deterministic* when δ does not contain two rules of the form $(q_1, \ldots, q_p) \xrightarrow{f} q$ and $(q_1, \ldots, q_p) \xrightarrow{f} q'$ with $q \neq q'$.

Intuitively, the automaton A takes a tree $T \in T(\Sigma)$ as input. It proceeds from the leaves to the root (that explains why it is called bottom-up), annotating states to the nodes of T. A transition rule of the form shown above tells us that if the children of a node n are already annotated from left to right with $q_1, \ldots, q_p$ respectively, and if $\lambda(n) = f$, then the node n can be annotated by q. As a special case, a transition rule of the form $\xrightarrow{f} q$ implies that a leaf labeled with $f \in \Sigma_0$ can be annotated by q.

Formally, a *run* r of A on a tree $T = (S, \lambda) \in T(\Sigma)$ is a mapping from S to Q such that for each node $n \in T$ with children $n_1, \ldots, n_k$ we have

$$\left((r(n_1), \ldots, r(n_k)) \xrightarrow{\lambda(n)} r(n) \right) \in \delta.$$

For a state q, we let $T \xRightarrow{r}_A q$ denote that r is a run of A on T such that $r(\epsilon) = q$. We use $T \Rightarrow_A q$ denote that $T \xRightarrow{r}_A q$ for some r. For a set $S \subseteq Q$ of states, we let $T \xRightarrow{r}_A S$ $(T \Rightarrow_A S)$ denote that $T \xRightarrow{r}_A q$ $(T \Rightarrow_A q)$ for some $q \in S$. We say that A *accepts* T if $T \Rightarrow_A F$. We define $L(A) = \{T | \ T \text{ is accepted by } A\}$. A tree language K is said to be *regular* if there is a tree automaton A such that $K = L(A)$.

We now define the notion of context. Intuitively, a context is a tree with "holes" instead of leaves. Formally, we consider a special symbol $\square \notin \Sigma$ with arity 0. A *context* over Σ is a tree (S_C, λ_C) over $\Sigma \cup \{\square\}$ such that for all leaves $n_c \in S_C$, we have $\lambda_C(n_c) = \square$. For a context $C = (S_C, \lambda_C)$ with holes at leaves $n_1, \ldots, n_k \in S_C$, and trees $T_1 = (S_1, \lambda_1), \ldots, T_k = (S_k, \lambda_k)$, we define $C[T_1, \ldots, T_k]$ to be the tree (S, λ), where

- $S = S_C \cup \bigcup_{i \in \{1, \ldots, k\}} \{n_i \cdot n' | \ n' \in S_i\}$;
- for each $n = n_i \cdot n'$ with $n' \in S_i$ for some $1 \leq i \leq k$, we have $\lambda(n) = \lambda_i(n')$;
- for each $n \in S_C - \{n_1, \ldots, n_k\}$, we have $\lambda(n) = \lambda_C(n)$.

Intuitively, $C[T_1, \ldots, T_k]$ is the result of appending the trees $T_1, \ldots, T_k$ to the holes of C. Consider a tree automaton $A = (Q, F, \delta)$ over a ranked alphabet Σ. We extend the notion of runs to contexts. Let $C = (S_C, \lambda_C)$ be a context with leaves $n_1, \ldots, n_k$. A *run* r of A on C from $(q_1, \ldots, q_k)$ is defined in a similar manner to a run except that for leaf n_i, we have $r(n_i) = q_i$. In other words, each leaf labeled with $\square$ is annotated by one q_i. We use $C[q_1, \ldots, q_k] \xRightarrow{r}_A q$ to denote that r is a run of A on C from $(q_1, \ldots, q_k)$ such that $r(\epsilon) = q$. The notation $C[q_1, \ldots, q_k] \Rightarrow_A q$ and its extension to sets of states are explained in a similar manner to runs on trees.

Definition 3. [Suffix and Prefix]
For an automaton $A = (Q, F, \delta)$, we define the suffix *of a tuple of states $(q_1, \ldots, q_n)$ to be* $\text{suff}(q_1, \ldots, q_n) = \{C : \text{context} | \ C[q_1, \ldots, q_n] \Rightarrow_A F\}$. *For a state $q \in Q$, its* prefix *is the set of trees* $\text{pref}(q) = \{T : \text{tree} | \ T \Rightarrow_A q\}$.

Remark. Our definition of a context coincides with the one of [BT03] where all leaves are holes. On the other hand, a context in [CDG+99] and [AJMd02] is a tree with a *single* hole.

3 Tree Relations and Transducers

In this section we introduce tree relations and transducers.

For a binary relation R, we use R^+ to denote the transitive closure of R.

For a ranked alphabet Σ and $m \geq 1$, we let $\Sigma^\bullet(m)$ be the ranked alphabet which contains all tuples $(f_1, \ldots, f_m)$ such that $f_1, \ldots, f_m \in \Sigma_p$ for some p. We define $\rho((f_1, \ldots, f_m)) = \rho(f_1)$. In other words, the set $\Sigma^\bullet(m)$ contains the m-tuples, where all the elements in the same tuple have equal arities. Furthermore, the arity of a tuple in $\Sigma^\bullet(m)$ is equal to the arity of any of its elements. For trees $T_1 = (S_1, \lambda_1)$ and $T_2 = (S_2, \lambda_2)$, we say that T_1 and T_2 are *structurally equivalent*, denoted $T_1 \cong T_2$, if $S_1 = S_2$.

Consider structurally equivalent trees $T_1, \ldots, T_m$ over an alphabet Σ, where $T_i = (S, \lambda_i)$ for $i : 1 \leq i \leq m$. We let $T_1 \times \cdots \times T_m$ be the tree $T = (S, \lambda)$ over $\Sigma^\bullet(m)$ such that $\lambda(n) = (\lambda_1(n), \ldots, \lambda_m(n))$ for each $n \in S$. An m-ary *relation* on the alphabet Σ is a set of tuples of the form $(T_1, \ldots, T_m)$, where $T_1, \ldots, T_m \in T(\Sigma)$ and $T_1 \cong \cdots \cong T_m$. A tree language K over $\Sigma^\bullet(m)$ characterizes an m-ary tree relation $[K]$ on $T(\Sigma)$ as follows: $(T_1, \ldots, T_m) \in [K]$ iff $T_1 \times \cdots \times T_m \in K$.

We use tree automata also to characterize tree relations: an automaton A over $\Sigma^\bullet(m)$ characterizes an m-ary relation on $T(\Sigma)$, namely the relation $[L(A)]$. A tree relation is said to be *regular* if it is equal to $[L(A)]$, for some tree automaton A. In such as case, we denote this relation by $R(A)$.

Definition 4. [Tree Transducers]
In the special case where D is a tree automaton over $\Sigma^\bullet(2)$, we call D a tree transducer over Σ.

Remark. Our definition of tree transducers is a restricted version of the one considered in [BT02] in the sense that we only consider transducers that do not modify the structure of the tree. In [BT02], such transducers are called relabeling transducers.

4 Tree Regular Model Checking

We use the following framework known as *tree regular model checking* [AJMd02, BT02, KMM+01]:

Definition 5. [Program]
A program is a triple $P = (\Sigma, \phi_I, D)$ where

- Σ *is a ranked alphabet, over which the program configurations are encoded as trees;*

- ϕ_I *is a set of initial configurations represented by a tree automaton over* Σ;
- D *is a transducer over* Σ *characterizing a transition relation* $R(D)$.

In a similar manner to the the case of words (see [BJNT00]), the problems we are going to consider are the following:

- *Computing the transitive closure:* The goal is to compute a new tree transducer D^+ representing the transitive closure of D, i.e., $R(D^+) = (R(D))^+$. Such a representation can be used for computing the reachability set of the program or for finding cycles between reachable program configurations.
- *Computing the reachable states:* The goal is to compute a tree automaton representing $R(D^+)(\phi_I)$. This set can be used for checking safety properties of the program.

We will first provide a technique for computing D^+. Then, we will show the modifications needed for computing $R(D^+)(\phi_I)$ without computing D^+.

5   Computing the Transitive Closure

In this section we introduce the notion of *history transducer*. With a transducer D we associate a *history transducer* H which corresponds to the transitive closure of D. Each state of H is a word of the form $q_1 \cdots q_k$ where $q_1, \ldots, q_k$ are states of D. For a word w, we let $w(i)$ denote the i-th symbol of w. Intuitively, for each $(T, T') \in D^+$, the history transducer H encodes the successive runs of D needed to derive T' from T. The term "history transducer" reflects the fact that the transducer encodes the histories of all such derivations.

Definition 6. [History Transducer]
Consider a tree transducer $D = (Q, F, \delta)$ *over a ranked alphabet* Σ. *The history (tree) transducer* H *for* D *is an (infinite) transducer* (Q_H, F_H, δ_H), *where* $Q_H = Q^+$, $F_H = F^+$, *and* δ_H *contains all rules of the form*

$$(w_1, \ldots, w_p) \xrightarrow{(f, f')} w$$

such that there is $k \geq 1$ *where the following conditions are satisfied*

- $|w_1| = \cdots = |w_p| = |w| = k$;
- *there are* $f_1, f_2, \ldots, f_{k+1}$, *with* $f = f_1$, $f' = f_{k+1}$, *and*
  $(w_1(i) \ldots, w_p(i)) \xrightarrow{(f_i, f_{i+1})} w(i)$ *belongs to* δ, *for each* $i : 1 \leq i \leq k$.

Observe that all the symbols $f_1, \ldots, f_{k+1}$ are of the same arity p. Also, notice that if $(T \times T') \xRightarrow{r}_H w$, then there is a $k \geq 1$ such that $|r(n)| = k$ for each $n \in (T \times T')$. In other words, any run of the history transducer assigns states (words) of the same length to the nodes. From the definition of H we derive the following lemma (proved in [AJMd02]) which states that H characterizes the transitive closure of the relation of D.

Lemma 1. *For a transducer D and its history transducer H, we have that* $R(H) = R(D^+)$.

The problem with H is that it has infinitely many states. Therefore, we define an *equivalence* $\simeq$ on the states of H, and construct a new transducer where equivalent states are merged. This new transducer will hopefully only have a finite number of states.

Given an equivalence relation $\simeq$, the symbolic transducer $D_{\simeq}$ obtained by merging states of H according to $\simeq$ is defined as $(Q/\simeq, F/\simeq, \delta_{\simeq})$, where:

- $Q/\simeq$ is the set of equivalence classes of Q_H w.r.t. $\simeq$;
- $F/\simeq$ is the set of equivalence classes of F_H w.r.t. $\simeq$ (this will always be well-defined, see sufficient condition 5 of Theorem 1);
- $\delta_{\simeq}$ contains rules of the form $(x_1, \ldots, x_n) \xrightarrow{f}_{\simeq} x$ iff there are states $q_1 \in x_1, \ldots, q_n \in x_n, q \in x$ such that there is a rule $(q_1, \ldots, q_n) \xrightarrow{f} q$ of H.

Since H is infinite we cannot derive $D_{\simeq}$ by first computing H. Instead, we compute $D_{\simeq}$ on-the-fly collapsing states which are equivalent according to $\simeq$. In other words, we perform the following *procedure* (which need not terminate in general).

- The procedure computes successive reflexive powers of D: $D^{\leq 1}, D^{\leq 2}, D^{\leq 3}, \ldots$ (where $D^{\leq i} = \bigcup_{n=1}^{n=i} D^n$), and collapses states[4] according to $\simeq$. We thus obtain $D^{\leq 1}_{\simeq}, D^{\leq 2}_{\simeq}, \ldots$
- The procedure terminates when the relation R^+ is accepted by $D^{\leq i}_{\simeq}$. This can be tested by checking if the language $D^{\leq i}_{\simeq} \circ D$ is included in $D^{\leq i}_{\simeq}$.

6 Soundness, Completeness, and Computability

In this section, we describe how to derive equivalence relations on the states of the history transducer which can be used in the procedure given in Section 5. A *good* equivalence relation $\simeq$ satisfies the following two conditions:

- It is sound and complete, i.e., $R(D_{\simeq}) = R(H)$. This means that $D_{\simeq}$ characterizes the same relation as D^+.
- It is computable. This turns the procedure of Section 5 into an *implementable algorithm*, since it allows on-the-fly merging of equivalent states.

We provide a methodology for deriving good equivalence relations as follows: we define two simulation relations; namely a downward simulation relation $\preccurlyeq_{down}$ and an *upward simulation relation* $\preccurlyeq_{up}$, which together induce an equivalence relation $\simeq$. Then, we give sufficient conditions of the simulation relations which guarantee that the induced equivalence $\simeq$ is a good one.

6.1 Downward and Upward Simulation

We start by giving the definitions.

---

[4] The states of $D^{\leq i}$ are by construction states of the history transducer.

Definition 7. [Downward Simulation]
Let $A = (Q, F, \delta)$ be a tree automaton. A binary relation $\preccurlyeq_{down}$ is a downward simulation iff for any $n \geq 1$ and any symbol $f \in \Sigma_n$, for all states $q, q_1, \ldots, q_n, r$, the following holds:
Whenever $q \preccurlyeq_{down} r$ and $(q_1, \ldots, q_n) \xrightarrow{f} q$, then there exist states $r_1, \ldots, r_n$ such that $q_1 \preccurlyeq_{down} r_1, \ldots, q_n \preccurlyeq_{down} r_n$ and $(r_1, \ldots, r_n) \xrightarrow{f} r$.

Definition 8. [Upward Simulation]
Let $A = (Q, F, \delta)$ be a tree automaton. Given a downward simulation $\preccurlyeq_{down}$, a binary relation $\preccurlyeq_{up}$ is an upward simulation w.r.t. $\preccurlyeq_{down}$ iff for any $n \geq 1$ and any symbol $f \in \Sigma_n$, for all states $q, q_1, \ldots, q_i, \ldots, q_n, r_i \in Q$, the following holds:
Whenever $q_i \preccurlyeq_{up} r_i$ and $(q_1, \ldots, q_n) \xrightarrow{f} q$, then there exist states $r_1, \ldots, r_{i-1}, r_{i+1}, \ldots, r_n, r \in Q$ such that $q \preccurlyeq_{up} r$ and $\forall j \neq i : q_j \preccurlyeq_{down} r_j$ and $(r_1, \ldots, r_n) \xrightarrow{f} r$.

While the notion of a downward simulation is a straightforward extension of the word case, the notion of an upward simulation is not as obvious. This comes from the asymmetric nature of trees. If we follow the execution of a tree automaton downwards, it is easy to see that all respective children of two nodes related by simulation should continue to be related pairwise. If we now consider how a tree automaton executes when going upwards, we are confronted to the problem that the parent of the current node may have several children. The question is then how to characterize the behavior of such children. The answer lies in constraining their prefixes, i.e. using a downward simulation.

We state some elementary properties of the simulation relations.

Lemma 2. The reflexive closure and the transitive closure of a downward simulation $\preccurlyeq_{down}$ are both downward simulations. Furthermore, there is a unique maximal downward simulation.

Lemma 3. Let $\preccurlyeq_{down}$ be a reflexive (transitive) downward simulation. The reflexive (transitive) closure of an upward simulation w.r.t to $\preccurlyeq_{down}$ is also an upward simulation w.r.t $\preccurlyeq_{down}$. Furthermore there exists a unique maximal upward simulation w.r.t. any downward simulation.

Observe that both for downward simulations, and upward simulations, maximality implies transitivity and reflexivity.

We now define an equivalence relation derived from two simulation relations.

Definition 9. [Independence]
Two binary relations $\preceq_1$ and $\preceq_2$ are said to be independent iff whenever $q \preceq_1 r$ and $q \preceq_2 r'$, there exists s such that $r \preceq_2 s$ and $r' \preceq_1 s$.

Definition 10. [Induced Relation]
The relation $\simeq$ induced by two binary relations $\preceq_1$ and $\preceq_2$ is defined as:

$$\preceq_1 \circ \preceq_2^{-1} \cap \preceq_2 \circ \preceq_1^{-1}$$

The following Lemma gives sufficient conditions for two relations to induce an equivalence relation.

Lemma 4. *Let $\preceq_1$ and $\preceq_2$ be two binary relations. If $\preceq_1$ and $\preceq_2$ are reflexive, transitive, and independent, then their induced relation $\simeq$ is an equivalence relation.*

6.2 Sufficient Conditions for Soundness and Completeness

We give sufficient conditions for the two simulation relations to induce a sound and complete equivalence relation on states of a tree automaton.

We assume a tree automaton $A = (Q, F, \delta)$. We now define a relation $\simeq$ induced by the two relations $\preceq$ and $\preccurlyeq_{down}$ satisfying the following *sufficient* conditions:

1. $\preccurlyeq_{down}$ is a downward simulation;
2. $\preceq$ is a reflexive and transitive relation included in $\preccurlyeq_{up}$ which is an upward simulation w.r.t. $\preccurlyeq_{down}$;
3. $\preccurlyeq_{down}$ and $\preceq$ are independent;
4. whenever $x \in F$ and $x \preccurlyeq_{up} y$, then $y \in F$;
5. F is a union of equivalence classes w.r.t. $\simeq$;
6. whenever $\xrightarrow{f} x$ and $x \preccurlyeq_{down} y$, then $\xrightarrow{f} y$.

□

We first obtain the following Lemma which shows that if the simulations satisfy the sufficient conditions, then the induced relation is indeed an equivalence.

Lemma 5. *Let $A = (Q, F, \delta)$ be a tree automaton. Consider two binary relations $\preccurlyeq_{down}$ and $\preceq$ which satisfies the above sufficient conditions, as well as their induced relation $\simeq$. We have that $\simeq$ is an equivalence relation on states of A.*

The above Lemma holds since Conditions 1 through 3 imply directly that $\preccurlyeq_{down}$ and $\preceq$ satisfy the premises needed by Lemma 4.

Next, we state that such an equivalence relation is sound and precise.

Theorem 1. *Let $A = (Q, F, \delta)$ be a tree automaton. Consider two binary relations $\preccurlyeq_{down}$ and $\preceq$ satisfying the above sufficient conditions, and let $\simeq$ be their induced relation. Let $A_{\simeq} = (Q/\simeq, F/\simeq, \delta_{\simeq})$ be the automaton obtained by merging the states of A according to $\simeq$. Then, $L(A_{\simeq}) = L(A)$.*

Theorem 1 can be used to relate the languages of H and $D_{\simeq}$.

We are now ready to prove the soundness and the completeness of our on-the-fly algorithm (assuming a computable equivalence relation $\simeq$).

Theorem 2. *Consider two binary relations on the states of H $\preccurlyeq_{down}$ and $\preceq$, satisfying the hypothesis of Theorem 1. Let $\simeq$ be their induced equivalence relation. If the algorithm terminates at step i, then the transducer $D_{\simeq}^{\leq i}$ accepts the same relation as $D_{\simeq}$.*

6.3   Sufficient Condition for Computability

The next step is to give conditions on the simulations which ensure that the induced equivalence relation is computable.

Definition 11. [Effective Relation]
A relation $\preceq$ is said to be effective if the image of a regular set w.r.t. $\preceq$ and w.r.t. $\preceq^{-1}$ is regular and computable.

Effective relations induce an equivalence relation which is also computable.

Theorem 3. *Let $\preceq_1$ and $\preceq_2$ be both reflexive, transitive, effective and independent. Let $\simeq$ be their induced equivalence. Then for any state x of H, we can compute its equivalence class $[x]$ w.r.t. $\simeq$.*

The theorem follows by definition of $\simeq$, and effectiveness [5] of $\preceq_1$ and $\preceq_2$.   □

An equivalence relation that satisfies hypothesis of Theorem 1 and Theorem 3 can be used in the on-the-fly algorithm of Section 5 to compute the transitive closure of a tree transducer. The next step is to provide a concrete example of such an equivalence. Because we are not able to compute the infinite representation of H, the equivalence will be directly computed from the powers of D provided by the on-the-fly algorithm.

7   Good Equivalence Relation

In this section, we provide concrete relations satisfying Theorem 1 and Theorem 3. We first introduce prefix- and suffix-copying states.

Definition 12. [Prefix-Copying State]
Given a transducer D, and a state q, we say that q is a prefix-copying state if for any tree $T = (S, \lambda) \in \mathrm{pref}(q)$, then for any node $n \in S$, $\lambda(n) = (f, f)$ for some symbol $f \in \Sigma$.

Definition 13. [Suffix-Copying State]
Given a transducer D, and a state q, we say that q is a suffix-copying state if for any context $C = (S_C, \lambda_C) \in \mathrm{suff}(q)$, then for any node $n \in S_C$ with $\lambda_C(n) \neq \square$, we have $\lambda_C(n) = (f, f)$ for some symbol $f \in \Sigma$.

We let Q_{pref} (resp. Q_{suff}) denote the set of prefix-copying states (resp. the set of suffix-copying states) of D and we assume that $Q_{pref} \cap Q_{suff} = \emptyset$. We let $Q_N = Q - Q_{pref} \cup Q_{suff}$.

We now define relations by the means of rewriting relation on the states of the history transducer.

---

[5] A state x of the history transducer is a word. The set $\{x\}$ is regular.

Definition 14. [Generated Relation]
Given a set S of pairs of states of H, we define the relation $\mapsto$ generated by S to be the smallest reflexive and transitive relation such that $\mapsto$ contains S, and $\mapsto$ is a congruence w.r.t. concatenation (i.e. if $x \mapsto y$, then for any w_1, w_2, we have $w_1 \cdot x \cdot w_2 \mapsto w_1 \cdot y \cdot w_2$).

Next, we find relations $\preceq$ and $\preccurlyeq_{down}$ that satisfy the sufficient conditions for computability (Theorem 3) and conditions for exactness of abstraction (Lemma 6.2).

Definition 15. [Simulation Relations]

- *We define $\preccurlyeq_{down}$ to be the downward simulation generated by all pairs of the form $(q_{pref} \cdot q_{pref}, q_{pref})$ and $(q_{pref}, q_{pref} \cdot q_{pref})$, where $q_{pref} \in Q_{pref}$.*
- *Let $\preccurlyeq_{up}^1$ be the maximal upward simulation computed on $D \cup D^2$. Then, we define $\preceq$ to be the relation generated by the maximal set $S \subseteq \preccurlyeq_{up}^1$ such that*
  - $(q_{suff} \cdot q_{suff}, q_{suff}) \in S$ iff $(q_{suff}, q_{suff} \cdot q_{suff}) \in S$
  - $(q \cdot q_{suff}, q) \in S$ iff $(q, q \cdot q_{suff}) \in S$
  - $(q_{suff} \cdot q, q) \in S$ iff $(q, q_{suff} \cdot q) \in S$

  where $q_{suff} \in Q_{suff}$, and $q \in Q_N$.

In the full version of the paper, we provide efficient algorithms for computing the simulations needed for Definition 15. Those algorithms are adapted from those provided by Henzinger *et al.* [HHK95] for the case of finite words.

Let us state that the simulations of Definition 15 satisfy the hypothesis needed by Theorems 1 and 3.

Lemma 6. *The following properties of $\preccurlyeq_{down}$ hold:*

1. *$\preccurlyeq_{down}$ is a downward simulation;*
2. *$\preccurlyeq_{down}$ is effective.*

Lemma 7. *The following properties of $\preceq$ hold:*

1. *$\preceq$ is included in an upward simulation;*
2. *$\preceq$ is effective.*

We now state that $\preceq$ and $\preccurlyeq_{down}$ are independent.

Lemma 8. *$\preceq$ and $\preccurlyeq_{down}$ are independent.*

Lemma 9. *The following holds:*

- *whenever $x \in F_H$ and $x \preccurlyeq_{up} y$, then $y \in F_H$;*
- *F_H is a union of equivalence classes w.r.t. $\simeq$;*
- *whenever $\xrightarrow{f} x$ and $x \preccurlyeq_{down} y$, then $\xrightarrow{f} y$.*

We conclude that $\preceq$ and $\preccurlyeq_{down}$ satisfy the hypothesis of Theorem 1 and Theorem 3 and can thus be used by the on-the-fly procedure presented in Section 5.

8   Computing Reachable Configurations

We now sketch the modifications needed to compute $R(D^+)(\phi_I)$ without computing D^+. When checking for safety properties, such a computation is known to be sufficient. Computing $R(D^+)(\phi_I)$ rather than D^+, can simply be done by lightly modifying the definition of the history transducer. Assume that we have constructed a tree automaton A_{ϕ_I} for ϕ_I, we replace the transducer run in the first "row" of the history transducer by a transducer that only accept trees from A_{ϕ_I} in input. Such a transducer can easily by constructed. Let D be the transducer representing the transition of the system, the restricted transducer is obtained by taking the intersection between D and $A_{\phi_I} \times T(\Sigma)$ where Σ is the ranked alphabet of the system. Computing $R(D^+)(\phi_I)$ is often less expensive than computing D^+ because it only considers reachable sets of states (see Section 9 for a time comparison). We have an example for which our technique can compute $R(D^+)(\phi_I)$ but cannot compute D^+.

9   Experimental Results

The techniques presented in this paper have been applied on several case studies using a prototype implementation that relies in part on the regular model checking tool (see www.regularmodelchecking.com).

In Table 1 we report the result of running our implementation on a number of parametrized protocols for which we have computed the set of reachable states as well as the transitive closure of their transition relation. A full description of the protocols is given in the full version of the paper.

In our previous work [AJMd02], we were able to handle the first three protocols of the table (computation times were very long, however).

The technique of [BT02] was manually applied to compute the set of reachable states of the tree-arbiter protocol (and of smaller examples). But, the reachability computation was done by first computing the transitive closure for each individual action, and then applying a classical forward reachability algorithm using these results. However, such an approach requires manual intervention: to make the reachability analysis terminate, it is often necessary to combine actions in a certain order, or even to accelerate combinations of individual actions. In our approach, all computations are entirely automatic.

Observe that we are not able to compute the transitive closure of the transition relation of the tree-arbiter protocol (in fact, we do not know if it is regular

Table 1. Results

Relation	$|D|$	$|D^+|$	max size	$|D^+(\phi_I)|$	max size
Simple Token Protocol	3	4	15	3	17
Two-Way Token Protocol	4	6	28	3	26
Percolate Protocol	4	6	40	3	21
Tree-arbiter Protocol	8	-	-	10	246
Leader Election Protocol	6	9	105	10	150

or not). However, we are already able to compute transitive closure of individual actions for this protocol as well as the reachable set of states with the technique of Section 8.

10 Conclusions and Future Work

In this paper, we have presented a technique for computing the transitive closure of a tree transducer.

This technique has been implemented and successfully tested on a number of protocols, several of which are beyond the capabilities of existing tree regular model checking techniques.

We believe that substantial efficiency improvement can be achieved by considering more general equivalence relations than the one defined in Section 7, and by refining our algorithms for computing simulation relations.

The restriction to structure-preserving tree transducers might be seen as a weakness of our approach. However, structure-preserving tree transducers can model the relation of many interesting parametrized network protocols. In the future, we plan to investigate the case of non structure-preserving tree transducers. One possible solution would be to use *padding* to simulate a structure-preserving behavior. This would allow us to extend our method to work on such systems as Process Rewrite Systems (PRS). PRS are useful when modeling systems with a dynamic behavior [BT03].

Finally, it would also be interesting to see if one can extend our simulations, as well as the algorithms for computing them, in order to efficiently implement the technique presented in [BT02] (the detection of an increment can be done by isolating part of the automaton with the help of (bi)simulations).

References

[ABH+97] R. Alur, R.K. Brayton, T.A. Henzinger, S. Qadeer, and S.K. Rajamani. Partial-order reduction in symbolic state space exploration. In O. Grumberg, editor, *Proc. 9th Int. Conf. on Computer Aided Verification*, volume 1254, pages 340–351, Haifa, Israel, 1997. Springer Verlag.

[AJMd02] P. A. Abdulla, B. Jonsson, P. Mahata, and J. d'Orso. Regular tree model checking. In *Proc. 14th Int. Conf. on Computer Aided Verification*, volume 2404 of *Lecture Notes in Computer Science*, 2002.

[AJNd03] P. A. Abdulla, B. Jonsson, M. Nilsson, and J. d'Orso. Algorithmic improvements in regular model checking. In *Proc. 15th Int. Conf. on Computer Aided Verification*, volume 2725 of *Lecture Notes in Computer Science*, pages 236–248, 2003.

[BHV04] A. Bouajjani, P. Habermehl, and T. Vojnar. Abstract regular model checking. In *CAV04*, Lecture Notes in Computer Science, Boston, July 2004. Springer-Verlag.

[BJNT00] A. Bouajjani, B. Jonsson, M. Nilsson, and T. Touili. Regular model checking. In Emerson and Sistla, editors, *Proc. 12th Int. Conf. on Computer Aided Verification*, volume 1855 of *Lecture Notes in Computer Science*, pages 403–418. Springer Verlag, 2000.

[BLW03]   B. Boigelot, A. Legay, and P. Wolper. Iterating transducers in the large. In *Proc.* 15th *Int. Conf. on Computer Aided Verification*, volume 2725 of *Lecture Notes in Computer Science*, pages 223–235, 2003.

[BLW04]   B. Boigelot, A. Legay, and P. Wolper. Omega regular model checking. In *Proc. TACAS '04,* 10th *Int. Conf. on Tools and Algorithms for the Construction and Analysis of Systems*, Lecture Notes in Computer Science, 2004.

[BT02]   A. Bouajjani and T. Touili. Extrapolating Tree Transformations. In *Proc.* 14th *Int. Conf. on Computer Aided Verification*, volume 2404 of *Lecture Notes in Computer Science*, 2002.

[BT03]   A. Bouajjani and T. Touili. Reachability analysis of process rewrite systems. In *Proc. Int. Conf. on Foundations of Software Technology and Theoritical Computer Science (FSTTCS'03)*, Lecture Notes in Computer Science, 2003.

[CDG⁺99] H. Common, M. Dauchet, R. Gilleron, F. Jacquemard, D. Lugiez, S. Tison, and M. Tommasi. *Tree Automata Techniques and Applications.* not yet published, October 1999.

[DLS01]   D. Dams, Y. Lakhnech, and M. Steffen. Iterating transducers. In G. Berry, H. Comon, and A. Finkel, editors, *Computer Aided Verification*, volume 2102 of *Lecture Notes in Computer Science*, 2001.

[HHK95]   M. Henzinger, T. Henzinger, and P. Kopke. Computing simulations on finite and infinite graphs. In *Proc.* 36th *Annual Symp. Foundations of Computer Science*, pages 453–463, 1995.

[KMM⁺01] Y. Kesten, O. Maler, M. Marcus, A. Pnueli, and E. Shahar. Symbolic model checking with rich assertional languages. *Theoretical Computer Science*, 256:93–112, 2001.

[Tho90]   W. Thomas. Automata on infinite objects. In *Handbook of Theoretical Computer Science, Volume B: Formal Methods and Semantics*, pages 133–192, 1990.

Using Language Inference to Verify Omega-Regular Properties

Abhay Vardhan, Koushik Sen, Mahesh Viswanathan, and Gul Agha *

Dept. of Computer Science, Univ. of Illinois at Urbana-Champaign, USA
{vardhan, ksen, vmahesh, agha}@cs.uiuc.edu

Abstract. A novel machine learning based approach was proposed recently as a complementary technique to the acceleration based methods for verifying infinite state systems. In this method, the set of states satisfying a fixpoint property is learnt as opposed to being iteratively computed. We extend the machine learning based approach to verifying general ω-regular properties that include both safety and liveness. To achieve this, we first develop a new fixpoint based characterization for the verification of ω-regular properties. Using this characterization, we present a general framework for verifying infinite state systems. We then instantiate our approach to the context of regular model checking where states are represented as strings over a finite alphabet and the transition relation of the system is given as a finite state transducer; unlike previous learning based algorithms, we make no assumption about the transducer being length-preserving. Using Angluin's L* algorithm for learning regular languages, we develop an algorithm for verification of ω-regular properties of such infinite state systems. The algorithm is a complete verification procedure for systems for whom the fixpoint can be represented as a regular set. We have implemented the technique in a tool called LEVER and use it to analyze some examples.

1 Introduction

Automated verification of systems with respect to temporal properties involves computing fixpoints of functionals on sets of states of the system. This is often calculated by iteratively computing approximations to the fixpoint, until the process converges. When verifying infinite state systems, this iterative computation must necessarily be performed symbolically, using a suitably chosen representation for sets of states. However, since fixpoint computations are no longer guaranteed to converge within finitely many steps, a variety of *acceleration methods*, such as widening [15, 4] and abstraction [3], have been proposed. These methods have been used successfully to verify many practical examples

---

* The third author was supported in part by DARPA/AFOSR MURI Award F49620-02-1-0325 and NSF 04-29639. The other three authors were supported in part by DARPA IPTO TASK Program (contract F30602-00-2-0586), ONR Grant N00014-02-1-0715, and Motorola Grant MOTOROLA RPS #23 ANT.

N. Halbwachs and L. Zuck (Eds.): TACAS 2005, LNCS 3440, pp. 45–60, 2005.

and can be used to obtain complete verification procedures for special subclasses of systems (such as bounded local depth or simple transition relations [10]).

Recently, a complementary, machine learning based approach has been independently proposed in [17] and [9]. In this approach, the fixpoint is *learnt* from examples of states belonging to the fixpoint and states not belonging to the fixpoint. The advantage of the learning based approach is that termination does not depend on how long it takes to converge to the fixpoint, and hence this approach yields a complete verification procedure even when the fixpoint does not converge within a finite bound. Second, because intermediate approximations to the fixpoint are never computed, it avoids the space overhead of storing fixpoint approximations that may have a large symbolic representation. Preliminary experimental results based on this approach are promising [17, 9, 16].

In this paper, we present a general framework to verify infinite state systems with respect to specifications presented as non-deterministic Büchi automata. One of the central requirements of our framework is a learning algorithm that can learn concepts encoded using a chosen symbolic representation. The learning algorithm is used to learn the fixpoint of a specific function, such that the initial state of the system belongs to the learnt set if and only if the system satisfies the specification. This yields a complete verification procedure, *provided* the fixpoint can be represented in the chosen representation. We then instantiate the framework to the specific context of regular model checking, where states are encoded as strings over some finite alphabet, and the system's transition relation is presented as a transducer over such strings. Unlike previous work in this area, we *do not* assume that the transducer is length preserving. If the fixpoint of our functional can be expressed as a regular language, then our algorithm is guaranteed to terminate and either prove the system to be correct or demonstrate that it is faulty. We use Angluin's L* [2] algorithm to learn the regular set representation of the fixpoint.

The results presented here significantly advance the state of the art in learning based verification. First, our method verifies ω-regular properties which can express safety as well as liveness properties. This generalizes our previous work on safety properties reported in [17, 16]. Second, our instantiation to regular model checking is not confined to analyzing systems such as FIFO automata. We also do not need the transition relation to be restricted to be length-preserving as has been assumed in some other approaches such as [9]. Moreover, our general framework can potentially be used to verify systems symbolically represented using *polyhedra* or *ellipsoids*, not just regular languages, provided appropriate learning algorithms can be plugged in. Third, our algorithm for checking containment of the system's trace language in the specification automata's language, is not based on discovering loops where final states of the automata are visited infinitely often (as is the case in [9]). Thus, our algorithm will successfully identify faulty systems, even when there is no ultimately periodic execution that witnesses the violation. This is important because for general infinite state systems, it is often the case that there is no such ultimately periodic execution witnessing the violation of a liveness property. Finally, since we use Angluin's L* algorithm, we are guaranteed to not only learn the smallest automaton representing the fixpoint, but are also guaranteed to only make polynomially many calls to the learning algorithm.

The rest of the paper is organized as follows. We first outline results that are closely related to this paper. In Section 2, we introduce basic concepts and notation that are used in the paper. The general learning based verification framework for ω-regular languages is presented in Section 3. We first identify a functional whose fixpoint helps us verify ω-regular properties (Section 3.1) and then show how a learning algorithm can be used to compute the fixpoint of this functional (Section 3.2). In Section 4, we instantiate this general framework to the specific context of regular model checking, where states are represented as strings over a finite alphabet and the system's transition relation is represented as a transducer. We give detailed algorithms for the various operations that are needed in the learning based algorithm. Finally, in Section 5 we discuss the analysis of two examples using the implementation of this verification method in a tool called LEVER and present our conclusions in Section 6.

Related Work. We introduced the learning to verify approach in [17], where we used RPNI [12] to learn the regular set from positive and negative examples without active queries. In [16], we improved our learning procedure for FIFO automata by using a more powerful active learning framework and a better encoding for witnesses for membership queries. Concurrently and independently of our work, Habermehl *et al.* [9] have also proposed a learning based approach for verification of systems whose transition can be represented by a length-preserving transducer. The algorithm presented there crucially depends on the length-preserving nature of the transition relation for its completeness. An earlier use of regular inference techniques for reachability in parameterized rings of processes also appears in [8]. Verification of ω-regular properties for infinite state systems has also been addressed in [4] and [13]. Abdulla *et al.* [1] present a "two-dimensional" modal logic called LTL(MSO) for verification of liveness properties. The above approaches rely on loop detection for checking liveness and assume that the transition relation is length preserving. Recently, Bouajjani *et al.* [5] have analyzed liveness properties of non-length preserving systems using a notion of simulation between states.

2   Preliminaries

In this section, we present the learning framework that we will consider in this paper and basic definitions of Kripke structures and Büchi automata.

2.1   Learning with Membership and Equivalence Queries

A learning algorithm is usually set in a framework which describes the types of input data and queries available to the learner. In the framework of *active learning* [2]), the learning algorithm is given access to a knowledgeable teacher, often called a *minimally adequate teacher*. The knowledgeable teacher can be thought of as a pair of oracles: a *membership oracle* and an *equivalence oracle*. The membership oracle provides answers to queries about whether an example belongs to the concept being learnt or not. The equivalence oracle is a more powerful oracle which answers question about whether a hypothesis proposed by the learning algorithm is indeed equivalent to the concept being learnt. If at some point the learning algorithm's hypothesis is deemed correct by the equivalence oracle then the learning process stops. If on the other hand, the learner submits a hypothesis which is not equivalent to the target concept, the equivalence oracle not only says no, but also provides a counter-example to demonstrate when the hypothesis is wrong. The counter-example is either an example belonging to the hypothesis but not to the target concept, or it is an example belonging to the target concept but not to the submitted hypothesis. The active learning framework can be contrasted with the *passive learning* framework where the learner is simply provided a set of examples labeled as either belonging to the target concept or not; there is no knowledgeable teacher involved. The active learning algorithm is a powerful framework that in many cases admits efficient learning of concepts which otherwise cannot be learnt passively.

Our learning based verification approach uses a learning algorithm in the active learning framework. In particular, when we instantiate our learning based approach to verify a class of infinite state systems, we use a classical algorithm due to Angluin [2] which learns the smallest automaton recognizing the regular language, when it is allowed to interact with a knowledgeable teacher. Angluin's L* algorithm is also highly efficient; it can be shown that the number of queries made to the membership and equivalence oracles by the learning algorithm is bounded by a polynomial in the size of the smallest DFA recognizing the regular language. The main idea behind Angluin's L* algorithm is to systematically explore strings in the alphabet for membership and create a DFA with minimum number of states to make a conjecture for the target set. If the conjecture is incorrect, the string returned by the teacher is used to make corrections, possibly after more membership queries. The algorithm maintains a prefix closed set S representing different possible states of the target DFA, a set SA for the transition function consisting of strings from S extended with one letter of the alphabet, and a suffix closed set E denoting *experiments* to distinguish between states. An *observation table* with rows from $(S \cup SA)$ and columns from E stores results of the membership queries for strings in $(S \cup SA).E$ and is used to create the DFA for a conjecture.

2.2   Kripke Structures and Büchi Automaton

We use Kripke structure to model the system being verified and Büchi automaton for the specification. We now formally define these.

Kripke Structure. A *Kripke structure* K is a quintuple $(S^k, \Sigma, R^k, S_0^k, \mathcal{L})$ where S^k is the set of (possibly infinite) states, Σ is a finite alphabet, $R^k \subseteq S^k \times S^k$ is the (total) transition relation, $S_0^k \subseteq S^k$ is the set of initial states and $\mathcal{L} : S^k \to \Sigma$ is the labeling function. We restrict ourselves to Kripke structures that are finitely branching, *i.e.*, for any state s, the set $\{s' \mid R^k(s, s')\}$ is finite. We say $s \to s'$ iff $(s, s') \in R^k$. A *path starting from state* s is an infinite sequence $s_0, s_1, s_2 \ldots$ such that $s = s_0$ and for every i, $(s_i, s_{i+1}) \in R^k$. A *path* of a Kripke structure K is just a path starting from some initial state $s \in S_0^k$. The set of all paths of K will be denoted by $\mathcal{P}(K)$. For a path $\pi = s_0, s_1, s_2, \ldots$, $KTrace(\pi)$ is the sequence of labels $\ell_0, \ell_1, \ell_2, \ldots$ such that for every i, $\mathcal{L}(s_i) = \ell_i$. For a set of paths Π, $KTrace(\Pi)$ is taken to be $\{KTrace(\pi) \mid \pi \in \Pi\}$.

Büchi Automaton. A *Büchi automaton* [14] M is a quintuple $(S^m, \Sigma, S_0^m, \delta, F^m)$ where S^m is a finite set of states, $S_0^m \subseteq S^m$ is the set of initial states, δ : $S^m \times \Sigma \to 2^{S^m}$ is the transition function, $F^m \subseteq S^m$ is a set of *accepting* states. For an infinite word $v = v_0, v_1, v_2, \ldots \in \Sigma^\omega$, the run of M on v is a sequence of states $\rho = s_0, s_1, s_2, \ldots$, such that $s_{i+1} \in \delta(s_i, v_i)$ for every i. An infinite word v is accepted by M if there is some run ρ of M on v such that some state $s \in F^m$ appears infinitely often in ρ. The language accepted by M, which we denote by $\mathcal{S}(M)$, is the set of all words v accepted by M. A set of infinite words L is said to be ω-*regular* if there is some Büchi automaton such that $L = \mathcal{S}(M)$.

CTL* Various modal and temporal logics such as CTL^* are often used for specifying the acceptable behaviors of a system. For a comprehensive introduction to this subject, the reader is referred to [7]. In this paper we will be concerned with only one specific CTL^* property, namely $EGFp$. A state s in a Kripke structure K satisfies $EGFp$ if and only if there exists a path $\pi = s_0, s_1, s_2, \ldots$ starting from s such that for all i, $\mathcal{L}(s_j) = p$ for some $j \geq i$; in other words, the path encounters states labelled p infinitely often. When s satisfies $EGFp$, we will say $s, K \models EGFp$; when K is clear from the context we will simply write this as $s \models EGFp$. We will denote by $[EGFp]_K$ the set of all states s, such that $s, K \models EGFp$.

Satisfying Specifications. Similar to the traditional approach used in model checking using automata theory, we assume that the system specification is given in terms of the *bad behaviors* that the implementation must not exhibit. The bad behaviors are specified using a Büchi automaton. For a Kripke structure K and a Büchi automaton M, K is said to be *correct* with respect to M iff $KTrace(\mathcal{P}(K)) \cap \mathcal{S}(M) = \emptyset$. Since Büchi automata are closed under complementation even if we are given the specification as an automaton M_g specifying the *good behaviors*, we can complement M_g to get M which specifies the bad behaviors.

We will reduce the problem of checking if the system satisfies the specification to the problem of checking if the CTL^* formula $EGFp$ is satisfied. In order to do this, we first define the Kripke structure obtained by taking the cross product of a Kripke structure and a Büchi automaton.

Definition 1. *The cross-product of a Büchi automaton* $M = (S^m, \Sigma, S_0^m, \delta, F^m)$ *and a Kripke structure* $K = (S^k, \Sigma, R^k, S_0^k, \mathcal{L})$ *is the Kripke structure* $M \times K = (S^m \times S^k, \{f, \tilde{f}\}, R', S_0^m \times S_0^k, \mathcal{L}')$. *Here,* $((s_1^m, s_1^k), (s_2^m, s_2^k)) \in R'$ *if and only if* $(s_1^k, s_2^k) \in R^k$ *and* $s_2^m \in \delta(s_1^m, \mathcal{L}(s_1^k))$. *A state* (s^m, s^k) *in* $M \times K$ *is labelled by* f *if* $s^m \in F^m$ *and by* $\tilde{f}$ *otherwise.*

Lemma 1. *There is a path* $\pi = (s_0^m, s_0^k)(s_1^m, s_1^k)(s_2^m, s_2^k)\ldots$ *in the product Kripke structure* $M \times K$ *if and only if* $s_0^m s_1^m s_2^m \ldots$ *is a run in the Büchi automaton* M *on* $KTrace(s_0^k s_1^k s_2^k \ldots)$ *where* $s_0^k s_1^k s_2^k \ldots$ *is a path in* K.

Proposition 1. *For an automaton* M, $KTrace(\mathcal{P}(K)) \cap \mathcal{S}(M) = \emptyset$ *if and only if* $[\![EGFf]\!]_{M \times K} \cap (S_0^m \times S_0^k) = \emptyset$ *(In other words, no initial state of* $M \times K$ *satisfies* $EGFf$*).*

Proof. Suppose $KTrace(\mathcal{P}(K)) \cap \mathcal{S}(M) \neq \emptyset$. Then there is a path $\pi \in \mathcal{P}(K)$ such that $KTrace(\mathcal{P}(K))$ is accepted by M. Let $s_0^m s_1^m s_2^m \ldots$ be the accepting run in M. By Lemma 1, there is a path $\pi = (s_0^m, s_0^k)(s_1^m, s_1^k)(s_2^m, s_2^k)\ldots$ in $M \times K$. But since an accepting run of a Büchi automata visits a accepting state infinitely often, then by the product construction, the path $\pi = (s_0^m, s_0^k)(s_1^m, s_1^k)(s_2^m, s_2^k)\ldots$ in $M \times K$ visits states labelled f infinitely often. Thus, $M \times K$ satisfies $EGFf$.

If $M \times K$ satisfies $EGFf$ then there is a path $\pi = (s_0^m, s_0^k)(s_1^m, s_1^k)(s_2^m, s_2^k)\ldots$ which infinitely often visits states labeled f. By Lemma 1, there is a run $s_0^m s_1^m s_2^m \ldots$ in M on $KTrace(s_0^k s_1^k s_2^k \ldots)$. This is an accepting run because the product construction labels a state $(s^m, s^k) \in M \times K$ as f only if s^m is an accepting state. But then M accepts $KTrace(s_0^k s_1^k s_2^k \ldots)$. Hence, $KTrace(\mathcal{P}(K)) \cap \mathcal{S}(M) \neq \emptyset$. ∎

3 Learning to Verify ω-Regular Properties

In this section, we present a general framework to verify a system described as a Kripke structure K. We assume that we are given a Büchi automaton M that describes the set of behaviors that the system K *must not* exhibit. Recall, that in Section 2.2, we observed that the problem of checking if $KTrace(\mathcal{P}(K)) \cap \mathcal{S}(M) = \emptyset$ can be reduced to the problem of checking if an initial state of $M \times K$ satisfies $EGFf$. We first characterize $[\![EGFf]\!]$ using fixpoints of a functional that we define in Section 3.1. Next, we show that the fixpoint is unique and has certain key properties that we need for our problem. Finally, we will show how a learning algorithm can be used to learn the fixpoint, and therefore help verify if K satisfies M.

3.1 Fixpoint Characterization of $EGFf$

From now on, we assume that we are interested in checking if some initial state of a Kripke structure $K = (S, \{f, \tilde{f}\}, R, S_0, \mathcal{L})$ satisfies $EGFf$. Traditionally, the fixpoint characterization of $EGFf$ is given by $\nu Z_1.EX(\mu Z_2.Z_1 \wedge (f \vee EXZ_2))$ (see [6]). Notice that this formula involves nesting of the fixpoint operators which we wish to avoid in our learning-based technique for technical reasons. Therefore, we develop a novel characterization of $EGFf$ that does not use nesting. Further, we also obtain a unique fixpoint which make it possible to answer equivalence queries exactly. As far as we know, this is a new characterization and may be of independent interest. We now proceed to describe this fixpoint.

Let X be a set of triples (s, i, j) such that $s \in S$ and $i, j \in \mathbb{N}$, where $\mathbb{N}$ denotes the set of natural numbers. We define the functional $\Gamma : 2^{S \times \mathbb{N} \times \mathbb{N}} \to 2^{S \times \mathbb{N} \times \mathbb{N}}$ such that $\Gamma(X) = \Gamma_1(X) \cup \Gamma_2(X) \cup \Gamma_3(X)$, where

$$\Gamma_1(X) = \{(s, 0, j) \mid \mathcal{L}(s) = f \text{ and } j \in \mathbb{N}\}$$
$$\Gamma_2(X) = \{(s, i, j) \mid \mathcal{L}(s) = \tilde{f} \text{ and } \exists s'. s \to s' \ \exists j' < j. (s', i, j') \in X\}$$
$$\Gamma_3(X) = \{(s, i, j) \mid \mathcal{L}(s) = f \text{ and } \exists s'. s \to s' \ \exists j' < j. (s', i - 1, j') \in X\}$$

The intuition behind the definition of Γ is as follows. Consider a property $\eta_f^{i,j}$ such that a state s satisfies $\eta_f^{i,j}$ if there is a path of length j such that we encounter (at least) $i+1$ states that are labeled f. Formally, $s \models \eta_f^{i,j}$ iff there is a finite path $s_0, s_1, s_2, \ldots, s_j$ from state s such that there are indices $k_1, k_2, \ldots k_{i+1}$ such that $\mathcal{L}(s_{k_\ell}) = f$ for every $1 \le \ell \le i + 1$. Now the intuition behind Γ is that if X is a fixpoint of Γ and $(s, i, j) \in X$ then $s \models \eta_f^{i,j}$.

Clearly, Γ is monotonic and hence has fixpoints. In addition, we can show that Γ has a unique fixpoint. This is the objective of the next few observations.

Lemma 2. *Let X be a fixpoint of Γ. The following two facts hold about elements of X.*

1. *If $\mathcal{L}(s) = \tilde{f}$ then $\forall i \ge 0. \forall j. (s, i, j) \in X$ if and only if $\exists s'. s \to s' \ \exists j' < j. (s', i, j') \in X$*
2. *If $\mathcal{L}(s) = f$ then $\forall i \ge 1. \forall j. (s, i, j) \in X$ if and only if $\exists s'. s \to s' \ \exists j' < j. (s', i - 1, j') \in X$*

Proof. The results follow from the definition of the fixpoint under Γ. We illustrate this for one direction of 1; the proof for other cases is similar. Suppose $\mathcal{L}(s) = \tilde{f}$ and suppose $(s, i, j) \in X$. If $\exists s'. s \to s' \ \exists j' < j. (s', i, j') \in X$ does not hold then $(s, i, j) \notin \Gamma(X)$ which contradicts the fact that X is a fixpoint.

Proposition 2. *If X_1 is a fixpoint of Γ and X_2 is also a fixpoint of Γ then $X_1 \subseteq X_2$. Hence there is a unique fixpoint of Γ.*

Proof. Let $(s, i, j) \in X_1$. We show that then $(s, i, j) \in X_2$. The proof will proceed by induction on i and j.

Consider the base case when $i = 0$. We will prove the claim by induction on j. Clearly $(s, 0, 0) \in X_1$ iff $\mathcal{L}(s) = f$ iff $(s, 0, 0) \in X_2$. Suppose the claim holds for $(s, 0, j')$ for all $j' < j$. Consider $(s, 0, j) \in X_1$. If $\mathcal{L}(s) = f$ then $(s, 0, j) \in X_2$ for every j by the definition of Γ_1. Now if $\mathcal{L}(s) = \tilde{f}$ then by Lemma 2, it must be the case that there is s' and j' such that $s \to s'$, $j' < j$ and $(s', 0, j') \in X_1$. By the induction hypothesis, we know that $(s', 0, j') \in X_2$. Again, by Lemma 2, this means that $(s, 0, j) \in X_2$.

Assume that for every $i' < i$ and for every j', if $(s, i', j') \in X_1$ then $(s, i', j') \in X_2$. The induction step for (s, i, j) is proved by induction on j. For the base case when $j = 0$, we observe that $(s, i, 0)$ is not a member of any fixpoint of Γ (Lemma 2). The proof of the induction step is similar to the case of $i = 0$, and is skipped in the interests of space.

By symmetry, $X_2 \subseteq X_1$, hence $X_1 = X_2$ giving the uniqueness of the fixpoint for Γ.

Henceforth, we use X to denote the *unique* fixpoint of Γ. We are now ready to state the proposition that formally proves our intuition behind defining Γ.

Proposition 3. *Suppose X is the fixpoint of Γ. Then, $(s, i, j) \in X$ if and only if $s \models \eta_f^{i,j}$.*

Proof. ($\Rightarrow$) We prove this by induction on i and j. For the base case consider $i = 0$. We now induct on j. When $j = 0$, $(s, 0, 0) \in X$ iff $\mathcal{L}(s) = f$, which means that there is a path of length 0 starting from s where we encounter one state labeled f. Now suppose $j > 0$. If $\mathcal{L}(s) = f$ then it trivially follows that there is a path of length $j > 0$ starting from s where we encounter at least one state labeled f. Suppose $\mathcal{L}(s) = \tilde{f}$. Then by Lemma 2, there is s' and $j' < j$ such that $s \to s'$ and $(s', 0, j') \in X$. Then by induction hypothesis, $s' \models \eta_f^{0,j'}$ which then implies that $s \models \eta_f^{0,j}$.

Consider $i > 0$. Once again we induct on j. Observe that since by Lemma 2, $(s, i, 0)$ is not in any fixpoint when $i > 0$, the claim holds vacuously. The induction step goes through in manner similar to the case of $i = 0$ and the proof is therefore skipped.

($\Leftarrow$) We prove the converse direction also by induction. Consider $i = 0$. If $j = 0$ and $s \models \eta_f^{0,0}$ then it must be the case that $\mathcal{L}(s) = f$. This means that $(s, 0, 0) \in X$. Suppose $j > 0$ and $s \models \eta_f^{0,j}$. If $\mathcal{L}(s) = f$ then once again $(s, 0, j) \in X$. If $\mathcal{L}(s) = \tilde{f}$ then it must be the case that there is some s' such that $s \to s'$ and $s' \models \eta_f^{0,j-1}$. Thus by induction hypothesis $(s', 0, j - 1) \in X$ and therefore by Lemma 2, $(s, 0, j) \in X$.

Consider $i > 0$ and $s \models \eta_f^{i,j}$. If $\mathcal{L}(s) = f$ then it is definitely the case that there is s' such that $s \to s'$ and $s' \models \eta_f^{i-1,j-1}$. By induction hypothesis, $(s', i - 1, j - 1) \in X$, and that implies (by Lemma 2) that $(s, i, j) \in X$. On the other hand, if $\mathcal{L}(s) = \tilde{f}$ then we can conclude that there is s' such that $s \to s'$ and $s' \models \eta_f^{i,j-1}$. By induction hypothesis this means that $(s', i, j - 1) \in X$, and by this we can conclude that $(s, i, j) \in X$ because of Lemma 2.

We are now ready to characterize $[\![EGFf]\!]$ in terms of the fixpoint X of Γ. This is the formal content of Proposition 4. But before presenting that proposition, we need a technical definition.

Definition 2. $\sigma(X) = \{s \mid \forall i \exists j.(s, i, j) \in X\}$.

Proposition 4. *Suppose X is the fixpoint of Γ. Then $s \in \sigma(X)$ if and only if $s \models EGFf$.*

Proof. ($\Leftarrow$) Suppose $s \models EGFf$. Then there is a path $\pi = s_0, s_1, s_2, \ldots$ starting from s, such that for infinitely many k, $\mathcal{L}(s_k) = f$. Define j_i to be the least k such that $\mathcal{L}(s_k) = f$ and there are $i + 1$ states before s_k on π that are also labeled f. It is clear that $s \models \eta_f^{i,j_i}$ and therefore by Proposition 3, $(s, i, j_i) \in X$. Hence $s \in \sigma(X)$.

($\Rightarrow$) Suppose $s \in \sigma(X)$. By definition, for every i, there is some j such that $(s, i, j) \in X$. Hence, by Proposition 3, $s \models \eta_f^{i,j}$. Construct a tree with root s, containing edges appearing in all shortest paths that witness s satisfying $\eta_f^{i,j}$. A few observations about this tree are in order. First, the tree is finite branching; an immediate consequence of the Kripke structure being finite branching. Second, all leaves are labeled f since the tree is constructed using the shortest witnesses. Third, if s' is an internal node in the tree then every path from s' in the tree will reach a state labeled f. Finally, this tree has infinitely many vertices. By König's Lemma, there must be an infinite path in the tree. Let us call this infinite path π. We claim that this infinite path witnesses $EGFf$. Consider any state s' on path π. Since s' is an internal node in the tree, it must be the case that on every path from s' in the tree we encounter a state labeled f. In particular on the path π, we encounter a state labeled f beyond s'. Thus π has infinitely many states labeled f.

3.2 Learning Fixpoints

We are now ready to present our general framework for verifying ω-regular properties using learning. We make the following assumptions about the system K being verified.

1. The system K can be simulated from any state.
2. There is a convenient symbolic representation $\mathcal{R}$ for sets consisting of triples (s, i, j), where s is a state and i, j are natural numbers. This means that the representation is closed under complementation and decision procedures are available for membership in a set, containment of one set in another, and emptiness of a set.
3. Given the representation of a set Y of triples (s, i, j) and a state s it is possible to check if $s \in \sigma(Y)$
4. Given a representation of a set Y of triples (s, i, j) it is possible to compute the representation of $\Gamma(Y)$
5. There is an active learning algorithm for concepts encoded in the symbolic representation.

Based on these assumptions, we show how learning can be used to verify ω-regular properties. The central idea is to use the learning algorithm to learn the fixpoint X of Γ. After we learn the fixpoint, based on Propositions 1 and 4, we can reliably answer whether or not the system satisfies the specification. Thus to verify ω-regular properties using learning, we need to implement the membership and equivalence oracles that the learning algorithm needs.

Proposition 3 suggests a method to answer membership queries about whether (s, i, j) belongs to the fixpoint X of Γ. To check if (s, i, j) belongs to X, we will simulate the system for j steps starting from state s and check if on some path, we encounter $i + 1$ states labeled f. Further, given a representation for a set Y, we can also answer whether Y is in fact equal to X. Since Γ has a unique fixpoint, all we need to do is check if $\Gamma(Y) = Y$. If $\Gamma(Y) \neq Y$ then the equivalence query must provide a counterexample. In other words, we need to produce an element in the symmetric difference of Y and X. This can be done as follows for the different possible cases.

- $\Gamma(Y) \setminus Y \neq \emptyset$. Let $l = (s, i, j)$ be some element in this set. If $l = (s, 0, 0)$ then $l \in X$, because the only way we can have any $(s, 0, 0)$ in $\Gamma(Y)$ is if $\mathcal{L}(s) = f$.

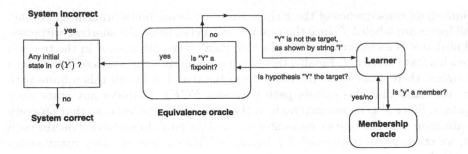

Fig. 1. Verification procedure

In this case, l is in X and hence in $X \oplus Y$. If $l = (s, 0, j)$ and $\mathcal{L}(s) = f$ then once again $l \in X$ and hence in $X \oplus Y$. If $l = (s, i, j)$ for some $j \neq 0$, we can check if $l \in X$ using the membership query. If yes, then l is also in $X \oplus Y$ and we are done. Otherwise, $l \in \Gamma(Y)$ because of the existence of some triple $(s', i', j') \in Y$ which satisfies the conditions Γ_2 or Γ_3. (s', i', j') cannot be in X otherwise (s, i, j) would have to be in X. Hence $(s', i', j') \in X \oplus Y$.

– $\Gamma(Y) \subsetneq Y$. From standard fixpoint theory, since X happens to also be the least fixpoint under Γ, it must be the intersection of all prefixpoints of Γ (a set Z is a prefixpoint if it *shrinks* under the functional Γ, i.e. $\Gamma(Z) \subseteq Z$). Now, Y is clearly a prefixpoint. Applying Γ to both sides of the equation $\Gamma(Y) \subsetneq Y$ and using monotonicity of Γ, we get $\Gamma(\Gamma(Y)) \subsetneq \Gamma(Y)$. Thus, $\Gamma(Y)$ is also a prefixpoint. Let l be some string in the set $Y \setminus \Gamma(Y)$. Since l is outside the intersection of two prefixpoints, it is not in the least fixpoint X. Hence, l is in $X \oplus Y$.

Once we have learned the fixpoint X, we can verify if the initial states of the Kripke structure satisfy $EGFf$ using Proposition 4. By Proposition 1, this provides an answer to the verification problem. The overall procedure is summarized in Figure 1. This procedure yields a complete verification method when the fixpoint X of Γ can be symbolically represented in the chosen representation. This is the content of the following theorem.

Theorem 1. *If the fixpoint X of Γ can be represented using the chosen symbolic data structure and a learning algorithm using membership and equivalence queries is available for this data structure, the verification procedure is guaranteed to terminate and correctly infer whether the system satisfies the specification.*

The theorem follows from observations made in this section.

4   Infinite State Systems Using Regular Languages

In Section 3.2 we presented a general set of conditions under which we can use a learning based approach to verify systems with respect to ω-regular properties.

In this section, we demonstrate this can be achieved within the context of using regular languages to represent sets of states.

Regular sets are a popular symbolic representation for sets of states of for infinite state systems. *Regular model checking* [4] has been applied to modeling *parameterized systems, FIFO automata, systems with integer variables* and *push down stacks*. Based on the practical success that has been enjoyed by *regular model checking* and the efficient learning algorithms available for regular languages, we apply our learning technique on regular sets. As mentioned before, we use Angluin's L^* [2] algorithm.

We assume that the states of the system can be encoded as strings over some finite alphabet ρ^k. The transition relation is given as a transducer τ^k which takes an input string corresponding to some state s and outputs a string for the state related to s. The transition relation is assumed to be total. The set of initial states is given by a regular set S_0^k and the set of states with a label a is given as regular sets S_a^k. Let K be the Kripke structure defined by the above sets.

4.1 Construction of the Product Kripke Structure

Let M be the Büchi automaton specifying the bad behaviors that must not be exhibited by the system. Since ω-regular languages are powerful enough to express fairness constraints, we assume that such constraints, if any, are already embodied in the Büchi automaton. We now show how to construct the product Kripke structure $M \times K$. We extend the alphabet ρ^k to $\rho^{M \times K}$ with new symbols b_{s^m}, one for each state s^m in M. A state (s^m, s^k) in $M \times K$ is encoded as a string with the first letter as b_{s^m} and the remaining part of the string as the original string encoding s^k. Initial states in $S_0^{M \times K}$ are given by concatenating a letter b_{s_0} for $s_0 \in S_0^m$ and a string in S_0^k. The set of states $S_{\tilde{f}}$ (resp. S_f) labelled with $\tilde{f}$ (resp. f) is given by a DFA which looks at the first letter of the input string and accepts if this is b_{s^m} for some $s^m \notin F^m$ (resp. $s^m \in F^m$). The transducer $\tau^{M \times K}$ representing the transition relation for $M \times K$ is a bit more tedious but can be constructed using standard automata operations.

Henceforth, we restrict our attention to the Kripke structure $M \times K$. For ease of notation, we drop the superscript $M \times K$ in τ, S_0, ρ and so on.

4.2 Symbolic Representation for the Fixpoint X

As discussed in Section 3.2, we now need to learn the fixpoint X of the functional Γ. In general, X is a subset of $\rho^* \times \mathbb{N} \times \mathbb{N}$. To encode X as a regular set we use the alphabet ρ^X given by $(\rho \cup \{\bot\}) \times \{0, \bot\} \times \{0, \bot\}$. This is the alphabet that will be used by Angluin's L^* learning algorithm. Here 0 is a unary symbol for natural numbers and $\bot$ is a new "filler" symbol. An element (s, i, j) is encoded as string over ρ^X such that projecting the symbols on the first component gives us s (the $\bot$ symbols are ignored); and projecting on the second and third components gives i and j respectively in unary notation.

4.3   Membership and Equivalence Queries

As discussed before, membership queries for X can be answered using Proposition 3. For answering equivalence queries, we need a symbolic way to calculate $\Gamma(X)$. Apart from the standard operations on regular set we define the following.

Definition 3. *Given Y a set of strings in the alphabet of ρ^X, define*

$$Inc^i(Y) = \{(s,i,j) \mid (s,i-1,j) \in Y\}$$
$$Inc^j(Y) = \{(s,i,j) \mid (s,i,j-1) \in Y\}$$

Given a DFA M_Y for Y, the DFA for $Inc^i(Y)$ can be constructed as follows. $Inc^i(Y)$ keeps two copies of M_Y, with initial states in the first copy and final states in the second copy. Any transition t with the $\perp$ symbol for the i component in the first copy is changed to a transition to the state corresponding to the target of t in the second copy and the i component symbol is changed to 0. We also add a transition from a state in the first copy which used to be final in M_Y to the corresponding state in the second copy with symbol $(\perp, 0, \perp)$. A similar construction can be used for $Inc^j(Y)$.

Checking Hypothesis for Upward Closure in j. A property that we will find useful in answering equivalence queries is that by definition of Γ, its fixpoint X is upward closed in the j component, i.e., if (s,i,j) in X then for all $j' > j$, (s,i,j') is also in X. A set Y is upward closed in the j component if and only if $Inc^j(Y) \subseteq Y$. If Y is not upward closed then let (s,i,j) be the string in $Inc^j(Y) \setminus Y$. Clearly, $(s,i,j) \notin Y$. Now we use membership query to check if $(s,i,j) \in X$. If (s,i,j) is indeed in X then (s,i,j) is in the symmetric difference $X \oplus Y$. Otherwise $(s,i,j-1)$ is also not in X (since X has the upward closed property). In this case $(s,i,j-1) \in X \oplus Y$.

Symbolic Computation of Γ_1. A finite automaton for $\Gamma_1(Y)$ is obtained by taking the DFA for f and taking its cross product with a DFA that accepts 0 for the i component and another DFA which accepts any j.

Symbolic Computation of Γ_2. If we always first check for upward closure in j, we can assume that we would need to compute Γ_2 only for sets which are upward closed. Let $\tau^{-1}(Y)$ be the inverse of τ lifted to the triples (s,i,j) so that it simply copies the second and the third components. It can be seen that if Y is upward closed then $\Gamma_2(Y) = S_{\bar{f}} \cap Inc^j(\tau^{-1}(Y))$.

Symbolic Computation of Γ_3. For Γ_3, $\tau^{-1}(Y)$ gives the set of states which have a successor in Y. It is easy to see that $\Gamma_3(Y) = S_f \cap Inc^i(Inc^j(\tau^{-1}(Y)))$.

Using the Fixpoint Check. From the previous paragraphs, we have a symbolic method to compute $\Gamma(Y) = \Gamma_1(Y) \cup \Gamma_2(Y) \cup \Gamma_3(Y)$. Now, the equivalence oracle simply needs to check if $Y = \Gamma(Y)$. We also need a method of extracting strings in the symmetric difference of Y and the fixpoint in case Y is not the fixpoint. It can be seen that the approach outlined in Section 3.2 can be applied to regular sets.

4.4   Checking for $s_0 \in \sigma(X)$.

Proposition 5. $\sigma(X) = \overline{Proj_1(\overline{Proj_{1,2}(X)})}$. Here, $Proj_1$ is the projection to the first component and $Proj_{1,2}$ the projection to the first and second components.

Proof (Sketch). Recall that $\sigma(X) = \{s \mid \forall i \exists j.(s,i,j) \in X\}$. Equivalently, $\sigma(X) = \{s \mid \neg(\exists i \neg(\exists j.(s,i,j) \in X))\}$. The claim follows from the fact that $\exists$ can be eliminated using projection and the $\neg$ operator corresponds to taking the complement.

Given a regular representation of X we can calculate $\sigma(X)$ using standard regular set operations. Then the system is correct if and only if $S_0 \cap \sigma(X) = \emptyset$. The verification algorithm is summarized in Figure 2.

algorithm *learner*
begin
Angluin's L^* algorithm
end

algorithm *isMember*
Input: (s,i,j)
Output: is $(s,i,j) \in X$?
begin
From s simulate system for j steps
  Does any path in above encounter
  at least $i + 1$ states labelled f?
If yes *return* true
else *return* false
end

algorithm *Equivalence Check*
Input: Hypothesis Y
Output: For fixpoint X, is $Y = X$?
If not, then some string in $Y \oplus X$
begin
  If $Inc^j(Y) \setminus Y \neq \emptyset$ {upward closure check}
    let $(s,i,j) \in Inc^j(Y) \setminus Y$
    if isMember$((s,i,j))$
      return (no, (s,i,j))
    else
      return (no, $(s,i,j-1)$)
  else if $\Gamma(Y) \setminus Y \neq \emptyset$ {fixpoint check}
    let $(s,i,j) \in \Gamma(Y) \setminus Y$
    Find (s',i',j') which causes (s,i,j) to be
                              in $\Gamma(Y)$
    if isMember$((s,i,j))$
      return (no, (s,i,j))
    else
      return (no, (s',i',j'))
  else if $\Gamma(Y) \subsetneq Y$
    return (no, $l \in (Y \setminus \Gamma(Y))$)
  else {found fixpoint}
    if $S_0 \cap \overline{Proj_1(\overline{Proj_{1,2}(X)})} \neq \emptyset$
      print "System incorrect"
    else
      print "System correct"
end

Fig. 2. Verifying ω-regular properties for regular set based systems

4.5   Complexity Analysis

Let m be the length of the longest string returned by the teacher in a negative answer to an equivalence query, n be the number of states of the minimal automaton representing the fixpoint X, k be the size of the alphabet of the learned language and t be the number of states of the automaton representing the transducer for the transition relation. As shown in [2], Angluin's algorithm makes $O(kmn^2)$ membership queries and $O(n)$ equivalence queries. The worst case for the equivalence query for a hypothesis Y occurs when we look for a string in the difference of Y and $\Gamma(Y)$. The size of DFA representing Y is bounded by n. Looking at Γ, it can be seen that the DFA representing the difference of Y and $\Gamma(Y)$ would be $O(nt)$. Thus the length of the longest string returned by an equivalence query is $m = O(nt)$.

The cost of answering membership queries dominates the total runtime cost of the algorithm. Using $m = O(nt)$, the number of membership queries is $O(ktn^3)$. For efficiency, given a query for (s, i, j), we build a DFA D_j for $\Gamma^{j+1}(\emptyset)$ where Γ^{j+1} denotes the composition of Γ $j + 1$ times with itself. Once D_j has been built, all queries with the same value of j can be answered by checking if the queried element is accepted by D_j. Thus the cost of the membership queries is equal to the number of membership queries and the cost of building the DFAs. The cost for D_j is $(O(t))^j$ which leads to the total cost of membership queries of $O(t^{O(nt)} + ktn^3)$ (using maximum value of j to be $m = O(nt)$).

5   Examples

We have extended our learning based verification tool suite called LEVER [11] with the algorithm presented in this paper and have successfully analyzed liveness properties for two examples of infinite state systems. The Büchi automaton forms the specification and also describes the fairness constraints on the system. The states of the system considered are encoded as strings over an alphabet as described in [4]. We now briefly discuss the examples analyzed.

Token passing. We consider a parameterized system of processes in which each process can send a token to the process to its right. There is a single token in the system and initially it rests with the leftmost process. The liveness property that is encoded with the Büchi automaton is, "every process eventually receives a token". The fixpoint for Γ is found to be regular and the system shown to be correct using our verification procedure.

Producer consumer. This consists of a FIFO automata with a single channel, in which one part of the system constantly produces messages while another part consumes them. We verify the property, "a message produced by the producer is eventually consumed". Again, the fixpoint for Γ is found to be regular and the system verified to be correct.

Both the examples take just a few seconds to analyze on a 1.5 GHz computer. We continue to optimize the implementation in LEVER, and in future plan on analyzing more examples of infinite state systems and comparing our running time with other tools that are available.

6 Conclusion

In this paper we presented a general learning based verification framework to verify ω-regular properties of infinite state systems. We instantiated the framework in the context of regular model checking giving detailed algorithms for the various primitive operations that are needed in order to perform the learning based verification procedure. The algorithm is a significant improvement in the current state of the art in learning based verification, as it verifies general ω-regular properties, while not making restrictive assumptions about the way the transition relation of the system is represented as a transducer. Furthermore, the algorithm can detect buggy implementations, even when the implementations do not have an ultimately periodic counter-example for the property.

References

1. P. A. Abdulla, B. Jonsson, M. Nilson, J. d'Orso, and M. Saksena. Regular model checking for LTL(MSO). In *Proc. of CAV'04, USA, LNCS 3114*, 2004.
2. D. Angluin. Learning regular sets from queries and counterexamples. *Inform. Comput.*, 75(2):87–106, Nov. 1987.
3. A. Bouajjani, P. Habermehl, and T. Vojnar. Abstract regular model checking. In *CAV'04, LNCS 3114*, 2004.
4. A. Bouajjani, B. Jonsson, M. Nilsson, and T. Touili. Regular model checking. In E. A. Emerson and A. P. Sistla, editors, *Proceedings of the 12th International Conference on Computer-Aided Verification (CAV'00)*, volume 1855 of *LNCS*, pages 403–418. Springer, 2000.
5. A. Bouajjani, A. Legay, and P. Wolper. Handling liveness properties in (ω-)regular model-checking. In *Proc. of Infinity'04, London, UK*, 2004.
6. E.A. Emerson and C.-L. Lei. Efficient model checking in fragments of the propositional mucalculus. In *Proccedings of the First Annual Symposium on Logic in Computer Science*, pages 267–278, Washington, D.C., 1986. IEEE Computer Society Press.
7. E. A. Emerson. Temporal and modal logic. In J. V. Leeuwen, editor, *Handbook of Theoretical Computer Science*, volume B, pages 995–1072. Elsevier, Amsterdam, 1990.
8. L. Fribourg and H. Olsén. Reachability sets of parametrized rings as regular languages. In *Proc. 2nd Int. Workshop on Verification of Infinite State Systems (INFINITY'97), Bologna, Italy, July 1997*, volume 9. Elsevier Science, 1997.
9. P. Habermehl and T. Vojnar. Regular model checking using inference of regular languages. In *Proc. of Infinity'04, London, UK*, 2004.
10. B. Jonsson and M. Nilsson. Transitive closures of regular relations for verifying infinite-state systems. In *6th International Conference on Tools and Algorithms for Construction and Analysis of Systems (TACAS'00)*, volume 1785 of *LNCS*, pages 220–234. Springer, 2000.
11. LEVER. Learning to verify tool. http://osl.cs.uiuc.edu/~vardhan/lever.html, 2004.
12. J. Oncina and P. Garcia. Inferring regular languages in polynomial update time. In *Pattern Recognition and Image Analysis*, volume 1 of *Series in Machine Perception and Artificial Intelligence*, pages 49–61. World Scientific, Singapore, 1992.

13. A. Pnueli and E. Shahar. Liveness and acceleration in parameterized verification. In *CAV'00*, 2000.
14. W. Thomas. Automata on infinite objects. In J. V. Leeuwen, editor, *Handbook of Theoretical Computer Science*, volume B, pages 133–191. Elsevier, Amsterdam, 1990.
15. T. Touili. Regular model checking using widening techniques. In *ENTCS*, volume 50. Elsevier, 2001.
16. A. Vardhan, K. Sen, M. Viswanathan, and G. Agha. Actively learning to verify safety for fifo automata. In *LNCS 3328, Proc. of FSTTCS'04, Chennai, India*, pages 494–505, 2004.
17. A. Vardhan, K. Sen, M. Viswanathan, and G. Agha. Learning to verify safety properties. In *LNCS 3308, Proc. of ICFEM'04, Seattle, USA*, pages 274–288, 2004.
18. A. Vardhan, K. Sen, M. Viswanathan, and G. Agha. Using language inference to verify omega-regular properties (full version). http://osl.cs.uiuc.edu/docs/omega/omegaLearn2.pdf, 2004.

On-the-Fly Reachability and Cycle Detection for Recursive State Machines *

Rajeev Alur[1], Swarat Chaudhuri[1], Kousha Etessami[2], and P. Madhusudan[3]

[1] University of Pennsylvania, USA
[2] University of Edinburgh, UK
[3] University of Illinois at Urbana-Champaign, USA

Abstract. Searching the state space of a system using enumerative and on-the-fly depth-first traversal is an established technique for model checking finite-state systems. In this paper, we propose algorithms for on-the-fly exploration of recursive state machines, or equivalently push-down systems, which are suited for modeling the behavior of procedural programs. We present algorithms for reachability (is a bad state reachable?) as well as for fair cycle detection (is there a reachable cycle with progress?). We also report on an implementation of these algorithms to check safety and liveness properties of recursive boolean programs, and its performance on existing benchmarks.

1 Introduction

Recursive state machines (RSM) can model control flow in typical sequential imperative programming languages with recursive procedure calls, and are equivalent to pushdown systems [1]. Even though the state-space of an RSM is infinite due to recursion, model checking problems for RSMs are decidable [6, 7, 15, 12, 1, 5]. *Extended RSMs* (ERSM) augment RSMs with global and local variables that can be tested and updated along the edges of the control structure. Contemporary tools for software verification employ abstraction to automatically extract ERSMs from code written in languages such as C, and then use ERSM model checking algorithms to check temporal requirements [4, 17]. The complexity of the key analysis problems for ERSMs, such as reachability, is polynomial in the number of states [12, 1], where a state needs to encode the control location and the values of all the global and in-scope local variables. To cope with the state-space explosion due to the variables, existing implementations of ERSM model checkers such as BEBOP [3] and MOPED [12] use symbolic encoding using automata and binary decision diagrams. In this paper, we propose *on-the-fly* explicit-state search algorithms as a viable alternative.

An on-the-fly algorithm explores the reachable states starting from initial states by computing the successors of a state only when needed, typically using

---

* This research was partially supported by ARO URI award DAAD19-01-1-0473, and NSF awards ITR/SY 0121431 and CCR-0306382.

N. Halbwachs and L. Zuck (Eds.): TACAS 2005, LNCS 3440, pp. 61–76, 2005.

depth-first traversal, and terminates as soon as it finds a counterexample to the property being verified. While the effectiveness of this technique is limited by the number of states that can be stored and processed, it has its own advantages over the symbolic approach. The guards and updates on an edge can be complex, and can even include calls to library functions. It does not require an *a priori* encoding of the states, and hence, can support complex and unbounded data types and dynamic creation of data. Early termination allows discovery of shallow bugs rapidly. Finally, the performance is more predictable as more states are guaranteed to be searched with an increase in the available memory and time. Consequently, tools such as SPIN [18] and MURφ [10] that rely on on-the-fly explicit-state search algorithms have been very effective for classical model checking problems. More recent tools like ZING [2] and BANDERA [8] are also explicit-state, support complex data types, concurrency, and recursion, but do not offer any termination guarantees.

We first consider the *reachability* problem for ERSMs: starting from an initial state, can control reach one of the target locations along some execution of the ERSM? Our algorithm combines on-the-fly traversal of extended state machines with early termination used in explicit-state model checkers and a summarization algorithm used in interprocedural data-flow analysis [20].

We build on our reachability algorithm to arrive at a novel solution to the *fair cycle detection* problem for ERSMs: starting from an initial state, is there an execution of the ERSM that visits one of the target locations infinitely often? This fair cycle detection problem is central to the algorithmic verification of liveness requirements. The known solution to this problem is most naturally viewed in two phases [1]. In the first phase, all the summary edges are computed, and the second phase reduces to fair cycle detection in an ordinary graph containing these summary edges. Since we desire an on-the-fly solution with the possibility of early termination, we do not want to compute all the summary edges first, and wish to interleave the two phases. We can view this problem as fair cycle detection in a graph (second phase) in which the edges, namely, the summary edges discovered by the first phase, are inserted dynamically. For on-the-fly fair cycle detection in ordinary graphs, tools such as SPIN employ the so-called *nested depth-first-search* algorithm [9], but this algorithm relies on the ordering of states in a depth-first traversal, which fails if we allow dynamic insertion of (summary) edges. In the proposed solution, we use a path-based algorithm for computing the strongly-connected-components (SCC) of a graph [16]. Every time the first phase discovers a summary transition, the SCC discovery algorithm processes the newly reachable states. As a new SCC is discovered, early termination is possible if it contains a state with the target location or a summary transition representing a path through such a state, and if not, all vertices in the SCC can be collapsed to a single vertex for efficiency. Cycle detection (but not *fair* cycle detection) is interesting in program analysis in the context of *points-to* analysis and cycle detection in dynamic graphs has been studied [19, 14].

For analysis of worst-case time bounds, let us assume that the ERSM has k components, has no variables and has total size n (control locations plus transitions). Then, the time bounds for non-on-the-fly explicit-state algorithms for reachability and fair cycle detection are $O(n)$ [1], while the symbolic algorithms for reachability and fair cycle detection are $O(n^2)$ [13]. The newly proposed reachability algorithm is $O(n)$ and the new fair cycle detection algorithm is $O(kn)$.

To test the performance of the proposed algorithms, we implemented them in the tool VERA. The ERSM model is described in an input language that extends the boolean programs of BEBOP [3] with additional types such as bounded integers. The specifications can be written as monitors, and the tool performs on-the-fly reachability and fair cycle detection on the product of the model and the monitor. The regression test suite of SLAM contains boolean programs obtained from abstractions of real-world C code [4], and while VERA performs well on examples that contain a bug, it performs poorly compared to symbolic checkers such as MOPED [12] when forced to search the entire space. On examples such as Quicksort from MOPED's benchmarks that need manipulation of integer variables, VERA performs significantly better than MOPED. Finally, we manually abstracted a Linux driver code in which METAL had found a double locking error using static analysis [11]. VERA performs well on this example, and can also prove the liveness requirement that "every lock should eventually be released."

2   Extended Recursive State Machines

In this section, we introduce the formalism of extended recursive state machines (ERSMs). We start with the language we use to specify guarded commands.

Expressions and Assignments. Let us have a set T of types and a domain D_t associated with each type $t \in T$. In particular, we allow a *boolean* type with the domain $\{T, F\}$. Let V be a finite set of variables where each variable is associated with a type, and let $Expr(V)$ be a set of typed expressions. We refer to the set of expressions of boolean type as $BoolExp(V)$.

An *interpretation* of V is a map $\sigma : v \in V \mapsto d \in D_t$, where v is of type t. Every interpretation can be extended to a unique semantic map $\sigma : expr \in Expr \mapsto d \in D_t$, where $expr$ is of type t.

An *assignment* over V has the form $[x_1, x_2, \ldots, x_l] := [exp_1, exp_2, \ldots, exp_l]$, where $x_j \in V$ are distinct variables, and for all j, $exp_j \in Expr(V)$ is an expression of the same type as x_j. We refer to the set of assignments over V as $Assgn(V)$. The semantics of assignments are defined over pairs (σ_1, σ_2) of interpretations of V. Given an assignment α of the above form, we say $\sigma_2 = \alpha(\sigma_1)$ if (1) $\sigma_2(x_j) = \sigma_1(exp_j)$ for all x_j, and (2) $\sigma_1(y) = \sigma_2(y)$ for all variables $y \in V \setminus \{x_1, x_2, \ldots, x_l\}$.

Syntax of ERSMs. An *extended recursive state machine (ERSM)* A is a tuple $\langle G, \gamma_{in}, p, (A_1, A_2, \ldots, A_k) \rangle$, where G is a finite set of global variables, γ_{in} is an *initial* interpretation of G, $p \in \{1, \ldots, k\}$ is the index of the initial component, and each *component state machine* $A_i = \langle L_i, I_i, O_i, \lambda_{i_{in}}, N_i, en_i, ex_i, \delta_i \rangle$ consists of

- a finite set L_i of local variables, a set $I_i \subseteq L_i$ of input variables, and a set $O_i \subseteq L_i$ of output variables. The sets I_i and O_i are totally ordered, the j-th variables in these orders being given by $I_i(j)$ and $O_i(j)$ respectively. Also, we require that $I_p = \emptyset$;
- an *initial* interpretation $\lambda_{i_{in}}$ of L_i;
- a finite set N_i of nodes;
- two special nodes $en_i, ex_i \in N_i$, known respectively as the *entry node* and the *exit node*; [1]
- A set δ_i of *edges*, where an edge can be one of two forms:
  - Internal edge: A tuple (u, v, g, α). Here u and v are nodes in N_i, $g \in BoolExp(G \cup L_i)$ is a *guard* on the edge, and $\alpha \in Assgn(G \cup L_i)$ is an assignment. Intuitively, such an edge will be taken only if the guard g is true, and if it is taken, the assignments will be applied to the current variables. The set of internal edges in component i is denoted by δ_i^I.
  - Call edge: A tuple (u, v, g, m, in, out). Here u and v are nodes in N_i, $g \in BoolExp(G \cup L_i)$ is an edge guard, $m \in \{1, 2, \ldots, k\}$ is the index of the *called* component, and $in \in L_i^r$ and $out \in L_i^q$, for $r = |I_m|$ and $q = |O_m|$, are two lists of local variables. Intuitively, in is the list of parameters passed to the call, and out is the list of variables where the outputs of the call are stored on return from the call. We require that all variables in out are distinct.

    The set of call edges in component i is denoted by δ_i^C. The function $Y_i : \delta_i^C \to \{1, 2, \ldots, k\}$ maps call edges to indices of the components they call, so that, for a call edge e such as above, $Y_i(e) = m$.

We assume that entry nodes en_i do not have incoming edges and exit nodes ex_i do not have outgoing edges.   □

We designate the component A_p as the *initial component*. This component, where runs of A begin, models the "main" procedure in procedural programs.

Example: Figure 1 shows a sample ERSM with one global variable a, and components A_1 and A_2. Component A_1 has an input variable i, and an output variable x. Component A_2, also the initial component, has no inputs and one local/output variable y. All variables are of boolean type, and initially, we have $a = F$, $x = T$, and $y = T$.

In the diagram, an internal edge (u, v, g, α) is drawn as a solid arrow from node u to node v annotated by $(g \Rightarrow \alpha)$ (we will omit the guard g and the assignment α if, respectively, g is always true and the assignment α is empty). A call edge (u, v, g, m, in, out) is a dashed arrow annotated by $(g \Rightarrow out := m(in))$ (we omit out if it is empty, and leave out the guard g if it is trivially true).

---

[1] The usual definition of RSMs [1] allows components to have multiple entry and exit nodes. In this paper, we model entries and exits by input and output variables, so it suffices to let each component have one entry and one exit node.

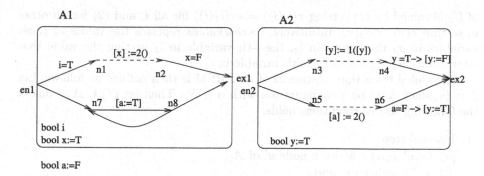

Fig. 1. A sample ERSM

Semantics of ERSMs. ERSMs model procedural programs written in C-like imperative languages and resemble the latter in operational semantics. Components, nodes, internal edges, and call edges in ERSMs respectively model procedures, control locations, intraprocedural control flow, and procedure invocations in procedural programs, and *configurations* and *runs* of ERSMs are the equivalents of program states and program executions. A *configuration* of an ERSM consists of a call stack, a current node, and a current interpretation of the global and in-scope local variables. The transition relation on configurations has three kinds of transitions: *internal steps*, *calls*, and *returns*. At an internal step, control follows an internal edge, reaches a new node, and applies the assignments on the edge to the variables in scope, the stack remaining unaffected. During a call, a call edge and the current interpretation of the local variables in scope are pushed onto the call stack, control reaches the entry node of the called component, and a new set of local variables are initialized. At a return, we pop a calling context off the stack, reinstate the popped local variables (after adjusting for possible output values), and proceed to the node to which the popped call edge leads.

We now formally define the configuration space Q of an ERSM A. A *configuration* of A is a tuple $\psi = \langle \gamma, stack, u, \lambda \rangle$, where γ is an interpretation of G, and $stack$ is either of the form $\langle (e_1, \lambda_1), (e_2, \lambda_2), \ldots, (e_r, \lambda_r) \rangle$ or the empty list. Here, $e_1, e_2, \ldots, e_r$ are call edges of A, λ_1 is an interpretation of L_p, e_1 is a call edge in A_p, and, for every $i > 1$, λ_i is an interpretation of L_c and e_i is a call edge in A_c, where $c = Y(e_{i-1})$. Finally, u is a node in N_j and λ is an interpretation of L_j, where j equals p if $stack$ is empty, and $Y(e_r)$ otherwise.

In a configuration of the above form, we define the node u to be the *current node* in ψ. We refer to this node as $Currnode(\psi)$.

We need some more notation before we can define the transition relation on these configurations. Let σ_1 and σ_2 be interpretations of disjoint sets of variables V_1 and V_2. Then $\sigma_1 \sqcup \sigma_2$ is the interpretation of $(V_1 \cup V_2)$ that agrees with σ_1 and σ_2 on variables from V_1 and V_2 respectively.

Now let $l_1 \in U_1^q$ and $l_2 \in U_2^q$ be two lists of variables such that $U_1 \cap U_2 = \emptyset$ and members of l_2 are all distinct. Let us also have interpretations σ_1 and σ_2 of U_1 and U_2 respectively. Then $\tau = borrowValues(\sigma_2, l_2, \sigma_1, l_1)$ is an interpretation of U_2 obtained by (1) setting $\tau(l_2(i)) = \sigma_1(l_1(i))$ for all i, and (2) for all other v, setting $\tau(v) = \sigma_2(v)$. Intuitively, *borrowValues* replaces the values of those variables in σ_2 that occur in l_2, the i-th variable in l_2 getting the value that interpretation σ_1 gives to the i-th variable in l_1.

The global transition relation Δ of an ERSM is then defined as follows. Let $\psi = \langle \gamma, stack, u, \lambda \rangle$ be a configuration with $u \in N_j$. Then $(\psi, \psi') \in \Delta$ iff one of the following sets of conditions holds:

1. Internal step
   (a) $(u, u', g, \alpha) \in \delta_j^I$ for a node u' of A_j,
   (b) $\gamma \sqcup \lambda$ satisfies g, and
   (c) $\psi' = \langle \gamma', stack, u', \lambda' \rangle$, where $\gamma' \sqcup \lambda' = \alpha(\gamma \sqcup \lambda)$.
2. Call
   (a) $e = (u, u', g, m, in_m, out_m) \in \delta_j^C$ for a node u' of A_j,
   (b) $\gamma \sqcup \lambda$ satisfies g, and
   (c) $\psi' = \langle \gamma, \langle stack, (e, \lambda) \rangle, en_m, \lambda' \rangle$, where $\lambda' = borrowValues(\lambda_{m_{in}}, I_m, \lambda, in_m)$.
3. Return
   (a) u is the exit node ex_j of A_j,
   (b) *stack* is of the form $\langle stack', (e_r, \lambda_r) \rangle$
   (c) $e_r = (v, u', g, j, in_j, out_j)$ for some v, u', g, in_j, and out_j, and
   (d) $\psi' = \langle \gamma, stack', u', \lambda' \rangle$, where $\lambda' = borrowValues(\lambda_r, out_j, \lambda, O_j)$.

Note that the configurations Q and the transition relation Δ define an ordinary (and in general infinite) transition system T_A. A *run* of A is a (finite or infinite) sequence $\rho = \psi_0 \psi_1 \psi_2 \ldots$, where $\psi_0 = \langle \gamma_{in}, \bot, en_p, \lambda_{p_{in}} \rangle$ ($\bot$ being the empty stack sequence), and for all i, $\psi_i \in Q$ and $(\psi_i, \psi_{i+1}) \in \Delta$. The semantics of A are defined by its set of runs.

Given an ERSM A, we are interested in two central algorithmic questions:

1. *Reachability:* Given an ERSM A and a set of *target nodes* T of A, does A have a run $\rho = \psi_0 \psi_1 \psi_2 \ldots$ such that $Currnode(\psi_j) \in T$ for some j?
2. *Fair cycle detection:* Given an ERSM A and a set R of *repeating nodes* of A, does A have a run $\rho = \psi_0 \psi_1 \psi_2 \ldots$ such that $Currnode(\psi_j) \in R$ for *infinitely many* $j \in \mathbb{N}$?

In this paper, we present two algorithms that search the set of local states enumeratively to solve these problems. These algorithms differ from previous work in two important respects:

1. *On-the-fly search:* We generate states "on demand", as we explore the state space, and only store the visited states.
2. *Early termination:* Our algorithms terminate as soon as a reachability witness or a cycle containing a repeating state occurs in the visited state space. Consequently, our algorithms do not necessarily have to generate the entire state space in order to terminate.

3   Reachability

We now describe an on-the-fly, early-terminating algorithm to check if a given set T of target nodes is reachable in an ERSM A.

A *state* of an ERSM A is a tuple of the form $s = \langle v, \gamma, \lambda \rangle$, where v is a node, and γ and λ are interpretations of global and local variables. Note that a state is different from a configuration in that it does not include the stack. An *entry state* for component A_i is a state $s = \langle v, \gamma, \lambda \rangle$ where $v = en_i$. Likewise, $s = \langle v, \gamma, \lambda \rangle$ is an *exit state* if $v = ex_i$. A *summary* is a pair (s_{en}, s_{ex}), where s_{en} is an entry state and s_{ex} is an exit state in the same component.

Let us now define a state graph S corresponding to A. The vertices of S are the states of A and the set of transitions of S is the smallest set E of transitions satisfying the following conditions:

- **Internal Transitions.** Let $s = \langle u, \gamma, \lambda \rangle$ be a state. If A_i has an internal edge (u, v, g, α) and the interpretation $\gamma \sqcup \lambda$ satisfies g, then E has a internal transition (s, s'), where $s' = \langle v, \gamma', \lambda' \rangle$, where $\gamma' \sqcup \lambda' = \alpha(\gamma \sqcup \lambda)$.
- **Call and Summary Transitions.** Let $s = \langle u, \gamma, \lambda \rangle$ be a state. Assume A_i has a call edge $(u, v, g, m, in_m, out_m)$ and the interpretation $\gamma \sqcup \lambda$ satisfies g. Let $s_{en} = \langle en_m, \gamma, \lambda_{en} \rangle$, where $\lambda_{en} = borrowValues(\lambda_{m_{in}}, I_m, \lambda, in_m)$. Then (s, s_{en}) is a call transition in E.
  If $s_{ex} = \langle ex_m, \gamma', \lambda_{ex} \rangle$ is some exit state in A_m and s_{ex} is reachable from s_{en} using only internal and summary transitions, then (s, s') is a *summary transition* in E where $s' = \langle v, \gamma', \lambda' \rangle$ and $\lambda' = borrowValues(\lambda, out_m, \lambda_{ex}, O_m)$.

For a set of repeating nodes R, let us also define S_R, which is defined exactly as S is defined above except that summary transitions can be of two kinds, *fair* or *not fair*. When a summary transition is added, it is set to be fair if the run from s_{en} to s_{ex} goes through a state involving R or uses a fair summary transition.

The key to checking reachability and cycles in an ERSM is given by the following lemma:

Lemma 1 ([1]). *Let A be an ERSM and let S be its associated state-graph. For a given set of target nodes T, T is reachable in A iff there is a node of the form (u, γ, λ) with $u \in T$ reachable in S. Similarly, given a set of repeating nodes R, there is run of A that visits R infinitely often iff there is a path in S_R that visits the set $\{(u, \gamma, \lambda) | u \in R\}$ infinitely often or uses fair summary edges infinitely often.*

Note that if local and global variables are finite-domain, then S is finite as well, and the above lemma shows checking reachability and fair cycles are decidable. We refer to the subgraph of S induced by the nodes belonging to A_i, i.e. nodes of the form (u, γ, λ) where $u \in N_i$, as S_i; the graphs S_i contain only internal and summary transitions. Our reachability algorithm explores S on-the-fly looking for a state of the form (u, γ, λ), where $u \in T$. It can be in fact viewed as an interleaving of k separate depth-first searches, the i-th search taking place in the transition system S_i.

REACHABILITY(s, s_{en})

```
 1    Visited ← Visited ∪ {(s, s_en)}
 2    if Currnode(s) ∈ T
 3      then print ("Target reached") ;  break
 4    if s is an exit state in component i
 5      then VisitedExits[i, s_en] ← VisitedExits[i, s_en] ∪ {s}
 6          for (s', s'_en) ∈ VisitedCalls[i, s_en]
 7          do s_ret = GETRETURNSTATE(s', s)
 8              if (s_ret, s'_en) ∉ Visited
 9                  then REACHABILITY(s_ret, s'_en)
10      else for e ∈ Edges_I(s)
11          do if s satisfies guard of e
12              then s' ← APPLY(e, s)
13                  if (s', s_en) ∉ Visited
14                      then REACHABILITY(s', s_en)
15          for e ∈ Edges_C(s)
16          do if s satisfies guard of e
17              then m ← Y(e);  s' ← GETENTRYSTATE(e, s)
18                  VisitedCalls[m, s'] ← VisitedCalls[m, s'] ∪ {(s, s_en)}
19                  if (s', s_en) ∉ Visited
20                      then REACHABILITY(s', s_en)
21                      else for s_ex ∈ VisitedExits[Y(e), s']
22                          do s_ret = GETRETURNSTATE(s, s_ex)
23                              if (s_ret, s_en)) ∉ Visited
24                                  then REACHABILITY(s_ret, s_en)
```

Fig. 2. On-the-fly reachability in ERSMs

Our search begins from the initial state $\langle en_p, \gamma_{in}, \lambda_{p_{in}} \rangle$, in the initial component A_p. The search proceeds depth-first following edges in A_p. If, during this search, we are at a state s_1 in S_p and find a call edge calling component A_q, we would need to search along a summary transition in S_p. To discover this transition, however, we would need to know the reachability relation between the corresponding entry and exit states in A_q, and to compute this relation, we must search S_q.

The crux of the algorithm is to view S_p as an *incompletely specified* transition system and *suspend* the search in S_p when such a situation occurs. Given s_1 and the call edge in question, we can compute the entry state s_2 in S_q reached following the corresponding call transition. If s_2 has not been visited so far, we search S_q starting from s_2; if a search from s_2 has previously been started, we simply suspend searching and wait for future "updates". As we learn more about reachability between entry and exit states in S_q, we may add corresponding summary transitions in S_p and resume the search in S_p. If all local searches terminate, then we have explored all of the reachable part of S, and can terminate.

Figure 2 describes the algorithm more formally. Given a state $s = \langle v, \gamma, \lambda \rangle$, we refer to the set of internal and call edges going out of v as $Edges_I(s)$ and $Edges_C(s)$ respectively. If the variables in s satisfy the guard g on an internal edge e, the function $Apply(e, s)$ returns the state s' to which the corresponding internal transition leads. If s satisfies the guard g on a call edge e, the function $GetEntryState(e, s)$ returns the entry state s' that is the target of the corresponding call transition. Finally, suppose s is an exit state in component A_m and s' is a state with a call transition to component A_m; also suppose there exists a summary transition (s', s'') corresponding to s', e and s. Then the function $GetReturnState(s', s)$ returns the state s''.

The function $Reachability$ has two inputs: a state s in component A_i and an entry state s_{en}. The pair of states (s, s_{en}) forms a *context* if s is reachable from s_{en}. The set $VisitedCalls[i, s_{en}]$ stores the set of "calling contexts": contexts (s', s'_{en}) where control switched to component A_i and entry state s_{en}. Then, if an exit state s_{ex} in A_i is reachable from state s_{en}, a summary transition between states s' and $s'' = GetReturnState(s', s_{ex})$ has been discovered.

To solve the reachability problem, we call $Reachability(s_{init}, s_{init})$, where $s_{init} = \langle en_p, \gamma_{in}, \lambda_{p_{in}} \rangle$. Termination of this algorithm is guaranteed if the set of states reachable from the initial states is finite; one such special case is when all types are finite-domain. We omit the detailed proof of correctness.

Theorem 1. *Let A be an ERSM, T be a set of target nodes, and $s_{init} = \langle en_p, \gamma_{in}, \lambda_{p_{in}} \rangle$. Then if the algorithm $Reachability(s_{init}, s_{init})$ halts, it prints "Target reached" iff there is a run of A that reaches a configuration ψ with $Currnode(\psi) \in T$. Moreover, if the set of states reachable from s_{en} in S is finite, then $Reachability(s_{init}, s_{init})$ is guaranteed to halt.* □

This algorithm has some of the nicer, "on-the-fly" properties of DFS. We start with an initial state, only store the "visited" state space, make a switch to a different component only when a call edge requires it, and, even when such a switch is made, "discover" entry states only when necessary. Moreover, we can terminate as soon as we encounter a target state.

If s'_{en} is an entry state of S_i reachable in S and s' is reachable from s'_{en} using edges in S_i only, then when calling $Reachability(s_{init}, s_{init})$, the recursive procedure $Reachability(s', s'_{en})$ will be called at most once. This observation leads to the following complexity of the reachability algorithm in terms of the number of discovered states and transitions in S:

Theorem 2. *Let $Reachability$ terminate on a given ERSM A. Let n and m be the number of states and edges in the explored part of S. Let β be a bound on the maximum number of reachable entry or exit states in any component S_i. Then $Reachability(s_{init}, s_{init})$ takes $O(m\beta + n\beta^2)$ time to terminate and space $O(n\beta)$.* □

4 Fair Cycle Detection

Let us fix an ERSM A and a set of repeating nodes R of A. Let S_R be the associated state-graph of A and R as defined in the previous section. In this section, we present an on-the-fly fair cycle detection algorithm for ERSMs that searches the transition system $\mathcal{S}_R$ for a cycle containing a repeating state or a fair summary edge. If the domains of the types are finite, Lemma 1 guarantees that A has a run visiting infinitely many repeating states if and only if such a cycle exists. Our core idea is to view $\mathcal{S}_R$ as an incomplete transition system to which edges are added dynamically, and to use an *online cycle detection algorithm for dynamically presented graphs* to find such a cycle.

The following are a few ways in which this can be implemented:

- The most naive algorithm would be to search the state-space of A using REACHABILITY, postponing cycle detection until we know all states and transitions in $\mathcal{S}_R$. At that point, we may detect cycles in $\mathcal{S}_R$ using an algorithm (such as nested DFS [9]) for cycle detection in finite graphs. This algorithm, however, is inherently a two-phase algorithm and does not have the early termination property.
- Another possibility is to adapt the nested DFS algorithm [9] to a setting where summary transitions are dynamically presented and early termination is required. This turns out to be difficult. The problem is that in the nested DFS algorithm, the secondary search follows the DFS order computed by the primary search: if s and s' are two states such that s is an ancestor of s' in the primary DFS tree, the secondary search from s' must terminate *before* the secondary search from s may start. However, in our context, we may discover a summary transition from s' (that can possibly introduce cycles) while searching a different branch of the primary DFS tree rooted at s. A conceivable way of adapting this algorithm to our setting would be to start a new instance of REACHABILITY each time we reach a repeating state s_r, to check if s_r is reachable from itself. However, the time complexity of such an algorithm would be N_F times the size of $\mathcal{S}_R$, where N_F is the number of repeating states; note that due to data interpretations, N_F can be very large.
- A third option, which is what we follow, is to maintain strongly connected components (SCCs) in $\mathcal{S}_R$ dynamically using an incremental algorithm. We terminate, reporting a cycle, as soon as the explored part of $\mathcal{S}_R$ starts containing a non-trivial SCC with a repeating state or a fair summary transition in it. However, linear time incremental algorithms for maintaining SCCs are not known. While we could use heuristically tuned online algorithms such as in [19], we have chosen instead to use an adaptation of Gabow's algorithm as it uses simpler data-structures.

Our algorithm FAIR-CYCLE-DETECT consists of two subroutines: one explores the state space of the ERSM and discovers new transitions in $\mathcal{S}_R$ (including summary transitions), while the other updates the SCCs in the discovered graph. The former algorithm is essentially the algorithm REACHABILITY of the previous section while the latter is an adaptation of a path-based DFS algorithm by Gabow [16] that finds SCCs in a graph.

Gabow's algorithm finds SCCs in a graph via a DFS on it. As soon as a back edge is identified, it contracts the cycle formed by it into an SCC, and, finally, outputs the SCCs in a topological order. This algorithm has an early termination property, because if an SCC introduced by a back edge contains a repeating state or a fair summary transition, we can terminate immediately.

Let us now describe an optimization that changes the structure of our algorithm. Since Gabow's algorithm essentially explores its graph using a depth-first search and the state-space exploration of the ERSM done by REACHABILITY is also essentially a DFS, these two can be combined easily. However, in REACHABILITY, when a new summary is discovered, the control shifts to the returns corresponding to this summary, which can be in an entirely different part of the graph. Since such a 'jump' requires us to restart our SCC algorithm, we prefer to process the summary transitions later, after the current DFS is over.

Consequently, our search-space exploration algorithm is the same as REACHABILITY, except that when a summary is discovered, the returns corresponding to it are not pursued and instead the new summary transitions are recorded in a set $Summ$. The dynamic SCC algorithm processes these transitions and updates the SCCs. When the exploration stops (or the current *search phase* ends), we add the summary transitions in $Summ$ and run the dynamic SCC algorithm once more to effect the changes. Then we call the exploration algorithm again and ask it to proceed from the return states corresponding to the newly discovered summary transitions in $Summ$. We terminate, concluding that there is no fair cycle, if no new summary is found at the end of a search phase. Figure 3 and Figure 4 give the pseudocode of the entire algorithm FAIR-CYCLE-DETECT.

SCC-SEARCH explores the transition system S_R recursively, feeding every new transition to the procedure UPDATE-SCCs, which uses two stacks [16] to update the data structures it uses to remember the SCCs, and halts if the new transition introduces a fair cycle. To perform this update, it may have to do a DFS on the graph of discovered SCCs; however, since the edges fed to it in a phase are in DFS order, it only needs one cache of "visited" SCCs per phase.

While backtracking from the search, the procedure CREATE-COMPONENT, which marks an SCC to be used in the next phase, is called. Finally, the procedure COLLAPSE-SCCs takes in a set of summary edges found in the previous search phase (fair summaries are kept track of using a special bit b) and updates the current graph G of SCCs with them, terminating if it finds a fair cycle.

The correctness of this algorithm is guaranteed by the following theorem:

Theorem 3. *Given an ERSM A, a set R of repeating nodes, and the entry state $s_{init} = \langle en_p, \gamma_{in}, \lambda_{p_{in}} \rangle$, if the algorithm FAIR-CYCLE-DETECT halts, then it prints "Fair cycle found" iff there is a run of A that has infinitely many configurations ψ' with $Currnode(\psi') \in R$. Furthermore, if the state-graph S_R corresponding to A is finite, then FAIR-CYCLE-DETECT always halts.* $\square$

Recall that in every search phase, we need to perform a search on the graph of SCCs. The total number of search phases in FAIR-CYCLE-DETECT is bounded by the number of possible summaries in S_R. Let N be the maximum, over all component graphs S_i, of the number of pairs (s_{en}, s_{ex}), where s_{ex} is an exit state in S_i and is reachable from entry state s_{en} of S_i. Then S_R can have at most kN search phases, where k is the number of components in A. Hence, we have:

FAIR-CYCLE-DETECT()
```
 1    graph G ← ({s_in}, ∅); Visited ← ∅; S_in = {(s_in, s_in, (s_in ∈ R))}
 2    repeat
 3            Summ ← ∅; INITIALIZE-SCC-UPDATE()
 4            for (s, s_en, b) ∈ S_in
 5            do SCC-SEARCH (s, s_en, b)
 6            COLLAPSE-SCCs (Summ)
 7            if COLLAPSE-SCCs finds a fair nontrivial SCC
 8                then print ("Fair cycle found") ; break
 9            S_in ← {(s_ret, s', b) : ∃s.(s'_en, (s, s_ret), b) ∈ Summ}
10    until Summ = ∅
11    print ("No fair cycle")
```

Fig. 3. Fair cycle detection algorithm

SCC-SEARCH(s, s_en, b)
```
 1    Visited ← Visited ∪ {(s, s_en, b)}
 2    if s is an exit state in component i
 3    then VisitedExits[i, s_en] ← VisitedExits[i, s_en] ∪ {(s, b)}
 4            for (s', s'_en, b') ∈ VisitedCalls[i, s_en]
 5            do s_ret = GETRETURNSTATE(s', s); b_ret = b ∨ b' ∨ (s_ret ∈ R)
 6                if (s_ret, s'_en, b_ret) ∉ Visited
 7                    then Summ ← Summ ∪ {((s', s_ret), s'_en, b_ret)}
 8    else for e ∈ Edges_I(s)
 9            do if s satisfies guard of e
10                then s' ← APPLY(e, s); b' = b ∨ (s' ∈ R); UPDATE-SCCs(s, s', b');
11                    if UPDATE-SCCs finds a fair nontrivial SCC
12                        then print ("Fair cycle found") ; break
13                    if (s', s_en, b') ∉ Visited
14                        then SCC-SEARCH(s', s_en, b')
15            for e ∈ Edges_C(s)
16            do if s satisfies guard of e
17                then m ← Y(e); s' ← GETENTRYSTATE(e, s);
18                    b' = (s' ∈ R); UPDATE-SCCs(s, s', b')
19                    VisitedCalls[m, s'] ← VisitedCalls[m, s'] ∪ {(s, s_en, b)}
20                    if (s', s_en, b') ∉ Visited
21                        then SCC-SEARCH(s', s_en, b')
22                        else for (s_ex, b_ex) ∈ VisitedExits[Y(e), s']
23                            do s_ret = GETRETURNSTATE(s, s_ex)
24                                b_ret = b_ex ∨ b' ∨ (s_ret ∈ R)
25                                if (s_ret, s_en, b_ret) ∉ Visited
26                                    then SCC-SEARCH(s_ret, s_en, b_ret)
27    CREATE-COMPONENT ()
```

Fig. 4. Procedure SCC-Search

Theorem 4. *Let A be an ERSM, R be a set of repeating nodes and S_R be the associated state graph. Let n and m be the number of states and edges, β be* *a bound on the maximum number of reachable entry states* and *reachable exit states in any* S_i, *in the reachable part of* $\mathcal{S}_R$. *Then* FAIR-CYCLE-DETECT *takes* $O(kN(m\beta + n\beta^2))$ *time to terminate and uses space* $O(n\beta^2 + m)$.   □

Note that N is bounded by β^2. While FAIR-CYCLE-DETECT does not run in time linear in the size of $\mathcal{S}_R$, it has the early-termination property and some "on-the-fly" properties.

5   VERA

VERA is a Java implementation of the algorithms for reachability and fair cycle detection presented in this paper. In this section, we highlight its main features and compare it with MOPED [13], a popular BDD-based LTL model checker for pushdown systems.

Input Language. *Boolean programs*, introduced in [3] and used in the SLAM verification process [4], are abstractions of imperative programs that retain most of the control structures available in a C-like language but only allow variables and expressions of boolean type. These abstractions permit procedure calls with call-by-value parameter passing and recursion; procedures can return vectors of expressions. Global and local declarations of variables are permitted. Allowed statements include parallel assignment (where a list of variables may be assigned in parallel, either by a list of expressions or by a vector returned by a proce-dure), "goto" jumps, "if-else" branches, and "while" loops. Non-determinism is permitted both in branches and loops.

VERA accepts boolean programs as inputs; it also admits a bounded-integer data type and arithmetic expressions on variables declared as such. These ab-stractions are translated into ERSMs internally before the algorithms for reach-ability and fair cycle detection are applied.

Specifying Properties. One way to specify target (or repeating) nodes in VERA is to list a set of *target (or repeating) labels* along with the input. Any control location marked by such a label translates into a target or repeating node. The target (repeating) set may also be specified by a *monitor*.

A *monitor*, in our context, is a finite automaton M with edges labeled by guards on global and local variables in A, and a set of states identified as target states. The definition of the product P of M and A is standard: a configuration of P consists of a configuration of A and the current state of M, and progress along a monitor is allowed only if the current variables satisfy the guard on it. A target (or repeating) node in P is one where the current state of M is a target. Given a monitor and the ERSM underlying an input program, VERA can perform reachability (cycle) analysis for the product ERSM P.

5.1   Experiments

SLAM **Regression Testing Examples.** We ran VERA on the regression test suite for SLAM: a collection of 64 C programs which, after abstraction in SLAM,

Example	Lines	Globals	Locals	Reachable	Visited	VERA time(s)	MOPED time (s)
n-mutex1	439	3	13	Yes	274	0.06	0.04
p-mutex33	460	6	21	Yes	702	0.21	0.14
n-i2o-simple	347	2	3	Yes	94	0.08	0.01
n-list-22	305	0	15	Yes	316	0.07	0.02
p-mutex34	466	6	21	No	14144	6.17	0.08
p-farray	306	0	8	No	1304	0.18	0.01
p-nbebop-test	239	0	16	No	75524	151.85	0.04
p-srdriver	1454	10	36	No	-	-	0.29

Fig. 5. Experiments on the SLAM regression test suite

N	VERA runtime(s)	VERA visited states	MOPED runtime(s)	MOPED BDD nodes
4	0.08	95	0.16	40880
6	0.08	95	4.01	1.91×10^5
8	0.08	95	260.35	2.12×10^6
10	0.10	95	-	-
32	0.15	95	-	-

Fig. 6. Buggy quicksort

give boolean programs whose lengths range between 80 and 1450 lines. In each case, the query was: *is the control location labeled as SLIC_ERROR reachable?* The experiments were run on a machine with 2GB of RAM and two 1.4 GHz CPUs. Measurements on a few representative examples are tabulated in Figure 5. The first three columns show the number of lines of code, the number of global variables, and the maximum number of local variables in a procedure (recall that the number of ERSM states is exponential in the last two parameters). The next column gives the answer to the query. The next two columns give the number of visited states at termination, and total runtime in seconds. The final column shows the runtime of the MOPED model checker on the same example.

In the first four examples, where the target set is reachable, VERA seems to find a reachability witness easily. In the next four cases, where it has to generate the entire reachable state space, it performs much worse than MOPED. Particularly, in the last case, where there there may be as many as 10 uninitialized globals and 36 uninitialized locals in any procedure, the state space is too large for our procedure to terminate. On the other hand, in examples such as p-mutex34 where VERA works better, there are complex conditions on edges but the number of uninitialized variables is not very high.

Quicksort. Among the examples that come with MOPED is an abstraction of a buggy quicksort routine (quicksort_error.pds). The routine has two non-deterministically chosen integer inputs and can run into an infinite loop for some input values. While there exists a short witness to this error, it is by no means trivial.

We use MOPED and VERA to find this witness. To do this in VERA, we write a simple monitor and run the fair cycle detection module. We find that VERA's early termination capability lets it identify a cycle very fast, even when inputs have large ranges and, consequently, the set of reachable states is very large. The symbolic algorithm for MOPED, however, becomes prohibitively expensive as the number of bits in an integer (N) is increases, and does not terminate for $N = 10$ or above (see Figure 6).

We also compared VERA and MOPED on a trivial reachability property: whether the program has *some* terminating run. VERA identifies a witness immediately, whereas in MOPED, an effect similar to Figure 6 is observed.

Abstraction of a Linux Driver. Finally, we ran VERA's reachability and cycle detection algorithms on a manual abstraction of the Perle Specialix RIO driver for Linux. This driver, 1100 lines long and previously identified as buggy by the Stanford metacompilation project [11], contains a double locking error. We abstract it manually into a 220-line VERA input file, keeping the basic control structure intact, modeling locks and process id-s by VERA variables, and replacing many of the control-flow conditions by nondeterminism. We write simple monitors to answer the following questions:

(1) Is there an execution where the same lock is acquired twice in a row?
(2) Is every lock that is acquired also released?

In the former case, there exists a reachability witness to an error state. For 4-bit integers, VERA detects the error in 0.18s after visiting 15 states (this figure stays more or less the same even as the size of the integer type is made larger). In the second case, our abstraction satisfies the property, and VERA has to generate the entire state space before it terminates. Because of a few uninitialized integer variables, this space is quite large. For $N = 2$, it takes 50.92s. For higher values of N, VERA does not terminate.

6   Conclusions

We have presented algorithms for on-the-fly reachability and fair cycle detection for extended recursive state machines. Algorithmically, on-the-fly detection of cycles deserves further exploration. It is closely related to the problem of dynamic data structures for graphs where insertions are allowed, and queries check existence of cycles containing repeating nodes. It is open whether the worst-case quadratic bound of our cycle-detection algorithms can be improved. It would be interesting to know whether online SCC algorithms are essential to detect fair cycles in ERSMs on-the-fly, i.e. whether faster algorithms for on-the-fly traversal of ERSMs would necessarily imply faster online algorithms for cycle detection. Our implementation in VERA and experimentation support the hypothesis that on-the-fly model checking is a viable, and sometimes more effective, alternative to symbolic checkers for verifying ERSMs. Future work will focus on optimizations, alternative strategies for cycle detection, and applications to program analysis problems.

Acknowledgements. We thank Mihalis Yannakakis for useful discussions, Sriram Rajamani and Stefan Schwoon for the SLAM regression test suite, and an anonymous referee for several relevant references in program analysis.

References

1. R. Alur, K. Etessami, and M. Yannakakis. Analysis of recursive state machines. In *Proc. Computer-Aided Verification*, LNCS 2102: 207–220, 2001.

2. T. Andrews, S. Qadeer, S.K. Rajamani, J. Rehof, and Y. Xie. Zing: A model checker for concurrent software. In *Proc. CAV'04*, LNCS 3114: 484–487, 2004.

3. T. Ball and S. Rajamani. Bebop: A symbolic model checker for boolean programs. In *SPIN Workshop on Model Checking of Software*, LNCS 1885: 113–130, 2000.

4. T. Ball and S. Rajamani. The SLAM toolkit. In *Proc. CAV'01*, LNCS 2102, 2001.

5. M. Benedikt, P. Godefroid, and T. Reps. Model checking of unrestricted hierarchical state machines. In *Proc. ICALP '01*, LNCS 2076: 652–666, 2001.

6. A. Boujjani, J. Esparza, and O. Maler. Reachability analysis of pushdown automata: Applications to model checking. In *CONCUR'97*, LNCS 1243, 1997.

7. O. Burkart and B. Steffen. Model checking the full modal mu-calculus for infinite sequential processes. *Theoretical Computer Science*, 221:251–270, 1999.

8. J.C. Corbett, M.B. Dwyer, J. Hatcliff, S. Laubach, C.S. Pasareanu, Robby, and H. Zheng. Bandera: Extracting finite-state models from Java source code. In *Proc. of Intl. Conf. on Software Engg.*, pages 439–448. 2000.

9. C. Courcoubetis, M.Y. Vardi, P. Wolper, and M. Yannakakis. Memory efficient algorithms for the verification of temporal properties. *Formal Methods in System Design*, 1:275–288, 1992.

10. D.L. Dill, A.J. Drexler, A.J. Hu, and C.H. Yang. Protocol verification as a hardware design aid. In *IEEE International Conference on Computer Design: VLSI in Computers and Processors*, pages 522–525, 1992.

11. D. Engler, B. Chelf, A. Chou, and S. Hallem. Checking system rules using system-specific, programmer-written compiler extensions. In *Proc. 4th USENIX OSDI*, pages 1–16, 2000.

12. J. Esparza, D. Hansel, P. Rossmanith, and S. Schwoon. Efficient algorithms for model checking pushdown systems. In *Computer Aided Verification, 12th International Conference*, LNCS 1855, pages 232–247. Springer, 2000.

13. J. Esparza and S. Schwoon. A BDD-based model checker for recursive programs. *Lecture Notes in Computer Science*, 2102:324+, 2001.

14. M. Fähndrich, J.S. Foster, Z. Su, and A. Aiken. Partial online cycle elimination in inclusion constraint graphs. *Proc. PLDI '98*, pages 85–96, 1998.

15. A. Finkel, B. Willems, and P. Wolper. A direct symbolic approach to model checking pushdown systems. In *Proc. Workshop on Verification of Infinite State Systems*, volume 9 of *Electronic Notes in Theor. Comp. Sci.* Elsevier, 1997.

16. H. Gabow. Path-based depth-first search for strong and biconnected components. *Inf. Process. Lett.*, 74(3-4):107–114, 2000.

17. T.A. Henzinger, R. Jhala, R. Majumdar, G.C. Necula, G. Sutre, and W. Weimer. Temporal-safety proofs for systems code. In *CAV 02: Proc. of 14th Conf. on Computer Aided Verification*, LNCS 2404, pages 526–538, 2002.

18. G.J. Holzmann. The model checker SPIN. *IEEE Transactions on Software Engineering*, 23(5):279–295, 1997.

19. D.J. Pearce, P.H.J. Kelly, and C. Hankin. Online cycle detection and difference propagation for pointer analysis. *Software Quality Journal*, 12(4):311–337, 2004.

20. T. Reps, S. Horwitz, and M. Sagiv. Precise interprocedural dataflow analysis via graph reachability. *POPL '95*, pages 49–61, 1995.

Empirically Efficient Verification for a Class of Infinite-State Systems*

Jesse Bingham and Alan J. Hu

Department of Computer Science, University of British Columbia

Abstract. *Well-structured transition systems* (WSTS) are a broad and well-studied class of infinite-state systems, for which the problem of verifying the reachability of an upward-closed set of error states is decidable (subject to some technicalities). Recently, Bingham proposed a new algorithm for this problem, but applicable only to the special cases of broadcast protocols and petri nets. The algorithm exploits finite-state symbolic model checking and was shown to outperform the classical WSTS verification algorithm on a contrived example family of petri nets.

In this work, we generalize the earlier results to handle a larger class of WSTS, which we dub *nicely sliceable*, that includes broadcast protocols, petri nets, context-free grammars, and lossy channel systems. We also add an optimization to the algorithm that accelerates convergence. In addition, we introduce a new reduction that soundly converts the verification of parameterized systems with unbounded conjunctive guards into a verification problem on nicely sliceable WSTS. The reduction is complete if a certain decidable side condition holds. This allows us to access industrially relevant challenge problems from parameterized memory system verification. Our empirical results show that, although our new method performs worse than the classical approach on small petri net examples, it performs substantially better on the larger examples based on real, parameterized protocols (e.g., German's cache coherence protocol, with data paths).

1   Introduction

The widespread practical success of finite-state model checking [9, 29] has stimulated interest in the algorithmic verification of infinite-state systems. The goal is to verify systems that are naturally modelled as infinite state as well as systems that might be finite-state in practice, but that are too large to be verified via finite-state methods in the foreseeable future (e.g., pushdown automata to model a program's call stack, parameterized memory system protocols to model a realistically-sized memory system).

Well-structured transition systems (WSTS) [19, 2, 20] are a broad class of infinite-state systems, for which an extensive and elegant body of research has developed. In particular, the verification problem of determining the reachability of an upward-closed set of error states is decidable (provided some side conditions are satisfied) via an algorithmic framework we call the *classical approach* [2, 20, 18].

---

* This work was supported in part by a UBC Li Tze Fong Memorial Fellowship and a grant from the Natural Sciences and Engineering Research Council of Canada.

N. Halbwachs and L. Zuck (Eds.): TACAS 2005, LNCS 3440, pp. 77–92, 2005.

Recently, Bingham proposed a new algorithm for this problem [4]. Unlike the classical approach, the new algorithm works by computing fix-points over a series of finite-state systems of increasing size, allowing the leveraging of sophisticated techniques from finite-state model checking. However, the theory was developed only for a special case of WSTS, namely, broadcast protocols (which subsume petri nets). Using finite-state symbolic model checking [7], Bingham demonstrated a contrived family of petri nets for which the new algorithm substantially outperformed the classical approach.

This paper generalizes and extends the earlier work in several ways. We introduce a new subclass of WSTS and generalize the earlier theory and algorithms to apply to the subclass. We show how the new subclass subsumes petri nets, broadcast protocols, lossy channel systems, and context-free grammars. We introduce an optimization to the algorithm that accelerates convergence. We also provide a new reduction that allows soundly applying our verification method to certain protocols with unbounded conjunctive guards, which are not WSTS, as commonly occurs in memory system protocols. Finally, we give experimental evidence on a variety of infinite-state systems, including German's parameterized cache coherence protocol [23], a widely cited verification challenge problem.

Because of space constraints, all proofs have relegated to the appendix of the electronic version of this paper [5].

2   Preliminaries

Let $\mathbb{N}$ denote the natural numbers. We use various notations for orderings: $\preceq$ will denote an arbitrary reflexive and transitive relation (which may satisfy stronger requirements depending on context), and we write $x \prec y$ to mean $x \preceq y \wedge y \npreceq x$. The symbol $\leq$ will denote the usual ordering on the reals and subsets thereof, and for any positive dimension m, we extend $\leq$ to be the usual point-wise vector ordering over $\mathbb{N}^m$ defined by $v \leq u$ iff $v_i \leq u_i$ for all $1 \leq i \leq m$. We also employ $\leq$ as the covering relation between petri net markings.

The systems we consider are a certain type of *well-structured transition system*, and the "bad" states will be characterized by an *upward-closed* set. These and other relevant notions are now defined, mostly following the terminology of [20].

Definition 1 (upward-closure,basis,upward-closed set). *Let $\preceq$ be a reflexive and transitive relation over a set X. For $Y \subseteq X$, the* upward-closure *of Y is the set $\uparrow Y = \{x \mid \exists y \in Y : y \preceq x\}$. When $U = \uparrow Y$ we say that Y is a basis for U. A set U is said to be $\preceq$-upward-closed (or simply upward-closed if $\preceq$ is clear from context) if $U = \uparrow U$.*

Definition 2 (well-quasi-ordering). *A* well-quasi-ordering (wqo) *is a reflexive and transitive relation $\preceq$ over a set X such that for any infinite sequence $x_0, x_1, x_2, \dots$ over X, there exists $i, j \in \mathbb{N}$ such that $i < j$ and $x_i \preceq x_j$.*

Lemma 1. *[25] If $\preceq$ is a wqo, then any $\preceq$-upward-closed set has a unique finite basis B such that for all $x, y \in B$ we have $x \npreceq y \wedge y \npreceq x$.*

Given upward-closed U, we let basis(U) denote the unique finite basis of U, the existence of which is guaranteed by Lemma 1.

```
previous_reach, reach : finite subset of S
previous_reach := ∅
reach := gen(U)
while ↑reach ⊄ ↑previous_reach do
    if I ∩ ↑reach ≠ ∅ then
        exit with verification failure
    previous_reach := reach
    reach := reach ∪ Pred(↑reach)
exit with verification success
```

Fig. 1. The classical algorithm

Definition 3 (well-structured transition system). *A well-structured transition system (WSTS) is a triple* $(S, \rightarrow, \preceq)$ *such that*

1. *S is a (possibly infinite) state space*
2. $\rightarrow \subseteq S \times S$ *is called the transition relation*
3. $\preceq$ *is a wqo over S*
4. *For all* $x, x', y \in S$ *such that* $x \rightarrow x'$ *and* $x \preceq y$, *there exists* $y' \in S$ *such that* $y \rightarrow y'$.[1]

The covering relation $\leq$ between petri net markings is a wqo. Given a finite set of markings M, the set $\uparrow M$ includes all markings that cover at least one $m \in M$. Petri nets are WSTS (with respect to $\leq$) [20].

The decision problem regarding WSTS we aim to solve is as follows.

Definition 4 (WSTS Safety Problem). *Given a WSTS* $S = (S, \rightarrow, \preceq)$, *an* $\preceq$-*upward-closed set* $U \subseteq S$, *and a set of* initial states $I \subseteq S$, *does there exists a sequence* $x_0 \rightarrow \cdots \rightarrow x_\ell$ *such that* $x_0 \in I$ *and* $x_\ell \in U$? *We write* Safe(S, I, U) *(resp.,* ¬Safe(S, I, U)*) if the answer is "no" (resp. "yes").*

We have intentionally omitted any restrictions on the initial state set I to avoid needlessly complicating this paper. In general I can be infinite, hence a symbolic representation is necessary; for example, [2, 4] require that I be a so-called *parametric set*. Decidability of the WSTS Safety Problem depends (in part) on the form of I.

The *classical approach* to this problem is given in Fig. 1 [2, 18, 20]. On the surface, this algorithm resembles the well-known finite-state backward reachability analysis, i.e. *least fix-point computation*, the difference being that the involved sets are upward-closed (and hence infinite), so a symbolic representation (i.e. finite basis) is necessary. For the approach to work, the following conditions are necessary:

- Given finite *reach* $\subseteq S$, we must be able to compute another finite set X such that $\uparrow X = \{x \mid \exists y \in \uparrow reach : x \rightarrow y\}$. We denote X by Pred($\uparrow reach$).
- I must be represented in a form that permits the intersection checks of the if conditional.

---

[1] This requirement is called *monotonicity* in [2] and *strong compatibility* in [20]. The latter paper gives a slightly weaker definition of WSTS, requiring that y' only satisfy $y \rightarrow^* y'$.

Necessary for practical implementation of the classical algorithm is an efficient representation of *reach*, since this set can become very large. Delzanno et al. propose using a data structure called *covering sharing trees* (CST) for this purpose [12]. One drawback of this technique is that checking for convergence is co-NP hard in the size of the involved CSTs.

3   Nicely Sliceable WSTS

Our algorithm works on a subclass of WSTS we call *nicely sliceable WSTS* (NSW). To be deemed a NSW, a WSTS must satisfy three properties. We first describe each intuitively and provide some motivation for why they are required, and then we present the formal definitions.

- **Discrete:** The wqo must be discrete, meaning that for any element x, there is a bound on the length of any strictly decreasing sequence starting with x. We call the length of the longest such sequence x's *weight*. Furthermore, discreteness requires that the number of elements of a given weight be finite. Discreteness allows for finite-state model checking to be applied to the subsystem formed by bounding the weight of states.
- **Weight-Respecting:** When a transition changes the weight, the same change in weight can be effected by the transition relation for elements greater than the starting state of the transition. Weight-respectfulness is a technical requirement needed for the proof of the Convergence Theorem, which gives a termination condition for our algorithm.
- **Deflatable:** Whenever we have a transition from outside an upward-closed set U to a state in U, deflatability asserts the existence of a similar transition involving states of bounded weight. Deflatability is similar to downward compatibility [20], though the two are incomparable. Deflatability, like weight-respectfulness, is essential in the proof of our Convergence Theorem.

Definition 5 (dwqo, weight function, base weight). *A wqo is a* discrete wqo *(dwqo) over X if for all $x \in X$ there exists $k \in \mathbb{N}$ such for any sequence $x_0 \prec x_1 \prec \cdots \prec x_\ell = x$ we have $\ell \leq k$. Associated with a dwqo $\preceq$ is the* weight function $w : X \to \mathbb{N}$ *that maps each x to the minimum such k. We also require that $\{x \in X \mid w(x) = i\}$ be finite for each $i \in \mathbb{N}$. For $\preceq$-upward-closed U, the* base weight *of U is $\mathrm{bw}(U) = \max(\{w(x) \mid x \in \mathrm{basis}(U)\})$.*

Example 1. For $m \geq 1$, the point-wise vector ordering $\leq$ over $\mathbb{N}^m$ is a dwqo, and for each $v \in \mathbb{N}^m$ we have $w(v) = \sum_{i=1}^{m} v_i$. The set $\{0, 1/2, 2/3, 3/4, \ldots\} \cup \{1\}$ along with $\leq$ is an example of a wqo that is not a dwqo, since taking $x = 1$ violates Def. 5.

Definition 6 (discrete WSTS). *A discrete WSTS (DWSTS) is a WSTS $(S, \to, \preceq)$ where $\preceq$ is a dwqo.*

In a DWSTS, the weight function slices the state space into a countable number of finite partitions $S_0, S_1, S_2, \ldots$, where $S_i = \{x \in S \mid w(x) = i\}$.

Example 2. Petri nets along with the marking dominance relation $\leq$ are an example of DWSTSs; the induced weight function simply counts the number of tokens.

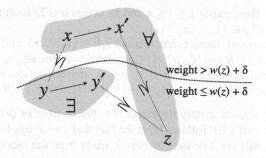

Fig. 2. A diagrammatic presentation of Def. 8. A DWSTS $(S, \rightarrow, \preceq)$ is said to be δ-deflatable (for $\delta \in \mathbb{N}$) if for all $x, x', z \in S$ that satisfy the depicted relations, there exists $y, y' \in S$ that satisfy the depicted relations, and also both $w(y)$ and $w(y')$ are not greater than $w(z) + \delta$.

Definition 7 (weight respecting DWSTS). *A DWSTS is said to be* weight respecting *if we may strengthen condition 4 of Def. 3 to require that* $w(x') - w(x) = w(y') - w(y)$.

Example 3. Petri nets are weight respecting DWSTSs. Suppose $x \rightarrow x'$ by firing transition t, and $x \preceq y$. Since firing t always changes the total number of tokens by the same amount, we can obtain the appropriate y' by firing t from y.

Definition 8 (δ-deflatable DWSTS). *A DWSTS* $(S, \rightarrow, \preceq)$ *is said to be* δ-deflatable *for* $\delta \in \mathbb{N}$ *if whenever* $x \rightarrow x'$ *and* $z \preceq x'$, *there exists* y *and* y' *such that all of the following hold: 1)* $y \preceq x$, *2)* $y \rightarrow y'$, *3)* $z \preceq y'$, *4)* $w(y) \leq w(z) + \delta$, *and 5)* $w(y') \leq w(z) + \delta$. *(See Fig. 2.)*

Example 4. Petri nets are δ-deflatable, where δ is the maximum over all in-degrees and out-degrees of the petri net transitions. A suitable $y \rightarrow y'$ can be constructed by taking only the tokens involved in the firing that takes $x \rightarrow x'$ and adding them to z.

Definition 9 (NSW). *A δ-NSW is a DWSTS that is weight-respecting and δ-deflatable. A NSW is a δ-NSW for some δ.*

We now give three examples of systems that are NSW.

Example 5. Broadcast protocols (BP), which model the composition of identical finite-state processes, are 2-NSW. Here we roughly follow the definition of [18, 17]. A BP is a triple (L, Σ, R), where L is the set of *local states*, Σ is the set of *labels*, and $R \subseteq L \times \Sigma \times L$. Σ is required to be of the form $\Sigma_l \cup \Sigma_r \times \{!, ?\} \cup \Sigma_b \times \{!!, ??\}$, where Σ_l, Σ_r, and Σ_b are disjoint sets of *actions*, respectively called *local*, *rendez-vous*, and *broadcast* actions. Labels of the form (a, d) are written simply as ad, i.e. $(a, ??)$ is written $a??$. Intuitively, labels of the form $a!$ and $a!!$, are outputs, while those of the form $a?$ and $a??$ are inputs. We make the following restriction on R: for any $a!! \in \Sigma$ and any $s \in L$, there exists $s' \in L$ such that $(s, a??, s') \in R$.

The semantics of a BP (L, Σ, R) is the transition system $(S, \rightarrow)$ where the state space S is the set of all nonempty finite words over L, and $s \rightarrow s'$ iff $s = \ell_1 \ldots \ell_n$ and $s' = \ell'_1 \ldots \ell'_n$, and one of the following hold.

- *local transition*: there exists $1 \leq i \leq n$ and an action $a \in \Sigma_l$ such that $(\ell_i, a, \ell'_i) \in R$, and $\ell'_j = \ell_j$ for all $j \in \{1, \ldots, n\} \setminus \{i\}$.
- *rendez-vous transition*: there exists distinct $i, k \in \{1, \ldots, n\}$ and an action $a \in \Sigma_r$ such that $(\ell_i, a!, \ell'_i) \in R$ and $(\ell_k, a?, \ell'_k) \in R$, and $\ell'_j = \ell_j$ for all $j \in \{1, \ldots, n\} \setminus \{i, k\}$.
- *broadcast transition*: there exists $1 \leq i \leq n$ and an action $a \in \Sigma_b$ such that $(\ell_i, a!!, \ell'_i) \in R$ and, for each $j \in \{1, \ldots, n\} \setminus \{i\}$, $(\ell_j, a??, \ell'_j) \in R$.

The weight of a BP state is simply its length (i.e. the number of processes involved). Weight respectfulness of a BP follows from the fact that $s \rightarrow s'$ implies that s and s' are of the same weight. BPs are 2-deflatable; here 2 arises from the fact that a rendez-vous transition is guarded by 2 processes.

Example 6. Lossy Channel Systems (LCS) [1] are 1-NSW. The state of a lossy LCS is a pair[2] (s, σ), where s an element in a finite state space, and $\sigma \in \Sigma^*$ is a string over the channel alphabet Σ. The usual wqo defined by $(s_1, \sigma_1) \preceq (s_2, \sigma_2)$ if $s_1 = s_2$ and σ_1 is a (not necessarily contiguous) substring of σ_2 is a dwqo[3]. The associated weight function is $w((s, \sigma)) = length(\sigma)$. A transition of a LCS can manipulate the channel string by appending a symbol to the tail, removing a symbol from the head, or nondeterministically deleting a symbol from anywhere in the string. The reader may verify that these systems are 1-deflatable and weight-respecting.

Example 7. Context-free grammars (CFG) are NSW. A CFG is a triple $G = (N, T, R)$ where N and T are disjoint, finite sets of *nonterminal symbols* and *terminal symbols*, respectively, and $R \subseteq N \times \Sigma^*$ is a finite set of *production rules*, where $\Sigma = N \cup T$. A CFG corresponds to the NSW $(\Sigma^*, \rightarrow, \preceq)$, where $x \rightarrow y$ iff there exist $x_1, x_2 \in \Sigma^*$ and $(\alpha, \beta) \in R$ such that $x = x_1 \alpha x_2$ and $y = x_1 \beta x_2$. The dwqo $\preceq \subseteq \Sigma^* \times \Sigma^*$ is such that $x \preceq y$ iff x can be obtained by deleting zero or more symbols from[3] y. The weight function is $w(x) = length(x)$. The system is δ-deflatable, where $\delta = \max(\{length(x) \mid \exists y \in N : (y, x) \in R\})$. Weight respectfulness comes from the fact that each production rule induces a fixed weight change.

4 Our Algorithm

This section develops our algorithm, which is shown in Fig. 3. The inputs are a δ-NSW $(S, \rightarrow, \preceq)$, a set of initial states I, and an $\preceq$-upward-closed set of target states U. For each $i = i_0, i_0 + 1, i_0 + 2, \ldots$, (where $i_0 = \text{bw}(U)$) the algorithm computes the backward reachable set $\text{br}(U, i)$, which is the set of states from which U is reachable along a path that never exceeds weight i. Formally, we have the following definition.

Definition 10 (br). *Given a WSTS $(S, \rightarrow, \preceq)$, an upward closed set $U \subseteq S$, and $i \in \mathbb{N}$ we let $\text{br}(U, i)$ denote the set of all $x \in S$ such that there exists a sequence $x_0 \rightarrow x_1 \rightarrow \cdots \rightarrow x_\ell$ such that $x_0 = x$, $x_\ell \in U$, and for all $0 \leq j \leq \ell$ we have $w(x_j) \leq i$. We also define $\text{br}(U) = \bigcup_{i=0}^{\infty} \text{br}(U, i)$.*

---

[2] For simplicity we include only a single channel, the usual definition allows for an arbitrary (but finite) number of channels.

[3] That this relation is a wqo is known as *Higman's Lemma*[25].

Since $br(U,i)$ is necessarily finite for all $i \geq 0$, this set can be computed using classical finite-state symbolic model checking [7] based on BDDs [6]. The algorithm terminates upon either of the following events:

- Convergence occurs. By *convergence*, we mean that we have reached an n such that $\uparrow br(U,n) = br(U)$. How this is done is articulated in our Theorem 1 below. The existence of such an n is guaranteed by Theorem 2.
- Intersection with the initial states is detected. Since we have left the requirements of the initial states undefined, we have necessarily left this check undefined in our algorithm. In general, for this check to be computable, we must be able to decide if $I \cap br(U) = \emptyset$, given $br(U,n)$, where n is as in the previous item.

We now present two theorems. Theorem 1 gives us a necessary and sufficient condition for convergence, while Theorem 2 guarantees that our algorithm will always terminate.

Theorem 1 (Convergence). *For a δ-NSW, an upward-closed set U, and $n \geq bw(U)$,*

$$br(U, n + \delta) \subseteq \uparrow br(U, n) \tag{1}$$

if and only if

$$br(U) = \uparrow br(U, n) \tag{2}$$

Theorem 2. *For any DWSTS and upward-closed set U, there exists an n satisfying (2).*

In order to use Theorem 1 in our algorithm, we must have a means to decide (1). Our approach requires the use of a computable *lifting operator*, which intuitively "lifts" a set $br(U,i)$ to a truncated version of its upward-closure. The truncation omits everything with weight strictly greater than some given $d \in \mathbb{N}$; hence finiteness is preserved.

Definition 11 (lifting operator). *Given a dwqo $\preceq$ over a set X, the associated* lifting operator *is the function* $\text{Lift} : X \times \mathbb{N} \to 2^X$ *defined by*

$$\text{Lift}(x,d) = \{y \mid x \preceq y \wedge w(y) \leq d\}$$

We extend Lift *to act on sets by decreeing* $\text{Lift}(Y,d) = \bigcup_{y \in Y} \text{Lift}(y,d)$.

The following theorem explains how the lifting operator is relevant to deciding containments along the lines of (1). For a finite set X, let $\text{maxw}(X) = \max(\{w(x) \mid x \in X\})$.

Theorem 3. *Let $\preceq$ be a dwqo over a set X, and let X_{i-1} and X_i be finite subsets of X such that $\text{maxw}(X_{i-1}) \leq i - 1$ and $\text{maxw}(X_i) \leq i$. Then $X_i \subseteq \uparrow X_{i-1}$ if and only if $X_i \subseteq \text{Lift}(X_{i-1}, i)$.*

```
1    i := bw(U)
2    n := i
3    Γ_{i-1} := ∅
4    while (n ≥ i − δ) do
5        compute Γ_i := br(U,i)
6        if intersection(Γ_i,I) then
7            exit with verification failure
8        if (Γ_i ⊄ Lift(Γ_{i-1},i)) then
9            n := i
10       i := i+1
11   exit with verification success
```

Fig. 3. Our algorithm, which, given a δ-NSW S, an upward-closed set U, and a set of initial states I, decides $\mathsf{Safe}(S,I,U)$ using finite-state model checking. The variable i represents the maximum weight of the states computed in each iteration of the while-loop. i is initially the base weight of U and is incremented each iteration. The variable n tracks the last value of i for which "new" states were found in $\mathsf{br}(U,i)$ (see Def. 10), i.e. states x that weren't already "covered" by the existence of $y \in \mathsf{br}(U,i-1)$ such that $y \preceq x$. The condition of the while loop (line 4) will only fail when (1) holds, which by Theorem 1 indicates convergence. Each iteration of the loop involves computing $\mathsf{br}(U,i)$, which is done in a nested backward reachability loop (implicit in line 5). Line 6 tests to see if the initial states have been reached, and line 7 terminates if so. Line 8 determines if something "new" was found this iteration, if so n is updated to be i. If the condition of line 8 fails δ times consecutively, by Theorem 3 we have $\Gamma_{n+\delta} \subseteq \Gamma_{n+\delta-1} \subseteq \cdots \subseteq \Gamma_n$ and thus (1) holds and verification is successful. Theorem 2 guarantees that this will eventually happen

4.1 An Optimization

In this section we propose an optimization to the algorithm of Fig. 3. Note that in Fig 3, the computation of $\mathsf{br}(U,i)$ involves an iterative fix-point computation, starting with set $U_{\leq i} = \{x \in U \mid w(x) \leq i\}$. In some sense, much of the work of this computation was already performed when computing $\mathsf{br}(U,i-1)$; since this is a subset of $\mathsf{br}(U,i)$, it is redundant to "rediscover" these states. Also note that

$$U_{\leq i} \subseteq \mathsf{Lift}(\mathsf{br}(U,i-1),i) \subseteq \mathsf{br}(U)$$

It follows that we can eliminate the unnecessary overhead by starting the fix-point computation from $\mathsf{Lift}(\mathsf{br}(U,i-1),i)$, a set which we need to compute anyway for the containment check of line 8. Our optimization involves replacing lines 3 and 5 of Fig. 3 with the following, respectively:

$$\begin{aligned}
&3'\quad \Gamma_{i-1} := \mathsf{basis}(U)\\
&5'\qquad \text{compute } \Gamma_i := \mathsf{br}(\mathsf{Lift}(\Gamma_{i-1},i),i)
\end{aligned} \tag{3}$$

This optimization has the potential to greatly reduce the number of iterations performed in the fix-point computations. As an extreme example, in an iteration of the outer loop for which $\mathsf{br}(U,i) \subseteq \mathsf{Lift}(\mathsf{br}(U,i-1),i)$ holds, the computation of Γ_i will involve only a single backward image computation.

Theorem 4. *The optimization (3) preserves correctness of our algorithm.*

5   Implementation Using Symbolic Model Checking

Given an NSW $(S, \rightarrow, \preceq)$, our algorithm manipulates finite subsets of S, so, in theory, we can directly apply standard finite-state symbolic model checking. In practice, we must provide a state encoding for the the finite-state subsets and a way to compute the tasks needed by our algorithm:

- the fix-point computation of line 5 or $5'$
- the intersection check of line 6
- the lifting operation of line 8
- the containment check of line 8

This section sketches how we implemented the algorithm for various types of NSW. Our current implementation uses a very straightforward BDD-based approach, but our algorithm should be able to harness the many advances in symbolic model checking.

5.1   Parameterized Protocols

For petri nets and extensions such as broadcast protocols, there is a natural notion of *local state*, i.e., the (finite) state of each process in the broadcast protocol, or the place (out of a finite number) occupied by each token in a petri net. Our encoding follows [4] and uses *concrete global states*, i.e. tuples over local states. The weight is simply the number of processes, so we can represent subsets of S_i by sets over L^i, where L is the local state space. It is straightforward to construct a BDD for the transition relation in this framework, and hence the fix-point computation. The lifting operation is called *existential lifting* and can be computed using standard BDD operations. Finally, [4] shows that when I is a so-called *parametric set*, the intersection check of line 6 can also be performed using standard operations.

5.2   Lossy Channel Systems

As explained in Example 6, the infinite state space of a LCS is $S = C \times \Sigma^*$, where C is the finite state space of the control, and Σ is the channel alphabet. Let $S_{\leq i} = \{(c, \sigma) \in S \mid length(\sigma) \leq i\}$. Similarly to our encoding for parameterized protocols, we represent a subset of $S_{\leq i}$ by a collection of tuples of the form $(s, c_1, c_2, \ldots, c_i)$, where $s \in S$ and each $c_j \in \Sigma \cup \{empty\}$. Here $c_1, \ldots, c_i$ stores the contents of the channel, and the new symbol *empty* indicates that the channel "slot" does not contain a message. The lifting operator simply inserts an element of $\Sigma \cup \{empty\}$ nondeterministically into the channel, hence (possibly) increasing the number of non-*empty* slots by 1. The intersection and containment checks are also straightforward in this representation.

5.3   Comparison to Standard Approach

Comparing our approach to the classical approach (i.e., CSTs) provides intuition about when each approach is likely to perform better.

Convergence. Given two CSTs C_1 and C_2, the problem of checking if C_1 *subsumes* C_2 (i.e. if the upward-closed set represented by C_1 is a superset of that of C_2) is co-NP hard in the size of the involved CSTs [12]. Unfortunately, checking subsumption is an integral part of the classical algorithm (cf. the while condition in Fig. 1). To combat this problem, Delzanno et al. develop a sophisticated heuristic solution in which certain CST simulation relations facilitate pruning of an (exponential time) exact subsumption check [13]. In contrast, subsumption between two BDDs can be decided in time proportional to the product of their sizes [6]. In fact, we can correctly replace the containment of line 8 of Fig. 3 with an equality test: $\Gamma_i \neq \text{Lift}(\Gamma_{i-1}, i)$. This test can be done *in constant time* using a reasonable BDD library, such as CUDD [30].

Data Structure Size. The main efficiency difference is likely to derive from the sizes of the underlying data structures. Predicting the dynamics of the sizes is a complex problem. Though BDDs compactly represent many practical boolean functions, the worst case size is exponential in their height (i.e. the number of boolean variables). Similarly, although bounds on the size of CST have not been derived in the literature (to our knowledge), any such bound is at least exponential in the height of the structure. Here, we consider data structure height as a coarse measure of worst-case size.

The CST-based approach is applicable to both petri nets and broadcast protocols. Let L be the set of local states (i.e. petri net places). Then we call $|L|$ the *dimensionality* of a parameterized protocol. The height of the CSTs is fixed and equal to the dimensionality, while the height of the BDDs is at most $(n_f + \delta) \lceil \log_2 |L| \rceil$, where n_f is the final value of n in our algorithm. This suggests that our approach might be superior when $(n_f + \delta) \lceil \log_2 |L| \rceil$ is much less than the dimensionality, since under such circumstances the CSTs are more likely to blow-up.

For other NSW, such as LCS and CFG, we expect our ability to encode large control states spaces and/or large alphabets compactly using BDDs to provide our approach with an advantage for systems with these characteristics.

6   Conjunctive Guard Reduction

Though WSTS (and indeed NSW) encompass a broad and important class of infinite state systems, there are common system attributes that preclude well-structuredness. An example of such an attribute is the so-called *conjunctive guard* (CG). CG are used in parameterized systems of processes when a transition is to be enabled only if the local states of *all* processes satisfy some predicate. This contrasts with petri net or broadcast protocols, in which only a fixed, finite number of processes may guard a transition. Unfortunately, endowing petri nets or broadcast protocols with CG renders even safety property verification undecidable [15]. In this section we develop a sound reduction that reduces a BP with conjunctive guards with to a BP.

Emerson and Kahlon have proposed a sound *and complete* verification technique for a class of protocols with CG [16], however it is unclear if the approach will scale beyond systems with small local state. For example, their subsequent treatment of German's protocol requires a nontrivial amount of manual reasoning [14].

BPs were defined formally in Example 5; here we extend that definition to define *conjunctively guarded broadcast protocols* (CGBP). A CGBP is a tuple (L, Σ, R, g), where (L, Σ, R) is a BP, and $g : \Sigma_l \rightarrow 2^L$. For each action $a \in \Sigma_l$, $g(a)$ is called the *conjunctive guard*. The semantics are changed so that a local transition a may occur only if all other processes are in states that satisfy the conjunctive guard of a^4. Formally, we conjoin the following condition to the local transition semantics presented in Example 5: $\ell_j \in g(a)$ for all $j \in \{1, \ldots, n\} \setminus \{i\}$.

Local action a is said to be *conjunctively guarded* if $g(a) \neq L$. Hence a BP is a CGBP in which no action is conjunctively guarded, since in this case the additional requirement on each local transition is tautological.

Our reduction transforms a CGBP $\mathcal{B} = (L, \Sigma, R, g)$ into a BP $\mathcal{B}' = (L', \Sigma', R')$. Intuitively $\mathcal{B}'$ replaces conjunctively guarded local actions with broadcasts. These new broadcasts allow all processes to check if they *would have* permitted the transition in $\mathcal{B}$, i.e. if their local state satisfies the CG. Whenever a process detects a violation of a CG in this manner, it refuses to participate in any future actions by "resigning"; resigned processes are stuck in that state forever.

Formally, we define $\mathcal{B}'$ as follows. We denote by Σ_{cg} the set of conjunctively guarded actions in $\mathcal{B}$, i.e. $\Sigma_{cg} = \{a \mid a \in \Sigma_l \wedge g(a) \neq L\}$.

- $L' = L \cup \{resigned\}$, where *resigned* is a new local state not in L. A process will enter *resigned* if it notices (through a broadcast) that a conjunctive guard was violated.
- Σ' is defined by $\Sigma'_l = \Sigma_l \setminus \Sigma_{cg}$, $\Sigma'_r = \Sigma_r$, and $\Sigma'_b = \Sigma_b \cup \Sigma_{cg}$, i.e. all conjunctively guarded local actions are replaced with broadcasts.
- R' contains exactly the following transitions
  - for each $(\ell, \alpha, \ell') \in R$ such that $\alpha \in \{a!, a?, a!!, a??\} \cup \Sigma'_l$ we have $(\ell, \alpha, \ell') \in R'$. Hence all rendez-vous, broadcast, and non-conjunctively guarded local actions are unchanged.
  - for each $(\ell, a, \ell') \in R$ such that $a \in \Sigma_{cg}$ we have $(\ell, a!!, \ell') \in R'$. Hence conjunctively guarded local actions become broadcasts.
  - for each $a \in \Sigma_{cg}$ $(\ell, a??, \ell') \in R'$, where $\ell' = \ell$ if $\ell \in g(a)$ otherwise $\ell' = resigned$. Hence, upon receiving a broadcast corresponding to a CG transition, a process is unaffected if it satisfied the conjunctive guard, otherwise it enters *resigned*.
  - for each $a \in \Sigma'_b$ we have $(resigned, a??, resigned) \in R'$. These transitions serve only to satisfy the restriction that broadcasts must always be received.

The following theorem states that $\mathcal{B}'$ is a sound reduction of $\mathcal{B}$, and can be proved by observing that any reachable state of $\mathcal{B}$ corresponds to a reachable state of $\mathcal{B}'$ in which no process is in local state *resigned*.

Theorem 5. *For CGBP $\mathcal{B}$, $\mathsf{Safe}(\mathcal{B}', I, U)$ implies $\mathsf{Safe}(\mathcal{B}, I, U)$.*

This reduction is "complete" if a certain decidable side condition holds. For each conjunctively guarded local transition a of $\mathcal{B}$, let $\widehat{g}(a) \subseteq L$ be the set of local states ℓ such that there exists a sequence of zero or more non-conjunctively guarded local transitions taking ℓ to a state $\ell' \in g(a)$; note that $g(a) \subseteq \widehat{g}(a)$. We construct a broadcast protocol

---

[4] Our definition of CGBP allows only local actions to have conjunctive guards. The definition and the reduction can be generalized to support conjunctively guarded rendez-vous and broadcasts.

$\mathcal{B}''$ that modifies $\mathcal{B}'$ as follows. A new local state *error* is added, and when a process in local state ℓ receives broadcast a (corresponding to a conjunctively guarded local action in $\mathcal{B}$), its next state is ℓ', defined by

$$\ell' = \begin{cases} error & \text{if } \ell \notin \widehat{g}(a) \\ resigned & \text{if } \ell \in \widehat{g}(a) \wedge \ell \notin g(a) \\ \ell & \text{if } \ell \in g(a) \end{cases}$$

Let *Error* be the set of all broadcast protocol states such that at least one process is in local state *error*. We note that *Error* is upward-closed. The following theorem states that if *Error* is unreachable in $\mathcal{B}''$, then the conjunctive guard reduction is both sound and complete.

Theorem 6. *For CGBP $\mathcal{B}$, suppose* $\mathsf{Safe}(\mathcal{B}'',I,Error)$. *Then* $\mathsf{Safe}(\mathcal{B},I,U)$ *if and only if* $\mathsf{Safe}(\mathcal{B}',I,U)$.

7 Experiments

In this section, we present experimental results for several petri nets, a MESI cache protocol, a lossy channel system, and a more elaborate caching protocol. All experiments were run on a machine with an Intel Pentium 4 at 2.6GHz and 4GB total memory. The implementation of the classical approach we compare against is based on an extension of CSTs called *interval sharing trees* [21].

7.1 Petri Nets

In [13], Delzanno et al. run their CST-based implementation of the classical approach against several petri nets. These nets have small dimensionality, so, as discussed in Sect. 5.3, we do not expect our approach to perform well. Indeed, Table 1 shows that the CST-based implementation outperforms our approach by several orders of magnitude. Recall from Sect. 5.3 that we anticipated that our approach would have an advantage when the height of our BDDs is dwarfed by the height of the CSTs, which is not the case here. In fact, for all three petri nets, the CSTs enjoy a shorter height than the BDDs.

7.2 MESI Protocol

MESI is a common variety of cache coherence protocol. In a MESI protocol, each client has a cache block in one of four states: *modified* (M), *exclusive* (E), *shared* (S), or

Table 1. Experiments involving selected petri nets from [13]. For Mesh(2×2), our tool spaced out

Petri net	Our runtime	CST runtime	Max BDD height	CST height (dimensionality)
Multipool	3010	2.09	50	18
CSM	95	0.06	36	14
Mesh(2×2)	>1300	1.30	>40	32

Table 2. Results for the MESI protocol with conjunctive guards over multiple blocks. Run times are in seconds. The column *dimension* indicates the height of the CST data structures in the CST approach, and also the width of the real vectors processed by Hytech in Delzanno's polyhedral approach

# of blocks	Our runtime	CST runtime	Hytech runtime	Max BDD height	dimension
1	0.0	0.0	0.0	9	5
2	0.1	0.2	380.0	18	25
3	0.7	131.9	>7989.0	27	125
4	4.6			36	625

invalid (I). Although many MESI protocols are conceivable, here we use the standard version used by computer architects (e.g., [10]), which has a conjunctive guard, so we use our reduction from Sect. 6.

We wanted a "knob" that would give us some control over the size of the local state space. Since cache protocols are typically used to orchestrate the sharing of multiple blocks, we instantiated the MESI protocol over m blocks[5], for $m \in \{1, 2, 3, 4\}$.

Results are given in Table 2. Our CG reduction allowed the verification to succeed, so there was no need to verify the side condition. We compare our result against both the CST-based classical approach and another variant of the classical approach based on the polyhedral model checker hytech [11, 24]. The results clearly indicate the superior scalability of our approach as the local state grows. The Hytech-based approach aborts even for $m = 3$, reporting "Out of memory". The parser of the CST tool cannot handle the size of the description of MESI with 4 blocks, which is 5.9 MBs. This large size arises because the broadcast matrices used by the classical approach grow quadratically in the dimension of the problem. This contrasts with the mere 30 KB of SMV that constitutes our tool's input.

7.3 Alternating Bit Protocol

As an experiment with lossy channel systems, we selected the alternating bit protocol (ABP). ABP involves two unbounded, lossy channels, one that carries data and sequence bits from the sender to the receiver, and another that carries acknowledgements from the receiver to the sender. Our ABP model is based on the presentation in [27], and we verify that whenever the sender receives an acknowledgement, the previously sent data (a copy of which is saved by the sender) matches the receiver's data buffer. As a complexity knob, we vary the number *data_count*, which specifies the number of different data values that may be sent. Results are shown in Table 3.

---

[5] In this case, since the "sub-protocols" controlling each block are independent, correctness for $m = 1$ entails correctness for all $m \geq 1$. In practice, however, such a simplification is often not possible, because real protocols can exhibit nontrivial interactions between different blocks. This experiment measures how our approach handles the explosive growth in local state resulting from analyzing multiple blocks.

Table 3. Alternating Bit Protocol Results. As a rough comparison, we ran preliminary experiments with TReX, a state-of-the-art verification tool for lossy channel systems [3]. We do not intend a direct comparison, because of our inexperience with TReX (e.g., an internal data structure overflowed when we tried *data_count* = 6). However, the pattern is clear: TReX is faster when the alphabet (analogous to dimensionality in broadcast protocols) is small, but the run time is growing exponentially; our tool scales more gracefully

data_count	our runtime
3	0.2
7	0.6
15	1.9
31	5.7
63	23.1
127	90.0
255	340.7

data_count	TReX runtime
1	0.01
2	0.02
3	0.05
4	0.08
5	0.15

7.4   German's Protocol

German's protocol [23] is a challenge problem for parameterized verification that has been previously tackled in several papers [28, 26, 8]. As in [8], we include a one bit data path. The original description [23] is a Murφ model, and is almost a CGBP: the Murφ description involves a variable of type *client ID*. We've encoded this variable by simply giving each process an extra bit, which is true iff the original variable would point to the process. This system is a CGBP, and our CG reduction is applied.

As mentioned in Sect. 7.2, even *describing* a BP in a format suitable for the classical approach is problematic when the dimension is large. Due to its various channels and the presence of data variables, our model of German's protocol has a dimensionality of 6144. For this reason, we were unable even to run the CST-tool against this example. The results for our tool are given in Table 4.

Table 4. Results for German's Protocol. To convert the protocol to a CGBP, we needed to re-encode the curPtr variable. Although this encoding was straightforward, we verified the encoding as a sanity check. The main verification task was "data coherence", which verified that the value of each read is the most recently written data value. Since the CG reduction is sound and the verification succeeded, we actually did not need to run the "conjunctive guard reduction" verification task. We have provided the run time simply to illustrate that the side condition is verifiable in practice

Property (all passed)	Runtime (sec)
Encoding of curPtr	3
Conjunctive guard reduction	214
Data coherence	63

8   Conclusions and Future Work

We have introduced the concept of NSW and provided a new algorithm for verification of these transition systems. The algorithm harnesses the power of finite-state symbolic model checking. We have also introduced a new reduction for systems with unbounded conjunctive guards. As predicted by our theory, experimental results show that our new verification algorithm greatly outperforms existing approaches for systems that involve large local state spaces, control state spaces, channel alphabets, etc. We attribute this to the ability of BDDs to encode such sets succinctly.

Our current implementation is fairly naive. We believe more sophisticated symbolic model checking techniques can produce still better results. Other avenues for future work include computing bounds on BDD sizes, finding additional NSW applications, and finding ways to apply our method semi-algorithmically to systems that are not NSW.

Very recently, Geeraerts et al. [22] have proposed a compelling approach to verification of WSTS based on forward reachability. This is the first sound and complete algorithm that performs forward analysis of WSTS. Similar to our approach, theirs is based on a framework in which a sequence of finite-state subsystems of increasing size are examined until either a counterexample is found, or a certain convergence condition is reached. Convergence occurs when an abstraction, which becomes more and more precise, is tight enough to verify non-reachability. Obvious directions for future work include comparing our approach with that of Geeraerts et al., and investigating the possibility of employing BDDs as we do for backward reachability in their forward framework.

References

1. P. Abdulla and B. Jonsson. Verifying programs with unreliable channels. In *Proceedings of the Eighth Annual IEEE Symposium on Logic in Computer Science*, pages 160–170, 1993.
2. P. A. Abdulla, K. Cerans, B. Jonsson, and T. Yih-Kuen. General decidability theorems for infinite-state systems. In *10th Annual IEEE Symp. on Logic in Computer Science (LICS'96)*, pages 313–321, 1996.
3. A. Annichini, A. Bouajjani, and M. Sighireanu. TReX: A tool for reachability analysis of complex systems. In *Proc. 13th Intern. Conf. on Computer Aided Verification (CAV'01)*, 2001.
4. J. Bingham. A new approach to upward closed set backward reachability analysis. In *6th International Workshop on Verification of Infinite-State Systems (INFINITY)*, 2004.
5. J. Bingham and A. J. Hu. Empirically efficient verification for a class of infinite-state systems. Extended electronic version of this paper, Lecture Notes in Computer Science number 3440, http://www.springerlink.com/.
6. R. E. Bryant. Graph-based algorithms for boolean function manipulation. *IEEE Transactions on Computers*, C-35(8):677–691, August 1986.
7. J. R. Burch, E. M. Clarke, K. L. McMillan, D. L. Dill, and L. J. Hwang. Symbolic model checking: 10^{20} states and beyond. *Information and Computation*, 98(2), 1992.
8. C.T. Chou, P. K. Mannava, and S. Park. A simple method for parameterized verification of cache coherence protocols. In *Formal Methods in Computer-Aided Design*, 2004.
9. E. M. Clarke and E. A. Emerson. Design and synthesis of synchronization skeletons using branching time temporal logic. In Dexter Kozen, editor, *Workshop on Logics of Programs*, pages 52–71, May 1981. Published 1982 as Lecture Notes in Computer Science Number 131.

10. D. E. Culler, J. P. Singh, and A. Gupta. *Parallel Computer Architecture: A Hardware/Software Approach.* Morgan Kaufmann, 1998.
11. G. Delzanno. Automatic verification of parameterized cache coherence protocols. In *Proceedings of the 12th International Conference on Computer Aided Verification*, July 2000.
12. G. Delzanno and J. F. Raskin. Symbolic representation of upward-closed sets. In *6th International Conference Tools and Algorithms for Construction and Analysis of Systems (TACAS)*, pages 426–440, 2000.
13. G. Delzanno, J. F. Raskin, and L. Van Begin. Attacking symbolic state explosion. In *Proceedings of the 13th International Conference on Computer-Aided Verification (CAV)*, pages 298–310, 2001.
14. E. A. Emerson and V. Kahlon. Exact and efficient verification of parameterized cache coherence protocols. In *12th IFIP Advanced Research Working Conference on Correct Hardware Design and Verification Methods (CHARME)*, October 2003.
15. E. A. Emerson and V. Kahlon. Model checking guarded protocols. In *Eighteenth Annual IEEE Symposium on Logic in Computer Science (LICS)*, pages 361–370, June 2003.
16. E. A. Emerson and V. Kahlon. Rapid parameterized model checking of snoopy cache protocols. In *9th International Conference on Tools and Algorithms for Construction and Analysis of Systems (TACAS)*, pages 144–159, April 2003.
17. E. A. Emerson and K. S. Namjoshi. On model checking for non-deterministic infinite-state systems. In *Proceedings of LICS 1998*, pages 70–80, 1998.
18. J. Esparza, A. Finkel, and R. Mayr. On the verification of broadcast protocols. In *Proceedings of LICS '99*, pages 352–359, 1999.
19. A. Finkel. Reduction and covering of infinite reachability trees. *Information and Computation*, 89(2):144–179, 1990.
20. A. Finkel and Ph. Schnoebelen. Well structured transition systems everywhere! *Theoretical Computer Science*, 256(1-2):63–92, 2001.
21. P. Ganty and L. Van Begin. Non deterministic automata for the efficient verification of infinite-state. presented at: CP+CV Workshop at European Joint Conferences on Theory and Practice of Software (ETAPS), 2004.
22. G. Geeraerts, J.-F. Raskin, and L. Van Begin. Expand, Enlarge and Check: new algorithms for the coverability problem of WSTS. In *Proceedings of FSTTCS'04, 24th International Conference on Foundations of Software Technology and Theoretical Computer Science, Chennai, India*, pages 287–298, 2004.
23. S. German. Personal correspondence. 2003.
24. T. A. Henzinger, P.-H. Ho, and H. Wong-Toi. Hytech: A model checker for hybrid systems. *Software Tools for Technology Transfer*, 1:110–122, 1997.
25. G. Higman. Ordering by divisibility in abstract algebras. *Proceedings of the London Mathematical Society (3)*, 2(7):326–336, 1952.
26. S. K. Lahiri and R. E. Bryant. Constructing quantified invariants via predicate abstraction. In *Proc. of 5th Intl. Conference on Verification, Model Checking and Abstract Interpretation (VMCAI)*, pages 267–281, 2004. LNCS 2937.
27. L. Lamport. *Specifying Systems: The TLA+ Language and Tools for Hardware and Software Engineers*. Addision-Wesley, 2002.
28. A. Pnueli, S. Ruah, and L. Zuck. Automatic deductive verification with invisible invariants. In *Proceedings of Tools and Algorithms for the Construction and Analysis of Systems (TACAS)*, pages 82–97, 2001.
29. J.-P. Queille and J. Sifakis. Specification and verification of concurrent systems in Cesar. In *5th International Symposium on Programming*, pages 337–351. Springer, 1981. Lecture Notes in Computer Science Number 137.
30. F. Somenzi. Colorado university decision diagram package (CUDD) webpage. http://vlsi.colorado.edu/~fabio/CUDD/cuddIntro.html.

Context-Bounded Model Checking of Concurrent Software

Shaz Qadeer and Jakob Rehof

Microsoft Research
{qadeer, rehof}@microsoft.com

Abstract. The interaction among concurrently executing threads of a program results in insidious programming errors that are difficult to reproduce and fix. Unfortunately, the problem of verifying a concurrent boolean program is undecidable [24]. In this paper, we prove that the problem is decidable, even in the presence of unbounded parallelism, if the analysis is restricted to executions in which the number of context switches is bounded by an arbitrary constant. Restricting the analysis to executions with a bounded number of context switches is unsound. However, the analysis can still discover intricate bugs and is sound up to the bound since within each context, a thread is fully explored for unbounded stack depth. We present an analysis of a real concurrent system by the ZING model checker which demonstrates that the ability to model check with arbitrary but fixed context bound in the presence of unbounded parallelism is valuable in practice. Implementing context-bounded model checking in ZING is left for future work.

1 Introduction

The design of concurrent programs is difficult due to interaction between concurrently executing threads, leading to programming errors that are difficult to reproduce and fix. Therefore, analysis techniques that can automatically detect errors in concurrent programs can be invaluable. In this paper, we present a novel interprocedural static analysis based on model checking [8, 23] for finding subtle safety errors in concurrent programs with unbounded parallelism.

Algorithms exist for checking assertions in a single-threaded boolean program with procedures (and consequently an unbounded stack) [28, 25] and form the basis of a number of efficient static analysis tools [4, 10] for sequential programs. But the same problem is undecidable for multi-threaded programs [24]. As a result, most previous analyses for concurrent programs have suffered from two limitations. Some restrict the synchronization model, which makes the analysis inapplicable to most common concurrent software applications. Other analyses are imprecise either because they are flow-insensitive or because they use decidable but coarse abstractions. This limitation makes it extremely difficult to report errors accurately to programmers. As a result, these analyses have seen limited use in checking tools for concurrent software. We present a more detailed discussion of related work in Section 6.

N. Halbwachs and L. Zuck (Eds.): TACAS 2005, LNCS 3440, pp. 93–107, 2005.
© Springer-Verlag Berlin Heidelberg 2005

In this paper, we take a different approach and focus on the following decision problem:

> Given a multithreaded boolean program P and a positive integer k, does P go wrong by failing an assertion via an execution with at most k contexts?

A *context* is an uninterrupted sequence of actions by a *single* thread. Thus, in an execution with k contexts execution switches from one thread to another $k - 1$ times. We prove that this problem is decidable and present an algorithm that is polynomial in the size of P and exponential in the parameter k.

Our technique, although unsound in general, is both sound and precise for context-bounded executions of concurrent programs. We believe that it can catch nontrivial safety errors caused by concurrency. First, even though our analysis bounds the number of contexts in an execution, it fully explores a thread within each context. Due to recursion within a thread, the number of stack configurations explored within a context is potentially unbounded. Our analysis considers each such reachable configuration as a potential point for a context switch and schedules all other threads from it. Second, our experience analyzing low-level systems code with the KISS checker [22] indicates that a variety of subtle bugs caused by concurrency are manifested by executions with few contexts.

Our work is inspired by the KISS project but significantly extends its scope by employing entirely different techniques. The KISS checker simulates executions of a concurrent program P with the executions of a sequential program P' derived from P. The various threads in P are scheduled using the single stack of P'. The use of a single stack fundamentally limits the number of context switches that can be explored. KISS is unable to explore more than two context switches for a concurrent program with two threads and cannot handle an unbounded number of threads. This paper presents a general algorithm for exploring an arbitrary number of context switches, even in the presence of unbounded parallelism, in a way that is sound and precise up to the bound.

The main difficulty with context-bounded model checking is that in each thread context, an unbounded number of stack configurations could be reachable due to recursion. Since a context switch may happen at any time, a precise analysis must schedule other threads from each of these configurations. To guarantee termination, a systematic state exploration algorithm must use a finite representation of an unbounded set of stack configurations. Our previous algorithm based on transactions and procedure summaries [20] is not guaranteed to terminate for context-bounded model checking because it keeps an explicit representation of the stack of each thread. Summarization [20] may still be useful as an optimization technique that is complementary to the techniques presented in this paper.

We achieve a finite representation of an unbounded set of stack configurations by appealing to the result that the reachable configurations (sometimes called the pushdown store language) of a pushdown system is regular [3, 12, 27] and consequently representable by a finite automaton. We use this fact to design an algorithm for context-bounded model checking for a concurrent boolean program with a finite but arbitrary number of threads. We then consider the main problem of this paper, context-bounded model checking of dynamic concurrent boolean programs. A dynamic concurrent boolean program is allowed to use two new operators. The *fork* operator creates a new thread and returns an integer identifying the new thread. The *join* operator blocks until the thread identified by an argument to the operation has terminated. We assume that *fork*, *join*, and copy from one variable to another are the only operations on thread identifiers. We show that for any context bound k and for any dynamic concurrent boolean program P, we can construct a concurrent boolean program Q with $k+1$ threads such that it suffices to check Q rather than P. Since concurrent software invariably uses dynamic thread creation, this result significantly increases the applicability of context-bounded model checking.

Proofs of the theorems in this paper can be found in our report [21].

2   Example

In this section, we present an example of a real concurrency error that requires four context switches to manifest itself. The error was found by model checking a large transaction management system written in C# with a bounded number of threads, using the model checker ZING [2] after compiling 10,000 lines of C# code into ZING. Since the error cannot manifest itself with fewer than four context switches, it could not be discovered by the techniques of KISS [22] which are inherently limited to two context switches.

The code shown in Figure 1 contains excerpts from two methods of a hashtable class that is part of the transaction manager implementing the two-

```
void Remove( LtmInternalTransaction tx )
{
  if( !tx.inTimerList )
  {
    // This transaction is not in the list.
    return;
  }
POINT 1:
  lock( this ) // lock bucket of hash table
  {
    if( tx.nextLink != null )
    {
POINT 3:
      tx.nextLink.prevLink = tx.prevLink;
    }
    if( tx.prevLink != null )
    {
      // ERROR: null pointer dereference
      tx.prevLink.nextLink = tx.nextLink;
    }
    ...
}
```

```
bool ProcessList()
{
  LtmInternalTransaction tx;
  long expirationTime = DateTime.UtcNow.Ticks;

  do
  {
    tx = null;
    lock( this )  // lock bucket of hash table
    {
      ... // remove transaction from timeout list
      ... // tx is made non-null here
    }
    if( tx != null )
    {
      tx.prevLink = null;
POINT 2:
      tx.nextLink = null;
POINT 4:
      ...
    }
  } while( tx != null );
}
```

Fig. 1. Example

phase commit protocol. The methods `Remove` and `ProcessList` are found within
a class that implements a bucket of the hashtable. When a client thread is registered with the transaction manager, a reference to the thread is stored in the
hashtable. The error arises when a thread T_c has comitted a transaction `tx` and
executes in the `Remove` method in order to remove the finished transaction from
the appropriate bucket of the hashtable. At the same time, a timer thread T_t is
executing in the `ProcessList` method to determine if any of the transactions
referenced in the bucket of the hashtable has timed out. Thread T_c gets interrupted at `POINT 1` in the `Remove` method, just after it has tested that `tx` has
not already been removed by the timer and just before it tries to acquire a lock
on the bucket in order to remove the transaction. Thread T_t acquires the lock
on the same bucket inside `ProcessList`, and it decides that transaction `tx` has
timed out. It goes on to remove `tx` by setting the bucket links in `tx` to `null` (the
bucket is a doubly-linked list). Just before setting `tx.nextLink` to `null`, another
context switch occurs, at `POINT 2`. Thread T_c resumes execution at `POINT 1` and
learns that `tx.nextLink` is non-`null`. It gets interrupted by thread T_t at `POINT`
`3` which resumes execution at `POINT 2` and sets `tx.nextLink` to `null`. It gets
interrupted by thread T_c at `POINT 4`. Thread T_c resumes execution at `POINT`
`3` and dereferences the `null` pointer `tx.nextLink`. The error can be fixed by
extending the scope of the `lock` statement in the `ProcessList` method down to
`POINT 4`.

We have been able to discover several other bugs in the system of the same
nature. However, we have not been able to check the system under scenarios
in which asynchronous calls and dynamically created timers may create new
threads, because ZING may not terminate on programs with unbounded parallelism. The results of this paper show that we can achieve a finite abstraction
by bounding the number of contexts to an arbitrary constant, even in the presence of dynamic thread creation. It is an important problem for future work to
integrate our algorithm in ZING, thereby enabling us to find deep errors such as
the one shown above, even in the presence of unbounded parallelism.

3   Pushdown Systems

Domains

$\gamma \in \Gamma$	*Stack alphabet*
$w \in \Gamma^*$	*Stack*
$g \in G$	*Global state*
$\Delta \subseteq (G \times \Gamma) \times (G \times \Gamma^*)$	*Transition relation*
$c \in G \times \Gamma^*$	*Configuration*
$\longrightarrow_\Delta \subseteq (G \times \Gamma^*) \times (G \times \Gamma^*)$	*Pds transition*

Let G and Γ be arbitrary fixed finite sets. We refer to G as the set of *global
states*, and we refer to Γ as the *stack alphabet*. We let g range over elements of
G, and we let γ range over elements of Γ. A *stack w* is an element of Γ^*, the

set of finite strings over Γ, including the empty string ϵ. A *configuration* c is an element of $G \times \Gamma^*$; we write configurations as $c = \langle g, w \rangle$ with $g \in G$ and $w \in \Gamma^*$.

A *transition relation* Δ over G and Γ is a finite subset of $(G \times \Gamma) \times (G \times \Gamma^*)$. A *pushdown system* $P = (G, \Gamma, \Delta, g_{in}, w_{in})$ is given by G, Γ, a transition relation Δ over G and Γ, and an initial configuration $\langle g_{in}, w_{in} \rangle$. The transition relation Δ determines a transition system on configurations, denoted $\longrightarrow_\Delta$, as follows: $\langle g, \gamma w' \rangle \longrightarrow_\Delta \langle g', ww' \rangle$ for all $w' \in \Gamma^*$, if and only if $(\langle g, \gamma \rangle, \langle g', w \rangle) \in \Delta$. We write $\longrightarrow_\Delta^*$ to denote the reflexive, transitive closure of $\longrightarrow_\Delta$. Notice that, by the signature of Δ, there are no transitions $\longrightarrow_\Delta$ from a configuration whose stack is empty. Hence, a pushdown system as defined here halts when the stack becomes empty.

A configuration c of a pushdown system is called *reachable* if and only if $c_{in} \longrightarrow_\Delta^* c$, where c_{in} is the initial configuration of the pushdown system. In general, there are inifinitely many reachable configurations of a pushdown system, because the stack is unbounded.

The reachability problem for pushdown systems is decidable because the set of reachable configurations (sometimes called the pushdown store language) of a pushdown system is regular [3, 12]. A *regular pushdown store automaton* $A = (Q, \Gamma, \delta, I, F)$ is a finite automaton with states Q, alphabet Γ, transition relation $\delta \subseteq Q \times \Gamma \times Q$, initial states I and final states F. The automaton may contain ϵ-transitions. The sets Q and I satisfy $G \subseteq Q$ and $I \subseteq G$. Such an automaton defines a language of pushdown configurations by the rule [27]:

- A accepts a pushdown configuration $\langle g, w \rangle$, if and only if A accepts the word w when started in the state g.

A subset $S \subseteq G \times \Gamma^*$ of pushdown configurations is called *regular*, if and only if there exists a regular pushdown store automaton A such that $S = L(A)$.

For a pushdown system $P = (G, \Gamma, \Delta, g_{in}, w_{in})$ and a set of configurations $S \subseteq G \times \Gamma^*$, let $Post_\Delta^*(S)$ be the set of configurations reachable from S, i.e., $Post_\Delta^*(S) = \{c \mid \exists c' \in S. \ c' \longrightarrow_\Delta^* c\}$. The following theorem [27] shows that the set of reachable configurations from a regular set of configurations is again regular. For details on the construction leading to this result we refer the reader to [27].

Theorem 1 ([27]). *Let $P = (G, \Gamma, \Delta, g_{in}, w_{in})$ be a pushdown system, and let A be a regular pushdown store automaton. There exists a regular pushdown store automaton A' such that $Post_\Delta^*(L(A)) = L(A')$. The automaton A' can be constructed from P and A in time polynomial in the size of P and A.*

4   Concurrent Pushdown Systems

A *concurrent pushdown system* is a tuple $P = (G, \Gamma, \Delta_0, \ldots, \Delta_N, g_{in}, w_{in})$ with transition relations $\Delta_0, \ldots, \Delta_N$ over G and Γ, $N \geq 0$, an initial state g_{in} and an initial stack w_{in}. A configuration of a concurrent pushdown system is a tuple $c = \langle g, w_0, \ldots, w_N \rangle$ with $g \in G$ and $w_i \in \Gamma^*$, that is, a global state g followed by

Input: Concurrent pushdown system $(G, \Gamma, \Delta_0, \ldots, \Delta_N, g_{in}, w_{in})$ and bound k

0. **let** $A_{in} = (Q, \Gamma, \delta, \{g_{in}\}, F)$ such that $L(A_{in}) = \{\langle g_{in}, w_{in}\rangle\}$;

1. $WL := \{(\langle g, A_{in}, \ldots, A_{in}\rangle, 0)\}$;   // There are N copies of A_{in}
2. $Reach := \{\langle g, A_{in}, \ldots, A_{in}\rangle\}$;

3. **while** (WL **not empty**)
4.   **let** $(\langle g, A_0, \ldots, A_N\rangle, i) = $ REMOVE(WL) **in**
5.   **if** ($i < k$)
6.   **forall** ($j = 0 \ldots N$)
7.   **let** $A'_j = Post^*_{\Delta_j}(A_j)$ **in**
8.   **forall** ($g' \in G(A'_j)$) {
9.   **let** $x = \langle g', \text{RENAME}(A_0, g'), \ldots, \text{ANONYMIZE}(A'_j, g'), \ldots,$
                                                          $\text{RENAME}(A_N, g')\rangle$ **in**
10.   ADD($WL, (x, i + 1)$);
11. $Reach := Reach \cup \{x\}$;
                  }
Output : $Reach$

Fig. 2. Algorithm

a sequence of stacks w_i, one for each constituent transition relation. The initial configuration of P is $\langle g_{in}, w_{in}, \ldots, w_{in}\rangle$ where all $N + 1$ stacks are initialized to w_{in}. The transition system of P, denoted $\longrightarrow_P$, rewrites configurations of P by rewriting the global state together with any one of the stacks, according to the transition relations of the constituent pushdown systems. Formally, we define $\langle g, w_0, \ldots, w_i, \ldots w_N\rangle \longrightarrow_i \langle g', w_0, \ldots, w'_i, \ldots w_N\rangle$ if and only if $\langle g, w_i\rangle \longrightarrow_{\Delta_i} \langle g', w'_i\rangle$. We define the transition relation $\longrightarrow_P$ on configurations of P by the union of the $\longrightarrow_i$, i.e., $\longrightarrow_P = \bigcup_{i=0}^{N} \longrightarrow_i$.

4.1   Bounded Reachability

A configuration c is called reachable, if and only if $c_{in} \longrightarrow_P^* c$, where c_{in} is the initial configuration. The reachability problem for concurrent pushdown systems is undecidable [24]. However, as we will show below, bounding the number of context switches allowed in a transition leads to a decidable restriction of the reachability problem.

For a positive natural number k, we define the k-bounded transition relation $\overset{k}{\longrightarrow}$ on configurations c inductively, as follows:

$$c \overset{1}{\longrightarrow} c' \text{ iff there exists } i \text{ such that } c \longrightarrow_i^* c'$$
$$c \overset{k+1}{\longrightarrow} c' \text{ iff there exist } c'' \text{ and } i \text{ such that } c \overset{k}{\longrightarrow} c'' \text{ and } c'' \longrightarrow_i^* c'$$

Thus, a k-bounded transition contains at most $k - 1$ "context switches" in which a new relation $\longrightarrow_i$ can be chosen. Notice that the full transitive closure of each transition relation $\longrightarrow_i$ is applied within each context. We say that a configuration c is k-reachable if $c_{in} \overset{k}{\longrightarrow} c$. The k-bounded reachability problem for a concurrent pushdown system P is: Given configurations c_0 and c_1, is it the case that $c_0 \overset{k}{\longrightarrow} c_1$?

For fixed k, the lengths and state spaces of k-bounded transition sequences may be unbounded, since each constituent transition relation $\longrightarrow_i^*$ may generate infinitely many transitions containing infinitely many distinct configurations. Therefore, decidability of k-bounded reachability requires an argument. In order to formulate this argument, we will define a transition relation over *aggregate configurations* of the form $\langle\!\langle g, R_0, \ldots, R_N \rangle\!\rangle$, where R_i are regular subsets of Γ^*.

For a global state $g \in G$ and a regular subset $R \subseteq \Gamma^*$, we let $\langle\!\langle g, R \rangle\!\rangle$ denote the set of configurations $\{\langle g, w \rangle \mid w \in R\}$. Notice that $\langle\!\langle g, \emptyset \rangle\!\rangle = \emptyset$. For $G = \{g_1, \ldots, g_m\}$, any regular set of configurations $S \subseteq G \times \Gamma^*$ can evidently be written as a disjoint union: $(*)$ $S = \biguplus_{i=1}^m \langle\!\langle g_i, R_i \rangle\!\rangle$ for some regular sets of stacks $R_i \subseteq \Gamma^*$, $i = 1 \ldots m$ (if there is no configuration with global state g_j in S, then we take $R_j = \emptyset$.) By Theorem 1, the set $Post_\Delta^*(S)$ for regular S can also be written in the form $(*)$, since it is a regular set. We abuse set membership notation to denote that $\langle\!\langle g', R' \rangle\!\rangle$ is a component of the set $Post_\Delta^*(S)$ as represented in the form $(*)$, writing $\langle\!\langle g', R' \rangle\!\rangle \in Post_\Delta^*(S)$ if and only if $Post_\Delta^*(S) = \biguplus_{i=1}^m \langle\!\langle g_i, R_i \rangle\!\rangle$ with $\langle\!\langle g', R' \rangle\!\rangle = \langle\!\langle g_j, R_j \rangle\!\rangle$ for some $j \in \{1, \ldots, m\}$.

Given a concurrent pushdown system $P = (G, \Gamma, \Delta_0, \ldots, \Delta_N, g_{in}, w_{in})$, we define relations $\Longrightarrow_i$ on aggregate configurations, for $i = 0 \ldots N$, by $\langle\!\langle g, R_0, \ldots, R_i, \ldots, R_N \rangle\!\rangle \Longrightarrow_i \langle\!\langle g', R_0, \ldots, R_i', \ldots, R_N \rangle\!\rangle$ if and only if $\langle\!\langle g', R_i' \rangle\!\rangle \in Post_{\Delta_i}^*(\langle\!\langle g, R_i \rangle\!\rangle)$. Finally, define the transition relation $\Longrightarrow$ on aggregate configurations by the union of the $\Longrightarrow_i$, i.e., $\Longrightarrow = (\bigcup_{i=0}^N \Longrightarrow_i)$. For aggregate configurations a_1 and a_2, we write $a_1 \overset{k}{\Longrightarrow} a_2$, if and only if there exists a transition sequence using $\Longrightarrow$ starting at a_1 and ending at a_2 with at most k transitions. Notice that each relation $\Longrightarrow_i$ contains the full transitive closure computed by the $Post_{\Delta_i}^*$ operator.

The following theorem reduces k-bounded reachability in a concurrent pushdown system to repeated applications of the sequential $Post^*$ operator.

Theorem 2. *Let $P = (G, \Gamma, \Delta_0, \ldots, \Delta_N, g_{in}, w_{in})$ be a concurrent pushdown system. Then, for any k, we have $\langle g, w_0, \ldots, w_N \rangle \overset{k}{\longrightarrow} \langle g', w_0', \ldots, w_N' \rangle$ if and only if $\langle\!\langle g, \{w_0\}, \ldots, \{w_N\} \rangle\!\rangle \overset{k}{\Longrightarrow} \langle\!\langle g', R_0', \ldots, R_N' \rangle\!\rangle$ for some $R_0', \ldots, R_N'$ such that $w_i' \in R_i'$ for all $i \in \{0, \ldots, N\}$.*

4.2 Algorithm

Theorem 1 and Theorem 2 together give rise to an algorithm for solving the context-bounded reachability problem for concurrent pushdown systems. The algorithm is shown in Figure 2.

The algorithm processes a worklist WL containing a set of items of the form $(\langle g, A_0, \ldots, A_N \rangle, i)$, where $g \in G$ is a global state, the A_j are pushdown store automata, and i is an index in the range $\{0, \ldots, k-1\}$. The operation REMOVE(WL) removes an item from the worklist and returns the item; ADD(WL, *item*) adds the item to the worklist. The initial pushdown store automaton $A_{in} = (Q, \Gamma, \delta, \{g_{in}\}, F)$ has initial state g_{in} and accepts exactly the initial configuration $\langle g_{in}, w_{in} \rangle$. In the line numbered 7 of the algorithm in Figure 2, the pushdown store automaton $A'_j = Post^*_{\Delta_j}(A_j)$ is understood to be constructed according to Theorem 1 so that $L(A'_j) = Post^*_{\Delta_j}(L(A_j))$. In line 8, $G(A'_j) = \{g' \mid \exists w.\langle g', w \rangle \in L(A'_j)\}$. All pushdown store automata A_j constructed by the algorithm have at most one start state $g \in G$. When applied to such an automaton RENAME(A, g') returns the result of renaming the start state if any of A to g'. The operation ANONYMIZE(A, g') is obtained from A by renaming all states of A except g' to fresh states that are not in G.

The algorithm in Figure 2 works by repeatedly applying the $Post^*$ operator to regular pushdown store automata that represent components in aggregate configurations. The operations RENAME and ANONYMIZE are necessary for applying Theorem 1 repeatedly, since the construction of pushdown store automata [27] uses elements of G as states in these automata. In order to avoid confusion between such states across iterated applications of Theorem 1, renaming on states from G is necessary, and hence successive pushdown store automata constructed by the algorithm in Figure 2 may grow for increasing values of the bound k. This factunderlies the undecidability of the unbounded reachability problem.

Theorem 3. *Let* $P = (G, \Gamma, \Delta_0, \ldots, \Delta_N, g_{in}, w_{in})$ *be a concurrent pushdown system. For any k, the algorithm in Figure 2 terminates on input P and k, and $\langle\langle g_{in}, \{w_{in}\}, \ldots, \{w_{in}\}\rangle\rangle \stackrel{k}{\Longrightarrow} \langle\langle g', R'_0, \ldots, R'_N \rangle\rangle$ if and only if the algorithm outputs Reach with $\langle g', A'_0, \ldots, A'_N \rangle \in$ Reach such that $L(A'_i) = \langle\langle g', R'_i \rangle\rangle$ for all $i \in \{0, \ldots, N\}$.*

Theorem 2 together with Theorem 3 imply that the algorithm in Figure 2 solves the context-bounded model checking problem, since Theorem 2 shows that aggregate configurations correctly represent reachability in the relation $\stackrel{k}{\longrightarrow}$.

For a concurrent pushdown system $P = (G, \Gamma, \Delta_0, \ldots, \Delta_N, g_{in}, w_{in})$ we measure the size of P by $|P| = \max(|G|, |\Delta_0|, |\Delta_1|, \ldots, |\Delta_N|, |\Gamma|)$. For a pushdown store automaton $A = (Q, \Gamma, \delta, I, F)$ we measure the size of A by $|A| = \max(|Q|, |\delta|, |\Gamma|)$.

Theorem 4. *For a concurrent pushdown system $P = (G, \Gamma, \Delta_0, \ldots, \Delta_N, g_{in}, w_{in})$ and a bound k, the algorithm in Figure 2 decides the k-bounded reachability problem in time $\mathcal{O}(k^3(N|G|)^k|P|^5)$.*

5   Dynamic Concurrent Pushdown Systems

In this section, we define a dynamic concurrent pushdown system with operations for forking and joining on a thread. To allow for dynamic fork-join parallelism, we allow program variables in which thread identifiers can be stored. Thread identifiers are members of the set $Tid = \{0, 1, 2, \ldots\}$. The identifier of a forked thread may be stored by the parent thread in such a variable. Later, the parent thread may perform a join on the thread identifier contained in that variable.

Formally, a dynamic concurrent pushdown system is a tuple

$$(GBV, GTV, LBV, LTV, \Delta, \Delta_F, \Delta_J, g_{in}, \gamma_{in}).$$

The various components of this tuple are described below.

- GBV is the set of global variables containing boolean values and GTV is the set of global variables containing thread identifiers. Let G be the (infinite) set of all valuations to the global variables.
- LBV is the set of local variables containing boolean values and LTV is the set of local variables containing thread identifiers. Let Γ be the (infinite) set of all valuations to the local variables.
- $\Delta \subseteq (G \times \Gamma) \times (G \times \Gamma^*)$ is the transition relation describing a single step of any thread.
- $\Delta_F \subseteq Tid \times (G \times \Gamma) \times (G \times \Gamma^*)$ is the fork transition relation. If $(t, \langle g, \gamma \rangle, \langle g', w \rangle) \in \Delta_F$, then in the global store g a thread with γ at the top of its stack may fork a thread with identifier t modifying the global store to g' and replacing γ at the top of the stack with w.
- $\Delta_J \subseteq LTV \times (G \times \Gamma) \times (G \times \Gamma^*)$ is the join transition relation. If $(x, \langle g, \gamma \rangle, \langle g', w \rangle) \in \Delta_J$, then in the global store g a thread with γ at the top of its stack blocks until the thread with identifier $\gamma(x)$ finishes execution. On getting unblocked, this thread modifies the global store to g' and replaces γ at the top of the stack with w.
- g_{in} is a fixed valuation to the set of global variables such that $g_{in}(x) = 0$ for all $x \in GTV$.
- γ_{in} is a fixed valuation to the set of local variables such that $\gamma_{in}(x) = 0$ for all $x \in LTV$.

Domains

$ss \in Stacks = Tid \to (\Gamma \cup \{\$\})^*$
$c \in C = G \times Tid \times Stacks \qquad Configuration$
$\leadsto \subseteq C \times C$

Every dynamic concurrent pushdown system is equipped with a special symbol $\$ \notin \Gamma$ to mark the bottom of the stack of each thread. A configuration of the system is a triple $\langle g, n, ss \rangle$, where g is the global state, n is the identifier of the last thread to be forked, and $ss(t)$ is the stack for thread $t \in Tid$. The execution of the dynamic concurrent pushdown system starts in the configuration $\langle g_{in}, 0, ss_0 \rangle$, where $ss_0(t) = \gamma_{in}\$$ for all $t \in Tid$. The rules shown below define the transitions that may be performed by thread t from a configuration $\langle g, n, ss \rangle$.

Operational Semantics

(SEQ)
$$\frac{t \leq n \quad ss(t) = \gamma w' \quad (\langle g, \gamma \rangle, \langle g', w \rangle) \in \Delta}{\langle g, n, ss \rangle \leadsto_t \langle g', n, ss[t := ww'] \rangle}$$

(SEQEND)
$$\frac{t \leq n \quad ss(t) = \$}{\langle g, n, ss \rangle \leadsto_t \langle g, n, ss[t := \epsilon] \rangle}$$

(FORK)
$$\frac{t \leq n \quad ss(t) = \gamma w' \quad (n+1, \langle g, \gamma \rangle, \langle g', w \rangle) \in \Delta_F}{\langle g, n, ss \rangle \leadsto_t \langle g', n+1, ss[t := ww'] \rangle}$$

(JOIN)
$$\frac{t \leq n \quad ss(t) = \gamma w' \quad x \in LTV \quad (x, \langle g, \gamma \rangle, \langle g', w \rangle) \in \Delta_J \quad ss(\gamma(x)) = \epsilon}{\langle g, n, ss \rangle \leadsto_t \langle g', n, ss[t := ww'] \rangle}$$

All rules are guarded by the condition $t \leq n$ indicating that thread t must have already been forked. Thus, only thread 0 can make a move from the initial configuration $\langle g_{in}, 0, ss_0 \rangle$. The rule (SEQ) allows thread t to perform a transition according to the transition relation Δ. The rule (SEQEND) is enabled if the top (and the only) symbol on the stack of thread t is $\$$. The transition pops the $\$$ symbol from the stack of thread t without changing the global state so that thread t does not perform any more transitions. The rule (FORK) creates a new thread with idenfier $n+1$. The rule (JOIN) is enabled if thread $\gamma(x)$, where γ is the symbol at the top of the stack of thread t, has terminated. The termination of a thread is indicated by an empty stack.

5.1   Assumptions

In realistic concurrent programs with fork-join parallelism, the usage of thread identifiers (and consequently variables containing thread identifiers) is restricted. A thread identifier is created by a fork operation and stored in a variable. Then, it may be copied from one variable to another. Finally, a join operation may look at a thread identifier contained in such a variable. In a nutshell, no control flow other than that implicit in a join operation depends on thread identifiers. We exploit the restricted use of thread identifiers in concurrent systems to devise an algorithm for solving the k-bounded reachability problem.

To formalize the assumptions about the restricted use of thread identifiers, we need the notion of a renaming function. A renaming function is a partial function from Tid to Tid. When a renaming function f is applied to a global store g, it returns another store in which the value of each variable of type Tid is transformed by an application of f. If f is undefined on the value of some global variable in g, it is also undefined on g. Similarly, a renaming function can be applied to a local store as well. A renaming function is extended to a sequence of local stores by pointwise application to each element of the sequence.

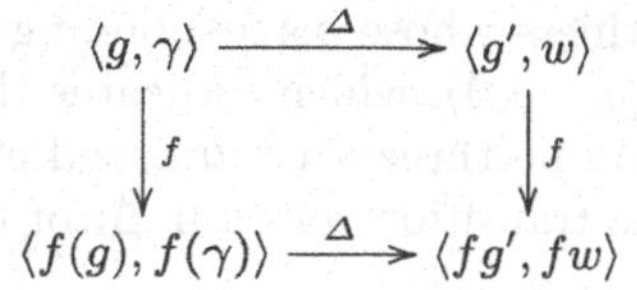

$$\langle g, \gamma \rangle \xrightarrow{\ \Delta\ } \langle g', w \rangle$$

$$\Big\downarrow f \qquad\qquad \Big\downarrow f$$

$$\langle f(g), f(\gamma) \rangle \xrightarrow{\ \Delta\ } \langle fg', fw \rangle$$

Fig. 3. Pictorial view of assumption about Δ

Figure 3 presents a pictorial view of assumption about Δ. This view shows four arrows, two horizontal labeled with the transition relation Δ and two vertical labeled with the renaming function f. The assumption on Δ expresses two requirement on tuples (g, γ) for which the left vertical arrow holds: (1) If the top horizontal arrow holds in addition, then the remaining two arrows hold. (2) If the bottom horizontal arrow holds in addition, then the remaining two arrows hold. Assumptions about Δ_F and Δ_J are similar in spirit to Δ. For lack of space, we leave the formal statements of these assumptions in our technical report [21].

5.2   Reduction to Concurrent Pushdown Systems

In this section, we show how to reduce the problem of k-bounded reachability on a dynamic concurrent pushdown system to a concurrent pushdown system with $k+1$ threads. Given a dynamic concurrent pushdown system P and a positive integer k, our method produces a concurrent pushdown system P_k containing $k+1$ threads with identifiers in $\{0, 1, \ldots, k\}$ such that it suffices to verify the k-bounded executions of P_k. The latter problem can be solved using the algorithm in Figure 2.

The key insight behind our approach is that in a k-bounded execution, at most k different threads may perform a transition. We would like to simulate transitions of these k threads with transitions of threads in P_k with identifiers in $\{0, \ldots, k-1\}$. The last thread in P_k with identifier k never performs a transition; it exists only to simulate the presence of the remaining threads in P.

Let $Tid_k = \{0, 1, \ldots, k\}$ be the set of the thread identifiers bounded by k. Let $AbsG_k$ and $Abs\Gamma_k$ be the set of all valuations to global and local variables respectively, where the variables containing thread identifiers only take values from Tid_k. Note that both $AbsG_k$ and $Abs\Gamma_k$ are finite sets.

Given a dynamic concurrent pushdown system

$$P = (GBV, GTV, LBV, LTV, \Delta, \Delta_F, \Delta_J, g_{in}, \gamma_{in})$$

and a positive integer k, we define a concurrent pushdown system

$$P_k = (AbsG_k \times Tid_k \times \mathcal{P}(Tid_k), Abs\Gamma_k \cup \{\$\}, \Delta_0, \ldots, \Delta_k, (g_{in}, 0, \emptyset), \gamma_{in}\$).$$

The concurrent pushdown system P_k has $k+1$ threads. A global state of P_k is 3-tuple (g, n, α), where g is a valuation to the global variables, n is the largest thread identifier whose corresponding thread is allowed to make a transition, and

α is the set of thread identifiers whose corresponding threads have terminated. The initial global state is $(g_{in}, 0, \emptyset)$, which indicates that initially only thread 0 can perform a transition and no thread has finished execution. The rules below define the transitions in the transition relation Δ_t of thread t.

Definition of Δ_t

$$\text{(ABSSEQ)} \quad \frac{t \leq n \quad (\langle g, \gamma \rangle, \langle g', w \rangle) \in \Delta}{(\langle (g, n, \alpha), \gamma \rangle \,,\, \langle (g', n, \alpha), w \rangle) \in \Delta_t}$$

$$\text{(ABSSEQEND)} \quad \frac{t \leq n}{(\langle (g, n, \alpha), \$ \rangle \,,\, \langle (g, n, \alpha \cup \{t\}), \epsilon \rangle) \in \Delta_t}$$

$$\text{(ABSFORK)} \quad \frac{t \leq n \quad n+1 < k \quad (n+1, \langle g, \gamma \rangle, \langle g', w \rangle) \in \Delta_F}{(\langle (g, n, \alpha), \gamma \rangle \,,\, \langle (g', n+1, \alpha), w \rangle) \in \Delta_t}$$

$$\text{(ABSFORKNONDET)} \quad \frac{t \leq n \quad (k, \langle g, \gamma \rangle, \langle g', w \rangle) \in \Delta_F}{(\langle (g, n, \alpha), \gamma \rangle \,,\, \langle (g', n, \alpha), w \rangle) \in \Delta_t}$$

$$\text{(ABSJOIN)} \quad \frac{t \leq n \quad x \in LTV \quad (x, \langle g, \gamma \rangle, \langle g', w \rangle) \in \Delta_J \quad \gamma(x) \in \alpha}{(\langle (g, n, \alpha), \gamma \rangle \,,\, \langle (g', n, \alpha), w \rangle) \in \Delta_t}$$

Note that all rules above are guarded by the condition $t \leq n$ to indicate that no transition in thread t is enabled in $\langle (g, n, \alpha), \gamma \rangle$ if $t > n$. The rule (ABSSEQ) adds transitions in Δ to Δ_t. The rule (ABSSEQEND) adds thread t to the set of terminated threads. The rules (ABSFORK) and (ABSFORKNONDET) handle thread creation in P and are the most crucial part of our transformation. The rule (ABSFORK) handles the case when the new thread being forked participates in a k-bounded execution. This rule increments the counter n allowing thread $n+1$ to begin simulating the newly forked thread. The rule (ABSFORKNONDET) handles the case when the new thread being forked does not pariticipate in a k-bounded execution. This rule leaves the counter n unchanged thus conserving the precious resource of thread identifiers in P_k. Both these rules add the transitions of the forking thread in Δ_F to Δ. The rule (ABSJOIN) handles the join operator by using the fact that the identifiers of all previously terminated threads are present in α. Again, this rule adds the transitions of the joining thread in Δ_J to Δ.

We can now state the correctness theorems for our transformation. To simplify the notation required to state these theorems, we write a configuration $\langle (g', n', \alpha), w_0, w_1, \ldots, w_k \rangle$ of P_k as $\langle (g', n', \alpha), ss' \rangle$, where ss' is a map from Tid_k to $(Abs\Gamma_k \cup \$)^*$.

First, our transformation is sound which means that by verifying P_k, we do not miss erroneous k-bounded executions of P.

Theorem 5 (Soundness). *Let P be a dynamic concurrent pushdown system and k be a positive integer. Let $\langle g, n, ss \rangle$ be a k-reachable configuration of P. Then there is a total renaming function $f : Tid \rightarrow Tid_k$ and a k-reachable configuration $\langle (g', n', \alpha), ss' \rangle$ of the concurrent pushdown system P_k such that $g' = f(g)$ and $ss'(f(j)) = f(ss(j))$ for all $j \in Tid$.*

Second, our transformation is precise which means that every erroneous k-bounded execution of P_k corresponds to an erroneous execution of P.

Theorem 6 (Completeness). *Let P be a dynamic concurrent pushdown system and k be a positive integer. Let $\langle (g', n', \alpha), ss' \rangle$ be a k-reachable configuration of the concurrent pushdown system P_k. Then there is a total renaming function $f : Tid \to Tid_k$ and a k-reachable configuration $\langle g, n, ss \rangle$ of P such that $g' = f(g)$ and $ss'(f(j)) = f(ss(j))$ for all $j \in Tid$.*

Thus, with Theorems 5 and 6, we have successfully reduced the problem of k-bounded reachability on a dynamic concurrent pushdown system to a concurrent pushdown system with $k + 1$ threads.

6   Related Work

We are not aware of any previous work that develops a theory of context-bounded analysis of concurrent software that is sound and complete up to the bound. Our techniques exploit results from model checking of sequential pushdown systems, in particular, Schwoon's generalization [27] of regular representation of sequential pushdown store languages [3, 12]. We have discussed the relation to our previous work on procedure summaries [20] and the KISS checker [22] in Section 1.

The notion of bounded-depth model checking, popular in hardware verification, can also be used for software verification [7]. These techniques bound the execution depth resulting in analysis of finite executions. In contrast, due to unbounded exploration within a thread context, our work allows analysis of unbounded execution sequences.

A number of model checkers have been developed for concurrent software [17, 14, 29, 9, 26, 18, 30]. All of these checkers keep explicit representation of the thread stacks, which might result in non-termination. Our analysis maintains a symbolic representation of the thread stacks and is guaranteed to terminate.

A variety of automated compositional techniques for verifying concurrent software have been developed [6, 16, 13, 15]. These techniques verify each process separately in an automatically constructed abstraction of the environment. The constructed abstraction is typically stackless and imprecise. As a result, these techniques are sound but not complete.

The idea of abstracting an unbounded number of processes into a single process has been used in verification of cache-coherence protocols [19] and compositional verification of software [15].

For restricted models of synchronization, assertion checking is decidable even with both concurrency and procedure calls. Esparza and Podelski present an algorithm for this restricted class of programs [11]. Alur and Grosu have studied the interaction between concurrency and procedure calls in the context of refinement between STATECHART programs [1]. At each step of the refinement process, their system allows either the use of nesting (the equivalent of procedures) or parallelism, but not both. Also, recursively nested modes are not allowed. In contrast, we place no restrictions on how parallelism interacts with procedure calls, and allow recursive procedures.

Bouajjani, Esparza, and Touili present an analysis that constructs abstractions of context-free languages [5]. The abstractions are chosen so that the emptiness of the intersection of the abstractions is decidable. Their analysis is sound but incomplete due to overapproximation in the abstractions.

7   Conclusion

In this paper we give for the first time a theory of context-bounded model checking for concurrent software that is sound up to the bound in the sense that it explores each context to full depth. Our algorithm finds any error that can possibly manifest itself in an error trace with a number of context switches within the bound, even in the presence of unbounded parallelism. It is an important research problem for future work to integrate our algorithm into explicit state model checking frameworks such as ZING [2].

References

1. R. Alur and R. Grosu. Modular refinement of hierarchic reactive machines. In *POPL 00: Principles of Programming Languages*, pages 390–402. ACM, 2000.
2. T. Andrews, S. Qadeer, S. K. Rajamani, J. Rehof, and Y. Xie. Zing: Exploiting program structure for model checking concurrent software. In *CONCUR 2004: Fifteenth International Conference on Concurrency Theory, London, U.K., September 2004*, LNCS. Springer-Verlag, 2004. Invited paper.
3. J-M. Autebert, J. Berstel, and L. Boasson. Context-free languages and pushdown automata. In *Handbook of Formal Languages, vol. 1 (Eds.: G. Rozenberg and A. Salomaa)*, pages 111 – 174. Springer-Verlag, 1997.
4. T. Ball and S. K. Rajamani. The SLAM project: Debugging system software via static analysis. In *POPL 02: Principles of Programming Languages*, pages 1–3. ACM, January 2002.
5. A. Bouajjani, J. Esparza, and T. Touili. A generic approach to the static analysis of concurrent programs with procedures. In *POPL 03: Principles of Programming Languages*, pages 62–73. ACM, 2003.
6. S. Chaki, E. M. Clarke, A. Groce, S. Jha, and H. Veith. Modular verification of software components in C. *IEEE Transactions on Software Engineering*, 30(6):388–402, 2004.
7. E. M. Clarke, A. Biere, R. Raimi, and Y. Zhu. Bounded model checking using satisfiability solving. *Formal Methods in System Design*, 19(1):7–34, 2001.
8. E. M. Clarke and E. A. Emerson. Synthesis of synchronization skeletons for branching time temporal logic. In *Logic of Programs*, LNCS 131, pages 52–71. Springer-Verlag, 1981.
9. J. Corbett, M. Dwyer, John Hatcliff, Corina Pasareanu, Robby, S. Laubach, and H. Zheng. Bandera : Extracting finite-state models from Java source code. In *ICSE 00: Software Engineering*, 2000.
10. M. Das, S. Lerner, and M. Seigle. ESP: Path-sensitive program verification in polynomial time. In *PLDI 02: Programming Language Design and Implementation*, pages 57–69. ACM, 2002.

11. J. Esparza and A. Podelski. Efficient algorithms for pre* and post* on interprocedural parallel flow graphs. In *POPL 00: Principles of Programming Languages*, pages 1–11. ACM, 2000.
12. A. Finkel, B. Willems, and P. Wolper. A direct symbolic approach to model checking pushdown systems. *Electronic Notes in Theoretical Computer Science*, 9, 1997.
13. D. Giannakopoulou, C. S. Pasareanu, and H. Barringer. Assumption generation for software component verification. In *ASE 02: Automated Software Engineering*, pages 3–12, 2002.
14. P. Godefroid. Model checking for programming languages using verisoft. In *POPL 97: Principles of Programming Languages*, pages 174–186, 1997.
15. T. A. Henzinger, R. Jhala, and R. Majumdar. Race checking by context inference. In *PLDI 04: Programming Language Design and Implementation*, pages 1–13, 2004.
16. T. A. Henzinger, R. Jhala, R. Majumdar, and S. Qadeer. Thread-modular abstraction refinement. In *CAV 03: Computer-Aided Verification*, pages 262–274, 2003.
17. G. Holzmann. The model checker SPIN. *IEEE Transactions on Software Engineering*, 23(5):279–295, May 1997.
18. M. Musuvathi, D. Park, A. Chou, D. Engler, and D. L. Dill. CMC: A pragmatic approach to model checking real code. In *OSDI 02: Operating Systems Design and Implementation*, 2002.
19. F. Pong and M. Dubois. Verification techniques for cache coherence protocols. *ACM Computing Surveys*, 29(1):82–126, 1997.
20. S. Qadeer, S. K. Rajamani, and J. Rehof. Summarizing procedures in concurrent programs. In *POPL 04: ACM Principles of Programming Languages*, pages 245–255. ACM, 2004.
21. S. Qadeer and J. Rehof. Context-bounded model checking of concurrent software. Technical Report MSR-TR-2004-70, Microsoft Research, 2004.
22. S. Qadeer and D. Wu. KISS: Keep it simple and seqeuential. In *PLDI 04: Programming Language Design and Implementation*, pages 14–24. ACM, 2004.
23. J. Queille and J. Sifakis. Specification and verification of concurrent systems in CESAR. In M. Dezani-Ciancaglini and U. Montanari, editors, *Fifth International Symposium on Programming*, Lecture Notes in Computer Science 137, pages 337–351. Springer-Verlag, 1981.
24. G. Ramalingam. Context sensitive synchronization sensitive analysis is undecidable. *ACM Trans. on Programming Languages and Systems*, 22:416–430, 2000.
25. T. Reps, S. Horwitz, and M. Sagiv. Precise interprocedural dataflow analysis via graph reachability. In *POPL 95: Principles of Programming Languages*, pages 49–61. ACM, 1995.
26. Robby, M. Dwyer, and J. Hatcliff. Bogor: An extensible and highly-modular model checking framework. In *FSE 03: Foundations of Software Engineering*, pages 267–276. ACM, 2003.
27. S. Schwoon. *Model-Checking Pushdown Systems*. PhD thesis, Lehrstuhl für Informatik VII der Technischen Universität München, 2000.
28. M. Sharir and A. Pnueli. Two approaches to interprocedural data flow analysis. In *Program Flow Analysis: Theory and Applications*, pages 189–233. Prentice-Hall, 1981.
29. W. Visser, K. Havelund, G. Brat, and S. Park. Model checking programs. In *ASE 00: Automated Software Engineering*, pages 3–12, 2000.
30. E. Yahav. Verifying safety properties of concurrent Java programs using 3-valued logic. In *POPL 01: Principles of Programming Languages*, pages 27–40, 2001.

A Generic Theorem Prover of CSP Refinement*

Yoshinao Isobe[1] and Markus Roggenbach[2]

[1] AIST, Japan
y-isobe@aist.go.jp
[2] University of Wales Swansea, United Kingdom
M.Roggenbach@Swan.ac.uk

Abstract. We describe a new tool called CSP-Prover which is an inter-active theorem prover dedicated to refinement proofs within the process algebra CSP. It aims specifically at proofs for infinite state systems, which may also involve infinite non-determinism. Semantically, CSP-Prover supports both the theory of complete metric spaces as well as the theory of complete partial orders. Both these theories are implemented for infinite product spaces. Technically, CSP-Prover is based on the theorem prover Isabelle. It provides a deep encoding of CSP. The tool's architecture follows a generic approach which makes it easy to adapt it for various CSP models besides those studied here: the stable failures model $\mathcal{F}$ and the traces model $\mathcal{T}$.

1 Introduction

Among the various frameworks for the description and modelling of reactive systems, process algebra plays a prominent rôle. It has proved to be suitable at the level of requirement specification, at the level of design specifications, and also for formal refinement proofs [2]. In this context, the process algebra CSP [11, 21] has successfully been applied in various areas, ranging from train control systems [5] over software for the international space station [3, 4] to the verification of security protocols [23].

Concerning tool support for CSP, the model checker FDR [15] is without doubt the standard proof tool for CSP. It allows for refinement proofs as well as for deadlock and livelock analysis. However, in general FDR restricts CSP specifications to finite state systems[1] and allows only the use of concrete data types. Furthermore, in practical applications it is often hard to deal with the state explosion problem. In this context, the use of theorem provers has been suggested e.g. by [26, 25, 8, 24] in order to complement the well-established technique of model checking.

---

* Supported by Royal Society with Short Visit Grants.
[1] On the LHS of a refinement check, see [22] for a precise characterisation of the possible infinite state processes on the RHS.

N. Halbwachs and L. Zuck (Eds.): TACAS 2005, LNCS 3440, pp. 108–123, 2005.

In this paper we describe a new tool CSP-Prover. Its generic architecture makes it suitable for various denotational CSP models. The implemented theories of complete metric spaces and complete partial orders allow CSP-Prover to deal with infinite state systems with unbounded non-determinism. Using the theorem prover Isabelle [16], CSP-Prover can also analyse specifications in CSP based on abstract data types. We demonstrate the relevance of these properties by proofs in the context of an industrial case study.

The paper is organised as follows: First, we describe the theorem prover Isabelle and give a short overview on the process algebra CSP. Then, the generic architecture of CSP-Prover is discussed in detail. Sect. 5 demonstrates how to apply CSP-Prover in various settings. Finally, we relate CSP-Prover to similar tools.

2   The Theorem Prover Isabelle

Isabelle [18] is an interactive theorem prover. Theorems to be proved are entered as *goals*. A goal can be manipulated by proof-commands referring to a set of predefined inference *rules* producing new goals. Such rules can be combined to form *proof tactics*. A proof is completed, if by application of rules and tactics the only open goal is the truth value **True**. Successfully proved theorems can be stored and used later as new rules.

To extend an existing logic, Isabelle offers mechanisms to define new types, functions, predicates etc. The keyword **typedef** defines a new type as a non-empty subset of an existing type:

```
typedef SubType = {x::SuperType. P(x)}
```

Here, P is a predicate over the existing type SuperType, and SubType is the newly defined type by the subset. In addition, the keyword **datatype** is used for recursive type definitions with type-constructors, for example,

```
datatype 'a list = Nil  |  Cons 'a "'a list"
```

where Nil and Cons are type constructors, and 'a is a type variable. Type classes can be defined by

```
axclass SubClass < SuperClass
    name₁: (a condition)   name₂: (a condition) ···
```

where SubClass is included in SuperClass and contains only types which satisfy conditions named $name_{1,2,...}$. Everything in SuperClass is inherited by SubClass. Another possibility to use this inheritance is to declare that a type forms an instance of SubClass by the keyword **instance**. Such a declaration requires a proof that the type satisfies the conditions of SubClass and all its super classes.

Theorems, together with definitions and proof-commands needed for their proof, can be stored in *theory-files*. Isabelle organises such files in a rule-database, to which other theory files may refer. Such a theory-file generally has the format

> **theory** T = B_1 + $\cdots$ + B_n :   *declarations, definitions, and proofs*   **end**

where $B_1, \cdots, B_n$ are names of *parent theories* of theory T. Everything used in parent theories is available in their children. This allows for a hierarchical organisation of theory-files.

3   The CSP Dialect Chosen for CSP-Prover

This section briefly summarises CSP syntax, CSP semantics and how to analyse process equations in CSP, following closely [21]. It also gives a first overview on what has been implemented in CSP-Prover.

```
P ::=  SKIP                    %% successful terminating process
    |  STOP                    %% deadlock process
    |  a -> P                  %% action prefix
    |  c ! v -> P              %% sending v over channel c (*)
    |  c ? x : X -> P(x)       %% receiving x∈X on channel c (*)
    |  c !! x : X -> P(x)      %% non-deterministic sending x∈X on channel c (*)
    |  c !! x -> P(x)          %% non-deterministic sending x on channel c (*)
    |  ? x : X -> P(x)         %% external prefix choice
    |  ! x : X -> P(x)         %% internal prefix choice (*)
    |  P [+] P                 %% external choice
    |  P |~| P                 %% internal choice
    |  ! x : X .. P(x)         %% replicated internal choice
    |  IF b THEN P ELSE P      %% conditional
    |  P |[X]| P               %% generalized parallel
    |  P ||| P                 %% interleaving (*)
    |  P || P                  %% synchronous parallel (*)
    |  P -- X                  %% hiding
    |  P [[r]]                 %% relational renaming
    |  P ;; P                  %% sequential composition
    |  P [> P                  %% (untimed) timeout (*)
    |  <C>                     %% process name
```

Fig. 1. Syntax of basic CSP processes in CSP-Prover

3.1   Syntax

The process algebra CSP [11, 21] is defined relative to a given set of communications. Its *basic processes* are built from primitive processes like SKIP and STOP. CSP includes communication primitives like sending and receiving values over a communication channel, distinguishes between internal and external choice between two processes, offers a variety of parallel operators, sequential composition of processes, and various other features like renaming and hiding. Fig. 1 shows that the CSP dialect implemented by CSP-Prover covers all these features[2]. This syntax definition involves certain Isabelle notations: given a type 'a as set of communications, a:'a is a single communication, c:('v⇒'a) denotes a channel name, v:'v is a passed value, b:bool stands

---

[2] The syntactical differences to CSP-M, as e.g. in the sequential composition P ;; P, avoid overloading of symbols also used by Isabelle.

for a boolean value, X:'a set is a subset of 'a, and r:('a * 'a) set denotes a binary relation over communications. Derived operators are marked by (*) . In CSP, *recursive processes* are either defined by process equations or by so-called μ-recursion. Here, CSP-Prover currently offers only the former mechanism. Each recursive process has the form LET df IN P, where the body process P can contain process names whose behaviours are defined by fixed points of the function df. The most convenient way to define this function is to use Isabelle's keyword **primrec** for defining recursive functions. For example, a process Inc which iteratively sends an increasing natural number n to a channel c is defined as follows:

```
primrec df      (Loop n) = c ! n -> <Loop (n+1)>
defs "Inc_def:      Inc == LET df IN <Loop 0>"
```

Such parametrised process expressions can – on the semantical side of CSP – give rise to infinite systems of equations.

3.2   Semantics

CSP is a language with many semantics, different in their style as well as in their ability to distinguish between different reactive behaviour. There are operational, denotational and algebraic approaches, ranging from the simple finite traces model T to such complex semantics as the infinite traces model with failures/divergences U. For a general theorem prover on CSP the denotational semantics are of special interest. Even under the restriction to finitely nondeterministic CSP the algebraic approach does not work quite cleanly for the three main models: the traces model T, the failure-divergence model N, and the stable failures model F (see [21] for the details).

The current prototype of CSP-Prover concentrates on the denotational stable-failures semantics F: This semantics allows for analysis of deadlock-freedom and of liveness properties (for which the traces model T is too weak). Furthermore, the semantic domain of F is a complete metric space (cms) as well as complete partial order (cpo) even in the case of infinite alphabets[3]. For recursively defined processes, both approaches, cms and cpo, allow to prove the existence of solutions and to analyse these solutions by powerful induction principles.

Given a set of communications A, the domain of the *stable failures model* F is a set of pairs (T, F) satisfying certain healthiness conditions, where $T \subseteq A^{*\checkmark}$ and $F \subseteq A^{*\checkmark} \times \mathbb{P}(A^\checkmark)$[4]. In such a pair (T, F), T is the set of traces a process can execute, while the elements $(s, X) \in F$ describe sets of communications X which a process can fail to accept after executing the trace s. The healthiness conditions state e.g. that the sets T need to be non-empty and prefix-closed,

---

[3] The semantic domain of the failure-divergence model N is not a cpo on refinement order for infinite alphabets; however it is a cms independent of the alphabet size. Another problem is that in N the semantics clauses for hiding work only under special conditions.

[4] $A^\checkmark := A \cup \{\checkmark\}$, $A^{*\checkmark} := A^* \cup \{s \frown \langle\checkmark\rangle \mid s \in A^*\}$.

that a trace occurring in F needs to be a trace in T, that after termination a process may refuse to engage in any events.

Typical examples of the semantic clauses of $\mathcal{F}$ are:

$$
\begin{aligned}
&traces(\texttt{STOP}) = \{\langle\rangle\} \\
&failures(\texttt{STOP}) = \{(\langle\rangle, X) \mid X \subseteq A^{\checkmark}\} \\
&traces(\texttt{a -> P}) = \{\langle\rangle\} \cup \{\langle\texttt{a}\rangle \frown s \mid s \in traces(\texttt{P})\} \\
&failures(\texttt{a -> P}) = \{(\langle\rangle, X) \mid \texttt{a} \notin X\} \cup \{(\langle\texttt{a}\rangle \frown s, X) \mid (s, X) \in failures(\texttt{P})\}
\end{aligned}
$$

Our implementation uses the traces semantics and the stable-failures semantics as they are defined in [21]. As Isabelle allows only for consistent theories, our encoding can also be seen as a proof for the well-formedness of these semantics[5].

3.3   Analysing CSP Recursion

Consider the recursive equations in CSP defined by the following functions:

```
primrec df1    (P) = a -> <P> |~| b -> SKIP
primrec df2    (Q) = a -> <Q>
```

For such equations the natural questions are: (1) Do there exist solutions for P and Q in, say, the CSP model $\mathcal{F}$? (2) Are these solutions uniquely determined? (3) How to prove properties on these solutions, e.g. that Q refines P? To deal with these questions, CSP employs two different techniques: complete metric spaces (cms) and complete partial orders (cpo) which are both implemented in CSP-Prover. These two approaches follow a similar pattern: the first step consists of proving that the domain of a given CSP model is a cms or a cpo, respectively. As a particularity of CSP, metric spaces are introduced in terms of so-called restriction spaces. The second step consists of proving that the various CSP operators satisfy the pre-requisite properties, namely contractiveness for cms and continuity for cpo. Finally, a fixed point theorem is used to deal with question (1). In the case of cms this is Banach's theorem, while it is Tarski's theorem within the cpo approach. For question (2) Banach's theorem leads to a unique fixed point, while Tarski's theorem does not guarantee uniqueness. Here, the least fixed point is chosen in the CSP models T and $\mathcal{F}$. To answer question (3) both the cms and the cpo approach offer as a technique the so-called fixed point induction.

Up to now the described framework works only for one *single equation*. But how about an *infinite system of equations* like the recursive process Inc illustrated in Sect. 3.1? For such infinite systems, infinite products of cms and cpo, respectively, are required. Furthermore, the pre-requisite properties of the fixed point theorems need to be proved only on the base of component functions.

---

[5] In an earlier encoding of CSP in Isabelle [26] it was necessary to correct an up-to-then established CSP semantics.

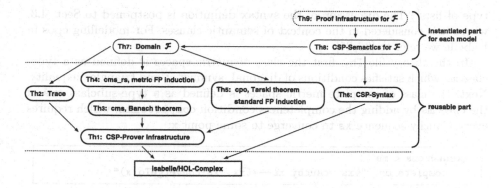

Fig. 2. The theory map of CSP-Prover instantiated with the stable-failures model $\mathcal{F}$

4   A Generic Theorem Prover for CSP Refinement

CSP-Prover extends the Isabelle [18] theory HOL-Complex (which is HOL [16] extended with a definitional development of the real and complex numbers) by a hierarchy of theory-files encoding CSP, see Fig. 2. The prototype discussed here supports the stable-failures model $\mathcal{F}$ as well as the traces model $\mathcal{T}$. CSP-Prover has a generic architecture divided into a large *reusable part* $Th_{1,...,6}$ independent of specific CSP models and an *instantiated part* $Th_{7,8,9}$ for each specific CSP model.

The reusable part contains Banach's fixed point theorem and the metric fixed point induction rule based on complete metric spaces (cms) as well as Tarski's fixed point theorem and the standard fixed point induction rule based on complete partial orders (cpo). Furthermore, it provides infinite product constructions for these spaces. Thus, when CSP-Prover is instantiated with the domain of a new CSP model, the fixed point theorems, the induction rules, as well as the product constructions are available for free, provided the domain is a cms or a cpo. Additionally, the reusable part provides guidelines in form of proof obligations on how to show that a domain is a cms or a cpo. Here, especially the theory on restriction spaces plays an important rôle for proofs concerning cms.

Another contribution of the reusable part is the definition of the CSP syntax as a recursive type. Here, instantiating CSP-Prover with a new model requires to provide its semantic clauses defined inductively over this type. This means that the syntax is *deeply encoded*, thus structural induction on processes is supported.

4.1   Reusable Part

The reusable part consists of a theory of traces (Th_2), fixed point theories on cms and cpo ($Th_{3,4,5}$), the definitions of the CSP syntax (Th_6), and fundamental theorems on limits and least upper bounds (Th_1). In this Section, we concentrate on how to encode cms and restriction spaces. Trace theory is similar to the data type of lists[6]. The discussion of the syntax definition is postponed to Sect. 4.3, where it is considered in the context of semantic clauses. For modelling cpos in Isabelle we refer to [26, 25].

In the theory file Th$_3$, first the class of metric spaces is defined as a type-class ms which satisfies conditions of diagonal, symmetry, and triangle inequality. Next, the class of complete metric spaces is defined as a type-subclass cms of the class ms by adding the completeness condition complete_ms, which requires every Cauchy sequence xs to converge to some point x:

```
axclass cms < ms
    complete_ms: "∀xs. cauchy xs⟶(∃x. xs convergeTo x)"
```

Then, Banach's fixed point theorem is proved, i.e. that any contraction map f over cms has a unique fixed point and the sequence obtained by iteratively applying f to any value x0 converges to the fixed point.

```
theorem Banach_thm: "contraction (f::('a::cms⇒'a))
    ⟹ (f hasUFP ∧ (λn. (f^n) x0) convergeTo (UFP f))"
```

A way for deriving a metric space from a restriction space is given in [21]. Thus, if a space is an instance of the class rs of restriction spaces then the space is also an instance of ms_rs which is the multiple-inheritance from ms and rs. An important result on ms_rs is that the completeness of ms_rs is preserved by the constructors * (binary product) and fun (function space). For example, if type T is an instance of cms_rs, then the function type I ⇒ T is also an instance of cms_rs for an arbitrary type I. This theorem is expressed in Isabelle by

```
instance fun :: (type,cms_rs) cms_rs
```

The function type I ⇒ T1 is used to deal with infinite product spaces whose index set is I, which are required to deal with infinite state systems (see Sect. 3.3). Take for example the CSP model $\mathcal{F}$. Here we need that $\mathcal{F}^I$ is a cms for any infinite index set I, which is intuitively the set of (infinitely many) process names. The above property expresses: if $\mathcal{F}$ is an instance of cms_rs then $\mathcal{F}^I$ is also an instance of cms_rs.

Finally, the following metric fixed point induction rule on cms_rs is proved (see [21] on continuity and constructiveness for restriction spaces).

```
theorem cms_fixpoint_induction: "[| (R::'a::cms_rs⇒bool) x ;
    continuous_rs R ; constructive_rs f ; inductivefun R f |]
        ⟹ f hasUFP ∧ R (UFP f)"
```

---

[6] The event type of CSP consists of communications (Ev a) and the event ✓ for successful termination. The trace type is defined as the subset of event lists such that ✓ cannot occur except in the last place of a list.

4.2   Instantiated Part

The instantiated part consists of instantiated domain theories (Th_7 in Fig. 2), semantic clauses (Th_8), and a proof infrastructure (Th_9). The proof infrastructure contains many CSP laws such as step laws, distributive laws, fixed-point induction rules, etc. Furthermore, it provides a powerful tactic `csp_hnf_tac` for translating any expression to a head normal form. As these rules and tactics are proved in Isabelle, they are guaranteed to be sound with respect to the chosen CSP semantics.

In the current CSP-Prover, the domains of the stable-failures model $\mathcal{F}$ and the traces model $\mathcal{T}$ are instantiated as types `'a domSF` and `'a domT`, respectively, where `'a` is the type of communications. Here, the type `'a domT` can be reused for defining `'a domSF`:

```
typedef 'a domT = "{T::('a trace set). HC_T1(T)}"
types 'a failure = "'a trace * 'a event set"
typedef 'a domF = "{F::('a failure set). HC_F2(F)}"
types 'a domTF = "'a domT * 'a domF"
typedef 'a domSF = "{SF::('a domTF). HC_T2(SF) & HC_T3(SF)
                                      & HC_F3(SF) & HC_F4(SF)}"
```

where HC_T1, $\cdots$, HC_F4 are predicates which exactly represent the healthiness conditions T1, $\cdots$, F4 given in [21].

In order to apply Banach's theorem and the metric induction rule to the model $\mathcal{F}$, it is required to prove that the infinite product `('i,'a) domSF_prod` of `'a domSF` is an instance of `cms_rs`, where `('i,'a) domSF_prod` is a synonym of `('i ⇒ 'a domSF)` and the type `'i` represents the indexing set of the product space. This is proved as follows: (1) domT and domF are instances of `cms_rs`, (2) domTF is also an instance of `cms_rs`, thus there exists a limit of each Cauchy sequence in domSF ($\subset$ domTF), (3) the limit is contained in domSF, thus domSF is also an instance of `cms_rs`, and (4) domSF_prod is an instance of `cms_rs`. Here, the proofs of (2) and (4) follow by preservation of `cms_rs` under the constructors * and `fun` as mentioned in Sect. 4.1. This example shows how the provided infrastructure in terms of restriction spaces discharges certain proof obligations when a new CSP model is integrated in CSP-Prover.

4.3   Deep Encoding

The CSP syntax is defined as a recursive type `('n,'a) proc` by the command **datatype** as shown in Fig. 3, where `'n` and `'a` are type variables for process-names and communications, respectively. This syntax encoding style implies that structural induction over processes is available by the Isabelle's proof command `induct_tac`. Recursive processes take the form LET:fp df IN P, their type is `('n,'a) procRC`. Here, the function df binds process names to processes, it has the type `('n,'a) procDF`. And fp is a variable instantiated by either Ufp or Lfp, and specifies which fixed point of df is used for giving the meaning of process names: i.e. the unique fixed point by Ufp and the least fixed point by Lfp. In the current CSP-Prover, LET df IN P is an abbreviation of LET:Ufp df IN P.

```
datatype ('n,'a) proc = STOP
                      | SKIP
                      | Act_prefix "'a" "('n,'a) proc"      ("_ -> _")
                      | ...
                      | Proc_name  "'n"                     ("<_>")

type ('n,'a) procDF = "'n => ('n,'a) proc"

datatype fp_type = Ufp | Lfp

datatype
  ('n,'a) procRC = Letin "fp_type" "('n,'a) procDF" "('n,'a) proc"    ("LET:_ _ IN _")
```

Fig. 3. Syntax definition of processes

```
consts
  evalT  :: "'a proc => ('n,'a) domSF_prod => 'a domT"     ("[_]_T")
  evalF  :: "'a proc => ('n,'a) domSF_prod => 'a domF"     ("[_]_F")
  evalSF :: "'a proc => ('n,'a) domSF_prod => 'a domSF"    ("[_]_SF")

primrec
  "[STOP]_T    = (λe. {[]_t}_t)"
  "[SKIP]_T    = (λe. {[]_t, [√]_t}_t)"
  "[a -> P]_T  = (λe. {t. t=[]_t ∨ (∃s. t=[Ev a]_t @_t s ∧ s ∈_t [P]_T e) }_t)"
                  ⋮
  "[<C>]_T     = (λe. fstSF (e C))"             (* note: fstSF (T ,, F) = T *)

primrec
  "[STOP]_F    = (λe. {f. ∃X. f=([]_t, X) }_f)"
  "[SKIP]_F    = (λe. {f. (∃X. f=([]_t, X) ∧ X ⊆ Evset) ∨ (∃X. f=([√]_t, X)) }_f)"
  "[a -> P]_F  = (λe. {f. (∃X. f=([]_t,X) ∧ Ev a ∉ X) ∨
                      (∃s X. f=([Ev a]_t @_t s, X) ∧ (s, X) ∈_f [P]_F e) }_f)"
                  ⋮
  "[<C>]_F     = (λe. sndSF (e C))"             (* note: sndSF (T ,, F) = F *)

defs evalSF_def :
  "[P]_SF == (λe. ([P]_T e ,, [P]_F e))"

consts
  evalDF :: "('n=>('m,'a) proc)=>('m,'a) domSF_prod =>('n,'a) domSF_prod"   ("[_]_DF")
  evalRC :: "('n,'a) procRC=>'a domSF"                                       ("[_]_RC")

defs evalDF_def :
  "[df]_DF == (λe. (λC. ([df C]_SF e)))"

recdef evalRC "measure (λx. 0)"
  "[LET:Ufp df IN P]_RC = [P]_SF (UFP [df]_DF)"     (* based on cms *)
  "[LET:Lfp df IN P]_RC = [P]_SF (LFP [df]_DF)"     (* based on cpo *)
```

Fig. 4. Semantics definition of processes

The CSP semantics is defined by translating process-expressions into elements of the model $\mathcal{F}$ by a mapping ($[P]_{SF}$ e) as shown in Fig. 4, where e is an evaluation function for process names in P. The mapping ($[P]_{SF}$ e) is a pair of mappings ($[P]_T$ e ,, $[P]_F$ e), where (T ,, F) requires T and F to satisfy healthiness conditions T1 and F2, respectively, and the pair of them to satisfy T2, T3, F3, and F4. The mappings ($[P]_T$ e) and ($[P]_F$ e) are defined by the same semantic clauses of the model $\mathcal{F}$ in [21], where subscripts t and f (e.g. in $[\,]_t$ and $\in_f$) are attached to operators on domT and domF, in order to avoid conflicts with the operators on Isabelle's built-in types such as list and set. Furthermore, the meaning $[\![df]\!]_{DF}$ of each defining function is defined such that the meaning of each process name C is $[\![df\ C]\!]_{SF}$. Finally, the meaning $[\![LET\!:\!fp\ df\ IN\ P]\!]_{RC}$ of each recursive process is defined by $[\![P]\!]_{SF}$, where the meaning of each process name in P is given by a suitable fixed point of $[\![df]\!]_{DF}$.

5   Applications

In this section we demonstrate how CSP-Prover can be used for the verification of reactive systems. First, we discuss deadlock analysis and a refinement proof in the context of an industrial case study. Then we study a mutual exclusion problem arising in the classical example of the dining mathematicians.

5.1   Verification in the Context of an Industrial Case Study

The EP2 system[7] is a new industrial standard of electronic payment systems. It consists of seven autonomous entities centred around the EP2 *Terminal*: Cardholder (i.e., customer), Point of Service (i.e., cash register), Attendant, POS Management System, Acquirer, Service Center, and Card, see Fig. 5. These en-

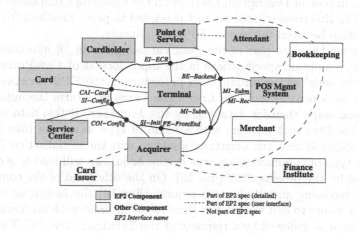

Fig. 5. Overview of the EP2 System

tities communicate with the Terminal and, to a certain extent, with one another via *XML-messages* in a fixed format.

---

[7] EP2 is a joint project established by a number of (mainly Swiss) financial institutes and companies in order to define infrastructure for credit, debit, and electronic purse terminals in Switzerland (www.eftpos2000.ch).

```
 1  (* data part *)
 2  typedecl init_d        typedecl request_d
 3  typedecl response_d   typedecl exit_d
 4  datatype Data = Init init_d | Exit exit_d | Request request_d | Response response_d
 5  datatype Event = c Data
 6
 7  (* process part *)
 8  datatype ACName = Acquirer | AcConfM | Terminal | TerminalConfM
 9  consts ACDef :: "(ACName, Event) procDF"
10  primrec
11    "ACDef (Terminal) = c !! init:(range Init) -> <TerminalConfM>"
12    "ACDef (TerminalConfM) =
13      c ? x -> IF (x:range Request)
14            THEN c !! response:(range Response) -> <TerminalConfM>
15            ELSE IF (x:range Exit) THEN SKIP ELSE STOP"
16    "ACDef (Acquirer) = c ? x:(range Init) -> <AcConfM>"
17    "ACDef (AcConfM) =
18      c !! exit:(range Exit) -> SKIP |~|
19      c !! request:(range Request) -> c ? response:(range Response) -> <AcConfM>"
20
21  constdefs AC :: "(ACName, Event) procRC"
22    "AC == LET ACDef IN (<Acquirer> |[range c]| <Terminal>)"
```

Fig. 6. EP2 Specification at the Abstract Component Description Level

In [9], major parts of the EP2 system have been formalised in CSP-CASL [20]. Following the structure of the original EP2 documents, the specifications presented in [9] can be classified to be e.g. on the Architectural Level, on the Abstract Component Description Level, or on the Concrete Component Description Level. In this context, tool support is needed to prove deadlock freedom for the interaction between the various EP2 components.

Translating the data part of the specifications given in [9] into adequate Isabelle code, we obtain specifications in the input format of CSP-Prover. Fig. 6 shows the nucleus[8] of the initialisation procedure of the EP2 Terminal at the Abstract Component Description Level. The Terminal starts the initialisation (line 11) and waits then for data sent by the Acquirer. If this data is of type Request, the Terminal answers with a value of type Response (line 14). Another possibility is that the Acquirer wants to exit the initialisation (line 15). Any other type of communication sent by the Acquirer will lead to a deadlock represented by the process STOP (line 15). On the other end of the communication, after receiving an initialisation request (line 16) the Acquirer internally decides if it wants to exit the process (line 18) or interact with the Terminal by sending a request followed by a response of the Terminal (line 19). The system AC to be analysed here consists of the parallel composition of the Terminal and the Acquirer synchronised on the channel c (line 22).

It is the defining characteristic of the Abstract Component Description Level that the data involved is *loosely* specified. No specific values are defined (lines 2–5). Semantically this means that – depending on the interpretation of e.g. the type init_d – the described systems might involve infinite non-determinism,

---

[8] For the purpose of this paper, the specification text has been simplified. The complete formalisation and proof can be found in [12].

```
1    datatype AbsName = Abstract | Loop
2    consts AbsDef :: "(AbsName, Event) procDF"
3    primrec
4      "AbsDef (Abstract) = c !! init:(range Init) -> <Loop>"
5      "AbsDef (Loop) =
6          c !! exit:(range Exit) -> SKIP |~|
7          c !! request:(range Request) -> c !! response:(range Response) -> <Loop>"
8
9    constdefs Abs :: "(AbsName, Event) procRC"
10     "Abs == LET AbsDef IN <Abstract>"
```

Fig. 7. An abstraction of the process shown in Fig. 6

e.g. if the type init_d has infinitely many values, the Terminal process of Fig. 6 chooses internally between sending any of these values (line 11). Thus, CSP-Prover has simultaneously to deal with a *class* of specifications: it has to prove that a certain property holds for any possible interpretation of the types involved.

Using CSP-Prover, we can show the above described process AC to be stable-failure equivalent to the process Abs of Fig. 7. Note that Abs is a sequential, i.e. by syntactic characterisation deadlock-free process. As stable failure equivalence preserves deadlocks, establishing this equivalence proves that the interaction of Terminal and Acquirer on the Abstract Component Description Level is deadlock free[9]. Fig. 8 shows the complete script to prove the stable-failure equivalence Abs =F AC (line 14) in CSP-Prover. First, a mapping is defined from the process-names of Abs to process expressions in AC (line 3-5)[10]. Next, it is shown that the involved recursive processes are guarded and do not use the hiding operator. This is fully automated routine (lines 8–11). After these preparations, Abs =F AC is given as a goal (line 14). Using the above mapping, now the recursive processes are unfolded to a base case and step cases by fixed point induction (line 16). Since a step case is produced for each of the process names of Abs, the step cases are instantiated by induction on AbsName (line 17). Finally, the theorem is proven by Isabelle's tactic auto, CSP-Prover's tactic csp_hnf_tac, which transforms any expression into a head normal form, and csp_decompo, which decomposes CSP-operators (line 18).

5.2   The Dining Mathematicians

The dining mathematicians [7] are a classical mutual exclusion problem: There are two mathematicians living at the same place, whose life is focused on two activities, namely thinking (TH0 and TH1, respectively) and eating (EAT0 and EAT1, respectively). As they have a strong dislike for each other, they want never to eat at the same time. To ensure this, they agreed to the following protocol. They both have access to a common variable (VAR n) storing integer

---

[9] In this example, abstraction is convenient to establish deadlock-freedom; in general, CSP-Prover is capable to support e.g. the various deadlock rules stated in [21].

[10] It is hard to automatically derive such correspondences. However, CSP-Prover can assist users to derive them.

```
 1   (* expected correspondence of process-names in Abs to AC *)
 2   consts Abs_to_AC :: "AbsName ⇒ (ACName, Event) proc"
 3   primrec
 4     "Abs_to_AC (Abstract) = (<Acquirer> |[range c]| <Terminal>)"
 5     "Abs_to_AC     (Loop) = (<AcConfM> |[range c]| <TerminalConfM>)"
 6
 7   (* guarded and no hiding operator *)
 8   lemma guard_nohide[simp]:
 9     "!! C. guard (ACDef C) & nohide (ACDef C)"
10     "!! C. guard (AbsDef C) & nohide (AbsDef C)"
11   by (induct_tac C, simp_all, induct_tac C, simp_all)
12
13   (* the main theorem *)
14   theorem ep2: "Abs =F AC"
15   apply (unfold Abs_def AC_def)
16   apply (rule csp_fp_induct_cms[of _ _ _ "Abs_to_AC"], simp_all)
17   apply (induct_tac C)
18   by (auto simp add: image_iff | tactic {* csp_hnf_tac 1 *} | rule csp_decompo)+
```

Fig. 8. The complete proof script for AC =F Abs

```
datatype Event = Eat0 | Back0 | End0 | RD0 int | WR0 int
               | Eat1 | Back1 | End1 | RD1 int | WR1 int | NUM int
syntax      "_CH0" :: "Event set" ("CH0")         "_CH1" :: "Event set" ("CH1")
translations "CH0" == "(range RD0) ∪ (range WR0)"  "CH1" == "(range RD1) ∪ (range WR1)"

datatype SysName = VAR int | TH0 | EAT0 int | TH1 | EAT1 int
consts SysDef :: "(SysName, Event) procDF"
primrec
  "SysDef     (TH0) = RD0 ? n -> IF (EVEN n) THEN Eat0 -> <EAT0 n> ELSE Back0 -> <TH0>"
  "SysDef     (TH1) = RD1 ? n -> IF (ODD n) THEN Eat1 -> <EAT1 n> ELSE Back1 -> <TH1>"
  "SysDef (EAT0 n) = End0 -> WR0 ! (n div 2) -> <TH0>"
  "SysDef (EAT1 n) = End1 -> WR1 ! (3 * n + 1) -> <TH1>"
  "SysDef  (VAR n) =   WR0 ? n -> <VAR n> [+] WR1 ? n -> <VAR n>
                   [+] RD0 ! n -> <VAR n> [+] RD1 ! n -> <VAR n>"
constdefs Sys :: "int ⇒ (SysName, Event) procRC"
  "Sys == (λn. LET SysDef IN (<TH0> |[CH0]| <VAR n> |[CH1]| <TH1>) -- (CH0 ∪ CH1))"
```

Fig. 9. The dining mathematicians: Csp-Prover description of the concrete system

values. If the stored integer (n) is even, the first mathematician is allowed to start eating. When finished, the first mathematician sets the stored value to (n/2). A similar procedure holds for the second mathematician, where the check is if the value of the stored variable is odd, and the value written back after eating is (3n+1)[11]. Fig. 9 shows this system described in Csp-Prover. Here, each of the process definitions (EAT0 n), (EAT1 n), and (VAR n) describes infinitely many equations. The question is: does this now precisely described system exclude the situation where both mathematicians eat together? Or, on a more formal level: has this system a trace where Eat1 appears between consecutive communications Eat0 and End0 (or vice versa)?

The classical argument in analysing this system is to provide an abstraction of the dining mathematicians which clearly has the desired exclusion property. This

---

[11] The function involved here is the so-called *Collatz function* which is studied in the context of the $3x + 1$ problem, see [13] for a survey.

abstraction Spc consists only of three states, which stand for the situations 'both mathematicians think' THO_TH1 and 'one mathematician eats while the other is thinking' (EATO_TH1 and THO_EAT1, respectively). With CSP-Prover we can show that (Sys n) is a stable-failures refinement of Spc for any integer n, thus "ALL n. Spc <=F Sys n". The respective proof script is substantially longer than the proof of Abs =F AC shown in Sec. 5.1. But it follows the same strategy: First, the goal is unfolded by fixed point induction. In a second step the resulting proof obligations are translated to head normal forms and automatically discharged. The details are omitted here, the full script as well as the abstraction Spc are available at [12]. As Spc is again a sequential process, this refinement result also establishes deadlock-freedom of (Sys n).

6   Related Work

Based on general purpose theorem provers like Isabelle [18], HOL [10] or PVS [17], various tools for theorem proving over process algebras have been presented.

Closest to our approach are the CSP encodings of Tej/Wolff [26, 25] and Schneider/Dutertre [8, 24]. *Tej/Wolff* suggest a shallow encoding of CSP in Isabelle/HOL based on the cpo approach. Their encoding HOL-CSP is focused on the failure-divergence model of CSP. To deal with recursion it introduces a new process order that implies the standard refinement order. HOL-CSP lacks the possibility of proofs on the syntactic process structure. Thus, powerful tactics as csp_hnf_tac in CSP-Prover for transforming process expressions to head normal form are not available. *Schneider/Dutertre*'s encoding of the CSP traces model $\mathcal{T}$ in PVS is tailored to the verification of security protocols. Semantically it uses the cpo approach. It does not consider process termination. Due to its clear focus, refinement proofs of the nature shown in the previous section are out of its scope. Compared to these two encodings, a major advantage of CSP-Prover is its genericity. It is easy to adapt CSP-Prover to any other denotational CSP model. Furthermore, in offering both, the cms and the cpo approach, it allows to use the more convenient and the more promising setting for any proof step.

Alternative to encoding a denotational semantics, [6, 19, 1] base their encodings on an axiomatic semantics of the process algebra. As discussed in Sect. 3.2, such an approach is not an option in the context of CSP.

7   Conclusion and Future Work

We have shown a new tool CSP-Prover which supports refinement proofs over various CSP models. Thanks to its powerful semi-automatic and automatic tactics, CSP-Prover has successfully been applied in an industrial case study as well as for a complex example tailored to be a benchmark for refinement proofs.

In the future, we intend to include the failure-divergence model $\mathcal{N}$ in CSP-Prover. Furthermore, we will integrate CSP-Prover with the model checker FDR. In this context the theory of data independence, see e.g. [14], will play an important rôle. Continuing the work on EP2 and applying CSP-Prover to other case studies, e.g. of the area of train control systems, will help to develop more proof infrastructure to further automate refinement proofs.

Acknowledgement

The authors would like to thank AIST (Japan) and the Royal Society (UK) for financial support; Faron G. Moller and Kazuhito Ohmaki for initiating our cooperation; Erwin R. Catesbeiana (jr.) for advice on semantical questions; as well as Christoph Lüth, Ranko Lazic, Jan Peleska, Bill Roscoe, and Holger Schlingloff for valuable feedback and advice on our tool.

References

1. T. Basten and J. Hooman. Process algebra in PVS. In W. Cleaveland, editor, *TACAS'99*, LNCS 1579, pages 270–284. Springer, 1999.
2. J. Bergstra, A. Ponse, and S. Smolka. *Handbook of Process Algebra*. Elsevier, 2001.
3. B. Buth, M. Kouvaras, J. Peleska, and H. Shi. Deadlock analysis for a fault-tolerant system. In *AMAST'97*, LNCS 1349, pages 60–75. Springer, 1997.
4. B. Buth, J. Peleska, and H. Shi. Combining methods for the livelock analysis of a fault-tolerant system. In A. M. Haeberer, editor, *AMAST'98*, LNCS 1548, pages 124–139. Springer, 1998.
5. B. Buth and M. Schrönen. Model-checking the architectural design of a fail-safe communication system for railway interlocking systems. In J. M. Wing, J. Woodcock, and J. Davies, editors, *FM'99*, LNCS 1709. Springer, 1999.
6. A. Camilleri. Combining interaction and automation in process algebra verification. In G. Goos and J. Hartmanis, editors, *TAPSOFT 1991*, LNCS 494, pages 283–295. Springer, 1991.
7. E. M. Clarke and H. Schlingloff. Model checking. In A. Robinson and A. Voronkov, editors, *Handbook of Automated Reasoning*. Elsevier, 2001.
8. B. Dutertre and S. Schneider. Using a PVS embedding of CSP to verify authentication protocols. In E. L. Gunter and A. Felty, editors, *TPHOL 1997*, LNCS 1275, pages 121–136. Springer, 1997.
9. A. Gimblett, M. Roggenbach, and H. Schlingloff. Towards a formal specification of an electronic payment system in CSP-CASL. In J. L. Fiadeiro, P. Mosses, and F. Orejas, editors, *WADT 2004*, LNCS. Springer, to appear.
10. M. Gordon and T. Melham. *Introduction to HOL*. Cambrige University Press, 1993.
11. C. A. R. Hoare. *Communicating Sequential Processes*. Prentice Hall, 1985.
12. Y. Isobe and M. Roggenbach. Webpage on CSP-Prover. http://staff.aist.go.jp/y-isobe/CSP-Prover/CSP-Prover.html.
13. J. C. Lagarias. The $3x + 1$ problem and its generalizations. *Amer. Math. Monthly*, 92:3–23, 1985.
14. R. Lazic. *A Semantic Study of Data Independence with Applications to Model Checking*. PhD thesis, Oxford University Computing Laboratory, 1999.
15. F. S. E. Limited. Failures-divergence refinement: FDR2. http://www.fsel.com/.
16. T. Nipkow, L. C. Paulon, and M. Wenzel. *Isabelle/HOL*. LNCS 2283. Springer, 2002.

17. S. Owre, J. M. Rushby, and N. Shankar. PVS: A prototype verification system. In D. Kapur, editor, *CADE'92*, LNAI 607, pages 748–752. Springer, 1992.
18. L. C. Paulson. *A Generic Theorem Prover*. LNCS 828. Springer, 1994.
19. I. P. Rix Groenboom, Chris Hendriks. Algebraic proof assistants in HOL. In B. Möller, editor, *MPC'95*, LNCS 947, pages 305–321. Springer, 1995.
20. M. Roggenbach. CSP-CASL – A new integration of process algebra and algebraic specification. *Theoretical Computer Science*, to appear.
21. A. Roscoe. *The Theory and Practice of Concurrency*. Prentice Hall, 1998.
22. A. Roscoe. On the expressive power of CSP refinement. In *Proceedings of AV-oCS'03*, Technical Report. Southampton University, 2003.
23. P. Ryan, S. Schneider, M. Goldsmith, G. Lowe, and B. Roscoe. *The Modelling and Analysis of Security Protocols: the CSP Approach*. Addison-Wesley, 2001.
24. S. Schneider. Verifying authentication protocol implementations. In B. Jacobs and A. Rensink, editors, *FMOODS 2002, IFIP Conference Proceedings* Vol. 209, pages 5–24. Kluwer, 2002.
25. H. Tej. *HOL-CSP: Mechanised Formal Development of Concurrent Processes*. BISS Monograph Vol. 19. Logos Verlag Berlin, 2003.
26. H. Tej and B. Wolff. A corrected failure-divergence model for CSP in Isabelle/HOL. In J. Fitzgerald, C. B. Jones, and P. Lucas, editors, *FME'97*, LNCS 1313, pages 318–337. Springer, 1997.

Separating Fairness and Well-Foundedness for the Analysis of Fair Discrete Systems[*]

Amir Pnueli[1], Andreas Podelski[2], and Andrey Rybalchenko[2]

[1] New York University, New York
[2] Max-Planck-Institut für Informatik, Saarbrücken

Abstract. Fair discrete systems (FDSs) are a computational model of concurrent programs where fairness assumptions are specified in terms of sets of states. The analysis of fair discrete systems involves a non-trivial interplay between fairness and well-foundedness (ranking functions). This interplay has been an obstacle for automation. The contribution of this paper is a new analysis of temporal properties of FDSs. The analysis uses a domain of binary relations over states labeled by sets of indices of fairness requirements. The use of labeled relations separates the reasoning on well-foundedness and fairness.

1 Introduction

Fair discrete systems provide a computational model of concurrent programs where fairness assumptions are specified in terms of sets of states [8]. The analysis of fair discrete systems involves a non-trivial interplay between fairness and well-foundedness (ranking functions). Its automation is a difficult task. One particular difficulty is the design of an abstract domain that accounts for well-foundedness and fairness.

We propose an analysis that avoids such an interplay by separating the reasoning on well-foundedness and fairness. The analysis is based on binary relations over states that are labeled by sets of indices of fairness requirements. We design an operator F_{FDS} on a (concrete) domain D_{FDS} of such labeled relations. We use least fixed points of F_{FDS} to establish the validity of temporal FDS properties. Furthermore, we design an abstract domain $D_{\mathsf{FDS}}^{\#}$ on which approximations of least fixed points of F_{FDS} are effectively computable. The formalization of our analysis follows the framework of abstract interpretation [3].

The starting point for the design of our analysis is a domain D that consists of binary relations over states, together with an operator F that composes relations with the transition relation of the system. This domain allows us to reason about well-foundedness [18], but it does not account for justice and compassion requirements of FDSs. We extend the domain D to account for fairness by labeling its elements with sets of indices of fairness requirements. We extend the composition operator F by taking the labeling into

---

[*] The second and third author were supported in part by the German Research Foundation (DFG) as a part of the Transregional Collaborative Research Center "Automatic Verification and Analysis of Complex Systems" (SFB/TR 14 AVACS), by the German Federal Ministry of Education and Research (BMBF) in the framework of the Verisoft project under grant 01 IS C38.

N. Halbwachs and L. Zuck (Eds.): TACAS 2005, LNCS 3440, pp. 124–139, 2005.

account, and obtain the operator F_{FDS}, whose least fixed points allow us to reason about well-foundedness and fairness. Given a set of labeled relations L that constitute the least fixed point of F_{FDS}, we account for well-foundedness by considering the relations that appear in the elements of L. We reason about fairness by considering the sets of labels.

We provide an abstract domain $D^{\#}_{\text{FDS}}$ on which approximations of least fixed points of F_{FDS} can be computed. We abstract the part of labeled relations that may cause the iterative fixed point computation to diverge. This means that the abstract domain $D^{\#}_{\text{FDS}}$ consists of abstractions of binary relations over states labeled by sets of indices of fairness requirements. We assume that the correspondence between the domain of relations and their abstractions is given by a Galois connection, which is left as a parameter of our analysis.

Our analysis accounts for general temporal properties by applying the automata-theoretic framework for the verification of concurrent programs [23]. We encode the temporal property into a specification automaton. We translate the acceptance condition of the product of the automata-theoretic construction into additional fairness requirements, which we handle in the same way as the fairness requirements of the FDS. Then, we apply our analysis on the product FDS.

For proving the soundness and partial completeness [2] of our analysis we develop a corresponding proof rule whose auxiliary assertions are labeled relations.

We have implemented the analysis in a prototype tool, and applied it on interesting examples of concurrent programs. We proved an eventual reachability property for a concurrent program that evolves the inter-process communication via an asynchronous, lossy, and corrupting channel. The property relies on the eventual reliability of the channel, which we model by a compassion requirement. We also considered the mutual exclusion protocols BAKERY and TICKET. For each protocol, we proved the non-starvation property, *i.e.* the accessibility of the critical section, for the first process. Justice requirements are needed to deal with the process idling in all examples.

Our main contribution is the analysis of temporal properties of fair discrete systems, and the proof of its soundness and partial completeness. The analysis is based on separating the reasoning on well-foundedness and fairness, which facilitates its automation. We achieve the separation by building the analysis on the domain of binary relations labeled by sets of indices of fairness requirements.

Related Work. The framework of abstract interpretation provides a basis for the systematic design of a program analysis [3]. It is difficult to integrate fairness into the definition of abstract domains.

There exist verification methods for finite-state systems with state-based fairness requirements that account for justice and compassion on the algorithmic level, *e.g.* [8, 13]. Experimental evaluation has confirmed the advantage of the direct treatment of fairness (as opposed to the automata-theoretic translation into a Büchi acceptance condition).

For dealing with infinite-state systems, there exist proof rules for the verification of termination [12] and general temporal properties [14] under justice and compassion requirements that account for the fairness requirements without applying the automata-theoretic encoding. The proof rules rely on well-founded orderings, which must be supplied by the user. Justice requirements are handled directly by the proof rules; verification under compassion requirements is done by recursive application of the proof rule to a transformed program. Our proof rule treats justice and compassion in a uniform way, without program transformation.

The uniform liveness-verification of parameterized FDSs [5, 6] requires construction of auxiliary assertions that account for well-foundedness and fairness. The construction of such assertions can be effectively automated by applying "instantiate-project-and-generalize" heuristic, which allows for the treatment of several classes of parameterized communication protocols. Our approach relies on least fixed point computations, where heuristics can be applied to find abstractions.

Transition invariants provide a basis for reasoning about well-foundedness [18]. They can account for the fairness given by a Büchi accepting condition. Labeled relations extend transition invariant to account for justice and compassion requirements imposed on sets of states, *i.e.*, for the generalized Büchi and Streett acceptance conditions.

Abstract-transition programs, introduced in [19], provide a basis for an automated method for the verification of programs with the *transition*-based fairness requirements. Its accounting for well-foundedness is similar to the one via labeled relations, whereas the treatment of fairness is based on graphs underlying abstract-transition programs.

The automata-theoretic framework of [23] is the basis of our analysis for the verification of general temporal properties. For infinite-state concurrent programs, the Büchi and the Streett acceptance conditions are translated to the Wolper (*i.e.* all states are accepting) acceptance condition. Thus, a proof of fair termination is reduced to a proof of termination of a program obtained from the original one by a transformation that encodes the fairness requirements into the state space. This approach is converse to ours.

The stack assertions based method of [9] for proving fair termination accounts for justice and compassion requirements directly. The method requires identification of tuples of well-founded mappings (stacks assertions), one element for each fairness requirement, which must by supplied by the user. The method keeps track of fairness through the tuple structure. No automation is described.

2   Preliminaries

Fair Discrete Systems. Following [8], a fair discrete system (FDS) $S = \langle \Sigma, \Theta, T, J, C \rangle$ consists of:

- Σ: a set of *states*,
- Θ: a set of *initial* states such that $\Theta \subseteq \Sigma$,
- T: a finite set of *transitions* such that each transition $\tau \in T$ is associated with a *transition relation* $\rho_\tau \subseteq \Sigma \times \Sigma$,
- $J = \{J_1, \ldots, J_k\}$: a set of *justice* requirements, such that $J_i \subseteq \Sigma$ for each $i \in \{1, \ldots, k\}$,
- $C = \{\langle p_1, q_1 \rangle, \ldots, \langle p_m, q_m \rangle\}$: a set of *compassion* requirements, such that $p_i, q_i \subseteq \Sigma$ for each $i \in \{1, \ldots, m\}$.

A *computation* σ is a maximal sequence of states $s_1, s_2, \ldots$ such that s_1 is an *initial* state, *i.e.* $s_1 \in \Theta$, and for each $i \geq 1$ there exists a transition $\tau \in T$ such that s_i goes to s_{i+1} under ρ_τ, *i.e.* $(s_i, s_{i+1}) \in \rho_\tau$. A finite segment $s_i, s_{i+1}, \ldots, s_j$ of a computation where $i < j$ is called a *computation segment*. The set *Acc* of *accessible states* consists of all states that appear in computations of S.

A computation $\sigma = s_1, s_2, \ldots$ satisfies the set of justice requirements $\mathcal{J}$ when for each $J \in \mathcal{J}$ there exist infinitely many positions i in σ such that $s_i \in J$. The computation σ satisfies the set of compassion requirements $\mathcal{C}$ when for each $\langle p, q \rangle \in \mathcal{C}$ either σ contains only finitely many positions i such that $s_i \in p$, or σ contains infinitely many positions j such that $s_j \in q$.

We observe that justice requirements can be translated into compassion requirements as follows. For every justice requirement J we extend the set of compassion requirements by the pair $\langle \Sigma, J \rangle$. We assume that all justice requirements are translated into the compassion requirements, and that the set of compassion requirements $\mathcal{C}$ contains the translated justice requirements. A specialization of the analysis presented in this paper for an explicit treatment of justice requirements is straightforward.

Automata-Theoretic Approach to Temporal Verification. Given a FDS S, we verify a temporal property Ψ under the compassion requirements $\mathcal{C}$ by applying the automata-theoretic framework [23]. We assume that the property is given by a (possibly infinite-state) specification automaton $\mathcal{A}_\Psi$ that accepts exactly the infinite sequences of states that violate the property Ψ. We do not encode the compassion requirements into the automaton.

Let $\mathcal{A}_\Psi$ be a Büchi automaton with the set of states Q and the acceptance condition $F \subseteq Q$. Let the FDS $S \||| \mathcal{A}_\Psi$ be the product of the synchronous parallel composition of S and $\mathcal{A}_\Psi$.

Remark 1. The FDS S with the compassion requirements $\mathcal{C}$ satisfies the property Ψ given by the Büchi automaton $\mathcal{A}_\Psi$ if and only if the FDS $S \||| \mathcal{A}_\Psi$ terminates under the compassion requirements $\mathcal{C}_\||| $ shown below.

$$\mathcal{C}_\||| = \{ \langle p \times Q, q \times Q \rangle \mid \langle p, q \rangle \in \mathcal{C} \} \cup \{ \langle \Sigma \times Q, \Sigma \times F \rangle \}$$

Domain of Transition Invariants. Following [18], we define a domain $D = 2^{\Sigma \times \Sigma}$ of binary relations over states ordered by the subset inclusion ordering $\subseteq$. On this domain, we define an operator $F_\tau : D \to D$, where $\tau \in T$ and the symbol $\circ$ denotes the relational composition (*i.e.* $R_1 \circ R_2 = \{ (s, s'') \mid (s, s') \in R_1 \text{ and } (s', s'') \in R_2 \}$):

$$F_\tau(T) = T \circ \rho_\tau .$$

We will use the domain D and the operator F_τ as a starting point for the development our analysis.

3   Analysis

We fix a FDS S with the set of compassion requirements $\mathcal{C}$. We define an analysis that allows one to prove that S terminates under $\mathcal{C}$. We apply the Galois connection approach for abstract interpretation [3] as a basis for our analysis. We assume an abstract domain $D^\#$, partially ordered by a relation $\sqsubseteq$, that contains abstractions of elements (binary relations) from the domain D. Let a Galois connection (α, γ) formalize the correspondence between the domains D and $D^\#$, formally:

$$\forall T \in D \; \forall T^\# \in D^\#. \; \alpha(T) \sqsubseteq T^\# \Leftrightarrow T \subseteq \gamma(T^\#) .$$

Let $|\mathcal{C}|$ be the set of the indices of all compassion requirements:

$$|\mathcal{C}| = \{1, \ldots, m\} .$$

We obtain a domain D_{FDS} that accounts for compassion requirements by an extension of D with sets of compassion requirements:

$$D_{\mathsf{FDS}} = D \times 2^{|\mathcal{C}|} \times 2^{|\mathcal{C}|} .$$

We define an ordering $\subseteq_{\mathsf{FDS}}$ on elements (T_1, P_1, Q_1) and (T_2, P_2, Q_2) of D_{FDS}:

$$(T_1, P_1, Q_1) \subseteq_{\mathsf{FDS}} (T_2, P_2, Q_2) = T_1 \subseteq T_2 \text{ and } P_1 \subseteq P_2 \text{ and } Q_1 \subseteq Q_2 .$$

We define the following auxiliary functions that map sets of states into sets of indices of compassion requirements. For a set of states $S \subseteq \Sigma$ we have

$$\mathsf{None}(S) = \{j \in |\mathcal{C}| \mid S \cap p_j = \emptyset\} , \qquad \mathsf{Some}(S) = \{j \in |\mathcal{C}| \mid S \cap q_j \neq \emptyset\} .$$

We extend the functions None and Some to binary relations. Given a relation $T \subseteq \Sigma \times \Sigma$, we have

$$\mathsf{None}(T) = \bigcup_{(s_1, s_2) \in T} \mathsf{None}(\{s_1, s_2\}) , \qquad \mathsf{Some}(T) = \bigcup_{(s_1, s_2) \in T} \mathsf{Some}(\{s_1, s_2\}) .$$

We define an operator $F_{\mathsf{FDS}, \tau} : D_{\mathsf{FDS}} \to D_{\mathsf{FDS}}$, which is an extension of the operator F_τ that accounts for compassion requirements, as follows:

$$F_{\mathsf{FDS}, \tau}(T, P, Q) = (F_\tau(T), P \cap \mathsf{None}(F_\tau(T)), Q \cup \mathsf{Some}(F_\tau(T))) .$$

Theorem 1. *The operator $F_{\mathsf{FDS}, \tau}$ is monotonic. Formally,*

$$(T_1, P_1, Q_1) \subseteq_{\mathsf{FDS}} (T_2, P_2, Q_2) \implies F_{\mathsf{FDS}, \tau}(T_1, P_1, Q_1) \subseteq_{\mathsf{FDS}} F_{\mathsf{FDS}, \tau}(T_2, P_2, Q_2) .$$

Proof. Let (T_1, P_1, Q_1) and (T_2, P_2, Q_2) be two elements of D_{FDS} such that $(T_1, P_1, Q_1) \subseteq_{\mathsf{FDS}} (T_2, P_2, Q_2)$. Since $T_1 \subseteq T_2$ we have

$$\bigcup_{(s, s') \in T_1 \circ \rho_\tau} \mathsf{None}(\{s, s'\}) \subseteq \bigcup_{(s, s') \in T_2 \circ \rho_\tau} \mathsf{None}(\{s, s'\}) ,$$

i.e., we have $\mathsf{None}(F_\tau(T_1)) \subseteq \mathsf{None}(F_\tau(T_2))$. Analogously, we have $\mathsf{Some}(F_\tau(T_1)) \subseteq \mathsf{Some}(F_\tau(T_2))$. We conclude $F_{\mathsf{FDS}, \tau}(T_1, P_1, Q_1) \subseteq_{\mathsf{FDS}} F_{\mathsf{FDS}, \tau}(T_2, P_2, Q_2)$. $\qquad \square$

We define an abstract counterpart $D_{\mathsf{FDS}}^{\#}$ of the domain D_{FDS} as follows:

$$D_{\mathsf{FDS}}^{\#} = D^{\#} \times 2^{|\mathcal{C}|} \times 2^{|\mathcal{C}|} .$$

We define an ordering $\subseteq_{\mathsf{FDS}}^{\#}$ on elements $(T_1^{\#}, P_1, Q_1)$ and $(T_2^{\#}, P_2, Q_2)$ of $D_{\mathsf{FDS}}^{\#}$:

$$(T_1^{\#}, P_1, Q_1) \subseteq_{\mathsf{FDS}}^{\#} (T_2^{\#}, P_2, Q_2) = T_1^{\#} \sqsubseteq T_2^{\#} \text{ and } P_1 \subseteq P_2 \text{ and } Q_1 \subseteq Q_2 .$$

Note that we only abstract a component of D_{FDS}-elements that may potentially allow for infinite, strictly increasing chains $(T_1, P_1, Q_1) \sqsubseteq_{\mathsf{FDS}} (T_2, P_2, Q_2) \sqsubseteq_{\mathsf{FDS}} \ldots$. We define a pair of functions $(\alpha_{\mathsf{FDS}}, \gamma_{\mathsf{FDS}})$ that connect the domains D_{FDS} and $D_{\mathsf{FDS}}^{\#}$:

$$\alpha_{\mathsf{FDS}}(T, P, Q) = (\alpha(T), P, Q), \qquad \gamma_{\mathsf{FDS}}(T^{\#}, P, Q) = (\gamma(T^{\#}), P, Q).$$

Lemma 1. *The pair of functions* $(\alpha_{\mathsf{FDS}}, \gamma_{\mathsf{FDS}})$ *is a Galois connection between* D_{FDS} *and* $D_{\mathsf{FDS}}^{\#}$.

Proof. From the monotonicity of γ and α follows that α_{FDS} and γ_{FDS} are monotonic. We carry out the following transformations:

$$\alpha_{\mathsf{FDS}}(\gamma_{\mathsf{FDS}}(T^{\#}, P, Q)) = \alpha_{\mathsf{FDS}}(\gamma(T^{\#}), P, Q)$$
$$= (\alpha(\gamma(T^{\#})), P, Q).$$

Since (α, γ) is a Galois connection, by Theorem 5.3.0.4 in [4], we have that $\alpha(\gamma(T^{\#})) \subseteq T^{\#}$ and hence $\alpha_{\mathsf{FDS}}(\gamma_{\mathsf{FDS}}(T^{\#}, P, Q)) \sqsubseteq_{\mathsf{FDS}} (T^{\#}, P, Q)$. Similarly, we obtain $(T, P, Q) \sqsubseteq_{\mathsf{FDS}} \gamma_{\mathsf{FDS}}(\alpha_{\mathsf{FDS}}(T, P, Q))$. By Theorem 5.3.0.4 in [4], we conclude that $(\alpha_{\mathsf{FDS}}, \gamma_{\mathsf{FDS}})$ is a Galois connection. $\square$

The abstract operator $F_{\mathsf{FDS},\tau}^{\#} : D_{\mathsf{FDS}}^{\#} \rightarrow D_{\mathsf{FDS}}^{\#}$ is defined below:

$$F_{\mathsf{FDS},\tau}^{\#}(T^{\#}, P, Q) = \alpha_{\mathsf{FDS}}(F_{\mathsf{FDS},\tau}(\gamma_{\mathsf{FDS}}(T^{\#}, P, Q))).$$

We extend $F_{\mathsf{FDS},\tau}^{\#}$ to the full set of transitions T:

$$F_{\mathsf{FDS}}^{\#}(T^{\#}, P, Q) = \{F_{\mathsf{FDS},\tau}^{\#}(T^{\#}, P, Q) \mid \tau \in T\}.$$

The monotonicity of the fixed point operator $F_{\mathsf{FDS}}^{\#}$ is a direct consequence of Theorem 1 and the monotonicity of the abstraction/concretization functions. By Tarski's fixed point theorem, the least fixed point of $F_{\mathsf{FDS}}^{\#}$ exists. We denote the least fixed point of $F_{\mathsf{FDS}}^{\#}$ above the basis $\{(\alpha(\rho_\tau), \mathsf{None}(\rho_\tau), \mathsf{Some}(\rho_\tau)) \mid \tau \in T\}$ by $\mathsf{lfp}(F_{\mathsf{FDS}}^{\#}, T)$. We compute $\mathsf{lfp}(F_{\mathsf{FDS}}^{\#}, T)$ in the usual fashion. If the range of the abstraction function α does not allow infinite, strictly increasing chains then the fixed point computation always terminates after finitely many iterations.

We show our analysis for termination of the FDS S under the compassion requirements C on Figure 1. For proving the soundness and partial completeness of the analysis we will develop a corresponding proof rule, whose auxiliary assertions denote elements of the domain D_{FDS}. The partial completeness property, following [2], requires that the analysis gives a positive answer for a FDS that terminates under compassion requirements C in case the abstract domain $D_{\mathsf{FDS}}^{\#}$ satisfies the following property. The domain $D_{\mathsf{FDS}}^{\#}$ contains an abstract value $L^{\#}$ that satisfies the condition imposed by the analysis.

```
input
    FDS S with:
        states Σ,
        transitions T,
        compassion requirements C,
    abstract domain D# with:
        abstraction function α : 2^{Σ×Σ} → D#,
        concretization function γ : D# → 2^{Σ×Σ}
begin
    F#_FDS  =  λ(T#, P, Q). {(α(ρ_τ ∘ γ(T#)),
                            P ∩ None(ρ_τ ∘ γ(T#)),
                            Q ∪ Some(ρ_τ ∘ γ(T#))) | τ ∈ T}
    L#  =  lfp(F#_FDS, T)
    if foreach (T#, P, Q) in L#
        P ∪ Q ≠ |C|  or  well-founded(γ(T#))
    then
        return("FDS S terminates under C")
end.
```

Fig. 1. Analysis of termination for a fair discrete system S under compassion requirements C

Theorem 2. *The analysis shown on Figure 1 is sound and partially complete.*

Proof. See Section 5.   □

We apply our analysis on general temporal properties of fair discrete systems as follows. Let Ψ be a temporal property given by a Büchi automaton $\mathcal{A}_\Psi$. Note that we do not encode the fairness requirements into $\mathcal{A}_\Psi$. Following Remark 1, we construct a FDS $S |||\mathcal{A}_\Psi$ together with the set of compassion requirements $C_{|||}$. For proving that the FDS S satisfies the property Ψ under the compassion requirements C we apply our analysis on $S|||\mathcal{A}_\Psi$ (with compassion requirements $C_{|||}$).

We account for temporal properties given by generalized Büchi and Streett automaton in a straightforward way. For this purpose, we use a direct translation of the generalized Büchi and Streett acceptance conditions into compassion requirements, following the lines of the translation shown in Remark 1.

4   Proof Rule

In this section, we show a proof rule for the verification of fair discrete systems. The auxiliary assertions of the proof rule, called *labeled relations*, denote elements of the domain D_{FDS} used by our analysis. The correspondence between the proof rule and the analysis will allow us to prove Theorem 2, which states the analysis' correctness.

Informally, a labeled relation is a triple (T, P, Q) consisting of a binary relation T over states together with two sets of compassion requirements P and Q. Labeled relations capture sets of computations segments. A computation segment $s_1, \ldots, s_n$ is captured by (T, P, Q) if the pair (s_1, s_n) is an element of T, and the infinite sequence $(s_1, \ldots, s_n)^\omega$, *i.e.* the infinite concatenation of the segment with itself, satisfies only those compassion requirements whose indices are in the set $P \cup Q$. We give a formal definition of labeled relations below.

Definition 1 (Labeled Relation). *A labeled relation* (T, P, Q) *consists of a binary relation* $T \subseteq \Sigma \times \Sigma$ *and two sets of indices (labels)* $P, Q \subseteq |\mathcal{C}|$. *The labeled relation* (T, P, Q) *captures a computation segment* $s_1, \ldots, s_n$ *if the following conditions hold:*

$$(s_1, s_n) \in T, \qquad \text{None}(\{s_1, \ldots, s_n\}) \subseteq P, \qquad \text{Some}(\{s_1, \ldots, s_n\}) \subseteq Q.$$

We write $\text{seg}(T, P, Q)$ *for the set of all computation segments that are captured by the labeled relation* (T, P, Q).

The following theorem allows us to separate the reasoning about well-foundedness and fairness.

Theorem 3. *The FDS S terminates under the set of compassion requirements $\mathcal{C}$ if and only if there exist labeled relations* $(T_1, P_1, Q_1), \ldots, (T_n, P_n, Q_n)$ *such that 1) every computation segment of S is captured by some labeled relation from the set, and 2) for every labeled relation (T, P, Q) in the set either $|\mathcal{C}| \neq P \cup Q$ or the relation T is well-founded.*

Proof. (**if**-direction) For a proof by contraposition, assume that 1) a finite set L of labeled relations captures every computation segment, 2) for each $(T, P, Q) \in L$ holds that either $|\mathcal{C}| \neq P \cup Q$ or the relation T is well-founded, and 3) S does not terminate under the compassion requirements $\mathcal{C}$. We will show that there exists a labeled relation (T, P, Q) in L such that the relation T is not well-founded and $|\mathcal{C}| = P \cup Q$.

By the assumption that S does not terminate under $\mathcal{C}$, there exists an infinite computation $\sigma = s_1, s_2, \ldots$ that satisfies all compassion requirements.

We partition the set $|\mathcal{C}|$ of indices of compassion requirements into two subsets $|\mathcal{C}|^p$ and $|\mathcal{C}|^q$ as follows. An index j (of the compassion requirement $\langle p_j, q_j \rangle$) is an element of the subset $|\mathcal{C}|^p$ if there exist only finitely many positions i in σ such that $s_i \in p_j$; otherwise, j is an element of the subset $|\mathcal{C}|^q$. There exists a position r such that for each $i \geq r$ and for each $j \in |\mathcal{C}|^p$ we have $s_i \notin p_j$.

Let $H = h_1, h_2, \ldots$ be an infinite ordered set of positions in σ such that $h_1 = r$ and for each $i \geq 1$ and for each $j \in |\mathcal{C}|^q$ there exist a position h between the positions h_i and h_{i+1} with $s_h \in q_j$. Since σ satisfies all compassion requirements such a set H exists.

For the fixed σ and the fixed H, we choose a function f that maps an ordered pair (k, l), where $k < l$, of indices in H to one of the labeled relations in L as follows:

$$f(k, l) = (T, P, Q) \in L \quad \text{such that } (s_k, \ldots, s_l) \in \text{seg}(T, P, Q).$$

Such a function f exists since every computation segment is captured by some labeled relation in L. The function f induces an equivalence relation $\sim$ on ordered pairs of elements from H:

$$(k, l) \sim (k', l') \quad = \quad f(k, l) = f(k', l').$$

The equivalence relation $\sim$ has finite index since the range of f is finite.

By Ramsey's theorem [20], there exists an infinite ordered set of positions $K = k_1, k_2, \ldots$, where $k_i \in H$ for all $i \geq 1$, with the following property. All pairs of elements in K belong to the same equivalence class, say $[(m, n)]_\sim$ with $m, n \in K$. That is, for all $k, l \in K$ such that $k < l$ we have $(k, l) \sim (m, n)$. We fix m and n. Let (T_{mn}, P_{mn}, Q_{mn}) denote the labeled relation $f(m, n)$.

Since for all $i \geq 1$ we have $(k_i, k_{i+1}) \sim (m, n)$, the function f maps the pair (k_i, k_{i+1}) to (T_{mn}, P_{mn}, Q_{mn}) for all $i \geq 1$. Hence, the infinite sequence $s_{k_1}, s_{k_2}, \ldots$ is induced by the relation T_{mn}, i.e., for all $i \geq 1$ we have $(s_{k_i}, s_{k_{i+1}}) \in T_{mn}$. We conclude that the relation T_{mn} is not well-founded.

By the choice of H the following claims hold. For every $i \geq k_1$ and for every $j \in |\mathcal{C}|^p$ the state s_i is not an element of p_j. For every $i \geq 1$ and for every $j \in |\mathcal{C}|^q$ there exists a position k between the positions k_i and k_{i+1} such that $s_k \in q_j$. Hence, for every $i \geq 1$ the infinite sequence $(s_{k_i}, \ldots, s_{k_{i+1}})^\omega$ satisfies all compassion requirements. We conclude $|\mathcal{C}| = P_{mn} \cup Q_{mn}$.

(**only if**-direction) is shown after the proof of Theorem 4 in this section.   □

We formalize the correspondence between labeled relations and the ingredients of our analysis by the lemmas below. The ordering $\subseteq_{\mathsf{FDS}}$ approximates the subset inclusion ordering between the sets of computation segments captured by labeled relations, as shown in Lemma 2.

Lemma 2. *The relation $\subseteq_{\mathsf{FDS}}$ is an approximation of the entailment relation between the sets of computation segments that are captured by two labeled relations. Formally,*

$$(T_1, P_1, Q_1) \subseteq_{\mathsf{FDS}} (T_2, P_2, Q_2) \implies \mathsf{seg}(T_1, P_1, Q_1) \subseteq \mathsf{seg}(T_2, P_2, Q_2) .$$

Proof. Let the computation segment $s_1, \ldots, s_n$ be captured by the labeled relation (T_1, P_1, Q_1). From $(T_1, P_1, Q_1) \subseteq_{\mathsf{FDS}} (T_2, P_2, Q_2)$ and the definition of labeled relations, we directly obtain $(s_1, \ldots, s_n) \in \mathsf{seg}(T_2, P_2, Q_2)$.   □

The operator $F_{\mathsf{FDS}, \tau}$ is 'compatible' with the composition of computation segments, as formalized in Lemma 3.

Lemma 3. *Every extension of a computation segment that is captured by a labeled relation (T, P, Q) by a segment consisting of a pair of states in a transition relation ρ_τ is captured by the application of the operator $F_{\mathsf{FDS}, \tau}$ on (T, P, Q). Formally,*

$$(s_1, \ldots, s_n) \in \mathsf{seg}(T, P, Q) \text{ and } (s_n, s_{n+1}) \in \rho_\tau \implies$$
$$(s_1, \ldots, s_n, s_{n+1}) \in \mathsf{seg}(F_{\mathsf{FDS}, \tau}(T, P, Q)) .$$

Proof. Let $s_1, \ldots, s_n$ be a computation segment that is captured by the labeled relation (T, P, Q), and let (s_n, s_{n+1}) be an element of the transition relation ρ_τ. By the definition of labeled relations, for the set of indices of compassion requirements $P_n = \mathsf{None}(\{s_1, \ldots, s_n\})$ we have $P_n \subseteq P$. Furthermore, for the set of indices $P_{n+1} = \mathsf{None}(\{s_1, \ldots, s_n, s_{n+1}\})$ holds $P_{n+1} \subseteq \mathsf{None}(\{s_1, s_{n+1}\}) \subseteq \mathsf{None}(T \circ \rho_\tau)$ and $P_{n+1} \subseteq P_n$. Hence, we have $P_{n+1} \subseteq P$ and $P_{n+1} \subseteq \mathsf{None}(T \circ \rho_\tau)$. We conclude $P_{n+1} \subseteq P \cap \mathsf{None}(F_\tau(T))$.

Analogously, we have $\mathsf{Some}(\{s_1, \ldots, s_n\}) \subseteq Q$, and, hence, for the set of indices $Q_{n+1} = \mathsf{Some}(\{s_1, \ldots, s_n, s_{n+1}\})$ holds $Q_{n+1} \subseteq Q \cup \mathsf{Some}(F_\tau(T))$.

The pair of states (s_1, s_{n+1}) is an element of the relational composition $T \circ \rho_\tau$, since (s_1, s_n) is an element of the relation T. We conclude that $s_1, \ldots, s_n, s_{n+1}$ is captured by $F_{\text{FDS},\tau}(T, P, Q)$. $\qquad\qquad\qquad\qquad\qquad\qquad\qquad\qquad\qquad\qquad\qquad\qquad\qquad\qquad\quad\square$

We canonically extend the ordering $\subseteq_{\text{FDS}}$ to sets of labeled relations:

$$L \subseteq_{\text{FDS}} M = \forall (T_1, P_1, Q_1) \in L\, \exists (T_2, P_2, Q_2) \in M.\, (T_1, P_1, Q_1) \subseteq_{\text{FDS}} (T_2, P_2, Q_2)\,.$$

We canonically extend the operator $F_{\text{FDS},\tau}$ to sets of labeled transitions:

$$F_{\text{FDS},\tau}(L) = \{F_{\text{FDS},\tau}(T, P, Q) \mid (T, P, Q) \in L\}\,.$$

We show a proof rule COMP-TERM for verifying the termination of fair discrete systems under compassion requirements on Figure 2. By applying Theorem 3, we reduce this termination proof to the problem of identifying of a set of labeled relation that captures every computation segment of S. The premises P1 and P2 identify such sets of labeled relations, which is justified by Lemma 4. The premise P3 accounts for well-foundedness and fairness.

Lemma 4. *A set of labeled relations L for the FDS S that satisfies the premises* P1 *and* P2 *of the proof rule* COMP-TERM *captures every computation segment.*

Proof. Given a set of labeled relations L that satisfies the premises P1 and P2 of the proof rule COMP-TERM, we show that every computation segment is captured by some labeled relation in L by the induction over the segment length.

Let s_1, s_2 such that $(s_1, s_2) \in \rho_\tau$, where τ is a transition, be a computation segment. From $\text{None}(\{s_1, s_2\}) \subseteq \text{None}(\rho_\tau)$ and $\text{Some}(\{s_1, s_2\}) \subseteq \text{Some}(\rho_\tau)$ follows directly that the segment s_1, s_2 is captured by the labeled relation $(\rho_\tau, \text{None}(\rho_\tau), \text{Some}(\rho_\tau))$. By Lemma 2 and the premise P1, the segment s_1, s_2 is captured by some labeled relation in L, which is $\subseteq_{\text{FDS}}$-greater than $(\rho_\tau, \text{None}(\rho_\tau), \text{Some}(\rho_\tau))$.

The induction assumption is that the computation segment $s_1, \ldots, s_n$ is captured by a labeled relation (T, P, Q) from L. Let (s_n, s_{n+1}) be an element of ρ_τ. By Lemma 3, we have $(s_1, \ldots, s_n, s_{n+1}) \in \text{seg}(F_{\text{FDS},\tau}(T, P, Q))$. Analogously to the base case, the segment $s_1, \ldots, s_n, s_{n+1}$ is captured by some labeled relation in L, which is $\subseteq_{\text{FDS}}$-greater than $F_{\text{FDS},\tau}(T, P, Q)$. $\qquad\qquad\qquad\qquad\square$

Theorem 4. *The proof rule* COMP-TERM *is sound and complete.*

Proof. The soundness of the proof rule follows directly from the **if**-direction of Theorem 3, and Lemma 4.

For proving completeness, we assume that the FDS S terminates under the compassion requirements $\mathcal{C}$. We construct a set L of labeled relations that satisfies all premises of the proof rule COMP-TERM. Let L be the set of labeled relations defined as follows. For each pair of sets of indices $P \subseteq |\mathcal{C}|$ and $Q \subseteq |\mathcal{C}|$ let (T, P, Q) be a labeled relation in L such that a pair of states (s, s') is an element of the relation T if there exists a computation segment $s_1, \ldots, s_n$ such that $s_1 = s$, $s_n = s'$, $P = \text{None}(\{s_1, \ldots, s_n\})$, and $Q = \text{Some}(\{s_1, \ldots, s_n\})$.

We prove that L satisfies all premises of the proof rule COMP-TERM. We make the following assumptions on the transition relations ρ_τ, where $\tau \in \mathcal{T}$.

FDS S with:

    states Σ,

    compassion requirements C,

    transitions T,

Set of labeled relations $L = \{(T_1, P_1, Q_1), \ldots, (T_n, P_n, Q_n)\}$ such that:

    $T_i \subseteq \Sigma \times \Sigma$ and $P_i, Q_i \subseteq |C|$ for all $i \in \{1, \ldots, n\}$

    P1: $(\rho_\tau, \mathsf{None}(\rho_\tau), \mathsf{Some}(\rho_\tau)) \sqsubseteq_{\mathsf{FDS}} L$ for each $\tau \in T$

    P2: $F_{\mathsf{FDS},\tau}(L) \sqsubseteq_{\mathsf{FDS}} L$ for each $\tau \in T$

    P3: $P_i \cup Q_i \neq |C|$ or T_i well-founded   for each $i \in \{1, \ldots, n\}$

FDS S terminates under compassion requirements C

Fig. 2. Proof rule COMP-TERM

Assumption 1. *For every pair (s, s') of states in the transition relation ρ_τ, where $\tau \in T$, the sequence s, s' is a computation segment.*

This assumption is not a proper restriction. We can assume that the transition relations are restricted to the accessible states. Alternatively, we may use a weaker version of the proof rule that restricts the transition relations ρ_τ in the premise P1 to the accessible states Acc.

Assumption 2. *For each transition $\tau \in T$ there exists two sets of indices P and Q of compassion requirements such that for every pair (s, s') of states in ρ_τ we have $P = \mathsf{None}(\{s, s'\})$ and $Q = \mathsf{Some}(\{s, s'\})$.*

This assumption can be fulfilled by splitting every transition relation according to the sets that appear in the fairness requirements. Now we prove that L satisfies every premise of the proof rule.

Premise P1: We show that for every program transition $\tau \in T$ the condition $(\rho_\tau, \mathsf{None}(\rho_\tau), \mathsf{Some}(\rho_\tau)) \sqsubseteq_{\mathsf{FDS}} (T, P, Q)$ holds for the labeled relation $(T, P, Q) \in L$ such that $P = \mathsf{None}(\rho_\tau)$ and $Q = \mathsf{Some}(\rho_\tau)$. We need to prove $\rho_\tau \subseteq T$. For every pair of states (s, s') in ρ_τ the sequence s, s' is a computation segment, by Assumption 1. Furthermore, we have $\mathsf{None}(\{s, s'\}) = P$ and $\mathsf{Some}(\{s, s'\}) = Q$, by Assumption 2. Hence, by construction of the labeled relation (T, P, Q), the pair (s, s') is an element of the relation T.

Premise P2: We show that for every labeled relation $(T_1, P_1, Q_1) \in L$ and for every transition $\tau \in T$ it holds $F_{\mathsf{FDS},\tau}(T_1, P_1, Q_1) \sqsubseteq_{\mathsf{FDS}} (T_2, P_2, Q_2)$, where (T_2, P_2, Q_2) is the labeled relation in L such that $P_2 = P_1 \cap \mathsf{None}(F_\tau(T_1))$ and $Q_2 = Q_1 \cup \mathsf{Some}(F_\tau(T_1))$. We need to prove $T_1 \circ \rho_\tau \subseteq T_2$.

We note the following auxiliary statement. For every pair (s, s') of states in T_1 we have $P_1 \subseteq \mathsf{None}(\{s\})$, $\mathsf{Some}(\{s\}) \subseteq Q_1$, $P_1 \subseteq \mathsf{None}(\{s'\})$, and $\mathsf{Some}(\{s'\}) \subseteq Q_1$. To justify the statement above for the pair $(s, s') \in T_1$, we consider a computation segment $s, \ldots, s'$ that is captured by (T_1, P_1, Q_1) such that $\mathsf{None}(\{s, \ldots, s'\}) = P_1$

and $\mathsf{Some}(\{s, \ldots, s'\}) = Q_1$, which exists by construction of (T_1, P_1, Q_1). From the definitions of None and Some, our auxiliary statement follows directly.

Now we are ready to prove $T_1 \circ \rho_\tau \subseteq T_2$. For a pair of states $(s_1, s_n) \in T_1$ there exists a computation segment $s_1, \ldots, s_n$ that is captured by the labeled relation (T_1, P_1, Q_1) such that $\mathsf{None}(\{s_1, \ldots, s_n\}) = P_1$ and $\mathsf{Some}(\{s_1, \ldots, s_n\}) = Q_1$, by construction of (T_1, P_1, Q_1). By Lemma 3, for a pair of states $(s_n, s_{n+1}) \in \rho_\tau$ the computation segment $s_1, \ldots, s_n, s_{n+1}$ is captured by the labeled relation $F_{\mathsf{FDS},\tau}(T_1, P_1, Q_1)$. Next, we prove the equalities

$$\mathsf{None}(\{s_1, \ldots, s_n, s_{n+1}\}) = P_1 \cap \mathsf{None}(F_\tau(T_1)),$$

$$\mathsf{Some}(\{s_1, \ldots, s_n, s_{n+1}\}) = Q_1 \cup \mathsf{Some}(F_\tau(T_1)),$$

from which $(s_1, s_{n+1}) \in T_2$ follows directly, by construction of (T_2, P_2, Q_2). We follow the chain of observations below:

$\mathsf{None}(\{s_1, \ldots, s_n, s_{n+1}\})$

$= P_1 \cap \mathsf{None}(\{s_n, s_{n+1}\})$

$= P_1 \cap \mathsf{None}(\{s_n, s_{n+1}\}) \cap \displaystyle\bigcup_{(s,s') \in T_1, (s',s'') \in \rho_\tau} \mathsf{None}(\{s\}) \qquad$ since $P_1 \subseteq \mathsf{None}(\{s\})$

$= P_1 \cap \displaystyle\bigcup_{(s,s') \in T_1, (s',s'') \in \rho_\tau} (\mathsf{None}(\{s\}) \cap \mathsf{None}(\{s_n, s_{n+1}\}))$

$= P_1 \cap \displaystyle\bigcup_{(s,s') \in T_1, (s',s'') \in \rho_\tau} (\mathsf{None}(\{s\}) \cap \mathsf{None}(\{s', s''\})) \qquad$ by Assumption 2

$= \displaystyle\bigcup_{(s,s') \in T_1, (s',s'') \in \rho_\tau} (\mathsf{None}(\{s, s''\}) \cap \mathsf{None}(\{s'\}) \cap P_1)$

$= \displaystyle\bigcup_{(s,s') \in T_1, (s',s'') \in \rho_\tau} (\mathsf{None}(\{s, s''\}) \cap P_1) \qquad$ since $P_1 \subseteq \mathsf{None}(\{s'\})$

$= P_1 \cap \mathsf{None}(F_\tau(T_1)) .$

The proof of $\mathsf{Some}(\{s_1, \ldots, s_n, s_{n+1}\}) = Q_1 \cup \mathsf{Some}(F_\tau(T_1))$ is analogous.

Premise P3: We show, by contraposition, that for every labeled relation (T, P, Q) in L such that $P \cup Q = |\mathcal{C}|$ we have that the relation T is well-founded.

Assume that there exists an infinite sequence of states $s^1, s^2, \ldots$ such that for all $i \geq 1$ the pair (s^i, s^{i+1}) is an element of T, i.e., the relation T is not well-founded. By construction of (T, P, Q), the state s^1 is accessible from some initial state $s_1 \in \Theta$. Furthermore, for all $i \geq 1$ there exists a computation segment $(s^i, \ldots, s^{i+1}) \in \mathsf{seg}(T, P, Q)$ that connects the states s^i and s^{i+1}. For connecting the states s^i and s^{i+1} we choose a computation segment such that $\mathsf{None}(\{s^i, \ldots, s^{i+1}\}) = P$ and $\mathsf{Some}(\{s^i, \ldots, s^{i+1}\}) = Q$. Such a segment exists by construction of (T, P, Q). We conclude that there exists an infinite computation $\sigma = s_1, \ldots, s^1, \ldots, s^2, \ldots$. Next, we prove that σ satisfies all compassion requirements.

For each $j \in P$ we have that p_j-states does not appear in σ after the state s^1. For each $j \in Q$ and each $i \geq 1$ we have that some q_j-state appear in the segment $s^i, \ldots, s^{i+1}$. Since $P \cup Q = |\mathcal{C}|$, the computation σ satisfies all compassion requirements.

There is a contradiction to our assumption that S terminates under the compassion requirements C. □

Proof. Theorem 3 (**only if**-direction) The set of labeled relations constructed in the completeness part of the proof of Theorem 4 satisfies all premises of the proof rule COMP-TERM. By Lemma 4, such a set captures all computation segments. Hence, whenever the FDS S terminates under the compassion requirements C, there exists a set of labeled relations L such that for each $(T, P, Q) \in L$ we have either $P \cup Q \neq |C|$ or the relation T is well-founded. □

We obtain a proof rule for the verification of general temporal properties of fair discrete systems by following Remark 1. We account for temporal properties given by a generalized Büchi automaton or a Streett automaton in a straightforward way, since generalized Büchi and Streett acceptance conditions are directly expressible as compassion requirements.

5   Correctness of the Analysis

We prove the soundness of the analysis as follows. First, we observe that the abstract least fixed point $\mathsf{lfp}(F_{\mathsf{FDS}}^{\#}, \mathcal{T})$ represents a finite set L of labeled relations:

$$L = \{(\gamma(T), P, Q) \mid (T, P, Q) \in \mathsf{lfp}(F_{\mathsf{FDS}}^{\#}, \mathcal{T})\}.$$

that satisfies the premises P1 and P2 of the proof rule COMP-TERM. This observation holds since the operator $F_{\mathsf{FDS}}^{\#}$ is a conservative approximation of the operator F_{FDS}, due to the Galois connection $(\alpha_{\mathsf{FDS}}, \gamma_{\mathsf{FDS}})$. Hence, whenever the analysis gives the positive answer then the set L satisfies all premises of the proof rule. By Theorem 4, we conclude the analysis is sound.

The partial completeness of the analysis follows from the completeness of the proof rule. We assume that the FDS S terminates under the compassion requirements C. Let L be a finite set of labeled relations that satisfies all premises of the proof rule. Such a set exists, by Theorem 4. Let the abstract domain $D_{\mathsf{FDS}}^{\#}$ contains an abstract value $L^{\#}$ such that $L = \gamma_{\mathsf{FDS}}(L^{\#})$. By Theorem 13 in [2], we conclude that the least fixed point $\mathsf{lfp}(F_{\mathsf{FDS}}^{\#}, \mathcal{T})$ computed on $D_{\mathsf{FDS}}^{\#}$ satisfies the condition that leads to the positive answer.

6   Applications

We have implemented the analysis in a prototype tool using SICStus Prolog [10] and its built-in solver for linear arithmetic [7]. We applied the tool on several examples, described below.

In our implementation, we have instantiated the abstract domain $D_{\mathsf{FDS}}^{\#}$ by a set of abstract transitions. Abstract transitions are conjunctions built from some fixed, finite set of transition predicates [19]. A transition predicate denotes a binary relation over states, and is represented by an atomic assertion over unprimed and primed program variables,

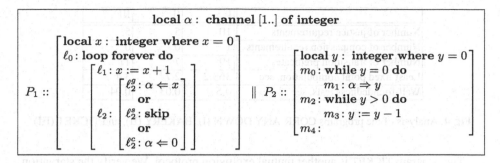

Fig. 3. Program CORR-ANY-DOWN

e.g. $x' \leq x - 1$. The abstraction of a relation T is the abstract transition $T^\#$ such that T entails the relation denoted by $T^\#$. The meaning of the concretization function γ is identity. We represent the relations $\gamma(T^\#)$ by a 'simple' program that consists of a single while loop with only update statements in the loop body, following [18, 19]. There exist a number of well-foundedness tests for the class of simple while programs that are built using linear arithmetic expressions [1, 17, 22]. Our tool implements the test described in [17].

We give a brief description of the example programs. We start with the program CORR-ANY-DOWN, shown on Figure 3. The communication between the processes of the program CORR-ANY-DOWN takes place over an asynchronous channel α. The channel α is unreliable. Messages sent over the channel can be transmitted correctly, get lost or corrupted during the transmission. The transition $\alpha \Leftarrow x$ models a correct transmission, **skip** models the message loss, and $\alpha \Leftarrow 0$ models the message corruption [16]. We prove the eventual reachability of the location m_4.

This property relies on the assumption that the value of the variable x is eventually communicated to the variable y, i.e., that the channel α is eventually reliable. We model the eventual reliability by a compassion requirement $\langle at\_\ell_1, at\_\ell_2^g \rangle$ that ensures a successful transmission if there are infinitely many attempts to send a message.

The eventual reliability of the communication channel is in fact not sufficient for proving termination. We also need to exclude computations in which one of the processes idles forever in some location. Hence, we introduce a justice requirement for each location, e.g. $\neg at\_\ell_1$ and $\neg(at\_m_0 \land y = 0)$.

We model the asynchronous communication channel α by an integer array of infinite size. We keep track of the positions in the array at which the read and write operations take place, as well as the position at which the first successfully transmitted value is written.

The program BAKERY is a simplified version [15] of the Bakery mutual exclusion protocol [11] for two processes. We verify the starvation freedom for the first process. This means that whenever it leaves the non-critical section, it will eventually reach the critical section. The property relies on justice assumptions that none of the processes idles forever in some location.

	I	II	III
Number of justice requirements	10	5	5
Number of compassion requirements	1	0	0
Number of transition predicates	19	7	11
Least fixed point computation, sec	363.2	2.7	3.4
Well-foundedness tests, sec	0.5	0.03	0.04

Fig. 4. Analysis of the programs CORR-ANY-DOWN (I), BAKERY (II), and TICKET (III)

The program TICKET is another mutual exclusion protocol. We verify the starvation freedom property for the first process. It requires the same kind of fairness requirements as the program BAKERY.

Figure 4 shows the collected statistics. For each program we give the number of justice and compassion requirements that were necessary to prove the property, and the number of transition predicates that induce the abstract domain $D^{\#}$. We measured the time spent on the fixed point computation $\mathsf{lfp}(F_{\mathsf{FDS}}^{\#}, \mathcal{T})$, and the well-foundedness checks well-founded($\gamma(T^{\#})$) (see the analysis on Figure 1).

7   Conclusion

We have presented an analysis of temporal properties of fair discrete systems. Our analysis relies on the domain of labeled relations, which provides the separation of well-foundedness and fairness. We have successfully applied our analysis to verify temporal properties of interesting programs. The verified properties rely on justice and compassion requirements.

References

1. M. Colón and H. Sipma. Synthesis of linear ranking functions. In *Proc. of TACAS'2001: Tools and Algorithms for the Construction and Analysis of Systems*, volume 2031 of *LNCS*, pages 67–81. Springer, 2001.
2. P. Cousot. Partial completeness of abstract fixpoint checking. In *Proc. of SARA'2000: Abstraction, Reformulation, and Approximation*, volume 1864 of *LNCS*, pages 1–15. Springer, 2000.
3. P. Cousot and R. Cousot. Abstract interpretation: a unified lattice model for static analysis of programs by construction or approximation of fixpoints. In *Proc. of POPL'1977: Principles of Programming Languages*, pages 238–252. ACM Press, 1977.
4. P. Cousot and R. Cousot. Systematic design of program analysis frameworks. In *Proc. of POPL'1979: Principles of Programming Languages*, pages 269–282. ACM Press, 1979.
5. Y. Fang, N. Piterman, A. Pnueli, and L. D. Zuck. Liveness with incomprehensible ranking. In *Proc. of TACAS'2004: Tools and Algorithms for the Construction and Analysis of Systems*, volume 2988 of *LNCS*, pages 482–496. Springer, 2004.
6. Y. Fang, N. Piterman, A. Pnueli, and L. D. Zuck. Liveness with invisible ranking. In Steffen and Levi [21], pages 223–238.
7. C. Holzbaur. *OFAI clp(q,r) Manual, Edition 1.3.3*. Austrian Research Institute for Artificial Intelligence, Vienna, 1995. TR-95-09.

8. Y. Kesten, A. Pnueli, and L. Raviv. Algorithmic verification of linear temporal logic specifications. In *Proc. of ICALP'1998: Int. Colloq. on Automata, Languages and Programming*, volume 1443 of *LNCS*, pages 1–16. Springer, 1998.

9. N. Klarlund. Progress measures and stack assertions for fair termination. In *Proc. of PODC'1992: Principles of Distributed Computing*, pages 229–240. ACM Press, 1992.

10. T. I. S. Laboratory. *SICStus Prolog User's Manual*. Swedish Institute of Computer Science, PO Box 1263 SE-164 29 Kista, Sweden, October 2001. Release 3.8.7.

11. L. Lamport. A new solution of Dijkstra's concurrent programming problem. *Communications of the ACM*, 17(8):453–455, 1974.

12. D. Lehmann, A. Pnueli, and J. Stavi. Impartiality, justice and fairness: The ethics of concurrent termination. In *Proc. of ICALP'1981: Int. Colloq. on Automata, Languages and Programming*, volume 115 of *LNCS*, pages 264–277. Springer, 1981.

13. O. Lichtenstein and A. Pnueli. Checking that finite state concurrent programs satisfy their linear specification. In *Proc. of POPL'1985: Principles of Programming Languages*, pages 97–107. ACM Press, 1985.

14. Z. Manna and A. Pnueli. Completing the temporal picture. *Theoretical Computer Science*, 83(1):91–130, 1991.

15. Z. Manna and A. Pnueli. *Temporal verification of reactive systems: Safety*. Springer, 1995.

16. Z. Manna and A. Pnueli. Temporal verification of reactive systems: Progress. Draft, 1996.

17. A. Podelski and A. Rybalchenko. A complete method for the synthesis of linear ranking functions. In Steffen and Levi [21], pages 239–251.

18. A. Podelski and A. Rybalchenko. Transition invariants. In *Proc. of LICS'2004: Logic in Computer Science*, pages 32–41. IEEE, 2004.

19. A. Podelski and A. Rybalchenko. Transition predicate abstraction and fair termination. In *Proc. of POPL'2005: Principles of Programming Languages*. ACM Press, 2005. To appear.

20. F. P. Ramsey. On a problem of formal logic. In *Proc. London Math. Soc.*, volume 30, pages 264–285, 1930.

21. B. Steffen and G. Levi, editors. *Proc. of VMCAI'2004: Verification, Model Checking, and Abstract Interpretation*, volume 2937 of *LNCS*. Springer, 2004.

22. A. Tiwari. Termination of linear programs. In *Proc. of CAV'2004: Computer Aided Verification*, volume 3114 of *LNCS*, pages 70–82. Springer, 2004.

23. M. Y. Vardi. Verification of concurrent programs — the automata-theoretic framework. *Annals of Pure and Applied Logic*, 51:79–98, 1991.

An Abstract Interpretation-Based
Refinement Algorithm for Strong Preservation

Francesco Ranzato and Francesco Tapparo

Dipartimento di Matematica Pura ed Applicata,
Università di Padova, Italy

Abstract. The Paige and Tarjan algorithm (PT) for computing the coarsest refinement of a state partition which is a bisimulation on some Kripke structure is well known. It is also well known in abstract model checking that bisimulation is equivalent to strong preservation of CTL and in particular of Hennessy-Milner logic. Building on these facts, we analyze the basic steps of the PT algorithm from an abstract interpretation perspective, which allows us to reason on strong preservation in the context of generic inductively defined (temporal) languages and of abstract models specified by abstract interpretation. This leads us to design a generalized Paige-Tarjan algorithm, called GPT, for computing the minimal refinement of an abstract interpretation-based model that strongly preserves some given language. It turns out that PT can be obtained by instantiating GPT to the domain of state partitions for the case of strong preservation of Hennessy-Milner logic. We provide a number of examples showing that GPT is of general use. We show how two well-known efficient algorithms for computing simulation and stuttering equivalence can be viewed as simple instances of GPT. Moreover, we instantiate GPT in order to design a $O(|\,Transitions\,||States|)$-time algorithm for computing the coarsest refinement of a given partition that strongly preserves the language generated by the reachability operator **EF**.

1   Introduction

Motivations. The Paige and Tarjan [15] algorithm — in the paper denoted by PT — for efficiently computing the coarsest refinement of a given partition which is *stable* for a given state transition relation is well known. Its importance stems from the fact that PT actually computes *bisimulation equivalences*, because a partition P of a state space Σ is stable for a transition relation $R \subseteq \Sigma \times \Sigma$ if and only if P is a bisimulation equivalence on the transition system $\langle \Sigma, R \rangle$. In particular, PT is widely used in model checking for reducing the state space of a Kripke structure $\mathcal{K}$ because it turns out that the quotient of $\mathcal{K}$ w.r.t. bisimulation equivalence *strongly preserves* branching-time temporal languages like CTL and CTL* [2, 3]. Paige and Tarjan first provide the basic $O(|R||\Sigma|)$-time PT algorithm and then exploit a computational logarithmic improvement in order to design a $O(|R| \log |\Sigma|)$-time algorithm, which is usually referred to as Paige-Tarjan algorithm. It is important to remark that the logarithmic Paige-Tarjan algorithm is derived as a computational refinement of PT that does not affect the correctness of the procedure which is instead proved for the PT algorithm. As shown in [16], it turns out that state partitions can be viewed as *domains in abstract interpretation* and strong preservation can

N. Halbwachs and L. Zuck (Eds.): TACAS 2005, LNCS 3440, pp. 140–156, 2005.

be cast as *completeness in abstract interpretation*. Thus, our first aim was to understand, from an abstract interpretation perspective, why PT is a correct procedure for computing strongly preserving partitions.

The PT Algorithm. Let us recall how PT works. Let $\text{pre}_R = \lambda X.\{s \in \Sigma \mid \exists x \in X. s \xrightarrow{R} x\}$ denote the usual predecessor transformer on $\wp(\Sigma)$. A partition $P \in \text{Part}(\Sigma)$ is PT stable for R when for any block $B \in P$, if $B' \in P$ then either $B \subseteq \text{pre}_R(B')$ or $B \cap \text{pre}_R(B') = \varnothing$. For a given subset $S \subseteq \Sigma$, we denote by $\text{PTsplit}(S, P)$ the partition obtained from P by replacing each block $B \in P$ with the blocks $B \cap \text{pre}_R(S)$ and $B \smallsetminus \text{pre}_R(S)$, where we also allow no splitting, namely that $\text{PTsplit}(S, P) = P$. When $P \neq \text{PTsplit}(S, P)$ the subset S is called a *splitter* for P. Splitters(P) denotes the set of splitters of P, while PTrefiners$(P) \stackrel{\text{def}}{=} \{S \in \text{Splitters}(P) \mid \exists\{B_i\} \subseteq P. S = \cup_i B_i\}$. Then, the PT algorithm goes as follows.

```
while (P is not PT stable) do
    choose S ∈ PTrefiners(P);
    P := PTsplit(S, P);
endwhile                          PT
```

An Abstract Interpretation Perspective of PT. Our work originated from a number of observations on the above PT algorithm. Firstly, we may view the output $\text{PT}(P)$ as the coarsest refinement of a partition P that strongly preserves CTL. For standard abstract models which are partitions, it is known that strong preservation of CTL is equivalent to strong preservation of (finitary) Hennessy-Milner logic HML [12], i.e., the language generated by the grammar: $\varphi ::= p \mid \varphi_1 \wedge \varphi_2 \mid \neg\varphi \mid \text{EX}\varphi$, where p ranges over atomic propositions in AP such that $\{[\![p]\!] \subseteq \Sigma \mid p \in AP\} = P$ and the semantic interpretation of EX is $\text{pre}_R : \wp(\Sigma) \to \wp(\Sigma)$. Thus, we observe that $\text{PT}(P)$ indeed computes the coarsest partition P_{HML} that refines P and strongly preserves HML. Moreover, the partition P_{HML} corresponds to the state equivalence $\equiv_{\text{HML}}$ induced by the semantics of HML: $s \equiv_{\text{HML}} s'$ iff $\forall\varphi \in \text{HML}. s \in [\![\varphi]\!] \Leftrightarrow s' \in [\![\varphi]\!]$. Hence, we also observe that P_{HML} is an abstraction of the state semantics of HML on the domain $\text{Part}(\Sigma)$ of partitions of Σ. Thus, our starting point was that PT can be viewed as an algorithm for computing the most abstract object on the particular domain $\text{Part}(\Sigma)$ that strongly preserves the particular language HML. We made this view precise within Cousot and Cousot's abstract interpretation framework [4, 5].

We introduced in [16] an abstract interpretation-based framework for reasoning on strong preservation of abstract models w.r.t. generic inductively defined languages. We showed that the lattice $\text{Part}(\Sigma)$ of partitions of the state space Σ can be viewed as an abstraction of the lattice $\text{Abs}(\wp(\Sigma))$ of abstract interpretations of $\wp(\Sigma)$. Thus, a partition $P \in \text{Part}(\Sigma)$ is here viewed as a particular abstract domain $\gamma(P) \in \text{Abs}(\wp(\Sigma))$. This leads to a precise correspondence between *forward complete* abstract interpretations and strongly preserving abstract models. Let us recall that completeness in abstract interpretation [4, 5, 10] encodes an ideal situation where no loss of precision occurs by approximating concrete computations on the abstract domain. The problem of minimally refining an abstract model in order to get strong preservation of some language $\mathcal{L}$ can be cast as the problem of making an abstract interpretation $\mathcal{A}$ forward complete for the semantic operators of $\mathcal{L}$ through a minimal refinement of the abstract domain of $\mathcal{A}$. It turns out that this latter completeness problem always admits a fixpoint solution.

Hence, in our abstract interpretation framework, it turns out that for any $P \in \mathrm{Part}(\Sigma)$, the output $\mathrm{PT}(P)$ is the partition abstraction in $\mathrm{Part}(\Sigma)$ of the minimal refinement of $\gamma(P) \in \mathrm{Abs}(\wp(\Sigma))$ which is complete for the set F of semantic operators of the language HML, where $F_{\mathrm{HML}} = \{\cap, \complement, \mathrm{pre}_R\}$ is the set of operators on $\wp(\Sigma)$ of HML. In particular, it turns out that a partition P is PT stable iff $\gamma(P)$ is complete for the operators in F_{HML}. Also, the following observation is crucial in our approach. The splitting operation $\mathrm{PTsplit}(S, P)$ can be viewed as the *best correct approximation* on $\mathrm{Part}(\Sigma)$ of a refinement operation $\mathrm{refine}_f(S, \cdot) : \mathrm{Abs}(\wp(\Sigma)) \rightarrow \mathrm{Abs}(\wp(\Sigma))$ on abstract domains: given an operator $f : \wp(\Sigma) \rightarrow \wp(\Sigma)$, $\mathrm{refine}_f(S, A)$ refines an abstract domain A through a "f-refiner" $S \in A$ to the most abstract domain containing both A and $f(S)$. In particular, P results to be PT stable iff the abstract domain $\gamma(P)$ cannot be refined w.r.t. the function pre_R. Thus, if $\mathrm{refine}_f^{\mathrm{Part}}$ denotes the best correct approximation in $\mathrm{Part}(\Sigma)$ of refine_f then the PT algorithm can be formulated as follows.

> **while** the set of pre_R-refiners of $P \neq \varnothing$ **do**
>   **choose** some pre_R-refiner $S \in \gamma(P)$;
> $P := \mathrm{refine}_{\mathrm{pre}_R}^{\mathrm{Part}}(S, P)$;
> **endwhile**

Main Results. This abstract interpretation-based view of PT leads us to generalize PT to: (1) a generic domain $\mathcal{A}$ of abstract models generalizing the domain of state partitions $\mathrm{Part}(\Sigma)$ and (2) a generic set F of operators on $\wp(\Sigma)$ providing the semantics of some language $\mathcal{L}_F$ and generalizing the set F_{HML} of operators of HML. We design a generalized Paige-Tarjan refinement algorithm, called GPT, which, for any abstract model $A \in \mathcal{A}$, is able to compute the most abstract refinement of A in $\mathcal{A}$ which is strongly preserving for the language $\mathcal{L}_F$. The correctness of GPT is guaranteed by some completeness conditions on $\mathcal{A}$ and F. We provide a number of applications showing that GPT is an algorithmic scheme of general use. We prove that two well-known algorithms computing *simulation* and *stuttering* equivalence can be obtained as simple instances of GPT. First, we show that the algorithm by Henzinger et al. [13] that computes simulation equivalence in $O(|R||\Sigma|)$-time (as far as time-complexity is concerned, this is the best available algorithm) corresponds to the instance of GPT where the set of operators is $F = \{\cap, \mathrm{pre}_R\}$ and the abstract domain $\mathcal{A}$ is the lattice of disjunctive (i.e. precise for least upper bounds [5]) abstract domains of $\wp(\Sigma)$. We obtain this as a consequence of the fact that simulation equivalence corresponds to strong preservation of the language $\varphi ::= p \mid \varphi_1 \wedge \varphi_2 \mid \mathbf{EX}\varphi$. Second, we show that GPT can be instantiated in order to get the Groote-Vaandrager algorithm [11] that computes divergence blind stuttering equivalence in $O(|R||\Sigma|)$-time (again, this is the best known time bound). Let us recall that the Groote-Vaandrager algorithm can be also used for computing branching bisimulation equivalence, which is the state equivalence induced by CTL*-X [2,7,11]. In this case, the set of operators is $F = \{\cap, \complement, \mathbf{EU}\}$, where $\mathbf{EU}$ is the standard semantic interpretation of the existential until, while $\mathcal{A}$ is the domain of partitions $\mathrm{Part}(\Sigma)$. Moreover, we instantiate GPT in order to design a new partition refinement algorithm for the language inductively generated by the reachability operator $\mathbf{EF}$ and propositional logic, namely with $F = \{\cap, \complement, \mathbf{EF}\}$. In this case, we describe a simple implementation for this instance of GPT that leads to a $O(|R||\Sigma|)$-time algorithm.

2   Basic Notions

Notation. Let X be any set. $\mathrm{Fun}(X)$ denotes the set of all the functions $f : X^n \to X$, where $\mathrm{ar}(f) = n > 0$ is the the the arity of f. For a set $S \in \wp(\wp(X))$, we write the sets in S in a compact form like $\{1, 12, 123\} \in \wp(\wp(\{1, 2, 3\}))$. We denote by $\complement$ the complement operator w.r.t. some universe set. A function $f : C \to C$ on a complete lattice C is additive when f preserves least upper bounds. We denote by $\mathrm{Part}(X)$ the set of partitions on X. $\mathrm{Part}(X)$ is endowed with the following standard partial order $\preccurlyeq$: given $P_1, P_2 \in \mathrm{Part}(X)$, $P_1 \preccurlyeq P_2$, i.e. P_2 is coarser than P_1 (or P_1 refines P_2) iff $\forall B \in P_1.\exists B' \in P_2.B \subseteq B'$. It turns out that $\langle \mathrm{Part}(X), \preccurlyeq, \curlywedge, \curlyvee, \{X\}, \{\{x\}\}_{x \in X}\rangle$ is a complete lattice. We consider transition systems (Σ, R) where the relation $R \subseteq \Sigma \times \Sigma$ (also denoted by $\xrightarrow{R}$) is total. A Kripke structure (Σ, R, AP, ℓ) consists of a transition system (Σ, R) together with a set AP of atomic propositions and a labelling function $\ell : \Sigma \to \wp(AP)$. For any $s \in \Sigma$, $[s]_\ell \overset{\mathrm{def}}{=} \{s' \in \Sigma \mid \ell(s) = \ell(s')\}$. Also, $P_\ell \overset{\mathrm{def}}{=} \{[s]_\ell \mid s \in \Sigma\} \in \mathrm{Part}(\Sigma)$. A transition relation $R \subseteq \Sigma \times \Sigma$ defines the usual pre/post transformers on $\wp(\Sigma)$: pre_R, post_R, $\widetilde{\mathrm{pre}}_R$, $\widetilde{\mathrm{post}}_R$. When clear from the context, subscripts R are sometimes omitted.

Abstract Interpretation and Completeness. In standard abstract interpretation, abstract domains can be equivalently specified either by Galois connections/insertions (GCs/GIs) or by (upper) closure operators (uco's) [5]. Closure operators have the advantage of being independent from the representation of domain's objects and are therefore appropriate for reasoning on abstract domains independently from their representation. We will denote by (α, C, A, γ) a GC/GI of the abstract domain A into the concrete domain C through the abstraction and concretization maps $\alpha : C \to A$ and $\gamma : A \to C$. Recall that $\mu : C \to C$ is a uco when μ is monotone, idempotent and extensive (i.e., $x \leq \mu(x)$). If μ is reductive (i.e., $\mu(x) \leq x$) instead of extensive then μ is a lower closure operator (lco), namely a uco on the dual lattice $C_\geq$. It is known that the set $\mathrm{uco}(C)$ of uco's on C, endowed with the pointwise ordering $\sqsubseteq$, gives rise to the complete lattice $\langle \mathrm{uco}(C), \sqsubseteq, \sqcup, \sqcap, \lambda x.\top_C, id\rangle$. We have that $\mu \sqsubseteq \rho$ iff $\rho(C) \subseteq \mu(C)$; in this case, we say that μ is a refinement of ρ. Also, $\langle \mathrm{lco}(C), \sqsubseteq\rangle$ denotes the complete lattice of lower closure operators on C. It turns out that $\mathrm{uco}(C)$ and $\mathrm{lco}(C)$ are dual isomorphic, namely $\mathrm{uco}(C)_\sqsupseteq$ and $\mathrm{lco}(C)_\sqsubseteq$ are isomorphic. Hence, notions and results concerning uco's can be stated dually for lco's. Each closure is uniquely determined by the set of its fixpoints, which is also its image. Also, a subset $X \subseteq C$ is the set of fixpoints of some uco on C iff X is meet-closed, i.e. $X = \mathcal{M}(X) \overset{\mathrm{def}}{=} \{\wedge Y \mid Y \subseteq X\}$ (where $\top_C = \wedge_C \varnothing \in \mathcal{M}(X)$). Often, we will identify closures with their sets of fixpoints because this does not give rise to ambiguity. In view of the above equivalence, throughout the paper $\langle \mathrm{uco}(C), \sqsubseteq\rangle$ will play the role of the (complete) lattice of abstract domains of the concrete domain C [4, 5]. The ordering on $\mathrm{uco}(C)$ corresponds to the standard order that compares abstract domains with regard to their precision: A_1 is more precise than A_2 (or A_2 is more abstract than A_1) iff $A_1 \sqsubseteq A_2$ in $\mathrm{uco}(C)$. Let (α, C, A, γ) be a GI, $f : C \to C$ be some concrete semantic function — for simplicity, we consider here 1-ary functions — and $f^\sharp : A \to A$ be a corresponding abstract function. Then, $\langle A, f^\sharp\rangle$ is a sound abstract interpretation when $\alpha \circ f \sqsubseteq f^\sharp \circ \alpha$. The abstract function $f^A \overset{\mathrm{def}}{=} \alpha \circ f \circ \gamma : A \to A$ is called the best correct approximation of f in A. Completeness in abstract interpretation corresponds to require the following strengthening of soundness: $\alpha \circ f = f^\sharp \circ \alpha$. This is called *backward* completeness because a dual *forward* completeness may be considered. The soundness equation $\alpha \circ f \sqsubseteq f^\sharp \circ \alpha$ is equivalent to $f \circ \gamma \sqsubseteq \gamma \circ f^\sharp$, so that forward completeness for $f^\sharp$ corresponds to strengthen soundness by requiring: $f \circ \gamma = \gamma \circ f^\sharp$. Giacobazzi et al. [10] observed that both backward and forward completeness uniquely depend upon the abstraction map, namely they are abstract domain properties. These domain properties can be formulated through uco's as follows: an abstract domain $\mu \in \mathrm{uco}(C)$ is backward complete for f iff $\mu \circ f = \mu \circ f \circ \mu$ holds, while μ is forward complete for f iff $f \circ \mu = \mu \circ f \circ \mu$.

Shells. Refinements of abstract domains have been much studied in abstract interpretation [4, 5] and led to the notion of shell of an abstract domain [10]. Given a generic poset $P_\leq$ of semantic objects — where $x \leq y$ intuitively means that x is a "refinement" of y, i.e. x is more precise than y — and a property $\mathcal{P} \subseteq P$ of these objects, the generic notion of *shell* goes as follows: the $\mathcal{P}$-shell of an object $x \in P$ is defined to be an object $s_x \in P$ such that: (i) s_x satisfies the property $\mathcal{P}$, (ii) s_x is a refinement of x, and (iii) s_x is the greatest among the objects satisfying (i) and (ii). Note that if a $\mathcal{P}$-shell exists then it is unique. We will be particularly interested in shells of abstract domains and partitions. Given a state space Σ and a partition property $\mathcal{P} \subseteq \mathrm{Part}(\Sigma)$, the $\mathcal{P}$-shell of $P \in \mathrm{Part}(\Sigma)$ is the coarsest refinement of P that satisfies $\mathcal{P}$, when this exists. Given a concrete domain C and an abstract domain property $\mathcal{P} \subseteq \mathrm{uco}(C)$, the $\mathcal{P}$-shell of $\mu \in \mathrm{uco}(C)$, when this exists, is the most abstract domain that refines μ and satisfies $\mathcal{P}$. Giacobazzi et al. [10] show that backward complete shells always exist when the concrete operations are continuous.

Let us now consider the property of forward completeness. Let $F \subseteq \mathrm{Fun}(C)$ (thus functions in F may have any arity) and $S \in \wp(C)$. We denote by $F(S) \in \wp(C)$ the image of F on S, i.e. $F(S) \overset{\text{def}}{=} \{f(\vec{s}) \mid f \in F, \ \vec{s} \in S^{\mathrm{ar}(f)}\}$, and we say that S is F-closed when $F(S) \subseteq S$. An abstract domain $\mu \in \mathrm{uco}(C)$ is forward F-complete when μ is forward complete for any $f \in F$. Thus, the (forward) F-complete shell operator $\mathrm{S}_F : \mathrm{uco}(C) \to \mathrm{uco}(C)$ is defined as follows: $\mathrm{S}_F(\mu) \overset{\text{def}}{=} \sqcup \{\eta \in \mathrm{uco}(C) \mid \eta \sqsubseteq \mu, \ \eta \text{ is forward } F\text{-complete}\}$. As already observed by Giacobazzi and Quintarelli [9], it is easy to show that for any domain μ, $\mathrm{S}_F(\mu)$ is forward F-complete, namely forward complete shells always exist. It is worth noting that $\mathrm{S}_F \in \mathrm{lco}(\mathrm{uco}(C)_\sqsubseteq)$ and that $\mathrm{S}_F(\mu)$ is the smallest (w.r.t. set inclusion) set that contains μ and is both F-closed and meet-closed. When C is finite, note that for the meet operator $\wedge : C^2 \to C$ we have that, for any F, $\mathrm{S}_F = \mathrm{S}_{F \cup \{\wedge\}}$, because uco's are meet-closed.

We define $F^{\mathrm{uco}} : \mathrm{uco}(C) \to \mathrm{uco}(C)$ as $F^{\mathrm{uco}} \overset{\text{def}}{=} \mathcal{M} \circ F$, namely $F^{\mathrm{uco}}(\rho) = \mathcal{M}(\{f(\vec{x}) \mid f \in F, \ \vec{x} \in \rho^{\mathrm{ar}(f)}\})$. This operator characterizes forward F-completeness because it turns out that ρ is forward F-complete iff $\rho \sqsubseteq F^{\mathrm{uco}}(\rho)$. Moreover, given $\mu \in \mathrm{uco}(C)$, we consider the operator $F_\mu : \mathrm{uco}(C) \to \mathrm{uco}(C)$ defined by $F_\mu(\rho) \overset{\text{def}}{=} \mu \sqcap F^{\mathrm{uco}}(\rho)$ and we also note that $F_\mu(\rho) = \mathcal{M}(\mu \cup F(\rho))$. Observe that F_μ is monotone on $\mathrm{uco}(C)$ and therefore it admits (least and) greatest fixpoint. It turns out that we may constructively characterize the shell $\mathrm{S}_F(\mu)$ as the greatest fixpoint (denoted by gfp) in $\mathrm{uco}(C)$ of the operator F_μ.

Lemma 2.1. $S_F(\mu) = \text{gfp}(F_\mu)$.

Example 2.2. Let $\Sigma = \{1, 2, 3, 4\}$ and $f_o : \Sigma \to \Sigma$ be the function $\{1 \mapsto 2, 2 \mapsto 3, 3 \mapsto 4, 4 \mapsto 4\}$. Let $f : \wp(\Sigma) \to \wp(\Sigma)$ be the lifting of f_o to the powerset, i.e., $f \stackrel{\text{def}}{=} \lambda S.\{f_o(s) \mid s \in S\}$. Consider the abstract domain $\mu = \{\varnothing, 2, 1234\} \in \text{uco}(\wp(\Sigma)_\subseteq)$. By Lemma 2.1, $S_f(\mu) = \{\varnothing, 2, 3, 4, 34, 234, 1234\}$ because:

$$\rho_0 = \{1234\} \quad \text{(top uco)}$$

$$\rho_1 = \mathcal{M}(\mu \cup f(\rho_0)) = \mathcal{M}(\mu \cup \{234\}) = \{\varnothing, 2, 234, 1234\}$$

$$\rho_2 = \mathcal{M}(\mu \cup f(\rho_1)) = \mathcal{M}(\mu \cup \{\varnothing, 3, 34, 234\}) = \{\varnothing, 2, 3, 34, 234, 1234\}$$

$$\rho_3 = \mathcal{M}(\mu \cup f(\rho_2)) = \mathcal{M}(\mu \cup \{\varnothing, 3, 4, 34, 234\}) = \{\varnothing, 2, 3, 4, 34, 234, 1234\}$$

$$\rho_4 = \mathcal{M}(\mu \cup f(\rho_3)) = \mathcal{M}(\mu \cup \{\varnothing, 3, 4, 34, 234\}) = \rho_3 \quad \text{(greatest fixpoint).} \quad \square$$

3 Generalized Strong Preservation

Partitions as Abstract Domains. Let Σ be any (possibly infinite) set of system states. We recall from [16] how the the lattice of state partitions $\text{Part}(\Sigma)$ can be viewed as an abstraction of the lattice of abstract domains $\text{uco}(\wp(\Sigma))$. Our goal is to perform a *complete abstract computation* of a forward complete shell $S_F(\mu) = \text{gfp}(F_\mu)$ (cf. Lemma 2.1) on the lattice of partitions. Thus, we need to approximate a greatest fixpoint computation from above so that, as usual in abstract interpretation in these cases, we consider concrete and abstract domains with their dual ordering relations. Hence, we are looking for a GI of $\text{Part}(\Sigma)_\succeq$ into $\text{uco}(\wp(\Sigma))_\sqsupseteq$.

We define a mapping par : $\text{uco}(\wp(\Sigma)) \to \text{Part}(\Sigma)$ by $\text{par}(\mu) \stackrel{\text{def}}{=} \{[s]_\mu \mid s \in \Sigma\}$, where $[s]_\mu \stackrel{\text{def}}{=} \{s' \in \Sigma \mid \mu(\{s'\}) = \mu(\{s\})\}$. On the other hand, pcl : $\text{Part}(\Sigma) \to \text{uco}(\wp(\Sigma))$ is defined by $\text{pcl}(P) \stackrel{\text{def}}{=} \lambda X \in \wp(\Sigma). \cup \{B \in P \mid X \cap B \neq \varnothing\}$, i.e. $\text{pcl}(P)(X)$ is the minimal covering of the set $X \subseteq \Sigma$ through blocks in P. Observe that $\text{pcl}(P)$ is indeed a uco whose set of fixpoints is given by all the unions of blocks in P, i.e. $\text{pcl}(P) = \{\cup_i B_i \mid \{B_i\} \subseteq P\}$. It turns out that $(\text{par}, \text{uco}(\wp(\Sigma))_\sqsupseteq, \text{Part}(\Sigma)_\succeq, \text{pcl})$ is a GI. An abstract domain $\mu \in \text{uco}(\wp(\Sigma))$ is *partitioning* — meaning that it represents exactly a partition; also, pcl stands for "partitioning closure" — when $\text{pcl}(\text{par}(\mu)) = \mu$ holds. We denote by $\text{puco}(\wp(\Sigma))$ the set of partitioning abstract domains. As a consequence, the mappings pcl and par give rise to an order isomorphism allowing to view state partitions as partitioning uco's: $\text{Part}(\Sigma)_\preceq \cong \text{puco}(\wp(\Sigma))_\sqsubseteq$. It turns out that an abstract domain $\mu \in \text{uco}(\wp(\Sigma))$ is partitioning iff $\forall S \in \mu. \complement(S) \in \mu$ iff (i) μ is additive and (ii) $\{\mu(\{s\})\}_{s \in \Sigma} \in \text{Part}(\Sigma)$. Therefore, the partition associated to some $\mu \in \text{puco}(\wp(\Sigma))$ is the set of μ-images of singletons, i.e. $\text{par}(\mu) = \{\mu(\{s\}) \mid s \in \Sigma\}$.

Example 3.1. Consider $\Sigma = \{1, 2, 3, 4\}$ and the corresponding lattice $\text{Part}(\Sigma)_\preceq$. The uco's $\mu_1 = \{\varnothing, 12, 3, 4, 1234\}$, $\mu_2 = \{\varnothing, 12, 3, 4, 34, 1234\}$, $\mu_3 = \{\varnothing, 12, 3, 4, 34, 123, 124, 1234\}$, $\mu_4 = \{12, 123, 124, 1234\}$ and $\mu_5 = \{\varnothing, 12, 123, 124, 1234\}$ all induce the same partition $P = \text{par}(\mu_i) = \{12, 3, 4\} \in \text{Part}(\Sigma)$. Observe that μ_3 is the only partitioning closure because $\text{pcl}(P) = \mu_3$. $\square$

Abstract Semantics and Generalized Strong Preservation. Let us now recall from [16] how to cast strong preservation in standard abstract model checking as forward completeness of abstract interpretations. We consider languages $\mathcal{L}$ whose syntactic state formulae φ are inductively defined by a BNF grammar: $\varphi ::= p \mid f(\varphi_1, ..., \varphi_n)$, where $p \in AP$ ranges over a set of atomic propositions that is left unspecified while f ranges over a finite set Op of operators (each $f \in Op$ has an arity $\mathrm{ar}(f) > 0$).

The interpretation of formulae in $\mathcal{L}$ is determined by a *semantic structure* $\mathcal{S} = (\Sigma, I, AP, \ell)$ where: Σ is any set of states, $I : Op \rightarrow \mathrm{Fun}(\wp(\Sigma))$ is an interpretation function such that for any $f \in Op$, $I(f) : \wp(\Sigma)^{\mathrm{ar}(f)} \rightarrow \wp(\Sigma)$, AP is a set of atomic propositions and $\ell : \Sigma \rightarrow \wp(AP)$ is a labelling function. Semantic structures generalize the role of Kripke structures by requiring that the semantic interpretation of a n-ary syntactic state operator is given by any n-ary mapping on $\wp(\Sigma)$. For $p \in AP$ and $f \in Op$ we will also use p and f to denote, respectively, $\{s \in \Sigma \mid p \in \ell(s)\}$ and $I(f)$. Also, $Op \stackrel{\mathrm{def}}{=} \{f \in \mathrm{Fun}(\wp(\Sigma)) \mid f \in Op\}$. The *concrete state semantic function* $[\![\cdot]\!]_{\mathcal{S}} : \mathcal{L} \rightarrow \wp(\Sigma)$ evaluates a formula $\varphi \in \mathcal{L}$ to the set of states making φ true on the semantic structure $\mathcal{S}$, namely it is inductively defined as follows:

$$[\![p]\!]_{\mathcal{S}} = p \text{ and } [\![f(\varphi_1, ..., \varphi_n)]\!]_{\mathcal{S}} = f([\![\varphi_1]\!]_{\mathcal{S}}, ..., [\![\varphi_n]\!]_{\mathcal{S}}).$$

In the following, we will freely use standard logical and temporal operators together with their corresponding usual interpretations: for example, $I(\wedge) = \cap$, $I(\neg) = \complement$, $I(\mathrm{EX}) = \mathrm{pre}_R$, etc. We say that a language $\mathcal{L}$ is closed under a semantic operation $g : \wp(\Sigma)^n \rightarrow \wp(\Sigma)$ when for any $\varphi_1, ..., \varphi_n \in \mathcal{L}$, there exists some $\psi \in \mathcal{L}$ such that $g([\![\varphi_1]\!]_{\mathcal{S}}, ..., [\![\varphi_n]\!]_{\mathcal{S}}) = [\![\psi]\!]_{\mathcal{S}}$. It is straightforward to extend this notion to infinitary operators, e.g. infinite logical conjunction.

The state semantics $[\![\cdot]\!]_{\mathcal{S}}$ induces a state logical equivalence $\equiv_{\mathcal{L}}^{\mathcal{S}} \subseteq \Sigma \times \Sigma$ as usual: $s \equiv_{\mathcal{L}}^{\mathcal{S}} s'$ iff $\forall \varphi \in \mathcal{L}. s \in [\![\varphi]\!]_{\mathcal{S}} \Leftrightarrow s' \in [\![\varphi]\!]_{\mathcal{S}}$. The corresponding state partition is denoted by $P_{\mathcal{L}} \in \mathrm{Part}(\Sigma)$ (the index $\mathcal{S}$ for the underlying semantic structure is omitted).

For a number of well known temporal languages like CTL*, ACTL*, CTL*-X, it turns out that if a partition is more refined than $P_{\mathcal{L}}$ then it induces a standard *strongly preserving* (s.p.) abstract model. This means that if we interpret $\mathcal{L}$ on a Kripke structure $\mathcal{K} = (\Sigma, R, AP, \ell)$ and $P \preceq P_{\mathcal{L}}$ then one can define an abstract Kripke structure $\mathcal{A} = (P, R^{\sharp}, AP, \ell^{\sharp})$ that strongly preserves $\mathcal{L}$: for any $\varphi \in \mathcal{L}$ and for any $s \in \Sigma$ and $B \in P$ such that $s \in B$, we have that $B \in [\![\varphi]\!]_{\mathcal{A}} \Leftrightarrow s \in [\![\varphi]\!]_{\mathcal{K}}$. For example, $R^{\sharp} = R^{\exists\exists}$ for CTL* and $R^{\sharp} = R^{\forall\exists}$ for ACTL*, while $\ell^{\sharp}(B) = \cup_{s \in B} \ell(s)$ (see e.g. [3, 6]). Moreover, it turns out that $P_{\mathcal{L}}$ is the smallest s.p. abstract state space, namely if $(A, R^{\sharp}, AP, \ell^{\sharp})$ is any abstract Kripke structure that strongly preserves $\mathcal{L}$ then $|P_{\mathcal{L}}| \leq |A|$. Thus, following Dams [6], the notion of strong preservation can be given for generic state partitions: given a language $\mathcal{L}$ and a semantic structure $\mathcal{S}$, $P \in \mathrm{Part}(\Sigma)$ is strongly preserving for $\mathcal{L}$ (w.r.t. $\mathcal{S}$) when $P \preceq P_{\mathcal{L}}$. Recall that $P_{\ell} \in \mathrm{Part}(\Sigma)$ is the partition induced by the labeling ℓ and observe that $P_{\mathcal{L}} \preceq P_{\ell}$ always holds. Hence, it turns out that $P_{\mathcal{L}}$ is the coarsest refinement of P_{ℓ} which is s.p. for $\mathcal{L}$, namely $P_{\mathcal{L}}$ is the strongly preserving (for $\mathcal{L}$) shell of P_{ℓ}.

Abstract interpretation allows us to define *abstract semantics*. Consider any abstract domain $\mu \in \mathrm{uco}(\wp(\Sigma))$. The *abstract semantic function* $[\![\cdot]\!]_{\mathcal{S}}^{\mu} : \mathcal{L} \rightarrow \mu$ induced by μ evaluates any $\varphi \in \mathcal{L}$ to an abstract value $[\![\varphi]\!]_{\mathcal{S}}^{\mu} \in \mu$. The semantics $[\![\cdot]\!]_{\mathcal{S}}^{\mu}$ is compositionally defined by interpreting any $p \in AP$ and $f \in Op$ as best correct approximations on the abstract domain μ of their concrete interpretations p and f:

$$\llbracket p \rrbracket_S^\mu = \mu(p) \quad \text{and} \quad \llbracket f(\varphi_1, ..., \varphi_n) \rrbracket_S^\mu = \mu(f(\llbracket \varphi_1 \rrbracket_S^\mu, ..., \llbracket \varphi_n \rrbracket_S^\mu)).$$

Intuitively, the partition $P_{\mathcal{L}}$ induced by $\mathcal{L}$ is an abstraction of the semantics $\llbracket \cdot \rrbracket_S$. We make this observation precise as follows. We define an abstract domain $\mu \in \mathrm{uco}(\wp(\Sigma))$ as strongly preserving for $\mathcal{L}$ (w.r.t. $\mathcal{S}$) when for any $S \in \wp(\Sigma)$ and $\varphi \in \mathcal{L}$: $\mu(S) \subseteq \llbracket \varphi \rrbracket_S^\mu \Leftrightarrow S \subseteq \llbracket \varphi \rrbracket_S$. As shown in [16], it turns out that this generalizes the notion of strong preservation from partitions to abstract domains because, by exploiting the above isomorphism between partitions and partitioning abstract domains, it turns out that P is s.p. for $\mathcal{L}$ w.r.t. $\mathcal{S}$ iff $\mathrm{pcl}(P)$ is s.p. for $\mathcal{L}$ w.r.t. $\mathcal{S}$. This provides the right framework for viewing strong preservation as a forward completeness property. Given a state space Σ, we associate to any set $S \subseteq \wp(\Sigma)$ a set of atomic propositions $AP_S \stackrel{\text{def}}{=} \{p_X \mid X \in S\}$ and a corresponding labeling $\ell_S \stackrel{\text{def}}{=} \lambda s \in \Sigma. \{p_X \in AP_S \mid s \in X\}$. In particular, this can be done for any abstract domain $\mu \in \mathrm{uco}(\wp(\Sigma))$ by viewing μ as a set of sets. Hence, given a state space Σ and an interpretation function $I : Op \to \mathrm{Fun}(\wp(\Sigma))$, any abstract domain $\mu \in \mathrm{uco}(\wp(\Sigma))$ determines the semantic structure $\mathcal{S}_\mu = (\Sigma, I, AP_\mu, \ell_\mu)$. The following result shows that strongly preserving shells indeed coincide with forward complete shells.

Theorem 3.2 ([16]). *Let $\mathcal{L}$ be closed under infinite logical conjunction. Then, for any $\mu \in \mathrm{uco}(\wp(\Sigma))$, $S_{Op}(\mu)$ is the most abstract domain that refines μ and is strongly preserving for $\mathcal{L}$ w.r.t. $\mathcal{S}_\mu$.*

This allows to characterize the coarsest s.p. partition $P_{\mathcal{L}}$ as a forward complete shell when $\mathcal{L}$ is closed under logical conjunction and negation.

Corollary 3.3 ([16]). *Let $\mathcal{L}$ be closed under infinite logical conjunction and negation. Then, $P_{\mathcal{L}} = \mathrm{par}(S_{Op}(\mathrm{pcl}(P_\ell)))$.*

4   GPT: A Generalized Paige-Tarjan Refinement Algorithm

In order to emphasize the ideas leading to our generalized Paige-Tarjan algorithm, let us first sketch how some relevant points in PT can be viewed and generalized from an abstract interpretation perspective.

A New Perspective of PT. Consider a finite Kripke structure (Σ, R, AP, ℓ). In the following, we denote $\mathrm{Part}(\Sigma)$ simply by Part and pre_R by pre. As a consequence of Theorem 3.2, we showed in [16] that the output $\mathrm{PT}(P)$ of the Paige-Tarjan algorithm on input $P \in \mathrm{Part}$ is the abstraction through the map par of the forward $\{\mathrm{pre}, \complement\}$-complete shell of $\mathrm{pcl}(P)$, i.e. $\mathrm{PT}(P) = \mathrm{par}(S_{\{\mathrm{pre}, \complement\}}(\mathrm{pcl}(P)))$. Thus, $\mathrm{PT}(P)$ computes the partition abstraction of the most abstract domain that refines $\mathrm{pcl}(P)$ and is strongly preserving for Hennessy-Milner logic HML, namely, by Corollary 3.3, $\mathrm{PT}(P)$ computes the coarsest s.p. partition P_{HML}. On the other hand, Lemma 2.1 gives a constructive characterization of forward complete shells, meaning that it provides an iterative algorithm for computing a shell $S_F(\mu)$: begin with $\rho = \top_{\mathrm{uco}(\wp(\Sigma))}$ and iteratively, at each step, compute $F_\mu(\rho)$

until a fixpoint is reached. This scheme could be in particular applied for computing $S_{\{\text{pre},\mathbb{C}\}}(\text{pcl}(P))$. However, note that the algorithm induced by Lemma 2.1 is far from being efficient: at each step $F_\mu(\rho)$ always re-computes the images $f(\vec{s})$ that have been already computed at the previous step (cf. Example 2.2). Thus, in our abstract interpretation view, PT is an algorithm that computes *a particular abstraction of a particular forward complete shell*. Our goal is to analyze the basic steps of the PT algorithm in order to investigate whether it can be generalized from an abstract interpretation perspective to an algorithm that computes *a generic abstraction of a generic forward complete shell*. We isolate in our abstract interpretation framework the following key points concerning the PT algorithm. Let $P \in \text{Part}$ be any partition.

(i) $\text{PTsplit}(S, P) = \text{par}(\mathcal{M}(\text{pcl}(P) \cup \{\text{pre}(S)\})) = P \curlywedge \{\text{pre}(S), \mathbb{C}(\text{pre}(S))\} = P \curlywedge \text{par}(\mathcal{M}(\{\text{pre}(S)\}))$.
(ii) $\text{PTrefiners}(P) = \{S \in \text{pcl}(P) \mid \text{par}(\mathcal{M}(\text{pcl}(P) \cup \{\text{pre}(S)\})) \prec P\}$.
(iii) P is PT stable iff $\{S \in \text{pcl}(P) \mid \text{par}(\mathcal{M}(\text{pcl}(P) \cup \{\text{pre}(S)\})) \prec P\} = \varnothing$.

Point (i) provides a characterizaztion of the PT splitting step as best correct approximation on the abstract domain Part of the following domain refinement operation: given $S \subseteq \Sigma$, $\text{refine}_{\text{pre}}(S, \cdot) \stackrel{\text{def}}{=} \lambda\mu.\mathcal{M}(\mu \cup \{\text{pre}(S)\}) : \text{uco}(\wp(\Sigma)) \to \text{uco}(\wp(\Sigma))$. In turn, Points (ii) and (iii) yield a characterization of PTrefiners and PT stability based on this best correct approximation on Part of $\text{refine}_{\text{pre}}(S, \cdot)$. Thus, if $\text{refine}_{\text{pre}}^{\text{Part}} : \text{Part} \to \text{Part}$ denotes the best correct approximation of $\text{refine}_{\text{pre}}(S, \cdot)$ on Part, we may

```
while {T ∈ pcl(P) | refine_pre^Part(T, P) ≺ P} ≠ ∅ do
    choose S ∈ {T ∈ pcl(P) | refine_pre^Part(T, P) ≺ P};
    P := refine_pre^Part(S, P);
endwhile
```

view PT as follows. In the following, we generalize this view of PT to generic abstract domains of $\text{uco}(\wp(\Sigma))$ and isolate some conditions ensuring the correctness of this generalized algorithm.

Generalizing PT. We generalize Points (i)-(iii) above as follows. Let $F \subseteq \text{Fun}(\wp(\Sigma))$. We define a family of refinement operators of abstract domains $\text{refine}_f : \wp(\Sigma)^{\text{ar}(f)} \to (\text{uco}(\wp(\Sigma)) \to \text{uco}(\wp(\Sigma)))$ indexed on functions $f \in F$ and tuples of sets $\vec{S} \in \wp(\Sigma)^{\text{ar}(f)}$:

(i) $\text{refine}_f(\vec{S}, \mu) \stackrel{\text{def}}{=} \mathcal{M}(\mu \cup \{f(\vec{S})\})$.

A tuple $\vec{S}$ is a F-refiner for an abstract domain μ when there exists $f \in F$ such that $\vec{S} \in \mu^{\text{ar}(f)}$ and indeed $\vec{S}$ contributes to refine μ w.r.t. f, i.e., $\text{refine}_f(\vec{S}, \mu) \sqsubset \mu$. Thus:

(ii) $\text{Refiners}_f(\mu) \stackrel{\text{def}}{=} \{\vec{S} \in \mu^{\text{ar}(f)} \mid \text{refine}_f(\vec{S}, \mu) \sqsubset \mu\}$;
$\text{Refiners}_F(\mu) \stackrel{\text{def}}{=} \cup_{f \in F} \text{Refiners}_f(\mu)$.
(iii) μ is F-stable iff $\text{Refiners}_F(\mu) = \varnothing$.

These simple observations lead us to design the following PT-like algorithm called CPT_F (Concrete PT), parameterized by F, taking as input an abstract domain $\mu \in \text{uco}(\wp(\Sigma))$ and computing the forward F-complete shell of μ.

```
while (Refiners_F(μ) ≠ ∅) do
    choose for some f ∈ F, S⃗ ∈ Refiners_f(μ);
    μ := refine_f(S⃗, μ);
endwhile                                        CPT_F
```

Lemma 4.1. *Let Σ be finite.* CPT_F *always terminates and, for any* $\mu \in \text{uco}(\wp(\Sigma))$, $\text{CPT}_F(\mu) = S_F(\mu)$.

Example 4.2. Let us illustrate CPT on $\mu = \{\varnothing, 2, 1234\}$ of Example 2.2.

$$\mu_0 = \mu = \{\varnothing, 2, 1234\} \qquad\qquad S_0 = \{2\} \in \text{Refiners}_f(\mu_0)$$
$$\mu_1 = \mathcal{M}(\mu_0 \cup \{f(S_0)\}) = \{\varnothing, 2, 3, 1234\} \qquad S_1 = \{3\} \in \text{Refiners}_f(\mu_1)$$
$$\mu_2 = \mathcal{M}(\mu_1 \cup \{f(S_1)\}) = \{\varnothing, 2, 3, 4, 1234\} \qquad S_2 = \{1234\} \in \text{Refiners}_f(\mu_2)$$
$$\mu_3 = \mathcal{M}(\mu_2 \cup \{f(S_2)\}) = \{\varnothing, 2, 3, 4, 234, 1234\} \quad S_3 = \{234\} \in \text{Refiners}_f(\mu_3)$$
$$\mu_4 = \mathcal{M}(\mu_3 \cup \{f(S_3)\}) = \{\varnothing, 2, 3, 4, 34, 234, 1234\} \;\Rightarrow\; \text{Refiners}_f(\mu_4) = \varnothing$$

Let us note that while in Example 2.2 each step consists in computing the images of f for the sets belonging to the whole domain at the previous step and this gives rise to re-computations, here instead an image $f(S_i)$ is never computed twice because at each step we nondeterministically choose a refiner S and apply f to S. $\qquad\square$

Our goal is to provide an abstract version of CPT_F that works on a generic abstraction A of the lattice $\text{uco}(\wp(\Sigma))$. As recalled at the beginning of Section 3, since we aim at designing an algorithm for computing an abstract greatest fixpoint, viz. $\alpha(\text{CPT}_F(\mu))$ for some abstraction map α, we need to approximate this greatest fixpoint computation "from above" instead of "from below" as it happens for least fixpoint computations. Thus, we consider a Galois insertion $(\alpha, \text{uco}(\wp(\Sigma))_\sqsupseteq, A_\geq, \gamma)$ of an abstract domain $A_\geq$ into the dual lattice of abstract domains $\text{uco}(\wp(\Sigma))_\sqsupseteq$. We denote by $\geq$ the ordering relation of the abstract domain A, because this makes the concrete and abstract ordering notations uniform. Notice that since we consider a Galois insertion of A into the complete lattice $\text{uco}(\wp(\Sigma))$, by standard results [5], it turns out that A must be a complete lattice as well. Also, we denote by $\rho_A \stackrel{\text{def}}{=} \gamma \circ \alpha$ the corresponding uco on $\text{uco}(\wp(\Sigma))_\sqsupseteq$. For any $f \in F$, the best correct approximation $\text{refine}_f^A : \wp(\Sigma)^{\text{ar}(f)} \to (A \to A)$ of refine_f on A is therefore defined as usual:

(i) $\text{refine}_f^A(\vec{S}, a) \stackrel{\text{def}}{=} \alpha(\text{refine}_f(\vec{S}, \gamma(a)))$.

Accordingly, abstract refiners and stability go as follows:

(ii) $\text{Refiners}_f^A(a) \stackrel{\text{def}}{=} \{\vec{S} \in \gamma(a)^{\text{ar}(f)} \mid \text{refine}_f^A(\vec{S}, a) < a\}$;
   $\text{Refiners}_F^A(a) \stackrel{\text{def}}{=} \cup_{f \in F} \text{Refiners}_f^A(a)$.
(iii) An abstract object $a \in A$ is F-stable iff $\text{Refiners}_F^A(a) = \varnothing$.

It is worth remarking that $a \in A$ is F-stable iff $\gamma(a)$ is forward F-complete. We may now define the following abstract version of the above algorithm CPT_F, called GPT_F^A (Generalized PT), parameterized on the abstract domain A. $\text{GPT}_F^A(a)$ computes a sequence of abstract objects $\{a_i\}_{i \in \mathbb{N}}$

> **input:** abstract object $a \in A$
> **while** ($\text{Refiners}_F^A(a) \neq \varnothing$) **do**
>   **choose** for some $f \in F$, $\vec{S} \in \text{Refiners}_f^A(a)$;
> $a := \text{refine}_f^A(\vec{S}, a)$;
> **endwhile** $\qquad\qquad\qquad\boxed{\text{GPT}_F^A}$

which is a decreasing chain in A. Thus, in order to ensure termination of GPT_F^A it is enough to consider an abstract domain A satisfying the descending chain condition (DCC). Furthermore, let us remark that correctness for GPT_F^A means that for any $a \in A$,

$\mathrm{GPT}_F(a) = \alpha(\mathsf{S}_F(\gamma(a)))$. Note that, by Lemma 2.1, $\alpha(\mathsf{S}_F(\gamma(a))) = \alpha(\mathrm{gfp}(F_{\gamma(a)}))$. It should be clear that correctness for GPT is somehow related to backward completeness in abstract interpretation. In fact, if the abstract domain A is backward complete for $F_\mu = \lambda\rho.\mu \sqcap F^{\mathrm{uco}}(\rho)$ then, by Lemma 2.1, $\alpha(\mathrm{gfp}(F_\mu)) = \mathrm{gfp}(F_\mu^A)$, where F_μ^A is the best correct approximation of the operator F_μ on the abstract domain A, and $\mathrm{GPT}_F^A(a)$ intuitively is an algorithm for computing $\mathrm{gfp}(F_\mu^A)$. Indeed, the following result shows that GPT_F^A is correct when A is backward complete for F^{uco}, because this implies that A is backward complete for F_μ, for any μ. Moreover, we also isolate the following condition ensuring correctness for GPT_F^A: the forward F-complete shell of any concretization $\gamma(a)$ still belongs to $\gamma(A)$, namely A is forward complete for the forward F-complete shell S_F.

Theorem 4.3. *Let A be DCC and assume that one of the following conditions holds:*

(i) $\rho_A \circ F^{\mathrm{uco}} \circ \rho_A = \rho_A \circ F^{\mathrm{uco}}$.

(ii) $\rho_A \circ \mathsf{S}_F \circ \rho_A = \mathsf{S}_F \circ \rho_A$ *(i.e., $\forall a \in A.\, \mathsf{S}_F(\gamma(a)) \in \gamma(A)$).*

Then, GPT_F^A always terminates and for any $a \in A$, $\mathrm{GPT}_F^A(a) = \alpha(\mathsf{S}_F(\gamma(a)))$.

Corollary 4.4. *Under the hypotheses of Theorem 4.3, for any $a \in A$, $\mathrm{GPT}_F^A(a)$ is the F-stable shell of a.*

Example 4.5. Let us consider again Example 2.2. Recall that an abstract domain $\rho \in \mathrm{uco}(\wp(\Sigma))$ is disjunctive iff for any (possibly empty) $S \subseteq \rho$, $\cup S \in \rho$. We denote by $\mathrm{duco}(\wp(\Sigma))$ the set of disjunctive domains in $\mathrm{uco}(\wp(\Sigma))$. Thus, the disjunctive shell $\mathsf{S}_\cup : \mathrm{uco}(\wp(\Sigma)) \to \mathrm{duco}(\wp(\Sigma))$ maps any ρ to the well-known disjunctive completion $\mathsf{S}_\cup(\rho) = \{\cup S \mid S \subseteq \rho\}$ of ρ (see [5]). It turns out that $\mathrm{duco}(\wp(\Sigma))$ is indeed an abstract domain of $\mathrm{uco}(\wp(\Sigma))_\sqsupseteq$, namely $(\mathsf{S}_\cup, \mathrm{uco}(\wp(\Sigma))_\sqsupseteq, \mathrm{duco}(\wp(\Sigma))_\sqsupseteq, id)$ is a GI.

It turns out that condition (i) of Theorem 4.3 is satisfied for this GI. In fact, by exploiting the fact that, by definition, $f : \wp(\Sigma) \to \wp(\Sigma)$ is additive, it is not hard to verify that $\mathsf{S}_\cup \circ f^{\mathrm{uco}} \circ \mathsf{S}_\cup = \mathsf{S}_\cup \circ f^{\mathrm{uco}}$. Thus, let us apply $\mathrm{GPT}_f^{\mathrm{duco}}$ to the disjunctive abstract domain $\mu_0 = \{\varnothing, 2, 1234\} = \mathsf{S}_\cup(\{2, 1234\}) \in \mathrm{duco}(\wp(\Sigma))$.

$$\mu_0 = \mu = \{\varnothing, 2, 1234\} \qquad\qquad S_0 = \{2\} \in \mathrm{Refiners}_f^{\mathrm{duco}}(\mu_0)$$

$$\mu_1 = \mathsf{S}_\cup(\mathcal{M}(\mu_0 \cup \{f(S_0)\})) = \{\varnothing, 2, 3, 23, 1234\} \quad S_1 = \{3\} \in \mathrm{Refiners}_f^{\mathrm{duco}}(\mu_1)$$

$$\mu_2 = \mathsf{S}_\cup(\mathcal{M}(\mu_1 \cup \{f(S_1)\}))$$

$$= \{\varnothing, 2, 3, 4, 23, 24, 34, 234, 1234\} \qquad\qquad \Rightarrow \mathrm{Refiners}_f^{\mathrm{duco}}(\mu_2) = \varnothing$$

From Example 4.2 we know that $\mathsf{S}_f(\mu_0) = \{\varnothing, 2, 3, 4, 34, 234, 1234\}$. Thus, as expected from Theorem 4.3, $\mathrm{GPT}_f^{\mathrm{duco}}(\mu_0)$ coincides with $\mathsf{S}_\cup(\mathsf{S}_f(\mu_0)) = \{\varnothing, 2, 3, 4, 23, 24, 34, 234, 1234\}$. Note that we reached the abstract fixpoint in two iterations, whereas in Example 4.2 the concrete computation by CPT_f needed four iterations. $\square$

An Optimization of GPT. As pointed out in [15], PT works even if we choose splitters among blocks instead of unions of blocks, i.e., if we replace PTrefiners(P) with the subset of "block refiners" PTblockrefiners(P) $\overset{\text{def}}{=}$ PTrefiners(P) $\cap P$. This can be easily generalized as follows. Given $g \in F$, for any $a \in A$, let $\text{subRefiners}_g^A(a) \subseteq \text{Refiners}_g^A(a)$. We denote by IGPT_F^A (Improved GPT) the version of GPT_F^A where Refiners_g^A is replaced with subRefiners_g^A.

Corollary 4.6. *Let $g \in F$ be such that, for any $a \in A$, $\text{subRefiners}_g^A(a) = \varnothing \Leftrightarrow \text{Refiners}_g^A(a) = \varnothing$. Then, for any $a \in A$, $\text{GPT}_F^A(a) = \text{IGPT}_F^A(a)$.*

Instantiating GPT *with Partitions.* Let the state space Σ be finite. The following properties (1) and (2) are consequences of the fact that a partitioning abstract domain $\text{pcl}(P)$ is closed under complements, i.e. $X \in \text{pcl}(P)$ iff $\complement(X) \in \text{pcl}(P)$.

(1) $\text{Refiners}_\complement^{\text{Part}}(P) = \varnothing$.
(2) For any f and $\vec{S} \in \wp(\Sigma)^{\text{ar}(f)}$, $\text{refine}_f^{\text{Part}}(\vec{S}, P) = P \curlywedge \{f(\vec{S}), \complement(f(\vec{S}))\}$.

Thus, by Point (1), for any $F \subseteq \text{Fun}(\wp(\Sigma))$, a partition $P \in \text{Part}$ is F-stable iff P is $(F \cup \{\complement\})$-stable, that is complements can be left out. Hence, if $F^{-\complement}$ denotes $F \setminus \{\complement\}$ then $\text{GPT}_F^{\text{Part}}$ may be simplified as follows. Note that the number of iterations of $\text{GPT}_F^{\text{Part}}$ is bounded by the hei-

> **while** $(\text{Refiners}_{F^{-\complement}}^{\text{Part}}(a) \neq \varnothing)$ **do**
>   **choose** for some $f \in F^{-\complement}$, $\vec{S} \in \text{Refiners}_f^{\text{Part}}(a)$;
> $P := P \curlywedge \{f(\vec{S}), \complement(f(\vec{S}))\}$;
> **endwhile** $\text{GPT}_F^{\text{Part}}$

ght of the lattice Part, that is by the number of states $|\Sigma|$. Thus, if each refinement step involving some $f \in F$ takes $O(\text{cost}(f))$ time then the time complexity of $\text{GPT}_F^{\text{Part}}$ is bounded by $O(|\Sigma| \max(\{\text{cost}(f) \mid f \in F\}))$.

Let us now consider a language $\mathcal{L}$ with operators in Op and let (Σ, I, AP, ℓ) be a semantic structure for $\mathcal{L}$. If $\mathcal{L}$ is closed under logical conjunction and negation then, for any $\mu \in \text{uco}(\wp(\Sigma))$, $S_{Op}(\mu)$ is closed under complements and therefore it is a partitioning abstract domain. Thus, condition (ii) of Theorem 4.3 is satisfied. As a consequence of Corollary 3.3 we obtain the following characterization.

Corollary 4.7. *If $\mathcal{L}$ is closed under conjunction and negation then $\text{GPT}_{Op}^{\text{Part}}(P_\ell) = P_\mathcal{L}$.*

This provides a parameteric algorithm for computing the coarsest strongly preserving partition $P_\mathcal{L}$ induced by a generic language $\mathcal{L}$ including propositional logic.
PT *as an Instance of* GPT. It is now immediate to obtain PT as an instance of GPT. We know that $\text{GPT}_{\{\text{pre},\complement\}}^{\text{Part}} = \text{GPT}_{\text{pre}}^{\text{Part}}$. Moreover, by Points (i) and (ii) above:

$$P \curlywedge \{\text{pre}(S), \complement(\text{pre}(S))\} = \text{PTsplit}(S, P) \text{ and } \text{Refiners}_{\text{pre}}^{\text{Part}}(P) = \text{PTrefiners}(P).$$

Hence, by Point (iii), it turns out that $P \in \text{Part}$ is PT stable iff $\text{Refiners}_{\text{pre}}^{\text{Part}}(P) = \varnothing$. Thus, the instance $\text{GPT}_{\text{pre}}^{\text{Part}}$ provides *exactly* the PT algorithm. Also, correctness follows from Corollaries 4.4 and 4.7: $\text{GPT}_{\text{pre}}^{\text{Part}}(P)$ is both the coarsest PT stable refinement of P and the coarsest strongly preserving partition P_{HML}.

5 Applications

5.1 Simulation Equivalence and Henzinger et al.'s Algorithm

It is well known that simulation equivalence is an appropriate state equivalence to be used in abstract model checking because it strongly preserves ACTL* and provides a better state-space reduction than bisimulation equivalence. However, computing simulation equivalence is harder than bisimulation [14]. Henzinger et al. [13] provide an algorithm, here called HHK, for computing simulation equivalence which runs in $O(|R||\Sigma|)$-time. As far as time-complexity is concerned, HHK is the best available algorithm for this problem. We show here that HHK can be obtained as an instance of our algorithmic scheme GPT.

Consider a finite Kripke structure $\mathcal{K} = (\Sigma, R, AP, \ell)$ and let $\equiv_{\text{sim}}$ and P_{sim} denote, respectively, simulation equivalence on $\mathcal{K}$ and its corresponding partition. Henzinger et al.'s algorithm maintains, for any state $s \in \Sigma$, a set of states $\text{sim}(s) \subseteq \Sigma$. Initially, $\text{sim}(s) = [s]_\ell$ and at each iteration some $\text{sim}(s)$ is reduced, so that at the end $s \equiv_{\text{sim}} s'$ iff $s \in \text{sim}(s')$ and $s' \in \text{sim}(s)$. The algorithmic scheme HHK

---

for all $s \in \Sigma$ **do** $\text{sim}(s) := \{s' \in \Sigma \mid \ell(s') = \ell(s)\}$ **endfor**
while $(\exists u, v, w \in \Sigma. \; u \in \text{pre}(\{v\}) \; \& \; w \in \text{sim}(u) \; \& $
$\qquad\qquad\qquad\qquad\qquad w \notin \text{pre}(\text{sim}(v)))$ **do**
$\quad \text{sim}(u) := \text{sim}(u) \smallsetminus \{w\};$
endwhile   HHK

---

is as follows. Let us show how to cast HHK as an instance of GPT. In this case, we consider the abstraction of $\text{uco}(\wp(\Sigma))$ given by the disjunctive abstract domains $\text{duco}(\wp(\Sigma))$, namely additive closures, that we already defined in Example 4.5. Thus, $S_\cup : \text{uco}(\wp(\Sigma)) \to \text{duco}(\wp(\Sigma))$ is the disjunctive completion and $(S_\cup, \text{uco}(\wp(\Sigma))_\sqsupseteq, \text{duco}(\wp(\Sigma))_\sqsupseteq, id)$ is the corresponding Galois insertion. Any disjunctive abstract domain $\rho \in \text{duco}(\wp(\Sigma))$ is completely determined by the images of the singletons $\{s\}$ because, for any $X \in \wp(\Sigma)$, $\rho(X) = \cup_{x \in X} \rho(\{x\})$. Hence, any $\rho \in \text{duco}(\wp(\Sigma))$ can be represented by the set $\{\rho(\{s\})\}_{s \in \Sigma}$, and conversely any set of sets $\mathcal{S} = \{S_s\}_{s \in \Sigma}$ indexed on Σ determines a disjunctive abstract domain that we denote by $\rho_{\mathcal{S}}$. This shows that HHK can be viewed as an algorithm which maintains and refines a disjunctive abstract domain of $\wp(\Sigma)$ determined by the current $\{\text{sim}(s)\}_{s \in \Sigma}$.

On the other hand, it is known (see e.g. [17–Section 8]) that simulation equivalence on $\mathcal{K}$ coincides with the state equivalence induced by the following language $\mathcal{L}$: $\varphi ::= p \mid \varphi_1 \wedge \varphi_2 \mid \text{EX}\varphi$, namely, $P_{\text{sim}} = P_{\mathcal{L}}$. Moreover, as already observed in Example 4.5, it turns out that that $S_\cup \circ \text{pre}^{\text{uco}} \circ S_\cup = S_\cup \circ \text{pre}^{\text{uco}}$. Thus, by Theorem 4.3, $\text{GPT}_{\text{pre}}^{\text{duco}}(P_\ell) = S_\cup(S_{\text{pre}}(\text{pcl}(P_\ell)))$, and in turn $\text{par}(\text{GPT}_{\text{pre}}^{\text{duco}}(P_\ell)) = \text{par}(S_\cup(S_{\text{pre}}(\text{pcl}(P_\ell))))$. By Theorem 3.2, we know that $S_{\text{pre}}(\text{pcl}(P_\ell))$ is the most abstract domain which is strongly preserving for $\mathcal{L}$. As a consequence, it turns out that $\text{par}(S_\cup(S_{\text{pre}}(\text{pcl}(P_\ell)))) = P_{\mathcal{L}} = P_{\text{sim}}$. Thus, we showed that $\text{GPT}_{\text{pre}}^{\text{duco}}(P_\ell) = P_{\text{sim}}$, namely $\text{GPT}_{\text{pre}}^{\text{duco}}$ allows to compute simulation equivalence.

Even more, it turns out that $\text{GPT}_{\text{pre}}^{\text{duco}}$ exactly coincides with HHK and therefore admits the $O(|R||\Sigma|)$-time implementation described in [13]. In fact, if $\mathcal{S} = \{\text{sim}(s)\}_{s \in \Sigma}$ is the current set of sets maintained by HHK then it is possible to show that: (1) the condition of the while loop in HHK for $\mathcal{S}$ is exactly equivalent to pre-stability for the corresponding disjunctive abstract domain $\rho_{\mathcal{S}}$; (2) the refinement of $\mathcal{S}$ in HHK is precisely a step of pre-refinement of the additive uco $\rho_{\mathcal{S}}$ in $\text{GPT}_{\text{pre}}^{\text{duco}}$.

5.2   Stuttering Equivalence and Groote-Vaandrager Algorithm

Behavioural *stuttering*-based equivalences originated as state equivalences induced by languages without a next-time operator [7]. We are interested here in *divergence blind stuttering* (dbs for short) equivalence. Given a Kripke structure $\mathcal{K} = (\Sigma, R, AP, \ell)$, we denote by $P_{\mathrm{dbs}} \in \mathrm{Part}(\Sigma)$ the partition corresponding to the largest dbs equivalence on $\mathcal{K}$. We showed in [16] that P_{dbs} coincides with the coarsest strongly preserving partition $P_{\mathcal{L}}$ for the following language $\mathcal{L}$: $\varphi ::= p \mid \varphi_1 \wedge \varphi_2 \mid \neg\varphi \mid \mathrm{EU}(\varphi_1, \varphi_2)$, where the semantics $\mathrm{EU} : \wp(\Sigma)^2 \to \wp(\Sigma)$ of the existential until EU is as usual:

$$\mathrm{EU}(S_1, S_2) = S_2 \cup \{s \in S_1 \mid \exists s_0, ..., s_n \in \Sigma, \text{ with } n \geq 0, \text{ such that (i) } s_0 = s,$$
$$\text{(ii) } \forall i \in [0, n). \, s_i \in S_1, \, s_i \xrightarrow{R} s_{i+1}, \text{ (iii) } s_n \in S_2\}.$$

Therefore, as a straight instance of Corollary 4.7, it turns out that $\mathrm{GPT}_{\mathrm{EU}}^{\mathrm{Part}}(P_\ell) = P_{\mathcal{L}} = P_{\mathrm{dbs}}$. Groote and Vaandrager [11] designed the following partition refinement algorithm, here denoted by GV, for computing the partition P_{dbs}, where, for $B_1, B_2 \in P$,[1]

```
P := P_ℓ;
while GVrefiners(P) ≠ ∅ do
    choose ⟨B₁, B₂⟩ ∈ GVrefiners(P);
    P := GVsplit(⟨B₁, B₂⟩, P);
endwhile                              GV
```

$$\mathrm{GVsplit}(\langle B_1, B_2\rangle, P) \overset{\text{def}}{=} P \curlywedge \{\mathrm{EU}(B_1, B_2), \complement(\mathrm{EU}(B_1, B_2))\}$$
$$\mathrm{GVrefiners}(P) \overset{\text{def}}{=} \{\langle B_1, B_2\rangle \in P \times P \mid \mathrm{GVsplit}(\langle B_1, B_2\rangle, P) \prec P\}.$$

Groote and Vaandrager show how GV can be efficiently implemented in $O(|R||\Sigma|)$-time. Indeed, it turns out that GV *exactly* coincides with $\mathrm{IGPT}_{\mathrm{EU}}^{\mathrm{Part}}$. This is a consequence of the following two facts:

(1) $\mathrm{GVrefiners}(P) = \emptyset$ iff $\mathrm{Refiners}_{\mathrm{EU}}^{\mathrm{Part}}(P) = \emptyset$;
(2) $\mathrm{GVsplit}(\langle B_1, B_2\rangle, P) = \mathrm{refine}_{\mathrm{EU}}^{\mathrm{Part}}(\langle B_1, B_2\rangle, P)$.

Hence, by Corollary 4.6, Point (1) allows us to exploit the $\mathrm{IGPT}_{\mathrm{EU}}^{\mathrm{Part}}$ algorithm in order to choose refiners for EU among the pairs of blocks of the current partition, so that by Point (2) we obtain that $\mathrm{IGPT}_{\mathrm{EU}}^{\mathrm{Part}}$ exactly coincides with the GV algorithm.

5.3   A Language Expressing Reachability

Let us consider the following language $\mathcal{L}$ which is able to express propositional logic and reachability: $\varphi ::= p \mid \varphi_1 \wedge \varphi_2 \mid \neg\varphi \mid \mathrm{EF}\varphi$. Given a Kripke structure (Σ, R, AP, ℓ), the interpretation $\mathrm{EF} : \wp(\Sigma) \to \wp(\Sigma)$ of the reachability operator EF is as usual: $\mathrm{EF}(S) \overset{\text{def}}{=} \mathrm{EU}(\Sigma, S)$. Since $\mathcal{L}$ includes propositional logic, by Corollary 4.7, we have that the instance $\mathrm{GPT}_{\mathrm{EF}}^{\mathrm{Part}}$ allows to compute the coarsest strongly preserving partition $P_{\mathcal{L}}$, namely $\mathrm{GPT}_{\mathrm{EF}}^{\mathrm{Part}}(P_\ell) = P_{\mathcal{L}}$. Also, we may restrict ourselves to "block refiners", that is, $\mathrm{BlockRefiners}_{\mathrm{EF}}^{\mathrm{Part}}(P) = \{B \in P \mid P \curlywedge \{\mathrm{EF}(B), \complement(\mathrm{EF}(B))\} \prec P\}$. In fact, it turns out that $\mathrm{BlockRefiners}_{\mathrm{EF}}^{\mathrm{Part}}(P) = \emptyset$ iff $\mathrm{Refiners}_{\mathrm{EF}}^{\mathrm{Part}}(P) = \emptyset$. Therefore, by exploiting Corollary 4.6, we have that $\mathrm{IGPT}_{\mathrm{EF}}^{\mathrm{Part}}(P_\ell) = P_{\mathcal{L}}$, where $\mathrm{IGPT}_{\mathrm{EF}}^{\mathrm{Part}}$ is as follows. Our implementation of $\mathrm{IGPT}_{\mathrm{EF}}^{\mathrm{Part}}$ exploits the following "stability under refinement"

```
while (BlockRefiners_EF^Part(P) ≠ ∅) do
    choose B ∈ BlockRefiners_EF^Part(P);
    P := P ⋏ {EF(B), ∁(EF(B))};
endwhile                              IGPT_EF^Part
```

---

[1] In [11], $\mathrm{pos}(B_1, B_2)$ denotes $\mathrm{EU}(B_1, B_2) \cap B_1$.

property: if $Q \preceq P$ and B is a block of both P and Q then $P \lambda \{\mathbf{EF}(B), \complement(\mathbf{EF}(B))\} = P$ implies $Q \lambda \{\mathbf{EF}(B), \complement(\mathbf{EF}(B))\} = Q$. As a consequence, if some block B of the current partition P_{curr} is not a $\mathbf{EF}$-refiner for P_{curr} and B is also a block of the next partition P_{next} then B cannot be a $\mathbf{EF}$-refiner for P_{next}. This suggests an implementation of $\mathrm{IGPT}_{\mathbf{EF}}^{\mathrm{Part}}$ based on the following points:

(1) to represent the current partition P as a doubly linked *list* of blocks;
(2) to scan *list* from the beginning in order to find block refiners;
(3) when a block B of the current partition P is split in B_1 and B_2 then we remove B from *list* and we append B_1 and B_2 at the end of *list*.

This leads to the following refinement of $\mathrm{IGPT}_{\mathbf{EF}}^{\mathrm{Part}}$.

```
list := list of blocks in P;
scan B in list
  compute EF(B);
  current_end points to the end of list;
  scan B' in list up to current_end
    if (B' ∩ EF(B) ≠ ∅ and B' ∖ EF(B) ≠ ∅) then
      { remove B' from list;  append B' ∩ EF(B) and B' ∖ EF(B) to list; }
  endscan
endscan
```

It is not hard to devise a practical implementation of this algorithm requiring $O(|R||\Sigma|)$ time. As a preprocessing step we first compute the DAG of the strongly connected components (s.c.c.'s) of the directed graph (Σ, R) that we denote by $\mathrm{DAG}_{(\Sigma,R)}$. This can be done through a well-known algorithm (see e.g. [1]) running in $O(|\Sigma| + |R|)$-time, i.e. by totality of the transition relation R, in $O(|R|)$-time. Moreover, this algorithm returns the s.c.c.'s in $\mathrm{DAG}_{(\Sigma,R)}$ in topological order. This allows us to represent $\mathrm{DAG}_{(\Sigma,R)}$ through an adjacency list where the s.c.c.'s are recorded in reversed topological ordering in a list L. Thus, if S and S' are two s.c.c.'s of (Σ, R) such that there exists $s \in S$ and $s' \in S'$ with $s \xrightarrow{R} s'$ then S follows S' in the list L. By exploiting this representation of $\mathrm{DAG}_{(\Sigma,R)}$ we are able:

(1) to compute $\mathbf{EF}(B)$, for some block $B \in$ *list*, in $O(|R|)$-time;
(2) to execute the inner scan loop in $O(|\Sigma|)$-time.

Hence, each iteration of the outer scan loop costs $O(|R|)$-time, because, by totality of R, $|\Sigma| \leq |R|$. Moreover, it turns out that the number of iterations of the outer scan loop is in $O(|\Sigma|)$. We thus obtain that this implementation of $\mathrm{IGPT}_{\mathbf{EF}}^{\mathrm{Part}}$ runs in $O(|R||\Sigma|)$-time.

6   Related and Future work

Related Work. Dams [6–Chapter 5] presents a generic splitting algorithm which, for a given language $\mathcal{L} \subseteq \mathrm{ACTL}$, computes an abstract model $A \in \mathrm{Abs}(\wp(\Sigma))$ that strongly preserves $\mathcal{L}$. This technique is inherently different from ours, in particular because it is guided by a splitting operation of an abstract state that depends on a given formula of ACTL. Additionally, Dams' methodology does not guarantee optimality of the resulting strongly preserving abstract model, as instead we do, because his algorithm may provide strongly preserving models which are too concrete. Dams [6–Chapter 6] also presents a generic partition refinement algorithm that computes a given (behavioural) state equivalence and generalizes PT (i.e., bisimulation equivalence) and Groote and Vaandrager (i.e., stuttering equivalence) algorithms. This algorithm is parameterized on a notion of splitter corresponding to some state equivalence, while our algorithm is directly parameterized on a given language: the example given in [6] (a "flat" version of CTL-X) seems to indicate that finding the right definition of splitter for some language may be a hard task. Gentilini et al. [8] provide an algorithm that solves a so-called generalized coarsest partition problem, meaning that they generalize PT stability to partitions endowed with an acyclic relation. They show that this technique can be instantiated to obtain a logarithmic algorithm for PT stability and an efficient algorithm for simulation equivalence. This approach is very different from ours since the partition refinement algorithm is not driven by strong preservation w.r.t. some language.

Future Work. GPT is parameteric on a domain of abstract models which is an abstraction of the lattice of abstract domains $\mathrm{Abs}(\wp(\Sigma))$. We instantiated GPT to the lattice $\mathrm{Part}(\Sigma)$ of partitions and to the lattice $\mathrm{DisjAbs}(\wp(\Sigma))$ of disjunctive abstract domains. We plan to investigate whether the GPT scheme can be applied to new domains of abstract models. In particular, models which are abstractions of $\mathrm{Part}(\Sigma)$ could be useful for computing *approximations of strongly preserving partitions*. As an example, if we are interested in reducing only a portion $S \subseteq \Sigma$ of the state space Σ, we may consider the domain $\mathrm{Part}(S)$ as an abstraction of $\mathrm{Part}(\Sigma)$ in order to get strong preservation only on the portion S.

Acknowledgments. This work was partially supported by the FIRB Project "*Abstract interpretation and model checking for the verification of embedded systems*", by the COFIN2002 Project "COVER: *Constraint based verification of reactive systems*" and by the COFIN2004 Project "AIDA: *Abstract Interpretation Design and Applications*".

References

1. A.V. Aho, J.E. Hopcroft and J.D. Ullman. *Data Structures and Algorithms*. Addison-Wesley, 1983.
2. M.C. Browne, E.M. Clarke and O. Grumberg. Characterizing finite Kripke structures in propositional temporal logic. *Theor. Comp. Sci.*, 59:115-131, 1988.
3. E.M. Clarke, O. Grumberg and D.A. Peled. *Model Checking*. The MIT Press, 1999.
4. P. Cousot and R. Cousot. Abstract interpretation: a unified lattice model for static analysis of programs by construction or approximation of fixpoints. In *Proc. 4th ACM POPL*, 238-252, 1977.
5. P. Cousot and R. Cousot. Systematic design of program analysis frameworks. In *Proc. 6th ACM POPL*, 269-282, 1979.
6. D. Dams. *Abstract Interpretation and Partition Refinement for Model Checking*. PhD Thesis, Eindhoven Univ., 1996.
7. R. De Nicola and F. Vaandrager. Three logics for branching bisimulation. *J. ACM*, 42(2):458-487, 1995

8. R. Gentilini, C. Piazza and A. Policriti. From bisimulation to simulation: coarsest partition problems. *J. Automated Reasoning*, 31(1):73-103, 2003.
9. R. Giacobazzi and E. Quintarelli. Incompleteness, counterexamples and refinements in abstract model checking. In *Proc. 8ᵗʰ SAS*, LNCS 2126:356-373, 2001.
10. R. Giacobazzi, F. Ranzato and F. Scozzari. Making abstract interpretations complete. *J. ACM*, 47(2):361-416, 2000.
11. J.F. Groote and F. Vaandrager. An efficient algorithm for branching bisimulation and stuttering equivalence. In *Proc. 17ᵗʰ ICALP*, LNCS 443:626-638, 1990.
12. M. Hennessy and R. Milner. Algebraic laws for nondeterminism and concurrency. *J. ACM*, 32(1):137-161, 1985.
13. M.R. Henzinger, T.A. Henzinger and P.W. Kopke. Computing simulations on finite and infinite graphs. In *Proc. 36ᵗʰ FOCS*, 453-462, 1995.
14. A. Kucera and R. Mayr. Why is simulation harder than bisimulation? In *Proc. 13ᵗʰ CONCUR*, LNCS 2421:594-610, 2002.
15. R. Paige and R.E. Tarjan. Three partition refinement algorithms. *SIAM J. Comput.*, 16(6):973-989, 1987
16. F. Ranzato and F. Tapparo. Strong preservation as completeness in abstract interpretation. In *Proc. 13ᵗʰ ESOP*, LNCS 2986:18-32, 2004.
17. R.J. van Glabbeek. The linear time - branching time spectrum I: the semantics of concrete sequential processes. In *Handbook of Process Algebra*, pp. 3-99, Elsevier, 2001.

Dependent Types for Program Understanding

Raghavan Komondoor*, G. Ramalingam, Satish Chandra,
and John Field

IBM Research

Abstract. Weakly-typed languages such as Cobol often force programmers to represent distinct data abstractions using the same low-level physical type. In this paper, we describe a technique to recover implicitly-defined data abstractions from programs using type inference. We present a novel system of dependent types which we call *guarded types*, a path-sensitive algorithm for inferring guarded types for Cobol programs, and a semantic characterization of correct guarded typings. The results of our inference technique can be used to enhance program understanding for legacy applications, and to enable a number of type-based program transformations.

1   Introduction

Despite myriad advances in programming languages, libraries, and tools since business computing became widespread in the 1950s, large-scale legacy applications written in Cobol still constitute the computing backbone of many businesses. Such applications are notoriously difficult and time-consuming to update in response to changing business requirements. This difficulty very often stems from the fact that the logical structure of the code and data manipulated by these applications is not apparent from the program text. Two sources for this phenomenon are the lack in Cobol of modern abstraction mechanisms, and the fragmentation of the physical realization of logical abstractions due to repeated ad-hoc maintenance activities. In this paper, we focus on the problem of *recovering* certain data abstractions from legacy Cobol applications. By doing so, we aim to facilitate a variety of program maintenance activities that can benefit from a better understanding of logical data relationships.

Cobol is a *weakly-typed* language both in the sense that it has few modern type abstraction constructs[1], and because those types that it does have are for the most part not statically (or dynamically) enforced. For example:

- Cobol has no notion of scalar user-defined type; programmers can declare only the representation type of scalar variables (such variables are usually

---

* Contact author: komondoo@us.ibm.com.
[1] Modern versions of Cobol address some of these shortcomings; however, the bulk of existing legacy programs are written in early dialects of Cobol lacking type abstraction facilities.

N. Halbwachs and L. Zuck (Eds.): TACAS 2005, LNCS 3440, pp. 157–173, 2005.

character or digit sequences). Hence, there is no means to declaratively distinguish among variables that store data from distinct logical domains, e.g., quantities and serial numbers.

- Cobol allows allows multiple record-structured variables to be declared to occupy the same memory. This "redefinition" feature can be used both to create different "views" on the same runtime variable, or to store data from different logical domains at different times, often distinguished by a tag value stored elsewhere. However, there is no explicit mechanism to declare which idiom is actually intended.
- Cobol programmers routinely store values in variables whose declared structures do not fully reflect the logical structure of the values being stored. One reason why programmers do this is the one already mentioned: to simulate subtyping by storing data from different logical domains (that are subtypes of some base domain) in a variable at different times.

As part of the *Mastery* project at IBM Research our long-term goal is to recover logical data models from applications at a level of abstraction similar to that found in expressive design-level languages such as UML [8] or Alloy [5], to alleviate language limitations, and to address the physical fragmentation alluded to above. Here, we describe initial steps toward this goal by describing a *type inference* technique for recovering abstractions from Cobol programs in the form of *guarded types*. Guarded types may contain any of the following classes of elements:

Atomic types: Domains of scalar values. In many cases, distinct atomic types will share the same physical representation; e.g., Quantity and SerialNumber. Atomic types can optionally be constrained to contain only certain specific runtime values.

Records: Domains consisting of fixed-length sequences of elements from other domains.

Guarded disjoint unions: Domains formed by the union of two or more logically disjoint domains, where the constituent domains are distinguished by one or more atomic types constrained to contain distinct *guard* or tag values.

The principal contributions of the paper are the guarded type system used to represent data abstractions; a formal characterization of a correct guarded typing of a program; and a path-sensitive algorithm to infer a valid guarded typing for any program (path-sensitivity is crucial to inferring reasonably accurate guarded union types). Although our techniques are designed primarily to address data abstraction recovery for Cobol programs, we believe our approach may also be applicable to other weakly-typed languages; e.g., assembly languages.

1.1   Introduction to MiniCobol and Motivating Example

We will illustrate our typing language and inference algorithm using the example programs in Fig. 1. These examples are written in a simple language MiniCobol, which contains the essential features of Cobol relevant to this paper. Consider the

```
    01 PAY-REC.
      05 PAYEE-TYPE PIC X.
      05 DATA PIC X(13).
    01 IS-VISITOR PIC X.
    01 PAY PIC X(4).
/1/ READ PAY-REC FROM IN-F.              ['E':Emp ⊗ Eld ⊗ Salary ⊗ Unused ⊕
                                           !{'E'}:Vis ⊗ SSN5 ⊗ SSN4 ⊗ Stipend]
/2/ MOVE 'N' TO IS-VISITOR.              ['N':VisNo]
/3/ IF PAYEE-TYPE = 'E'                  ['E':Emp ⊕ !{'E'}:Vis]
/4/   MOVE DATA[8:11] TO PAY.            [Salary]
    ELSE
/5/   MOVE 'Y' TO IS-VISITOR.            ['Y':VisYes]
/6/   MOVE DATA[10:13] TO PAY.           [Stipend]
    ENDIF
/7/ WRITE PAY TO PAY-F.                  [Salary ⊕ Stipend]
/8/ IF IS-VISITOR = 'Y'                  ['N':VisNo ⊕ 'Y':VisYes]
/9/   WRITE DATA[6:9] TO VIS-F.          [SSN4]
                                      (a)
```

```
    01 ID.
      05 ID-TYPE PIC X(3).
      05 ID-DATA PIC X(9).
      05 SSN PIC X(9) REDEFINES ID-DATA.
      05 EMP-ID PIC X(7) REDEFINES ID-DATA.
/1/ READ ID.                             [ 'SSN':SSNTyp ⊗ SSN ⊕
                                           !{'SSN'}:EldTyp ⊗ Eld ⊗ Unused]
/2/ IF ID-TYPE = 'SSN'                   ['SSN':SSNTyp ⊕ !{'SSN'}:EldTyp]
/3/   WRITE SSN TO SSN-F                 [SSN]
    ELSE
/4/   WRITE EMP-ID TO EID-F.             [Eld]
    ENDIF
                                      (b)
```

```
    01 SSN.
    01 SSN-EXPANDED REDEFINES SSN.
      05 FIRST-5-DIGITS X(5).
      05 LAST-4-DIGITS X(4).
/1/ READ SSN FROM IDS-F.                 [SSN5 ⊗ SSN4]
/2/ WRITE LAST-4-DIGITS.                 [SSN4]
                                      (c)
```

Fig. 1. Example programs with guarded typing solutions produced by the inference algorithm of Sec. 3

fragment depicted in Fig. 1(a). The code for the program is shown in TYPEWRITER font, while the type annotations inferred by our inference algorithm are shown within square brackets. The initial part of the program contains variable declarations. Variables are prefixed by *level numbers*; e.g., 01 or 05. A variable with level 01 can represent either a scalar or a record; it is a record if additional variables with higher level numbers follow it, and a scalar otherwise. A variable with level greater than 01 denotes a record or scalar field nested within a previously-declared variable (with lower level). Clauses of the form PIC X(n) denote the fact that the corresponding variable is a character string of length n (n defaults to 1 when not supplied). A REDEFINES clause after a variable declaration indicates that two variables refer to the same storage. For example, in the program fragment in Fig. 1(b), variables ID-DATA, SSN, and EMP-ID all occupy the same storage. Note that the variable declarations reveal the total memory size required by a program (19 bytes, in the case of the example in Figure 1(a)), as well as the beginning and ending offset within memory of each variable.

The code following the data declarations contains the executable statements. MiniCobol contains MOVE statements, which represent assignments, READ and WRITE statements, as well as the usual control-flow constructs such as statement sequencing, conditional statements, loops, and go-to statements. During program execution the value of each variable is a string of 1-byte characters, as is each program constant and the contents of each file. (Cobol follows the same approach, for the most part, e.g., representing numbers as strings of decimal digits). In other words, the program state at any point during execution of a program P is represented by a string of size |P| (in addition to the "program counter"), where |P| is the total memory required by P. A program P's execution begins with an implicit READ of |P| characters which initializes the state of the program.

MOVE statements have operands of equal length. The statement READ *var* FROM *file* reads |*var*| bytes from *file*, where |*var*| is the declared length of *var*, and assigns this value to *var* (we assume in this paper that programs are always given inputs that are "long enough", so READ *var* FROM *file* always gets |*var*| bytes). Similarly, WRITE *var* TO *file* appends the contents of *var* to *file*. In MiniCobol a *data reference* is a reference to a variable, or to a part of a variable identified by an explicit range of locations within the variable; e.g., DATA[8:11] refers to bytes 8 through 11 in the 13 byte variable DATA. We will use the term *variable occurrence* to denote an occurrence of a data-reference in a program.

The program in Fig. 1(a) reads a payment record from file IN-F and processes it. A payment record may pertain to an employee (PAYEE-TYPE = 'E'), or to a visitor (PAYEE-TYPE ≠ 'E'). For an employee, the first 7 bytes of DATA contain the employee ID number, the next four bytes contain the salary, and the last two bytes are unused. For a visitor, however, the first 9 bytes of DATA contain a social security number, and the next four bytes contain a stipend. The program checks the type of the payment record and copies the salary/stipend into PAY accordingly; it writes out PAY to file PAY-F and, in the case of a visitor, writes the last four digits of the social security number to VIS-F.

1.2   Inferring Guarded Types

The right column of Fig. 1 depicts the guarded typing solutions inferred by the algorithm in Sec. 3. For each line, the type shown between square brackets is the type assigned to the underlined variable at the program point *after* the execution of the corresponding statement or predicate. Guarded types are built from an expression language consisting of *(constrained) atomic types* and the operators '⊗' (concatenation) and '⊕' (disjoint union), with '⊗' binding tighter than '⊕'. Constrained atomic types are represented by expressions of the form *constr* : tvar, where *constr* is a *value constraint* and tvar is a *type variable*. A value constraint is either a literal value (in MiniCobol, always a string literal), an expression of the form !(*some set of literals*) denoting the set of all values *except* those enumerated in the set, or an expression of the form !{} denoting the set of all values. If the value constraint is omitted, then it is assumed to be !{}. The atomic type variables in the example are shown in sans serif font; e.g., Emp, Eld, Salary, and Unused. Our type inference algorithm does not generate meaningful names for type variables (the names were supplied manually for expository purposes); however, heuristics could be used to suggest names automatically based on related variable names. The inference process assigns a type to each *occur-*

rence of a data reference; thus different occurrences in the program of the same data reference may be assigned different types. By inspecting the guarded types assigned to data references in Fig. 1, we can observe that the inference process recovers data abstractions *not evident from declared physical types*, as follows:

Domain Distinctions. The typing distinguishes among distinct logical domains not explicitly declared in the program. For example, the references to DATA[8:11] in statement 4 and DATA[6:9] in statement 9 are assigned distinct type variables Salary and SSN4, respectively, although the declaration of DATA makes no such distinction.

Occurrence Typing and Value Flow. Different *occurrences* of variable PAY have distinct types, specifically, type Salary at statement 4, Stipend at statement 6, and Salary $\oplus$ Stipend at statement 7. This indicates that there is no "value flow" between statements 4 and 6, whereas there is potential flow between statements 4 and 7 as well as statements 6 and 7.

Scalar Values vs. Records. The typing solution distinguishes scalar types from record types; these types sometimes differ from physical structure of the declared variable. For example, PAY-REC at statement 1 has a type containing the concatenation operator '$\otimes$', which means it (and DATA within it) store structured data at runtime, while other variables in the program store only scalars. Note that although DATA is declared to be a scalar variable, it really stores record-structured data (whose "fields" are accessed via explicit indices). Note that an occurrence type can contain information about record structure that is inferred from definitions or uses elsewhere in the program of the value(s) contained in the occurrence, including program points following the occurrence in question. So, for example, the record structure of the occurrence of PAY-REC is inferred from uses of (variables declared within) PAY-REC in subsequent statements.

Value Constraints and Disjoint Union Tags. The constraints for the atomic types inside the union type associated with IS-VISITOR in statement 8 indicate that the variable contains either 'N' or 'Y' (and no other value). More interestingly, constrained atomic types inside records can be interpreted as *tags* for the disjoint unions containing them. For example, consider the type assigned to PAY-REC in statement 1. That type denotes the fact that PAY-REC contains *either* an employee number (EId) followed by a Salary and two bytes of of unused space, where the PAYEE-TYPE field is constrained to have value 'E', *or* a social security number followed by a stipend, with with the PAYEE-TYPE field constrained to contain 'E'.

Overlay Idioms. Finally, we observe that the typing allows distinct data abstraction patterns, both of which use the REDEFINES overlay mechanism, to be distinguished by the inference process. Consider the example programs in Figures 1(b) and (c). Program (b) reads an ID record, and, depending on the value of the ID-TYPE field, interprets ID-DATA either as as a social security number or as an employee ID. Here, REDEFINES is used to store elements of a standard disjoint union type, and the type ascribed to ID makes this clear. By contrast, example (c) uses the overlay mechanism to to provide two *views* of the same social security number data: a "whole" view, and a 2-part (first 5 digits, last 4 digits) view.

1.3   Applications

In addition to facilitating program understanding, data abstraction recovery can also be used to facilitate certain common program transformations. For example, consider a scenario where employee IDs in example Fig. 1(a) must be expanded to accommodate an additional digit. Such *field expansion* scenarios are quite common. The guarded typing solution we infer helps identify variable occurrences that are affected by a potential expansion. For example, if we wish to expand the implicit "field" of DATA containing Eld, only those statements that have references to Eid or other type variables in the same union component as Eid (e.g., Salary) are affected. Note that the disjoint union information inferred by our technique identifies a smaller set of affected items than previous techniques (e.g., [7]) which do not infer this information.

A number of additional program maintenance and transformation tasks can be facilitated by guarded type inference, although details are beyond the scope of this paper. Such tasks include: separating code fragments into modules based on which fragments use which types (which is a notion of *cohesion*); porting from weakly-typed languages to object-oriented languages; refactoring data declarations to make them reflect better how the variables are used (e.g., the overlaid variables SSN and SSN-EXPANDED in the example in Fig. 1(c) may be collapsed into a single variable); and migrating persistent data access from flat files to relational databases.

1.4   Related Work

While previous work on recovering type abstractions from programs [6, 3, 10, 7] has addressed the problem of inferring atomic and record types, our technique adds the capability of inferring disjoint union types, with constrained atomic types serving as tags. To do this accurately, we use a novel *path sensitive* analysis technique, where value constraints distinguish abstract dataflow facts that are specific to distinct paths. Since the algorithm is flow-sensitive, it also allows distinct occurrences of the same variable to be assigned different types. To see the strengths of our approach, consider again the example in Fig. 1(a). The algorithm uses the predicate IF PAYEE-TYPE = 'E' to split the dataflow fact corresponding to PAY-REC into two facts, one for the "employee" case (PAYEE-TYPE = 'E') and the other for the "visitor" case (PAYEE-TYPE ≠ 'E'). As a result, the algorithm infers that DATA[8:11] (at one occurrence) stores a Salary while the DATA[10:13] stores a Stipend (at a different occurrence) even though these two memory intervals are overlapping. We are aware of no prior abstraction inference technique that is capable of making this distinction. Note that our approach can in many cases maintain correlations between values of variables, and hence correlate fragments of code that are not even controlled by predicates that have common variables. For example, our approach recognizes that statements 5 and

9 in Fig. 1(a) pertain to the "visitor" case, even though the controlling predicates for each statement do not share a common variable.

The flow-insensitive approach of [10] is able to infer certain subtyping relationships; these are similar in some respects to our union types. In particular, when a single variable is the target of assignments from different variables at different points, e.g., the variable PAY in statements 4 and 6 in Fig. 1(a), their approach infers that the types of the source variables are subtypes of the type of the target. Our approach yields similar information in this case. However, our technique uses path sensitivity to effectively identify subtyping relationships in additional cases; e.g., a supertype (in the form of a disjoint union) is inferred for PAY-REC in statement 1, even though this variable is explicitly assigned only once in the program.

Various approaches based on analysis techniques other than static type inference, e.g., concept analysis, dynamic analysis, and structural heuristics, have been proposed for the purpose of extracting logical data models (or aspects of logical data models) from existing code [1, 2, 4, 9]. Previous work in this area has not, to the best of our knowledge, addressed extraction of type abstractions analogous to our guarded types (in particular, extraction of union/tag information). However, much of this work is complementary in the sense that it recovers different classes of information (invariants, clusters, roles, etc.) that could be profitably combined with our types.

Our guarded types are *dependent types*, in the sense that they incorporate a notion of value constraint. While dependent types have been applied to a number of problems (see [11] for examples), we are unaware of any work that has used dependent types to recover data abstractions from legacy applications, or that combine structural inference with value flow information.

The rest of the paper is structured as follows. Section 2 specifies the guarded type language and notation. Section 3 presents our type inference algorithm. Following that, we present the correctness characterization for the guarded type system in Section 4, along with certain theorems concerning correct type solutions. We conclude the paper in Section 5 with a discussion on future work.

2   The Type System

Let $AtomicTypeVar = \cup_{i>0} V_i$ denote a set of type variables. A type variable belonging to V_i is said to have *length i*. We will use symbols α, β, γ, etc., (sometimes in subscripted form, as in α_i) to range over type variables. Type variables are also called atomic types.

As the earlier examples illustrated, often the specific value of certain *tag* variables indicate the type of certain other variables. To handle such idioms well, types in our type systems can capture information about the values of variables. We define a set of value constraints *ValueAbs* as follows, and use symbols c, d, c_1, d_2, etc., to range over elements of *ValueAbs*:

$$ValueAbs ::= s \mid !\{s_1, s_2, \ldots, s_k\}, \text{ where } s \text{ and each } s_i \text{ are } Strings$$

While the value constraint s is used to represent that a variable has the value s, the value constraint $!\{s_1, s_2, \ldots, s_k\}$ is used to represent that a variable has a value different from s_1 through s_k. In particular, the value constraint $!\{\}$ represents any possible value, and we will use the symbol $\top$ to refer to $!\{\}$.

We define a set of type expressions $\mathcal{TE}$, built out of type variables, and value constraints using *concatenation* and *union* operators, as follows:

$$\mathcal{TE} ::= (\textit{ValueAbs}, \textit{AtomicTypeVar}) \mid \mathcal{TE} \otimes \mathcal{TE} \mid \mathcal{TE} \oplus \mathcal{TE}$$

We refer to a type expression of the form $(\textit{ValueAbs}, \textit{AtomicTypeVar})$ as a *leaf* type-expression. We refer to a type expression containing no occurrences of the union operator '$\oplus$' as a *union-free* type expression.

We will use the notation $\alpha^{|i|}$ to indicate that variable α has length i, and the notation $c{:}\alpha^{|i|}$ to represent a leaf type-expression $(c, \alpha^{|i|})$. In contexts where there is no necessity to show the *ValueAbs* component we use the notation $\alpha^{|i|}$ to denote a leaf type-expression itself. Where there is no confusion we denote concatenation implicitly (without the $\otimes$ operator).

A *type mapping* for a given program is a function from variable occurrences in the program, denoted *VarOccurs*, to $\mathcal{TE}$.

3   Type Inference Algorithm

3.1   Introduction to Algorithm

Input: The input to our algorithm is a control flow graph, generated from the program and preprocessed as follows. All complex predicates (involving logical operators) are decomposed into simple predicates and appropriate control flow. Furthermore, predicates P of the form "X == s" or "X != s", where s is a constant string, are converted into a statement "Assume P" in the *true* branch and a statement "Assume $!P$" in the *false* branch. Other simple predicates are handled conservatively by converting them into no-op statements that contain references to the variables that occur in the predicate. The program has a single (structured) variable Mem (if necessary, a new variable is introduced that contains all of the program's variables as substructures or fields). We assume, without loss of generality, that a program has a single input file and a single output file.

Solution Computed by the Algorithm: For every statement S, the algorithm computes a set S.inType of union-free types (see Section 2), which describes the type of variable Mem before statement S. Specifically, the set $\{f_1, f_2, \cdots, f_k\}$, where each f_i is a union-free type, is the representation used by the algorithm for the type $f_1 \oplus f_2 \oplus \cdots \oplus f_k$. The algorithm represents each union-free type in right-associative normal form (i.e., as a sequence of leaf type-expressions). When the algorithm is finished each S.inType set contains the type of the variable Mem at the program point before statement S. Generating a type mapping for all variables from this is straightforward, and is based on the following characteristic of the computed solution: for each variable X that occurs in S and each union-free type f in S.inType, f contains a projection $f[X]$ (i.e., a subsequence of f, which itself is a sequence of leaf type-expressions) that begins (resp. ends) at the same offset position as X begins (resp. ends) within Mem. We omit the details of generating the type mapping due to space constraints.

Key Aspects of the Algorithm: We now describe the essential conceptual structure of our inference algorithm. The actual algorithm, which is presented in Figures 2 and 3, incorporates certain optimizations and, hence, has a somewhat different structure. Recall that READs and literal MOVEs (MOVE statements whose source operand is a constant string) are the only "origin" statements: i.e., these are the only statements that introduce new values during execution (other statements use values, or copy them, or write them to files). For each origin statement S, our algorithm maintains a set S.readType of union-free types, which represents the type of the values originating at this statement.

At the heart of our algorithm is an iterative, worklist-based, dataflow analysis that, given S.readType for every origin statement S, computes S1.inType for every statement S1 in the program. An element $\langle S, f \rangle$ in the worklist indicates that f belongs to S.inType. The analysis identifies how the execution of S transforms the type f into a type f' and propagates f' to the successors of S. We will refer to this analysis as the *inner loop analysis*.

The whole algorithm consists of an *outer loop* that infers S.readType (for every origin statement S) in an iterative fashion. Initially, the values originating at an origin statement S are represented by a single type variable α_S whose length is the same as that of the operand of S. In each iteration of the outer loop analysis, an inner loop analysis is used to identify how the values originating at statement S (described by the set S.readType) flow through the program. During this inner loop analysis, two situations (described below) identify a *refinement* to S.readType. When this happens, the inner loop analysis is (effectively) stopped, S.readType is refined as necessary, and the next iteration of the outer loop is started. The algorithm terminates when an instance of the inner loop analysis completes without identifying any further refinement to S.readType.

We now describe the two possible ways in which S.readType may be refined. The first type of refinement happens when the inner loop analysis identifies that there is a reference in a statement S2 to a *part* of a value currently represented by a type variable β. When this happens, the algorithm *splits* β into new variables of smaller lengths such that the portion referred to in S2 corresponds exactly to one of the newly obtained variables. More specifically, let S be the origin statement for β (i.e., S.readType includes some union-free type that includes β). Then, S.readType is refined by replacing β by a sequence $\beta_1\beta_2$ or a sequence $\beta_1\beta_2\beta_3$ as appropriate. The intuition behind splitting β is that the reference to the portion of β in S2 is an indication that β is really *not* an atomic type, but a structured type (that contains the β_i's as fields).

The second type of refinement happens when the inner loop analysis identifies that a value represented by a leaf type, say γ, may be compared for equality with a constant l. When this happens, the leaf type is *specialized* for constant l. Specifically, if the leaf type originates as part of a union-free type, say $\gamma\delta\rho$, in S.readType, then $\gamma\delta\rho$ is replaced by two union-free types $(l:\gamma_1)\delta_1\rho_1$ and

Procedure Main
    Initialize worklist to $\{\ \langle entry,\ \top : \alpha^{|m|}\rangle\}$, where *entry* is the entry statement of the program, α is a new type variable, and m is the size of memory. Initialize S.inType to ϕ for all statements S.
    for all statements S = READ Y **do** {X and Y are used to denote *variable occurrences* (see Sec. 1.1)}
        Create a new type variable $\alpha_S^{|l|}$, where l is the size of Y. Initialize S.readType to $\{\top : \alpha_S\}$.
    for all statements S = MOVE s TO Y, where s is a string literal **do**
        Create a new type variable $\alpha_S^{|l|}$, where l is the length of s (and of Y). From this point in the algorithm treat S as if it were the statement "READ Y". Initialize S.readType to $\{s : \alpha_S\}$.
    while worklist is not empty **do**
        Extract some $\langle S, t\rangle$ from worklist. Call Process(S, t).
Procedure Process(S : statement, ft : union-free type for Mem)
    for all variable occurrences X in S **do**
        if Subseq(ft, X) is undefined **then**
            Call Split(ft, X). Call Restart. **return**.
    if S = MOVE X TO Y **then**
        Call Propagate(Succ, Subst(ft, Y, Subseq(ft,X))), for all successors Succ of S.
    else if S = READ Y **then**
        for all union-free types ftY in S.readType **do**
            Call Propagate(Succ, Subst(ft, Y, ftY)), for all successors Succ of S.
    else if S = ASSUME X == s **then**
        Let ret = evalEquals(Subseq(ft,X), s).
        if ret = *true* **then**
            Call Propagate(Succ, ft), for all successors Succ of S.
        else if ret = *false* **then**
            do nothing {Subseq(ft,X) is *inconsistent* with s – hence no fact is propagated}
        else {ret is of the form (α, s_i)}
            Call Specialize(α, s_i). Call Restart. **return**.
    else if S = ASSUME X != s **then**
        Let ret = evalNotEquals(Subseq(ft, X), s).
        if ret = *true* **then**
            Call Propagate(Succ, ft), for all successors Succ of S.
        else {ret = *false*}
            do nothing {Subseq(ft,X) has the constant value s – hence no fact is propagated}
        else {ret is of the form (α, s_i)}
            Call Specialize(α, s_i). Call Restart. **return**.
Function Subseq(ft : union-free type for Mem, X : (portion of) program variable)
    if a sequence ftX of leaf type-expressions within ft begins (ends) at the same position within ft as X does within Mem **then return** ftX **else** *Undefined*
Function Subst(ft : union-free type for Mem, X : (portion of) program variable, ftX : union-free type)
{$|ft| = |Mem|$, $|ftX| = |X|$, and Subseq(ft, X) is defined. }
    Replace the subsequence Subseq(ft, X) within ft with ftX and return the resultant union-free type.
Procedure Propagate(S : statement, ft : union-free type for Mem)
    if $\langle S, ft\rangle \notin$ S.inType **then** Add $\langle S, ft\rangle$ to worklist, and to S.inType.
Procedure Restart
    for all READ statements S **do**
        for all union-free types ft_p in S.inType **do**
            add $\langle S, ft_p\rangle$ to the worklist

Fig. 2. Type inference algorithm – procedures Main, Process, Subseq, Subst, Propagate, and Restart

$(!l : \gamma_2)\delta_2\rho_2$ (consisting of new type variables) in S.readType. In the general case, repeated specializations can produce more complex value constraints (see Figures 2 and 3 for a complete description of specialization). The benefit of specializing a type by introducing copies is that variable occurrences in the *then* and *else* branches of IF statements cause the respective copies of the type to refined, thus improving precision.

    The algorithm infers a type mapping for every program. It always terminates, intuitively because the inner-loop analysis is monotonous, and because the mem-

Procedure Split(ft : union-free type for Mem, X : (portion of) program variable)

Let $a = \alpha^{|l|}$ be a leaf type-expr within ft and off be an offset within a such that the prefix or suffix of a bordering off occupies an interval within ft that is non-overlapping with the interval occupied by X within Mem. Create two new type variables $\alpha_1^{|l_1|}$ and $\alpha_2^{|l_2|}$, where $l_1 = $ off and $l_2 = l-$ off. Let S be the READ statement such that there exists a union-free type $ft_S \in$ S.readType such that a leaf type-expr $b = c{:}\alpha^{|l|}$ is in ft_S.
if c is a string s then
   Split s in to two strings s_1 and s_2 of lengths l_1 and l_2, respectively.
   Let $b_{split} = s_1{:}\alpha_1^{|l_1|} s_2{:}\alpha_2^{|l_2|}$.
else $\{c$ is of the form $!some\ set\}$
   Let $b_{split} = \top{:}\alpha_1^{|l_1|} \top{:}\alpha_2^{|l_2|}$.
Create a copy ft'_S of ft_S that is identical to ft_S except that b is replaced by b_{split}.
Call Replace(S, ft_S, $\{ft'_S\}$).

Procedure Specialize($\alpha^{|l|}$: type variable, s : string of length l)

Let S be the READ statement such that there exists a union-free type $ft_S \in$ S.readType such that a leaf type-expr $b = c{:}\alpha$ is in ft_S. Pre-condition: c is of the form !Q, where Q is a set that does not contain s. Create two new copies of ft_S, $ft1_S$ and $ft2_S$, such that each one is identical to ft_S except that it uses new type variable names. Replace the leaf type-expr corresponding to b in $ft1_S$ with $s{:}\alpha_1^{|l|}$, and the leaf type-expr corresponding to b in $ft2_S$ with $!(Q + \{s\}){:}\alpha_2^{|l|}$, where α_1 and α_2 are two new type variables. Call Replace(S, ft_S, $\{ft1_S, ft2_S\}$).

Procedure Replace(S : a READ statement, ft : a union-free type in S.readType, fts : a set of union-free types)

Set S.readType = S.readType − {ft} + fts.
for all all type variables α occurring in ft do
   Remove from S.inType, for all statements S, all union-free types that contain α. Remove from the worklist all facts $\langle Sa, fta\rangle$, where fta is a union-free type that contains α.

Procedure evalEquals(ft : union-free type, s : string of the same length as ft)

Say $ft = c_1{:}\alpha_1^{|l_1|} c_2{:}\alpha_2^{|l_2|} \ldots c_m{:}\alpha_m^{|l_m|}$.
Let $s_1, s_2, \ldots s_m$ be strings such that $s = s_1 s_2 \ldots s_m$ and s_i has length l_i, for all $1 \leq i \leq m$.
if for all $1 \leq i \leq m$: $c_i = s_i$ then
   return $true$ {ft's value is s}
else if for some $1 \leq i \leq m$: $c_i =!S$, where S is a set that contains s_i then
   return $false$ {ft is inconsistent with s}
else {ft is consistent with s − therefore, specialize ft}
   Let i be an integer such that $1 \leq i \leq m$ and c_i is !S, where S is a set that does not contain s_i.
   return (α_i, s_i).

Procedure evalNotEquals(ft : union-free type, s : string of the same length as ft)

Say $ft = c_1{:}\alpha_1^{|l_1|} c_2{:}\alpha_2^{|l_2|} \ldots c_m{:}\alpha_m^{|l_m|}$.
Let $s_1, s_2, \ldots s_m$ be strings such that $s = s_1 s_2 \ldots s_m$ and s_i has length l_i, for all $1 \leq i \leq m$.
if for all $1 \leq i \leq m$: $c_i = s_i$ then
   return $false$ {ft's value is equal to s}
else
   if $m > 1$ OR $m = 1$ and $c_1 =!(some\ set\ containing\ s_1)$ then return $true$ else return (α_1, s_1).

Fig. 3. Type inference algorithm − other procedures

ory requirement (and hence, the number of refinement steps) for any program is fixed. The actual algorithm described in Figures 2 and 3 differs from the above conceptual description as follows: Rather than perform an inner loop analysis from scratch in each iteration of the outer loop, results from the previous execution of the inner loop analysis that are still valid are reused. Therefore, the two loops are merged into a single loop.

3.2   Illustration of Algorithm Using Example in Figure 1(a)

Figure 4 illustrates a trace of the algorithm when applied to the example in Figure 1(a). Specifically, the figure illustrates (a subset of) the state of the

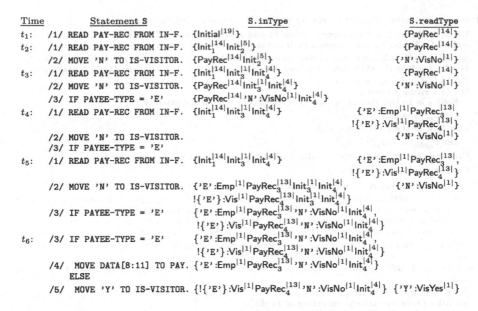

Fig. 4. Illustration of algorithm using example in Figure 1(a)

algorithm at selected seven points in time $(t_1, t_2, \ldots, t_7)$. The second column in the figure shows a statement S, the third column shows the value of S.inType, while the last column shows the value of S.readType if S is an origin statement.

Initially, a type variable is created for each origin statement. As explained in Section 1.1, a MiniCobol program has an implicit READ Mem at the beginning. Though we do not show this statement in Figure 4, it is an origin statement, with a corresponding type variable $\text{Initial}^{|19|}$, representing the initial state of memory, in its readType. In the figure /1/.inType represents the readType of the implicit READ. Similarly, /1/.readType contains $\text{PayRec}^{|14|}$, which is the initial type assigned by the algorithm to PAY-REC. (We use the notation /n/ to denote the statement labeled n in Figure 1(a).)

The first row shows the state at time point t_1, when the worklist contains the pair $\langle /1/, \text{Initial}^{|19|} \rangle$. Notice that statement 1 (READ PAY-REC) has a variable occurrence (PAY-REC) that corresponds to a portion (the first 14 bytes) of $\text{Initial}^{|19|}$, which is the type variable for the entire memory. Therefore, as described in Section 3.1, $\text{Initial}^{|19|}$ is "split" into $\text{Init}_1^{|14|}\text{Init}_2^{|5|}$. This split refinement updates the readType associated with the implicit initialization READ M and terminates the first inner loop analysis and initiates the second inner loop analysis.

In the next inner loop analysis, $\langle /1/, \text{Init}_1^{|14|}\text{Init}_2^{|5|} \rangle$ is placed in the worklist. Processing this pair requires no more splitting; therefore, $\text{Init}_1^{|14|}$ is replaced by $\text{PayRec}^{|14|}$, which is the type in /1/.readType. The resultant type $f = \text{PayRec}^{|14|}\text{Init}_2^{|5|}$ is placed in /2/.inType and is propagated to statement /2/ (by placing $\langle /2/, f \rangle$ in the worklist). The resulting algorithm state is shown in Figure 4 at time point t_2.

(In general, for any origin statement S that refers to a variable X, processing a pair $\langle S, f \rangle$ involves replacing the portion of f that corresponds to X ($f[X]$) with t_X, for each type t_X in S.readType, and propagating the resultant type(s) to the program point(s) that follow S.)

Next, the worklist item $\langle /2/, \mathsf{PayRec}^{|14|}\mathsf{Init}_2^{|5|}\rangle$ is processed. As statement /2/ refers to IS-VISITOR, which corresponds to a portion of $\mathsf{Init}_2^{|5|}$, this type variable is split into $\mathsf{Init}_3^{|1|}\mathsf{Init}_4^{|4|}$ and a new inner loop analysis is started.

This analysis propagates the newly split type through statements /1/ and /2/. The result is that the type $\mathsf{PayRec}^{|14|}$'N':$\mathsf{VisNo}^{|1|}\mathsf{Init}_4^{|4|}$ reaches /3/.inType. The resulting state is shown as time point t_3. Statement /3/ causes a split once again, meaning a new inner loop analysis starts.

The next inner loop analysis eventually reaches the state shown as time point t_4, where the algorithm is about to process the pair $\langle /3/, \ \mathsf{PayRec}_1^{|1|}\mathsf{PayRec}_2^{|13|}$'N': $\mathsf{VisNo}^{|1|}\mathsf{Init}_4^{|4|}\rangle$ from the worklist. Because PAYEE-TYPE, which is of type $\mathsf{PayRec}_1^{|1|}$, is compared with the constant 'E', the algorithm *specializes* the type variable $\mathsf{PayRec}_1^{|1|}$ by replacing, in its origin /1/.readType, its container type $\mathsf{PayRec}_1^{|1|}$ $\mathsf{PayRec}_2^{|13|}$ with two types $\{$'E' : $\mathsf{Emp}^{|1|}\mathsf{PayRec}_3^{|13|}$, !$\{$'E'$\}$: $\mathsf{Vis}^{|1|}\mathsf{PayRec}_4^{|13|}\}$. A new inner loop analysis now starts.

Using the predicate PAYEE-TYPE = 'E' to specialize /1/.readType is meaningful for the following reason: since statement /1/ is the *origin* of $\mathsf{PayRec}_1^{|1|}$ (the type of PAYEE-TYPE), the predicate implies that there are two kinds of records that are read in statement /1/, those with the value 'E' in the their PAYEE-TYPE field and those with some other value, and that these two types of records are handled differently by the program. The specialization of /1/.readType captures this notion.

Time point t_5 shows the algorithm state after the updated /1/.readType is propagated to /3/.inType by the new inner loop analysis. Notice that corresponding to the two types in /1/.readType, there are two types in /2/.inType and /3/.inType (previously there was only one type in those sets). The types in /3/.inType are (as shown): $f_1 = $ 'E' :$\mathsf{Emp}^{|1|}\mathsf{PayRec}_3^{|13|}$'N' :$\mathsf{VisNo}^{|1|}\mathsf{Init}_4^{|4|}$ and $f_2 =$!$\{$'E'$\}$:$\mathsf{Vis}^{|1|}\mathsf{PayRec}_4^{|13|}$'N' :$\mathsf{VisNo}^{|1|}\mathsf{Init}_4^{|4|}\}$.

The same inner loop analysis continues. Since f_1 and f_2 are now specialized wrt PAYEE-TYPE, the algorithm determines that type f_1 need only be propagated to the *true* branch of the IF predicate and that type f_2 need only be propagated to the *false* branch. The result is shown in time point t_6. This is an exhibition of path sensitivity, and it has two benefits. Firstly, the variables occurring in each branch cause only the appropriate type (f_1 or f_2) to be split (i.e, the two branches do not pollute each other). Secondly, the correlation between the values of the variables PAYEE-TYPE and IS-VISITOR is maintained, which enables the algorithm, when it later processes the final IF statement (statement /8/), to propagate only the type that went through the *true* branch of the first IF statement (i.e., f_1) to the *true* branch of statement /8/.

We finish our illustration of the algorithm at this point. The final solution, after the computed inType sets are converted into a type mapping for all variable occurrences is shown in Figure 1(a). Notice that each type in /1/.readType (shown to the right of Statement 1) reflects the structure inferred from only those variables that occur in the appropriate branch of the IF statements.

4   Type System: Semantics, Correctness, and Properties

In this section we define the notion of a "correct" type mapping, which we call a *typing solution*. We state certain properties of typing solutions, and illustrate that as a result typing solutions provide information about flow of values in the program. Note that a program may, in general, have a number of typing solutions; our type inference algorithm finds one of them.

4.1   An Instrumented Semantics for MiniCobol

Since we are interested in tracking the flow of values, we define an instrumented semantics where every input-file- and literal-character value is tagged with an unique integer that serves as its identifier. Let *IChar* denote the set of *instrumented characters*, and *IString* denote the set of instrumented strings (sequences of instrumented characters). Thus, every instrumented string *is* contains a character string, $charSeq(is)$, which is its actual value, as well as an *integer sequence*, $intSeq(is)$.

It is straightforward to define an instrumentation function that takes a program P and an input string I and returns $instr(P,I)$ – an instrumented program and an instrumented string – by converting every character in every string literal occurring in P as well as every character in I into an instrumented character with a unique id. Thus, $instr(P,I)$ contains a set of instrumented strings, one corresponding to I, and the others corresponding to the string literals in P.

We define a collecting instrumented semantics $\mathcal{M}$ with the following signature:

$$\mathcal{M} : Program \to String \to VarOccurs \to 2^{IString}$$

Given a program P and an input (*String*) I, the instrumented semantics executes the instrumented program and input $instr(P,I)$ much like in the standard semantics, except that every location now stores an instrumented character, and the instrumented program state is represented by an instrumented string. The collecting semantics $\mathcal{M}$ identifies the set of all values (*IStrings*) each variable occurrence in the program can take.

4.2   Semantics for Type Expressions

We can give type-expressions a meaning with the signature

$$\mathcal{T} : \mathcal{TE} \to (AtomicTypeVar \to 2^{IString}) \to 2^{IString}$$

as follows: this definition extends a given $\sigma : AtomicTypeVar \to 2^{IString}$ that maps a type variable to a set of values (instrumented strings) of the same length as the type variable, to yield the set of values represented by a $\mathcal{TE}$. Before defining $\mathcal{T}$, we define the meaning of value constraints via a function $\mathcal{C}$ which maps *ValueAbs* to 2^{String}:

$$\mathcal{C}(s) = \{s\}$$
$$\mathcal{C}(!\{s_1, s_2, \ldots, s_k\}) = \{s \mid s \in String \wedge s \notin \{s_1, s_2, \ldots, s_k\}\}$$
$$\mathcal{T}[c{:}\alpha]\sigma = \{v \mid v \in \sigma(\alpha) \wedge charSeq(v) \in \mathcal{C}(c)\}$$
$$\mathcal{T}[\tau_1 \otimes \tau_2]\sigma = \{i_1 @ i_2 \mid i_i \in \mathcal{T}[\tau_1]\sigma, i_2 \in \mathcal{T}[\tau_2]\sigma\}$$
$$(@ \text{ represents concatenation})$$
$$\mathcal{T}[\tau_1 \oplus \tau_2]\sigma = \mathcal{T}[\tau_1]\sigma \cup \mathcal{T}[\tau_2]\sigma$$

4.3   Correct Type Mappings

Definition 1 (Atomization). *An* atomization *of an instrumented string s is a list of instrumented strings whose concatenation yields s: i.e., a list* $[s_1, s_2, \cdots, s_k]$ *such that* $s_1 @ s_2 @ \cdots @ s_k = s$. *We refer to the elements of an instrumented string's atomization as* atoms.

Definition 2 (Atomic Type Mapping). *Given a program P and an input string I, an* atomic type mapping π *for (P,I) consists of an atomization of each instrumented string in instr(P,I), along with a function mapping every atom to a type variable. We denote the set of atoms produced by* π *by atoms(π), and denote the type variable assigned to an atom a by just* $\pi(a)$. *Also,* π^{-1} *is the inverse mapping, from type variables to sets of atoms, induced by* π.

Definition 3 (Correct Atomic Type Mapping). *Let* Γ *be a type mapping for a program P, and let* π *be an atomic type mapping for instr(P,I), where I is an input string. (Γ, π) is said to be* correct *for (P,I) if for every variable occurrence v in P,*

$$\mathcal{T}[\Gamma(v)]\pi^{-1} \supseteq \mathcal{M}[P](I)(v).$$

For example, consider the given program P and type mapping Γ_b in Figure 1(b), and let input string I = 'EID1234567'. In this case *instr*(P,I) contains two instrumented strings, 'SSN' from P and 'EID1234567' from I; we omit, for brevity, the (unique) integer tags on the characters, and use an overline to indicate their presence. A candidate atomization and atomic type mapping π_b for this example is ['$\overline{\text{SSN}}$': SSNTyp, '$\overline{\text{EID}}$':EIdTyp, '$\overline{1234567}$':EId]. (Γ_b, π_b) is correct for the given (P, I).

Definition 4 (Typing Solution). *A type mapping* Γ *for a program P is said to be* correct *if for every input I there exists an atomic type mapping* π *such that (Γ, π) is correct for (P,I). We will refer to a type mapping that is correct as a* typing solution.

Because π maps each atom in the input string and program to a single type variable, it follows that in a typing solution distinct type variables correspond to distinct domains of values (atoms).

4.4   Properties of Correct Type Mappings

Theorem 1 (Atoms are Indivisible). *If* (Γ, π) *is correct for (P,I), then during execution of P on I no variable occurrence ever contains a part of an atom without containing the whole atom.*

For example, recall the pair (Γ_b, π_b) mentioned earlier, and recall that it was correct for the program in Figure 1(b) with input string 'EID1234567'. Then, the above theorem asserts that no variable occurrence in the program ever takes on a value that contains a proper substring of any of the atoms $'\overline{\mathrm{SSN}}'$, $'\overline{\mathrm{EID}}'$, and $'\overline{1234567}'$ during execution of the program on the given input string. Thus, an atomization helps identify indivisible units of "values" that can be meaningfully used to talk about the "flow of values". The indivisibility also implies that in a typing solution each type variable corresponds to a *scalar* domain.

We now show how typing solutions tell us whether, for any two variable occurrences, there is *no* execution in which some instrumented value flows to both occurrences. The following definition formalizes this notion of "disjointedness".

Definition 5 (Disjointedness). *Two variable occurrences v and w in a program P are said to be disjoint if for any input I, for any* $s_1 \in \mathcal{M}[P](I)(v)$ *and* $s_2 \in \mathcal{M}[P](I)(w)$, s_1 *and* s_2 *do not have any instrumented character in common.*

We now introduce the notion of *overlap*, and then show how typing solutions yield information about disjointness.

Definition 6 (Overlap). *(a) Two value constraints* c_1 *and* c_2 *are said to overlap if they are not of the form* s_1 *and* s_2, *where* $s_1 \neq s_2$ *and not of the form* s_1 *and* $!S$, *where* $s_1 \in S$. *(b) Two leaf type-expressions* $c_1 : \alpha_1$ *and* $c_2 : \alpha_2$ *are said to overlap if* $\alpha_1 = \alpha_2$ *and* c_1 *and* c_2 *overlap.*

Theorem 2 (Typing Solutions Indicate Disjointedness). *Let* Γ *be a typing solution for a program P and let v and w be two variable occurrences in P. If* $\Gamma(v)$ *and* $\Gamma(w)$ *have no overlapping leaf type-expressions, then v and w are strongly disjoint.*

Consider the example program and typing solution in Figure 1(a). The two occurrences of PAY in lines 4 and 6, respectively, have non-overlapping types (Salary and Stipend, respectively). Theorem 2 thus tells us that these two occurrences are disjoint (even though they refer to the same variable). On the other hand each of these two occurrences is *non-disjoint* with the occurrence of PAY-REC in line 1; this is because the type expression assigned to the occurrence of PAY-REC in line 1 contains both Salary and Stipend.

5   Future Work

This paper describes an approach for inferring several aspects of logical data models such as atomic types, record structure based on usage of variables in the code, and guarded disjoint unions. In the future we plan to work on inferring additional desirable aspects of logical data models such as associations between types (e.g., based on foreign keys).

Within the context of the approach described in this paper, future work includes expanding upon the range of idioms that programmers use to implement union types that the algorithm addresses, expanding the power of the type system and algorithm, e.g., by introducing more expressive notions of value constraints, handling more language constructs (e.g., arrays, procedures), improving the efficiency of the algorithm, and generating "factored" types in the algorithm instead of sets of union-free types (e.g., $\alpha(\beta \oplus \gamma)\delta$, instead of $\{\alpha\beta\delta, \alpha\gamma\delta\}$).

References

1. G. Canfora, A. Cimitile, and G. A. D. Lucca. Recovering a conceptual data model from cobol code. In *Proc. 8th Intl. Conf. on Softw. Engg. and Knowledge Engg. (SEKE '96)*, pages 277–284. Knowledge Systems Institute, 1996.
2. B. Demsky and M. Rinard. Role-based exploration of object-oriented programs. In *Proc. 24th Intl. Conf. on Softw. Engg.*, pages 313–324. ACM Press, 2002.
3. P. H. Eidorff, F. Henglein, C. Mossin, H. Niss, M. H. Sorensen, and M. Tofte. Annodomini: from type theory to year 2000 conversion tool. In *Proc. 26th ACM SIGPLAN-SIGACT Symp. on Principles of Programming Languages*, pages 1–14. ACM Press, 1999.
4. M. D. Ernst, J. Cockrell, W. G. Griswold, and D. Notkin. Dynamically discovering likely program invariants to support program evolution. In *Proc. 21st Intl. Conf. on Softw. Engg.*, pages 213–224. IEEE Computer Society Press, 1999.
5. D. Jackson. Alloy: A lightweight object modelling notation. *ACM Transactions on Software Engineering and Methodology*, 11(2):256–290, 2002.
6. R. O'Callahan and D. Jackson. Lackwit: a program understanding tool based on type inference. In *Proc. 19th intl. conf. on Softw. Engg.*, pages 338–348. ACM Press, 1997.
7. G. Ramalingam, J. Field, and F. Tip. Aggregate structure identification and its application to program analysis. In *Proc. 26th ACM SIGPLAN-SIGACT Symp. on Principles of Programming Languages*, pages 119–132. ACM Press, 1999.
8. J. Rumbaugh, I. Jacobson, and G. Booch. *The Unified Modeling Language Reference Manual (2nd Edition)*. Addison-Wesley Professional, 2004.
9. A. van Deursen and T. Kuipers. Identifying objects using cluster and concept analysis. In *Proc. 21st Intl. Conf. on Softw. Engg.*, pages 246–255. IEEE Computer Society Press, 1999.
10. A. van Deursen and L. Moonen. Understanding COBOL systems using inferred types. In *Proc. 7th Intl. Workshop on Program Comprehension*, pages 74–81. IEEE Computer Society Press, 1999.
11. H. Xi. *Dependent Types in Practical Programming*. PhD thesis, Carnegie-Mellon University, 1998.

A Note on On-the-Fly Verification Algorithms*

Stefan Schwoon and Javier Esparza

Institut für Formale Methoden der Informatik, Universität Stuttgart
{schwoosn, esparza}@informatik.uni-stuttgart.de

Abstract. The automata-theoretic approach to LTL verification relies on an algorithm for finding accepting cycles in a Büchi automaton. Explicit-state model checkers typically construct the automaton "on the fly" and explore its states using depth-first search. We survey algorithms proposed for this purpose and identify two good algorithms, a new algorithm based on nested DFS, and another based on strongly connected components. We compare these algorithms both theoretically and experimentally and determine cases where both algorithms can be useful.

1 Introduction

The model-checking problem for finite-state systems and linear-time temporal logic (LTL) is usually reduced to checking the emptiness of a Büchi automaton, i.e. the product of the system and an automaton for the negated formula [24]. Various strategies exist for reducing the size of the automaton. For instance, *symbolic* model checking employs data structures that compactly represent large sets of states. This strategy combines well with breadth-first search, leading to solutions whose worst-case time is essentially $\mathcal{O}(n^2)$ or $\mathcal{O}(n \log n)$, if n is the size of the product. A survey of symbolic emptiness algorithms can be found in [8].

Explicit-state model checkers, on the other hand, construct the product automaton 'on the fly', i.e. while searching the automaton. Thus, the model checker may be able to find a counterexample without ever constructing the complete state space. This technique can be combined with partial order methods [18, 15] to reduce the state-explosion effect. The best known on-the-fly algorithms use depth-first-search (DFS) strategies to explore the state space; their running times are linear in the size of the product (i.e. the number of states plus the number of transitions). These algorithms can be partitioned into two classes:

Nested DFS, originally proposed by Courcoubetis et al [5], conducts a first search to find and sort the accepting states. A second search, interleaved with the first, checks for cycles around accepting states. Holzmann et al's modification of this algorithm [15] is widely regarded as the state-of-the-art algorithm for

---

* This work is supported by EPSRC Grant GR/93346 (*An Automata-theoretic Approach to Software Model Checking*) and the DFG project *Algorithms for Software Model Checking*.

N. Halbwachs and L. Zuck (Eds.): TACAS 2005, LNCS 3440, pp. 174–190, 2005.

on-the-fly model checking and is used in Spin [14]. The advantage of this algorithm is its memory efficiency. On the downside, it tends to produce rather long counterexamples. Recently, Gastin et al [10] proposed two modifications to [5]: one to find counterexamples faster, and another to find the minimal counterexample. Another problem with Nested DFS is that its extension to generalised Büchi automata creates significant additional effort, see Subsection 5.2.

The other class can be characterised as *SCC-based algorithms*. Clearly, a counterexample exists if and only if there is a strongly connected component (SCC) that is reachable from the initial state and contains at least one accepting state and at least one transition. SCCs can be identified using, e.g., Tarjan's algorithm [22]. Tarjan's algorithm can easily accomodate generalised Büchi automata, but uses much more memory than Nested DFS. Couvreur [6] and Geldenhuys and Valmari [11] have proposed modifications of Tarjan's algorithm, whose common feature is that they recognize an accepting cycle as soon as all transitions on the cycle are explored. Thus, the search may explore a smaller part of the automaton and tends to produce shorter counterexamples.

In this paper, we survey existing algorithms of both classes and discuss their relations to each other. This discussion leads to the following contributions:

- We propose an improved Nested-DFS algorithm. The algorithm finds counterexamples with less exploration than [15] and [10] and needs less memory.
- We analyse a simplified version of Couvreur's algorithm [6] and show that it has advantages over the more recently proposed algorithm from [11]. We make several other interesting observations about this algorithm that were missed in [6]. With these, we reinforce the argument made in [11], i.e. that SCC-based algorithms are competitive with Nested DFS.
- As a byproduct, we propose an algorithm for finding SCCs, which, to the best of our knowledge, has not been considered previously. This algorithm can be used to improve model checkers for CTL.
- Having identified one dominating algorithm in each class, we discuss their relative advantages for specialised classes of automata. It is known that model checking can be done more efficiently for automata with certain structural properties [2]. Our observations sharpen the results from [2] and provide a guideline on which algorithms should be used in which case.
- We suggest a modification to the way partial-order reduction can be combined with depth-first search.
- Finally, we illustrate our findings by experimental results.

We proceed as follows: Section 2 establishes the notation used in the algorithms. Sections 3 and 4 discuss nested and SCC-based algorithms, respectively. Section 5 takes a closer look at the pros and cons of both classes, while Section 6 discusses the combination with partial order methods. Section 7 reports some experiments, and Section 8 contains the conclusions and an open question.

A slightly extended version of this paper is available as a technical report [19].

2   Notation

The accepting cycle problem can be stated in many different variants. For now, we concentrate on its most basic form in order to present the algorithms in a simple and uniform manner. Thus, our problem is as follows:

Let $B = (S, T, A, s_0)$, where $T \subseteq S \times S$, be a *Büchi automaton* (or just *automaton*) with *states* S and *transitions* T. We call $s_0 \in S$ the *initial state*, and $A \subseteq S$ the set of *accepting states*. A *path* is a sequence of states $s_1 \cdots s_k$, $k \geq 1$, such that $(s_i, s_{i+1}) \in T$ for all $1 \leq i < k$. Let d_B denote the length of the longest path of B in which all states are different. A *cycle* is a path with $s_1 = s_k$; the cycle is *accepting* if it contains a state from A. An *accepting run* (or *counterexample*) is a path $s_0 \cdots s_k \cdots s_l$, $l > k$, where $s_k \cdots s_l$ forms an accepting cycle. The *cycle detection problem* is to determine whether a given automaton B has an accepting run.

Extensions of the problem, such as generalised Büchi automata, production of counterexamples (as opposed to merely reporting that one exists), partial-order reduction, and exploiting additional knowledge about the automaton are discussed partly along with the algorithms, and partly in Sections 5 and 6.

All algorithms presented below use depth-first-search strategies and are designed to work 'on the fly', i.e. B can be constructed during the search. In the presentation of all algorithms, we make the following assumptions:

- Initially, the state s_0 is known.
- Given a state s, we can compute the set $post(s) := \{ t \mid (s, t) \in T \}$.
- For each state s, $s \in A$ can be decided (in constant time).
- The statement **report cycle** ends the algorithm with a positive answer. When the algorithm ends normally, no accepting run is assumed to exist.

3   Algorithms Based on Nested DFS

The first Nested-DFS algorithm was proposed by Courcoubetis, Vardi, Wolper, and Yannakakis [5]. It can be said to consist of a *blue* and a *red* search procedure, both of which visit any state at most once. It requires two bits per state, a 'blue' and a 'red' bit. We assume that when a state is generated by *post* for the first time, both bits are false. The algorithm is shown in Figure 1. Procedure *dfs_blue* conducts a depth-first search and sets the blue bit in all visited states. When the search from an accepting state s finishes, *dfs_red* is invoked. This procedure sets the red bit in all states it encounters and avoids visiting states twice. If *dfs_red* finds that s can be reached from itself, an accepting run is reported.

3.1   Known Improvements on Nested DFS

The algorithm from [5] can be improved to find counterexamples earlier under certain circumstances. Consider the automaton shown in Figure 2 (a). To find the counterexample, the blue DFS must first reach the accepting state s_1, and then the red DFS needs to go from s_1 to s_0 and back again to s_1, even though an

```
1   procedure nested_dfs ()        10   procedure dfs_blue (s)
2     call dfs_blue(s0);           11     s.blue := true;
                                   12     for all t ∈ post(s) do
3   procedure dfs_red (s)          13       if ¬t.blue then
4     s.red := true;               14         call dfs_blue(t);
5     for all t ∈ post(s) do       15     if s ∈ A then
6       if ¬t.red then             16       seed := s;
7         call dfs_red(t);         17       call dfs_red(s);
8       else if t = seed then
9         report cycle;
```

Fig. 1. The Nested-DFS algorithm from [5]

(a)   (b)

Fig. 2. Two examples for improvements on the Nested-DFS algorithm

accepting run is already completed at s_0. A modification suggested by Holzmann, Peled, and Yannakakis [15] eliminates this situation: As soon as a red DFS initiated at s finds a state t such that t is on the call stack of the blue DFS, the search can be terminated, because t is obviously guaranteed to reach s. To check in constant time whether a state is on the call stack, one additional bit per state is used (or, alternatively, a hash table containing the states on the stack).

Another improvement on Nested DFS was recently published by Gastin, Moro, and Zeitoun [10], who suggested the following additions:

1. The blue DFS can detect an accepting run if it finds an edge back to an accepting state that is currently on the call stack. Consider Figure 2 (b): in [15], both the blue and the red procedure need to search the whole automaton to find the accepting cycle. With the suggestion in [10], the cycle is found without entering the red search. We note that this improvement can be slightly generalized to include the case where the *current* search state is accepting and finds an edge back to a state on the stack.
2. States are marked *black* during the blue DFS if they have been found not to be part of an accepting run. Thus, the red search can ignore black states. However, the computational effort required to make states black is asymptotically as big as the effort expended in the red search: one additional visit to every successor state. Moreover, the effort is necessary for *every* blue state, even if the state is never going to be touched by the red search. Therefore, the use of black states is not necessarily an improvement.[1]

The algorithm from [10] requires three bits per state.

---

[1] [10] also proposes an algorithm for finding minimal counterexamples, which has exponential worst-time complexity, and for which the black search can provide useful preprocessing. As the scope of this paper is on linear-time algorithms, this matter is not considered here.

3.2   A New Proposal

We now formulate a version of Nested DFS that includes the improvements for early detection of cycles from [15, 10], but without the extra memory requirements. This is based on the observation that, out of the eight cases that could be encoded in [15] with the three bits *blue*, *red*, and *stack*, four can never happen:

- A state with its *blue* and *red* bit false cannot have its *stack* bit set to true.
- By induction, we show that no state can have its *red* bit set to true and its *blue* bit set to false, independently of its *stack* bit. When the red search is initiated, all successors of *seed* have appeared in the blue search. Later, if the red search encounters a blue state t with non-blue successor u, we can conclude that t has not yet terminated its blue search. Thus, t must be on the call stack, and the improvement of [15] will cause the red search to terminate before considering u.
- The case where a state has both its *red* and *stack* bit set does not have not be considered: With the improvement from [15], the red search terminates as soon as it encounters a state with the *stack* bit.

The remaining four cases can be encoded with two bits. The algorithm in Figure 3 assigns one of four colours to each state:

- *white*: We assume that states are white when they are first generated by a call to *post*.
- *cyan*: A state whose blue search has not yet terminated.
- *blue*: A state that has finished its blue search and has not yet been reached in a red search.
- *red*: A state that has been considered in both the blue and the red search.

The seed state of the red search is treated specially: It remains cyan during the red search and is made red afterwards. Thus, it matches the check at line 18, and the need for a *seed* variable is eliminated. Like in the other algorithms based on Nested DFS, the counterexample can be obtained from the call stack at the time when the cycle is reported.

```
 1  procedure new_dfs ()
 2      call dfs_blue(s0);

 3  procedure dfs_blue (s)
 4      s.colour := cyan;
 5      for all t ∈ post(s) do
 6          if t.colour = cyan
 7              ∧ (s ∈ A ∨ t ∈ A) then
 8              report cycle;
 9          else if t.colour = white then
10              call dfs_blue(t);
11      if s ∈ A then
12          call dfs_red(s);
13          s.colour := red;
14      else
15          s.colour := blue;

16  procedure dfs_red (s)
17      for all t ∈ post(s) do
18          if t.colour = cyan then
19              report cycle;
20          else if t.colour = blue then
21              t.colour := red;
22              call dfs_red(t);
```

Fig. 3. New Nested-DFS algorithm

4   Algorithms Based on SCCs

The algorithms in this class are based on the notion of *strongly-connected components* (SCCs). Formally, an SCC is a maximal subset of states C such that for every pair $s, t \in C$ there is a path from s to t and vice versa. The first state of C entered during a depth-first search is called the *root* of C. An SCC is called *trivial* if it consists of a single state, and if this single state does not have a transition to itself. An accepting run exists if and only if there exists a non-trivial SCC that contains at least one accepting state and whose states are reachable from s_0. In the following we present the main ideas behind three SCC-based algorithms. These explanations are not intended as a full proof, but should serve to explain the relationship between the algorithms.

Tarjan [22] first developed an algorithm for identifying SCCs in linear time in the size of the automaton. His algorithm uses depth-first search and is based on the following concepts: Every state is annotated with a *DFS number* and a *lowlink number*. DFS numbers are assigned in the order in which states appear in the DFS; we assume that the DFS number is 0 when a state is first generated by *post*. The lowlink number of a state s is the lowest DFS number of a state t in the same SCC as s such that t was reachable from s via states that were not yet explored when the search reached s. Moreover, Tarjan maintains a set called *Current* to which states are added when they are first detected by the DFS. A state is removed from *Current* when its SCC is completely explored, i.e. when the DFS of its root concludes. *Current* is represented twice, as a bit-array and as a stack. The following properties hold:

(1) *Current* contains only states from partially explored SCCs whose roots are still on the call stack. Thus, every state in *Current* has a path to a state on the call stack (e.g., its root).
(2) Therefore, if t is in *Current* when the DFS at state s detects a transition to t, t has a path to its root, from there to s, so both are in the same SCC.
(3) Roots have the lowest DFS number within their SCC and are the only states whose DFS number equals their lowlink number.
(4) A root r is the first state of its SCC to be added to *Current*. At the time when the DFS at r concludes, all other SCCs reachable from r have been completely explored and removed from *Current*. Thus, the nodes belonging to the SCC can be identified by removing nodes from the stack representation of *Current* until r is found. At the same time, one can check whether the SCC is non-trivial and contains an accepting state.

For the purpose of finding accepting cycles, the use of Tarjan's algorithm has several drawbacks compared to Nested-DFS algorithms: It uses more memory per state (one bit plus two integers as opposed to two bits), and a larger stack: In Nested DFS, the stack may grow as large as d_B whereas in Tarjan's algorithm *Current* may at worst contain all states, even if d_B is small. Moreover, it may take longer to find a counterexample, because an SCC cannot be checked for acceptance until itself and all SCCs reachable from it have been completely explored. In Nested DFS, a red search may be started even before an SCC has

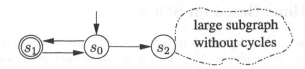

Fig. 4. Nested DFS may outperform Tarjan's algorithm on this automaton

been completely explored. Figure 4 illustrates this: Nested-DFS algorithms may find the cycle $s_0 s_1 s_0$ and stop without examining the right part of the automaton provided that edge (s_0, s_1) is explored before (s_0, s_2); Tarjan's algorithm is bound to explore the whole automaton regardless of the order of exploration.

Recent developments, however, have shown that Tarjan's algorithm can be modified to eliminate or reduce some of these disadvantages, and that SCC-based algorithms can be competitive to Nested DFS. Two modifications are presented below. Their common feature is that they can detect a counterexample as soon as all transitions along an accepting run have been explored. In other words, their amount of exploration is *minimal* (i.e., minimal among all DFS algorithms that follow the search order provided by *post*).

4.1   The Geldenhuys-Valmari Algorithm

The algorithm recently proposed by Geldenhuys and Valmari [11] extends Tarjan's algorithm with the following idea: Suppose that the DFS starts exploring an accepting state s. At this point, all states in *Current* (including s) have a path to s (property (1)). Moreover, the states that are in *Current* at this point can be characterised by the fact that their lowlink number is less than or equal to the DFS number of s. Thus, to find a cycle including s, we need to find a state with such a lowlink number in the DFS starting at s. To this end, the DFS in [11] always keeps track of the deepest accepting state currently in the DFS stack. When a cycle is found, the search is terminated immediately.

This algorithm requires slightly more memory than Tarjan's because it must remember the deepest accepting state for each position in the stack. However, if a counterexample exists, the algorithm may find it earlier than Nested DFS.

4.2   Couvreur's Algorithm

Couvreur [6] proposed (in his own words) "a simple variation of the Tarjan algorithm" that solves the accepting cycle problem on generalised automata (see Subsection 5.2), but where acceptance conditions are associated with transitions. This algorithm has the advantage of detecting counterexamples early, as in [11]. Here, we translate and simplify the algorithm for the problem stated in Section 2 and then show that it has a number of additional benefits that were not considered in [6]. The following ideas, which improve upon Tarjan's algorithm, are relevant for the algorithm:

```
1   procedure couv ()                    12   for all t ∈ post(s) do
2     count := 0; Roots := ∅;            13     if t.dfsnum = 0 then
3     call couv_dfs(s₀);                 14       call couv_dfs(t);
                                         15     else if t.current then
4   procedure remove (s):                16       repeat
5     if ¬s.current then return;         17         u := pop(Roots);
6     s.current := false;                18         if u ∈ A then report cycle;
7     for all t ∈ post(s) do remove(t);  19       until u.dfsnum ≤ t.dfsnum;
                                         20       push(Roots, u);
8   procedure couv_dfs(s):               21     if top(Roots) = s then
9     count := count + 1;                22       pop(Roots);
10    s.dfsnum := count;                 23       call remove(s);
11    push(Roots, s); s.current := true;
```

Fig. 5. Translation of Couvreur's algorithm

- *The stack representation of Current is unnecessary.* By property (4), when the DFS of a root r finishes, all other SCCs reachable from the root have already been removed from *Current*. Therefore, the SCC of r consists of all nodes that are reachable from r and still in *Current*. These can be found by a second DFS starting at r, using the bit-array representation of *Current*.
- *Lowlink numbers can be avoided.* The purpose of lowlink numbers is to test whether a given state is a root. However, the DFS number already contains partial knowledge about the lowlink: it is greater than or equal to it. Couvreur's algorithm maintains a stack (called *Roots*) of potential roots to which a state is added when it appears on the call stack. Recall property (2): when the DFS sees a transition from s to t after the DFS of t, and t is still in *Current*, then s and t are in the same SCC. A root has the lowest DFS number in its SCC. Thus, all states in the call stack with a DFS number greater than that of t cannot be roots and are removed from *Roots*. Moreover, these states are part of a cycle around s; if one of them is accepting, then a counterexample exists. Finally, a node r can now be identified as a root by checking whether r is still in *Roots* when its DFS finishes. At this point, r can also be removed from *Roots*.

Figure 5 presents the algorithm. The transformation from the algorithm in [6] is quite straightforward, even though a slightly different problem is solved.

The issue of generating an actual counterexample was not considered in [6]. Fortunately, adding this is relatively easy: At line 18, the call stack plus the transition (s, t) provide a path from s_0 via u to t. To complete the cycle, we need a path from t to u, which can be found with a simple DFS within the non-removed states starting at u (the *current* bit can be abused to avoid exploring states twice in this DFS). Alternatively, we could search for *any* state on the call stack of the DFS whose number is at most $t.dfsnum$, which may lead to slightly smaller counterexamples, but requires an additional '*on_stack*' bit for each state.

4.3   Comparison

The algorithms presented in Subsections 4.1 and 4.2 report a counterexample as soon as all the transitions belonging to it have been explored. Thus, they find the same counterexamples with the same amount of exploration. However, Couvreur's algorithm has several advantages to those of both Tarjan and Geldenhuys and Valmari [11]:

- It needs just one integer per state instead of two.
- *Current* is a *superset* of the call stack and contains at worst all the states ([11] mentions the use of stack space as a drawback). The *Roots* stack, however, is only a *subset* of the call stack. This eliminates one disadvantage of SCC-based algorithms when compared to Nested DFS.
- Couvreur's algorithm can be easily extended to multiple acceptance conditions (see Subsection 5.2). It is not clear how such an extension could be done with the algorithm of Geldenhuys and Valmari.

Note that the first two advantages are not pointed out in [6]. It seems that this has caused Couvreur's algorithm to remain largely unappreciated (as evidenced by the fact that [11] does not seem to be aware of [6]).

On the downside, Couvreur's algorithm may need two calls to *post* per state whereas the others need only one.

4.4   On Identifying Strongly Connected Components

The algorithm in Figure 5 can be easily transformed into an algorithm for identifying the SCCs of the automaton. All that is required is to remove line 18 and to output the nodes as they are processed in the *remove* procedure.

To the best of our knowledge, this algorithm is superior to previously known algorithms for identifying SCCs: The advantages over Tarjan's algorithm [22] have already been pointed out. Gabow [9] avoids computing lowlink numbers, but still uses the stack representation of *Current*. Nuutila and Soisalon-Soininen [17] reduce stack usage in special cases only, and still use lowlink numbers. Sharir's algorithm [20] has none of these drawbacks, but requires reversed edges. Surprisingly, the issue of detecting SCCs was not considered in [6].

Compared to the algorithms that use a stack representation of *Current*, the new algorithm explores edges twice, whereas the others explore edges only once. This might be a disadvantage if the calls to *post* are computationally expensive. However, the algorithm remains linear in the size of B, and the memory savings can be significant (see Section 7).

In the model-checking world, SCC decomposition is used in CTL for computing the semantics of the *EG* operator [4] or for adding fairness constraints [3]. Therefore, this algorithm can benefit explicit-state CTL model checkers.

5   Nested DFS Versus SCC-Based Algorithms

In Sections 3 and 4 we have shown that the new Nested-DFS algorithm (Figure 3) and the modification of Couvreur's algorithm (Figure 5) dominate the other algo-

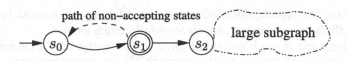

Fig. 6. SCC-based algorithms outperform Nested DFS on this automaton

rithms in their class. Of these two, the nested algorithm is more memory-efficient: While the difference in stack usage, where the SCC algorithm consumes at most twice as much as the nested algorithm, is relatively harmless, the difference in memory needed *per state* can be more significant: the nested algorithm needs only two bits, the SCC algorithm needs an integer.

Nested DFS therefore remains the best alternative for combination with the bitstate hashing technique [13], which allows to analyse very large systems while potentially missing parts of the state space. If traditional, lossless hashing techniques are used, the picture is different: State descriptors even for small systems often include dozens of bytes, so that an extra integer becomes negligible. In addition, this small disadvantage of the SCC algorithm is offset by its earlier detection of counterexamples: the SCC algorithm always detects a counterexample as soon as all transitions on a cycle have been explored (i.e. with minimal exploration), while the nested algorithm may take arbitrarily longer.

For instance, assume that in the automaton shown in Figure 6, the path from s_1 back to s_0 is explored before the subgraph starting at s_2. Then, the SCC algorithm reports a counterexample as soon as the cycle is closed, without visiting s_2 and the states beyond. The nested search, however, needs to explore the large subgraph before the second DFS can start at s_1 and detect the cycle.

In Subsection 5.1, we examine how this advantage of the SCC-based algorithm is related to structural properties of the automaton. It turns out that for an important class of automata (namely *weak* automata), nested DFS avoids the disadavantage (and can in fact be replaced by a simple, non-nested DFS).

5.1   Exploiting Structural Properties

In [2], Černá and Pelánek defined the following structural hierarchy of Büchi automata (see also [16, 1]):

- Any Büchi automaton is an *unrestricted* automaton.
- A Büchi automaton is *weak* if and only if its states can be partitioned into sets $Q_1, \ldots, Q_n$ such that each Q_i, $1 \leq i \leq n$ is either contained in A or disjoint from it; moreover, if there is a transition from a state in Q_i to a state in Q_j, then $i \leq j$.
- A weak automaton is *terminal* if and only if the partitions containing accepting states have no transitions into other partitions.

The automata encountered in LTL model checking are the products of a system and a Büchi automaton specifying some (un)desirable property. Clearly, if the specification automaton is weak or terminal, then so is its product with the system. Thus, the type of the product can be safely approximated by the type of the specification automaton, which is usually much smaller.

Accepting runs of weak automata have the property that all states in their cycle part (which all belong to the same SCC) are accepting states. We now prove that the nested DFS algorithm (Figure 3) discovers an accepting run in procedure *blue_dfs* as soon as all of its transitions have been explored. Assume that no counterexample has been completely explored so far, that the blue DFS is currently at state s, and that (s, t) is the last transition in a counterexample that has not been explored. We can assume that (s, t) is in the cycle part of the counterexample (otherwise a complete reachable cycle would have been explored before, violating the assumption), so both s and t must be accepting states. Then, the blue DFS will report a counterexample at line 8 if and only if t is cyan when (s, t) is explored. We prove that t is cyan by contradiction: Being an accepting state, t cannot be blue; if t is white, then discovering (s, t) will not close a cycle; and if t is red, then by construction t is not part of a counterexample.

A consequence of this is that the nested algorithm, when processing a weak automaton, *always* finds cycles in line 8 (when they exist). Thus, when examining weak automata, the algorithm of Figure 3 can be improved by disabling the red search (if an accepting state reaches line 11, it is not part of an accepting cycle, because such a cycle would have been found during the blue search). Thus, we end up with a simple, non-nested DFS. Černá and Pelánek [2] previously proposed simple DFS on weak systems because of its efficiency; we point out that it also finds counterexamples with minimal exploration.

Weak automata are important because they can represent (the negation of) many 'popular' properties, e.g. invariants ($\mathbf{G}\,p$), progress ($\mathbf{G}\,\mathbf{F}\,p$), or response ($\mathbf{G}(p \rightarrow \mathbf{F}\,q)$). In fact, [2] claims that 95% of the formulas in a well-known specification patterns database lead to weak automata, and propose a method that generates weak automata for a suitably restricted subset of LTL formulas. Somenzi and Bloem [21] propose an algorithm for unrestricted formulas that attempts to produce automata that are 'as weak as possible'.

For terminal automata, [2] proposes to use simple reachability checks. For correctness, this requires the assumption that every state has a successor.

For unrestricted automata, the new nested-DFS algorithm can be combined with the changes proposed by Edelkamp et al [7], which further exploit structural properties of the system and allow to combine the approach with guided search.

5.2   Handling Generalised Büchi Automata

The accepting cycle problem can also be posed for *generalised* Büchi automata, in which A is replaced by a *set of* acceptance sets $\mathcal{A} \subseteq 2^S$. Here, a cycle is accepting if it intersects all sets $A \in \mathcal{A}$. Generalised Büchi automata arise naturally during the translation of LTL into Büchi automata (see, e.g., [12, 6]). Moreover, fairness constraints of the form $\mathbf{G}\,\mathbf{F}\,p$ can be efficiently encoded with acceptance sets. Generalised Büchi automata can be translated into (normal) Büchi automata, but checking them directly may lead to more efficient procedures. The following paragraph briefly reviews the solutions proposed for this method:

Let n be the number of acceptance sets in $\mathcal{A}$. For nested DFS, Courcoubetis et al [5] proposed a method with at worst $2n$ traversals of each state. Tauriainen's solution [23] reduces the number of traversals to $n + 1$. Couvreur's algorithm [6] works directly on generalised automata; the number of traversals is at most 2, independently of n. This is accomplished by implementing the elements of *Roots* as tuples (*state*, *set*), where *set* contains the acceptance sets that intersect the SCC of *state*; these sets are merged during pop sequences.

Thus, Couvreur's algorithm has a clear edge over nested DFS in the generalised case: It can detect accepting runs with minimal exploration *and* with less runtime overhead.

5.3   Summary

The question of optimised algorithms for specialised classes of Büchi automata has been addressed before in [2], as pointed out in Subsection 5.1. Likewise, [6] and [11] previously raised the point that SCC-based algorithms may be faster than nested DFS, but without addressing the issue of *when* this was the case. Our results show that these issues are related, which leads to the following picture:

- For weak automata, simple DFS should be used by default: it is simpler and more memory-efficient than SCC algorithms *and* finds counterexamples with minimal exploration.
- For unrestricted automata, an SCC-based algorithm should be used unless bit hashing is required. The memory overhead of Couvreur's algorithm (Figure 5) is not significant, and it can find counterexamples with less exploration than nested DFS (and often shorter ones, see Section 7). If *post* is computationally expensive, Geldenhuys and Valmari's algorithm may be preferable.
- The improved nested DFS algorithm (Figure 3) should be used for unrestricted automata if bitstate hashing is needed.

Note also that when generalised Büchi automata can be used, the balance shifts in favour of Couvreur's algorithm.

6   Compatibility with Partial Order Reduction

DFS-based model checking may be combined with partial-order reduction to alleviate the state-explosion problem. This technique tries not to explore all successors of a state, but only a subset matching certain conditions. In the practical approach of Peled [18], several candidate subsets of successors are tried until one is found that matches the conditions. Crucially, the chosen subset at state s depends on the DFS call stack at s. For correctness, one must ensure that each call to $post(s)$ chooses the same subset. This can be done by (i) ensuring that the call stack is always the same for any given state, or (ii) remembering the chosen successor set, which costs extra memory. Holzmann et al [15] describe memory-efficient methods for (ii), which, however, constrain the kinds of candidate successor sets that can be used. We show that there is an alternative solution for both nested DFS and SCC-based algorithms that does not require to remember successor sets, and does not constrain the candidate sets.

Note first that the nested DFS algorithms do not have property (i); the call stack in the red DFS may differ from the one in the blue DFS. In [6], Couvreur claims that his algorithm satisfies property (i). However, adding counterexample generation destroys this property: a state *can* be entered with a different call stack during the extra DFS needed for generating a counterexample, see Subsection 4.2. In both cases, the solutions of [15] can be used as a remedy.

The alternative solution is based on the following observations: The red search of the new nested algorithm (Figure 3) only explores cyan or blue states. The extra DFS in the SCC-based algorithm touches only states in the explored, but unremoved part of the automaton. Thus, if the partial-order reduction produces an unexplored successor during these searches, that successor can be discarded, because it cannot have been generated during the first search. In other words, one may simply generate *all* successor states and then discard those that were not explored before. Note that this may still produce some transitions that were not explored in the first search – however, it is easy to show that these extra transitions never lead to false results and at best to earlier detection of cycles.

As this solution does not impose constraints on candidate successor sets, it could lead to larger reductions at a (probably small) run-time price. We have not yet tried whether this leads to improvements in practice. No partial-order-related precautions are required when simple DFS is used for weak automata (see Section 5.1), as was already observed in [2].

7   Experiments

For experimental comparisons, we replicated two of the three variants from Geldenhuys and Valmari's example [11], a leader election protocol with extinction for arbitrary networks. In both variants, the election restarts after completion; in Variant 1, the same node wins every time, in Variant 2, each node gets a turn at becoming the leader. Like in [11], the network specified in the model consisted of three nodes.

Both variants were modelled in Promela. Spin [14] was used to generate the complete product state space (with partial-order reduction), and the result was given as input to our own implementation of the algorithms.

The results are summarized in Table 1. The first two sections of the table contain the results for the instances in which accepting cycles were found (for nested and SCC-based algorithms, resp.), whereas the third section contains the examples that did not contain accepting cycles. In all tables, ϕ indicates the LTL properties that were checked, which were taken from [11]. The 'weak' column indicates whether the resulting automaton was weak or not, 'states' is the total number of states in the product, and 'trans' the total number of transitions. (Note that the exact numbers differ from [11] because we used our own models of the algorithms.) The algorithms that were compared were:

Table 1. Experimental results on leader election example

Ex. w/ cycles (nested)			HPY			GMZ			New		
φ	weak	states	trans	st	tr	dp	st	tr	dp	st	tr	dp
				Variant 1								
B	no	16685	31405	385	409	386	371	392	372	214	215	215
E	yes	4849	6081	129	130	130	129	129	130	129	129	130
H	no	29564	46059	17658	21769	582	17658	42916	582	17658	21769	582
I	no	29564	46059	17658	21769	582	17658	42916	582	17658	21769	582
				Variant 2								
A	no	42564	77358	7218	16485	740	7218	16498	740	5786	13398	557
B	no	49256	93765	721	746	722	707	729	708	439	440	440
E	yes	14115	17794	367	368	368	367	367	368	367	367	368
G	yes	28126	37457	3982	4589	1040	3982	8130	1040	3982	4588	1040
H	no	111094	181559	33128	53575	906	33128	106364	906	33128	53575	906

Ex. w/ cycles (SCC)				Couv/GV		Couv		GV	
φ	weak	states	trans	st	dp	tr	$|Roots|$	tr	$|Current|$
				Variant 1					
B	no	16685	31405	214	215	215	129	215	214
E	yes	4849	6081	129	130	129	129	129	129
H	no	29564	46059	16132	328	38249	129	20009	4825
I	no	29564	46059	16132	328	38249	129	20009	4825
				Variant 2					
A	no	42564	77358	5786	557	13398	367	6983	561
B	no	49256	93765	439	440	440	354	440	439
E	yes	14115	17794	367	368	367	367	367	367
G	yes	28126	37457	3982	1040	4588	379	4588	3982
H	no	111094	181559	15259	798	36791	367	18998	14091

Ex. w/o cycles			transitions explored					stack size	
φ	states	depth	HPY	GMZ	New	Couv	GV	$|Roots|$	$|Current|$
			Variant 1						
A	13057	312	30554	41600	30554	41600	20800	129	4825
C	3925	113	9372	9372	9372	9372	4686	113	113
D	8964	312	20822	31868	20822	31868	15394	129	4825
F	8964	312	20822	31868	20822	31868	15394	129	4825
G	4849	312	6081	12162	6081	12162	6081	129	4825
			Variant 2						
C	3925	113	9372	9372	9372	9372	4686	113	113
D	27323	825	66522	100724	66522	100724	50362	367	14091
F	27323	825	64512	96704	64512	96704	48352	367	14091
I	83658	900	173557	247748	173557	247748	123874	367	14091

- HPY: the algorithm of Holzmann et al [15], see Subsection 3.1;
- GMZ: the algorithm of Gastin et al [10], see Subsection 3.1;
- New: the new nested algorithm from Figure 3, see Subsection 3.2;
- Couv: the simplified algorithm of Couvreur [6], see Subsection 4.2;
- GV: the algorithm of Geldenhuys and Valmari [11], see Subsection 4.1.

To ensure comparable results, the order of successors given by *post* was the same in all algorithms and was always followed. The following (implementation-independent) statistics are provided: Columns marked 'st' indicate the number of *distinct* states visited during the search; 'tr' indicates how many transitions were generated by calls to *post*, i.e. individual transitions may count more than once. 'dp' indicates the maximal depth of the call stack. The length of counterexamples was almost always equal to the value of 'dp', and only slightly less otherwise. For the SCC-based algorithms, we also provide the maximal size of their explicit state stacks. In the last section, the whole graph is explored, therefore the only differences are in the transition count, and the size of the explicit state stacks.

The results demonstrate the most important observations made in the theoretical discussion of the algorithms, in particular:

- The new nested-DFS algorithm finds counterexamples faster than the other nested algorithms in three cases. In those cases, the counterexamples are found as fast as in the SCC algorithms, but that is just a lucky coincidence.
- The GMZ algorithm was never faster than the new algorithm, i.e. its extra black search did not provide an advantage.
- The SCC-based algorithms found counterexamples earlier than HPY and GMZ on *all* weak automata, and earlier than the new nested algorithm in three cases. In all cases, earlier detection of counterexamples also translated to *shorter* counterexamples, but this is not guaranteed in general.
- The *Roots* stack of Couvreur's algorithm is often *much* smaller than the *Current* stack of the GV algorithm; in return, it may touch transitions twice.

The relative differences between the algorithms could be made arbitrarily large by choosing suitable examples – the purpose of this set of examples was just to provide experimental evidence that the differences do exist. For a more meaningful comparison in practice (i.e. in actual time and memory requirements) one would have to integrate these algorithms into an actual model checker (e.g. Spin), which would be a possible next step.

8   Conclusions

We have portrayed and compared a number of algorithms for finding accepting cycles in Büchi automata. A new nested-DFS algorithm was proposed, which was experimentally shown to perform better than existing ones. Moreover, we have presented an adaptation of Couvreur's SCC-based algorithm and shown that it has important advantages, some of which were not previously observed. Thus, we believe that both nested DFS and SCC algorithms have their place in LTL verification; the one uses less memory, the other finds counterexamples faster. Moreover, we provide a refined judgement that takes into account structural properties of the Büchi automaton.

There remains an interesting open question: Is there a linear-time algorithm that combines the advantages of nested DFS and SCC-based algorithms, i.e. one that finds counterexamples with minimal exploration *and* uses only a constant number of bits per state?

References

1. R. Bloem, K. Ravi, and F. Somenzi. Efficient decision procedures for model checking of linear time logic properties. In *CAV'99*, LNCS 1633, pages 222–235, 1999.
2. I. Černá and R. Pelánek. Relating hierarchy of linear temporal properties to model checking. In *Proc. of MFCS*, LNCS 2747, pages 318–327, 2003.
3. E. Clarke, A. Emerson, and P. Sistla. Automatic verification of finite-state concurrent systems using temporal logic specifications. *TOPLAS*, 8:244–263, 1986.
4. E. M. Clarke, O. Grumberg, and D. A. Peled. *Model Checking*. MIT Press, 1999.
5. C. Courcoubetis, M. Y. Vardi, P. Wolper, and M. Yannakakis. Memory-efficient algorithms for the verification of temporal properties. *Formal Methods in System Design*, 1(2/3):275–288, 1992.
6. J.-M. Couvreur. On-the-fly verification of linear temporal logic. In *Proc. Formal Methods*, LNCS 1708, pages 253–271, 1999.
7. S. Edelkamp, A. Lluch-Lafuente, and S. Leue. Directed explicit-state model checking in the validation of communication protocols. *STTT*, 2004.
8. K. Fisler, R. Fraer, G. Kamhi, M. Y. Vardi, and Z. Yang. Is there a best symbolic cycle-detection algorithm? In *Proc. of TACAS*, LNCS 2031, pages 420–434, 2001.
9. H. N. Gabow. Path-based depth-first search for strong and biconnected components. *Information Processing Letters*, 74(3–4):107–114, 2000.
10. P. Gastin, P. Moro, and M. Zeitoun. Minimization of counterexamples in SPIN. In *Proc. 11th SPIN Workshop*, LNCS 2989, pages 92–108, 2004.
11. J. Geldenhuys and A. Valmari. Tarjan's algorithm makes on-the-fly LTL verification more efficient. In *Proc. of TACAS*, LNCS 2988, pages 205–219, 2004.
12. R. Gerth, D. A. Peled, M. Y. Vardi, and P. Wolper. Simple on-the-fly automatic verification of linear temporal logic. In *Proc. of PSTV*, pages 3–18. IFIP, 1996.
13. G. J. Holzmann. An analysis of bitstate hashing. *Formal Methods in System Design*, 13(3):289–307, 1998.
14. G. J. Holzmann. *The Spin Model Checker: Primer and Reference Manual*. Addison-Wesley, 2003.
15. G. J. Holzmann, D. A. Peled, and M. Yannakakis. On nested depth first search. In *Proc. 2nd SPIN Workshop*, pages 23–32, 1996.
16. O. Kupferman and M. Y. Vardi. Freedom, weakness, and determinism: From linear-time to branching-time. In *Proc. of LICS*, pages 81–92. IEEE, 1998.
17. E. Nuutila and E. Soisalon-Soininen. On finding the strongly connected components in a directed graph. *Information Processing Letters*, 49:9–14, 1994.
18. D. A. Peled. Combining partial order reductions with on-the-fly model-checking. *Formal Methods in System Design*, 8(1):39–64, January 1996.
19. S. Schwoon and J. Esparza. A note on on-the-fly verification algorithms. Technical Report 2004/06, Universität Stuttgart, November 2004.

20. M. Sharir. A strong-connectivity algorithm and its applications in data flow analysis. *Computers and Mathematics with Applications*, 7(1):67–72, 1981.
21. F. Somenzi and R. Bloem. Efficient Büchi automata from LTL formulae. In *Proc. of CAV*, LNCS 1855, pages 248–263, 2000.
22. R. Tarjan. Depth-first search and linear graph algorithms. *SIAM Journal on Computing*, 1(2):146–160, 1972.
23. H. Tauriainen. Nested emptiness search for generalized Büchi automata. Technical Report A79, Helsinki University of Technology, July 2003.
24. M. Y. Vardi and P. Wolper. Automata theoretic techniques for modal logics of programs. *Journal of Computer and System Sciences*, 32:183–221, 1986.

Truly On-the-Fly LTL Model Checking

Moritz Hammer[1], Alexander Knapp[1], and Stephan Merz[2]

[1] Institut für Informatik, Ludwig-Maximilians-Universität München
{Moritz.Hammer, Alexander.Knapp}@pst.ifi.lmu.de
[2] INRIA Lorraine, LORIA, Nancy
Stephan.Merz@loria.fr

Abstract. We propose a novel algorithm for automata-based LTL model checking that interleaves the construction of the generalized Büchi automaton for the negation of the formula and the emptiness check. Our algorithm first converts the LTL formula into a linear weak alternating automaton; configurations of the alternating automaton correspond to the locations of a generalized Büchi automaton, and a variant of Tarjan's algorithm is used to decide the existence of an accepting run of the product of the transition system and the automaton. Because we avoid an explicit construction of the Büchi automaton, our approach can yield significant improvements in runtime and memory, for large LTL formulas. The algorithm has been implemented within the SPIN model checker, and we present experimental results for some benchmark examples.

1   Introduction

The automata-based approach to linear-time temporal logic (LTL) model checking reduces the problem of deciding whether a formula φ holds of a transition system $\mathcal{T}$ into two subproblems: first, one constructs an automaton $\mathcal{A}_{\neg\varphi}$ that accepts precisely the models of $\neg\varphi$. Second, one uses graph-theoretical algorithms to decide whether the product of $\mathcal{T}$ and $\mathcal{A}_{\neg\varphi}$ admits an accepting run; this is the case if and only if φ does not hold of $\mathcal{T}$. On-the-fly algorithms [2] avoid an explicit construction of the product and are commonly used to decide the second problem. However, the construction of a non-deterministic Büchi (or generalized Büchi) automaton $\mathcal{A}_{\neg\varphi}$ is already of complexity exponential in the length of φ, and several algorithms have been suggested [3,4,5,7,18,20] that improve on the classical method for computing Büchi automata [9]. Still, there are applications, for example when verifying liveness properties over predicate abstractions [13], where the construction of $\mathcal{A}_{\neg\varphi}$ takes a significant fraction of the overall verification time. The relative cost of computing $\mathcal{A}_{\neg\varphi}$ is particularly high when φ does not hold of $\mathcal{T}$, because acceptance cycles are often found rather quickly when they exist.

In this paper we suggest an algorithm for LTL model checking that interleaves the construction of (a structure equivalent to) the automaton and the test for non-emptiness. Technically, the input to our algorithm is a transition system $\mathcal{T}$ and a linear weak alternating automaton (LWAA, alternatively known as a very weak alternating automaton) corresponding to $\neg\varphi$. The size of the LWAA is linear in the length of the LTL formula,

N. Halbwachs and L. Zuck (Eds.): TACAS 2005, LNCS 3440, pp. 191–205, 2005.

and the time for its generation is insignificant. It can be considered as a symbolic representation of the corresponding generalized Büchi automaton (GBA). LWAA have also been employed as an intermediate format in the algorithms suggested by Gastin and Oddoux [7], Fritz [5], and Schneider [17]. Our main contribution is the identification of a class of "simple" LWAA whose acceptance criterion is defined in terms of the sets of locations activated during a run, rather than the standard criterion in terms of automaton transitions. To explore the product of the transition system and the configuration graph of the LWAA, we employ a variant of Tarjan's algorithm to search for a strongly connected component that satisfies the automaton's acceptance condition.

We have implemented the proposed algorithm as an alternative verification method in the SPIN model checker [12], and we discuss some implementation options and report on experimental results. Our implementation is available for download at http://www.pst.ifi.lmu.de/projekte/lwaaspin/.

2   LTL and Linear Weak Alternating Automata

We define alternating ω-automata, especially LWAA, and present the translation from propositional linear-time temporal logic LTL to LWAA. Throughout, we assume a fixed finite set $\mathcal{V}$ of atomic propositions.

2.1   Linear Weak Alternating Automata

We consider automata that operate on temporal structures, i.e. ω-sequences of valuations of $\mathcal{V}$. Alternating automata combine the existential branching mode of nondeterministic automata (i.e., choice) with its dual, universal branching, where several successor locations are activated simultaneously. We present the transitions of alternating automata by associating with every location $q \in Q$ a propositional formula $\delta(q)$ over $\mathcal{V}$ and Q. For example, we interpret

$$\delta(q_1) \;=\; (v \wedge q_2 \wedge (q_1 \vee q_3)) \vee (\neg w \wedge q_1) \vee w$$

as asserting that if location q_1 is currently active and the current input satisfies v then the automaton should simultaneously activate the locations q_2 and either q_1 or q_3. If the input satisfies $\neg w$ then q_1 should be activated. If the input satisfies w then no successor locations need to be activated from q_1. Otherwise (i.e., if the input satisfies $\neg v$), the automaton blocks because the transition formula can not be satisfied. At any point during a run, a set of automaton locations (a *configuration*) will be active, and transitions are required to satisfy the transition formulas of all active locations. Locations $q \in Q$ may only occur positively in transition formulas: locations cannot be inhibited. We use the following generic definition of alternating ω-automata:

Definition 1. *An* alternating ω-automaton *is a tuple* $\mathcal{A} = (Q, q_0, \delta, Acc)$ *where*

- Q *is a finite set (of locations) where* $Q \cap \mathcal{V} = \emptyset$,
- $q_0 \in Q$ *is the initial location,*
- $\delta : Q \to \mathcal{B}(Q \cup \mathcal{V})$ *is the transition function that associates a propositional formula* $\delta(q)$ *with every location* $q \in Q$; *locations in* Q *can only occur positively in* $\delta(q)$,
- *and* $Acc \subseteq Q^{\omega}$ *is the acceptance condition.*

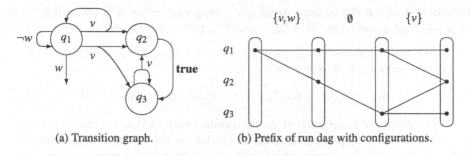

(a) Transition graph.   (b) Prefix of run dag with configurations.

Fig. 1. Visualization of alternating automata and run dags

When the transition formulas $\delta(q)$ are written in disjunctive normal form, the alternating automaton can be visualized as a hypergraph. For example, Fig. 1(a) shows an alternating ω-automaton and illustrates the above transition formula. We write $q \to q'$ if q may activate q', i.e. if q' appears in $\delta(q)$.

Runs of an alternating ω-automaton over a temporal structure $\sigma = s_0 s_1 \ldots$ are not just sequences of locations but give rise to trees, due to universal branching. However, different copies of the same target location can be identified, and we obtain a more economical dag representation as illustrated in Fig. 1(b): the vertical "slices" of the dag represent configurations that are active before reading the next input state.

We identify a set and the Boolean valuation that makes true precisely the elements of the set. For example, we say that the sets $\{v, w, q_2, q_3\}$ and $\{w\}$ satisfy the formula $\delta(q_1)$ above. For a relation $r \subseteq S \times T$, we denote its domain by $\mathrm{dom}(r)$. We denote the image of a set $A \subseteq S$ under r by $r(A)$; for $x \in S$ we sometimes write $r(x)$ for $r(\{x\})$.

Definition 2. *Let* $\mathcal{A} = (Q, q_0, \delta, Acc)$ *be an alternating ω-automaton and* $\sigma = s_0 s_1 \ldots$, *where* $s_i \subseteq \mathcal{V}$, *be a temporal structure. A* run dag *of $\mathcal{A}$ over σ is represented by the ω-sequence* $\Delta = e_0 e_1 \ldots$ *of its edges* $e_i \subseteq Q \times Q$. *The* configurations $c_0 c_1 \ldots$ *of Δ, where* $c_i \subseteq Q$, *are inductively defined by* $c_0 = \{q_0\}$ *and* $c_{i+1} = e_i(c_i)$. *We require that for all* $i \in \mathbb{N}$, $\mathrm{dom}(e_i) \subseteq c_i$ *and that for all* $q \in c_i$, *the valuation* $s_i \cup e_i(q)$ *satisfies* $\delta(q)$. *A finite* run dag *is a finite prefix of a run dag.*

A path *in a run dag Δ is a (finite or infinite) sequence* $\pi = p_0 p_1 \ldots$ *of locations* $p_i \in Q$ *such that* $p_0 = q_0$ *and* $(p_i, p_{i+1}) \in e_i$ *for all i. A run dag Δ is* accepting *iff* $\pi \in Acc$ *holds for all infinite paths π in Δ. The language* $\mathcal{L}(\mathcal{A})$ *is the set of words that admit some accepting run dag.*

Because locations do not occur negatively in transition formulas $\delta(q)$, it is easy to see that whenever $s_i \cup X$ satisfies $\delta(q)$ for some set X of locations, then so does $s_i \cup Y$ for any superset Y of X. However, the dag resulting from replacing X by Y will have more paths, making the acceptance condition harder to satisfy. It is therefore enough to consider only run dags that arise from minimal models of the transition formulas w.r.t. the states of the temporal structure, activating as few successor locations as possible.

LWAA are alternating ω-automata whose accessibility relation determines a partial order: q' is reachable from q only if q' is smaller or at most equal to q. We are interested in LWAA with a co-Büchi acceptance condition:

Definition 3. *A (co-Büchi) linear weak alternating automaton $\mathcal{A} = (Q, q_0, \delta, F)$ is a tuple where Q, q_0, and δ are as in Def. 1 and $F \subseteq Q$ is a set of locations, such that*

- *the relation $\preceq_{\mathcal{A}}$ defined by $q' \preceq_{\mathcal{A}} q$ iff $q \to^* q'$ is a partial order on Q and*
- *the acceptance condition is given by*

$$Acc = \{p_0 p_1 \ldots \in Q^\omega : p_i \in F \text{ for only finitely many } i \in \mathbb{N}\}.$$

In particular, the hypergraph of the transitions of an LWAA does not contain cycles other than self-loops, and run dags of LWAA do not contain "rising edges" as in Fig. 1. It follows that every infinite path eventually remains stable at some location q, and the acceptance condition requires that $q \notin F$ holds for that "limit location". LWAA characterize precisely the class of star-free ω-regular languages, which correspond to first-order definable ω-languages and therefore also to the languages definable by propositional LTL formulas [16, 22].

2.2   From LTL to LWAA

Formulas of LTL (over atomic propositions in $\mathcal{V}$) are built using the connectives of propositional logic and the temporal operators **X** (next) and **U** (until). They are interpreted over a temporal structure $\sigma = s_0 s_1 \ldots \in (2^{\mathcal{V}})^\omega$ as follows; we write $\sigma|_i$ to denote the suffix $s_i s_{i+1} \ldots$ of σ from state s_i:

$$
\begin{array}{llll}
\sigma \models p & \text{iff } p \in s_0 & \sigma \models \varphi \wedge \psi & \text{iff } \sigma \models \varphi \text{ and } \sigma \models \psi \\
\sigma \models \neg\varphi & \text{iff } \sigma \not\models \varphi & \sigma \models \mathbf{X}\varphi & \text{iff } \sigma|_1 \models \varphi \\
\sigma \models \varphi \, \mathbf{U} \, \psi & \text{iff} & \multicolumn{2}{l}{\text{for some } i \in \mathbb{N}, \sigma|_i \models \psi \text{ and for all } j < i, \sigma|_j \models \varphi}
\end{array}
$$

We freely use the standard derived operators of propositional logic and the following derived temporal connectives:

$$
\begin{array}{ll}
\mathbf{F}\varphi \equiv \mathbf{true} \, \mathbf{U} \, \varphi & \text{(eventually } \varphi) \\
\mathbf{G}\varphi \equiv \neg\mathbf{F}\neg\varphi & \text{(always } \varphi) \\
\varphi \, \mathbf{V} \, \psi \equiv \neg(\neg\varphi \, \mathbf{U} \, \neg\psi) & \text{(} \varphi \text{ releases } \psi)
\end{array}
$$

An LTL formula φ can be understood as defining the language

$$\mathcal{L}(\varphi) = \{\sigma \in (2^{\mathcal{V}})^\omega : \sigma \models \varphi\},$$

and the automata-theoretic approach to model checking builds on this identification of formulas and languages, via an effective construction of automata $\mathcal{A}_\varphi$ accepting the language $\mathcal{L}(\varphi)$. The definition of an LWAA $\mathcal{A}_\varphi$ is particularly simple [15]: without loss of generality, we assume that LTL formulas are given in negation normal form (i.e., negation is applied only to propositions), and therefore include clauses for the dual operators $\vee$ and **V**. The automaton is $\mathcal{A}_\varphi = (Q, q_\varphi, \delta, F)$ where Q contains a location q_ψ for every subformula ψ of φ, with q_φ being the initial location. The transition formulas $\delta(q_\psi)$ are defined in Fig. 2(a); in particular, LTL operators are simply decomposed according to their fixpoint characterizations. The set F of co-final locations consists of all locations $q_{\psi \mathbf{U} \chi} \in Q$ that correspond to "until" subformulas of φ. It is easy to verify

location q	$\delta(q)$
q_ψ (ψ a literal)	ψ
$q_{\psi \wedge \chi}$	$\delta(q_\psi) \wedge \delta(q_\chi)$
$q_{\psi \vee \chi}$	$\delta(q_\psi) \vee \delta(q_\chi)$
$q_{\mathbf{X}\psi}$	q_ψ
$q_{\psi \mathbf{U} \chi}$	$\delta(q_\chi) \vee (\delta(q_\psi) \wedge q_{\psi \mathbf{U} \chi})$
$q_{\psi \mathbf{V} \chi}$	$\delta(q_\chi) \wedge (\delta(q_\psi) \vee q_{\psi \mathbf{V} \chi})$

(a) Transition formulas of $\mathcal{A}_\varphi$

(b) $\mathcal{A}_{\mathbf{GF}p}$

(c) $\mathcal{A}_{p\mathbf{U}(q\mathbf{U}r)}$

Fig. 2. Translation of LTL formulas into LWAA

that the resulting automaton $\mathcal{A}_\varphi$ is an LWAA: for any locations q_ψ and q_χ, the definition of $\delta(q_\psi)$ ensures that $q_\psi \to q_\chi$ holds only if χ is a subformula of ψ. Correctness proofs for the construction can be found in [15, 23]; conversely, Rohde [16] and Löding and Thomas [14] prove that for every LWAA $\mathcal{A}$ there is an LTL formula $\varphi_\mathcal{A}$ such that $\mathcal{L}(\varphi_\mathcal{A}) = \mathcal{L}(\mathcal{A})$.

The number of subformulas of an LTL formula φ is linear in the length of φ, and therefore so is the size of $\mathcal{A}_\varphi$. However, in practice the automaton should be minimized further. Clearly, unreachable locations can be eliminated. Moreover, whenever there is a choice between activating sets X or Y of locations where $X \subseteq Y$ from some location q, the smaller set X should be preferred, and Y should be activated only if X cannot be. As a simple example, we can define $\delta(q_{\mathbf{F}p}) = p \vee (\neg p \wedge q_{\mathbf{F}p})$ instead of $\delta(q_{\mathbf{F}p}) = p \vee q_{\mathbf{F}p}$.

Figure 2 shows two linear weak alternating automata obtained from LTL formulas by applying this construction (the locations in F are indicated by double circles).

Further minimizations are less straightforward. Because the automaton structure closely resembles the structure of the LTL formula, heuristics to minimize the LTL formula [4, 18] are important. Fritz and Wilke [6] discuss more elaborate optimizations based on simulation relations on the set Q of locations.

3   Deciding Language Emptiness for LWAA

In general, it is nontrivial to decide language emptiness for alternating ω-automata, due to their intricate combinatorial structure: a configuration consists of a set of automaton locations that have to "synchronize" on the current input state during a transition to a successor configuration. The standard approach is therefore based on a translation to non-deterministic Büchi automata, for which emptiness can be decided in linear time. Unfortunately, this translation is of exponential complexity.

Linear weak alternating automata have a simpler combinatorial structure: the transition graph contains only trivial cycles, and therefore a run dag is non-accepting only if it contains a path that ends in a self-loop at some location $q \in F$. This observation gives rise to the following non-emptiness criterion for LWAA, which is closely related to Theorem 2 of [7]:

Theorem 4. *Assume that $\mathcal{A} = (Q, q_0, \delta, F)$ is an LWAA. Then $L(\mathcal{A}) \neq \emptyset$ if and only if there exists a finite run dag $\Delta = e_0 e_1 \ldots e_n$ with configurations $c_0 c_1 \ldots c_{n+1}$ over a finite sequence $s_0 \ldots s_n$ of states and some $k \leq n$ such that*

1. *$c_k = c_{n+1}$ and*
2. *for every $q \in F$, one has $(q, q) \notin e_j$ for some j where $k \leq j \leq n$.*

Proof. "If": Consider the infinite dag $\Delta' = e_0 \ldots e_{k-1}(e_k \ldots e_n)\omega$. Because $c_k = c_{n+1}$, it is obvious that Δ' is a run dag over $\sigma = s_0 \ldots s_{k-1}(s_k \ldots s_n)^{\omega}$; we now show that Δ' is accepting. Assume, to the contrary, that $\pi = p_0 p_1 \ldots$ is some infinite path in Δ' such that $p_i \in F$ holds for infinitely many $i \in \mathbb{N}$. Because $\mathcal{A}$ is an LWAA, there exists some $m \in \mathbb{N}$ and some $q \in Q$ such that $p_i = q$ for all $i \geq m$. It follows that $(q, q) \in e_i$ holds for all $i \geq m$, which is impossible by assumption (2) and the construction of Δ'. Therefore, Δ' must be accepting, and $L(\mathcal{A}) \neq \emptyset$.

"Only if": Assume that $\sigma = s_0 s_1 \ldots \in L(\mathcal{A})$, and let $\Delta' = e_0 e_1 \ldots$ be some accepting run dag of $\mathcal{A}$ over σ. Since Q is finite, Δ' can contain only finitely many different configurations $c_0, c_1, \ldots$, and there is some configuration $c \subseteq Q$ such that $c_i = c$ for infinitely many $i \in \mathbb{N}$. Denote by $i_0 < i_1 < \ldots$ the ω-sequence of indexes such that $c_{i_j} = c$. If there were some $q \in F$ such that $q \in e_j(q)$ for all $j \geq i_0$ (implying in particular that $q \in c_j$ for all $j \geq i_0$ by Def. 2) then Δ' would contain an infinite path ending in a self-loop at q, contradicting the assumption that Δ' is accepting. Therefore, for every $q \in F$ there must be some $j_q \geq i_0$ such that $(q, q) \notin e_{j_q}$. Choosing $k = i_0$ and $n = i_m - 1$ for some m such that $i_m > j_q$ for all (finitely many) $q \in F$, we obtain a finite run dag Δ as required. □

Observe that Thm. 4 requires to inspect the *transitions* of the dag and not just the configurations. In fact, a run dag may well be accepting although some location $q \in F$ is contained in all (or almost all) configurations. For example, consider the LWAA for the formula **G X F** p: the location $q_{\mathbf{F}p}$ will be active in every run dag from the second configuration onward, even if the run dag is accepting. We now introduce a class of LWAA for which it is enough to inspect the configurations.

Definition 5. *An LWAA $\mathcal{A} = (Q, q_0, \delta, F)$ is simple if for all $q \in F$, all $q' \in Q$, all states $s \subseteq \mathcal{V}$, and all $X, Y \subseteq Q$ not containing q, if $s \cup X \cup \{q\} \models \delta(q')$ and $s \cup Y \models \delta(q)$ then $s \cup X \cup Y \models \delta(q')$.*

In other words, if a co-final location q can be activated from some location q' for some state s while it can be exited during the same transition, then q' has an alternative transition that avoids activating q, and this alternative transitions activates only locations that would anyway have been activated by the joint transitions from q and q'. For simple LWAA, non-emptiness can be decided on the basis of the visited configurations alone, without memorizing the graph structure of the run dag.

Theorem 6. *Assume that $\mathcal{A} = (Q, q_0, \delta, F)$ is a simple LWAA. Then $L(\mathcal{A}) \neq \emptyset$ if and only if there exists a finite run dag $\Delta = e_0 e_1 \ldots e_n$ with configurations $c_0 c_1 \ldots c_{n+1}$ over a finite sequence $s_0 \ldots s_n$ of states and some $k \leq n$ such that*

1. *$c_k = c_{n+1}$ and*
2. *for every $q \in F$, one has $q \notin c_j$ for some j where $k \leq j \leq n$.*

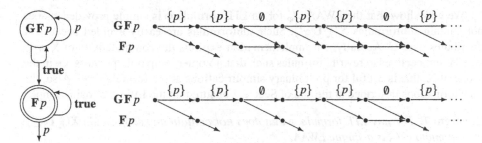

Fig. 3. Illustration of the construction of Thm. 6

Proof. "If": The assumption $q \notin c_j$ and the requirement that $\text{dom}(e_j) \subseteq c_j$ imply that $(q, q) \notin e_j$, and therefore $L(\mathcal{A}) \neq \emptyset$ follows using Thm. 4.

"Only if": Assume that $L(\mathcal{A}) \neq \emptyset$, obtain a finite run dag Δ satisfying the conditions of Thm. 4, and let $l = n - k + 1$ denote the length of the loop. "Unwinding" Δ, we obtain an infinite run dag $e_0 e_1 \ldots$ over the temporal structure $s_0 s_1 \ldots$ whose edges are $e_i = e_{k+((i-k) \bmod l)}$ for $i > n$, and similarly for the states s_i and the configurations c_i. W.l.o.g. we assume that the dag contains no unnecessary edges, i.e. that for all $e_i \in \Delta$, $(q, q') \in e_i$ holds only if $q \to q'$.

We inductively construct an infinite run dag $\Delta' = e'_0 e'_1 \ldots$ with configurations $c'_0 c'_1 \ldots$ such that $c'_i \subseteq c_i$ as follows: let $c'_0 = c_0$ and for $i < k$, let $e'_i = e_i$ and $c'_{i+1} = c_{i+1}$. For $i \geq k$, assume that c'_i has already been defined. Let F_i denote the set of $q \in c'_i \cap F$ such that $(q, q) \notin e_i$ but $q \in e_i(c'_i)$, and for any $q \in F_i$ let Q'_q denote the set of locations $q' \in c'_i$ such that $(q', q) \in e_i$ and let $Y_q = e_i(q)$. Because $\mathcal{A}$ is simple, it follows that $s_i \cup (e_i(q') \setminus \{q\}) \cup Y_q \models \delta(q')$, for all $q \in F_i$ and $q' \in Q'_q$. We let e'_i be obtained from the restriction of e_i to c'_i by deleting all edges (q', q) for $q \in F_i$ and adding edges (q', q'') for all $q' \in Q'_q$ and $q'' \in Y_q$, for $q \in F_i$. Clearly, this ensures that $c'_{i+1} \subseteq c_{i+1}$ holds for the resulting configuration and that $c'_{i+1} \cap F_i = \emptyset$.

For any $q \in F_i$, the definition of an LWAA and the assumption that $q \notin Y_q$ ensure that $q'' \prec_{\mathcal{A}} q$ holds for all $q'' \in Y_q$, as well as $q \preceq_{\mathcal{A}} q'$ for all $q' \in Q'_q$. In particular, we must have $q'' \neq q'$ for all $q'' \in Y_q$ and $q' \in Q'_q$, and therefore e'_i does not contain more self loops than e_i: for all $p \in Q$, we have $(p, p) \in e'_i$ only if $(p, p) \in e_i$.

Consequently, Δ' is an accepting infinite run dag such that for every $q \in F$ there exists some $j \geq k$ such that $q \notin c'_j$. It now suffices to pick some $n \geq k$ satisfying the conditions of the theorem; such an n exists because F is finite and Δ' can contain only finitely many different configurations. □

Fig. 3 illustrates two accepting run dags for a simple LWAA: the dag shown above satisfies the criterion of Thm. 4 although the co-final location corresponding to $\mathbf{F}\,p$ remains active from the second configuration onward. The dag shown below is the result of the transformation described in the proof, and indeed the location $\mathbf{F}\,p$ is infinitely often inactive.

We now show that the LWAA $\mathcal{A}_\varphi$ for an LTL formula φ is simple provided φ does not contain subformulas $\mathbf{X}(\chi \mathbf{U} \chi')$. Such subformulas are easily avoided because $\mathbf{X}$ distributes over $\mathbf{U}$. Actually, our implementation exploits the commutativity of $\mathbf{X}$ with all LTL connectives to rewrite formulas such that no other temporal operators are in the scope of $\mathbf{X}$; this is useful for preliminary simplifications at the formula level. Also, the transformations described at the end of Sect. 2.2 ensure that the LWAA remains simple.

Theorem 7. *For any LTL formula φ that does not contain any subformula $\mathbf{X}(\chi \mathbf{U} \chi')$, the automaton $\mathcal{A}_\varphi$ is a simple LWAA.*

Proof. Let $\mathcal{A}_\varphi = (Q, q_\varphi, \delta, F)$ and assume that $q \in F$, $q' \in Q$, and $X, Y \subseteq Q$ are as in Def. 5, in particular $s \cup X \cup \{q\} \models \delta(q')$ and $s \cup Y \models \delta(q)$. The proof is by induction on ψ where $q' = q_\psi$.

$\psi \equiv (\neg)v$: $\delta(q') = \psi$, so we must have $s \models \delta(q')$, and the assertion $s \cup X \cup Y \models \delta(q')$ follows trivially.

$\psi \equiv \chi \otimes \chi'$, $\otimes \in \{\wedge, \vee\}$: $\delta(q') = \delta(q_\chi) \otimes \delta(q_{\chi'})$, and the assertion follows easily from the induction hypothesis.

$\psi \equiv \mathbf{X}\chi$: $\delta(q') = q_\chi$, and by assumption χ is not an $\mathbf{U}$ formula, so $q_\chi \notin F$. In particular, $q_\chi \neq q$, and so the assumption $s \cup X \cup \{q\} \models \delta(q')$ implies that $s \cup X \models \delta(q')$, and the assertion $s \cup X \cup Y \models \delta(q')$ follows by monotonicity.

$\psi \equiv \chi \mathbf{U} \chi'$: $\delta(q') = \delta(q_{\chi'}) \vee (\delta(q_\chi) \wedge q')$. In case $s \cup X \cup \{q\} \models \delta(q_{\chi'})$, the induction hypothesis implies $s \cup X \cup Y \models \delta(q_{\chi'})$, hence also $s \cup X \cup Y \models \delta(q')$.

If $s \cup X \cup \{q\} \models \delta(q_\chi) \wedge q'$, we consider two cases: if $q = q'$ then $s \cup Y \models \delta(q')$ holds by assumption. Moreover, $s \cup X \cup Y \models \delta(q_\chi)$ holds by induction hypothesis, and the assertion follows.

Otherwise, we must have $q' \in X$. Again, $s \cup X \cup Y \models \delta(q_\chi)$ follows from the induction hypothesis, and since $q' \in X$ it follows that $s \cup X \cup Y \models \delta(q_\chi) \wedge q'$.

$\psi \equiv \chi \mathbf{V} \chi'$: $\delta(q') = \delta(q_{\chi'}) \wedge (\delta(q_\chi) \vee q')$. In particular, $s \cup X \cup \{q\} \models \delta(q_{\chi'})$, and we obtain $s \cup X \cup Y \models \delta(q_{\chi'})$ by induction hypothesis.

If $s \cup X \cup \{q\} \models \delta(q_\chi)$, we similarly obtain $s \cup X \cup Y \models \delta(q_\chi)$. Otherwise, note that $q \neq q'$ because $q \in F$ and $q' \notin F$ (since it is not an $\mathbf{U}$ formula). Therefore, we must have $s \cup X \models q'$, and a fortiori $s \cup X \cup Y \models q'$, completing the proof. $\square$

Let us note in passing that simple LWAA are as expressive as LWAA, i.e. they also characterize the class of star-free ω-regular languages: from [14, 16] we know that for every LWAA $\mathcal{A}$ there is an LTL formula $\varphi_\mathcal{A}$ such that $L(\varphi_\mathcal{A}) = L(\mathcal{A})$. Since $\mathbf{X}$ distributes over $\mathbf{U}$, $\varphi_\mathcal{A}$ can be transformed into an equivalent formula φ' of the form required in Thm. 7, and $\mathcal{A}_{\varphi'}$ is a simple LWAA accepting the same language as $\mathcal{A}$.

4   Model Checking Algorithm

We describe a model checking algorithm based on the nonemptiness criterion of Thm. 6, and we discuss some design decisions encountered in our implementation. The algorithm has been integrated within the LTL model checker SPIN, and we present some results that have been obtained on benchmark examples.

```
procedure Visit(s, C):
  let c = (s,C) in
    inComp[c] := false; root[c] := c; labels[c] := 0;
    cnt[c] := cnt; cnt := cnt+1; seen := seen U {c};
    push(c, stack);
    forall c' = (s',C') in Succ(c) do
      if c' ∉ seen then Visit(s',C') end if;
      if ¬inComp[c'] then
        if cnt[root[c']] < cnt[root[c]] then
          labels[root[c']] := labels[root[c']] U labels[root[c]];
          root[c] := root[c']
        end if;
        labels[root[c]] := labels[root[c]]
                         U (f_lwaa \ C); // f_lwaa ≡ co-final locations
        if labels[root[c]] = f_lwaa then raise Good_Cycle end if;
      end if;
    end forall;
    if root[c]=c then
      repeat
        d := pop(stack);
        inComp[d] := true;
      until d=c;
    end if;
  end let;
end Visit;

procedure Check:
  stack := empty; seen := 0; cnt := 0;
  Visit(init_ts, {init_lwaa});    // start with initial location
end Check;
```

Fig. 4. LWAA-based model checking algorithm

4.1   Adapting Tarjan's Algorithm

Theorem 6 contains the core of our model checking algorithm: given the simple LWAA $\mathcal{A}_{\neg\varphi}$ corresponding to the negation $\neg\varphi$ of the property to be verified, we explore the product of the transition system $\mathcal{T}$ and the graph of configurations of $\mathcal{A}_{\neg\varphi}$, searching for a strongly connected component that satisfies the acceptance condition. In fact, in the light of Thm. 6 a simple LWAA $\mathcal{A}$ can alternatively be viewed as a symbolic representation of a GBA whose locations are sets of locations of $\mathcal{A}$, and that has an acceptance condition per co-final location of $\mathcal{A}$.

The traditional CVWY algorithm [2] for LTL model checking based on Büchi automata has been generalized for GBA by Tauriainen [21], but we find it easier to adapt Tarjan's algorithm [19] for finding strongly connected components in graphs. Figure 4 gives a pseudo-code representation of our algorithm. The depth-first search operates on pairs (s,C) where s is a state of the transition system and C is a configuration of the LWAA. Given a pair $c = (s,C)$, the call to Succ computes the set $succ_{\mathcal{T}}(s) \times succ_{\mathcal{A}}(s,C)$ containing all pairs $c' = (s',C')$ of successor states s' of the transition system and successor configurations C' of the LWAA, i.e. those C' which satisfy $s \cup C' \models \delta(q)$ for all $q \in C$. Tarjan's algorithm assigns a so-called root candidate root to each node of the graph, which is the oldest node on the stack known to belong to the same SCC.

In model checking, we are not so much interested in actually computing SCCs: it is sufficient to verify that the acceptance criterion of Thm. 6 is met for some strongly connected subgraph (SCS). To do so, we associate a `labels` field with the root candidate of each SCC that accumulates the locations $q \in F$ that have been found absent in some pair (s, C) contained in the SCC. Whenever `labels` is found to contain all co-final states of the LWAA (denoted by `f_lwaa`), the SCS must be accepting and the search is aborted. Note that we need to maintain two stacks: one for the depth-first search recursion, and one for identifying SCCs.

If an accepting SCS is found, we also want to produce a counter-example, and Tarjan's algorithm is less convenient for this purpose than the CVWY algorithm whose recursion stack contains the counter-example once a cycle has been detected. In our case, neither the recursion stack nor the SCC stack represent a complete counter-example. A counter-example can still be obtained by traversing the nodes of an accepting SCS that have already been visited, without re-considering the transition system. We add two pointers to our node representation in the SCC stack, representing "backward" and "forward" links that point to the pair from which the current node was reached and to the oldest pair on the stack that is a successor of the current pair. Indeed, one can show that the subgraph of nodes on the SCC stack with neighborhood relation

$$\{(c, c') : c' = forward(c) \text{ or } c = backward(c')\}$$

also forms an SCS of the product graph. A counter-example can now be produced by enforcing a visit to all the pairs that satisfy some acceptance condition.

4.2   Computation of Successor Configurations

The efficient generation of successor configurations in $succ_{\mathcal{A}}(s, C)$ is a crucial part of our algorithm. Given a configuration $C \subseteq Q$ of the LWAA and a state s of the transition system (which we identify with a valuation of the propositional variables), we need to compute the set of all C' such that $s \cup C' \models \delta(q)$ holds for all $q \in C$. Moreover, we are mainly interested in finding minimal successor configurations.

An elegant approach towards computing successor configurations makes use of BDDs [1]. In fact, the transitions of an LWAA can be represented by a single BDD. The set of minimal successor configurations is obtained by conjoining this BDD with the BDD representations of the state s and the source configuration C, and then extracting the set of all satisfying valuations of the resulting BDD. Some experimentation convinced us, however, that the resulting BDDs become too big for large LTL formulas. Alternatively, one can store BDDs representing $\delta(q)$ for each location q and form the conjunction of all $\delta(q)$ for $q \in C$. Again, this approach turned out to consume too much memory.

We finally resorted to using BDDs only as a representation of configurations. To do so, we examine the hyperedges of the transition graph of the LWAA, which correspond to the clauses of the disjunctive normal form of $\delta(q)$. For every location $q \in C$, we compute the disjunction of its enabled transitions, and then take the conjunction over all locations in C. We thus obtain

$$succ_{\mathcal{A}}(s, C) = \bigwedge_{q \in C} (\bigvee_{t \in enabled(s, q)} (t \setminus \mathcal{V}))$$

as the BDD representing the set of successor configurations, where $enabled(s,q)$ denotes the set of enabled transitions of q for state s, i.e. those transitions t for which $s \cup Q \models t$. Although this requires pre-computing a potentially exponentially large set of transitions, this approach appears to be fastest for BDD-based calculation of successor nodes.

We compare this approach to a direct calculation of successor configurations that stores them as a sorted list, which is pruned to remove non-minimal successors. Although the pruning step is of quadratic complexity in our implementation (it could be improved to $O(n \log n)$ time), experiments showed that it pays off handsomely because fewer nodes need to be explored in the graph search.

4.3   Adapting Spin

Either approach to computing successors works best if we can efficiently determine the set of enabled transitions of an LWAA location. One way to do this is to generate C source code for a given LWAA and then use the CPU arithmetics. The SPIN model checker employs a similar approach, albeit for Büchi automata, and this is one of reasons why we adapted it to use our algorithm.

SPIN [10, 12], is generally considered as one of the fastest and most complete tools for protocol verification. For a given model (written in Promela) and Büchi automaton (called "never-claim"), it generates C sources that are then compiled to produce a model-specific model checker. SPIN also includes a translation from LTL formulas to Büchi automata, but for our comparisons we used the LTL2BA tool due to Gastin and Oddoux [7], which is faster by orders of magnitude for large LTL formulas.

Our adaptation, called LWAASPIN, adds the generation of LWAA to SPIN, and modifies the code generation to use Tarjan's algorithm and on-the-fly calculation of successor configurations. This involved about 150 code changes, and added about 2600 lines of code. SPIN includes elaborate optimizations, such as partial-order reduction, that are independent of the use of non-deterministic or alternating automata and that can therefore be used with our implementation as well. We have not yet adapted SPIN's optimizations of memory usage such as bitstate hashing to our algorithm, although we see no obstacle in principle to do so.

4.4   Experimental Results

Geldenhuys and Valmari [8] have recently proposed to use Tarjan's algorithm, but for non-deterministic Büchi automata, and we have implemented their algorithm for comparison. We have not been able to reproduce their results indicating that Tarjan's algorithm outperforms the CVWY algorithm on nondeterministic Büchi automata (their paper does not indicate which implementation of CVWY was used). In our experiments, both algorithms perform head-to-head on most examples. We now describe the results for the implementation based on LWAA.

For most examples, the search for an accepting SCS in the product graph is slower than the runtime of the model checker produced by SPIN after LTL2BA has generated the Büchi automaton. However, our algorithm can be considerably faster than generating the Büchi automaton and then checking the emptiness of the product automaton, for large LTL formulas. However, note that both SPIN and our implementation use unguided search, and we can thus not exactly compare single instances of satisfiable problems.

Large LTL formulas are not as common as one might expect. SPIN's implementation of the CVWY algorithm can handle weak fairness of processes directly; such conditions do not have to be added to the LTL formula to be verified. We present two simple and scalable examples: the dining philosophers problem and a binary semaphore protocol.

For the dining philosophers example, we want to verify that if every philosopher holds exactly one fork infinitely often, then philosopher 1 will eventually eat:

$$\mathbf{GF}\,hasFork_1 \wedge \ldots \wedge \mathbf{GF}\,hasFork_n \;\Rightarrow\; \mathbf{GF}\,eat_1$$

The model dinphil$n$ denotes the situation where all n philosophers start with their right-hand fork, which may lead to a deadlock. The model dinphil$n$i avoids the deadlock by letting the n-th philosopher start with his left-hand fork.

For the binary semaphore example we claim that if strong fairness is ensured for each process, all processes will eventually have been in their critical section:

$$(\mathbf{GF}\,canenter_1 \Rightarrow \mathbf{GF}\,enter_1) \wedge \ldots \wedge (\mathbf{GF}\,canenter_n \Rightarrow \mathbf{GF}\,enter_n) \;\Rightarrow\; \mathbf{F}\,allcrit$$

By sfgood$n$, we denote a constellation with n processes and strong fairness assumed for each of them, while sfbad$n$ denotes the same constellation, except with weak fairness for process p_n, which will allow the process to starve.

Table 1 contains timings (in seconds) for the different steps of the verification process for SPIN 4.1.1 and for our LWAASPIN implementation. SPIN requires successive invocations of ltl2ba, spin, gcc and pan; LWAASPIN combines the first two stages. The times were measured on an Intel Pentium® 4, 3.0 GHz computer with 1GB main memory running Linux and without other significant process activity. Entries "o.o.t." indicate that the computation did not finish within 2 hours, while "o.o.m." means "out of memory".

We can see that most of the time required by SPIN is spent on preparing the pan model checker, either by calculating the non-deterministic Büchi automata for the dining philosophers, or by handling the large automata sources for the binary semaphore example. LWAASPIN significantly reduces the time taken for pre-processing.

The sizes of the generated automata are indicated in Tab. 2. "States seen" denotes the number of distinct states (of the product automaton) encountered by LWAASPIN using the direct successor configuration calculation approach. It should be noted that the Büchi automata for the dining philosophers example are very small compared to the size of the formula, and are in fact linear; even for the dinphil10i case, the automaton contains only 12 locations. This is not true for the semaphore example: the Büchi automaton for sfgood7 contains 3025 locations and 23391 transitions. Still, one advantage of using LTL2BA is that a Büchi automaton that has been computed once can be stored and reused; this could reduce the overall verification time for the dining philosophers example where the same formula is used for both the valid and the invalid model.

We can draw two conclusions from our data: first, the preprocessing by lwaaspin uses very little time because we do not have to calculate the Büchi automaton (although strictly speaking our implementation is also exponential because it transforms the transition formulas into disjunctive normal form). This makes up for the usually inferior

Table 1. Comparison of SPIN and LWAASPIN (BDD-less successor calculation)

Problem	Counter-example	SPIN				LWAASPIN		
		lt12ba	spin	gcc	pan	lwaaspin	gcc	pan
dinphil6	yes	0.431	0.019	0.601	0.079	0.019	0.579	0.163
dinphil8	yes	35.946	0.02	0.671	0.133	0.027	0.818	0.166
dinphil10	yes	3611.724	0.025	0.767	1.642	0.057	1.899	0.170
dinphil12	yes	o.o.t.				0.141	6.644	0.206
dinphil14	yes					0.499	28.082	0.431
dinphil15	yes					0.972	o.o.m.	
dinphil6i	no	0.431	0.024	0.639	0.244	0.020	0.616	0.569
dinphil8i	no	35.946	0.021	0.711	7.309	0.028	0.861	20.177
dinphil10i	no	3611.724	0.025	0.807	722.874	0.070	2.623	623.760
dinphil11i	no	o.o.t.				0.099	3.438	o.o.m.
sfbad6	yes	1.904	0.912	7.284	0.025	0.066	2.211	1.312
sfbad7	yes	27.674	42.525	o.o.m.		0.179	7.423	7.848
sfbad8	yes					0.784	43.472	7.000
sfbad9	yes					2.627	o.o.m.	
sfgood6	no	2.292	17.329	27.608	2.193	0.064	2.227	2.540
sfgood7	no	36.306	417.485	o.o.m.		0.357	8.214	15.940
sfgood8	no					0.718	42.688	140.130
sfgood9	no					2.634	o.o.m.	

Table 2. Comparison of successor calculation, and sizes of the automata

Problem	Successor calculation		LWAA		Büchi		States seen
	BDD	direct	Locations	Transitions	Locations	Transitions	
dinphil6	0.834	0.761	10	207	8	36	105
dinphil8	1.194	1.011	12	787	10	55	119
dinphil10	2.803	2.126	14	3095	12	78	133
dinphil6i	1.291	1.205	10	207	8	36	46165
dinphil8i	21.802	21.021	12	787	10	55	$1.2 \cdot 10^6$
dinphil10i	643.006	626.453	14	3095	12	78	$1.5 \cdot 10^7$
sfbad6	16.664	3.589	26	4140	252	1757	137882
sfbad7	354.874	15.461	30	16435	1292	8252	597686
sfgood6	32.261	4.831	26	4139	972	5872	221497
sfgood7	115.539	24.511	30	16434	3025	23391	872589

performance of our pan version. It also means that we can at least start a model checking run, even for very large LTL formulas, in the hope of finding a counter-example. Second, we can check larger LTL formulas. Ultimately, we encounter the same difficulties as SPIN during both the gcc and the pan phases; after all, we are confronted with a PSPACE-complete problem. The pre-processing phase could be further reduced by avoiding the generation of an exponential number of transitions in the C sources, postponing more work to the pan executable. Besides, the bitstate hashing technique as implemented in SPIN [11] could also be applied to Tarjan's algorithm.

Table 2 also compares the two approaches to computing successor configurations described in Sect. 4.2. The BDD-based approach appears to be less predictable and never outperforms the direct computation, but further experience is necessary to better understand the tradeoff.

5   Conclusion and Further Work

We have presented a novel algorithm for the classical problem of LTL model checking. It uses an LWAA encoding of the LTL property as a symbolic representation of the corresponding GBA, which is effectively generated on the fly during the state space search, and never has to be stored explicitly. By adapting the SPIN model checker to our approach, we validate that, for large LTL formulas, the time gained by avoiding the expensive construction of a non-deterministic Büchi automaton more than makes up for the runtime penalty due to the implicit GBA generation during model checking, and this advantage does not appear to be offset by the simplifications applied to the intermediate automata by algorithms such as LTL2BA. However, we do not yet really understand the relationship between minimizations at the automaton level and the local optimizations applied in our search.

We believe that our approach opens the way to verifying large LTL formulas by model checking. Further work should investigate the possibilities that arise from this opportunity, such as improving techniques for software model checking based on predicate abstraction. Also, our implementation still leaves room for performance improvements. In particular, the LWAA should be further minimized, the representation of transitions could be reconsidered, and the memory requirements could be reduced by clever coding techniques.

References

1. R. E. Bryant. Graph-based algorithms for boolean function manipulation. *IEEE Trans. Computers*, C-35(8):677–691, 1986.
2. C. Courcoubetis, M. Y. Vardi, P. Wolper, and M. Yannakakis. Memory-efficient algorithms for the verification of temporal properties. *Formal methods in system design*, 1:275–288, 1992.
3. M. Daniele, F. Giunchiglia, and M. Y. Vardi. Improved automata generation for linear temporal logic. In N. Halbwachs and D. Peled, editors, *11th Intl. Conf. Computer Aided Verification (CAV'99)*, volume 1633 of *Lect. Notes in Comp. Sci.*, pages 249–260, Trento, Italy, 1999. Springer-Verlag.
4. K. Etessami and G. Holzmann. Optimizing Büchi automata. In C. Palamidessi, editor, *CONCUR 2000 - Concurrency Theory: 11th International Conference*, volume 1877 of *Lect. Notes in Comp. Sci.*, pages 153–167, University Park, PA, 2000. Springer-Verlag.
5. C. Fritz. Constructing Büchi automata from linear temporal logic using simulation relations for alternating Büchi automata. In O. Ibarra and Z. Dang, editors, *8th Intl. Conf. Implementation and Application of Automata (CIAA 2003)*, volume 2759 of *Lect. Notes in Comp. Sci.*, pages 35–48, Santa Barbara, CA, USA, 2003. Springer-Verlag.

6. C. Fritz and T. Wilke. State space reductions for alternating Büchi automata: Quotienting by simulation equivalences. In M. Agrawal and A. Seth, editors, *22nd Conf. Found. Software Tech. and Theor. Comp. Sci. (FSTTCS 2002)*, volume 2556 of *Lect. Notes in Comp. Sci.*, pages 157–168, Kanpur, India, 2002. Springer-Verlag.

7. P. Gastin and D. Oddoux. Fast LTL to Büchi automata translation. In G. Berry, H. Comon, and A. Finkel, editors, *13th Intl. Conf. Computer Aided Verification (CAV'01)*, volume 2102 of *Lect. Notes in Comp. Sci.*, pages 53–65, Paris, France, 2001. Springer-Verlag.

8. J. Geldenhuys and A. Valmari. Tarjan's algorithm makes LTL verification more efficient. In K. Jensen and A. Podelski, editors, *10th Intl. Conf. Tools and Algorithms for the Construction and Analysis of Systems (TACAS'04)*, volume 2988 of *Lect. Notes in Comp. Sci.*, pages 205–219, Barcelona, Spain, 2004. Springer-Verlag.

9. R. Gerth, D. Peled, M. Y. Vardi, and P. Wolper. Simple on-the-fly automatic verification of linear temporal logic. In P. Dembinski and M. Sredniawa, editors, *Protocol Specification, Testing, and Verification*, pages 3–18, Warsaw, Poland, 1995. Chapman & Hall.

10. G. Holzmann. The Spin model checker. *IEEE Trans. on Software Engineering*, 23(5):279–295, 1997.

11. G. Holzmann. An analysis of bitstate hashing. *Formal Methods in System Design*, 13(3):289–307, 1998.

12. G. Holzmann. *The SPIN Model Checker*. Addison-Wesley, 2003.

13. Y. Kesten and A. Pnueli. Verifying liveness by augmented abstraction. In J. Flum and M. Rodríguez-Artalejo, editors, *Computer Science Logic (CSL'99)*, volume 1683 of *Lect. Notes in Comp. Sci.*, pages 141–156, Madrid, Spain, 1999. Springer-Verlag.

14. C. Löding and W. Thomas. Alternating automata and logics over infinite words. In J. van Leeuwen et al., editor, *IFIP Intl. Conf. Theor. Comp. Sci. (TCS 2000)*, volume 1872 of *Lect. Notes in Comp. Sci.*, pages 521–535, Sendai, Japan, 2000.

15. D.E. Muller, A. Saoudi, and P.E. Schupp. Weak alternating automata give a simple explanation of why most temporal and dynamic logics are decidable in exponential time. In *3rd IEEE Symp. Logic in Computer Science (LICS'88)*, pages 422–427, Edinburgh, Scotland, 1988. IEEE Press.

16. S. Rohde. *Alternating automata and the temporal logic of ordinals*. PhD thesis, Dept. of Math., Univ. of Illinois, Urbana-Champaign, IL, 1997.

17. K. Schneider. Yet another look at LTL model checking. In L. Pierre and T. Kropf, editors, *IFIP Work. Conf. Correct Hardware Design and Verification Methods (CHARME'99)*, volume 1703 of *Lect. Notes in Comp. Sci.*, pages 321–326, Bad Herrenalb, Germany, 1999. Springer-Verlag.

18. F. Somenzi and R. Bloem. Efficient Büchi automata from LTL formulae. In E.A. Emerson and A.P. Sistla, editors, *12th Intl. Conf. Computer Aided Verification (CAV 2000)*, volume 1633 of *Lect. Notes in Comp. Sci.*, pages 257–263, Chicago, IL, 2000. Springer-Verlag.

19. R. E. Tarjan. Depth first search and linear graph algorithms. *SIAM Journal of Computing*, 1:146–160, 1972.

20. H. Tauriainen. On translating linear temporal logic into alternating and nondeterministic automata. Research Report A83, Helsinki Univ. of Technology, Lab. Theor. Comp. Sci., Espoo, Finland, December 2003.

21. H. Tauriainen. Nested emptiness search for generalized Büchi automata. In M. Kishnevsky and Ph. Darondeau, editors, *4th Intl. Conf. Application of Concurrency to System Design (ACSD 2004)*, pages 165–174, Hamilton, Ontario, 2004. IEEE Computer Society.

22. W. Thomas. Languages, automata, and logic. In G. Rozenberg and A. Salomaa, editors, *Handbook of Formal Language Theory*, volume III, pages 389–455. Springer-Verlag, 1997.

23. M. Y. Vardi. Alternating automata and program verification. In J. van Leeuwen, editor, *Computer Science Today*, volume 1000 of *Lect. Notes in Comp. Sci.*, pages 471–485. Springer-Verlag, 1995.

Complementation Constructions for Nondeterministic Automata on Infinite Words

Orna Kupferman[1],[*] and Moshe Y. Vardi[2],[**]

[1] Hebrew University, School of Engineering and Computer Science,
Jerusalem 91904, Israel
orna@cs.huji.ac.il,
http://www.cs.huji.ac.il/~orna
[2] Rice University, Department of Computer Science, Houston,
TX 77251-1892, U.S.A
vardi@cs.rice.edu,
http://www.cs.rice.edu/~vardi

Abstract. The complementation problem for nondeterministic automata on infinite words has numerous applications in formal verification. In particular, the language-containment problem, to which many verification problems are reduced, involves complementation. Traditional optimal complementation constructions are quite complicated and have not been implemented. Recently, we have developed an analysis techniques for runs of co-Büchi and generalized co-Büchi automata and used the analysis to describe simpler optimal complementation constructions for Büchi and generalized Büchi automata. In this work, we extend the analysis technique to Rabin and Streett automata, and use the analysis to describe novel and simple complementation constructions for them.

1 Introduction

The complementation problem for nondeterministic automata on infinite words has numerous applications in formal verification. In order to check that the language of an automaton $\mathcal{A}_1$ is contained in the language of a second automaton $\mathcal{A}_2$, one checks that the intersection of $\mathcal{A}_1$ with an automaton that complements $\mathcal{A}_2$ is empty. Many problems in verification and design are reduced to language containment. In model checking, the automaton $\mathcal{A}_1$ corresponds to the system, and the automaton $\mathcal{A}_2$ corresponds to the specification [Kur94, VW94]. While it is easy to complement specifications given in terms of formulas in temporal logic, complementation of specifications given in terms of automata is so problematic, that in practice the user is required to describe the specification in terms of a deterministic automaton (it is easy to complement a deterministic automaton) [Kur87, HHK96], or to supply the automaton for the negation of the specification [Hol97]. Language containment is also useful in the context of abstraction,

---

[*] Supported in part by BSF grant 9800096, and by a grant from Minerva.
[**] Supported in part by NSF grants CCR-9988322, CCR-0124077, CCR-0311326, IIS-9908435, IIS-9978135, EIA-0086264, and ANI-0216467, by BSF grant 9800096, by Texas ATP grant 003604-0058-2003, and by a grant from the Intel Corporation.

N. Halbwachs and L. Zuck (Eds.): TACAS 2005, LNCS 3440, pp. 206–221, 2005.

where a large system is replaced by an abstraction whose language is richer, yet its state space is smaller. Such abstractions are particularly useful in the context of parametric verification, where a parallel composition of an unbounded number of processes is abstracted by a composition of a finite number of them [KP00, KPP03], and in the context of inheritance and behavioral conformity in object-oriented analysis and design [HK02]. Other applications have to do with the fact that language equivalence is checked by two language-containment tests. For example, the translators from LTL into automata have reached a remarkable level of sophistication (cf. [GBS02]), and it is useful to check their correctness, which involves a language-equivalence test.

Efforts to develop simple complementation constructions for nondeterministic automata started early in the 60s, motivated by decision problems of second order logics. Büchi suggested a complementation construction for nondeterministic Büchi automata that involved a complicated combinatorial argument and a doubly-exponential blow-up in the state space [Büc62]. Thus, complementing an automaton with n states resulted in an automaton with $2^{2^{O(n)}}$ states. In 1988, Safra introduced an optimal determinization construction, which also enabled a $2^{O(n \log n)}$ complementation construction [Saf88], matching the known lower bound [Mic88]. Another $2^{O(n \log n)}$ construction was suggested by Klarlund in [Kla91], which circumvented the need for determinization. The optimal constructions in [Saf88, Kla91] found theoretical applications in the establishment of decision procedures (cf. [EJ91]), but the intricacy of the constructions makes their implementation difficult. We know of no implementation of Klarlund's algorithm, and the implementation of Safra's algorithm [THB95] has to cope with the rather involved structure of the states in the complementary automaton. In [KV01] we described a simple, optimal complementation of nondeterministic Büchi automata, based on the analysis of runs of universal co-Büchi automata. A report on an implementation of this construction can be found in [GKSV03]. The construction was extended to nondeterministic generalized Büchi automata in [KV04]. Beyond its simplicity, the construction has other attractive properties: it can be implemented symbolically [Mer00, KV01], it is amenable to optimizations [GKSV03] and improvements [FKV04], and it naturally generates certificates to the verification task [KV04].

Many of the applications described above for the language-containment problem involve Rabin and Streett automata; cf. [LPS81, KPSZ02]. In particular, applications that involve the composition of processes and objects are typically applied to systems augmented with a strong-fairness condition, which corresponds to the Streett acceptance condition. Since nondeterministic Büchi automata recognize all the ω-regular languages, the complementation procedure in [KV01] can be used in order to complement richer classes of automata on infinite words, like nondeterministic Rabin and Streett automata: given a Rabin or Streett automaton $\mathcal{A}$, one can first translate $\mathcal{A}$ to a nondeterministic Büchi automaton $\mathcal{A}'$, and then complement $\mathcal{A}'$. While such an approach is reasonable for Rabin automata, it is not reasonable for Streett automata. Indeed, given a Rabin automaton $\mathcal{A}$ with n states and index k, the automaton $\mathcal{A}'$ has $O(nk)$ states, resulting in a complementary Büchi automaton with $2^{O(nk \log nk)}$ states. When $\mathcal{A}$ is a Streett automaton, however, $\mathcal{A}'$ has $O(n2^k)$ states [SV89], resulting in a complementary Büchi automaton with $2^{O(nk2^k \log n)}$ states. The fact that going through Büchi automata leads to a doubly-exponential construction makes the complementation problem for nondeterministic Streett automata much harder than the corresponding problem for Rabin automata. The first exponential complementation construction for Streett automata was given in [SV89]. their bound for the size of complementary automaton is 2^{m^5}, where m is the size of the input automaton. Only in [Kla91, Saf92], Klarlund and Safra came up with an improved construction, where the complementary automaton has $2^{O(nk \log nk)}$ states (optimality of this bound is still open). As has been the case with the early optimal constructions for Büchi automata, the constructions in [Kla91, Saf92] are quite complicated, and quite difficult to understand and teach.

In this work, we generalize the approach of [KV01, KV04] to nondeterministic Rabin and Streett automata, and describe novel and simple complementation construction for them. Given a nondeterministic Rabin automaton A with n states and index k, the complementary automaton $\tilde{A}$ we construct is a nondeterministic Büchi automaton with $2^{O(nk \log n)}$ states. When A is a Streett automaton, $\tilde{A}$ has $2^{O(nk \log nk)}$ states. Our construction is based on an analysis of the runs of the universal dual of A, by means of ranks associated with states. In this sense, it is closely related to the *progress-measures* introduced in [Kla90]. Note that while the constructions (Theorems 2 and 4) are simple, the analysis (Lemmas 3 and 4) is quite nontrivial. As in the case of Büchi, the state space of the complementary automaton consists of subsets of the state space of original automaton and ranking functions for them, thus our constructions can be implemented symbolically[1], and we expect them to be optimizable. Note that in the case of Streett automata, our blow-up matches the one of Klarlund and Safra, whereas in the case of Rabin automata, we improve the known $2^{O(nk \log nk)}$ bound exponentially. At any rate, the main advantage of our approach is in the simplicity of the construction; the complexity analysis shows that, furthermore, there is no "penalty" for this simplicity.

2   Preliminaries

Automata on Infinite Words. Given an alphabet Σ, an *infinite word over* Σ is an infinite sequence $w = \sigma_0 \cdot \sigma_1 \cdot \sigma_2 \cdots$ of letters in Σ. We denote by w^l the suffix $\sigma_l \cdot \sigma_{l+1} \cdot \sigma_{l+2} \cdots$ of w. An *automaton on infinite words* is $A = \langle \Sigma, Q, Q_{in}, \rho, \alpha \rangle$, where Σ is the input alphabet, Q is a finite set of states, $\rho : Q \times \Sigma \to 2^Q$ is a transition function, $Q_{in} \subseteq Q$ is a set of initial states, and α is an acceptance condition (a condition that defines a subset of Q^ω). Intuitively, $\rho(q, \sigma)$ is the set of states that A can move into when it is in state q and it reads the letter σ. Since the transition function of A may specify many possible transitions for each state and letter, A is not *deterministic*. If ρ is such that for every $q \in Q$ and $\sigma \in \Sigma$, we have that $|\rho(q, \sigma)| = 1$, then A is a deterministic automaton.

A *run* of A on w is a function $r : \mathbb{N} \to Q$ where $r(0) \in Q_{in}$ and for every $l \geq 0$, we have $r(l+1) \in \rho(r(l), \sigma_l)$. In automata over finite words, acceptance is defined according to the last state visited by the run. When the words are infinite, there is no such thing "last state", and acceptance is defined according to the set $Inf(r)$ of states that r visits *infinitely often*, i.e., $Inf(r) = \{q \in Q : \text{for infinitely many } l \in \mathbb{N}, \text{ we have } r(l) = q\}$. As Q is finite, it is guaranteed that $Inf(r) \neq \emptyset$. The way we refer to $Inf(r)$ depends on

---

[1] In contrast, the state space of the complementary automata in [Kla91, Saf92] consist of labeled ordered trees, making a symbolic implementation difficult.

the acceptance condition of $\mathcal{A}$. Several acceptance conditions are studied in the literature. We consider here five:

- *Büchi automata*, where $\alpha \subseteq Q$, and r is accepting iff $Inf(r) \cap \alpha \neq \emptyset$.
- *co-Büchi automata*, where $\alpha \subseteq Q$, and r is accepting iff $Inf(r) \cap \alpha = \emptyset$.
- *Generalized Büchi automata*, where $\alpha = \{G_1, G_2, \ldots, G_k\}$ and r is accepting iff $Inf(r) \cap G_i \neq \emptyset$ for all $1 \leq i \leq k$.
- *Generalized co-Büchi automata*, where $\alpha = \{B_1, B_2, \ldots, B_k\}$ and r is accepting iff $Inf(r) \cap B_i = \emptyset$ for some $1 \leq i \leq k$.
- *Rabin automata*, where $\alpha = \{\langle G_1, B_1\rangle, \langle G_2, B_2\rangle, \ldots, \langle G_k, B_k\rangle\}$, and r is accepting iff for some $1 \leq i \leq k$, we have that $Inf(r) \cap G_i \neq \emptyset$ and $Inf(r) \cap B_i = \emptyset$.
- *Streett automata*, where $\alpha = \{\langle B_1, G_1\rangle, \langle B_2, G_2\rangle, \ldots, \langle B_k, G_k\rangle\}$, and r is accepting iff for all $1 \leq i \leq k$, if $Inf(r) \cap B_i \neq \emptyset$, then $Inf(r) \cap G_i \neq \emptyset$.

The number k of sets in the generalized Büchi and co-Büchi acceptance conditions or pairs in the Rabin and Streett acceptance conditions is called the *index* of α (or $\mathcal{A}$). Note that the Büchi and the co-Büchi conditions are dual, in the sense that a run r satisfies a Büchi condition α iff r does not satisfy α when regarded as a co-Büchi condition. Similarly, generalized Büchi and generalized co-Büchi are dual, and so are Rabin and Streett.

Since $\mathcal{A}$ is not deterministic, it may have many runs on w. In contrast, a deterministic automaton has a single run on w. There are two dual ways in which we can refer to the many runs. When $\mathcal{A}$ is a *nondeterministic* automaton, it accepts an input word w iff there exists an accepting run of $\mathcal{A}$ on w. When $\mathcal{A}$ is a *universal* automaton, it accepts an input word w iff all the runs of $\mathcal{A}$ on w are accepting.

We use three-letter acronyms to describe types of automata. The first letter describes the transition structure and is one of "D" (deterministic), "N" (nondeterministic), and "U" (universal). The second letter describes the acceptance condition and is one of "B" (Büchi), "C" (co-Büchi), "GB" (generalized Büchi), "GC" (generalized co-Büchi), "S" (Streett), and "R" (Rabin). The third letter designates the objects accepted by the automata; in this paper we are only concerned with "W" (infinite words). Thus, for example, NBW designates a nondeterministic Büchi word automaton and UCW designates a universal co-Büchi word automaton. For the case of Streett and Rabin automata we sometimes also indicate the index of the automaton. For example, USW[1] is a universal Streett word automaton with one pair in its acceptance condition.

In [KV01], we suggested the following approach for complementing nondeterministic automata: in order to complement a nondeterministic automaton, first dualize the transition function and the acceptance condition, and then translate the resulting universal automaton back to a nondeterministic one. By [MS87], the dual automaton accepts the complementary language, and so does the nondeterministic automaton we end up with. In the special case of Büchi automata, one starts with an NBW, dualize it to a UCW, which accepts the complementary language, and then translates the UCW to an equivalent NBW. Thus, rather than determinization, complementation is based on a translation of universal automata to nondeterministic ones, which turned out to be much simpler. In this paper, we extend this approach to Rabin and Streett automata.

Run DAGs Consider a universal word automaton $\mathcal{A} = \langle \Sigma, Q, Q_{in}, \delta, \alpha \rangle$. Let $|Q| = n$. The runs of $\mathcal{A}$ on a word $w = \sigma_0 \cdot \sigma_1 \cdots$ can be arranged in an infinite DAG (directed acyclic graph) $\mathcal{G}_r = \langle V, E \rangle$, where

- $V \subseteq Q \times \mathbb{N}$ is such that $\langle q, l \rangle \in V$ iff some run of $\mathcal{A}$ on w has $r(l) = q$. For example, the first level of $\mathcal{G}_r$ contains the vertices $Q_{in} \times \{0\}$.
- $E \subseteq \bigcup_{l \geq 0} (Q \times \{l\}) \times (Q \times \{l+1\})$ is such that $E(\langle q, l \rangle, \langle q', l+1 \rangle)$ iff $\langle q, l \rangle \in V$ and $q' \in \delta(q, \sigma_l)$.

Thus, $\mathcal{G}_r$ embodies exactly all the runs of $\mathcal{A}$ on w. We call $\mathcal{G}_r$ the *run* DAG of $\mathcal{A}$ on w, and we say that $\mathcal{G}_r$ is *accepting* if all its paths satisfy the acceptance condition α. Note that $\mathcal{A}$ accepts w iff $\mathcal{G}_r$ is accepting. We say that a vertex $\langle q', l' \rangle$ is a *successor* of a vertex $\langle q, l \rangle$ iff $E(\langle q, l \rangle, \langle q', l' \rangle)$. We say that $\langle q', l' \rangle$ is *reachable* from $\langle q, l \rangle$ iff there exists a sequence $\langle q_0, l_0 \rangle, \langle q_1, l_1 \rangle, \langle q_2, l_2 \rangle, \ldots$ of successive vertices such that $\langle q, l \rangle = \langle q_0, l_0 \rangle$, and there exists $i \geq 0$ such that $\langle q', l' \rangle = \langle q_i, l_i \rangle$. For a set $S \subseteq Q$, we say that a vertex $\langle q, l \rangle$ of $\mathcal{G}_r$ is an *S-vertex* if $q \in S$.

Consider a (possibly finite) DAG $\mathcal{G} \subseteq \mathcal{G}_r$. We say that a vertex $\langle q, l \rangle$ is *finite* in $\mathcal{G}$ if only finitely many vertices in $\mathcal{G}$ are reachable from $\langle q, l \rangle$. For a set $S \subseteq Q$, we say that a vertex $\langle q, l \rangle$ is *S-free* in $\mathcal{G}$ if all the vertices in $\mathcal{G}$ that are reachable from $\langle q, l \rangle$ are not *S*-vertices. Note that, in particular, an *S*-free vertex is not an *S*-vertex. Finally, we say that the *width* of $\mathcal{G}$ is d if d is the maximal number for which there are infinitely many levels l such that there are d vertices of the form $\langle q, l \rangle$ in $\mathcal{G}$. Note that the width of $\mathcal{G}_r$ is at most n.

Runs of UCW and UGCW were studied in [KV01, KV04]. For $x \in \mathbb{N}$, let $[x]$ denote the set $\{0, 1, \ldots, x\}$, and let $[x]^{odd}$ and $[x]^{even}$ denote the set of odd and even members of $[x]$, respectively. Consider a generalized co-Büchi condition $\alpha = \{B_1, \ldots, B_k\}$. Let $I = \{1, \ldots, k\}$, and let $\Omega_I = [2n]^{even} \cup ([2n]^{odd} \times I)$. We refer to the members of Ω_I in $[2n]^{even}$ as *even ranks* and refer to the members of Ω_I in $[2n]^{odd} \times \{j\}$ as *odd ranks with index j*. The members of Ω_I are ordered according to their element in $[2n]$. Thus, $r \leq r'$, $\langle r, i \rangle \leq r'$, and $r \leq \langle r', i' \rangle$ iff $r \leq r'$. In addition, $\langle r, i \rangle \leq \langle r', i' \rangle$ iff $r < r'$ or $\langle r, i \rangle = \langle r', i' \rangle$.

Generalized Co-Büchi Ranking. Recall that a run r satisfies α if there is some $j \in I$ such that $inf(r) \cap B_j = \emptyset$. A *generalized co-Büchi ranking* (GC-ranking, for short) for $\mathcal{G}_r$ is a function $f : V \to \Omega_I$ that satisfies the following conditions:

1. For all vertices $\langle q, l \rangle \in V$, if $f(\langle q, l \rangle) = \langle r, j \rangle$, then $q \notin B_j$.
2. For all edges $\langle \langle q, l \rangle, \langle q', l+1 \rangle \rangle \in E$, we have $f(\langle q', l+1 \rangle) \leq f(\langle q, l \rangle)$.

Thus, a ranking associates with each vertex in $\mathcal{G}_r$ a rank in Ω_I so that ranks along paths are not increased, and B_j-vertices cannot get an odd rank with index j. Note that each path in $\mathcal{G}_r$ eventually gets trapped in some rank. We say that the ranking f is an *odd GC-ranking* if all the paths of $\mathcal{G}_r$ eventually get trapped in an odd rank. Formally, f is odd iff for all paths $\langle q_0, 0 \rangle, \langle q_1, 1 \rangle, \langle q_2, 2 \rangle, \ldots$ in $\mathcal{G}_r$, there is $l \geq 0$ such that $f(\langle q_l, l \rangle)$ is odd, and for all $l' \geq l$, we have $f(\langle q_{l'}, l' \rangle) = f(\langle q_l, l \rangle)$. Note that, equivalently, f is odd if every path of $\mathcal{G}_r$ has infinitely many vertices with odd ranks.

Lemma 1. [KV04] *The following are equivalent.*

1. *All the paths of $\mathcal{G}_r$ satisfy the generalized co-Büchi condition $\{B_1, \ldots, B_k\}$.*
2. *There is an odd GC-ranking for $\mathcal{G}_r$.*

Proof: Assume first that there is an odd GC-ranking for $\mathcal{G}_r$. Then, every path in $\mathcal{G}_r$ eventually gets trapped in an odd rank with index j, for some $j \in I$. Hence, as B_j-vertices cannot get an odd rank with index j, all the paths of $\mathcal{G}_r$ has some $j \in I$ for which they visit B_j only finitely often, and we are done.

For the other direction, given an accepting run DAG $\mathcal{G}_r$, we define an infinite sequence $\mathcal{G}_0 \supseteq \mathcal{G}_1 \supseteq \mathcal{G}_2 \supseteq \ldots$ of DAGs inductively as follows. For $\mathcal{G} \subseteq \mathcal{G}_r$ and $j \in I$, we say that j is *helpful* for $\mathcal{G}$ if $\mathcal{G}$ contains a B_j-free vertex.

- $\mathcal{G}_0 = \mathcal{G}_r$.
- $\mathcal{G}_{2i+1} = \mathcal{G}_{2i} \setminus \{\langle q, l \rangle \mid \langle q, l \rangle \text{ is finite in } \mathcal{G}_{2i}\}$.
- Let $j \in I$ be the minimal[2] index helpful for $\mathcal{G}_{2i+1}$, if exists.
  Then, $\mathcal{G}_{2i+2} = \mathcal{G}_{2i+1} \setminus \{\langle q, l \rangle \mid \langle q, l \rangle \text{ is } B_j\text{-free in } \mathcal{G}_{2i+1}\}$.

It can be shown that for every $i \geq 0$, unless the DAG $\mathcal{G}_{2i+1}$ is empty, then there is some $j \in I$ that is helpful for $\mathcal{G}_{2i+1}$. Since the successors of a B_j-free vertex are also B_j-free, and since all the vertices in $\mathcal{G}_{2i+1}$ have at least one successor, the transition from $\mathcal{G}_{2i+1}$ to $\mathcal{G}_{2i+2}$ involves the removal of an infinite path from $\mathcal{G}_{2i+1}$. Since the width of $\mathcal{G}_0$ is bounded by n, it follows that the width of $\mathcal{G}_{2i}$ is at most $n - i$. Hence, $\mathcal{G}_{2n}$ is finite, and $\mathcal{G}_{2n+1}$ is empty.

Each vertex $\langle q, l \rangle$ in $\mathcal{G}_r$ has a unique index $i \geq 1$ such that $\langle q, l \rangle$ is either finite in $\mathcal{G}_{2i}$ or B_j-free in $\mathcal{G}_{2i+1}$, for some $j \in I$. Thus, the sequence of DAGs induces a function $f : V \to \Omega_I$, where $f(\langle q, l \rangle)$ is $2i$, if $\langle q, l \rangle$ is finite in $\mathcal{G}_{2i}$, and is $\langle 2i + 1, j \rangle$, if j is the minimal index helpful for $\mathcal{G}_{2i+1}$ and $\langle q, l \rangle$ is B_j-free in $\mathcal{G}_{2i+1}$. It can be shown that the function f is an odd GC-ranking[3]. □

A *co-Büchi-ranking* for $\mathcal{G}_r$ (*C-ranking*, for short) can be defined as a special case of GC-ranking. Since $I = \{1\}$, we omit the indices from the odd ranks, thus a C-ranking is a function $f : V \to [2n]$. It can be shown (a special case of Lemma 1, see [KV01] for details) that all the paths of $\mathcal{G}_r$ have only finitely many α-vertices iff there is an odd C-ranking for $\mathcal{G}_r$.

3 NRW Complementation

In this section we analyze runs of USW and use the analysis in order to translate USW to NBW. The translation is then used for NRW complementation. We start with USW[1], and then generalize to USW with an arbitrary index.

---

[2] The fact that j is minimal is not important, any choice will do.

[3] The proof in [KV04] refers to a slightly different definition of GC-ranking, but it is easy to modify it to the definition we use here.

Streett[1]-ranking. We first consider USW[1], where $\alpha = \{\langle B, G \rangle\}$ contains a single pair, and $\mathcal{G}_r$ is accepting iff all paths in $\mathcal{G}_r$ have finitely many B-vertices or infinitely many G-vertices.

A *Streett[1]-ranking* for $\mathcal{G}_r$ (*S[1]-ranking*, for short) is a function $f : V \rightarrow [2n]$ that satisfies the following two conditions:

1. For all vertices $\langle q, l \rangle \in V$, if $f(\langle q, l \rangle)$ is odd, then $q \notin B$.
2. For all edges $\langle \langle q, l \rangle, \langle q', l+1 \rangle \rangle \in E$, either $f(\langle q', l+1 \rangle) \leq f(\langle q, l \rangle)$ or $q \in G$.

Thus, an S[1]-ranking associates with each vertex in $\mathcal{G}_r$ a rank in $[2n]$ so that the ranks along paths may increase only when a G-vertex is visited, and no B-vertex is odd. Note that each path in $\mathcal{G}_r$ either visit G-vertices infinitely often or eventually gets trapped in some rank. We say that the S[1]-ranking f is an *odd S[1]-ranking* if all the paths of $\mathcal{G}_r$ either visit G-vertices infinitely often or eventually gets trapped in an odd rank. Formally, f is odd iff for all paths $\langle q_0, 0 \rangle, \langle q_1, 1 \rangle, \langle q_2, 2 \rangle, \ldots$ in $\mathcal{G}_r$, either $q_l \in G$ for infinitely many $l \geq 0$ or there is $l \geq 0$ such that $f(\langle q_l, l \rangle)$ is odd, and for all $l' \geq l$, we have $f(\langle q_{l'}, l' \rangle) = f(\langle q_l, l \rangle)$. Note that, equivalently, f is odd if every path of $\mathcal{G}_r$ has infinitely many G-vertices or infinitely many odd vertices.

Lemma 2. *The following are equivalent.*

1. *All the paths of $\mathcal{G}_r$ satisfy the Streett[1] condition $\{\langle B, G \rangle\}$.*
2. *There is an odd S[1]-ranking for $\mathcal{G}_r$.*

Lemma 2 implies that $\mathcal{A}$ accepts a word w iff there is a ranking for the run DAG $\mathcal{G}_r$ of $\mathcal{A}$ on w such that every infinite path in $\mathcal{G}_r$ has infinitely many G-vertices or infinitely many odd vertices. Intuitively, the lemma suggests that the two requirements that the Streett[1] condition involves (finitely many B or infinitely many G) can be reduced to a new condition of only one type (infinitely often, for odd or G-vertices). This intuition is formalized in the translation of USW[1] to NBW, which is described (as a special case of a translation of USW to NBW) in Theorem 2.

Theorem 1. *Let $\mathcal{A}$ be a USW[1] with n states. There is an NBW $\mathcal{A}'$ with $2^{O(n \log n)}$ states such that $\mathcal{L}(\mathcal{A}') = \mathcal{L}(\mathcal{A})$.*

Streett-ranking. We now turn to consider a general Streett condition $\alpha = \{\langle B_1, G_1 \rangle, \ldots, \langle B_k, G_k \rangle\}$, where $\mathcal{G}_r$ is accepting iff all paths in $\mathcal{G}_r$ have, for all $1 \leq i \leq k$, finitely many B_i-vertices or infinitely many G_i-vertices.

Consider a function $f : V \rightarrow [2n]^k$. For an index $1 \leq i \leq k$, we use $f(v)[i]$ to denote the i-th element in $f(v)$. We call $f(v)[i]$ the *i-rank of v* (according to f). A *Streett-ranking* (*S-ranking*, for short) for $\mathcal{G}_r$ is a function $f : V \rightarrow [2n]^k$ that satisfies the following two conditions:

1. For all vertices $\langle q, l \rangle \in V$ and $1 \leq i \leq k$, if $f(\langle q, l \rangle)[i]$ is odd, then $q \notin B_i$.
2. For all edges $\langle \langle q, l \rangle, \langle q', l+1 \rangle \rangle \in E$ and $1 \leq i \leq k$, either $f(\langle q', l+1 \rangle)[i] \leq f(\langle q, l \rangle)[i]$ or $q \in G_i$.

Thus, an S-ranking f associates with each vertex in $\mathcal{G}_r$ a vector of k ranks in $[2n]$ so that for all $1 \leq i \leq k$, the projection $f[i]$ of f is an S[1]-ranking with respect to $\langle B_i, G_i \rangle$.

We say that the ranking f is an *odd S-ranking* if, for all $1 \leq i \leq k$, the S[1]-ranking $f[i]$ is odd. Thus, for all $1 \leq i \leq k$, all the paths of $\mathcal{G}_r$ either visit G_i-vertices infinitely often or eventually get trapped in an odd i-rank. Formally, f is odd iff for all paths $\langle q_0, 0 \rangle, \langle q_1, 1 \rangle, \langle q_2, 2 \rangle, \ldots$ in $\mathcal{G}_r$ and for all $1 \leq i \leq k$, either $q_l \in G_i$ for infinitely many $l \geq 0$ or there is $l \geq 0$ such that $f(\langle q_l, l \rangle)[i]$ is odd, and for all $l' \geq l$, we have $f(\langle q_{l'}, l' \rangle)[i] = f(\langle q_l, l \rangle)[i]$. Note that, equivalently, f is odd if every path of $\mathcal{G}_r$ has, for all $1 \leq i \leq k$ infinitely many G_i-vertices or infinitely many vertices with an odd i-rank.

Lemma 3. *The following are equivalent.*

1. *All the paths of $\mathcal{G}_r$ satisfy the Streett condition $\{\langle B_1, G_1 \rangle, \ldots, \langle B_k, G_k \rangle\}$.*
2. *There is an odd S-ranking for $\mathcal{G}_r$.*

Proof: Immediate from Lemma 2 and the definition of an odd S-ranking as the composition of k odd S[1]-rankings for the pairs in the Streett condition.   □

From USW to NBW. A USW $\mathcal{A}$ with $\alpha = \{\langle B_1, G_1 \rangle, \langle B_2, G_2 \rangle, \ldots, \langle B_k, G_k \rangle\}$ is equivalent to the intersection of the k USW[1] $\mathcal{A}_i$ obtained from $\mathcal{A}$ by taking the acceptance condition to be $\langle B_i, G_i \rangle$. It is not surprising, then, that the definition of an odd S-ranking f requires f to be an odd S[1]-ranking with respect to all pairs in α. Following this approach, translating $\mathcal{A}$ to an NBW $\mathcal{A}'$ can proceed by first translating each USW[1] $\mathcal{A}_i$ into an equivalent NBW $\mathcal{A}_i'$ as described in Theorem 1, and then defining $\mathcal{A}'$ as the product of the $\mathcal{A}_i'$'s (see [Cho74] for the product construction for NBW). Such a product would have at most $k \cdot 3^{nk} \cdot (2n+1)^{nk}$ states. We now describe a direct construction, which follows from the analysis of S-ranking, and which is exponentially better.

Theorem 2. *Let $\mathcal{A}$ be a USW with n states and index k. There is an NBW $\mathcal{A}'$ with $2^{O(nk \log n)}$ states such that $\mathcal{L}(\mathcal{A}') = \mathcal{L}(\mathcal{A})$.*

Proof: Let $\mathcal{A} = \langle \Sigma, Q, Q_{in}, \delta, \{\langle B_1, G_1 \rangle, \ldots, \langle B_k, G_k \rangle\}\rangle$ When $\mathcal{A}'$ reads a word w, it guesses an odd S-ranking for the run DAG $\mathcal{G}_r$ of $\mathcal{A}$ on w. At a given point of a run of $\mathcal{A}'$, it keeps in its memory a whole level of $\mathcal{G}_r$ and a guess for the rank of the vertices at this level. In order to make sure that for all $1 \leq i \leq k$, all the paths of $\mathcal{G}_r$ either visit i-odd or G_i-vertices infinitely often, $\mathcal{A}'$ has a flag $1 \leq i \leq k$ and it remembers the set of states that owe a visit to i-odd or G_i-vertices. Once the set becomes empty, i is changed to $(i \bmod k) + 1$.

Before we define $\mathcal{A}'$, we need some notations. A *level ranking* for $\mathcal{A}$ is a function $g : Q \to [2n]^k$, such that for all $1 \leq i \leq k$, if $g(q)[i]$ is odd, then $q \notin B_i$. Let $\mathcal{R}$ be the set of all level rankings. For a subset S of Q and a letter σ, let $\delta(S, \sigma) = \bigcup_{s \in S} \delta(s, \sigma)$. Note that if level l in $\mathcal{G}_r$, for $l \geq 0$, contains the states in S, and the $(l+1)$-th letter in w is σ, then level $l + 1$ of $\mathcal{G}_r$ contains the states in $\delta(S, \sigma)$.

For two level rankings g and g' in $\mathcal{R}$ and a letter σ, we say that g' *covers* $\langle g, \sigma \rangle$ if for all q and q' in Q, if $q' \in \delta(q, \sigma)$, then for all $1 \leq i \leq k$, either $q \in G_i$ or $g'(q')[i] \leq g(q)[i]$. Thus, if g describes the ranks of the vertices of level l, and the $(l+1)$-th letter in w is σ, then g' is a possible level ranking for level $l + 1$. Finally, for $g \in \mathcal{R}$ and $1 \leq i \leq k$, let $good(g, i) = G_i \cup \{q : g(q)[i] \in [2n]^{odd}\}$. Thus, a state of Q is in $good(g, i)$ if it belongs to G_i or has an i-odd rank.

Now, $\mathcal{A}' = \langle \Sigma, Q', Q'_{in}, \delta', \alpha' \rangle$, where

- $Q' = 2^Q \times 2^Q \times \mathcal{R} \times \{1, \ldots, k\}$, where a state $\langle S, O, g, i \rangle \in Q'$ indicates that the current level of the DAG contains the states in S, the pair that is now examined is i, the set $O \subseteq S$ contains states along paths that have not visited a G_i-vertex or an i-odd vertex since the last time O has been empty, and g is the guessed level ranking for the current level.[4]
- $Q'_{in} = Q_{in} \times \{\emptyset\} \times \mathcal{R} \times \{1\}$.
- δ' is defined, for all $\langle S, O, g, i \rangle \in Q'$ and $\sigma \in \Sigma$, as follows.
    - If $O \neq \emptyset$, then $\delta'(\langle S, O, g, i \rangle, \sigma) = \{\langle \delta(S, \sigma), \delta(O, \sigma) \setminus good(g', i), g', i \rangle : g' \text{ covers } \langle g, \sigma \rangle\}$.
    - If $O = \emptyset$, then $\delta'(\langle S, O, g, i \rangle, \sigma) = \{\langle \delta(S, \sigma), \delta(S, \sigma) \setminus good(g', (i \bmod k) + 1), g', (i \bmod k) + 1 \rangle : g' \text{ covers } \langle g, \sigma \rangle\}$.
- $\alpha' = 2^Q \times \{\emptyset\} \times \mathcal{R} \times \{1, \ldots, k\}$.

Since there are at most $(2n + 1)^{nk}$ level rankings, the number of states in $\mathcal{A}'$ is at most $k \cdot 3^n \cdot (2n + 1)^{nk} = 2^{O(nk \log n)}$. □

For the proof of Theorem 1, note that when $\mathcal{A}$ is a USW[1], there is no need for the index component in the state space, and $\mathcal{A}'$ has $2^{O(n \log n)}$ states.

Theorem 3. *Let $\mathcal{A}$ be an NRW with n states and index k. There is an NBW $\tilde{\mathcal{A}}$ with $2^{O(nk \log n)}$ states such that $\mathcal{L}(\tilde{\mathcal{A}}) = \Sigma^\omega \setminus \mathcal{L}(\mathcal{A})$.*

Proof: The automaton $\tilde{\mathcal{A}}$ is obtained by translating the USW that dualizes $\mathcal{A}$ to an NBW. □

Note that the previous complementation constructions for NRW involve a $2^{O(nk \log nk)}$ blow up, as they first translate the NRW into an NBW with $O(nk)$ states, and complementing an NBW with m states results in an NBW with $2^{O(m \log m)}$ states [Saf88]. Thus, our construction eliminates the term k from the exponent. In addition, the constants hiding in the $O()$ notation are exponentially better in our approach. Indeed, the number of states of an NBW equivalent to an NRW[k] with n states may be $2nk$. On the other hand, our ranks refer to the original state space of the automaton, and there is no need to double it for each pair. For example, when $k = 1$, going through NBW results in a complementary NBW with at most $3^{2n} \cdot (4n + 1)^{2n}$ states, whereas our direct construction results in an NBW with at most $3^n \cdot (2n + 1)^n$ states.

4   NSW Complementation

In this section we analyze runs of URW and use the analysis in order to translate URW to NBW. The translation is then used for NSW complementation.

---

[4] Note that a naive direct construction results in an NBW whose state space contains k subsets of Q, each acting as the "O component" of a pair in α. Since, however, the O component of all pairs should become empty infinitely often, it is possible to optimize the naive construction and keep track of a single pair (and its corresponding O component) at a time.

Rabin-ranking. Consider a Rabin condition $\alpha = \{\langle G_1, B_1 \rangle, \langle G_2, B_2 \rangle, \ldots, \langle G_k, B_k \rangle\}$. Let $I = \{1, \ldots, k\}$, and let $\Omega_I = [2n]^{even} \cup ([2n]^{odd} \times I)$. Recall that a run r satisfies α iff there is $1 \leq i \leq k$ such that $Inf(r) \cap G_i \neq \emptyset$ and $Inf(r) \cap B_i = \emptyset$. A *Rabin rank* is a tuple $\langle \langle r_1, i_1 \rangle, \ldots, \langle r_{m-1}, i_{m-1} \rangle, r_m \rangle$ of m ranks in Ω_I, for $1 \leq m \leq k + 1$. The i_j's are distinct, and except for the last rank, which is even, all the ranks are odd. We refer to m as the *width* of the rank, and to the j-th element of a Rabin rank γ as $\gamma[j]$. Let $\mathcal{D}_I$ denote the set of Rabin ranks (with respect to α).

A *Rabin ranking* (*R-ranking*, for short) for $\mathcal{G}_r$ is a function $f : V \to \mathcal{D}_I$ that satisfies the following conditions:

1. For all $\langle q, l \rangle \in V$, let m be the width of $f(\langle q, l \rangle)$. Then,
   (a) For all $1 \leq j < m - 1$, if $f(\langle q, l \rangle)[j] = \langle r_j, i_j \rangle$, then $q \notin G_{i_j}$.
   (b) For all $1 \leq j < m$, if $f(\langle q, l \rangle)[j] = \langle r_j, i_j \rangle$, then $q \notin B_{i_j}$.
2. For all edges $\langle \langle q, l \rangle, \langle q', l + 1 \rangle \rangle \in E$, let m and m' be the widths of $f(\langle q, l \rangle)$ and $f(\langle q', l + 1 \rangle)$, respectively, and let $m'' = \min\{m, m'\}$. Then,
   (a) For all $1 \leq j \leq m'' - 1$, if $f(\langle q', l + 1 \rangle)[h] = f(\langle q, l \rangle)[h]$ for all $1 \leq h < j$, then $f(\langle q', l + 1 \rangle)[j] \leq f(\langle q, l \rangle)[j]$.
   (b) If $f(\langle q', l + 1 \rangle)[h] = f(\langle q, l \rangle)[h]$ for all $1 \leq h < m''$, then either $f(\langle q', l + 1 \rangle)[m''] \leq f(\langle q, l \rangle)[m'']$, or $m'' > 1$, $f(\langle q, l \rangle)[m'' - 1] = \langle r_{m''-1}, i_{m''-1} \rangle$, and $q \in G_{i_{m''-1}}$.

Thus, if $f(\langle q, l \rangle) = \gamma$ and $f(\langle q', l + 1 \rangle) = \gamma'$, then Condition 2 guarantees that for all $1 \leq j \leq m'' - 1$, if $\gamma'[j] > \gamma[j]$, then there is $1 \leq h < j$ such that $\gamma'[h] \neq \gamma[h]$. In addition, if $\gamma'[m''] > \gamma[m'']$, then either there is $1 \leq h < j$ such that $\gamma'[h] \neq \gamma[h]$, or $m'' > 1$, $f(\langle q, l \rangle)[m'' - 1] = \langle r_{m''-1}, i_{m''-1} \rangle$, and $q \in G_{i_{m''-1}}$. We refer to the latter conjunction as the *bridge disjunct* of Condition 2b.

For a vertex $v \in V$, the width of v, denoted $width(v)$, is the width of $f(v)$. A vertex with width 1 is *even*, and a vertex with width at least 2 is *odd*. We say that a vertex $\langle q, l \rangle$ is *happy* (with respect to f) if $f(\langle q, l \rangle) = \langle \langle r_1, i_1 \rangle, \ldots, \langle r_{m-1}, i_{m-1} \rangle, r_m \rangle$ for some $m > 1$ and $q \in G_{i_{m-1}}$. Note that all happy vertices are odd. An *R-ranking* is an *odd R-ranking* if all infinite paths have infinitely many happy vertices.

Lemma 4. *The following are equivalent.*

1. *All the paths of $\mathcal{G}_r$ satisfy the Rabin condition $\{\langle G_1, B_1 \rangle, \ldots, \langle G_k, B_k \rangle\}$.*
2. *There is an odd R-ranking for $\mathcal{G}_r$.*

Intuitively, Lemma 4 suggests that the requirements that the Rabin condition involves, which are of different types (infinitely often, for the G_i elements, and finitely often, for the B_i elements), can be reduced to a new condition of only one type (infinitely often, for happy vertices). This intuition is formalized in the construction below. Note that while the proof of Lemma 4 is complicated, the construction that follows is simple.

Theorem 4. *Let $\mathcal{A}$ be a URW with n states and index k. There is an NBW $\mathcal{A}'$ with $2^{O(nk \log nk)}$ states such that $\mathcal{L}(\mathcal{A}') = \mathcal{L}(\mathcal{A})$.*

Proof: Let $\mathcal{A} = \langle \Sigma, Q, Q_{in}, \delta, \{\langle G_1, B_1 \rangle, \ldots, \langle G_k, B_k \rangle\}\rangle$ When $\mathcal{A}'$ reads a word w, it guesses an odd R-ranking for the run DAG $\mathcal{G}_r$ of $\mathcal{A}$ on w. At a given point of a run of

$\mathcal{A}'$, it keeps in its memory a whole level of $\mathcal{G}_r$ and a guess for the ranks of the vertices at this level. In order to make sure that all the infinite paths of $\mathcal{G}_r$ visit happy vertices infinitely often, $\mathcal{A}'$ remembers the set of states that owe a visit to happy vertices.

Before we define $\mathcal{A}'$, we need to adjust our notations to ranks in $\mathcal{D}_I$. A *level ranking* for $\mathcal{A}$ is a function $g : Q \to \mathcal{D}_I$, such that for all $q \in Q$ with $width(g(q)) = m$, and for all $1 \le j < m - 1$, if $g(q)[j] = \langle r_j, i_j \rangle$, then $q \notin G_{i_j}$. Also, for all $1 \le j < m$, if $g(q)[j] = \langle r_j, i_j \rangle$, then $q \notin B_{i_j}$. The correspondence between the above conditions and Condition 1 in the definition of R-ranking guarantees that g describes possible ranks for vertices in some level of $\mathcal{G}_r$. Let $\mathcal{R}$ be the set of all level rankings. Note that since a Rabin rank in $\mathcal{D}_I$ can be characterized by at most k elements in $[2n]^{odd}$, one element in $[2n]^{even}$, and a permutation of I, the size of $\mathcal{D}_I$ is at most $n^k \cdot (n+1) \cdot k!$. Accordingly, there are at most $2^{O(nk \log nk)}$ level rankings. For two level rankings g and g' in $\mathcal{R}$, a subset $S \subseteq Q$, and a letter σ, we say that g' *covers* $\langle g, S, \sigma \rangle$ if for all $q \in S$ and $q' \in \delta(q, \sigma)$, the following holds. Let m and m' be the widths of $g(q)$ and $g(q')$, respectively, and let $m'' = \min\{m, m'\}$. Then,

1. For all $1 \le j \le m'' - 1$, if $g'(q')[h] = g(q)[h]$ for all $1 \le h < j$, then $g'(q')[j] \le g(q)[j]$.
2. If $g(q')[h] = g(q)[h]$ for all $1 \le h < m''$, then either $g'(q')[m''] \le g(q)[m'']$, or $m'' > 1$, $g(q)[m'' - 1] = \langle r_{m''-1}, i_{m''-1} \rangle$, and $q \in G_{i_{m''-1}}$.

The correspondence between the above conditions and Condition 2 in the definition of R-ranking guarantees that if S is the set of states in level l, the $(l + 1)$-th letter in the word is σ, g describes the ranks of vertices of level l, and g' covers $\langle g, S, \sigma \rangle$, then g' is a possible level ranking for level $l + 1$. Finally, for $g \in \mathcal{R}$, let $good(g) \subseteq Q$ be the set of states q such that the width of $g(q)$ is $m > 1$, $g(q)[m - 1] = \langle r_{m-1}, i_{m-1} \rangle$ for some $r_{m-1} \in [2n]^{odd}$, and $q \in G_{i_{m-1}}$.

Now, $\mathcal{A}' = \langle \Sigma, Q', Q'_{in}, \delta', \alpha' \rangle$, where

- $Q' = 2^Q \times 2^Q \times \mathcal{R}$, where a state $\langle S, O, g \rangle \in Q'$ indicates that the current level of the DAG contains the states in S, the set $O \subseteq S$ contains states along paths that have not visited a happy vertex since the last time O has been empty, and g is the guessed level ranking for the current level.
- $Q'_{in} = Q_{in} \times \{\emptyset\} \times \mathcal{R}$.
- δ' is defined, for all $\langle S, O, g \rangle \in Q'$ and $\sigma \in \Sigma$, as follows.

  - If $O \ne \emptyset$, then $\delta'(\langle S, O, g \rangle, \sigma) = \{\langle \delta(S, \sigma), \delta(O, \sigma) \setminus good(g'), g' \rangle : g'$ covers $\langle g, S, \sigma \rangle\}$.
  - If $O = \emptyset$, then $\delta'(\langle S, O, g \rangle, \sigma) = \{\langle \delta(S, \sigma), \delta(S, \sigma) \setminus good(g'), g' \rangle : g'$ covers $\langle g, S, \sigma \rangle\}$.

- $\alpha' = 2^Q \times \{\emptyset\} \times \mathcal{R}$.

Since there are at most $2^{O(nk \log nk)}$ level rankings, the number of states in $\mathcal{A}'$ is at most $3^n \cdot 2^{O(nk \log nk)} = 2^{O(nk \log nk)}$.   □

Remark 1. Below we discuss some variants of R-ranking, which still satisfy Lemma 4, and therefore, with a corresponding adjustment of the definition of "covers", can be used in order to translate URW to NBW. First, it can be shown that Condition 1a is not essential. In other words, the proof of Lemma 4 stays valid when we allow a vertex $\langle q, l \rangle$ with $q \in G_{i_j}$ to have $f(\langle q, l \rangle)[j] = \langle r_j, i_j \rangle$, for $j < width(\langle q, l \rangle)$. Condition 1a, however, has the advantage that it restricts the state space of the NBW. Second, the indices i_j of a Rabin rank $\langle \langle r_1, i_1 \rangle, \ldots, \langle r_{m-1}, i_{m-1} \rangle, r_m \rangle$ need not be distinct. Again, the proof stays valid if we allow an index to repeat. As with Condition 1a, the fact the indices are distinct restricts the state space. On the other hand, in a symbolic implementation, such a restriction may cause complications.

Theorem 5. *Let $\mathcal{A}$ be an NSW with n states and index k. There is an NBW $\tilde{\mathcal{A}}$ with $2^{O(nk \log nk)}$ states such that $\mathcal{L}(\tilde{\mathcal{A}}) = \Sigma^\omega \setminus \mathcal{L}(\mathcal{A})$.*

Proof: The automaton $\tilde{\mathcal{A}}$ is obtained by translating the URW that dualizes $\mathcal{A}$ to an NBW. $\qquad\square$

5   Language Containment

Recall that a primary application of complementation constructions is language containment: in order to check that the language of an automaton $\mathcal{A}_1$ is contained in the language of a second automaton $\mathcal{A}_2$, one checks that the intersection of $\mathcal{A}_1$ with an automaton that complements $\mathcal{A}_2$ is empty. In this section we demonstrate the simplicity and advantage of our construction with respect to this application. We first show how an automaton that complements $\mathcal{A}_2$, when constructed using our construction, can be optimized in the process of its intersection with $\mathcal{A}_1$. We then describe the product $\mathcal{P}$ of $\mathcal{A}_1$ with the complementing automaton, namely the automaton whose emptiness should be tested in order to check whether $\mathcal{L}(\mathcal{A}_1) \subseteq \mathcal{L}(\mathcal{A}_2)$. Our goal in describing $\mathcal{P}$ is to highlight the simplicity of the language-containment algorithm. To the best of our knowledge, this is the first time that such a product $\mathcal{P}$ is described in a few lines.

5.1   Optimizations That Depend on $\mathcal{A}_1$

Consider a language-containment problem $\mathcal{L}(\mathcal{A}_1) \subseteq \mathcal{L}(\mathcal{A}_2)$. The solution that follows from our approach is to start by dualizing $\mathcal{A}_2$, translate the result (a universal automaton $\tilde{\mathcal{A}}_2$) to a nondeterministic automaton $\tilde{\mathcal{N}}_2$, which complements $\mathcal{A}_2$, and check the emptiness of the product $\mathcal{A}_1 \times \tilde{\mathcal{N}}_2$. Consider the universal automaton $\tilde{\mathcal{A}}_2$. Our translation of $\tilde{\mathcal{A}}_2$ to $\tilde{\mathcal{N}}_2$ is based on ranks we associate with vertices that appear in run DAGs of $\tilde{\mathcal{A}}_2$. Let n be the number of states on $\mathcal{A}_2$. The range of the ranks is $0, \ldots, 2n$, and, depending on the type of $\tilde{\mathcal{A}}_2$, they may be associated with indices, and/or arranged in tuples. The bound $2n$ on the maximal rank follows from the fact that the width of the run DAG is bounded by n. To see the latter, consider a run DAG $\mathcal{G}_r$ that embodies all the runs of $\tilde{\mathcal{A}}_2$ on a word $w = \sigma_0 \cdot \sigma_1 \cdots$. A level $l \geq 0$ of $\mathcal{G}_r$ contains exactly all vertices $\langle q, l \rangle$ such that a run of $\mathcal{A}_2$ on w visits q after reading the prefix $\sigma_0 \cdot \sigma_1 \ldots \sigma_{l-1}$. Thus, since there are n different states, there may be at most n different such vertices in each level.

In fact, we can tighten the width of $\mathcal{G}_r$ further. Indeed, the structure of $\mathcal{A}_2$ may guarantee that some states may not appear together in the same level. For example, if q_0 and q_1 are reachable only after reading even-length and odd-length prefixes of w, respectively, then q_0 and q_1 cannot appear together in the same level in the run DAG of $\mathcal{A}_2$ on w, which enables us to bound its width by $n-1$. In general, since the construction of $\tilde{\mathcal{N}}_2$ takes into an account all words $w \in \Sigma^\omega$, we need to check the "mutual exclusiveness" of q_0 and q_1 with respect to all words. This can be done using the subset construction [RS59]: let $\mathcal{A}_2 = \langle \Sigma, Q_2, Q_{in}^2, \delta_2, \alpha_2 \rangle$, and let $\mathcal{A}_2^d = \langle \Sigma, 2^{Q_2}, \{Q_{in}^2\}, \delta_2^d \rangle$ be the automaton without acceptance condition obtained by applying the subset construction to $\mathcal{A}_2$. Thus, for all $S \in 2^{Q_2}$, we have that $\delta_2^d(S, \sigma) = \bigcup_{s \in S} \delta_2(s, \sigma)$. Now, let $reach(\mathcal{A}_2) \subseteq 2^{Q_2}$ be the set of states reachable in $\mathcal{A}_2^d$ from $\{Q_{in}^2\}$. Thus, $S \subseteq Q_2$ is in $reach(\mathcal{A}_2)$ iff there is a finite word $w \in \Sigma^*$ such that $\delta_2^d(\{Q_{in}^2\}, w) = S$. Then, $reach(\mathcal{A}_2)$ contains exactly all sets S of states such that all the states in S may appear in the same level of some run DAG of $\mathcal{A}_2$. Accordingly, we can tighten our bound on the maximal width a run DAG may have to $r^{max} = \max_{S \in reach(\mathcal{A}_2)} |S|$, and tighten our bound on the maximal rank to $2r^{max}$. If $Q_2 \in reach(\mathcal{A}_2)$, then $r^{max} = n$, and we do not optimize. Often, however, the structure of $\mathcal{A}_2$ does prevent some states to appear together on the same level. As we shall explain now, the presence of $\mathcal{A}_1$ can make the above optimization even more effective.

It is easy to see that some states may be mutual exclusive (i.e., cannot appear in the same level in the run DAG) with respect to some words and not be mutual exclusive with respect to other words. The definition of r^{max} requires mutual exclusiveness with respect to all words. On the other hand, checking $\mathcal{L}(\mathcal{A}_1) \subseteq \mathcal{L}(\mathcal{A}_2)$, we only have to consider mutual exclusiveness with respect to words in $\mathcal{L}(\mathcal{A}_1)$. Note that the fewer words we have to consider, the more likely we are to get mutual exclusiveness, and then tighten the bound further. Checking mutual exclusiveness with respect to $\mathcal{L}(\mathcal{A}_1)$ can be done by taking the product of $\mathcal{A}_1$ with $\mathcal{A}_2^d$. Formally, let $\mathcal{A}_1 = \langle \Sigma, Q_1, Q_{in}^1, \delta_1, \alpha_1 \rangle$, and let $reach(\mathcal{A}_{2|\mathcal{A}_1}) \subseteq 2^{Q_2}$ be the set of states that are reachable in the product of $\mathcal{A}_1$ with $\mathcal{A}_2^d$, projected on the state space of $\mathcal{A}_2^d$. Thus, $S \subseteq Q_2$ is in $reach(\mathcal{A}_{2|\mathcal{A}_1})$ iff there is a finite word $w \in \Sigma^*$ and a state $s' \in Q_1$ such that $s' \in \delta_1(Q_{in}^1, w)$ and $\delta_2^d(\{Q_{in}^2\}, w) = S$. Note that $reach(\mathcal{A}_{2|\mathcal{A}_1})$ excludes from $reach(\mathcal{A}_2)$ sets that are reachable in $\mathcal{A}_2$ only via words that are not reachable in $\mathcal{A}_1$. Accordingly, we can tighten our bound on the maximal width a run DAG of $\mathcal{A}_2$ on a word in $\mathcal{L}(\mathcal{A}_1)$ may have to $r_{\mathcal{A}_1}^{max} = \max_{S \in reach(\mathcal{A}_{2|\mathcal{A}_1})} |S|$, and tighten our bound on the maximal rank in the construction of $\tilde{\mathcal{N}}_2$, which is designated for checking the containment of $\mathcal{L}(\mathcal{A}_1)$ in $\mathcal{L}(\mathcal{A}_2)$, to $2r_{\mathcal{A}_1}^{max}$.

Note that since we actually need to consider only accepting run DAGs, we can optimize further by removal of empty states from the participating automata. For example, if a state $s \in Q_2$ is such that $\mathcal{L}(\mathcal{A}_2^s) = \emptyset$, we remove s from the range of δ_2. In particular, it follows that $\mathcal{A}_2$ has no rejecting sinks, and the range of δ_2 may contain the empty set. This removes from $reach(\mathcal{A}_2)$ sets S that may appear in the same level in a rejecting run DAG of $\mathcal{A}_2$ but cannot appear in the same level in an accepting run DAG. Consequently, r^{max} may become smaller. Similarly, by removing (in addition) empty states from $\mathcal{A}_1$, we restrict $reach(\mathcal{A}_{2|\mathcal{A}_1})$ to sets S of states such that all the states in S may appear in the same level of some (accepting) run DAG of $\mathcal{A}_2$ on a word in $\mathcal{L}(\mathcal{A}_1)$. Finally, we can also remove from $reach(\mathcal{A}_{2|\mathcal{A}_1})$ sets S induced only by pairs $\langle s, S \rangle \in Q_1 \times 2^{Q_2}$ for which the product of $\mathcal{A}_1$ and $\mathcal{A}_2^d$ with initial state $\langle s, S \rangle$ is empty. Indeed, such sets cannot appear in the same level of an accepting run DAG of $\mathcal{A}_2$ on a word in $\mathcal{L}(\mathcal{A}_1)$.

5.2   The Product Automaton

We describe the construction for the most complicated case, where $\mathcal{A}_1$ and $\mathcal{A}_2$ are Streett automata. Other cases are similar, with modified definitions for $\mathcal{R}$, *covers*, and *good*, as in the proofs of Theorems 3 and 5.

Let $\mathcal{A}_1 = \langle \Sigma, Q_1, Q_{in}^1, \delta_1, \alpha_1 \rangle$ and $\mathcal{A}_2 = \langle \Sigma, Q_2, Q_{in}^2, \delta_2, \alpha_2 \rangle$. Also, let $\mathcal{R}$, *covers*, and *good*, be as in the proof Theorem 5, with respect to the components of $\mathcal{A}_2$. As explained in Section 5.1, the ranks in the range $\mathcal{D}_I$ of the level rankings in $\mathcal{R}$ can be restricted to Rabin ranks in which $\Omega_I = [2r_{\mathcal{A}_1}^{max}]^{even} \cup ([2r_{\mathcal{A}_1}^{max}]^{odd} \times I)$. We define the product of $\mathcal{A}_1$ and $\tilde{\mathcal{N}}_2$ as an NSW $\mathcal{P} = \langle \Sigma, Q', Q_{in}', \delta', \alpha' \rangle$, where

- $Q' = Q_1 \times 2^{Q_2} \times 2^{Q_2} \times \mathcal{R}$.
- $Q_{in}' = Q_{in}^1 \times \{Q_{in}^2\} \times \{\emptyset\} \times \mathcal{R}$.
- δ' is defined, for all $\langle q, S, O, g \rangle \in Q'$ and $\sigma \in \Sigma$, as follows.
  - If $O \neq \emptyset$, then $\delta'(\langle q, S, O, g \rangle, \sigma) =$
    $\{\langle q', \delta(S, \sigma), \delta(O, \sigma) \setminus good(g'), g' \rangle : q' \in \delta_1(q, \sigma) \text{ and } g' \text{ covers } \langle g, S, \sigma \rangle\}$.
  - If $O = \emptyset$, then $\delta'(\langle q', S, O, g \rangle, \sigma) =$
    $\{\langle q', \delta(S, \sigma), \delta(S, \sigma) \setminus good(g'), g' \rangle : q' \in \delta_1(q, \sigma) \text{ and } g' \text{ covers } \langle g, S, \sigma \rangle\}$.
- $\alpha' = (\bigcup_{\langle G, B \rangle \in \alpha_1} \{\langle G \times 2^{Q_2} \times 2^{Q_2} \times \mathcal{R}, B \times 2^{Q_2} \times 2^{Q_2} \times \mathcal{R} \rangle\}) \times \{\langle Q', Q_1 \times 2^{Q_2} \times \{\emptyset\} \times \mathcal{R} \rangle\}$.

6   Discussion

Complementation is a key construction in formal verification. At the same time, complementation of automata on infinite words is widely perceived to be rather difficult, unlike the straightforward subset construction for automata on finite words [RS59]. Checking the syllabi of several formal-verification courses, one finds that while most mention the closure under complementation for automata on infinite words, only a few actually teach a complementation construction. Indeed, not too many researchers are sufficiently familiar with the details of known constructions, and many believe that most of the students would not be able to follow the intricate technical details.

This situation has led to a perception that complementation constructions for automata on infinite words are rather impractical. Indeed, an attempt to implement Safra's construction led support to this perception [THB95]. Consequently, there is extensive work on simulation-based abstraction and refinement, cf. [LT87, AL91, DHW91], and research has focused on ways in which fair simulation can approximate language containment [HKR02], and ways in which the complementation construction can be circumvented by manually bridging the gap between fair simulation and language containment [Att99, KPP03].

We believe that this perception ought to be challenged. It is true that language containment is PSPACE-complete [MS73], whereas simulation can be solved in polynomial time [HHK95]. Nevertheless, the exponential blow-up of complementation, which is the reason underlying the PSPACE-hardness of language containment, is a worst-case analysis. As we have learned recently in the context of reasoning about automata on finite words, worst-case blow-ups rarely occur in typical practice [EKM98]. This is confirmed

220   O. Kupferman and M.Y. Vardi

by our recent experience with the complementation construction for Büchi automata [GKSV03]. It is worth remembering also that the translation from LTL to Büchi automata [VW94] was for several years considered impractical because of its worst-case exponential blow-up. We also found the construction of [KV01] quite easy to teach, covering it in a two-hour lecture[5]. We believe that the complementation problem for automata on infinite words ought to be investigated further by the research community, in order to make complementation constructions routinely applicable in formal verification. We hope that our results here for Rabin and Streett automata would constitute a significant contribution in that direction.

References

[AL91]   M. Abadi and L. Lamport. The existence of refinement mappings. *TCS*, 82(2):253–284, 1991.
[Att99]   P. Attie. Liveness-preserving simulation relations. In *Proc. 18th PODC*, pages 63–72, 1999.
[Büc62]   J.R. Büchi. On a decision method in restricted second order arithmetic. In *Proc. Internat. Congr. Logic, Method. and Philos. Sci. 1960*, pages 1–12, Stanford, 1962.
[Cho74]   Y. Choueka. Theories of automata on ω-tapes: A simplified approach. *Journal of CSS*, 8:117–141, 1974.
[DHW91]   D.L. Dill, A.J. Hu, and H. Wong-Toi. Checking for language inclusion using simulation relations. In *Proc. 3rd CAV*, LNCS 575, pages 255–265, 1991
[EJ91]   E.A. Emerson and C. Jutla. Tree automata, μ-calculus and determinacy. In *Proc. 32nd FOCS* pages 368–377, 1991.
[EKM98]   J. Elgaard, N. Klarlund, and A. Möller, Mona 1.x: new techniques for WS1S and WS2S. In *Proc. 10th CAV*, LNCS 1427, pages 516–520, 1998.
[FKV04]   E. Friedgut, O. Kupferman, and M.Y. Vardi. Büchi complementation made tighter. In *Proc. 2nd ATVA*, LNCS 3299, pages 64–78, 2004.
[GBS02]   S. Gurumurthy, R. Bloem, and F. Somenzi. Fair simulation minimization. In *Proc. 14th CAV*, LNCS 2404, pages 610–623, 2002.
[GKSV03] S. Gurumurthy, O. Kupferman, F. Somenzi, and M.Y. Vardi. On complementing nondeterministic Büchi automata. In *Proc. 12th CHARME*, LNCS 2860, pages 96–110, 2003.
[HHK95]   M.R. Henzinger, T.A. Henzinger, and P.W. Kopke. Computing simulations on finite and infinite graphs. In *Proc. 36th FOCS*, pages 453–462, 1995.
[HHK96]   R.H. Hardin, Z. Har'el, and R.P. Kurshan. COSPAN. In *Proc. 8th CAV*, LNCS 1102, pages 423–427, 1996.
[HK02]   D. Harel and O. Kupferman. On the behavioral inheritance of state-based objects. *IEEE TSE*, 28(9):889–903, 2002.
[HKR02]   T.A. Henzinger, O. Kupferman, and S. Rajamani. Fair simulation. *I&C*, 173(1):64–81, 2002.
[Hol97]   G.J. Holzmann. The model checker SPIN. *IEEE TSE*, 23(5):279–295, May 1997.
[Kla90]   N. Klarlund. *Progress Measures and finite arguments for infinite computations*. PhD thesis, Cornell University, 1990.

---

[5] Lecture notes can be found in www.wisdom.weizmann.ac.il/~vardi/av (Moshe Vardi) and. www7.in.tum.de/lehre/automaten2/SS99/ (Javier Esparza).

[Kla91]   N. Klarlund. Progress measures for complementation of ω-automata with applications to temporal logic. In *Proc. 32nd FOCS*, pages 358–367, 1991.

[KP00]   Y. Kesten and A. Pnueli. Verification by augmented finitary abstraction. *I&C*, 163(1):203–243, 2000.

[KPP03]   Y. Kesten, N. Piterman, and A. Pnueli. Bridging the gap between fair simulation and trace containment. In *Proc. 15th CAV*, LNCS 2725, pages 381–393, 2003.

[KPSZ02] Y. Kesten, A. Pnueli, E. Shahar, and L. Zuck. Network invariant in action. In *Proc. 13th CONCUR*, LNCS 2421, pages 101–115, 2002.

[Kur87]   R.P. Kurshan. Complementing deterministic Büchi automata in polynomial time. *Journal of CSS*, 35:59–71, 1987.

[Kur94]   R.P. Kurshan. *Computer Aided Verification of Coordinating Processes*. Princeton Univ. Press, 1994.

[KV01]   O. Kupferman and M.Y. Vardi. Weak alternating automata are not that weak. *ACM ToCL*, 2001(2):408–429, 2001.

[KV04]   O. Kupferman and M.Y. Vardi. From complementation to certification. In *10th TACAS*, LNCS 2988, pages 591–606, 2004.

[LPS81]   D. Lehman, A. Pnueli, and J. Stavi. Impartiality, justice, and fairness – the ethics of concurrent termination. In *Proc. 8th ICALP*, LNCS 115, pages 264–277, 1981.

[LT87]   N. A. Lynch and M.R. Tuttle. Hierarchical correctness proofs for distributed algorithms. In *Proc. 6th PODC*, pages 137–151, 1987.

[Mer00]   S. Merz. Weak alternating automata in Isabelle/HOL. In *Proc. 13th TPiHOL*, LNCS 1869, pages 423–440, 2000.

[Mic88]   M. Michel. Complementation is more difficult with automata on infinite words. CNET, Paris, 1988.

[MS73]   A.R. Meyer and L.J. Stockmeyer. Word problems requiring exponential time: Preliminary report. In *Proc. 5th STOC*, pages 1–9, 1973.

[MS87]   D.E. Muller and P.E. Schupp. Alternating automata on infinite trees. *TCS*, 54:267–276, 1987.

[RS59]   M.O. Rabin and D. Scott. Finite automata and their decision problems. *IBM Journal of Research and Development*, 3:115–125, 1959.

[Saf88]   S. Safra. On the complexity of ω-automata. In *29th FOCS*, pages 319–327, 1988.

[Saf92]   S. Safra. Exponential determinization for ω-automata with strong-fairness acceptance condition. In *Proc. 24th STOC*, 1992.

[SV89]   S. Safra and M.Y. Vardi. On ω-automata and temporal logic. In *Proc. 21st STOC*, pages 127–137, 1989.

[THB95]   S. Tasiran, R. Hojati, and R.K. Brayton. Language containment using nondeterministic ω-automata. In *Proc. 8th CHARME*, LNCS 987, pages 261–277, 1995.

[VW94]   M.Y. Vardi and P. Wolper. Reasoning about infinite computations. *I&C*, 115(1):1–37, November 1994.

Using BDDs to Decide CTL

Will Marrero

DePaul University, Chicago, IL 60604, USA
wmarrero@cs.depaul.edu

Abstract. Computation Tree Logic (CTL) has been used quite extensively and successfully to reason about finite state systems. Algorithms
have been developed for checking if a particular model satisfies a CTL
formula (model checking) as well as for deciding if a CTL formula is
valid or satisfiable. Initially, these algorithms explicitly constructed the
model being checked or the model demonstrating satisfiability. A major
breakthrough in CTL model checking occurred when researchers started
representing the model implicitly via Boolean formulas. The use of ordered binary decision diagrams (OBDDs) as an efficient representation
for these formulas led to a large jump in the size of the models that can
be checked. This paper presents a way to encode the satisfiability algorithms for CTL in terms of Boolean formulas as well, so that symbolic
model checking techniques using OBDDs can be exploited.

Keywords: CTL, satisfiability, validity, BDDs, tableau

1   Introduction

Temporal logic has been used quite extensively and successfully to reason about
finite state systems, including both hardware and software systems. While there
are different logics to choose from, this discussion focuses on Computation Tree
Logic (CTL) proposed by Clarke and Emerson [1]. (For a survey of various
temporal logics, see Chapter 16 of *Handbook of Theoretical Computer Science,
Volume B* [2].)

Initial efforts with CTL focused on algorithms for checking if a particular
structure satisfies a formula (model checking) as well as algorithms for checking if there exists a structure that satisfies a formula (satisfiability) [1]. These
algorithms required the explicit construction of a finite-state transition system
either to check that it satisfies the formula or in an attempt to prove that the
formula is satisfiable. In general, the size of the finite-state transition system is
exponential in the number of atomic propositions in the case of model checking
and exponential in the size of the formula in the case of satisfiability. This placed
a severe limitation on the size of the problems that could be handled by these
algorithms.

A major breakthrough occurred when researchers started using boolean formulas to represent the transition relation of the finite-state system as well as
sets of states in the system implicitly. This technique, called symbolic model

N. Halbwachs and L. Zuck (Eds.): TACAS 2005, LNCS 3440, pp. 222–236, 2005.

checking, avoids explicitly constructing the graph for the system [3, 4]. The key was to use Ordered Binary Decision Diagrams (OBDDs), which are a canonical representation for quantified boolean formulas [5]. This allowed researchers to verify systems with more than 10^{20} states [3].

While much effort continued to be focused on symbolic model checking, very little effort was placed on using these symbolic techniques in the area of CTL satisfiability checking. In particular, the algorithms for CTL satisfiability rely on the construction of an explicit model for the formula in question either by constructing a *tableau* [1] or by constructing a *Hintikka structure* [6]. This paper presents a satisfiability algorithm for CTL which uses OBDDs to implicitly construct a model satisfying the formula. This work depends heavily on the explicit-state Hintikka structure algorithm presented in [6] and is inspired by a similar use of OBDDs for LTL satisfiability and model checking presented in [3, 7].

2 Syntax and Semantics

2.1 Syntax

We provide the syntax and semantics of CTL in a slightly non-standard way which will be useful later when describing the algorithm. The set of well formed formulas (hereafter shortened to formulas) are defined inductively as follows:

- The constants **tt**(true) and **ff**(false) are formulas.
- If p is an atomic proposition, then p is a formula.
- If f is a formula, then so is $\neg f$.
- If f and g are formulas, then so are $f \wedge g$ and $f \vee g$.
- If f is a formula, then so are **EX**f and **AX**f.
- If f and g are formulas, then so are **E**$[f$ **U** $g]$, **A**$[f$ **U** $g]$, **E**$[f$ **R** $g]$, and **A**$[f$ **R** $g]$.

We will also use the following common abbreviations: $f \rightarrow g$ for $\neg f \vee g$, $f \leftrightarrow g$ for $(f \rightarrow g \wedge g \rightarrow f)$, **EF**$f$ for **E**$[$**tt U** $f]$, **AF**f for **A**$[$**tt U** $f]$, **EG**f for **E**$[$**ff R** $f]$, and **AG**f for **A**$[$**ff R** $f]$.

2.2 Structures

CTL formulas are interpreted over Kripke structures. A Kripke structure $M = (S, L, R)$ consists of

- S - a set of states
- $L : S \rightarrow 2^{AP}$ - a labeling of each state with atomic propositions true in the state
- $R \subseteq S \times S$ - a transition relation

Note that the transition relation R is required to be *total* which means every state has a successor. (In other words $\forall s \in S$. $\exists s' \in S$. $R(s, s')$). A *path*, $\pi = s_0, s_1, s_2, \ldots$ is an infinite sequence of states such that $(s_i, s_{i+1}) \in R$ for all $i \geq 0$.

2.3   Semantics

The truth or falsity of a formula f in a state s of a structure $M = (S, L, R)$ is given by the inductively defined relation $\models$. In the definition below, p is an atomic proposition while f and g are arbitrary formulas.

- $M, s \models p$ iff $p \in L(s)$.
- $M, s \models \neg f$ iff $M, s \not\models f$.
- $M, s \models f \wedge g$ iff $M, s \models f$ and $M, s \models f$.
- $M, s \models f \vee g$ iff $M, s \models f$ or $M, s \models f$.
- $M, s \models \mathbf{EX} f$ iff there exists a state s' such that $R(s, s')$ and $M, s' \models f$.
- $M, s \models \mathbf{AX} f$ iff for all states s', $R(s, s')$ implies $M, s' \models f$.
- $M, s \models \mathbf{E}[f \ \mathbf{U} \ g]$ iff there exists a path $s_0, s_1, s_2, \ldots$ where $s_0 = s$ and there exists $k \geq 0$ such that $M, s_k \models g$ and $M, s_i \models f$ for all $0 \leq i < k$.
- $M, s \models \mathbf{A}[f \ \mathbf{U} \ g]$ iff for all paths $s_0, s_1, s_2, \ldots$ where $s_0 = s$, there exists $k \geq 0$ such that $M, s_k \models g$ and $M, s_i \models f$ for all $0 \leq i < k$.
- $M, s \models \mathbf{E}[f \ \mathbf{R} \ g]$ iff there exists a path $s_0, s_1, s_2, \ldots$ where $s_0 = s$, such that for all $k > 0$, if $M, s_i \not\models f$ for all $0 \leq i < k$, then $M, s_k \models g$
- $M, s \models \mathbf{A}[f \ \mathbf{R} \ g]$ iff for all paths $s_0, s_1, s_2, \ldots$ where $s_0 = s$, and for all $k > 0$, if $M, s_i \not\models f$ for all $0 \leq i < k$, then $M, s_k \models g$

Note that we have the following dualities:

- $\neg(f \wedge g) \equiv \neg f \vee \neg g$
- $\neg \mathbf{EX} f \equiv \mathbf{AX} \neg f$
- $\neg \mathbf{E}[f \ \mathbf{U} \ g] \equiv \mathbf{A}[\neg f \ \mathbf{R} \ \neg g]$
- $\neg \mathbf{E}[f \ \mathbf{R} \ g] \equiv \mathbf{A}[\neg f \ \mathbf{U} \ \neg g]$

Also note the following semantic identities which will be used when trying to construct a model that satisfies a formula.

- $\mathbf{E}[f \ \mathbf{U} \ g] \equiv g \vee (f \wedge \mathbf{EX} \mathbf{E}[f \ \mathbf{U} \ g])$
- $\mathbf{A}[f \ \mathbf{U} \ g] \equiv g \vee (f \wedge \mathbf{AX} \mathbf{A}[f \ \mathbf{U} \ g])$
- $\mathbf{E}[f \ \mathbf{R} \ g] \equiv g \wedge (f \vee \mathbf{EX} \mathbf{E}[f \ \mathbf{R} \ g])$
- $\mathbf{A}[f \ \mathbf{R} \ g] \equiv g \wedge (f \vee \mathbf{AX} \mathbf{A}[f \ \mathbf{R} \ g])$

The modalities $\mathbf{EU}$ and $\mathbf{AU}$ are the until operator. For example, $\mathbf{E}[f \ \mathbf{U} \ g]$ is interpreted to mean there is a path on which g eventually holds and on which f holds *until* g holds. The abbreviation $\mathbf{EF} f$ ($\mathbf{AF} f$) is interpreted to mean that along some path (along all paths) f eventually holds at some point in the future while the abbreviation $\mathbf{EG} f$ ($\mathbf{AG} f$) means that there along some path (along on all paths) f holds globally. The modalities $\mathbf{ER}$ and $\mathbf{AR}$ are not as common nor as intuitive as the other modalities. The modality $\mathbf{R}$ is often translated as "release". $\mathbf{E}[f \ \mathbf{R} \ g]$ can be understood to mean that along some path g is required to be true unless f becomes true in which case g is no longer required to be true after that state. In other words, $\mathbf{E}[f \ \mathbf{R} \ g]$ has the same meaning as $\mathbf{EG} g \vee \mathbf{E}[g \ \mathbf{U} \ f \wedge g]$. The importance of $\mathbf{ER}$ and $\mathbf{AR}$ is that they are the duals of the until operator and they can be used to define $\mathbf{EG}$ and $\mathbf{AG}$. The $\mathbf{R}$ modality was introduced in [8] (although $\mathbf{V}$ was used instead of the currently popular $\mathbf{R}$) precisely because a dual for the until operator was required.

3   Hintikka Structures

We now proceed to describe the algorithm for trying to construct a satisfying model for a formula f given in [2]. First, we assume that the formula f is in *negation normal form*, which means all negations are pushed inward as far as possible using the dualities in Section 2.3. For any formula g, we will use $\sim g$ to represent the formula $\neg g$ after being converted into negation normal form.

The *closure* of a formula f, denoted $cl(f)$, is the smallest set of formulas such that

- Every subformula of f is a member of $cl(f)$.
- If $\mathbf{E}[f\ \mathbf{U}\ g] \in cl(f)$ or $\mathbf{E}[f\ \mathbf{R}\ g] \in cl(f)$, then, $\mathbf{EXE}[f\ \mathbf{U}\ g] \in cl(f)$ or $\mathbf{EXE}[f\ \mathbf{R}\ g] \in cl(f)$ respectively.
- If $\mathbf{A}[f\ \mathbf{U}\ g] \in cl(f)$ or $\mathbf{A}[f\ \mathbf{R}\ g] \in cl(f)$, then, $\mathbf{AXA}[f\ \mathbf{U}\ g] \in cl(f)$ or $\mathbf{AXA}[f\ \mathbf{R}\ g] \in cl(f)$ respectively.

For example,

$$cl(\mathbf{AF}p \wedge \mathbf{EX}q) = \{\mathbf{AF}p \wedge \mathbf{EX}q, \mathbf{AF}p, \mathbf{AXAF}p, p, \mathbf{EX}q, q\}$$

We will use $\phi = \mathbf{AF}p \wedge \mathbf{EX}q$ as a running example. The *extended closure* of f, denoted $ecl(f)$, is defined to be $cl(f) \cup \{\ \sim g \mid g \in cl(f)\ \}$. For example,

$$ecl(\phi) = cl(\phi) \cup \{\mathbf{EG}\neg p \vee \mathbf{AX}\neg q, \mathbf{EG}\neg p, \mathbf{EXEG}\neg p, \neg p, \mathbf{AX}\neg q, \neg q\}$$

An *elementary* formula is one which is either a literal, a negated literal, or a formula whose main connective is $\mathbf{EX}$ or $\mathbf{AX}$. We will use $el(f)$ to denote the elementary formulas of f (the members of $ecl(f)$ that are elementary). Any other formula is said to be *nonelementary*. For example,

$$el(\phi) = \{\mathbf{AXAF}p, p, \mathbf{EX}q, q, \mathbf{EXEG}\neg p, \neg p, \mathbf{AX}\neg q, \neg q\}$$

Recall that all formulas are assumed to be in negation normal form, so all nonelementary formulas have a binary main connective. By using the semantic identities from Section 2.3, every nonelementary formula can be viewed as either a conjunctive formula $\alpha \equiv \alpha_1 \wedge \alpha_2$ or as a disjunctive formula $\beta \equiv \beta_1 \vee \beta_2$. Table 1 contains the classifications for all nonelementary formulas.

Table 1. Classification of nonelementary formulas

$\alpha = f \wedge g$	$\alpha_1 = f$	$\alpha_2 = g$
$\alpha = \mathbf{E}[f\ \mathbf{R}\ g]$	$\alpha_1 = g$	$\alpha_2 = f \vee \mathbf{EXE}[f\ \mathbf{R}\ g]$
$\alpha = \mathbf{A}[f\ \mathbf{R}\ g]$	$\alpha_1 = g$	$\alpha_2 = f \vee \mathbf{AXA}[f\ \mathbf{R}\ g]$
$\beta = f \vee g$	$\beta_1 = f$	$\beta_2 = g$
$\beta = \mathbf{E}[f\ \mathbf{U}\ g]$	$\beta_1 = g$	$\beta_2 = f \wedge \mathbf{EXE}[f\ \mathbf{U}\ g]$
$\beta = \mathbf{A}[f\ \mathbf{U}\ g]$	$\beta_1 = g$	$\beta_2 = f \wedge \mathbf{AXA}[f\ \mathbf{U}\ g]$

The model we will try to build for the formula f will have states labeled with subsets of $ecl(f)$. We will need to impose certain consistency requirements when constructing the model. The labeling $L : S \to 2^{ecl(f)}$ must satisfy the following consistency rules for all states s in the model:

- *Propositional Consistency Rules:*
  (PC0) $\sim p \in L(s)$ implies $p \notin L(s)$.
  (PC1) $\alpha \in L(s)$ implies $\alpha_1 \in L(s)$ and $\alpha_2 \in L(s)$.
  (PC2) $\beta \in L(s)$ implies $\beta_1 \in L(s)$ or $\beta_2 \in L(s)$.
  (PC3) $\mathbf{tt} \in L(s)$
  (PC4) $\mathbf{ff} \notin L(s)$
- *Local Consistency Rules:*
  (LC0) $\mathbf{AX}f \in L(s)$ implies that for every successor t of s, $f \in L(t)$.
  (LC1) $\mathbf{EX}f \in L(s)$ implies that there exists a successor t of s, such that $f \in L(t)$.

A *fragment* is a triple $(\hat{S}, \hat{R}, \hat{L})$. It is similar to a structure, except that $\hat{R}$ need not be total. Nodes that do not have successors are called *frontier nodes* while nodes with at least one successor are called *interior nodes*. The fragments we choose will be directed acyclic graphs contained within a particular structure $M = (S, R, L)$ that is under consideration. So $\hat{S} \subseteq S$, $\hat{R} \subseteq R$, and $\hat{L} = L|_{\hat{S}}$. In addition, all nodes in a fragment satisfy rules **PC0-PC4** and **LC0** above, and all interior nodes also satisfy **LC1**.

It turns out that we do not have to construct the full model for a formula f to determine satisfiability. Instead, we will construct a *pseudo-Hintikka structure* for f. A pseudo-Hintikka structure for f is a structure $M = (S, R, L)$ where:

1. $f \in L(s)$ for some state $s \in S$.
2. All states satisfy the consistency rules **PC0-PC4** and **LC0-LC1**.
3. All eventualities are *pseudo-fulfilled* as follows:
   - $\mathbf{A}[f \mathbf{\ U\ } g] \in L(s)$ implies there is a fragment contained in M and rooted at s such that for all frontier nodes t, $g \in L(t)$ and for all interior nodes u, $f \in L(u)$.
   - $\mathbf{E}[f \mathbf{\ U\ } g] \in L(s)$ implies there is a fragment contained in M and rooted at s such that for some frontier node t, $g \in L(t)$ and for all interior nodes u, $f \in L(u)$.

In [2], Emerson proves that a formula f is satisfiable if and only if there is a finite pseudo-Hintikka structure for f. He proceeds to give the following algorithm for deciding the satisfiability of a formula f:

1. Build an initial tableau $T = (S, R, L)$ for f as follows:
   - Define S to be the collection of maximal, propositionally consistent subsets of $ecl(f)$. In other words, $\forall s \in S$. $\forall g \in ecl(f)$. $\{g, \sim g\} \cap s \neq \emptyset$ and s satisfies **PC0 - PC4**.
   - Define R to be $S \times S - \{ (s,t) \mid$ for some $\mathbf{AX}g \in ecl(f)$, $\mathbf{AX}g \in s$ and $g \notin t \}$. This ensures that T satisfies **LC0**.
   - Define $L(s) = s$ for all $s \in S$.

2. Ensure the tableau also satisfies pseudo-fulfillment of eventualities and **LC1**. This can be done by repeatedly applying the following rules until a fixpoint is reached:
   - Delete any state that has no successors.
   - Delete any state that violates **LC1**.
   - Delete any state s that is labeled with an eventuality that does not have a fragment certifying pseudo-fulfillment of r.
3. The formula f is satisfiable if and only if the final tableau has a state labeled with f.

It is important to note that the final tableau is *not* necessarily a model for the formula, although Emerson does describe how a satisfying model could be extracted from this final tableau [2].

4 OBDD Encoding

The algorithm presented in Section 3 assumes an explicit representation of the tableau as a finite-state transition system. OBDDs have been used as an efficient, implicit representation for transition systems and for sets of states in both CTL and LTL model checking as well as in deciding satisfiability for LTL formulas [3, 7]. We use similar techniques to decide satisfiability for CTL formulas by encoding the initial tableau (step 1) and the fixpoint computation (step 2) in terms of OBDDs. When the final tableau is computed, its states and transition relation will also be represented as OBDDs and we can simply ask if the conjunction of the OBDD for the states with the OBDD for the formula f is satisfiable (is not the false OBDD).

First, we observe that when constructing the initial tableau $T = (S, R, L)$ for a formula f, the propositional consistency rules **PC0-PC2** mean that the labeling on the elementary formulas in a state completely determines the labeling on all formulas in $ecl(f)$ in that state, so we could define S to be $2^{ecl(f)}$. In fact, we only need half of the elementary formulas since the label on g also determines the label on $\sim g$. (Recall that $\sim g$ is the result of pushing in the negation in the formula $\neg g$.) Therefore, we can use $S = 2^{el^+(f)}$ where $el^+(f)$ are the formulas in $ecl(f)$ that are either atomic propositions or have **EX** as the main connective. Again, using $\phi = \mathbf{AF}p \wedge \mathbf{EX}q$, we have

$$el^+(\phi) = \{p, \mathbf{EXEG}\neg p, q, \mathbf{EX}q\}$$

The set $el^+(f)$ forms the set of boolean state variables. Each unique assignment to these state variables yields a unique state in the tableau. To help avoid confusion, we use $\langle g \rangle$ to denote the state variable for $g \in el^+(f)$ and $\mathcal{V}_f = \{ \langle g \rangle \mid g \in el^+(f) \}$ to denote the set of all state variables in the tableau for f. We then encode states of the tableau as well as the transition relation of the tableau using quantified boolean formulas (QBF) over $\mathcal{V}_f$ which will be represented using OBDDs. For example, any QBF formula over $\mathcal{V}_f$ can be used to encode the set of states in which that formula evaluates to true.

The labeling function L can easily be implemented using OBDDs. Using Table 1, and the fact that all **EX** and all **AX** formulas will correspond to variables (possibly negated) in $\mathcal{V}_f$, we can translate any formula in $g \in ecl(f)$ into an equivalent boolean formula $\overline{g}$ over $\mathcal{V}_f$ without temporal operators as follows:

- $\overline{p} = \langle p \rangle$ for all atomic propositions p.
- $\overline{\neg p} = \neg \langle p \rangle$ for all atomic propositions p.
- $\overline{g \wedge h} = \overline{g} \wedge \overline{h}$
- $\overline{g \vee h} = \overline{g} \vee \overline{h}$
- $\overline{\mathbf{EX}g} = \langle \mathbf{EX}g \rangle$
- $\overline{\mathbf{AX}g} = \neg \langle \mathbf{EX} \sim g \rangle$
- $\overline{\mathbf{E}[g \ \mathbf{U} \ h]} = \overline{h} \vee (\overline{g} \wedge \langle \mathbf{EXE}[g \ \mathbf{U} \ h] \rangle)$
- $\overline{\mathbf{A}[g \ \mathbf{U} \ h]} = \overline{h} \vee (\overline{g} \wedge \neg \langle \mathbf{EXE}[\sim g \ \mathbf{R} \ \sim h] \rangle)$
- $\overline{\mathbf{E}[g \ \mathbf{R} \ h]} = \overline{h} \wedge (\overline{g} \vee \langle \mathbf{EXE}[g \ \mathbf{R} \ h] \rangle)$
- $\overline{\mathbf{A}[g \ \mathbf{R} \ h]} = \overline{h} \wedge (\overline{g} \vee \neg \langle \mathbf{EXE}[\sim g \ \mathbf{U} \ \sim h] \rangle)$

With this translation, we can determine if a state is labeled with g by checking if $\overline{g}$ evaluates to true in the state. In other words, $L(s) = \{ g \mid s \models \overline{g} \}$. Clearly, this definition for L satisfies the propositional consistency rules **PC0-PC4**.

We now have constructed S and L for the tableau. To construct the transition relation R, we create a second copy of state variables, $\mathcal{V}'_f = \{ v' \mid v \in \mathcal{V}_f \}$, to represent the next state in a transition. In what follows, V and V' are boolean vectors representing a truth assignment to the variables in V_f and V'_f respectively. A boolean vector V is identified with the state s that is equal to the set of variables in V_f assigned true by V. (Recall that in our tableau, $S = 2^{el^+(f)}$ and so each state is a subset of $el^+(f)$). The tableau transition relation $\overline{R}(V, V')$ is encoded as a QBF formula over $V_f \cup V'_f$ that evaluates to true whenever there is a transition from the state encoded by the assignment V to the state encoded by the assignment V'.

Recall that the transition relation for the tableau has a transition between every pair of states except where this would violate rule **LC0**. In other words, there should be a transition from s to s' whenever

$$\bigwedge_{\mathbf{AX}g \in ecl(f)} \mathbf{AX}g \in L(s) \Rightarrow g \in L(s')$$

is satisfied. This can be translated into a boolean formula over $\mathcal{V}_f \cup \mathcal{V}'_f$ as

$$R(V, V') = \bigwedge_{\langle \mathbf{EX}g \rangle \in \mathcal{V}_f} \langle \mathbf{EX}g \rangle \vee \overline{\sim g}'$$

where for any QBF formula h over $\mathcal{V}_f$, h' is identical to h except that every occurrence of a variable $v \in \mathcal{V}_f$ is replaced by the corresponding next state variable $v' \in \mathcal{V}'_f$. So $\langle \mathbf{EX}g \rangle$ is a variable in $\mathcal{V}_f$ and would have a value assigned to it by the boolean vector V while $\overline{\sim g}'$ is a formula over the variables in $\mathcal{V}'_f$ which would be assigned values from the boolean vector V'. Note that this formula for R restricts outgoing transitions from any state s labeled with $\mathbf{AX}g$, since then

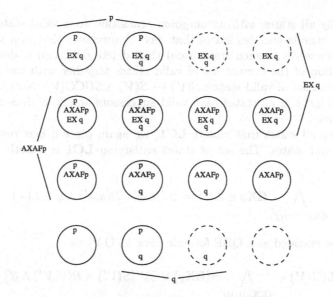

Fig. 1. Constructing a tableau for $\phi = \mathbf{AF}p \wedge \mathbf{EX}q$

$\overline{\mathbf{AX}g} = \neg\langle\mathbf{EX}\sim g\rangle$ would be true. This would require all outgoing transitions from the state to satisfy $\overline{\sim\sim g'} = \overline{g}'$ thus satisfying rule **LC0**.

Figure 1 shows the states in the initial tableau for $\phi = \mathbf{AF}p \wedge \mathbf{EX}q$. So that it is easier to follow the discussion, the figure uses the label $\mathbf{AXAF}p$ which is actually not in $el^+(\phi)$ instead of $\mathbf{EXEG}\neg p$ which is. Since $\mathbf{AXAF}p \equiv \neg\mathbf{EXEG}\neg p$, states in which $\mathbf{AXAF}p$ does *not* appear are exactly the states where $\mathbf{EXEG}\neg p$ should appear. Recall that $\mathbf{AF}p$ is characterized by the disjunctive formula $p \vee \mathbf{AXAF}p$. Therefore, states which are labeled with neither p nor $\mathbf{AXAF}p$ (and which are drawn with dashed lines for ease of identification) are the states that would also not be labeled with $\mathbf{AF}p$. In this example, there is a transition from every state to every state, except that states labeled with $\mathbf{AXAF}p$ do not have transitions to dashed states (states that would not be labeled with $\mathbf{AF}p$). Also, states not labeled with $\mathbf{EX}q$ would be labeled with $\mathbf{AX}\neg q$ and so would have no outgoing transitions to q labeled states.

Step two of the satisfiability algorithm requires us to remove "bad" states from the tableau. We use a QBF formula to encode the states of the original tableau that have not been removed. Let $S(V)$ be a QBF formula over $\mathcal{V}_f$ encoding all the currently valid states in the tableau. The initial value for $S(V)$ is the formula **tt**. We now show how to update $S(V)$ to remove "bad" states as defined in the explicit tableau algorithm. In what follows, $R(V, V')$ is the QBF encoding of the transition relation described earlier.

To remove all states that have no successors, we place a new restriction on valid states. The formula

$$SUCC(V) = \exists V' \, . \, R(V, V') \wedge S(V')$$

is satisfied by all states with an outgoing transition to a valid state. In other words, this formula encodes states that have a successor that is a valid state. To restrict ourselves to such states (and thus delete dead end nodes), we take the conjunction of the current set of valid states together with the formula to get an updated set of valid states: $S(V) \leftarrow S(V) \wedge SUCC(V)$. Note that in our example in Figure 1, all states have valid successors and so S does not change in this example.

To remove all states that violate **LC1**, we again place a new restriction on the set of valid states. The set of states satisfying **LC1** is exactly the states satisfying:

$$\bigwedge_{\mathbf{EX}g \in ecl(f)} \mathbf{EX}g \in L(s) \Rightarrow \exists s' \in S \ . \ R(s, s') \wedge g \in L(s')$$

which can be encoded as a QBF formula over $\mathcal{V}_f \cup \mathcal{V}'_f$ as

$$LC1(V) = \bigwedge_{\langle \mathbf{EX}g \rangle \in \mathcal{V}_f} \neg \langle \mathbf{EX}g \rangle \vee \exists V'[S(V') \wedge R(V, V') \wedge \overline{g}']$$

Again, to update the set of valid states, simply take the conjunction of the current valid states with this formula and so the update becomes

$$S(V) \leftarrow S(V) \wedge SUCC(V) \wedge LC1(V).$$

Again, in our example, all states labeled with **EX**q have at least one transition to a state labeled with q and so again S does not change.

Finally, to remove all states that are labeled with eventualities that are not pseudo-fulfilled, we need predicates for states labeled with eventualities and predicates for states at the root of a fragment certifying pseudo-fulfillment. Assume that a predicate $frag_{\mathbf{E}[g \ \mathbf{U} \ h]}$ $(frag_{\mathbf{A}[g \ \mathbf{U} \ h]})$ over the state variables $\mathcal{V}_f$ exists such that $frag_{\mathbf{E}[g \ \mathbf{U} \ h]}$ $(frag_{\mathbf{A}[g \ \mathbf{U} \ h]})$ evaluates to true exactly in those states which are roots of fragments certifying pseudo-fulfillment of the formula $\mathbf{E}[g \ \mathbf{U} \ h]$ $(\mathbf{A}[g \ \mathbf{U} \ h])$. To encode the states labeled with an eventuality, we must recall that there are no variables associated with formulas of the form $\mathbf{E}[g \ \mathbf{U} \ h]$ or $\mathbf{A}[g \ \mathbf{U} \ h]$ since neither is an elementary formula. However, states satisfying $\langle \mathbf{EXE}[g \ \mathbf{U} \ h] \rangle \wedge \overline{g}$ would be labeled with $\mathbf{E}[g \ \mathbf{U} \ h]$ in the original algorithm. Similarly, states satisfying $\neg \langle \mathbf{EXE}[g \ \mathbf{R} \ h] \rangle \wedge \overline{\sim g}$ would be labeled with $\mathbf{A}[\sim g \ \mathbf{U} \ \sim h]$ in the original algorithm. Such states also need to satisfy $frag_{\mathbf{E}[g \ \mathbf{U} \ h]}$ or $frag_{\mathbf{A}[\sim g \ \mathbf{U} \ \sim h]}$ respectively. The corresponding formulas for states that respect the pseudo-fulfillment requirement are:

$$E(V) = \bigwedge_{\langle \mathbf{EXE}[g \ \mathbf{U} \ h] \rangle \in \mathcal{V}_f} \left[\neg \langle \mathbf{EXE}[g \ \mathbf{U} \ h] \rangle \vee \neg \overline{g} \vee frag_{\mathbf{E}[g \ \mathbf{U} \ h]} \right]$$

$$A(V) = \bigwedge_{\langle \mathbf{EXE}[g \ \mathbf{R} \ h] \rangle \in \mathcal{V}_f} \left[\langle \mathbf{EXE}[g \ \mathbf{R} \ h] \rangle \vee \overline{g} \vee frag_{\mathbf{A}[\sim g \ \mathbf{U} \ \sim h]} \right]$$

Note that states satisfying $\overline{h}$ would also be labeled with $\mathbf{E}[g \ \mathbf{U} \ h]$ and states satisfying $\sim h$ would also be labeled with $\mathbf{A}[\sim g \ \mathbf{U} \ \sim h]$, but these states have the trivial fragment consisting only of the state itself and so do not need to be checked. Once again, the current set of valid states is restricted to those satisfying these predicates and update becomes

$$S(V) \leftarrow S(V) \wedge SUCC(V) \wedge LC1(V) \wedge E(V) \wedge A(V)$$

Once again, S does not change in this example, and the fixpoint is reached immediately.

Recall that in our example there are no elementary formulas of the form $\mathbf{EXE}[g \ \mathbf{U} \ h]$. The only eventuality, $\mathbf{AF}p$, results in the elementary formula $\neg\mathbf{EXE}[\mathbf{ff} \ \mathbf{R} \ \neg p]$. Therefore, $E(V) = \mathbf{tt}$ since the conjunction is empty. There is only one elementary formula of the form $\mathbf{EXE}[g \ \mathbf{R} \ h]$ and so

$$A(V) = \langle \mathbf{EXE}[\mathbf{ff} \ \mathbf{R} \ \neg p] \rangle \vee frag_{\mathbf{A}[\mathbf{tt} \ \mathbf{U} \ p]}$$

In our example, states in which the variable $\langle \mathbf{EXE}[\mathbf{ff} \ \mathbf{R} \ \neg p] \rangle$ is assigned true are the ones that are not labeled with $\mathbf{AXAF}p$. In other words, in order for a state in our example to satisfy $A(V)$, it must either not be labeled with $\mathbf{AXAF}p$ or it must satisfy the predicate $frag_{\mathbf{A}[\mathbf{tt} \ \mathbf{U} \ p]}$ It turns out that every state in the initial tableau satisfies $frag_{\mathbf{A}[\mathbf{tt} \ \mathbf{U} \ p]}$. Figure 2 illustrates certifying fragments for two states in the tableau. Along the bottom is a fragment rooted at the bottom right node certifying pseudo-fulfillment of $\mathbf{AF}p$ for that node. The fragment consists of only three nodes and two transitions even though in the original tableau, all three nodes had transitions to every state in the tableau. Similarly, near the top right is a fragment consisting of three nodes that is rooted at the rightmost node in the second row and certifying pseudo-fulfillment of $\mathbf{AF}p$ for that node. Note that in both cases, many other certifying fragments were possible, and some would have been smaller (would have only contained 2 states). For example, in the top fragment, the leftmost transition could be removed and what remains is a valid 2 state fragment rooted at the same node. Note that because of the $\mathbf{EX}q$ label in the root node, we could not keep the left transition and remove the right transition instead.

All that remains is to give definitions for $frag_{\mathbf{E}[g \ \mathbf{U} \ h]}$ and $frag_{\mathbf{A}[\sim g \ \mathbf{U} \ \sim h]}$. These predicates cannot be encoded directly in QBF; however, they can be encoded as fixpoints of QBF formulas. These fixpoints can then be computed iteratively as is done for μ-calculus model checking [3]. The correct definitions for $frag_{\mathbf{E}[g \ \mathbf{U} \ h]}$ and $frag_{\mathbf{A}[g \ \mathbf{U} \ h]}$ are given in the theorems stated below which are proved in the full version of this paper [9].

Theorem 1. *The set of states at the root of a fragment certifying pseudo-fulfillment of $\mathbf{E}[g \ \mathbf{U} \ h]$ equals the set of states satisfying the fixpoint equation:*

$$frag_{\mathbf{E}[g \ \mathbf{U} \ h]} = \mu Z \ . \ \left[\overline{h} \vee \left(\overline{g} \wedge \exists V'[R(V,V') \wedge S(V') \wedge Z(V')] \right) \right]$$

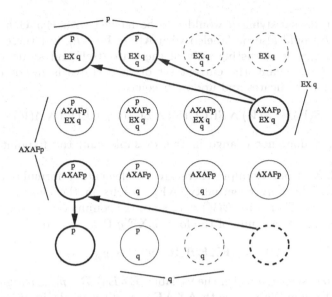

Fig. 2. Example fragments certifying pseudo-fulfillment of **AF**p

Readers familiar with modal μ-calculus model checking may be more familiar with the following formulation

$$frag_{\mathbf{E}[g \ \mathbf{U} \ h]} = \mu Z \ . \ \overline{[h} \vee (\overline{g} \wedge \Diamond Z)]$$

where for any formula f, $\Diamond f$ is true in a state if there exists a next state where f is true. The μ-calculus formula $\Diamond f$ can be translated into a QBF formula as $\exists V' \ . \ R(V, V') \wedge S(V') \wedge f'$. The extra term $S(V')$ is required to ensure the next state satisfying f is also a valid state, since unlike in model checking, the structure is not fixed. Recall that the satisfiability algorithm begins with a tableau that includes too many states. As states are pruned, we need to ensure that these pruned states are not used to satisfy the predicate for pseudo-fulfillment. Therefore, the entire formula reads as follows: a state is at the root of a certifying fragment for $\mathbf{E}[g \ \mathbf{U} \ h]$ iff

- the state satisfies h or
- the state
  1. satisfies g and
  2. the state has a successor that is a valid state at the root of a certifying fragment for $\mathbf{E}[g \ \mathbf{U} \ h]$.

The definition for $frag_{\mathbf{A}[g \ \mathbf{U} \ h]}$ is a little more complicated. The difference arises because in the case of $frag_{\mathbf{E}[g \ \mathbf{U} \ h]}$, states serving as witnesses to **EX** formulas did not themselves have to satisfy $\mathbf{E}[g \ \mathbf{U} \ h]$. But for $frag_{\mathbf{A}[g \ \mathbf{U} \ h]}$, any state witnessing an **EX** formula must also satisfy $\mathbf{A}[g \ \mathbf{U} \ h]$. The theorem below provides the correct μ-calculus formula to use.

Theorem 2. *The set of states at the root of a fragment certifying pseudo-fulfillment of* $\mathbf{A}[g \ \mathbf{U} \ h]$ *equals the set of states satisfying the fixpoint equation:*

$$
\text{frag}_{\mathbf{A}[g \ \mathbf{U} \ h]} = \mu Z \cdot \left[\begin{array}{c} \overline{h} \\ \vee \\ \left(\overline{g} \wedge \exists V' \big[R(V, V') \wedge S(V') \wedge Z(V') \big] \right. \\ \wedge \\ \left. \bigwedge_{\langle \mathbf{EX}i \rangle \in \mathcal{V}_f} \left(\langle \mathbf{EX}i \rangle \to \exists V' \big[R(V, V') \wedge S(V') \wedge Z(V') \wedge \overline{i'} \big] \right) \right) \end{array} \right]
$$

The corresponding modal μ-calculus formula is

$$
\text{frag}_{\mathbf{A}[g \ \mathbf{U} \ h]} = \mu Z \cdot \overline{h} \vee \left(\overline{g} \wedge \Diamond Z \wedge \bigwedge_{\langle \mathbf{EX}i \rangle \in \mathcal{V}_f} \big[\langle \mathbf{EX}i \rangle \to \Diamond(Z \wedge \overline{i}) \big] \right)
$$

This formula reads as follows: a state is at the root of a certifying fragment for $\mathbf{A}[g \ \mathbf{U} \ h]$ iff

- the state satisfies h or
- the state
   1. satisfies g and
   2. the state has at least one successor that is a valid state at the root of a certifying fragment for $\mathbf{A}[g \ \mathbf{U} \ h]$ and
   3. for every label of the form $\mathbf{EX}i$ in the state, there is a valid successor that satisfies i and that is at the root of a certifying fragment for $\mathbf{A}[g \ \mathbf{U} \ h]$.

It seems counterintuitive that the predicate for $\text{frag}_{\mathbf{A}[g \ \mathbf{U} \ h]}$, should contain existential quantification. However the first one appears because the models for CTL formulas are Kripke structures which must have a transition relation that is *total*. Without the first existential, any $\mathbf{AU}$ eventuality could be trivially certified by not including any outgoing transitions; however, such dead end states are not allowed in a Kripke structure. The second existential is required because of the presence of other existential formulas ($\mathbf{EX}$ formulas) in the label for the state.

We now have all the machinery we need to give a fixpoint characterization for the full algorithm. Given the construction of the QBF transition relation described earlier, the states in the final tableau can be computed as the greatest fixpoint of the predicate transformer:

$$
T(S) = S(V) \wedge SUCC(V) \wedge LC1(V) \wedge E(V) \wedge A(V).
$$

This means that the original CTL formula f is satisfiable if and only if some state in the intial tableau satisfies

$$
\overline{f} \wedge \nu S \cdot S(V) \wedge SUCC(V) \wedge LC1(V) \wedge E(V) \wedge A(V).
$$

The BDD for this formula encodes the constraints on states that satisfy theformula, so once the BDD is constructed, we need only verify that it is not the *false* BDD.

Table 2. Experimental Results

Experiment	Time (sec.)	BDD Variables	BDD Memory (KB)
induction_16	30.3	100	544
induction_20	111	124	608
induction_24	286	148	736
induction_28	710	172	960
precede_16	0.6	102	544
precede_32	11.3	198	544
precede_64	101	390	992
precede_128	794	774	2912
fair_8	0.2	50	512
fair_16	1.9	98	512
fair_32	20	194	576
fair_64	166	386	672
fair_128	1370	770	1856
nobase_16	33.9	100	544
nobase_20	106	124	608
nobase_24	308	148	768
nobase_28	728	172	960

5   Experimental Results

Satisfiability for CTL is known to be EXPTIME complete [2]. The μ-calculus formula we need to check has alternation depth 2 and can be checked in time $O(|f| \cdot |M|^3)$ using the result in [10]. Note that the f here is our μ-calculus formula and not the original f we were checking for satisfiability. Also, M is the initial tableau whose size is exponential in the size of the CTL formula we are checking. Like model checking, the limiting factor is really the exponential size of the model. As is the case for symbolic model checking, the practicality of the technique is supported by experimental results.

Table 2 contains the results of some experiments conducted with our satisfiability checker. The first column contains the name of the experiment. The second column lists the amount of time taken in seconds. The third column lists the number of BDD variables required (twice the size of $el^+(f)$). The last column displays how much memory was allocated by the BDD library while running the experiment. All experiments were performed on a 600MHz Pentium III machine with 512 MB running Linux. Experiments consisted of checking for the validity of a formula by checking that its negation is not satisfiable. The experiments named induction_n successfully verified the validity of formulas of the form

$$\left[p_0 \wedge \bigwedge_{i=0}^{n-1} \mathbf{AG}\left(p_i \rightarrow \mathbf{AX}p_{[i+1]_n} \right) \right] \rightarrow \mathbf{AGAF}p_0$$

The experiments named precede_n successfully verified the validity of formulas of the form

$$\left[\mathbf{AF} p_n \wedge \bigwedge_{i=0}^{n} \neg p_i \wedge \bigwedge_{i=0}^{n-1} \mathbf{AG}(\neg p_i \rightarrow \mathbf{AX} \neg p_{i+1}) \right] \rightarrow \mathbf{AF} p_0$$

The experiments named fair_n successfully verified the validity of formulas of the form

$$\left[\mathbf{AGAF} p_0 \wedge \bigwedge_{i=0}^{n-1} \mathbf{AG}(p_i \rightarrow \mathbf{AXAF} p_{[i+1]_n}) \right] \rightarrow \mathbf{AGAF} p_{n-1}$$

Finally, the experiments named nobase_n verified that the induction formulas were not valid without the base case. In other words, these experiments successfully verified that the formulas

$$\neg \left[\bigwedge_{i=0}^{n-1} \mathbf{AG}(p_i \rightarrow \mathbf{AX} p_{[i+1]_n}) \rightarrow \mathbf{AGAF} p_0 \right]$$

are satisfiable.

6   Conclusion

We have implemented a symbolic algorithm for determining whether a CTL formula is satisfiable or not. The algorithm avoids constructing an explicit pseudo-Hintikka structure for the formula by using OBDDs (boolean formulas) to encode the structure. The procedure has exponential time complexity; however, we have been able to use it to check a number of complex formulas (on the order of 100 atomic propositions). We are confident that this algorithm will work for other non-trivial formulas.

While this algorithm seems sufficient to check the very structured formulas in the experiments, it remains to be seen how practical this approach is if used on formulas that may arise from some problem domain. Identifying problem domains where this kind of satisfiability checker would prove useful would be an excellent avenue for future work.

Perhaps the most obvious avenue for future work is the development of a model synthesis facility for CTL. Not only could it be useful to be able to construct concrete models that satisfy certain properties, but it would also be very useful to be able to construct a concrete model that fails to satisfy some property. This could serve as a counterexample facility while doing validity checking (a feature usually not available in theorem provers). In other words, to check the validity of f, one checks if $\neg f$ is satisfiable. If $\neg f$ is not satisfiable, then f is valid. However, if $\neg f$ is satisfiable, an example model satisfying $\neg f$ would help us to understand why f is not valid. Often when trying experiments, we would try to verify formulas we thought were valid. When our algorithm reported back that the formula was not valid, it often took a significant amount of work to determine if this was an error in our algorithm or a mistake in our formula. In all cases, it was a mistake in the formula. However, an automatically generated

Fig. 3. Minimal model for $\phi = \mathbf{AF}p \wedge \mathbf{EX}q$

counter-example would have drastically reduced the time and thought involved in trying to uncover the mistake. It must be noted that there is some cause for concern regarding the practicality of synthesizing the model. In particular, the size of the model generated by Emerson's algorithm is bounded by $m2^n$ where n is the length of the formula and m is the number of eventualities appearing in the formula [2]. Some minimization would most likely be necessary. In particular, it would be extremely helpful to be able to find small certifying fragments. In our running example, the smallest fragment for $\mathbf{AF}p$ for a state that also satisfies $\mathbf{EX}q$ is shown in Figure 3 which is clearly much smaller than the initial tableau. In the model checking community, there is already a need to find small counterexamples and perhaps we can once again build on their work.

References

1. Clarke, E.M., Emerson, E.A.: Design and synthesis of synchronization skeletons using branching time temporal logic. In: Proceedings of Logics of Programs. Volume 131 of Lecture Notes in Computer Science., Springer-Verlag (1981) 52–71
2. Emerson, E.A.: Temporal and modal logic. In van Leeuwen, J., ed.: Handbook of Theoretical Computer Science. Volume B. MIT Press (1990) 995–1072
3. Burch, J.R., Clarke, E.M., McMillan, K.L., Dill, D.L., Hwang, J.: Symbolic model checking: 10^{20} states and beyond. Information and Computation **98** (1992) 142–170
4. Coudert, O., Madre, J.C., Berthet, C.: Verification of synchronous sequential machines based on symbolic execution. In: Proceedings of Automatic Verification Methods for Finite State Systems. (1989) 365–373
5. Bryant, R.E.: Graph-based algorithms for boolean function manipulation. IEEE Transactions on Computers **C-35** (1986) 677–691
6. Emerson, E.A., Halpern, J.Y.: Decision procedures and expressiveness in the temporal logic of branching time. In: Proceedings of the ACM Symposium on Theory of Computing. (1982) 169–180
7. Clarke, E., Grumberg, O., Hamaguchi, K.: Another look at LTL model checking. Formal Methods in System Design **10** (1997) 47–71
8. Clarke, E.M., Grumberg, O., Long, D.E.: Model checking and abstraction. ACM Transactions on Programming Languages and Systems **16** (1994) 1512–1542
9. Marrero, W.: Using BDDs to decide CTL. Technical Report 04-005, DePaul University (2004)
10. Emerson, E.A., Lei, C.L.: Efficient model checking in fragments of the propositional mu-calculus. In: Proceedings of the 1st Annual Symposium on Logic in Computer Science, IEEE Computer Society Press (1986) 267–278

Model Checking Infinite-State Markov Chains*

Anne Remke, Boudewijn R. Haverkort, and Lucia Cloth

University of Twente, Faculty for Electrical Engineering,
Mathematics and Computer Science
{anne, brh, lucia}@cs.utwente.nl

Abstract. In this paper algorithms for model checking CSL (continuous stochastic logic) against infinite-state continuous-time Markov chains of so-called quasi birth-death type are developed. In doing so we extend the applicability of CSL model checking beyond the recently proposed case for finite-state continuous-time Markov chains, to an important class of infinite-state Markov chains. We present syntax and semantics for CSL and develop efficient model checking algorithms for the steady-state operator and the time-bounded next and until operator. For the former, we rely on the so-called matrix-geometric solution of the steady-state probabilities of the infinite-state Markov chain. For the time-bounded until operator we develop a new algorithm for the transient analysis of infinite-state Markov chains, thereby exploiting the quasi birth-death structure. A case study shows the feasibility of our approach.

1   Introduction

Continuous-time Markov chains are a widely spread modeling formalism for performance and dependability evaluation of computer and communication systems. Recently, various researchers have adopted CTMCs as "stochastic extension" of finite-state automata and have proposed new logics to express quantitative properties for them. Most notably is the work on CSL for CTMCs [2, 4] as stochastic extension of CTL, and the work on CSRL for Markov reward models (CTMCs enhanced with a state reward) [3]. Efficient computational algorithms have been developed for checking these models against formally specified properties expressed in these logics, cf. [3, 4], as well as supporting tools, cf. PRISM [13] and ETMC² [11].

All of the above work, however, has focused on *finite*-state models. In this paper we will extend model checking CSL towards *infinite*-state CTMCs. It is then possible to assess infinite-state systems, or to approximate the behavior of very large-but-finite systems. The analysis of general infinite-state CTMCs is, however, beyond reach. Therefore, we restrict the class of infinite-state CTMCs

* The work presented in this paper has been performed in the context of the MC=MC project (612.000.311), financed by the Netherlands Organization for Scientific Research (NWO) and is based on the diploma thesis [18], supported by the German Academic Exchange Service (DAAD).

N. Halbwachs and L. Zuck (Eds.): TACAS 2005, LNCS 3440, pp. 237–252, 2005.
© Springer-Verlag Berlin Heidelberg 2005

to the class of so-called *quasi birth-death models* (QBDs) [16], for which, despite their infinite state space, efficient algorithms exist to compute steady-state probabilities. As we will see in the course of the paper, we also require the transient, i.e., time-dependent, analysis of the infinite-state QBDs; we develop new algorithms for that purpose in this paper as well.

The paper is further organized as follows. We introduce labeled infinite-state CTMCs, and QBDs in particular, in Section 2. We then describe syntax and semantics of CSL in Section 3. Section 4 addresses in detail the model checking algorithms for the CSL operators. The feasibility of the approach is illustrated in Section 5 with a small case study, and the paper is concluded in Section 6.

2   Infinite-State CTMCs

For a fixed set of AP of atomic propositions a labeled infinite-state CTMC is defined as follows:

Definition 1. *A **labeled infinite-state CTMC** $\mathcal{M}$ is a tuple $(S, \mathbf{Q}, L)$ with an infinite countable set of states S, a square generator matrix[1] $\mathbf{Q} : S \times S \to \mathbb{R}$, and labeling function $L : S \to 2^{AP}$.*

The value $\mathbf{Q}(i, j) \geq 0$, for $i \neq j$, equals the rate at which a transition from state i to state j occurs in the CTMC, whereas $\mathbf{Q}(i, i)$ denotes the negative sum of the off-diagonal entries in the same row of $\mathbf{Q}$; its value represents the rate of leaving state i (in the sense of an exponentially distributed residence time). The labeling function L assigns to each state the set of valid atomic propositions in that state.

A special case of infinite-state CTMCs are CTMCs with quasi birth-death structure [16]. Informally speaking, the infinite state space of a QBD can be viewed as a two-dimensional strip, which is finite in one dimension and infinite in the other. Furthermore, the states in this strip can be grouped in so-called levels, according to their value or identity in the infinite dimension. Thus, the state space of a QBD consist of neighboring levels, which are all alike, except for the first one (level 0). The first level is called *boundary level* and all the others *repeating levels*. The first repeating level is sometimes called the *border level* as it separates the boundary level from the repeating levels.

Transitions, represented by positive entries in the matrix $\mathbf{Q}$, can only occur between states of the same level or between states of neighboring levels. All repeating levels have the same inter- and intra-level transition structure. The state space of a QBD can be partitioned into an infinite number of finite sets $S^j, j = \{0, 1, \ldots\}$, each containing the states of one level, such that $S = \bigcup_{j=0}^{\infty} S^j$. Figure 1(a) gives a graphical representation of a QBD, where level 0 is the boundary level and the levels from level 1 onwards are repeating levels. The inter-level transitions can be represented through matrices $\mathbf{B}_{0,1}, \mathbf{B}_{1,0}, \mathbf{A}_0, \mathbf{A}_2$, whereas

---

[1] Note that $\mathcal{M}$ does not contain self loops. Residence times in a CTMC obey a memoryless distribution, hence, self loops can be eliminated.

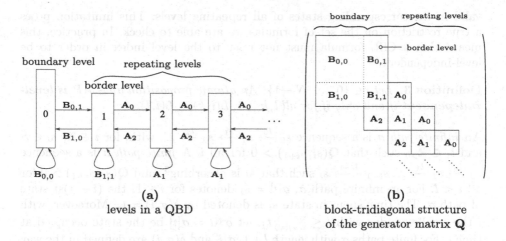

(a)
levels in a QBD

(b)
block-tridiagonal structure
of the generator matrix $\mathbf{Q}$

Fig. 1. Regular structure of QBDs

the intra-level transitions can be represented through the matrices $\mathbf{B}_{0,0}$, $\mathbf{B}_{1,1}$ and $\mathbf{A}_1$ (cf. Figure 1(b)).

Although QBDs are introduced here at the state level, high-level formalisms, e.g., based on stochastic Petri nets [17] or stochastic process algebras [7, 15], do exist.

Definition 2. *A **labeled QBD** $\mathcal{Q}$ of order (N_0, N) (with $N, N_0 \in \mathbb{N}^+$) is a labeled infinite-state CTMC, cf. Def. 1. The set of states is composed as $S = \{0, \dots, N_0 - 1\} \times \{0\} \cup \{0, \dots, N - 1\} \times \mathbb{N}^+$, where the first part represents the boundary level with N_0 states, and the second part the infinite number of repeating levels, each with N states. The block-tridiagonal generator matrix $\mathbf{Q}$ consists of the following finite matrices describing the inter- and intra-level transitions:*

$\mathbf{B}_{0,0} \in \mathbb{R}^{N_0 \times N_0}$: *intra-level transition structure of the boundary level,*
$\mathbf{B}_{0,1} \in \mathbb{R}^{N_0 \times N}$: *inter-level transitions from the boundary level to the border level,*
$\mathbf{B}_{1,0} \in \mathbb{R}^{N \times N_0}$: *inter-level transitions from the border level to the boundary level,*
$\mathbf{B}_{1,1} \in \mathbb{R}^{N \times N}$: *intra-level transition structure of the border level.*
$\mathbf{A}_0 \in \mathbb{R}^{N \times N}$: *inter-level transitions from one repeating level to the next higher repeating level,*
$\mathbf{A}_1 \in \mathbb{R}^{N \times N}$: *intra-level transitions for the repeating levels[2], and*
$\mathbf{A}_2 \in \mathbb{R}^{N \times N}$: *inter-level transitions from one repeating level to the next lower repeating level.*

In the following we limit ourselves to strongly connected CTMCs and to so-called *level-independent* atomic propositions. That is, if an atomic proposition $ap \in AP$ is valid in a certain state of an arbitrary repeating level, it has to be

---

[2] Note that $\mathbf{B}_{1,1}$ differs from $\mathbf{A}_1$ only in the diagonal entries.

valid in the corresponding states of all repeating levels. This limitation poses a true restriction on the set of formulas we are able to check. In practice, this means that a CSL formula must not refer to the level index in order to be level-independent.

Definition 3. *Let $i \in \{0, \ldots, N - 1\}$. An atomic proposition $ap \in AP$ is **level-independent** if and only if for all $l, k \geq 1, L(i, k) = L(i, l)$.*

An *infinite path* σ is a sequence $s_0 \xrightarrow{t_0} s_1 \xrightarrow{t_1} s_2 \xrightarrow{t_2} \ldots$ with, for $i \in \mathbb{N}$, $s_i \in S$ and $t_i \in \mathbb{R}_{>0}$ such that $\mathbf{Q}(s_i, s_{i+1}) > 0$ for all i. A *finite path* σ is a sequence $s_0 \xrightarrow{t_0} s_1 \xrightarrow{t_1} \ldots s_{l-1} \xrightarrow{t_{l-1}} s_l$ such that s_l is absorbing[3], and $\mathbf{Q}(s_i, s_{i+1}) > 0$ for all $i < l$. For an infinite path σ, $\sigma[i] = s_i$ denotes for $i \in \mathbb{N}$ the $(i + 1)$st state of path σ. The time spent in state s_i is denoted by $\delta(\sigma, i) = t_i$. Moreover, with i the smallest index with $t \leq \sum_{j=0}^{i} t_j$, let $\sigma@t = \sigma[i]$ be the state occupied at time t. For finite paths σ with length $l + 1$, $\sigma[i]$ and $\delta(\sigma, i)$ are defined in the way described above for $i < l$ only and $\delta(\sigma, l) = \infty$ and $\delta@t = s_l$ for $t > \sum_{j=0}^{l-1} t_j$.

$Path^{\mathcal{Q}}(s_i)$ is the set of all finite and infinite paths of the QBD $\mathcal{Q}$ that start in state s_i and $Path^{\mathcal{Q}}$ includes all (finite and infinite) paths of the QBD $\mathcal{Q}$. The superscript $\mathcal{Q}$ will be omitted whenever it is clear to which QBD the paths refer.

As for finite CTMCs, a probability measure Pr on paths can be defined [4]. Starting from there, two different types of state probabilities can be distinguished for QBDs.

The **transient state probability** is a time-dependent measure that considers the QBD at an exact time instant t. The probability to be in state s' at time instant t, given the initial state s is denoted as $\pi^{\mathcal{Q}}(s, s', t) = \Pr(\sigma \in Path(s) \mid \sigma@t = s')$. The transient probabilities are characterized by a linear system of differential equations of infinite size. Let $\underline{\pi}(t)$ be the vector of transient state probabilities at time t for all possible states (we omit the superscript $\mathcal{Q}$ as well as the starting state s for brevity here), we have $\underline{\pi}'(t) = \underline{\pi}(t) \cdot \mathbf{Q}$, given starting state s. Using a standard differential equation solver is difficult since we deal with an infinite number of differential equations. An approach using Laplace transforms and exploiting the tri-diagonal structure of the matrix $\mathbf{Q}$ has been presented in [20], however, this approach does not lead to practically feasible algorithms. Instead, it is better to resort to a technique known as uniformization, cf. [8, 9]. This will be elaborated upon in Section 4.

The **steady-state probabilities** to be in state s', given initial state s, are then defined as $\pi^{\mathcal{Q}}(s, s') = \lim_{t \to \infty} \pi^{\mathcal{Q}}(s, s', t)$, and indicate the probabilities to be in some state s' "in the long run". If steady-state is reached, the above mentioned derivatives will approach zero. Furthermore, if the QBD is ergodic, the initial state does not influence the steady-state probabilities (we therefore often write $\pi(s')$ instead of $\pi(s, s')$ for brevity). Thus, the steady-state probability vector $\underline{\pi}$ then follows from the infinite system of linear equations $\underline{\pi} \cdot \mathbf{Q} = \underline{0}$, and $\sum_s \pi_s = 1$ (normalization). This system of equations can be solved using so-called matrix-geometric methods which exploit the repetitive structure in the

---

[3] A state s is called absorbing if for all s' the rate $\mathbf{Q}(s, s') = 0$.

matrix $\mathbf{Q}$ [9, 16]. The idea is that the steady-state probabilities are found in a level-wise fashion, starting from the boundary and the border level. In order to do so, one first has to find the smallest square matrix $\mathbf{R}$ that satisfies the matrix-quadratic equation $\mathbf{A}_0\mathbf{R}^2 + \mathbf{A}_1\mathbf{R} + \mathbf{A}_2 = 0$. Efficient algorithms to do so exist, cf. [14]. Then, a system of linear equations can be set up that involves only the steady-state probabilities of the boundary and the border level, as well as a normalization equation with respect to these two levels. This system of linear equations can be solved with known iterative techniques like the Gauss-Seidel iterative method. Let $\underline{v}_0$ and $\underline{v}_1$ denote the steady-state probabilities of the first two levels, then, the matrix-geometric result [16] states that for $i = 1, 2, \cdots$, we have $\underline{v}_{i+1} = \underline{v}_i \cdot \mathbf{R}$.

A final remark should be made about stability. Since a QBD has an infinite state space, the transition rates can be such that all probability mass in steady state resides in levels that are "infinitely far away" from level 0. This, often undesirable situation, can be detected solely on the basis of the matrices $\mathbf{A}_0, \mathbf{A}_1$ and $\mathbf{A}_2$, hence, before any (expensive) computations on $\mathbf{R}$ start. Notice that in such cases, computing steady-state probabilities does not make sense; transient probabilities can still be computed.

3   The Logic CSL

We apply the logic CSL [4] on QBDs. Syntax and semantics are the same for the only difference that we now interpret the formulas over QBDs.

Syntax. Let $p \in [0, 1]$ be a real number, $\bowtie \in \{\leq, <, >, \geq\}$ a comparison operator, $I \subseteq \mathbb{R}_{\geq 0}$ a nonempty interval and AP a set of atomic propositions with $ap \in AP$.

Definition 4. *CSL state formulas Φ are defined by*

$$\Phi ::= \mathtt{tt} \mid ap \mid \neg\Phi \mid \Phi \wedge \Phi \mid S_{\bowtie p}(\Phi) \mid \mathcal{P}_{\bowtie p}(\phi),$$

where ϕ is a path formula constructed by

$$\phi ::= \mathcal{X}^I \Phi \mid \Phi \mathcal{U}^I \Phi.$$

The steady-state operator $S_{\bowtie p}(\Phi)$ denotes that the steady-state probability for a Φ-state meets the bound p. $\mathcal{P}_{\bowtie p}(\phi)$ asserts that the probability measure of the paths satisfying ϕ meets the bound p. The next operator $\mathcal{X}^I \Phi$ states that a transition to a Φ-state is made at some time instant $t \in I$. The until operator $\Phi \mathcal{U}^I \Psi$ asserts that Ψ is satisfied at some time instant in the interval I and that at all preceding time instants Φ holds.

Semantics. For a CSL state formula Φ on a QBD Q, the satisfaction set contains all states of Q that fulfill Φ. The satisfaction set can be considered as the infinite union of finite *level satisfaction sets*: $Sat(\Phi) = Sat^0(\Phi) \cup \bigcup_{j=1}^{\infty} Sat^j(\Phi)$. $Sat^j(\Phi)$ contains only those Φ-states that are situated in level j. Satisfaction is stated in terms of a satisfaction relation $\models$, which is defined as follows.

Definition 5. *The relation* $\models$ *for states and CSL state formulas is defined as:*

$$s \models \text{tt} \quad \text{for all } s \in S, \qquad s \models \Phi \wedge \Psi \quad \text{iff } s \models \Phi \text{ and } s \models \Psi,$$
$$s \models ap \quad \text{iff } ap \in L(s) \qquad s \models \mathcal{S}_{\bowtie p}(\Phi) \text{ iff } \pi^{\mathcal{Q}}(s, Sat(\Phi)) \bowtie p,$$
$$s \models \neg \Phi \quad \text{iff } s \not\models \Phi \qquad s \models \mathcal{P}_{\bowtie p}(\phi) \text{ iff } Prob^{\mathcal{Q}}(s, \phi) \bowtie p.$$

where $\pi^{\mathcal{Q}}(s, Sat(\Phi)) = \sum_{s' \in Sat(\Phi)} \pi^{\mathcal{Q}}(s, s')$, *and* $Prob^{\mathcal{Q}}(s, \phi)$ *describes the probability measure of all paths* $\sigma \in Path(s)$ *that satisfy* ϕ *when the system is starting in state* s, *that is,* $Prob^{\mathcal{Q}}(s, \phi) = Pr\{\sigma \in Path^{\mathcal{Q}}(s) \mid \sigma \models \phi\}$.

Definition 6. *The relation* $\models$ *for paths and CSL$^{\infty}$ path formulas is defined as:*

$$\sigma \models \mathcal{X}^{I} \Phi \qquad \text{iff } \sigma[1] \text{ is defined and } \sigma[1] \models \Phi \text{ and } \delta(\sigma, 0) \in I,$$

$$\sigma \models \Phi \, \mathcal{U}^{I} \Psi \qquad \text{iff } \exists t \in I \, (\sigma @ t \models \Psi \wedge (\forall t' \in [0, t)(\sigma @ t' \models \Phi))).$$

4 Model Checking Algorithms

In order to develop a model checking algorithm for QBDs, we need to focus on the connection between the validity of state formulas and the special birth-death structure of QBDs. At first glance, one could think that in corresponding states of all repeating levels the same CSL formulas hold. Model checking a QBD would then be reducible to model checking the boundary level and one repeating level representative for all others. Unfortunately this is not the case, as can be explained considering the time-bounded next and until operator. In order to check CSL properties that contain these path formulas, we need to examine all possible paths in a level-wise fashion. Considering time-bounded next, note that in the border level other next-formulas might be satisfied than in the other repeating levels, because the boundary level is still reachable from the border level but not from any other repeating level. Thus, if we want to check for example the formula $\phi = \mathcal{X}^{I}$ *red* and the property *red* is only valid in the boundary level, this property ϕ can be fulfilled by a path starting in the border level, but not when starting in any other repeating level. A similar reasoning holds for the until operator, where not only the border level is concerned but even more repeating levels, because with the until operator not just one step is considered, but potentially infinitely many. Thus, for path-formulas no two repeating levels can a priori be considered the same.

4.1 Level Independence of CSL Formulas

Even though CSL formulas are not level independent in general, their validity does not change arbitrarily between levels. Remember that we assume level independence of atomic propositions for the QBDs we consider. For CSL formulas, we generalize the idea of level independence: we only require that the validity in a state is level independent for repeating levels with an index of at least k. Thus, we allow the validity of a CSL formula to change between corresponding states of repeating levels, but only up to repeating level $k - 1$. From level k onwards, the validity must remain unchanged.

Definition 7. *Let Q be a QBD of order (N_0, N). A CSL state formula Φ is level independent as of level $k \geq 1$ (in QBD Q) if and only if for levels above and including k, the validity of Φ in a state does not depend on the level, that is,*

$$\text{for all } i \in \{0, \ldots, N-1\} \text{ and for all } l \geq k: \quad (i, l) \models \Phi \iff (i, k) \models \Phi.$$

The following proposition states, under the assumption of level independent atomic propositions, that such a k exists for any CSL state formula.

Proposition 1 Let Q be a QBD with level independent atomic properties and let Φ be a CSL state formula. Then there exists a $k \in \mathbb{N}$, such that Φ is level independent as of level k in Q.

We will justify this proposition inductively in the sections that discuss the model checking of the different types of CSL state formulas.

For model checking a property Φ, we will compute the set $Sat(\Phi)$ with a recursive descent procedure over the parse tree of Φ. To do so, the CSL formula Φ is split into its sub-formulas and for every sub-formula the model checker is invoked recursively. For a state formula Φ that is level independent as of level k, cf. Definition 7, only the first k level satisfaction sets have to be computed. $Sat^k(\Phi)$ then acts as a representative for all following levels. In what follows we discuss the required computations for one such invocation, for each of the operators in the logic CSL.

4.2   Atomic Propositions and Logical Operators

Computing the satisfaction set for an atomic proposition ap proceeds as follows. $Sat^0(ap)$ consists of those states of the boundary level where ap is contained in the labeling. We test all states in the border level in order to obtain $Sat^1(ap)$, and, hence, $Sat^j(ap)$ for $j \geq 1$ (as per Definition 3).

Let Φ be a CSL state formula that is level independent as of level k. Its negation $\neg\Phi$ is clearly also level independent as of level k. The level satisfaction sets of $\neg\Phi$ are computed by complementing the corresponding satisfaction set of Φ:

$$Sat^j(\neg\Phi) = S^j \setminus Sat^j(\Phi), \text{for all } j \geq 0.$$

Let Φ and Ψ be two CSL state formulas, level independent as of level k_Φ and k_Ψ, respectively. The conjunction $\Phi \wedge \Psi$ is level independent as of level $\max(k_\Phi, k_\Psi)$. The level satisfaction sets are computed by intersecting the corresponding satisfaction sets of Φ and Ψ:

$$Sat^j(\Phi \wedge \Psi) = Sat^j(\Phi) \cap Sat^j(\Psi), \text{for all } j \geq 0.$$

4.3   Steady-State Operator

A state s satisfies $\mathcal{S}_{\bowtie p}(\Phi)$ if the accumulated steady state probability of all Φ-states reachable from s meets the bound p. Since we assume a strongly connected QBD, the steady-state probabilities are independent of the starting state. It follows that either all states satisfy a steady-state formula or none of the states does, which implies that a steady-state formula is always level independent as of level 1. We first determine the satisfaction set $Sat(\Phi)$ and then compute the accumulated steady-state probability. If the accumulated steady-state probability meets the bound p, we have $Sat(S_{\bowtie p}(\Phi)) = S$, otherwise, $Sat(S_{\bowtie p}(\Phi)) = \varnothing$. Exploiting the special structure of QBDs, the accumulated probability is given by

$$\pi(Sat(\Phi)) = \sum_{s \in Sat(\Phi)} \pi(s) = \sum_{j=0}^{\infty} \sum_{s \in Sat^j(\Phi)} \underline{v}_j(s),$$

where the vectors $\underline{v}_j = (\cdots, \underline{v}_j(s), \cdots)$ can be computed one after the other, using the matrix-geometric method, as discussed in Section 2.

In order to deal with the infinite sum we iterate through the repeating levels and accumulate the steady-state probabilities in a level-wise fashion. Denote with $\tilde{\pi}^l(Sat(\Phi))$ the accumulated steady-state probabilities of all Φ-states up to level l, that is,

$$\tilde{\pi}^l(Sat(\Phi)) = \sum_{j=0}^{l} \sum_{s \in Sat^j(\Phi)} \underline{v}_j(s).$$

Starting with $l = 0$, we iterate through the levels and compute $\tilde{\pi}^l(Sat(\Phi))$ and $\tilde{\pi}^l(Sat(\neg\Phi))$, respectively. The computation of the steady-state probabilities of $\neg\Phi$-states introduces no additional cost, since they are computed anyway. In every step we have to check whether we can already decide on the validity of the steady-state formula $S_{\bowtie p}(\Phi)$. The following implications hold:

(a) $\qquad \tilde{\pi}^j(Sat(\Phi)) > p \Rightarrow \pi(Sat(\Phi)) > p,$
(b) $\qquad \tilde{\pi}^j(Sat(\neg\Phi)) > 1 - p \Rightarrow \pi(Sat(\Phi)) < p.$

As soon as one of the left hand side inequalities becomes true, the iteration stops. For the interpretation we distinguish the cases $S_{<p}(\Phi)$ and $S_{>p}(\Phi)$. For $S_{\geq p}(\Phi)$ or $S_{\leq p}(\Phi)$ the equations need to be modified accordingly. For $S_{<p}(\Phi)$ the interpretation is as follows. If inequality (a) holds, the condition $\pi(Sat(\Phi)) < p$ is clearly not accomplished and $Sat(S_{<p}(\Phi)) = \varnothing$. If inequality (b) holds, the condition $\pi(Sat(\Phi)) < p$ is accomplished and $Sat(S_{<p}(\Phi)) = S$. For $S_{>p}(\Phi)$ the same conditions need to be checked in every iteration step j, but they need to be interpreted differently. If inequality (a) holds, the probability bound is met and $Sat(S_{>p}(\Phi)) = S$. If inequality (b) holds, the bound is not met and $Sat(S_{>p}(\Phi)) = \varnothing$.

The satisfaction set of Φ might be finite. For a CSL formula Φ that is level independent as of level k, this is the case when no state in level k satisfies Φ. The iteration then ends at level $k - 1$ and $\pi(Sat(\Phi)) = \tilde{\pi}^{k-1}(Sat(\Phi))$. In case $Sat(\Phi)$ is infinite, the iterations stop as soon as one of the inequalities is satisfied. Unfortunately, if the probability p is exactly equal to the steady-state probability $\pi(Sat(\Phi))$, the approximations $\tilde{\pi}^l(Sat(\Phi))$ and $\tilde{\pi}^l(Sat(\neg\Phi))$ will never fulfill one of the inequalities. In an implementation of this algorithm some care must be taken to detect this case in order to avoid a non-stopping iteration.

Instead of the just-sketched iterative process, we can also develop a closed-form matrix expression for the probability $\pi(Sat(\Phi))$ by exploiting properties of the matrix-geometric solution, i.e., by using the fact that $\sum_i \mathbf{R}^i = (\mathbf{I} - \mathbf{R})^{-1}$. In doing so, the infinite summation disappears, however, it comes at the cost of a required matrix inversion. In practice, this is therefore not always a more efficient approach, but it avoids the stopping problem.

4.4   Time-Bounded Next Operator

Recall that a state s satisfies $\mathcal{P}_{\bowtie p}(\mathcal{X}^I \Phi)$ if the one-step probability to reach a state that fulfills Φ within a time in $I = [a, b]$, outgoing from s meets the bound p, that is,

$$s \models \mathcal{P}_{\bowtie p}(\mathcal{X}^I \Phi) \Leftrightarrow \Pr\{\sigma \in Path(s) \mid \sigma \models \mathcal{X}^I \Phi\} \bowtie p$$

$$\Leftrightarrow \left(\left(e^{Q(s,s) \cdot a} - e^{Q(s,s) \cdot b} \right) \cdot \sum_{\substack{s' \in Sat(\Phi) \\ s' \neq s}} \frac{Q(s,s')}{-Q(s,s)} \right) \bowtie p, \qquad (1)$$

where $e^{Q(s,s) \cdot a} - e^{Q(s,s) \cdot b}$ is the probability of residing at s for a time in I, and $\frac{Q(s,s')}{-Q(s,s)}$ specifies the probability to step from state s to state s'. Note that the above inequality contains a (possibly infinite) summation over all Φ-states. However, we only need to sum over the states of $Sat(\Phi)$ that are reachable from s in one step. That is, for $s = (i, j)$, we only have to consider the Φ-states from levels $j-1, j$, and $j+1$. For all states of all other levels the one-step probabilities are zero anyway. The infinite set $Sat(\Phi)$ ruling the summation in (1) can thus be replaced by the finite set $Sat_{\mathcal{X},(i,j)}(\Phi)$ containing only the states from level $j-1, j, j+1$ that fulfill Φ, that is,

$$Sat_{\mathcal{X},(i,j)}(\Phi) = \begin{cases} Sat^0(\Phi) \cup Sat^1(\Phi), & j = 0, \\ Sat^{j-1}(\Phi) \cup Sat^j(\Phi) \cup Sat^{j+1}(\Phi), & \text{otherwise.} \end{cases}$$

Now, let the inner formula Φ of the next-formula be level independent as of level k. Hence, the validity of the state formula $\mathcal{P}_{\bowtie p}(\mathcal{X}^I \Phi)$ might be different in corresponding states for all levels up to $k - 1$. Therefore, unfortunately, level k can still have different states satisfying $\mathcal{P}_{\bowtie p}(\mathcal{X}^I \Phi)$ since level $k - 1$ is reachable in one step. But, as of level $k+1$, only levels can be reached where the validity of state formula Φ is equal for corresponding states. Hence, if Φ is level independent as of level k, $\mathcal{P}_{\bowtie p}(\mathcal{X}^I \Phi)$ is level independent as of level $k+1$. For the construction of the satisfaction set of such a formula, we therefore have to compute explicitly the satisfying states up to level $k + 1$. Subsequently, $Sat^{k+1}(\mathcal{P}_{\bowtie p}(\mathcal{X}^I \Phi))$ can be seen as a representative for all following repeating levels.

4.5   Time-Bounded Until Operator

For model checking $\mathcal{P}_{\bowtie p}(\Phi \, \mathcal{U}^I \Psi)$ we adopt the general approach for finite CTMCs [4]. The idea is to use a transformed QBD where several states are made absorbing. We focus on the case where $I = [0, t]$. The CSL path formula $\varphi = \Phi \, \mathcal{U}^{[0,t]} \Psi$ is valid if a Ψ-state is reached on a path, before time t via only Φ-states. As

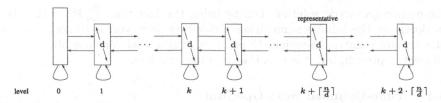

Fig. 2. Finite fraction of the QBD needed for the transient solution

soon as a Ψ-state is reached, the future behavior of the QBD is irrelevant for the validity of φ. Thus all Ψ-states can be made absorbing without affecting the satisfaction set of formula φ. On the other hand, as soon as a $(\neg\Phi \wedge \neg\Psi)$ state is reached, φ will be invalid, regardless of the future evolution of the system. As a result we may switch from checking the Markov chain $\mathcal{Q}$ to the Markov chain $\mathcal{Q}[\Psi][\neg\Phi \wedge \neg\Psi] = \mathcal{Q}[\neg\Phi \vee \Psi]$, where the states satisfying the formula in $[\cdot]$ are made absorbing. Model checking a formula involving the until operator then reduces to calculating the transient probabilities $\pi^{\mathcal{Q}[\neg\Phi\vee\Psi]}(s, s', t)$ for all Ψ-states s'. Exploiting the special structure of QBDs yields

$$s \models \mathcal{P}_{\bowtie p}(\Phi \, \mathcal{U}^{[0,t]}\Psi) \Leftrightarrow Prob^{\mathcal{Q}}(s, \Phi \, \mathcal{U}^{[0,t]}\Psi) \bowtie p$$

$$\Leftrightarrow \left(\sum_{i=0}^{\infty} \sum_{s' \in Sat^i(\Psi)} \pi^{\mathcal{Q}[\neg\Phi\vee\Psi]}(s, s', t) \right) \bowtie p.$$

Making the QBD Finite. Uniformization [8] is an often used method to compute transient probabilities in finite CTMCs. The continuous-time model is transformed into a discrete-time model together with a Poisson process with rate λ. The uniformization constant λ must be at least equal to the maximum absolute value of the diagonal entries of the generator $\mathbf{Q}$. Since for a QBD the matrix $\mathbf{Q}$ has only finitely many different diagonal entries (originating from the matrices $\mathbf{B}_{0,0}, \mathbf{B}_{1,1}$, and $\mathbf{A}_1$), λ can be determined even though $\mathbf{Q}$ has an infinite number of entries. For an allowed numerical error ε_t, uniformization requires a finite number n of steps (state changes) to be taken into account in order to compute the transient probabilities. Note that n can be computed *a priori*, given ε_t, λ and t.

Let $d \geq 1$ be the so-called *level diameter*, that is, the minimum number of state transitions that is needed to cross a complete repeating level. If n steps are to be taken into account, only $\lceil \frac{n}{d} \rceil$ levels can be reached from a state in level l in either direction.

Thus, for model checking the formula $\mathcal{P}_{\bowtie p}(\Phi \, \mathcal{U}^{[0,t]}\Psi)$, first all $\neg\Phi \vee \Psi$-states have to be made absorbing. If $\neg\Phi \vee \Psi$ is level-independent as of level k, then, using uniformization with n steps, we obtain the same transient probabilities for corresponding states as of level $k + \lceil \frac{n}{d} \rceil$, since only equivalent repeating levels are seen when stepping through the QBD.

In order to compute the transient probabilities for all states of the QBD, it suffices to compute them for the first $k + \lceil \frac{n}{d} \rceil$ levels only. Hence, only a finite part of the infinite QBD is needed. Outgoing from level $k + \lceil \frac{n}{d} \rceil$ there must still be the possibility to undertake $\lceil \frac{n}{d} \rceil$ steps "to the right". The total number of levels we have to consider therefore is $k + 2 \cdot \lceil \frac{n}{d} \rceil$ (cf. Figure 2). Thus, we reduced the task of computing transient probabilities for an infinite QBD to the computation of transient probabilities in a finite CTMC.

Interpretation of the Transient Probabilities. For all states in the first $k + \lceil \frac{n}{d} \rceil$ levels, we add the computed transient probabilities to reach any Ψ-state and check whether the accumulated probability meets the bound p. When using uniformization, the computed accumulated probability

$$\tilde{\pi}^{\mathcal{Q}[\neg \Phi \vee \Psi]}(s, Sat(\Psi), t) = \sum_{s' \in Sat(\Psi)} \tilde{\pi}^{\mathcal{Q}[\neg \Phi \vee \Psi]}(s, s', t)$$

is always an underestimation of the actual probability. Fortunately, we are able to indicate a maximum error ε_m (depending on ε_t) such that

$$\pi^{\mathcal{Q}[\neg \Phi \vee \Psi]}(s, Sat(\Psi), t) \leq \tilde{\pi}^{\mathcal{Q}[\neg \Phi \vee \Psi]}(s, Sat(\Psi), t) + \varepsilon_m.$$

The value of ε_m decreases as n increases. Applying the above inequality, we obtain the following implications:

$$\text{(a)} \quad \tilde{\pi}^{\mathcal{Q}[\neg \Phi \vee \Psi]}(s, Sat(\Psi), t) > p \Rightarrow \pi^{\mathcal{Q}[\neg \Phi \vee \Psi]}(s, Sat(\Psi), t) > p$$
$$\text{(b)} \quad \tilde{\pi}^{\mathcal{Q}[\neg \Phi \vee \Psi]}(s, Sat(\Psi), t) < p - \varepsilon_m \Rightarrow \pi^{\mathcal{Q}[\neg \Phi \vee \Psi]}(s, Sat(\Psi), t) < p$$

If one of these inequalities (a) or (b) holds, we can decide whether the bound $< p$ or $> p$ is met. For the bounds $\leq p$ and $\geq p$, similar implications can be derived. If $\tilde{\pi}^{\mathcal{Q}[\neg \Phi \vee \Psi]}(s, Sat(\Psi), t) \in [p, p - \varepsilon_m]$, then we cannot decide whether $\pi^{\mathcal{Q}[\neg \Phi \vee \Psi]}(s, Sat(\Psi), t)$ meets the bound p. The number of steps n considered when computing the transient probabilities via uniformization has been too small in that case. Decreasing ε_t, hence, increasing n, might resolve this problem.

As already mentioned, for all levels $\geq k + \lceil \frac{n}{d} \rceil$, the transient probabilities computed with n steps will be the same. If we can decide whether the bound p is met (case (a) or (b) above), we can be sure that $\mathcal{P}_{\bowtie p}(\Phi \, \mathcal{U}^{[0,t]} \Psi)$ is level independent as of level $k + \lceil \frac{n}{d} \rceil$. It might actually be the case that level independence starts at a smaller level.

If n is large enough we check for all states in levels up to $k + \lceil \frac{n}{d} \rceil$ whether the accumulated transient probability of reaching a Ψ-state meets the bound p. These states form the subsequent level satisfaction sets $Sat^j(\mathcal{P}_{\bowtie p}(\Phi \, \mathcal{U}^{[0,t]} \Psi))$. The satisfaction set for level $k + \lceil \frac{n}{d} \rceil$ is representative for all following levels.

The more general case where $I = [t_1, t_2]$ for $0 < t_1 < t_2$ can be treated by following the procedure given in [4]. It requires the computation of transient probabilities in two "versions" of the QBD, where different states are made absorbing. The number of levels to be considered must be adapted accordingly. Details of this procedure are omitted for brevity here, but can be found in [18].

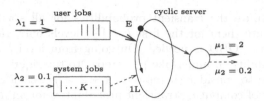

Fig. 3. Dual-Job-Class Cyclic-Server System

The case where $I = [0, \infty]$ can be addressed similarly as in the finite-state case, cf. [4–Corollary 1], except for the fact that it leads to a system of linear equations of infinite size. Given the special (QBD) structure of this system of linear equations, it appears that also in this case a matrix-geometric solution approach might be applicable, but this remains to be investigated.

Complexity. For model checking the until operator we need to consider $k + \frac{2n}{d}$ levels with N states, respectively N_0 states for the boundary level. ν denotes the average number of transitions originating from a single state of the QBD. To compute the transient probabilities we require the sum of $\mathcal{O}(\lambda t)$ matrices, each of which is the result of a matrix-matrix multiplication. This results in an overall computational complexity of $\mathcal{O}(\lambda t \cdot \nu (N_0 + kN + nN)^2)$. Regarding storage complexity, we require $\mathcal{O}(3(N_0 + kN + nN))$ storage for the probability matrices and $\mathcal{O}(\nu(N_0^2 + NN_0 + N^2))$ for the transition matrix of the underlying DTMC.

5   Case Study: A Dual-Job-Class Cyclic-Server System

System Description. We analyze a system with two sorts of jobs, as depicted in Figure 4. User jobs, having high priority, are served according to an exhaustive scheduling strategy. System jobs, having low priority, are served with a 1-limited scheduling strategy. In the beginning, the server always starts serving user jobs and a system job can only be served after at least one user job has been served. As long as there are user jobs in the queue, the server first serves these jobs. System jobs can only be served, if all user jobs have been served and at least one system job is waiting for service. If the server changes to system jobs, only one job is served and afterwards the server polls the user jobs queue again. We can have an infinite number of user jobs and at most K system jobs in the system. We have modeled this system as iSPN [17]; from this iSPN the underlying QBD is automatically generated. The order of this QBD depends on the actual value of K; each level of the underlying QBDs consists of $2K + 1$ states that model the number of system jobs in the queue and the presence of the server at the system-job queue. The QBD for $K = 1$ is given in Figure 4.

Its states can be interpreted as follows: j indicates the number of user jobs currently in the system, $i = 0$ means that a system job is being served, $i = 1$ means that no system job is waiting, and $i = 2$ means that a system job just arrived but is not being served yet.

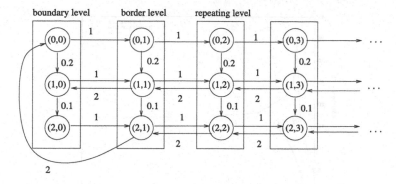

Fig. 4. QBD of the Dual-Job-Class Cyclic-Server System

Steady-State Property. We want to know whether the steady-state probability of having a full system-job queue is greater than 0.1. As CSL formula, this property can be stated as $S_{>0.1}(Q_{Sys}full)$, where $Q_{Sys}full$ is the atomic proposition that is valid in all states where the system-job queue is full.

For any K, every level contains exactly two states satisfying atomic proposition $Q_{Sys}full$, being the state with K system jobs present (queued), and with the server active with either a system job or a user job. In case of $K = 1$, we see in Figure 4 that these are the states $(0, \cdot)$ and $(2, \cdot)$. Hence, $Sat(Q_{Sys}full)$ has infinite size. For $K < 11$, $Sat(S_{>0.1}(Q_{Sys}full)) = S$, thus, the formula holds in all states. For $K \geq 11$, $Sat(S_{>0.1}(Q_{Sys}full)) = \varnothing$.

Figure 5 shows the number of iterations (as discussed in Section 4.3), needed to verify the property, depending on the system parameter K. If the actual steady-state probability of $Q_{Sys}full$-states comes close to the given bound 0.1, more iterations are needed. This explains the peak at $K = 11$. Figure 5 also gives the computation time for different K. Note that the smaller number of iterations for $K > 11$ does not lead to a smaller computation time, since more time is needed per iteration (as the matrices become larger).

Time-Bounded Until Property. As system jobs have a low priority compared to the user jobs, we would like to know for which states of the QBD the probability of the system-job queue to become empty in a certain time interval is greater than 0.1. Stated in CSL, we analyze $\Phi = P_{>0.1}(\neg Q_{Sys}Empty\ U^{[0,t]}Q_{Sys}Empty)$.

For $K = 1$ the formula Φ can be interpreted as follows: Is the probability greater than 0.1 that a waiting system job is served in a certain time interval? For a time interval $I = [0, 2]$, a given error $\varepsilon = 10^{-7}$, uniformization considers 23 steps. As Φ is level-independent as of level 1 and we have a level-diameter of 1, level 24 can serve as a representative for the higher repeating levels. Analyzing the resulting satisfaction set $Sat(P_{>0.1}(\neg Q_{Sys}Empty\ U^{[0,2]}Q_{Sys}Empty))$ shows the following.

All states with first index $i = 1$ are trivially included in the satisfaction set, because $Q_{Sys}Empty$ is already valid in these states. States with first index $i = 0$ are included as they model a situation in the system where the server is serving

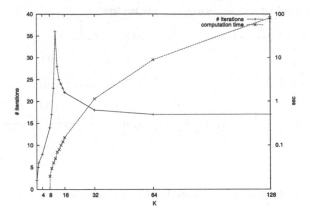

Fig. 5. Number of iterations and computation time required for checking $\mathcal{S}_{>0.1}(\mathtt{Q_{Sys}full})$, as a function of the maximum number of system jobs K

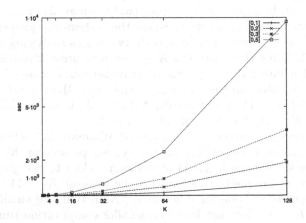

Fig. 6. Computation time required for checking $\mathcal{P}_{>0.1}(\neg\mathtt{Q_{Sys}Empty}\ \mathcal{U}^{[0,t]}\mathtt{Q_{Sys}Empty})$, as a function of the maximum number of system jobs K

a system job. Hence, for those states the probability for the system job to be served in time interval $[0,2]$ is greater than 0.1. If the system job just arrived in the queue ($i = 2$), model checking shows that the probability for this job to be served in time is only greater than 0.1 if less than three user jobs are waiting for service.

For the computation of the satisfaction sets, we have to deal with state spaces of the size $(2K+1)\cdot(2n+2)$. The left-hand term accounts for the size of one level and the right-hand term for the number of levels considered by uniformization. n gives the number of steps which is considered by uniformization, depending on the error ε_t. In Figure 6 the computation time is depicted for different time intervals. For larger time intervals the state space grows as uniformization needs to consider more steps which results in larger computation times.

6   Conclusions

In this paper we have presented model-checking algorithms for checking CSL properties against infinite-state CTMCs, in particular for QBDs. The model checking algorithms make extensive use of uniformization for transient analysis (for time-bounded until) and matrix-geometric methods for determining steady-state probabilities (for the steady-state operator). The model checking algorithms as presented are new. Our approach to analyze the transient state probabilities of infinite-state CTMC is also new. We have shown the feasibility of the model checking algorithms by a case study.

We are aware of the fact that when checking nested formulas, the number of levels that have level-dependent properties grows, which makes the algorithms less efficient. On the other hand, practice reveals that the nesting depth of logical expressions to be checked is typically small [6], so that this is not so much of a disadvantage after all.

At various points, the presented algorithms can be made more efficient. For instance, for checking time-bounded until we have introduced the notion of level diameter. In practice, there might be two different diameters, depending on the direction of crossing a level (to higher or to lower levels). Exploiting this fact might lead to smaller finite-state Markov chains to be considered.

We also required the QBD under study to be strongly connected, in order to make use of the fact that the steady-state probabilities do not depend on the starting state. It is left for further investigation how the model checking algorithms have to be adapted to account for non-strongly connected QBDs.

By restricting ourselves to level-independent formulas, we restrict the set of CSL formulas that can be checked. For model checking level-*dependent* CSL formulas new model checking algorithms will be needed, since in that case we cannot exploit the level-independent QBD structure to cut the infinite set of states.

We note that there has been done a substantial amount of work on model checking infinite-state systems, e.g., on regular model checking [1] and probabilistic lossy channel systems [19], however, not in the context of continuous-time Markov chains, as we have presented here. It remains to be investigated whether and how we can exploit these results in our context.

Finally, we need to complete our work on the tool chain for specifying and model checking infinite-state systems, and possibly will integrate it into other model checking tools for CTMCs. First details on this, and on many of the other issues addressed in this paper, can be found in the recently completed diploma thesis [18].

References

1. P. Abdulla, B. Jonsson, M. Nilsson, and M. Saksena. A survey of regular model checking. In P. Gardner and N. Yoshida, editors, *Proc. Concur 2004*, number 3170 in Lecture Notes in Computer Science, pages 35–48, 2004.
2. A. Aziz, K. Sanwal, and R. Brayton. Model checking continuous-time Markov chains. *ACM Transactions on Computational Logic*, 1(1):162–170, 2000.

3. C. Baier, B.R. Haverkort, H. Hermanns, and J.-P. Katoen. On the logical characterisation of performability properties. In *Proc. 27th Int. Colloquium on Automata, Languages and Programming (ICALP'00)*, number 1853 in Lecture Notes in Computer Science, pages 780–792, 2000.
4. C. Baier, B.R. Haverkort, H. Hermanns, and J.-P. Katoen. Model-checking algorithms for continuous-time Markov chains. *IEEE Transactions on Software Engineering*, 29(7):524–541, July 2003.
5. A. Bell. *Distributed evaluation of stochasic Petri nets*. PhD thesis, Dept. of Computer Science, RWTH Aachen, 2004.
6. M.B. Dwyer, G.S. Avrunin, and J.C. Corbett. Patterns in property specification for finite-state verification. In *Proc. 21st Int. Conf. on Software Engineering*, pages 411–420. IEEE CS Press, 1999.
7. A. El-Rayes, M. Kwiatkowska, and G. Norman. Solving infinite stochastic process algebra models through matrix-geometric methods. In *Proc. 7th Process Algebras and Performance Modelling Workshop (PAPM'99)*, pages 41–62. University of Zaragoza, 1999.
8. D. Gross and D.R. Miller. The randomization technique as a modeling tool and solution procedure for transient Markov processes. *Operations Research*, 32(2):343–361, 1984.
9. B.R. Haverkort. *Performance of Computer Communication Systems*. John Wiley & Sons, 1998.
10. B.R. Haverkort, H. Hermanns, and J.-P. Katoen. On the use of model checking techniques for dependability evaluation. In *Proc. 19th IEEE Symposium on Reliable Distributed Systems (SRDS'00)*, pages 228–237. IEEE CS Press, 2000.
11. H. Hermanns, J.-P. Katoen, J. Meyer-Kayser, and M. Siegle. A tool for model-checking Markov chains. *International Journal on Software Tools for Technology Transfer*, 4(2):153–172, 2003.
12. J.-P. Katoen. *Concepts, Algorithms, and Tools for Model Checking*. Arbeitsberichte des IMMD 32(1), Friedrich-Alexander Universität Erlangen Nürnberg, June 1999.
13. M. Kwiatkowska, G. Norman, and D. Parker. Probabilistic symbolic model checking with PRISM: a hybrid approach. *International Journal on Software Tools for Technology Transfer*, 6(2):128–142, 2004.
14. G. Latouche and V. Ramaswami. A logarithmic reduction algorithm for quasi birth and death processes. *Journal of Applied Probability*, 30:650–674, 1993.
15. I. Mitrani, A. Ost, and M. Rettelbach. TIPP and the spectral expansion method. In F. Baccelli, A. Jean-Marie, and I. Mitrani, editors, *Quantitative Models in Parallel Systems*, pages 99–113. Springer, 1995.
16. M.F. Neuts. *Matrix Geometric Solutions in Stochastic Models: An Algorithmic Approach*. Johns Hopkins University Press, 1981.
17. A. Ost. *Performance of Communication Systems. A Model-Based Approach with Matrix-Geometric Methods*. PhD thesis, Dept. of Computer Science, RWTH Aachen, 2001.
18. A. Remke. Model Checking Quasi Birth Death Processes. Master's thesis, Dept. of Computer Science, RWTH Aachen, 2004 (http://www.cs.utwente.nl/~anne/pub/modelchecking.pdf).
19. Ph. Schnoebelen. The verification of probabilistic lossy channel systems. In C. Baier, B.R. Haverkort, H. hermanns, J.-P. Katoen, and M. Siegle, editors, *Validation of Stochastic Systems*, volume 2925 of *Lecture Notes in Computer Science*, pages 445–465, 2004.
20. J. Zhang and E.J. Coyle. Transient analysis of quasi-birth-death processes. *Stochastic Models*, 5(3):459–496, 1989.

Algorithmic Verification of Recursive Probabilistic State Machines

Kousha Etessami[1] and Mihalis Yannakakis[2]

[1] School of Informatics, University of Edinburgh
[2] Department of Computer Science, Columbia University

Abstract. Recursive Markov Chains (RMCs) ([EY05]) are a natural abstract model of procedural probabilistic programs and related systems involving recursion and probability. They succinctly define a class of denumerable Markov chains that generalize multi-type branching (stochastic) processes. In this paper, we study the problem of model checking an RMC against a given ω-regular specification. Namely, given an RMC A and a Büchi automaton B, we wish to know the probability that an execution of A is accepted by B. We establish a number of strong upper bounds, as well as lower bounds, both for *qualitative* problems (is the probability = 1, or = 0?), and for *quantitative* problems (is the probability $\geq p$?, or, approximate the probability to within a desired precision). Among these, we show that qualitative model checking for general RMCs can be decided in PSPACE in $|A|$ and EXPTIME in $|B|$, and when A is either a single-exit RMC or when the total number of entries and exits in A is bounded, it can be decided in polynomial time in $|A|$. We then show that quantitative model checking can also be done in PSPACE in $|A|$, and in EXPSPACE in $|B|$. When B is deterministic, all our complexities in $|B|$ come down by one exponential.

For lower bounds, we show that the qualitative model checking problem, even for a fixed RMC, is EXPTIME-complete. On the other hand, even for reachability analysis, we showed in [EY05] that our PSPACE upper bounds in A can not be improved upon without a breakthrough on a well-known open problem in the complexity of numerical computation.

1 Introduction

Recursive Markov Chains (RMCs) are a natural abstract model of procedural probabilistic programs. They succinctly define a natural class of denumerable Markov chains that generalize multi-type branching (stochastic) processes. Informally, an RMC consists of a collection of finite state component Markov chains (MC) that can call each other in a potentially recursive manner. Each component MC has a set of *nodes* (ordinary states), a set of *boxes* (each mapped to a component MC), a well-defined interface consisting of a set of *entry* and *exit* nodes (nodes where it may start and terminate), and a set of probabilistic transitions connecting the nodes and boxes. A transition to a box specifies the entry node and models the invocation of the component MC associated with the

N. Halbwachs and L. Zuck (Eds.): TACAS 2005, LNCS 3440, pp. 253–270, 2005.

box; when (and if) the component MC terminates at an exit, execution of the calling MC resumes from the corresponding exit of the box.

RMCs are a probabilistic version of Recursive State Machines (RSMs). RSMs ([AEY01, BGR01]) and closely related models like Pushdown Systems (PDSs) (see, e.g., [EHRS00, BR00]) have been studied extensively in recent research on model checking and program analysis, because of their applications to verification of sequential programs with procedures. Recursive Markov Chains generalize other well-studied models involving probability and recursion: *Stochastic Context-Free Grammars* (SCFGs) have been extensively studied, mainly in natural language processing (NLP) (see [MS99]). *Multi-Type Branching Processes* (MT-BPs), are an important family of stochastic processes with many applications in a variety of areas (see, e.g., [Har63]). Both SCFG's and MT-BP's are essentially equivalent to *single-exit* RMC's: the special case of RMC's in which all components have one exit. Probabilistic models of programs and systems are of interest for several reasons. First, a program may use randomization, in which case the transition probabilities reflect the random choices of the algorithm. Second, we may want to model and analyse a program or system under statistical conditions on its behaviour (e.g., based on profiling statistics or on statistical assumptions), and to determine the induced probability of properties of interest

We introduced RMCs in [EY05] and developed some of their basic theory, focusing on algorithmic reachability analysis: what is the probability of reaching a given state starting from another? In this paper we study the more general problem of model checking an RMC against an ω-regular specification: given an RMC A and a Büchi automaton B, what is the probability that an execution of A is accepted by B? The techniques we develop in this paper for model checking go far beyond what was developed in [EY05] for reachability analysis.

General RMCs are intimately related to probabilistic Pushdown Systems (pPDSs), and there are efficient translations between RMCs and pPDSs. There has been some recent work on model checking of pPDSs ([EKM04, BKS05]). As we shall describe shortly, our results yield substantial improvements, when translated to the setting of pPDSs, on the best algorithmic upper and lower bounds known for ω-regular model checking of pPDSs.

We now outline the main results in this paper. We are given an RMC A and a property in the form of a (non-deterministic) Büchi automaton (BA) B, whose alphabet corresponds to (labels on) the vertices of A. Let $P_A(L(B))$ denote the probability that an execution of A is accepted by B (i.e., satisfies the property). The *qualitative* model checking problems are: (1) determine whether almost all executions of A satisfy the property B (i.e. is $P_A(L(B)) = 1$?, this corresponds to B being a desirable correctness property), and (2) whether almost no executions of A satisfy B (i.e. is $P_A(L(B)) = 0$?, corresponding to B being an undesirable error property). In the *quantitative* model checking problems we wish to compare $P_A(L(B))$ to a given rational threshold p, i.e., is $P_A(L(B)) \geq p$?, or alternatively, we may wish to approximate $P_A(L(B))$ to within a given number of bits of precision. Note that in general $P_A(L(B))$ may be irrational or may not even be expressible by radicals [EY05]. Hence it cannot be computed exactly.

Qualitative:		reachability	det. Büchi	nondet. Büchi
	1-exit	P	P	P in RMC, EXPTIME in Büchi
	Bd	P	P	P in RMC, EXPTIME in Büchi
	general	PSPACE	PSPACE	PSPACE in RMC, EXPTIME in Büchi

Quantitative:		reachability	det. Büchi	nondet. Büchi
	1-exit	PSPACE	PSPACE	PSPACE in RMC, EXPSPACE in Büchi
	Bd	P	P in RMC for fixed Büchi	P in RMC, for fixed Büchi
	general	PSPACE	PSPACE	PSPACE in RMC, EXPSPACE in Büchi

Fig. 1. Complexity of Qualitative and Quantitative problems

We show that the qualitative model checking problems can be solved in PSPACE in $|A|$ and EXPTIME in $|B|$. More specifically, in a first phase the algorithm analyzes the RMC A by itself (using PSPACE only in $|A|$). In a second phase, it further analyses A in conjunction with B, using polynomial time in A and exponential time in B. If the automaton B is deterministic then the time is polynomial in B. Furthermore, if A is a single-exit RMC (which corresponds to SCFG's and MT-BP's), then the first phase, and hence the whole algorithm, can be done in polynomial time in A. Another such case, where we can model-check qualitatively in polynomial time in A, is when the total number of entries and exits in A is bounded (we call them Bd-RMCs). In terms of probabilistic program abstractions, this class of RMC's corresponds to programs with a bounded number of distinct procedures, each of which has a bounded number of input/output parameter values. The internals of the components of the RMCs (i.e., the procedures) can be arbitrarily large and complex.

For quantitative model checking, we show that deciding whether $P_A(L(B)) \geq p$, given a rational $p \in [0, 1]$, can be decided in PSPACE in $|A|$ and EXPSPACE in $|B|$. When B is deterministic, the space is polynomial in both A and B. Moreover, for A a Bd-RMC, and when B is fixed, there is an algorithm that runs in P-time in $|A|$; however, in this case (unlike the others) the exponent of the polynomial depends on B. Table 1 summarizes our complexity upper bounds (the "reachability" columns are from [EY05]; all the other results are new).

For lower bounds, we prove that the qualitative model checking problem, even for a fixed, single entry/exit RMC, is already EXPTIME-complete. On the other hand, even for reachability analysis, we showed in [EY05] that our PSPACE upper bounds in A, even for the quantitative 1-exit problem, and the general qualitative problem, can not be improved without a breakthrough on the complexity of the *square root sum* problem, a well-known open problem in the complexity of exact numerical computation (see Section 2.2).

Related Work. Model checking of flat Markov chains has received extensive attention both in theory and practice (e.g. [CY95, Kwi03, PZ93, Var85]). It is known that model checking of a Markov chain A with respect to a Büchi automaton B is PSPACE-complete, and furthermore the probability $P_A(L(B))$ can be computed exactly in time polynomial in A and exponential in B. Recursive Markov chains were introduced recently in [EY05], where we developed some of their basic theory and investigated the termination and reachability problems; we summarize the main results in Section 2.2. Recursion introduces a number of new difficulties that are not present in the flat case. For example, in the flat case, the qualitative problems depend only on the structure of the Markov chain (which transitions are present) and not on the precise values of the transition probabilities; this is not any more the case for RMC's and numerical issues have to be dealt with even in the qualitative problem. Furthermore, unlike the flat case, the desired probabilities cannot be computed exactly.

The closely related model of probabilistic Pushdown Systems (pPDS) was introduced and studied recently in [EKM04, BKS05]. They largely focus on model checking against branching-time properties, but they also study deterministic ([EKM04]) and non-deterministic ([BKS05]) Büchi automaton specifications. There are efficient (linear time) translations between RMCs and pPDSs, similar to translations between RSMs and PDSs (see [AEY01, BGR01]). Our upper bounds, translated to pPDSs, improve those obtained in [EKM04, BKS05] by an exponential factor in the general setting, and by more for specific classes like single-exit and Bd-RMCs. Specifically, [BKS05], by extending results in [EKM04], show that qualitative model checking for pPDSs can be done in PSPACE in the size of the pPDS and 2-EXPSPACE in the size of the Büchi automaton, while quantitative model checking can be decided in EXPTIME in the size of the pPDS and in 3-EXPTIME in the size of the Büchi automaton. They do not obtain stronger complexity results for the class of pBPAs (equivalent to single-exit RMCs). Also, the class of Bd-RMCs has no direct analog in pPDSs, as the total number of entries and exits of an RMC gets lost in translation to pPDSs. Reference [EE04] is a survey paper that predates this paper and summarizes only the results in prior papers [EKM04, EY05, BKS05].

The paper is organized as follows. Section 2 gives necessary definitions and background on RMC's from [EY05]. Section 3 shows how to construct from an RMC, A, a flat Markov chain M'_A which in some sense "summarizes" A; this chain plays a central role analogous to the "summary graph" for RSMs [AEY01, BGR01]. Section 4 addresses the qualitative model checking problems, presenting both upper and lower bounds. Section 5 addresses the quantitative model checking problem; a fundamental "unique fixed point theorem" is proved for RMC's, and plays a crucial role in our quantitative algorithms.

Due to space limitations, we have removed almost all proofs from this paper.

2   Definitions and Background

A *Recursive Markov Chain (RMC)*, A, is a tuple $A = (A_1, \ldots, A_k)$, where each *component chain* $A_i = (N_i, B_i, Y_i, En_i, Ex_i, \delta_i)$ consists of:

- A set N_i of *nodes*
- A subset of *entry* nodes $En_i \subseteq N_i$, and a subset of *exit* nodes $Ex_i \subseteq N_i$.
- A set B_i of *boxes*. Let $B = \cup_{i=1}^{k} B_i$ be the (disjoint) union of all boxes of A.

- A mapping $Y_i : B_i \mapsto \{1, \ldots, k\}$ assigns a component to every box.
  Let $Y = \cup_{i=1}^k Y_i$ be $Y : B \mapsto \{1, \ldots, k\}$ where $Y|_{B_i} = Y_i$, for $1 \leq i \leq k$.
- To each box $b \in B_i$, we associate a set of *call ports*, $Call_b = \{(b, en) \mid en \in En_{Y(b)}\}$, and a set of *return ports*, $Return_b = \{(b, ex) \mid ex \in Ex_{Y(b)}\}$.
- A transition relation δ_i, where transitions are of the form $(u, p_{u,v}, v)$ where:
  1. the source u is either a non-exit node $u \in N_i \setminus Ex_i$, or a return port $u = (b, ex) \in Return_b$, where $b \in B_i$.
  2. The destination v is either a non-entry node $v \in N_i \setminus En_i$, or a call port $v = (b, en) \in Call_b$, where $b \in B_i$.
  3. $p_{u,v} \in \mathbb{R}_{>0}$ is the probability of transition from u to v. (We assume $p_{u,v}$ is rational.)
  4. *Consistency of probabilities*: for each u, $\sum_{\{v' \mid (u, p_{u,v'}, v') \in \delta_i\}} p_{u,v'} = 1$, unless u is a call port or exit node; neither have outgoing transitions, in which case $\sum_{v'} p_{u,v'} = 0$.

We will use the term *vertex* of A_i to refer collectively to its set of nodes, call ports, and return ports, and we denote this set by Q_i, and we let $Q = \cup_{i=1}^k Q_i$ be the set of all vertices of the RMC A. That is, the transition relation δ_i is a set of probability-weighted directed edges on the set Q_i of vertices of A_i. Let $\delta = \cup_i \delta_i$ be the set of all transitions of A.

An RMC A defines a global denumerable Markov chain $M_A = (V, \Delta)$ as follows. The global *states* $V \subseteq B^* \times Q$ are pairs of the form $\langle \beta, u \rangle$, where $\beta \in B^*$ is a (possibly empty) sequence of boxes and $u \in Q$ is a *vertex* of A. More precisely, the states $V \subseteq B^* \times Q$ and transitions Δ are defined inductively as follows:

1. $\langle \epsilon, u \rangle \in V$, for $u \in Q$. (ϵ denotes the empty string.)
2. if $\langle \beta, u \rangle \in V$ and $(u, p_{u,v}, v) \in \delta$, then $\langle \beta, v \rangle \in V$ and $(\langle \beta, u \rangle, p_{u,v}, \langle \beta, v \rangle) \in \Delta$
3. if $\langle \beta, (b, en) \rangle \in V$ and $(b, en) \in Call_b$, then
   $\langle \beta b, en \rangle \in V$, & $(\langle \beta, (b, en) \rangle, 1, \langle \beta b, en \rangle) \in \Delta$.
4. if $\langle \beta b, ex \rangle \in V$ and $(b, ex) \in Return_b$, then
   $\langle \beta, (b, ex) \rangle \in V$ & $(\langle \beta b, ex \rangle, 1, \langle \beta, (b, ex) \rangle) \in \Delta$.

Item 1 corresponds to the possible initial states, 2 corresponds to a transition within a component, 3 is when a new component is entered via a box, 4 is when the process exits a component and control returns to the calling component.

Some states of M_A are *terminating*, i.e., have no outgoing transitions. Namely, states $\langle \epsilon, ex \rangle$, where ex is an exit. We want M_A to be a proper Markov chain, so we consider terminating states as *absorbing*, with a self-loop of probability 1.

A *trace* (or *trajectory*) $t \in V^\omega$ of M_A is an infinite sequence of states $t = s_0 s_1 s_2 \ldots$ such that for all $i \geq 0$, there is a transition $(s_i, p_{s_i, s_{i+1}}, s_{i+1}) \in \Delta$, with $p_{s_i, s_{i+1}} > 0$. Let $\Omega \subseteq V^\omega$ denote the set of traces of M_A. For a state $s = \langle \beta, v \rangle \in V$, let $Q(s) = v$ denote the vertex at state s. Generalizing this to traces, for a trace $t \in \Omega$, let $Q(t) = Q(s_0) Q(s_1) Q(s_2) \ldots \in Q^\omega$. We will consider M_A with *initial states* from $Init = \{\langle \epsilon, v \rangle \mid v \in Q\}$. More generally we may have a probability distribution $p_{\text{init}} : V \mapsto [0, 1]$ on initial states (we usually assume p_{init} has support only in $Init$, and we always assume it has finite support). This induces a probability distribution on traces generated by random walks on M_A. Formally, we have a probability space $(\Omega, \mathcal{F}, \mathbf{Pr}_\Omega)$, parametrized by p_{init}, where $\mathcal{F} = \sigma(\mathcal{C}) \subseteq 2^{\Omega}$ is the σ-field generated by the set of *basic cylinder sets*, $\mathcal{C} = \{C(x) \subseteq \Omega \mid x \in V^*\}$, where for $x \in V^*$ the cylinder at x is $C(x) = \{t \in \Omega \mid t = xw, \ w \in V^{\omega}\}$. The probability distribution $\mathbf{Pr}_{\Omega} : \mathcal{F} \mapsto [0,1]$ is determined uniquely by the probabilities of cylinder sets, which are:

$$\mathbf{Pr}_{\Omega}(C(s_0 s_1 \ldots s_n)) = p_{\text{init}}(s_0) p_{s_0,s_1} p_{s_1,s_2} \cdots p_{s_{n-1},s_n}$$

See, e.g., [Bil95]. RMCs where every component has at most one exit are called *1-exit* RMCs. RMCs where the total number of entries and exits is bounded by a constant c, (i.e., $\sum_{i=1}^{k} |En_i| + |Ex_i| \leq c$) are called *Bounded total entry-exit* RMCs (Bd-RMCs, for short).

2.1   The Central Questions for Model Checking of RMCs

We first define reachability probabilities that play an important role in our analysis. Given a vertex $u \in Q_i$ and an exit $ex \in Ex_i$, both in the same component A_i, let $q^*_{(u,ex)}$ denote the probability of eventually reaching the state $\langle \epsilon, ex \rangle$, starting at the state $\langle \epsilon, u \rangle$. Formally, we have $p_{\text{init}}(\langle \epsilon, u \rangle) = 1$, and $q^*_{(u,ex)} \doteq \mathbf{Pr}_{\Omega}(\{t = s_0 s_1 \ldots \in \Omega \mid \exists\, i\,, s_i = \langle \epsilon, ex \rangle\})$. As we shall see, the probabilities $q^*_{(u,ex)}$ will play an important role in obtaining other probabilities.

Recall that a Büchi automaton $B = (\Sigma, S, q_0, R, F)$, has an alphabet Σ, a set of states S, an initial state $q_0 \in S$, a transition relation $R \subseteq S \times \Sigma \times S$, and a set of accepting states $F \subseteq S$. A *run* of B is a sequence $\pi = q_0 v_0 q_1 v_1 q_2 \ldots$ of alternating states and letters such that for all $i \geq 0$ $(q_i, v_i, q_{i+1}) \in R$. The ω-word associated with run π is $w_{\pi} = v_0 v_1 v_2 \ldots \in \Sigma^{\omega}$. The run π is *accepting* if for infinitely many i, $q_i \in F$. Define the ω-language $L(B) = \{w_{\pi} \mid \pi \text{ is an accepting run of } B\}$. Note that $L(B) \subseteq \Sigma^{\omega}$. Let $\mathcal{L} : Q \mapsto \Sigma$, be a given Σ-labelling of the vertices v of RMC A. $\mathcal{L}$ naturally generalizes to $\mathcal{L} : Q^{\omega} \mapsto \Sigma^{\omega}$: for $w = v_0 v_1 v_2 \ldots \in Q^{\omega}$, $\mathcal{L}(w) = \mathcal{L}(v_0)\mathcal{L}(v_1)\mathcal{L}(v_2)\ldots$. Given RMC A, with initial state $s_0 = \langle \epsilon, u \rangle$, and given a BA B over the alphabet Σ, let $P_A(L(B))$ denote the probability that a trace of M_A is in $L(B)$. More precisely: $P_A(L(B)) \doteq \mathbf{Pr}_{\Omega}(\{t \in \Omega \mid \mathcal{L}(Q(t)) \in L(B)\})$. One needs to show that the sets $\{t \in \Omega \mid \mathcal{L}(Q(t)) \in L(B)\}$ are measurable (in $\mathcal{F}$). This is not difficult (see similar proofs in [CY95, Var85]). The *model checking* problems for ω-regular properties of RMCs are:

(1) *Qualitative* model checking problems: Is $P_A(L(B)) = 1$? Is $P_A(L(B)) = 0$?
(2) *Quantitative* model checking problems: given $p \in [0,1]$, is $P_A(L(B)) \geq p$? Also, we may wish to approximate $P_A(L(B))$ to within a given number of bits of precision.

Note, with a routine for the problem $P_A(L(B)) \geq p$?, we can approximate $P_A(L(B))$ to within i bits using binary search with i calls to the routine. Thus, for quantitative model checking the first problem entails the second. Note that probabilistic reachability is a special case of model checking: given vertex u of RMC A and a subset of vertices F, the probability that the RMC starting at u visits some vertex in F (in some stack context) is equal to $P_A(L(B))$, where we let the labelling $\mathcal{L}$ map vertices in F to 1 and the other vertices to 0, and B is the 2-state automaton that accepts strings that contain a 1. Similarly, for the *repeated reachability* problem, where we are interested whether a trajectory from u infinitely often visits a vertex of F, we can let B be the (2-state deterministic) automaton that accepts strings with an infinite number of 1's.

To simplify the descriptions of our results, we assume henceforth that $\Sigma = Q$, the vertices of A. This is w.l.o.g. since the problem can be reduced to this case by relabelling the RMC A and modifying the automaton B (see, e.g., [CY95]), however care is needed when measuring complexity separately in RMC, A, and BA, B, since typically B and Σ are small in relation to A. Our complexity results are all with respect to the standard sizes of A and B.

2.2   Basic RMC Theory and Reachability Analysis (From [EY05])

We recall some of the basic theory of RMCs developed in [EY05], where we studied reachability analysis. Considering the probabilities $q^*_{(u,ex)}$ as unknowns, we can set up a system of (non-linear) polynomial equations, such that the probabilities $q^*_{(u,ex)}$ are the *Least Fixed Point* (LFP) solution of this system. Use a variable $x_{(u,ex)}$ for each unknown probability $q^*_{(u,ex)}$. We will often find it convenient to index the variables $x_{(u,ex)}$ according to a fixed order, so we can refer to them also as $x_1, \ldots, x_n$, with each $x_{(u,ex)}$ identified with x_j for some j. We thus have a vector of variables: $\mathbf{x} = (x_1\, x_2 \ldots x_n)^T$.

Definition 1. *Given RMC $A = (A_1, \ldots, A_k)$, define the system of polynomial equations, S_A, over the variables $x_{(u,ex)}$, where $u \in Q_i$ and $ex \in Ex_i$, for $1 \leq i \leq k$. The system contains one equation $x_{(u,ex)} = P_{(u,ex)}(\mathbf{x})$, for each variable $x_{(u,ex)}$. $P_{(u,ex)}(\mathbf{x})$ denotes a multivariate polynomial with positive rational coefficients. There are 3 cases, based on the "type" of vertex u:*

1. *Type I: $u = ex$. In this case: $x_{(ex,ex)} = 1$.*
2. *Type II: either $u \in N_i \setminus \{ex\}$ or $u = (b, ex')$ is a return port. In these cases:*
$$x_{(u,ex)} = \textstyle\sum_{\{v \mid (u,p_{u,v},v) \in \delta\}} p_{u,v} \cdot x_{(v,ex)}.$$
3. *Type III: $u = (b, en)$ is a call port. In this case:*
$$x_{((b,en),ex)} = \textstyle\sum_{ex' \in Ex_{Y(b)}} x_{(en,ex')} \cdot x_{((b,ex'),ex)}$$

In vector notation, we denote $S_A = (x_j = P_j(\mathbf{x}) \mid j = 1, \ldots, n)$ by: $\mathbf{x} = P(\mathbf{x})$.

Given A, we can construct $\mathbf{x} = P(\mathbf{x})$ in P-time: $P(\mathbf{x})$ has size $O(|A|\theta^2)$, where θ denotes the maximum number of exits of any component. For vectors $\mathbf{x}, \mathbf{y} \in \mathbb{R}^n$, define $\mathbf{x} \preceq \mathbf{y}$ to mean that $x_j \leq y_j$ for every coordinate j. For $D \subseteq \mathbb{R}^n$, call a mapping $H : \mathbb{R}^n \mapsto \mathbb{R}^n$ *monotone* on D, if: for all $\mathbf{x}, \mathbf{y} \in D$, if $\mathbf{x} \preceq \mathbf{y}$ then $H(\mathbf{x}) \preceq H(\mathbf{y})$. Define $P^1(\mathbf{x}) = P(\mathbf{x})$, and $P^k(\mathbf{x}) = P(P^{k-1}(\mathbf{x}))$, for $k > 1$. Let $\mathbf{q}^* \in \mathbb{R}^n$ denote the n-vector of probabilities $q^*_{(u,ex)}$, using the same indexing as used for $\mathbf{x}$. Let $\mathbf{0}$ denote the all 0 n-vector. Define $\mathbf{x}^0 = \mathbf{0}$, and $\mathbf{x}^k = P(\mathbf{x}^{k-1}) = P^k(\mathbf{0})$, for $k \geq 1$. The map $P : \mathbb{R}^n \mapsto \mathbb{R}^n$ is monotone on $\mathbb{R}^n_{\geq 0}$.

Theorem 1. *([EY05], see also [EKM04]) $\mathbf{q}^* \in [0,1]^n$ is the <u>Least Fixed Point</u> solution, LFP(P), of $\mathbf{x} = P(\mathbf{x})$. Thus, $\mathbf{q}^* = P(\mathbf{q}^*)$ and $\mathbf{q}^* = \lim_{k \to \infty} \mathbf{x}^k$, and for all $k \geq 0$, $\mathbf{x}^k \preceq \mathbf{x}^{k+1} \preceq \mathbf{q}^*$, and for all $\mathbf{q}' \in \mathbb{R}^n_{\geq 0}$, if $\mathbf{q}' = P(\mathbf{q}')$, then $\mathbf{q}^* \preceq \mathbf{q}'$.*

There are already 1-exit RMCs for which the probability $q^*_{(en,ex)}$ is irrational and not "solvable by radicals" ([EY05]). Thus, we can't compute probabilities exactly. Given a system $x = P(x)$, and a vector $q \in [0,1]^n$, consider the following sentence in the *Existential Theory of Reals* (which we denote by $\boldsymbol{ExTh}(\mathbb{R})$):

$$\varphi \equiv \exists x_1, \ldots, x_m \bigwedge_{i=1}^{m} P_i(x_1, \ldots, x_m) = x_i \wedge \bigwedge_{i=1}^{m} 0 \leq x_i \wedge \bigwedge_{i=1}^{m} x_i \leq q_i$$

φ is true precisely when there is some $z \in \mathbb{R}^m$, $0 \preceq z \preceq q$, and $z = P(z)$. Thus, if we can decide the truth of this sentence, we could tell whether $q^*_{(u,ex)} \leq p$, for some rational p, by using the vector $q = (1, \ldots, p, 1, \ldots)$. We will rely on decision procedures for $\boldsymbol{ExTh}(\mathbb{R})$. It is known that $\boldsymbol{ExTh}(\mathbb{R})$ can be decided in PSPACE and in exponential time, where the time exponent depends (linearly) only on the number of variables; thus for a fixed number of variables the algorithm runs in polynomial time [Can88, Ren92, BPR96]. As a consequence:

Theorem 2. *([EY05]) Given RMC A and rational ρ, there is a PSPACE algorithm to decide whether $q^*_{(u,ex)} \leq \rho$, with running time $O(|A|^{O(1)} \cdot 2^{O(m)})$ where m is the number of variables in the system $x = P(x)$ for A. Moreover $q^*_{(u,ex)}$ can be approximated to within j bits of precision within PSPACE and with running time at most j times the above.*

For Bd-RMCs, as shown in [EY05] it is possible to construct efficiently a system of equations in a *bounded* number of variables, whose LFP yields the entry-exit probabilities $q^*_{(en,ex)}$. Since $\boldsymbol{ExTh}(\mathbb{R})$ is decidable in P-time when the number of variables is bounded, this yields:

Theorem 3. *([EY05]) Given Bd-RMC, A & rational $p \in [0,1]$, there is a P-time algorithm to decide whether, for a vertex u & exit ex, $q^*_{(u,ex)} \geq p(or < p)$.*

For 1-exit RMCs (SCFGs), the qualitative termination/reachability problem can be solved efficiently, via an eigenvalue characterization and other techniques.

Theorem 4. *([EY05]) There is a P-time algorithm that for a 1-exit RMC, vertex u and exit ex, decides which of the following holds:(1) $q^*_{(u,ex)} = 0$,(2) $q^*_{(u,ex)} = 1$,or (3) $0 < q^*_{(u,ex)} < 1$.*

Hardness, such as NP-hardness, is not known for RMC reachability. However, in [EY05] we gave strong evidence of "difficulty": the square-root sum problem is P-time reducible to deciding whether $q^*_{(u,ex)} \geq p$, in a 1-exit RMC, and to deciding whether $q^*_{(u,ex)} = 1$ for a 2-exit RMC. *Square-root sum* is the following decision problem: given $(d_1, \ldots, d_n) \in \mathbb{N}^n$ and $k \in \mathbb{N}$, decide whether $\sum_{i=1}^{n} \sqrt{d_i} \leq k$. It is solvable in PSPACE, but it has been a major open problem since the 1970's (see, e.g., [GGJ76, Tiw92]) whether it is solvable even in NP.

As a practical efficient numerical algorithm for computing the probabilities $q^*_{(u,ex)}$, it was proved in [EY05] that a multi-dimensional Newton's method converges monotonically to the LFP of $\mathbf{x} = P(\mathbf{x})$, and constitutes a rapid acceleration of iterating $P^k(\mathbf{0})$, $k \to \infty$.

3   The Conditioned Summary Chain M'_A

For an RMC A, suppose we somehow have the probabilities $q^*_{(u,ex)}$ "in hand". Based on these, we construct a *conditioned summary chain*, M'_A, a finite Markov chain that will allow us to answer repeated reachability questions. Extensions of M'_A will later be a key to model checking RMCs. Since probabilities $q^*_{(u,ex)}$ are potentially irrational, we can not compute M'_A exactly. However, M'_A will be important in our correctness arguments, and we will in fact be able to compute the "structure" of M'_A, i.e., what transitions have non-zero probability. The structure of M'_A will be sufficient for answering various "qualitative" questions.

We will assume, w.l.o.g., that each RMC has one initial state $s_0 = \langle \epsilon, en_{init} \rangle$, with en_{init} the only entry of a component that does not contain any exits. Any RMC can readily be converted to an "equivalent" one in this form.

Before describing M'_A, let us recall from [AEY01], the construction of a "summary graph", $H_A = (Q, E_{H_A})$, which ignores probabilities and is based only on information about reachability in the underlying RSM of A. Let R be the binary relation between entries and exits of components such that $(en, ex) \in R$ precisely when there exists a path from $\langle \epsilon, en \rangle$ to $\langle \epsilon, ex \rangle$, in the underlying graph of M_A. The edge set E_{H_A} is defined as follows. For $u, v \in Q$, $(u, v) \in E_{H_A}$ iff one of the following holds:

1. u is not a call port, and $(u, p_{u,v}, v) \in \delta$, for $p_{u,v} > 0$.
2. $u = (b, en)$ is a call port, and $(en, ex) \in R$, and $v = (b, ex)$ is a return port.
3. $u = (b, en)$ is a call port, and $v = en$ is the corresponding entry.

For each vertex $v \in Q_i$, let us define the probability of *never exiting*: $ne(v) = 1 - \sum_{ex \in Ex_i} q^*_{(v,ex)}$. Call a vertex v *deficient* if $ne(v) > 0$, i.e. there is a nonzero probability that if the RMC starts at v it will never terminate (reach an exit of the component).

We define $M'_A = (Q_{M'_A}, \delta_{M'_A})$ as follows. The set of states $Q_{M'_A}$ of M'_A is the set of deficient vertices: $Q_{M'_A} = \{v \in Q \mid ne(v) > 0\}$. For $u, v \in Q_{M'_A}$, there is a transition $(u, p'_{u,v}, v)$ in $\delta_{M'_A}$ if and only if one of the following conditions holds:

1. $u, v \in Q_i$ and $(u, p_{u,v}, v) \in \delta_i$, and $p'_{u,v} = \frac{p_{u,v} \cdot ne(v)}{ne(u)}$.
2. $u = (b, en) \in Call_b$, $v = (b, ex) \in Return_b$, $q^*_{(en,ex)} > 0$, & $p'_{u,v} = \frac{q^*_{(en,ex)} \, ne(v)}{ne(u)}$.
3. $u = (b, en) \in Call_b$ and $v = en$, and $p'_{u,v} = \frac{ne(v)}{ne(u)}$. We call these transitions, from a call port to corresponding entry, special *red* transitions.

Note that in all three cases, $p'_{u,v}$ is well-defined (the denominator is nonzero) and it is positive. Recall that we assumed that the initial vertex en_{init} is the entry of a component A_0, and A_0 has no exits. Thus for all $v \in Q_0$, $ne(u) = 1$, and thus $Q_0 \subseteq Q_{M'_A}$, and if $(u, p_{u,v}, v) \in \delta_0$, then $(u, p_{u,v}, v) \in \delta_{M'_A}$.

Proposition 1. *Probabilities on transitions out of each state in $Q_{M'_A}$ sum to 1.*

M'_A is an ordinary (flat) Markov chain. Let $(\Omega', \mathcal{F}', \mathbf{Pr}_{\Omega'})$ denote the probability space on traces of M'_A. We now define a mapping $\rho : \Omega \mapsto \Omega' \cup \{\star\}$, that maps every trace t of the original (infinite) Markov chain M_A, either to a unique trajectory $\rho(t) \in \Omega'$ of the MC M'_A, or to the special symbol $\star$. Trajectories mapped to $\star$ will be precisely those that go through missing vertices $u \in Q$ that are not in $Q_{M'_A}$, i.e., with ne(u) = 0. We show the total probability of all these trajectories is 0, i.e., $\mathbf{Pr}_\Omega(\rho^{-1}(\star)) = 0$, and moreover, M'_A preserves the probability measure of M_A: for all $D \in \mathcal{F}'$, $\rho^{-1}(D) \in \mathcal{F}$, and $\mathbf{Pr}_{\Omega'}(D) = \mathbf{Pr}_\Omega(\rho^{-1}(D))$. We define ρ in two phases. We first define a map $\rho^H : \Omega \mapsto Q^\omega$, where every trajectory $t \in \Omega$ is mapped to an infinite path $\rho^H(t)$ in the summary graph H_A. Thereafter, we let $\rho(t) = \rho^H(t)$ if all vertices of $\rho^H(t)$ are in M'_A, and let $\rho(t) = \star$ otherwise. We define ρ^H for a trace $t = s_0 s_1 \ldots s_i \ldots$, sequentially based on prefixes of t, as follows. By assumption, $s_0 = \langle \epsilon, en_{\text{init}} \rangle$. ρ^H maps s_0 to en_{init}. Suppose $s_i = \langle \beta, u \rangle$, and, inductively, suppose that ρ^H maps $s_0 \ldots s_i$ to $en_{\text{init}} \ldots u$. First, suppose u is not a call port, and that $s_{i+1} = \langle \beta, v \rangle$, then $s_0 \ldots s_i s_{i+1}$ maps to $en_{\text{init}} \ldots uv$. Next, suppose $u = (b, en)$ is a call port and $s_{i+1} = \langle \beta b, en \rangle$. If the trace eventually returns from this call (i.e., there exists $j > i+1$, such that $s_j = \langle \beta b, ex \rangle$ and $s_{j+1} = \langle \beta, (b, ex) \rangle$, and such that each of the states $s_{i+1} \ldots s_j$, have βb as a prefix of the call stack), then $s_0 \ldots s_j$ is mapped by ρ^H to $en_{\text{init}} \ldots u(b, ex)$. If the trace never returns from this call, then $s_0 \ldots s_i s_{i+1}$ maps to $en_{\text{init}} \ldots u\, en$. This concludes the definition of ρ^H. We show that the mapping ρ is measure preserving.

Lemma 1. $\mathbf{Pr}_\Omega(\rho^{-1}(\star)) = 0$. *Moreover, for all $D \in \mathcal{F}'$, $\rho^{-1}(D) \in \mathcal{F}$ and* $\mathbf{Pr}_\Omega(\rho^{-1}(D)) = \mathbf{Pr}_{\Omega'}(D)$.

Let $H'_A = (Q_{H'_A}, E_{H'_A})$ be the underlying directed graph of M'_A. In other words, $Q_{H'_A} = Q_{M'_A}$, and $(u, v) \in E_{H'_A}$ iff $(u, p'_{u,v}, u) \in \delta_{M'_A}$. We show we can compute H'_A in P-time for 1-exit RMCs and Bd-RMCs, and in PSPACE for arbitrary RMCs. The basic observation is: the structure of M'_A depends only on qualitative facts about the probabilities $q^*_{(en,ex)}$ and ne(u), for $u \in Q$.

Proposition 2. *For a RMC A (respectively, 1-exit or Bd-RMC), and $u \in Q$, we can decide whether ne(u) > 0 in PSPACE (respectively, P-time).*

Proof. Suppose u is in a component A_i where $Ex_i = \{ex_1, \ldots, ex_k\}$. Clearly, ne($u$) > 0 iff $\sum_{j=1}^k q^*_{(u,ex_j)} < 1$. Consider the following sentence, φ, in **ExTh**($\mathbb{R}$).

$$\varphi \equiv \exists x_1, \ldots, x_n \bigwedge_{i=1}^n P_i(x_1, \ldots, x_n) = x_i \wedge \bigwedge_{i=1}^n 0 \leq x_i \wedge \sum_{j=1}^k x_{(u,ex_j)} < 1$$

Since $\mathbf{q}^*$ is the LFP solution of $\mathbf{x} = P(\mathbf{x})$, φ is true in the reals if and only if $\sum_{j=1}^k q^*_{(u,ex_j)} < 1$. This query can be answered in PSPACE. In the special case of a 1-exit RMC, we have $Ex_i = \{ex_1\}$, and ne(u) > 0 iff $q^*_{(u,ex_1)} < 1$. As mentioned in section 2.2, this can be answered in P-time for 1-exit RMCs ([EY05]). Similarly, for Bd-RMCs the question can be answered in P-time by the techniques developed in [EY05]. $\square$

Corollary 1. *For a RMC A (respectively, 1-exit or Bd-RMC), we can compute H'_A in PSPACE (respectively, in polynomial time).*

Proof. Recall that $u \in Q_{H'_A}$ precisely when $u \in Q$ and $\mathrm{ne}(u) > 0$. Thus we can determine the set of nodes with the said complexities, respectively. The transitions of type 1 and 3 in the definition of M'_A are immediately determined. For the type 2 transitions, where $u = (b, en)$ and $v = (b, ex)$, in order to determine whether to include the corresponding summary edge (u, v) we need to decide whether $q^*_{(en,ex)} > 0$. This can be done in polynomial time by invoking the reachability algorithm for RSM's [AEY01, BGR01]. □

4   Qualitative Model Checking

Upper Bounds. Given an RMC $A = (A_1, \ldots, A_k)$ and a (nondeterministic) Büchi automaton $B = (\Sigma, S, q_0, R, F)$ whose alphabet Σ is the vertex set of A, we wish to determine whether $P_A(L(B)) = 1$, $= 0$, or is in-between. We will construct a finite Markov chain $M'_{A,B}$ such that $P_A(L(B))$ is equal to the probability that a trajectory of $M'_{A,B}$ starting from a given initial state reaches one of a designated set of "accepting" bottom SCCs.

First, let $B' = (\Sigma, 2^S, \{q_0\}, R', F')$ be the deterministic automaton obtained by the usual subset construction on B. In other words, states of B' are subsets $T \subseteq S$, and the transition function $R' : (2^S \times \Sigma) \mapsto 2^S$ is given by: $R'(T_1, v) = \{q' \in S \mid \exists q \in T_1 \text{ s.t. } (q, v, q') \in R\}$. (We make no claim that $L(B) = L(B')$.)

Next we define the standard *product* RMC, $A \otimes B'$, of the RMC A, and the deterministic Büchi automaton B'. $A \otimes B'$ has the same number of components as A. Call these $A'_1, \ldots, A'_k$. The vertices in component A'_i are pairs (u, T), where $u \in Q_i$ and $T \in 2^S$, and (u, T) is an entry (exit) iff u is an entry (exit). The transitions of A'_i are as follows: there is a transition $((u, T), p_{u,v}, (v, R'(T, v)))$ in A'_i iff there is a transition $(u, p_{u,v}, v)$ in A_i.

Define $M'_{A,B}$ as $M'_{A,B} = M'_{A \otimes B'}$. Thus $M'_{A,B}$ is the conditioned summary chain of RMC $A \otimes B'$. For qualitative analysis on $M'_{A,B}$, we need the underlying graph $H'_{A,B}$. Importantly for the complexity of our algorithms, we do not have to explicitly construct $A \otimes B'$ to obtain $H'_{A,B}$. Observe that states of $M'_{A,B} = (Q \times 2^S, \delta_{M'_{A,B}})$ are pairs (v, T) where v is a state of M'_A, and T a state of B'. The initial state of $M'_{A,B}$ is $(v_0, \{q_0\})$, where v_0 is the initial state of M'_A and q_0 of B. The transitions of $M'_{A,B}$ from a state (v, T) are as follows:

- Case 1: v is not a call port. Then for every transition $(v, p'_{v,v'}, v') \in \delta_{M'_A}$, we have a corresponding transition $((v, T), p'_{v,v'}, (v', R'(T, v'))) \in \delta_{M'_{A,B}}$.
- Case 2: v is a call port, $v = (b, en)$ where v is vertex in component A_i and box b is mapped to component A_j. If there is a *red* transition $(v, p_{v,en}, en) \in \delta_{M'_A}$ then there is a *red* transition $((v, T), p_{v,en}, (en, R'(T, en)) \in \delta_{M'_{A,B}}$ with the same probability.
- Case 3: If v has a summary transition $(v, p_{v,v'}, v')$ in M'_A, where $v' = (b, ex)$, then we have summary transitions of the form $((v, T), p'', (v', T'))$ in $M'_{A,B}$

to states of the form (v', T') iff there exists a path in M_A from $\langle \epsilon, en \rangle$ to $\langle \epsilon, ex \rangle$ which, viewed as a string, drives B' from T to T'; the probability p'' of the transition is $p'' = p' \cdot \text{ne}(v')/\text{ne}(v)$ where p' is the probability of all such v-v' paths that drive B' from T to T'.

$M'_{A,B}$ is a well-defined Markov chain, which is a refinement of M'_A. That is, every trajectory of $M'_{A,B}$ projected on the first component is a trajectory of M'_A and the projection preserves probabilities. We can define a mapping σ from the trajectories t of the original (infinite) Markov chain M_A to the trajectories of $M'_{A,B}$, or the special symbol $\star$, in a similar manner as we defined the mapping ρ from trajectories of M to M'_A. For a trajectory t of M_A, it is easy to see that if $\rho(t) \neq \star$ then also $\sigma(t) \neq \star$. Thus, with probability 1 a trajectory of M_A is mapped to one of $M'_{A,B}$. Furthermore, we can show along similar lines the analogue of Lemma 2, i.e. the mapping σ preserves probabilities.

Consider a product graph (without probabilities) $M'_A \otimes B$ between the Markov chain M'_A and the given nondeterministic BA B (not B') as follows: $M'_A \otimes B$ has nodes (v, q), for all vertices v of M'_A and states q of B, and an edge $(v, q) \to (v', q')$ if either (i) $v \to v'$ is an ordinary edge or a red edge of M'_A and q has a transition to q' on input v', or (ii) $v \to v'$ is a summary edge and the RMC has a path from v to v' that corresponds to a run of B from q to q'; if any such run goes through an accepting state then we mark the edge $(v, q) \to (v', q')$ as an *accepting* edge. Also, call a node (v, q) *accepting* if $q \in F$ is an accepting state of B.

With every transition (edge) of $M'_{A,B}$ and every edge of $M'_A \otimes B$ we associate a string γ over Σ (the vertex set of A) that caused the edge to be included; i.e., if edge $(v, T) \to (v', T')$ of $M'_{A,B}$ (respectively, edge $(v, q) \to (v', q')$ of $M'_A \otimes B$) corresponds to an ordinary or red edge of M'_A then $\gamma = v'$. If it corresponds to a summary edge then we let γ be any string that corresponds to a $v - v'$ path that drives B' from T to T' (resp., for which B has a path from q to q'; if the edge $(v, q) \to (v', q')$ is marked as accepting then we pick a path that goes through an accepting state of B). In the case of a summary edge, there may be many strings γ as above; we just pick anyone of them.

Let t be any trajectory of M_A starting from $\langle \epsilon, v \rangle$, for some vertex v of M'_A and let r be a corresponding run of B starting from a state q. With probability 1, t maps to a trajectory $t' = \rho(t)$ of M'_A. The mapping ρ can be extended to pairs (t, r), where r is a run of B on t, i.e., the pair (t, r) is mapped to a run $r' = \rho(t, r)$ of $M'_A \otimes B$. If r is an accepting run of B then r' goes infinitely often through an accepting node or an accepting edge. The converse does not hold necessarily: a non-accepting run r of B corresponding to a trajectory t may be mapped to a run r' of $M'_A \otimes B$ that traverses infinitely often an accepting edge.

If B is a deterministic BA, then $M'_{A,B}$ and $M'_A \otimes B$ are clearly the same (except that in $M'_A \otimes B$ we did not include the probabilities of the edges). In this case, the analysis is simpler. Let us say that a bottom strongly connected component (SCC) of $M'_{A,B}$ (and $M'_A \otimes B$) is *accepting* iff it contains an accepting node or an accepting edge.

Theorem 5. *For a RMC A and a deterministic BA B, the probability $P_A(L(B))$ that a trajectory of A is accepted by B is equal to the probability that a trajectory of $M'_{A,B}$ starting from the initial node (v_0, q_0) reaches an accepting bottom SCC.*

Suppose now that B is nondeterministic. We will follow the approach of [CY95] for flat Markov chains, except that here we have to deal with recursive calls and with the summary edges of the constructed Markov chain $M'_{A,B}$ which correspond to sets of paths in the original chain M_A rather than single steps. This complicates things considerably.

Let v be a vertex of M'_A and $q \in F$ an accepting state of B. Let $D(v, q)$ be the subgraph of $M'_{A,B}$ induced by the node $(v, \{q\})$ and all nodes reachable from it . We say that the pair (v, q) is *special of type 1* if some bottom SCC C of $D(v, q)$ contains a state (v, T) with $q \in T$. We associate with such a pair (v, q) a string $\gamma(v, q) \in \Sigma^*$ that is the concatenation of the strings associated with the edges of $D(v, q)$ on a path from $(v, \{q\})$ to a node of C. (There may be many such paths; just pick anyone.) Let $v = (b, en)$ be a vertex of M'_A that is a call port of a box b of A and let $q \notin F$ be a non-accepting state of B. Define a graph $D(v, q)$ as follows. The graph contains a root node vq and a subgraph of $M'_{A,B}$ consisting of the nodes reachable from vq after we add the following edges. We add an edge from vq to a node $(v', \{q'\})$ of $M'_{A,B}$, where $v' = (b, ex)$ is a return port of the same box b as v, iff there is a path γ from $\langle \epsilon, en \rangle$ to $\langle \epsilon, ex \rangle$ such that B has a run from q to q' on γ that goes through an accepting state; we label the edge $vq \to (v', \{q'\})$ with such a string γ. The graph $D(v, q)$ consists of the root vq and the subgraph of $M'_{A,B}$ induced by all the nodes that are reachable from vq after adding the above edges. We call the pair (v, q) *special of type 2* if some bottom SCC C of $D(v, q)$ contains a state (v, T) with $q \in T$. As in the previous case, we associate with the pair (v, q) a string $\gamma(v, q) \in \Sigma^*$ that is the concatenation of the strings associated with the edges of $D(v, q)$ on a path from vq to a node of C. Special pairs have the following important properties.

Lemma 2. *Suppose (v, q) is special and that RMC A starts at $\langle \epsilon, v \rangle$ and first performs the transitions in $\gamma(v, q)$. Then with probability 1 such a trajectory t of the RMC is accepted by B with initial state q. Specifically, there is a corresponding accepting run r of B such that $\rho(t, r)$ is a run of $M'_A \otimes B$ starting from (v, q) that infinitely repeats node (v, q) if (v, q) is special of type 1, or repeats an accepting edge out of (v, q) if (v, q) is special of type 2.*

Lemma 3. *Suppose there is non-zero probability that a trajectory of the RMC A starting at any vertex $u \in M'_A$ has a corresponding run in $M'_A \otimes B$ starting from any node (u, p) which repeats an accepting state (v, q) infinitely often or repeats an accepting edge $(v, q) \to (v', q')$ infinitely often. Then (v, q) is special.*

Proposition 3. *$P_A(L(B)) > 0$ iff from (v_0, q_0) in $M'_A \otimes B$ we can reach a special (v, q).*

Call a bottom SCC of the flat Markov chain $M'_{A,B}$ *accepting* if it contains a state (v, T), with some $q \in T$ such that (v, q) is special; otherwise call it *rejecting*.

Theorem 6. $P_A(L(B))$ *is equal to the probability that a trajectory of* $M'_{A,B}$ *starting from the initial state* $(v_0, \{q_0\})$ *reaches an accepting bottom SCC.*

Thus, $P_A(L(B)) = 1$ iff all bottom SCCs of $M'_{A,B}$ reachable from $(v_0, \{q_0\})$ are accepting, and $P_A(L(B)) = 0$ iff no reachable bottom SCC is accepting (i.e., by Prop. 3, there is no path in $M'_A \otimes B$ from $(v_0, \{q_0\})$ to a special node (v, q)).

As with M'_A and H'_A, let $H'_{A,B}$ denote the underlying directed graph of $M'_{A,B}$. For the qualitative problem, we only need (1) to construct $H'_{A,B}$ and thus only need to know which nodes and edges are present, and (2) to determine which pairs (v, q) are special, and hence which bottom SCCs are accepting. Thus we first have to identify the vertices u of the RMC A for which $ne(u) > 0$, which can be done in PSPACE for general RMCs and P-time for 1-exit RMCs and for Bd-RMCs. Then, the edges of $H'_{A,B}$ can be determined by the standard reachability algorithm for RSMs ([AEY01]). This works by first constructing the genuine product of the underlying RSM of A (ignoring probabilities on transitions) together with the Büchi automaton B'. This defines a new RSM $A \otimes B'$ (no probabilities), whose size is polynomial in A and B', and thus is exponential in the original non-deterministic Büchi automaton B. The time required for reachability analysis for RSMs is polynomial ([AEY01]). Thus, once we have identified the deficient vertices of the RMC, the rest of the construction of $H'_{A,B}$ takes time polynomial in A and B'.

To determine which pairs (v, q) are special, we construct for each candidate (v, q) the graph $D(v, q)$. For (v, q) with $q \in F$, this is immediate from $H'_{A,B}$. For (v, q) with $q \notin F$ and $v = (b, en)$ a call port of a box b, we test for each return port $v' = (b, ex)$ of the box and each state q' of B whether there should be an edge $vq \rightarrow (v', \{q'\})$; this involves a call to the RSM algorithm of [AEY01] to determine whether there is a path in the RSM $A \otimes B$ from (en, q) to (ex, q') (with empty stack) that goes through a vertex whose second component is an accepting state of B. Once we determine these edges, we can construct $D(v, q)$. This takes time polynomial in A and B'. Then compute the SCCs of $D(v, q)$, examine the bottom SCCs and check if one of them contains (v, T) with $q \in T$.

Finally, once we have identified the special pairs, we examine the reachable bottom SCCs of $H'_{A,B}$ and determine which ones are accepting and which are rejecting. The dependence of the time complexity on the size of the given RMC A is polynomial except for the identification of the vertices u for which $ne(u) > 0$. The dependence on $|B|$ is exponential because of the subset construction. If B is deterministic to begin with, we avoid the exponential blow-up and thus have polynomial complexity in B. Thus we have:

Theorem 7. *Given RMC* A *& Büchi automaton* B, *we can decide whether* $P_A(L(B)) = 0$, $P_A(L(B)) = 1$, *or* $0 < P_A(L(B)) < 1$ *in PSPACE in* A, *and EXPTIME in* B. *For a 1-exit RMC or Bd-RMC, the time complexity is polynomial in* $|A|$. *And, if* B *is deterministic, the time complexity in* $|B|$ *is also polynomial.*

Lower Bounds. We show conversely that the exponential time complexity of qualitative model checking for a nondeterministic BA is in general unavoidable.

Theorem 8. *Deciding whether a given RMC A satisfies a property specified by a Büchi automaton B with probability $= 1$, (i.e., whether $P_A(L(B)) = 1$) is EXPTIME-complete. Furthermore, this holds even if the RMC is fixed and each component has 1 entry and 1 exit. Moreover, the qualitative "emptiness" problem, namely deciding whether $P_A(L(B)) = 0$, is also EXPTIME-complete, again even when the RMC is fixed and each component has 1 entry and 1 exit.*

5   Quantitative Model Checking

As mentioned, the transition probabilities of the chain $M'_{A,B}$ cannot be computed exactly, but instead have to be determined implicitly. To do quantitative model checking in PSPACE in $|A|$, it will be crucial to use $\boldsymbol{ExTh}(\mathbb{R})$ to uniquely identify LFP(P) for the systems $x = P(x)$. The following key theorem enables this.

Theorem 9. *(Unique Fixed Point Theorem) The equations $x = P(x)$ have a unique solution q^* that satisfies $\sum_{ex} q^*_{(u,ex)} < 1$ for every deficient vertex u, and $\sum_{ex} q^*_{(u,ex)} \leq 1$ for every other vertex u. (Of course, $q^* = $ LFP(P).)*

Theorem 10. *Given RMC, A, and BA, B, and a rational value $p \in [0,1]$, we can decide whether $P_A(L(B)) \geq p$ in PSPACE in $|A|$ and in EXPSPACE in B, specifically in space $O(|A|^{c_1} 2^{c_2|B|})$ for some constants c_1, c_2. Furthermore, if B is deterministic we can decide this in PSPACE in both A and B.*

Proof. We make crucial use of Theorem 9, and we combine this with use of the summary chain $M'_{A,B}$, and queries to $\boldsymbol{ExTh}(\mathbb{R})$. Observe that by Theorem 6, all we need to do is "compute" the probability that a trajectory of $M'_{A,B}$, starting from the initial state $(v_0, \{q_0\})$ reaches an accepting bottom SCC. We can not compute $M'_{A,B}$ exactly, however, we will be able to identify the transition probabilities uniquely inside a $\boldsymbol{ExTh}(\mathbb{R})$ query, and will, inside the same query identify the probability of reaching an accepting bottom SCC.

Let $\mathbf{q}^* = $ LFP(P) be the solution vector of probabilities for the system $\mathbf{x} = P(\mathbf{x})$ associated with RMC A. Recall that by Proposition 2, we can compute in PSPACE in $|A|$ the set $Q' = \{u \in Q \mid ne(u) > 0\}$ of deficient vertices. We do this as a first step. Consider next the following quantifier-free formula, where $c(u)$ is the index of the component of a vertex u:

$$\varphi_1(\mathbf{x}) \equiv \mathbf{x} = P(\mathbf{x}) \wedge 0 \preceq \mathbf{x} \wedge \bigwedge_{u \in Q'} \sum_{ex \in Ex_{c(u)}} x_{(u,ex)} < 1 \wedge \bigwedge_{u \in Q \setminus Q'} \sum_{ex \in Ex_{c(u)}} x_{(u,ex)} = 1$$

By Theorem 9, the only vector $\mathbf{x}$ in $\mathbb{R}^n$ for which $\varphi_1(\mathbf{x})$ holds true is $\mathbf{q}^*$. In other words, φ_1 uniquely identifies LFP(P). Recall that $ne(u) = 1 - \sum_{ex \in Ex_{c(u)}} q^*_{(u,ex)}$. Now, let $\mathbf{y}$ be a vector of variables indexed by vertices of A, and let $\varphi_2(\mathbf{x}, \mathbf{y}) \equiv \bigwedge_{u \in Q} y_u = 1 - \sum_{ex \in Ex_{c(u)}} x_{(u,ex)}$. The only vector of reals $(\mathbf{x}, \mathbf{y})$ that satisfies $\varphi_1 \wedge \varphi_2$ is the one where $x_{(u,ex)} = q^*_{(u,ex)}$ and $y_u = ne(u)$. Recall the construction of $M'_{A,B}$. The states of $M'_{A,B}$ are pairs (v, T), where $v \in Q'$, and $T \subseteq S$ is a set of states of B. The transitions of $M'_{A,B}$ come in three varieties.

Case 1: v is not a call port, and $(v, p'_{v,v'}, v') \in \delta_{M'_A}$. Then we have a corresponding transition $((v,T), p'_{v,v'}, (v', R'(T,v'))) \in \delta_{M'_{A,B}}$, where $p'_{v,v'} = p_{v,v'} \, \mathrm{ne}(v')/\mathrm{ne}(v)$, and thus $p'_{v,v'} \, \mathrm{ne}(v) = p_{v,v'} \, \mathrm{ne}(v')$. Associate a variable $z_{v,v'}$ with each such probability $p'_{v,v'}$, and define the formula: $\varphi_3(\mathbf{y}, \mathbf{z}) \equiv \bigwedge_{(v,v') \in \mathrm{Case1}} z_{v,v'} y_v = p_{v,v'} y_{v'}$.

Case 2: v is a call port, $v = (b, en)$ where v is vertex in component A_i and box b is mapped to component A_j, and $v' = en$, and there is a *red* transition $(v, p'_{v,v'}, v') \in \delta_{M'_A}$. Then there is a *red* transition $((v,T), p'_{v,v'}, (v', R'(T,v')) \in \delta_{M'_{A,B}}$ with the same probability. Here $p'_{v,v'} = \mathrm{ne}(v')/\mathrm{ne}(v)$, and thus $p'_{v,v'} \, \mathrm{ne}(v) = \mathrm{ne}(v')$. Associate a variable $z_{v,v'}$ with each such probability $p'_{v,v'}$, and define: $\varphi_4(\mathbf{y}, \mathbf{z}) \equiv \bigwedge_{(v,v') \in \mathrm{Case2}} z_{v,v'} y_v = y_{v'}$.

Case 3: v is a call port that has a summary transition $(v, p'_{v,v'}, v')$ in M'_A to a vertex $v' = (b, ex)$, then we have summary transitions of the form $((v,T), p'', (v', T'))$ in $M'_{A,B}$ to the following set of states of the form (v', T'): If there exists a path of M_A that starts at the entry en of A_j and ends at the exit ex (with empty call stack) which, viewed as a string drives B' from T to T', then we include the edge $((v,T), p'_{(v,T),(v',T')}, (v', T'))$ in $\delta_{M'_{A,B}}$, where $p'_{(v,T),(v',T')} = q^*_{((en,T),(ex,T'))} \cdot \mathrm{ne}(v')/\mathrm{ne}(v)$, and where $q^*_{((en,T),(ex,T'))}$ is the probability of reaching $\langle \epsilon, (ex, T') \rangle$ from $\langle \epsilon, (en, T) \rangle$ in the product RMC $A \otimes B'$. First, compute $A \otimes B'$ and its associated equations $\mathbf{w} = P^\otimes(\mathbf{w})$ explicitly. Note that $|A \otimes B'| = O(|A||B'|)$. Let $Q^\otimes$ be the set of vertices of $A \otimes B'$. We can compute the set $Q'^\otimes$ of vertices v of $A \otimes B'$, for which $\mathrm{ne}(v) > 0$ in PSPACE in $|A \otimes B'|$. Consider now the quantifier-free formula:

$$\varphi_5(\mathbf{w}) \equiv \mathbf{w} = P^\otimes(\mathbf{w}) \wedge 0 \preceq \mathbf{w} \wedge \bigwedge_{u \in Q'^\otimes} \sum_{ex \in Ex_{c(u)}} w_{(u,ex)} < 1 \wedge \bigwedge_{u \in Q^\otimes \setminus Q'^\otimes} \sum_{ex \in Ex_{c(u)}} w_{(u,ex)} = 1$$

By Theorem 9, $\mathrm{LFP}(P^\otimes)$, is the only vector in $\mathbb{R}^n$ for which $\varphi_5(\mathbf{w})$ holds true. In other words, φ_5 uniquely identifies $\mathrm{LFP}(P^\otimes)$. Now, associate a variable $z_{(v,T),(v',T')}$ with each probability $p'_{(v,T),(v',T')}$, where $v = (b, en)$ and $v' = (b, ex)$, and define: $\varphi_6(\mathbf{y}, \mathbf{w}, \mathbf{z}) \equiv \bigwedge_{((v,T),(v',T')) \in \mathrm{Case3}} z_{(v,T),(v',T')} y_v = w_{((en,T),(ex,T'))} y_{v'}$.

Observe, $\bigwedge_{j=1}^{6} \varphi_j$ has a unique solution, and the values of variables $\mathbf{z}$ in this solution identify the probabilities p' on transitions of $M'_{A,B}$. By the methods of section 4, we compute the underlying graph $H'_{A,B}$ of $M'_{A,B}$ and compute the SCCs of $H'_{A,B}$ that contain either an accepting node or an accepting edge. Let us define a revised finite Markov chain, $M''_{A,B}$, in which we remove all SCCs in $M'_{A,B}$ that contain an accepting node or edge, and replace them by a new absorbing node v^*, with a probability 1 transition to itself. Furthermore, in $M''_{A,B}$ we also remove all nodes that can not reach v^*, and all transitions into those nodes. (Technically, some nodes of $M''_{A,B}$ may no longer have full probability on the transitions leaving them, but that is ok for our purposes.)

Now, recall from Markov chain theory (see, e.g., [Bil95]) that for such a finite (sub-)Markov chain $M''_{A,B}$, there is a *linear* system of equations $\mathbf{t} = F(\mathbf{t})$, over variables t_{u,v^*}, where u is any node of $M''_{A,B}$, and where the coefficients in the linear system $F(\mathbf{t})$ are the probabilties p' on transitions of $M''_{A,B}$ such that the least fixed point solution, LFP(F), of $\mathbf{t} = F(\mathbf{t})$ assigns to variable t_{u,v^*} the probability that v^* is reachable from u. (In particular, one of the linear equations is $t_{v^*,v^*} = 1$.) Moreover, because we have eliminated from $M''_{A,B}$ all nodes that can not reach v^*, LFP(F) is the *unique* solution to this system. Thus consider the formula: $\varphi_7(\mathbf{w},\mathbf{t}) \equiv \mathbf{t} = F(\mathbf{t})$. Thus the formula $\bigwedge_{j=1}^{7} \varphi_j$ has a unique solution in the reals, and the values assigned to variables $t_{(u,v^*)}$ in this solution identify the probability of reaching an accepting SCC from node u in $M'_{A,B}$.

For initial node $u^* = (v_0, \{q_0\})$ of $M'_{A,B}$, and $p \in [0,1]$, the following sentence, ψ, is true in $\mathbb{R}$ iff $P_A(L(B)) \geq p$: $\psi \equiv \exists \mathbf{x}, \mathbf{y}, \mathbf{z}, \mathbf{w}, \mathbf{t} \bigwedge_{j=1}^{7} \varphi_j \wedge t_{u^*,v^*} \geq p$. $\quad\square$

Theorem 11. *For a fixed BA, B, given a Bd-RMC, A, and a rational value $p \in [0,1]$, we can decide whether $P_A(L(B)) \geq p$ in time polynomial in $|A|$.*

Proof. (idea) The proof is a modification of Theorem 10. We extend a technique developed in [EY05]. We use variables only for entry-exit pairs of A and $A \otimes B'$, express all other variables as rational functions of those, and transform the system to one of polynomial constraints in a bounded number of variables. $\quad\square$

References

[AEY01] R. Alur, K. Etessami, and M. Yannakakis. Analysis of recursive state machines. In *Proc. of 13th Int. Conf. on Computer-Aided Verification*, pages 304–313, 2001.

[BGR01] M. Benedikt, P. Godefroid, and T. Reps. Model checking of unrestricted hierarchical state machines. In *Proc. of ICALP'01*, volume 2076 of *LNCS*, pages 652–666, 2001.

[Bil95] P. Billingsley. *Probability and Measure*. J. Wiley and Sons, 3rd edition, 1995.

[BKS05] T. Brázdil, A. Kučera, and O. Stražovský. Decidability of temporal properties of probabilistic pushdown automata. In *Proc. of 22nd STACS'05*. Springer, 2005.

[BPR96] S. Basu, R. Pollack, and M. F. Roy. On the combinatorial and algebraic complexity of quantifier elimination. *J. of the ACM*, 43(6):1002–1045, 1996.

[BR00] T. Ball and S. Rajamani. Bebop: A symbolic model checker for boolean programs. In *SPIN'2000*, volume 1885 of *LNCS*, pages 113–130, 2000.

[Can88] J. Canny. Some algebraic and geometric computations in PSPACE. In *Prof. of 20th ACM STOC*, pages 460–467, 1988.

[CY95] C. Courcoubetis and M. Yannakakis. The complexity of probabilistic verification. *Journal of the ACM*, 42(4):857–907, 1995.

[EE04] J. Esparza and K. Etessami. Verifying probabilistic procedural programs. In *Proc. FSTTCS'04*, 2004. (Invited survey paper).

[EHRS00] J. Esparza, D. Hansel, P. Rossmanith, and S. Schwoon. Efficient algorithms for model checking pushdown systems. In *12th CAV*, volume 1855, pages 232–247. Springer, 2000.

[EKM04] Javier Esparza, Antonín Kučera, and Richard Mayr. Model checking probabilistic pushdown automata. In *Proc. of 19th IEEE LICS'04*, 2004.

[EY05]   K. Etessami and M. Yannakakis. Recursive markov chains, stochastic grammars, and monotone systems of non-linear equations. In *Proc. of 22nd STACS'05*. Springer, 2005. (Tech. Report, U. Edinburgh, June 2004).

[GGJ76]   M. R. Garey, R. L. Graham, and D. S. Johnson. Some NP-complete geometric problems. In *8th ACM STOC*, pages 10–22, 1976.

[Har63]   T. E. Harris. *The Theory of Branching Processes*. Springer-Verlag, 1963.

[Kwi03]   M. Kwiatkowska. Model checking for probability and time: from theory to practice. In *Proc. 18th IEEE LICS*, pages 351–360, 2003.

[MS99]   C. Manning and H. Schütze. *Foundations of Statistical Natural Language Processing*. MIT Press, 1999.

[PZ93]   A. Pnueli and L. D. Zuck. Probabilistic verification. *Inf. and Comp.*, 103(1):1–29, 1993.

[Ren92]   J. Renegar. On the computational complexity and geometry of the first-order theory of the reals. parts i,ii, iii. *J. of Symbolic Computation*, pages 255–352, 1992.

[Tiw92]   P. Tiwari. A problem that is easier to solve on the unit-cost algebraic ram. *Journal of Complexity*, pages 393–397, 1992.

[Var85]   M. Vardi. Automatic verification of probabilistic concurrent finite-state programs. In *Proc. of 26th IEEE FOCS*, pages 327–338, 1985.

Monte Carlo Model Checking

Radu Grosu and Scott A. Smolka

Dept. of Computer Science, Stony Brook Univ., Stony Brook, NY, 11794, USA
{grosu, sas}@cs.sunysb.edu

Abstract. We present MC^2, what we believe to be the first randomized, Monte Carlo algorithm for temporal-logic model checking. Given a specification S of a finite-state system, an LTL formula φ, and parameters ϵ and δ, MC^2 takes $M = \ln(\delta)/\ln(1 - \epsilon)$ random samples (random walks ending in a cycle, i.e *lassos*) from the Büchi automaton $B = B_S \times B_{\neg\varphi}$ to decide if $L(B) = \emptyset$. Let p_Z be the expectation of an accepting lasso in B. Should a sample reveal an accepting lasso l, MC^2 returns false with l as a witness. Otherwise, it returns true and reports that the probability of finding an accepting lasso through further sampling, under the assumption that $p_Z \geq \epsilon$, is less than δ. It does so in time $O(MD)$ and space $O(D)$, where D is B's recurrence diameter, using an optimal number of samples M. Our experimental results demonstrate that MC^2 is fast, memory-efficient, and scales extremely well.

1 Introduction

Model checking [7, 23], the problem of deciding whether or not a property specified in temporal logic holds of a system specification, has gained wide acceptance within the hardware and protocol verification communities, and is witnessing increasing application in the domain of software verification. The beauty of this technique is that when the state space of the system under investigation is finite-state, model checking may proceed in a fully automatic, push-button fashion. Moreover, should the system fail to satisfy the formula, a counter-example trace leading the user to the error state is produced.

Model checking, however, is not without its drawbacks, the most prominent of which is *state explosion*: the phenomenon where the size of a system's state space grows exponentially in the size of its specification. See, for example, [27], where it is shown that the problem is PSPACE-complete for LTL (Linear Temporal Logic). Over the past two decades, researchers have developed a plethora of techniques (heuristics) aimed at curtailing state explosion, including symbolic model checking, partial-order reduction methods, symmetry reduction, and bounded model checking. A comprehensive discourse on model checking, including a discussion of techniques for state explosion, can be found in [6].

We present in this paper an alternative approach to coping with state explosion based on the technique of *random sampling* by executing a random walk through the system's state transition graph. Such a technique was first advocated by West [31, 32] and Rudin [24] to find errors (safety violations) in communication protocols. We show how this this technique can be extended and formalized in the context of LTL model checking.

N. Halbwachs and L. Zuck (Eds.): TACAS 2005, LNCS 3440, pp. 271–286, 2005.
© Springer-Verlag Berlin Heidelberg 2005

Our approach makes use of the following idea from the automata-theoretic technique of Vardi and Wolper [30] for LTL model checking: given a specification S of a finite-state system and an LTL formula φ, $S \models \varphi$ (S models φ) if and only if the language of the Büchi automaton $B = B_S \times B_{\neg\varphi}$ is empty. Here B_S is the Büchi automaton representing S's state transition graph, and $B_{\neg\varphi}$ is the Büchi automaton for the negation of φ. Call a cycle reachable from an initial state of B a *lasso*, and say that a lasso is *accepting* if the cycle portion of the lasso contains a final state of B. The presence in B of an accepting lasso means that S is *not* a model of φ. Moreover, such an accepting lasso can be viewed as a *counter-example* to $S \models \varphi$.

To decide if $L(B)$ is empty, we have developed the MC^2 Monte Carlo model-checking algorithm. Underlying the execution of MC^2 is a Bernoulli random variable Z that takes value 1 with probability p_Z and value 0 with probability $q_Z = 1 - p_Z$. Intuitively, p_Z is the probability that a random walk in B, starting from an initial state and terminating at a cycle, is an accepting lasso. MC^2 takes $M = \ln(\delta)/\ln(1 - \epsilon)$ such random walks through B, each of which can be understood as a random sample Z_i. The random walks are constructed *on-the-fly* in order to avoid the *a priori* construction of B, which would immediately lead to state explosion. Should a sample Z_i correspond to an accepting lasso l, MC^2 returns false with l as a witness. Otherwise, it returns true and reports that the probability of finding an accepting lasso through further sampling, under the assumption that $p_Z \geq \epsilon$, is less than δ.

The main features of our MC^2 algorithm are the following.

- To the best of our knowledge, MC^2 is the first randomized, Monte Carlo algorithm to be proposed in the literature for the classical problem of temporal-logic model checking.
- MC^2 performs random sampling of lassos in the Büchi automaton $B = B_S \times B_{\neg\varphi}$ to yield a one-sided error Monte Carlo decision procedure for the LTL model-checking problem $S \models \varphi$.
- Unlike other model checkers,[1] MC^2 also delivers *quantitative* information about the model-checking problem. Should the random sampling performed by MC^2 not reveal an accepting lasso in $B = B_S \times B_{\neg\varphi}$, MC^2 returns true and reports that the probability of finding an accepting lasso through further sampling, under the assumption that $p_Z \geq \epsilon$, is less than δ.
- MC^2 is very efficient in both time and space. Its time complexity is $O(MD)$ and its space complexity is $O(D)$, where D is B's recurrence diameter. Moreover, the number of samples $M = \ln(\delta)/\ln(1 - \epsilon)$ taken by MC^2 is optimal.
- Although we present MC^2 in the context of the classical LTL model-checking problem, the algorithm works with little modification on systems specified using stochastic modeling formalisms such as discrete-time Markov chains.
- We have implemented MC^2 in the context of the JMOCHA model checker for Reactive Modules [2]. Our experimental results demonstrate that MC^2 is

---

[1] We are referring here strictly to model checkers in the classical sense, i.e., those for nondeterministic/concurrent systems and temporal logics such as LTL, CTL, and the mu-calculus. Model checkers for probabilistic systems and logics, a topic discussed in Section 7, also produce quantitative results.

fast, memory-efficient, and scales extremely well. It consistently outperforms
JMOCHA's LTL enumerative model checker, which uses a form of partial-order
reduction.

The rest of the paper develops along the following lines. Section 2 considers
the requisite probability theory of geometric random variables and hypothesis
testing. Section 3 presents MC^2, our Monte Carlo model-checking algorithm. Section 4 describes our JMOCHA implementation of MC^2. Section 5 summarizes our
experimental results. Section 6 considers alternative random-sampling strategies
to the one currently used by MC^2. Section 7 discusses related work. Section 8 contains our conclusions and directions for future work. Appendix A of [10] provides
an overview of automata-theoretic LTL model checking.

2   Random Sampling and Hypothesis Testing

As we will show in Section 3, to each instance $S \models \varphi$ of the LTL model-checking
problem, one may associate a Bernoulli random variable Z that takes value 1
with probability p_Z and value 0 with probability $q_Z = 1 - p_Z$. Intuitively, p_Z is
the probability that an arbitrary run of S is a counter-example to φ. Since p_Z
is hard to compute, one can use Monte Carlo techniques to derive a one-sided
error randomized algorithm for LTL model checking.

Given a Bernoulli random variable Z, define the *geometric* random variable
X with parameter p_Z whose value is the number of independent trials required
until success, i.e., until $Z = 1$. The *probability mass function* of X is $p(N) =$
$\mathbf{Pr}[X = N] = q_Z^{N-1} p_Z$ and the *cumulative distribution function* (CDF) of X is

$$F(N) = \mathbf{Pr}[X \leq N] = \sum_{n \leq N} p(n) = 1 - q_Z^N$$

Requiring that $F(N) = 1 - \delta$ for *confidence ratio* δ yields:

$$N = \ln(\delta) / \ln(1 - p_Z)$$

which provides the number of attempts N needed to achieve success (find a
counter-example) with probability $1 - \delta$.

In our case, p_Z is in general unknown. However, given an *error margin* ϵ and
assuming that $p_Z \geq \epsilon$ we obtain that

$$M = \ln(\delta) / \ln(1 - \epsilon) \geq N = \ln(\delta) / \ln(1 - p_Z)$$

and therefore that $\mathbf{Pr}[X \leq M] \geq \mathbf{Pr}[X \leq N] = 1 - \delta$. Summarizing:

$$p_Z \geq \epsilon \quad \Rightarrow \quad \mathbf{Pr}[X \leq M] \geq 1 - \delta \quad \text{where} \quad M = \ln(\delta) / \ln(1 - \epsilon) \quad (1)$$

In equation 1 gives us the minimal number of attempts M needed to achieve
success with confidence ratio δ, under the assumption that $p_Z \geq \epsilon$.

The standard way of discharging such an assumption is to use *statistical hypothesis testing* (see e.g. [21]). To understand how this technique works, consider
the following example.

Example 1 (Fair versus biased coin). Suppose there are two coins in a hat. One is fair and the other is biased towards tails. The task is to randomly select one of them and determine which one it is. To do this, one can proceed as follows: (i) Define the *null hypothesis* H_0 as "the fair coin was selected"; (ii) Perform N trials noting each time whether a heads or tails occurred; (iii) If the number of heads is "low", reject H_0. Else, fail to reject H_0. Two types of errors can occur in this scenario as shown in the following table:

	H_0 is true	H_0 is false
Reject H_0	Type-I error (probability α)	Correct to reject H_0
Fail to reject H_0	Correct to fail to reject H_0	Type-II error (probability β)

A type-I error occurs when H_0 is rejected even though it is true and a type-II error occurs when H_0 is not rejected even though it is false. A type-I error can be thought of as a false positive in the setting of abstract interpretation, while a type-II error can be viewed as a false negative. The probability of a type-I error is denoted by α and that of a type-II error by β; common practice is to find appropriate bounds for each of these error probabilities.

In our case, H_0 is the assumption that $p_Z \geq \epsilon$. Rewriting inequation 1 with respect to H_0 we obtain:

$$\mathbf{Pr}[X \leq M \mid H_0] \geq 1 - \delta \qquad (2)$$

We now perform M trials. If no counterexample is found, i.e. if $X > M$, we reject H_0. This may introduce a type-I error: H_0 may be true even though we did not find a counter-example. However, the probability of making this error is bounded by δ; this is shown in inequation 3 which is obtained by taking the complement of $X \leq M$ in inequation 2:

$$\mathbf{Pr}[X > M \mid H_0] < \delta \qquad (3)$$

Because we seek to attain a one-sided error decision procedure, we do not consider type-II errors in our application of hypothesis testing: as soon as we find a counter-example, we stop sampling and decide (with probability 1) that $S \models \varphi$ is false. To estimate the error probability and obtain a corresponding bound on the probability β of a type-II error,[2] we would need to continue sampling no matter how early on in the sampling process the first counter-example is encountered.

Such an approach is put forth by us in [11] where we show how to compute an (ϵ, δ)-approximation $\widetilde{p}_Z$ of p_Z; i.e., $\widetilde{p}_Z$ is such that:

$$\mathbf{Pr}[p_Z(1 - \epsilon) \leq \widetilde{p}_Z \leq p_Z(1 + \epsilon)] \geq 1 - \delta$$

---

[2] A type-II error arises in our setting when $p_Z < \epsilon$ even though we find a counter-example within M samples, thereby leading us to believe incorrectly that $p_Z \geq \epsilon$. Given that p_Z represents the probability that an arbitrary run of S is a counter-example to φ, one could say that we were "fortunate" to find a counter-example in this many samples.

As shown in [11], this can be done in a number of samples that is optimal to within a constant factor by appealing to the optimal approximation algorithm (OAA) of [8].

The approach taken here, in contrast, appeals to basic probability theory of Bernoulli and geometric random variables to derive a decision procedure for the LTL model-checking problem. The number of samples taken by MC^2 is therefore usually an order of magnitude smaller than that required by OAA. This is to be expected as the theory underlying OAA is based on the more general Chernoff bounds, which are applicable to any random variable encoding a Poisson trial.

MC^2 returns false at the first sample corresponding to an accepting lasso; i.e., it's tolerance level for errors is one. Relaxing this condition would allow MC^2 to continue sampling until an upper bound U on the number of counter-examples sampled is reached. Such an approach is related to the statistical quality control process used in manufacturing, where a batch of N items is rejected when more than U of them are found to be defective out of M randomly and sequentially chosen samples. This process is known in the literature as a *single acceptance plan with curtailed sampling* [9]. The computation of M is considerably more involved in this case, as it depends on the cumulative distribution function of a random variable with a negative binomial distribution.

3   Monte Carlo Model-Checking Algorithm

In this section, we present our randomized, automata-theoretic approach to model checking based on the DDFS algorithm given in Appendix A of [10] and the theory of geometric random variables and hypothesis testing presented in Section 2. The *samples* we are interested in are the reachable cycles (or "lassos") of a Büchi automaton B.[3] Should B be the product automaton $B_S \times B_{\neg\varphi}$ defined in Appendix A of [10], then a lasso containing a final state of B inside the cycle (an "accepting lasso") can be interpreted as a *counter-example* to $S \models \varphi$. A lasso of B is sampled via a random walk through B's transition graph, starting from a randomly selected initial state of B.

Definition 1 (Lasso Sample Space). *A finite run $\sigma = s_0 x_0 \ldots s_n x_n s_{n+1}$ of a Büchi automaton $B = (\Sigma, Q, Q_0, \Delta, F)$, is called a* lasso *if $s_0 \ldots s_n$ are pairwise distinct and $s_{n+1} = s_i$ for some $0 \leq i \leq n$. Moreover, σ is said to be an* accepting lasso *if some $s_j \in F$, $i \leq j \leq n$; otherwise it is a* non-accepting lasso. *The* lasso sample space L of B is the set of all lassos of B, while L_a and L_n are the sets of all accepting and non-accepting lassos of B, respectively.*

To define a probability space over L we show how to compute the probability of a lasso.

Definition 2 (Run Probability). *The* probability $\mathbf{Pr}[\sigma]$ *of a finite run $\sigma = s_0 x_0 \ldots s_{n-1} x_{n-1} s_n$ of a Büchi automaton B is defined inductively as follows:*

---

[3] We assume without loss of generality that every state of a Büchi automaton B has at least one outgoing transition, even if this transition is a self-loop.

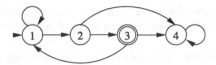

Fig. 1. Example lasso probability space

$\mathbf{Pr}[s_0] = k^{-1}$ *if* $|Q_0| = k$ *and* $\mathbf{Pr}[s_0x_0 \ldots s_{n-1}x_{n-1}s_n] = \mathbf{Pr}[s_0x_0 \ldots s_{n-1}] \cdot \pi[s_{n-1}x_{n-1}s_n]$ *where* $\pi[s\,x\,t] = m^{-1}$ *if* $(s, x, t) \in \Delta$ *and* $|\Delta(s)| = m$.

Note that the above definition explores uniformly outgoing transitions. An alternative definition might explore uniformly successor states.

Example 2 (Probability of lassos). Consider the Büchi automaton B of Figure 1. It contains four lassos, 11, 1244, 1231 and 12344, having probabilities 1/2, 1/4, 1/8 and 1/8, respectively. Lasso 1231 is accepting.

Proposition 1 (Lasso Probability Space). *Given a Büchi automaton B, the pair $(\mathcal{P}(L), \mathbf{Pr})$ defines a discrete probability space.*

The proof of this proposition considers the infinite tree T corresponding to the infinite unfolding of Δ. T' is the (finite) tree obtained by making a cut in T at the first repetition of a state along any path in T. It is easy to show by induction on the height of T' that the sum of the probabilities of the runs (lassos) associated with the leaves of T' is 1.

Definition 3 (Lasso Bernoulli Variable). *The random variable Z associated with the probability space $(\mathcal{P}(L), \mathbf{Pr})$ of a Büchi automaton B is defined as follows: $p_Z = \mathbf{Pr}[Z = 1] = \sum_{\lambda_a \in L_a} \mathbf{Pr}[\lambda_a]$ and $q_Z = \mathbf{Pr}[Z = 0] = \sum_{\lambda_n \in L_n} \mathbf{Pr}[\lambda_n]$.*

Example 3 (Lassos Bernoulli Variable). For the Büchi automaton B of Figure 1, the lassos Bernoulli variable has associated probabilities $p_Z = 1/8$ and $q_Z = 7/8$.

Having defined Z, we now present our Monte Carlo decision procedure, which we call MC^2, for the LTL model-checking problem. Its pseudo-code is as follows, where $\texttt{rInit(B)=random}(S_0)$, $\texttt{rNext(B,s)=t'}$, $(\texttt{s}, \alpha', \texttt{t'}) = \texttt{random}(\{\tau \in \Delta \mid \exists \alpha, \texttt{t}. \tau = (\texttt{s}, \alpha, \texttt{t})\})$ and $\texttt{acc(s,B)=(s} \in \texttt{F})$. The main routine consists of three statements, the first of which uses inequation 1 of Section 2 to determine the value for M, given parameters ϵ and δ. The second statement is a for-loop that successively samples up to M lassos by calling the *random lasso* (RL) routine. If an accepting lasso l is found, MC^2 decides false and returns l as a counter-example. If no accepting lasso is found within M trials, MC^2 decides true, and reports that with probability less than δ, p_Z is greater than ϵ.

The RL routine generates a random lasso by using the *randomized init* (rInit) and *randomized next* (rNext) routines. To determine if the generated lasso is accepting, it stores the index i of each encountered state s in HashTbl and records the index of the most recently encountered accepting state in f. Upon detecting a cycle, i.e., the state $\texttt{s := rNext(B,s)}$ is in HashTbl, it checks if $\texttt{HashTbl(s)} \leq \texttt{f}$;

MC² algorithm
input: $B = (\Sigma, Q, Q_0, \Delta, F)$; $0 < \epsilon < 1$; $0 < \delta < 1$.
output: Either (false, accepting lasso 1) or (true, "$\mathbf{Pr}[X > M \mid H_0] < \delta$")

(1)   M := $\ln \delta$ / $\ln(1 - \epsilon)$;
(2)   for (i := 1; i ≤ M; i++) if (RL(B)==(1,1)) return (false,1);
(3)   return (true,"$\mathbf{Pr}[X > M \mid H_0] < \delta$");

RL algorithm
input: Büchi automaton B;
output: Samples a RL 1. Returns (1,1) if accepting; (0,Null) otherwise

(1)   s := rInit(B); i := 0; f := 0;
(2)   while (s ∉ HashTbl) {
(3)   HashTbl(s) := ++i;
(4)   if (acc(s,B)) f := i;
(5)   s := rNext(B,s); }
(6)   if (HashTbl(s) ≤ f) return (1,lasso(HashTbl)) else return (0,Null);

the cycle is an accepting cycle if and only if this is the case. The function lasso() extracts a lasso from the states stored in HashTbl.

As with DDFS, one can avoid the explicit construction of B, by generating random states rInit(B) and rNext(B,s) on demand and performing the test for acceptance acc(B,s) symbolically. In the next section we present such a succinct representation and show how to efficiently generate random initial and successor states.

Theorem 1 (MC² Correctness). *Given a Büchi automaton B and parameters ϵ and δ, if MC² returns false, then $L(B) \neq \emptyset$. Otherwise, $\mathbf{Pr}[X > M \mid H_0] < \delta$ where $M = \ln(\delta)/\ln(1 - \epsilon)$ and $H_0 \equiv p_Z \geq \epsilon$.*

Proof. If RL finds an accepting lasso then $L(B) \neq \emptyset$ by definition. Otherwise, each call to RL can be shown to be an independent Bernoulli trial and the result follows from inequation 3 of Section 2.

MC² is very efficient in both time and space. The *recurrence diameter* of a Büchi automaton B is the longest loop-free path in B starting from an initial state.

Theorem 2 (MC² Complexity). *Let B be a Büchi automaton, D its recurrence diameter and $M = \ln(\delta)/\ln(1-\epsilon)$. Then MC² runs in time $O(MD)$ and uses $O(D)$ space. Moreover, M is optimal.*

Proof. The length of a lasso is bounded by D; the number of samples taken is bounded by M. That M is optimal follows from inequation 3, which provides a tight lower bound on the number of trials needed to achieve success with confidence ratio δ and lower bound ϵ on p_Z.

It follows from Theorems 1 and 2 that MC² is a one-sided error, Monte Carlo decision procedure for the emptiness-checking problem for Büchi automata. For $B = B_S \times B_{\neg \varphi}$, MC² yields a Monte Carlo decision procedure for the LTL model-checking problem $S \models \varphi$ requiring $O(MD)$ time and $O(D)$ space. In the worst case, D is exponential in $|S| + |\varphi|$ and thus MC²'s asymptotic complexity would match that of DDFS. In practice, however, we can expect MC^2 to perform better than this. For example, for the problem of N dining philosophers, our experimental results of Section 5 indicate that $D = O(N \cdot 1.4^N)$.

4   Implementation

We have implemented the DDFS and MC^2 algorithms as an extension to JMOCHA [2], a model checker for synchronous and asynchronous concurrent systems specified using *reactive modules* [3]. An LTL formula $\neg\varphi$ is specified in our extension of JMOCHA as a pair consisting of a reactive module monitor and a boolean formula defining its set of accepting states. By selecting the new enumerative or randomized LTL verification option, one can check whether $S \models \varphi$: JMOCHA takes the composition of the system and formula modules and applies either DDFS or MC^2 on-the-fly to check for accepting lassos.

An example reactive module, for a "fair stick" in the dining philosophers problem, is shown below. It consists of a collection of typed variables partitioned into *external* (input), *interface* (output), and *private*. For this example, rqL, rqR, rlL, rlR, grL, grR, pc, and pr denote left and right request, left and right release, left and right grant, program counter, and priority, respectively. The priority variable pr is used to enforce fairness.

```
type stickType is {free,left,right}
module Stick is
   external rqL,rqR,rlL,rlR:event; interface grL,grR:event;
   private pc,pr:stickType;
atom STICK
   controls pc,pr,grL,grR; reads pc,pr,grL,grR,rqL,rqR,rlL,rlR
   awaits rqL,rqR,rlL,rlR
init
[] true -> pc' := free; pr' := left;
update
[] pc = free & rqL? & ¬rqR? -> grL!; pc':= left; pr' := right;
[] pc = free & rqL? & rqR? & pr = left -> grL!; pc':= left; pr' := right;
[] pc = free & rqL? & rqR? & pr = right -> grR!; pc':= right; pr' := left;
[] pc = free & rqR? & ¬rqL? -> grR!; pc':= right; pr' := left;
[] pc = left & rlL? -> pc' := free;
[] pc = right & rlR? -> pc' := free;
```

In JMOCHA, variables change their values in a sequence of rounds: an *initialization* round followed by *update* rounds. Initialization and updates of controlled (interface and private) variables are specified by *actions* defined as a set of *guarded parallel assignments*. Controlled variables are partitioned into *atoms*: each variable is initialized and updated by exactly one atom.

The initialization round and all update rounds are divided into sub-rounds, one for the environment and one for each atom A. In an A-sub-round of the initialization round, all variables controlled by A are initialized simultaneously, as defined by an initial action. In an A-sub-round of each update round, all variables controlled by A are updated simultaneously, as defined by an update action.

In a round, each variable x has two values: the value at the beginning of the round, written as x and called the *read value*, and the value at the end of the round written as x' and called the *updated value*. *Events* are modeled by toggling boolean variables. For example rqL? $\overset{\text{def}}{=}$ rqL' $\neq$ rqL and grL! $\overset{\text{def}}{=}$ grL' := ¬grL. If a variable x controlled by an atom A depends on the updated value y' of a variable controlled by atom B, then B has to be executed before A. We say that A *awaits* B and that y is an awaited variable of A. The await dependency defines a partial order $\succ$ among atoms.

Operators on modules include *renaming*, *hiding* of output variables, and *parallel composition*. Parallel composition is defined only when the modules update disjoint sets of variables and have a joint acyclic await dependency. In this case, the composition takes the union of the private and interface variables, the union of the external variables (minus the interface variables), the union of the atoms, and the union of the await dependencies.

A feature of our JMOCHA implementation of MC^2 is that, given a Reactive module M, the next state along a random walk through M, s'=rNext(s,M), is generated randomly both for the external variables M.extl and for the controlled variables M.ctrl. For the former, we randomly generate a state s.extl' from the set of all input valuations Q.M.extl. For the latter, we proceed for each atom A in a linear order $\succ_M^L$ compatible with $\succ_M$ as follows: We first randomly choose a guarded assignment A.upd(i) with true guard A.upd(i).grd(s), where i is less than the number |A.upd| of guarded assignments in A. We then randomly generate a state s.ctrl' from the set of all states returned by its parallel (nondeterministic) assignment A.upd(i).ass(s). If no guarded assignment is enabled, we keep the current state s.ctrl. The routine rInit is implemented in a similar way.

5   Experimental Results

We compared the performance of MC^2 and DDFS by applying our implementation of these algorithms in JMOCHA to the Reactive-Modules specification of two well known model-checking benchmarks: the *dining philosophers* problem and the *Needham Schroeder* mutual authentication protocol. All reported results were obtained on a PC equipped with an Athlon 2100+ MHz processor and 1GB RAM running Linux 2.4.18 (Fedora Core 1).

For dining philosophers, we considered two LTL properties: *deadlock freedom* (DF), which is a safety property, and *starvation freedom* (SF), which is a liveness property. For a system of n philosophers, their specification is as follows:

$$DF : G\,\neg\,(pc_1 = \texttt{wait} \,\&\, \ldots \,\&\,pc_n = \texttt{wait})$$
$$SF : G\,F\,(pc_1 = \texttt{eat})$$

We considered Reactive-Modules specifications of both a symmetric and asymmetric solution to the problem. In the symmetric case, all philosophers can simultaneously pick up their right forks, leading to deadlock. Lockout-freedom is also violated since no notion of fairness has been incorporated into the solution. That both properties are violated is intentional, as it allow us to compare the relative performance of DDFS and MC^2 on finding counter-examples.

Table 1. Deadlock and starvation freedom for symmetric (unfair) version

ph	DDFS time	entr	MC² time	mxl	cxl	M		ph	DDFS time	entr	MC² time	mxl	cxl	M
4	0.02	31	0.08	10	10	3		4	0.17	29	0.02	8	8	2
8	1.62	511	0.20	25	8	7		8	0.71	77	0.01	7	7	1
12	3:13	8191	0.25	37	11	11		12	1:08	125	0.02	9	9	1
16	>20:0:0	–	0.57	55	8	18		16	7:47:0	173	0.11	18	18	1
20	–	oom	3.16	484	9	20		20	–	oom	0.06	14	14	1
30	–	oom	35.4	1478	11	100		30	–	oom	1.12	223	223	1
40	–	oom	11:06	13486	10	209		40	–	oom	1.23	218	218	1

Table 2. Deadlock and starvation freedom for fair asymmetric version

ph	DDFS time	entr	MC² time	mxl	avl		ph	DDFS time	entr	MC² time	mxl	avl
4	0:01	178	0:20	49	21		4	0:01	538	0:20	50	21
6	0:03	1772	0:45	116	42		6	0:17	9106	0:46	123	42
8	0:58	18244	2:42	365	99		8	7:56	161764	2:17	276	97
10	16:44	192476	7:20	720	234		10	–	oom	7:37	760	240
12	–	oom	21:20	1665	564		12	–	oom	21:34	1682	570
16	–	oom	3:03:40	7358	3144		16	–	oom	2:50:50	6124	2983
20	–	oom	19:02:00	34158	14923		20	–	oom	22:59:10	44559	17949

For the symmetric case, we chose $\delta = 10^{-1}$ and $\epsilon = 1.8 \cdot 10^{-3}$ which yields $M = 1257$. This number of samples proved sufficiently large in that for each instance of dining philosophers on which we ran our implementation of MC², a counter-example was detected. The results for the symmetric unfair case are given in Table 1. The meaning of the column headings is the following: ph is the number of philosophers; time is the time to find a counter-ex. in hrs:mins:secs; entr is the number of entries in the hash table; mxl is the maximum length of a sample; cxl is the length of the counter-example; N is the no. samples to find a counter-ex. As the data demonstrate, DDFS runs out of memory for 20 philosophers, while MC² not only scales up to a larger number of philosophers, but also outperforms DDFS on the smaller numbers. This is especially the case for starvation freedom where one sample is enough to find a counter-example.

To avoid storing a large number of states in temporary variables, one might attempt to generate successor states one at a time (which is exactly what rNext(B,s) of MC² does). However, the constraint imposed by DDFS to generate *all* successor states in sequential order inevitably leads to the additional time and memory consumption.

In the asymmetric case, a notion of fairness has been incorporated into the specification and, as a result, deadlock and starvation freedom are preserved. Specifically, the specification uses a form of round-robin scheduling to explicitly

Table 3. Needham-Schroeder protocol

mr	DDFS		MC^2				mr	DDFS		MC^2			
	time	entr	time	mxl	cxl	M		time	entr	time	mxl	cxl	M
4	0.38	607	1.68	87	87	103	40	1:11	158431	1:46	325	117	7818
8	1.24	2527	11.3	208	65	697	48	2:03	264607	1:45	232	25	6997
16	5.87	13471	10.2	223	61	612	56	3:24	409951	6:54	278	133	28644
24	18.7	39007	3:06	280	44	12370	64	5:18	600607	7:12	347	32	29982
32	36.2	85279	2:54	269	63	11012	72	–	oom	11:53	336	63	43192

encode weak fairness. As in the symmetric case, we chose $\delta = 10^{-1}$ and $\epsilon = 1.8 \cdot 10^{-3}$. Our results are given in Table 2, where columns mxl and avl represent the maximum and average length of a sample, respectively.

The next model-checking benchmark we considered was the Needham-Schroeder public-key authentication protocol; first published in 1978 [22], this protocol initiated a large body of work on the design and analysis of cryptographic protocols. In 1995, Lowe published an attack on the protocol that had apparently been undiscovered for the previous 17 years [17]. The following year, he showed how the flaw could be discovered mechanically by model checking [18].

The intent of the Needham-Schroeder protocol is to establish mutual authentication between principals A and B in the presence of an intruder who can intercept, delay, read, copy, and generate messages, but who does not know the private keys of the principals. The flaw discovered by Lowe uses an interleaving of two runs of the protocol.

To illustrate MC^2's ability to find attacks in security protocols like Needham-Schroeder when traditional model checkers fail due to state explosion, we encoded the original (incorrect) Needham-Schroeder protocol as a Reactive-Modules specification and checked if it is free from intruder attacks. Our results are shown in Table 3 where column mr represents the maximum nonce range;[4] i.e., a value of n for mr means that a nonce used by the principals can range in value from 0 to n, and also corresponds to the maximum number of runs of the protocol. The meaning of the other columns are the same as those in Table 1 for the symmetric (incorrect) version of dining philosophers.

In the case of Needham-Schroeder, counter-examples have a lower probability of occurrence and DDFS outperforms MC^2 when the range of nonces is relatively small. However, MC^2 scales up to a larger number of nonces whereas DDFS runs out of memory.

6   Alternative Random-Sampling Strategies

To take a random sample, which in our case is a random lasso, MC^2 performs a "uniform" random walk through the product Büchi automaton $B = B_S \times B_{\neg\varphi}$.

---

[4] The principals in the Needham-Schroeder protocol use nonces—previously unused and unpredictable identifiers—to ensure secrecy.

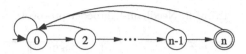

Fig. 2. Adversarial Büchi automaton B

In order to decide which transition to take next, a fair, k-sided coin is tossed when a state of B is reached having k outgoing transitions. No attempt is made to bias the sampling towards accepting lassos, which is the notion of success for the Bernoulli random variable Z upon which MC^2 is based. We are currently experimenting with alternative sampling strategies that favor accepting lassos.

Multi-Lassos. The *multi-lasso* sampling strategy ignores back-edges that do not lead to an accepting lasso if there are still forward edges to be explored. As shown below, this may have dramatic consequences.

In the case where the out-degree of B's states is nearly uniform, the sampling currently performed by MC^2 is biased toward shorter paths. To see this, consider for simplicity, the case where the out-degree is constant at $k > 1$. Then, the probability of a random lasso of length l is $(\frac{1}{k})^l$ and the shorter the lasso, the higher its probability. Thus, when S is *not* a model of φ, MC^2 is likely to first sample, and hence identify, a *shorter* counter-example sequence rather than a longer one. Given that shorter counter-examples are easier to decode and understand than longer ones, the advantage of this form of biased sampling becomes apparent.

On the other hand, one can construct an automaton that is adversarial to the type of sampling performed by MC^2. For example, consider the Büchi automaton B of Figure 2 consisting of a chain of $n+1$ states, such that for each state there is also a transition going back to the initial state. Furthermore, the only final state of B is the last state of the chain. Then there are $n+1$ lassos $l_0, \ldots, l_n$ in B, only one of which, l_n, is accepting. Moreover, according to Definition 2, the probability assigned to l_n is $1/2^n$, requiring $O(2^n)$ samples to be taken to sample l_n with high probability.

Interpreting automaton B of Figure 2 as the state-transition behavior of some system S, observe that B itself is not probabilistic even if the sampling performed on it by MC^2 is. In fact, it might even be the case that lasso l_n corresponds to a "normal" or likely behavioral pattern of S, making its detection essential. In this case, the adversarial nature of B is evident. Using a multi-lasso strategy however, dramatically increases the probability of l_n to 1, as the size of the multi-lasso space of B is 1.

Probabilistic Systems. In *probabilistic model checking* (see, for example, [16]), the state-transition behavior of a system S is prescribed by a probabilistic automaton such as a discrete-time Markov chain (DTMC). In this case, there is a natural way to assign a probability to a random walk σ: it is simply the product of the state-transition probabilities p_{ij} for each transition from state i to j along σ. This implies that MC^2 extends with little modification to the case of LTL model checking over DTMCs. Also, the example of Figure 2 becomes less adversarial as l_n would indeed in a probabilistic model be one of very low probability.

Input Partitioning. When the probabilities of outgoing transitions are not known in advance, it seems reasonable to assign a uniform probability to transitions involving internal nondeterminism. This justifies the use of a sampling strategy based on uniform random walks for closed systems as discussed above. For open systems, however, assigning a uniform probability to transitions involving external nondeterminism seems to be less than optimal: in practice, an attacker might use the same input to trigger a faulty behavior of the system over and over again. Since the external probabilities are in general unknown, a reasonable sampling strategy for open systems would be to partition (or abstract) the input into equivalence classes that trigger essentially the same behavior, and randomly choose a representative of each class when generating successor states.

7   Related Work

The Lurch debugger [14] performs random search on models of concurrent systems given as AND-OR graphs. Each iteration of the search function finds one global-state path, storing a hash value for each global state it encounters. The random search is terminated when the percentage of new states to old states reaches a "saturation point" or a user-defined limit on time or memory is reached. In [5] randomization is used to decide which visited states should be stored, and which should be omitted, during LTL model checking, with the goal of reducing memory requirements.

Probabilistic model checkers cater to stochastic models and logics, including, but not limited to, those for discrete- and continuous-time Markov chains [16, 4], Probabilistic I/O Automata [28], and Probabilistic Automata [25]. Examples logics treated by these model checkers include PCTL [12] and CSL [1]. Stochastic modeling formalisms and logics are also considered in [33, 15, 26]; these researchers, like us, advocate an approach to model checking based on random sampling of execution paths and hypothesis testing. The logics treated by these approaches, however, are restricted to time-bounded safety properties. Also, the number of samples taken by our algorithm—arrived at by appealing directly to the theory of geometric random variables—is optimal and therefore significantly smaller than the number of samples taken in [15].

Several techniques have been proposed for the automatic verification of safety and reachability properties of concurrent systems based on the use of random walks to uniformly sample the system state space [19, 13, 29]. In contrast, MC^2 performs random sampling of lassos for general LTL model checking. In [20], Monte Carlo and abstract interpretation techniques are used to analyze programs whose inputs are divided into two classes: those that behave according to some fixed probability distribution and those considered nondeterministic.

8   Conclusions

We have presented MC^2, what we believe to be the first randomized, Monte Carlo decision procedure for classical temporal-logic model checking. Utilizing basic probability theory of geometric random variables, MC^2 performs random sampling of lassos in the Büchi automaton $B = B_S \times B_{\neg \varphi}$ to yield a one-sided error Monte Carlo decision procedure for the LTL model-checking problem $S \models \varphi$. It does so using an optimal number of samples M. Benchmarks show that MC^2 is fast, memory-efficient, and scales extremely well.

In terms of ongoing and future work, we are implementing the alternative sampling strategies discussed in Section 6. Also, we are seeking to improve the time and space efficiency of our JMOCHA implementation of MC^2 by "compiling" it into a BDD representation. This involves encoding the current state, hash table, and guarded assignments of each atom in a reactive module as BDDs, and implementing the next-state computation and the containment (in the hash table) check as BDD operations.

As an open problem, it would be interesting to extend our techniques to the model-checking problem for branching-time temporal logics, such as CTL and the modal mu-calculus. This extension appears to be non-trivial since the idea of sampling accepting lassos in the product graph will no longer suffice.

Acknowledgments. We would like to thank Rajeev Alur, Javier Esparza, Richard Karp, Michael Luby, and Eugene Stark for helpful discussions. We are also grateful to the anonymous referees for their valuable comments.

References

1. A. Aziz, K. Sanwal, V. Singhal, and R. K. Brayton. Verifying continuous-time Markov chains, 1996.
2. R. Alur, L. de Alfaro, R. Grosu, T. A. Henzinger, M. Kang, C. M. Kirsch, R. Majumdar, F. Mang, and B. Y. Wang. JMOCHA: A model checking tool that exploits design structure. In *Proceedings of the 23rd international conference on Software engineering*, pages 835–836. IEEE Computer Society, 2001.
3. R. Alur and T. A. Henzinger. Reactive modules. *Formal Methods in System Design*, 15(1):7–48, July 1999.
4. C. Baier, B. Haverkort, H. Hermanns, and J.-P. Katoen. Efficient computation of time-bounded reachability probabilities in uniform continuous-time Markov decision processes. In *Proc. of TACAS*, 2004.
5. L. Brim, I. Černá, and M. Nečesal. Randomization helps in LTL model checking. In *Proceedings of the Joint International Workshop, PAPM-PROBMIV 2001*, pages 105–119. Springer, LNCS 2165, September 2001.
6. E. M. Clarke, O. Grumberg, and D. Peled. *Model Checking*. MIT Press, 1999.
7. E.M. Clarke and E.A. Emerson. Design and synthesis of synchronization skeletons using branching time temporal logic. In *Proc. Workshop on Logic of Programs*, LNCS 131, pages 52–71. Springer, 1981.
8. P. Dagum, R. Karp, M. Luby, and S. Ross. An optimal algorithm for Monte Carlo estimation. *SIAM Journal on Computing*, 29(5):1484–1496, 2000.
9. A. J. Duncan. *Quality Control and Industrial Statistics*. Irwin-Dorsley, 1974.

10. R. Grosu and S. A. Smolka. Monte carlo model checking (extended version). In LNCS 3440 on SpringerLink. Springer-Verlag, 2005.
11. R. Grosu and S. A. Smolka. Quantitative model checking. In *First Intl. Symp. on Leveraging Applications of Formal Methods (Participants Proceedings)*, 2004. Also available from http://www.cs.sunysb.edu/~sas/papers/GS04.pdf.
12. H. Hansson and B. Jonsson. A logic for reasoning about time and reliability. *Formal Aspects of Computing*, 6(5):512–535, 1994.
13. P. Haslum. Model checking by random walk. In *Proc. of 1999 ECSEL Workshop*, 1999.
14. M. Heimdahl, J. Gao, D. Owen, and T. Menzies. On the advantages of approximate vs. complete verification: Bigger models, faster, less memory, usually accurate. In *Proc. of 28th Annual NASA Goddard Software Engineering Workshop (SEW'03)*, 2003.
15. T Hérault, R. Lassaigne, F. Magniette, and S. Peyronnet. Approximate probabilistic model checking. In *Proc. Fifth International Conference on Verification, Model Checking, and Abstract Interpretation (VMCAI 2004)*, 2004.
16. M. Z. Kwiatkowska, G. Norman, and D. Parker. PRISM: Probabilistic symbolic model checker. In *Proceedings of the 12th International Conference on Computer Performance Evaluation, Modelling Techniques and Tools*, pages 200–204. Springer-Verlag, 2002.
17. G. Lowe. An attack on the Needham-Schroeder public-key authentication protocol. *Information Processing Letters*, pages 131–133, 1995.
18. G. Lowe. Breaking and fixing the Needham-Schroeder public-key protocol using FDR. In *Proceedings of the Second International Workshop on Tools and Algorithms for Construction and Analysis of Systems*, pages 147–166. Springer-Verlag, 1996.
19. M. Mihail and C. H. Papadimitriou. On the random walk method for protocol testing. In *6th International Conference on Computer Aided Verification (CAV)*, pages 132–141. Springer, LNCS 818, 1994.
20. D. Monniaux. An abstract monte-carlo method for the analysis of probabilistic programs. In *Proc. 28th ACM SIGPLAN-SIGACT symposium on Principles of programming languages*, pages 93–101. ACM Press, 2001.
21. A. M. Mood, F.A. Graybill, and D.C. Boes. *Introduction to the Theory of Statistics*. McGraw-Hill Series in Probability and Statistics, 1974.
22. R. Needham and M. D. Schroeder. Using encryption for authentication in large networks of computers. *Communications of the ACM*, 21(12):993–999, 1978.
23. J. P. Queille and J. Sifakis. Specification and verification of concurrent systems in Cesar. In *Proceedings of the International Symposium in Programming*, volume 137 of *Lecture Notes in Computer Science*, Berlin, 1982. Springer-Verlag.
24. H. Rudin. Protocol development success stories: Part 1. In *Proc. 12th Int. Symp. on Protocol Specification, Testing and Verification*, pages 149–160. North Holland, 1992.
25. R. Segala and N. A. Lynch. Probabilistic simulations for probabilistic processes. In B. Jonsson and J. Parrow, editors, *Proceedings of CONCUR '94 — Fifth International Conference on Concurrency Theory*, pages 481–496. Volume 836 of *Lecture Notes in Computer Science*, Springer-Verlag, 1994.
26. K. Sen, M. Viswanathan, and G. Agha. Statistical model checking of black-box probabilistic systems. In *16th International Conference on Computer Aided Verification (CAV 2004)*, 2004.
27. A. P. Sistla and E. M. Clarke. The complexity of propositional linear temporal logic. *Journal of the ACM*, 32:733–749, 1985.

28. E. W. Stark and S. A. Smolka. Compositional analysis of expected delays in networks of probabilistic I/O automata. In *Proc. 13th Annual Symposium on Logic in Computer Science*, pages 466–477, Indianapolis, IN, June 1998. IEEE Computer Society Press.

29. E. Tronci, G., D. Penna, B. Intrigila, and M. Venturini. A probabilistic approach to automatic verification of concurrent systems. In *Proc. of 8th IEEE Asia-Pacific Software Engineering Conference (APSEC)*, 2001.

30. M. Vardi and P. Wolper. An automata-theoretic approach to automatic program verification. In *Proc. IEEE Symposium on Logic in Computer Science*, pages 332–344, 1986.

31. C. H. West. Protocol validation by random state exploration. In *Proc. Sixth IFIP WG 6.1 Int. Workshop on Protocol Specification, Testing, and Verification*. North Holland, 1986.

32. C. H. West. Protocol validation in complex systems. In *SIGCOMM '89: Symposium proceedings on Communications architectures & protocols*, pages 303–312. ACM Press, 1989.

33. H. L. S. Younes and R. G. Simmons. Probabilistic verification of discrete event systems using acceptance sampling. In *Proc. 14th International Conference on Computer Aided Verification*, 2002.

Efficient Conflict Analysis for Finding All Satisfying Assignments of a Boolean Circuit*

HoonSang Jin, HyoJung Han, and Fabio Somenzi

University of Colorado at Boulder

{Jinh, Hhhan, Fabio}@Colorado.EDU

Abstract. Finding all satisfying assignments of a propositional formula has many applications to the synthesis and verification of hardware and software. An approach to this problem that has recently emerged augments a clause-recording propositional satisfiability solver with the ability to add "blocking clauses." One generates a blocking clause from a satisfying assignment by taking its complement. The resulting clause prevents the solver from visiting the same solution again. Every time a blocking clause is added the search is resumed until the instance becomes unsatisfiable. Various optimization techniques are applied to get smaller blocking clauses, since enumerating each satisfying assignment would be very inefficient.

In this paper, we present an improved algorithm for finding all satisfying assignments for a generic Boolean circuit. Our work is based on a hybrid SAT solver that can apply conflict analysis and implications to both CNF formulae and general circuits. Thanks to this capability, reduction of the blocking clauses can be efficiently performed without altering the solver's state (e.g., its decision stack). This reduces the overhead incurred in resuming the search. Our algorithm performs conflict analysis on the blocking clause to derive a proper conflict clause for the modified formula. Besides yielding a valid, nontrivial backtracking level, the derived conflict clause is usually more effective at pruning the search space, since it may encompass both satisfiable and unsatisfiable points. Another advantage is that the derived conflict clause provides more flexibility in guiding the score-based heuristics that select the decision variables. The efficiency of our new algorithm is demonstrated by our preliminary results on SAT-based unbounded model checking of VIS benchmark models.

1   Introduction

Many applications in computer science rely on the ability to solve large instances of the propositional satisfiability (SAT) problem. Examples include bounded and unbounded model checking [2, 20, 21], equivalence checking [11] and various other forms of automated reasoning [1, 17], test generation, and placement and routing of circuits [23]. While some of these applications only require a yes-no answer, an increasing number of them relies on the solver's ability to provide a proof of unsatisfiability [10, 29], a satisfying assignment that is minimal according to some metric [5, 24], or an enumeration of all satisfying assignments to a propositional formula [20].

---

* Work supported in part by SRC contract 2004-TJ-920.

N. Halbwachs and L. Zuck (Eds.): TACAS 2005, LNCS 3440, pp. 287–300, 2005.

Specifically, the systematic exploration of all satisfying assignments is important for unbounded SAT-based model checking, for decision procedures for arithmetic constraints, Presburger arithmetic, and various fragments of first order logic, and in the optimization of logic circuits. The problem is computationally hard because listing all the solutions requires exponential time in the worst case. All efforts should be made to present (and compute) the set of satisfying assignment in a concise form. Normally, the desired format is a disjunctive normal form (DNF) formula, which should consist of as few terms as it is feasible without compromising the speed of the solver. Recent advances in the design of SAT solvers like non-chronological backtracking and conflict analysis based on unique implication points, and efficient implementations like those based on two-watched literal schemes have inspired new approaches to the solution enumeration problem as well [20]. In this paper, in particular, we show how to take full advantage of sophisticated conflict analysis techniques to substantially increase both the speed of enumeration and the conciseness of the solution.

Conventional SAT solvers are targeted to computing just one solution, but they can be augmented to get all solutions. We call the problem of finding all satisfying assignments *AllSat*. In principle, to solve AllSat, it is enough to force the SAT solver to continue the search after getting each satisfying assignment.

In previous work [20, 16, 6], once a satisfying assignment is found then a *blocking clause* is generated by taking its complement. Blocking clauses are added to the function being examined to prevent the SAT solver from finding the same solution again. They represent the natural way to force a SAT solver based on conflict clause recording to continue the search. Various optimization techniques are applied to get smaller blocking clauses, since enumerating each satisfying assignment would be very inefficient. In applications like unbounded model checking [20], one seeks to enumerate the assignments to a propositional formula originally given in the form of a circuit. The translation of this circuit to conjunctive normal form (CNF) introduces auxiliary variables whose values are determined by those of the inputs of the circuit. The solutions that are enumerated should only be in terms of these input variables, and the minimization of the blocking clauses should take this feature into account. One way to achieve this objective is to use a so-called *auxiliary implication graph* to determine a subset of the input assignments sufficient to justify the output of the circuit.

The approach of [16] uses an external two-level minimization program to get a minimized form for sets of satisfying assignments instead of finding a minimized blocking clause internally on the fly. Every time a solution is identified then it is saved in DNF in addition to adding its negation as a blocking clause. The accumulated DNF is periodically fed to a two-level minimizer. All recent advances in propositional SAT [22, 9, 15] based on DPLL [8, 7] can be adopted to enhance performance of these AllSat methods, since they use exactly the same SAT algorithm except for the addition of the blocking clauses as additional constraints.

In [19, 12], the authors point out that the size of the instance may be increased significantly by the addition of the blocking clauses. Consequently, the speed of finding one solution is decreased because of the time spent in implications for those blocking clauses. They propose to save solutions in a decision tree by restricting non-chronological

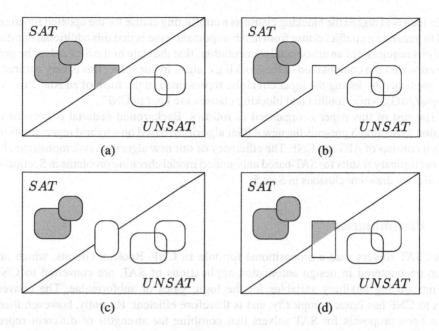

Fig. 1. Illustration of AllSat solving

backtracking. The decision heuristic also is restricted to increase the chance of saving solutions into the decision tree.

A simple algorithm for AllSat based on adding blocking clauses is illustrated in Fig. 1. For a given SAT instance, the search space can be divided into SAT and UNSAT subspaces. In the figure, the filled rectangles represent the blocking clauses created from satisfying assignments and the unfilled rectangles represent the conflict clauses generated from conflict analysis. In conventional SAT solving, if the satisfying assignment is identified on the SAT side, then the search is terminated. By contrast, in AllSat, the search is continued to cover all SAT and UNSAT points. When all the search space is covered by blocking clauses and conflict clauses then AllSat solving is finished. Minimization techniques can enlarge the filled rectangles as in [20, 16, 6]. Since large rectangles can prune large parts of the search space, these minimization techniques are beneficial.

Suppose that while solving AllSat, we have a blocking clause close to the UNSAT side, as illustrated in Part (a) of the figure. By adding the blocking clause, the corresponding satisfying assignments are moved to the UNSAT side as in (b). In the future, the solver may find a conflict such that the conflict-learned clause prunes this part of search space as in (c). Since finding blocking clauses and conflict analysis can only be applied on the SAT and UNSAT sides, respectively, these conventional solvers cannot apply powerful pruning techniques on both SAT and UNSAT side simultaneously as in (d). That is, they cannot add clauses that prevent the future exploration of both SAT and UNSAT points of the search space. In this paper we propose an efficient conflict analysis that removes this limitation. This technique improves the effectiveness of non-chronological backtracking, and of the heuristic that chooses the decision variables. The main idea is to regard the blocking clause as a conflicting clause for the updated function, and to generate a conflict clause from it. An important issue is that this additional conflict analysis requires, for an efficient implementation, that the state of the SAT solver be preserved across the computation of the blocking clause. In our solver this is very naturally accomplished by letting the input circuit be represented in the form of an And-Inverter Graph (AIG), while conflict and blocking clauses are kept in CNF.

The rest of this paper is organized as follows. Background material is covered in Section 2. Section 3 presents the new AllSat algorithm based on a hybrid representation, which consists of AIG and CNF. The efficiency of our new algorithm is demonstrated by our preliminary results for SAT-based unbounded model checking problems in Section 4. Finally, we draw conclusions in Sect.5.

2   Preliminaries

Most SAT solvers read a propositional formula in CNF. Boolean circuits, which are often encountered in design automation applications of SAT, are converted to CNF by introducing auxiliary variables for the logic gates or subformulae. The conversion to CNF has linear complexity, and is therefore efficient. Recently, however, there have been proposals for SAT solvers that combine the strengths of different representations, including circuits, CNF formulae, and Binary Decision Diagram (BDD [4]) [18, 14].

In this paper we rely on both CNF and AIGs to solve the AllSat problem. An *And-Inverter Graph* (AIG) is a Boolean circuit such that each internal node ν has exactly two predecessors, and if the predecessor variables are v_1 and v_2, its function $\phi(\nu)$ is one of $v_1 \wedge v_2$, $v_1 \wedge \neg v_2$, $\neg v_1 \wedge v_2$, and $\neg v_1 \wedge \neg v_2$. A *Conjunctive Normal Form* (CNF) is a set of *clauses*; each clause is a set of *literals*; each literal is either a variable or its complement. The function of a clause is the disjunction of its literals, and the function of a CNF formula is the conjunction of its clauses.

Figure 2 shows the pseudocode for the DPLL procedure. Procedure CHOOSENEX-TASSIGNMENT checks the implication queue. If the queue is empty, the procedure makes a *decision*: it chooses one unassigned variable and a value for it, and adds the assignment

```
1   DPLL() {
2       while (CHOOSENEXTASSIGNMENT()) {
3           while (DEDUCE() == CONFLICT) {
4               blevel = ANALYZECONFLICT();
5               if (blevel ≤ 0) return UNSATISFIABLE;
6               else BACKTRACK(blevel);
7           }
8       }
9       return SATISFIABLE;
10  }
```

Fig. 2. DPLL algorithm

```
 1   AllSat() {
 2      while  (1) {
 3         while  (CHOOSENEXTASSIGNMENT()) {
 4            while  (DEDUCE() == CONFLICT) {
 5               blevel = ANALYZECONFLICT();
 6               if (blevel ≤ 0) return UNSATISFIABLE;
 7               else BACKTRACK(blevel);
 8            }
 9         }
10         FINDANDADDBLOCKINGCLAUSE();
11         BACKTRACK();
12      }
13   }
```

Fig. 3. AllSat algorithm

to the implication queue. If none can be found, it returns false. This causes DPLL to return an affirmative answer, because the assignment to the variables is complete.

If a new assignment has been chosen, its implications are added by DEDUCE to the queue. Efficient computation of implications for clauses is discussed in [25, 27, 22, 9]; implications in AIGs are described in [18];

If the implications yield a conflict, ANALYZECONFLICT() is launched. Conflict analysis relies on the (implicit) construction of an *implication graph*. Each literal in the conflicting clause has been assigned at some level either by a decision, or by an implication. If there are multiple literals from the current decision level, at least one of them is implied. Conflict analysis locates the source of that implication—it may be a clause or an AIG node—and extends the implication graph by adding arcs from the antecedents of the implication to the consequent. This process continues until there is exactly one assignment for the current level among the leaves of the tree. The disjunction of the negation of the leaf assignments gives then the conflict clause. The highest level of the assignments in the conflict clause, excluding the current one, is the backtracking level. The single assignment at the current level is known as first *Unique Implication Point* (UIP). Conflict clauses based on the first UIP have been empirically found to work well [28].

Conflict analysis produces two important results. The first is a clause implied by the given circuit and objectives. This *conflict clause* is added to the clauses of the circuit. Termination relies on it, because it causes the search to continue in a different direction. The second result of conflict analysis is the *backtracking level*: Each assignment to a variable has a *level* that starts from 0 and increases with each new decision. When a conflict is detected, the algorithm determines the lowest level at which a decision was made that eventually caused the conflict. The search for a satisfying assignment resumes from this level by deleting all assignments made at higher levels. This *non-chronological backtracking* allows the decision procedure to ignore inconsequential decisions that have provably no part in the conflict being analyzed.

Figure 3 shows the basic algorithm to get all satisfying assignments to a propositional formula. The DPLL procedure is extended with the ability to add *blocking clauses* as in [20, 6]. One generates a blocking clause from a satisfying assignment by taking the

complement of the conjunction of all the literals in the assignment. Procedure FIND-
ANDADDBLOCKINGCLAUSE() finds a blocking clause and adds it to the database. The
resulting clause prevents the solver from visiting the same solution again. Every time a
blocking clause is added, the search is resumed at some safe backtracking level until the
instance becomes unsatisfiable.

3   Algorithm

In the technique we propose, an AIG is used to represent the Boolean circuit whose
satisfying assignments must be enumerated, while the result of a conflict analysis is
represented as one clause. In our framework, conflict analysis and implications can be
applied to both CNF formulae and AIGs. Figure 4 shows the pseudocode for the proposed
algorithm. The naive algorithm of Figure 3 can be improved by replacing lines 10 and
11 with the procedure in Figure 4.

In the algorithm description, C is a Boolean circuit in the form of an AIG, which is
given as an input together with obj; obj is the *objective*, which is a node of C. We want to
find the all the assignments over V that satisfy obj. F is the formula resulting from conjoining C with the conflict clauses and the blocking clauses generated while solving the
AllSat problem. Therefore, initially F is C and when F becomes 0 AllSat is completed.

Procedure BLOCKINGCLAUSEANALYSIS is called when a satisfying assignment is
found in F. To get a blocking clause B over the variables in V, Boolean constraint
propagation is applied on C, which is the original Boolean circuit, disregarding conflict
learned clauses and blocking clauses. This is to get a smaller assignment from this
analysis. Figure 5 shows the reason why C is used for finding minimized assignments.
Suppose we have 4 variables in our SAT instance, and $a \wedge c$ is the off-set. $\neg a \wedge b \wedge \neg c \wedge d$
is a satisfying assignment that was detected at an earlier stage. It is possible to get such
an assignment if we use a heuristic minimization algorithm, but with small changes,

```
1    BlockingClauseAnalysis(F, C, A, V, obj) {
2        B = ∅;
3        for each v ∈ V {
4            B = B ∪ v;
5            BCPONCIRCUIT(C, v, A(v));
6            if (VALUE(obj) == A(obj)) break ;
7        }
8        MINIMIZATIONBASEDONANTECEDENT(C, B, obj);
9        ADDBLOCKINGCLAUSE(F, ¬B);
10       if (CHECKUIP(F, B) == 0)
11           bLevel = CONFLICTANALYSIS(F, ¬B);
12       else
13           bLevel = GETSAFEBACKTRACKLEVEL(F, ¬B);
14       BACKTRACK(bLevel);
15   }
```

Fig. 4. Blocking clause analysis algorithm

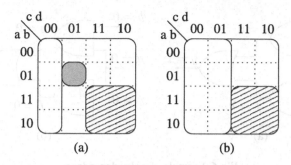

Fig. 5. Example of minimization

the example could be adapted to the case in which exact minimization is applied. Now suppose that satisfying assignment $\neg c \land \neg d$ is found. If we try to expand $\neg c \land \neg d$ with respect to F, which is $C \land (a \lor \neg b \lor c \lor \neg d)$, it cannot be expanded further as in (a). But if we apply minimization with respect to C, it can be expanded to $\neg c$ as in (b). Therefore heuristic minimization on C instead of F will give us a chance to get further minimization, since the expansion on C may give us a cover made up of prime implicants instead of a disjoint cover. In our framework, implications on either the AIG or the CNF clauses can be disabled. Since the conflict clauses and blocking clauses are saved as clauses, the implication on C can be done without extra effort by enabling the implication on AIGs only.

While applying Boolean constraints propagation (BCP) based on valuations of the variables in V, if the objective obj is satisfied then a sufficient satisfying assignment is identified. There is still room to improve because different orders of application of Boolean constraint propagation may result in different sufficient sets of variables. The assignments are further minimized by checking the implication graph C. Figure 6 (a) shows a small example that illustrates order dependency. If we check if y is implied while applying BCP with the order of a, b, c, d then $\neg a \land \neg b \land c \land d$ is identified as a satisfying assignment. If we check if y is implied while applying BCP with the order of c, d, a, b then $c \land d$ is a sufficient assignment. To reduce this inefficiency caused by the order of BCP, we traverse the implication graph after the implication on y has been obtained. Even though we apply BCP with the order of a, b, c, d, $c \land d$ is detected as sufficient assignment by traversing implication graph on C even with inefficient order of BCP. This is done in MINIMIZATIONBASEDONANTECEDENT. This procedure is similar to the techniques used in [20, 13]. It should be noted that this method does not guarantee minimality of satisfying assignment. Figure 6 (b) shows a case in which we may not get a minimal assignment with this method. In this example $a = 0$ is a minimal assignment. If the implication order is b, a, c, the sufficient assignment is found to be $\neg b \land \neg a$. Only when a is implied first the minimal assignment is detected.

Thanks to our solver's hybrid capability, reduction of the blocking clauses can be efficiently performed on C without altering the solver's state (e.g., its decision stack for F and the two-watched literal lists). Therefore the blocking clause is added to F, immediately generating a conflict on F. If a blocking clause has only one variable assignment at the maximum decision level of the implication graph of F, then it already

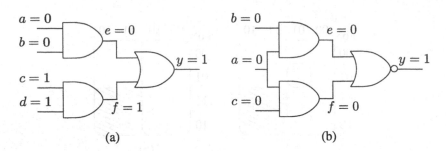

Fig. 6. Example of order dependency

has a unique implication point in it. Otherwise the conflict analysis is applied to get a conflict-learned clause.

Since the solver's state is not altered during the minimization procedure as opposed to implementations based on CNF solver [20, 6], this eliminates a reason for restarting the solver every time a blocking clause is added. One can avoid the restart by duplicating the whole solver data base so as not to alter the solver's state. However, it is not efficient to find an appropriate backtracking level where the search should be resumed based on blocking clause. Our algorithm, on the other hand, performs conflict analysis on the blocking clause to derive a proper conflict clause for the modified formula. Besides yielding a valid, nontrivial backtracking level, the derived conflict clause is usually more effective at pruning the search space, since it often encompasses both satisfiable and unsatisfiable points as shown in Figure 1. It is also unrestricted in the sense that both input and internal variables of the Boolean circuit may appear in it.

A final advantage of our analysis is that the derived conflict clause provides more flexibility in guiding the score-based heuristics that select the decision variables. If the blocking clauses are used to update the variable scores, the scores of the variables in V will unduly increase, since the variables in the blocking clauses are restricted to variables in that set. This will cause the solver to make decisions almost only on those variables. The result may be beneficial for the pruning of the SAT part of the search space, but not for the UNSAT part. The conflict clauses generated by the proposed algorithm still contain a lot of variables from V. The variables implied earlier than at the current decision level in a conflicting clause are immediately added to the conflict learned clause. Since a conflicting clause—in this case, the blocking clause that was added to F—consists of those variables, the resulting conflict clause still contains a lot of variables in V. To avoid increasing the score of those variables, we use the Deepest Variable Hiking (DVH) decision heuristics [15]. Boosting only the score of the most recent decision variable among the literals in the conflict-learned clause results in a more balanced approach at letting the blocking clauses influence the search direction.

With proof identical to that of Proposition 1 in [29] one shows that the improved All-Sat procedure that performs conflict analysis on the blocking clauses does not require the addition of either blocking clauses or conflict clauses to F to guarantee termination. However, as in standard SAT solvers, these additional clauses may prove useful by causing implications during BCP. Many tradeoffs are possible. In our current implementation we keep both blocking and conflict clauses.

We show that the conflict clauses generated by the proposed algorithm never block other satisfying assignment as follows.

Lemma 1. *For formula F, the conflict learned clause γ generated by conflict analysis on blocking clause β is implied by $F \wedge \beta$.*

Proof. Since the conflict occurred after adding blocking clause to F, $F \wedge \beta \rightarrow \gamma$.   □

Theorem 1. *For formula F, the conflict learned clause γ generated by conflict analysis on blocking clause β never blocks satisfying assignments not in β.*

Proof. Since $F \wedge \beta$ does not block any satisfying assignments except $\neg\beta$, γ cannot block other satisfying assignments by Lemma 1.   □

All satisfying assignments produced by the algorithms are satisfying assignments of C, because at all times $F \rightarrow C$. In summary, the AllSat algorithm terminates after having enumerated all satisfying assignments of C, and is therefore correct.

4   Experimental Results

We have implemented the proposed all satisfying assignments algorithm in VIS-2.1 [3, 26]. To show the efficiency of the proposed algorithm on various examples, we implemented a SAT-based unbounded model checker that uses the AX operator as described in [20].

Our algorithm should already be faster than the one described in [20] because of the hybrid capability and minimization technique discussed in Section 3. Therefore we

Table 1. Performance comparison for reaching a given pre-image step

Design	# latches	pre-image steps	With CA		Without	
			CPU time	# blocking	CPU time	# blocking
synch_bakery	22	49	676.7	37651	2398.9	67280
itc-b07	45	20	628.0	492	1607.2	870
solitaireVL	22	12*	2155.2	17754	15698.5	44693
heap	24	4*	847.4	34815	3028.4	78654
eight	27	2*	487.7	99992	1939.5	144563
buf_bug	27	8*	3128.9	26343	4160.6	39266
swap	27	5*	1893.7	16224	15808.3	24234
two	30	15*	3414.7	28866	10537.5	48961
luckySevenONE	30	24*	6846.2	40963	17657.0	70465
cube	32	10*	4498.9	46214	8013.5	47018
bpb	36	6*	103.3	5648	3823.8	79946
huff	37	9*	7787.1	100855	13441.5	113222
ball	86	6*	46.8	26659	176.8	52772
s1423	74	2*	2039.0	64097	7153.7	78928
Ifetchprod	147	3*	233.1	47103	716.5	57278

Table 2. Performance comparison until reaching timeout

Design	# latches	With CA		Without	
		pre-image steps	CPU time	pre-image steps	CPU time
vsa16a	172	2	1086	0*	≥20000
swap	27	6	3458	4*	≥20000
solitaireVL	22	46	6695	13*	≥20000
eight	27	4*	≥20000	3*	≥20000
two	30	18*	≥20000	16*	≥20000
luckySevenONE	30	27*	≥20000	25*	≥20000
cube	32	11*	≥20000	11*	≥20000
heap	32	6*	≥20000	5*	≥20000
huff	37	17*	≥20000	10*	≥20000
s1423	74	4*	≥20000	2*	≥20000
ball	86	8*	≥20000	7*	≥20000

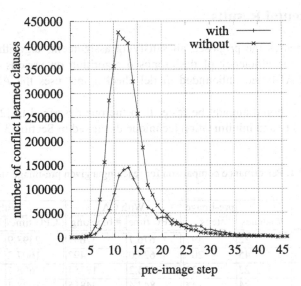

Fig. 7. Number of conflict learned clauses

compare the proposed algorithm with and without conflict analysis on blocking clauses on our hybrid solver rather than comparing with a CNF SAT based implementation. The experimental setup is as follows. The inputs, that is, the transition relation and the invariant property, are given as Boolean circuits. At every iteration of the AX operation, the frontier is extracted and expressed as a circuit in terms of next state variables. A new objective is created to satisfy the set of states in the frontier. The iteration is continued until convergence.

The model checking examples are selected from the VIS benchmark suite [26]. The examples that could be solved in a few seconds were removed from the set. There is not

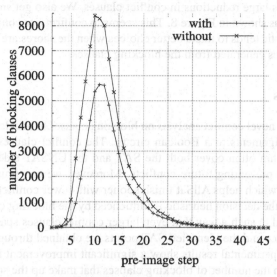

Fig. 8. Number of blocking clauses

direct correlation between the size of the model and its difficulty for model checking. In several of the large examples we considered, the cones of influence of the given properties are small so that the pre-images based on AllSat are trivial. By contrast, most of the selected examples are small, but notoriously difficult for SAT-based methods.

The experiments have been performed on 1.7 GHz Pentium IV with 1 GB of RAM running Linux. We have set the time out limit to 20,000 s.

Table 1 compares the CPU time spent and the number of blocking clauses generated until the same number of pre-image steps is reached. The number is the one that the slower method can complete within the allotted time. The column labeled 'With CA' shows the performance of the proposed algorithm that applies conflict analysis on the blocking clauses. The column labeled 'Without' shows the performance of AllSat without having conflict analysis on the blocking clauses. All other features described in Sect. 3 are still applied for the results shown in this column. The comparison of the two sets of results highlights consistent speed-up (up to 20 times). A '*' after the number of pre-image steps signals that the performed pre-image steps did not suffice for convergence. Even though we have consistent speed-up, some examples benefit more than others from the improved algorithm. We conjecture that this is mainly due to the distribution of satisfying and unsatisfying assignments over the search space.

Table 2 compares the numbers of pre-image steps that can be completed in a given amount of time. The proposed algorithm never finishes fewer pre-image steps. Again, a '*' after the number of pre-image steps indicates that convergence was not reached. For example, 'vsa16a' converges in two pre-image steps with the proposed conflict analysis, while it times out in the first iteration without the proposed conflict analysis.

Figures 7 and 8 show the numbers of conflict learned clauses and the numbers of blocking clauses of the 'solitaireVL' example. Figure 7 supports our claim that the proposed algorithm generates conflict clauses encompassing both SAT and UNSAT points, since it shows large reductions in conflict clauses. We also get smaller numbers of blocking clauses as shown in Figure 8. This seems to confirm our conjecture that the DVH decision heuristic tends to make better choices when the scores are updated based on the conflict clauses generated from the blocking clauses.

5   Conclusions

We have presented a novel conflict analysis on blocking clauses to accelerate the search of all satisfying assignments to a Boolean circuit. The conflict clauses generated by the proposed algorithm often cover both the SAT and the UNSAT side of the search space. This helps in preventing future conflicts. Moreover, we can prune larger parts of the search space, which helps AllSat finish sooner with fewer conflicts. Since in the proposed algorithm the decision heuristic is influenced by the blocking clauses as well, the search is directed in such a way that even larger conflict clauses spanning both the original UNSAT space and the identified SAT points are obtained through the standard conflict analysis. Experimental results show a significant improvement in the speed of AllSat solving and in the number of blocking clauses that make up the solution.

An improved solver for AllSat will benefit many applications that use it directly, like the SAT-based model checker we used to validate our implementation, or that use it as the basis of another algorithm. Examples of the latter that we plan to investigate are decision procedures for various fragments of first order logic.

Acknowledgment

We thank Ken McMillan for clarifying to us the details of his implementation.

References

[1] G. Audemard, P. Bertoli, A. Cimatti, A. Kornilowicz, and R. Sebastiani. A SAT based approach for solving formulas over boolean and linear mathematical propositions. In *International Conference on Automated Deduction*, July 2002.

[2] A. Biere, A. Cimatti, E. Clarke, and Y. Zhu. Symbolic model checking without BDDs. In *Fifth International Conference on Tools and Algorithms for Construction and Analysis of Systems (TACAS'99)*, pages 193–207, Amsterdam, The Netherlands, March 1999. LNCS 1579.

[3] R. K. Brayton et al. VIS: A system for verification and synthesis. In T. Henzinger and R. Alur, editors, *Eighth Conference on Computer Aided Verification (CAV'96)*, pages 428–432. Springer-Verlag, Rutgers University, 1996. LNCS 1102.

[4] R. E. Bryant. Graph-based algorithms for Boolean function manipulation. *IEEE Transactions on Computers*, C-35(8):677–691, August 1986.

[5] D. Chai and A. Kuehlmann. A fast pseudo-Boolean constraint solver. In *Proceedings of the Design Automation Conference*, pages 830–835, Anaheim, CA, June 2003.

[6] P. Chauhan, E. M. Clarke, and D. Kroening. Using SAT based image computation for reachability analysis. In *Technical Report CMU-CS-03-151*, 2003.

[7] M. Davis, G. Logemann, and D. Loveland. A machine program for theorem proving. *Communications of the ACM*, 5:394–397, 1962.

[8] M. Davis and H. Putnam. A computing procedure for quantification theory. *Journal of the Association for Computing Machinery*, 7(3):201–215, July 1960.

[9] E. Goldberg and Y. Novikov. BerkMin: A fast and robust SAT-solver. In *Proceedings of the Conference on Design, Automation and Test in Europe*, pages 142–149, Paris, France, March 2002.

[10] E. Goldberg and Y. Novikov. Verification of proofs of unsatisfiability for CNF formulas. In *Design, Automation and Test in Europe (DATE'03)*, pages 886–891, Munich, Germany, March 2003.

[11] E. Goldberg, M. Prasad, and R. Brayton. Using SAT for combinational equivalence checking. In *Proceedings of the Conference on Design, Automation and Test in Europe*, pages 114–121, June 2001.

[12] O. Grumberg, A. Schuster, and A. Yadgar. Memory efficient all-solutions SAT solver and its application for reachability analysis. In *Proceedings of FMCAD*, Austin, TX, 2004. To appear.

[13] M. K. Iyer, G. Parthasarathy, and K.-T. Cheng. SATORI – a fast sequential SAT engine for circuits. In *Proceedings of the International Conference on Computer-Aided Design*, pages 320–325, San Jose, CA, November 2003.

[14] H. Jin, M. Awedh, and F. Somenzi. CirCUs: A satisfiability solver geared towards bounded model checking. In R. Alur and D. Peled, editors, *Sixteenth Conference on Computer Aided Verification (CAV'04)*. Springer-Verlag, Berlin, July 2004. To appear.

[15] H. Jin and F. Somenzi. CirCUs: A hybrid satisfiability solver. In *International Conference on Theory and Applications of Satisfiability Testing (SAT 2004)*, Vancouver, Canada, May 2004.

[16] H.-J. Kang and I.-C. Park. SAT-based unbounded symbolic model checking. In *Proceedings of the Design Automation Conference*, pages 840–843, Anaheim, CA, June 2003.

[17] D. Kroening, J. Ouaknine, S. A. Seshia, , and O. Strichman. Abstraction-based satisfiability solving of Presburger arithmetic. In *Sixteenth Conference on Computer Aided Verification (CAV'04)*, pages 308–320, July 2004.

[18] A. Kuehlmann, M. K. Ganai, and V. Paruthi. Circuit-based Boolean reasoning. In *Proceedings of the Design Automation Conference*, pages 232–237, Las Vegas, NV, June 2001.

[19] B. Li, M. S. Hsiao, and S. Sheng. A novel SAT all-solutions for efficient preimage computation. In *Proceedings of the Conference on Design, Automation and Test in Europe*, pages 380–384, March 2004.

[20] K. L. McMillan. Applying SAT methods in unbounded symbolic model checking. In E. Brinksma and K. G. Larsen, editors, *Fourteenth Conference on Computer Aided Verification (CAV'02)*, pages 250–264. Springer-Verlag, Berlin, July 2002. LNCS 2404.

[21] K. L. McMillan. Interpolation and SAT-based model checking. In W. A. Hunt, Jr. and F. Somenzi, editors, *Fifteenth Conference on Computer Aided Verification (CAV'03)*, pages 1–13. Springer-Verlag, Berlin, July 2003. LNCS 2725.

[22] M. Moskewicz, C. F. Madigan, Y. Zhao, L. Zhang, and S. Malik. Chaff: Engineering an efficient SAT solver. In *Proceedings of the Design Automation Conference*, pages 530–535, Las Vegas, NV, June 2001.

[23] G. Nam, F. Aloul, K. Sakallah, and R. Rutenbar. A comparative study of two boolean formulations of FPGA detailed routing constaraints. In *IEEE Transactions on Computer-Aided Design of Integrated Circuits*, pages 688–696, June 2004.

[24] K. Ravi and F. Somenzi. Minimal assignments for bounded model checking. In *International Conference on Tools and Algorithms for Construction and Analysis of Systems (TACAS'04)*, pages 31–45, Barcelona, Spain, March-April 2004. LNCS 2988.

[25] J. P. M. Silva and K. A. Sakallah. Grasp—a new search algorithm for satisfiability. In *Proceedings of the International Conference on Computer-Aided Design*, pages 220–227, San Jose, CA, November 1996.

[26] URL: http://vlsi.colorado.edu/~vis.

[27] H. Zhang. SATO: An efficient propositional prover. In *Proceedings of the International Conference on Automated Deduction*, pages 272–275, July 1997. LNAI 1249.

[28] L. Zhang, C. Madigan, M. Moskewicz, and S. Malik. Efficient conflict driven learning in Boolean satisfiability solver. In *Proceedings of the International Conference on Computer-Aided Design*, pages 279–285, San Jose, CA, November 2001.

[29] L. Zhang and S. Malik. Validating SAT solvers using an independent resolution-based checker: Practical implementations and other applications. In *Design, Automation and Test in Europe (DATE'03)*, pages 880–885, Munich, Germany, March 2003.

Bounded Validity Checking of Interval Duration Logic

Babita Sharma[1], Paritosh. K. Pandya[2], and Supratik Chakraborty[1]

[1] Indian Institute of Technology, Bombay, India
babita@cfdvs.iitb.ac.in, supratik@cse.iitb.ac.in
[2] Tata Institute of Fundamental Research, India
pandya@tifr.res.in

Abstract. A rich dense-time logic, called Interval Duration Logic (IDL), is useful for specifying quantitative properties of timed systems. The logic is undecidable in general. However, several approaches can be used for checking validity (and model checking) of IDL formulae in practice. In this paper, we propose bounded validity checking of IDL formulae by polynomially reducing this to checking unsatisfiability of *lin-sat* formulae. We implement this technique and give performance results obtained by checking the unsatisfiability of the resulting *lin-sat* formulae using the ICS solver. We also perform experimental comparisons of several approaches for checking validity of IDL formulae, including (a) digitization followed by automata-theoretic analysis, (b) digitization followed by pure propositional SAT solving, and (c) *lin-sat* solving as proposed in this paper. Our experiments use a rich set of examples drawn from the Duration Calculus literature.

1 Introduction

Interval Duration Logic (IDL)[16] is a highly expressive logic for specifying properties of real-time systems. It is a variant of Duration Calculus (DC) [20] with finite *timed state sequences* as its models. IDL, like DC, is a dense-time interval temporal logic, incorporating the notion of cumulative amount of time (duration) for which a condition holds in a given time interval. Because of this, IDL is well-suited for describing complex properties of real-time systems, including scheduling and planning constraints. A large number of case studies have exemplified the expressive power of the logic [19].

It has been shown that because of its rich expressive power, the problem of satisfiability (validity) checking of IDL (and DC) formulae is undecidable [16]. In spite of this, for reasons of practical applicability, there has been interest in developing tools and techniques for validity and model checking of various duration logics [5, 8, 16]. One approach has been to work with discrete-time versions of duration calculus [14, 9, 18]. More recently, a digitization approach which approximates dense-time validity of IDL by discrete-time validity has been proposed [6]. But model checking of dense-time interval logics like DC and IDL remains a challenging problem. So far, there have been no tools available for model checking

N. Halbwachs and L. Zuck (Eds.): TACAS 2005, LNCS 3440, pp. 301–316, 2005.
© Springer-Verlag Berlin Heidelberg 2005

these logics and very few experimental results profile the proposed techniques. In this paper, we address both these issues.

In recent years, bounded model checking (BMC) [3] has emerged as a practically useful method, especially for detecting shallow bugs in complex systems. BMC exhaustively explores the system behaviour up to a bounded depth k in the state transition graph. Typically such exploration is reduced to solving satisfiability of a propositional formula. Inspired by the success of the BMC approach, we apply it to the problem of validity checking of IDL formulae. We consider the question 'Does there exist a model (timed state sequence) of length k that violates a given IDL formula?' or 'Is the given IDL formula k-valid?'. As in the BMC approach, we reduce the problem of checking k-bounded validity of an IDL formula to checking unsatisfiability of a *lin-sat* formula, which is a Boolean combination of propositional variables and mathematical constraints over real variables. We then use 'Integrated Canonizer and Solver (ICS)[1]' [7], a SAT-based solver to check the *lin-sat* formula for satisfiability.

As our primary contribution, we propose an efficient encoding of k-validity of IDL into unsatisfiability of *lin-sat*. Our encoding is is linear in the size of the IDL formula and cubic in k. Since the unsatisfiability of *lin-sat* is in Co-NP, this provides a Co-NP algorithm for deciding k-validity of IDL formula. We also give experimental evidence of the effectiveness of the proposed technique.

It must be noted that Fränzle [9] was the first to suggest bounded validity checking of a discrete-time duration calculus without timing constraints by polynomial-sized reduction to propositional SAT solving. In this paper, we extend Fränzle's techniques to deal with discrete and dense-time duration constructs in an efficient manner.

As our second contribution, we implement some alternative methods for checking the validity of IDL formulae. These are based on the digitization technique of Chakravorty and Pandya [6] combined with automata-theoretic analysis [14], as well as propositional SAT solving [9]. We provide experimental results on the relative performance of these techniques on several problems drawn from the Duration Calculus literature.

The remainder of this paper is organized as follows. In Section 2, we recall from [16] the basics of Interval Duration Logic. In Section 3, we present a polynomial-time reduction of the bounded validity checking problem for IDL formulae to the problem of checking unsatisfiability of *lin-sat* formulae, and prove the correctness of our reduction. In Section 4, we compare our approach with digitization based approaches and give experimental results. We end the paper with some conclusions and a discussion of related work in Section 5.

2   Interval Duration Logic: An Overview

Let *Pvar* be the set of propositional variables. The set of states, Σ, is given by 2^{Pvar}, *i.e.*, the set of all subsets of *Pvar*. Let $\mathbb{R}$ denote the set of real numbers and $\mathbb{R}^0$ denote the set of non-negative real numbers.

---

[1] ICS is developed by SRI International.

Definition 1. *A* **timed state sequence** *over Pvar is a pair* $\theta = (\sigma, \tau)$, *where* $\sigma = s_0\, s_1\, \ldots\, s_{n-1}$ *is a finite non-empty sequence of states with* $s_i \in 2^{Pvar}$, *and* $\tau = t_0\, t_1\, \ldots\, t_{n-1}$ *is a finite non-decreasing sequence of time-stamps such that* $t_i \in \mathbb{R}^0$ *with* $t_0 = 0$.

A timed state sequence gives a sampled view of timed behaviour. It is assumed that the system evolves by discrete transitions. Let $dom(\theta) = \{0, \ldots, n-1\}$ be the set of positions within the sequence θ. Let the length, n, of θ be denoted by $\#\theta$. Let $\theta[i]$ denote the timed state at the ith position of θ. Element s_i denotes the ith state and t_i gives the time at which this state is entered. Thus the system remains in state s_i for the duration $[t_i, t_{i+1})$, which includes t_i but excludes t_{i+1}. The set of intervals in θ is given by $Intv(\theta) = \{[b, e] \in dom(\theta)^2 \mid b \leq e\}$, where each interval $[b, e]$ identifies a sub-sequence of θ between positions b and e. We use the notation $\theta, i \models P$ to denote that proposition P evaluates to true at state $\theta[i]$.

Syntax of IDL.[2] Let Π be a set of propositions over a finite set of propositional variables $Pvar$ and let c range over non-negative integer constants. The set of formulae of IDL is inductively defined as follows:

- $\eta \bowtie c$ and $\ell \bowtie c$ are formulae, where $\bowtie \in \{<, =, >, \geq, \leq\}$.
- If $P \in \Pi$ then $\lceil P \rceil^0$, $\lceil\lceil P \rceil\rceil$, $\sum P \bowtie c$, and $\int P \bowtie c$ are formulae.
- If D, D_1 and D_2 are formulae, then so are $D_1 {}^\frown D_2$, $D_1 \wedge D_2$ and $\neg D$.

Semantics of IDL. The satisfaction of an IDL formula D for behaviour θ and interval $[b, e] \in Intv(\theta)$ is denoted as $\theta, [b, e] \models D$, and is defined as follows.

$$\theta, [b, e] \models \lceil P \rceil^0 \quad \text{iff} \quad b = e \text{ and } \theta, b \models P$$
$$\theta, [b, e] \models \lceil\lceil P \rceil\rceil \quad \text{iff} \quad b < e \text{ and } \theta, i \models P \text{ for all } i \text{ such that } b \leq i < e$$
$$\theta, [b, e] \models \neg D \quad \text{iff} \quad \theta, [b, e] \not\models D$$
$$\theta, [b, e] \models D_1 \wedge D_2 \quad \text{iff} \quad \theta, [b, e] \models D_1 \text{ and } \theta, [b, e] \models D_2$$
$$\theta, [b, e] \models D_1 {}^\frown D_2 \quad \text{iff} \quad \exists m : b \leq m \leq e : \theta, [b, m] \models D_1 \text{ and } \theta, [m, e] \models D_2$$

Entities η, ℓ, $\sum P$ and $\int P$ are called *measurements*. The entity η, called the *step length*, denotes the number of steps within a given interval, while the *time length* ℓ gives the amount of real-time spanned by a given interval. $\sum P$, called the *step count*, denotes the number of states for which proposition P is true within the interval $[b, e)$. *Duration* $\int P$ gives the amount of real-time for which proposition P holds in the given interval. η and $\sum P$ are called *discrete measurements*, while ℓ and $\int P$ are called *dense measurements*. The value of a measurement term t in a timed state sequence θ and an interval $[b, e]$, denoted as $eval(t, \theta, [b, e])$, is defined as follows:

- $eval(\eta, \theta, [b, e]) = e - b$
- $eval(\ell, \theta, [b, e]) = t_e - t_b$
- $eval(\sum P, \theta, [b, e]) = \displaystyle\sum_{i=b}^{e-1} \begin{cases} 1 & if \quad \theta, i \models P \\ 0 & otherwise \end{cases}$

---

[2] Here we consider the version of IDL without quantification $\exists p.D$.

$$- \quad eval(\textstyle\int P, \theta, [b, e]) = \sum_{i=b}^{e-1} \begin{cases} t_{i+1} - t_i & \text{if } \theta, i \models P \\ 0 & \text{otherwise} \end{cases}$$

We say that $\theta, [b, e] \models t \bowtie c$ iff $eval(t, \theta, [b, e]) \bowtie c$.

Derived Operators. Let $\Diamond D \stackrel{\text{def}}{=} true \frown D \frown true$ and $\Box D \stackrel{\text{def}}{=} \neg \Diamond \neg D$. Then, $\Diamond D$ holds for an interval $[b, e]$ if for some sub-interval of $[b, e]$, the formula D holds. Similarly, $\Box D$ holds for $[b, e]$ if for all sub-intervals of $[b, e]$, the formula D is true.

Definition 2 (k-Bounded Validity of IDL Formulae). *Let* $D \in IDL$, *and let* $k \in \mathbb{N}$ *be a natural number. We define the following terminology.*

- **Validity in behaviour:** $\theta \models D$ iff $\theta, [0, \#\theta - 1] \models D$
- **Validity:** $\models D$ iff $\theta \models D$ *for all* θ
- **k-satisfiability:** $sat_k(D)$ iff $\theta \models D$ *for some* θ *such that* $\#\theta = k + 1$
- **k-validity:** $\models_k D$ iff $\theta \models D$ *for all* θ *such that* $\#\theta = k + 1$ □

Example 1 (Gas Burner). Consider a simplified version of the gas burner problem from [21]. Formula $des1 \stackrel{\text{def}}{=} \Box(\lceil\lceil Leak \rceil\rceil \Rightarrow \ell \leq maxleak)$ states that any occurrence of gas leakage, *Leak*, will be stopped (by turning off *Gas* in full design) within $maxleak$ seconds. Formula $des2 \stackrel{\text{def}}{=} \Box((\lceil\lceil Leak \rceil\rceil \frown \lceil\lceil \neg Leak \rceil\rceil \frown \lceil Leak \rceil^0) \Rightarrow \ell \geq minsep)$ states that between two occurrences of *Leak* there will be at least $minsep$ seconds. In its full version, this is achieved by keeping *Gas* off for at least $minsep$ time. The safety requirement here is that "gas must never leak for more than *leakbound* seconds in any period of at most *winlen* seconds". This is captured by the formula $concl \stackrel{\text{def}}{=} \Box(\ell \leq winlen \Rightarrow \textstyle\int Leak \leq leakbound)$. To establish the safety requirement, we must prove the validity of the following IDL formula for the given values of constants $maxleak$, $minsep$, $winlen$ and $leakbound$:

$$G(maxleak, minsep, winlen, leakbound) \stackrel{\text{def}}{=} des1 \wedge des2 \Rightarrow concl \qquad \Box$$

2.1   Sub-logics and Decidability

Let DDC be the subset of IDL where dense-time measurement constructs of the form $\ell \bowtie c$ or $\int P \bowtie c$ are not used. Let DDCR be a further subset of DDC where even the discrete-time measurement constructs $\eta \bowtie c$ or $\Sigma P \bowtie c$ are not used. For DDC formulae, the time-stamps τ in behaviour $\theta = (\sigma, \tau)$ do not play any role. We can therefore define $\sigma \models D$. The following theorem establishes the decidability of DDC and DDCR.

Theorem 1. *[14] For every DDC formula D over propositional variables Pvar, we can effectively construct a finite state automaton $A(D)$ over the alphabet 2^{Pvar} such that for all state sequences $\sigma \in (2^{Pvar})^*$, $\sigma \models D$ iff $\sigma \in L(A(D))$. Hence, satisfiability (validity) checking of DDC and DDCR formulae are decidable, and can be reduced to checking the existence of an accepting (rejecting) path in $A(D)$.*   □

A tool, called DCVALID, based on the above automata-theoretic decision procedure for DDC has been implemented earlier, and has been found to be effective on many significant examples [14]. Although the lower bound on the size of automaton $A(D)$ is non-elementary in the worst-case, such blowup is rarely observed in practice (see [14]).

If, however, we consider the full dense-time logic IDL, its rich expressive power comes at the cost of decidability.

Theorem 2. *[16] The satisfiability (and hence validity) checking of IDL formulae is undecidable .* □

In spite of this, for practical applicability, there has been interest in developing partial techniques for checking validity of IDL formulae. One such partial technique was the digitization approach of Chakravorty and Pandya [6]. In the next section, we present a new approach to deciding k-validity of IDL formulae.

3   From IDL to *lin-sat*

As mentioned earlier, a *lin-sat* formula is a Boolean combination of propositional variables and linear constraints over real variables. Each linear constraint is restricted to be in one of the forms: (a) $(x - y) \bowtie c$, (b) $\sum_{x_i \in V} x_i \bowtie c$ or (c) $(x - y) = z$, where x, x_i, y and z are real variables, V is a finite set of real variables, c is an integer constant and $\bowtie \in \{<, >, \geq, \leq, =\}$. For example, $(x_1 + x_3) \leq 3 \wedge (b_2 \vee (x_2 - x_3 = x_1))$ is a *lin-sat* formula.

Let the sets of propositional and real variables appearing in a *lin-sat* formula ϕ be denoted by *Pvar* and *Rvar* respectively. An *interpretation* $\mathcal{I}$ consists of (i) a mapping of variables in *Pvar* to {True, False} and (ii) a mapping of variables in *Rvar* to $\mathbb{R}$. A *lin-sat* formula ϕ is *satisfiable* if there exists an *interpretation* for which ϕ evaluates to True. A *lin-sat* formula is *valid* if it is satisfiable for all interpretations. We denote this by $\models_{linsat} \phi$.

Theorem 3. *The satisfiability problem for lin-sat is NP-complete. Hence, validity (unsatisfiability) checking for lin-sat is co-NP-complete.*

Proof: Given a *lin-sat* formula ϕ, let $Constr(\phi)$ denote the set of syntactically distinct linear constraints in ϕ. For each constraint $\chi_i \in Constr(\phi)$, let v_{χ_i} be a propositional variable distinct from all variables in *Pvar*. The resulting set of variables, $\{v_{\chi_i} \mid \chi_i \in Constr(\phi)\}$, is denoted *Auxvar*. Let $\phi^a = \phi[v_{\chi_i}/\chi_i]$ be the propositional formula obtained by replacing each linear constraint χ_i in the formula ϕ by v_{χ_i}. Let μ be an assignment of truth values to variables in *Pvar* $\cup$ *Auxvar*. We denote by $LinSys(\mu)$ the set $\{\chi_i \mid \mu(v_{\chi_i}) = \text{True}\} \cup \{\neg \chi_j \mid \mu(v_{\chi_j}) = \text{False}\}$. We call μ consistent if all constraints in $LinSys(\mu)$ are simultaneously satisfiable. It is straightforward to see that ϕ is satisfiable if and only if there is a consistent μ such that $\mu \models \phi^a$. Thus, we can non-deterministically guess an assignment μ, and then verify in polynomial-time that it is consistent and satisfies ϕ^a. Since the size of ϕ^a, henceforth denoted as $|\phi^a|$, is linear in $|\phi|$, checking if $\mu \models \phi^a$ requires time linear in $|\phi|$. The check for consistency of μ reduces to determining the feasibility of the set, $LinSys(\mu)$, of linear constraints. Since the size of $LinSys(\mu)$ is linear in $|\phi|$, this check also requires time polynomial (grows as the fifth power) in $|\phi|$ [12]. Thus, satisfiability for *lin-sat* is in NP. To see that it is also NP-hard, we note that an arbitrary instance of 3-SAT is also an instance of satisfiability of *lin-sat*.

3.1   An Encoding Scheme

Given an IDL formula D and an integer bound $k \geq 0$, we now describe a technique to construct a *lin-sat* formula, $compile(D, k)$, such that D is k-valid *if and only if* $compile(D, k)$ is an unsatisfiable *lin-sat* formula.

We first define the sets of variables used in $compile(D, k)$, which are different from those used in D. (i) Let $Pvar$ be the set of propositional variables of D. Let $LSatPvar(k) = \{x_0, \ldots, x_k \mid x \in Pvar\}$, where x_i represents the value of x in state $\theta[i]$. Moreover, for a proposition P over $Pvar$, let P_i be obtained by replacing each x by x_i in P. Then, P_i represents the value of P in state $\theta[i]$. (ii) Let $LSatTvar(k) = \{t_0, \ldots, t_k\}$, where the t_i are fresh real variables representing time-stamps in the timed state sequence θ. (iii) For every proposition P that occurs in a measurement sub-formula, *i.e.*, $\int P \bowtie c$ and/or $\Sigma P \bowtie m$, we introduce k real variables, dur_P_i and/or c_Q_i for i in $0 \ldots (k-1)$. We call this set of variables as $LSatMvar(D, k)$.

In order to correctly capture the semantics of IDL in *lin-sat*, we need to introduce some constraints on the variables defined above. Specifically, time must not flow backward. Moreover, variables dur_P_i and c_P_i are intended to represent the values of $\int P$ and ΣQ in the interval $[i, i+1]$. Thus, we have the following invariants.

$$INVT(k) \stackrel{\text{def}}{=} (t_0 = 0) \wedge \bigwedge_{i=0}^{k-1} (t_i \leq t_{i+1})$$

$$INVD(k) \stackrel{\text{def}}{=} \bigwedge_{i=0}^{k-1} \left(\bigwedge_{c\_Q_i \in LSatMvar(D,k)} (Q_i \wedge (c\_Q_i = 1)) \vee (\neg Q_i \wedge (c\_Q_i = 0)) \right) \wedge$$

$$\bigwedge_{i=0}^{k-1} \left(\bigwedge_{dur\_P_i \in LSatMvar(D,k)} (P_i \wedge (dur\_P_i = t_{i+1} - t_i)) \vee (\neg P_i \wedge (dur\_P_i = 0)) \right)$$

$$FINV(k) \stackrel{\text{def}}{=} INVT(k) \wedge INVD(k)$$

Given an IDL formula D and an integer $k \geq 0$, we define the syntactic encoding of k-validity of D as unsatisfiability of the following *lin-sat* formula.

$$compile(D, k) \stackrel{\text{def}}{=} FINV(k) \wedge \neg\beta^{[0,k]}(D).$$

Here, $\beta^{[0,k]}(D)$ is computed recursively using the translation scheme shown in Table 1. In this table, column 2 gives an IDL sub-formula, D', and column 3 gives its encoding for subinterval $[b, e]$, where $0 \leq b \leq e \leq k$. For notational convenience, we denote this encoding as $\beta^{[b,e]}(D')$.

Table 1. Translation of IDL to *lin-sat*

No.	IDL : D'	*lin-sat*: $\beta^{[b,e]}(D')$
1	$\lceil P \rceil^0$	$P_b \wedge (b = e)$
2	$\lceil P \rceil$	$\bigwedge_{i=b}^{e-1} P_i \wedge (e > b)$
3	$\eta \bowtie m$	$(e - b) \bowtie m$
4	$\ell \bowtie m$	$(t_e - t_b) \bowtie m$
5	$\Sigma P \bowtie m$	$\sum_{i=b}^{e-1} c\_P_i \bowtie m$
6	$\int P \bowtie m$	$\sum_{i=b}^{e-1} dur\_P_i \bowtie m$
7	$\neg D_1$	$\neg(\beta^{[b,e]}(D_1))$
8	$D_1 \wedge D_2$	$\beta^{[b,e]}(D_1) \quad \wedge \quad \beta^{[b,e]}(D_2)$
9	$D_1 \frown D_2$	$\bigvee_{j=b}^{e}\left[(\beta^{[b,j]}(D_1)) \quad \wedge \quad (\beta^{[j,e]}(D_2)) \right]$

3.2 Proof Outline for Correctness of *lin-sat* Reduction

In this Section, we will use $\models_{lin}$ for satisfaction in *lin-sat* to distinguish it from $\models$ which denotes satisfaction in IDL. Given a timed state sequence θ of length $k + 1$ and an IDL formula D, we restrict ourselves to *lin-sat* formulae over variables in $LSatPvar(k) \cup LSatTvar(k) \cup LSatMvar(D, k)$. We define $\mathcal{I}_\theta$ as an interpretation of *lin-sat* in which each propositional variable x_i in $LSatPvar(k)$ is assigned the value of x in state $\theta[i]$, and each t_i in $LSatTvar(k)$ is assigned the time-stamp τ_i of state $\theta[i]$. In addition, each variable c_P_i in $LSatMvar(D, k)$ is assigned 1 if $\theta, i \models P$, and is assigned 0 otherwise. Similarly, each variable dur_Q_i in $LSatMvar(D, k)$ is assigned $(\tau_{i+1} - \tau_i)$ if $\theta, i \models Q$, and is assigned 0 otherwise. Thus, by definition, $\mathcal{I}_\theta \models_{lin} FINV(k)$.

Similarly, given an interpretation $\mathcal{I}$ of *lin-sat* that satisfies $FINV(k)$, we define $\theta_\mathcal{I}$ as a timed state sequence in which (i) the value of propositional variable x in state $\theta_\mathcal{I}[i]$ is the same as that of x_i in $\mathcal{I}$, and (ii) the time-stamp of $\theta_\mathcal{I}[i]$ is equal to the value of t_i in $\mathcal{I}$, for all i in 0 through k.

Lemma 1. *There is a bijection between the set of timed state sequences, θ, of length $k + 1$ and the set of interpretations, $\mathcal{I}$, of lin-sat that satisfy $FINV(k)$.*

The proof for the lemma follows from the fact that the definitions of $\mathcal{I}_\theta$ and $\theta_\mathcal{I}$ are injections. We will denote the bijective pair as $(\theta, \mathcal{I}_\theta)$ or $(\mathcal{I}, \theta_\mathcal{I})$, as convenient.

Theorem 4. *Let $D \in IDL$ and θ be a timed state sequence with $\#\theta = k + 1$. For all $[b, e] \in Intv(\theta)$ we have $\theta, [b, e] \models D$ iff $\mathcal{I}_\theta \models_{lin} \beta^{[b,e]}(D)$.*

Proof: The proof is by induction on the structure of D.

Base Cases: We prove only one case, that of $D = \ell \bowtie m$. The proof for the other cases, where D is $\lceil P \rceil^0$, $\lceil\lceil P \rceil\rceil$, $\eta \bowtie c$, $\sum P \bowtie c$ or $\int P \bowtie c$ are omitted for lack of space. The full proof can be found in [17].

- Let $D = \ell \bowtie m$. Then,

$\theta, [b, e] \models \ell \bowtie m$
iff $\tau_e - \tau_b \bowtie m$ ... from IDL semantics
iff $\mathcal{I}_\theta \models_{lin}$ $((t_e - t_b) \bowtie m)$ ... as $\mathcal{I}_\theta(t_b) = \tau_b$ and $\mathcal{I}_\theta(t_e) = \tau_e$.
iff $\mathcal{I}_\theta \models_{lin}$ $\beta^{[b,e]}(D)$ ... from Table 1

Induction Step: We prove only one case, that of $D = D_1 \frown D_2$. The proof for the other cases where D is $D_1 \wedge D_2$ or $\neg D_1$ are similar and are omitted for lack of space.

- Let $D = D_1 \frown D_2$. Then,

$\theta, [b, e] \models D_1 \frown D_2$
iff   ... from IDL semantics
        for some $m : b \leq m \leq e$, $\theta, [b, m] \models D_1$ and $\theta, [m, e] \models D_2$
iff   ... by the induction hypothesis
        for some $m : b \leq m \leq e$, $\mathcal{I}_\theta \models_{lin}$ $(\beta^{[b,m]}(D_1))$ and $\mathcal{I}_\theta \models_{lin}$ $(\beta^{[m,e]}(D_2))$
iff   ... from semantics of $\vee$
        $\mathcal{I}_\theta \models_{lin}$ $\bigvee_{m=b}^{e}$ $[(\beta^{[b,m]}(D_1))$ $\wedge$ $(\beta^{[m,e]}(D_2))]$
iff   ... from Table 1
        $\mathcal{I}_\theta \models_{lin}$ $\beta^{[b,e]}(D)$ $\square$

Corollary 1. $\models_k D$ **iff** $compile(D, k)$ *is unsatisfiable for all interpretations in lin-sat. Moreover,* $\mathcal{I} \models compile(D, k)$ **implies** $\theta_\mathcal{I} \not\models D$. $\square$

3.3   Optimizing the Encoding

In the above encoding scheme, the same *lin-sat* sub-formula may be replicated at several places when generating $\beta^{[0,k]}(D)$ due to repeated evaluation of $\beta^{[i,j]}(D')$. This can lead to an exponential blowup in the size of the output formula (see [17,9] for concrete instances). In order to address this problem, following Fränzle [9], we introduce auxiliary variables for denoting potentially common sub-formulae.

Let $SubForm(D)$ be the set of sub-formulae of D. Then, $LSatAux(D, k) = \{\gamma_\psi^{[b,e]} \mid 0 \leq b \leq e \leq k, \psi \in SubForm(D)\}$ gives the set of auxiliary variables used for the optimized encoding. We now reuse the notation of Table 1, and modify column 3 of rows numbered 7, 8 and 9 in this table by replacing all occurrences of $\beta^{[b,e]}(D_i)$ with $\gamma_{D_i}^{[b,e]}$. Let the new encoding scheme, represented by the modified table, be called $\delta^{[b,e]}(D)$. Given an IDL formula D and an integer $k > 0$, the optimized *lin-sat* encoding can now be obtained as

$$compile\_opt(D, k) \stackrel{\text{def}}{=} FINV(k) \wedge \neg \gamma_D^{[0,k]} \wedge$$
$$\bigwedge_{\gamma_\psi^{[b,e]} \in LSatAux(D,k)} (\gamma_\psi^{[b,e]} \Leftrightarrow \delta^{[b,e]}(\psi)).$$

It is straightforward to see that $compile\_opt(D, k)$ is equisatisfiable to the formula $compile(D, k)$, and therefore the correctness proof of Section 3.2 applies here as well. The number of auxiliary variables in $LSatAux(D, k)$ is $O(k^2.|D|)$, and the worst-case size of $\delta^{[b,e]}(\psi)$ is $O(k)$ (from rows 2, 5, 6 and 9 of Table 1). Also, the size $|FINV(k)|$ is $|INVT(k)|+|INVD(k)|+1$. From the definitions of these invariants, $|INVT(k)|$ is $O(k)$ and $|INVD(k)|$ is $O(k.|D|)$. Thus, the size of $compile\_opt(D, k)$ is $O(k^3.|D|)$.

As a further optimization, we note that auxiliary variables need not be introduced for every sub-formula and sub-interval combination. Therefore, we have implemented our encoding tool, *idl2ics*, as a two-pass translator. In the first pass, we identify all sub-formulae and sub-interval combinations that repeat in the encoding scheme, and introduce auxiliary variables only for these combinations. This effectively reduces the size of $LSatAux(D, k)$. In the second pass, the translator uses these auxiliary variables to generate $compile\_opt(D, k)$.

3.4   A Comparison of IDL Validity Checking Approaches

In this section, we give a comparative overview of several approaches proposed in the literature for checking (bounded) validity of IDL formulae.

Approach A: This is the bounded validity checking approach proposed in Corollary 1 of this paper. Checking k-validity of an IDL formula D is polynomially reduced to checking unsatisfiability of the *lin-sat* formula $compile\_opt(D, k)$. The size of $compile\_opt(D, k)$ is at most $O(k^3.|D|)$ where $|D|$ includes the size of binary encoding of integer constants occurring in D. Formula $compile\_opt(D, k)$ can be checked for unsatisfiability using a Co-NP algorithm based on Theorem 3.

Theorem 5. *Using approach A, k-validity checking of IDL formula D is decidable with Co-NP complexity. The complement problem, that of finding a satisfying assignment of $compile\_opt(D, k)$, is solvable by an NP algorithm with input size $O(k^3.|D|)$, i.e. polynomial in both k and $|D|$.* □

Approach B: Chakravorty and Pandya [6] have proposed a *digitization technique* for reducing validity checking of IDL formulae to validity checking of formulae in the discrete-timed logic DDC (see Section 2.1). They have defined a translation $dig : IDL \rightarrow DDC$ such that $\models_{DDC} dig(D)$ implies $\models_{IDL} D$. They have also proposed simple structural tests to identify a subclass $SYNCID \subset IDL$ for which $\models_{DDC} dig(D)$ if and only if $\models_{IDL} D$. The size of $dig(D)$ is $O(|D|)$, and validity of $dig(D)$ can be checked using the automata-theoretic decision procedure implemented in the tool DCVALID [14]. The worst case complexity of validity checking of DDC formulae is non-elementary in the size of the formula.

Theorem 6. *Using approach B, the validity of $D \in SYNCID(\subset IDL)$ is decidable by an algorithm with non-elementary worst-case complexity.* □

Approach C: Recall from Section 2.1 that the subset $DDCR$ of DDC consists of formulae without any quantitative measurements. It has been shown by earlier researchers [14, 8, 19] that every formula $D \in DDC$ can be effectively transformed to an equivalent formula $untime(D) \in DDCR$. The worst-case size of $untime(D)$ is $O(2^{|D|})$, where $|D|$ includes the size of binary encoding of constants occurring in D. In approach C, a formula $D \in SYNCID(\subset IDL)$ is first digitized to a validity preserving formula $dig(D) \in DDC$. This is then reduced to an equivalent DDCR formula, $untime(dig(D))$, which can be checked for bounded validity. Note that for $D' \in DDCR$, the translation $compile\_opt(D', m)$ gives a purely propositional formula whose unsatisfiability can be established by *propositional SAT-solving*. The size of the propositional formula $compile\_opt(untime(dig(D)), m)$ is $O(m^3.|untime(dig(D))|)$, which is $O(m^3.2^{|D|})$ in the worst-case. Fränzle [9] first suggested checking m-validity of DDC formulae using propositional SAT solving. Hence, approach C is an extension of his work.

In the context of bounded validity checking, the effect of digitization on the length of counter-models is an important factor to consider. Let D be digitizable, i.e. $D \in SYNCID$. Chakravorty and Pandya [6] have shown that every timed state sequence θ of logic IDL can be represented by a state sequence $\hat{\theta}$ of DDC such that $\theta \models_{IDL} D$ iff $\hat{\theta} \models_{DDC} dig(D)$. The encoding of time in $\hat{\theta}$ is achieved by having exactly one unit of time elapse between successive states in the sequence. In contrast, the elapse of an arbitrary length of time between successive states can be represented in the timed state sequence θ by using appropriate time-stamps. Thus, a discretized (counter-)model $\hat{\theta}$ is typically much longer than the corresponding time-stamped (counter-)model θ. Let k be the length of the shortest (counter-)model of D and let k' be the length of shortest (counter-)model of $dig(D)$. While it is difficult to estimate k' directly from k and D, it is easy to see that $k \leq k'$. This follows from the fact that the bijective mapping $\theta \rightarrow \hat{\theta}$ does not reduce the length of the model [6]. We will present experimental results comparing k and k' on several benchmark problems later in the paper.

Theorem 7. *Using approach C, k-validity of $D \in SYNCID(\subset IDL)$ is decidable with Co-NEXP complexity. The complement problem, that of finding a satisfying assignment of $compile\_opt(untime(dig(D)), k')$ is solvable by an NP algorithm with input size $O(k'^3.2^{|D|})$. i.e., polynomial in k' (with $k' \geq k$) and **exponential** in $|D|$.*   □

4   Implementation and Experimental Results

The three approaches outlined in the previous section have widely differing theoretical complexities. Moreover, each of them gives a partial solution to the problem of checking whether an IDL formula D is valid. Hence, an experimental evaluation of their effectiveness and efficiency is needed.

Implementation: For realizing approach A, we have implemented a translator, *idl2ics*, from IDL to *lin-sat*, giving the formula $compile\_opt(D, k)$. The resulting *lin-sat* formula is checked for unsatisfiability using the ICS solver [7]. Using Corollary 1, if a satisfying assignment is found by ICS, a counter-example for the original IDL formula is obtained in an encoded form. If the *lin-sat* formula is found to be unsatisfiable, the original IDL formula is declared k-valid. We have also conducted preliminary experiments with other solvers like UCLID and CVClite for checking unsatisfiability of *lin-sat* formulae. However, ICS significantly outperformed both CVClite and UCLID for our benchmarks [17]. Hence our detailed experiments were conducted with the ICS solver.

For implementing digitization-based approaches B and C, we have developed a translator, *idl2ddc*, that takes a formula $D \in IDL$ and returns $dig(D)$ along with an indication of whether $D \in SYNCID$. In approach B, the formula $dig(D)$ is checked for validity using the DCVALID tool. In approach C, we further translate $dig(D)$ to *untime*$(dig(D))$ using a translator, *ddc2ddcr*, that transforms a formula $D \in SYNCID$ to a validity-preserving formula *untime*$(D) \in DDCR$. The formula *untime*$(dig(D))$ is then checked for bounded validity by translating it using *idl2ics* with a suitable bound k' for the model length. The resulting propositional formula is then checked for unsatisfiability using the ICS solver.

We draw our set of benchmarks from the Duration Calculus literature. We refer the reader to [11, 17] for the detailed IDL specification of each problem. Each problem was formulated such that the IDL formula is in $SYNCID$. Owing to space limitations, we simply list the formula name for each problem here along with a list of its parameters (time constants) below. In each case, the aim is to check the validity of the IDL specification for some given values of time constants.

1. G($maxleak, minsep, winlen, leakbound$) denotes a **gas burner** specification [21], given earlier as Example 1.
2. M($\delta, \omega, \epsilon, \zeta, \kappa$) denotes a **minepump controller** specification [16, 13].
3. L(t_s, t_0, t_{max}, t_m) denotes a **lift controller** specification [4, 17].
4. J24 and J44 denote **job-shop scheduling** problems on 4 machines with 2 and 4 jobs respectively [17].

Experimental Results: Table 2 gives our experimental results comparing the performance of the three approaches. Here, "CE len" denotes the length of the smallest counter-example found by the various approaches. In case the formula is valid (as detected by approach B), we use the entry V for "CE len". For such formulae, we do not apply approaches A and C, since these bounded validity checking techniques are useful only for invalid formulae. The corresponding rows in Table 2 are therefore marked "Valid - BVC Not Applied". The various columns under each approach show the translation times and the time taken to check validity (unsatisfiability) of the resulting formulae using ICS or DCVALID. In Approach B, a "↓" entry denotes an abort due to the BDD-nodes for the automata representation exceeding a fixed threshold. An entry >26h denotes that the corresponding computation was aborted after 26 hours since it did not terminate in that time. A "-" entry denotes non-applicability due to the failure of the preceding stage. Counter-example generation is not applicable to valid formulae and this is denoted by an 'NA" entry. All our experiments were performed on a 1 GHz i686 PC with 1GB RAM running RedHat Linux 7.3.

Note on DCVALID: In approach B above, the validity of $dig(D)$ is checked using the tool DCVALID [14]. In Table 2, column 3 under approach B gives the time taken

Table 2. Comparative Performance of IDL Validity Checking Approaches

Example	Approach A			Approach C			Approach B				
	CE len	idl2*lin-sat* +ICS time (secs)		CE len	idl2ddcr + ddcr2sat + ICS time(secs)			CE len	idl2ddc + Dcvalid time(secs)	OPT-CTLDC time(secs)		
										T	R	C
M(2,12,5,20,2)	7	0.01	2.28	-	0.01	>26h	-	30	0.01	39.62	1.76	2.99	5m35
M(20,120,50,100,20)	7	0.02	2.30	-	0.06	>24h	-	-	0.01	↓	↓	-	-
M(3,25,5,27,5)	Valid - BVC not applicable							V	0.01	2m	2.08	1.52	NA
M(4,30,5,35,7)	Valid - BVC not applicable							V	0.01	↓	2.48	1.77	NA
G(1,2,11,3)	7	0.1	0.52	8	0.0	33.87	25.58	8	0.0	18.24	0.37	0.08	0.15
G(1,2,15,4)	9	0.0	4.41	10	0.1	1m17	16m34	10	0.0	↓	0.43	0.11	0.20
G(10,5,50,30)	7	0.01	1.00	-	0.02	>24h	-	35	0.01	↓	3.82	2.03	2.81
G(15,10,80,35)	5	0.0	0.22	-	0.0	>24h	-	39	0.01	↓	35.07	20.75	28.49
G(20,10,100,50)	5	0.0	0.22	-	0.0	>24h	-	-	0.01	↓	↓	-	-
G(20,10,70,45)	5	0.0	0.21	-	0.0	>24h	-	-	0.01	↓	↓	-	-
G(1,4,12,4)	Valid - BVC not applicable							V	0.0	↓	0.43	0.11	NA
L(10,3,5,10)	2	0.01	0.09	13	0.02	0.19	231m	-	0.01	↓	9.9	>1h	-
L(100,30,50,70)	3	0.02	0.12	-	0.08	>24h	-	-	0.0	↓	↓	-	-
J24	7*	0.01	0.30	-	0.02	>19h	-	33	0.0	10.01	1.29	8.44	3m18
J44	10*	0.05	259m	-	0.01	>24h	-	-	0.0	↓	2.95	1m4	>9h

Table 3. Growth of Computation time (in seconds) with k in k-Validity Checking

k	Mine1	Mine2	Gas1	Gas2	Gas3	Gas4	Gas5	Lift1	Lift2	Job24	Job44
1	0.10	0.08	0.09	0.09	0.09	0.09	0.08	0.08	0.09	0.09	0.09
2	0.10	0.10	0.08	4.73	0.08	0.09	0.09	**0.09**	0.10	0.09	0.10
3	0.17	0.16	0.07	4.73	0.12	0.12	0.13	0.12	**0.12**	0.09	0.12
4	0.32	0.29	0.08	4.74	0.18	0.16	0.17	0.15	0.17	0.12	0.16
5	0.81	0.58	0.08	4.79	0.33	**0.22**	**0.22**	-	0.23	0.20	0.26
6	1.31	1.07	0.67	4.67	0.71	0.25	0.25	-	-	0.48	0.69
7	**2.28**	**2.30**	**0.52**	1.68	**1.00**	0.30	0.29	-	-	**0.3**	2.96
8	6.47	4.96	0.65	4.43	0.77	-	-	-	-	0.28	15.8
9	10.02	9.98	0.75	**4.41**	0.84	-	-	-	-	0.63	8m23.65
10	-	-	-	5.38	-	-	-	-	-	-	**258m66.69**
11	-	-	-	6.47	-	-	-	-	-	-	Aborts
12	-	-	-	-	-	-	-	-	-	-	Aborts
Sum upto CE	5.09	4.58	1.59	29.86	2.51	0.68	0.69	0.17	0.31	1.37	16070.52

by the currently released version (1.4) of DCVALID. However, this tool suffers from several inefficiencies and a more optimized version of the automata-theoretic analysis has been implemented by us. This is denoted by "OPT-CTLDC" and columns 4-6 under approach B of Table 2 give the time taken using OPT-CTLDC. The optimized analysis works in the following steps: (i) it applies a few validity preserving transformations to the QDDC formula, (ii) it translates the formula into a synchronous product of several sub-automata (taking time T), which are output as SMV modules [15], (iii) it performs reachability analysis of the SMV model (taking time R) to detect a counter-example of the original formula, and (iv) it performs a forward search (taking time C) to explicitly generate the shortest counter-example, if one exists. Step (ii) is performed using the tool CTLDC [15, 14] and steps (iii) and (iv) are performed using the tool NuSMV. Details of this optimized approach will be addressed in a future paper. However, it can be seen from Table 2 that the OPT-CTLDC based approach is significantly more efficient vis-a-vis the DCVALID based approach.

Table 3 profiles the time taken by ICS for checking satisfiability of formula $compile\_opt(k, D)$ for different values of k, as used in approach A. The entries in bold correspond to the shortest counter-example. It can be seen that the computation time grows smoothly with the value of k with no significant jump between valid and invalid instances.

5   Conclusions and Discussion

The dense-time logic IDL is undecidable in general (see Theorem 2). Hence, all algorithmic approaches to its validity checking are doomed to be incomplete. In this paper, we have presented a technique for bounded validity checking of IDL by reducing it to checking unsatisfiability of $lin\text{-}sat$. We have compared this technique to methods based on digitization of IDL, both theoretically and experimentally. Our experimental comparison used a variety of well-known examples. In the process, we have created tools [11] which allow such examples to be verified. We now discuss the relative merits of the three approaches (A, B and C) based on the results of Sections 3.4 and 4, and draw some conclusions.

Digitization (used in approaches B and C) reduces the validity of dense-time IDL to the validity of discrete-time DDC. While it is sound for all formulae (i.e. $\models_{DDC} dig(D) \Rightarrow \models_{IDL} D$), it is complete only for the sub-class $SYNCID \subset IDL$. We believe that this is not a crippling restriction in practice (see [6]).

In approach B, the digitized formula is checked for validity using the automata-theoretic decision procedure for DDC (see Theorem 6) implemented in the tool DCVALID as well as in its optimized version, OPT-CTLDC. While the worst-case complexity of this approach is non-elementary, this is rarely observed in practice. As shown in Table 2, this approach succeeds in proving validity/invalidity of several examples when the constants in the formulae are relatively small. Moreover, this approach can establish unbounded validity of a formula, while approaches A and C can only check bounded validity. Unfortunately, for many problem instances with large constants, approach B fails to succeed within reasonable time and space constraints.

Approach A checks k-validity of an IDL formula D by checking unsatisfiability of a $lin\text{-}sat$ formula (see Theorem 5). While it cannot establish the validity of

Table 4. Gas Burner for different constants using Approach A

Constants	CE Len	Translation Time(secs)	ICS Time(secs)
G(5, 7, 69, 28)	11	0.01	18.43
G(10, 15, 137, 53)	11	0.01	18.24
G(210, 534, 4000, 1225)	11	0.01	18.39
G(7400, 9535, 93010, 44341)	11	0.01	18.66

an IDL formula D, like bounded model checking, it is useful for finding shallow counter-examples of invalid IDL formulae. As Table 2 shows, when used in this fashion, approach A is much more effective compared to the other approaches. Counter-examples (timed state sequences) of lengths up to 11 could be found relatively efficiently for almost all our benchmarks. When large constants are present in the formula, approach A clearly outperforms the other approaches. This is because the time taken for *lin-sat* solving is relatively insensitive to the scaling of constants. This is clearly borne out in Table 4. In contrast, digitization-based approaches, like B and C, that model the passage of time in steps of one unit, are very sensitive to scaling of constants.

Approach C combines digitization and SAT solving for bounded validity checking (see Theorem 7). Theoretically, it suffers from an exponential increase in the worst-case complexity over approach A. However, it uses propositional SAT solving instead of the more complicated *lin-sat* solving of approach A. Despite this, our experiments show that in most cases, approach C is not very effective and is outperformed by approaches A and B (OPT-CTLDC). One reason for this is the exponential increase in the size of the propositional SAT formula compared to the *lin-sat* formula of approach A. Another significant factor is the need for using a larger bound, k', for finding the shortest counter-example in approach C, as compared to the bound k used in approach A. The experimental results on the shortest counter-example lengths in Table 2 clearly point to this factor.

While we have presented a technique for bounded validity checking of IDL formulae, this can be easily extended to perform bounded model-checking of timed-automata [1] against an IDL specification D. Following the approach of Audemard et al [1], this can be achieved by checking the unsatisfiability of $compile\_opt(D, k)$ conjuncted with a *lin-sat* formula representing the k-step behaviour of the timed automaton. We propose to extend our tool with this capability in the future.

Comparison with Related Work: Bounded model checking of LTL formulae using SAT solving was proposed by Bierre et al [3] as an efficient method for finding shallow counter examples. Audemard et al [1] extended this to timed systems using MATHSAT solving. Fränzle [9] first proposed bounded validity checking of Discrete Duration Calculus without timing constructs (i.e., the same as DDCR) by a polynomial-sized reduction to propositional SAT solving. When used with the timing constructs ΣP and η, this reduction has an exponential blowup, assuming binary encoding of constants in the formula (see Theorem 7). Fränzle demonstrated that for simple instances of the discrete-time version of the gas burner problem, his technique was superior to the automata-theoretic procedure DCVALID. In this paper, we have extended Fränzle's technique to the dense-time logic IDL including the *duration* and *count* constructs. We have given an encoding of k-validity of IDL into unsatisfiability of *lin-sat*, where the size of the encoding is polynomial in the size of the IDL formula D, with constants encoded in binary. We believe that our generalization of Fränzle's work is practically significant and advantageous, as demonstrated by our experimental evaluation. More recently, Fränzle and Herde have investigated efficient SAT-solving techniques for 0-1 linear constraints which arise in the translation of the discrete-time *count* construct [10].

Fränzle was influenced by the prior work of Ayari and Basin [2], who gave a polynomial-time encoding of the logic ML2STR (monadic logic of finite words) into Quantified Boolean Formulae for bounded validity checking. Ayari and Basin demonstrated that on many problems, the automata-theoretic decision procedure for ML2STR (using the MONA tool) performed better than the QBF SAT solving technique. But on some complex problems, QBF SAT solving was able to find counter-examples faster. Approach B in our experiments uses a similar automata-theoretic technique, but it handles the dense-time logic IDL using digitization. Moreover, the tool OPT-CTLDC considerably improves the automata based analysis.

Acknowledgments. The authors thank Martin Fränzle and A. Cimatti for their helpful comments, and Dina Thomas and S. N. Krishna for their help in conducting experiments.

References

1. G. Audemard, A. Cimatti, A. Kornilowicz, and R. Sebastiani. Bounded Model Checking for Timed Systems. In *FORTE*, volume 2529 of *LNCS*. Springer, 2002.
2. A. Ayari and D. Basin. Bounded Model Construction for Monadic Second-Order Logics. In *CAV*, volume 1855 of *LNCS*. Springer, 2000.
3. A. Bierre, A. Cimatti, E. Clarke, and Y. Zhu. Symbolic Model Checking without BDDs. In *TACAS*, volume 1579 of *LNCS*. Springer, 1999.
4. Dines Bjørner. Trusted computing systems: The procos experience. In *ICSE*, pages 15–34, 1992.
5. A. Bouajjani, Y. Lakhnech, and R. Robbana. From Duration Calculus to Linear Hybrid Automata. In *CAV*, volume 939 of *LNCS*. Springer, 1995.
6. G. Chakravorty and P.K. Pandya. Digitizing Interval Duration Logic. In *CAV*, volume 2725 of *LNCS*. Springer, 2003.
7. J. Filliâtre, S. Owre, H. Rueß, and N. Shankar. ICS: Integrated Canonizer and Solver. In *CAV*, volume 2102 of *LNCS*. Springer, 2001.
8. M. Fränzle. Model-Checking Dense-Time Duration Calculus. In *M.R. Hansen (ed.), Duration Calculus: A Logical Approach to Real-Time Systems Workshop proceedings of ESSLLI X*, 1998.
9. M. Fränzle. Take it NP-easy: Bounded Model Construction for Duration Calculus. In *FTRTFT*, volume 2469 of *Lecture Notes in Computer Science*. Springer, 2002.
10. M. Fränzle and C. Herde. Efficient SAT engines for concise logics: Accelerating proof search for zero-one linear constraint systems. In M. Vardi and A. Voronkov, editors, *LPAR*, volume 2850 of *LNAI*, pages 302–316. Springer, 2003.

11. IDLVALID: Model Checking Dense-time Duration Logics. WWW page, 2004. http://www.tcs.tifr.res.in/~pandya/idlvalid.html.
12. N. Karmarkar. A new polynomial-time algorithm for linear programming. *Combinatorica*, 4(4):373–395, 1984.
13. Z. Liu. Specification and Verification in the Duration Calculus. In M. Joseph, editor, *Real-time Systems: Specification, Verification and Analysis*, pages 182–228. Prentice Hall, 1996.
14. P.K. Pandya. Specifying and Deciding Quantified Discrete-Time Duration Dalculus Formulae using DCVALID. In Paul Pettersson and Wang Yi, editors, *RTTools*, Uppsala University Technical Report Series, 2000.
15. P.K. Pandya. Model checking CTL[DC]. In *TACAS*, volume 2031 of *LNCS*. Springer, 2001.
16. P.K. Pandya. Interval Duration Logic: Expressiveness and Decidability. In E. Asarin, O. Maler, and S. Yovine, editors, *TPTS'02*, volume 65 of *ENTCS*. Elsevier Science Publishers, 2002.
17. B. Sharma. *SAT Based Validity Checking of Interval Duration Logic Formuale*. M.Tech Dissertation, Dept. of Computer Science and Engineering, IIT Bombay, June 2004.
18. J.U. Skakkebæk and P. Sestoft. Checking Validity of Duration Calculus Formulas. ESPRIT project PROCOS II. Technical report, Department of Computer Science, Technical University of Denmark, 1996.
19. Chaochen Zhou and M.R. Hansen. *Duration Calculus*. Springer, 2003.
20. Chaochen Zhou, C.A.R. Hoare, and A.P. Ravn. A Calculus of Durations. *Information Processing Letters*, 40(5):269–276, 1991.
21. Chaochen Zhou, A. Ravn, and M.R. Hansen. An Extended Duration Calculus for Hybrid Real-Time Systems. In *Hybrid Systems*, pages 36–59. Springer, 1993.

An Incremental and Layered Procedure for the Satisfiability of Linear Arithmetic Logic*

Marco Bozzano[1], Roberto Bruttomesso[1], Alessandro Cimatti[1], Tommi Junttila[2], Peter van Rossum[1], Stephan Schulz[3], and Roberto Sebastiani[4]

[1] ITC-IRST, Via Sommarive 18, 38050 Povo, Trento, Italy
{bozzano,bruttomesso,cimatti,vanrossum}@itc.it
[2] Helsinki University of Technology, P.O.Box 5400, FI-02015 TKK, Finland
Tommi.Junttila@tkk.fi
[3] University of Verona, Strada le Grazie 15, 37134 Verona, Italy
schulz@eprover.org
[4] Università di Trento, Via Sommarive 14, 38050 Povo, Trento, Italy
rseba@dit.unitn.it

Abstract. In this paper we present a new decision procedure for the satisfiability of Linear Arithmetic Logic (LAL), i.e. boolean combinations of propositional variables and linear constraints over numerical variables. Our approach is based on the well known integration of a propositional SAT procedure with theory deciders, enhanced in the following ways.

First, our procedure relies on an *incremental* solver for linear arithmetic, that is able to exploit the fact that it is repeatedly called to analyze sequences of increasingly large sets of constraints. Reasoning in the theory of LA interacts with the boolean top level by means of a stack-based interface, that enables the top level to add constraints, set points of backtracking, and backjump, without restarting the procedure from scratch at every call. Sets of inconsistent constraints are found and used to drive backjumping and learning at the boolean level, and theory atoms that are consequences of the current partial assignment are inferred.

Second, the solver is *layered*: a satisfying assignment is constructed by reasoning at different levels of abstractions (logic of equality, real values, and integer solutions). Cheaper, more abstract solvers are called first, and unsatisfiability at higher levels is used to prune the search. In addition, theory reasoning is partitioned in different clusters, and tightly integrated with boolean reasoning.

We demonstrate the effectiveness of our approach by means of a thorough experimental evaluation: our approach is competitive with and often superior to several state-of-the-art decision procedures.

* This work has been sponsored by the CALCULEMUS! IHP-RTN EC project, contract code HPRN-CT-2000-00102, and has thus benefited of the financial contribution of the Commission through the IHP programme. It has also been partly supported by ESACS, an European sponsored project, contract no. G4RD-CT-2000-00361, by ORCHID, a project sponsored by Provincia Autonoma di Trento, and by a grant from Intel Corporation. The work of T. Junttila has also been supported by the Academy of Finland, project 53695. S. Schulz has also been supported by a grant of the Italian Ministero dell'Istruzione, dell'Universit e della Ricerca and the University of Verona. R. Sebastiani is also sponsored by a MIUR COFIN02 project, code 2002097822_003.

N. Halbwachs and L. Zuck (Eds.): TACAS 2005, LNCS 3440, pp. 317–333, 2005.

1   Motivations and Goals

Many practical domains require a degree of expressiveness beyond propositional logic. For instance, timed and hybrid systems have a discrete component as well as a dynamic evolution of real variables; proof obligations arising in software verification are often boolean combinations of constraints over integer variables; circuits described at Register Transfer Level, even though expressible via booleanization, might be easier to analyze at a higher level of abstraction (see e.g. [15]). Many of the verification problems arising in such domains can be naturally modeled as satisfiability in Linear Arithmetic Logic (LAL), i.e., the boolean combination of propositional variables and linear constraints over numerical variables. For its practical relevance, LAL has been devoted a lot of interest, and several decision procedures exist that are able to deal with it (e.g., SVC [17], ICS [24, 19], CVCLITE [17, 10], UCLID [36, 33], HDPLL [30]).

In this paper, we propose a new decision procedure for the satisfiability of LAL, both for the real-valued and integer-valued case. We start from a well known approach, previously applied in MATHSAT [26, 4] and in several other systems [24, 19, 17, 10, 35, 3, 21]: a propositional SAT procedure, modified to enumerate propositional assignments for the propositional abstraction of the problem, is integrated with dedicated theory deciders, used to check consistency of propositional assignments with respect to the theory.

In this paper, we extend the MATHSAT approach in the following directions. First, the linear arithmetic solver is *incremental*: since the theory solver is called to analyze increasingly large sets of constraints, theory reasoning interacts with the boolean top level by means of a stack-based interface, that enables the top level to add constraints, set points of backtracking, and backjump. In addition, sets of inconsistent constraints are identified and used to drive backjumping and learning at the boolean level, and theory atoms that are consequences of the current partial assignment are automatically inferred. Second, we make aggressive use of *layering*: a satisfying assignment is incrementally constructed by reasoning at different levels of abstractions (logic of equality, real values, and integer solutions). Cheaper, more abstract solvers are called first, and unsatisfiability at higher levels is used to prune the search. In addition, theory reasoning is partitioned in different *clusters*, and tightly integrated with boolean reasoning.

We evaluated our approach by means of a thorough experimental comparison: the MATHSAT solver is compared against the state-of-the-art systems ICS, CVCLITE, and UCLID [33] on a large set of benchmarks proposed in the literature. We show that our approach is able to deal effectively with a wide class of problems, with performances comparable with and often superior to the other systems.

This paper is structured as follows. In Sect. 2 we define Linear Arithmetic Logic. In Sect. 3 we describe the basic algorithm, the interplay between boolean and theory reasoning, and the incrementality of the theory solver. In Sect. 4 we describe the internal structure of the solver, focusing on the ideas of layering and clustering. In Sect. 5 we describe the MATHSAT system, and in Sect. 6 we present the result of the experimental evaluation. In Sect. 7 we discuss some related work; finally, in Sect. 8 we draw some conclusions and outline the directions for future work.

2   Background

Let $\mathbb{B} := \{\bot, \top\}$ be the domain of boolean values. Let $\mathcal{D}$ be the domain of either real numbers $\mathbb{R}$ or integers $\mathbb{Z}$. By *math-terms* and *math-formulas* on $\mathcal{D}$ we denote respectively the quantifier-free linear mathematical expressions and formulas built on constants, variables and arithmetical operators over $\mathcal{D}$ and on boolean propositions, closed on boolean connectives. Math-terms are either constants $c_i \in \mathcal{D}$, or variables v_i over $\mathcal{D}$, possibly with coefficients (i.e. $c_i \cdot v_j$), or applications of the arithmetic operators $+$ and $-$ to math-terms. Atomic math-formulas are either boolean propositions A_i over $\mathbb{B}$, or applications of the arithmetic relations $=, \neq, >, <, \geq, \leq$ to math-terms. Such formulas are also called *atoms*. Math formulas are either atoms or combinations of math formulas by means of the standard boolean connectives $\wedge, \neg, \vee, \rightarrow, \leftrightarrow$. For instance, $A_1 \wedge ((v_1 + 5) \leq 2v_3)$ is a math-formula on either $\mathbb{R}$ or $\mathbb{Z}$; an atom is called *boolean* if it is a boolean proposition, otherwise it is called a *mathematical* atom. A *literal* is either an atom (a *positive* literal) or its negation (a *negative* literal). Examples of literals are $A_1, \neg A_2, (v_1 + 5v_2 \leq 2v_3 - 2), \neg(2v_1 - v_2 = 5)$. If l is a negative literal $\neg \psi$, then by "$\neg l$" we mean ψ rather than $\neg \neg \psi$. We denote by $Atoms(\phi)$ the set of mathematical atoms of a math-formula ϕ.

We introduce a bijective function $\mathcal{M2B}$ (for "Math-to-Boolean"), also called *boolean abstraction* function, that maps boolean atoms into themselves, math-atoms into fresh boolean atoms —so that two atom instances in φ are mapped into the same boolean atom iff they are syntactically identical— and distributes over sets and boolean connectives. Its inverse function $\mathcal{B2M}$ (for "Boolean-to-Math") is respectively called *refinement*.

An *interpretation* in $\mathcal{D}$ is a map I which assigns values in $\mathcal{D}$ to math-terms and truth values in $\mathbb{B}$ to math-formulas, and interprets mathematical constants, arithmetical and boolean operators according to the usual semantics of arithmetical and logical symbols. We say that I *satisfies* a math-formula ϕ, written $I \models \phi$, iff $I(\phi)$ evaluates to true. E.g., the math-formula $\varphi := (A_1 \rightarrow (v_1 - 2v_2 \geq 4)) \wedge (\neg A_1 \rightarrow (v_1 = v_2 + 3))$ is satisfied by an interpretation I in $\mathbb{Z}$ s.t. $I(A_1) = \top$, $I(v_1) = 8$, and $I(v_2) = 1$. We say that a math-formula φ is *satisfiable* in $\mathcal{D}$ if there exists an interpretation in $\mathcal{D}$ which satisfies φ.

We address the problem of checking the satisfiability of math-formulas. As standard boolean formulas are a strict sub-case of math-formulas, it follows trivially that the problem is NP-hard. Thus the problem is theoretically "at least as hard" as standard boolean satisfiability, and much harder in practice.

A total (resp. partial) *truth assignment* for a math-formula ϕ is a truth value assignment μ to all (resp. a subset of) the atoms of ϕ. We represent truth assignments as set of literals $\mu = \{\alpha_1, \ldots, \alpha_N, \neg\beta_1, \ldots, \neg\beta_M, A_1, \ldots, A_R, \neg A_{R+1}, \ldots, \neg A_S\}, \alpha_1, \ldots, \alpha_N, \beta_1, \ldots, \beta_M$ being mathematical atoms and $A_1, \ldots, A_S$ being boolean atoms, with the intended meaning that positive and negative literals represent atoms assigned to true and to false respectively.

We say that μ *propositionally satisfies* ϕ, written $\mu \models_p \phi$, iff $\mathcal{M2B}(\mu) \models \mathcal{M2B}(\phi)$. Intuitively, if we see a math-formula ϕ as a propositional formula in its atoms, then $\models_p$ is the standard satisfiability in propositional logic.

We say that an interpretation I satisfies μ iff I satisfies all the elements of μ. For instance, the assignment $\{A_1, (v_1 - 2v_2 \geq 4), \neg(v_1 = v_2 + 3)\}$ propositionally satisfies

$(A_1 \rightarrow (v_1 - 2v_2 \geq 4)) \wedge (\neg A_1 \rightarrow (v_1 = v_2 + 3))$, and it is satisfied by I s.t. $I(A_1) = \top$, $I(v_1) = 8$, and $I(v_2) = 1$. We say that an assignment or a math-formula is *LAL-satisfiable* if there is an interpretation I satisfying if, *LAL-unsatisfiable* otherwise.

Example 1. Consider the following math-formula φ:

$$\varphi = (\neg \underline{(2v_2 - v_3 > 2)} \vee A_1) \wedge (\underline{\neg A_2} \vee (2v_1 - 4v_5 > 3))$$
$$\wedge ((3v_1 - 2v_2 \leq 3) \vee A_2) \wedge (\neg(2v_3 + v_4 \geq 5) \vee \neg \underline{(3v_1 - v_3 \leq 6)} \vee \neg A_1)$$
$$\wedge (A_1 \vee \underline{(3v_1 - 2v_2 \leq 3)}) \wedge (\underline{(v_1 - v_5 \leq 1)} \vee (v_5 = 5 - 3v_4) \vee \neg A_1)$$
$$\wedge (A_1 \vee \underline{(v_3 = 3v_5 + 4)} \vee A_2).$$

The truth assignment given by the underlined literals above is:

$$\mu = \{\neg(2v_2 - v_3 > 2), \neg A_2, (3v_1 - 2v_2 \leq 3), \neg(3v_1 - v_3 \leq 6), (v_1 - v_5 \leq 1), (v_3 = 3v_5 + 4)\}.$$

μ propositionally satisfies φ as it sets to true one literal of every disjunction in φ. Notice that μ is not satisfiable, as both the following sub-assignments of μ

$$\{\neg(2v_2 - v_3 > 2), (3v_1 - 2v_2 \leq 3), \neg(3v_1 - v_3 \leq 6)\} \tag{1}$$
$$\{\neg(3v_1 - v_3 \leq 6), (v_1 - v_5 \leq 1), (v_3 = 3v_5 + 4)\} \tag{2}$$

do not have any satisfying interpretation.   ◇

Given a LAL-unsatisfiable assignment μ, we call a *conflict set* any LAL-unsatisfiable sub-assignment $\mu' \subseteq \mu$; we say that μ' is a *minimal* conflict set if all subsets of μ' are LAL-satisfiable. E.g., both (1) and (2) are minimal conflict sets of μ.

3   The Top Level Algorithm: Boolean+Theory Solving

This section describes the MATHSAT algorithm [4] (see Fig. 1), and its extensions. MATHSAT takes as input a math-formula ϕ, and returns $\top$ if ϕ is LAL-satisfiable (with I containing a satisfying interpretation), and $\bot$ otherwise. (Without loss of generality, ϕ is assumed to be in conjunctive normal form (CNF).) MATHSAT invokes MATHDPLL on the boolean formula $\varphi := \mathcal{M2B}(\phi)$. (Both $\mathcal{M2B}$ and $\mathcal{B2M}$ can be implemented so that they require constant time in mapping one atom.)

MATHDPLL tries to build an assignment μ satisfying φ, such that its refinement is LAL-satisfiable, and the interpretation I satisfying $\mathcal{B2M}(\mu)$ (and ϕ). This is done recursively, with a variant of DPLL modified to enumerate assignments, and trying to refine them according to LAL:

base. If $\varphi == \top$, then μ propositionally satisfies $\mathcal{M2B}(\phi)$. In order to check if μ is LAL-satisfiable, which shows that φ is LAL-satisfiable, MATHDPLL invokes the linear mathematical solver MATHSOLVE on the refinement $\mathcal{B2M}(\mu)$, and returns a *Sat* or *Unsat* value accordingly.

backtrack. If $\varphi == \bot$, then μ has lead to a propositional contradiction. Therefore MATHDPLL returns *Unsat* and backtracks.

unit. If a literal l occurs in φ as a unit clause, then l must be assigned a true value. Thus, MATHDPLL is invoked recursively with *assign(l, φ)* and the assignment obtained

function MATHSAT *(Math-formula* ϕ, *interpretation* & I)
   return MATHDPLL *($\mathcal{M}2\mathcal{B}(\phi), \{\}, I$);*

function MATHDPLL *(Boolean-formula* φ, *assignment* & μ, *interpretation* & I)
   if ($\varphi == \top$)   /* base   */
      then return MATHSOLVE *($\mathcal{B}2\mathcal{M}(\mu), I$)* ;
   if ($\varphi == \bot$)   /* backtrack */
      then return *Unsat;*
   if {l occurs in φ as a unit clause}   /* unit prop. */
      then return MATHDPLL *($assign(l, \varphi), \mu \cup \{l\}, I$);*
   if (MATHSOLVE *($\mathcal{B}2\mathcal{M}(\mu), I$) == Unsat*)   /* early pruning */
      then return *Unsat;*
   l := *choose-literal*(φ);   /* split   */
   if (MATHDPLL *($assign(l, \varphi), \mu \cup \{l\}, I$) == Sat*)
      then return *Sat;*
      else return MATHDPLL *($assign(\neg l, \varphi), \mu \cup \{\neg l\}, I$);*

Fig. 1. High level view of the MATHSAT algorithm

by adding l to μ. *assign(l, φ)* substitutes every occurrence of l in φ with $\top$ and propositionally simplifies the result.

early pruning MATHSOLVE is invoked on (the refinement of) the current assignment μ. If this is found unsatisfiable, then there is no need to proceed, and the procedure backtracks.

split If none of the above situations occurs, then *choose-literal(φ)* returns an unassigned literal l according to some heuristic criterion. Then MATHDPLL is first invoked recursively with arguments *assign(l, φ)* and $\mu \cup \{l\}$. If the result is *Unsat*, then MATHDPLL is invoked with arguments *assign($\neg l, \varphi$)* and $\mu \cup \{\neg l\}$.

The schema of Fig. 1 is over-simplified for explanatory purposes. However, it can be easily adapted to exploit advanced SAT solving techniques (see [38] for an overview). In the rest of this section, we will focus on the interaction between boolean reasoning (carried out by MATHDPLL) and theory reasoning (carried out by MATHSOLVE) instead of on the details underlying the boolean search.

Theory-Driven Backjumping and Learning. [23, 37]. When MATHSOLVE finds the assignment μ to be LAL-unsatisfiable, it also returns a conflict set η causing the unsatisfiability. This enables MATHDPLL to backjump in its search to the most recent branching point in which at least one literal $l \in \eta$ is not assigned a truth value, pruning the search space below. We call this technique *theory-driven backjumping*. Clearly, its effectiveness strongly depends on the conflict set generated.

Example 2. Consider the formula φ and the assignment μ of Ex. 1. Suppose that MATHDPLL generates μ following the order of occurrence within φ, and that MATHSOLVE(μ) returns the conflict set (1). Thus MATHDPLL can jump back directly to the branching point $\neg(3v_1 - v_3 \leq 6)$ without exploring the right branches of ($v_3 = 3v_5 + 4$) and

$(v_1 - v_5 \leq 1)$. If instead MATHSOLVE(μ) returns the conflict set (2), then MATHSAT backtracks to $(v_3 = 3v_5 + 4)$. Thus, (2) causes no reduction in search. $\diamond$

When MATHSOLVE returns a conflict set η, the clause $\neg\eta$ can be added in conjunction to φ: this will prevent MATHDPLL from generating again any branch containing η. We call this technique *theory-driven learning*.

Example 3. As in Ex. 2, suppose MATHSOLVE(μ) returns the conflict set (1). Then the clause $(2v_2 - v_3 > 2) \vee \neg(3v_1 - 2v_2 \leq 3) \vee (3v_1 - v_3 \leq 6)$ is added in conjunction to φ. Thus, whenever a branch contains two elements of (1), then MATHDPLL will assign the third to false by unit propagation. $\diamond$

As in the boolean case, learning must be used with some care, since it may cause an explosion in the size of φ. Therefore, some techniques can be used to discard learned clauses when necessary [11]. Notice however the difference with standard boolean backjumping and learning [11]: in the latter case, the conflict set propositionally falsifies the formula, while in our case it is inconsistent from the mathematical viewpoint.

Theory-Driven Deduction. [2, 4, 21]. With early pruning, MATHSOLVE is used to check if μ is LAL-satisfiable, and possibly close whole branches of the search. It is also possible to use MATHSOLVE to reduce the remaining boolean search: in fact, the mathematical analysis of μ performed by MATHSOLVE can allow for discovering that the value of some mathematical atoms $\psi \notin \mu$ is already determined, based on some subset $\mu' \in \mu$ being part of the current assignment. For instance, consider the case where the literals $(v_1 - v_2 \leq 4)$ and $(v_2 = v_3)$ are in the current (partial) assignment μ, while $(v_1 - v_3 \leq 5)$ is currently unassigned. Since $\{(v_1 - v_2 \leq 4), (v_2 = v_3)\} \models (v_1 - v_3 \leq 5)$, atom $(v_1 - v_3 \leq 5)$ can not be assigned to $\bot$, since this would make μ LAL-inconsistent. MATHSOLVE is therefore used to detect and suggest to the boolean search which unassigned literals have forced values. This kind of deduction is often very useful, since it can trigger new boolean constraint propagation: the search is deepened without the need to split. Moreover, the implication clauses (e.g. $\neg(v_1 - v_2 \leq 4) \vee \neg(v_2 = v_3) \vee (v_1 - v_3 \leq 5)$) can be learned and added to the main formula: this constrains the remaining boolean search in the event of backtracking.

Incremental and Backtrackable Theory Solver. [5, 17, 24]. Given the stack-based nature of the boolean search, the MATHSOLVE can significantly exploit previous computations. Consider the following trace (left column, then right):

MATHSOLVE (μ_1)	$\Longrightarrow$ *Sat*	Undo μ_2	
MATHSOLVE $(\mu_1 \cup \mu_2)$	$\Longrightarrow$ *Sat*	MATHSOLVE $(\mu_1 \cup \mu_2')$	$\Longrightarrow$ *Sat*
MATHSOLVE $(\mu_1 \cup \mu_2 \cup \mu_3)$	$\Longrightarrow$ *Sat*	MATHSOLVE $(\mu_1 \cup \mu_2' \cup \mu_3')$	$\Longrightarrow$ *Sat*
MATHSOLVE $(\mu_1 \cup \mu_2 \cup \mu_3 \cup \mu_4)$	$\Longrightarrow$ *Unsat*	MATHSOLVE $(\mu_1 \cup \mu_2' \cup \mu_3' \cup \mu_4')$	$\Longrightarrow$ *Sat*

On the left, an assignment is repeatedly extended until a conflict is found. We notice that MATHSOLVE is invoked (during early pruning calls) on *incremental* assignments. When a conflict is found, the search backtracks to a previous point (on the right), and MATHSOLVE is then restarting from a previously visited state. Based on these considerations, our MATHSOLVE is not a function call: it has a persistent state, and is *incremental* and *backtrackable*. Incremental means that it avoids restarting the computation from scratch whenever it is given as input an assignment μ' such that $\mu' \supset \mu$ and μ has already been proved satisfiable. Backtrackable means that it is possible to return to a previous state on the stack in a relatively efficient manner. In fact, MATHSOLVE mimics the stack based behaviour of the boolean search.

4   Clustering and Layering in MATHSOLVE

In this section, we discuss how to optimize MATHSOLVE, based on two main ideas: *clustering* and *layering*.

Clustering. At the beginning of the search, the set $Atoms(\phi)$ of all atoms occurring in the formula is partitioned into disjoint *clusters*: intuitively, two atoms (literals) belong to the same cluster if they share a variable. Say $Lits(\phi) = L_1 \cup \cdots \cup L_k$ is the so-obtained static partitioning of the literals. Because no two L_i have a variable in common, the assignment μ is satisfiable if and only if each $\mu \cap L_i$ is satisfiable.

Based on this idea, instead of having a single, monolithic solver for linear arithmetic, k different solvers are constructed, each responsible for the handling of a single cluster. The advantage of this approach is not only that running k solvers on k disjoint problems is faster then running one solver on the union of those k problems, but also a significant gain is obtained by the potential construction of smaller conflict sets. Additionally, we are hashing the results of calls to the linear solvers; if there are more linear solvers, then the likelihood of a hit increases.

Layering. In many calls to MATHSOLVE, a general solver for linear constraints is not needed: very often, the unsatisfiability of the current assignment μ can be established in less expressive, but much easier, sub-theories. Thus, MATHSOLVE is organized in a *layered hierarchy* of solvers of increasing solving capabilities. If a higher level solver finds a conflict, then this conflict is used to prune the search at the boolean level; if it does not, the lower level solvers are activated.

Layering can be explained as trying to privilege faster solvers for more abstract theories over slower solvers for more general theories. Fig. 2 shows a rough idea of the structure of MATH-SOLVE, and highlights the two places in MATH-SOLVE where this layering is taking place. Firstly, the current assignment μ is passed to the *equa-*

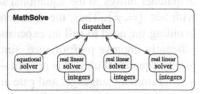

Fig. 2. Clustering and layering

tional solver, described in more detail in Sect. 4.1, that only deals with (positive and negative) equalities. Only if this solver does not find a conflict is a full-blown solver for linear arithmetic invoked. Secondly, the *solver for linear arithmetic*, described in Sect. 4.2, is itself layered: when reasoning about integer variables, it first tries to find a conflict over the real numbers, and looks for a conflict over the integers only in case of satisfiability.

4.1   The Equational Satisfiability Procedure

The first layer of MATHSOLVE is provided by the equational solver, a satisfiability checker for the logic of unconditional ground equality over uninterpreted function symbols. It is incremental and supports efficient backtracking. The solver generates conflict sets, deduces assignments for equational literals, and can provide explanations for its deductions. Thanks to the equational solver, MATHSAT can be used as an efficient decision procedure for the full logic of *equality over uninterpreted function symbols* (EUF). However, in this section we focus on the way the equational solver is used to improve the performance on LAL.

The solver is based on the congruence closure algorithm suggested in [28], and reuses some of the data structures of the theorem prover E [32] to store and process terms and atoms. It internally constructs a congruence data structure that can determine if two arbitrary terms are necessarily forced to be equal by the currently asserted constraints, and can thus be used to determine the value of (some) equational atoms.

It also maintains a list of asserted *disequations*, and signals unsatisfiability if one of these is violated by the current congruence. Similarly, the solver implicitly knows that syntactically different constants in $\mathcal{D}$ are semantically distinct, and efficiently detects and signals if a new equation forces the identification of distinct domain elements.

If two terms are equal, an auxiliary proof tree data structure allows us to extract the reason, i.e. the original constraints (and just those) that forced this equality. If a disequality constraint is violated, we can return the reason (together with the violated inequality) as a *conflict set*.

Similarly, we can perform *forward deduction*: for each unassigned equational atom, we can determine if the two sides are already forced to be equal by the current assignment, and hence whether the atom has to be asserted as true or false. Again, we can extract the reason for this deduction and use it to represent the deduction as a learned clause on the Boolean level.

There are two ways in which the equational solver can be used: as a solver for equational clusters, or as a layer in the arithmetic reasoning process. In the first case, only those clusters not involving any arithmetic at all are given to the equational solver: the dispatcher moves to the equational solver only equations of the form $v_i \bowtie v_j$, $v_i \bowtie c_j$, with $\bowtie \in \{=, \neq\}$. Thus, the equational solver provides a full solver for some clusters, avoiding the need to call an expensive linear solver on an easy problem. This can significantly improve performance, since in practical examples it is often the case that a purely equational cluster is present – typical examples are modeling of assignments in a programming language, and gate and multiplexer definitions in circuits.

In the second case, the dispatcher also passes constraints involving arithmetic operators to the equational solver. While arithmetic functions are treated as fully uninterpreted, the equational solver has a limited interpretation of $<$ and $\leq$, knowing only that $s < t$ implies $s \neq t$, and $s = t$ implies $s \leq t$ and $\neg(s < t)$. However, all deductions and conflicts under EUF semantics are also valid under fully interpreted semantics. Thus, the efficient equational solver can be used to prune the search space. Only if the equational solver cannot deduce any new assignments and reports a tentative model, this model has to be verified (or rejected) by lower level solvers.

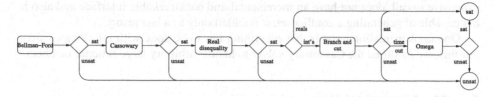

Fig. 3. Control flow of linear solver

4.2   The Solver for Linear Arithmetic

The task of the linear solver is to check a given assignment μ of linear constraints ($\sum_i c_i v_i \bowtie c_j$, with $\bowtie \in \{=, \neq, >, <, \geq, \leq\}$) for satisfiability and, as appropriate, return a model or a conflict set.

The linear solver itself is also layered, running faster, more general solvers first and using slower, more specialized solvers only if the early ones do not detect an inconsistency. The control flow through the linear solver is given in Fig. 3.

First, we consider only those constraints that are in the difference logic fragment, i.e., the subassignment of μ consisting of all constraints of the forms $v_i - v_j \bowtie c$ and $v_i \bowtie c$, with $\bowtie \in \{=, \neq, <, >, \leq, \geq\}$. Satisfiability checking for this subassignment is reduced to a negative-cycle detection problem in the graph whose nodes correspond to variables and whose edge correspond to the constraints. We use an incremental version of the Bellman-Ford algorithm to search for a negative-cycle and hence for a conflict [16].

Second, we try to determine if the current assignment μ is consistent over the reals, by means of the Cassowary constraint solver. Cassowary [13, 8] is a simplex-based solver over the reals, using slack variables to efficiently allow the addition and removal of constraints and the generation of a minimal conflict set.

Cassowary is called on μ minus the disequalities (i.e., with $\bowtie$ equal to $\neq$). When Cassowary does not find a conflict, its incremental and backtrackable machinery is used to check for each disequality $\sum c_i v_i \neq c_j$ in μ separately if it is consistent with the non-disequality constraints in μ. We do so by adding and retracting both $\sum c_i v_i < c_j$ and $\sum c_i v_i > c_j$. Of course, if one of the disequalities is inconsistent, the whole assignment μ is inconsistent. However, if each disequality separately is consistent, then by dimensionality reasons all of μ is consistent.[1]

Whenever the variables are interpreted over the reals, MATHSOLVE is done at this point. If the variables are interpreted over the integers, and the problem is unsatisfiable in the reals, then it is so in the integers. When the problem is satisfiable in the reals, a simple form of branch-and-cut is carried out, to search for solutions over the integers, using Cassowary's incremental and backtrackable machinery. If branch-and-cut does not find either an integer solution or a conflict within a small, predetermined amount of search, the Omega constraint solver [29] is called on the current assignment. Omega is a constraint solver over the integers based on Fourier-Motzkin. Since it is computationally

---

[1] Basically because it is impossible to write an affine subspace A of $\mathbb{R}^k$ as a finite union of proper affine subspaces of A.

expensive to call, does not have an incremental and backtrackable interface and also is not capable of generating a conflict set, it is called only as a last resort.

One implementation issue is that everything has to be done with infinite precision. For this, we modified the Cassowary solver to handle arbitrary large rational numbers.

5   The MATHSAT System

The actual MATHSAT system has three components: (i) a preprocessor, (ii) a boolean satisfiability solver, and (iii) the MATHSOLVE theory solver described in Sect. 4.

Preprocessor. MATHSAT allows the input formulas to contain constructions that cannot be handled directly by the MATHDPLL algorithm. These features and some optimizations are handled by a *preprocessor*. First, MATHSAT allows the input formulas to be in non-clausal form and to include boolean operators such as $\rightarrow$ and ternary if-then-else. Thus the last step in the preprocessor is to translate the formula into CNF by using a standard linear-time satisfiability preserving translation. Second, the input formulas may contain uninterpreted functions and predicates. If they are used in a mixed way that cannot be handled either by the EUF solver or linear arithmetic solver alone (e.g. an atom $f(x) + f(z) = c$), the preprocessor uses Ackermann's reduction to eliminate them [1].

In addition, the preprocessor uses a form of *static learning* to add some satisfiability preserving constraints that help to prune the search space in the boolean level. For instance, if a formula ϕ contains a set of math-atoms of form $\{(t = c_1), ..., (t = c_n)\}$, where t is a math-term and c_i are mutually disjoint constants, then ϕ is conjuncted with constraints enforcing that at most one of the atoms can be true. Similarly, a linear number of constraints encoding the basic mathematical relationships between simple (in)equalities of the form $t \bowtie c_i$, $\bowtie \in \{<, \leq, =\geq, >\}$, are added. E.g. if $(t \leq 2), (t = 3), (t > 5)$ are math-atoms in ϕ, then ϕ is conjuncted with the constraints $(t = 3) \rightarrow \neg(t > 5)$, $(t = 3) \rightarrow \neg(t \leq 2)$, and $(t \leq 2) \rightarrow \neg(t > 5)$. Furthermore, some facts between difference constraints of form $t_1 - t_2 \bowtie c$, where $\bowtie \in \{<, \leq, \geq, >\}$ and c is a constant, are included: (i) mutual exclusion of conflicting constraints is forced, e.g. for $(t_1 - t_2 \leq 3)$ and $(t_2 - t_1 < -4)$, the constraint $\neg(t_1 - t_2 \leq 3) \vee \neg(t_2 - t_1 < -4)$ is added, and (ii) constraints corresponding to triangle inequalities are added, e.g. for $(t_1 - t_2 \leq 3)$, $(t_2 - t_3 < 5)$, and $(t_1 - t_3 < 9)$, the constraint $(t_1 - t_2 \leq 3) \wedge (t_2 - t_3 < 5) \rightarrow (t_1 - t_3 < 9)$ is included.

Boolean Solver. The math-formula in CNF produced by the preprocessor is given to the boolean satisfiability solver extended to implement the MATHDPLL algorithm in Sect. 3. In MATHSAT, the boolean solver is built upon the MINISAT solver [18]. Thus it inherits conflict-driven learning and back-jumping, restarts [34, 11, 22], optimized boolean constraint propagation based on the two-watched literal scheme, and an effective splitting heuristics VSIDS [27] for free. It communicates with MATH-SOLVE through an interface (resembling the one in [21]) that passes assigned literals, LAL-consistency queries and backtracking commands to MATHSOLVE and gets back answers to the queries, mathematical conflict sets and implied literals (Sect. 3). The boolean solver is also extended to handle some optimization options relevant when dealing with math-formulas. For instance, MATHSAT inherits MINISAT's feature of periodically discarding some of the learned clauses to prevent explosion of the formula size. But because clauses generated by theory-driven learning and forward deduction mechanisms (Sect. 3) may have required a lot of work in MATHSOLVE, as a default option they are never discarded. As a second example, it is possible to initialize the VSIDS heuristics weights of literals so that either boolean or mathematical atoms are preferred as splitting choices early in the MATHDPLL search.

Furthermore, as the theory of linear arithmetic on $\mathbb{Z}$ is much harder, in theory and in practice, than that on $\mathbb{R}$ [12], in early pruning calls we only use weaker but faster versions of MATHSOLVE, which look for a solution on the reals only. This is based on the heuristic consideration that, in practice, if an assignment is consistent in $\mathbb{R}$ it is often also consistent in $\mathbb{Z}$, and that early pruning checks are not necessary for the correctness and completeness of the procedure.

6   Experimental Evaluation

In this section we report on the experiments we have carried out to evaluate the performance of our approach. The experiments were run on a 4-processor PentiumIII 700 MhZ machine with more than 6 Gb of memory, running Linux RedHat 7.1. An executable version of MATHSAT and the source files of all the experiments performed in the paper are available at [26].

Description of the Test Cases. The first set of experiments was performed on the SAL suite [31], a set of benchmarks for ground decision procedures. The suite is derived from bounded model checking of timed automata and linear hybrid systems, and from test-case generation for embedded controllers. The problems are represented in non-clausal form, and constraints are in linear arithmetic. This suite contains 217 problems, 110 of which are in the separation logic fragment.

The second set of experiments was performed on a benchmark suite (called RTLC hereafter) formalizing safety properties for RTL circuits, provided to us by the authors of [30] (see [30] for a more detailed description of the benchmarks).

Finally, we used a benchmark suite (CIRC) generated by ourselves, verifying properties for some simple circuits. The suite is composed of three different kinds of benchmarks, all of them being parametric in (and scaling up with) N, where $[0..2^N - 1]$ is the range of an integer variable. In the first benchmark, the modular sum of two integers is checked for equality against the bit-wise sum of their bit decomposition. The negation of the resulting formula is therefore unsatisfiable. In the second benchmark, two identical shift-and-add multipliers and two integers a and b are given; a and the bit decomposition of b (respectively b and the bit decomposition of a) are given as input to the first (respectively, the second) multiplier, and the outputs of the two multipliers are checked for equality. The negation of the resulting formula is therefore unsatisfiable. In the third benchmark, an integer a and the bitwise decomposition of an integer b are given as input to a shift-and-add multiplier; the output of the multiplier is compared

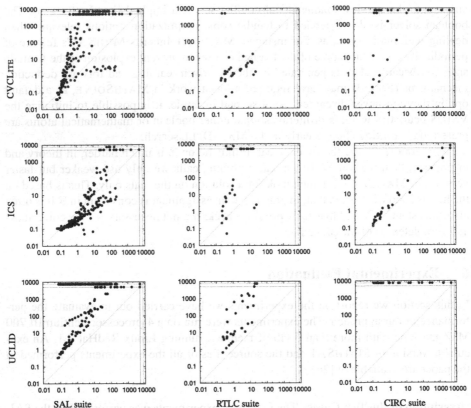

Fig. 4. Execution time ratio: the X and Y axes report MATHSAT and each competitor's times respectively

with the constant integer value p^2, p being the biggest prime number strictly smaller than 2^N. The resulting formula is satisfiable, but it has only one solution: $a = b = p$ and corresponding bit values.

Comparison with Other State-of-the-Art Tools. We evaluated the performance of MATHSAT with respect to other state-of-the-art tools, namely ICS, CVCLITE and UCLID. For ICS and UCLID, the latest officially released versions were used for the comparative evaluation. For CVCLITE, we used the latest available version on the online repository, given that the latest officially released version showed a bug related to the management of integer variables. Moreover, the version we used turned out to be much faster than the other one. The time limit for these experiments was set to 1800 seconds (only one processor was allowed to run for each run) and the memory limit was set to 500 MB.

The overall results are reported in Fig. 4. The rows show the comparison between MATHSAT and, respectively, CVCLITE, ICS and UCLID, whereas the columns correspond to the different test suites. The X and Y axes show, respectively, MATHSAT

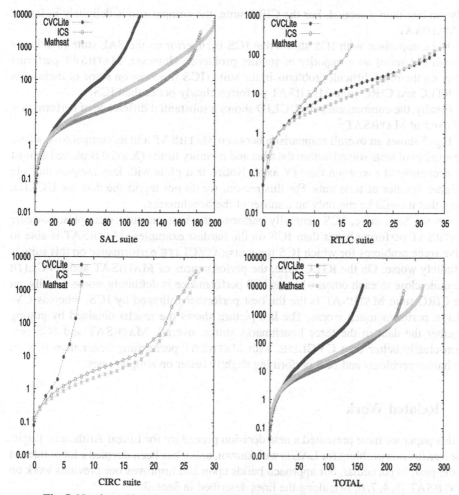

Fig. 5. Number of benchmarks solved (X axis) versus accumulated time (Y axis)

and each of the competitor's execution times. A dot in the upper part of a picture, i.e. above the diagonal, means a better performance of MATHSAT and viceversa. The two uppermost horizontal lines and the two rightmost vertical lines represent, respectively, benchmarks that ended in out-of-memory (higher) or timed-out (lower) for, respectively, each of the competitors and MATHSAT.

For the UCLID tests only, the dots on the uppermost horizontal line represent problems on which UCLID could not be run on, because it does not support full LAL; thus, these points are significant only for MATHSAT.

The comparison with CVCLITE shows that MATHSAT performs generally better on the majority of the benchmarks in the SAL suite (CVCLITE timeouts on several of them). On the RTLC suite, the comparison is slightly in favour of CVCLITE for some of the problems whose time ratio is close to 1, however CVCLITE has high computation times and even timeouts a couple of times for a few problems which MATHSAT can solve in less than a second. For the CIRC suite, the comparison is definitely in favour of MATHSAT.

The comparison with ICS shows that ICS is superior on the SAL suite (that is, on its own test suite) on a majority of smaller problems. However, MATHSAT performs better on the most difficult problems in the suite (ICS timeouts on some of them). On the RTLC and CIRC suite MATHSAT performs clearly better than ICS.

Finally, the comparison with UCLID shows a substantial difference of performance in favour of MATHSAT [2].

Fig. 5 shows an overall comparison between MATHSAT and its competitors, where the number of tests solved within the time and memory limits (X axis) is plotted against the accumulated execution time (Y axis). Notice that plots with less samples indicate a higher number of time outs. For this reason, we do not report the data for UCLID, given that it could be run only on a subset of the benchmarks.

On the SAL suite, ICS generally performs the best on most examples; however MATHSAT performs better than ICS on the hardest examples (MATHSAT is able to solve some problems for which ICS timeouts); CVCLITE performance on this suite is definitely worse. On the RTLC suite, the performances of MATHSAT and CVCLITE are quite close to each other, whereas ICS performance is definitely worse. Finally, on the CIRC suite MATHSAT is the the best performer followed by ICS, whereas CV-CLITE performs much worse. The last picture shows the results obtained by putting together the data in the three benchmarks suites: overall, MATHSAT and ICS perform clearly better than CVCLITE, with MATHSAT performing better than ICS on the harder problems and ICS performing slightly better on simpler ones.

7   Related Work

In this paper we have presented a new decision procedure for Linear Arithmetic Logic. The verification problem for LAL is well known, and it has been devoted a lot of interest in the past. In particular, our approach builds upon and improves our previous work on MATHSAT [5, 4, 7, 6, 14], along the lines described in Sect. 3.

Other related decision procedures are the ones considered in Sect. 6, namely CV-CLITE [17, 10], ICS [24, 19] and UCLID [36, 33]. CVCLITE is a library for checking validity of quantifier-free first-order formulas over several interpreted theories, including real and integer linear arithmetic, arrays and uninterpreted functions. CVCLITE replaces the older tools SVC and CVC [17]. ICS is a decision procedure for the satisfiability of formulas in a quantifier-free, first-order theory containing both uninterpreted function symbols and interpreted symbols from a set of theories including arithmetic, tuples, arrays, and bit-vectors. Finally, UCLID is a tool incorporating a decision procedure for arithmetic of counters, the theories of uninterpreted functions and equality (EUF), separation predicates and arrays. It can also handle limited forms of quantification. In this paper these tools have been compared using the benchmarks falling into the class of linear arithmetic logic (in the case of UCLID the subset of arithmetic of

---

[2] UCLID could not be run on some of the problems in SAL and RTLC and on all of the problems in CIRC, because it does not support full LAL, hence the emptiness of the bottom-right picture.

counters). A comparison on the benchmarks dealing with the theory of EUF is part of our future work.

Other relevant systems are Verifun [20], a tool using lazy-theorem proving based on SAT-solving, supporting domain-specific procedures for the theories of EUF, linear arithmetic and the theory of arrays, and the tool ZAPATO [9], a tool for counterexample-driven abstraction refinement whose overall architecture is similar to Verifun. The DPLL(T) [21] tool is a decision procedure for the theory of EUF, which, similarly to MATHSAT, is based on a DPLL-like SAT-solver engine coupled with a specialized solver for EUF. A comparison with DPLL(T) in the case of EUF is also planned as future work. ASAP [25], is a decision procedure for quantifier-free Presburger arithmetic (that is, the theory of LAL over non-negative integers) implemented on top of UCLID; a comparison was not possible given that the system is not publicly available. A further relevant system is TSAT++ [35, 3], which is limited, however, to the separation logic fragment of LAL.

Finally, we mention [30], which presents HDPLL, a decision procedure for LAL, specialized to the verification of circuits at RTL level. The procedure is based on DPLL-like Boolean search engine integrated with a constraint solver based on Fourier-Motzkin elimination and finite domain constraint propagation. According to the experimental results in [30], HDPLL seems to be very competitive, at least for property verification of circuits at RTL level. It would be very interesting to perform a thorough experimental evaluation wrt. MATHSAT (at the moment this was not possible due to unavailability of the tool) and also to investigate the possibility of tuning MATHSAT using some ideas mentioned in the paper.

8 Conclusions and Future Work

In this paper we have presented a new decision procedure for the satisfiability of Linear Arithmetic Logic. The work is carried out within the (known) framework of integration between off-the-shelf SAT solvers, and specialized theory solvers. We proposed several improvements. First, the theory solver is incremental and backtrackable, and therefore able to tightly interact with the boolean top level by mimicking its stack-based behaviour; furthermore, it provides explanations in case of conflict, and can carry out deductions that provide truth values to unassigned atoms. Second, we heavily exploit the idea of layering: the satisfiability of theory constraints is evaluated in theories of increasing strength (Equality, Separation logic, Linear Arithmetic over the reals, and Linear Arithmetic over the integers). The idea is to privilege less expensive solvers (for weaker theories), thus reducing the use of more expensive solvers. Finally, static learning and weakened early pruning are also used. We carried out a thorough experimental evaluation of our approach: the MATHSAT solver is able to tackle effectively a wide class of problems, with performance comparable with and often superior to the state-of-the-art competitors.

Besides the experiments shown in this paper, we have performed an additional set of experiments to evaluate the impact of the above mentioned improvements on the overall performance of MATHSAT. The results of this evaluation are reported in an extended version of this paper, available at [26].

As future work, we plan to further tune MATHSAT, to investigate the impact of different splitting heuristics taking into account the internal nature of constraints. In addition, we plan to extend MATHSAT to deal with other theories, including non-linear arithmetics, arrays, bitvectors, and a model of memory access. We are investigating an extension of MATHSAT to combinations of theories, in particular EUF and LAL. Finally, we plan to lift SAT-based model checking beyond the boolean case, to the verification of sequential RTL circuits and of hybrid systems.

References

1. W. Ackermann. *Solvable Cases of the Decision Problem.* North Holland Pub. Co., Amsterdam, 1954.
2. A. Armando, C. Castellini, and E. Giunchiglia. SAT-based procedures for temporal reasoning. In *Proc. European Conference on Planning, CP-99*, 1999.
3. A. Armando, C. Castellini, E. Giunchiglia, and M. Maratea. A SAT-based Decision Procedure for the Boolean Combination of Difference Constraints. In *Proc. Conference on Theory and Applications of Satisfiability Testing (SAT'04)*, 2004.
4. G. Audemard, P. Bertoli, A. Cimatti, A. Korniłowicz, and R. Sebastiani. A SAT Based Approach for Solving Formulas over Boolean and Linear Mathematical Propositions. In *Proc. CADE'2002.*, volume 2392 of *LNAI*. Springer, July 2002.
5. G. Audemard, P. Bertoli, A. Cimatti, A. Korniłowicz, and R. Sebastiani. Integrating boolean and mathematical solving: Foundations, basic algorithms and requirements. In *Proc. AISC-Calculemus 2002*, volume 2385 of *LNAI*, pages 231–245. Springer, 2002.
6. G. Audemard, M. Bozzano, A. Cimatti, and R. Sebastiani. Verifying Industrial Hybrid Systems with MathSAT. In *Proc. of the 1st CADE-19 Workshop on Pragmatics of Decision Procedures in Automated Reasoning (PDPAR'03)*, 2003.
7. G. Audemard, A. Cimatti, A. Korniłowicz, and R. Sebastiani. SAT-Based Bounded Model Checking for Timed Systems. In *Proc. FORTE'02*, volume 2529 of *LNCS*. Springer, 2002.
8. G.J. Badros and A. Borning. The Cassowary linear arithmetic constraint solving algorithm: Interface and implementation. Technical Report UW-CSE-98-06-04, Jun 1998.
9. T. Ball, B. Cook, S.K. Lahiri, and L. Zhang. Zapato: Automatic Theorem Proving for Predicate Abstraction Refinement. In *Proc. CAV'04*, pages 457–461. Springer, 2004.
10. C. Barrett and S. Berezin. CVC Lite: A New Implementation of the Cooperating Validity Checker. In *Proc. CAV'04*, volume 3114 of *LNCS*, pages 515–518. Springer, 2004.
11. R. J. Bayardo, Jr. and R. C. Schrag. Using CSP Look-Back Techniques to Solve Real-World SAT instances. In *Proc. AAAI/IAAI'97*, pages 203–208. AAAI Press, 1997.
12. A. Bockmayr and V. Weispfenning. Solving Numerical Constraints. In *Handbook of Automated Reasoning*, pages 751–842. MIT Press, 2001.
13. A. Borning, K. Marriott, P. Stuckey, and Y. Xiao. Solving linear arithmetic constraints for user interface applications. In *Proc. UIST'97*, pages 87–96. ACM, 1997.
14. M. Bozzano, A. Cimatti, G. Colombini, V. Kirov, and R. Sebastiani. The MathSat solver – a progress report. In *Proc. Workhop on Pragmatics of Decision Procedures in Automated Reasoning 2004 (PDPAR 2004)*, 2004.
15. R. Brinkmann and R. Drechsler. RTL-datapath verification using integer linear programming. In *Proc. ASP-DAC 2002*, pages 741–746. IEEE, 2002.
16. Boris V. Cherkassky and Andrew V. Goldberg. Negative-cycle detection algorithms. *Mathematical Programming*, 85(2):277–311, 1999.
17. CVC, CVCLITE and SVC. http://verify.stanford.edu/{CVC,CVCL,SVC}.

18. N. Eén and N. Sörensson. An extensible SAT-solver. In *Theory and Applications of Satisfiability Testing (SAT 2003)*, volume 2919 of *LNCS*, pages 502–518. Springer, 2004.
19. J.-C. Filliâtre, S. Owre, H. Ruess, and N. Shankar. ICS: Integrated Canonizer and Solver. In *Proc. Conference on Computer Aided Verification (CAV'01)*, pages 246–249, 2001.
20. C. Flanagan, R. Joshi, X. Ou, and J.B. Saxe. Theorem Proving using Lazy Proof Explication. In *Proc. CAV'03*, volume 2725 of *LNCS*, pages 355–367. Springer, 2003.
21. H. Ganzinger, G. Hagen, R. Nieuwenhuis, A. Oliveras, and C. Tinelli. DPLL(T): Fast decision procedures. In *Proc. CAV'04*, volume 3114 of *LNCS*, pages 175–188. Springer, 2004.
22. C. Gomes, B. Selman, and H. Kautz. Boosting Combinatorial Search Through Randomization. In *Proceedings of the Fifteenth National Conference on Artificial Intelligence*, 1998.
23. I. Horrocks and P. F. Patel-Schneider. FaCT and DLP. In *Proc. Tableaux'98*, pages 27–30, 1998.
24. ICS. http://www.icansolve.com.
25. D. Kroening, J. Ouaknine, S. Seshia, and O. Strichman. Abstraction-Based Satisfiability Solving of Presburger Arithmetic. In *Proc. CAV'04*, pages 308–320. Springer, 2004.
26. MATHSAT. http://mathsat.itc.it.
27. M. W. Moskewicz, C. F. Madigan, Y. Z., L. Zhang, and S. Malik. Chaff: Engineering an efficient SAT solver. In *Design Automation Conference*, 2001.
28. R. Nieuwenhuis and A. Oliveras. Congruence Closure with Integer Offsets. In *Proc. 10th LPAR*, number 2850 in LNAI, pages 77–89. Springer, 2003.
29. Omega. http://www.cs.umd.edu/projects/omega.
30. G. Parthasarathy, M.K. Iyer, K.-T. Cheng, and Li-C. Wang. An efficient finite-domain constraint solver for circuits. In *Proc. DAC'04*, pages 212–217. IEEE, 2004.
31. SAL Suite. http://www.csl.sri.com/users/demoura/gdp-benchmarks.html.
32. S. Schulz. E – A Brainiac Theorem Prover. *AI Communications*, 15(2/3):111–126, 2002.
33. S.A. Seshia, S.K. Lahiri, and R.E. Bryant. A hybrid SAT-based decision procedure for separation logic with uninterpreted functions. In *Proc. DAC'03*, pages 425–430. ACM, 2003.
34. J. P. M. Silva and K. A. Sakallah. GRASP - A new Search Algorithm for Satisfiability. In *Proc. ICCAD'96*, 1996.
35. TSAT++. http://www.ai.dist.unige.it/Tsat.
36. UCLID. http://www-2.cs.cmu.edu/~uclid.
37. S. Wolfman and D. Weld. The LPSAT Engine & its Application to Resource Planning. In *Proc. IJCAI*, 1999.
38. L. Zhang and S. Malik. The quest for efficient boolean satisfiability solvers. In *Proc. CAV'02*, volume 2404 of *LNCS*, pages 17–36. Springer, 2002.

A Two-Tier Technique for Supporting Quantifiers in a Lazily Proof-Explicating Theorem Prover

K. Rustan M. Leino[1], Madan Musuvathi[1], and Xinming Ou[2]

[1] Microsoft Research, Redmond, WA, USA
{leino,madanm}@microsoft.com
[2] Princeton University, Princeton, NJ, USA
xou@cs.princeton.edu

Abstract. Lazy proof explication is a theorem-proving architecture that allows a combination of Nelson-Oppen-style decision procedures to leverage a SAT solver's ability to perform propositional reasoning efficiently. The SAT solver finds ways to satisfy a given formula propositionally, while the various decision procedures perform theory reasoning to block propositionally satisfied instances that are not consistent with the theories. Supporting quantifiers in this architecture poses a challenge as quantifier instantiations can dynamically introduce boolean structure in the formula, requiring a tighter interleaving between propositional and theory reasoning.

This paper proposes handling quantifiers by using two SAT solvers, thereby separating the propositional reasoning of the input formula from that of the instantiated formulas. This technique can then reduce the propositional search space, as the paper demonstrates. The technique can use off-the-shelf SAT solvers and requires only that the theories are checkpointable.

1   Introduction

Automatic verification of hardware and software systems requires a good decision procedure for the conditions to be verified. Verification conditions generated for the verification of software involve functions and predicates for many types of values, including those of the source programming language. Designing decision procedures for these individual theories may be easier than designing a decision procedure that handles all of them. Nelson and Oppen [12, 11] developed a famous method for combining decision procedures of a class of first-order theories. Because of its modular architecture, theorem provers based on this method can readily support many interesting theories that are useful in practice. Many theorem provers are based on such combinations, for example Simplify [5], Verifun [7], ICS [3], and CVC Lite [2], and these have been applied to the verification of hardware and software systems.

Software verification conditions also involve quantified formulas. For example, the verification conditions generated by the program checker ESC/Java [9] use quantified formulas in several ways: (0) to specify a partial set of properties of otherwise uninterpreted functions, (1) to axiomatize properties guaranteed by Java and its type system, (2) to describe a procedure call's effect on the program heap, (3) to state object invariants

N. Halbwachs and L. Zuck (Eds.): TACAS 2005, LNCS 3440, pp. 334–348, 2005.

for all objects of a class, and (4) to support quantifiers, usually over array elements, supplied by the user. Unfortunately, the Nelson-Oppen combination method is applicable only to quantifier-free first-order formulas. Reasoning about quantifiers in this setting cannot be handled as an ordinary theory, but instead needs special support. Another problem is that it is not always possible to have a terminating decision procedure when the input formulas contain quantifiers, but the prevalence of quantified formulas in important problems demands that the theorem provers handle them effectively in practice.

The Simplify theorem prover [5] provides support for quantified formulas that has been shown to be effective for software verification applications, for example in extended static checking [6, 9]. Simplify uses a kind of pattern matching of ground terms to trigger the instantiation of universally quantified formulas. However, Simplify does not handle propositional search very efficiently. A new generation of theorem provers, including Verifun [7], ICS [3], and CVC Lite [2], attempt to speed up the propositional search by leveraging the last decade's advances in SAT solving and using a *lazy-proof-explication* architecture. In such an architecture, a Nelson-Oppen combination of decision procedures interacts with an off-the-shelf SAT solver: the SAT solver finds ways to satisfy a given formula propositionally, while the combination of other decision procedures performs theory reasoning to block propositionally satisfied instances that are not consistent with the theories.

To use such a new-generation theorem prover in software verification applications, we seek to incorporate support for quantified formulas in the lazy-proof-explication architecture. This poses the following key challenges. First, quantified formulas typically involve propositional connectives. As a result, quantifier instantiations performed during theory reasoning can dynamically introduce boolean structure in the formula. This requires tighter interleaving between propositional and theory reasoning. Second, most quantifier instantiations are not useful in proving the validity of the formula. Blindly exposing such redundant instantiations to the SAT solver could drastically reduce the performance of the propositional search.

Support for quantified formulas in a lazy-proof-explication prover has been incorporated into Verifun [8]. When the quantifier instantiations result in formulas with propositional structure, Verifun augments the original formula with such instantiations so that the SAT solver can find ways to satisfy these instantiations in the context of the original formula. However, the added disjunctions then persist in the prover's state.

As an alternative approach, we propose a *two-tier* technique in this paper. This technique involves two off-the-shelf SAT solvers, a *main* solver that performs the propositional reasoning of the input formula, and a *little* solver that reasons over the quantifier instantiations. When the main SAT solver produces a propositionally satisfying instance that is consistent with the decision procedures, a pattern matching algorithm, similar to the one in Simplify, generates a set of quantifier instantiations. The little SAT solver, along with the decision procedures, tries to falsify the satisfying instance with the instantiations produced. If successful, the little SAT solver then generates a blocking clause that only contains literals from the input formula. By thus separating the propositional reasoning of the input formula from that of the instantiated formulas, this technique reduces the propositional search space.

Section 2 introduces some preliminaries and reviews the architecture of theorem provers based on lazy proof explication. Section 3 discusses the main problem in handling quantifiers in lazy-proof-explication theorem provers. The quantifier algorithm is presented in Section 4. We trace through an example in Section 5 and report on our preliminary experience with an implementation of the algorithm in Section 6. The final sections offer a discussion, some related work, and a conclusion.

2 Theorem Proving Using Lazy Proof Explication

In this section, we review in more detail the architecture and main algorithm of a theorem prover based on lazy proof explication.

2.1 Terminology

A *formula* is constructed from an arbitrary combination of function and predicate symbols, propositional connectives, and first-order quantifier bindings. The following is an example formula:

$$(\forall\, a, i, v \bullet 0 \leqslant i \wedge i < Length(a) \Rightarrow read(write(a, i, v), i) = v\,) \wedge$$
$$Length(b) > 0$$
$$\Rightarrow read(write(b, 0, 10), 0) = 10$$

An *atom* is a formula that does not start with a propositional connective. Propositional connectives include conjunction ($\wedge$), disjunction ($\vee$), negation ($\neg$), and implication ($\Rightarrow$). For example, the following are all atoms:

$$(\forall\, a, i, v \bullet 0 \leqslant i \wedge i < Length(a) \Rightarrow read(write(a, i, v), i) = v\,),$$
$$Length(b) > 0,$$
$$read(write(b, 0, 10), 0) = 10.$$

A *quantifier atom* is an atom that starts with a quantifier. A *literal* is either an atom or its negation. A *quantifier literal* is either a quantifier atom or its negation. A *monome* is a set of literals. If $\mathcal{P}$ is a set of formulas, we sometimes write just $\mathcal{P}$ when we mean the conjunction of the formulas in $\mathcal{P}$.

A theorem prover can be equivalently viewed either as a validity checker or a satisfiability checker: establishing the validity of a given conjecture P is equivalent to showing a satisfying assignment does not exist for $\neg P$. For the theorem provers discussed in this paper, we take the second view, thinking of the input as a formula (the negation of a conjecture) to be satisfied or shown unsatisfiable. We define three notions of satisfiability for a formula Φ: propositional satisfiability ($PSat(\Phi)$), satisfiability with theories ($TSat(\Phi)$), and satisfiability with theories and quantifiers ($QSat(\Phi)$).

1. $PSat(\Phi) = True$ if there exists a satisfying truth value assignment to every atom in Φ.
2. $TSat(\Phi) = True$ if $PSat(\Phi) = True$ and the truth value assignment to the non-quantifier atoms is consistent with the underlying theories.
3. $QSat(\Phi) = True$ if $PSat(\Phi) = True$ and the truth value assignment to the atoms is consistent with both the underlying theories and the semantics of quantifiers.

Proposition 1 *QSat(Φ) implies TSat(Φ), which in turn implies PSat(Φ).*

We define a *lemma* to be a formula that does not affect the satisfiability of any formula. That is, if P is a lemma and $Φ$ is any formula, then $QSat(Φ)$ iff $QSat(Φ \wedge P)$. Note that if both P and Q are lemmas, then so is $P \wedge Q$. And if P is a lemma and P implies Q, then Q is also a lemma. In this paper, we use three kinds of lemmas:

1. a tautology generated by the theories,
2. a quantifier instantiation lemma of the form $(\forall x \bullet P(x)) \Rightarrow P(a)$, which is also a tautology,
3. a quantifier skolemization lemma of the form $(\exists x \bullet P(x)) \Rightarrow P(K)$ for an appropriate skolem function K, as defined later.

2.2   Lazy Proof Explication

In a lazy-proof-explication theorem prover, an off-the-shelf SAT solver conducts propositional reasoning of an input formula $Φ$. The SAT solver treats each atom in $Φ$ as an opaque propositional variable. When possible, the SAT solver returns a truth value assignment m of these atoms that propositionally satisfies $Φ$. The theorem prover then invokes the theory-specific decision procedures to determine if the monome m is consistent with the underlying theories. If so, the input formula $Φ$ is satisfiable. If not, the theories are responsible for producing a lemma that shows the monome m to be inconsistent. By conjoining this lemma to $Φ$—which by the definition of lemma does not change the satisfiability of $Φ$—the theorem prover blocks the assignment m.

For example, suppose a theorem prover is asked about the satisfiability of the following formula:

$$([\![x \leqslant y]\!] \vee [\![y = 5]\!]) \wedge ([\![x < 0]\!] \vee [\![y \leqslant x]\!]) \wedge \neg[\![x = y]\!]$$

where for clarity we have enclosed each atom within special brackets. As (the propositional projection of) this formula is passed to the SAT solver, the SAT solver may return a monome containing the following three literals (corresponding to the truth value assignment to three atoms):

$$[\![x \leqslant y]\!], \ [\![y \leqslant x]\!], \ \neg[\![x = y]\!] \tag{1}$$

This monome is then passed to the theories, where the theory of arithmetic detects an inconsistency and return the following lemma:

$$[\![x \leqslant y]\!] \wedge [\![y \leqslant x]\!] \ \Rightarrow \ [\![x = y]\!] \tag{2}$$

By conjoining this lemma to the original formula, the propositional assignment (1) is explicitly ruled out in the further reasoning performed by the SAT solver. Since (2) is a lemma, it could have been generated and conjoined to the input even before the first invocation of the SAT solver, but the strategy of generating this lemma on demand—that is, lazily—is the reason the architecture is called *lazy* proof explication.

Figure 1 outlines the algorithm of a theorem prover using lazy proof explication. $PSat(F)$ is implemented by calling an off-the-shelf SAT solver (after projecting the atoms onto propositional variables). If the result is *True*, a monome m is returned as

```
Input: formula F
Output: satisfiability of F
while (PSat(F)) {
  let monome m be the satisfying assignment ;
  P := CheckMonome(m) ;
  if (P = ∅) {
    return True ;
  } else {
    F := F ∧ P ;
  }
}
return False ;
```

Fig. 1. Lazy-proof-explication algorithm without support for quantifiers

the satisfying assignment. Then, *CheckMonome* is called to determine if m is consistent with the underlying theories. *CheckMonome*(m) returns a set of lemmas that are sufficient to refute monome m. An empty set indicates that the theories are unable to detect any inconsistency, in which case the algorithm reports that the original formula is satisfiable. Otherwise, the lemmas are conjoined to F and the loop continues until either the formula becomes propositionally unsatisfiable or the theories are unable to find inconsistency in the monome returned by *PSat*.

3   Handling Quantifiers

When a formula contains quantifiers, usually the information expressed by the quantifiers must be used in showing a formula is unsatisfiable. This section discusses some basic notation and challenges for handling quantifiers. The main quantifier algorithm is presented in Section 4.

3.1   Terminology

A quantified formula has the form ($\delta x \bullet F$), where δ is either $\forall$ or $\exists$. Quantifiers can be arbitrarily nested. Provided all the bound variables have been suitably α-renamed, the following three equations hold:

$$\neg(\delta x \bullet F) \equiv (\bar{\delta} x \bullet \neg F)$$
$$(\delta x \bullet F) \wedge G \equiv (\delta x \bullet F \wedge G)$$
$$(\delta x \bullet F) \vee G \equiv (\delta x \bullet F \vee G)$$

Here $\bar{\forall} = \exists$ and $\bar{\exists} = \forall$. By repeatedly applying the above three equations, we can move all the quantifiers in a quantifier atom to the front and convert it to the prenex form ($\delta_1 x_1 \bullet$ ($\delta_2 x_2 \bullet \ldots$ ($\delta_n x_n \bullet F$))), where F does not contain any quantifier.

   The existentially bound variables in the prenex form can be eliminated by skolemization. Skolemization replaces each existential variable x in the quantified body with a term $K(\Psi)$, where K is a fresh function symbol that is unique to the quantified formula and the existential variable x, and Ψ is the list of universally bound variables that appear before x. The skolem term $K(\Psi)$ is interpreted as the "existing term" determined by Ψ. We say the resulting purely universal formula is in *canonical form*. We use $Canon(Q)$ to denote the canonical form of a formula Q. Note that $Q \Rightarrow Canon(Q)$ is a lemma.

For any quantified formula C in canonical form and any substitution θ that maps each universal variable to a ground term, we write $C[\theta]$ to denote the formula obtained by taking C's body and applying θ to it.

3.2   Challenges in Handling Quantifiers

In order to reason about quantifiers, one can instantiate the universal variables with some concrete terms. This will introduce new facts that contain boolean structures, which cannot be directly used in the theory reasoning to refute the current monome. Neither can one only rely on propositional reasoning to handle these new facts because some inconsistency has to be determined by the theories. This means that in order to reason about quantifiers, both propositional reasoning and theory reasoning are necessary. This poses a challenge to theorem provers with lazy proof explication, where the two are clearly separated.

One approach is to conjoin the original formula with lemmas of instantiating universal quantifiers. Let Q be a quantifier literal in a formula F and let θ be a substitution that maps each universal variable in $Canon(Q)$ to a concrete term. Then, the following is a lemma for F:

$$Q \Rightarrow Canon(Q)[\theta]$$

It is a lemma because $Q \Rightarrow Canon(Q)$ and $Canon(Q) \Rightarrow Canon(Q)[\theta]$ are lemmas.

Conjoining these lemmas puts more constraints on the original formula. If the instantiations are properly chosen, more inconsistencies can be detected and eventually the formula can be shown to be unsatisfiable. Simplify [5] uses a matching heuristic to return a set of instantiations that will likely be useful in refuting the formula. However, there may still be too many useless instantiations returned by the matcher. This may blow up the SAT solver, because those lemmas can have arbitrary propositional structure, causing more case splits.

The quantifier algorithm we present in this paper adopts a different approach. First, the matching heuristic in Simplify is still used to return likely-useful instantiations. Then, the little SAT solver performs the propositional reasoning for those instantiated formulas. During the reasoning process, many new instantiations are generated, but only some of them are relevant in refuting the monome. Once the monome is refuted, our algorithm returns an appropriate lemma. The rationale of using the little SAT solver is to separate the propositional reasoning for finding a satisfying monome from the propositional reasoning for refuting a monome. Once a monome is refuted, many of the instantiations are not useful anymore. Without this two-tier approach, they would remain in the formula and introduce many unnecessary case splits in the future rounds of reasoning.

4   Quantifier Algorithm

The quantifier reasoning is performed in the *CheckMonome* function in the algorithm shown in Figure 1. We show the quantifier algorithm in two steps. In section 4.1, we present the simple one mentioned in Section 3.2. In Section 4.2, we show how to use the little SAT solver in *CheckMonome* to perform both propositional and theory reasoning.

4.1   One-Tier Quantifier Algorithm

Figure 2 shows the *CheckMonome* algorithm with the simple quantifier support discussed in Section 3.2. We call this the *one-tier* quantifier algorithm. The quantifier module is invoked only when the other theories cannot detect any inconsistency in the given monome. As discussed in Section 3.2, the lemmas are generated by instantiating universal quantifications. The instantiations are returned from a matching algorithm similar to that of Simplify. To avoid generating duplicate instantiations, the quantifier module remembers the instantiations it has produced. When no more lemmas can be generated, *CheckMonome* will return an empty set, in which case the algorithm in Figure 1 will terminate with the result of *True*. To guarantee termination (at the cost of completeness), an implementation limits the number of times the quantifier module can be called for each run of the theorem prover and simply return an empty set when the limit is exceeded.

Unlike the lemmas output by the theories after discovering an inconsistency, the lemmas generated by the quantifier module generally are not guaranteed to refute the monome. There are two reasons for this. First, many inconsistencies involve both quantifier reasoning and theory reasoning. Without cooperating with the other theories, the lemmas returned by instantiating quantifiers alone may not be sufficient to propositionally block the monome. Second, the instantiations returned by the matching algorithm depend on the monome. Since instantiating quantifiers may produce more atoms to appear in a monome, it is possible that the matcher can provide the "right" instantiation only after several rounds.

As a result of *CheckMonome* returning a set of lemmas insufficient to refute the monome, the next round may call *CheckMonome* with the same monome, plus some extra literals coming from the quantifier instantiation. This is undesirable, because the SAT solver repeats its work to find the same monome again. A more serious problem

```
Input: monome m
Output: a set of lemmas P

procedure CheckMonome(m) ≡
    Assert m to the theories ;
    if (m is inconsistent with the theories) {
        Theories output a lemma P that refutes m ;
    } else {
        Quantifier module generates lemmas P ;
    }
    return P ;
```

Fig. 2. *CheckMonome* algorithm in the one-tier technique

Input: monome m
Output: a set of lemmas that can refute m, or $\emptyset$ when m is satisfiable

```
0.  procedure CheckMonome(m) ≡
1.      Assert m to theories ;
2.      Checkpoint all theories ;
3.      P := ∅ ;
4.      loop {
5.          if (the theories report inconsistency) {
6.              Theories output a lemma P₀ that refutes current monome ;
7.          } else {
8.              Quantifier module generates new lemmas P₀ ;
9.              if (P₀ = ∅) {
10.                 return ∅ ;
11.             }
12.         }
13.         P := P ∪ P₀ ;
14.         if (PSat(m ∧ P) = False) {
15.             return FindUnsatCore(m, P) ;
16.         }
17.         let m ∧ m' be the satisfying monome ;
18.         Restore checkpoints in all the theories ;
19.         Assert m' to theories ;
20.     }
```

Fig. 3. The $CheckMonome$ algorithm using the two-tier technique

of this simple algorithm is that many of the returned lemmas are not even relevant in refuting the monome. Those useless lemmas remain in the formula during the proving process, and without removing them, the SAT solver will eventually be overwhelmed by many unnecessary case splits.

4.2   Two-Tier Quantifier Algorithm

In order to use quantifier instantiations to refute a monome, propositional reasoning is needed. The key problem of the simple $CheckMonome$ algorithm is: by directly returning the lemmas generated from quantifiers, it essentially relies on the main SAT solver to perform the propositional reasoning of those newly generated formulas. This causes repetitive and unnecessary work in the main SAT solver. To address this problem, we separate the propositional reasoning of the instantiated formula from that of the original formula by using a little SAT solver in our $CheckMonome$ algorithm (Figure 3).

Set P records all the lemmas generated so far. Some of the lemmas are generated by the quantifier module (line 8), while the others are generated by the theories (line 6). When new lemmas are added into P, the little SAT solver performs propositional reasoning on $m \wedge P$ (line 14). For every satisfying assignment $m \wedge m'$ produced by the little SAT solver, the algorithm invokes the theories to check if the assignment is consistent. To avoid redundant work, the algorithm checkpoints the state of the theories before entering the loop (line 2). As a result, the algorithm only needs to assert m' to the theories in each iteration (line 19).

The loop continues as long as $\mathcal{P}$ does not propositionally refute m and new lemmas are still being generated. If no more lemmas can be generated, either by the quantifier module or by the theories, and $m \wedge \mathcal{P}$ is still satisfiable, the algorithm terminates and returns an empty set, indicating failure to refute monome m.

Once $\mathcal{P}$ can refute m, the function $FindUnsatCore(m, \mathcal{P})$ is called to extract a good-quality lemma from $\mathcal{P}$. $FindUnsatCore(F, G)$ requires that $F \wedge G$ is propositionally unsatisfiable. It returns a formula H such that $G \Rightarrow H$, $F \wedge H$ is still unsatisfiable, and the atoms in H all occur in F.

Function $FindUnsatCore$ can be implemented in various ways. Modern SAT solvers can extract a small unsatisfiable core of a propositional formula [14] and this seems to be useful in $FindUnsatCore$. Alternatively, interpolants [10] may be used here, because any interpolant of G and F satisfies the specification of $FindUnsatCore(F, G)$. For our preliminary experiments, we have the following naive implementation of the $FindUnsatCore$ function for the particular kind of arguments that show up in the algorithm:

For a monome m and a formula P, if $PSat(m \wedge P) = False$, then there exists a minimal subset m_0 of m such that $PSat(m_0 \wedge P) = False$. Such a m_0 can be obtained by trying to take out one literal from m at a time and discard the literal if the formula remains propositionally unsatisfiable. It is easy to see that $P \Rightarrow \neg m_0$. We just return $\neg m_0$ as the result of $FindUnsatCore(m, P)$.

Correctness. The correctness of the two-tier algorithm hinges on the fact that every formula in $\mathcal{P}$ is a lemma for the monome m. The correctness of the algorithm is formalized as the following theorem.

Theorem 1. *Let $\mathcal{P}$ be the set of all lemmas generated during the run of the algorithm. Then, the algorithm refutes the monome m iff $TSat(m \wedge \mathcal{P}) = False$.*

Intuitively, the result of the algorithm is the same as if we had generated all the lemmas $\mathcal{P}$ up front and run a standard Nelson-Oppen theorem prover on the formula $m \wedge \mathcal{P}$. Since conjoining lemmas does not change the satisfiability of a formula, the theorem shows our algorithm to be sound:

Corollary 2. *If the algorithm refutes m, then $QSat(m) = False$.*

This is because $\neg TSat(m \wedge \mathcal{P}) \Rightarrow \neg QSat(m \wedge \mathcal{P})$ by Proposition 1, and $QSat(m \wedge \mathcal{P}) = QSat(m)$ by the definition of lemma. On the other hand, the algorithm is not complete, since we cannot always generate all the lemmas relevant to the formula. When the algorithm fails to refute a monome, all that is known is $TSat(m \wedge \mathcal{P}) = True$, that is, even with all the information in $\mathcal{P}$, a Nelson-Oppen theorem prover cannot refute the monome either.

5   Example

In this section, we demonstrate how our algorithm works on a small example.

Let P and Q be two quantified formulas:

$$P : \quad (\forall x \bullet x < 10 \Rightarrow R(f(x)))$$
$$Q : \quad (\forall y \bullet R(f(y)) \Rightarrow S(g(y)))$$

where the match patterns to be used for P and Q are $x: f(x)$ and $y: g(y)$, respectively. A pattern ρ is a lambda term such that if a subterm t of the formula matches it, i.e. $\exists t_0 . t = \rho(t_0)$, t_0 will be used to instantiate the universal variable ρ is associated with. In our current implementation, the patterns are specified by the user, although they could be automatically inferred in most cases. We now trace our algorithm through the request of determining whether or not the following formula is satisfiable:

$$[\![P]\!] \wedge [\![Q]\!] \wedge ([\![b = 1]\!] \vee [\![b = 2]\!]) \wedge \neg[\![S(f(b))]\!] \wedge \neg[\![S(g(0))]\!]$$

In the first round, the main SAT solver returns a monome m, say

$$\{ [\![P]\!], [\![Q]\!], [\![b = 1]\!], \neg[\![S(f(b))]\!], \neg[\![S(g(0))]\!] \}$$

Since no theory can detect inconsistency, the quantifier module is invoked to generate lemmas. According to the match pattern, x is instantiated with b in P and y is instantiated with 0 in Q:

$$[\![P]\!] \Rightarrow ([\![b < 10]\!] \Rightarrow [\![R(f(b))]\!]) \tag{3}$$
$$[\![Q]\!] \Rightarrow ([\![R(f(0))]\!] \Rightarrow [\![S(g(0))]\!]) \tag{4}$$

The lemmas (3) and (4) are conjoined to the monome and the little SAT solver is called. The extended monome m' for the newly-introduced atoms might be:

$$\{ \neg[\![b < 10]\!], \neg[\![R(f(0))]\!] \}$$

At this point the theories detect an inconsistency between $[\![b = 1]\!]$ and $\neg[\![b < 10]\!]$. So a new lemma is added:

$$[\![b = 1]\!] \wedge \neg[\![b < 10]\!] \Rightarrow \textit{False} \tag{5}$$

In the next iteration, m' is

$$\{ [\![R(f(b))]\!], \neg[\![R(f(0))]\!] \}$$

The theories are unable to detect inconsistency in the monome $m \wedge m'$. The quantifier module is invoked again to generate lemmas. This time the term $f(0)$ in the newly generated formulas matches the pattern, so x in P is instantiated by 0.

$$[\![P]\!] \Rightarrow ([\![0 < 10]\!] \Rightarrow [\![R(f(0))]\!]) \tag{6}$$

The next m' is

$$\{ [\![R(f(b))]\!], \neg[\![R(f(0))]\!], \neg[\![0 < 10]\!] \}$$

The theory then detects an inconsistency:

$$\neg[\![0 < 10]\!] \Rightarrow \textit{False} \tag{7}$$

After conjoining (7), the original monome m will be propositional refuted. The lemma constructed is

$$[\![P]\!] \wedge [\![Q]\!] \wedge \neg[\![S(g(0))]\!] \Rightarrow \textit{False}$$

After conjoining this lemma to the original formula, it becomes propositionally unsatisfiable.

If we use the simple algorithm, lemma (3) would be conjoined to the input formula, even though it has nothing to do with the contradiction. In the subsequent solving, this unnecessary lemma could introduce a case split on ($[\![b = 1]\!] \lor [\![b = 2]\!]$), if the SAT solver happens to assign $[\![b < 10]\!]$ False. The theories would have to consider both in order to block the truth value assignment $\neg[\![b < 10]\!]$. By separating the two SAT solvers, our algorithm only needs to consider one of them.

6   Experimental Results

We have implemented the two-tier quantifier algorithm in a lazy-proof-explication theorem prover in development at Microsoft Research. For a comparison, we also implemented the one-tier algorithm. This section describes the results from our preliminary evaluation of the algorithm.

Figure 4 shows the number of SAT-solver case splits required for some small examples. In addition to showing the case splits by the main and little SAT solvers in the two-tier approach, we show the number of case splits performed by our implementation of *FindUnsatCore*. We used two sets of examples, explained next.

The first set of formulas was designed to show how the two-tier approach can save case splits over the one-tier approach. Formula $ex2$ is the example from Section 5, and $ex9$ and $ex100$ are the same example but with 9 and 100 different disjuncts instead of 2. The number of case splits for these examples (Figure 4) confirm that the two-tier approach can indeed reduced the number of case splits.

The second set of formulas was constructed to look like (the negations of) typical verification conditions of method bodies in an object-oriented program (*cf.* [9, 1]): on entry to the method body, one gets to assume that an object invariant holds for all allocated objects; on return from the method, one needs to show that the object invariant holds for all allocated objects; in between, the method body contains control structure and calls to other methods. In our example, we used an object invariant that puts an integer constraint on a field f of objects. In our example, the method body to be verified makes calls of

formula	one-tier SAT solver case splits	two-tier main SAT case splits	little SAT case splits	*FindUnsatCore* case splits
ex2	7	1	1	9
ex9	44	9	3	23
ex100	428	106	2	104
prog.1.1	116	0	116	51
prog.2.2	547	4	491	277
prog.3.4	1919	13	1505	919
prog.3.4.err	2000	11	1312	218

Fig. 4. Results from running some preliminary experiments, showing the number of SAT solver case splits performed by the one-tier and two-tier approaches on some small examples

/* axioms about operations that read and write the heap */
$(\forall\, h, x, F, y, G, a \bullet\ x \neq y \lor F \neq G \Rightarrow$
$$sel(upd(h, x, F, a), y, G) = sel(h, y, G)\ )\ \land$$
$(\forall\, h, x, F, a \bullet\ sel(upd(h, x, F, a), x, F) = a\ )\ \land$
/* fields names are distinct (only two distinctions are needed for this example) */
$f \neq g \land g \neq alloc\ \land$
/* object invariants hold initially, where H is the name of the heap */
$(\forall\, o \bullet\ o \neq null \land is(o, T) \land sel(H, o, alloc) \Rightarrow sel(H, o, f) < 7\ )\ \land$
/* encoding of the call, where K is the name of the heap in the post-state */
$(\forall\, o, F \bullet\ sel(H, o, F) = sel(K, o, F)\ \lor$
$\quad (o = p \land F = g) \lor (o = p \land F = f)\ \lor$
$\quad \neg sel(H, o, alloc)\ )\ \land$
$(\forall\, o \bullet\ sel(H, o, alloc) \Rightarrow sel(K, o, alloc)\ )\ \land$
$(\forall\, o \bullet\ \neg sel(H, o, alloc) \land sel(K, o, alloc) \Rightarrow sel(K, o, f) < 7\ )\ \land$
$sel(K, p, f) = 3\ \land$
/* the (negation of the) postcondition to be proved */
$\neg(\forall\, o \bullet\ o \neq null \land is(o, T) \land sel(K, o, alloc) \Rightarrow sel(K, o, f) < 7\ )$

Fig. 5. A formula showing a typical structure of verification conditions of methods in an object-oriented program

the form $p.M(x)$, where p is some object and x is an integer. The semantics of the calls come from the specification of the callee. We used a specification for M that says that $p.M(x)$ sets the field $p.f$ to x, arbitrarily assigns to the field $p.g$, and allocates an arbitrary number of objects and changes the fields of those objects in arbitrary ways that satisfy the object invariant.

Formula $prog.1.1$ is (the negation of) the verification condition for a method whose body simply calls $p.M(3)$. It is shown in Figure 5. Formulas $prog.2.2$ and $prog.3.4$ are similar, but correspond to method bodies containing 2 and 4 calls (with various parameters) and with if statements that give rise to 2 and 3 execution paths, respectively. Formula $prog.3.4.err$ corresponds to the same program as $prog.3.4$, but with an inserted program error; thus, $prog.3.4.err$ is the only one of our small formulas that is satisfiable.

Since $prog.1.1$ is a straight-line program, there are no case splits to be done by the main SAT solver, so the little SAT solver performs roughly the same work as the SAT solver in the one-tier approach. Verification conditions produced from method bodies with more than one possible control-flow path contain disjunctions at the top level of the formula. As soon as there are such disjunctions in our examples, the two-tier approach performs fewer case splits not just in the main SAT solver, but in the main and little SAT solvers combined.

When the two-tier approach refutes a monome produced by the main SAT solver, the lemma returned to the main SAT solver has been pruned to contain a minimal number of literals. This keeps the state of the main SAT solver small, but the pruning has a price. The pruning may be done directly by the SAT solver, but our implementation performs the pruning using the *FindUnsatCore* function described above. Figure 4 shows that this function performs a rather large number of case splits. We do not yet know the actual cost of these case splits relative to everything else in our implementation.

7   Discussion

7.1   Detecting Useful Quantifier Instantiations

The two-tier technique separates the propositional reasoning of the input formula from
the propositional reasoning of the quantifier instantiations. By doing so, this technique
prevents useless instantiations from blowing up the propositional search of the input
formula. However, it is possible for some instantiations to be repeatedly useful in refuting
many propositionally satisfying assignment of the input formula. In such cases, it could
be advantageous to expose this instantiation to the main SAT solver.

As an example, consider the following input formula:

$$[\![(\forall x \bullet\ P(x)\ \Rightarrow\ x \leqslant a\ )]\!]\ \wedge\ [\![P(2)]\!]\ \wedge\ ([\![a = 0]\!] \vee [\![a = 1]\!])$$

Suppose the main SAT solver picks a satisfying assignment consisting of the first two
conjuncts and the disjunct $[\![a = 0]\!]$. The following instantiation

$$[\![(\forall x \bullet\ P(x)\ \Rightarrow\ x \leqslant a\ )]\!]\ \Rightarrow\ [\![P(2)]\!]\ \Rightarrow\ [\![2 \leqslant a]\!]$$

is sufficient to refute the current satisfying assignment. Consequently, the two-tier technique returns the following lemma:

$$[\![(\forall x \bullet\ P(x)\ \Rightarrow\ x \leqslant a\ )]\!] \wedge [\![P(2)]\!]\ \Rightarrow\ \neg[\![a = 0]\!]$$

However, the instantiation above is also sufficient to refute the (only) other satisfying
assignment of the input formula.

If it is possible to detect such reuse of instantiations, the algorithm can expose these
instantiations to the main SAT solver. We are currently exploring different heuristics to
identify such useful instantiations.

7.2   Handling Non-convex Theories

For efficiency, it is best if theories combined using Nelson-Oppen are *convex*. Informally,
a convex theory will never infer a disjunction of equalities without inferring one of them.
Thus the decision procedures only need to propagate single equalities. For non-convex
theories, sometimes it is necessary for the decision procedure to propagate a disjunction
of equalities. For example, the integer arithmetic theory can infer the following fact:

$$0 \leqslant x \wedge x \leqslant 3\ \Rightarrow\ x = 0 \vee x = 1 \vee x = 2 \vee x = 3.$$

This fact should be added as a lemma in the proving process. Like the lemmas generated
by quantifier instantiation, there is a risk that useless lemmas increase the work required
of the propositional search. The same technique discussed in this paper is readily applied
to those non-convex theories. In this sense, our algorithm in Figure 3 actually provides
a unified approach to handle both quantifiers and non-convex theories—they can both
be viewed as a theory that can generate lemmas of arbitrary forms.

8   Related Work

Among decision-procedure based theorem provers, besides our work, Simplify [5], Verifun [7], and CVC Lite [2] all provide some degree of quantifier support.

Simplify's method of using triggering patterns to find instantiations [11, 5] has proved quite successful in practice. Once an instantiation is generated, it remains in the prover until the search backtracks from the quantifier atom. We implemented a similar triggering algorithm and used a second SAT solver to reason about the instantiated formulas so that useful instantiations can be identified.

Our handling of quantifiers is based on Verifun's early work [8]. Some attempts have been made in Verifun to identify useful lemmas from instantiations of quantifiers. However, it seems that it is an optimization that works only when the instantiations alone can propositionally refute the current monome. In most scenarios, we believe, the quantifier module needs to cooperate with other theories to find out the instantiations that are useful to refute the monome.

In CVC Lite, each term is given a type and the formula is type checked. Types give hints about which terms can be used to instantiate a universal variable. However, instantiating a variable with every term whose type matches may be unrealistic for large problems.

Apart from the decision-procedure based theorem provers that rely on heuristic instantiations of quantified formulas, many automated first-order theorem provers including the resolution-based theorem provers (such as Vampire [13]) and the superposition theorem provers (such as HaRVey [4]) can handle quantifiers.

9   Conclusion

In this paper, we have proposed a two-tier technique for handling quantifiers in a lazy-proof-explication theorem prover. The propositional reasoning of the original formula and that of the instantiated formulas are handled by two SAT solvers. The major purpose of this separation is to avoid unnecessary case splits caused by intertwining useless instantiations and the original formula. The *FindUnsatCore* method can extract, from a set of lemmas generated during quantifier reasoning, a "good lemma" that is both relevant to the problem and sufficient to refute the given monome. We also use checkpointable theories to improve efficiency during the quantifier reasoning.

Acknowledgments. We thank the referees for their many useful comments on a previous version of this paper.

References

1. Mike Barnett, Robert DeLine, Manuel Fähndrich, K. Rustan M. Leino, and Wolfram Schulte. Verification of object-oriented programs with invariants. *Journal of Object Technology*, 3(6):27–56, 2004.
2. Clark Barrett and Sergey Berezin. CVC Lite: A new implementation of the cooperating validity checker. In *Proceedings of the 16th International Conference on Computer Aided Verification (CAV)*, Lecture Notes in Computer Science. Springer, July 2004.

3. Leonardo de Moura and Harald Rueß. Lemmas on demand for satisfiability solvers. In *Fifth International Symposium on the Theory and Applications of Satisfiability Testing (SAT'02)*, May 2002.
4. David Déharbe and Silvio Ranise. Light-weight theorem proving for debugging and verifying units of code. In *Proc. of the International Conference on Software Engineering and Formal Methods (SEFM03)*, Camberra, Australia, September 2003.
5. David Detlefs, Greg Nelson, and James B. Saxe. Simplify: A theorem prover for program checking. Technical Report HPL-2003-148, HP Labs, July 2003.
6. David L. Detlefs, K. Rustan M. Leino, Greg Nelson, and James B. Saxe. Extended static checking. Research Report 159, Compaq Systems Research Center, December 1998.
7. Cormac Flanagan, Rajeev Joshi, Xinming Ou, and James B. Saxe. Theorem proving using lazy proof explication. In *15th Computer-Aided Verification conference (CAV)*, July 2003.
8. Cormac Flanagan, Rajeev Joshi, and James B. Saxe. An explicating theorem prover for quantified formulas. Technical Report HPL-2004-199, HP Labs, 2004.
9. Cormac Flanagan, K. Rustan M. Leino, Mark Lillibridge, Greg Nelson, James B. Saxe, and Raymie Stata. Extended static checking for Java. In *Proceedings of the 2002 ACM SIGPLAN Conference on Programming Language Design and Implementation (PLDI)*, volume 37, number 5 in *SIGPLAN Notices*, pages 234–245. ACM, May 2002.
10. Kenneth L. McMillan. Interpolation and SAT-based model checking. In *15th International Conference on Computer Aided Verification*, Lecture Notes in Computer Science. Springer, 2003.
11. Charles Gregory Nelson. *Techniques for Program Verification*. PhD thesis, Stanford University, 1980. Also available as Xerox PARC technical report CSL-81-10, 1981.
12. Greg Nelson and Derek C. Oppen. Simplification by coorperating decision procedures. *ACM Transactions on Programming Languages and Systems*, 1(2):245–57, 1979.
13. Alexandre Riazanov and Andrei Voronkov. The design and implementation of vampire. *AI Commun.*, 15(2):91–110, 2002.
14. Lintao Zhang and Sharad Malik. Extracting small unsatisfiable cores from unsatisfiable boolean formulas. In *Sixth International Conference on Theory and Applications of Satisfiability Testing (SAT2003)*, May 2003.

Symbolic Test Selection
Based on Approximate Analysis*

Bertrand Jeannet, Thierry Jéron, Vlad Rusu, and Elena Zinovieva

IRISA/INRIA, Campus de Beaulieu, Rennes, France
{bjeannet, jeron, rusu, lenaz}@irisa.fr

Abstract. This paper addresses the problem of generating symbolic test cases for testing the conformance of a black-box implementation with respect to a specification, in the context of reactive systems. The challenge we consider is the selection of test cases according to a test purpose, which is here a set of scenarios of interest that one wants to observe during test execution. Because of the interactions that occur between the test case and the implementation, test execution can be seen as a game involving two players, in which the test case attempts to satisfy the test purpose.

Efficient solutions to this problem have been proposed in the context of finite-state models, based on the use of fixpoint computations. We extend them in the context of infinite-state symbolic models, by showing how approximate fixpoint computations can be used in a conservative way. The second contribution we provide is the formalization of a quality criterium for test cases, and a result relating the quality of a generated test case to the approximations used in the selection algorithm.

1 Introduction

In this paper we address the generation of test cases in the framework of conformance testing of reactive systems [1]. In this context, a Test Case (TC) is a program run in parallel with a black-box Implementation Under Test (IUT), that stimulates the IUT by repeatedly sending inputs and checking that the observed outputs of the IUT are in conformance with a given specification S. In case the IUT exhibits a conformance error, the execution is immediately interrupted. However, in addition to checking the conformance of the IUT, the goal of the test case is to guide the parallel execution towards the satisfaction of a test purpose, typically a set of scenarios of interest. Because of this second feature, test execution can be seen as a game between two programs, the test case and the IUT. The test case wins if it succeeds to make the parallel execution realize one of the interesting scenarios specified by the test purpose; the IUT wins if the execution cannot be extended any more to one that realizes an interesting scenario. If a conformance error is detected, the game terminates with a tie.

The *test selection* problem consists in finding a strategy that minimizes the likelihood for the test case to lose the game. Indeed, it is generally not possible

---

* The full version of this paper is available as Irisa report [11].

N. Halbwachs and L. Zuck (Eds.): TACAS 2005, LNCS 3440, pp. 349–364, 2005.

to ensure that the test case wins, because IUT is unknown: it is a black-box program that may behave in a non-controllable way. This problem has been previously addressed in a context where the specifications, the test cases and the test purposes are modeled with finite Labelled Transition Systems (LTS) [9].

Finding a suitable strategy for the test case is decomposed in two steps:

1. One first performs an *off-line* selection of a Test Case that detects when the game is lost by the tester and stops the execution in this case. This is done by static analysis of the specification S and the test purpose TP.
2. Then, during the execution of the obtained test case in parallel with the IUT, one performs an *on-line* selection of the inputs that the test case sends to the IUT. This on-line selection is based on the history of the current execution.

A previous paper [14] extends these principles and algorithmic methods to the case where specifications, test purposes and test cases are modeled with Input-Output Symbolic Transition Systems (ioSTS), which are automata that operate on variables (integers, booleans, aggregate types, ...) and communicate with the environment by means of input and output actions carrying parameters. For undecidability reason, the static analysis used for the off-line selection (Step 1) is approximated. [14] considers only a specific analysis (moreover restricted to the control structure) and does not study the effect of the approximations on the generated test cases.

The contributions of this paper are twofold. First we describe a general test selection method parameterized by an approximate analysis, in the context of Input-Output Symbolic Transition Systems. Compared to [14], we allow for the use of more precise analyses that perform both control and data based selection. We show that the test cases obtained by this method are sound. Second, we investigate the effect of the approximations of the analysis from the point of view of test execution as a game: in which way do they degrade the winning capabilities of the obtained test case? This leads us to define an accuracy ordering between test cases, to formalize the notion of optimal test case, and to compare the test cases generated by our method using these notions.

Context and Related Work

Conformance testing: Testing is the most used validation technique to assess the quality of software systems. Among the aspects of software that can be tested, *e.g.*, functionality, performance, timing, robustness, etc, we focus here on conformance testing and specialize it to reactive systems. In this approach, the software is specified in a behavioral model which serves both as a basis for test generation and for verdicts assignment. Testing theories based on models such as automata associated to fault models (see *e.g.* the survey [13]), or labelled transition systems with conformance relations (see *e.g.* [16]) are now well understood. Test generation algorithms have been designed based on these theories, and tools like TorX [2], TGV [9] have been developed and used on industrial-size systems.

Test selection: The test selection problem consits of choosing some test cases among many possible, according to a given criterion. Most approaches are based on variants of classical control and data-flow coverage criteria [8, 3], while others focus on specific functionalities using test purposes [6]. Although this is not always made explicit, test generation typically relies on reachability and coreachability analyses [9] based on pre- and post- predicate transformers.

Symbolic models: Many of the existing test generation algorithms and tools operate on variants of labeled transition systems (LTS). High-level specifications (written in languages such as SDL, Lotos, or UML) can be treated as well, via a translation (by state-space exploration) to the more basic labeled transition systems. More recently, attempts have been made in the direction of *symbolic* test generation [14] which works directly on the higher-level specifications without enumerating their state-space, thus avoiding the state-space explosion problem.

Outline: In Section 2, we recall ioLTS model, the corresponding testing theory and the principles of test generation using test purposes. In Section 3, we define the syntax of the symbolic model of ioSTS and its ioLTS semantics. In Section 4, we propose an off-line test selection algorithm for ioSTS based on syntactical transformations and parameterized by an approximate fixpoint analysis. Section 5 describes the on-line test selection that occurs during test execution. Section 6 defines qualitative properties on tests cases concerning their ability to satisfy the test purpose, and shows how the approximations used in the off-line test generation step influence those qualities.

2 Testing with Input/Output Labeled Transition Systems

Specification languages for reactive systems can often be given a semantics in terms of labelled transition systems. For test generation, we use the following version where actions are explictly partitioned into *inputs*, which are controlled by the environment, and *outputs*, which the environment may only observe. This model also serves as a semantic model for our symbolic automata (cf. Section 3).

Definition 1 (ioLTS). *An Input/Output Labelled Transition System is a tuple* $(Q, Q_0, \Lambda, \rightarrow)$ *where Q is a set of states, Q_0 the set of initial states, $\Lambda = \Lambda_? \cup \Lambda_!$ is a set of actions partitioned into inputs ($\Lambda_?$) and outputs ($\Lambda_!$) and $\rightarrow \subseteq Q \times \Lambda \times Q$ is the transition relation.*

We write $q \overset{\alpha}{\rightarrow} q'$ in place of $(q, \alpha, q') \in \rightarrow$ and note $q \overset{\alpha}{\rightarrow}$ when $\exists q' : q \overset{\alpha}{\rightarrow} q'$.

For the sake of simplicity, we consider only *deterministic* ioLTS: the alphabet does not contain internal actions and $\forall q \in Q, q \overset{\alpha}{\rightarrow} q' \wedge q \overset{\alpha}{\rightarrow} q'' \Rightarrow q' = q''$.

A *run* is a finite sequence $\rho = q_0 \overset{\alpha_0}{\rightarrow} q_1 \overset{\alpha_1}{\rightarrow} \ldots \overset{\alpha_{n-1}}{\rightarrow} q_n$ such that $q_0 \in Q_0$ and $\forall i < n, (q_i, \alpha_i, q_{i+1}) \in \rightarrow$. Its projection onto actions is the *trace* $\sigma = trace(\rho) = \alpha_0 \ldots \alpha_{n-1}$. We denote by $Runs(M) \subseteq Q_0 \cdot (\Lambda \cdot Q)^*$ the set of runs of M and by $Traces(M) \subseteq \Lambda^*$ the set of traces of M. An ioLTS M can be seen as an automaton if it is equipped with a set of marked states $X \subseteq Q$. A run $\rho = q_0 \overset{\alpha_0}{\rightarrow} q_1 \overset{\alpha_1}{\rightarrow} \ldots \overset{\alpha_{n-1}}{\rightarrow} q_n$ is *accepted in* X iff $q_n \in X$. We denote $Runs_X(M) \subseteq Runs(M)$ the set of runs accepted by X. Similarly, the set of accepted traces $Traces_X(M) \subseteq Traces(M)$ is obtained by projecting $Runs_X(M)$ on Λ^*. An ioLTS M is *complete in a state* q if $\forall \alpha \in \Lambda : q \xrightarrow{\alpha}$; it is *complete* if it is complete in all states. Similarly, the notion of *input*-completeness is defined by replacing Λ with $\Lambda_?$.

The *synchronous product* of two ioLTS $M = (Q, Q_0, \Lambda, \to^M)$ and $M' = (Q', Q'_0, \Lambda, \to^{M'})$ with same alphabet is the ioLTS $M \times M' = (Q \times Q', Q_0 \times Q'_0, \Lambda, \to^{M \times M'})$ where $\to^{M \times M'}$ is defined by the inference rule:

$$\frac{q_1 \xrightarrow{\alpha}{}^M q_2 \quad q'_1 \xrightarrow{\alpha}{}^{M'} q'_2}{(q_1, q'_1) \xrightarrow{\alpha}{}^{M \times M'} (q_2, q'_2)} \quad \text{(Sync)}$$

As usual, we get $Traces(M \times M') = Traces(M) \cap Traces(M')$ and $Traces_{X \times X'}(M \times M') = Traces_X(M) \cap Traces_{X'}(M')$ for $X \subset Q$ and $X' \subset Q'$.

For a set of traces $W \subseteq \Lambda^*$, we denote respectively by $pref_{\le}(W)$ and $pref_{<}(W)$ the set of prefixes (resp. strict prefixes) of W. For $X \subseteq Q$, we denote by $post(X) = \{q' \mid \exists q \in X, \exists \alpha \in \Lambda : q \xrightarrow{\alpha} q'\}$ and $pre(X) = \{q \mid \exists q' \in X, \exists \alpha \in \Lambda : q \xrightarrow{\alpha} q'\}$ the pre- and post-condition operators. The set of states *reachable* from a subset Q' of Q in M may then be defined by $reach(Q') = \text{lfp}(\lambda X.Q' \cup post(X))$ where lfp is the least fixpoint operator. Similarly, the set of states *coreachable* from a set of states Q' may be defined as $coreach(Q') = \text{lfp}(\lambda X.Q' \cup pre(X))$.

2.1   Testing Theory

The testing theory we consider is based on the notions of *specification, implementation*, and *conformance relation* between them [16]. The specification is an ioLTS $S = (Q^S, Q_0^S, \Lambda, \to^S)$. The Implementation Under Test (*IUT*) is also assumed to be an ioLTS $IUT = (Q^{IUT}, Q_0^{IUT}, \Lambda, \to^{IUT})$ which is unknown except for its alphabet, which is assumed to be the same as that of the specification. Moreover, it is assumed that the *IUT* is *input-complete*, which reflects the hypothesis that the implementation cannot refuse an input from its environment.

Definition 2 (Conformance relation). *A trace σ is conformant to S, denoted by σ conf S, iff $pref_{\le}(\sigma) \cap (Traces(S) \cdot \Lambda_!) \subseteq Traces(S)$. IUT is conformant to S, denoted by IUT conf S, iff $Traces(IUT) \cap Traces(S) \cdot \Lambda_! \subseteq Traces(S)$.*

Intuitively, *IUT conf S* if after each trace of S, *IUT* may emit only outputs that S can emit as well while its inputs are unconstrained. For readers familiar with ioco [16], note that *conf* can be interpreted as ioco if S makes *quiescence* (absence of output) explicit. For instance on the figure $\neg(\sigma_1$ conf $S)$, σ_2 conf S, and σ_0 conf S as σ_0 diverges from S by an *input*.

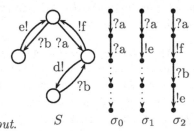

2.2   Test Cases and Test Purposes

A test case is an ioLTS able to interact with an implementation and to emit verdicts about the implementation's conformance with respect to the specification.

Table 1. Properties of Test Cases

Property	Explanations
(1) TC is output-complete, verdict states are sink	always, def 3
(2) $Traces(TC) \subseteq Traces(S) \cdot (\{\epsilon\} \cup \Lambda_!)$	always, def 3
(3) $Traces_{Fail}(TC) = Traces(TC) \cap ((Traces(S) \cdot \Lambda_!) \setminus Traces(S))$	soundness, def 5
(4) $Traces_{Pass}(TC) = Traces(TC) \cap ATraces(S, TP)$	soundness, def 5
(5) $Traces_{Inconc}(TC) \subseteq RTraces(S, TP)$	soundness, def 5
(6) $Traces_{Inconc}(TC) = Traces(TC) \cap RTraces(S, TP)$ $\cap pref_<(ATraces(S, TP)) \cdot \Lambda_!$	optimality, def 10
(7) $Traces(TC) \cap \Lambda^* \cdot \Lambda_? \subseteq pref_<(ATraces(S, TP))$	optimality, def 10

In our approach, a test case is an ioLTS implementing a strategy for satisfying a given *test purpose* (typically, staying within a (finite or infinite) set of traces). The test case takes into account output choices of the specification (observable non-determinism) and anticipates incorrect outputs of the implementation.

Definition 3 (Test Case). *A* test case *for a specification S is an ioLTS $TC = (Q^{TC}, Q_0^{TC}, \Lambda^{TC}, \rightarrow^{TC})$ equipped with 3 disjoint subsets of sink states* Pass, Fail, Inconc $\subseteq Q^{TC}$ *(corresponding to the verdicts it may emit) such that*

- *its alphabet is the mirror of that of S ($\Lambda_?^{TC} = \Lambda_!^S$ and $\Lambda_!^{TC} = \Lambda_?^S$) and it is input-complete (outputs of IUT are not refused) except in verdict states;*
- *$Traces(TC) \subseteq Traces(S) \cdot (\{\epsilon\} \cup \Lambda_!)$: as soon as a conformance error cannot occur any more the test case stops (cf. Definition 2).*

The specification S contains all the information relevant to conformance, and its mirror followed by *input-completion* constitutes a test case by itself. However, such a test case is typically too large and is not focused on any part of the system. It is more interesting in practice to test what happens in the course of a given scenario (or set thereof), and if no error has been detected, to end the test successfully when the scenario is completed. This is precisely the reason for introducing *test purposes*.

Definition 4 (Test Purpose). *A* test purpose *TP for a specification S is an ioLTS $TP = (Q^{TP}, Q_0^{TP}, \Lambda, \rightarrow^{TP})$ equipped with a subset* Accept $\subseteq Q^{TP}$ *of accepting states, which are sink. TP is complete except in* Accept *states. TP defines a set $ATraces(S, TP)$ of accepted traces of S which induces a set $RTraces(S, TP)$ of refused traces (traces of S that cannot be extended to accepted traces):*

$$ATraces(S, TP) = Traces_{Q^S \times Accept}(S \times TP) \tag{1}$$

$$RTraces(S, TP) = Traces(S) \setminus pref_\leq(ATraces(S, TP)) \tag{2}$$

Observe that *both accepted and refused traces are conformant*. More elaborate test purposes can be defined which may choose traces based on internal actions and states. We do not describe them here for simplicity.

A test case TC should emit the appropriate verdicts in the appropriate situations. Fail verdicts should be emitted if and only if a non conformance is observed. This requirement depends only on S. Additionally, since a test purpose TP is used for selection, TC and IUT can be viewed as players in a game. In this context, Pass verdicts should reflect success of the game for the test case, while Inconc verdicts should reflect defeat for the test case. These requirements are made explicit in the following definition:

Definition 5 (Soundness of test case verdicts). *The verdicts of TC are sound w.r.t. S and TP whenever the following properties of Table 1 are satisfied:*

- *(3): Fail is emitted iff TC observes an unspecified output after a trace of S.*
- *(4): Pass is emitted iff TC observes a trace of S accepted by TP.*
- *(5): Inconc may be emitted only if the trace observed by TC belongs to S (thus, it is conformant) but is refused by TP. In this case, the test execution can be interrupted, as Pass cannot be emitted any more.*

Notice that for test cases satisfying Definition 5, Fail and Pass verdicts are uniquely defined, so that they are emitted appropriately and as soon as possible. In particular for Fail, the requirement is stronger than the usual notion of soundness [16] which says that only non conformant IUTs can be rejected. On the other hand, Definition 5 does not uniquely define the Inconc verdict. We have adopted this definition in anticipation of the general (symbolic) test selection algorithm (addressed in Section 4) where checking whether a trace is refused is undecidable.

2.3 Off-line Test Selection Algorithm

For finite ioLTS, the principles of test generation using test purposes [12] are described by Table 2. Explanations and sketch of proof are given below.

1. After Step 1, by properties of $\times$, $Traces_{\mathsf{Pass}}(P) = ATraces(S, TP)$, implying Property (4) of Table 1, and $Traces(P) \subseteq Traces(S)$, implying Property (2). Intuitively, the product P combines information about conformance, coming from S, and information about the game with the IUT, coming from TP.
2. After Step 2, we have $Traces_{\mathsf{Inconc}}(P') \subseteq RTraces(S, TP)$, implying Property (5) of Table 1. Properties (2) and (4) from the previous step are preserved. This *selection* step is based on the definition of $RTraces(S, TP)$ and the following property: $pref_<(Traces_{\mathsf{Pass}}(P)) = Traces_{coreach(\mathsf{Pass})}(P)$. The exact knowledge of $coreach(\overline{\mathsf{Pass}})$ allows to detect when an action extends a trace and causes it to be refused (*i.e.*, not a prefix any more of accepted traces).
3. After Step 3, we have $Traces_{\mathsf{Fail}}(TC) = Traces(TC) \cap (Traces(S) \cdot \Lambda_! \setminus Traces(S))$, which is Property (3) of Table 1. Moreover, Property (1) becomes true (rule (Fail)). Properties (2), (4), (5) are preserved by the transformation.

The TGV tool [9] is based on the above algorithm. The main optimization, consists in performing these operations on the fly. This means that S, P, P', and TC are built in a lazy way, from a high level specification, thus avoiding the state explosion problem. This involves both a reachability and coreachability

Table 2. Off-line test selection algorithm

{ 1. Product and Pass verdict }
 $P := S \times TP$; Pass $:= Q^S \times Accept^{TP}$;
{ 2. Selection and Inconc verdict }
 $P' = (Q^P, Q_0^P, \Lambda, \to^{P'})$ is equipped with Inconc $\subseteq Q^P$ and $\to^{P'}$ is defined by:

$$\frac{q, q' \in coreach(\mathsf{Pass})}{q \xrightarrow{\alpha}_P q' \quad \alpha \in \Lambda_? \cup \Lambda_!}{q \xrightarrow{\alpha}_{P'} q'} \quad (\text{KeepI})$$

$$\frac{q \in coreach(\mathsf{Pass}), q' \notin coreach(\mathsf{Pass})}{q \xrightarrow{\alpha}_P q' \quad \alpha \in \Lambda_!}{q \xrightarrow{\alpha}_{P'} q' \quad q' \in \mathsf{Inconc}} \quad (\text{Inconc})$$

{ 3. Input-completion and Fail verdict }
 $TC = (Q^{P'} \cup \{\mathsf{Fail}\}, Q_0^P, \Lambda^{TC}, \to^{TC})$ with $\Lambda_?^{TC} = \Lambda_!$ and $\Lambda_!^{TC} = \Lambda_?$, and
$\to^{TC}$ is defined by:

$$\frac{q \xrightarrow{\alpha}_{P'} q'}{q \xrightarrow{\alpha}_{TC} q'} \quad (\text{KeepF})$$

$$\frac{\neg(q \xrightarrow{\alpha}_{P'}) \quad \alpha \in \Lambda_!}{q \xrightarrow{\alpha}_{TC} \mathsf{Fail} \quad (\alpha \in \Lambda_?^{TC})} \quad (\text{Fail})$$

analysis of P that do not modify the soundness of the test case. A test case
generated as above is called a *complete test graph* as it contains all traces
accepted by TP. This notion will be formalized in Section 6. TGV also allows
to generate other test cases that are less complete, by pruning some outputs
and the corresponding subgraphs.

We do not describe the *on-line* selection phase, that occurs during the parallel
execution of the test case with the IUT. It is described later for ioSTS.

3   ioSTS: Input/Output Symbolic Transition Systems

In this section, we introduce a model of symbolic automata with a finite set of
locations and typed variables, which communicates with its environment through
actions carrying values. We call it ioSTS for Input/Output Symbolic Transition
Systems. Figure 1 gives an example of such an ioSTS.

Variables, Predicates, Assignments. In the sequel we shall assume a set of
typed variables. We note $\mathcal{D}_v$ the domain in which a variable v takes its values.
For a set of variables $V = \{v_1, \ldots, v_n\}$, we note $\mathcal{D}_V$ the product domain $\mathcal{D}_{v_1} \times \ldots \times \mathcal{D}_{v_n}$. An element of $\mathcal{D}_V$ is thus a vector of values for the variables in V. We
use also the notation $\mathcal{D}_v$ for a vector v of variables. Depending on the context, a
predicate $P(V)$ on a set of variables V may be considered either as a set $P \subseteq \mathcal{D}_V$,
or as a logical formula, the semantics of which is a function $\mathcal{D}_V \to \{true, false\}$.
An assignment for a variable v depending on the set of variables V is a function
of type $\mathcal{D}_V \to \mathcal{D}_v$. An assignment for a set X of variables is then a function
of type $\mathcal{D}_V \to \mathcal{D}_X$. We do not specify the syntactical constructions used for
building predicates and assignments. They are discussed in the full paper.

Definition 6 (ioSTS). *An Input/Output Symbolic Transition System $\mathcal{M}$ is defined by a tuple (V, Θ, Σ, T) where:*

- $V = V_p \cup V_o$ is the set of variables, partitioned into a set V_p of proper variables and a set V_o of observed variables.
- Θ is the initial condition: a predicate $\Theta \subseteq \mathcal{D}_{V_p}$ defined on proper variables.
- $\Sigma = \Sigma_? \cup \Sigma_!$ is the finite alphabet of actions. Each action a has a signature $\text{sig}(a)$, which is a tuple of types $\text{sig}(a) = \langle t_1, \ldots, t_k \rangle$ specifying the types of the communication parameters carried by the action.
- T is a finite set of symbolic transitions. A symbolic transition $t = (a, \boldsymbol{p}, G, A)$, also noted $\left[a(\boldsymbol{p}) : G(\boldsymbol{v}, \boldsymbol{p}) ? \boldsymbol{v}'_p := A(\boldsymbol{v}, \boldsymbol{p}) \right]$, is defined by (i) an action $a \in \Sigma$ and a tuple of (formal) communication parameters $\boldsymbol{p} = \langle p_1, \ldots, p_k \rangle$, which are local to a transition; without loss of generality, we assume that each action a always carries the same vector $\boldsymbol{p}$, which is supposed to be well-typed w.r.t. the signature $\text{sig}(a) = \langle t_1, \ldots, t_k \rangle$; $\mathcal{D}_{\boldsymbol{p}}$ is denoted by $\mathcal{D}_{\text{sig}(a)}$; (ii) a guard $G \subseteq \mathcal{D}_V \times \mathcal{D}_{\text{sig}(a)}$, which is a predicate on the variables and the communication parameters, and (iii) an assignment $A : \mathcal{D}_V \times \mathcal{D}_{\text{sig}(a)} \to \mathcal{D}_{V_p}$, which defines the evolution of the proper variables. We denote by A_v the function in A defining the evolution of the variable $v \in V_p$.

This model is rather standard, except for the distinction between proper and observed variables. The observed variables allow an observer ioSTS $\mathcal{M}_1$ to inspect the variables of another ioSTS $\mathcal{M}_2$ when composed together with it. Note also that there is no explicit notion of control location, since the control structure of an automaton can be encoded by a specific program counter variable.

The *semantics* of an ioSTS $\mathcal{M} = (V, \Theta, \Sigma, T)$ is an ioLTS $\llbracket \mathcal{M} \rrbracket = (Q, Q_0, \Lambda, \to)$:
- $Q = \mathcal{D}_V$, $Q_0 = \{ \boldsymbol{\nu} = \langle \boldsymbol{\nu}_p, \boldsymbol{\nu}_o \rangle \mid \boldsymbol{\nu}_p \in \Theta \wedge \boldsymbol{\nu}_o \in \mathcal{D}_{V_o} \}$;
- $\Lambda = \{ \langle a, \boldsymbol{\pi} \rangle \mid a \in \Sigma \wedge \boldsymbol{\pi} \in \mathcal{D}_{\text{sig}(a)} \}$;
- $\to$ is defined by

$$\frac{(a, \boldsymbol{p}, G, A) \in T \quad \boldsymbol{\nu} = \langle \boldsymbol{\nu}_p, \boldsymbol{\nu}_o \rangle \in \mathcal{D}_V \quad \boldsymbol{\pi} \in \mathcal{D}_{\text{sig}(a)} \quad G(\boldsymbol{\nu}, \boldsymbol{\pi})}{\boldsymbol{\nu}' = \langle \boldsymbol{\nu}'_p, \boldsymbol{\nu}'_o \rangle \in \mathcal{D}_V \quad \boldsymbol{\nu}'_p = A(\boldsymbol{\nu}, \boldsymbol{\pi})} \qquad \text{(Sem)}$$
$$\boldsymbol{\nu} \xrightarrow{\langle a, \boldsymbol{\pi} \rangle} \boldsymbol{\nu}'$$

The rule says that a transition $(a, \boldsymbol{p}, G, A)$ of an ioSTS is fireable in the current state $\boldsymbol{\nu} = \langle \boldsymbol{\nu}_p, \boldsymbol{\nu}_o \rangle$, if there exists a valuation $\boldsymbol{\pi}$ of the communication parameters $\boldsymbol{p}$ such that $\langle \boldsymbol{\nu}, \boldsymbol{\pi} \rangle$ satisfies the guard G; in such a case, the valued action $\langle a, \boldsymbol{\pi} \rangle$ is taken, the proper variables are assigned new values as specified by the assignment A, whereas observed variables take arbitrary values. Such a behaviour for observed variables reflects the fact that their value is defined by another ioSTS.

Given this semantics, most notions and properties of ioSTS are defined in terms of their underlying ioLTS semantics. For example, a run (resp. a trace) of an ioSTS $\mathcal{M}$ is a run (resp. a trace) of its ioLTS semantics $\llbracket \mathcal{M} \rrbracket$. An ioSTS $\mathcal{M}$ is *deterministic* if $\llbracket \mathcal{M} \rrbracket$ is deterministic. Whether an ioSTS is deterministic or not cannot be decided for ioSTS in the general case, as it implies the knowledge of reachable states. Sufficient conditions for an ioSTS to be deterministic exist (mutual exclusion of guards of all transitions labeled by the same action).

The *product* of ioSTS is more complex than that of ioLTS: ioSTS synchronize on actions, but also via observed variables, which observe *runs* (not only traces).

Definition 7 (Product). *Two ioSTS $\mathcal{M}^i = (V^i, \Theta^i, \Sigma, T^i), i = 1, 2$ with the same alphabet are* compatible for product *if $V_p^1 \cap V_p^2 = \emptyset$ (proper variables are disjoint). In this case, their product $\mathcal{M}^1 \times \mathcal{M}^2 = \mathcal{M} = (V, \Theta, \Sigma, T)$ is defined by*

- $V = V_p \cup V_o$, with $V_p = V_p^1 \cup V_p^2$ and $V_o = (V_o^1 \cup V_o^2) \setminus V_p$;
- $\Theta(\langle v^1, v^2 \rangle) = \Theta^1(v^1) \wedge \Theta^2(v^2)$;
- *T is defined by the following inference rule:*

$$\frac{\left[a(p) \ : \ G^1(v^1, p) \, ? \, (v_p^1)' := A^1(v^1, p) \right] \in T^1 \qquad \left[a(p) \ : \ G^2(v^2, p) \, ? \, (v_p^2)' := A^2(v^2, p) \right] \in T^2}{\left[a(p) \ : \ G^1(v^1, p) \wedge G^2(v^2, p) \, ? \, (v_p^1)' := A^1(v^1, p), (v_p^2)' := A^2(v^2, p) \right]}$$

If $V_o^1 \cap V_p^2 \neq \emptyset$, G^1 and A^1 may depend on proper variables of $\mathcal{M}_2$ (cf. Figure 3). Let $\mathcal{M}^1$ and $\mathcal{M}^2$ be two ioSTS compatible for product, and $\mathcal{M} = \mathcal{M}^1 \times \mathcal{M}^2$. Then $Traces(\mathcal{M}) \subseteq Traces(\mathcal{M}^1) \cap Traces(\mathcal{M}^2)$. Let also $F^i = X^i \times \mathcal{D}_{V_o^i}$, where $i = 1, 2$ and $X^i \subseteq \mathcal{D}_{V_p^i}$, be sets of accepting states of ioSTS $\mathcal{M}^i$. By taking as set of accepting states $F = X^1 \times X^2 \times \mathcal{D}_{V_o}$ for $\mathcal{M}$, we have $Traces_F(\mathcal{M}) \subseteq Traces_{F^1}(\mathcal{M}^1) \cap Traces_{F^2}(\mathcal{M}^2)$. It is not hard to see that the two trace inclusions are obtained from corresponding equalities for runs and accepting runs, which become inclusions by projection on observable actions.

The testing theory for ioLTS developed in Section 2.1 also applies to ioSTS. Specifications, test purposes and test cases are assumed to be ioSTS; moreover

- A specification is supposed to be an ioSTS $S = (V^S, \Theta^S, \Sigma, T^S)$ with only proper variables and no observed variable ($V^S = V_p^S$);
- A test purpose for S is an ioSTS $TP = (V^{TP}, \Theta^{TP}, \Sigma, T^{TP})$ such that $V_o^{TP} = V_p^S$ (symbolic test purposes are allowed to observe the internal state of S). The set of accepting states is defined by the truth value of a Boolean variable Accept $\in V_p^{TP}$. TP should be *complete* except when Accept = true, which means that for any action a, $\bigcup_{(a,p,G,A) \in T^{TP}} G \Leftrightarrow \neg$Accept. This condition can be enforced syntactically by completion of TP. It ensures that TP does not restrict the runs of S before they are accepted (if ever).
- A test case is an ioSTS $TC = (V^{TC}, \Theta^{TC}, \Sigma, T^{TC})$ with a variable Verdict $\in V^{TC}$ of the enumerated type $\{\texttt{none}, \texttt{fail}, \texttt{pass}, \texttt{inconc}\}$.

The set of accepted traces is defined as $ATraces(S, TP) = Traces_{\mathsf{Accept}}(S \times TP)$ (as in Definition 4, except that the product is now the ioSTS product).

4   Off-line Test Selection for ioSTS

The aim of this section is to extend the test generation principles of ioLTS to *symbolic* test generation, taking into account the following difficulties:

1. Ensuring semantic transformations through operations on ioSTS;
2. Relying on approximate coreachability analysis instead of exact analysis, due to undecidability issues in the (infinite-state) symbolic case.

Table 3. Off-line symbolic test selection algorithm

{ 1. Product and Pass verdict }

$P := S \times TP$

$P' = (V^P \cup \{\text{Verdict}\}, \Theta^P \wedge \text{Verdict} = \text{none}, \Sigma, T^{P'})$ is defined by

$$\frac{[\,a(p) \,:\, G(v,p)\,?\,v' = A(v,p)\,] \in T^P}{\left[\begin{array}{c} a(p) \,:\, G(v,p) \wedge \text{Verdict} = \text{none}\,? \\ v' := A(v,p), \text{Verdict}' := \text{if } A_{\text{Accept}} \text{ then pass else Verdict} \end{array}\right] \in T^{P'}} \quad (3)$$

{ 2. Selection and Inconc verdict }

$P'' = (V^{P'}, \Theta^{P'}, \Sigma, \to^{P''})$ is defined by

$$\frac{[\,a(p) \,:\, G(v,p)\,?\,v' = A(v,p)\,] \in T^{P'}}{[\,a(p) \,:\, G(v,p) \wedge pre^\alpha(A)(coreach^\alpha)\,?\,v' = A(v,p)\,] \in T^{P''}} \quad (\text{KeepI})$$

$$\frac{[\,a(p) \,:\, G(v,p)\,?\,v' = A(v,p); \text{Verdict}' := A_{\text{Verdict}}\,] \in T^{P'} \quad a \in \Sigma_!}{[\,a(p) \,:\, G(v,p) \wedge \neg pre^\alpha(A)(coreach^\alpha)\,?\,v' = A(v,p); \text{Verdict}' := \text{inconc}\,] \in T^{P''}}$$
$$(\text{Inconc})$$

{ 3. Input-completion and Fail verdict }

$TC = (V^{P'}, \Theta^{P'}, \Sigma, T^{TC})$ is defined by

$$\frac{t \in T^{P''}}{t \in T^{TC}} \quad (\text{KeepF}) \qquad \frac{a \in \Sigma_! \quad G_a = \bigwedge\{\neg G(v,p) \mid (a,p,G,A) \in T^{P''}\}}{[\,a(p) \,:\, G_a(v,p)\,?\,\text{Verdict}' := \text{fail}\,] \in T^{TC}} \quad (\text{Fail})$$

We consider again the simple case where the specification S and the test purpose TP do not contain internal actions or non-determinism. Our running example is depicted on Figure 1–6. The selection algorithm is given in Table 3. The first step is the symbolic version of Step 1 for ioLTS (cf. Table 2). The same invariants hold. The transformation from P to P' specifies the behavior of the Verdict variable and makes states with Verdict $\neq$ none sink.

Step 2 is the main step of the selection. As the coreachability problem is now undecidable, coreachability analysis should be approximated. Fixpoint computations on ioSTS or similar models can indeed be overapproximated by classical Abstract Interpretation techniques [4, 7, 10]. We consider here an overapproximation $coreach^\alpha \supseteq coreach(\text{Pass})$ of the exact set of coreachable states (see Figure 7(b)). It can be represented by a logical formula to be used in syntactical operations on ioSTS. Moreover, $pre^\alpha(A)(X)$ denotes a formula representing an overapproximation of the precondition $pre(A)(X) = A^{-1}(X)$ of states in X by the assignement A. In this context, $pre^\alpha(A)(coreach^\alpha)$ is an overapproximation of the set of values for variables and parameters which allow to stay in $coreach(\text{Pass})$ when taking the transition, or in other words it is a *necessary condition*. Its negation is thus a *sufficient condition* to leave $coreach(\text{Pass})$, and to lose the game for the test case. Hence, rule (KeepI) discards all (semantic) transitions labeled by a (controllable) input that *certainly* exit $coreach(\text{Pass})$, and rule (KeepI) "redirects" to Inconc all transitions labelled by an (uncontrollable) output that *certainly* exit $coreach(\text{Pass})$.

Finally, Step 3 is the symbolic version of the corresponding step in Table 2.

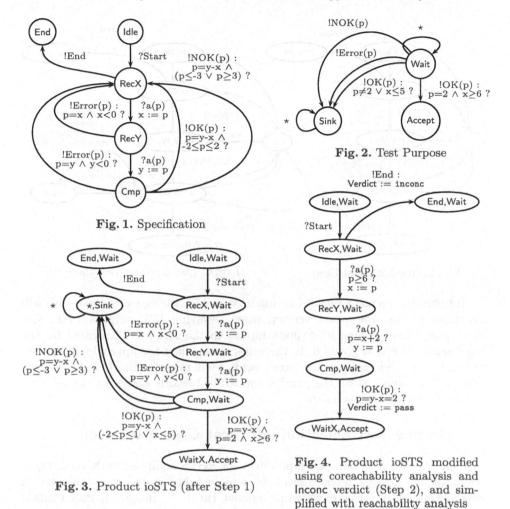

Fig. 1. Specification

Fig. 2. Test Purpose

Fig. 3. Product ioSTS (after Step 1)

Fig. 4. Product ioSTS modified using coreachability analysis and Inconc verdict (Step 2), and simplified with reachability analysis

Example: The specification describes a program which is waiting for two successive inputs $?a(p_1)$ and $?a(p_2)$, and emits $!OK(p_2 - p_1)$ when their difference is less than 2 in absolute value, and $!NOK$ otherwise. If the value held by the channel $?a$ is negative, the message $!Error$ is emitted. The program may also emit $!End$ and ends its execution. The test purpose specifies that a test of interest is one that terminates with the first emission of $!OK(p)$, and with $p = 2$, from a state of the specification where $x \geq 6$. A $!NOK(p)$ message is forbidden. This implies that we should have $p \geq 6$ (resp. $p = x+2$) in $?a(p)$ from location RecX (resp. RecY), facts which are discovered by a coreachability analysis using convex polyhedra [7] and taken into account in Figure 4. The resulting test case is depicted in Figure 5.

In contrast, if the analysis performed on the product of Figure 3 is a more simple interval analysis, it would only detects that we should have $p \geq 6$ in $?a(p)$ from location RecY, and we would obtain the test case depicted in Figure 6. Here, we avoid to lose the game by receiving a conformant $?Error(p)$ messages (because we emit $!a(p)$ with $p \geq 0$) but we can lose the game with conformant $?OK(p)$ or $?NOK(p)$ messages.

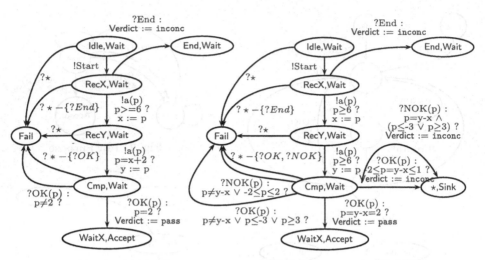

Fig. 5. Resulting Test Case   **Fig. 6.** Less accurate Test Case

Intuitively, the main effect of approximations for the generated test case will be either to miss the Inconc verdict, when receiving *IUT* outputs, or to lose the game, when sending inadequate inputs to the *IUT*, as illustrated by the comparison of Figure 5 and 6. In the worst case, when the approximation does not deliver any information, the Inconc verdict will never be emitted and the test case will not guide at all the parallel execution towards accepting states. This will be formalized in Section 6.

5   On-line Test Selection and Test Case Execution

The off-line test selection phase produces an ioSTS equipped with verdicts, in which (some) losing strategies has been removed, but it does not implement a single strategy, in terms of its game against the *IUT*. Indeed, it may contain choices between several outputs that may be sent to the *IUT*. For instance, in Figure 5, from the location RecY,Wait, the action $a(p)$ may be emitted for any $p \geq 6$. This illustrates the fact that the test case has to assign values to the formal communication parameters carried by the actions.

As a consequence, test case execution implies *on-line constraint solving*. A test case is then executed as follows. At any point of the parallel execution of *TC* with *IUT*, *TC* is in a known state $\nu \in \mathcal{D}_V$. It may then have the choice between observing an output of the *IUT*, or controling an input of the *IUT*:

- *TC* observes an output a of the *IUT* with actual values of parameters $\pi \in \mathcal{D}_{sig(a)}$. As *TC* is input-complete and deterministic, exactly one transition $(a, \boldsymbol{p}, G, A) \in T^{TC}$ satisfies $\langle \nu, \pi \rangle \in G$. It then performs the assignments $\nu' = A(\nu, \pi)$, and checks the value of Verdict.
- *TC* controls an input a in a transition $(a, \boldsymbol{p}, G, A)$. By constraint solving, it chooses π such that $\langle \nu, \pi \rangle \in G$, sends $a(\pi)$ to *IUT*, performs $\nu' = A(\nu, \pi)$, and finally checks the verdict.

A test execution driver thus needs to implement the choice between observing or controlling, the evaluation of guards on outputs of the IUT, constraint solving for the choice of values of parameters on inputs of the IUT, and evaluation of assignments. Evaluation of a formula is never a problem, however the use of constraint solving techniques to instantiate input parameters imposes restrictions into a decidable theory, such as Presburger arithmetic.

6   Quality of Generated Test Cases

As sketched during the off-line test selection algorithm of Section 4, test case verdicts are sound, which implies the usual soundness property of test cases — only non-conformant IUT can be rejected, like for ioLTS. Exhaustiveness — every non conformant IUT may be rejected [16], can also be proved, but this is out of the scope of the present paper.

These properties are related to conformance or to soundness of verdicts. They do not say whether test cases are good players in the game against the IUT. In this section we formalize qualitative properties of test cases relative to their ability to satisfy the test purpose during test execution, and show how the precision of the approximate analysis during the off-line selection algorithm influences them. We consider a fixed specification S and test purpose TP.

We can first compare two test cases in terms of their sets of traces leading to Pass. The requirement (4) of Table 1 only relates $Traces_{Pass}(TC)$ and $Traces(TC)$. However, a test case can be pruned in any state where there exists a choice between several outputs (inputs of IUT). Such an operation may reduce the sets $Traces(TC)$ and $Traces_{Pass}(TC)$.

Definition 8 (Completeness ordering; completeness of a test case). *Let TC and TC' be two test cases with sound verdicts (Definition 5), both generated from same S and TP. TC' is less complete than TC, denoted by $TC' \preceq^{comp} TC$, if $Traces_{Pass}(TC') \subseteq Traces_{Pass}(TC)$. TC is a complete test case if $Traces_{Pass}(TC) = ATraces(S, TP)$.*

The test cases produced by the off-line test selection algorithms of Sections 2.3 and 4 are complete. In the TGV tool however [9], they are pruned to remove the choices between inputs to be sent to the IUT. Thus, in this case the on-line test selection (described in section 5 for ioSTS) is partly performed off-line.

The (partial) completeness of a test case is not directly related to its quality as a player in the game for satisfying the test purpose. However, we are only able to compare the quality of test cases when they are equivalent with respect to the completeness ordering. Otherwise, two test cases may have disjoint sets of traces, which makes their comparison as players difficult. We now define an accuracy ordering between test cases that are equivalent with respect to the completeness ordering. The definition seems simplistic, however it makes sense when examining its consequences, by taking the properties of Table 1 into account.

Definition 9 (Accuracy ordering). *Let TC and TC' be two test cases with sound verdicts that are equivalent for the completeness ordering. TC is more accurate than TC', denoted by $TC \preceq^{acc} TC'$, if $Traces(TC) \subseteq Traces(TC')$.*

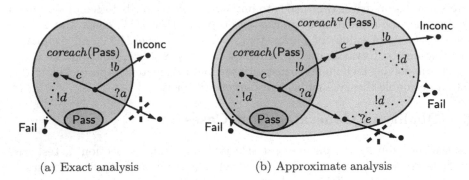

(a) Exact analysis   (b) Approximate analysis

Fig. 7. Control and inconclusiveness: Step 2 of off-line selection algorithms

In particular, using properties of Table 1, $TC \preceq^{acc} TC'$ implies

1. $Traces_{Inconc}(TC) \subseteq Traces(TC')$: TC' detects inconclusives later than TC, if ever;
2. $Traces_{Fail}(TC) \subseteq Traces_{Fail}(TC')$: TC' emits more Fail verdicts than TC,

The second consequence may seem paradoxical: an accurate test case detects less conformance errors than a less accurate one! In fact, two test cases that are equivalent for the completeness ordering have same accepted traces and detect exactly the same errors along prefixes of those accepted traces. But a less accurate test case (i) exercices weaker control on the inputs of the IUT and (ii) emits Inconc verdicts later, which gives more opportunity to the IUT to exhibit non-conformance. Figure 5 and 6 illustrates point (i).

Now, among sound and completeness-equivalent test cases, the optimal test case can be defined as the test case where refused traces of S w.r.t. TP are never entered by a controllable input of the IUT and where Inconc verdict is emitted as soon as an output of IUT enters these refused traces.

Definition 10 (Optimal test case). *TC is optimal w.r.t. S and TP if:*

1. $Traces(TC) \cap \Lambda^* \cdot \Lambda_? \subseteq pref_{\leq}(ATraces(S, TP))$: *TC does not lose the game on a controllable action;*
2. $Traces_{Inconc}(TC) = Traces(TC) \cap RTraces(S, TP) \cap pref_{<}(ATraces(S, TP)) \cdot \Lambda_!$: *TC immediately detects refused traces.*

These conditions correspond to properties (7) and (6) of Table 1, respectively.

In the case of finite ioLTS it is not hard to see that the algorithm in Section 2.3 builds sound, complete and optimal test cases. Completeness is obtained at Step 1 of the algorithm. Optimality is obtained at Step 2, as Inconc is reached exactly when leaving $coreach(Pass)$. Both properties are preserved by Step 3. In the case of ioSTS, we also build sound and complete test cases. However, the effect of the approximate coreachability analysis is to relax the optimality (see also Figure 6). The following theorem confirms the relevance of the accuracy ordering of test cases (Definition 9) and identifies the consequences of an approximate analysis in the off-line test selection algorithm.

Theorem 1 (Relating accuracy to precision). *Let TC and TC' be two test cases generated by the algorithm described in Table 3, where TC was generated using a more precise approximation α than the approximation α' used for generating TC', i.e., $pre^\alpha(A)(coreach^\alpha) \subseteq pre^{\alpha'}(A)(coreach^{\alpha'})$. Then $TC \preceq^{acc} TC'$.*

Proof. We need only to consider Step 2. For inputs, only the rule (KeepI) of Step 2 of the algorithm applies. In this case, a better precision for $pre^\alpha(A)(coreach^\alpha)$ strengthens the guards of the symbolic transitions, implying that fewer semantic transitions will be inferred in the underlying ioLTS. For outputs, both inference rules apply. For any state q of the underlying ioLTS, a better precision for $pre^\alpha(A)(coreach^\alpha)$ means that more semantic transitions from q leading to Inconc (which is sink) will be inferred by the rule (Inconc) while less transitions from q to its "normal" successors (which are generally not sink) will be inferred by the rule (KeepI). This implies that $Traces(TC^1) \subseteq Traces(TC^2)$. Moreover, $Traces_{\text{Pass}}(TC^1) = Traces_{\text{Pass}}(TC^2)$, hence the conclusion of the theorem.

The two extreme cases are actually the following:

- The computation is exact; an *optimal* test case is obtained, as in Section 2.3;
- The approximation is maximal ($pre^\alpha(A)(coreach^\alpha) = true$), thus delivers no information: Step 2 of the algorithm has no effect and the test case is unable to control the implementation to satisfy the test purpose, nor to detect when Inconc should be emitted.

7   Conclusion

In this paper, we have presented a symbolic test generation algorithm for specifications and test purposes given as symbolic automata. Test generation has been decomposed into an off-line selection of test cases and an on-line execution on the *IUT*. The off-line selection is based on syntactical transformations and is parameterized by an approximate fixpoint analysis. We have showed how the precision of the analysis influences the accuracy of selected test cases. The on-line execution is based on constraint solving. These algorithms have been implemented in our tool STG, STG relies on NBac (http://www.irisa.fr/prive/bjeannet/nbac/nbac.html) for the approximate fixpoint analysis and Omega (http://www.cs.umd.edu/projects/omega/) for constraint resolution in Presburger arithmetic. STG uses a more general model than the one presented here, in particular admitting non-deterministic specifications under some restrictions. While most other works are limited to controlable (and deterministic) systems, we are able to generate test cases for non-controllable (and non-deterministic) specifications. Moreover, we believe that our framework can be generalized to other models that cannot be analyzed in an exact way.

In a sense, our approach is an improvement of strictly on-line approaches (as e.g. TorX [2, 5]), which lack control of the test cases on the *IUT*. Off-line symbolic selection seriously improves this feature. In fact, off-line selection based on test purposes can be seen as a syntactic slicing of the specification w.r.t. particular scenarios, preserving the capability to generate sound test cases on line.

Several extensions of our work can be investigated. We have presented this work in the context of conformance testing, but similar techniques could be used in structural testing for the selection of test cases based on the source code. Also, other models can be considered, such as programs with recursive calls modelled as pushdown automata. One problem is then to decide what is observable and controlable by a tester. Finally, other selection criteria can benefit from our techniques, like safety properties [15] or standard structural coverage criteria.

References

1. ISO/IEC 9646. Conformance Testing Methodology and Framework, 1992.
2. A. Belinfante, J. Feenstra, R.G. de Vries, J. Tretmans, N. Goga, L. Feijs, S. Mauw, and L. Heerink. Formal test automation: A simple experiment. In 12th Int. Workshop on Testing of Communicating Systems. Kluwer Academic Publishers, 1999.
3. M. Benjamin, D. Geist, A. Hartman, G. Mas, R. Smeets, and Y. Wolfsthal. A feasibility study in formal coverage driven test generation. In DAC99, 1999.
4. P. Cousot and R. Cousot. Abstract intrepretation: a unified lattice model for static analysis of programs by construction or approximation of fixpoints. In 4th ACM Symposium on Principles of Programming Languages, Los Angeles, CA, 1977.
5. L. Frantzen, J. Tretmans, and T. Willemse. Test generation based on symbolic specifications. In FATES 2004, Linz, Austria, 2004.
6. J. Grabowski, D. Hogrefe, and R. Nahm. Test Case Generation with Test Purpose Specification by MSCs. In 6th SDL Forum, Darmstadt (Germany). North-Holland, 1993.
7. N. Halbwachs, Y.E. Proy, and P. Roumanoff. Verification of real-time systems using linear relation analysis. Formal Methods in System Design, 11(2), 1997.
8. H.S. Hong, I. Lee, O. Sokolsky, and H. Ural. A temporal logic based theory of test coverage and generation. In TACAS '02, Grenoble, France, LNCS 2280. Springer-Verlag, 2002.
9. C. Jard and T. Jéron. TGV: theory, principles and algorithms. International Journal on Software Tools for Technology Transfer, 6, 2004.
10. B. Jeannet. Dynamic partitioning in linear relation analysis. application to the verification of reactive systems. Formal Methods in System Design, 23(1), 2003.
11. B. Jeannet, T. Jéron, V. Rusu, and E. Zinovieva. Symbolic test selection using approximate analysis. Technical Report 1649, INRIA, 2004. Available at http://www.irisa.fr/bibli/publi/pi/2004/1649/1649.html.
12. T. Jéron and P. Morel. Test generation derived from model-checking. In CAV'99, Trento, Italy, LNCS 1633. Springer-Verlag, 1999.
13. D. Lee and M. Yannakakis. Principles and Methods of Testing Finite State Machines - A Survey. Proceedings of the IEEE, 84(8), 1996.
14. V. Rusu, L. du Bousquet, and T. Jéron. An approach to symbolic test generation. In Integrated Formal Methods (IFM'00), Dagstuhl, Allemagne, LNCS 1945. Springer Verlag, 2000.
15. V. Rusu, H. Marchand, and T. Jéron. Verification and symbolic test generation for safety properties. Technical Report 5285, INRIA, 2004. Available at http://www.inria.fr/rrrt/rr-5285.html.
16. J. Tretmans. Test generation with inputs, outputs and repetitive quiescence. Software—Concepts and Tools, 17(3), 1996.

Symstra: A Framework for Generating Object-Oriented Unit Tests Using Symbolic Execution

Tao Xie[1], Darko Marinov[2], Wolfram Schulte[3], and David Notkin[1]

[1] Dept. of Computer Science & Engineering, Univ. of Washington, Seattle, WA 98195, USA
[2] Department of Computer Science, University of Illinois, Urbana-Champaign, IL 61801, USA
[3] Microsoft Research, One Microsoft Way, Redmond, WA 98052, USA
{taoxie, notkin}@cs.washington.edu, marinov@cs.uiuc.edu,
schulte@microsoft.com

Abstract. Object-oriented unit tests consist of sequences of method invocations. Behavior of an invocation depends on the method's arguments and the state of the receiver at the beginning of the invocation. Correspondingly, generating unit tests involves two tasks: generating method sequences that build relevant receiver-object states and generating relevant method arguments. This paper proposes Symstra, a framework that achieves both test generation tasks using symbolic execution of method sequences with symbolic arguments. The paper defines symbolic states of object-oriented programs and novel comparisons of states. Given a set of methods from the class under test and a bound on the length of sequences, Symstra systematically explores the object-state space of the class and prunes this exploration based on the state comparisons. Experimental results show that Symstra generates unit tests that achieve higher branch coverage faster than the existing test-generation techniques based on concrete method arguments.

1 Introduction

Object-oriented unit tests are programs that test classes. Each test case consists of a fixed sequence of method invocations with fixed arguments that explores a particular aspect of the behavior of the class under test. Unit tests are becoming an important component of software development. The Extreme Programming discipline [5], for instance, leverages unit tests to permit continuous and controlled code changes. Unlike in traditional testing, it is developers (not testers) who write tests for every aspect of the classes they develop. However, manual test generation is time consuming, and so typical unit test suites cover only some aspects of the class.

Since unit tests are gaining importance, many companies now provide tools, frameworks, and services around unit tests. Tools range from specialized test frameworks, such as JUnit [18] or Visual Studio's new team server [25], to automatic unit-test generation, such as Parasoft's Jtest [27]. However, existing test-generation tools typically do not provide guarantees about the generated unit-test suites. In particular, the suites rarely satisfy the branch-coverage test criterion [6], let alone a stronger criterion, such as the bounded intra-method path coverage [3] of the class under test. We present an approach that uses symbolic execution to exhaustively explore bounded method sequences of the

N. Halbwachs and L. Zuck (Eds.): TACAS 2005, LNCS 3440, pp. 365–381, 2005.

class under test and to generate tests that achieve high branch and intra-method path coverage for complex data structures such as container implementations.

1.1   Background

Generating test sequences involves two tasks: generating method sequences that build relevant receiver-object state and generating relevant method arguments. Researchers have addressed this problem several times. Most tools generate test sequences using concrete representations. A popular approach is to use (smart) random generation; this approach is embodied in tools such as Jtest [27] (a commercial tool for Java) or JCrasher [13] and Eclat [26] (two research prototypes for Java). Random tests generated by these tools often execute the same sequences [34] and are not covering (do not cover all sequences). The AsmLT model-based testing tool [16, 15] uses concrete-state space-exploration techniques [12] to generate covering method sequences. But AsmLT requires the user to carefully choose sufficiently large concrete domains for method arguments and the right abstraction functions to guarantee the covering. Tools such as Korat [8] are able to generate non-isomorphic object graphs that can be used for testing, but they do not generate covering test sequences.

King proposed in the 70's to use symbolic execution for testing and verification [20]. Because of the advances in constraint solvers, this technique recently regained the attention for test generation. For example, the BZ-TT tool uses constraint solving to derive method sequences from B specifications [22]. However, the B specifications are not object-oriented. Khurshid et al. [19, 33] proposed an approach for generating tests for Java classes based on symbolic execution. They show that their generation based on symbolic execution generates tests faster than their model checking of method sequences with concrete arguments. This is expected: symbolic representations describe not only single states, but sets of states, and when applicable, symbolic representations can yield large improvements, witnessed for example by symbolic model checking [24]. The approach of Khurshid et al. [19,33], however, generates the receiver-object states, similar to Korat [8], only as object graphs, not through method sequences. Moreover, it requires the user to provide specially constructed class invariants [23], which effectively describe an over-approximation of the set of reachable object graphs.

Symbolic execution is the foundation of static code analysis tools. These tools typically do not generate test data, but automatically verify simple properties of programs. These properties often allow merging symbolic states that stem from different execution paths. However, for test generation, states have to be kept separate, since different tests should be used for different paths. Recently, tools such as SLAM [4,2] and Blast [17,7] were adapted for test generation. However, neither of them can deal with complex data structures, which are the focus of this paper.

1.2   Contributions

This paper makes the following contributions.

Symbolic Sequence Exploration: We propose Symstra, a framework that uses symbolic execution to generate method sequences. When applicable, Symstra uses an exhaustive exploration of method sequences with symbolic variables for primitive-type arguments.

(We also discuss how Symstra can handle reference-type arguments.) Each symbolic argument represents a set of all possible concrete values for the argument. Symstra uses symbolic execution to operate on symbolic states that include symbolic variables.

Symbolic State Comparison: We present novel techniques for comparison of symbolic states of object-oriented programs. Our techniques allow Symstra to prune the exploration of the object state and thus generate tests faster, without compromising the exhaustiveness of the exploration. In particular, the pruning preserves the intra-method path coverage of the generated test suites.

Implementation: We describe an implementation of a test-generation tool for Symstra. Our implementation handles dynamically allocated structures, method pre- and post-conditions, and symbolic data. Our current implementation does not support concurrency, but such support can be added by reimplementing Symstra in a Java model checker, such as Java Pathfinder [32] or Bogor [29].

Evaluation: We evaluate Symstra on seven subjects, most of which are complex data structures. The experimental results show that Symstra generates tests faster than the existing test-generation techniques based on exhaustive exploration of sequences with concrete method arguments [33, 16, 15, 34]. Further, given the same time for generation, Symstra can generate tests that achieve better branch coverage than the existing techniques. Finally, Symstra works on ordinary Java implementations and does not require the user to provide the additional methods required by some other approaches [33, 8].

2   Example

This section illustrates how Symstra explores method sequences and generates tests. Figure 1 shows a binary search tree class BST that implements a set of integers. Each tree has a pointer to the root node. Each node has an element and pointers to the left and right children. The class also implements the standard set operations: insert adds an element, if not already in the tree, to a leaf; remove deletes an element, if in the tree, replacing it with the smallest larger child if necessary; and contains checks if an element is in the tree. The class also has a default constructor that creates an empty tree.

Some tools such as Jtest [27] or JCrasher [13] test a class by generating random sequences of methods; for BST, they could for example generate the following tests:

```
Test 1:                               Test 2:
  BST t1 = new BST();                   BST t2 = new BST();
  t1.insert(0);                         t2.insert(2147483647);
  t1.insert(-1);                        t2.remove(2147483647);
  t1.remove(0);                         t2.insert(-2147483648);
```

Each test has a method sequence on the objects of the class, e.g., Test 1 creates a tree t1, invokes two insert methods on it, and then one remove. Typically, checking the correctness (of outputs) for such tests relies on design-by-contract annotations translated into run-time assertions [27, 10] or on model-based testing [16]. If there are no annotations or models, the tools check only the code robustness: execute the tests and check for uncaught exceptions [13].

```
class BST implements Set {
    Node root;
    static class Node {
        int value;
        Node left;
        Node right;
    }
    void insert(int value) { ... }
    void remove(int value) { ... }
    bool contains(int value) { ... }
}
```

Fig. 1. A set implemented as a binary search tree

Some other tools [33, 16, 15, 34] can exhaustively explore all method sequences up to a given length. Such exploration raises two questions: (1) what arguments to use for method calls, and (2) how to determine equivalent tests? These tools typically require the user to provide a sufficiently good set of concrete values for each argument, or based on the argument type, use a set of default values that may miss relevant behaviors. These tools check equivalence of test sequences by comparing the states that the sequences build; the comparison uses either user-provided functions or defaults, such as identity or isomorphism. This generation is similar to explicit-state model checking [12].

Symstra also explores all sequences, but using *symbolic values* for primitive-type arguments in method calls. Such exploration relieves Symstra users from the burden of providing concrete values: Symstra determines the relevant values during the execution. Having symbolic arguments necessitates symbolic execution [20]. It operates on a symbolic state that consists of two parts: (1) a *constraint*, known as the *path condition*, that must hold for the execution to reach a certain point and (2) a heap that contains symbolic variables. When the symbolic execution encounters a branch, it explores both outcomes, appropriately adding the branch condition or its negation to the constraint. Symbolic state exploration in Symstra is conceptually similar to symbolic model checking [24].

Let us consider the symbolic execution of the following sequence:

```
BST t = new BST();
t.insert(x₁);
t.insert(x₂);
t.insert(x₃);
t.remove(x₄);
```

This sequence has four method calls whose arguments are symbolic variables x_1, x_2, x_3, and x_4. While an execution of a sequence with concrete arguments produces one state, symbolic execution of a sequence with symbolic arguments can produce several states, thus resulting in an execution tree. Figure 2 shows a part of the execution tree for this example. Each state has a heap and a constraint that must hold for that heap to be created. The constructor first creates an empty tree. The first insert then adds the element x_1 to the tree.

The second insert produces states s_3, s_4, and s_5: if $x_1 = x_2$, the tree does not change, and if $x_2 > x_1$ (or $x_2 < x_1$), x_2 is added in the right (or left) subtree. Note that the symbolic states s_2 and s_4 are *syntactically* different: s_2 has the constraint true, while s_4 has $x_1 = x_2$. However, these two symbolic states are *semantically* equivalent: they can be instantiated into the same set of concrete heaps by giving to x_1 and x_2

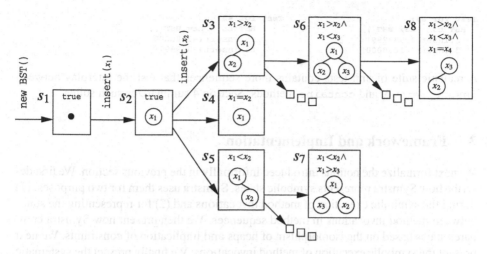

Fig. 2. A part of the symbolic execution tree

concrete values that satisfy the constraints; since x_2 does not appear in the heap in s_4, the constraint in s_4 is "irrelevant". Instead of state equivalence, it suffices to check state *subsumption*: we say that s_2 subsumes s_4 because the set of concrete heaps of s_4 is a subset of the set of concrete heaps of s_2. Hence, Symstra does not need to explore s_4 after it has already explored s_2. Symstra detects this by checking that the implication of constraints $x_1 = x_2 \Rightarrow$ true holds. Our current Symstra implementation uses the Omega library [28] and CVC Lite [11] to check the validity of the implication.

The third insert again produces several symbolic states. Symstra applies insert only on s_3 and s_5 (and not on s_4). In particular, we focus on s_6 and s_7, two of the symbolic states that these executions produce. These two states are syntactically different, but semantically equivalent: we can exchange the variables x_2 and x_3 to obtain the same symbolic state. Symstra detects this by checking that s_6 and s_7 are *isomorphic* (Section 3.2). Symstra finally applies remove. Note again that one of the symbolic states produced, s_8, is subsumed by a previously explored state, s_3.

This example has illustrated how Symstra would explore symbolic execution for one particular sequence. Symstra actually exhaustively explores the symbolic execution tree for all sequences up to a given length, pruning the exploration based on subsumption. These sequences consists of all specified methods of the class under test, i.e., insert, remove, and contains for BST.

After producing a symbolic state s, Symstra can generate a specific test with concrete arguments to produce a concrete heap of s. Symstra generates the test by traversing the shortest path from the root of the symbolic execution tree to s and outputting the method calls that it encounters. To generate concrete arguments for these calls, Symstra uses a constraint solver. Our current implementation uses the POOC solver [31]. For example, the tests that it generates for s_3 and s_5 are:

```
Test for s3:                      Test for s5:
  BST t3 = new BST();               BST t5 = new BST();
  t3.insert(-999999);               t5.insert(-1000000);
  t3.insert(-1000000);              t5.insert(-999999);
```

A realistic suite of unit tests contains more sequences that test the interplay between insert, remove, and contains methods. Section 4 summarizes such suites.

3   Framework and Implementation

We next formalize the notions introduced informally in the previous section. We first describe how Symstra represents symbolic states. Symstra uses them for two purposes: (1) during the symbolic execution of method invocations and (2) for representing the states between method invocations in method sequences. We then present how Symstra compares states based on the isomorphism of heaps and implication of constraints. We next present the symbolic execution of method invocations. We finally present the systematic exploration of method sequences and how Symstra uses symbolic state comparison to prune this exploration. We present the Symstra technique itself as well as our current implementation.

3.1   Symbolic State

Symbolic states differ from concrete states, on which the usual program executions operate, in that symbolic states contain symbolic expressions with symbolic variables and also constraints on these variables [20]. Symstra uses the following symbolic expressions and constraints:

- A symbolic variable is a symbolic expression. Each symbolic variable has a type, which is one of the Java types. For example, x_1 and x_2 may be each a symbolic variable (and thus also a symbolic expression) of type int.
- A Java constant of some type is a symbolic expression of that type.
- For each Java operator $\odot$ with n operands, n symbolic expressions of the appropriate operand types connected with $\odot$ are a symbolic expression of the result type. For example, $x_1 + x_2$ and $x_1 > x_2$ are expressions of type int and boolean, respectively.
- Symbolic expressions of type boolean are constraints.

Let P be the set of all primitive values, including integers, true, false, etc. Let V be a set of infinite number of symbolic variables of each type and U a set of all possible expressions formed from V and P. Given a valuation for the variables, $\eta : V \to P$, we extend it to evaluate all expressions $\eta : U \to P$ as follows: $\eta(p) = p$ for all $p \in P$, and $\eta(\odot u_1, \ldots, u_n) = \mathrm{eval}(\odot, \eta(u_1), \ldots, \eta(u_n))$ for all $u_1, \ldots, u_n \in U$ and operations $\odot$, where eval evaluates operations on primitive values according to the Java semantics.

In object-oriented programs, a concrete state consists of a global heap and a stack (in general one stack for each thread, but we consider here only single-threaded programs), as well as several other parts, such as metadata for classes and program counters. Symbolic states in Symstra have the same parts as concrete states, but the heaps and stacks in symbolic states can contain symbolic expressions; additionally, each symbolic state has a constraint. We focus on the symbolic state between method sequences.

Definition 1. *A symbolic state $\langle C, H \rangle$ is a pair of a constraint and a symbolic heap.*

We view each heap as a graph: nodes represent objects (as well as primitive values and symbolic expressions) and edges represent object fields. Let O be some set of objects whose fields form a set F. Each object has a field that represents its class. We consider arrays as objects whose fields are labelled with (integer) array indexes and point to the array elements.

Definition 2. *A symbolic heap is an edge-labelled graph $\langle O, E \rangle$, where $E \subseteq O \times F \times (O \cup \{\texttt{null}\} \cup U)$ such that for each field f of each $o \in O$ exactly one $\langle o, f, o' \rangle \in E$. A concrete heap has only concrete values: $o' \in O \cup \{\texttt{null}\} \cup P$.*

3.2 Heap Isomorphism

We define heap isomorphism as graph isomorphism based on node bijection [8]. We are interested in detecting isomorphic heaps because they lead to equivalent method behaviors; hence, it suffices to explore only one representative from each isomorphism partition. Nodes in symbolic heaps contain symbolic variables, so we first define a renaming of symbolic variables. Given a bijection $\tau : V \rightarrow V$, we extend it to the whole $\tau : U \rightarrow U$ as follows: $\tau(p) = p$ for all $p \in P$, and $\tau(\odot u_1, \ldots, u_n) = \odot \tau(u_1), \ldots, \tau(u_n)$ for all $u_1, \ldots, u_n \in U$ and operations $\odot$. We further extend τ to substitute free variables in formulas with bound variables, avoiding capture as usual.

Definition 3. *Two heaps $\langle O_1, E_1 \rangle$ and $\langle O_2, E_2 \rangle$ are isomorphic iff there are bijections $\rho : O_1 \rightarrow O_2$ and $\tau : V \rightarrow V$ such that:*

$$E_2 = \{\langle \rho(o), f, \rho(o') \rangle | \langle o, f, o' \rangle \in E_1, o' \in O_1\} \cup \{\langle \rho(o), f, \texttt{null} \rangle | \langle o, f, \texttt{null} \rangle \in E_1\} \cup$$
$$\{\langle \rho(o), f, \tau(o') \rangle | \langle o, f, o' \rangle \in E_1, o' \in U\}.$$

Note that the definition allows only object identities and symbolic variables to vary: two isomorphic heaps have the same fields for all objects and equal (up to renaming) symbolic expressions for all primitive fields.

The state exploration in Symstra focuses on the state of several objects and does not consider the entire heap; in this context, the state of an object o consists of the values of the fields of o and fields of all objects *reachable* from o. From a program heap $\langle O, E \rangle$ and a tuple $\langle v_0, \ldots, v_n \rangle$ of pointers and symbolic expressions $v_i \in O \cup U$, where $0 \leq i \leq n$, Symstra constructs a *rooted heap* [34] $\langle O_h, E_h \rangle$ that has a unique root object $r \in O_h$: Symstra first creates the heap $\langle O', E' \rangle$, where $O' = O \cup \{r\}$, $r \notin O$, and $E' = E \cup \{\langle r, i, v_i \rangle | 0 \leq i \leq n\}$, and then creates $\langle O_h, E_h \rangle$ as the subgraph of $\langle O', E' \rangle$ such that $O_h \subseteq O'$ is the set of all objects reachable from r within E' and $E_h = \{\langle o, f, o' \rangle \in E' | o \in O_h\}$.

We can efficiently check isomorphism of rooted heaps, even though for general graphs it is unknown whether checking isomorphism can be done in polynomial time. Symstra *linearizes* heaps into integer sequences such that checking heap isomorphism corresponds to checking sequence equality. Figure 3 shows the linearization algorithm.

```
Map<Object,int> objs; // maps objects to unique ids
Map<SymVar,int> vars; // maps symbolic variables to unique ids

int[] linearize(Object root, Heap <O,E>) {
  objs = new Map();  vars = new Map();
  return lin(root, <O,E>>;
}

int[] lin(Object root, Heap <O,E>) {
  if (objs.containsKey(root))
    return singletonSequence(objs.get(root));
  int id = objs.size() + 1;  objs.put(root, id);
  int[] seq = singletonSequence(id);
  Edge[] fields = sortByField({ <root, f, o> in E });
  foreach (<root, f, o> in fields) {
    if (isSymbolicExpression(o)) seq.append(linSymExp(o));
    elseif (o == null) seq.append(0);
    else seq.append(lin(o, <O,E>)); // pointer to an object
  }
  return seq;
}

int[] linSymExp(SymExp e) {
  if (isSymVar(e)) {
    if (!vars.containsKey(e))
      vars.put(e, vars.size() + 1);
    return singletonSequence(vars.get(e));
  } elseif (isPrimitive(e)) return uniqueRepresentation(e);
  else { // operation with operands
    int[] seq = singletonSequence(uniqueRepresentation(e.getOperation()));
    foreach (SymExp e' in e.getOperands())
      seq.append(linSymExp(e'));
    return seq;
  }
}
```

Fig. 3. Pseudo-code of linearization for a symbolic rooted heap

It starts from the root and traverses the heap depth first. It assigns a unique identifier to each object, keeps this mapping in objs and reuses it for objects that appear in cycles. It also assigns a unique identifier to each symbolic variable, keeps this mapping in vars and reuses it for variables that appear several times in the heap.

A similar linearization is used to represent concrete heaps in model checking [1, 30, 32]. This paper extends the linearization from our previous work [34] with linSymExp that handles symbolic expressions; this improves on the approach of Khurshid et al. [19, 33] that does not use any comparison for symbolic expressions. It is easy to show that our linearization normalizes rooted heaps.

Theorem 1. *Two rooted heaps* $\langle O_1, E_1 \rangle$ *(with root* r_1*) and* $\langle O_2, E_2 \rangle$ *(with root* r_2*) are isomorphic iff* linearize$(r_1, \langle O_1, E_1 \rangle)$=linearize$(r_2, \langle O_2, E_2 \rangle)$.

3.3   State Subsumption

We define symbolic state subsumption based on the concrete heaps that each symbolic state represents. Symstra uses state subsumption to prune the exploration. To instantiate

```
boolean checkSubsumes(Constraint C1, Heap H1,
                      Constraint C2, Heap H2) {
    int[] i1 = linearize(root(H1), H1);
    Map<SymVar,int> v1 = vars; // at the end of previous linearization
    Set<SymVar> n1 = variables(C1) - v1.keys(); // variables not in the heap
    int[] i2 = linearize(root(H2), H2);
    Map<SymVar,int> v2 = vars; // at the end of previous linearization
    Set<SymVar> n2 = variables(C2) - v2.keys(); // variables not in the heap
    if (i1 <> i2) return false;
    Renaming τ = v2 o v1⁻¹ // compose v2 and the inverse of v1
    return checkValidity(τ(∃n2. C2) ⇒ ∃n1. C1);
}
```

Fig. 4. Pseudo-code of subsumption checking for symbolic states

a symbolic heap into a concrete heap, we replace the symbolic variables in the heap with primitive values that satisfy the constraint in the symbolic state.

Definition 4. *An* instantiation $\mathcal{I}(\langle C, H \rangle)$ *of a symbolic state* $\langle C, H \rangle$ *is a set of concrete heaps* H' *such that there exists a valuation* $\eta : V \to P$ *for which* $\eta(C)$ *is true and* H' *is the evaluation* $\eta(H)$ *of all expressions in* H *according to* η.

Definition 5. *A symbolic state* $\langle C_1, H_1 \rangle$ subsumes *another symbolic state* $\langle C_2, H_2 \rangle$, *in notation* $\langle C_1, H_1 \rangle \supseteq \langle C_2, H_2 \rangle$, *iff for each concrete heap* $H'_2 \in \mathcal{I}(\langle C_2, H_2 \rangle)$, *there exists a concrete heap* $H'_1 \in \mathcal{I}(\langle C_1, H_1 \rangle)$ *such that* H'_1 *and* H'_2 *are isomorphic.*

Symstra uses the algorithm in Figure 4 to check if the constraint of $\langle C_1, H_1 \rangle$, after suitable renaming, implies the constraint of $\langle C_2, H_2 \rangle$. Note that the implication is universally quantified over the (renamed) symbolic variables that appear in the heaps and existentially quantified over the symbolic variables that do not appear in the heaps (more precisely only in H_1, because the existential quantifier for n_2 in the premise of the implication becomes a universal quantifier for the whole implication). We can show that this algorithm is a conservative approximation of subsumption.

Theorem 2. *If* checkSubsumes($\langle C_1, H_1 \rangle$, $\langle C_2, H_2 \rangle$) *then* $\langle C_1, H_1 \rangle$ *subsumes* $\langle C_2, H_2 \rangle$.

Symstra gains the power and inherits the limitations from the technique used to check the implication on the (renamed) constraints. The current Symstra prototype uses the Omega library [28], which provides a complete decision procedure for Presburger arithmetic, and CVC Lite [11], an automatic theorem prover, which has decision procedures for several types of constraints, including real linear arithmetic, uninterpreted functions, arrays, etc. Since these checks can consume a lot of time, Symstra further uses the following conservative approximation: if free-variables($\exists n_1. C_1$) are not a subset of free-variables($\tau(\exists n_2. C_2)$), return false without checking the implication.

3.4 Symbolic Execution

We next discuss the symbolic execution of one method in a method sequence. Each method execution starts with one symbolic state and produces several symbolic states. We use the notation $\sigma_m(\langle C, H \rangle)$ to denote the set $\{\langle C_1, H_1 \rangle, \ldots, \langle C_n, H_n \rangle\}$ of states that the symbolic execution, σ, of the method m produces starting from the state $\langle C, H \rangle$.

Following the typical symbolic executions [20, 33], Symstra symbolically explores both branches of if statements, modifying the constraint with a conjunct that needs to hold for the execution to take a certain branch. In this context, the constraint is called *path condition*, because it is a conjunction of conditions that need to hold for the execution to take a certain path and reach the current address. This symbolic execution directly explores every path of the method under consideration. The common issue in the symbolic execution is that the number of paths may be infinite (or too large as it grows exponentially with the number of branches) and thus $\sigma_m(\langle C, H \rangle)$ may be (practically) unbounded. In such cases, Symstra can use the standard set of heuristics to explore only some of the paths [33, 9].

The current Symstra prototype implements the execution steps on symbolic state by rewriting the code to operate on symbolic expressions. Further, Symstra implements the exploration of different branches by re-executing the method from the beginning for each path, without storing any intermediate states. Note that Symstra re-executes only one method (for different paths), not the whole method sequence. (This effectively produces a depth-first exploration of paths within one method, while the exploration of states between methods is breadth-first as explained in the next section.)

Our Symstra prototype also implements the standard optimizations for symbolic execution. First, Symstra simplifies the constraints that it builds at branches; specifically, before conjoining the path condition so far C and the current branch condition C' (where C' is a condition from an if or its negation), Symstra checks if some of the conjuncts in C implies C'; if so, Symstra does not conjoin C'. Second, Symstra checks if the constraint $C\&\&C'$ is unsatisfiable; if so, Symstra stops the current path of symbolic execution, because it is an infeasible path. The current Symstra prototype can use the Simplify [14] theorem prover or the Omega library [28] to check unsatisfiability. We have found that Omega is faster, but it handles only linear arithmetic constraints.

Given a symbolic state at the entry of a method execution, Symstra uses symbolic execution to achieve structural coverage within the method, because symbolic execution systematically explores all feasible paths within the method. If the user of Symstra is interested in only the tests that achieve new branch coverage, our Symstra prototype monitors the branch coverage during symbolic execution and selects a symbolic execution for concrete test generation (Section 3.6) when the symbolic execution covers a new branch. The Symstra prototype can also be extended for selecting symbolic executions that achieve new bounded intra-method path coverage [3].

3.5   Symbolic State Exploration

We next present the symbolic state space for method sequences and how Symstra systematically explores this state space. The state space consists of all states that are reachable with the symbolic execution of all possible method sequences for the class under test. Let C and M be a set of the constructor and non-constructor methods of this class. Each method sequence starts with a constructor from C followed by several methods from M. We denote with $\Sigma_{C,M}$ the state space for these sequences. The initial symbolic state is $s_0 = \langle \text{true}, \{\} \rangle$: the constraint is true, and the heap is empty. The state space includes the states that the symbolic execution produces for the constructors and methods: $\bigcup_{c \in \mathcal{C}} \sigma_c(s_0) \subset \Sigma_{\mathcal{C},\mathcal{M}}$ and $\forall s \in \Sigma_{\mathcal{C},\mathcal{M}}. \bigcup_{m \in \mathcal{M}} \sigma_m(s) \subset \Sigma_{\mathcal{C},\mathcal{M}}$. As usual [12], $\Sigma_{\mathcal{C},\mathcal{M}}$ is the least fixed point of these equations. The state space is typically infinite.

The current Symstra prototype exhaustively explores a bounded part of the symbolic state space using a breadth-first search. The inputs to Symstra are a set of constructor $\mathcal{C}$ and non-constructor methods $\mathcal{M}$ of the class under test and a bound on the length of sequences. Symstra maintains a set of explored states and a processing queue of states. Symstra processes the queue in a breadth-first manner: it takes one state and symbolically executes each method under test (constructor at the beginning of the sequence and a non-constructor after that) for each path on this state. Every such execution yields a new symbolic state. Symstra adds the new state to the queue for further exploration only if it is not subsumed by an already explored state from the set. Otherwise, Symstra prunes the exploration: the new symbolic state represents only a subset of the concrete heaps that some explored symbolic state represents; it is thus unnecessary to explore the new state further. Pruning based on subsumption plays the key role in enabling Symstra to explore large state spaces.

3.6   Concrete Test Generation

During the symbolic state exploration, Symstra also builds specific concrete tests that lead to the explored states. Whenever Symstra finishes a symbolic execution of a method that generates a new symbolic state $\langle C, H \rangle$, it also generates a *symbolic test*. This test consists of the constraint C and the shortest method sequence that reaches $\langle C, H \rangle$. (Symstra associates such a method sequence with each symbolic state and dynamically updates it during execution). Symstra then instantiates a symbolic test using the POOC constraint solver [31] to solve the constraint C over the symbolic arguments for methods in the sequence. Based on the produced solution, Symstra obtains concrete arguments for the sequence leading to $\langle C, H \rangle$. Symstra exports such concrete test sequences into a JUnit test class [18]. It also exports the constraint C associated with the test as a comment for the test in the JUnit test class.

At the class-loading time, Symstra instruments each branching point of the class under test for measuring branch coverage at the bytecode level. It also instruments each method of the class to capture uncaught exceptions at runtime. The user can configure Symstra to select only those generated tests that increase branch coverage or throw new uncaught exceptions.

4   Evaluation

This section presents our evaluation of Symstra for exploring method sequences and generating tests. We compare Symstra with Rostra [34], our previous framework that generates tests using bounded-exhaustive exploration of sequences with concrete arguments. We have developed Symstra on top of Rostra, so that the comparison does not give an unfair advantage to Symstra because of unrelated improvements. In these experiments, we have used the Simplify [14] theorem prover to check unsatisfiability of path conditions, the Omega library [28] to check implications, and the POOC constraint solver [31] to solve constraints. We have performed the experiments on a Linux machine

Table 1. Experimental subjects

class	methods under test	some private methods	#ncnb lines	# branches
IntStack	push,pop	–	30	9
UBStack	push,pop	–	59	13
BinSearchTree	insert,remove	removeNode	91	34
BinomialHeap	insert,extractMin delete	findMin,merge unionNodes,decrease	309	70
LinkedList	add,remove,removeLast	addBefore	253	12
TreeMap	put,remove	fixAfterIns fixAfterDel,delEntry	370	170
HeapArray	insert,extractMax	heapifyUp,heapifyDown	71	29

with a Pentium IV 2.8 GHz processor using Sun's Java 2 SDK 1.4.2 JVM with 512 MB allocated memory.

Table 1 lists the seven Java classes that we use in the experiments. The first six classes were previously used in evaluating Rostra [34], and the last five classes were used in evaluating Korat [8]. The columns of the table show the class name, the public methods under test (that the generated sequences consist of), some private methods invoked by the public methods, the number of non-comment, non-blank lines of code in all those methods, and the number of branches for each subject.

We use Symstra and Rostra to generate test sequences with up to N methods. Rostra also requires concrete values for arguments, so we set it to use N different arguments (the integers from 0 to $N - 1$) for methods under test. Table 2 shows the comparison between Symstra and Rostra. We range N from five to eight. (For $N < 5$, both Symstra and Rostra generate tests really fast, usually within a couple of seconds, but those tests do not have good quality.) We tabulate the time to generate the tests (measured in seconds, Columns 3 and 7), the number of explored symbolic and concrete object states (Columns 4 and 8), the number of generated tests (Columns 5 and 9), and the branch coverage[1] achieved by the generated tests (Columns 6 and 10). In Columns 5 and 9, we report the total number of generated tests and, in the parentheses, the cumulative number of tests that increase the branch coverage.

During test generation, we set a three-minute timeout for each iteration of the breadth-first exploration: when an iteration exceeds three minutes, the exhaustive exploration of Symstra or Rostra is stopped and the system proceeds with the next iteration. We use a "*" mark for each entry where the test-generation process timed out; the state exploration of these entries is no longer exhaustive. We use a "–" mark for each entry where Symstra or Rostra exceeded the memory limit.

The results indicate that Symstra generates method sequences of the same length N often much faster than Rostra, thus enabling Symstra to generate longer method sequences within a given time limit. Both Symstra and Rostra achieve the same branch

---

[1] We measure the branch coverage at the bytecode level during the state exploration of both Symstra and Rostra, and calculate the total number of branches also at the bytecode level.

Table 2. Experimental results of test generation using Symstra and Rostra

class	N	Symstra				Rostra			
		time	states	tests	%cov	time	states	tests	%cov
UBStack	5	0.95	22	43(5)	92.3	4.98	656	1950(6)	92.3
	6	4.38	30	67(6)	100.0	31.83	3235	13734(7)	100.0
	7	7.20	41	91(6)	100.0	*269.68	*10735	*54176(7)	*100.0
	8	10.64	55	124(6)	100.0	-	-	-	-
IntStack	5	0.23	12	18(3)	55.6	12.76	4836	5766(4)	55.6
	6	0.42	16	24(4)	66.7	-	-	-	-
	7	0.50	20	32(5)	88.9	*689.02	*30080	*52480(5)	*66.7
	8	0.62	24	40(6)	100.0	-	-	-	-
BinSearchTree	5	7.06	65	350(15)	97.1	4.80	188	1460(16)	97.1
	6	28.53	197	1274(16)	100.0	23.05	731	7188(17)	100.0
	7	136.82	626	4706(16)	100.0	-	-	-	-
	8	*317.76	*1458	*8696(16)	*100.0	-	-	-	-
BinomialHeap	5	1.39	6	40(13)	84.3	4.97	380	1320(12)	84.3
	6	2.55	7	66(13)	84.3	50.92	3036	12168(12)	84.3
	7	3.80	8	86(15)	90.0	-	-	-	-
	8	8.85	9	157(16)	91.4	-	-	-	-
LinkedList	5	0.56	6	25(5)	100.0	32.61	3906	8591(6)	100.0
	6	0.66	7	33(5)	100.0	*412.00	*9331	*20215(6)	*100.0
	7	0.78	8	42(5)	100.0	-	-	-	-
	8	0.95	9	52(5)	100.0	-	-	-	-
TreeMap	5	3.20	16	114(29)	76.5	3.52	72	560(31)	76.5
	6	7.78	28	260(35)	82.9	12.42	185	2076(37)	82.9
	7	19.45	59	572(37)	84.1	41.89	537	6580(39)	84.1
	8	63.21	111	1486(37)	84.1	-	-	-	-
HeapArray	5	1.36	14	36(9)	75.9	3.75	664	1296(10)	75.9
	6	2.59	20	65(11)	89.7	-	-	-	-
	7	4.78	35	109(13)	100.0	-	-	-	-
	8	11.20	54	220(13)	100.0	-	-	-	-

coverage for method sequences of the same length N. However, Symstra achieves higher coverage faster. It also takes less memory and can finish generation in more cases than Rostra. These results are due to the fact that each symbolic state, which Symstra explores at once, actually describes a set of concrete states, which Rostra must explore one by one. Rostra often exceeds the memory limit when $N = 7$ or $N = 8$, which is often not enough to guarantee full branch coverage.

5   Discussion and Future Work

Specifications. Symstra uses specifications, i.e., method pre- and post-conditions and class invariants, written in the Java Modelling Language (JML) [21]. The JML tool-set transforms these constructs into run-time assertions that throw JML-specific exceptions when violated. Generating method sequences for methods with JML specifications amounts to generating *legal* method sequences that satisfy pre-conditions and class invariants, i.e., do not throw exceptions for these constructs. If during the exploration Symstra finds a method sequence that violates a post-condition or invariant, Symstra has discovered a bug; Symstra can be configured to generate such tests and continue or stop test generation. If a class implementation is correct with respect to its specification, paths that throw post-condition or invariant exceptions should be infeasible.

Symstra operates on the bytecode level. It can perform testing of the specifications woven into method bytecode by the JML tool-set or by similar tools. Note that in this setting Symstra essentially uses black-box testing [33] to explore only those symbolic states that are produced by method executions that satisfy pre-conditions and class invariants; conditions that appear in specifications simply propagate into the constraints associated with a symbolic state explored by Symstra. Using symbolic execution, Symstra thus obtains the generation of legal test sequences "for free".

Performance. Based on state subsumption, our current Symstra prototype explores one or more symbolic states that have the isomorphic heap. We plan to evaluate an approach that explores exactly one *union* symbolic state for each isomorphic heap. We can create a union state using a disjunction of the constraints for all symbolic states with the isomorphic heap. Each union state subsumes all the symbolic states with the isomorphic heap, and thus exploring only union states can further reduce the number of explored states without compromising the exhaustiveness of the exploration. (Subsumption is a special case of union; if $C_2 \Rightarrow C_1$, then $C_1 \vee C_2$ simplifies to C_1.)

Symstra enables exploring longer method sequences than the techniques based on concrete arguments. However, users may want to have an exploration of even longer sequences to achieve some test purpose. In such cases, the users can apply several techniques that trade the guarantee of the intra-method path coverage for longer sequences. For example, the user may provide abstraction functions for states [23], as used for instance in the AsmLT generation tool [15], or binary methods for comparing states (e.g. `equals`), as used for instance in Rostra. Symstra can then generate tests that instead of subsumption use these user-provided functions for comparing state. This leads to a potential loss of intra-method path coverage but enables faster, user-controlled exploration. To explore longer sequences, Symstra can also use standard heuristics [33,9] for selecting only a set of paths instead of exploring all paths.

Limitations. The use of symbolic execution has inherent limitations. For example, it cannot precisely handle array indexes that are symbolic variables. This situation occurs in some classes, such as `DisjSet` and `HashMap` used previously in evaluating Rostra [34]. One solution is to combine symbolic execution with (exhaustive or random) exploration based on concrete arguments: a static analysis would determine which arguments can be symbolically executed, and for the rest, the user would provide a set of concrete values [15].

So far we have discussed only methods that take primitive arguments. We cannot directly transform non-primitive arguments into symbolic variables of primitive type. However, we can use the standard approach for generating non-primitive arguments: generate them also as sequences of method calls that may recursively require more sequences of method calls, but eventually boil down to methods that have only primitive values (or null). (Note that this also handles mutually recursive classes.) JCrasher [13] and Eclat [26] take a similar approach. Another solution is to transform these arguments into reference-type symbolic variables and enhance the symbolic execution to support heap operations on symbolic references. Concrete objects representing these variables can be generated by solving the constraints and setting the instance fields using reflection. However, the collected constraints are often not sufficient to generate legal instances, in which case an additional object invariant is required.

6   Conclusion

We have proposed Symstra, a novel framework that uses symbolic execution to generate a small number of method sequences that reach high branch and intra-method path coverage for complex data structures. Symstra exhaustively explores method sequences with symbolic arguments up to a given length. It prunes the exploration based on state subsumption; this pruning speeds up the exploration, without compromising its exhaustiveness. We have implemented a test-generation tool for Symstra and evaluated it on seven subjects, most of which are complex data structures. The results show that Symstra generates tests faster than the existing test-generation techniques based on exhaustive exploration of sequences with concrete method arguments, and given the same time limit, Symstra can generate tests that achieve better branch coverage than these existing techniques.

Acknowledgments

We thank Corina Pasareanu and Willem Visser for their comments on our implementation of subsumption checking, help in using symbolic execution, and valuable feedback on an earlier version of this paper. We also thank Wolfgang Grieskamp, Sarfraz Khurshid, Viktor Kuncak, and Nikolai Tillmann for useful discussions on this work and anonymous reviewers for the comments on a previous version of this paper. Darko Marinov would like to thank his advisor, Martin Rinard, for supporting part of this work done at MIT. This work was funded in part by NSF grant CCR00-86154. We also acknowledge support through the High Dependability Computing Program from NASA Ames cooperative agreement NCC-2-1298.

References

1. T. Andrews, S. Qadeer, S. K. Rajamani, J. Rehof, and Y. Xie. Zing: A model checker for concurrent software. In *Proc. 6th International Conference on Computer Aided Verification*, pages 484–487, 2004.
2. T. Ball. A theory of predicate-complete test coverage and generation. Technical Report MSR-TR-2004-28, Microsoft Research, Redmond, WA, April 2004.
3. T. Ball and J. R. Larus. Using paths to measure, explain, and enhance program behavior. *IEEE Computer*, 33(7):57–65, 2000.
4. T. Ball, R. Majumdar, T. Millstein, and S. K. Rajamani. Automatic predicate abstraction of C programs. In *Proc. the ACM SIGPLAN 2001 Conference on Programming Language Design and Implementation*, pages 203–213, 2001.

5. K. Beck. *Extreme programming explained*. Addison-Wesley, 2000.
6. B. Beizer. *Software Testing Techniques*. International Thomson Computer Press, 1990.
7. D. Beyer, A. J. Chlipala, T. A. Henzinger, R. Jhala, and R. Majumdar. Generating tests from counterexamples. In *Proc. 26th International Conference on Software Engineering*, pages 326–335, 2004.
8. C. Boyapati, S. Khurshid, and D. Marinov. Korat: automated testing based on Java predicates. In *Proc. International Symposium on Software Testing and Analysis*, pages 123–133, 2002.
9. W. R. Bush, J. D. Pincus, and D. J. Sielaff. A static analyzer for finding dynamic programming errors. *Softw. Pract. Exper.*, 30(7):775–802, 2000.
10. Y. Cheon and G. T. Leavens. A simple and practical approach to unit testing: The JML and JUnit way. In *Proc. 16th European Conference Object-Oriented Programming*, pages 231–255, June 2002.
11. S. B. Clark W. Barrett. CVC Lite: A new implementation of the cooperating validity checker. In *Proc. 16th International Conference on Computer Aided Verification*, pages 515–518, July 2004.
12. E. M. Clarke, O. Grumberg, and D. A. Peled. *Model Checking*. The MIT Press, Cambridge, MA, 1999.
13. C. Csallner and Y. Smaragdakis. JCrasher: an automatic robustness tester for Java. *Software: Practice and Experience*, 34:1025–1050, 2004.
14. D. Detlefs, G. Nelson, and J. B. Saxe. Simplify: a theorem prover for program checking. Technical Report HPL-2003-148, HP Laboratories, Palo Alto, CA, 2003.
15. Foundations of Software Engineering, Microsoft Research. The AsmL test generator tool. http://research.microsoft.com/fse/asml/doc/AsmLTester.html.
16. W. Grieskamp, Y. Gurevich, W. Schulte, and M. Veanes. Generating finite state machines from abstract state machines. In *Proc. International Symposium on Software Testing and Analysis*, pages 112–122, 2002.
17. T. A. Henzinger, R. Jhala, R. Majumdar, and G. Sutre. Software verification with BLAST. In *Proc. 10th SPIN Workshop on Software Model Checking*, pages 235–239, 2003.
18. JUnit, 2003. http://www.junit.org.
19. S. Khurshid, C. S. Pasareanu, and W. Visser. Generalized symbolic execution for model checking and testing. In *Proc. 9th International Conference on Tools and Algorithms for the Construction and Analysis of Systems*, pages 553–568, April 2003.
20. J. C. King. Symbolic execution and program testing. *Commun. ACM*, 19(7):385–394, 1976.
21. G. T. Leavens, A. L. Baker, and C. Ruby. Preliminary design of JML: A behavioral interface specification language for Java. Technical Report TR 98-06i, Department of Computer Science, Iowa State University, June 1998.
22. B. Legeard, F. Peureux, and M. Utting. A comparison of the LIFC/B and TTF/Z test-generation methods. In *Proc. 2nd International Z and B Conference*, pages 309–329, January 2002.
23. B. Liskov and J. Guttag. *Program Development in Java: Abstraction, Specification, and Object-Oriented Design*. Addison-Wesley, 2000.
24. K. L. McMillan. *Symbolic Model Checking*. Kluwer Academic Publishers, 1993.
25. Microsoft Visual Studio Developer Center, 2004. http://msdn.microsoft.com/vstudio/.
26. C. Pacheco and M. D. Ernst. Eclat documents. Online manual, Oct. 2004. http://people.csail.mit.edu/people/cpacheco/eclat/.
27. Parasoft. Jtest manuals version 5.1. Online manual, July 2004. http://www.parasoft.com/.
28. W. Pugh. A practical algorithm for exact array dependence analysis. *Commun. ACM*, 35(8):102–114, 1992.
29. Robby, M. B. Dwyer, and J. Hatcliff. Bogor: an extensible and highly-modular software model checking framework. In *Proc. 9th ESEC/FSE*, pages 267–276, 2003.

30. Robby, M. B. Dwyer, J. Hatcliff, and R. Iosif. Space-reduction strategies for model checking dynamic systems. In *Proc. 2003 Workshop on Software Model Checking*, July 2003.
31. H. Schlenker and G. Ringwelski. POOC: A platform for object-oriented constraint programming. In *Proc. 2002 International Workshop on Constraint Solving and Constraint Logic Programming*, pages 159–170, June 2002.
32. W. Visser, K. Havelund, G. Brat, and S. Park. Model checking programs. In *Proc. 15th IEEE International Conference on Automated Software Engineering*, pages 3–12, 2000.
33. W. Visser, C. S. Pasareanu, and S. Khurshid. Test input generation with Java PathFinder. In *Proc. 2004 ACM SIGSOFT International Symposium on Software Testing and Analysis*, pages 97–107, 2004.
34. T. Xie, D. Marinov, and D. Notkin. Rostra: A framework for detecting redundant object-oriented unit tests. In *Proc. 19th IEEE International Conference on Automated Software Engineering*, pages 196–205, Sept. 2004.

Dynamic Symmetry Reduction*

E. Allen Emerson and Thomas Wahl

Department of Computer Sciences and Computer Engineering Research Center,
The University of Texas, Austin/TX 78712, USA
{emerson, wahl}@cs.utexas.edu

Abstract. *Symmetry reduction* is a technique to combat the state explosion problem in temporal logic model checking. Its use with symbolic representation has suffered from the prohibitively large BDD for the *orbit relation*. One suggested solution is to pre-compute a mapping from states to possibly *multiple representatives* of symmetry equivalence classes. In this paper, we propose a more efficient method that determines representatives dynamically during fixpoint iterations. Our scheme preserves the uniqueness of representatives. Another alternative to using the orbit relation is *counter abstraction*. It proved efficient for the special case of full symmetry, provided a conducive program structure. In contrast, our solution applies also to systems with less than full symmetry, and to systems where a translation into counters is not feasible. We support these claims with experimental results.

1 Introduction

Model checking [CE81, QS82] is a successful approach to formal verification of finite-state concurrent systems. Numerous attempts have been made to combat its main obstacle, the state space explosion problem. *Symmetry reduction* is a technique that exploits replication. The state space is reduced by considering global states equivalent that are identical up to applications of structure automorphisms, for example permutations that interchange the identities of participating components. This equivalence, the *orbit relation*, gives rise to a bisimilar quotient structure over the equivalence classes (orbits) [ES96, CEFJ96].

Symmetry reduction was first successfully incorporated into explicit-state verifiers, such as Murφ [ID96]. Disappointingly, it was discovered that *symbolic representation* using BDDs, by then becoming a standard in large-scale system verification, seemed not to combine favorably with symmetry reduction [CEFJ96]. The reason is that the BDD for the orbit relation is provably intractably large.

In this paper we present a strategy of bypassing the orbit relation. To perform symmetry reduction, it is not necessary to build a representation of the quotient structure. Instead, the reduction can be achieved by computing transition images

---

* This work was supported in part by NSF grants CCR-009-8141 and CCR-020-5483, and SRC contract 2002-TJ-1026.

N. Halbwachs and L. Zuck (Eds.): TACAS 2005, LNCS 3440, pp. 382–396, 2005.

with respect to the unreduced structure, and immediately afterwards mapping the new states to their respective representatives. The main contribution of this paper is to provide an efficient *symbolic* algorithm for a function that takes a set of states and computes their representatives, given the underlying symmetry group and the permutation action. We first concentrate on full component symmetry, the most frequent and beneficial case in practice. We go on to show how to extend our algorithm to other symmetry groups and to *data symmetry* (see section 2).

Our solution compares with previous approaches as follows. Clarke et. al. [CEFJ96] proposed the admission of *multiple* orbit representatives. This affords the possibility to map a state to that representative of its orbit for which this mapping is most efficient. The relation ξ associating states with their representatives is pre-computed in a BDD. This method, albeit an improvement, was not effective enough for systems of interesting size. This is in part because the BDD for ξ is generally still huge, and in part due to the multiplicity of the representatives, such that symmetry is not exploited to the fullest extent. In comparison, our method *dynamically* computes representatives of states, i.e. embedded in the model checking process. In addition to preserving the uniqueness of orbit representatives, this has the important advantage that there is no need to compute, let alone store for the lifetime of the program, the representative mapping ξ. Further, for reachability analysis we only maintain representatives actually encountered during the computation, which might be few. In contrast, pre-computing representatives (irrespective of reachability) may consume a lot of resources, only to find afterwards that a state close to an initial state already has a bug.

Another technique, *generic representatives* [ET99], applies to the special case of fully symmetric systems. The idea is that two global states are symmetry-equivalent exactly if for every *local* state L, the number of components residing in L is the same in both global states. This approach requires a translation of the original program text into one that represents global states as vectors of counters, one counter for each local state. The Kripke structure derived from the new program can then be model-checked without further symmetry considerations. This method, more generally known as *counter abstraction* [PXZ02], proved to be very efficient—if applicable: it is limited to full component symmetry, its performance degrades if there are too many local states, and the translation to counters can be non-trivial [EW03]. Our new reduction algorithm is not based on counting processes in local states and thus does not suffer from any of these problems.

In summary, this paper presents an exact, yet flexible and efficient response to the orbit relation dilemma of symbolic symmetry reduction. It works with many common symmetry groups and even applies to data symmetry. It requires no expensive up-front computation of a representative mapping and no translation of the input program, nor does it depend unreasonably on the number of local states. Experimental results document the superiority of our approach to existing ones, often by orders of magnitude.

2   Background: Symmetry Reduction

Intuitively, the Kripke model $M = (S, R)$ of a system is symmetric if it is invariant under certain transformations of its state space S. In general, such a transformation is a bijection $\pi \colon S \to S$. The precise definition of π depends on the type of symmetry; common ones are discussed in the next paragraph. Given π, we derive a mapping at the transition relation level by defining $\pi(R) = \{(\pi(s), \pi(t)) \colon (s, t) \in R\}$. Structure M is said to be *symmetric* with respect to a set G of bijections if $\pi(R) = R$ for all $\pi \in G$. The bijections with this property are called *automorphisms* of M and form a group under function composition, M's *symmetry group*.

The most common type of symmetry is known as *component symmetry*. In this case, the automorphism π takes over the task of permuting the components. For example, if l_i denotes the local state of component $i \in [1..n]$, π is derived from a permutation on $[1..n]$ and acts on a state s as $\pi(s) = \pi(l_1, \ldots, l_n) = (l_{\pi(1)}, \ldots, l_{\pi(n)})$. Under *data symmetry* [ID96], an automorphism acts directly on the variable values, in the form $\pi(l_1, \ldots, l_n) = (\pi(l_1), \ldots, \pi(l_n))$. For example, the permutation π on $\{a, b\}$ that flips a and b acts on state (a, a) under component symmetry by exchanging *positions* 1 and 2 in the pair to yield the same state (a, a). Under data symmetry, π exchanges the *values* a and b to yield (b, b).

2.1   Exploiting Symmetry

Given a group G of automorphisms $\pi \colon S \to S$, the relation $\theta := \{(s, t) \colon \exists \pi \in G \colon \pi(s) = t\}$ on S defines an equivalence between states, known as *orbit relation*; the equivalence classes it entails are called *orbits* [CEFJ96]. Relation θ induces a quotient structure $\bar{M} = (\bar{S}, \bar{R})$, where $\bar{S}$ is a chosen set of representatives of the orbits, and $\bar{R}$ is defined as

$$\bar{R} = \{(\bar{s}, \bar{t}) \in \bar{S} \times \bar{S} \colon \exists s, t \in S \colon (s, \bar{s}) \in \theta \wedge (t, \bar{t}) \in \theta \wedge (s, t) \in R\}. \quad (1)$$

Depending on the size of G, $\bar{M}$ can be up to exponentially smaller than M. In case of symmetry, i.e. given $\pi(R) = R$ for all $\pi \in G$, $\bar{M}$ is bisimulation equivalent to M; the bisimulation relation is $\xi = (S \times \bar{S}) \cap \theta$. Relation ξ is actually a function and maps a state s to the unique representative $\bar{s}$ of its equivalence class under θ. Summarizing, for two states s, $\bar{s}$ with $(s, \bar{s}) \in \xi$ and any *symmetric* formula f, i.e. such that $p \Leftrightarrow \pi(p)$ is a tautology for every propositional subformula p of f and every $\pi \in G$,

$$M, s \models f \quad \text{iff} \quad \bar{M}, \bar{s} \models f. \quad (2)$$

2.2   Unique Versus Multiple Representatives

Equation 1 defining the quotient transition relation makes use of the orbit relation θ. Clarke et. al. [CEFJ96] show that computing this relation can be expensive in both time and space, especially in a symbolic context. There is currently no polynomial-time algorithm for deciding, for an arbitrary symmetry group G, whether there is a permutation mapping a given state to another. In addition, a symbolic representation of the orbit relation using BDDs can be shown to require space exponential in the smaller of the number of components and the number of local states per component. This is even true for special symmetries, such as the important full symmetry group.

An alternative that avoids the orbit relation is provided by the same authors [CEFJ96]. In their approach, the quotient structure is allowed to have more than one representative per orbit. The programmer supplies a choice of representative states Rep. In [CEFJ96], precise conditions are given for the existence of a set $C \subset G$ of permutations such that

$$\xi := \{(s, r) : r \in Rep \land \exists \pi \in C : \pi(s) = r\}$$

is a suitable representative relation from which a bisimulation equivalent quotient structure can be derived. This quotient is the structure $\bar{M} = (Rep, \bar{R})$, where $\bar{R}$ is defined as before in equation 1, except that $\bar{S}$ is replaced by Rep, and θ by ξ. The intuition behind this is that for any state s, in order to find a representative r for it (i.e. $(s, r) \in \xi$), it suffices to try applying permutations from C to s, instead of all permutations from G. If C is exponentially smaller than G, this is a big win in the search for a representative of s. Indeed, as experiments have shown, avoiding the orbit relation this way certainly outweighs the cost of extra representative states.

2.3   Counter Abstraction of Fully Symmetric Systems

For the case of fully symmetric systems of concurrently executing components, one can make use of the following observation in order to represent orbits. Two global states, viewed as vectors of local state identifiers, are identical up to permutation exactly if for every local state L, the frequency of occurrence of L is the same in the two states—permutations only change the order of elements, not the elements themselves. An orbit can therefore be represented as a vector of counters, one for each local state, that records how many of the components are in the corresponding local state. For example, in a system with local states N, T and C, the states (N, N, T, C), (N, C, T, N), and (T, N, N, C) are all symmetry-equivalent; their orbit (which contains other states as well) can be represented compactly as $(2N, 1T, 1C)$ or just $(2, 1, 1)$.

In practice, it may be possible to rewrite the program describing a fully component-symmetric system such that its variables are local state counters in the first place (before building a Kripke structure). This procedure is known as counter abstraction [PXZ02]. The advantage of the counter notation is that the symmetry is implicit in the representation; the very act of rewriting the program from the *specific* notation of local state variables into the *generic* [ET99] notation of local state counters implements symmetry reduction. Subsequently, model checking can be applied to the structure derived from the counter-based program without further considerations of symmetry.

In addition to being applicable only to fully symmetric systems, counter abstraction requires that automorphisms act on states only by changing the order of state components, not their values (as they do under data symmetry), since only then counters are insensitive to automorphism application. Further, since rewriting the program in terms of counters in fact anonymizes the components, variables containing component identifiers complicate matters, for example turn variables and pointers to other components [EW03].

3   Dynamically Computing Representatives

Symmetry reduction and model checking can be combined in two principally different ways. The straightforward method seems to be to build a representation of the quotient structure $\bar{M}$ and then model check it. Fig. 1 (a) shows the standard fixpoint routine to compute the representative states satisfying EF *bad*, assuming we have a BDD representation of the quotient transition relation $\bar{R}$. We use $\overline{bad}$ to denote the representatives of *bad* states of M.

In practice, this algorithm is usually not the method of choice for symbolic model checking. The reason is that direct computation of the BDD for the quotient transition relation $\bar{R}$ is very expensive. Equation 1 involves the orbit relation directly and is thus intractable as an algorithm. In our experiments, we were only able to compute this BDD in a reasonable amount of time for very simple examples. An intuitive argument for the complexity is that the orbit relation, even if not used during the computation of $\bar{R}$, is essentially embedded in the BDD for $\bar{R}$.

An alternative is to modify the model checking algorithm. Consider the version in fig. 1 (b). It is identical to (a), except that it uses the operation $\alpha(\text{EX}_R\, Z)$ in the computation of the next iterate: It first applies to Z the backward image operator with respect to R, rather than with respect to $\bar{R}$. It then employs some mechanism α that maps the results to representatives, formally defined as

$$\alpha(T) = \{\bar{t} \in \bar{S} : \exists t \in T : (t, \bar{t}) \in \theta\}. \tag{3}$$

Viewing the quotient $\bar{M}$ as an abstraction of the concrete system M, α precisely denotes the abstraction function, mapping concrete to abstract states. The algorithm in fig. 1 (b) is an instance of the *abstract interpretation* framework [CC77]. Generally, abstract images can be computed by mapping the given

<table>
<tr><td>

$Y := \emptyset$
repeat
   $Y' := Y$
   $Y := \overline{bad} \vee \text{EX}_{\bar{R}}\, Y$
until $Y = Y'$
return Y

</td><td>

$Z := \emptyset$
repeat
   $Z' := Z$
   $Z := \overline{bad} \vee \alpha(\text{EX}_R\, Z)$
until $Z = Z'$
return Z

</td></tr>
<tr><td align="center">(a)</td><td align="center">(b)</td></tr>
</table>

Fig. 1. Two ways to compute the representative states satisfying EF *bad*

abstract state to the concrete domain using the concretization function γ, then applying the concrete image, and finally mapping the result back to the abstract domain using α. Symmetry affords the simplification that γ can be chosen to be the identity function, since abstract states (i.e. representatives) are embedded in the concrete state space. We can thus apply EX_R (the concrete backward image operator) directly to a set of abstract states (Z, in fig. 1 (b)), obtaining the set of concrete successor states. Applying α produces the final abstract backward image result.

Given different realizations of α, fig. 1 (b) actually represents a family of symmetry reduction algorithms. The definition of α (3) is based on the orbit relation and is therefore inappropriate as a recipe for an algorithm. Another way to compute α is as forward image under a precomputed representative relation $\xi \subset S \times \bar{S}$. This technique was used by Clarke et. al. [CEFJ96] in connection with multiple representatives; the authors describe ways to obtain such a relation without explicitly using the orbit relation θ. In contrast, we propose in this paper to compute the set of representatives of a set of states *dynamically* during the execution of symbolic fixpoint algorithms, instead of a priori *statically*. This has two advantages:

1. We avoid computing, and storing at all times, the table ξ associating states with representatives, which is expensive.
2. For reachability analysis, we do not need the complete set of representatives $\bar{S}$, which is required for the computation of ξ. Rather we only maintain representatives encountered during the computation.

The algorithm to compute α depends on the type and underlying group of symmetry. In the following section, we first describe in detail the algorithm for the most common and important case of full component symmetry. Later, in section 6, we present extensions to other symmetries and also generalize our algorithm to full CTL model checking.

4   Computation of α Under Full Component Symmetry

A scheme for defining representatives frequently used in the case of full component symmetry is the following. Recall that an orbit consists of all states that are identical up to permutations of components, which amounts to permutations of the local states of the components. Given some total ordering among the local states, there is a unique state in each orbit where the local states appear in ascending order. Thus, the unique representative of a state can be chosen to be the lexicographically least element of the state's orbit. This element can be computed by *sorting* the local state vector representing the given state[1].

How can this be accomplished symbolically? Not every sorting algorithm lends itself to symbolic implementation. Compared to an explicit-state algorithm,

---

[1] We assume for now that there are no symmetry-relevant global variables; section 6 below generalizes.

instead of sorting one vector of local states, we want to sort an entire set of local state vectors in one fell swoop. One algorithm that allows this efficiently is *bubble sort*. It is a comparison-based sorting procedure that rearranges the input vector in-place by swapping out-of-order elements. To symbolically bubble-sort a set of vectors simultaneously, we remark: Instead of comparing two elements of *the* input vector, the algorithm forms a sub*set* of vectors for which the two elements in question are out of order. Instead of swapping one pair of out-of-order elements, we apply the swap operation to all vectors in the subset, in one step.

The operation of swapping two items turns out to be the factor dominating efficiency. Its complexity depends heavily on the distance, in the BDD variable ordering, of the bits involved in the swap. In order to keep this distance small, we exploit one key feature of bubble sort: it is optimal in the *locality* of swap operations—it swaps only adjacent elements.

The lexicographical order of global states is based on a total order $\leq$ on the local states of the components. For a fixed global state z, this order $\leq$ induces a total order $\leq_z$ on the components via

$$p \leq_z q \quad \text{iff} \quad l_p(z) \leq l_q(z),$$

where $l_i(z)$ is the local state of component i in global state z. Given $\leq_z$, and denoting by n the total number of components, the set of representative states (the lexicographically least members of some orbit) is defined as

$$\bar{S} = \{z \in S : \forall p < n : p \leq_z p + 1\} = \bigcap_{p < n} \{z \in S : p \leq_z p + 1\}. \tag{4}$$

For our algorithm, the exact definition of $\leq_z$ is irrelevant; we only need it to be a total order on the components. This flexibility turns out to be useful in situations where considering just the local states of components is not enough to characterize representative states; these situations are discussed in section 6. Our sorting algorithm looks for states z with components that are not in correct order with respect to $\leq_z$, and swaps them. This is repeated until a fixpoint is reached, cf. fig. 2.

For p ranging from 1 to $n - 1$, the predicate transformer τ in (b) computes Z_{bad}, the set of states in Z in which components p and $p + 1$ are not in the correct order (line 2). If Z_{bad} is non-empty, the algorithm first saves the set of states in Z in which p and $p + 1$ are in correct order (line 4) and then swaps components p and $p + 1$ in all states in Z_{bad} (line 5). The simultaneous swapping can be achieved by swapping the bits that store components p and $p + 1$ in the BDD for Z_{bad}, which effects all states in Z_{bad}. This is the expensive step of the algorithm; it profits from the fact that these bits are nearby (see section 5). Finally, the untouched and the swapped states in Z are combined to give the new value for Z (line 6).

$$\alpha(T): \quad \boxed{\begin{array}{l} \text{1. } Z := T \\ \text{2. repeat} \\ \text{3. } \quad Z' := Z \\ \text{4. } \quad Z := \tau(Z) \\ \text{5. until } Z = Z' \\ \text{6. return } Z \end{array}}$$

$$\tau(Z): \quad \boxed{\begin{array}{l} \text{1. for } p := 1 \text{ to } n-1 \text{ do} \\ \text{2. } \quad Z_{bad} := Z \wedge \neg\{z : p \leq_z p+1\} \\ \text{3. } \quad \text{if } Z_{bad} \neq \emptyset \text{ then} \\ \text{4. } \quad \quad Z_{good} := Z \setminus Z_{bad} \\ \text{5. } \quad \quad Z_{swapped} := swap(p, p+1, Z_{bad}) \\ \text{6. } \quad \quad Z := Z_{good} \vee Z_{swapped} \\ \text{7. return } Z \end{array}}$$

(a)   (b)

Fig. 2. Computing the representative mapping α using subroutine τ

5   Correctness and Efficiency of the Algorithm

Our algorithm is an instance of the template shown in fig. 1 (b). We first show more generally that the template computes the same result as the algorithm (a) in the same figure. We only assume that α maps the states of its argument set to representatives.

Lemma 1. Let α satisfy

$$\alpha(T) = \{\bar{t} \in \bar{S} : \exists t \in T : (t, \bar{t}) \in \theta\}. \tag{5}$$

Then, for an arbitrary set $P \subset \bar{S}$ of representatives, $\mathsf{EX}_{\bar{R}} P = \alpha(\mathsf{EX}_R P)$.

Proof: In the following, we also use the notation $\alpha(t)$ for the unique representative of a single state t, i.e. the unique element of $\alpha(\{t\})$.

$\bar{s} \in \alpha(\mathsf{EX}_R P)$
$\Leftrightarrow$ ⟨def. of backward image and function application⟩
$\exists s, \bar{t} : \bar{s} = \alpha(s) \wedge (s, \bar{t}) \in R \wedge \bar{t} \in P$
$\Leftrightarrow$ ⟨"$\Rightarrow$": $t := \bar{t}$ and note $\bar{t} \in P \subset \bar{S}$, so $\bar{t} = \alpha(\bar{t}) = \alpha(t)$⟩
    ⟨"$\Leftarrow$": $s := \pi(s')$ for $\pi : \pi(t) = \bar{t}$. Then $\alpha(s') = \alpha(s)$, $\pi(s', t) = (s, \bar{t}) \in R$⟩
$\exists s', t, \bar{t} : \bar{s} = \alpha(s') \wedge \bar{t} = \alpha(t) \wedge (s', t) \in R \wedge \bar{t} \in P$
$\Leftrightarrow$ ⟨def. of $\bar{R}$⟩
$\exists \bar{t} : (\bar{s}, \bar{t}) \in \bar{R} \wedge \bar{t} \in P$
$\Leftrightarrow$ ⟨def. of backward image⟩
$\bar{s} \in \mathsf{EX}_{\bar{R}} P$.   □

Corollary 2. The two algorithms in fig. 1 return the same set (and they do so with the same number of iterations of the **repeat** loop).

Proof: Let Y_i and Z_i denote the ith iterates of the two algorithms. Then for all i, $Y_i \subset \bar{S}$, $Z_i \subset \bar{S}$ (by the definitions of $\overline{bad}$, backward image in $\bar{R}$ and α). Thus, utilizing lemma 1, for all i, $Y_i = Z_i$, from which the two claims follow.   □

Lemma 3. The algorithm in fig. 2 computes α satisfying equation 5.

Proof: We will show termination and partial correctness.

Termination: The argument is essentially the same as for standard bubble sort. Every call to $swap(p, p+1, Z_{bad})$ brings the local state of at least one of the components p and $p+1$ closer to its correct position. Hence, after about n^2 swaps, there is no pair $(p, p+1)$ left with $\neg(p \leq_z p+1)$. Thus, Z_{bad} as computed in line 2 (fig. 2 (b)) is empty in every iteration of the **for** loop, Z remains unchanged, and the condition $Z = Z'$ in line 5 (a) is true.

Partial correctness: We use two observations.

(I) When the algorithm terminates, we know that for all values of p, Z_{bad} as computed in line 2 (b) is empty. Hence, $Z \subset \bigcap_{p<n}\{z : p \leq_z p+1\} = \bar{S}$ (equation 4), so $Z = \alpha(T) \subset \bar{S}$.

(II) Predicate transformer τ manipulates the set Z by applying transpositions ($swap$) to states in Z. Hence, at the end T and $\alpha(T)$ contain the same states up to permutations[2].

These observations allow us to prove $\alpha(T) = \{\bar{t} \in \bar{S} : \exists t \in T : (t, \bar{t}) \in \theta\}$ as two inclusions:

$\subset$: Consider $\bar{t} \in \alpha(T)$. From (I) we know $\bar{t} \in \bar{S}$. From (II) we conclude that there exists t in T with $(t, \bar{t}) \in \theta$.

$\supset$: Consider $\bar{t} \in \bar{S}$, $t \in T$ such that $(t, \bar{t}) \in \theta$. From (II) we conclude that there exists π such that $\pi(t) \in \alpha(T)$. From (I) we conclude $\pi(t) \in \bar{S}$. Since there is exactly one representative of t in $\bar{S}$, we derive $\pi(t) = \bar{t}$, so $\bar{t} \in \alpha(T)$. $\square$

Corollary 4. The algorithm in fig. 1 (b), using the computation of α in fig. 2, correctly implements backward reachability analysis on the quotient structure.

Efficiency Considerations

The set $\{z : p \leq_z p+1\}$, which is by definition $\{z : l_p(z) \leq l_{p+1}(z)\}$, needs to be calculated only once for each p. The condition that the local state of component p is at most that of component $p+1$ can be expressed symbolically with a BDD of size $\mathcal{O}(l^2)$, for the number l of possible local states.

As indicated earlier, the $swap$ operation in line 5, fig. 2 (b), is the bottleneck of the algorithm. In BDD terms, it corresponds to pairwise swapping of all bits that represent the two items to be swapped. The complexity of swapping two bits in all elements of a set T, i.e. computing

$$\{(\ldots x_j \ldots x_i \ldots) : (\ldots x_i \ldots x_j \ldots) \in T\},$$

depends exponentially on the distance d of x_i and x_j in the BDD variable ordering. To illustrate this claim, we observe that in the BDD for T, every subtree rooted at a node labeled x_i contains at most 2^d nodes labeled x_j. Each such node labeled x_j has an immediate subtree that corresponds to one of the cases

---

[2] There is, however, in general no single π such that $\alpha(T) = \pi(T)$, i.e. α by itself is not just a permutation.

affected by the swap, namely $(x_i, x_j) = (0, 1)$ and $(x_i, x_j) = (1, 0)$. These 2^d subtrees must be moved.

BDD variable orderings usually have the property that it is possible to index the components as $1, \ldots, n$ such that the distance between corresponding bits of components p and q is proportional to $|p - q|$. Consider, for example, the following frequently used orderings:

> **concatenated:** $b_{11} \ldots b_{1 \log l}$ $b_{21} \ldots b_{2 \log l}$ $\cdots$ $\cdots$ $b_{n1} \ldots b_{n \log l}$
>
> **interlaced:** $b_{11} \ldots b_{n1}$ $b_{12} \ldots b_{n2}$ $\cdots$ $\cdots$ $b_{1 \log l} \ldots b_{n \log l}$

where b_{ij} denotes the jth bit of component i. For the concatenated ordering, the distance between the jth bit of component p and the jth bit of component q is $\log l \cdot |p - q|$; for the interlaced ordering, it is $|p - q|$.

Bubble sort, among the numerous sorting procedures, enjoys the unique feature of swapping only adjacent components. The distance $|p - q|$ is hence 1, for every swap operation, thus minimizing the complexity of swapping. This proves bubble sort optimal for our purpose of symbolic sorting.

6   Generalizations

6.1   Other Types of Symmetry

The idea of sorting to obtain unique orbit elements only works for the case of full component symmetry. Without proof, we give here the idea of how to compute α for other, less lucrative, but still somewhat common types of symmetry.

Consider first the case of component symmetries. Permutations act on states in the form $\pi(l_1, \ldots, l_n) = (l_{\pi(1)}, \ldots, l_{\pi(n)})$. Our solution for full symmetry generalizes as follows. Call a symmetry group G of permutations on $[1..n]$ *nice* if there exists a "small" subset F of G with the following property: *A state z is lexicographically least in its orbit exactly if there is no $\pi \in F$ with $\pi(z) <_{lex} z$.* Many common symmetry groups are nice. For full symmetry, F can be chosen as the set of $n - 1$ transpositions $(i \; i + 1)$ $(1 \le i < n)$. Set F also happens to be a generating set for the full symmetry group. If the group G itself is small, $F := G$ is a viable choice. This is, for example, the case for the n rotations generated by the left shift cycle $(1 \; 2 \; \ldots \; n)$. Note that in this case the generating set $\{(1 \; 2 \; \ldots \; n)\}$ is not a valid choice for F: The vector $z := (BCA)$ is not lexicographically least, yet applying the generating permutation does not make z smaller (applying it twice does).

Given a nice group G, consider the algorithm for α as before in fig. 2 (a), but with subroutine τ as shown in fig. 3. Again, Z_{bad} in line 2 selects the states z in Z that are not lexicographically least. By the niceness of G, this means that for some $\pi \in F$, $\pi(z) <_{lex} z$. Line 5 applies π element-wise to Z_{bad}. This algorithm terminates, since $<_{lex}$ is a well-order on the set of local state vectors. Hence, eventually there will be no π such that for some z, $\pi(z) <_{lex} z$. Partial correctness follows from an argument similar to that in lemma 3.

If G is nice, we expect to have a small set F of permutations that can be traversed in line 1. The direct application of π in line 5 may be expensive.

$$\tau(Z): \quad \begin{array}{ll} \text{1. } & \textbf{for } \pi \text{ in } F \textbf{ do} \\ \text{2. } & \quad Z_{bad} := Z \wedge \{z : \pi(z) <_{\text{lex}} z\} \\ \text{3. } & \quad \textbf{if } Z_{bad} \neq \emptyset \textbf{ then} \\ \text{4. } & \quad\quad Z_{good} := Z \setminus Z_{bad} \\ \text{5. } & \quad\quad Z_{swapped} := \{\pi(z) : z \in Z_{bad}\} \\ \text{6. } & \quad\quad Z := Z_{good} \vee Z_{swapped} \\ \text{7. } & \textbf{return } Z \end{array}$$

Fig. 3. Subroutine τ for "nice" symmetry groups

However, π can be expressed as a product of at most $1/2n(n-1)$ transpositions of *adjacent* elements. As argued in section 5, transpositions of neighbors are the least expensive permutations, as for implementation using BDDs. The important point is that the algorithm for τ in fig. 3 resembles bubble sort, in that it is in-place, and it only swaps neighboring processes, if the π's in F are rewritten as products of transpositions.

For data symmetry (see section 2), the idea of lexicographically least orbit elements no longer applies. A set of unique representatives can be defined as $\{(l_1, \ldots, l_n) : \forall i : l_i \leq i\}$. To compute the mapping α, the algorithm in fig. 2 can still be used, with only slight modifications. Set Z_{bad} (line 2) contains the states from Z that satisfy $l_p > p$. Line 5 swaps the values p and l_p in all states in Z_{bad}. Since l_p may vary from state to state in Z_{bad} (even for fixed p), a loop over the possible values of l_p is required.

6.2   Process Id Variables

Often, systems have *id-sensitive* global variables containing component ids, such as the identity of a process holding a token or a reference to a process having an exclusive copy of some cache data. In this case, the condition $\forall p : p < n : l_p(z) \leq l_{p+1}(z)$ is not enough to guarantee that z is a unique representative state. Consider, for instance, the two states $(A, A, B, 1)$ and $(A, A, B, 2)$ of a three-process system with one id-sensitive global variable (listed last). Since components 1 and 2 are both in local state A in both states, the permutation that flips 1 and 2 proves the states equivalent[3] The local states appear in ascending order: AAB. Yet, the states differ, compromising uniqueness. The solution is to define the unique representative as the orbit element with ascending local states where the id-sensitive variables have minimal values (1, in the example above). In this case, $p \leq_z p+1$ means for state z and the local states of p and $p+1$ that either $l_p(z) < l_{p+1}(z)$, **or** $l_p(z) = l_{p+1}(z)$ and none of the id-sensitive variables has value $p+1$. This condition is violated for $z := (A, A, B, 2)$ and $p := 1$. Thus, the permutation (1 2) will be applied to z, whereupon it turns into $(A, A, B, 1)$.

This solution can be extended to the more challenging case of id-sensitive *local* variables, the general treatment of which is beyond the scope of this paper.

---

[3] This permutation acts on (permutes) the id-sensitive variable; see [EW03] for details.

6.3   Full CTL Model Checking

Section 4 can be summarized as having presented an efficient algorithm for the computation of $\mathsf{EX}_{\bar{R}}\, Z$, used in backward reachability analysis. This algorithm generalizes to all CTL formulas as follows. Existential modalities (EG, EF, EU) have a fixpoint characterization based on existential backward images. For example, $\mathsf{EG}\, f$ can be calculated as the greatest fixpoint of the predicate transformer $\lambda(Z) = f \wedge \mathsf{EX}\, Z$. For the quotient structure, an algorithm similar to that in fig. 1 (b) can be used.

The universal backward image $\mathsf{AX}_{\bar{R}}\, Z$ cannot be replaced by an analogous construct involving α. Suppose we wish to compute the representative states satisfying AG *good* on the quotient structure. An algorithm similar to that in fig. 1 (a) exists, which computes the greatest fixpoint of $\lambda(Z) = \overline{good} \wedge \mathsf{AX}_{\bar{R}}\, Z$. However, in general $\alpha(\mathsf{AX}_R\, Z) \subsetneq \mathsf{AX}_{\bar{R}}\, Z$. The underlying problem is that the abstraction function α distributes over set union, but not intersection:

$$\alpha(P \cup Q) = \alpha(P) \cup \alpha(Q), \quad \text{but}$$
$$\alpha(P \cap Q) \subsetneq \alpha(P) \cap \alpha(Q) \quad \text{(in general)}.$$

The solution is to reduce universal to existential modalities. Care must be taken in that negation over the quotient structure is with respect to $\bar{S}$, the set of representatives. Thus, in a context where states are encoded as elements of S, we have to compute $\{\bar{s} \in \bar{S} : \bar{s} \notin Z\}$ as $\bar{S} \wedge \neg Z$. We obtain

$$\mathsf{AX}_{\bar{R}}\, Z = \bar{S} \wedge \neg(\mathsf{EX}_{\bar{R}}(\bar{S} \wedge \neg Z)) = \bar{S} \wedge \neg(\alpha(\mathsf{EX}_R(\bar{S} \wedge \neg Z))).$$

The above solutions for the EG modality—a *greatest* fixpoint—and the universal modalities require the set $\bar{S}$ of all representatives (unlike the case of EF [reachability] and EU, where only representatives encountered during the computation are stored). Depending on the application and the definition of representatives, the BDD for this set can be (but is not always) costly. It can be computed as $\alpha(true)$, but the "direct" way based on the expression $\bigcap_{p<n} p \leq_z p+1$ is often more efficient. Other than $\bar{S}$, the above equations only involve boolean primitives, existential backward image with respect to R, and the abstraction function α. This makes our technique complete for CTL.

7   Experimental Results

We present results of verifying example systems using our technique, with respect to properties that came along with the system specification. Our tool uses the CUDD BDD package [Som01]. We ran the examples on an i686/1400 Mhz PC with 256MB main memory. In tables, the figure behind the name of an example indicates the number of components involved. "Number of BDD Nodes" refers to the peak number of BDD nodes allocated at any time during execution. It represents the memory bottleneck of the verification run. The abbreviations s, m, h, M stand for seconds, minutes, hours, and million, respectively.

Table 1. Comparison to Multiple Representatives and Counter Abstraction

Problem	Multiple Representatives		Counter Abstraction		Dynamic Symmetry Reduction	
	Number of BDD Nodes	Time	Number of BDD Nodes	Time	Number of BDD Nodes	Time
MsLock 10	369,239	1:15m	68,154	29s	24,092	15s
MsLock 20	4,407,127	4:05h	325,325	7:06m	139,990	9:35m
MsLock 30	(>13M)	(>28h)	725,672	24:26m	375,649	1:23h
CCP 03	16,522,710	13:12h	1,988,991	7:55m	14,088	1s
CCP 05	(>12M)	(>35h)	4,001,573	1:49h	74,754	14s
CCP 10	—	—	(>14M)	(>18h)	1,075,206	26:35m
CCP 15	—	—	—	—	4,947,726	6:17h

Table 2. Comparison to unreduced Model Checking and Multiple Representatives

Problem	Without Symmetry Reduction		Multiple Representatives		Dynamic Symmetry Reduction	
	Number of BDD Nodes	Time	Number of BDD Nodes	Time	Number of BDD Nodes	Time
Comp&Swap 40	376,681	1m	157,470	25s	48,433	10s
Comp&Swap 50	(>14M)	(>24h)	4,259,627	37:34m	419,529	4:03m
Comp&Swap 60	—	—	(>10M)	(>24h)	6,246,717	2:10h
Fetch&Store 40	1,083,830	4:12m	413,036	2:02m	160,628	40s
Fetch&Store 50	(>12M)	(>24h)	(>11M)	(>24h)	2,017,634	29:43m
Fetch&Store 60	—	—	—	—	(>12M)	(>24h)
Distrib. List 30	861,158	28s	708,339	20s	60,394	2s
Distrib. List 40	6,380,209	4:35m	2,963,024	2:37m	213,448	5s
Distrib. List 50	(>15M)	(>24h)	13,580,042	29:30m	271,366	11s

In Table 1, we compare our dynamic symmetry reduction technique to the aforementioned alternative methods, Multiple Representatives and Counter Abstraction. To ensure fair comparison, we set various BDD parameters individually for each technique such that it performed best. The MsLock example is a simplified model of a queuing lock algorithm [MS91]. The simplification was necessary to make the system amenable to counter abstraction. The example denoted CCP refers to a buggy version of a cache coherence protocol suggested by S. German, see for example [LS03]. Due to the presence of errors, parameterized model checking (for arbitrary n) initially fails on this protocol (an inductive invariant proving the safety property does not exist). Model checkers such as our tool can then be used to provide an error trace for fixed values of the size parameter. This example is characterized by a large number of local states, which is why counter abstraction performs much worse on it than our dynamic technique.

The Multiple Representatives approach suffers from the high cost of building the representative mapping ξ.

The second table presents examples to which counter abstraction can not be applied. The reason is that here permutations act upon states by not only changing the order of local state components, but also their values. "Comp&Swap" and "Fetch&Store" are two versions of the queuing lock [MS91], a simplification of which was used in the MsLock example above. The "Distrib. List" example is a distributed protocol for processes in a FIFO queue sending and receiving messages, acting as a relay if asked to do so [MD96]. Symmetry exists in both the processes and the messages. In this table we also show results of the verification run *without* symmetry reduction, where the intermediate BDDs become huge quickly. Our technique invariably outperforms the other two, for large problem instances by orders of magnitude.

8   Summary

In this paper, we have presented a dynamic symmetry reduction technique that surpasses, to the best of our knowledge, previously known techniques dramatically. Multiple Representatives suffer from symptoms similar to those of orbit relation-based approaches (although alleviated). Counter abstraction is often efficient if operative, but does not scale well for systems of components with a large local state space, requires full symmetry, and is only applicable to symmetries with "simple" permutation action. In contrast, our solution is not based on counters and thus more flexible, yet it does not suffer from the problems associated with storing pairs of states and their representatives.

Our method can generally be seen as a symbolic abstraction technique that avoids pre-computing the abstraction function, but rather offers an efficient symbolic algorithm to map concrete to abstract states *on the fly*. In connection with symmetry reduction, there was a need for such a technique, due to the ongoing difficulties with the orbit relation.

Bubble sort is traditionally regarded naive and not successful on large sorting problems. Our decision to use it in the representative mapping under full symmetry is an instance of a phenomenon often seen in parallel programming: The most clever and sophisticated sequential algorithms are not always the best in a new computational model. Instead, a simple-minded routine can prove very suitable. In our case, we believe that the *locality* of bubble sort, i.e. its affecting only nearby elements and being in-place, is paramount.

Related Work. In addition to the references mentioned in the introduction, the work closest to ours is the paper by Barner and Grumberg [BG02], who considered combining symmetry and symbolic representation using BDDs mainly for falsification. If too large, the set of reached representatives is under-approximated, which renders the algorithm inexact. Also, their work uses multiple representatives and therefore forgoes some of the symmetry reduction possible. Finally, there is a lot of other work on symmetry not directly related to symbolic representation [PB99, God99, SGE00, HBL$^+$03–among many].

References

[BG02]   Sharon Barner and Orna Grumberg. Combining symmetry reduction and under-approximation for symbolic model checking. *Computer-Aided Verification (CAV)*, 2002.

[Bry86]   Randy E. Bryant. Graph-based algorithms for boolean function manipulation. *IEEE Transactions on Computers*, 1986.

[CC77]   Patrick Cousot and Radhia Cousot. Abstract interpretation: a unified lattice model for static analysis of programs by construction or approximation of fixpoints. *Principles of Programming Languages (POPL)*, 1977.

[CE81]   Edmund M. Clarke and E. Allen Emerson. The design and synthesis of synchronization skeletons using temporal logic. *Logic of Programs (LOP)*, 1981.

[CEFJ96]   Edmund M. Clarke, Reinhard Enders, Thomas Filkorn, and Somesh Jha. Exploiting symmetry in temporal logic model checking. *Formal Methods in System Design (FMSD)*, 1996.

[ES96]   E. Allen Emerson and A. Prasad Sistla. Symmetry and model checking. *Formal Methods in System Design (FMSD)*, 1996.

[ET99]   E. Allen Emerson and Richard J. Trefler. From asymmetry to full symmetry: New techniques for symmetry reduction in model checking. *Conference on Correct Hardware Design and Verification Methods (CHARME)*, 1999.

[EW03]   E. Allen Emerson and Thomas Wahl. On combining symmetry reduction and symbolic representation for efficient model checking. *Conference on Correct Hardware Design and Verification Methods (CHARME)*, 2003.

[God99]   Patrice Godefroid. Exploiting symmetry when model-checking software. *Formal Methods for Protocol Engineering and Distributed Systems (FORTE)*, 1999.

[HBL+03]   Martijn Hendriks, Gerd Behrmann, Kim Guldstrand Larsen, Peter Niebert, and Frits W. Vaandrager. Adding symmetry reduction to uppaal. *Formal Modeling and Analysis of Timed Systems (FORMATS)*, 2003.

[ID96]   C. Norris Ip and David L. Dill. Better verification through symmetry. *Formal Methods in System Design (FMSD)*, 1996.

[LS03]   Shuvendu Lahiri and Sanjit Seshia. *UCLID: A Verification Tool for Infinite-State Systems*. http://www-2.cs.cmu.edu/~uclid/, 2003.

[MD96]   Ralph Melton and David L. Dill. *Murφ Annotated Reference Manual, rel. 3.1*. http://verify.stanford.edu/dill/murphi.html, 1996.

[MS91]   John M. Mellor-Crummey and Michael L. Scott. Algorithms for scalable synchronization on shared-memory multiprocessors. *ACM Transactions on Computer Systems (TOCS)*, 1991.

[PB99]   Manish Pandey and Randal E. Bryant. Exploiting symmetry when verifying transistor-level circuits by symbolic trajectory evaluation. *IEEE Transactions on Computer-Aided Design*, 1999.

[PXZ02]   Amir Pnueli, Jessie Xu, and Leonore Zuck. Liveness with $(0, 1, \infty)$-Counter abstraction. *Computer-Aided Verification (CAV)*, 2002.

[QS82]   Jean-Pierre Quielle and Joseph Sifakis. Specification and verification of concurrent systems in cesar. *5th International Symposium on Programming*, 1982.

[SGE00]   A. Prasad Sistla, Viktor Gyuris, and E. Allen Emerson. Smc: a symmetry-based model checker for verification of safety and liveness properties. *ACM Transactions on Software Engineering and Methodology*, 2000.

[Som01]   Fabio Somenzi. *The CU Decision Diagram Package, release 2.3.1.* http://vlsi.colorado.edu/~fabio/CUDD/, 2001.

Localization and Register Sharing for Predicate Abstraction

Himanshu Jain*, Franjo Ivančić, Aarti Gupta, and Malay K. Ganai

NEC Laboratories America, 4 Independence Way,
Suite 200, Princeton, NJ 08540

Abstract. In the domain of software verification, predicate abstraction has e-merged to be a powerful and popular technique for extracting finite-state models from often complex source code. In this paper, we report on the application of three techniques for improving the performance of the predicate abstraction re-finement loop. The first technique allows faster computation of the abstraction. Instead of maintaining a global set of predicates, we find predicates relevant to various basic blocks of the program by weakest pre-condition propagation along spurious program traces. The second technique enables faster model checking of the abstraction by reducing the number of state variables in the abstraction. This is done by re-using Boolean variables to represent different predicates in the abstraction. However, some predicates are useful at many program locations and discovering them lazily in various parts of the program leads to a large number of abstraction refinement iterations. The third technique attempts to identify such predicates early in the abstraction refinement loop and handles them separately by introducing dedicated state variables for such predicates. We have incorporated these techniques into NEC's software verification tool F-SOFT, and present promising experimental results for various case studies using these techniques.

1 Introduction

In the domain of software verification, *predicate abstraction* [2, 7, 9, 11] has emerged to be a powerful and popular technique for extracting finite-state models from often complex source code. It abstracts data by keeping track of certain predicates on the data. Each predicate is represented by a Boolean variable in the abstract program, while the original data variables are eliminated. The application of predicate abstraction to large programs depends crucially on the choice and usage of the predicates. If all predicates are tracked globally in the program, the analysis often becomes intractable due to the large number of predicate relationships. In Microsoft's SLAM [4] toolkit, this problem is handled by generating coarse abstractions using techniques such as *Cartesian approximation* and the *maximum cube length approximation* [3]. These techniques limit the number of predicates in each theorem prover query. The refinement of the abstraction is carried out by adding new predicates. If no new predicates are found, the spurious behavior is due to inexact predicate relationships. Such spurious behavior is removed by a separate refinement algorithm called CONSTRAIN [1].

---

* The author is now at the School of Computer Science, Carnegie Mellon University.

N. Halbwachs and L. Zuck (Eds.): TACAS 2005, LNCS 3440, pp. 397–412, 2005.

The BLAST toolkit [13] introduced the notion of *lazy abstraction*, where the abstraction refinement is completely demand-driven to remove spurious behaviors. Recent work [14] describes a new refinement scheme based on interpolation [8], which adds new predicates to some program locations only, which we will call henceforth *localization of predicates*. On average the number of predicates tracked at a program location is small and thus, the localization of predicates enables predicate abstraction to scale to larger software programs. In this paper we describe three novel contributions:

- Our first contribution is inspired by the lazy abstraction approach and the localization techniques implemented in BLAST. While BLAST makes use of interpolation, we use weakest pre-conditions to find predicates relevant at each program location. Given an infeasible trace $s_1; \ldots; s_k$, we find predicates whose values need to be tracked at each statement s_i in order to eliminate the infeasible trace. For any program location we only need to track the relationship between the predicates relevant at that location. Furthermore, since we use predicates based on weakest pre-conditions along infeasible traces, most of the predicate relationships are obtained from the refinement process itself. This enables us to significantly reduce the number of calls to back-end decision procedures leading to a much faster abstraction computation.
- The performance of BDD-based model checkers depends crucially on the number of state variables. Due to predicate localization most predicates are useful only in certain parts of the program. The state variables corresponding to these predicates can be *reused* to represent different predicates in other parts of the abstraction, resulting in a reduction of the total number of state variables needed. We call this *abstraction with register sharing*. This constitutes our second technique which reduces the number of state variables, enabling more efficient model checking of the abstract models.
- While the above techniques speed up the individual computations and the model checking runs of the abstractions, they might result in too many abstraction refinement iterations. This can happen if the value of a certain predicate needs to be tracked at multiple program locations, i.e., if the predicate is useful *globally* or at least in some large part of the program. Since we add predicates lazily only along infeasible traces, the fact that a predicate is globally useful for checking a property will be learned only through multiple abstraction refinement iterations. We make use of a simple heuristic for deciding when the value of a certain predicate may need to be tracked globally or in a complete functional scope. If the value of a predicate needs to be tracked in a large scope, then it is assigned a *dedicated* state variable which is not reused for representing the value of other predicates in the same scope.

Further Related Work: Rusu et al. [20] present a framework for proving safety properties that combines predicate abstraction, refinement using weakest pre-conditions and theorem proving. However, no localization of predicates is done in their work. Namjoshi et al. [18] use weakest pre-conditions for extracting finite state abstractions, from possibly infinite state programs. They compute the weakest pre-conditions starting from an initial set of predicates derived from the specification, control guards etc. This process is iterated until a fix-point is reached, or a user imposed bound on the number of iterations is reached. In the latter case, the abstraction might be too coarse to prove the given property. However, no automatic refinement procedure is described. The MAGIC tool [5] also makes use of weakest pre-conditions in a similar way. Both approaches have the disadvantage that the number of predicates tracked at each program location can be much higher, which may make the single model checking step difficult. In contrast, we propagate the weakest pre-conditions lazily, that is, only to the extent needed to remove infeasible traces. In order to check if a sequence of statements in the C program is (in)feasible we use a SAT-solver as in [16]. The relationships between a set of predicates is found by making use of SAT-based predicate abstraction [6, 17]. We further improve the performance of SAT-based simulation of counterexamples and abstraction computation by making use of range analysis techniques [19, 21] to determine the maximum number of bits needed to represent each variable in the given program.

In the experiments presented in Section 5, F-SOFT computes a single BDD representing the reachable set of states. As is done in SLAM for example, F-SOFT is able to partition the BDD into subsets according to the basic blocks. However, the effects discussed in this paper still carry over to such a scheme as the individual BDDs will be smaller and contain fewer state variables in the support set. This is due to the fact that prior approaches cannot quantify out uninteresting predicates since their value may be important in following basic blocks. The information computed in our approach gives us a more accurate classification of which predicates are useful in a given basic block.

Outline: The following section describes the pre-processing of the source code with our software verification tool F-SOFT [15] and the localized abstraction refinement framework based on weakest pre-condition propagation. F-SOFT allows both SAT-based and BDD-based bounded and unbounded model checking of C. Here, we focus on our BDD-based model checker since BDDs often work well enough for abstract models with few state variables. The third section presents an overview of the computation of the abstraction with and without register sharing, while the fourth section describes our approach of dedicating abstract state variables to predicates. Section 5 discusses the experimental results, and we finish this paper with some concluding remarks.

2   A Localized Abstraction-Refinement Framework

2.1   Software Modeling

In this section, we briefly describe our software modeling approach that is centered around basic blocks as described in [15]. The preprocessing of the source code is performed before the abstraction refinement routine is invoked. A program counter variable is introduced to monitor progress in the control flow graph consisting of basic blocks. Our modeling framework allows *bounded recursion* through the introduction of a fixed depth function call stack, when necessary, and introduces special variables representing function return points for non-recursive functions. Due to space limitation, we omit the details of our handling of pointer variables, which can be found in [15]. It is based on adding simplified *pointer-free* assignments in the basic blocks.

2.2   Localization Information

The formula ϕ describes a set of program states, namely, the states in which the value of program variables satisfy ϕ. The *weakest pre-condition* [10] of a formula ϕ with respect to a statement s is the weakest formula whose truth before the execution of s entails the truth of ϕ after s terminates. We denote the weakest pre-condition of ϕ with respect to s by $WP(\phi, s)$. Let s be an assignment statement of the form v = e; and ϕ be a C expression. Then the weakest pre-condition of ϕ with respect to s, is obtained from ϕ by replacing every occurrence of v in ϕ with e.

Given an if statement with condition p, we write assume p or assume ¬p, depending upon the branch of the if statement that is executed. The weakest pre-condition of ϕ with respect to assume p, is given as $\phi \wedge p$. As mentioned earlier, pointer assignments are rewritten early on in our tool chain, thus allowing us to focus here on only the above cases. The weakest pre-condition operator is extended to a sequence of statements by $WP(\phi, s_1; s_2) = WP(WP(\phi, s_2), s_1)$. A sequence of statements $s_1; \ldots; s_k$ is said to be *infeasible*, if $WP(true, s_1; \ldots; s_k) = false$. Note that for ease of presentation, we present the following material using individual statements while the actual implementation uses a control flow graph consisting of basic blocks.

We define $child(s)$ to denote the set of statements reachable from s in one step in the control flow graph. Each statement s in the program keeps track of the following information: (1) A set of predicates denoted as $local(s)$ whose values need to be tracked before the execution of s. We say a predicate p is *active* at the statement s, if $p \in local(s)$. (2) A set of predicate pairs denoted as $transfer(s)$. Intuitively, if $(p_i, p_j) \in transfer(s)$, then the value of p_j after s terminates is equal to the value of p_i before the execution of s. Formally, a pair $(p_i, p_j) \in transfer(s)$ satisfies the following conditions:

- $p_i \in \{True, False\} \cup local(s)$.
- There exists $s' \in child(s)$, such that $p_j \in local(s')$.
- If s is an assignment statement, then $p_i = WP(p_j, s)$.
- If s is an assume statement, then $p_i = p_j$.

We refer to the sets $local(s)$ and $transfer(s)$ together as the *localization information* at the statement s. This information is generated during the refinement step, and is used for creating refined abstractions which eliminate infeasible traces.

Example: Consider the code in Fig. 1(a) and the localization information in Fig. 1(d). Since $(p_4, p_3) \in transfer(s_1)$ and s_1 is an assignment, it means that $p_4 (c = m)$ is the weakest pre-condition of $p_3 (x = m)$ with respect to statement s_1. The value of predicate p_4 is useful only before the execution of s_1. After the execution of s_1, predicate p_3 becomes useful.

2.3   Refinement Using Weakest Pre-condition Propagation

Let $s_1; \ldots; s_k$ be an infeasible program trace. If s_i is of the form assume p_i, then the weakest pre-condition of p_i is propagated backwards from s_i until s_1. When computing the weakest pre-condition of a predicate p_i with respect to a statement s_j of the form assume p_j, we propagate the weakest pre-conditions of p_i and p_j separately. That is,

```
s
1: x = c;
2: y = c + 1;
3: if (x == m);
4:     if (y != m+1);
5:         ERROR: ;
```
(a)

```
s
1: x = c;
2: y = c + 1;
3: assume (x == m);
4: assume (y != m+1);
```
(b)

s	local(s)	transfer(s)
1:	$\{p_2\}$	$\{(p_2,p_2)\}$
2:	$\{p_2\}$	$\{(p_2,p_1)\}$
3:	$\{p_1\}$	$\{(p_1,p_1)\}$
4:	$\{p_1\}$	

(c)

s	local(s)	transfer(s)
1:	$\{p_2,p_4\}$	$\{(p_2,p_2),(p_4,p_3)\}$
2:	$\{p_2,p_3\}$	$\{(p_2,p_1),(p_3,p_3)\}$
3:	$\{p_1,p_3\}$	$\{(p_1,p_1)\}$
4:	$\{p_1\}$	

(d)

Fig. 1. (a) A simple C program. (b) An infeasible program trace. (c) Status of $local(s)$ and $transfer(s)$ sets after the first iteration of the refinement algorithm (see Fig. 2). Predicates p_1, p_2 denote $y \neq m+1$ and $c \neq m$, respectively. (d) New additions to the $local(s)$ and $transfer(s)$ in the second iteration. p_3, p_4 denote $x = m$ and $c = m$, respectively

we do not introduce a new predicate for $p_i \wedge p_j$. This is done to ensure that the predicates remain atomic. The $local$ and the $transfer$ sets for the various statements are updated during this process. The complete algorithm is given in Fig. 2.

Example: Consider the C program in Fig. 1(a) and an infeasible trace in Fig. 1(b). Assume that initially $local(s)$ and $transfer(s)$ sets are empty for each s. The refinement algorithm in Fig. 2 is applied to the infeasible trace. The localization information after the first iteration ($i = 4$) and second iteration ($i = 3$) of the outer loop in the refinement algorithm, is shown in Fig. 1(c) and Fig. 1(d), respectively. No change occurs to the localization information for $i = 2$ and $i = 1$, since s_2 and s_1 do not correspond to assume statements.

If $s_1; \ldots; s_k$ is infeasible, then $WP(true, s_1; \ldots; s_k) = false$ by definition. Intuitively, the atomic predicates in $WP(true, s_1; \ldots; s_k)$ appear in $local(s_1)$. Thus, by finding the relationships between the predicates in $local(s_1)$, it is possible to construct a refined model which eliminates the infeasible trace. When an infeasible trace $s_1; \ldots; s_k$ is refined using the algorithm in Fig. 2, s_1 is stored into a set of statements denoted by $marked$. If a statement s is in the $marked$ set, and the size of $local(s)$ is less than a certain threshold, then the abstraction routine computes the relationships between the predicates in $local(s)$ using SAT-based predicate abstraction [6, 17]. Otherwise, these relationships are determined lazily by detection of spurious abstract states [1].

Proof Based Analysis: The refinement algorithm described in Fig. 2 performs a backward weakest pre-condition propagation for each assume statement in the infeasible trace. However, neither all assume statements nor all assignments may be necessary for the infeasibility of the given trace. Propagating the weakest pre-conditions for all such statements results in an unnecessary increase in the number of predicates active at each

Input: An infeasible trace $s_1; \ldots; s_k$
Algorithm:

```
1: for i = k downto 1                                    //outer for loop
2:     if s_i is of form (assume φ_i) then               //propagate weakest pre-conditions
3:         local(s_i) = local(s_i) ∪ {φ_i}               //localize φ_i at s_i
4:         seed = φ_i
5:         for j = i − 1 downto 1                         //inner for loop
6:             if s_j is an assignment statement then
7:                 wp = WP(seed, s_j)
8:             else
9:                 wp = seed
10:            local(s_j) = local(s_j) ∪ {wp}            //localize wp at s_j
11:            transfer(s_j) = transfer(s_j) ∪ {(wp, seed)}//store predicate relationships
12:            seed = wp
13:            if seed is constant (i.e, true or false) then exit inner for loop
14:        end for
15:    end if
16: end for
17: marked = marked ∪ {s_1}
```

Fig. 2. Predicate localization during refinement

statement in the infeasible trace. We make use of the SAT-based proof of infeasibility of the given trace to determine the statements for which the weakest pre-condition propagation should be done [12]. Thus, the localization information is updated partially, in a way that is sufficient to remove the spurious behavior. The computation of an abstract model using the localization information is described in the next section.

3 Computing Abstractions

We describe the abstraction of the given C program by defining a transition system T. The transition system $T = (Q, I, R)$ consists of a set of states Q, a set of initial states $I \subseteq Q$, and a transition relation $R(q, q')$, which relates the current state $q \in Q$ to a next-state $q' \in Q$. The abstract model preserves the control flow in the original C program. Let $P = \{p_1, \ldots, p_k\}$ denote the union of the predicates active at various program locations. We first describe an abstraction scheme where each predicate p_i is assigned one unique Boolean variable b_i in the abstract model. The state space of the abstract model is $|L| \cdot 2^k$, where L is the set of control locations in the program. We call this scheme *abstraction without register sharing*. Next, we describe a scheme where the number of Boolean variables needed to represent the predicates in P is equal to the maximum number of predicates active at any program location. The size of the abstract model is given by $|L| \cdot 2^{k'}$, where $k' = max_{1 \leq i \leq |L|} |local(s_i)|$. We call this scheme *abstraction with register sharing*. Due to the localization of predicates, k' is usually much smaller than k, which enables faster model checking of the abstraction obtained using register sharing.

3.1   Abstraction Without Register Sharing

Let PC denote the vector of state variables used to encode the program counter. In abstraction without register sharing each predicate p_i has a state variable b_i in the abstract model. Each state in the abstraction corresponds to the valuation of $|PC| + k$ state variables, where k is the total number of predicates. In the initial state PC is equal to the value of the entry location in the original program. The state variables corresponding to the predicates are initially assigned non-deterministic Boolean values. Given a statement s_l and a predicate p_i the following cases are possible:

- s_l is either an assume statement or an assignment statement that does not assign to any variable in p_i. That is, after executing s_l the value of predicate p_i remains unchanged. Thus, in the abstract model the value of the state variable b_i remains unchanged after executing s_l. We denote the set of all statements where p_i is unchanged as $unc(p_i)$.
- s_l assigns to some variable in p_i. Let p_j denote the weakest pre-condition of p_i with respect to s_l. If the predicate p_j is active at s_l, that is $p_j \in local(s_l)$, and $(p_j, p_i) \in transfer(s_l)$, then after executing s_l, the value of predicate p_i is the same as the value of predicate p_j before executing s_l. In the abstract model this simply corresponds to transferring the value of b_j to b_i at s_l. If the predicate p_j is not active at s_l, then the abstract model assigns a non-deterministic Boolean value to b_i at s_l. This is necessary to ensure that the abstract model is an over-approximation of the original program.

We denote the set of all statements that can update the value of a predicate p_i as $update(p_i)$. The set of statements where the weakest pre-condition of p_i is available is denoted by $wpa(p_i)$. Using the localization information from Sec. 2.2, $wpa(p_i)$ is defined as follows: $wpa(p_i) := \{s_l | s_l \in update(p_i) \wedge \exists p_j. (p_j, p_i) \in transfer(s_l)\}$.

We use $inp(p_i)$ to denote the set of statements that assign a non-deterministic value v_i to the state variable b_i. This set is defined as $update(p_i) \backslash wpa(p_i)$. Let c_{il} denote the state variable corresponding to the weakest pre-condition of predicate p_i with respect to s_l. We use pc_l to denote that the program counter is at s_l, that is $PC = l$, and v_i to denote a non-deterministic input variable. The next state function for the variable b_i is then defined as follows:

$$b'_i := \left[\bigvee_{s_l \in unc(p_i)} (pc_l \wedge b_i) \right] \vee \left[\bigvee_{s_l \in wpa(p_i)} (pc_l \wedge c_{il}) \right] \vee \left[\bigvee_{s_l \in inp(p_i)} (pc_l \wedge v_i) \right] \quad (1)$$

Note that no calls to a decision procedure are needed when generating the next-state functions. All the required information is gathered during the refinement step itself by means of weakest pre-condition propagation.

Example: Consider the abstraction of the program in Fig. 3(a) with respect to the localization information given in Fig. 3(b). The predicate p_1 ($y \neq m + 1$) is updated at statement s_2, and its weakest pre-condition p_2 ($c \neq m$) is active at s_2, and $(p_2, p_1) \in transfer(s_2)$. So the next state function for the state variable representing p_1 is given as follows: $b'_1 := (pc_2 \wedge b_2) \vee ((pc_1 \vee pc_3 \vee pc_4) \wedge b_1)$. The other next state functions are given as follows: $b'_2 := b_2$, $b'_4 := b_4$, and $b'_3 := (pc_1 \wedge b_4) \vee ((pc_2 \vee pc_3 \vee pc_4) \wedge b_3)$. The resulting abstraction is shown in Fig. 3 (c). For simplicity the control flow is shown explicitly in the abstraction.

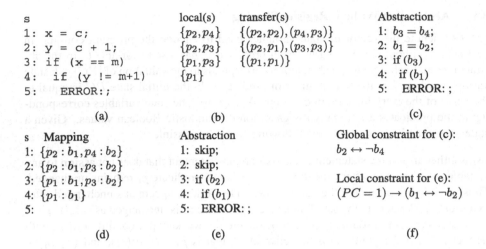

Fig. 3. (a) C program. (b) Localization information for the program where p_1, p_2, p_3, p_4 denote the predicates $y \neq m + 1, c \neq m, x = m, c = m$, respectively. (c) Abstraction with no register sharing. Boolean variable b_i represents the value of p_i in the abstraction. (d) Mapping of predicates in $local(s)$ for each s to the Boolean variables (register sharing). (e) Abstraction with register sharing. (f) Global constraint and Local constraint for abstractions in (c) and (e) , respectively

Global Constraint Generation: The precision of the abstraction can be increased by finding the relationships between the predicates in $local(s)$ for some s. For example, in Fig. 3(b) the relationship between the predicates in $local(s_1)$ results in a *global constraint*, $b_2 \leftrightarrow \neg b_4$. This constraint holds in all states of the abstract model of Fig. 3 (c) as the Boolean variables b_2 and b_4 always represent the same predicate throughout the abstraction without register sharing. The abstraction without register sharing given in Fig. 3(c) combined with the global constraint in Fig. 3(f) is sufficient to show that the ERROR label is not reachable in the C program given in Fig. 3(a). Note that we could have simplified the computation here by recognizing that $p_4 = \neg p_2$, which we omit for presentation purposes only.

The constraint generation is done only for some of the statements which are marked during the refinement (Fig. 2, line no. 17). We use SAT-based predicate abstraction [6, 17] to find the relationships between the predicates in $local(s)$ for such statements. This is the only time we use any decision procedure other than checking for the feasibility of traces. Due to the computational cost of enumerating the set of solutions, we only perform this computation for very small sets of predicates. Other relationships are then discovered on demand based on spurious abstract states [1].

3.2   Abstraction with Register Sharing

In abstraction with no register sharing, the state-space of the abstract model is $|L| \cdot 2^{|P|}$, where P is the set of predicates, and L is the set of locations in the given program. Thus, when the number of predicates is large, model checking of the abstraction can become a bottleneck even with a symbolic representation of the state space. We make use of the locality of predicates to speed up the model checking of the abstraction. This is done by reducing the number of (Boolean) state variables in the abstraction. The fact that each state variable in the abstract model is only locally useful can be used to represent different predicates in different parts of the program using the same state variable. We call the reuse of state variables in the abstract model *register sharing*.

Example: Consider the C program in Fig. 3(a) and the localization information in Fig. 3(b). The abstraction of this program with *no* register sharing in Fig. 3(c), contains four state variables, one for each predicate. However, the number of predicates active at any program statement is $max_{1 \leq i \leq 4}|local(s_i)| = 2$. Intuitively, it should be possible to create an abstraction with just two state variables.

The predicates p_2, p_4 are active at program location 1, so we introduce two Boolean variables b_1, b_2, to represent each of these predicates, respectively. After the execution of s_1, predicate p_4 is no longer active, and the state variable b_2 can be used to represent some other predicate. Predicate p_3 becomes active at s_2, so we can reuse the abstract variable b_2 to represent p_3 at s_2. In a similar fashion, b_1 can be reused to represent predicate p_1 at program locations s_3 and s_4. We use $p : b$ to denote that the predicate p is represented by the state variable b. The mapping of active predicates at each program location to the state variables is given in Fig 3(d).

The abstraction with register sharing is obtained by translating the predicate relationships in $transfer(s)$ for each s, according to the mapping discussed above. Continuing our example, $(p_4, p_3) \in transfer(s_1)$ in Fig. 3(b), the value of the state variable representing p_4 at s_1, must be transferred to the state variable representing p_3, afterwards. Since both p_4 and p_3 are represented by the same state variable b_2, the abstraction for s_1 does not alter the value of b_2. The abstraction using only two state variables (b_1, b_2) is shown in Fig 3(e). The `skip` statement means that the values of the state variables b_1 and b_2 remain unchanged for that statement.

Mapping Predicates to State Variables: Recall, that $p = \{p_1, \ldots, p_k\}$ denotes the set of predicates. Let $B = \{b_1, \ldots, b_l\}$ be the set of state variables in the abstraction, where l equals the maximum number of active predicates at any program location. For every statement s, the predicates relevant at s are mapped to unique state variables in B. Let map be a function that takes a statement s and a predicate p as arguments. If $p \in local(s)$, then the result of $map(s, p)$ is a state variable $b \in B$; otherwise, the result is $\perp$. Recall that $child(s)$ denotes the set of statements reachable from s in one step in the control flow graph. The constraints to be satisfied by map are as follows:

– Two distinct predicates which are active together at the same statement should not be assigned the same Boolean variable in the abstraction for that statement.

$$\forall s \forall p_i, p_j \in local(s) \; [p_i \neq p_j \rightarrow map(s, p_i) \neq map(s, p_j)]$$

– Consider statement s and $(p_1, p_2) \in transfer(s)$. By definition there exists $s' \in child(s)$ where p_2 is active, that is $p_2 \in local(s')$. This case is shown in Fig. 4(a). Suppose the predicate p_1 is mapped to b_i in s and p_2 is mapped to b_j in s'. The abstraction for the statement s will assign the value of b_i to b_j. So b_j should not be

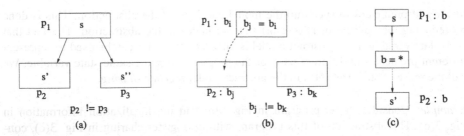

Fig. 4. (a) Statement s and two successors s' and s''. Predicates p_1, p_2, p_3 are active at s, s', and s'', respectively. (b) Abstraction with register sharing, where $(p_1, p_2) \in transfer(s)$. Predicate p_1, p_2 are mapped to b_i, b_j, respectively, in the abstraction. Predicate $p_3 \neq p_2$ should not be mapped to b_j for safe abstraction i.e., an over-approximation of the original program. (c) Boolean variable b is used to represent two distinct predicates p_1 and p_2 on the same path. It is set to a * (non-deterministic value) between s and s' to ensure safe abstraction

used to represent a predicate p_3, where $p_3 \neq p_2$, in any other successor of s. This is because there is no relationship between the value of the predicate p_1 at s and the predicate p_3 at s''. This constraint is shown in Fig. 4(b).

We now describe the algorithm which creates an abstraction in the presence of register sharing. Let $abs(s)$ be a set of Boolean pairs associated with each statement s. Intuitively, if $(b_l, b_m) \in abs(s)$, then in the abstraction the value of b_m after s terminates is equal to the value of b_l before the execution of s. Formally, $abs(s)$ is defined as follows:

$$abs(s) := \{(b_l, b_m) | \exists (p_i, p_j) \in transfer(s). \ b_l = map(s, p_i) \ \wedge$$
$$\exists s' \in child(s). \ b_m = map(s', p_j)\}.$$

Given a Boolean variable b_i and a statement s_l, the following cases are possible:

- s_l updates the value of b_i. That is, there exists a $b_j \in B$ such that $(b_j, b_i) \in abs(s_l)$. We denote the set of all statements which update b_i as $update(b_i)$. The function $rhs(s_l, b_i)$ returns the Boolean variable which is assigned to b_i in the statement s_l.
- s_l assigns a non-deterministic value to b_i. The set of all such statements is denoted by $nondet(b_i)$. In order to understand the use of this set, consider a Boolean variable b which is used to represent two distinct predicates p_1 and p_2 on the same path. Assume that b is not used to represent any other predicate between the statements s and s'. Since p_1 and p_2 are not related, the value of b when it is representing p_1 should not be used when b is representing p_2. So b is assigned a non-deterministic value between the path starting from s to s'. This is necessary to ensure that the abstraction is an over-approximation of the original program. This case is shown in Fig. 4(c).
- The value of b_i is a don't-care at statement s_l. The value of b_i is a don't care for all the statements which are not present in $update(b_i)$ or $nondet(b_i)$. In such cases, we set the value of b_i to false at these statements, in order to simplify its conjunction with the program counter variable to false. This simplifies the overall transition relation.

Given the above information the next state function for the variable b_i is defined as follows (we use an input v_i for introducing non-determinism and pc_l to denote $PC = l$):

$$b_i' := \Big[\bigvee_{s_l \in update(b_i)} (pc_l \wedge rhs(s_l, b_i)) \Big] \vee \Big[\bigvee_{s_l \in nondet(p_i)} (pc_l \wedge v_i) \Big]. \qquad (2)$$

Local constraint generation: The abstraction can be made more precise by relating the predicates in $local(s)$ for some s. For example, in Fig. 3(b) the predicates in $local(s_1)$ satisfy the constraint that $p_2 \leftrightarrow \neg p_4$. In order to add this constraint to the abstraction, we need to translate it in terms of the Boolean variables. The mapping given in Fig. 3(d) assigns Boolean variables b_1, b_2 to p_2, p_4, at s_1 respectively. This leads to a constraint $(PC = 1) \rightarrow (b_1 \leftrightarrow \neg b_2)$. This is called a *local constraint* as it is useful only when $PC = 1$. We cannot omit the $PC = 1$ term from the constraint as this would mean that $b_1 \leftrightarrow \neg b_2$ holds throughout the abstraction. The abstraction with register sharing in Fig. 3(e) combined with the local constraint in Fig. 3(f) is sufficient to show that the ERROR label is not reachable in the C program given in Fig. 3(a).

4   Dedicated State Variables

Register sharing enables the creation of abstract models with as few Boolean variables as possible which enables more efficient model checking of the abstractions. However, register sharing might also result in a large number of refinement iterations as described in the following. Consider a sequence SE of statements from s to s', which does not modify the value of a predicate p. Suppose p is localized at the statements s, s', but not at any intermediate statement in SE. In abstraction with register sharing, it is possible that p is represented by two different Boolean variables b_1 and b_2 at s and s', respectively. Because the value of p remains unchanged along SE, the value of b_1 at s should be equal to the value of b_2 at s'. If this is not tracked, we may obtain a spurious counterexample by assigning different values to b_1 at s and b_2 at s'. This leads to a refinement step, which localizes the predicate p at every statement in SE, to ensure that the value of predicate p does not change along SE in subsequent iterations. We should note that such behavior is handled in the abstraction *without* register sharing approach through the use of the *unchanged* set denoted by *unc* in Eqn. (1) described earlier.

If p is discovered frequently in different parts of the program through various spurious counterexamples, then using the abstraction with register sharing will lead to many abstraction refinement iterations. This problem can be avoided, if p is represented by exactly one Boolean variable b in a large scope of the abstraction. This is because the value of b will not be changed by any statement in SE, and thus, the value of b at s' will be the same as that at s. We call a Boolean variable which represents only one predicate for a large scope a *dedicated state variable*. The next state function for a dedicated state variable b is computed using Eqn. (1).

Hybrid Approach: Initially, when a predicate is discovered it is assigned a Boolean variable, which can be reused for representing different predicates in other parts of the abstraction. If the same predicate is discovered through multiple counterexamples in the various parts of the program, then it is assigned a dedicated Boolean variable for a global or functional scope of the program depending on the variables used in the predicate. The decision about when to assign a dedicated Boolean variable to a predicate is done by making use of the following heuristic.

For each predicate p, let $usage(p, i)$ denote the number of statements where p is localized in the iteration number i of the abstraction refinement loop. If $usage(p, i)$ exceeds a certain user-defined threshold TH, then p is assigned a dedicated Boolean variable. If $TH = 0$, then every predicate will be assigned a dedicated state variable as soon as it is discovered. This is similar to performing abstraction with no register sharing for all state variables. On the other hand, if $TH = |L| + 1$, where $|L|$ is the total number of statements in the program, then none of the predicates will be assigned a dedicated state variable. This allows complete reuse of the abstract variables, which is similar to abstraction with register sharing. For any intermediate value of TH we have a *hybrid* of abstraction with and without register sharing.

In the hybrid approach, it is possible to have global constraints on the dedicated state variables. This saves refinement iterations where the same constraint is added locally in various parts by means of counterexamples. We can still have local constraints on the state variables which are reused. Furthermore, we hope to discover as early as possible whether a predicate should be given a dedicated state variable by having a low threshold for the early iterations of the abstraction refinement loop, which increases as the number of iterations increases. Predicting early on that a predicate may need a dedicated state variable reduces the number of abstraction refinement iterations substantially.

5   Experimental Results

We have implemented these techniques in NEC's F-SOFT [15] verification tool. All experiments were performed on a $2.8GHz$ dual-processor Linux machine with 4GB of memory. We report our experimental results on the TCAS and Alias case studies. TCAS (Traffic Alert and Collision Avoidance System) is an aircraft conflict detection and resolution system used by all US commercial aircrafts. We used an ANSI-C version of a TCAS component available from Georgia Tech. Even though the pre-processed program has only 1652 lines of code, the number of predicates needed to verify the properties is non-trivial for both F-SOFT and BLAST. We checked 10 different safety properties of the TCAS system. Alias is an artificial benchmark which makes extensive use of pointers. Each property was encoded as a certain error label in the code. If the label is not reachable, then the property is said to hold. Otherwise, we report the length of the counterexample in the "Bug" column in Table 1. CPU times are given in seconds, and we set a time limit of one hour for each analysis. Note, that many implementation details of F-SOFT and BLAST not discussed here may impact the measured runtimes.

5.1   Predicate Localization, Register Sharing, and Dedicated State Variables

We first experimented with no localization of predicates. However, this approach did not scale, as the abstraction computation becomes a bottleneck. We next experimented with localization of predicates using weakest pre-conditions. The results of applying only localization and abstraction without register sharing is shown under the "Localize" heading in the Table 1. The "Time Abs MC" column gives the total time, followed by the breakup of total time into the time taken by abstraction (Abs), model checking (MC), respectively. We omit the time taken by refinement, which is equal to Time - (Abs + MC) for each row. The "P" and the "I" columns give the total number of predicates, and the total number of iterations, respectively. Two observations can be made from the "Localize" results: 1) Due to the localization of predicates, the abstraction computation is no longer a bottleneck. 2) Model checking takes most of the time, since for each predicate a state variable is created in the abstract model. Note that the model checking step is the cause of the timeouts in three rows under the "Localize" results.

Next, we experimented with register sharing. The number of state variables in the abstraction was reduced, and the individual model-checking steps became faster. However, as discussed in Sec. 4 this approach resulted in too many abstraction refinement iterations. This problem was solved by discovering on-the-fly whether a predicate should be assigned a dedicated state variable, that is, a state variable which will not be reused. A dedicated state variable is introduced for a predicate whose usage exceeds a progressively increasing threshold, starting at 5% of the total number of program locations.

The results of combining these multiple techniques is given under the "Combined" heading in Table 1. The "P Max Ded" column gives the total number of predicates (P), followed by the maximum number of predicates active at any program location (Max), and the total number of state variables which represent exactly one predicate, that is, dedicated state variables (Ded). Observe that the time spent during model checking (MC) has reduced significantly as compared to the "Localize" column.

We also experimented with the TH (threshold) parameter, which is used to determine when a predicate is assigned a dedicated state variable. Fig. 5(a) shows the variation of the total runtime with the initial value for the threshold. When the threshold is equal to zero every predicate is assigned a dedicated state variable. This results in too many state variables in the abstract model causing the total runtime to be high. However, as the

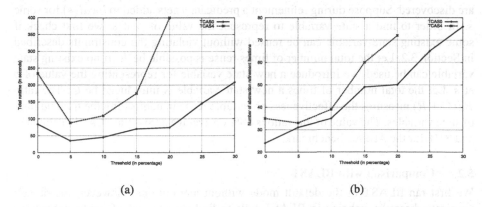

(a)   (b)

Fig. 5. (a) Variation in the total runtime with the threshold. (b) Variation in the total number of abstraction refinement iterations with the threshold

Table 1. Results for: 1) Localization, abstraction without register sharing ("Localize"). 2) Localization, abstraction with register sharing, dedicated state variables ("Combined"). 3) BLAST with interpolation ("BLAST"). A "-" indicates that the property holds. A "·" indicates that the benchmark could not be handled properly. A "TO" indicates a timeout of 1hr. We report the statistics observed before timeout occurs

Bench-mark	Localize					Combined							BLAST					Bug
	Time	Abs	MC	P	I	Time	Abs	MC	P	Max	Ded	I	Time	P	Max	Avg	I	
TCAS0	245	7	196	71	32	**36**	5	15	65	26	18	31	96	85	24	10	33	-
TCAS1	1187	15	1069	108	44	**161**	9	118	96	35	25	38	256	137	43	17	42	-
TCAS2	952	10	882	74	38	**104**	25	51	95	31	24	36	148	108	31	11	40	-
TCAS3	940	15	864	91	36	**46**	17	17	73	22	15	33	172	101	26	10	44	152
TCAS4	1231	13	1111	97	39	**88**	9	48	90	34	25	32	182	149	38	13	51	166
TCAS5	1222	11	1128	79	41	141	8	98	98	37	29	31	**105**	114	31	10	33	-
TCAS6	TO	20	2270	117	49	330	16	266	109	40	33	40	**293**	158	41	14	69	179
TCAS7	1758	16	1627	79	47	**64**	10	29	94	28	21	33	287	125	30	11	63	160
TCAS8	TO	21	1988	84	51	**119**	13	68	106	34	27	41	181	116	31	11	46	-
TCAS9	TO	26	3349	113	58	**250**	14	186	106	34	27	44	322	140	40	14	61	179
ALIAS	50	6	33	61	11	**6**	2	1	55	25	15	9	·	·	·	·	·	-

threshold is increased, the number of abstraction refinement iterations starts to increase as shown in Fig. 5(b). The best runtime in our experiments has so far been obtained for an initial threshold of 5%. Even such a small value for the threshold is effective in separating the predicates which are *globally* relevant from those which are *locally* useful. As the threshold is further increased very few predicates are assigned dedicated state variables. One of the main advantages of choosing a small initial threshold is that we are able to decide early on whether a predicate may need a dedicated state variable. If we start with a higher initial threshold, the number of additional iterations needed for a single predicate to receive a dedicated state variable increases too much.

The map function (see Section 3.2) is computed incrementally, as new predicates are discovered. Suppose during refinement a predicate p gets added to $local(s)$ for some s. In order to find a state variable to represent the value of p at s, we first check if some existing state variable can be reused without violating the constraints described in Section 3.2. Let the total number of times reuse is possible be R. If no existing state variable can be used, we introduce a new state variable for representing the value of p at s. Let the total number of times a new state variable is introduced be C. The ratio $R/(C+R)$ measures the effectiveness of variable reuse in controlling the total number of state variables. The value of this ratio is 88% on average across the TCAS benchmarks and 81% for the ALIAS benchmark.

5.2   Comparison with BLAST

We first ran BLAST in the default mode without any options. However, the default predicate discovery scheme in BLAST fails to find the new set of predicates during refinement, and terminates without (dis)proving any of the TCAS properties. Next, we tried the Craig interpolation [14] options (craig1 and craig2) provided by BLAST. The BLAST manual recommends the use of predH7 heuristic with Craig interpolation.

Of the various options to BLAST, `craig2` and `predH7` result in the best performance when checking the TCAS properties. Table 1 gives the result of running BLAST with these options under the "BLAST" heading. The "P Max Avg" column gives the total number of predicates (P), followed by the maximum (Max) and the average (Avg) number of predicates active at any program location (rounded to the nearest integer).

The best runtimes are shown in bold in Table 1. Note that the "Combined" technique of F-SOFT outperforms BLAST on 9 out of 11 benchmarks, and the number of iterations required by "Combined" is less than that for "BLAST" in all cases. Recall that the size of the abstraction is exponential in the maximum number of active predicates (Max). This number is comparable for both BLAST and F-SOFT, even though BLAST makes use of a more complex refinement technique based on the computation of interpolants.

6   Conclusions and Future Work

The application of the predicate abstraction paradigm to large software depends crucially on the choice and usage of the predicates. If all predicates are tracked globally in the program, the analysis often becomes intractable due to the large number of predicate relationships. In this paper we described various techniques for improving the overall performance of the abstraction refinement loop. We presented experimental results in our F-SOFT [15] toolkit using the techniques of predicate localization, register sharing and dedicated state variables, and showed how a combination of these techniques allowed us to check properties requiring a large number of predicates.

There are a number of interesting avenues for future research. Theoretical comparison between the use of interpolants [14] and the use of weakest pre-conditions for localization of predicates will be useful. Other techniques for finding the right balance between the predicates whose values are tracked locally and the predicates whose values are tracked globally are worth further investigation. Furthermore, we need to experiment with these heuristics for more and larger case studies as well.

Acknowledgment. We thank Rupak Majumdar and Ranjit Jhala for their help with BLAST.

References

1. T. Ball, B. Cook, S. Das, and S. Rajamani. Refining approximations in software predicate abstraction. In *TACAS 04*, pages 388–403. Springer, 2004.
2. T. Ball, R. Majumdar, T.D. Millstein, and S.K. Rajamani. Automatic predicate abstraction of C programs. In *Programming Language Design and Implementation*, pages 203–213, 2001.
3. T. Ball, A. Podelski, and S.K. Rajamani. Boolean and Cartesian abstraction for model checking C programs. In *TACAS 01*, volume 2031, 2001.
4. T. Ball and S.K. Rajamani. Automatically validating temporal safety properties of interfaces. In *SPIN Workshop on Model Checking of Software*. Springer, 2001.
5. S. Chaki, E. Clarke, A. Groce, S. Jha, and H. Veith. Modular verification of software components in C. In *ICSE 03*, pages 385–395. IEEE, 2003.
6. E. Clarke, D. Kroening, N. Sharygina, and K. Yorav. Predicate abstraction of ANSI–C programs using SAT. *Formal Methods in System Design*, 25:105–127, Sep–Nov 2004.

7. P. Cousot and R. Cousot. Abstract interpretation: a unified lattice model for static analysis of programs by construction or approximation of fixpoints. In *Proceedings of the 4th ACM Symposium on Principles of Programming Languages*, pages 238–252, 1977.

8. William Craig. Linear reasoning. In *Journal of Symbolic Logic*, pages 22:250–268, 1957.

9. S. Das, D. Dill, and S. Park. Experience with predicate abstraction. In *Computer Aided Verification*, LNCS 1633, pages 160–171. Springer, 1999.

10. E. Dijkstra. *A Discipline of Programming*. Prentice Hall, 1976.

11. S. Graf and H. Saidi. Construction of abstract state graphs with PVS. In *CAV 97*, pages 72–83. Springer, 1997.

12. A. Gupta, M.K. Ganai, P. Ashar, and Z. Yang. Iterative abstraction using SAT-based BMC with proof analysis. In *International Conference on Computer Aided Design (ICCAD)*, 2003.

13. T. A. Henzinger, R. Jhala, R. Majumdar, and G. Sutre. Lazy abstraction. In *POPL 02*, pages 58–70, 2002.

14. T.A. Henzinger, R. Jhala, R. Majumdar, and K.L. McMillan. Abstractions from proofs. In *POPL 04*, pages 232–244. ACM Press, 2004.

15. F. Ivančić, Z. Yang, M. Ganai, A. Gupta, and P. Ashar. Efficient SAT-based bounded model checking for software verification. In *Symposium on Leveraging Applications of Formal Methods*, 2004.

16. H. Jain, D. Kroening, and E. Clarke. Verification of SpecC using predicate abstraction. In *MEMOCODE 04*, pages 7–16. IEEE, 2004.

17. S. K. Lahiri, R. E. Bryant, and B. Cook. A symbolic approach to predicate abstraction. In *CAV 03*, pages 141–153. Springer, 2003.

18. Kedar S. Namjoshi and Robert P. Kurshan. Syntactic program transformations for automatic abstraction. In *CAV 00*, number 1855 in LNCS, 2000.

19. R. Rugina and M.C. Rinard. Symbolic bounds analysis of pointers, array indices, and accessed memory regions. In *PLDI 00*, pages 182–195, 2000.

20. Vlad Rusu and Eli Singerman. On proving safety properties by integrating static analysis, theorem proving and abstraction. In *TACAS 99*, pages 178–192, 1999.

21. A. Zaks, F. Ivančić, H. Cadambi, I. Shlyakhter, Z. Yang, M. Ganai A. Gupta, and P. Ashar. Range analysis for software verification. *Submitted for publication*, 2005.

On Some Transformation Invariants
Under Retiming and Resynthesis*

Jie-Hong R. Jiang

Department of Electrical Engineering and Computer Sciences,
University of California, Berkeley

Abstract. Transformations using retiming and resynthesis operations
are the most important and practical (if not the only) techniques used in
optimizing synchronous hardware systems. Although these transformations have been studied extensively for over a decade, questions about
their *optimization capability* and *verification complexity* are not answered
fully. Resolving these questions may be crucial in developing more effective synthesis and verification algorithms. This paper settles the above
two open problems. The optimization potential is resolved through a constructive algorithm which determines if two given finite state machines
(FSMs) are transformable to each other via retiming and resynthesis operations. Verifying the equivalence of two FSMs under such transformations, when the history of iterative transformation is unknown, is proved
to be PSPACE-complete and hence just as hard as general equivalence
checking, contrary to a common belief. As a result, we advocate a conservative design methodology for the optimization of synchronous hardware
systems to ameliorate verifiability. Our analysis reveals some properties
about initializing FSMs transformed under retiming and resynthesis. On
the positive side, established is a lag-independent bound on the length
increase of initialization sequences for FSMs under retiming. It allows a
simpler incremental construction of initialization sequences compared to
prior approaches. On the negative side, we show that there is no analogous transformation-independent bound when resynthesis and retiming
are iterated. Fortunately, an algorithm computing the exact length increase is presented.

1 Introduction

Retiming [7, 8] is an elementary yet effective technique in optimizing synchronous
hardware systems. By simply repositioning registers, it is capable of reschedul-
ing computation tasks in an optimal way subject to some design criteria. As
both an advantage and a disadvantage, retiming preserves the circuit structure
of the system under consideration. It is an advantage in that it supports incremental engineering change with good predictability, and a disadvantage in that

---

* This work was supported in part by NSF grant CCR-0312676, the California Micro
program, and our industrial sponsors, Fujitsu, Intel, Magma and Synplicity.

N. Halbwachs and L. Zuck (Eds.): TACAS 2005, LNCS 3440, pp. 413–428, 2005.

the optimization capability is somewhat limited. Therefore, resynthesis [9, 1, 10] was proposed to be combined with retiming, allowing modification of circuit structures. This combination of retiming and resynthesis certainly extends the optimization power of retiming, but to what extent remains an open problem, even though some notable progress has been made since [9], e.g. [14, 15, 20]. Fully resolving this problem is crucial in understanding the complexity of verifying the equivalence of systems transformed by retiming and resynthesis and in constructing correct initialization sequences. In fact, despite its effectiveness, the transformation of retiming and resynthesis is not widely used in hardware synthesis flows due to the verification hindrance and the initialization problem. Progress in these areas could enhance the practicality and application of retiming and resynthesis, and advance the development of more effective synthesis and verification algorithms.

This paper tackles three main problems regarding retiming and resynthesis:

Optimization power: What is the transformation power of retiming and resynthesis? How can we tell if two synchronous systems are transformable to each other with retiming and resynthesis operations?

Verification complexity: What is the computational complexity of verifying if two synchronous systems are equivalent under retiming and resynthesis?

Initialization: How does the transformation of retiming and resynthesis affect the initialization of a synchronous system? How can we correct initialization sequences?

Our main results include

- (Section 3) Characterize constructively the transformation power of retiming and resynthesis.
- (Section 4) Prove the PSPACE-completeness of verifying the equivalence of systems transformed by retiming and resynthesis operations when the transformation history is lost.
- (Section 5) Demonstrate the effects of retiming and resynthesis on the initialization sequences of synchronous systems. Present an algorithm correcting initialization sequences.

2   Preliminaries

In this paper, to avoid later complication we shall not restrict ourselves to binary variables and Boolean functions. Thus, we assume that variables can take values from arbitrary finite domains, and similarly functions can have arbitrary finite domains and co-domains. When (co)domains are immaterial in the discussion, we shall omit specifying them. We introduce the following notational conventions. Let $\mathcal{V}_1$ be a set of variables. Notation $[\![\mathcal{V}_1]\!]$ represents the set of all possible valuations over $\mathcal{V}_1$. Let $\mathcal{V}_2 \subseteq \mathcal{V}_1$. For $x \in [\![\mathcal{V}_1]\!]$, we use $x[\mathcal{V}_2] \in [\![\mathcal{V}_2]\!]$ to denote the valuation over variables $\mathcal{V}_2$ which agrees with x on $\mathcal{V}_2$. Suppose s is a (current-)state variable. Its primed version s' denotes the corresponding next-state variable.

Synchronous Hardware Systems. Based on [7], a syntactical definition of *synchronous hardware systems* can be formulated as follows. A hardware system is abstracted as a directed graph, called a *communication graph*, $G = (V, E)$ with *typed* vertices V and *weighted* edges E. Every vertex $v \in V$ represents either the environment or a functional element. The vertex representing the environment is the *host*, which is of type undefined; a vertex is of type f if the functional element it represents is of function f (which can be a multiple-output function consisting of $f_1, f_2, \ldots$). Every edge $e\langle w \rangle = (u, v)\langle w \rangle \in E$ with a non-negative integer-valued weight w corresponds to the interconnection from vertex u to vertex v interleaved by w state-holding elements (or registers). (From the viewpoint of hardware systems, any component in a communication graph disconnected from the host is redundant. Hence, in the sequel, we assume that a communication graph is a single connected component.) A hardware system is *synchronous* if, in its corresponding communication graph, every cycle contains at least one positive-weighted edge. This paper is concerned with synchronous hardware systems whose registers are all triggered by the same clock ticks. Moreover, according to the initialization mechanism, a register can be reset either explicitly or implicitly. For registers with explicit reset, their initial values are determined by some reset circuitry when the system is powered up. In contrast, for registers with implicit reset, their initial values can be arbitrary, but can be brought to an identified set of states (i.e. the set of *initial states*[1]) by applying some input sequences, the so-called *initialization* (or *reset*) *sequences* [13]. It turns out that explicit-reset registers can be replaced with implicit-reset ones plus some reset circuitry [10, 17]. (Doing so admits a more systematic treatment of retiming synchronous hardware systems because retiming explicit-reset registers needs special attention to maintain equivalent initial states.) Without loss of generality, this paper assumes that all registers have implicit reset. In addition, we are concerned with initializable systems, that is, there exist input sequences which bring the systems from any state to some set of designated initial states.

The semantical interpretation of synchronous hardware systems can be modelled as *finite state machines* (FSMs). An FSM $\mathcal{M}$ is a tuple $(Q, I, \Sigma, \Omega, \delta, \lambda)$, where Q is a finite set of states, $I \subseteq Q$ is the set of initial states, Σ and Ω are the sets of input and output alphabets, respectively, and $\delta : \Sigma \times Q \to Q$ (resp. $\lambda : \Sigma \times Q \to \Omega$) is the transition function (resp. output function). Let $\mathcal{V}_S$, $\mathcal{V}_I$, and $\mathcal{V}_O$ be the sets of variables that encode the states, input alphabets, and output alphabets respectively. Then $Q = [\![\mathcal{V}_S]\!]$, $\Sigma = [\![\mathcal{V}_I]\!]$ and $\Omega = [\![\mathcal{V}_O]\!]$. To uniquely construct an FSM from a communication graph $G = (V, E)$, we divide each edge $(u, v)\langle w \rangle \in E$ into $w + 1$ edges separated by w registers and connected with the two end-vertices u and v. We then associate the outgoing (incoming) edges of registers with current-state variables $\mathcal{V}_S$ (next-state variables $\mathcal{V}_{S'}$); associate the outgoing (incoming) edges of the host with variables $\mathcal{V}_I$ ($\mathcal{V}_O$). All other edges are associated with internal variables. The transition and output functions

---

[1] When referring to "initial states," we shall mean the starting states of a system *after* initialization.

are obtained, starting from $\mathcal{V}_{S'}$ and $\mathcal{V}_O$, respectively, by a sequence of recursive substitutions of variables with functions of their input functional elements until the functions depend only on variables $\mathcal{V}_I \cup \mathcal{V}_S$.

We define a strong form of state equivalence which will govern the study of the transformation power of retiming.

Definition 1. *Given an FSM $\mathcal{M} = (Q, I, \Sigma, \Omega, \delta, \lambda)$, two states $q_1, q_2 \in Q$ are* **immediately equivalent** *if $\delta(\sigma, q_1) \equiv \delta(\sigma, q_2)$ and $\lambda(\sigma, q_1) \equiv \lambda(\sigma, q_2)$ for any $\sigma \in \Sigma$.*

Also, we define *dangling states* inductively as follows.

Definition 2. *Given an FSM, a state is* **dangling** *if either it has no predecessor state or all of its predecessor states are dangling. All other states are* **non-dangling**.

Retiming. A *retiming operation* over a synchronous hardware system consists of a series of atomic moves of registers across functional elements in either a forward or backward direction. (The relocation of registers is crucial in exploring optimal synchronous hardware systems with respect to various design criteria, such as area, performance, power, etc. As not our focus, the exposition of retiming in the optimization perspective is omitted in this paper. Interested readers are referred to [8].) Formally speaking, retiming can be described with a *retime function* [7] over a communication graph as follows.

Definition 3. *Given a communication graph $G = (V, E)$, a* **retime function** *$\rho : V \to \mathbb{Z}$ maps each vertex to an integer, called the* **lag** *of the vertex, such that $w + \rho(v) - \rho(u) \geq 0$ for any edge $(u, v)\langle w \rangle \in E$. If $\rho(\text{host}) \equiv 0$, ρ is called* **normalized**; *otherwise, ρ is* **unnormalized**.

Given a communication graph $G = (V, E)$, any retime function ρ over G uniquely determines a "legally" retimed communication graph $G^\dagger = (V, E^\dagger)$ in which $(u, v)\langle w \rangle \in E$ if, and only if, $(u, v)\langle w + \rho(v) - \rho(u) \rangle \in E^\dagger$. It is immediate that the retime function $-\rho$ reverses the retiming from $G^\dagger$ to G.

Retime functions can be naturally classified by calibrating their equivalences as follows.

Definition 4. *Given a communication graph G, two retime functions ρ_1 and ρ_2 are equivalent if they result in the same retimed communication graph.*

Proposition 1. *Given a retime function ρ with respect to a communication graph, offsetting ρ by an integer constant c results in an equivalent retime function.*

Hence any retime function can be normalized. This equivalence relation, which will be useful in the study of the increase of initialization sequences due to retiming, induces a partition over retime functions. Equivalent retime functions (with respect to some communication graph) form an equivalence class.

Proposition 2. *Given a communication graph G, any equivalence class of re-time functions is of infinite size; any equivalence class of normalized retime functions is of size either one or infinity (only when G contains components disconnected from the host). Furthermore, any equivalence class of retime functions has a normalized member.*

Resynthesis. A *resynthesis operation* over a function f rewrites the syntactical formula representation of f while maintaining its semantical functionality. Clearly, the set of all possible rewrites is infinite (but countable, namely, with the same cardinality as the set $\mathbb{N}$ of natural numbers). When a resynthesis operation is performed upon a synchronous hardware system, we shall mean that the transition and output functions of the corresponding FSM are modified in representations but preserved in functionalities. This modification in representations will be reflected in the communication graph of the system. (Again, such rewrites are usually subject to some optimization criteria. Since this is not our focus, the optimization aspects of resynthesis operations are omitted. See, e.g., [1] for further treatment.)

3 Optimization Capability

The transformation power of retiming and resynthesis can be understood best with state transition graphs (STGs) defined by FSMs. We investigate how retiming and resynthesis operations can alter STGs.

3.1 Optimization Power of Retiming

We study how the atomic forward and backward moves of retiming affect the corresponding FSM $\mathcal{M} = (\llbracket \mathcal{V}_S \rrbracket, I, \Sigma, \Omega, \delta, \lambda)$ of a given communication graph $G = (V, E)$.

To study the effect of an atomic backward move, consider a normalized retime function ρ with $\rho(v) = 1$ for some vertex $v \in V$ and $\rho(u) = 0$ for all $u \in V \backslash \{v\}$. (Because a retiming operation can be decomposed as a series of atomic moves, analyzing ρ defined above suffices to demonstrate the effect.) Let $\mathcal{V}_S = \mathcal{V}_{S^\natural} \cup \mathcal{V}_{S^*}$ be the state variables of $\mathcal{M}$, where $\mathcal{V}_{S^\natural} = \{s_1, \dots, s_i\}$ and $\mathcal{V}_{S^*} = \{s_{i+1}, \dots, s_n\}$ are disjoint. Suppose v is of type $f : \llbracket \{t_1, \dots, t_j\} \rrbracket \rightarrow \llbracket \{s'_1, \dots, s'_i\} \rrbracket$, where the valuation of next-state variables s'_k is defined by $f_k(t_1, \dots, t_j)$ for $k = 1, \dots, i$. Let $\mathcal{M}^\dagger = (\llbracket \mathcal{V}_S^\dagger \rrbracket, I^\dagger, \Sigma, \Omega, \delta^\dagger, \lambda^\dagger)$ be the FSM after retiming, where state variables $\mathcal{V}_S^\dagger = \mathcal{V}_T \cup \mathcal{V}_{S^*}$ with $\mathcal{V}_T = \{t_1, \dots, t_j\}$. For any two states $q_1^\dagger, q_2^\dagger \in \llbracket \mathcal{V}_S^\dagger \rrbracket$, if $q_1^\dagger[\mathcal{V}_{S^*}] \equiv q_2^\dagger[\mathcal{V}_{S^*}]$ and $f(q_1^\dagger[\mathcal{V}_T]) \equiv f(q_2^\dagger[\mathcal{V}_T])$, then $q_1^\dagger$ and $q_2^\dagger$ are immediately equivalent. This immediate equivalence results from the fact that the transition and output functions of $\mathcal{M}^\dagger$ can be valuated after the valuation of f, which filters out the difference between $q_1^\dagger$ and $q_2^\dagger$. Comparing state pairs between $\mathcal{M}$ and $\mathcal{M}^\dagger$, we can always find a relation $R \subseteq \llbracket \mathcal{V}_S \rrbracket \times \llbracket \mathcal{V}_S^\dagger \rrbracket$ such that

1. Pairs $(q_1, q_1^\dagger)$ and $(q_1, q_2^\dagger)$ are both in R for the state q_1 of $\mathcal{M}$ with $q_1[\mathcal{V}_{S^*}] \equiv q_1^\dagger[\mathcal{V}_{S^*}]$ and $q_1[\mathcal{V}_{S^\natural}] \equiv f(q_1^\dagger[\mathcal{V}_T])$.
2. It preserves the immediate equivalence, that is, $(q, q^\dagger) \in R$ if, and only if, $\lambda(\sigma, q) \equiv \lambda^\dagger(\sigma, q^\dagger)$ and $(\delta(\sigma, q), \delta^\dagger(\sigma, q^\dagger)) \in R$ for any $\sigma \in \Sigma$.

Since f is a total function, every state of $\mathcal{M}^\dagger$ has a corresponding state in $\mathcal{M}$ related by R. (It corresponds to the fact that backward moves of retiming cannot increase the length of initialization sequences, the subject to be discussed in Section 5.) On the other hand, since f may not be a surjective (or an onto) mapping in general, there may be some state q of $\mathcal{M}$ such that $\forall x \in [\![\mathcal{V}_T]\!]. q[\mathcal{V}_{S^\natural}] \not\equiv f(x)$, that is, no states can transition to q. In this case, q can be seen as being annihilated after retiming. To summarize,

Lemma 1. *An atomic backward move of retiming can 1) split a state into multiple immediately equivalent states and/or 2) annihilate states which have no predecessor states.*

With a similar reasoning by reversing the roles of $\mathcal{M}$ and $\mathcal{M}^\dagger$, one can show

Lemma 2. *An atomic forward move of retiming can 1) merge multiple immediately equivalent states into a single state and/or 2) create states which have no predecessor states.*

(Similar results of Lemmas 1 and 2 appeared in [15], where the phenomena of state creation and annihilation were omitted.)

Note that, in a single atomic forward move of retiming, transitions among the newly created states are prohibited. In contrast, when a sequence of atomic forward moves $m_1, \ldots, m_n$ are performed, the newly created states at move m_i can possibly have predecessor states created in later moves $m_{i+1}, \ldots, m_n$. Clearly all the newly created states not merged with original existing states due to immediate equivalence are dangling. However, to be shown in Section 5.1, the transition paths among these dangling states cannot be arbitrarily long.

Since a retiming operation consists of a series of atomic moves, Lemmas 1 and 2 set the fundamental rules of all possible changes of STGs by retiming. Observe that a retiming operation is always associated with some structure (i.e. a communication graph). For a fixed structure, a retiming operation has limited optimization power, e.g., the converses of Lemmas 1 and 2 are not true. That is, there may not exist atomic moves of retiming (over a communication graph) which meet arbitrary targeting changes on an STG. Unlike a retiming operation, a resynthesis operation provides the capability of modifying the vertices and connections of a communication graph.

3.2 Optimization Power of Retiming and Resynthesis

A resynthesis operation itself cannot contribute any changes to the STG of an FSM. However, when combined with retiming, it becomes a handy tool. In essence, the combination of retiming and resynthesis validates the converse of Lemmas 1 and 2 as will be shown in Theorem 1. Moreover, it determines the transitions of newly created states due to forward retiming moves, and thus has decisive effects on initialization sequences as will be discussed in Section 5.2. On the other hand, we shall mention an important property about retiming and resynthesis operations.

Lemma 3. *Given an FSM, the newly created states (not merged with original existing states due to immediate equivalence) due to atomic forward moves of retiming remain dangling throughout iterative retiming and resynthesis operations.*

Remark 1. As an orthogonal issue to our discussion on how retiming and resynthesis can alter the STG of an FSM, the transformation of retiming and resynthesis was shown [10] to have the capability of exploiting various state encodings (or assignments) of the FSM.

Notice that the induced state space of the dangling states originating from atomic moves of retiming is immaterial in our study of the optimization capability of retiming and resynthesis because an FSM after initialization never reaches such dangling states. An exact characterization of the optimization power of retiming and resynthesis is given as follows.

Theorem 1. *Ignoring the (unreachable) dangling states created due to retiming, two FSMs are transformable to each other through retiming and resynthesis if, and only if, their state transition graphs are transformable to each other by a sequence of splitting a state into multiple immediately equivalent states and of merging multiple immediately equivalent states into a single state.*

(A similar result of Theorem 1 appeared in [15], where however the optimization power of retiming and resynthesis was over-stated as will be detailed in Section 6.) From Theorem 1, one can relate two FSMs before and after the transformation of retiming and resynthesis as follows.

Corollary 1. *Given $\mathcal{M} = (Q, I, \Sigma, \Omega, \delta, \lambda)$ and $\mathcal{M}^\dagger = (Q^\dagger, I^\dagger, \Sigma, \Omega, \delta^\dagger, \lambda^\dagger)$, FSMs $\mathcal{M}$ and $\mathcal{M}^\dagger$ are transformable to each other through retiming and resynthesis operations if, and only if, there exists a relation $R \subseteq Q \times Q^\dagger$ satisfying*

1. *Any non-dangling state $q \in Q$ (resp. $q^\dagger \in Q^\dagger$) has at least one non-dangling state $q^\dagger \in Q^\dagger$ (resp. $q \in Q$) such that $(q, q^\dagger) \in R$.*
2. *State pair $(q, q^\dagger) \in R$ if and only if, for any $\sigma \in \Sigma$, $\lambda(\sigma, q) \equiv \lambda^\dagger(\sigma, q^\dagger)$ and $(\delta(\sigma, q), \delta^\dagger(\sigma, q^\dagger)) \in R$.*

Notice that the statements of Theorem 1 and Corollary 1 are nonconstructive in the sense that no procedure is given to determine if two FSMs are transformable to each other under retiming and resynthesis. This weakness motivates us to study a constructive alternative.

3.3 Retiming-Resynthesis Equivalence and Canonical Representation

Given an FSM, the transformation of retiming and resynthesis operations can rewrite it into a class of equivalent FSMs (constrained by Corollary 1). We ask

ConstructQuotientGraph
   input: a state transition graph G
   output: a state-minimized transition graph w.r.t. immediate equivalence
   begin
   01   remove dangling states from G
   02   **repeat**
   03   compute and merge immediately equivalent states of G
   04   **until** no merging performed
   05   **return** the reduced graph
   end

Fig. 1. Algorithm: Construct quotient graph

if there exists a computable canonical representative in each such class, and answer this question affirmatively by presenting a procedure constructing it. Rather than arguing directly over FSMs, we simplify our exposition by arguing over STGs.

Because retiming and resynthesis operations are reversible, we know

Proposition 3. *Given STGs G, G_1, and G_2. Suppose G_1 and G_2 are derivable from G using retiming and resynthesis operations. Then G_1 and G_2 are transformable to each other under retiming and resynthesis.*

We say that two FSMs (STGs) are *equivalent under retiming and resynthesis* if they are transformable to each other under retiming and resynthesis. Thus, any such equivalence class is *complete* in the sense that any member in the class is transformable to any member. To derive a canonical representative of any equivalence class, consider the algorithm outlined in Figure 1. Similar to the general state minimization algorithm [6], the idea is to seek a representative minimized with respect to the immediate equivalence of states. However, unlike the least-fixed-point computation of the general state minimization, the computation in Figure 1 looks for a greatest fixed point. Given an STG, the algorithm first removes all the dangling states, and then iteratively merges immediately equivalent states until no more states can be merged.

Theorem 2. *Given an STG G, Algorithm* ConstructQuotientGraph *produces a canonical state-minimized solution, which is equivalent to G under retiming and resynthesis.*

For a naïve explicit enumerative implementation, Algorithm *ConstructQuotientGraph* is of time complexity $O(kn^3)$, where k is the size of input alphabet and n is number of states. (Notice that the complexity is exponential when the input is an FSM, instead of an STG, representation.) For an implicit symbolic implementation, the complexity depends heavily on the internal symbolic representations. If Step 3 in Figure 1 computes and merges all immediately equivalent states at once in a breadth-first-search manner, then the algorithm converges in a minimum number of iterations.

VerifyEquivalenceUnderRetiming&Resynthesis
  input: two state transition graphs G_1 and G_2
  output: YES, if G_1 and G_2 are equivalent under retiming and resynthesis
          No, otherwise
  begin
  01    $G_{1/} := ConstructQuotientGraph(G_1)$
  02    $G_{2/} := ConstructQuotientGraph(G_2)$
  03   **if** $G_{1/}$ and $G_{2/}$ are isomorphic
  04   **then return** YES
  05   **else return** No
  end

Fig. 2. Algorithm: Verify equivalence under retiming and resynthesis

An algorithm outlined in Figure 2 can check if two STGs are transformable to each other under retiming and resynthesis.

Theorem 3. *Given two state transition graphs, Algorithm* VerifyEquivalence-UnderRetiming&Resynthesis *verifies if they are equivalent under retiming and resynthesis.*

The complexity of the algorithm in Figure 2 is the same as that in Figure 1 since the graph isomorphism check for STGs is $O(kn)$, which is not the dominating factor. With the presented algorithm, checking the equivalence under retiming and resynthesis is not easier than general equivalence checking. In the following section, we investigate its intrinsic complexity.

4   Verification Complexity

We show some complexity results of verifying if two FSMs are equivalent under retiming and resynthesis.

4.1   Verification with Unknown Transformation History

We investigate the complexity of verifying the equivalence of two FSMs with unknown history of (iterative) retiming and resynthesis operations.

Theorem 4. *Determining if two FSMs are equivalent under iterative retiming and resynthesis with unknown transformation history is PSPACE-complete.*

Proof. Certainly Algorithm *VerifyEquivalenceUnderRetiming&Resynthesis* can be performed in polynomial space (even with inputs in FSM representations).

On the other hand, we need to reduce a PSPACE-complete problem to our problem at hand. The following problem is chosen.

Given a total function $f : \{1, \dots, n\} \to \{1, \dots, n\}$, is there a composition of f such that, by composing f k times, $f^k(1) = n$?

In other words, the problem asks if n is "reachable" from 1 through f. It was shown [5] to be deterministic[2] LOGSPACE-complete in the unary representation and, thus, PSPACE-complete in the binary representation [12]. We show that the problem in the unary (resp. binary) representation is log-space (resp. polynomial-time) reducible to our problem with inputs in STG (resp. FSM) representations. We further establish that the answer to the PSPACE-complete problem is positive if and only if the answer to the corresponding equivalence verification problem (to be constructed) is negative. Since the complexity class of nondeterministic space is closed under complementation [4], the theorem follows.

To complete the proof, we elaborate the reduction. Given a function f as stated earlier, we construct two total functions $f_1, f_2 : \{0, 1, \ldots, n\} \to \{0, 1, \ldots, n\}$ as follows. Let f_1 have the same mapping as f over $\{1, \ldots, n-1\}$ and have $f_1(0) = 1$ and $f_1(n) = 1$. Also let f_2 have the same mapping as f with $f_2(0) = 1$ but $f_2(n) = 0$. Clearly the constructions of f_1 and f_2 can be done in log-space. Treating $\{0, 1, \ldots, n\}$ as the state set, f_1 and f_2 specify the transitions of two STGs, say G_1 and G_2, (which have empty input and output alphabets). Observe that any state of G_1 (similarly G_2) has exactly one next-state. Thus, every state is either in a single cycle or on a single path leading to a cycle. Observe also that two states of G_1 (similarly G_2) are immediately equivalent if and only if they have the same next-state. An important consequence of these observations is that all states not in cycles can be merged through iterative retiming and resynthesis due to immediate equivalence.

To see the relationship between reachability and equivalence under retiming and resynthesis, consider the case where n is reachable from 1 through f. States 1 and n of G_1 must be in a cycle excluding state 0; states 1 and n of G_2 must be in a cycle including state 0. Hence the state-minimized (with respect to immediate equivalence) graphs of G_1 and G_2 are not isomorphic. That is, G_1 and G_2 are not equivalent under retiming and resynthesis. On the other hand, consider the case where n is unreachable from 1 through f. Then state n of G_1 and state n of G_2 are dangling. From the mentioned observations, merging dangling states in G_1 and G_2 yields two isomorphic graphs. That is, G_1 and G_2 are equivalent under retiming and resynthesis. Therefore, n is reachable from 1 through f if, and only if, G_1 and G_2 are not equivalent under retiming and resynthesis. (Notice that, unlike the discussion of optimization capability, here we should not ignore the effects of retiming and resynthesis over the unreachable state space.)   ■

4.2   Verification with Known Transformation History

By Theorem 4, verifying if two FSMs are equivalent under retiming and resynthesis without knowing the transformation history is as hard as the general equivalence checking problem. Thus, we advocate a conservative design methodology optimizing synchronous hardware systems to ameliorate verifiability.

---

[2] It is a well-known result by Savitch [16] that deterministic and nondeterministic space complexities coincide.

An easy approach to circumvent the PSPACE-completeness is to record the history of retiming and resynthesis operations as verification checkpoints, or alternatively to perform equivalence checking after every retiming or resynthesis operation. The reduction in complexity results from the following well-known facts.

Proposition 4. *Given two synchronous hardware systems, verifying if they are transformable to each other with retiming is of the same complexity as checking graph isomorphism; verifying if they are transformable to each other with resynthesis is of the same complexity as combinational equivalence checking, which is NP-complete.*

Therefore, if transformation history is completely known, the verification complexity reduces to NP-complete.

5   Initialization Sequences

To discuss initialization sequences, we rely on the following proposition of Pixley [13].

Proposition 5. *([13]) An FSM is initializable only if its initial states are non-dangling. (In fact, any non-dangling state can be used as an initial state by suitably modifying initialization sequences.)*

By Lemma 3, Corollary 1 and Proposition 5, it is immediate that

Corollary 2. *The initializability of an FSM is an invariant under retiming and resynthesis.*

Hence we shall assume that the given FSM $\mathcal{M}$ is initializable. Furthermore, we assume that its initialization sequence is given as a black box. That is, we have no knowledge on how $\mathcal{M}$ is initialized. Under these assumptions, we study how the initialization sequence is affected when $\mathcal{M}$ is retimed (and resynthesized). As shown earlier, the creation and annihilation of dangling states are immaterial to the optimization capability of retiming and resynthesis. However, they play a decisive role in affecting initialization sequences. In essence, the longest transition path among dangling states determines how long the initialization sequences should be increased.

5.1   Initialization Affected by Retiming

Lag-dependent bounds. Effects of retiming on initialization sequences were studied by Leiserson and Saxe in [7], where their *Retiming Lemma* can be rephrased as follows.

Lemma 4. *([7]) Given a communication graph $G = (V, E)$ and a normalized retime function ρ, let $\ell = \max_{v \in V} -\rho(v)$ and let $G^\dagger$ be the corresponding retimed communication graph of G. Suppose $\mathcal{M}$ and $\mathcal{M}^\dagger$ are the FSMs specified by G and*

$G^\dagger$, respectively. Then after $\mathcal{M}^\dagger$ is initialized with an arbitrary input sequence of length ℓ, any state of $\mathcal{M}^\dagger$ has an equivalent[3] state in $\mathcal{M}$.

That is, ℓ (nonnegative for normalized ρ) gives an upper bound of the increase of initialization sequences under retiming. This bound was further tightened in [2, 18] by letting ℓ be the maximum of $-\rho(v)$ for all v of functional elements whose functions define non-surjective mappings. Unfortunately, this strengthening still does not produce an exact bound. Moreover, by Proposition 1, a normalized retime function among its equivalent retime functions may not be the one that gives the tightest bound. A derivation of exact bounds will be discussed in Section 5.2.

Lag-independent Bounds. Given a synchronous hardware system, a natural question is if there exists some bound which is universally true for all possible retiming operations. Even though the bound may be looser than lag-dependent bounds, it discharges the construction of new initialization sequences from knowing what retime functions have been applied. Indeed, such a bound does exist as exemplified below.

Proposition 6. *Given a communication graph $G = (V, E)$ and a normalized retime function ρ, let $r(v)$ denote the minimum number of registers along any path from the host to vertex v. Then $r(v)$ sets an upper bound of the number of registers that can be moved forward across v, i.e., $-r(v) \le \rho(v)$. (Similarly, $r(v)$ on G with reversed edges sets an upper bound of $\rho(v)$.)*

Thus, $\max_v r(v)$, which is intrinsic to a communication graph and is independent of retiming operations, yields a lag-independent bound.

When initialization delay is not a concern for a synchronous system, one can even relax the above lag-independent bound by saying that the total number of registers of the system is another lag-independent bound. As an example, suppose a system has one million registers and its retimed version runs at one gigahertz clock frequency. Then the initialization delay increased due to retiming is less than a thousandth of a second.

5.2   Initialization Affected by Retiming and Resynthesis

So far we have focused on initialization issues arising when a system is retimed only. Here we extend our study to issues arising when a system is iteratively retimed and resynthesized.

A difficulty emerges from directly applying Lemma 4 to bound the increase of initialization sequences under iterative retiming and resynthesis. Interleaving retiming with resynthesis makes the union bound $\sum_i u_i$ the only available bound from Lemma 4, where u_i denotes the lag-dependent bound for the ith retiming operation. Essentially, inaccuracies accumulate along with the summation of

---

[3] A state q of FSM $\mathcal{M}$ is equivalent to a state $q^\dagger$ of FSM $\mathcal{M}^\dagger$ if $\mathcal{M}$ starting from q, and $\mathcal{M}^\dagger$ starting from $q^\dagger$ have the same input-output behavior.

the union bound. Thus, the bound derived this way can be far beyond what is necessary. In the light of lag-independent bounds discussed earlier, one might hope that there may exist some constant which upper bounds the increase of initialization sequences due to any iterative retiming and resynthesis operations. (Notice that, when no resynthesis operation is performed, the transformation of a series of retiming operations can be achieved by a single retiming operation. Thus a lag-independent bound exists for *iterative* retiming operations.) Unfortunately, such a transformation-independent bound does not exist as shown in Theorem 5.

Lemma 5. *Any dangling state of an FSM (with implicit reset) is removable through iterative retiming and resynthesis operations.*

Theorem 5. *Given a synchronous hardware system and an arbitrary constant c, there always exist retiming and resynthesis operations on the system such that the length increase of the initialization sequence exceeds c.*

Since the mentioned union bound is inaccurate and requires knowing the applied retime functions, it motivates us to investigate the computation of exact[4] length increase of initialization sequences without knowing the history of retiming and resynthesis operations. The length increase can be derived by computing the length, say n, of the longest transition paths among the dangling states because applying an arbitrary[5] input sequence of length greater than n drives the system to a non-dangling state. The length n can be obtained using a symbolic computation. By breadth-first search, one can iteratively remove states without predecessor states until a greatest fixed point is reached. The number of the performed iterations is exactly n.

6   Related Work

Optimization Capability. The closest to our work on the optimization power of retiming and resynthesis is [15], where the optimization power was unfortunately over-stated contrary to the claimed exactness. The mistake resulted from the claim that any *2-way switch* operation is achievable using *2-way merge* and *2-way split* operations (see [15] for their definitions). (Essentially, a restriction needs to be imposed — under any input assignment, the next state of a current state to be split should be unique.) In fact, only 2-way merge and split operations are essential. Aside from this minor error, no constructive algorithm was known to determine if two given FSMs are equivalent under retiming and resynthesis. In addition, not discussed were the creation and annihilation of dangling states, which we show to be crucial in initializing synchronous hardware systems.

---

[4] The exactness is true under the assumption that the initialization sequence of the original FSM is given as a block box. If the initialization mechanism is explored, more accurate analysis may be achieved.

[5] Although exploiting some particular input sequence may shorten the length increase, it complicates the computation.

Verification Complexity. Ranjan in [14] examined a few verification complexities for cases under one retiming operation and up to two resynthesis operations with unknown transformation history. The complexity for the case under an arbitrary number of iterative retiming and resynthesis operations was left open, and was conjectured in [20] to be easier than the general equivalence checking problem. We disprove the conjecture.

Initialization Sequences. For systems with explicit reset, the effect of retiming on initial states was studied in [19, 3, 17]. In the explicit reset case, incorporating resynthesis with retiming does not contribute additional difficulty. Note that, for systems with explicit-reset registers, forward moves of retiming are preferable to backward moves in maintaining equivalent initial states, contrary to the case for systems with implicit-reset registers. To prevent backward moves, Even et al. in [3] proposed an algorithm to find a retime function such that the maximum lag among all vertices is minimized. Interestingly enough, their algorithm can be easily modified to obtain minimum lag-dependent bounds on the increase of initialization sequences. As mentioned earlier, explicit reset can be seen as a special case of implicit reset when reset circuitry is explicitly represented in the communication graph. Hence, the study of the implicit reset case is more general, and is subtler when considering resynthesis in addition to retiming.

Pixley in [13] studied the initialization of synchronous hardware systems with implicit reset in a general context. Leiserson and Saxe studied the effect of retiming on initialization sequences in [7], where a lag-dependent bound was obtained and was later improved by [2, 18]. We show a lag-independent bound instead. In recent work [11], a different approach was taken to tackle the initialization issue raised by retiming. Rather than increasing initialization sequence lengths, a retimed system was further modified to preserve its original initialization sequence. This modification might need to pay area/performance penalties and could nullify the gains of retiming operations. In addition, the modification requires expensive computation involving existential quantification, which limits the scalability of the approach to large systems. In comparison, prefixing an arbitrary input sequence of a certain length to the original initialization sequence provides a much simpler solution (without modifying the system) to the initialization problem.

7   Conclusions and Future Work

This paper demonstrated some transformation invariants under retiming and resynthesis. Three main results about retiming and resynthesis were established. First, an algorithm was presented to construct a canonical representative of an equivalence class of FSMs transformed under retiming and resynthesis. It was extended to determine if two FSMs are transformable to each other under retiming and resynthesis. Second, a PSPACE-complete complexity was proved for the above problem when the transformation history of retiming and resynthesis is unknown. Third, the effects of retiming and resynthesis on initialization sequences were studied. A lag-independent bound was shown on the length increase of initialization sequences of FSMs under retiming; in contrast, unboundability was shown for the case of iterative retiming and resynthesis. In addition, an exact analysis on the length increase was presented.

For future work, it is important to investigate more efficient computation, with reasonable accuracy, of the length increase of initialization sequences for FSMs transformed under retiming and resynthesis. Moreover, as the result of [3] can be modified to obtain a retime function targeting area optimization with minimum increase of initialization sequences, it would be useful to study retiming under other objectives while avoiding increasing initialization sequences.

Acknowledgements

The author wishes to thank Prof. Robert K. Brayton for helpful suggestions.

References

1. G. De Micheli. Synchronous logic synthesis: algorithms for cycle-time minimization. *IEEE Trans. on Computer-Aided Design*, vol. 10, pages 63–73, Jan. 1991.
2. A. El-Maleh, T. E. Marchok, J. Rajski, and W. Maly. Behavior and testability preservation under the retiming transformation. *IEEE Trans. on Computer-Aided Design*, vol. 16, pages 528–543, May 1997.
3. G. Even, I. Y. Spillinger, and L. Stok. Retiming revisited and reversed. *IEEE Trans. on Computer-Aided Design*, vol. 15, pages 348–357, March 1996.
4. N. Immerman. Nondeterministic space is closed under complementation. *SIAM Journal on Computing*. vol. 17, pages 935–938, 1988.
5. N. Jones. Space-bounded reducibility among combinatorial problems. *Journal of Computer and System Sciences*, vol. 11, pages 68–85, 1975.
6. Z. Kohavi, *Switching and Finite Automata Theory*. McGraw-Hill, 1978.
7. C. E. Leiserson and J. B. Saxe. Optimizing synchronous systems. *Journal of VLSI and Computer Systems*, 1(1):41–67, Spring 1983.
8. C. E. Leiserson and J. B. Saxe. Retiming synchronous circuitry. *Algorithmica*, vol. 6, pages 5–35, 1991.
9. S. Malik. *Combinational Logic Optimization Techniques in Sequential Logic Synthesis*. PhD thesis, University of California, Berkeley, 1990.
10. S. Malik, E. M. Sentovich, R. K. Brayton, A. Sangiovanni-Vincentelli. Retiming and resynthesis: optimization of sequential networks with combinational techniques. *IEEE Trans. Computer-Aided Design*, vol. 10, pages 74–84, Jan. 1991.
11. M. N. Mneimneh, K. A. Sakallah, and J. Moondanos. Preserving synchronizing sequences of sequential circuits after retiming. In *Proc. ASP-DAC*, Jan. 2004.
12. C. H. Papadimitriou. *Computational Complexity*. Addison-Wesley, 1994.
13. C. Pixley. A theory and implementation of sequential hardware equivalence. *IEEE Trans. Computer-Aided Design*, vol. 11, pages 1469–1478, Dec. 1992.
14. R. K. Ranjan. *Design and Implementation Verification of Finite State Systems*. Ph.D. thesis, University of California at Berkeley, 1997.
15. R. K. Ranjan, V. Singhal, F. Somenzi, and R. K. Brayton. On the optimization power of retiming and resynthesis transformations. In *Proc. Int'l Conf. on Computer-Aided Design*, pages 402–407, Nov. 1998.

16. W. Savitch. Relationships between nondeterministic and deterministic tape complexities. *Journal of Computer and System Sciences*, vol. 4, pages 177–192, 1970.
17. V. Singhal, S. Malik, and R. K. Brayton. The case for retiming with explicit reset circuitry. In *Proc. Int'l Conf. on Computer-Aided Design*, pages 618–625, 1996.
18. V. Singhal, C. Pixley, R. L. Rudell, and R. K. Brayton. The validity of retiming sequential circuits. In *Proc. Design Automation Conference*, pages 316–321, 1995.
19. H. J. Touati and R. K. Brayton. Computing the initial states of retimed circuits. *IEEE Trans. on Computer-Aided Design*, vol. 12, pages 157–162, Jan. 1993.
20. H. Zhou, V. Singhal, and A. Aziz. How powerful is retiming? In *Proc. IWLS*, 1998.

Compositional Message Sequence Charts (CMSCs) Are Better to Implement Than MSCs

Blaise Genest

LIAFA, Université Paris VII, 2 place Jussieu, 75251 Paris, France
& Departement of Computer Science, Warwick, Coventry, CV4 7AL, UK

Abstract. Communicating Finite States Machines (CFMs) and Message Sequence Graphs (MSC-graphs for short) are two popular specification formalisms for communicating systems. MSC-graphs capture requirements (scenarios), hence they are the starting point of the design process. Implementing an MSC-graph means obtaining an equivalent *deadlock-free* CFM, since CFMs correspond to distributed message-passing algorithms. Several partial answers for the implementation have been proposed. E.g., local-choice MSC-graphs form a subclass of deadlock-free CFM: Testing equivalence with some local-choice MSC-graph is thus a partial answer to the implementation problem. Using Compositional MSCs, we propose a new algorithm which captures more implementable models than with MSCs. Furthermore, the size of the implementation is reduced by one exponential.

1 Introduction

Specifying the behavior of software systems in such a way that formal methods can be applied and validation tasks can be automated, is a challenging goal. While research has brought strong results and tools for simple systems, complex systems still lack powerful techniques. For instance, concurrent systems such as message passing systems are still hard to cope with.

Concurrent languages such as Harel's Live Sequence Charts [11], UML sequence diagrams, interworkings..., have seen a growing interest this last decade. Among them, the ITU visual notation of *Message Sequence Charts* (*MSCs*, [14]) has received a lot of attention, both in the area of formal methods and in automatic verification [2, 13, 19, 18, 20]. MSCs can be considered as an abstract representation of communications between asynchronous processes. They are used as requirements, documentations, abstract test cases, and so on. *MSC-graphs* propose a way of modeling set of behaviors, combining parallel composition (processes) with sequential composition (transition system). The main advantage of such a visual representation is to have a local, explicit description of the communication and the causalities appearing in the system. On the other hand, SDL (ITU norm Z100) brings another formalism, namely *Communicating Finite States Machines* (*CFM* for short) [5]. Being really close to distributed algorithms, CFMs are the ideal model for modelling parallel programs. The absence of deadlock is crucial for communication protocols, where any blocking

N. Halbwachs and L. Zuck (Eds.): TACAS 2005, LNCS 3440, pp. 429–444, 2005.

execution means a failure in the system. That is, any concurrent system which has to be implemented must be turned into a deadlock-free CFM. Hence, we will consider only deadlock-free CFM implementations in this paper.

Our aim is to give a heuristic to implement MSC-graphs. That is, if a model passes the test, then it is implementable and we can provide an implementation. However, if it fails the test, it may be the case that it is implementable anyway. The important point is to understand which implementable systems are captured with this algorithm, the more the better. Our test captures every model which is equivalent to some *local-choice Compositional MSC-graph (local-choice CMSC-graphs for short)*. Every local-choice CMSC-graph is implementable, for its control is local (as for CFM), in contrast with the usual global control of MSC-graphs.

Implementation of MSC-graphs is a non trivial task, which has yet no definitive answer. The first implementation test, which was proposed by [1], captures a subclass of MSC-graphs which are equivalent to some deadlock-free CFM without adding control data to messages. This test covers only a subclass of the very restricted regular MSC-graphs. It was further extended to capture a subclass of globally-cooperative MSC-graphs [16], with the same EXPSPACE-complete complexity. With this same restriction of disallowing additional data, [12] characterizes the subclass of local-choice MSC-graph which is implementable. Since data parts are usually abstracted away in an MSC-graph specification, this restriction prevents many useful models from being implementable. For instance, as soon as we add data to messages, any local-choice MSC-graph is implementable [9]. The first paper to consider additional data was [13], giving the exact expressivity of a subclass of (not deadlock-free) CFMs in terms of MSC-graphs. [4] characterizes the expressivity of deadlock-free CFMs in terms of MSC-graphs, but no complete algorithm is provided. At last, an internal report [7] gives a PSPACE algorithm to test implementation into local-choice MSC-graph (thus into deadlock-free CFM), yielding an implementation of doubly exponential size.

In this paper, we extend the results of [7] in order to improve the complexity of the test to co-NP, yielding an implementation of single exponential size, instead of two exponentials. To achieve this goal, we use local-choice Compositional MSC-graphs. The implementation of this class follows easily from [9]. Using compositional MSCs instead of MSCs allows to capture more formalisms. CMSC-graphs were introduced by [10] to get rid of the finite generation restriction of MSC-graphs. Later, safe CMSC-graphs were shown to be model-checkable against MSO [18], temporal logic [8], and globally cooperative CMSC-graphs [6]. The important property used by these algorithms is that the events of any generated MSC can be scheduled using bounded communication channels, for a fixed bound (see section 3). Since nodes of a compositional MSC-graph need not be labeled by complete MSCs (there can be unmatched sends and receives), the time consuming test of [7] becomes irrelevant: Not only we show that we can still test whether a CMSC-graph is equivalent to some local-choice CMSC-graph (with a new algorithm), but the complexity is better than for local-choice

MSC-graphs (co-NP-complete vs PSPACE), improving the implementation size by one exponent, and thus making the test more practical.

Related Work: A new formalism, Triggered MSCs [22], was designed from the ground for the implementation purpose. It makes implementation easier than for MSC-graphs, but model-checking has not been studied yet. Also, Live Sequence Charts [11] use a different semantics to obtain implementability.

2   Message Sequence Charts (MSCs)

Message Sequence Charts (MSC for short) is a scenario language standardized by the ITU ([14]). They represent simple diagrams depicting the activity and communications in a distributed system. The entities participating in the interactions are called instances (or processes) and are represented by vertical lines. Message exchanges are depicted by arrows from the sender to the receiver. In addition to messages, atomic actions can also be represented.

Definition 1. *[10] A compositional MSC (CMSC) is a tuple $M=\langle \mathcal{P}, E, \mathcal{C}, t, m, < \rangle$ where:*

- $\mathcal{P}$ *is a finite set of processes,*
- E_p *is a finite set of events on process p, with $E = \bigcup_{p \in \mathcal{P}} E_p$*
- $\mathcal{C}$ *is a finite set of names for messages and local actions,*
- $t : E \to \mathcal{T} = \{p!q(a), p?q(a), p(a) \mid p \neq q \in \mathcal{P}, a \in \mathcal{C}\}$ *labels an event with its type: either a send $p!q(a)$ of message a on process p to q, a receive $p?q(a)$ on p from q, or a local event $p(a)$. We partition $E = S \cup R \cup L$ into sends, receives and local events.*
- $m : S \to R$ *is a partial and injective function matching a send to its corresponding receive. If $m(s) = r$, then $t(s) = p!q(a)$ and $t(r) = p?q(a)$ for some $p, q \in \mathcal{P}, a \in \mathcal{C}$.*
- $< \subseteq E \times E$ *is an acyclic relation between events consisting of:*
  - *a total order on E_p, for every process $p \in \mathcal{P}$, and*
  - *$s < r$, whenever $m(s) = r$.*

An MSC is a CMSC where the message function m is a total function that is one-to-one.

The event labeling t implicitly defines the process $P(e)$ for each event e: $P(e) = p$ if $t(e) \in \{p!q(a), p?q(a), p(a)\}$ for some $q \in \mathcal{P}, a \in \mathcal{C}$. We denote any pair $(p, q) \in \mathcal{P}^2$ of distinct processes as a channel. We assume that channels are FIFO, i.e., there is no overtaking on messages sent on the same channel.

The relation $<$ is called the *visual* order of the CMSC, since it corresponds to its graphical representation. It is comprised of the process ordering and the message ordering. Since $<$ is required to be acyclic, its reflexive-transitive closure $<^*$ is a partial order on the set E of events, which we will denote by $\leq$. An extension of $\leq$ to a total order is called a *linearization* of M. We consider labeled linearizations $t(e_1) \cdots t(e_n)$, with $e_1 \cdots e_n$ a linearization on events. One can

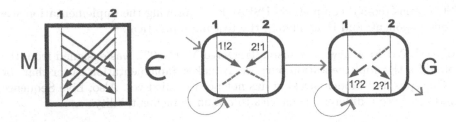

Fig. 1. The left part of the figure depicts an MSC scenario M. The two squares on the right are CMSCs involving actions $1!2, 2!1, 1?2, 2?1$

understand any linearization as some particular execution of the CMSC. Notice that because of the FIFO condition, one can retrieve an MSC from any of its linearizations.

Definition 2. *[17] We say that a linearization $t(e_1) \cdots t(e_n)$ is b-bounded if, for each channel (p,q), the difference between the number of sends $p!q$ and the number of receives $q?p$ in any prefix $t(e_1) \cdots t(e_i)$ is at most b, for any i. We say that an MSC M is existentially (respectively universally) b-bounded if some (resp. every) linearization of M is b-bounded .*

MSCs specify only finite behaviors. For describing sets of behaviors, we use MSC-graphs, which are the basic fragment of the High-level MSCs of the norm [14] (the norm allows hierarchy that we do not take into account here) that are just transition systems with nodes labeled by MSCs. They were extended to Compositional MSC-graphs (CMSC-graphs), where nodes are labeled by CMSCs [10].

Definition 3. *A CMSC-graph is a labeled transition system $G = (V, \rightarrow, v^0, F, \lambda)$ with set of nodes V, transition relation $\rightarrow \in V \times V$, initial node v^0 and set of final nodes F. Each node v is labeled by a CMSC $\lambda(v)$. An accepting path of G is defined as a sequence of transitions $\rho = (v_1 \rightarrow v_2 \cdots \rightarrow v_k)$ with $v_1 = v^0$ and $v_k \in F$.*

A composition of two CMSCs is one of the CMSCs defined by gluing together the processes axis, and extending the messages functions in any way such that the FIFO condition is preserved.

Definition 4. *A composition of CMSCs $M_1, \cdots, M_n$, where $M_i = \langle \mathcal{P}, E_i, A_i, t_i, m_i, <_i \rangle$ is a CMSC $M = \langle \mathcal{P}, E = \bigcup_i E_i, \mathcal{A} = \bigcup \mathcal{A}_i, t = \bigcup t_i, m, < \rangle$ such that:*

- *The message function m extends each m_i and it is required that m preserves the FIFO restriction on matched events. That is if $m(s) = r$ and $m(s') = r'$ are two messages from p to q and $s <_p s'$ then $r <_q r'$.*

- *The visual order $<$ is the union of $<_i$ and the set of (e, f) with $m(e) = f$ or $P(e) = P(f)$ and $e \in E_i, f \in E_j, j > i$.*

Notice that a sequence of given CMSCs $M_1, \ldots, M_n$ can admit several compositions. For instance, gluing together a CMSC composed by two send events from process 1 to 2 and a CMSC composed of two receives on 2 from 1 may yield the MSC consisting of two messages from 1 to 2. It can also yield a receive (which matchs a send which will be glued before), a message then a send to be matched. However, there can be at most one such composition that is an MSC, since the k-th send from p to q of an MSC is matched by the k-th receive on q from p. If it exists, we denote by $M_1 \cdots M_n$ the MSC which is a composition of $M_1, \cdots, M_n$. For instance, there exists only one MSC which is a composition of CMSCs seen along the path that loops three times around each node of figure 1. This MSC is depicted in the left part of figure 1. Since we will consider only the MSCs generated by a CMSC-graph, we are only interested in this unique composition, if it exists.

Definition 5. *The language of a CMSC-graph G is $\mathcal{L}(G) = \{\lambda(v_1) \cdots \lambda(v_k) \in \mathbb{MSC} \mid v_1 \cdots v_k$ is an accepting path of $G\}$, where $\mathbb{MSC}$ is the set of all MSCs.*

An MSC-graph is a CMSC-graph whose nodes are labeled by MSCs. Let G be an MSC-graph. The MSC-graph G is *finitely-MSC-generated*, that is any MSC generated by G is the composition of MSCs labeling the nodes of G. Hence, any $M \in \mathcal{L}(G)$ is existentially b-bounded, where b is the size of the largest MSC in the set L of MSCs labeling the nodes of G. We call G an $\exists$-*b-bounded* MSC-graph.

The right part of figure 1 depicts a CMSC-graph which is not existentially bounded, since iterating n times both loops gives an MSC which is not universally $n - 1$ bounded. In figure 2, we denote s for the send from host to function, and r for the receive on function from host. Then iterating n times the leftmost loop in figure 2 yields an MSC having the 1-bounded linearization $(sr)^{n+1}$, and having also the linearization $s^{n+1}r^{n+1}$ which is not $n - 1$-bounded. That is, this MSC-graph is existentially 1-bounded, but it is not universally bounded.

The size $|M|$ of a (C)MSC M is its number of events. The size $|G|$ of a (C)MSC-graph G is the sum of the sizes $|M|$ of the CMSCs labeling its nodes. The size of $\mathcal{P}$ is the number $\wp$ of processes.

A *Communicating finite-state machine* (CFM) $\mathcal{A} = (\mathcal{A}_p)_{p \in \mathcal{P}}$ [5] consists of finite automata $\mathcal{A}_p$ associated with processes $p \in \mathcal{P}$, that communicate over unbounded, error-free, FIFO channels. The content of a channel is a word over a finite alphabet $\mathcal{C}$. With each pair $(p, q) \in \mathcal{P}^2$ of distinct processes we associate a channel $C_{p,q}$. Each $\mathcal{A}_p$ is described by a tuple $\mathcal{A}_p = (S_p, A_p, \rightarrow_p, F_p)$ consisting of a set of local states S_p, a set of actions A_p, a set of local final states F_p and a transition relation $\rightarrow_p \subseteq S_p \times A_p \times S_p$. The computation begins in an initial state $s^0 \in \prod_{p \in \mathcal{P}} S_p$. The actions of $\mathcal{A}_p$ are either local actions or sending/receiving a message. We use the same notations as for MSCs. Sending message $p!q(a)$ means that a is appended to the channel $C_{p,q}$. Receiving message $p?q(a)$ means that a must be the first message in $C_{q,p}$, which will be then removed from $C_{q,p}$. A local action a on process p is denoted by $l_p(a)$. A run of a CFM is a linearization x

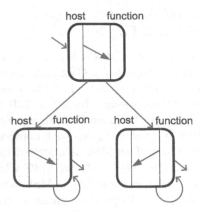

Fig. 2. MSC-graph depicting the isochronous transactions of usb 1.1

of some MSC such that the projection of x on process p is a run of A_p, for all p. In particular, x should not receive more messages than sent. We denote a run of the CFM as *successful*, if each process p can finish the run in some final state of F_p, and all channel are empty. The set of successful runs generated by A is denoted $L(A)$. It is easy to notice that if x is an accepting run of the MSC M, then any linearization of M is also a successful run. We will denote by $\mathcal{L}(A)$ the MSC-language of A, that is the set of MSCs whose linearizations are successful runs. Moreover, we say that a CFM is *deadlock-free* if every run can be extended to a successful run.

3   Existential Bound on Channels

CMSC-graphs are more expressive than CFMs [10], and thus most non trivial problems for CMSC-graphs are undecidable. The solution applied here to recover decidability is to consider representative linearizations, as what was done first for MSC-graphs by [20] and for CMSC-graphs by [18]. More precisely, if G is $\exists$-b-bounded, then every MSC $M \in \mathcal{L}(G)$ has a linearization in the set $\text{Lin}^b(G)$ of b-bounded linearizations of $\mathcal{L}(G)$. We call the set $\text{Lin}^b(G)$ a set of representatives for $\mathcal{L}(G)$, since any MSC of $\mathcal{L}(G)$ can be retrieved from a linearization of $\text{Lin}^b(G)$. To ensure an existential bound on channels, *safe CMSC-graphs* (called *realizable CMSC-graph* by [10], and simply CMSC-graphs by [18]) were defined.

Definition 6. *A CMSC-graph G is safe if every sequence of CMSCs labeling an accepting path of G can be composed as an MSC.*

Recall that it may be the case that among the CMSC-compositions of a path of a (non safe) CMSC-graph, none is an MSC (e.g. because number of sends and receives from p to q are not equal). Notice that safe CMSC-graphs contain the class of MSC-graphs. For instance, figure 2 depicts a safe CMSC-graph.

Being safe implies that each (looping) path $v_1 \cdots v_n, n \geq 1$ with $v_n \to v_1$ of the CMSC-graph G is labeled by the same number of sends and receives from p to q, for each pair of processes p, q. This is the key argument for the syntactical characterization of safe CMSC-graphs that can be checked in polynomial time [10]. For instance, the CMSC-graph depicted on the right part of figure 1 is not safe since loops are labeled with a different number of sends and receives.

Let K_G be the automaton obtained from G by replacing every node v of G by a sequence of $|\lambda(v)|$ transitions of the automaton, labeled by some linearization of $\lambda(v)$. The language $L(K_G)$ of this automaton is a set of representatives of $\mathcal{L}(G)$. Since each loop of the CMSC-graph G is labeled by the same number of sends and receives from p to q, for each pair of processes p, q, every $x \in L(K_G)$ is b-bounded, with $b \leq |G|$. Since this bound is important for G, we denote the b for which $L(K_G)$ is universally b-bounded as b_G. Hence, G is existentially b_G-bounded. We will use the class of globally-cooperative CMSC-graphs as a central class of our implementation algorithm. The reason is that this class ensures the existence of a regular set of representatives, namely $\text{Lin}^{b_G}(G)$.

Definition 7. *The communication graph of a CMSC M is a directed graph whose vertices are the processes involved in M, and there is an edge between vertices p, q iff M contains both a send $p!q$ from p to q and a receive $q?p$ on q from p (these send and receive may not define the same message).*

For instance, the communication graph of the MSC made of one message from process 3 to 2 and one message from process 1 to 2 is weakly connected. We recall that a loop in a CMSC-graph is a path starting and ending in the same node (we do not require that the loop is simple, that is, a loop can meet several times the same node).

Definition 8. *A CMSC-graph is loop-connected if every loop is labeled by a CMSC whose communication graph is weakly connected. A CMSC-graph is globally-cooperative (gc-CMSC-graph for short) if it is safe and loop-connected.*

In particular, if there is a loop labeled by two groups of processes without communication between the two groups, then G is not loop-connected, hence not globally-cooperative.

Proposition 1. *[6] The set $\text{Lin}^b(G)$ of b-bounded linearizations of every globally-cooperative CMSC-graph G is regular, for all $b \geq b_G$.*

4   Implementation by CFMs

It is easy to see that not every globally-cooperative CMSC-graph is implementable by a deadlock-free CFM (actually, they are always implementable by a CFM with possible deadlocks [6]). Since any specification should be implementable, we need a test for implementability.

Definition 9. *A CMSC-graph G is implementable without additional data iff there exists some deadlock-free CFM $\mathcal{A}$ with $\mathcal{L}(\mathcal{A}) = \mathcal{L}(G)$.*

There is an EXPSPACE-complete algorithm to test whether a globally-cooperative MSC-graph is implementable without additional data [1, 16]. Anyway, there are two drawbacks in such an approach. First, the algorithm is obviously time-consuming. Second, implementing directly an MSC-graph is too extreme, since some easily implementable MSC-graphs are said not to be, as the globally-cooperative MSC-graph of figure 2. The reason is that the data written in the first message is abstracted away, hence both host and function can choose to send the second message, yielding a scenario that is not possible in the system, thus a deadlock. The solution already used in [9, 13] is to allow data to be added to messages. For instance, we would add in the first message a bit to indicate which process (host or function) must send. A data projection function simply projects away the additional data from messages.

Definition 10. *A CMSC-graph G is implementable (with additional data) iff there exists some data projection Proj and some deadlock-free CFM A with $Proj(\mathcal{L}(A)) = \mathcal{L}(G)$.*

The problem is that we have no algorithm to test this implementability. Moreover, even if such an algorithm would exist, it would probably be too time consuming. We propose then an alternative approach to the problem, trying to go through a class which is easily implementable with additional data. The reason for non-implementability of an MSC-graph is the global control, whereas the choices in a CFM must be done locally. The idea is then to define local-choice MSC-graphs, that is, any node is controlled by a single process [3, 12].

Definition 11. *A CMSC-graph G is local-choice if*

- *G is safe*
- *For each transition $v \rightarrow w$, node w has a unique minimal event $\min(w)$. Moreover, the minimal process of w, denoted $pmin(w)$, appears in v.*
- *There exists a process p_0 such that the initial node of G has a unique minimal event on p_0.*

A local-choice MSC-graph is a local-choice CMSC-graph which is an MSC-graph.

Example 1. The MSC-graph in figure 2 is local-choice. The MSC-graph in figure 3 is not local-choice, since the looping node has two minimal events.

The next proposition follows easily from [9].

Proposition 2. *Any local-choice CMSC-graph is implementable. Moreover, the size of the CFM obtained is linear in the size of the local-choice CMSC-graph.*

The local-choice restriction appears to be a heuristics for implementation. That is, if a CMSC-graph is local-choice or equivalent to some local-choice CMSC-graph, then it is implementable (without deadlock). However, if it is not equivalent to a local-choice CMSC-graph, then this does not mean that it is not implementable.

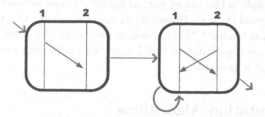

Fig. 3. A globally-cooperative MSC-graph universally bounded but not local-choice

4.1   A Concrete Protocol: USB

The protocol *USB* (Universal Serial Bus) describes several communication modes between two communicating processes, a master (called host), and a slave (called function) in the standard [21]. Every command is given by host. That is, the first message of each mode is from host to function, and contains the command (mode chosen, actions to perform, etc.). Three kinds of interactions can be done, Isochronous, Bulk and Setup.

The isochronous mode is described by the local-choice MSC-graph in figure 2. The first message tells function that host has chosen the isochronous mode, and whether host must send or receive information. Setup mode is a slight variation of the isochronous mode.

Bulk transfer looks like the alternated bit protocol. Every message received should be acknowledged with the parity of the message, such that the sender can be sure that his message was indeed received. In order to bound the channel, a limit for send events in transit is imposed. We represent a part of the Bulk protocol in the upper part of figure 4.

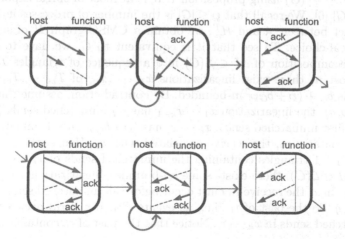

Fig. 4. Equivalent CMSC-graphs specifying the Bulk transactions of usb 1.1

The CMSC-graph in the upper part of figure 4 is not local-choice (the looping node has two minimal events). However, we can transform this CMSC-graph into the equivalent local-choice CMSC-graph depicted in the lower part of figure 4. We want to give an algorithm to build such an equivalent local-choice CMSC-graph, whenever it is possible.

5   Implementation Algorithms

A crucial notion related to local-choice are triangles. We call a CMSC T a *triangle* iff it has a unique minimal event $min(T)$ for the visual order. A triangle T is called an *MSC-triangle* iff it is an MSC. Let T_n be the set of triangles of size bounded by n. We define a generic CMSC-graph H_n^T: for each triangle $T \in T_n$, it has a node v_T labeled by T. There is a transition $v_T \rightarrow v_{T'}$ whenever $P(min(T')) \in P(T)$. We define in the same line the generic local-choice MSC-graph H_n^M on MSC-triangles of size at most n.

The next proposition shows that we must consider only globally-cooperative CMSC-graphs for our implementability test:

Proposition 3. [1] *Let G be a safe CMSC-graph that is not globally-cooperative. Then G is not equivalent to any local-choice CMSC-graph.*

Theorem 1. *A globally-cooperative CMSC-graph G is equivalent to some local-choice CMSC-graph iff there exists some n with $\mathcal{L}(G) \subseteq \mathcal{L}(H_n^T)$. If it is the case, then one can obtain some local-choice CMSC-graph equivalent to G, of size exponential in $|G|$ and n.*

Sketch of Proof. If $\mathcal{L}(G) \subseteq \mathcal{L}(H)$ for some local-choice CMSC-graph H, then $\mathcal{L}(G) \subseteq \mathcal{L}(H_n^T)$ with $n = |H|$.

Conversely, if $\mathcal{L}(G) \subseteq \mathcal{L}(H_n^T)$, then we compute an automaton $\mathcal{A}$ accepting $Lin^{b_G+(\wp+b_G\wp^2)n}(G)$ using proposition 1. It is at most of single exponential size in n and $|G|$ [6]. We recall that $\wp \leq |G|$ is the number of processes in $\mathcal{P}$. Making the product between $\mathcal{A}$ and H_n^T, we obtain a CMSC-graph H of size $|\mathcal{A}||H_n^T|$ that is local-choice. To see that it is equivalent to G, we have to show that for any decomposition of $M \in \mathcal{L}(G)$ into a sequence of triangles $T_1 \cdots T_m$ of size at most n, there exist linearizations $x_1, \cdots, x_m$ of $T_1, \cdots, T_m$ such that $x_1 \cdots x_m$ is $b_G + (\wp + b_G\wp^2)n$-bounded. By contradiction, assume that for some channel (p, q), the linearization $x_1 \cdots x_{k-1}$ has b_G unmatched sends (we denote by s_0 the first unmatched send), $x_k \cdots x_l$ has $(\wp + b_G\wp^2)n + 1$ unmatched sends, and x_{l+1} contains r_0, the receive associated with s_0. Hence, there are at least $(\wp + b_G\wp^2) + 1$ triangles containing the unmatched sends of $x_k \cdots x_l$ from p to q. Since $M \in \mathcal{L}(G)$, there exists some b_G-bounded linearization x equivalent to $x_1 \cdots x_{l+1}$. In x, the receive r_0 must occur before all unmatched sends in $x_k \cdots x_l$ from p to q. So the past of r_0 (i.e., all events e with $e \leq r_0$) occurs in x before the unmatched sends in $x_k \cdots x_l$. Notice that the past of r_0 contains the minimal

---

[1] This result is a slight variation over [7] which considered only MSC-graphs as input.

event of each triangle in $T_k, \ldots, T_l$ that has at least one unmatched send. It is now easy to check that the past of r_0 restricted to any of these triangles either eliminates some process from the past restricted to later triangles, or it contains an unmatched send. Since there are at most $\wp$ triangles of the first kind, there must be at least $b_G \wp^2 + 1$ triangles of the second kind, hence at least $b_G \wp^2 + 1$ unmatched sends in x before the unmatched sends of $x_k \cdots x_l$. So there is at least one channel with $b_G + 1$ unmatched sends, which contradicts the b_G-boundedness of x. $\qquad\square$

We can state theorem 1 similarly for local-choice MSC-graphs, by replacing H_n^T by H_n^M. Theorem 1 will give an algorithm for testing whether G is equivalent to some local-choice CMSC-graph as soon as we limit the value of n for which we must test $\mathcal{L}(G) \subseteq \mathcal{L}(H_n^T)$.

We show now some structural properties that must be satisfied by the CMSC-graphs we are interested in. We call two **MSCs** R, S *MSCs in parallel for G* if $P(R) \cap P(S) = \emptyset$ and there exist CMSCs L, N with $LRSN \in \mathcal{L}(G)$.

Proposition 4. [1] *Let G be a local-choice CMSC-graph. Let R, S be MSCs in parallel in G. Then either $|R| \leq 2\wp|G|$, or $|S| \leq 2\wp|G|$.*

We give another property that concerns only local-choice MSC-graphs, and not CMSC-graphs. Let M be an MSC and e be an event of M. We call e a *peak* of M if its future Future$(e) = \{f \in M \mid e \leq f\}$ for the visual order of M is an MSC (that is, if it contains some send or receive, it should also contain the associated event). In a local-choice **MSC**-graph, every event that starts a node is a peak, which is not always the case in a local-choice CMSC-graph. Let G be a CMSC-graph. We say that M is an *MSC-triangle without G-peak* if it exists an MSC-triangle L and an MSC N with $LMN \in \mathcal{L}(G)$ and LMN has a unique peak within M (which is min_M). It is worth noting that LMN can have peaks other than min_M, as soon as these peaks are not within M. Moreover, LM can have several peaks within M, but they will not be peaks anymore for LMN.

Proposition 5. [1] *Let G be a local-choice MSC-graph. Let M be an MSC-triangle without G-peak. Then $|M| \leq 2\wp|G|$.*

Using these notions, we can characterize the class of safe CMSC-graphs which are equivalent to any local-choice MSC-graph:

Theorem 2. [1] *Let G be a safe CMSC-graph. Then G is equivalent to some local-choice MSC-graph iff there exists some integer n such that:*

1. *G is globally cooperative.*
2. *Each $M \in \mathcal{L}(G)$ is a triangle.*
3. *Each MSCs M, N in parallel for G satisfies $|M| \leq n$, or $|N| \leq n$.*
4. *Each MSC-triangle M without G-peaks satisfies $|M| \leq n$.*

5.1   A Tractable Test Algorithm

The first test of theorem 2 is co-NP-complete [19]. The second test is NLOGSPACE [7]. The third test is co-NP [7]. The fourth test is PSPACE [7]. If the third and fourth tests are satisfied, then we have a value for n, such that $\mathcal{L}(G) \subseteq \mathcal{L}(H_{\wp n}^M)$, and then we can compute an equivalent local-choice MSC-graph using theorem 1. The problem is that the fourth test gives an exponential value to n (while the third gives a polynomial value to n), making the implementation potentially doubly exponential. However, the fourth test makes no sense for local-choice CMSC-graph, for which we can do better.

Example 2. The globally-cooperative MSC-graph in figure 3 is not equivalent to any local-choice MSC-graph, but it is not hard to show the equivalence with a local-choice CMSC-graph.

We turn now to the test whether a given safe CMSC-graph is equivalent to some local-choice CMSC-graph. We characterize triangles that cannot belong to $\mathcal{L}(H_n^T)$, that is which cannot be decomposed in a sequence of triangles of size at most n. Let $T = T_1 T_2$ be a decomposition of such a triangle into two triangles. We call the minimal events $\min(T) = \min(T_1) = e$ and $\min(T_2) = f$. In a CMSC, there are at most two immediate successors g, h of e (the event g on the same process as e, and the receive h of e if e is a send). Obviously, either $f \geq g$ or $f \geq h$. That is, if we want to minimize the size of T_1, an optimal choice is to take either $f = g$, or $f = h^2$. The triangle T_2 is defined as the set of events Future(f) in the future of f, and T_1 is the set of events that are not in Future(f), that is $F(f) =$ Future$(e) \setminus$ Future$(f) = T_1$. That is, if $|F(g)| > n$ and $|F(h)| > n$, then T is not decomposable into a sequence of triangles of size at most n. Furthermore, if T labels a path of a safe CMSC-graph G, and if $F(g)$ and $F(h)$ are large enough, then we can find a loop of G in $F(f)$ and one in $F(g)$ that we can iterate such that both $F(g)$ and $F(h)$ become as large as we want. That is, $\mathcal{L}(G) \not\subseteq \mathcal{L}(H_n^T)$ for any n.

Iterating one of these loops should not delete any event in $F(h)$ or in $F(g)$ because of a new dependency. To do so, we need to define the Ω-type, which is related to the existential bound b_G associated with G. The Ω-type of an event e is its type $t \in \{p!q, p?q\}$, plus the number modulo b_G of events of the same type that have happened before e, that is, $\Omega = \mathcal{T} \times \{0, \cdots, b_G - 1\}$. We denote by $type(X)$ the set of Ω-types of events in X.

Lemma 1. *Let MBN be an MSC that has two minimal events g, h, and assume that $type(Future(g) \cap M) = type(Future(g) \cap MB)$ and $type(Future(h) \cap M) = type(Future(h) \cap MB)$. We denote by $Future', F'$ and m' the functions corresponding to Future, F and m with respect to $MBBN$. Assume that M is existentially-b_G-bounded.*
  Then $F(g) \subseteq F'(g)$ and $F(h) \subseteq F'(h)$.

---

^{2} Actually, we take the only immediate successors of h instead of h since we want that the minimal process of a node belongs to any predecessor node.

Proof. Let $f \in \{g, h\}$. Assume by contradiction that Future$'(f) \cap F(f) \neq \emptyset$. We denote $d_1 \prec d_2 \prec \cdots \prec d_m$ a causality chain in $MBBN$ with $d_1 = f, d_m \in F(f)$, and where $d_i \prec d_{i+1}$ if $m'(d_i) = d_{i+1}$ or if $d_i <_p d_{i+1}$ for some process p.

We will show that $d_m \in$ Future(f), a contradiction with $d_m \in F(f)$. Assume that there is an i with d_i in the first B and d_{i+1} in the second B. We will delete the first B of $MBBN$ to obtain MBN. In MBN, we still have $d_{i+1} < d_m$. Since B conserves the Ω-types of Future(f), we have a $d_i' \in$ Future$(f) \cap M$, of same Ω-type as d_i. If $d_i <_p d_{i+1}$, then within MBN, we also have $d_i' <_p d_{i+1}$. Hence $d_m \in$ Future(f). Else, we have $m(d_i) = d_{i+1}$ in $MBBN$. Let d be the first event of B of same T-type as d_i (that is, the second component of its Ω-type can differs from d_i). We have $d_i' <_p d \leq_p d_i$ for some p. Hence $d \in$ Future$(f) \cap MB$ and there exists some $d' \in$ Future$(f) \cap M$, of same Ω-type as d. Hence, we have at least b_G sends of same T-type as d_i in $[d', d[$, that is in Future$(f) \cap M$.

Since M is existentially b_G-bounded, it has at most b_G unmatched sends: if we delete the first B, there exists some $d'' \in [d', d[\subseteq$ Future$(f) \cap M$ with $m(d'') = d_{i+1}$. Hence $d_m \in$ Future(f).

It remains to consider the case where there is one of the two occurrences of B that contains no $(d_i)_{i \leq m}$. We will then delete this occurrence of B to obtain MBN. We consider the new ordering relation in MBN. If $d_i <_p d_{i+1}$ in $MBBN$, then this is also true in MBN. If $m'(d_i) = d_{i+1}$, assume that $m(d_i) \neq d_{i+1}$. Else, $d_m \in$ Future(f). We have some d_i before the deleted B, and d_{i+1} after the deleted B. In the deleted B, there exists a send d of same T-type as d_i. We can apply the same arguments than above to prove that $d_m \in$ Future(f). $\square$

Let us recall that H_n^T is a CMSC-graph whose nodes are triangles of size at most n.

Proposition 6. *A globally-cooperative CMSC-graph G is equivalent to a local-choice CMSC-graph if and only if $\mathcal{L}(G) \subseteq \mathcal{L}(H_{b_0}^T)$, with $b_0 = 4b_G \wp^2 |G| + 1$. This test can be done in co-NP.*

Proof. Assume that $\mathcal{L}(G) \not\subseteq \mathcal{L}(H_{b_0}^T)$. It means that there exists an MSC $M \in \mathcal{L}(G)$ and a send $e \in M$ such that for all immediate $<$-successors $f \in \{g, h\}$ of e, we have $|F(f)| > b_0$. Else, we could decompose inductively any triangle $M \in \mathcal{L}(G)$ into triangles of size at most b_0. This test can be performed in co-NP.

We show now how to increase the size of $F(g)$ without decreasing the size of $F(h)$. By symmetry, we will do the same for augmenting $F(h)$. The MSC M labels a path of G. Since there are b_0 events in $F(g)$, there are at least $4b_G \wp^2 + 1$ occurrences of the same event $e_g \in F(g)$. Hence we can decompose M into a sequence $M = BB_1 \cdots B_n B'$ with B_i labeling a loop of G. Moreover, B_i begins and ends by e_g, and $n = 4b_G \wp^2 + 1$.

Among the loops $B_1 \cdots B_n$, at most $2b_G \wp^2$ can change the Ω-types of Future(g). More formally, let $Type_i(g)$ be the set of Ω-types of events in $(BB_1 \cdots B_i) \cap$ Future(g). There are at most $2b_G \wp^2$ loops B_i with $Type_{i-1}(f) \neq Type_i(f)$, since $Type_i(f)$ is an increasing sequence of sets of size at most $2b_G \wp^2$. In the same line, there are at most $2b_G \wp^2$ loops that can change the Ω-types of Future(h). That is, there is at least one loop, say B_k, that changes neither the Ω-type

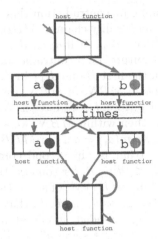

Fig. 5. globally-cooperative CMSC-graph hard to turn into a local-choice CMSC-graph

of Future(g), nor those of Future(h). We can then iterate the loop B_k without deleting any event from $F(g)$ or $F(h)$, applying the lemma 1.

Since B_k contains $e_g \in F(g)$ and does not change the Ω-types of Future(g), iterating the loop B_k makes $F(g)$ strictly grow.

In the same line, we can decompose M with respect to $F(h)$. Hence, we can iterate a loop that makes $F(h)$ strictly grow without shrinking $F(g)$. Since G is safe, we obtain an MSC of $\mathcal{L}(G)$ by iterating these two loops. Hence, we obtain for all k an MSC $M_k \in \mathcal{L}(G) \setminus \mathcal{L}(H_k^T)$. That is, G cannot be equivalent to any local-choice CMSC-graph.

□

Using theorem 1 and the previous proposition, we obtain:

Theorem 3. *Let G be a safe CMSC-graph. Then one can decide in co-NP whether G is equivalent to some local-choice CMSC-graph. If the answer is positive, then an equivalent local-choice CMSC-graph can be built of size exponential in $|G|$.*

Here is an example for which we need an exponential-blowup for coming from a globally-cooperative CMSC-graph to a local-choice CMSC-graph. Since there is a loop on host, we need to put the n local events on the same node. Since we have 2 choices for each local events, it yields 2^n nodes in any equivalent local-choice CMSC-graphs.

6   Conclusion

We presented an algorithm testing implementability of a scenario-based specification, CMSC-graphs, into local-choice CMSC-graphs, which is a strict subclass of deadlock-free CFMs. This test seems practical since it is co-NP and gives an implementation of size exponentially larger than the specification in the worst case.

This test is an improvement in both expressivity and complexity of the internal report [7], even when the model is given as an MSC-graph. That is, compositionality appears only as a technical step in our construction, and needs not to be known by the user.

There are two restrictions of local-choice MSC-graphs for turning them into CFMs. The first one is the need of numerous peaks, and the second one is a restriction on the number of events that are pairwise concurrent. We succeeded in getting rid of the first restriction using compositional MSC-graphs. A further work will consist in finding specification formalisms that allow more parallelism than local-choice CMSC-graphs.

Acknowledgments. I would like to thank Anca Muscholl for fruitful discussions, and anonymous referees for useful comments.

References

1. R. Alur, K. Etessami, and M. Yannakakis. Realizability and verification of MSC graphs. In *ICALP'01*, LNCS 2076, pp.797-808, 2001.
2. R. Alur and M. Yannakakis. Model checking of message sequence charts. In *CONCUR'99*, LNCS 1664, pp.114-129, 1999.
3. H. Ben-Abdallah and S. Leue. Syntactic detection of process divergence and non-local choice in MSCs. In *TACAS'97*, LNCS 1217, pp.259-274, 1997.
4. Nicolas Baudru and Rémi Morin. Safe implementability of regular message sequence chart specifications. In *(SNPD'03)*, pp 210–217. ACIS, 2003.
5. D. Brand and P. Zafiropulo. On communicating finite-state machines. *Journal of the ACM*, 30(2):pp.323-342, 1983.
6. Blaise Genest, Dietrich Kuske, and Anca Muscholl. A Kleene theorem for a class of communicating automata with effective algorithms, to appear in *DLT*, LNCS, 2004.
7. B. Genest and A. Muscholl. The structure of local choice in HMSC Internal report LIAFA, 2003 Available at http://www.crans.org/~genest/GM03.ps.
8. B. Genest, M. Minea, A. Muscholl, and D. Peled. Specifying and verifying partial order properties using template MSCs. In *FoSSaCS'04*, LNCS 2987, pp.195-210, 2004.
9. B. Genest, A. Muscholl, H. Seidl, and M. Zeitoun. Infinite-state High-level MSCs: Model-checking and realizability. In *ICALP'02*, LNCS 2380, pp.657-668, 2002.
10. E. Gunter, A. Muscholl, and D. Peled. Compositional Message Sequence Charts. In International Journal on Software Tools for Technology Transfer (STTT), Volume 5, Springer, 2003.
11. D. Harel and R. Marelly. Come, Let's Play: Scenario-Based Programming Using LSCs and the Play-Engine. Springer 2003.
12. Loïc Hélouët and Claude Jard. Conditions for synthesis of communicating automata from HMSCs. In *5th FMICS'00*, 2000.
13. J. G. Henriksen, M. Mukund, K. Narayan Kumar, M. Sohoni and P. Thiagarajan. A Theory of Regular MSC Languages To appear In *IC*, 2004, available at http://www.comp.nus.edu.sg/~thiagu/icregmsc.pdf.

14. ITU-TS recommendation Z.120, Message Sequence Charts, Geneva, 1999.
15. D. Kuske. Regular sets of infinite message sequence charts. In *Information and Computation 187*, Academic Press, pp.80-109, 2003.
16. M. Lohrey. Safe realizability of High-level Message Sequence Charts. In *CONCUR'02*, LNCS 2421, pp.177-192, 2002.
17. M. Lohrey and A. Muscholl. Bounded MSC communication In *Information and Computation 189*, Academic Press, pp.135-263, 2004.
18. P. Madhusudan and B. Meenakshi. Beyond Message Sequence Graphs In *FSTTCS'01*, LNCS 2245, pp.256-267, 2001.
19. A. Muscholl and D. Peled. Message Sequence Graphs and decision problems on Mazurkiewicz traces. In *MFCS'99*, LNCS 1672, pp.81-91, 1999.
20. D. Peled. Specification and verification of Message Sequence Charts. In *FORTE/PSTV'00*, pp.139-154, 2000.
21. USB 1.1 specification, available at http://www.usb.org/developers/docs/usbspec.zip
22. Bikram Sengupta and Rance Cleaveland. Triggered Message Sequence Charts. In *SIGSOFT 2002/FSE-10*. ACM Press, 2002.

Temporal Logic for Scenario-Based Specifications

Hillel Kugler[1], David Harel[2], Amir Pnueli[1,2,*], Yuan Lu[3], and Yves Bontemps[4]

[1] New York University, New York, NY, USA
{kugler, amir}@cs.nyu.edu
[2] The Weizmann Institute of Science, Rehovot, Israel
dharel@weizmann.ac.il
[3] Broadcom Corp., San Jose, CA, USA
ylu@broadcom.com
[4] University of Namur, Namur, Belgium
ybo@info.fundp.ac.be[**]

Abstract. We provide semantics for the powerful scenario-based language of live sequence charts (LSCs). We show how the semantics of live sequence charts can be captured using temporal logic. This is done by studying various subsets of the LSC language and providing an explicit translation into temporal logic. We show how a kernel subset of the LSC language (which omits variables, for example) can be embedded within the temporal logic CTL*. For this kernel subset the embedding is a strict inclusion. We show that existential charts can be expressed using the branching temporal logic CTL while universal charts are in the intersection of linear temporal logic and branching temporal logic LTL ∩ CTL. Since our translations are efficient, the work described here may be used in the development of tools for analyzing and executing scenario-based requirements and for verifying systems against such requirements.

1 Introduction

Understanding system and software behavior by looking at various "stories" or scenarios seems a promising approach, and it has focused intensive research efforts in the last few years. One of the most widely used languages for specifying scenario-based requirements is that of message sequence charts (MSCs), adopted long ago by the ITU [26], or its UML variant, sequence diagrams [25]. This paper addresses the relationship between scenario-based requirements and temporal logic [23]. As a scenario based language we focus on the language of live sequence charts (LSCs) [7] which is a powerful extension of classical message sequence charts.

LSCs distinguish between behaviors that may happen in the system (existential) from those that must happen (universal). A universal chart contains a

---

* This research was supported in part by the John von Neumann Minerva Center for the Verification of Reactive Systems, by the European Commission project OMEGA (IST-2001-33522) and by the Israel Science Foundation (grant No. 287/02-1).
** FNRS Research Fellow.

N. Halbwachs and L. Zuck (Eds.): TACAS 2005, LNCS 3440, pp. 445–460, 2005.
© Springer-Verlag Berlin Heidelberg 2005

prechart, which specifies the scenario which, if successfully executed, forces the system to satisfy the scenario given in the actual chart body.

Our contribution focuses on providing semantics for the powerful scenario-based language of live sequence charts, but the underlying approach and ideas are more general and can also be applied to other scenario based approaches including classical MSCs, UML sequence diagrams, triggered message sequence charts [24] and other variations. We show how the semantics of live sequence charts can be captured using temporal logics. This is done by studying various subsets of the LSC language and providing an explicit translation to temporal logic. We also show how some of the popular temporal logic "patterns" can be specified using live sequence charts.

In addition to gaining a better theoretical understanding of scenario-based languages, another motivation for this work is the development of tools for analyzing scenario based requirements and verifying systems against these requirements. Since our translations are efficient, the work described here may be used in tools that verify that a system satisfies a requirement specified using LSCs, in tools for executing scenarios directly, as suggested by the play-in/play-out approach [14, 15] and smart play-out [13], and in testing and synthesis tools.

2   Live Sequence Charts

2.1   Overview

Live sequence charts (LSCs) [7] have two types of charts: *universal* (annotated by a solid borderline) and *existential* (annotated by a dashed borderline). Universal charts are used to specify restrictions over all possible system runs. A universal chart typically contains a *prechart*, that specifies the scenario which, if successfully executed, forces the system to satisfy the scenario given in the actual chart body. Existential charts specify sample interactions between the system and its environment, and must be satisfied by at least one system run. They thus do not force the application to behave in a certain way in all cases, but rather state that there is at least one set of circumstances under which a certain behavior occurs. Existential charts can be used to specify system tests, or simply to illustrate longer (non-restricting) scenarios that provide a broader picture of the behavioral possibilities to which the system gives rise.

We will use an example of a cellular phone system to illustrate the main concepts and constructs of the language. The chart OpenCover appearing in Fig. 1 requires that whenever the user opens the Cover, as specified in the prechart (dashed hexagon), the Speaker must turn silent. Both the messages Open sent from the User to the Cover, and the self message Sound(Silent) of the Speaker are synchronous messages as denoted by the close triangular arrowheads.

The chart CloseCover appearing in Fig. 2 requires that whenever the user closes the Cover, The Chip will send the message MakeSound(Silent) to the Speaker and later the speaker will turn silent as designated by the self message Sound(Silent). The Display should set its state to Time and later set its background to Green. An LSC induces a partial order which is determined by the

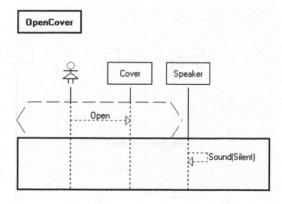

Fig. 1. Open Cover

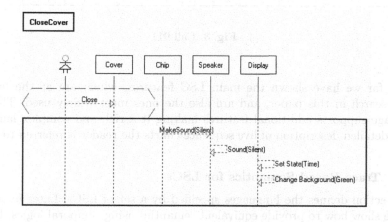

Fig. 2. Close Cover

order along an instance line, by the fact that a message can be received only after it is sent, and taking into account that a synchronous message blocks the sender until receipt. Thus in Fig. 2, message ChangeBackground(Green) must occur after message SetState(Time), but both are unordered with respect to messages MakeSound(Silent) and Sound(Silent). In the chart appearing in Fig. 2 all messages are synchronous, except message MakeSound(Silent) which is asynchronous, as denoted by the open arrowhead.

The chart Call911 appearing in Fig. 3 is an existential chart as denoted by the dashed borderline. It describes a scenario in which a user calls the number 911, opens the antenna and the call is answered. The chart in Fig. 3 introduces a new element – a condition – denoted by a hexagon. The conditions in this chart are hot conditions, specifying assertions that must hold for the scenario to be satisfied. Existential charts do not have a prechart, and the meaning is that this is a possible scenario, that should be satisfied by at least one system run.

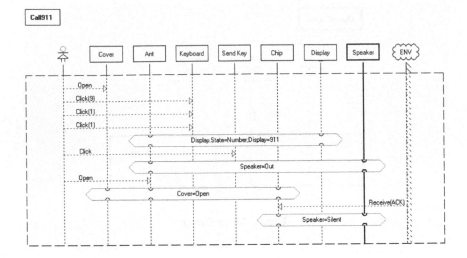

Fig. 3. Call 911

So far we have shown the main LSC features, which are at the focus of our research in this paper, and are also the ones most widely used. The LSC language supports additional features making it a rich and complex language. For a detailed description of live sequence charts the reader is referred to [7, 14].

2.2   Trace-Based Semantics for LSCs

This section defines the languages specified by a set of LSCs. Later in this paper we show how to provide equivalent semantics using temporal logics. For the ease of presentation and due to space limitations, the LSC definitions appearing here are a restricted and simplified version of the original LSC semantics [7]. These definitions provide the key ideas and concepts, allowing the reader to understand extensions that will be explained as we go along. The concept of an execution of a chart which is defined here will be used later in the temporal logic constructions.

We assume the LSC specification relates to an **object system** composed of a set of objects $\mathcal{O} = \{O_1 \ldots O_n\}$. An object system corresponds to an implementation, and our goal while providing semantics for LSCs is to define if a given object system satisfies an LSC specification. The instance identifiers in the LSC charts are objects from $\mathcal{O}$, and possibly also the environment denoted env. The LSC specifies the behavior of the system in terms of the message communication between the objects in the system. We want to define the notion of satisfiability of an LSC specification. In other words, we want to capture the languages $\mathcal{L} \subseteq A^* \cup A^\omega$ generated by the object systems that satisfy the LSC specification. The alphabet A used defines message communication between objects, $A = \mathcal{O} \times (\mathcal{O}.\Sigma)$ where Σ is the alphabet of messages.

Let $inst(m)$ be the set of all instance-identifiers referred to in chart m. With each instance i we associate a finite number of locations $dom(m, i) \subseteq \{0, ..., l\_max(i)\}$. We collect all locations of m in the set

$$dom(m) = \{< i, l >| \; i \in inst(m) \wedge l \in dom(m, i)\}$$

The messages appearing in m are triples

$$Messages(m) = dom(m) \times \Sigma \times dom(m),$$

where $(< i, l >, \sigma, < i', l' >)$ corresponds to instance i, while at location l, sending σ to instance i' at location l'. Each location can appear in at most one message in the chart. The relationship between locations and messages is given by the mapping

$$msg(m) : dom(m) \rightarrow Messages(m)$$

The msg function induces two Boolean predicates $send$ and $receive$. The predicate $send$ is true only for locations that correspond to the sending of a message, while the predicate $receive$ is true only for locations that correspond to the receiving of a message. We define the binary relation $R(m)$ on $dom(m)$ to be the smallest relation satisfying the following axioms and closed under transitivity and reflexivity:

– order along an instance line:

$$\forall < i, l >\in dom(m), l < l\_max(i) \Rightarrow < i, l > R(m) < i, l + 1 >$$

– order induced from message sending:

$$\forall msg \in Messages(m), msg = (< i, l >, \sigma, < i', l' >) \Rightarrow$$

$$< i, l > R(m) < i', l' >$$

– messages are synchronous; they block sender until receipt:

$$\forall msg \in Messages(m), msg = (< i, l >, \sigma, < i', l' >) \Rightarrow$$

$$< i', l' > R(m) < i, l + 1 >$$

We say that the chart m is **well-formed** if the relation $R(m)$ is acyclic. We assume all charts to be well-formed, and use $\leq_m$ to denote the partial order $R(m)$.

We denote the **preset** of a location $< i, l >$ containing all elements in the domain of a chart smaller than $< i, l >$ by

$$^\bullet < i, l >= \{< i', l' >\in dom(m)| \; < i', l' >\leq_m < i, l >\}.$$

We denote the partial order induced by the order along an instance line by $\prec_m$, thus $< i, l >\prec_m < i', l' >$ iff $i = i'$ and $l < l'$.

A **cut** through m is a set c of locations, one for each instance, such that for every location $< i, l >$ in c, the preset $^\bullet < i, l >$ does not contain a location $< i', l' >$ such that $< j, l_j > \prec_m < i', l' >$ for some location $< j, l_j >$ in c. A cut c is specified by the locations in all of the instances in the chart:

$$c = (< i_1, l_1 >, < i_2, l_2 >, ..., < i_n, l_n >)$$

For a chart m with instances $i_1, ..., i_n$ the **initial cut** c_0 has location 0 in all the instances. Thus, $c_0 = (< i_1, 0 >, < i_2, 0 >, ..., < i_n, 0 >)$. We denote $cuts(m)$ the set of all cuts through the chart m.

For chart m, some $1 \leq j \leq n$ and cuts c, c', with

$$c = (< i_1, l_1 >, < i_2, l_2 >, ..., < i_n, l_n >), c' = (< i_1, l'_1 >, < i_2, l'_2 >, ..., < i_n, l'_n >)$$

we say that c' is a $< j, l_j >$-**successor** of c, and write $succ_m(c, < j, l_j >, c')$, if c and c' are both cuts and

$$l'_j = l_j + 1 \wedge \forall i \neq j, l'_i = l_i$$

Notice that the successor definition requires that both c and c' are cuts, so that advancing the location of one of the instances in c is allowed only if the obtained set of locations remains unordered.

A **run** of m is a sequence of cuts, $c_0, c_1, ..., c_k$, satisfying the following:

- c_0 is an initial cut.
- for all $0 \leq i < k$, there is $1 \leq j_i \leq n$, such that $succ_m(c_i, < j_i, l_{j_i} >, c_{i+1})$.
- in the final cut c_k all locations are maximal.

Assume the natural mapping f between $(dom(m) \cup env) \times \Sigma \times dom(m)$ to the alphabet A, defined by

$$f(< i, l >, \sigma, < j, l' >) = (O_i, O_j.\sigma)$$

Intuitively, the function f maps a location to the sending object and to the message of the receiving object. Using this notation, $f(Messages(m))$ will be used to denote the letters in A corresponding to messages that are restricted by chart m:

$$f(Messages(m)) = \{f(v) \mid v \in Messages(m)\}$$

Definition 1. *Let $c = c_0, c_1, ..., c_k$ be a run. The **execution trace**, or simply the **trace** of c, written $w = trace(c)$, is the word $w = w_1 \cdot w_2 \cdots w_k$ over the alphabet A, defined by:*

$$w_i = \begin{cases} f(msg(m)(< j, l_j >)) & \text{if } succ_m(c_{i-1}, < j, l_j >, c_i) \wedge send(< j, l_j >) \\ \epsilon & \text{otherwise} \end{cases}$$

*We define the **trace language** generated by chart m, $\mathcal{L}_m^{trc} \subseteq A^*$, to be*

$$\mathcal{L}_m^{trc} = \{w \mid \exists (c_0, c_1, ..., c_k) \in \text{Runs}(m) \text{ s.t. } w = trace(c_0, c_1, ..., c_k)\}$$

There are two additional notions that we associate with an LSC, its **mode** and its **activation message**. These are defined as follows:

$$mod : m \rightarrow \{existential, universal\}$$

$$amsg : m \rightarrow dom(m) \times \Sigma \times dom(m)$$

The activation message of a chart designates when a scenario described by the chart should start, as we describe below. The charts and the two additional notions are now put together to form a specification. An **LSC specification** is a triple

$$LS = \langle M, amsg, mod \rangle,$$

where M is a set of charts, and $amsg$ and mod are the activation messages and modes of the charts, respectively.

The **language** of the chart m, denoted by $\mathcal{L}_m \subseteq A^* \cup A^\omega$, is defined as follows:

For an existential chart, $mod(m) = existential$, we require that the activation message is relevant (i.e., sent) at least once, and that the trace will then satisfy the chart:

$$\mathcal{L}_m = \{w = w_1 \cdot w_2 \cdots \mid \exists i_0, i_1, ..., i_k \text{ and } \exists v = v_1 \cdot v_2 \cdots v_k \in \mathcal{L}_m^{trc}, \text{ s.t.}$$
$$(i_0 < i_1 < ... < i_k) \wedge (w_{i_0} = f(amsg(m))) \wedge$$
$$(\forall j, 1 \leq j \leq k, w_{i_j} = v_j) \wedge$$
$$(\forall j', i_0 \leq j' \leq i_k, j' \notin \{i_0, i_1, ..., i_k\} \Rightarrow w_{j'} \notin f(Messages(m)))\}$$

The formula requires that the activation message is sent once ($w_{i_0} = f(amsg(m))$), and then the trace satisfies the chart; i.e., there is a subsequence belonging to the trace language of chart m ($v = v_1 \cdot v_2 \cdots v_k = w_{i_1} \cdot w_{i_2} \cdots w_{i_k} \in \mathcal{L}_m^{trc}$), and all the messages between the activation message until the end of the satisfying subsequence ($\forall j', i_0 \leq j' \leq i_k$) that do not belong to the subsequence ($j' \notin \{i_0, i_1, ..., i_k\}$) are not restricted by the chart m ($w_{j'} \notin f(Messages(m))$).

For a universal chart, $mod(m) = universal$, we require that each time the activation message is sent the trace will satisfy the chart:

$$\mathcal{L}_m = \{w = w_1 \cdot w_2 \cdots \mid \forall i, w_i = f(amsg(m)) \Rightarrow \exists i_1, i_2, ..., i_k \text{ and}$$
$$\exists v = v_1 \cdot v_2 \cdots v_k \in \mathcal{L}_m^{trc}, \text{ s.t. } (i < i_1 < i_2 < ... < i_k) \wedge$$
$$(\forall j, 1 \leq j \leq k, w_{i_j} = v_j) \wedge$$
$$(\forall j', i \leq j' \leq i_k, j' \notin \{i_1, ..., i_k\} \Rightarrow w_{j'} \notin f(Messages(m)))\}$$

The formula requires that after each time the activation message is sent ($\forall i, w_i = f(amsg(m))$), the trace will satisfy the chart m (this is expressed in the formula in a similar way to the case for an existential chart.)

Now come the main definitions, which finalize the semantics of our version of LSCs by connecting them with an object system:

Definition 2. *A system S **satisfies** the LSC specification $LS = \langle M, amsg, mod \rangle$, written $S \models LS$, if:*

1. $\forall m \in M, \quad mod(m) = universal \Rightarrow \mathcal{L}_S \subseteq \mathcal{L}_m$
2. $\forall m \in M, \quad mod(m) = existential \Rightarrow \mathcal{L}_S \cap \mathcal{L}_m \neq \emptyset$

3   Specifying Temporal Logic Patterns in LSCs

We show how to specify some important temporal logic formulas using LSCs. Apart from the interest in specifying the properties, this can help getting more familiar with LSCs by seeing several examples.

Consider the universal chart appearing in Fig. 4(a) specifying the temporal logic property Fp. The label Initial specifies that the chart can be activated only once, at the beginning of the system run. The prechart (top dashed hexagon)

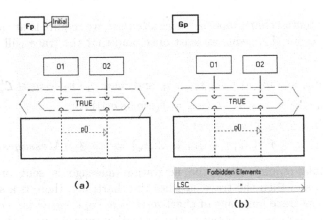

Fig. 4.

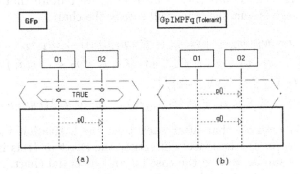

Fig. 5.

has the condition TRUE as activation condition, this implies the main chart consisting of the message p occur eventually. The chart appearing in Fig. 4(b) specifies the temporal logic property Gp. The default interpretation without the label Initial is that whenever the prechart is activated, the main chart follows so p eventually occurs, and the forbidden element restricts all other messages from occurring so p always occurs. The properties GFp and $G(p \to Fq)$ are specified in Fig. 5(a), (b). Note the label tolerant in Fig. 5(b) that allows p to occur more than once before q happens without causing a violation of the chart.

4   Basic Translation

Embedding LSCs into CTL*

As a starting point for studying the relationship between LSCs and temporal logic, we consider a subset of the LSC language including only messages, and with at most one message in a prechart. We show that these LSC specifications can be embedded in the branching temporal logic CTL* [9]. This translation was first proposed in [12]. In this paper we will show how to support a wider subset of LSCs compared to [12] and in a much more efficient way.

Definition 3. *Let $w = m_1 m_2 m_3 ... m_k$ be a finite trace. Let $R = \{e_1, e_2, e_3 \cdots e_l\}$ be a set of events. The temporal logic formula ϕ_w^R is defined as:*

$$\phi_w^R = NU(m_1 \wedge (X(NU(m_2 \wedge (X(NU(m_3...)))))))),$$

where the formula N is given by $N = \neg e_1 \wedge \neg e_2... \wedge \neg e_l$.

Definition 4. *Let $LS = \langle M, amsg, mod \rangle$ be an LSC specification. For a chart $m \in M$, we define the formula ψ_m as follows:*

- *If $mod(m) = universal$, then $\psi_m = AG(amsg(m) \to X(\bigvee_{w \in \mathcal{L}_m^{trc}} \phi_w^R))$.*
- *If $mod(m) = existential$, then $\psi_m = EF(\bigvee_{w \in \mathcal{L}_m^{trc}} \phi_w^R)$.*

Here for a universal chart m we take R to be the events appearing in the prechart and in the main chart.

The following can now be proved.

Proposition 1. *Given $LS = \langle M, amsg, mod \rangle$, let ψ be the CTL* formula $\bigwedge_{m \in M} \psi_m$, and let S be an object system. Then*

$$S \models \psi \quad \Leftrightarrow \quad S \models LS.$$

Proof. Follows from the definitions. Omitted from this version of the paper.

It is noteworthy that the reverse is not true: CTL* cannot be embedded in the language of LSCs. In particular, given the single level quantification mechanism of LSCs, the language cannot express general formulas with alternating path quantifiers. However, it shouldn't be too difficult to extend LSCs to allow certain kinds of quantifier alternation, as noted in [7]. This was not done there, since it was judged to have been too complex and unnecessary for real world usage of sequence charts.

5   Extending and Optimizing the Translation

5.1   Precharts with More Than One Message

In the language of live sequence charts, scenarios are a basic concept, so a prechart can itself describe a scenario which leads to the activation of the universal chart. We now consider the effect of this more general case on our translation. Since existential charts do not have precharts their translation is not affected, and we have to consider only the universal charts.

For a universal chart m we define the formula ψ_m as follows:

Definition 5.

$$\psi_m = G(\bigvee_{w \in \mathcal{L}^{trc}_{pch(m)}} \phi_w \rightarrow \bigvee_{w \in \mathcal{L}^{trc}_{pch(m)} \cdot \mathcal{L}^{trc}_m} \phi_w)$$

We denote $\mathcal{L}^{trc}_{pch(m)}$ the language of executions for the prechart m. The language $\mathcal{L}^{trc}_{pch(m)} \cdot \mathcal{L}^{trc}_m$ consists of concatenations of executions of the prechart and executions of the main chart.

Notice that this is a formula in linear temporal logic (LTL), as is the formula for a universal chart in the basic translation.

5.2   Improved Translation

The formula described in Definition 5 can be large, due to the possibility of having many different traces for the chart, which affects the number of clauses in the disjunction, and also due to the similarity of clauses at the different sides of the implication operator. We give an improved translation where the resulting temporal logic formulas are much more succinct (polynomial vs. exponential in the number of locations).

We consider the case where both the prechart and the main chart consist only of message communication, and denote $p_1, \cdots p_k$ the events appearing in the prechart, $m_1, \cdots m_l$ the events appearing in the main chart. Denote e_i any of these events, either in the prechart or in the main chart. Denote $e_i \prec e_j$ if e_i precedes e_j in the partial order induced by the chart and $e_i \not\prec e_j$ if e_i and e_j are unordered. We assume also that a message does not appear more than once in the same chart. It remains open whether an efficient translation exists for the most general case.

Definition 6.

$$\psi_m = G((\bigwedge_{p_i \prec p_j} \phi_{p_i, p_j} \wedge \bigwedge_{\forall p_i, m_j} \phi_{p_i, m_j} \wedge \bigwedge_{p_i \not\prec p_j} \neg \chi_{p_j, p_i}) \rightarrow$$

$$(\bigwedge_{m_i \prec m_j} \phi_{m_i, m_j} \wedge \bigwedge_{m_j \text{ is maximal}} F m_j \wedge \bigwedge_{\forall e_i, m_j} \neg \chi_{e_i, m_j}))$$

$$\phi_{x_i, x_j} = \neg x_j U x_i$$

$$\chi_{x_i, x_j} = (\neg x_i \wedge \neg x_j) U (x_i \wedge X((\neg x_i \wedge \neg x_j) U x_i))$$

Here the formula ϕ_{x_i,x_j} specifies that x_j must not happen before x_i which eventually occurs. The formula $\neg\chi_{x_i,x_j}$ specifies that x_i must not occur twice before x_j occurs. Note that this translation is polynomial in the number of messages appearing in the chart, while the translation in Definition 5 may be exponential in the number of messages appearing in the chart.

5.3   Past and Future

Another way to view LSCs is as a past formula implying a future formula, an approach similar to that of Gabbay [10]. An advantage of this view is that past formulas have simple and efficient canonical transformations to testers. A tester can be composed with a system and detect when a chart is activated due to the completion of the prechart. In this case the translation can be reduced to the simpler case of an activation message or activation condition rather than handling precharts explicitly. This view is formalized in the following definition:

Definition 7.

$$\psi_m = G((\bigwedge_{p_i \prec p_j} \tau_{p_i,p_j} \wedge \bigwedge_{\forall p_i,m_j} \tau_{m_j,p_i} \wedge \bigwedge_{p_i \not\prec p_j} \neg\xi_{p_j,p_i}) \rightarrow$$

$$(\bigwedge_{m_i \prec m_j} \phi_{m_i,m_j} \wedge \bigwedge_{m_j \ is \ maximal} Fm_j \wedge \bigwedge_{\forall e_i,m_j} \neg\chi_{e_i,m_j}))$$

$\phi_{x_i,x_j} = \neg x_j U x_i$

$\chi_{x_i,x_j} = (\neg x_i \wedge \neg x_j) U (x_i \wedge X((\neg x_i \wedge \neg x_j) U x_i))$

$\tau_{x_i,x_j} = \neg x_i S x_j$

$\xi_{x_i,x_j} = (\neg x_i \wedge \neg x_j) S (x_j \wedge Y((\neg x_i \wedge \neg x_j) S x_j))$

Here the formula τ_{x_i,x_j} specifies that x_i must not happen in the past before x_j which eventually occurs in the past. The formula $\neg\xi_{x_i,x_j}$ specifies that x_j must not occur twice in the past before x_i occurs. Y denotes the previous state, and is the past version of the operator X while S denotes the Since operator and is the past version of the Until operator U.

6   Expressing Formulas in CTL

In this section we investigate the possibilities of expressing LSCs using the branching time logic CTL. The logic CTL is a restricted subset of CTL*. In CTL the temporal operators G, F, X and U must be immediately preceded by a path quantifier. We now show that the formulas in Definition 4 are in CTL, i.e. although syntactically they are not CTL formulas (In ϕ_w the X and U operators are not immediately preceded by a path quantifier) they have equivalent formulas that are CTL formulas.

Proposition 2. *For any formula ψ_m in Definition 4 there exists an equivalent CTL formula ψ'_m.*

Proof. We consider the two cases of existential and universal charts.

Existential chart

The formula given is $\psi_m = EF(\bigvee_{w \in \mathcal{L}_m^{trc}} \phi_w)$ We can simplify it as follows:

$$EF(\bigvee_{w \in \mathcal{L}_m^{trc}} \phi_w) \equiv \bigvee_{w \in \mathcal{L}_m^{trc}} EF(\phi_w)$$

And then go on to show that ϕ_w is equivalent to the CTL formula where the E path quantifier is added before each X and U temporal operator.

Universal chart

The formula given is $\psi_m = AG(amsg(m) \rightarrow X(\bigvee_{w \in \mathcal{L}_m^{trc}} \phi_w))$.

We show a proof for the special case of a single disjunct:
$AG(amsg(m) \rightarrow X\phi_w)$. It illustrates the main ideas and results that can be applied to the general case.

In order to explain the proof we consider an example with messages m_0, m_1, m_2, m_3 and prove the following lemma:

Lemma 1.

$$G(m_0 \rightarrow (X(NU(m_1 \wedge X(NU(m_2 \wedge X(NUm_3))))))) \equiv$$

$$AG(m_0 \rightarrow (AX(A(NU(m_1 \wedge AX(A(NU(m_2 \wedge AX(A(NUm_3)))))))))))$$

Here $N = \neg m_0 \wedge \neg m_1 \wedge \neg m_2 \wedge \neg m_3$

In order to prove Lemma 1 we use a characterization obtained by Maidl of the common fragment of CTL and LTL [21]. In [21] an inductive definition of the ACTL [1] formulas that can be expressed in LTL is given. These formulas are called $ACTL^{det}$, and they are a restriction of ACTL.

$ACTL^{det}$ is inductively defined as follows:

Definition 8. $ACTL^{det}$

- *p is a predicate.*
- *For $ACTL^{det}$ formulas ϕ_1 and ϕ_2 and a predicate p:*
  $\phi_1 \wedge \phi_2$, $AX\phi_1$, $(p \wedge \phi_1) \vee (\neg p \wedge \phi_2)$, $A(p \wedge \phi_1)U(\neg p \wedge \phi_2)$, $A(p \wedge \phi_1)W(\neg p \wedge \phi_2)$.

Theorem 1. *(Maidl [21])*
Let ϕ be an ACTL formula. Then there exists an LTL formula ψ which is equivalent to ϕ iff ϕ can be expressed in $ACTL^{det}$.

We also use a theorem by Clarke and Draghicesku [6].

---

[1] ACTL is the fragment of those CTL formulas that contain, when in negation normal form, only A as a path quantifier.

Theorem 2. *(Clarke and Draghicesku [6]) For a CTL formula ϕ, we denote the result of removing all path quantifiers from ϕ by ϕ^d. Let ϕ be a CTL formula. Then there is an LTL formula ψ such that ϕ and ψ are equivalent iff ϕ is equivalent to ϕ^d.*

Proof. (of Lemma 1)

We now show that the formula in the right hand side of the equivalence in Lemma 1 is in ACTL^{det} by constructing it inductively according to Definition 8.

$\phi_0 = m_3$

$\phi_1 = A(\neg m_3 \wedge (\neg m_0 \wedge \neg m_1 \wedge \neg m_2))U(m_3 \wedge true) \equiv A(NU m_3)$

$\phi_2 = AX(\phi_1) \equiv AX(A(NU m_3))$

$\phi_3 = A((\neg m_2 \wedge (\neg m_0 \wedge \neg m_1 \wedge \neg m_3))U(m_2 \wedge \phi_2)) \equiv A(NU(m_2 \wedge AX(A(NU m_3))))$

$\phi_4 = AX(\phi_3) \equiv AX(A(NU(m_2 \wedge AX(A(NU m_3)))))$

$\phi_5 = A(\neg m_1 \wedge (\neg m_0 \wedge \neg m_2 \wedge \neg m_3))U(m_1 \wedge \phi_4)) \equiv A(NU(m_1 \wedge AX(A(NU(m_2 \wedge$
$AX(A(NU m_3))))))$

$\phi_6 = AX(\phi_5) \equiv AX(A(NU(m_1 \wedge AX(A(NU(m_2 \wedge AX(A(NU m_3))))))))$

$\phi_7 = (\neg m_0 \wedge TRUE) \vee (m_0 \wedge \phi_6) \equiv m_0 \rightarrow AX(A(NU(m_1 \wedge AX(A(NU(m_2 \wedge$
$AX(A(NU m_3))))))))$

$\phi_8 = A(true \wedge \phi_7)W(false) \equiv AG(m_0 \rightarrow AX(A(NU(m_1 \wedge AX(A(NU(m_2 \wedge$
$AX(A(NU m_3)))))))))$

This shows that the formula in the right hand side of the equivalence in Lemma 1 is in ACTL^{det}, and therefore according to Theorem 1 the formula is in the common fragment of LTL and CTL.

As we showed the formula:

$$AG(m_0 \rightarrow AX(A(NU(m_1 \wedge AX(A(NU(m_2 \wedge AX(A(NU m_3)))))))))$$

is in ACTL^{det} therefore by theorem 1 the formula can be expressed in LTL, and by theorem 2 it is equivalent to the formula obtained by removing all path quantifiers:

$$G(m_0 \rightarrow (X(NU(m_1 \wedge X(NU(m_2 \wedge X(NU m_3)))))))$$

thus completing the proof of Lemma 1.

□

The proof of an equivalence like that of Lemma 1 for an execution of arbitrary length k, $w = m_1 m_2 m_3 ... m_k$ is by induction on k and is straightforward.

7   Extension for Additional LSC Constructs

We briefly outline how our translations can be extended to handle additional LSC constructs. A detailed treatment will appear in the full version of the paper.

7.1   Conditions

The LSC language allows using conditions, which are assertions on the variables of the system. Variables may be local to an instance or globally known. Conditions can be handled within the framework described previously, the main effect of conditions on the translation is on the languages of executions. We consider generalized executions, $w = x_1 x_2 x_3 ... x_k$ is an execution of m, a sequence of events (send or receive) or conditions (or their negation) satisfying the requirements of m.

As before

$$\phi_w = NU(x_1 \wedge (X(NU(x_2 \wedge (X(NU(x_3 ...)))))))),$$

where the formula N is given by $N = \neg m_1 \wedge \neg m_2 ... \wedge \neg m_l$. Each m_i in the formula is a proposition indicating the occurrence of a send or receive event, the conditions do not appear in N. Each x_i in the formula ϕ_w is a proposition indicating the occurrence of a send or receive event m_i, a condition holding c_i or not holding $\neg c_i$. Conditions can come in two flavors: mandatory (hot) and provisional (cold). If a system run encounters a false mandatory condition the run aborts abnormally, while a false provisional condition induces a normal exit from the enclosing charts. Conditions can also be shared by several instances, forming a synchronization barrier. These issues can be treated by our translation but are beyond the scope of this version of the paper.

7.2   Iteration

A loop construct is a subchart that is iterated a number of times. Fixed loops are annotated by a number or variable name, while unbounded loops are performed an a priory unknown number of times. The subchart can be exited when a cold condition inside it is violated. Bounded loops can be treated by unfolding techniques. Unbounded loops enhance the expressive power of LSCs and cannot be expressed in propositional temporal logic (PTL), since PTL does not allow counting modulo n, which can be specified by an LSC with unbounded loop with a certain message appearing n times inside the loop.

8   Related Work

A large amount of work has been done on scenario-based specifications. We briefly discuss the ones most relevant to our work. The idea of using sequence charts to discover design errors at early stages of development has been investigated in [1, 22] for detecting race conditions, time conflicts and pattern matching. The language used in these papers is that of classical message sequence charts, with semantics being simply the partial order of events in a chart. In order to describe system behavior, such MSC's are composed into hierarchal message sequence charts (HMSC's) which are basically graphs whose nodes are MSC's. As has been observed in several papers, e.g. [2], allowing processes to progress along the HMSC with each chart being in a different node may introduce non-regular behavior and is the cause of undecidability of certain properties. Undecidability results and approaches to restrict HMSC's in order to avoid these problems appear in [16, 17, 11].

Live sequence charts have been used for testing and verification of system models. Lettrari and Klose [20] present a methodology supported by a tool called

TestConductor, which is integrated into Rhapsody [18]. The tool is used for monitoring and testing a model using a restricted subset of LSCs. Damm and Klose [8, 19] describe a verification environment in which LSCs are used to describe requirements that are verified against a Statemate model implementation. The verification is based on translating an LSC chart into a timed Büchi automaton, as described in [19], and it also handles timing issues. Standard translations from Büchi automata to temporal logic can then be applied. Previous work on optimizing temporal logic formulas for model-checking appears in [3]. LSCs have also been applied to the specification and verification of hardware systems [4, 5].

In [14] a methodology for specifying and validating requirements, termed "play-in/play-out" is described. According to this approach, requirements are captured by the user playing in scenarios using a graphical interface of the system to be developed or using an object model diagram. The user "plays" the GUI by clicking buttons, rotating knobs and sending messages (calling functions) to objects in an intuitive manner. As this is being done, the supporting tool, called the Play-Engine, constructs a formal version of the requirements in the form of LSCs. Play-out is a complementary idea to play-in, which makes it possible to execute the requirements directly. Smart play-out [13] is an extension of the play-out mechanism using verification methods to drive the execution. The semantics described in this paper follows that of [14, 13], but the translation to temporal logic described here is new and was not used as part of (smart) play-out, a direction that we plan to investigate in future work.

References

1. R. Alur, G.J. Holzmann, and D. Peled. An analyzer for message sequence charts. *Software Concepts and Tools*, 17(2):70–77, 1996.
2. R. Alur and M. Yannakakis. Model checking of message sequence charts. In *10th International Conference on Concurrency Theory (CONCUR99)*, volume 1664 of *Lect. Notes in Comp. Sci.*, pages 114–129. Springer-Verlag, 1999.
3. Yves Bontemps. Automated verification of state-based specifications against scenarios (a step toward relating inter-object to intra-object specifications). Master's thesis, University of Namur, Belgium, June 2001.
4. A. Bunker and G. Gopalakrishnan. Verifying a VCI Bus Interface Model Using an LSC-based Specification. In *Proceedings of the Sixth Biennial World Conference on Integrated Design and Process Technology*, pages 1–12, 2002.
5. A. Bunker and K. Slind. Property Generation for Live Sequence Charts. Technical report, University of Utah, 2003.
6. E.M. Clarke and I. A. Draghicescu. Expressibility results for linear-time and branching-time logics. In *Linear Time, Branching Time and Partial Order in Logics and Models for Concurrency*, vol. 354 of *LNCS*, pages 428–437, 1988.
7. W. Damm and D. Harel. LSCs: Breathing life into message sequence charts. *Formal Methods in System Design*, 19(1):45–80, 2001.
8. W. Damm and J. Klose. Verification of a radio-based signalling system using the statemate verification environment. *Formal Methods in System Design*, 19(2):121–141, 2001.
9. E.A. Emerson. Temporal and modal logics. In J. van Leeuwen, editor, *Handbook of theoretical computer science*, volume B, pages 995–1072. Elsevier, 1990.

10. D. Gabbay. The declarative past and imperative future. In *Temporal Logic in Specification*, volume 398 of *LNCS*, pages 407–448. Springer-Verlag, 1987.

11. E. L. Gunter, A. Muscholl, and D. Peled. Compositional message sequence charts. In *Proc. 7th Intl. Conf. on Tools and Algorithms for the Construction and Analysis of Systems (TACAS'01)*, vol. 2031 of LNCS, *Springer-Verlag*, pages 496–511, 2001.

12. D. Harel and H. Kugler. Synthesizing state-based object systems from LSC specifications. *Int. J. of Foundations of Computer Science (IJFCS).*, 13(1):5–51, Febuary 2002. (Also,*Proc. Fifth Int. Conf. on Implementation and Application of Automata (CIAA 2000)*, July 2000, Lecture Notes in Computer Science, Springer-Verlag, 2000.).

13. D. Harel, H. Kugler, R. Marelly, and A. Pnueli. Smart play-out of behavioral requirements. In *Proc. 4th Intl. Conference on Formal Methods in Computer-Aided Design (FMCAD'02)*, volume 2517 of *LNCS*, pages 378–398, 2002.

14. D. Harel and R. Marelly. *Come, Let's Play: Scenario-Based Programming Using LSCs and the Play-Engine.* Springer-Verlag, 2003.

15. D. Harel and R. Marelly. Specifying and Executing Behavioral Requirements: The Play In/Play-Out Approach. *Software and System Modeling (SoSyM)*, 2(2):82–107, 2003.

16. J.G. Henriksen, M. Mukund, K.N. Kumar, and P.S. Thiagarajan. On message sequence graphs and finitely generated regular MSC languages. In *Proc. 27th Int. Colloq. Aut. Lang. Prog.*, vol. 1853 of *LNCS*, pages 675–686. Springer-Verlag, 2000.

17. J.G. Henriksen, M. Mukund, K.N. Kumar, and P.S. Thiagarajan. Regular collections of Message Sequence Charts. In *Proceedings of the 25th International Symposium on Mathematical Foundations of Computer Science(MFCS'2000)*, volume 1893 of *Lect. Notes in Comp. Sci.*, pages 675–686. Springer-Verlag, 2000.

18. Rhapsody. I-Logix, Inc., products web page. http://www.ilogix.com/products/.

19. J. Klose and H. Wittke. An automata based interpretation of live sequence charts. In *Proc. 7th Intl. Conference on Tools and Algorithms for the Construction and Analysis of Systems (TACAS'01)*, volume 2031 of LNCS, *Springer-Verlag*, 2001.

20. M. Lettrari and J. Klose. Scenario-based monitoring and testing of real-time UML models. In *4th Int. Conf. on the Unified Modeling Language, Toronto*, October 2001.

21. M. Maidl. The common fragment of CTL and LTL. In *Proc. 41st IEEE Symp. Found. of Comp. Sci.*, pages 643–652, 2000.

22. A. Muscholl, D. Peled, and Z. Su. Deciding properties for message sequence charts. In *Proc. of the 1st Int. Conf. on Foundations of Software Science and Computation Structures (FOSSACS '98)*, vol. 1378 of *LNCS*, pages 226–242. Springer-Verlag, 1998.

23. A. Pnueli. The temporal logic of programs. In *Proc. 18th IEEE Symp. Found. of Comp. Sci.*, pages 46–57, 1977.

24. B. Sengupta and R. Cleaveland. Triggered message sequence charts. In *Proceedings of the tenth ACM SIGSOFT symposium on Foundations of software engineering*, pages 167–176. ACM Press, 2002.

25. UML. Documentation of the unified modeling language (UML). Available from the Object Management Group (OMG), http://www.omg.org.

26. Z.120 ITU-TS Recommendation Z.120: Message Sequence Chart (MSC). ITU-TS, Geneva, 1996.

Mining Temporal Specifications for Error Detection

Westley Weimer and George C. Necula

University of California, Berkeley
{weimer, necula}@cs.berkeley.edu

Abstract. Specifications are necessary in order to find software bugs using program verification tools. This paper presents a novel automatic specification mining algorithm that uses information about error handling to learn temporal safety rules. Our algorithm is based on the observation that programs often make mistakes along exceptional control-flow paths, even when they behave correctly on normal execution paths. We show that this focus improves the effectiveness of the miner for discovering specifications beneficial for bug finding.

We present quantitative results comparing our technique to four existing miners. We highlight assumptions made by various miners that are not always born out in practice. Additionally, we apply our algorithm to existing Java programs and analyze its ability to learn specifications that find bugs in those programs. In our experiments, we find filtering candidate specifications to be more important than ranking them. We find 430 bugs in 1 million lines of code. Notably, we find 250 more bugs using per-program specifications learned by our algorithm than with generic specifications that apply to all programs.

1 Introduction

Software remains buggy and testing is still the dominant approach for detecting software errors. The difficulties and costs of testing have helped to push forward techniques that automatically find classes of errors statically [4, 5, 6, 7, 13] or dynamically [10, 11, 12, 14]. Such program verification tools can point out bugs or provide guarantees about the absence of some mistakes.

Invariably, however, verification tools require *specifications* that describe some aspect of program correctness. Creating correct specifications is difficult, time-consuming and error-prone. Verification tools can only point out disagreements between the program and the specification. Even assuming a sound and complete tool, an imperfect specification can still yield false positives by pointing out non-bugs as bugs or false negatives by failing to point out real bugs. Crafting specifications typically requires program-specific knowledge.

One way to reduce the cost of writing specifications is to use implicit language-based specifications (e.g., null pointers should not be dereferenced) or to reuse standard library specifications (e.g., [4, 13]). More recently, however,

N. Halbwachs and L. Zuck (Eds.): TACAS 2005, LNCS 3440, pp. 461–476, 2005.

a variety of attempts have been made to infer program-specific temporal specifications and API usage rules [1, 2, 7, 14] automatically. These *specification mining* techniques take programs (and possibly dynamic traces, or other hints) as input and produce candidate specifications as output. In general, specifications could also be used for documenting, refactoring, testing, debugging, maintaining, and optimizing a program. We focus here on finding and evaluating specifications in a particular context: given a program and a generic verification tool, what specification mining technique should be used to find bugs in the program and thereby improve software quality? Thus we are concerned both with the number of "real" and "false positive" specifications produced by the miner and with the number of "real" and "false positive" bugs found using those "real" specifications.

We propose a novel technique for temporal specification mining that uses information about program error handling. Our miner assumes that programs will generally adhere to specifications along normal execution paths, but that programs will likely violate specifications in the presence of some run-time errors or exceptional situations. Intuitively, error-handling code may not be tested as often or the programmer may be unaware of sources of run-time errors. Taking advantage of this information is more important than ranking candidate policies.

The contributions of this paper are as follows:

- We propose a novel specification mining technique based on the observation that programmers often make mistakes in exceptional circumstances or along uncommon code paths.
- We present a qualitative comparison of five miners and show how some miner assumptions are not well-supported in practice.
- Finally, we give a quantitative comparison of our technique's bug-finding powers to generic "library" policies. For our domain of interest, mining finds 250 more bugs. We also show the relative unimportance of ranking candidate policies. In all, we find 69 specifications that lead to the discovery over 430 bugs in 1 million lines of code.

In Section 2 we describe temporal safety specifications. We present our specification mining algorithm in Section 3. In Section 4 we describe some existing specification mining algorithms, leading up to a qualitative comparison of various techniques in Section 5. We describe our experience running our miner in Section 6, comparing its bug-finding powers to another technique and to generic "library" specifications.

2   Temporal Safety Specifications

A specification miner takes a program as input and produces one or more candidate specifications with respect to a set of interesting program events. The program is presented as a set of static or dynamic *traces*, each of which is a sequence of events and annotations (e.g., data values, records of raised exceptions). Static traces are generated from the program source code. Dynamic traces are

```
Session sess = sfac.openSession();
Transaction tx;
try {
    tx = sess.beginTransaction();
    // do some work
    tx.commit();
} catch (Exception e) {
    if (tx != null) tx.rollback();
    throw e;
} finally
    sess.close();
```

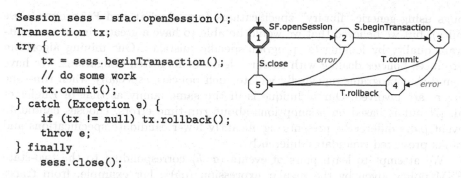

Fig. 1. hibernate2 Session class documentation pseudocode and temporal **safety policy**, given as an FSM over a six-event alphabet. Edge labels (events) are either successful method invocations or method *errors*. Other transitions involving these six events violate the policy, but other events (e.g., S.find) are not constrained produced by running the program against a workload. In practice, *events* are usually taken to be context-free function calls.

Mined *specifications* (or *policies*) are typically finite state machines with events as edges. A run of the program adheres to the policy if it generates a sequence of events accepted by the FSM. Such policies commonly limit how an interface may be invoked (e.g., close cannot be called before open and must be called after it). Many program verifiers can check such FSM properties, either per-object (as a form of typestate) or globally. Ammons et al. [2] present a more formal treatment of the mining problem.

As a concrete example, we consider a policy for the interfaces of the SessionFactory, Session and Transaction classes in the hibernate2 program, a 57k LOC framework that provides persistent Java objects [9]. The Session class is the central interface between hibernate2 and a client. The Session documentation includes explicit pseudocode and an injunction that clients should adhere to it. The code and five-state FSM specification are shown in Figure 1. We denote SessionFactory by SF, Session by S, and Transaction by T. A typical use of this interface would visit states 1 through 3, "do some work" there (involving events like S.flush and S.save that are not part of the input alphabet of the FSM and thus do not affect it), and then visit 5 and return to 1. In the next section we discuss our mining algorithm using this specification as a concrete example.

3   Specification Mining Algorithm

Our work on specification mining was motivated by observations of run-time error handling mistakes. Based on previous work examining such mistakes [13] we believe that client code frequently violates simple API specifications in exceptional situations (i.e., in the presence of run-time errors). We found such bugs using generic "library" specifications (e.g., Socket and File open/close rules), but we believed that we would be able to have a greater impact on software quality by looking for program-specific mistakes. Our mining algorithm produces policies dealing with resource leaks or forgotten obligations. We have found that programs repeatedly violate such policies, especially when run-time errors are involved. Our technique is in the same family as that of Engler et al. [7] but is based on assumptions about run-time errors, chooses candidate event pairs differently, presents significantly fewer candidate specifications and ranks presented candidates differently.

We attempt to learn pairs of events $\langle a, b \rangle$ corresponding to the two-state FSM policy given by the regular expression $(ab)*$. For example, from traces generated by the state machine in Figure 1 we might learn $\langle$SF.openSession, S.close$\rangle$, because every accepting sequence that transitions from state 1 to state 2 via SF.openSession must also transition from state 5 to state 1 via S.close. We learn multiple candidate specifications per program and present a ranked list to the user. For example, we might learn the candidate specification $\langle$SF.openSession, T.rollback$\rangle$. Unlike some mining algorithms that produce detailed policies that must be manually debugged or modified, we produce simple policies that are designed to be accepted or rejected. With this approach we will not be able to learn the "complete" policy in Figure 1. However, the full policy is closely approximated by $\langle$SF.openSession, S.close$\rangle$ and $\langle$S.beginTransaction, T.commit$\rangle$.

In a normal execution, events a and b may be separated by other events and difficult to discern as a pair. After an error has occurred, however, the cleanup code is usually much less cluttered and contains only operations required for correctness. Intuitively, a programmer who is aware of the specification will have included b in an exception handler, finally block, or other piece of cleanup code, making it easier to pick up than in a normal execution path. The pseudocode in Figure 1 demonstrates this sort of cleanup for the T.rollback and S.close events. If S.close is the only legal way to discharge a Session obligation, we expect to see S.close in well-written cleanup code.

We classify intra-procedural static traces as "error" traces if they involve exceptional control flow. These are the traces containing at least one method call that terminates with raising of an exception. Such exceptions are assumed to signal run-time errors or unusual situations. Traces in which no such exceptions are raised are "normal" traces. In Figure 1, a normal trace of events would involve the state sequence 1–2–3–5–1. An error trace would visit 1–2–5–1 or 1–2–3–4–5–1.

3.1   Filtering Candidate Specifications

Let N_{ab} be the number of normal traces that have a followed by b, and let N_a be the number that have a not followed by b. We define E_{ab} and E_a similarly for error traces. Given a set of traces, we consider all event pairs $\langle a, b \rangle$ from those traces such that all of the following occur:

Exceptional Control Flow (ex). Our novel filtering criterion is that event *b* must occur at least once in some cleanup code (e.g., a catch or finally block): we require $E_{ab} > 0$. We assume that if the policy is important to the programmer, language-level error handling will be used at least once to enforce it. In hibernate2, the SF.openSession and S.beginTransaction events never occur in cleanup code, thus ruling them out as the second event in a pair. The T.commit, T.rollback and S.close events all do occur in cleanup code, however. Other miners limit events to those on a user-specified list.[1] We prefer to automate the creation of this list because of the cost of acquiring specific knowledge about each target program. However, if such domain knowledge is available, it can be used instead of, or in addition to, the default from cleanup code. The occurrence of the event in normal execution traces will be used in Section 3.2 to rank candidate specifications.

One Error (oe). There must at least one *error* trace with *a* but without *b*: we require $E_a > 0$. We are here only interested in learning specifications that will lead to finding program errors, and we assume that the programmer will make mistakes in the handling of exceptional situations.

Same Package (sp). Events *a* and *b* must be declared in the same package. For example, we assume that no temporal specification will be concerned with the relative order of an invocation of an org.apache.xpath.Arg method and a net.sf.Hibernate.Session method from separate libraries. The user can specify wider or narrower related groups if such information is available.

Dataflow (df). Every value and receiver object expression in *b* must also be in *a*. When dealing with static traces we require that every non-primitive type in *b* also occur in *a*. We thus assume that Session SessionFactory.openSession() may be followed by void Session.close() but forbid the opposite ordering. Intuitively, this also corresponds to finding edges that share the same node in policies like Figure 1. This notion is in contrast to other miners where a more precise dataflow analysis rules out some unwanted specifications. In our experiments this lightweight dataflow requirement has been sufficient to capture our intuitive notion of correlated events.

3.2   Ranking Candidate Specifications

In order to improve the usability of this technique, we present to the user a ranked list of the candidate specifications that satisfy the criteria described above. Our heuristics will assign higher ranks to candidates that are more likely to be real policies. We do not rank policies based on the number of bugs the policy would find in the program. However, as we will see in Section 6, ranking plays a much smaller role than eliminating extraneous candidates.

---

[1] For example, in Engler et al. [7] the list includes functions whose names contain the substrings "lock", "unlock", "acquire", etc.

Event a	Event b	Real	N_a	N_{ab}	E_a	E_{ab}	Filters	rank	z-rank	z-rank$|_N$
SF.openSessi	S.close	Yes	3	100	1348	1040	ex oe sp df	0.971	-73.5	2.40
S.beginTrans	S.close	?	2	56	1037	501	ex oe sp df	0.966	-73.3	1.66
S.beginTrans	T.commit	Yes	2	56	565	973	ex oe sp df	0.966	-33.9	1.66
S.flush	S.close	no	9	39	200	473	ex oe sp df	0.812	-17.0	-2.02
T.commit	S.close	?	1	57	474	504	ex oe sp	0.983	-38.5	2.10
S.beginTrans	S.save	no	4	54	37	1501	oe sp df	0.931	9.90	0.788
SF.openSessi	T.commit	?	47	56	1415	973	ex oe sp	0.544	-81.0	-12.1
SF.openSessi	println	no	82	21	2121	267	ex oe df	0.204	-130	-23.4

Fig. 2. Static trace observations for Session events in hibernate2. The "real" column indicates whether $\langle a, b \rangle$ is definitely (Yes), possibly (?) or definitely not (no) a valid policy based on Figure 1. N_a is the number traces with a but not b, N_{ab} is the number of normal traces with a followed by b. E_a and E_{ab} measure the same figures for error traces. The "Filters" column indicates which of our filtering requirements the pair meets. Only the first four pairs qualify as candidates for our miner. The "rank" column reports $N_{ab}/(N_a + N_{ab})$ and high values indicate more likely specifications. The "z-rank" column shows the z-statistic applied to all traces as in Engler et al. [7], while the "z-rank$|_N$" column shows the z-statistic restricted to normal traces

We assume $\langle a, b \rangle$ is more likely to be a policy if the programmer intends to adhere to it many times. We assume that normal traces represent the intent of the programmer and that some error traces represent unforeseen circumstances likely to contain bugs; thus we rank pairs according to the fraction of *normal traces* in which a is followed by b.

Our ranking for a candidate $\langle a, b \rangle$ is $N_{ab}/(N_{ab} + N_a)$. The best ranking is 1, and a reported specification with rank 1 has a followed by b in all normal paths.

Figure 2 shows observations for Session-related events on a set of static traces. All eight pairs could potentially be policies, but our requirements in Section 3.1 filter out the last four. Since SF.openSession does not occur in any error-handling code, we do not consider pairs like $\langle$S.close, SF.openSession$\rangle$. As desired, we rule out pairs like $\langle$SF.openSession, T.commit$\rangle$ with our dataflow requirement (there is no Transaction object available in event a). Our package requirement correctly rules out policies involving printf-like logging methods. Finally, while we cannot rule out pairs like $\langle$S.flush, S.close$\rangle$ (where S.flush is one of the "do some work" options that would occur at state 3 of Figure 1), we rank it lower because a smaller fraction of normal paths have that pairing (e.g., in Figure 2 that pair ranks 0.812 while the best pair involving S.close ranks 0.971).

The z-rank and z-rank$|_N$ columns of Figure 2 show the result of using the z-statistic for proportions [8], an alternative ranking scheme, to rank candidate specifications, with the z-rank$|_N$ column being computed over normal traces only. The z-rank was used by Engler et al. [7]. The z-statistic increases with the total number of observations involving a and decreases with the number of observations involving a but not b. Ignoring some constant factors, z-rank$|_N$ is equal to our ranking multiplied by $\sqrt{N_a + N_{ab}}$. We provide an empirical comparison of these three rankings in Section 6.

4   Other Specification Mining Techniques

We now describe the main characteristics of several existing mining approaches.

Strauss. Ammons et al. [2] present a miner in which events from dynamic traces that are related by traditional dataflow dependencies form a *scenario*. The user provides a *seed* event and a maximum scenario size N. A scenario contains at most N ancestors and at most N descendants of the seed event. The seed can be any interesting event that is assumed to play a role in the specification. Such scenarios are fed to a probabilistic finite state machine learner. The output of the learner, a single policy, is minimized and may further be "cored" by removing infrequently traversed edges or "debugged" and simplified with the user's help [3].

WML-Static. Whaley et al. [14] propose two methods for deriving interface specifications for classes based on an explicit representation of typestate in member fields.

In the first (static) approach the user specifies a class in the program. Traces are generated statically by considering all pairs $\langle a, b \rangle$ of invocations for methods a and b of that class. If b conditionally raises an exception when a field has a certain constant value and a always sets that field to that value, $\langle a, b \rangle$ is considered a violation of the interface policy. For example, the `close` method might set the field `opened` to false, and the `read` method might raise an exception if `opened` is false. The single final specification consists of all other pairs $\langle a, b \rangle$, represented as a DFA with one state per method. This miner explicitly looks for "a must not be followed by b" requirements, and by considering all possible method pair interactions it discovers what can follow a as well. In our experiments, we used an extended version of the miner that considers multiple fields and inlines boolean methods.

JIST. The JIST tool of Alur et al. [1] refines the WML-static miner by using predicate abstraction for a more precise dataflow analysis. The user specifies a class and an undesired exception, as well as providing a set of predicates and a specification size k. A boolean model of the class is constructed based on the predicate set, and a model checker determines if invoking a sequence of methods raises the given exception. If it can, that sequence is removed from the specification. The process finds the most permissive policy of that size that is safe with respect to the predicates and the exception. As with Strauss, the output of the analysis is minimized using an off-the-shelf FSM library. In a WML-static policy, states represent the last invoked method. In JIST, states represent predicate valuations, which in turn represent object state. For example, JIST could produce a policy in which the sequence $\langle a, b \rangle$ is allowed but $\langle a, a, b \rangle$ is not. Thus, in JIST's more general policies, states do not correspond directly to the last method invocation.

WML-dynamic. Whaley et al. [14] also present a dynamic trace analysis that learns a *permissive* policy for a given class. Such a permissive specification is the most restrictive policy that accepts all of the training traces. Each field of the class is considered separately. Only events representing client calls to methods of that class that read or write that field are examined. If a is immediately followed by b in the trace, an edge from a to b is added to the policy. The single output policy for the class is formed from the per-field policies.

ECC. Engler et al. [7] describe a technique for mining rules of the form "b must follow a" as part of a larger work on may-must beliefs, bugs, and deviant behavior. If b follows a in any trace, the event pair $\langle a, b \rangle$ is considered as a candidate specification.

A pair $\langle a, b \rangle$ is a candidate policy if the events a and b are related by dataflow and if there are both traces in which a is followed by b and traces in which a is not followed by b. A series of dependency checks is employed: two events are related if they have either the same first argument, or have no arguments, or if the return value from the first passed as the sole argument to the second. The user may also restrict attention to a certain set of methods.

ECC produces a large number of candidate policies. Engler et al. use the z-statistic for proportions to hierarchically rank candidates. The z-statistic measures the difference between the observed ratio and an expected ratio p_0. Engler et al. use the ranking because it grows with the frequency with which the pair is observed together and decreases with the number of counter-examples observed. They take $p_0 = 0.9$ based on the assumption that perfect fits are uninteresting in bug-finding and that error cases are found near counter-examples. In our experiments we have found that ECC's assumptions tend to hold true for normal traces but not for error traces (where the frequency counts are quite high if the traces are static and often quite low if the traces are dynamic).

5   Qualitative Comparison of Mining Techniques

In this section we present experiments comparing these mining techniques. We evaluate a miner in terms of the policy it produces and later in terms of the number of bugs found by that policy. When comparing miners we abbreviate our miner (defined in Section 3) by WN.

The first experiment compares miner performance on policies governing hibernate2's SessionFactory, Session and Transaction classes, as described in Section 2. This example was chosen because one policy for it is clearly described in the documentation, and also because that policy is complex enough that none of the miners can expect to learn it perfectly (e.g., our technique is unable to find all of the pieces of the full specification because of its assumptions about run-time errors). ECC and WN both find policies about these classes (and others) automatically. For the purposes of comparison, however, we restrict all miners to policies about these three classes. For Strauss, WML and JIST we also provide all of the appropriate parameters (e.g., class names, predicates).

For the purposes of the comparison we present the same raw trace data to each algorithm that looks at client code. In addition, some amount of human help was given to every miner. For ECC and WN, two of the top seven candidate policies were manually selected. For Strauss and WML-dynamic, a slice or core of the learned policy was selected. For JIST and WML-static, all relevant predicates and fields were given.

5.1 Hibernate2 Session Specifications

Strauss, WML-dynamic, ECC, and our technique all learned policies similar to the documentation-based policy shown in Figure 1.

The Strauss policy (Figure 3) captures the beginning and the end of the Figure 1 closely but is less precise than Figure 1 in the middle. Strauss's use of frequency information means that common sequences of events like find and delete are included as part of the policy. Paths through states 2–6 are all particular instantiations of the "do some work" state 3 in Figure 1. Compared to Figure 1, a sequence of two flush events after an

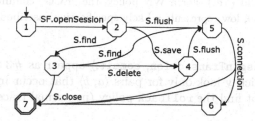

Fig. 3. A slice (the "hot core") of the Session policy learned by **Strauss**: the full learned specification has 10 states and 45 transitions

openSession is incorrectly rejected by the Strauss policy while a sequence that has beginTransaction but no rollback or commit is incorrectly accepted.

The WML-dynamic policy permissively accepts all of the input traces. A slice is shown in Figure 4, the full policy has 27 states and 117 transitions. The slice captures the highlights of Figure 1 (e.g., in states 1–2–3–5–6) but fails to reject observed illegal behavior (e.g., forgetting close) and rejects unobserved legal behavior (e.g., reconnect followed by close). WML-dynamic makes a strong frequency assumption: a transition is valid if and only if it is observed. By contrast, our algo-

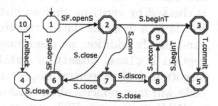

Fig. 4. A slice of the Session policy learned by **WML-dynamic**

rithm's ex and oe filters rule out some observed illegal behavior.

Figure 5 shows the top seven policies for these classes learned by ECC and our approach. ECC learned 350 such candidate policies. The z-statistic favors frequent pairs: the pair ⟨beginTransaction, save⟩ occurs on more than 1,500 traces, and is thus a common practice, but is not strictly required. Our approach learned 15 candidate policies, of which 2 are real. Two of the three main aspects of the documented specification, ⟨openSession, close⟩ and

ECC Policies					WN Policies				
#	z-rank	Event a	Event b	Real	Rank	Event a	Event b	Real	ECC
1	9.896	S.beginTrans	S.save	Yes	1.000	S.iterate	S.close	no	286
2	1.686	S.reconnect	S.load	no	1.000	S.getIdentifier	S.close	no	28
3	1.634	S.getLockMode	S.close	no	0.971	SF.openSession	S.close	Yes	256
4	0.609	SF.openConn	SF.closeConn	Yes	0.971	S.createQuery	S.close	no	269
5	0.430	S.disconnect	S.reconnect	no	0.969	S.find	S.close	no	290
6	0.309	S.getLockMode	S.load	no	0.966	S.beginTrans	T.commit	Yes	175
7	-0.430	S.disconnect	S.load	no	0.966	S.beginTrans	S.close	no	254

Fig. 5. The top seven `Session` policies learned by **ECC** and **WN**. Each policy requires an instance of "Event a" to be followed an instance of the corresponding "Event b". The "Real" column notes whether the policy is decidedly a false positive (no) or possibly valid (Yes). For a WN policy, the "ECC" column shows the ranked number (out of 350, low represents a likely specification) ascribed to it by the ECC algorithm

$\langle$`beginTransaction`, `commit`,$\rangle$ appear as #3 and #6 on the list. Since we explicitly look only for pairs $\langle a, b \rangle$ that occur in almost all normal traces we will not find the `rollback` policy (no normal traces include `rollback` events).

5.2   Hibernate2 `Session` Typestate Specifications

The `hibernate2` documentation mentions one notion of `Session` typestate. The code does contain defensive programming checks using this typestate that raise exceptions, just as WML-static and JIST assume. Unfortunately, neither WML-static nor JIST are able to learn this typestate because it is checked by verifying that an instance object is in a dynamic data structure kept at run-time. In addition, no check raises an exception if `close`, `commit` or `rollback` are forgotten, and in general inspecting library code will miss policies about such methods, so WML-static and JIST cannot learn the full specification in Figure 1.

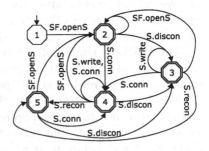

Fig. 6. `Session` policy learned by **WML-static**

WML-static (Figure 6) discovers five illegal sequences of `Session` methods. It finds a useful undocumented `Session` typestate: two variables track the state of a `Session` as it connects to a database. The `S.write` method checks these underlying typestate variables but does not set them. For WML-static and JIST, all unlisted events (e.g., `S.close`) are orthogonal to the learned policy.

JIST (Figure 7) produces a more precise policy (e.g., it discovers that `connection` cannot be followed by `writeObject`) because it does not require methods to have a uniform impact on the object's typestate. Each state in the JIST policy represents a distinct valuation of two variables. The `writeObject` method may only be called when both are false. The **reconnect** method always sets the second to true, so both techniques discover that it cannot be followed by **writeObject**. The **connection** method, however, has a different effect on the state variables depending on their current values, so WML-static cannot reason precisely about it.

In our experiments the important difference between JIST and WML-static was
not JIST's greater dataflow precision but
JIST's accurate characterization of interesting traces. All of the data manipulation was
either too complicated for both methods to
model (e.g., heap data structures) or simple enough to meet WML-static's assumptions (e.g., comparing fields and constant val-

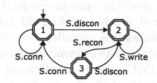

Fig. 7. JIST Session policy

ues). These observations support our algorithmic design choice to use a simple dataflow requirement but to pay careful attention to characterizing exceptional traces.

6   Experiments

We present bug-finding effectiveness results comparing the performance of all algorithms on the **Session** policy and results comparing our algorithm against ECC and generic "library" specifications for one million lines of code.

6.1   Comparison with Other Specification Miners

Given a candidate policy, we use an ESP-like tool [5] to find potential bugs by checking the policy against the source code [4, 5, 7, 13]. Each potential bug is classified as a false positive or a real error by manual inspection. For example, if an application fails to close a file but immediately shuts down as a result of the error, the "leaked" file is classed as a false positive. However, a leaked database lock between the JVM (held on behalf of the program) and an external database is a bug if no finalizers close the connection when the program (but not the JVM) shuts down.

In Figure 8 we present the results of using the mined specifications to find bugs in the **hibernate2** program. Each "false positive" or "real error" represents a method where a trace fails to adhere to the given policy. The WML-dynamic approach is not shown because its specification accepts all of the traces by construction (thus it finds no bugs but yields no false positives).

Strauss-Full, the entire 10-state policy learned by Strauss, yields too many false positives to be effective for bug-finding. Twenty-five of the false positives are from traces along which **S.close** occurs after a sequence of "work" that the specification fails to accept. However, since the specification also has many accepting states (in particular, the state after SF.openSession accepts), errors involving forgetting S.close are not reported.

Strauss-Cored, the sliced policy shown in Figure 3, gives a reduced number of false positives compared to Strauss-Full, but still suffers from the same problems. However, Strauss-Cored is able to find 46 methods in which openSession is called but close is not (and 4 false positives involving openSession).

ECC, using specification #1 (the policy with the highest z-rank, see Figure 5), finds 20 methods that deal with beginTransaction improperly, 3 false positives involving beginTransaction and 27 false positives involving save. ECC specification #4 turns out not to be useful for bug finding. Its z-rank is high (28 of 30 traces that mention a also mention b), but it only occurs at one point in the source code. Either the z-rank$|_N$ or our ranking would rank it much lower ($N_a = 1, N_{ab} = 1$).

Mining Technique	False Positives	Real Errors
Strauss-Full	27	0
Strauss-Cored	20	46
ECC #1	30	20
ECC #4	1	0
WN #3	4	46
WN #6	3	20
WML-static	9	0
JIST	1	0

Fig. 8. Comparison of miner bug-finding power for hibernate2 Session policies. "False Positives" are methods that violate the mined policy but are actually correct. "Real Errors" are buggy methods that violate the mined policy

Our method using specification #3 finds all 46 of the Session leaks found by Strauss-Cored (and the same four false positives). In fact, the Strauss-Cored report is a superset of the WN #3 report. Using specification #6 we are able to find the 20 methods with commit and rollback mistakes that are also found by ECC. Along 20 of the 23 error paths we report in which beginTransaction occurs but commit does not, rollback does not either. The ECC #1 report is a superset of the WN #6 report (but with additional false positives).

Neither the WML-static nor the JIST specification lead to the discovery of any bugs in this example. No traces contain S.discon followed by S.discon, for example (or indeed any other erroneous violations of this typestate specification). The JIST specification yields fewer false positives because it more accurately represents the underlying Session typestate.

We conclude from these experiments that (1) the various techniques produce different kinds of specifications, in accordance with their assumptions about how programmers make mistakes and (2) not all of the assumptions underlying these miners were born out by this example (such as the assumption that typestate would be explicitly and simply represented or assumptions about event frequency). WML-static and JIST were both able to find an undocumented typestate specification. Their low false positive count shows that they were able to form specifications that were permissive enough to accept most client behaviors. Strauss, ECC and our technique were all good at yielding specifications that found bugs. Our technique found all bugs reported by other techniques on this example and did so with the fewest false positives.

Program	Lines of Code	WN (our miner)		ECC			Library Policy Bugs
		Real Specs	Bugs via Specs	Real Specs	Total Specs	Bugs via Specs	
infinity 1.28	28k	1 / 10	4	0 / 227	6468	0	14
hibernate2 2.0b4	57k	9 / 51	93	3 / 424	9591	21	13
axion 1.0m2	65k	8 / 25	45	0 / 96	4159	0	15
hsqldb 1.7.1	71k	7 / 62	35	0 / 224	5032	0	18
cayenne 1.0b4	86k	5 / 35	18	3 / 311	8432	8	17
sablecc 2.17.4	99k	0 / 4	0	0 / 80	2506	0	3
jboss 3.0.6	107k	11 / 114	94	2 / 444	12852	4	40
mckoi-sql 1.0.2	118k	19 / 156	69	2 / 346	10860	5	37
ptolemy2 3.0.2	362k	9 / 192	72	3 / 656	23522	12	27
total	993k	69 / 649	430	13 / 2808	83422	50	172

Fig. 9. Bugs found with specifications mined by ECC and our technique. The "Real Specs" column counts valid specifications (determined by manual inspection) against candidate specifications. For WN, all candidate policies were inspected. For ECC, only candidates with non-negative z-rank were inspected. The "Total Specs" column counts all policies reported by ECC. The "Bugs via Specs" column counts methods that violate the "Real Specs". Finally, the last column counts methods violating a generic "library"-based policy that was applied equally to all programs

6.2   Bug Finding and Candidate Specification Ranking

Figure 9 compares our technique and the ECC technique on various benchmarks. The benchmarks were chosen for ease of comparison with previous work, and may favor the "a must be followed by b" specifications that both WN and ECC are designed to mine. We also compare the bugs found via specification mining to the bugs found via the generic "library" specifications we used in our previous work [13]. The library policies were two- to four-state FSMs describing network connections, database locks and file handles. We are unable to directly compare the other techniques because of the cost involved in manually specifying classes, predicates, and other parameters in advance.

ECC is able to find 4 specifications missed by our algorithm. In one of these examples, the b event never occurs in any error handling code (and thus does not meet our ex requirement). Removing the ex requirement causes our algorithm to produce 1,114 candidate specifications for hibernate2 alone. Given the paucity of real specifications that are filtered by the requirement and the plethora of false positives that it avoids, we believe that basing our algorithm on exceptional control flow paths was a good decision.

Of the 69 real specifications we found, 24 involved methods from separate classes, arguing against class-based module requirements. Only one valid specification involved methods from different libraries. On the other hand, for example, 30 of the first 100 false positive specifications reported by ECC for axion could have been avoided with our sp package-level module requirement. We believe these results argue strongly in favor of package-level requirements.

A common false positive for ECC paired the family of methods `ListIterator.hasNext` and `ListIterator.next`. The vast majority of paths that contain the former also contain the latter, and iterators occur frequently, causing the z-rank (whether restricted to normal traces or not) for such pairs to be high (`iterator` specifications occur as one of the top five candidates for ECC on six of our nine programs).

A common false positive for our technique paired `read` or `write` (instead of `open`) with `close`. As the ⟨`flush`, `close`⟩ data in Figure 2 demonstrate, work functions like `read` are almost invariably followed by `close` if they are present, but the more desirable `open`-based specification usually ranks higher.

Almost every valid specification our technique found was listed somewhere in ECC's voluminous output of candidate specifications. For example, our 59th candidate `jboss` policy finds four real errors and is #9522 on the ECC list (z-rank$= -54$, z-rank$|_N = -29$).

Figure 10 shows the number of bugs found as a function of the ranking used to sort candidate specifications produced by our algorithm. Compared to the z-rank, our ranking only required 42% of the specifications to be inspected (instead of 72%) in order to find two-thirds of the bugs. However, we conclude that since various rankings work only moderately better than a random shuffle, it is very important to produce a small number of extraneous candidates.

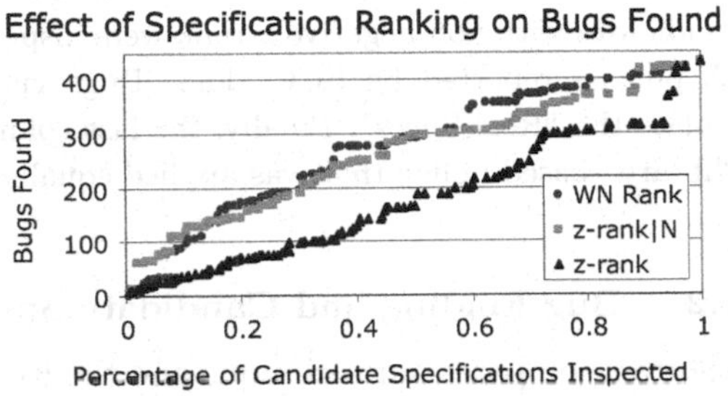

Our results for ECC are consistent with, but slightly better

Fig. 10. Bugs found as a function of the rank order in which candidate specifications are inspected. "WN Rank" is $N_{ab}/(N_a + N_{ab})$, the ranking used by our algorithm, "z-rank$|_N$" is the z-statistic restricted to normal traces and "z-rank" is the z-statistic

than, previously published figures in which 23 errors were found via specification mining on the Linux 2.4.1 kernel (about 840k LOC) [7]. ECC was designed to target C operating systems code. It actually performs better (in errors found per line of code) in this domain than in their reported experiments, although there is no reason to believe that the bug density should be the same.

One additional consideration is the utility of the found bugs. Evaluating the importance of a bug is beyond the scope of this work. Our mining technique favors resource leaks and forgotten obligations. One of the authors of `ptolemy2` was willing to rank resource leaks we found on his own scale. For that program, 11% of the bugs we reported were in tutorials or third-party code, 44% of them rated a 3 out of 5 for taking place in "little used, experimental code", 19% of them rated a 4 out of 5 and were "definitely a bug in code that is used more often", and 26% of them rated a 5 out of 5 and were "definitely a bug in code that is used often." We cannot claim that this breakdown generalizes, but it does provide one concrete example.

Using our miner to find bugs was decidely better than using generic library policies. We found 430 bugs using mined policies compared to 172 using generic ones. We found 380 more bugs and 56 more policies than ECC using 2000 fewer candidate specifications. This highlights the practical importance of our algorithmic assumptions, in particular our use of exceptional control flow.

7   Conclusions

As automatic program verification tools become more prevalent, specifications become the limiting factor in verification efforts, and specification mining for the purposes of finding bugs becomes more important. Given a program, a specification miner emits candidate policies that describe real or common program behavior. We propose a novel miner that uses information about exceptional paths. We compare the bug-finding power of various miners. In 1 million lines of Java code, we found 430 bugs using mined specifications compared to 172 using generic "library"-based ones, and we found more bugs than comparable mining algorithms. Our experiments highlighted the relative unimportance of candidate ranking and the practical importance of our algorithmic assumptions, in particular our use of exceptional control flow for specification mining.

Acknowledgments

We are indebted to Ras Bodik, Glenn Ammons and Dave Mandelin for insightful discussions and for setting up Strauss for our experiments. We thank Dawson Engler for enlightening discussions about his technique, z-ranking, and expected results. We thank John Whaley for providing us with the joeq source code and pointers for running WML. Finally, we thank Rajeev Alur for providing a number of examples of JIST in action.

References

1. R. Alur, P. Cerny, P. Madhusudan, and W. Nam. Synthesis of interface specifications for Java classes. In *Principles of Programming Languages*, 2005.
2. G. Ammons, R. Bodik, and J. R. Larus. Mining specifications. In *Principles of Programming Languages*, pages 4–16, 2002.
3. G. Ammons, D. Mandein, R. Bodik, and J. Larus. Debugging temporal specifications with concept analysis. In *Programming Language Design and Implementation*, San Diego, California, June 2003.
4. T. Ball and S. K. Rajamani. Automatically validating temporal safety properties of interfaces. In *SPIN 2001, Workshop on Model Checking of Software*, volume 2057 of *Lecture Notes in Computer Science*, pages 103–122, May 2001.
5. M. Das, S. Lerner, and M. Seigle. ESP: path-sensitive program verification in polynomial time. *SIGPLAN Notices*, 37(5):57–68, 2002.

6. R. DeLine and M. Fähndrich. Enforcing high-level protocols in low-level software. In *Programming Language Design and Implementation*, pages 59–69, 2001.
7. D. R. Engler, D. Y. Chen, and A. Chou. Bugs as inconsistent behavior: A general approach to inferring errors in systems code. In *Symposium on Operating Systems Principles*, pages 57–72, 2001.
8. D. Freedman, R. Pisani, and R. Purves. *Statistics*. W. W. Norton, 1998.
9. Hibernate. Object/relational mapping and transparent object persistence for Java and SQL databases. In *http://www.hibernate.org/*, July 2004.
10. B. Liblit, A. Aiken, A. X. Zheng, and M. I. Jordan. Bug isolation via remote program sampling. In *Programming Language Design and Implementation*, San Diego, California, June 9–11 2003.
11. G. C. Necula, S. McPeak, and W. Weimer. CCured: Type-safe retrofitting of legacy code. In *Principles of Programming Languages*, pages 128–139. ACM, Jan. 2002.
12. S. Savage, M. Burrows, G. Nelson, P. Sobalvarro, and T. Anderson. Eraser: A dynamic data race detector for multithreaded programs. *ACM Transactions on Computer Systems*, 15(4):391–411, 1997.
13. W. Weimer and G. Necula. Finding and preventing run-time error handling mistakes. In *Object-Oriented Programming, Systems, Languages, and Applications*, Vancouver, British Columbia, Canada, Oct. 2004.
14. J. Whaley, M. C. Martin, and M. S. Lam. Automatic extraction of object-oriented component interfaces. In *International Symposium of Software Testing and Analysis*, 2002.

A New Algorithm for Strategy Synthesis in LTL Games

Aidan Harding[1], Mark Ryan[1], and Pierre-Yves Schobbens[2]

[1] School of Computer Science, The University of Birmingham, Edgbaston,
Birmingham B15 2TT, UK
[2] Institut d'Informatique, Facultés Universitaires de Namur, Rue Grandgagnage 21,
5000 Namur, Belgium

Abstract. The automatic synthesis of programs from their specifications has been a dream of many researchers for decades. If we restrict
to open finite-state reactive systems, the specification is often presented
as an ATL or LTL formula interpreted over a finite-state game. The required program is then a strategy for winning this game. A theoretically
optimal solution to this problem was proposed by Pnueli and Rosner, but
has never given good results in practice. This is due to the 2EXPTIME-
complete complexity of the problem, and the intricate nature of Pnueli
and Rosner's solution. A key difficulty in their procedure is the determinisation of Büchi automata. In this paper we look at an alternative
approach which avoids determinisation, using instead a procedure that
is amenable to symbolic methods. Using an implementation based on
the BDD package CuDD, we demonstrate its scalability in a number of
examples. Furthermore, we show a class of problems for which our algorithm is singly exponential. Our solution, however, is not complete; we
prove a condition which guarantees completeness and argue by empirical
evidence that examples for which it is not complete are rare enough to
make our solution a useful tool.

1 Introduction

Finite-state reactive systems occur in many critical areas of computing. They can
be found in places such as network communication protocols, digital circuits, and
industrial control systems. Their use in systems which involve concurrency and
their interaction with unpredictable or hostile environments makes reactive systems notoriously hard to write correctly. By considering such systems as games
we can distinguish between events that we can control (inside the program) and
events that we cannot (the environment). This gives a more realistic framework
for reasoning about them than the conventional approach of "closing" the system
by adding a restricted environment and treating all choices uniformly.

We take the stance that closing an open system for verification or synthesis
is imprecise and that reasoning with game semantics provides a much better
solution. This stance has been advocated by many other researchers [1, 9, 10,
8], but there are some verification and synthesis problems that become much

N. Halbwachs and L. Zuck (Eds.): TACAS 2005, LNCS 3440, pp. 477–492, 2005.

harder in the game-theoretic world. In particular the problems of synthesis and verification for games with LTL winning conditions are 2EXPTIME-complete [12, 13]. This high complexity and the intricacy of the solution offered by Pnueli and Rosner have meant that despite the wealth of potential applications, there has been no implementation of synthesis for LTL games. We address this problem by providing a novel algorithm which avoids a major difficulty of the classical approach: the determinisation of Büchi automata. The best known method for this determinisation is due to Safra [14] and this method has been proven to be optimal [11] but has resisted efforts at efficient symbolic implementation [17]. Instead of trying to determinise a Büchi automaton, our algorithm uses a "shift automaton" to track the possible states that the Büchi automaton could be in and retake non-deterministic choices if they turn out to be wrong. The shift automaton is of roughly equal size to the deterministic automaton produced by Safra's algorithm, but it can be constructed symbolically. This has allowed for the construction of an efficient implementation using BDDs. In this paper we describe in detail a new algorithm for the synthesis of strategies in LTL games; we describe some small problems that can be solved by the implementation of this algorithm; and finally we give some performance data obtained by parameterising the given examples.

2 ω-Automata and Infinite Games

We quickly review the definitions and establish notations for writing about ω-automata and infinite games. Detailed information on ω-automata can be found in [18]; and information on infinite games can be found from [8] and [19].

Given an alphabet Σ, we denote the set of all finite words made from letters in Σ as Σ^*, and the set of all ω-words (infinte words) as Σ^ω. For a word $\lambda \in \Sigma^\omega$, we write $\lambda[i]$ for the i-th letter, $\lambda[i, j]$ for the finite section of the word from point i to j, and $\lambda[i, \infty]$ for the infinte suffix from point i. ω-automata provide a way of recognising sets of ω-words. An ω-automaton $\mathcal{A} = \langle Q_\mathcal{A}, i_\mathcal{A}, \delta_\mathcal{A}, Acc \rangle$ is a tuple where the component parts are as follows: $Q_\mathcal{A}$ is a finite set of states; $i_\mathcal{A}$ is an initial state; $\delta_\mathcal{A} : Q_\mathcal{A} \times \Sigma \mapsto 2^{Q_\mathcal{A}}$ is a transition function (we may define $\delta_\mathcal{A} : Q_\mathcal{A} \times \Sigma \mapsto Q_\mathcal{A}$ for deterministic automata); and Acc is an acceptance condition. A run ρ of an ω-automaton on a word λ is an infinite sequence of states such that $\rho[0] = i_\mathcal{A}$ and for all $i \geq 0$ $\rho[i + 1] \in \delta_\mathcal{A}(\rho[i], \lambda[i])$. We denote the set of states that occur infintely often on a run ρ by $In(\rho)$. In this paper we are concerned with two types of ω-automata: Büchi automata and Rabin automata. We write DB for a deterministic Büchi automaton and NB for a non-deterministic Büchi automaton. The acceptance condition in a Büchi automaton is a set $F \subseteq Q_\mathcal{A}$ and a word λ is accepted if and only if there is a run ρ on λ such that $In(\rho) \cap F \neq \emptyset$. The acceptance condition on a Rabin automaton is a set of pairs $\{(E_0, F_0), \ldots, (E_n, F_n)\}$ and a word λ is accepted if and only if there is a run ρ on λ such that there exists $i \in [0, n]$ such that $In(\rho) \cap F_i \neq \emptyset$ and $In(\rho) \cap E_i = \emptyset$.

An infinite game is a tuple $G = \langle Q_G, i_G, Q_P, Q_A, \delta_G \rangle$ representing a two-player game between the protagonist P and the antagonist A. Q_G is a set of states from which i_G is the initial one; Q_P and Q_A partition Q_G into turns for P and A, respectively; $\delta_G : Q_G \mapsto 2^{Q_G}$ is a transition function such that $\forall q \in Q_P \; \delta_G(q) \subseteq Q_A$ and $\forall q \in Q_A \; \delta_G(q) \subseteq Q_P$ i.e. the players alternate turns. A play of the game is an infinite sequence λ of states from Q_G such that $\lambda[0] = i_G$ and for all $i \geq 0 \; \lambda[i + 1] \in \delta_G(\lambda[i])$. We formalise the capabilites of players in the game with the notion of strategies. A strategy $f : Q_G^+ \mapsto 2^{Q_G}$ for P restricts the choices of P by prescribing how he should play his moves. We require that for any play λ and all $i \geq 0 \; f(\lambda[0, i]) \subseteq \delta_G(\lambda[i])$. The set of outcomes $out(f, q_0)$ of playing a strategy f from a state q_0 is defined as

$$out(f, q_0) = \{q_0, q_1, \ldots \mid \forall i \geq 0 \text{ if } (q_i \in Q_P) \; q_{i+1} \in f(q_0, \ldots, q_i)$$
$$\text{else } q_{i+1} \in \delta_G(q_i)\}$$

We also use partial strategies which are partial functions with the same type as a normal strategy. The set of outcomes of a partial strategy is defined as:

$$out(f, q_0) = \{q_0, q_1, \ldots \mid \forall i \geq 0 \text{ if } (q_i \in Q_P \wedge f(q_0, \ldots, q_i) \text{ defined})$$
$$q_{i+1} \in f(q_0, \ldots, q_i) \text{ else } q_{i+1} \in \delta_G(q_i)\}$$

When a game is provided with a winning condition $\widehat{W}$, we say that P can win the game if and only if there is a strategy (partial or complete) for P such that all outcomes of the strategy satisfy W.

3   Synthesis for NB Games

The main algorithm in our synthesis procedure takes as input a game $G = \langle Q_G, i_G, Q_P, Q_A, \delta_G \rangle$ and a winning condition in the form of a Büchi automaton, $B = \langle Q_B, i_B, \delta_B, F_B \rangle$. The algorithm identifies a set of states that are winning for P and produces a partial strategy (partial because it may be undefined from states which are not winning for P) such that the set of outcomes of the strategy from any winning state are accepted by B.

To see why the conventional approach uses determinisation, let us consider an approach which uses an obvious extension of the algorithm used for games with Büchi winning conditions [19]. A Büchi winning condition (as opposed to a winning condition specified by a NB) specifies a set $F_G \subseteq Q_G$ such that plays are winning for P if and only if they visit F_G infinitely often. The solution for these games offered in [19] is a game-theoretic extension of the algorithm proposed by Emerson and Lei for finding fair strongly connected components [7]. This algorithm is attractive as it has shown to be quite efficient when compared against other symbolic fair cycle detection algorithms [16]. It works by finding the set of states from where P has a strategy to reach F_G, then the states where P has a strategy to reach F_G and from there has a strategy to reach F_G again etc. An increasing number of visits to F_G are required until a fixed-point is achieved whereupon we know that P has a strategy to visit F_G infinitely often.

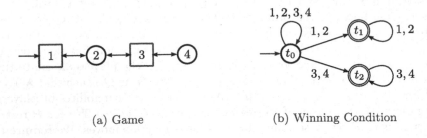

(a) Game   (b) Winning Condition

Fig. 1. A game where the winning condition "needs" determinisation. Square states are P's moves, circles are A's

The game-theoretic aspect of the algorithm in [19] works by adapting the notion of predecessor to enforce that a state in Q_P is winning if there exists a winning successor, and a state in Q_A is winning if all successors are winning.

We could try to perform the same computation over $G \times B$, always evaluating the B component existentially. However, there is an assumption in this algorithm that winning is transitive i.e. the states along a winning path are winning themselves. Whilst this may seem like a natural thing to expect, it is not actually true. The game and specification in Figure 1 give an example of how winning can fail to be transitive in this sense. P has only one choice which comes at state 3; he can win this game by always choosing $3 \rightarrow 4$ if he gets that choice. Although there is a winning strategy from $(1, t_0)$, if we follow that strategy and, at the same time, try to construct a winning run from the B part, we cannot be sure to reach a state from where there is another winning strategy. The opponent can stay in $\{(1, t_?), (2, t_?)\}$ as long as he likes and we must choose what to do with the Büchi component. We cannot allow the Büchi automaton to visit t_1 in case the opponent later chooses 3. So we either have a losing run in the Büchi component, $((1, t_0)(2, t_0))^\omega$ or reach $\{(1, t_1), (2, t_1)\}$ from where there is no winning strategy (A chooses 3 and B is stuck). On this basis, $(1, t_0)$ would not be identified as winning because P cannot be sure to reach a state in $Q_G \times F_B$ from where he has a winning strategy.

Our solution to this is to allow some "shifting" between Büchi states. If the Büchi automaton is in a dead-end state, we now allow the transition relation to be overridden by making a shift i.e make a transition as if the Büchi automaton were in a different state. We maintain the set of reachable Büchi states at all times, and this provides the justification for shifts – whenever a shift is made, it is made to some reachable state and, thus, is equivalent to retaking some earlier non-deterministic choices. The set of reachable states is provided by the shift automaton, $S = \langle Q_S, i_S, \delta_S \rangle$, a deterministic automaton derived from B with the subset construction where each state in Q_S represents a set of states from Q_B:

$$Q_S = \mathcal{P}(Q_B) \qquad i_S = \{i_B\} \qquad \delta_S(\phi, q) = \{t' \mid \exists t \in \phi. t' \in \delta_B(t, q)\} \qquad (1)$$

Accordingly, we define the synthesis algorithm over $G \times B \times S$. We call this product the *composite*, C, and define some shorthands to ease the burden of notation:

$$Q_C = Q_G \times Q_B \times Q_S \tag{2}$$

$$F_C = \{(q, t, \phi) \in Q_C \mid t \in F_B\} \tag{3}$$

$$Q_{CP} = \{(q, t, \phi) \in Q_C \mid q \in Q_{GP}\} \tag{4}$$

$$Q_{CA} = \{(q, t, \phi) \in Q_C \mid q \in Q_{GA}\} \tag{5}$$

Now, if we are in a situation such as the one in Figure 1, we can make winning transitive by allowing some shifts. The informal argument is as follows: From $(1, t_0, \{t_0\})$ we always go to $(2, t_1, \{t_0, t_1\})$ because we are optimistic about getting an accepting run in the B component. If the opponent always chooses $2 \to 1$, then we have an accepting run made up of $(1, t_0, \{t_0\})$ $((2, t_1, \{t_0, t_1\})$ $(1, t_0, \{t_0, t_1\}))^\omega$. If the opponent eventually chooses $2 \to 3$, then we take a shift: In state $(2, t_1, \{t_0, t_1\})$ the B component could have been in t_0, so when the opponent chooses 3 we make a shift and take the $t_0 \to^3 t_2$ transition i.e. we go to $(3, t_2, \{t_0, t_2\})$. From here, P can win and we end up with an overall winning path made up by $(1, t_0, \{t_0\})((2, t_1, \{t_0, t_1\})(1, t_0, \{t_0, t_1\}))^*(2, t_1, \{t_0, t_1\})$ $((3, t_2, \{t_0, t_2\})$ $(4, t_2, \{t_0, t_2\}))^\omega$.

Shifting helps the issue of completeness, but allowing an infinite number of shifts would be unsound. However, if shifting is only allowed finitely often, the language is not changed. Informally we justify this on the basis that acceptance is evaluated over infinite paths, and although shifting may allow finitely many extra visits to F_C, paths must eventually have no more shifts and thus would be accepting without any shifting. The soundness of finite shifting is implied by Theorem 2.

To write down the main synthesis algorithm with finite shifting, we first define two predecessor functions pre_P and pre_A. These are evaluated over the triple state-space of $G \times B \times S$, respecting the alternation of the game and allowing for shifting. Unlike a conventional predecessor function, two arguments are supplied. The second argument is a set that we allow shifts into. $pre_P(X, W)$ is the set of transitions which obey the game and shift automaton, and either have a transition in B to reach X ($t' \in \delta_B(t, q') \wedge (q', t', \phi') \in X$ in Equation 6) or have a shift justified by the shift automaton to reach W ($t' \in \phi' \wedge (q', t', \phi') \in W$ in Equation 6). $pre_A(X, W)$ simply uses $pre_P(X, W)$ as an approximation, and then makes sure that there is a good transition for every possible game-successor.

$$pre_P(X, W) = \{\langle (q, t, \phi), (q', t', \phi') \rangle \mid q' \in \delta_G(q), \phi' = \delta_S(\phi, q'),$$
$$(t' \in \delta_B(t, q') \wedge (q', t', \phi') \in X) \vee (t' \in \phi' \wedge (q', t', \phi') \in W)\} \tag{6}$$

$$pre_A(X, W) = \{\langle (q, t, \phi), (q', t', \phi') \rangle \in pre_P(X, W) \mid \forall q'_2 \in \delta_G(q)$$
$$\exists \langle (q, t, \phi), (q'_2, t'_2, \phi'_2) \rangle \in pre_P(X, W)\} \tag{7}$$

Using these definitions, we write the main algorithm in Figure 2[1]. To understand how the synthesis algorithm works, consider each of the variables in turn:

---

[1] We denote the k-th projection of a tuple T by $\pi_k(T)$

```
1    w_0 := ∅;
2    δ_{F,0,∞,∞} := ∅;
3    repeat counted by j = 1 ...
4        z_{j,0} := Q_C;
5        repeat counted by k = 1 ...
6            τ_{j,k} := z_{j,k-1} ∩ F_C;
7            s_{j,k,0} := ∅;
8            δ_{Fj,k,0} := δ_{Fj-1,∞,∞};
9            repeat counted by l = 1 ...
10               u_A := pre_A(τ_{j,k} ∪ s_{j,k,l-1}, w_{j-1}) ∩ (Q_{CA} × Q_{CV});
11               u_V := pre_V(τ_{j,k} ∪ s_{j,k,l-1}, w_{j-1}) ∩ (Q_{CV} × Q_{CA});
12               δ_{Fj,k,l} := δ_{Fj,k,l-1} ∪ {⟨(q,t,φ),(q',t',φ')⟩ ∈ u_A ∪ u_V
                                     | (q,t,φ) ∉ π_1(δ_{Fj,k,l-1})};
13               s_{j,k,l} := s_{j,k,l-1} ∪ π_1(u_A) ∪ π_1(u_V);
14           until s_{j,k,l} = s_{j,k,l-1}
15           z_{j,k} := z_{j,k-1} ∩ s_{j,k,∞};
16       until z_{j,k} = z_{j,k-1}
17       w_j := w_{j-1} ∪ z_{j,∞};
18   until w_j = w_{j-1}
```

Fig. 2. Synthesis algorithm with finite shifting

- w_j: At the end of the algorithm, this will contain the set of winning states. The j subscript is the maximum number of shifts required to win from a state in w_j.
- $z_{j,k}$: At the end of the middle loop, this is the set of states from where every outcome reaches $z_{j,k} \cap F_C$ infinitely often with no shifting or just reaches w_{j-1} (possibly by shifting). During the middle loop, every outcome reaches $z_{j,k-1} \cap F_C$ with no shifting or w_{j-1} (possibly by shifting).
- $τ_{j,k}$: The "target" for the innermost loop. This variable could be substituted for its definition at each use, it is clearer (and more efficient in implementation) to write separately.
- $s_{j,k,l}$: The set of states from where P can be sure to reach $τ_{j,k}$ in l steps with no shifting or w_{j-1} in l steps with a shift.
- $δ_{F,j,k,l}$: The partial strategy as it is synthesised. On the first j-loop it will be a strategy to win with no shifting. On line 12 we must be careful not to overwrite old moves. On iteration l of the inner loop, when a transition is first added to the strategy it must go into $s_{j,k,l-1} \cup τ_{j,k}$ or w_{j-1}. However, this state will be rediscovered on later iteration of the inner loop and u_P/u_A may contain transitions which do not make progress towards an accepting state and we must therefore keep the transition from the first discovery. Having built a strategy with no shifts, we carry this forward to the next iteration of the j-loop. Here another strategy is built up, but this time it allows the possibility of a shift to w_{j-1} since we already have a winning strategy from there. New moves are written for states in $w_j - w_{j-1}$, but as soon as the strategy reaches w_{j-1} the old strategy takes over.

The algorithm in Figure 2 is computing nested fixed-points which can be characterised as $\mu w.\nu z.\mu s.\pi_1((pre_P(s \vee (z \wedge F_C), w) \wedge (Q_{CP} \times Q_{CA})) \vee (pre_A(s \vee (z \wedge F_C), w) \wedge (Q_{CA} \times Q_{CP}))$. We note that on the first iteration of the outer loop in this algorithm, the computation performed is the naïve extension of the solution for Büchi games i.e. $\nu z.\mu s.\pi_1((pre_P(s \vee (z \wedge F_C), \bot) \wedge (Q_{CP} \times Q_{CA})) \vee (pre_A(s \vee (z \wedge F_C), \bot) \wedge (Q_{CA} \times Q_{CP}))$. This calculation does not depend on the shift automaton and, in this way, we are sometimes able to perform the strategy synthesis without having to generate the shift automaton. We can give a precise condition which assures this by first defining trivially determinisable Büchi automata.

Definition 1. *A Büchi automaton is trivially determinisable if and only if it can be made deterministic by removing 0 or more transitions without changing its language.*

Using this definition it is possible to prove the following theorem:

Theorem 1. *For any game G, with a winning condition specified by a Büchi automaton B, if B is trivially determinisable, then all winning states for P in Q_C satisfy $\nu z.\mu s.\pi_1((pre_P(s \vee (z \wedge F_C), \bot) \wedge (Q_{CP} \times Q_{CA})) \vee (pre_A(s \vee (z \wedge F_C), \bot) \wedge (Q_{CA} \times Q_{CP}))$.*

Whilst this definition includes the shift automaton, it is clear that the predecessor functions do not depend on the shift automaton when W is empty, so this proves that if B is trivially determinisable, the algorithm can succeed without generating the shift automaton. Intuitively, this theorem holds because the naïve algorithm is complete for deterministic Büchi automata and since the transitions of B are evaluated existentially, a trivially determinisable Büchi automaton is as good as a deterministic one. In the long version of this paper, this theorem and all the other theorems that follow are proven in the appendix.

Since pre_P and pre_A are monotonic functions and the state-spaces involved in the algorithm are finite, it follows that the algorithm terminates. The algorithm's soundness is asserted by the following theorem:

Theorem 2. *Once the algorithm has terminated, for all $(q, t, \phi) \in w_\infty$, $\delta_{\mathcal{F}\infty,\infty,\infty}$ is a partial strategy such that $\forall \lambda \in out(\delta_{\mathcal{F}\infty,\infty,\infty}, (q, t, \phi))\ \pi_1(\lambda[1, \infty])$ $\in \mathcal{L}(B, \phi)$.*

In much the same way as the completeness condition in Theorem 1, we can give a condition for the algorithm in Figure 2. To do this, we introduce the concept of the *generalised Rabin expansion* of a Büchi automaton. Intuitively, this automaton encodes the idea of finite shifting by its structure and winning condition.

Definition 2. *Let B be a Büchi automaton, and S be the corresponding shift automaton for B. The generalised Rabin expansion, $R = \langle Q_R, i_R, \delta_R, F_R, E_R \rangle$, of B and S is defined as*

$$Q_R = Q_B \times Q_S$$
$$i_R = i_B \times i_S$$
$$\delta_R = \{((t, \phi), a, (t', \phi')) \in Q_R \times \Sigma \times Q_R \mid \phi' \in \delta_S(\phi, a), t' \in \phi'\}$$
$$F_R = \{(t, \phi) \in Q_R \mid t \in F_B\}$$
$$E_R = \{((t, \phi), a, (t', \phi')) \in \delta_R \mid t' \notin \delta_B(t, a)\}$$

where, in the usual way, Q_R, i_R, and δ_R are the state-space, initial state, and transition function, respectively. F_R and E_R are used to define the winning condition of R: A run ρ on a word λ is winning if and only if $\exists^\infty i \geq 0.\rho[i] \in F_R$ and $\exists j \geq 0.\forall k \geq j \ (\rho[k], \lambda[k], \rho[k+1]) \notin E_R$.

It is convenient to specify a winning condition on transitions rather than states, but it is easy to translate such an automaton into a conventional Rabin automaton. The translation could be done as follows: create a second copy of every state; make every transition in E_R go instead to the copy; make every transition in the copy go back into the original; finally, set the Rabin condition to have infinitely many visits to F_R in the original and only finitely many visits to the copied states. We also note that for any reachable state (t, ϕ) in R, the invariant is maintained that $t \in \phi$.

With this definition in place, it is possible to prove the following theorem about completeness for the synthesis algorithm.

Theorem 3. *For any game G, with a winning condition specified by a Büchi automaton B, if B's generalised Rabin expansion is trivially determinisable then all winning states for P in Q_C satisfy $\mu w.\nu z.\mu s.\pi_1((pre_P(s \vee (z \wedge F_C), w) \wedge (Q_{CP} \times Q_{CA})) \vee (pre_A(s \vee (z \wedge F_C), w) \wedge (Q_{CA} \times Q_{CP}))$.*

We note that this is a safe approximation of the class of problems for which the algorithm will be complete. In fact, the structure of the game is also crucial to completeness. Providing a characterisation which uses the structure of both the game and the specification would be an interesting avenue for future research.

4   Synthesis for LTL Games

In the previous section we provided an algorithm for solving games with NB winning conditions that was complete under a condition on the form of the NB. We can perform synthesis for LTL games by using the tableau method to translate an LTL specification into a NB and then using the algorithm in Figure 2. With the restriction of Theorem 3 and our goal of symbolic implementation in mind, our choice of translation from LTL to NB must be made wisely. The method that we use is based on the symbolic construction of [4], with three changes: First, we deal with formulae in negation normal form rather than using a minimal set of temporal operators – as noted by [15], this provides us with a slight efficiency improvement as safety formulae do not have to be treated as negated liveness formulae. Secondly, we define a weaker transition formula than [4] – this allows some types of formulae to be translated into trivially determinisable Büchi automata and allows for the last change. Finally, we split variables into "required" and "optional" forms meaning that the fairness constraints of optional formulae do not necessarily have to be met as long as some other fairness constraints are whilst the constraints of required formulae must always be met.

First we recall the syntax and semantics of LTL, a more thorough review can be found in [6]. Syntactically, we consider an LTL formula ψ in negation normal form to obey the following grammar

$$\Pi ::= p \mid \neg \Pi \mid \Pi \vee \Pi \qquad \psi ::= \Pi \mid \psi \wedge \psi \mid \psi \vee \psi \mid X\psi \mid \psi \, \mathcal{U} \, \psi \mid \psi \, \mathcal{R} \, \psi$$

where p is a member of the set of atomic propositions. The semantics of LTL are defined inductively over infinite paths λ.

- $\lambda \vDash p$ iff $p \in \lambda[0]$.
- $\lambda \vDash \neg\psi$ iff $\lambda \nvDash \psi$.
- $\lambda \vDash \psi_1 \vee \psi_2$ iff $\lambda \vDash \psi_1$ or $\lambda \vDash \psi_2$.
- $\lambda \vDash \psi_1 \, \mathcal{U} \, \psi_2$ iff $\exists i \geq 0.\lambda[i,\infty] \vDash \psi_2$ and $\forall j \in [0, i-1]\ \lambda[j,\infty] \vDash \psi_1$.
- $\lambda \vDash \psi_1 \, \mathcal{R} \, \psi_2$ iff $\forall i \geq 0$ either $\lambda[i,\infty] \vDash \psi_2$ or there exists $j \in [0,i]$ such that $\lambda[j,\infty] \vDash \psi_1 \wedge \psi_2$.

Like [4], we define a function el() to return the set of elementary sub-formulae of an LTL formula. The set $\mathrm{el}(\psi)$ forms the set of propositions in the tableau for ψ.

- $\mathrm{el}(p) = \{p\}$
- $\mathrm{el}(\neg\psi) = \mathrm{el}(\psi)$
- $\mathrm{el}(\psi_1 \wedge \psi_2) = \mathrm{el}(\psi_1) \cup \mathrm{el}(\psi_2)$
- $\mathrm{el}(X\psi_1) = \{(X\psi_1)^r\} \cup \mathrm{el}(\psi_1)$
- $\mathrm{el}(\psi_1 \vee \psi_2) = \mathrm{el}(\psi_1) \cup \mathrm{el}(\psi_2) \cup \{x^o \mid x^r \in \mathrm{el}(\psi_1) \cup \mathrm{el}(\psi_2)\}$
- $\mathrm{el}(\psi_1 \, \mathcal{U} \, \psi_2) = \{(X(\psi_1 \, \mathcal{U} \, \psi_2))^r\} \cup \mathrm{el}(\psi_1) \cup \mathrm{el}(\psi_2)$
- $\mathrm{el}(\psi_1 \, \mathcal{R} \, \psi_2) = \{(X(\psi_1 \, \mathcal{R} \, \psi_2))^r\} \cup \mathrm{el}(\psi_1) \cup \mathrm{el}(\psi_2)$.

We see from this that the propositions arising from formulae under an $\vee$ appear in optional and required forms. This is how the optional formation is used – in a formula $\psi_1 \vee \psi_2$ the conventional tableau construction would generate an automaton which chooses between three covering formulae: $\psi_1 \wedge \neg\psi_2$, $\neg\psi_1 \wedge \psi_2$, and $\psi_1 \wedge \psi_2$. In a game where the opponent can infinitely often choose between satisfying the fairness constraints of ψ_1 or ψ_2, this splitting can necessitate infinite shifting for the algorithm in Figure 2. By making the fairness constraints optional, we allow the tableau to follow the $\psi_1 \wedge \psi_2$ path as long as the play is consistent with the safety requirements of $\psi_1 \wedge \psi_2$ and consider the play to be accepted if it satisfies either the fairness constraints of ψ_1 or the fairness constraints of ψ_2.

Again like [4], we define a function sat() which takes an LTL formula and returns a formula representing the set of states in the tableau for which outgoing fair paths are labelled by plays which satisfy the LTL formula. It works uniformly for all $t \in \{r, o\}$. The only change from the standard definition is in

$\text{sat}((\psi_1 \vee \psi_2)^r)$; here we always allow the possibility of the optional versions being taken instead of the required ones. Since the clause for the optional variables is $(\text{sat}(\psi_1^o) \wedge \text{sat}(\psi_2^o))$, the structure of the tableau ensures that paths are consistent with both formulae (i.e. they satisfy the non-fairness part of the formulae). Our new definition of the fairness constraints will allow one or the other to be satisfied. For all $t \in \{r, o\}$, $\text{sat}(\psi^t)$ is defined as:

- $\text{sat}(\Pi^t) = \Pi$
- $\text{sat}((\psi_1 \wedge \psi_2)^t) = \text{sat}(\psi_1^t) \wedge \text{sat}(\psi_2^t)$
- $\text{sat}((\psi_1 \vee \psi_2)^t) = \text{sat}(\psi_1^t) \vee \text{sat}(\psi_2^t) \vee (\text{sat}(\psi_1^o) \wedge \text{sat}(\psi_2^o))$
- $\text{sat}((X\psi_1)^t) = (X\psi_1)^t$
- $\text{sat}((\psi_1 \, \mathcal{U} \, \psi_2)^t) = \text{sat}(\psi_2^t) \vee (\text{sat}(\psi_1^t) \wedge X(\psi_1 \, \mathcal{U} \, \psi_2)^t)$
- $\text{sat}((\psi_1 \, \mathcal{R} \, \psi_2)^t) = (\text{sat}(\psi_1^t) \wedge \text{sat}(\psi_2^t)) \vee (\text{sat}(\psi_2^t) \wedge X(\psi_1 \, \mathcal{R} \, \psi_2)^t)$.

The transition relation ensures that if $X\psi$ occurs in a state, all fair paths from all successors of that state satisfy ψ.

$$\bigwedge_{t \in \{r, o\}} \bigwedge_{(X\psi_1)^t \in \text{el}(\psi^r)} (X\psi_1)^t \Rightarrow \text{sat}(\psi_1^t)'. \tag{8}$$

This differs from [4] by the inclusions of optional/required tags and by using $\Rightarrow$ instead of $\Leftrightarrow$. This relaxation is possible because the input formulae are in negation normal form and its soundness is implied by Theorem 4.

The fairness constraints on the tableau are defined by another new function, fsat(). Conventionally, the fairness constraints for a formula ψ would require that for each sub-formula of the form $\psi_1 \, \mathcal{U} \, \psi_2$ a fair path infinitely often has either $\neg X(\psi_1 \, \mathcal{U} \, \psi_2)$ or $\text{sat}(\psi_2)$ i.e. at any point, either $\psi_1 \, \mathcal{U} \, \psi_2$ is not required or it is eventually satisfied. Our definition of fsat is based on this notion, but allows for the special case of optional variables. Fairness on a path π is defined by the following function:

- $\text{fsat}(\Pi^t) = \top$
- $\text{fsat}((\psi_1 \vee \psi_2)^t) = \text{fsat}(\psi_1^t) \wedge \text{fsat}(\psi_2^t) \wedge (\text{fsat}(\psi_1^o) \vee \text{fsat}(\psi_2^o))$
- $\text{fsat}((\psi_1 \wedge \psi_2)^t) = \text{fsat}(\psi_1^t) \wedge \text{fsat}(\psi_2^t)$
- $\text{fsat}((X\psi_1)^t) = \text{fsat}(\psi_1^t)$
- $\text{fsat}((\psi_1 \, \mathcal{U} \, \psi_2)^t) = \text{fsat}(\psi_1^t) \wedge \text{fsat}(\psi_2^t)$

$$\wedge \, \exists^\infty i \geq 0. \pi[i] \in \text{sat}(\psi_2^t) \vee \neg(X(\psi_1 \, \mathcal{U} \, \psi_2))^t$$

- $\text{fsat}((\psi_1 \, \mathcal{R} \, \psi_2)^t) = \text{fsat}(\psi_1^t) \wedge \text{fsat}(\psi_2^t)$.

We see that the only departure from the conventional usage (a convention observed by [4]) is in allowing one or the other of a pair of optional variables to be satisfied.

Since our construction is a relaxation of the one given by [4], we do not prove its completeness. However, its soundness is asserted by the following theorem:

Theorem 4. *Let ψ be an LTL formula over a set, $\mathcal{P}$, of atomic propositions. Let T be the symbolic tableau automaton for ψ constructed as above. For any $\psi_1 \in \text{sub}(\psi)$, any $t \in \{r, o\}$ and any path, π, in T, for all $i \geq 0$ if $\pi[i] \in \text{sat}(\psi_1^t)$ and $\pi[i, \infty]$ satisfies $\text{fsat}(\psi_1^t)$ then $\pi[i, \infty] \models \psi_1$.*

Using this tableau construction we can perform the entire synthesis procedure symbolically. First the LTL formula is translated in the manner described above. This tableau is then used as the Büchi automaton in the algorithm from Figure 2 which can also be computed symbolically. Despite the doubly exponential worst-case complexity of this procedure we shall see in the following section that useful results can be computed. First, we note that for request-response specifications [20], strategies can be synthesised without generating a shift automaton i.e. the tableau for such specifications is trivially determinisable. Request-response specifications can be written in LTL as $G(p \land (r_0 \Rightarrow Fs_0) \land \ldots \land (r_n \Rightarrow Fs_n))$ and we prove the following proposition in the appendix.

Proposition 1. *The tableau for LTL formulae of the form $G(p \land (r_0 \Rightarrow Fs_0) \land \ldots \land (r_n \Rightarrow Fs_n))$ (where p, r_i, and s_i are propositional formulae) is always trivially determinisable.*

5   Implementation

The synthesis algorithm has been implemented in Java using native calls to the CuDD [5] library to handle BDDs. As input, the program takes an XML file containing a symbolic description of the game and an LTL specification. After successful synthesis, a number of output options are possible: the program can print the set of winning states; produce an explicit graph of the winning strategy with dot; show an interactive, expandable tree of the strategy so that the user can play it out; and convert the strategy into a program in the language of the Cadence SMV model checker [3]. The output to SMV can be used to check the correctness of the implementation by checking against the original LTL specification (once a winning strategy has been synthesised, it is possible to view the strategy as a closed system and check for correctness on all paths).

5.1   Examples

Mutual Exclusion. In this example we synthesise a controller to enforce mutual exclusion. We solve this problem for various numbers of processes in order to get a measure of the scalability of the implementation, using n as the parameter for size.

The game is modelled with the following boolean variables: u indicates the current turn and alternates between moves. When u is true, it is the user processes turn, when it is false it is the system's turn. $r1, r2, \ldots, rn$ indicate that a process requesting access to its critical section. When a request is made, it cannot be withdrawn until the critical section is reached. Furthermore, when it is the system's turn, the request variables must keep their old values. $c1, c2, \ldots, cn$ indicate that a process is in its critical section. ci can only become true if it is the system's turn and ri is true. When it is true, ci will become false in the next turn.

The specification of mutual exclusion and liveness can easily be written in in LTL as

$$G(\bigwedge_{i \in [1,n]} ((ri \Rightarrow Fci) \land \bigwedge_{j \in [i+1,n]} \neg(ci \land cj)))$$

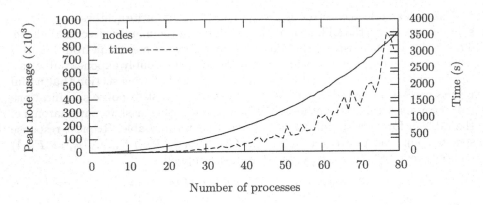

Fig. 3. Mutual exclusion performance data

For two processes, the synthesis implementation ran in about 30ms and produced a strategy which plays out Peterson's algorithm for mutual exclusion. Whenever both processes request at once, one process (say process 1) is chosen non-deterministically to proceed. From then until process 2 gets to enter its critical section, if both processes request at once then process 2 will be favoured. This behaviour is symmetric for both processes, guaranteeing that neither process starves. Strategies were found for problems with between 2 and 80 processes, recording the "peak live node usage" and time for each problem. The peak live node usage is a statistic gathered by the CuDD library denoting the maximum number of BDD nodes that have been used during a computation. The tests were run on a 1.5GHz Pentium 4 system with 256MB of RAM running Linux. The results are shown in Figure 3. We note that even with 80 processes, which gives a state-space of $2^{(80 \times 2)+1} \approx 10^{48}$ and a formula with 80 liveness sub-formulae, the time taken was about 50 minutes. This is quite reasonable for a model checking tool and the overall growth in the two plots shows the feasibility of the approach.

Lift System. Here we synthesise a controller for a lift (elevator) system. The game describes some general behaviour regarding the physical situation of a lift (there are user-controlled buttons, movement between floors is consecutive etc.), and the LTL specification puts requirements on the actual controller. We model the lift system with various numbers of floors, using n as a parameter for the size; the variables used to describe the system are: u which indicates the current turn and works as in mutual exclusion. f which indicates the current floor. This is modelled with $\lceil log(n) \rceil$ variables which we treat as a single integer variable. We write $f[0], f[1], \ldots f[n]$ to denote floors. Initially, the floor is 0; we require that transitions between floors are consecutive and that the floor does not change on users turns. $b[0], b[1], \ldots, b[n]$ are the button variables. These boolean variables are controlled by the users to simulate requests for the lift. Initially, all buttons

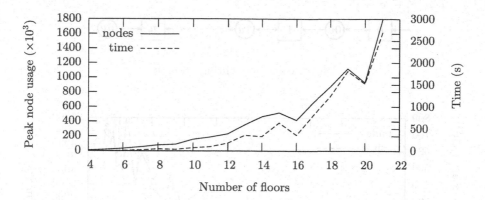

Fig. 4. Lift performance data

are off; once lit, a button stays on until the lift arrives and the buttons do not change on the system's turns. *up* is a boolean variable which observes the transition between floors and is true if the lift is going up. Initially *up* is false. The specification that we use for the lift system is as follows:

$$G\left(\left(\bigwedge_{i\in[0,n]} b[i] \Rightarrow Ff[i]\right) \wedge \bigwedge_{i\in[0,n]} f[i] \wedge \neg sb \Rightarrow f[i] \; \mathcal{U} \; (sb \; \mathcal{R} \; (F(f[0] \vee sb) \wedge \neg up))\right)\right)$$

Where *sb* is an abbreviation for $\bigvee_{i\in[1,n]} b[i]$ to mean "some button is lit". The first conjunct says that every request is eventually answered, the second demands that the lift should park when it is idle. If we synthesise a strategy without the parking specification, we find that the lift does answer all calls, but it does so by moving up and down continuously regardless of what calls are made (this was apparent from playing out the strategy and verified formally using SMV). In the second conjunct, the release formula is the actual parking action: the lift should go to $f[0]$ by going continuously down, unless some button is pressed. The rest of the formula can be read as: if the lift is on floor i and no button (other than 0) is pressed, then remain at floor i until parking can commence. Synthesising a strategy for the entire specification, we find that the lift now behaves as expected and, once again, we can verify that the strategy implements the specification by using SMV. The results for a range of sizes are plotted in Figure 4 – we see the time taken and the number of nodes used rising dramatically. This is due to the size and complexity of the specification resulting in an extremely large tableau. The fluctuations in time taken and nodes used are hard to explain. One possible cause could be the heuristic nature of the re-ordering algorithms in CuDD. Similar fluctuations are seen in the shifting example below, but they seem to be magnified here by the size of the state-space increase as each extra floor is added to the lift problem.

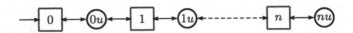

Fig. 5. Game for shifting example

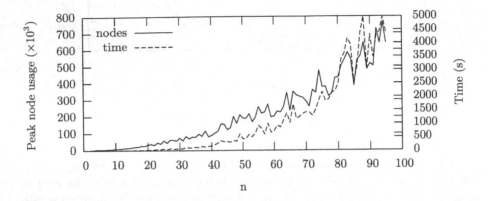

Fig. 6. Shift performance data

A Shifting Problem. The previous two examples were computed without having to use any shifting. Although a number of specifications were tried in the context of these systems, shifting was never required. It is clear that shifting is necessary for some specifications, though, so we use an abstract example based on the one from Figure 1 to measure performance in such cases. The game is shown in Figure 5.

The specification used is simply $FG0 \lor FG1 \lor \ldots \lor FGn$. For $n = 2$, this produces a tableau with the same property as the Büchi automaton in Figure 1 – it has two disjoint regions, one for $FG0$ and one for $FG1$. In order to solve this game, the algorithm needs to consider shifting. As expected, the synthesis algorithm generates a shift automaton and terminates using one shift. The winning strategy simply keeps play in 1 if the opponent ever chooses it, otherwise it has no choice but to stay in 0. Figure 6 shows the performance over a range of sizes. Even with a length of 95, and having to generate the doubly exponential shift automaton, the implementation ran in 1 hour 14 minutes.

6   Conclusion

We have provided a new algorithm and corresponding symbolic implementation to solve the problem of strategy synthesis in LTL games. Whilst this algorithm is not complete, it has performed well in the test-cases that were given to it and holds enough promise to warrant use on larger, real-world problems in the future. The separation between the partial solution to NB games and the symbolic tableau method itself offers the prospect of future improvements to the completeness result by changes to the tableau method. It would be interesting to see whether the completeness result given in terms of automata could be related back to a fragment of LTL so that it might be compared with such work as [2]. At present, there are formulae for which we know that the algorithm here does not perform optimally and there are formulae which cannot be dealt with in fragments solved by [2], but can be dealt with by our work.

References

1. R. Alur, T. A. Henzinger, and O. Kupferman. Alternating-time temporal logic. *Journal of the ACM*, 49(5):672–713, 2002.
2. R. Alur and S. La Torre. Deterministic generators and games for LTL fragments. *ACM Transactions on Computational Logic*, 5(1):1–25, January 2004.
3. SMV 10-11-02p1. http://www-cad.eecs.berkeley.edu/~kenmcmil/smv/, November 2002.
4. E. Clarke, O. Grumberg, and K. Hamaguchi. Another look at LTL model checking. In David L. Dill, editor, *CAV94*, volume 818, pages 415–427. Springer-Verlag, 1994.
5. CuDD: Colorado university decision diagram package, release 2.30. http://vlsi.colorado.edu/~fabio/CUDD/, February 2001.
6. E. A. Emerson. *Handbook of Theoretical Computer Science Volume B*, chapter Temporal and Modal Logic, pages 995–1072. Elsevier, 1990.
7. E. A. Emerson and C. Lei. Efficient model checking in fragments of the propositional model mu-calculus. In *IEEE Symposium on Logic in Computer Science*, pages 267–278, June 1986.
8. E. Grädel, W. Thomas, and T. Wilke, editors. *Automata, Logic, and Infinite Games*. Number 2500 in Lecture Notes In Computer Science. Springer, 2002.
9. S. Kremer and J.-F. Raskin. A game-based verification of non-repudiation and fair exchange protocols. *Journal Of Computer Security*, 11(3):399–429, 2003.
10. O. Kupferman and M. Y. Vardi. Module checking. In *8th Conference on Computer-Aided Verification*, volume 1102 of *LNCS*, pages 75–86, 1996.
11. C. Löding. Optimal bounds for the transformation of ω-automata. In *Proceedings of the 19th Conference on Foundations of Software Technology and Theoretical Computer Science*, number 1738 in LNCS, pages 97–109. Springer, 1999.
12. A. Pnueli and R. Rosner. On the synthesis of a reactive module. In *Proceedings Of 16th ACM Symposium On Principles Of Programming Languages*, pages 179–190, 1989.
13. R. Rosner. *Modular Synthesis of Reactive Systems*. PhD thesis, Weizmann Institute of Science, Rehovot, Israel, 1992.
14. S. Safra. *Complexity of Automata on Infinite Objects*. PhD thesis, The Weizmann Institute of Science, Rehovot, Israel, March 1989.
15. K. Schneider. Improving automata generation for linear temporal logic by considering the automaton hierarchy. *Lecture Notes in Computer Science*, 2250, 2001.
16. F. Somenzi, K. Ravi, and R. Bloem. Analysis of symbolic scc hull algorithms. In *Proceedings of the 4th International Conference on Formal Methods in Computer-Aided Design*, pages 88–105. Springer-Verlag, 2002.

17. S. Tasiran, R. Hojati, and R. K. Brayton. Language containment using nondeterministic omega-automata. In *Proceedings of Advanced Research Working Conference on Correct Hardware Design and Verification Methods, CHARME'95*, number 987 in Lecture Notes In Computer Science, pages 261–277, 1995.
18. W. Thomas. *Handbook of Theoretical Computer Science Volume B*, chapter Automata on Infinite Objects, pages 133–192. Elsevier, 1990.
19. W. Thomas. On the synthesis of strategies in infinite games. In *Symposium on Theoretical Aspects of Computer Science*, pages 1–13, 1995.
20. N. Wallmeier, P. Hütten, and W. Thomas. Symbolic synthesis of finite-state controllers for request-response specifications. In *Proceedings of the 8th International Conference on the Implementation and Application of Automata, CIAA*, volume 2759 of *Lecture Notes in Computer Science*, pages 11–22, 2003.

Shortest Counterexamples for Symbolic Model Checking of LTL with Past

Viktor Schuppan[1] and Armin Biere[2]

[1] ETH Zürich, Computer Systems Institute,
CH-8092 Zürich, Switzerland
Viktor.Schuppan@inf.ethz.ch

[2] Johannes Kepler University, Institute for Formal Models and Verification,
Altenbergerstrasse 69, A-4040 Linz, Austria
biere@jku.at

Abstract. Shorter counterexamples are typically easier to understand. The length of a counterexample, as reported by a model checker, depends on both the algorithm used for state space exploration and the way the property is encoded. We provide necessary and sufficient criteria for a Büchi automaton to accept shortest counterexamples. We prove that Büchi automata constructed using the approach of Clarke, Grumberg, and Hamaguchi accept shortest counterexamples of future time LTL formulae, while an automaton generated with the algorithm of Gerth et al. (GPVW) may lead to unnecessary long counterexamples. Optimality is lost in the first case as soon as past time operators are included. Adapting a recently proposed encoding for bounded model checking of LTL with past, we construct a Büchi automaton that accepts shortest counterexamples for full LTL. We use our method of translating liveness into safety to find shortest counterexamples with a BDD-based symbolic model checker without modifying the model checker itself. Though our method involves a quadratic blowup of the state space, it outperforms SAT-based bounded model checking on a number of examples.

1 Introduction

Counterexamples are a salient feature of model checking that help developers to understand the problem in a faulty design. Most counterexamples still need to be interpreted by humans, and shorter counterexamples will, in general, be easier to understand.

As LTL is defined over infinite paths counterexamples are, in principle, infinitely long. In a finite state system every failing LTL property also has a lasso-shaped counterexample $\beta\gamma^\omega$ [27]. Such a counterexample can be finitely represented, where its length is defined as the sum of the lengths of the stem β and loop γ [7]. Counterexamples to safety properties also have finite bad prefixes that are more useful for a developer than a corresponding infinite path. In [17] Kupferman and Vardi showed how to recognize the shortest bad prefix using an automaton of size doubly exponential in the size of the corresponding formula. In this paper we concentrate on shortest lasso-shaped counterexamples for general LTL properties.

BDD-based symbolic techniques usually proceed breadth first and can find shortest bad prefixes for many safety properties [17]. For more general specifications, finding

N. Halbwachs and L. Zuck (Eds.): TACAS 2005, LNCS 3440, pp. 493–509, 2005.

a shortest counterexample amounts to finding a shortest fair cycle, which is an NP-complete problem [7]. Most BDD-based model checkers offer only heuristics to minimize the length of counterexamples to such properties. For a comparative study on their performance and the length of the generated counterexamples see [20]. In explicit state model checking a double DFS [8] is typically used to search the state space. It does not find shortest counterexamples. Gastin et al. propose an algorithm [11] to minimize the length of counterexamples, which may visit a state an exponential number of times.

The first technique in widespread use that can produce shortest counterexamples for general LTL properties is SAT-based bounded model checking [3]. While [3] was restricted to future time LTL, more recent implementations cover full LTL [2], [5], [19]. Whether shortest counterexamples can be reported depends also on the encoding of the property. Both, [2] and [19] find shortest counterexamples. [5] achieves higher performance than [2] but sacrifices shortest counterexamples. A detailed experimental comparison of [5] and [19] is not yet available. As SAT-based model checking does not perform equally well on all examples as the BDD-based variant and vice versa [1], an efficient BDD-based technique that produces shortest counterexamples is desirable.

We recently proposed a method to translate liveness into safety [22], which finds shortest lassos and performs well on a number of examples in a BDD-based model checker. The automaton-based approach to model checking [27] employs such loop detection but requires translation of an LTL property into a Büchi automaton. Hence, not only must the shortest lasso be found, but the property automaton must also accept a shortest counterexample [11, 1]. So far, size of Büchi automata was a more important criterion than length of the resulting counterexamples, and little is known about the latter.

In this paper we establish necessary and sufficient criteria for Büchi automata to accept shortest counterexamples. We prove that the approach by Clarke et al. [6] generates Büchi automata that satisfy these criteria for future time LTL. This is not the case if past time is included, and we establish a quadratic bound on the excess length. We give an example that the algorithm by Gerth et al. [12] and many of its descendants do not generate shortest counterexamples even for future time LTL.

Past time operators do not add expressive power to future time LTL [15]. Still, a specification that includes past time operators may be more natural than the pure future variant, and it can be exponentially more succinct [18]. We are not aware of an efficient, easy-to-implement algorithm to translate a past time LTL formula into its future time equivalent. We instead construct a Büchi automaton that accepts shortest counterexamples for full LTL by adapting a recent, simple and efficient encoding for bounded model checking with past [19]. We then use our transformation from liveness to safety to find shortest counterexamples with a BDD-based symbolic model checker. The transformation itself does not require modifications to the model checker but is purely on the model and the specification to be checked. The only requirement is a breadth-first reachability check. Our experiments show that finding shortest counterexamples in the transformed model with the BDD-based algorithm of NuSMV [4] can be significantly faster than SAT-based bounded model checking of the original model.

In the following section we introduce our notation. In Sect. 3 we define shortest counterexamples and investigate which Büchi automata can accept them. We present our construction of a Büchi automaton that accepts shortest counterexamples in Sect. 4

and give some hints on our implementation in Sect. 5. Experimental results are reported in Sect. 6. The last section concludes.

2   Preliminaries

Let Σ be a finite set, let α be a finite or infinite sequence over Σ. The *length* of a sequence α is defined as $|\alpha| = n + 1$ if $\alpha = \sigma_0\sigma_1\ldots\sigma_n$ is finite, ∞ otherwise. $\alpha(i)$ denotes the element at index i, α_i is the suffix $\alpha(i)\alpha(i+1)\ldots$ of α with its first i states chopped off. We also call sequences over Σ *words* over Σ. The crossproduct of two sequences $\alpha \times \beta$ is defined componentwise.

Let β, γ be finite sequences. A sequence α is a $\langle\beta,\gamma\rangle$-*lasso* with *stem* β and *loop* γ iff $\alpha = \beta\gamma^\omega$. We sometimes write $\langle\alpha,\beta\rangle$ instead of $\alpha\beta^\omega$. The *length* of a lasso is defined as $|\langle\beta,\gamma\rangle| = |\beta| + |\gamma|$. A lasso $\langle\beta,\gamma\rangle$ is *minimal* for α iff $\alpha = \beta\gamma^\omega$ and $\forall\beta',\gamma'\,.\,\alpha = \beta'\gamma'^\omega \Rightarrow |\langle\beta,\gamma\rangle| \leq |\langle\beta',\gamma'\rangle|$. The *type* [18] of a $\langle\beta,\gamma\rangle$-lasso is defined as $type(\langle\beta,\gamma\rangle) = (|\beta|,|\gamma|)$. A sequence α can be mapped to a set of types: $type(\alpha) = \{type(\langle\beta,\gamma\rangle) \mid \alpha = \beta\gamma^\omega\}$. We state the following fact about sequences (proved in the full version of this paper [23]).

Lemma 1. *Let* $\langle\beta,\gamma\rangle$ *be a minimal lasso for* α, $\langle\beta',\gamma'\rangle$ *a minimal lasso for* α', *and* $\alpha'' = \alpha \times \alpha'$. *Then there are finite sequences* β'',γ'' *such that* $\langle\beta'',\gamma''\rangle$ *is a minimal lasso for* α'', $|\beta''| = max(|\beta|,|\beta'|)$, *and* $|\gamma''| = lcm(|\gamma|,|\gamma'|)^1$.

2.1   Kripke Structures

Following [16] we define a fair *Kripke structure* as tuple $K = (V,I,T,F)$. V is a finite set of *state variables* v_i, each ranging over a finite set V_i. A *state* s is a valuation of the variables in V, the set of all states is S. I is the *initial condition* that defines the set of initial states of K. The *transition relation* T is also given as a predicate, referring to valuations of the variables in the current state, s, and in the successor state, s'. $F = \{F_1,\ldots,F_n\}$ is a set of (weak) fairness constraints. The value of v in s is denoted by $v(s)$. If s is clear from the context, v also denotes the value of v in the current state, and v' that in the successor state. We assume a set of atomic propositions AP that relates variables to their potential valuations, each of the form $v_i = c_j$ with $c_j \in V_i$. A mapping L is implicitly given that maps a state s to the set of atomic propositions true in s.

A non-empty sequence of states is a *path* in K if $\forall 0 \leq i < |\pi|\,.\,(s_i,s_{i+1}) \models T$. If $s_0 \models I$, π is *initialized*. An infinite path π is *fair* if $\forall F_i \in F\,.\,\forall j\,.\,\exists k > j\,.\,\pi(k) \models F_i$. Π is the set of paths in K. Via L a path implicitly defines a sequence over 2^{AP}.

The synchronous product of two Kripke structures $K_1 = (V_1,I_1,T_1,F_1)$ and $K_2 = (V_2,I_2,T_2,F_2)$ is a Kripke structure $K_1 \times K_2 = (V_1 \cup V_2, I_1 \wedge I_2, T_1 \wedge T_2, F_1 \cup F_2)$. The projection of a state s onto a set of variables V' is denoted $s|_{V'}$.

2.2   PLTL

We consider specifications given in Propositional LTL with both future and past time operators (PLTLB) [9]. The syntax of PLTLB is defined over a set of atomic propositions

---

^{1} $lcm(a,b)$ denotes the *least common multiple* of a and b.

$$\pi_i \models p \quad \text{iff } p \in \pi_i \text{ for } p \in AP \qquad \pi_i \models \mathbf{X}\phi \quad \text{iff } \pi_{i+1} \models \phi$$

$$\pi_i \models \neg\phi \quad \text{iff } \pi_i \not\models \phi \qquad\qquad \pi_i \models \phi\,\mathbf{U}\,\psi \text{ iff } \exists j \geq i\,.\,(\pi_j \models \psi \wedge \forall i \leq k < j\,.\,\pi_k \models \phi)$$

$$\pi_i \models \phi \vee \psi \text{ iff } \pi_i \models \phi \text{ or } \pi_i \models \psi \qquad \pi_i \models \mathbf{Y}\phi \quad \text{iff } i > 0 \text{ and } \pi_{i-1} \models \phi$$

$$\pi_i \models \phi\,\mathbf{S}\,\psi \text{ iff } \exists 0 \leq j \leq i\,.\,(\pi_j \models \psi \wedge \forall j < k \leq i\,.\,\pi_k \models \phi)$$

Fig. 1. The semantics of PLTLB

AP. If ϕ and ψ are PLTLB formulae, so are $\neg\phi, \phi \vee \psi, \mathbf{X}\phi, \phi\,\mathbf{U}\,\psi, \mathbf{Y}\phi, \phi\,\mathbf{S}\,\psi$. The semantics of PLTLB is defined recursively on infinite sequences over 2^{AP} in Fig. 1.

If the past time operators $\mathbf{Y}$ and $\mathbf{S}$ are excluded, we obtain future time LTL formulae (PLTLF). Similarly, a past time formula (PLTLP) has no occurrences of $\mathbf{X}$ and $\mathbf{U}$. For this reason, when we speak about future or past we include present. We have the following usual abbreviations: $\top \equiv p \vee \neg p, \bot \equiv \neg\top, \phi \wedge \psi \equiv \neg(\neg\phi \vee \neg\psi), \phi \rightarrow \psi \equiv \neg\phi \vee \psi, \phi \leftrightarrow \psi \equiv (\phi \rightarrow \psi) \wedge (\psi \rightarrow \phi), \phi\,\mathbf{R}\,\psi \equiv \neg(\neg\phi\,\mathbf{U}\,\neg\psi), \mathbf{F}\phi \equiv \top\,\mathbf{U}\,\phi, \mathbf{G}\phi \equiv \neg\mathbf{F}\neg\phi, \mathbf{Z}\phi \equiv \neg\mathbf{Y}\neg\phi, \phi\,\mathbf{T}\,\psi \equiv \neg(\neg\phi\,\mathbf{S}\,\neg\psi), \mathbf{O}\phi \equiv \top\,\mathbf{S}\,\phi$, and $\mathbf{H}\phi \equiv \neg\mathbf{O}\neg\phi$.

A PLTLB property ϕ *holds universally* in a Kripke structure K, denoted $K \models_\forall \phi$, iff it holds for every initialized fair path. If $K \not\models_\forall \phi$, each initialized fair path π in K with $\pi \models \neg\phi$ is a *counterexample* for ϕ. ϕ *holds existentially*, $K \models_\exists \phi$, iff there exists an initialized fair path that fulfills ϕ. Each such path is a *witness* for ϕ. For every finite K, if $K \not\models_\forall \phi$, then there exists a fair $\langle \beta, \gamma \rangle$-lasso α in K such that $\alpha \not\models \phi$ [27]. A finite path π_{pre} is a *bad prefix* for ϕ iff $\forall \pi_{inf}\,.\,(|\pi_{inf}| = \infty \Rightarrow \pi_{pre}\pi_{inf} \not\models \phi)$ [17].

For $\mathbf{U}$ and $\mathbf{S}$ there exist recursive expansion formulae (e.g. [16]):

$$\phi = \psi_1\,\mathbf{U}\,\psi_2 : \pi_i \models \phi \text{ iff } (\pi_i \models \psi_2) \vee (\pi_i \models \psi_1) \wedge (\pi_{i+1} \models \phi)$$

$$\phi = \psi_1\,\mathbf{S}\,\psi_2 : \pi_i \models \phi \text{ iff } (\pi_i \models \psi_2) \vee (i > 0) \wedge (\pi_i \models \psi_1) \wedge (\pi_{i-1} \models \phi)$$

The expansion of $\mathbf{U}$ is not sufficient to guarantee proper semantics: additional measures must be taken to select the desired fixed point, e.g., by adding fairness constraints.

Finally, the *past operator depth* [2] of a formula ϕ, $h(\phi)$, is the maximal number of nested past operators in ϕ:

$$h(\phi) = \begin{cases} 0 & \text{iff } \phi \in AP \\ h(\psi) & \text{iff } \phi = \circ\psi\,, \text{where } \circ \in \{\neg, \mathbf{X}\} \\ max(h(\psi_1), h(\psi_2)) & \text{iff } \phi = \psi_1 \circ \psi_2\,, \text{where } \circ \in \{\vee, \mathbf{U}\} \\ 1 + h(\psi) & \text{iff } \phi = \mathbf{Y}\psi \\ 1 + max(h(\psi_1), h(\psi_2)) & \text{iff } \phi = \psi_1\,\mathbf{S}\,\psi_2 \end{cases}$$

The authors of [18, 2] proved independently that a PLTLB property ϕ can distinguish at most $h(\phi)$ loop iterations of a lasso. We restate Lemma 5.2 of [18] for PLTLB:

Lemma 2. *For any lasso π of type (l_s, l_l), for any PLTLB property ϕ with at most $h(\phi)$ nested past-time modalities, and any $i \geq l_s + l_l h(\phi)$, $\pi_i \models \phi \leftrightarrow \pi_{i+l_l} \models \phi$.*

2.3   Büchi Automata

A *Büchi automaton* over a set of variables V^K with a corresponding set of states S^K is a Kripke structure $B = (V, I, T, F)$, where $V = V^K \cup \hat{V}$. A *run* ρ of a Büchi automaton B

Table 1. Property-dependent part of a Büchi automaton constructed with CGH+

ψ	$V^\psi =$	$I^\psi =$	$T^\psi =$	$F^\psi =$
		definition		
p	$\{x_p\}$	$\top$	$x_p \leftrightarrow p$	$\emptyset$
$\neg\psi_1$	$V^{\psi_1} \cup \{x_\psi\}$	I^{ψ_1}	$T^{\psi_1} \wedge (x_\psi \leftrightarrow \neg x_{\psi_1})$	F^{ψ_1}
$\psi_1 \vee \psi_2$	$V^{\psi_1} \cup V^{\psi_2} \cup \{x_\psi\}$	$I^{\psi_1} \wedge I^{\psi_2}$	$T^{\psi_1} \wedge T^{\psi_2} \wedge$ $(x_\psi \leftrightarrow x_{\psi_1} \vee x_{\psi_2})$	$F^{\psi_1} \cup F^{\psi_2}$
$\mathbf{X}\psi_1$	$V^{\psi_1} \cup \{x_\psi\}$	I^{ψ_1}	$T^{\psi_1} \wedge (x_\psi \leftrightarrow x'_{\psi_1})$	F^{ψ_1}
$\psi_1 \mathbf{U} \psi_2$	$V^{\psi_1} \cup V^{\psi_2} \cup \{x_\psi\}$	$I^{\psi_1} \wedge I^{\psi_2}$	$T^{\psi_1} \wedge T^{\psi_2} \wedge$ $(x_\psi \leftrightarrow x_{\psi_2} \vee x_{\psi_1} \wedge x'_\psi)$	$F^{\psi_1} \cup F^{\psi_2} \cup$ $\{\{\neg x_\psi \vee x_{\psi_2}\}\}$
$\mathbf{Y}\psi_1$	$V^{\psi_1} \cup \{x_\psi\}$	$I^{\psi_1} \wedge (x_\psi \leftrightarrow \bot)$	$T^{\psi_1} \wedge (x'_\psi \leftrightarrow x_{\psi_1})$	F^{ψ_1}
$\psi_1 \mathbf{S} \psi_2$	$V^{\psi_1} \cup V^{\psi_2} \cup \{x_\psi\}$	$I^{\psi_1} \wedge I^{\psi_2} \wedge$ $(x_\psi \leftrightarrow x_{\psi_2})$	$T^{\psi_1} \wedge T^{\psi_2} \wedge$ $(x'_\psi \leftrightarrow x'_{\psi_2} \vee x'_{\psi_1} \wedge x_\psi)$	$F^{\psi_1} \cup F^{\psi_2}$

on an infinite word α over S^K, denoted $\rho \models \alpha$, is an initialized fair path in B such that $\forall i . \alpha(i) = \rho(i)|_{V^K}$. The set of all runs of B is $Runs(B)$. A word is *accepted* by B iff B has a run on α. The set of words accepted by B defines its *language* $Lang(B)$.

In the automaton-based approach to model checking [27] a Büchi automaton that recognizes counterexamples to the specification is constructed. In other words, the language of the automaton is precisely the set of witnesses for the negation of the specification. Then, an initialized fair path in the synchronous product of the model and that automaton indicates failure of the specification. Formally, to check whether $K \models_\forall \phi$ holds for some model K and LTL formula ϕ, we negate ϕ and construct a Büchi automaton $B^{\neg\phi}$ with $Lang(B^{\neg\phi}) = \{\alpha \mid \alpha \models \neg\phi\}$. Any initialized fair path in $K \times B^{\neg\phi}$ is a counterexample for ϕ.

In this scenario V^K corresponds to the set of atomic propositions in $\neg\phi$, whereas $\hat{V}$ depends on the specific algorithm used to obtain B. Our definition of a Büchi automaton is similar to a state-labeled, generalized Büchi automaton but splits states according to the variables in V^K. This is more convenient in a symbolic setting, where this split happens anyway when the synchronous product with the model automaton is formed. It does not restrict the generality of the results in Sect. 3 and 4.

An approach to construct a Büchi automaton tailored to symbolic model checking (used, e.g., in NuSMV [4]) is by Clarke, Grumberg, and Hamaguchi [6]. The original version deals only with future time formulae, but extensions to PLTLB are available, see. e.g., [16, 21]. We refer to this extended version as *CGH+* below. An automaton B^ϕ_{CGH+} is constructed as $B^\phi_{CGH+} = (V^\phi, I^\phi \wedge x_\phi, T^\phi, F^\phi)$ where V^ϕ, I^ϕ, T^ϕ, and F^ϕ are defined recursively in Tab. 1. All x_ψ are Boolean. On every run ρ on a word α the valuation of a state variable x_ψ of B^ϕ_{CGH+} reflects the validity of the corresponding subformula ψ of ϕ, i.e., $x_\psi(\rho(i)) \leftrightarrow \alpha_i \models \psi$. By [6, 16, 21] we have $Lang(B^\phi_{CGH+}) = \{\alpha \mid \alpha \models \phi\}$. Note that, for a uniform explanation, Tab. 1 uses state variables also for Boolean connectives. In [6, 16, 21] these are replaced by macros.

3   Büchi Automata to Detect Shortest Counterexamples

3.1   Shortest Counterexamples for PLTLB

We have defined PLTLB over infinite paths, hence we need to specify what should be considered a shortest counterexample. Given that we are only interested in finite representations, and a failing PLTLB property in a finite state system always has a lasso-shaped counterexample [27], we adopt the following definition from [7]: a shortest counterexample is one that has a most compact representation as a lasso.

Definition 1. *Let $K = (V,I,T,F)$ be a Kripke structure, let ϕ be a PLTLB property. A path α in K is a shortest counterexample for ϕ in K iff*

1. $\alpha \not\models \phi$
2. $\exists \beta,\gamma . (\alpha = \beta\gamma^{\omega} \wedge \forall \beta',\gamma' . (\beta'\gamma'^{\omega} \in \Pi \wedge \beta'\gamma'^{\omega} \not\models \phi \Rightarrow |\langle \beta,\gamma \rangle| \leq |\langle \beta',\gamma' \rangle|))$

This definition is not optimal. First, an early position of the violation (if that can be clearly attributed) need not coincide with the least number of states required to close a loop. Second, apart from length, ease of understanding is not a criterion either.

The first problem is most relevant for properties that also have finite bad prefixes, i.e., properties that are a subset of a safety property [17]. Finding the shortest bad prefix for safety formulae can be done in parallel, using the (doubly exponential) method proposed in [17]. The solution to the second problem is left as future work; for approaches and more references see [13].

3.2   Tight Büchi Automata

In the automaton-based approach to model checking, a PLTLB property is verified by searching for loops in the synchronous product of a Kripke structure K, representing the model, and a Büchi automaton B, accepting counterexamples for the property. Hence, if shortest counterexamples are desired, the product of the model and the Büchi automaton must have an initialized fair path $\lambda = \langle \mu, \nu \rangle$ that can be represented as lasso of the same length as the shortest counterexample $\alpha = \langle \beta, \gamma \rangle$. Kupferman and Vardi [17] call an automaton on finite words *tight* if it accepts shortest prefixes for violations of safety formulae. We extend that notion to Büchi automata on infinite words.

Definition 2. *Let B be a Büchi automaton. B is* tight *iff*

$$\forall \alpha \in Lang(B) . \forall \beta,\gamma . (\langle \beta,\gamma \rangle \text{ is minimal for } \alpha \Rightarrow$$
$$\exists \rho \in Runs(B) . \exists \lambda,\mu,\nu . (\rho \models \alpha \wedge \lambda = \alpha \times \rho = \mu\nu^{\omega} \wedge |\langle \mu,\nu \rangle| = |\langle \beta,\gamma \rangle|))$$

Consider the scenarios in Fig. 2. The automaton B in the left scenario has a run $\sigma\tau^{\omega}$ of the same structure as the counterexample $\beta\gamma^{\omega}$ in K, leading to an equally short counterexample $(\beta \times \sigma)(\gamma \times \tau)^{\omega}$ in the product $K \times B$. The run of the Büchi automaton in the right scenario has an unnecessarily long stem and loop.

From Lemma 1 it can be inferred that a path of the same length in $K \times B$ as the counterexample in K implies that the corresponding run $\rho = \sigma\tau^{\omega}$ in B can be represented as the same type as $\langle \beta, \gamma \rangle$. The left scenario in Fig. 2 suggests another, alternative formulation, which may be more intuitive and is easier to prove for some automata: the

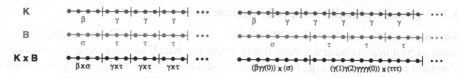

Fig. 2. Scenarios with shortest and non-optimal counterexample

subsequences of α starting at indices $4, 7, 10, \ldots$ are the same, as are those beginning at $5, 7, 11, \ldots$, and $6, 9, 12, \ldots$. On the other hand, the subsequences starting at the respective indices in a single iteration are all different — otherwise a part of the loop could be cut out, contradicting minimality. Hence, if B is tight, there must be a run ρ on α with the following property: for each pair of indices i, j, if the subsequences of α starting at i and j have the same future ($\alpha_i = \alpha_j$), then ρ maps i and j to the same state in B ($\rho(i) = \rho(j)$). Theorem 1 establishes the equivalence of the criteria.

Theorem 1. *Let B be a Büchi automaton. The following statements are equivalent:*

1. *B is tight.*
2. *$\forall \alpha \in Lang(B) . \forall \beta, \gamma . (\langle \beta, \gamma \rangle$ is minimal for $\alpha \Rightarrow$*
   $$\exists \rho \in Runs(B) . (\rho \models \alpha \wedge type(\langle \beta, \gamma \rangle) \in type(\rho)))$$
3. *$\forall \alpha \in Lang(B) . ((\exists \beta, \gamma . \alpha = \beta \gamma^\omega) \Rightarrow$*
   $$(\exists \rho \in Runs(B) . (\rho \models \alpha \wedge (\forall i, j . \alpha_i = \alpha_j \Rightarrow \rho(i) = \rho(j)))))$$

Proof. $1 \Rightarrow 2$: Assume a run $\rho = \sigma \tau^\omega$ such that $\lambda = \alpha \times \rho = \mu \nu^\omega$ with $|\langle \mu, \nu \rangle| = |\langle \beta, \gamma \rangle|$. Let $\langle \sigma', \tau' \rangle$ be minimal for ρ. Lemma 1 gives $|\sigma'| \leq |\beta|$ and $|\tau'|$ divides $|\gamma|$. Now it's easy to find σ'', τ'' with $\sigma'' \tau''^\omega = \sigma \tau^\omega$, and $type(\langle \sigma'', \tau'' \rangle) = type(\langle \beta, \gamma \rangle)$.

$2 \Rightarrow 1$: Assume a run ρ with $type(\langle \beta, \gamma \rangle) \in type(\rho)$. By definition of type, there exist σ, τ such that $\rho = \sigma \tau^\omega$, $|\beta| = |\sigma|$, and $|\gamma| = |\tau|$. Hence, with $\mu = \beta \times \sigma$ and $\nu = \gamma \times \tau$, we have $\lambda = \alpha \times \rho = \mu \nu^\omega$ and $|\langle \mu, \nu \rangle| = |\langle \beta, \gamma \rangle|$.

$2 \Rightarrow 3$: Let $\alpha \in Lang(B)$, assume $\langle \beta, \gamma \rangle$ minimal for α, and let $\rho = \sigma \tau^\omega$ be a run on α such that $|\beta| = |\sigma|$ and $|\gamma| = |\tau|$. Let i, j with $\alpha_i = \alpha_j$. It remains to show that $\rho(i) = \rho(j)$. This is done by case distinction according to the positions of i and j w.r.t. to β and γ in α. The case $i = j$ is obvious, the other cases either contradict the minimality of $\langle \beta, \gamma \rangle$ for α or can be reduced to a previous case. Details are given in the full version [23].

$3 \Rightarrow 2$: Let $\alpha = \beta \gamma^\omega \in Lang(B)$ and ρ a run on α with $\forall i, j . \alpha_i = \alpha_j \Rightarrow \rho(i) = \rho(j)$. Let $\langle \beta, \gamma \rangle$ be minimal for α.

$\quad \alpha = \beta \gamma^\omega \Rightarrow \forall i < |\gamma|, \forall k . \alpha_{|\beta|+i} = \gamma_i = \alpha_{|\beta|+i+|\gamma|k}$
$\quad\quad\quad\quad\quad \Rightarrow \forall i < |\gamma|, \forall k . \rho(|\beta|+i) = \rho(|\beta|+i+|\gamma|k)$

Let $\sigma = \rho(0), \ldots, \rho(|\beta|-1)$ and $\tau = \rho(|\beta|), \ldots, \rho(|\beta|+|\gamma|-1)$. Hence, $\rho = \sigma \tau^\omega$ such that $|\sigma| = |\beta|$ and $|\tau| = |\gamma|$. $\square$

3.3   (Non-) Optimality of Specific Approaches

The approach by Gerth et al. (GPVW) [12] for future time LTL forms the basis of many algorithms to construct small Büchi automata, which benefits explicit state model checking but is also used, e.g., for symbolic model checking in VIS [14]. Figure 3 shows an example that GPVW does not, in general, lead to tight automata. Subsequences starting from the initial state of the Büchi automaton fulfill $p \wedge \mathbf{X}\mathbf{G}q$, those starting from the other state satisfy $\mathbf{G}q$. The model has a single, infinite path satisfying $\mathbf{G}(p \wedge q)$ — a counterexample of length 1 to the specification $\neg(p \wedge \mathbf{X}\mathbf{G}q)$. Note that adding transitions or designating more initial states is not enough to make the automaton in Fig. 3 tight: an additional state is required. Non-optimality of GPVW is shared by many of its descendants, e.g., [26].

Fig. 3. Model and Büchi automaton to recognize counterexamples for $\neg(p \wedge \mathbf{X}\mathbf{G}q)$ resulting in non-optimal counterexample

In a Büchi automaton B^{ϕ}_{CGH+} each state variable corresponds to a subformula ψ of ϕ (see Tab. 1). This directly proves tightness of B^{ϕ}_{CGH+} for a PLTLF formula ϕ.

Proposition 1. *Let ϕ be a future time LTL formula, let B^{ϕ}_{CGH+} be defined as above. Then B^{ϕ}_{CGH+} is tight.*

Proof. Every two states in B^{ϕ}_{CGH+} differ in the valuation of at least one state variable, and therefore specify a different, non-overlapping future. According to Thm. 1, a Büchi automaton B is tight iff for each accepted word α there exists a run ρ on α in B with $\forall i, j . (\alpha_i = \alpha_j \Rightarrow \rho(i) = \rho(j))$. Clearly, $\alpha_i = \alpha_j$ have the same future, hence, on each run in B we have $\alpha_i = \alpha_j \Rightarrow \rho(i) = \rho(j)$.   □

What is useful for future time hurts tightness as soon as past operators are included: B^{ϕ}_{CGH+} may also distinguish states of an accepted word that have different past but same future. Lemma 2 states that a past time formula can distinguish only finitely many iterations of a loop. This can be used to establish an upper bound on the excess length of a counterexample produced by CGH+ for a PLTLB formula:

Proposition 2. *Let K be a Kripke structure, ϕ a PLTLB property with $K \not\models_{\forall} \phi$, and $B^{\neg\phi}_{CGH+}$ a Büchi automaton constructed with CGH+. Let $\alpha = \langle \beta, \gamma \rangle$ be a shortest counterexample in K. Then, there is an initialized fair lasso $\lambda = \langle \mu, \nu \rangle$ in $K \times B^{\neg\phi}_{CGH+}$ with $|\mu| \leq |\beta| + (h(\neg\phi) + 1)|\gamma|$ and $|\nu| = |\gamma|$.*

The proof is given in the full version [23]. For an example that exhibits excess length, which is quadratic in the length of the shortest counterexample, consider the simple modulo-n counter and property in Fig. 4 (adapted from [2]). The innermost formula $\mathbf{O}(c = n - 1)$ remains true from the end of the first loop iteration in the counter,

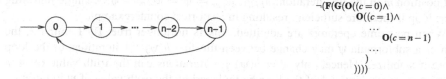

$$\neg(\mathbf{F}(\mathbf{G}(\mathbf{O}((c=0)\wedge \\
\mathbf{O}((c=1)\wedge \\
\dots \\
\mathbf{O}(c=n-1) \\
\dots \\
) \\
))))$$

Fig. 4. Simple modulo-n counter with property

$\mathbf{O}((c=n-2)\wedge(\mathbf{O}(c=n-1)))$ becomes and remains true $n-1$ steps later, etc. Hence, a loop in $B_{CGH+}^{\neg\phi}$ is only reached after $\mathbf{O}(n^2)$ steps of the counter have been performed. Clearly, the shortest counterexample is a single iteration of the loop with $\mathbf{O}(n)$ steps.

Every PLTLB formula can be transformed into a future time LTL formula equivalent at the beginning of a sequence [10]. Due to [18] we can expect an at least exponential worst-case increase in the size of the formula. Rather than translating an LTL formula with past into a pure future version, we follow a different path in the next section.

4   A Tight Look at LTL Model Checking

Proposition 2 states that a Büchi automaton constructed with CGH+ accepts a shortest counterexample with a run that may have an overly long stem but a loop of the same length as that of the counterexample. Bounded model checking [3] has been extended recently to include past time operators [2, 5, 19]. Of these, [2, 19] use *virtual unrolling* of the transition relation to find shortest counterexamples if past time operators are present. Inspired by [19], we adapt this approach to construct a tight Büchi automaton for PLTLB based on CGH+.

4.1   Virtual Unrolling for Bounded Model Checking of PLTLB

In bounded model checking, the model checking problem, which asks whether $K \models_\forall \phi$ holds, is translated into a sequence of propositional formulae of the form $\|[M,\phi,k]\|$ in the following way: $\|[M,\phi,k]\|$ is satisfiable iff a finite informative bad prefix [17] or lasso-shaped counterexample π of length k exists. In the case of a lasso-shaped counterexample, a loop is assumed to be closed between the last state $\pi(k)$ and some successor $\pi(l+1)$ of a previous occurrence of that last state $\pi(l)=\pi(k)$. The resulting formulae are then handed to a SAT solver for increasing bounds k until either a counterexample is found, absence of a counterexample is proved, or a user defined resource threshold is reached. Typically, one fresh Boolean variable $x_{j,\psi}$ is introduced for each pair of relative position in the path ($0 \le j \le k$) and subformula ψ of ϕ, such that $x_{j,\psi}$ is true iff ψ holds at position j.

On a lasso-shaped path, the truth of a future time formula ϕ at position k may depend on the truth of some of its subformulae ψ at positions $> k$. While those are not available directly, the truth of a future time formula at a given position within the loop does not change between different iterations of the loop. Hence, the truth value of ψ at position $0 \le m < k-l$ in any iteration $i \ge 0$ of the loop can be substituted with the truth value of

ψ at position m in the first iteration: $\pi_{l+i(k-l)+m} \models \psi \Leftrightarrow \pi_{l+m} \models \psi$. A single unrolling of the loop is therefore sufficient, resulting in a shortest counterexample.

When past time operators are admitted, this is no longer true. By Lemma 2, the truth of a subformula ψ may change between the first $h(\psi) + 1$ iterations of the loop before it stabilizes. Hence, only after $h(\psi) + 1$ iterations can the truth value of ψ in some iteration $i \geq h(\psi) + 1$ of the loop be replaced by the truth value of ψ in iteration $h(\psi) + 1$: $\pi_{l+i(k-l)+m} \models \psi \Leftrightarrow \pi_{l+(h(\psi)+1)(k-l)+m} \models \psi$. A naive approach for checking a past time formula ϕ would still have one Boolean variable per pair of relative position in the path and subformula. However, the approach would have to ensure that the path ends with $h(\phi) + 1$ copies of the loop. This would lead to a more complicated formulation of loop detection and would not allow to find shortest counterexamples. A less naive, but still suboptimal solution might not guarantee a high enough number of loop unrollings directly but could include the variables representing the truth of properties in the loop detection. That approach could not ensure shortest counterexamples either.

Benedetti and Cimatti [2] showed how to do better: note, that some subformulae ψ of ϕ have lower past operator depth, and, therefore, require fewer loop iterations to stabilize. In particular, atomic propositions remain stable from the first iteration onward. It is sufficient to perform a single unrolling of the loop. Rather than having only one Boolean variable $x_{j,\psi}$ per pair of relative position j in the path and subformula ψ, there are now as many variables per pair (j, ψ) as iterations of the loop are required for that subformula to stabilize. Each variable corresponds to the truth value of ψ at the same relative position j but in a different iteration i of the loop: $x_{j,\psi,i} \Leftrightarrow \pi_{j+i(k-l)} \models \psi$ with $0 \leq j \leq k \wedge 0 \leq i \leq h(\psi)$ (the value of $x_{j,\psi,i}$ may not be well-defined if $i > 0 \wedge j < l$). This *virtual unrolling* of the loop leads to shortest counterexamples.

4.2   A Tight Büchi Automaton for PLTLB

A Büchi automaton constructed with CGH+ suffers from similar problems as the naive approaches to bounded model checking of PLTLB. The automaton has a single variable representing the truth of a subformula in a given state. For a loop in the product of the model and the automaton to occur, the truth of all subformulae must have stabilized. Hence, we can adopt the same idea as outlined above to obtain a tight Büchi automaton.

We construct a Büchi automaton $B_{SB}^{\phi} = (V_{SB}^{\phi}, I_{SB}^{\phi}, T_{SB}^{\phi}, F_{SB}^{\phi})$ for a PLTLB formula ϕ as follows: $V_{SB}^{\phi} = V^{\phi} \cup \{lb, le\}$ with $LB = LE = \{\perp, \top\}$, $I_{SB}^{\phi} = I^{\phi} \wedge x_{\phi,0}$, $T_{SB}^{\phi} = T^{\phi} \wedge (lb \to lb')$, and $F_{SB}^{\phi} = F^{\phi} \cup \{\{lb \wedge le\}\}$, where V^{ϕ}, I^{ϕ}, T^{ϕ}, and F^{ϕ} are defined recursively in Tab. 2.

Each subformula ψ of ϕ is represented by $h(\psi) + 1$ state variables $x_{\psi,i}$. We refer to the i in $x_{\psi,i}$ as *generation* below. Two more state variables lb (for loop body) and le (for loop end) are added. As long as lb is false (on the stem), only variables in generation 0 are constrained according to the recursive definition of PLTLB. When lb becomes true (on the loop), the definitions apply to all generations. While le is false (the end of a loop iteration is not yet reached), $x_{\psi,i}$ is defined in terms of current and next-state values of variables in the same generation. When le is true (at the end of a loop iteration), the next-state values are obtained from the next generation of variables if the present generation is not already the last. The fairness constraints, which guarantee the correct

Table 2. Property-dependent part of a tight Büchi automaton

ψ	definition
p	$V^\Psi = \{x_{p,0}\}$, where $X_{p,0} = \{\bot, \top\}$ $T^\Psi = x_{p,0} \leftrightarrow p$ $I^\Psi = \top$ $\qquad\qquad\qquad\qquad\qquad\qquad F^\Psi = \emptyset$
$\neg\psi_1$	$V^\Psi = V^{\Psi_1} \cup \bigcup_{i=0}^{h(\psi)} \{x_{\psi,i}\}$, where $X_{\psi,i} = \{\bot, \top\}$ $T^\Psi = T^{\Psi_1} \wedge \bigwedge_{i=0}^{h(\psi)} (x_{\psi,i} \leftrightarrow \neg x_{\psi_1,i})$ $I^\Psi = I^{\Psi_1} \qquad\qquad\qquad\qquad\qquad F^\Psi = F^{\Psi_1}$
$\psi_1 \vee \psi_2$	$V^\Psi = V^{\Psi_1} \cup V^{\Psi_2} \cup \bigcup_{i=0}^{h(\psi)} \{x_{\psi,i}\}$, where $X_{\psi,i} = \{\bot, \top\}$ $T^\Psi = T^{\Psi_1} \wedge T^{\Psi_2} \wedge \bigwedge_{i=0}^{h(\psi)} (x_{\psi,i} \leftrightarrow x_{\psi_1,min(i,h(\psi_1))} \vee x_{\psi_2,min(i,h(\psi_2))})$ $I^\Psi = I^{\Psi_1} \wedge I^{\Psi_2} \qquad\qquad\qquad F^\Psi = F^{\Psi_1} \cup F^{\Psi_2}$
$X\psi_1$	$V^\Psi = V^{\Psi_1} \cup \bigcup_{i=0}^{h(\psi)} \{x_{\psi,i}\}$, where $X_{\psi,i} = \{\bot, \top\}$ $T^\Psi = T^{\Psi_1} \wedge (\neg lb \rightarrow (x_{\psi,0} \leftrightarrow x'_{\psi_1,0}))$ $\qquad\quad \wedge ((lb \wedge \neg le) \rightarrow \bigwedge_{i=0}^{h(\psi)-1} (x_{\psi,i} \leftrightarrow x'_{\psi_1,i}))$ $\qquad\quad \wedge ((lb \wedge le) \rightarrow \bigwedge_{i=0}^{h(\psi)-1} (x_{\psi,i} \leftrightarrow x'_{\psi_1,i+1}))$ $\qquad\quad \wedge (lb \rightarrow (x_{\psi,h(\psi)} \leftrightarrow x'_{\psi_1,h(\psi)}))$ $I^\Psi = I^{\Psi_1} \qquad\qquad\qquad\qquad\qquad F^\Psi = F^{\Psi_1}$
$\psi_1 \, U \, \psi_2$	$V^\Psi = V^{\Psi_1} \cup V^{\Psi_2} \cup \bigcup_{i=0}^{h(\psi)} \{x_{\psi,i}\}$, where $X_{\psi,i} = \{\bot, \top\}$ $T^\Psi = T^{\Psi_1} \wedge T^{\Psi_2} \wedge (\neg lb \rightarrow (x_{\psi,0} \leftrightarrow x_{\psi_2,0} \vee (x_{\psi_1,0} \wedge x'_{\psi,0})))$ $\qquad\quad \wedge ((lb \wedge \neg le) \rightarrow \bigwedge_{i=0}^{h(\psi)-1} (x_{\psi,i} \leftrightarrow x_{\psi_2,min(i,h(\psi_2))} \vee (x_{\psi_1,min(i,h(\psi_1))} \wedge x'_{\psi,i})))$ $\qquad\quad \wedge ((lb \wedge le) \rightarrow \bigwedge_{i=0}^{h(\psi)-1} (x_{\psi,i} \leftrightarrow x_{\psi_2,min(i,h(\psi_2))} \vee (x_{\psi_1,min(i,h(\psi_1))} \wedge x'_{\psi,i+1})))$ $\qquad\quad \wedge (lb \rightarrow (x_{\psi,h(\psi)} \leftrightarrow x_{\psi_2,h(\psi_2)} \vee (x_{\psi_1,h(\psi_1)} \wedge x'_{\psi,h(\psi)})))$ $I^\Psi = I^{\Psi_1} \wedge I^{\Psi_2} \qquad F^\Psi = F^{\Psi_1} \cup F^{\Psi_2} \cup \{\{\neg x_{\psi,h(\psi)} \vee x_{\psi_2,h(\psi_2)}\}\}$
$Y\psi_1$	$V^\Psi = V^{\Psi_1} \cup \bigcup_{i=0}^{h(\psi)} \{x_{\psi,i}\}$, where $X_{\psi,i} = \{\bot, \top\}$ $T^\Psi = T^{\Psi_1} \wedge (\neg lb \rightarrow (x'_{\psi,0} \leftrightarrow x_{\psi_1,0}))$ $\qquad\quad \wedge ((lb \wedge \neg le) \rightarrow \bigwedge_{i=0}^{h(\psi)-1} (x'_{\psi,i} \leftrightarrow x_{\psi_1,i}))$ $\qquad\quad \wedge ((lb \wedge le) \rightarrow \bigwedge_{i=0}^{h(\psi)-2} (x'_{\psi,i+1} \leftrightarrow x_{\psi_1,i}))$ $\qquad\quad \wedge (lb \rightarrow (x'_{\psi,h(\psi)} \leftrightarrow x_{\psi_1,h(\psi)}))$ $I^\Psi = I^{\Psi_1} \wedge (x_{\psi,0} \leftrightarrow \bot) \qquad F^\Psi = F^{\Psi_1}$
$\psi_1 \, S \, \psi_2$	$V^\Psi = V^{\Psi_1} \cup V^{\Psi_2} \cup \bigcup_{i=0}^{h(\psi)} \{x_{\psi,i}\}$, where $X_{\psi,i} = \{\bot, \top\}$ $T^\Psi = T^{\Psi_1} \wedge T^{\Psi_2} \wedge (\neg lb \rightarrow (x'_{\psi,0} \leftrightarrow x'_{\psi_2,0} \vee (x'_{\psi_1,0} \wedge x_{\psi,0})))$ $\qquad\quad \wedge ((lb \wedge \neg le) \rightarrow \bigwedge_{i=0}^{h(\psi)-1} (x'_{\psi,i} \leftrightarrow x'_{\psi_2,min(i,h(\psi_2))} \vee (x'_{\psi_1,min(i,h(\psi_1))} \wedge x_{\psi,i})))$ $\qquad\quad \wedge ((lb \wedge le) \rightarrow \bigwedge_{i=0}^{h(\psi)-1} (x'_{\psi,i+1} \leftrightarrow x'_{\psi_2,min(i+1,h(\psi_2))} \vee (x'_{\psi_1,min(i+1,h(\psi_1))} \wedge x_{\psi,i})))$ $\qquad\quad \wedge (lb \rightarrow (x'_{\psi,h(\psi)} \leftrightarrow x'_{\psi_2,h(\psi_2)} \vee (x'_{\psi_1,h(\psi_1)} \wedge x_{\psi,h(\psi)})))$ $I^\Psi = I^{\Psi_1} \wedge I^{\Psi_2} \wedge (x_{\psi,0} \leftrightarrow x_{\psi_2,0}) \qquad F^\Psi = F^{\Psi_1} \cup F^{\Psi_2}$

fixed point for **U** formulae, are only applied to the last generation of the corresponding variables.

The intuition is as follows. Starting with generation 0 on the stem and the first iteration of the loop, each generation i of $x_{\psi,i}$ represents the truth of ψ in one loop iteration, the end of which is signaled by $lb \wedge le$ being true. Formally, for $i < h(\psi)$, $x_{\psi,i}(j)$ holds the truth of ψ at position j of a word iff $lb \wedge le$ has been true on that path i times prior to the current state. From the $h(\psi)$-th occurrence of $lb \wedge le$, $x_{\psi,h(\psi)}$ continues to represent the truth of ψ.

Note that lb and le are oracles. The valuation of these variables on an arbitrary run may not correspond to the situations they are named after. However, for B^ϕ_{SB} to correctly recognize $\{\alpha \mid \alpha \models \phi\}$, it is not relevant which generation holds the truth at a given position. It is only required that at each position some generation represents truth correctly, each generation passes on to the next at some point, and ultimately, depending on ψ, the last generation $h(\psi)$ continues to hold the proper values.

For tightness, the variables of a given generation need to be able to take on the same values in every iteration of the loop, regardless of whether they currently hold the truth or not. This requires breaking the links to previous iterations for variables of generation 0 representing **Y** and **S** formulae at each start of a loop iteration after the first. In addition, **Y**- and **S**-variables of generations > 0 may not be constrained by past values at the beginning of the loop body. On a shortest run on some lasso-shaped word α, lb and le will correctly signal loop body and loop end.

Theorem 2. *Let ϕ be a PLTLB formula, let B^ϕ_{SB} be defined as above. Then, $Lang(B^\phi_{SB})$ $= \{\alpha \mid \alpha \models \phi\}$ and B^ϕ_{SB} is tight.*

Proof. By Lemma 3 and 4. $\square$

Lemma 3. $Lang(B^\phi_{SB}) = \{\alpha \mid \alpha \models \phi\}$

Proof. (Correctness) We show that on every fair path in $(V^\phi_{SB}, I^\phi, T^\phi_{SB}, F^\phi_{SB})$ the values of $x_{\psi,i_j}(j)$ represent the validity of the subformula ψ at position j, where i_j is either the number of le's seen so far or $h(\psi)$, whichever is smaller. Formally, let ρ be a run on α in $(V^\phi_{SB}, I^\phi, T^\phi_{SB}, F^\phi_{SB})$. For each position j in α, let $i_j = min(|\{k \mid (k \leq j-1) \wedge lb(\rho(k)) \wedge le(\rho(k))\}|, h(\psi))$. Inspection of Tab. 2 shows that the constraints on the $x_{\psi,i_j}(j)$ are the same as the constraints on the corresponding $x_\psi(j)$ in Tab. 1. Hence, $\alpha_j \models \psi \Leftrightarrow x_{\psi,i_j}(\rho(j))$.

(Completeness) We show that there is a run in $(V^\phi_{SB}, I^\phi, T^\phi_{SB}, F^\phi_{SB})$ for each word α. Choose a set of indices $U = \{j_0, j_1, \ldots\}$ such that $le(j) \leftrightarrow j \in U$. Further, choose $ls \leq j_0$ and set $lb(j) \leftrightarrow j \geq ls$. We inductively construct a valuation for $x_{\psi,i}(j)$ for each subformula ψ of ϕ, $i \leq h(\psi)$, and $j \geq 0$. If ψ is an atomic proposition p, set $x_{p,0}(j) \leftrightarrow (\alpha_j \models p)$. If the top level operator of ψ is Boolean, the valuation follows directly from the semantics of the operator. For **X**, each $x_{\psi,i}(j)$ is defined exactly once in Tab. 2. $\psi = \mathbf{Y}\psi_1$ is similar. Note that $h(\psi) = h(\psi_1) + 1$. Therefore, i runs only up to $h(\psi) - 2$ if $lb \wedge le$; $i = h(\psi) - 1$ is covered by the case for lb in the line below. $x_{\psi,i}(j)$ is unconstrained if $i = 0$ and $j - 1 \in U$ as well as if $i \geq 1$ and $j \leq ls$. For $\psi = \psi_1 \mathbf{U} \psi_2$, start with generation $h(\psi)$. If $x_{\psi_2,h(\psi_2)}$ remains false from some j_m on, assign $\forall j \geq j_m . x_{\psi,h(\psi)}(j) \leftrightarrow \bot$. Now work towards decreasing j from each j_n with $x_{\psi_2,h(\psi_2)}(j_n) \leftrightarrow \top$, using line 4 in the definition of T for **U**. Continue with generation $h(\psi) - 1$. Start at each $j \in U$ by obtaining $x_{\psi,h(\psi)-1}(j)$ from the previously assigned $x_{\psi,h(\psi)}(j+1)$ via line 3. Then work towards decreasing j again, using lines 1 or 2 in the definition of T until $x_{\psi,h(\psi)-1}$ is assigned for all j. This is repeated in decreasing order for each generation $0 \le i < h(\psi) - 1$. For **S**, start with $x_{\psi,0}(0)$ and proceed towards increasing j, also increasing i when $j \in U$ (lines 1 – 3 in the definition of T for **S**). When $i = h(\psi)$ is reached, assign $x_{\psi,h(\psi)}$ for all j using the fourth line in the definition of T. Then, similar to **U**, work towards decreasing i and j from each $j \in U$. Fairness follows from the definition of U, ls, and the valuation chosen for **U**.

The claim is now immediate by the definition of I_{SB}^ϕ. $\square$

Lemma 4. B_{SB}^ϕ *is tight.*

Proof. We show inductively that the valuations of the variables $x_{\psi,i}(j)$ can be chosen such that the valuation at a given relative position in a loop iteration is the same for each iteration in a generation i. Formally, let $\alpha = \beta\gamma^\omega$ with $\alpha \models \phi$. There exists a run ρ such that for all subformulae ψ of ϕ

$$\forall i \le h(\psi) . \forall j_1, j_2 \ge |\beta| . ((\exists k \ge 0 . j_2 - j_1 = k|\gamma|) \Rightarrow (x_{\psi,i}(\rho(j_1)) \leftrightarrow x_{\psi,i}(\rho(j_2))))$$

Atomic propositions, Boolean connectives, and **X** are clear. **Y** is also easy, we only have to assign the appropriate value from other iterations when $x_{\psi,i}(j)$ is unconstrained. For $\psi = \psi_1 \, \textbf{U} \, \psi_2$, by the induction hypothesis, $x_{\psi_2,h(\psi_2)}$ is either always false (in which case we assigned $x_{\psi,h(\psi)}(j)$ to false according to the proof of Lemma 3) or becomes true at the same time in each loop iteration. Hence, the claim holds for generation $h(\psi)$. From there we can proceed to previous generations in the same manner as in the proof of Lemma 3. For **S** we follow the order of assignments from the proof of Lemma 3. By induction, the claim holds for generation $h(\psi)$. From there, we proceed towards decreasing j and i. We use, by induction, the same valuations of subformulae and the same equations (though in reverse direction) as we used to get from $x_{\psi,0}(0)$ to generation $h(\psi)$. $\square$

B_{SB}^ϕ has $\textbf{O}(2^{|\phi|^2})$ states. A symbolic representation can be constructed in $\textbf{O}(|\phi|^2)$ time and space. Note, that the size of a Büchi automaton that is tight in the original sense of [17] (i.e., it recognizes shortest violating prefixes of safety properties) is doubly exponential in $|\phi|$ [17].

The same optimization as used in Sect. 2 for CGH+ can be applied. It replaces state variables for Boolean connectives with macros in order to reduce the number of BDD variables in the context of symbolic model checking with BDDs.

5   Finding Shortest Counterexamples with Symbolic Model Checking

We implemented the Büchi automaton described in the previous section for NuSMV [4]. We use our reduction of finite state model checking to reachability analysis [22] to find a shortest counterexample. For efficiency reasons, the encoding of the automaton is tightly integrated with the symbolic loop detection, which is at the heart of [22]. As an example, the signals for loop body and loop end are provided directly by the reduction rather than being separate input variables.

In fact, our implementation started as an adaptation of the very elegant encoding of PLTLB in [19] to our reduction. Only then we extracted a tight Büchi automaton from the construction. We kept our original implementation for its superior performance but chose to provide the more abstract view in the previous section, as, in our opinion, it provides better understanding and is also more widely applicable.

6   Experimental Results

In this section we compare our implementation to find shortest counterexamples with symbolic model checking from Sect. 5 with bounded model checking using the encoding of [19] and the standard LTL model checking algorithm of NuSMV [4]. For our translation, we performed invariant checking with NuSMV 2.2.2. For standard LTL, also in NuSMV 2.2.2, forward search on the reachable state space was applied. Bounded model checking was performed with the implementation of Timo Latvala in a modified NuSMV 2.1.2. If cone of influence reduction is to be used with our translation, the reduction must be applied before the translation. However, NuSMV 2.2.2 doesn't seem to provide a direct way to output the reduced model. Therefore, cone of influence reduction was disabled in all experiments. Otherwise, NuSMV 2.2.2 would find shorter loops, involving only the variables in the cone of the property, in the reduced model. Platform was an Intel Pentium IV at 2.8 GHz with 2 GB RAM running Linux 2.4.18. Timeout for each experiment was set to 1 hour, memory usage was limited to 1.5 GByte.

As the focus of this paper is on producing lasso-shaped counterexamples, only properties were chosen that proved false with such a counterexample. Results are shown in Tab. 3. The experiments include all real-world models used in [19]: abp4, brp, dme?, pci, and srg5. If the property checked in [19] has a lasso-shaped counterexample, it was used unmodified in our experiments ("L"). We also used the negated version of that property if that yields such a counterexample ("¬ L"). Some of the properties were made a liveness property by prefixing them with F (requiring a loop to prove false) or were enhanced to make part of the property non-volatile (yielding a more interesting counterexample), marked "nv". In addition, we chose some of the models from our previous work [22], with some properties already verified there and with new, more complicated properties. Templates of the properties are shown in the full version of this paper [23].

Columns 3 – 5 give the results for standard LTL model checking ("LTL"): l is the length of the counterexample, time is in seconds, and memory usage in thousand BDD nodes allocated. The 6th col. gives the length of a shortest counterexample as reported by our translation and bounded model checking. Columns 7 and 8 give run time and memory usage for our algorithm ("L2S"). The last three columns indicate run time for bounded model checking ("BMC"). The first of these is the time for the last unsuccessful iteration of the bounded model checker alone (not yet producing a counterexample), the second is the time for the first successful iteration alone (giving the shortest counterexample), and the last column is the time for all bounds from 1 until a counterexample is found. The implementation of [19] is not incremental [25], i.e., the SAT solver cannot benefit from results of previous iterations. We use the time required for the last unsuccessful iteration ("Time $l - 1$") to estimate the amount of work that an incremental implementation

Table 3. Real-world examples

model	property	LTL			L2S			BMC		
		l'	time	memory	l	time	memory	time $l-1$	time l	time $1\ldots l$
1394-3-2	0	16	72.8	119	11	**7.9**	1267	9.3	3.1	54.3
	1	12	17.0	157	11	**6.8**	1556	9.4	3.7	60.0
1394-4-2	0	t.o.	t.o.	t.o.	16	462.1	34695	**219.7**	13.6	1233.6
	1	20	812.6	2356	16	429.0	44177	**314.6**	14.9	1499.9
abp4	L	37	<1	234	16	**16.3**	844	78.8	8.4	340.2
brp	¬L	6	4.8	46	1	<1	192	<1	<1	<1
	¬L, nv	68	15.0	122	24	**104.9**	1560	1005.0	260.8	3171.0
dme2	¬L	1	<1	123	1	<1	128	<1	<1	<1
	¬L, nv	40	2.3	408	39	**1.2**	52	97.4	7.9	502.9
dme5	¬L	1	11.3	112	1	**1.1**	186	<1	<1	<1
	¬L, nv	344	1533.1	330	99	**384.8**	1396	t.o.	t.o.	t.o.
dme6	¬L	1	29.1	183	1	**1.6**	362	<1	<1	<1
	¬L, nv	t.o.	t.o.	t.o.	119	**926.4**	2093	t.o.	t.o.	t.o.
pci	F L	22	231.4	341	18	t.o.	t.o.	**771.2**	965.4	1879.6
prod-cons	0	69	3.1	311	26	**16.5**	722	442.4	41.7	551.8
	1	33	2.0	250	21	**1.8**	162	25.0	11.1	126.2
	2	58	71.0	216	24	**3.1**	221	7.6	10.9	178.8
	3	42	7.9	241	24	**2.6**	224	28.0	8.93	361.6
production-cell	0	85	<1	300	81	**9.8**	220	59.1	107.8	t.o.
	1	146	1.4	241	81	t.o.	t.o.	**23.4**	30.0	t.o.
bc57-sensors	0	112	141.3	213	103	**194.1**	4382	1143.1	201.9	t.o.
srg5	¬L	16	<1	120	1	<1	74	<1	<1	<1
	¬L, nv	15	<1	31	6	1.5	217	<1	<1	<1

would at least have to do. If our algorithm needs less time than that, we conclude that our algorithm is faster. "t.o." or "m.o." indicate time- or memory-out.

Both, L2S and BMC, find significantly shorter counterexamples than LTL. Our algorithm often outperforms BMC with respect to time. On the other hand, L2S needs more memory than standard LTL in most cases. L2S may even give a speed up when compared to the standard algorithm on some examples.

7   Conclusions

We have presented a method to find shortest lasso-shaped counterexamples for full LTL. Experimental results show competitive performance with bounded model checking. We have established general criteria for Büchi automata to accept shortest lasso-shaped counterexamples, extending the notion of a tight automaton from [17]. We have presented a construction of a Büchi automaton that is tight for full LTL.

Our construction generates Büchi automata with a high number of states. In ongoing work we apply virtual unrolling to obtain tight Büchi automata from the subclass of automata that, like automata constructed with CGH+, accepts counterexamples with an overly long stem but shortest loop. This should result in tight automata with fewer states and may help to facilitate application also in explicit state model checking employing, e.g., the algorithm of [11]. Further options include using transition-labeled instead of state-labeled automata [1] as well as more deterministic automata [24].

Acknowledgements. We thank Timo Latvala for providing us with his modified variant of NuSMV 2.1.2 including a very timely bug fix and Roderick Bloem for pointing us to the problem of a shortest informative vs. any shortest counterexample.

References

1. M. Awedh and F. Somenzi. Proving more properties with bounded model checking. In *CAV'04*, volume 3114 of *LNCS*, pages 96–108. Springer, 2004.
2. M. Benedetti and A. Cimatti. Bounded model checking for past LTL. In *TACAS'03*, volume 2619 of *LNCS*, pages 18–33. Springer, 2003.
3. A. Biere, A. Cimatti, E. Clarke, and Y. Zhu. Symbolic model checking without BDDs. In *TACAS'99*, volume 1579 of *LNCS*, pages 193–207. Springer, 1999.
4. A. Cimatti, E. Clarke, E. Giunchiglia, F. Giunchiglia, M. Pistore, M. Roveri, R. Sebastiani, and A. Tacchella. NuSMV 2: An opensource tool for symbolic model checking. In *CAV'02*, volume 2404 of *LNCS*, pages 359–364. Springer, 2002.
5. A. Cimatti, M. Roveri, and D. Sheridan. Bounded verification of past LTL. In *FMCAD'04*, volume 3312 of *LNCS*. Springer, 2004.
6. E. Clarke, O. Grumberg, and K. Hamaguchi. Another look at LTL model checking. *FMSD*, 10(1):47–71, 1997.
7. E. Clarke, O. Grumberg, K. McMillan, and X. Zhao. Efficient generation of counterexamples and witnesses in symbolic model checking. In *DAC'95*, pages 427–432. ACM, 1995.
8. C. Courcoubetis, M. Vardi, P. Wolper, and M. Yannakakis. Memory-efficient algorithms for the verification of temporal properties. *FMSD*, 1(2/3):275–288, 1992.
9. A. Emerson. Temporal and modal logic. In J. van Leeuwen, editor, *Handbook of Theoretical Computer Science: Volume B, Formal Methods and Semantics*, pages 995–1072. North-Holland Pub. Co., 1990.
10. D. Gabbay. The declarative past and imperative future. In *Temporal Logic in Specification*, volume 398 of *LNCS*, pages 409–448. Springer, 1989.
11. P. Gastin, P. Moro, and M. Zeitoun. Minimization of counterexamples in SPIN. In *SPIN'04*, volume 2989 of *LNCS*, pages 92–108. Springer, 2004.
12. R. Gerth, D. Peled, M. Vardi, and P. Wolper. Simple on-the-fly automatic verification of linear temporal logic. In *PSTV'95*, volume 38 of *IFIP Conference Proceedings*, pages 3–18. Chapman & Hall, 1996.
13. A. Groce and D. Kröning. Making the most of BMC counterexamples. In A. Biere and O. Strichman, editors, *BMC'04*, pages 71–84, 2004.
14. The VIS Group. VIS: A system for verification and synthesis. In *CAV'96*, volume 1102 of *LNCS*, pages 428–432. Springer, 1996.
15. J. Kamp. *Tense Logic and the Theory of Linear Order*. PhD thesis, University of California at Los Angeles, 1968.
16. Y. Kesten, A. Pnueli, and L. Raviv. Algorithmic verification of linear temporal logic specifications. In *ICALP'98*, volume 1443 of *LNCS*, pages 1–16. Springer, 1998.
17. O. Kupferman and M. Vardi. Model checking of safety properties. In *CAV'99*, volume 1633 of *LNCS*, pages 172–183. Springer, 1999.
18. F. Laroussinie, N. Markey, and P. Schnoebelen. Temporal logic with forgettable past. In *LICS'02*, pages 383–392. IEEE Computer Society, 2002.
19. T. Latvala, A. Biere, K. Heljanko, and T. Junttila. Simple is better: Efficient bounded model checking for past LTL. In *VMCAI'05*, volume 3385 of *LNCS*. Springer, 2005.
20. K. Ravi, R. Bloem, and F. Somenzi. A comparative study of symbolic algorithms for the computation of fair cycles. In *FMCAD'00*, volume 1954 of *LNCS*, pages 143–160. Springer, 2000.

21. K. Schneider. Improving automata generation for linear temporal logic by considering the automaton hierarchy. In *LPAR'01*, volume 2250 of *LNCS*, pages 39–54. Springer, 2001.

22. V. Schuppan and A. Biere. Efficient reduction of finite state model checking to reachability analysis. *International Journal on Software Tools for Technology Transfer (STTT)*, 5(2–3):185–204, 2004.

23. V. Schuppan and A. Biere. Shortest counterexamples for symbolic model checking of LTL with past. Technical Reports 470, ETH Zürich, Computer Systems Institute, 01 2005.

24. R. Sebastiani and S. Tonetta. "More deterministic" vs. "smaller" Büchi automata for efficient LTL model checking. In *CHARME'03*, volume 2860 of *LNCS*, pages 126–140. Springer, 2003.

25. O. Shtrichman. Pruning techniques for the SAT-based bounded model checking problem. In *CHARME'01*, volume 2144 of *LNCS*, pages 58–70. Springer, 2001.

26. F. Somenzi and R. Bloem. Efficient Büchi automata from LTL formulae. In *CAV'00*, volume 1855 of *LNCS*, pages 248–263. Springer, 2000.

27. M. Vardi and P. Wolper. An automata-theoretic approach to automatic program verification. In *LICS'86*, pages 332–344. IEEE Computer Society, 1986.

Snapshot Verification

Blaise Genest[1], Dietrich Kuske[2], Anca Muscholl[3], and Doron Peled[1]

[1]Department of Computer Science, University of Warwick,
Coventry CV4 7AL, United Kingdom
[2]Institut für Informatik, Universität Leipzig,
D-04009 Leipzig, Germany
[3]LIAFA, Université Paris 7, 2 place Jussieu,
75251 Paris Cedex 05, France

Abstract. The classical model for concurrent systems is based on observing execution sequences of global states, separated from each other by atomic transitions. This model is intuitively simple and enjoys a variety of mathematical tools, e.g., finite automata and linear temporal logic, and algorithms that can be applied in order to test and verify concurrent systems. Although this model is sufficient for most frequently used validation tasks, some phenomena of concurrent systems are difficult to express using its related formalisms. In particular, not all the global states (snapshots) related to an execution appear on a particular execution sequence; some appear on equivalent sequences. Previous attempts to move into formalisms that are based on a more detailed model of execution, e.g,. the causality based model, resulted in specification formalisms with inherently high complexity verification algorithms. We study here verification problems that involve allowing the execution sequences model to observe past global states from equivalent executions. We show various algorithms and complexity results related to our extension of the interleaving model.

1 Introduction

Several temporal logics are tailored to reason about partial order executions. With such logics, we are interested in local states of actions that occurred according to the partial order, or in the global states compatible with a partial order. A partial order among events can be completed into multiple total orders that are consistent with it, forming a set of *equivalent* execution sequences. As these equivalent sequences cannot be distinguished by an observer not capable of monitoring instantaneously concurrent processes, it is unnatural to distinguish between them. A specification that permits some interleaving sequence but forbids another equivalent one is possibly ambiguous. Local temporal logics like TLC [5], LocTL [8] and all MSO-definable temporal logics [12], do not distinguish equivalent sequences and allow model-checking in PSPACE. But expressing global properties of the system is notoriously hard in most of these formalisms. Alternatively, one can use global temporal logics that are tailored

N. Halbwachs and L. Zuck (Eds.): TACAS 2005, LNCS 3440, pp. 510–525, 2005.

to express global properties. The inherent problem of these logics is the very high computational complexity (e.g., EXSPACE-complete for the *UNTIL*-free fragment of ISTL [4] and non-elementary for LTrL [24, 26]).

In this paper, we consider a global temporal logic whose capability to talk about partial-order properties is restricted to expressing elementary properties of snapshots.

As a partial order execution model we select Mazurkiewicz traces. Namely, equivalence classes of sequences over some finite alphabet generated using a (fixed) independence relation over the alphabet. Two sequences are equivalent exactly when we can obtain one from the other by commuting adjacent independent occurrences of letters. Thus, if the alphabet includes a, b and c, where a and b are independent, but both interdependent with c, then we have $cabba \equiv caabb$, with $[cabba]$ denoting the trace (equivalence class) that includes the denoted sequence. A trace $[v]$ subsumes a trace $[u]$ if there is a sequence u' such that $v \equiv uu'$. In concurrency theory, this represents the fact that $[u]$ is a (possible) past of $[v]$. For example, $[cab]$ subsumes itself, $[ca]$, $[cb]$, $[c]$ and $[\epsilon]$ (the empty trace). Informally, we also say that the word cab subsumes cb.

We describe the Snapshot Linear Temporal Logic, a new temporal logic with propositions $[p]$, expressing that a state satisfying p has to be subsumed. Together with that logic, we give a model-checking algorithm, which is EXPSPACE only in the size of the alphabet, and has the same complexity as the model-checking of LTL otherwise. We further identify a fragment of the logic which is PSPACE-complete only in the size of the formula, extending the model-checking algorithm for LTL. In order to gain further insight of the model-checking problem (as we do not have a tight lower bound for it), we study the model-checking of snapshots of a word. The corresponding language theoretic problem is: given a word (which can represent an execution), we want to check whether it subsumes a word that is in some language $\mathcal{L}$ (where $\mathcal{L}$ can represent some property). To formalize the problem, we consider that the property is given by a trace-closed automaton. Hence, checking whether the snapshot of a word satisfies the property is equivalent to test whether $w \in [\mathcal{L}\Sigma^*]$, which is somehow related to pattern matching in traces. We later use a construction for the word problem for giving a more efficient model checking algorithm for a subset of our temporal logic.

Model-checking snapshots of a word can be seen as an extension of model-checking a word [19], which is an important task that has not received enough attention. For instance, model-checking a word is the core of runtime verification, but is also needed for DNA algorithms, or checking for a spurious counter-example in an abstracted model. We study variations of the problem, namely relaxing the dependencies and considering very long words. A case where the dependencies are not too complicated, is when the trace alphabet is series-parallel [9], that is, built on serial and parallel composition of letters. This kind of alphabets is often used to facilitate algorithms [7, 17]. To produce more efficient algorithms on very long words, we follow several papers [15, 19, 22] that consider that the word is given in a compressed way, by means of Straight Line Programs [22].

Related works deal with checking whether snapshots of an execution of a distributed system satisfy a given propositional predicate. Solutions for this appear e.g., in [11, 23]. In our work, we study the problem of checking whether such a word, or a finite state system, satisfy a given *temporal* property that also deals with snapshots.

2   Preliminaries

Let Σ be a finite alphabet. An *independence relation* is an irreflexive and symmetric relation $I \subseteq \Sigma \times \Sigma$. The pair (Σ, I) is called a *concurrency alphabet*.

For two words $u, v \in \Sigma^*$, write $u \overset{1}{\equiv} v$ if there exist words w_1, w_2 and letters a, b such that $(a, b) \in I$, $u = w_1 ab w_2$ and $v = w_1 ba w_2$, i.e., if u is obtained from v by exchanging the order of two adjacent independent letters. Let $\equiv$ be the reflexive and transitive closure of the relation $\overset{1}{\equiv}$. We say that u and v are *trace equivalent* [18] over (Σ, I) if $u \equiv v$. That is, u is trace equivalent to v if u can be obtained from v by repeatedly commuting adjacent independent letters.

We next want to extend this equivalence to infinite words. Denote by $u \prec v$ the fact that u is a finite prefix of v. For two infinite words $w_1, w_2 \in \Sigma^\omega$ over Σ, we write $w_1 \equiv^{\lim} w_2$ iff

- for every $u \in \Sigma^*$ such that $u \prec w_1$ there exist $v, v' \in \Sigma^*$ such that $v \prec w_2$ and $uv' \equiv v$, and
- for every $u \in \Sigma^*$ such that $u \prec w_2$ there exist $v, v' \in \Sigma^*$ such that $v \prec w_1$ and $uv' \equiv v$.

Since no confusion can arise, we abbreviate $w_1 \equiv^{\lim} w_2$ by $w_1 \equiv w_2$, i.e., we consider the *trace equivalence* $\equiv$ as an equivalence relation on the set of finite and infinite words. A *trace* is an equivalence class w.r.t. $\equiv$. It is usually denoted by writing one representative of the equivalence class in square brackets, e.g., $[abaac]$. The alphabet and independence relation should be clear from the context. Note that $u \equiv u'$ and $v \equiv v'$ imply $uv \equiv u'v'$ (for u, u' finite and v, v' possibly infinite). Thus, we can define a concatenation of traces simply by $[u][v] = [uv]$ for a finite word u and a finite or infinite word v. A trace $[u]$ *subsumes* $[v]$, denoted $[v] \sqsubseteq [u]$ if there exists some v' such that $u \equiv vv'$ (equivalently, if $[u] = [v][v']$). For a language L of finite and infinite words we write $[L]$ for the set $\{u \mid u \equiv v, v \in L\}$.

A (labeled) *transition system over* Σ is a tuple $\mathcal{A} = (S, E, \iota, \Sigma)$ with set of states S, transitions $E \subseteq S \times \Sigma \times S$, and initial state $\iota \in S$. An *automaton* is a transition system extended by a set of accepting states F. It is *trace-closed* if $[\mathcal{L}(\mathcal{A})] = \mathcal{L}(\mathcal{A})$, i.e., if its language is closed under the trace equivalence $\equiv$.

3   Snapshot Linear Temporal Logic

3.1   Syntax, Semantics, and Motivation

We extend the definition of Linear Temporal Logic (LTL) by adding a construct for dealing with snapshots. We call the new extension *Snapshot Linear Temporal Logic* or SLTL. Let $\mathcal{P}$ be a finite set of propositional formulas and $Bool(\mathcal{P})$ be the set of Boolean combinations of propositions over $\mathcal{P}$.

$$\varphi ::= p \mid [p] \mid (\neg\varphi) \mid (\varphi \vee \varphi) \mid (\bigcirc\varphi) \mid (\Box\varphi) \mid (\varphi\mathcal{U}\varphi)$$

where $p \in Bool(\mathcal{P})$. Note that the '[ ]' construct is applied only to a Boolean expression, never to a formula with modalities. Note also that we use square brackets for two different (although related) notions: for trace equivalence classes, as in the previous section, and in the logic to denote that a Boolean combination holds in a subsumed snapshot.

A *Kripke structure* $\mathcal{S} = (S, E, \iota, \Sigma, val)$ is a deterministic transition system (S, E, ι, Σ) together with a valuation function $val : S \rightarrow 2^{\mathcal{P}}$ assigning to a state s those atomic propositions that hold in this state. We now fix a Kripke structure $\mathcal{S}$. For a word $w \in \Sigma^*$, let $state(\iota, w)$ denote the unique state that is obtained by applying the actions of w to the initial state ι. The interpretation of SLTL-formulas is defined over a pair of sequences $u \in \Sigma^\star$ and $v \in \Sigma^\omega$.

- $(u, v) \models p$ iff $p \in val(state(\iota, u))$ for $p \in \mathcal{P}$.
- $(u, v) \models [p]$ iff there exists a sequence $u' \in \Sigma^\star$ such that $[u'] \sqsubseteq [u]$ and $state(\iota, u') \models p$ for $p \in Bool(\mathcal{P})$ (according to propositional logic).
- $(u, v) \models \neg\varphi$ iff $(u, v) \not\models \varphi$.
- $(u, v) \models \varphi \vee \psi$ iff $(u, v) \models \varphi$ or $(u, v) \models \psi$.
- $(u, v) \models \bigcirc\varphi$ iff $(ua, v') \models \varphi$ where $a \in \Sigma$ and $v' \in \Sigma^\omega$ with $v = av'$.
- $(u, v) \models \varphi\mathcal{U}\psi$ iff we can write $v = wv'$ such that $(uw, v') \models \psi$ and for any decomposition $w = w_1 w_2$ where w_2 is nonempty, $(uw_1, w_2v) \models \varphi$.

Based on these temporal operators, we can define (as usual) several other ones. In particular, $\varphi \wedge \psi = \neg((\neg\varphi) \vee (\neg\psi))$, $\varphi\mathcal{V}\psi = \neg((\neg\varphi)\mathcal{U}(\neg\psi))$, *true* $= p \vee \neg p$, *false* $= p \wedge \neg p$, $\Box\varphi = false\mathcal{V}\varphi$, and $\Diamond\varphi = true\mathcal{U}\varphi$.

It is not hard to verify that the following are tautologies involving the new snapshot operator:

$$\Box([p] \rightarrow \Box[p]) \qquad \Box(p \rightarrow [p]) \qquad \Box(([p \wedge q]) \rightarrow [p] \wedge [q])$$
$$\Box(([p] \vee [q]) \leftrightarrow [p \vee q]) \quad \Box(\neg[p] \rightarrow [\neg p])$$

To motivate such a logic, we describe a situation where an execution is a partial order of events, and a global state is a collection of local states of the different system components that are *history closed*. History closeness means that if the past or history (basically, a set of events) includes some event, then it must also include any event that happened previously. This notion of global states coincides with Chandy and Lamport's snapshot algorithm [6]. In an equivalent way, such a global state is related to snapshots as defined in Section 2. Thus, unlike interleaving semantics, we do not just have a simple sequence of global states. Snapshots are in particular important for achieving fault tolerance, where occasional snapshots of a distributed system are saved in order to allow the system to recover in a consistent way.

In our example, consider a bank with several branches, in different states. The bank operation hours in the different states accord with the local time. There is no global observation of the bank operation. Different branches can update each other by making phone calls. The bank employees are working according to some code of conduct that dictates what action to take in different situations. The customers can make various interactions with their branches (or even visit other branches), including deposits withdrawals and balance enquiries. Phone calls between branches are also actions of the system.

The bank analysts prepared a finite state model of the bank, and have written a specification of allowed behaviors of the bank system, using our specification formalism. The marked nodes in the graph correspond to some bank targets, e.g., having a certain balance, which is defined as the sum of money over the different branches in some global state. The bank lawyers can use histories of the executed actions to show that a balance existed. The bank does not stop everything in all branches to take frequent global and synchronized snapshots, e.g., printing the balance in each branch at exactly every hour. Hence snapshots are a good notion of balance that they can have.

We can express the fact that the bank has a positive balance snapshot for every (execution) sequence by $\Diamond[p]$, where p is a predicate denoting positive balance. This does not mean that p holds for some state in every execution sequence. We can also express the fact that q starts to hold for the minimal state that has a subsumed snapshot satisfying p by $(\neg q \wedge \neg[p])\mathcal{U}(q \wedge [p])$. We can extend the logic with related operators. For example, under the current definitions, $\Box\Diamond[p]$ does not mean under our semantics that there are infinitely many subsumed snapshots satisfying p, since $[p]$ is monotonic, thus one snapshot satisfying p suffices. Therefore, we can add an appropriate construct to capture such a property.

3.2 Model-Checking SLTL

In this section, we outline an algorithm that decides whether an SLTL-formula φ holds true for all words in a given Kripke structure $\mathcal{S} = (S, E, \iota, \Sigma, val)$. The idea is to construct a second Kripke structure $\mathcal{B}$ that includes the 'memory' which is required for deciding snapshot properties. While $\mathcal{P}$ is the set of atomic propositions of $\mathcal{S}$, we allow in $\mathcal{B}$ atomic propositions of the form p for $p \in \mathcal{P}$ as well as $[p]$ for $p \in Bool(\mathcal{P})$.

- The state set $S^{\mathcal{B}}$ equals $2^{S \times 2^{\Sigma}} \times S$. For $s = (\mathcal{X}, t) \in S^{\mathcal{B}}$, we write $current(s) = t \in S$ and $past(s) = \{s' \in S \mid \exists A \subseteq \Sigma : (s', A) \in \mathcal{X}\}$.
- The valuation function $val^{\mathcal{B}}$ is given by $val^{\mathcal{B}}(\mathcal{X}, s) = val(s) \cup \{[p] \mid \exists t \in past(\mathcal{X}, s) : t \models p\}$.
- There is an a-labeled edge in $E^{\mathcal{B}}$ from $(\mathcal{X}, s)$ to $(\mathcal{Y}, t)$ if

1. $(s, a, t) \in E$, and
2. $\mathcal{Y}$ is the set of all pairs $(t', B) \in S \times 2^{\Sigma}$ for which there is $(s', A) \in \mathcal{X}$ satisfying either
   (a) $s' = t'$ and $B = A \cup \{a\}$, or
   (b) $(s', a, t') \in E$, $A = B$, and $\{a\} \times A \subseteq I$.

- the initial state $\iota^{\mathcal{B}}$ is $(\{(\iota, \emptyset)\}, \iota)$

Intuitively, we keep in every state of $\mathcal{B}$ the current state s on $\mathcal{A}$ given the same sequence of letters from the initial state. In addition, we keep with s the set of states of subsumed traces. If t is a state of a subsumed trace, then we keep with it also the set A of letters (but not the actual sequence) that belong to the difference between the actual sequence and the subsumed one. Let $s \xrightarrow{a} r$ in E. Given a pair $\langle t, A \rangle$ kept as a past of s we generate the following pairs as a past of r: We add a to A and remain in state t, obtaining $\langle t, A \cup \{a\} \rangle$. This is because the set of subsumed traces is just extended, and if $t \xrightarrow{v} s$ then $t \xrightarrow{va} r$. Another pair is formed when a is independent of all letters in A. In this case we can also progress from t to r according to the transition relation of E obtaining $\langle r, A \rangle$. This is because if $u \equiv vv'$ (and hence $[v]$ is a prefix of $[u]$), and a is independent of the letters in v') then $[va]$ is a prefix of $[ua]$ and $t \xrightarrow{v'} r$.

A model-checking algorithm for SLTL uses the structure $\mathcal{B}$ instead of $\mathcal{S}$. Let φ be some SLTL-formula whose validity over $\mathcal{S}$ we want to check. Recall that the atomic propositions of $\mathcal{B}$ are of the form p for $p \in \mathcal{P}$ and $[p]$ for p a Boolean combination of elements from $\mathcal{P}$. Hence φ can be seen as a classical LTL-formula speaking about paths in the structure $\mathcal{B}$. Because of the construction of $\mathcal{B}$ from $\mathcal{S}$, we get for any infinite word v: $(\varepsilon, v) \models_{\mathcal{S}} \varphi$ (seen as SLTL-formula) iff $(\varepsilon, v) \models_{\mathcal{B}} \varphi$ (seen as LTL-formula). Now the well-known model-checking algorithm (i.e., translating the LTL-formula $\neg\varphi$ into an automaton and checking emptiness of the intersection of this automaton and $\mathcal{B}$) yields the following result

Theorem 1. Let $\mathcal{S}$ be a Kripke structure describing the system, and φ be an SLTL-formula of the Snapshot Linear Temporal Logic. Then one can check whether $\mathcal{S} \models \varphi$ in EXPSPACE, with a space complexity of $\mathcal{O}(|\mathcal{S}| \times 2^{|\Sigma|} \times |\varphi|)$, that is, in space complexity exponential only in the size of the alphabet.

4   Model-Checking Snapshots of a Word

We are given a language $L = [L]$ i.e., a language closed under trace equivalence w.r.t. some concurrency alphabet (Σ, I). We are also given an automaton $\mathcal{A}$ such that $L = \mathcal{L}(\mathcal{A})$, and a word $w \in \Sigma^*$. We want to check whether some snapshot of w fulfills the property given by $\mathcal{A}$, that is, whether $w \in [L\Sigma^*]$. Note that the language $[L\Sigma^*]$ consists of words from L where arbitrary letters are appended to them, and then shuffled to the left according to the independence relation I.

4.1   A Non deterministic Construction for the Membership Problem

Let $I \subseteq \Sigma^2$ be an independence relation and $\mathcal{A} = (S, E, \iota, \Sigma, F)$ be a trace-closed automaton.

For checking emptiness or inclusion of a word $w \equiv xy$ in the language $[\mathcal{L}(\mathcal{A})\Sigma^*]$ with $x \in \mathcal{L}(\mathcal{A})$, we can make the following construction. The idea is to guess the set of letters of the suffix of x that can still appear (as opposed to the previous automaton which kept what is used before from any point, hence had to keep many histories). Thus, the set of states is $S \times 2^\Sigma$ and a state $\langle s, A \rangle$ is accepting iff $s \in F$. The initial state is $\langle \iota, \Sigma \rangle$. Given a letter $a \in \Sigma$, there is a transition from state $\langle s, A \rangle$ labeled by a to $\langle s, B \rangle$, where $B \subseteq A$ excludes any letter from A that depends on a. If $a \in A$, we continue from a state $\langle s, A \rangle$ according to the transition relation of $\mathcal{A}$ to a state $\langle t, A \rangle$.

Formally, we define an automaton $\mathcal{D}$ with the following transitions:

- $\langle s, A \rangle \xrightarrow{a} \langle s, B \rangle$, when $B = A \setminus \{b \in A \mid (b, a) \in D\}$.
- $\langle s, A \rangle \xrightarrow{a} \langle t, A \rangle$, when $a \in A$ and $s \xrightarrow{a} t \in E$.

Basically, $\mathcal{D}$ is built on $2^{|\Sigma|}$ copies of $\mathcal{A}$. Now, consider that if a word belongs to $\mathcal{L}(\mathcal{D})$, then it will pass through at most $|\Sigma|$ of these copies. That is, these Σ automata can be non-deterministically guessed, together with the positions of w where the transition from one automaton to another is made. Then, it suffices to test whether each factor of w between two consecutive positions belongs to the automaton that was guessed, which can be easily performed in polynomial time.

Theorem 2. Let (Σ, I) be a concurrency alphabet. Let $\mathcal{A}$ be a trace-closed automaton and w a word of Σ^*. Then one can test in NP whether $w \in [\mathcal{L}(\mathcal{A})\Sigma^*]$. If the alphabet is fixed (not part of the input), then the problem is NLOGSPACE.

4.2   Lower Bound in the Deterministic Case

In this section, we show that the minimal deterministic automaton accepting $[L\Sigma^*]$ is exponential in the size of the automaton accepting L. To this aim, let $\Sigma = \{a, b, c, d\}$ with $I = \{a, b\} \times \{c, d\}$. We consider, for $p \in \mathbb{N}$, the language $L_p = [\{uavc \mid u \in \{a, b\}^*, v \in \{c, d\}^*, |u| \equiv |v| \mod p\}]$. Because of the special form of the independence relation I, a word $w \in \Sigma^*$ belongs to L_p iff its projection to $\{a, b\}$ ends with an a, its projection to $\{c, d\}$ ends with a c, and these two projections have the same length modulo p. Thus, in order to accept L_p, we need to count modulo p the occurrences of letters from $\{a, b\}$ and remember the last one of them, and similarly for $\{c, d\}$. Thus, we need $4 \cdot p^2$ many states.

Now let $u_1, \cdots, u_n \in \{a, b\}$ and $v_1, \cdots, v_m \in \{c, d\}$. Then the words $u_1 \ldots u_n v_1 \ldots v_m$ and $u_1 \ldots u_i v_1 \ldots v_j u_{i+1} \ldots u_n v_{j+1} \ldots v_m$ are equivalent for any i and j. Hence the former belongs to $[L_p \Sigma^*]$ iff there are $1 \leq i \leq n$ and $1 \leq j \leq m$ with $i = j \pmod p$, $u_i = a$ and $v_j = c$.

We want to show that in order to accept $[L_p \Sigma^*]$ with a deterministic automaton, we need exponentially many states (exponential in p): For a set $X =

$\{x_1, x_2, \ldots, x_n\} \subseteq \{0, 1, \ldots, p-1\}$ let $u_X = (b^{x_1} ab^{p-x_1-1})(b^{x_2} ab^{p-x_2-1}) \ldots$ $(b^{x_n} ab^{p-x_n-1})$. Then, by the observation in the previous paragraph, for $m < p$ we have $u_X d^m c \in [L_p \cdot \Sigma^*] \iff \exists i : m = x_i \pmod{p} \iff m \in X$.

Now suppose $\mathcal{A}$ is a deterministic automaton accepting $[L_p \Sigma^*]$ and let ι be its initial state. Furthermore, let X and X' be two distinct subsets of $\{0, 1, \ldots, p-1\}$ and suppose that they both lead to the same state when executed in the initial state of $\mathcal{A}$. Then there is (without loss of generality) $x \in S \setminus X'$. Since u_X and $u_{X'}$ lead to the same state, so do $u_X d^x c$ and $u_{X'} d^x c$. Since $u_X d^x c \in [L_p \Sigma^*]$ this state is accepting, implying that $u_{X'} d^x c$ is accepted by $\mathcal{A}$. Since this contradicts our assumption on $\mathcal{A}$ to accept $[L_p \Sigma^*]$, two distinct words of the form u_X cannot lead to the same state of $\mathcal{A}$ when executed in the initial state ι. Since there are exponentially many words u_X, the automaton $\mathcal{A}$ has exponentially many states.

Note that, in contrast to the exponential lower bound for a deterministic automaton, Theorem 2 gives a polynomial non deterministic automaton accepting $[L_p \Sigma^*]$ (since the alphabet is fixed).

5   A PSPACE-Complete Fragment of SLTL

We define now the 'negative' fragment of SLTL, whose model-checking exploits the model-checking of snapshots of a word (see section 4). Let us look at the usual normal form of LTL, that is when only the expression $\{p, [p]\}$ can use negation (negation is pushed the deepest possible). Then we say that a formula φ is a *negative* formula of SLTL if in the normal form of $\neg \varphi$, the negation is used only over Boolean combinations. That is, the snapshot expressions $[p]$ only appear in a positive form (in the negation of the formula). Note that negation may appear inside the '[ ]' operator. For instance, the property $\varphi = \Box \neg [p] \vee \Box \neg [q]$ is a negative formula of SLTL since $\neg \varphi = (\Diamond [p] \wedge \Diamond [q])$.

Notice that every LTL formula is a negative formula of SLTL since it does not use $[p]$. Hence, model-checking of negative SLTL formulas is already PSPACE-hard.

We show now how to do model-checking in PSPACE for such a formula. We use the LTL translation [14], except that subformulas of the form $[p]$ are kept as a whole (as in the construction for Theorem 1). This construction does not introduce new negations to propositional letters or snapshot subexpressions (as opposed e.g., to the construction in [25]). We know that there exists an automaton $\mathcal{B}_{\neg \varphi}$ accepting $\mathcal{L}(\neg \varphi)$, labeled by $p, \neg p$ and by *positive* $[p]$, whose size is exponential in $|\varphi|$.

We check each subformula $[p]$ on a separate automaton copy, computing the snapshots (trace prefixes) of $\mathcal{S}$, that is $[\mathcal{L}(\mathcal{S}) \Sigma^*]$, as constructed in Section 4.1. Note however that for two different $[p], [q]$, the prefixes need not be the same, and thus we need two different copies of the trace prefix automaton. Notice that once $[p]$ holds, it holds forever, so we need not have several copies for the same subformula $[p]$.

For every subformula $[p]$ (there are at most $|\varphi|$ such propositions), we create an automaton $\mathcal{S}_p$ from the Kripke structure $\mathcal{S}$ as follows: states, initial states, and transitions are those from S and a state is accepting iff it satisfies p; i.e., S_p accepts all those words that lead to a state in S satisfying p. There exists an automaton $\mathcal{A}_p$ of size exponential only in $|\Sigma|$ accepting $[\mathcal{L}(S_p)\Sigma^*]$ (see section 4.1). We just need to check whether there exists accepting paths $\rho_{\neg\varphi}, \rho, \rho_{p_1}, \cdots, \rho_{p_n}$ of $\mathcal{A}_{\neg\varphi}, S, \mathcal{A}_{p_1}, \cdots, \mathcal{A}_{p_n}$ labeled by the same word w (in the different copies), such that for every prefix u of w, the state $v_{\neg\varphi}, v, v_{p_1}, \cdots, v_{p_n}$ reached on u satisfy: if $v_{\neg\varphi} \models (\neg)p$, then $v \models (\neg)p$ and if $v_{\neg\varphi} \models [p]$, then $v_p \models p$. Hence,

Theorem 3. Let S be a Kripke structure describing the system, and φ be a negative formula of SLTL. Then the model-checking of $S \models \varphi$ is PSPACE-complete, with a space complexity of $\mathcal{O}(\log(|S|) \cdot |\varphi| \cdot |\Sigma|)$.

6   Efficient Model-Checking of a Word

Since model-checking snapshots of a word is important (see section 4 and 5), we propose here some variations to improve its efficiency.

6.1   Series-Parallel Alphabets

We show that the membership problem in $[\mathcal{L}(\mathcal{A})\Sigma^*]$ is in PTIME provided the independence alphabet is series-parallel (see also [7, 17] for algorithms on series-parallel alphabet). Actually, we consider the more general case of deciding membership in $[\mathcal{L}(\mathcal{A})\mathcal{L}(\mathcal{B})]$ in polynomial time provided $\mathcal{A}$ and $\mathcal{B}$ are trace-closed automata over a series-parallel independence alphabet (Σ, I).

In this section, we consider independence alphabets together with a chosen total order on the letters. Let $(\Sigma_1, I_1, \leq_1)$ and $(\Sigma_2, I_2, \leq_2)$ be disjoint independence alphabets where $\leq_1$ and $\leq_2$ are linear orders on Σ_1 and Σ_2, resp. A linear order $\leq$ is defined on $\Sigma_1 \cup \Sigma_2$ by $a \leq b$ iff $a \leq_1 b$ or $a \leq_2 b$ or $a \in \Sigma_1$ and $b \in \Sigma_2$. Then the serial composition $(\Sigma_1, I_1, \leq_1) \cdot (\Sigma_2, I_2, \leq_2)$ is $(\Sigma_1 \cup \Sigma_2, I_1 \cup I_2, \leq)$. The parallel composition $(\Sigma_1, I_1, \leq_1) \parallel (\Sigma_2, I_2, \leq_2)$ is defined to be $(\Sigma_1 \cup \Sigma_2, I_1 \cup I_2 \cup (\Sigma_1 \times \Sigma_2) \cup (\Sigma_2 \times \Sigma_1), \leq)$. A *series-parallel independence alphabet* is a tuple $(\Sigma, I, \leq)$ that can be constructed from ordered independence alphabets of the form $(\{\alpha\}, \emptyset, \leq)$. A *component* of $(\Sigma, I, \leq)$ is a set $\Gamma \subseteq \Sigma$ that occurs in this inductive construction. Note that any series-parallel independence alphabet has at most $|\Sigma|$ many components.

The linear order $\leq$ on Σ can be extended to words setting $x_1 x_2 \ldots x_m \leq y_1 y_2 \ldots y_n$ if $m < n$ or $m = n$ and $x_1 < y_1$ or $m = n$, $x_1 = y_1$ and $x_2 x_3 \ldots x_m \leq y_2 y_3 \ldots y_n$. Since this length-lexicographic order is a well order on Σ^*, any trace (i.e., any equivalence class of words) contains a minimal element. We call the minimal element of $[u]$ the lexicographic normal form LNF(u) of u.

From now on, we fix some series-parallel independence alphabet $(\Sigma, I, \leq)$ and two trace-closed automata $\mathcal{A} = (S^\mathcal{A}, E^\mathcal{A}, \iota^\mathcal{A}, \Sigma, F^\mathcal{A})$ and $\mathcal{B} = (S^\mathcal{B}, E^\mathcal{B}, \iota^\mathcal{B}, \Sigma, F^\mathcal{B})$. We will construct an automaton $\mathcal{C}(\Sigma)$ with states of the form (s, t, Γ, X) where $s \in S^\mathcal{A}$, $t \in S^\mathcal{B}$, $\Gamma \subseteq \Sigma$ is a component of $(\Sigma, I, \leq)$, and X is A or B with the following property:

Let $\Gamma \subseteq \Sigma$ be a component and $u \in \Gamma^*$ be in lexicographic normal form. Then $(s,t,\Gamma,X) \xrightarrow{u}_{\mathcal{C}} (s',t',\Gamma,Y)$ iff there exist $u_A, u_B \in \Gamma^*$ with $u \equiv u_A u_B$, $s \xrightarrow{u_A}_A s'$, $t \xrightarrow{u_B}_B t'$, and $u_B = \varepsilon$ provided $X = Y = A$ and $u_A = \varepsilon$ provided $X = Y = B$.

This automaton $\mathcal{C}$ will be constructed inductively following the inductive construction of the series-parallel independence alphabet $(\Sigma, I, \leq)$, i.e., we will have automata $\mathcal{C}(\Delta)$ for any component Δ such that the above invariant holds for all components $\Gamma \subseteq \Delta$ (and $\mathcal{C}(\Delta)$ does not have transitions labeled by letters outside of Δ).

In this construction, we will use the following automata $\mathcal{A}_\Gamma$ and $\mathcal{B}_\Gamma$ for Γ a component: The set of states of $\mathcal{A}_\Gamma$ is $S^A \times S^B \times \{\Gamma\} \times \{A\}$. There is transition $(s,t,\Gamma,A) \xrightarrow{a}_{\mathcal{A}_\Gamma} (s',t',\Gamma,A)$ iff $a \in \Gamma$, $s \xrightarrow{a}_A s'$ and $t = t'$. Symmetrically, the set of states of $\mathcal{B}_\Gamma$ is $S^A \times S^B \times \{\Gamma\} \times \{B\}$ and there is a transition $(s,t,\Gamma,B) \xrightarrow{a}_{\mathcal{B}_\Gamma} (s',t',\Gamma,B)$ in $\mathcal{B}$ iff $a \in \Gamma$, $s = s'$, and $t \xrightarrow{a}_B t'$.

The base case is simple: if $|\Gamma| = 1$, then $\mathcal{C}(\Gamma)$ is the union of $\mathcal{A}_\Gamma$ and $\mathcal{B}_\Gamma$, plus transitions from $\mathcal{A}_\Gamma$ to $\mathcal{B}_\Gamma$. That is, the set of states of $\mathcal{C}(\Gamma)$ equals $S^A \times S^B \times \{\Gamma\} \times \{A, B\}$ and there is a transition $(s,t,\Gamma,X) \xrightarrow{a}_{\mathcal{C}(\Gamma)} (s',t',\Gamma,Y)$ iff $a \in \Gamma$, $s \xrightarrow{a}_A s'$, $t = t'$, and $X = A$ or $s = s'$, $t \xrightarrow{a}_B t'$ and $X = Y = B$.

Now suppose that Γ is a component that is built as the parallel product of the components Γ_1 and Γ_2. Then we take as $\mathcal{C}(\Gamma)$ the union of the automata $\mathcal{C}(\Gamma_1)$ and $\mathcal{C}(\Gamma_2)$ together with transitions of the form $(s,t,\Gamma_1,X) \xrightarrow{a}_{\mathcal{C}(\Gamma)} (s',t',\Gamma_2,Y)$ provided $a \in \Gamma$, $s \xrightarrow{a}_A s'$ and $t = t'$ or $s = s'$ and $t \xrightarrow{a}_B t'$. Note that words over Γ in lexicographic normal form belong to $\Gamma_1^* \Gamma_2^*$. This allows to prove the invariant for $\mathcal{C}(\Gamma)$.

Finally, let Γ be a component that is built as the serial product of the components Γ_1 and Γ_2. Then $\mathcal{C}(\Gamma)$ is the union of the automata $\mathcal{A}_\Gamma$, $\mathcal{C}(\Gamma_1)$, $\mathcal{C}(\Gamma_2)$, and $\mathcal{B}_\Gamma$ together with transitions of the form $(s,t,\Delta_1,X) \xrightarrow{a}_{\mathcal{C}(\Gamma)} (s',t',\Delta_2,Y)$ provided Δ_1, Δ_2 are components of Γ (already seen by induction) and one of the following holds

(1) (s,t,Δ_1,X) is a state of $\mathcal{A}_\Gamma$ and
   − (s',t',Δ_2,Y) is a state of $\mathcal{C}(\Gamma_1)$ or of $\mathcal{B}_\Gamma$ and $a \in \Gamma_2$, or
   − (s',t',Δ_2,Y) is a state of $\mathcal{C}(\Gamma_2)$ or of $\mathcal{B}_\Gamma$ and $a \in \Gamma_1$
(2) (s',t',Δ_2,Y) is a state of $\mathcal{B}_\Gamma$ and
   − (s,t,Δ_1,X) is a state of $\mathcal{C}(\Gamma_1)$ and $a \in \Gamma_2$, or
   − (s,t,Δ_1,X) is a state of $\mathcal{C}(\Gamma_2)$ and $a \in \Gamma_1$.

This construction is visualized in Figure 1. To prove the invariant for $\mathcal{C}(\Gamma)$, let $u \in \Gamma^*$ be in lexicographic normal form. Write u as an alternating sequence of nonempty words u_i from Γ_1^+ and of Γ_2^+. For any trace equivalent factorization $v\,w \equiv u_1 u_2 \ldots u_n$, there exists i and a trace equivalent factorization $v'\,w' \equiv u_i$ with $v \equiv u_1 u_2 \ldots u_{i-1} v'$ and $w \equiv w' u_{i+1} \ldots u_n$. If $v' = \varepsilon$ or $w' = \varepsilon$, we go directly from $\mathcal{A}_\Gamma$ to $\mathcal{B}_\Gamma$. Otherwise, we go from $\mathcal{A}_\Gamma$ to $\mathcal{B}_\Gamma$ via $\mathcal{C}(\Gamma_k)$ with $u_i \in \Gamma_k^+$.

Proposition 1. Let $(\Sigma, I, \leq)$ be a series-parallel independence alphabet. Moreover, let $\mathcal{A}$ and $\mathcal{B}$ be automata such that $\text{LNF}(w)$ is accepted as soon as w is

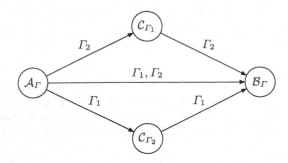

Fig. 1. Construction of $\mathcal{C}(\Gamma_1 \parallel \Gamma_2)$

accepted for any $w \in \Sigma^*$.[1] Then $u \in [\mathcal{L}(\mathcal{A})\mathcal{L}(\mathcal{B})]$ if and only if $\mathrm{LNF}(u) \in \mathcal{L}(\mathcal{C}(\Sigma))$ for any $u \in \Sigma^*$.

Note that $\mathcal{C}(\Gamma)$ is polynomial in $\mathcal{A}$ and $\mathcal{B}$ since there are only linearly many components of $(\Sigma, I, \leq)$. Since, in addition, $\mathrm{LNF}(u)$ can be constructed in polynomial time from u, we get the following improvement of Theorem 2:

Theorem 4. Let $(\Sigma, I, \leq)$ be a series-parallel independence alphabet and $\mathcal{A}$, $\mathcal{B}$ be trace-closed automata. Then we can test in polynomial time whether $w \in [\mathcal{L}(\mathcal{A})\, \Sigma^*]$.

Notice that if the automata $\mathcal{A}$ or $\mathcal{B}$ are not trace-closed, then the membership problem is NP-complete. Actually, a slightly easier problem, deciding whether there exists $v \equiv_I w$ such that $v \in \mathcal{L}(\mathcal{A})$, is already NP-complete [2]. The fact is that it remains NP-complete even if the alphabet is fully parallel, in particular even if it is series-parallel.

6.2   Compression

Usually, when one model-checks a word (see section 4), either this word comes from a very long log file (or DNA encoding), or it can be a looping run of some system: it is often very long. Having the most succinct representation for this word is then a big advantage, since it can severely decrease the runtime of the algorithm. We present here the idea of using words compressed by means of straight-line programs. If the word is not already compressed, then the tool from [1] can be used.

Straight-line programs. A straight-line program (SLP for short) over the alphabet Σ is a context-free grammar with variables $V = \{X_1, \ldots, X_k\}$, initial variable X_1 and rules from $V \times (V^* \cup \Sigma)$. The rules are such that there is exactly one rule for each left-hand side variable, and if $X_i \longrightarrow \alpha$, then each X_j in α satisfies $j > i$.

---

[1] This holds in particular if $\mathcal{A}$ and $\mathcal{B}$ are trace-closed.

The constraint on the rules makes that any variable X_i generates a unique word. For convenience, we denote the word generated by the variable X_i also as X_i. Without loss of generality, we can assume that rules are of size 2, that is of the form $X \longrightarrow YZ$ with $Y, Z \in (V \cup \{\epsilon\}) \cup \Sigma$. The size $|X|$ of an SLP X is its number of variables. Lately, algorithms on SLP-compressed objects have been intensively studied [1, 15, 19, 22]. We will used two known results, namely:

Proposition 2. Let w be an SLP, $\mathcal{A}$ an automaton and (Σ, I) a concurrency alphabet.

- The problem whether $w \in \mathcal{L}(\mathcal{A})$ is PTIME-complete [15, 19, 22], and solvable in time $\mathcal{O}(|w| \cdot |\mathcal{A}|^3)$.
- The problem whether there exists some $v \equiv_I w$ with $v \in \mathcal{L}(\mathcal{A})$ is PSPACE-complete [15].

Using the first part of proposition 2 and theorem 2, we can easily show that:

Proposition 3. Let w be an SLP and $\mathcal{A}, \mathcal{B}$ two trace-closed automata. The test whether $w \in [\mathcal{L}(\mathcal{A})\mathcal{L}(\mathcal{B})]$ is of complexity NP in the size of the alphabet (i.e., polynomial-time for a fixed alphabet).

We can restate the second result of proposition 2, showing that testing whether $w \in [\mathcal{L}(\mathcal{A})\mathcal{L}(\mathcal{B})]$ is PSPACE-complete if w is an SLP and $\mathcal{A}$ or $\mathcal{B}$ is not trace-closed. With more work, we can show that the complexity remains PSPACE-complete if the alphabet is series-parallel.

The interesting question is what happens when $\mathcal{A}, \mathcal{B}$ are both trace-closed and the alphabet is series-parallel. Actually, we manage to show that the problem is PTIME-complete in this case. That is, unlike the case where $\mathcal{A}$ or $\mathcal{B}$ is not trace-closed, compression does not increase the complexity.

Theorem 5. Let w be an SLP, (Σ, I) be a series-parallel alphabet, and $\mathcal{A}, \mathcal{B}$ be two trace-closed automata. Then testing whether $w \in [\mathcal{L}(\mathcal{A})\mathcal{L}(\mathcal{B})]$ is PTIME-complete, and solvable in time $\mathcal{O}(|w| \cdot (|\Sigma|^2 \cdot |\mathcal{A}| \cdot |\mathcal{B}|)^3)$.

Proof. Let w be an SLP. We use proposition 1 to obtain an automaton $\mathcal{C}$ that recognizes $\mathrm{LNF}(w)$ exactly when $w \in [\mathcal{L}(\mathcal{A})\mathcal{L}(\mathcal{B})]$. As soon as we obtain a polynomial-size SLP representation of $\mathrm{LNF}(w)$, we can use proposition 2 to have a PTIME algorithm for testing whether $\mathrm{LNF}(w) \in \mathcal{L}(\mathcal{C})$. It is PTIME-hard using [19].

The blow-up for obtaining an SLP representation of $\mathrm{LNF}(w)$ from an SLP w is likely to be exponential in general. Anyway, we are in the special case where the alphabet is series-parallel, for which we show now how to compute a polynomial SLP for $\mathrm{LNF}(w)$.

We first need to describe the SLP variables differently than for the SLP w. For any component alphabet Σ_i and rule $X = YZ$, we define the projection (X, Σ_i) of X on Σ_i by the rules:

- $(a, \Sigma_i) = a$ if $a \in \Sigma_i$, else $(a, \Sigma_i) = \epsilon$,
- $(X, \Sigma_i) = (Y, \Sigma_i)(Z, \Sigma_i)$.

Then, for $\Sigma_i = \Sigma_j \cdot \Sigma_k$ and $X = YZ$, we describe the longest prefix and suffix in Σ_j^* of the projection on Σ_i of X by $\mathrm{Pref}(X, \Sigma_j), \mathrm{Suf}(X, \Sigma_j)$.

The rules associated with $\mathrm{Pref}(X, \Sigma_j)$ are as follows:

- If $a \in \Sigma_j$, then $\mathrm{Pref}(a, \Sigma_j) = a$, else $\mathrm{Pref}(a, \Sigma_j) = \epsilon$.
- If $\mathrm{Pref}(Y, \Sigma_j)$ does not contain any letter from Σ_k, then
  $\mathrm{Pref}(X, \Sigma_j) = (Y, \Sigma_j)\mathrm{Pref}(Z, \Sigma_j)$, else $\mathrm{Pref}(X, \Sigma_j) = \mathrm{Pref}(Y, \Sigma_j)$.

The SLP (w, Σ) is defined using variables $(X, \Sigma_i), \mathrm{Pref}(X, \Sigma_i), \mathrm{Suf}(X, \Sigma_i)$. Then, for every rule $X = YZ$ of (w, Σ), we add the variable (XY) with the rule $(XY) = XY$. In particular, X, Y, Z can be a suffix or a prefix of variables of w. This gives an SLP of size $\mathcal{O}(2|\Sigma| \cdot |w|)$.

We can now describe the SLP $\mathrm{LNF}(w, \Sigma)$ computing $\mathrm{LNF}(w)$. For each component alphabet $\Sigma_i = \Sigma_j \cdot \Sigma_k$ and each variable $X = YZ$ of (w, Σ), we introduce new variables $\mathrm{Fact}(Y, \Sigma_h, \Sigma_l)$ for $h, l \in \{j, k\}$ representing the factor of $\mathrm{LNF}(Y, \Sigma_i)$ obtained by deleting the longest prefix of Y in Σ_h^* and the longest suffix of Y in Σ_l^*. In particular, $\mathrm{Fact}(Y, \emptyset, \Sigma_j)\mathrm{LNF}(\mathrm{Suf}(Y, \Sigma_j), \Sigma_j) = \mathrm{LNF}(Y, \Sigma_i)$.

Let $X = YZ$, $\Sigma_i = \Sigma_j \cdot \Sigma_k$ and $h, l, t \in \{j, k\}$ such that $\mathrm{Suf}(Y, \Sigma_t) \neq \epsilon$. The rule associated with $\mathrm{Fact}(X, \Sigma_h, \Sigma_l)$ is:

$\mathrm{Fact}(X, \Sigma_h, \Sigma_l) =$
$\quad \mathrm{Fact}(Y, \Sigma_h, \Sigma_t) \ \mathrm{LNF}((\mathrm{Suf}(Y, \Sigma_t)(\mathrm{Pref}(Z, \Sigma_t)), \Sigma_t) \ \mathrm{Fact}(Z, \Sigma_t, \Sigma_l)$

The rules associated with $\mathrm{LNF}(X, \Sigma_i)$ are

- $\mathrm{LNF}(a, \Sigma_i) = a$ if $a \in \Sigma_i$, else $\mathrm{LNF}(a, \Sigma_i) = \epsilon$,
- If $\Sigma_i = \Sigma_j \parallel \Sigma_k$ and $\Sigma_j \prec \Sigma_k$, then $\mathrm{LNF}(X, \Sigma_i) = \mathrm{LNF}(X, \Sigma_j)\mathrm{LNF}(X, \Sigma_k)$,
- If $\Sigma_i = \Sigma_j \cdot \Sigma_k$ with $\mathrm{Suf}(Y, \Sigma_j) \neq \epsilon$, then

  $\mathrm{LNF}(X, \Sigma_i) =$
  $\quad \mathrm{Fact}(Y, \emptyset, \Sigma_j) \ \mathrm{LNF}(\mathrm{Suf}(Y, \Sigma_j)\mathrm{Pref}(Z, \Sigma_j), \Sigma_j) \ \mathrm{Fact}(Z, \Sigma_j, \emptyset)$

Notice that in the description above, it might be the case that $\mathrm{Suf}(X, \Sigma_j)$ stands for $\mathrm{Suf}(\mathrm{Suf}(Y, \Sigma_l), \Sigma_j)$, because $X = \mathrm{Suf}(Y, \Sigma_l)$ is a variable of (w, Σ). Even though $\mathrm{Suf}(\mathrm{Suf}(Y, \Sigma_l), \Sigma_j)$ is not a variable of (w, Σ), we can express it with only one suffix, that is with variables of (w, Σ). Assume that $\Sigma_i = \Sigma_j \cdot \Sigma_k$. If $\mathrm{Suf}(Y, \Sigma_l)$ contains a letter of Σ_k, then $\mathrm{Suf}(\mathrm{Suf}(Y, \Sigma_l), \Sigma_j) = \mathrm{Suf}(Y, \Sigma_j)$. Else, $\mathrm{Suf}(\mathrm{Suf}(Y, \Sigma_l), \Sigma_j) = \mathrm{Suf}(Y, \Sigma_l)$. The case with two (or more) nested prefixes is symmetric. Notice moreover that a prefix of a suffix or a suffix of a prefix is not possible.

It is easy to show by induction that $\mathrm{LNF}(w, \Sigma)$ computes exactly the lexicographic normal form of the projection of w on Σ. Moreover, the size of the SLP $\mathrm{LNF}(w, \Sigma)$ is at most $\mathcal{O}(|\Sigma|^3 \cdot |w|)$.

Since the time complexity of checking whether an SLP S belongs to $\mathcal{L}(A)$ is $\mathcal{O}(|S| \cdot |A|^3)$, we get a complexity of $\mathcal{O}(|w| \cdot (|\Sigma|^2 \cdot |A| \cdot |B|)^3)$.   □

7   Conclusion

We described in this paper a new Linear Temporal Logic, the Snapshot LTL, which captures some properties of global logics on traces without the inherently high complexity. We proposed an EXPSPACE algorithm to do model-checking against this logic, based on a deterministic automaton construction. It would be interesting to compare the properties expressed by our logic with the one expressed by the EXPSPACE-complete fragment of LTrL [24] and of ISTL [21]. Moreover, the 'negative' fragment of SLTL is PSPACE-complete, yet more general than LTL.

We also considered model-checking for snapshots of a word, which is not easy to tackle either. For instance, the precise complexity is still unknown (but neither is known the precise complexity of model-checking a word against LTL properties [19]).

$w \in [\mathcal{L}(A)\Sigma^*]$	$\mathcal{A}$ trace-closed	$\mathcal{A}$
Normal case	NP	NP-complete
w compressed	NP	PSPACE-complete
Series-parallel	$2^{|\Sigma|} \times |\mathcal{A}|$	NP-complete
Series-parallel + compression	PTIME-complete	PSPACE-complete

Fig. 2. Complexity of the snapshot verification of a word

We studied the complexity when we vary slightly the problem (see figure 2), to understand the limits of our algorithms. We show that the time complexity becomes quickly polynomial, for instance when the alphabet is not too complex (series-parallel). Moreover, we show that the algorithms we proposed are pretty robust, since the complexity remains the same even in case where we use compressed words. On series-parallel alphabets and using compression, we obtained a PTIME-algorithm, which contrasts with the PSPACE-complete complexity as soon as $\mathcal{A}$ is not trace-closed.

Notice that this problem is somehow not complicated enough to get an NP-completeness result, since we would need for this more than a fixed number of automata. Indeed, the problem whether $w \in [\mathcal{L}(\mathcal{A}_1) \cdots \mathcal{L}(\mathcal{A}_n)]$ is NP-complete.

This work also shows that pattern matching a trace is PTIME in $|\Sigma|$ and NLOG in the size of the word (trace) if the alphabet is series-parallel, unlike the general case. In this case, our algorithm greatly simplifies the general pattern matching algorithm for compressed traces given in [15].

Acknowledgement. We would like to thank Christof Löding and Lenore Zuck for fruitful discussions and comments on this paper.

References

1. R. Alur, S. Chaudhuri, K. Etessami, S. Guha, and M. Yannakakis. Compression of Partially Ordered Strings. In *CONCUR 2003*, LNCS 2761, pp. 42-56.
2. R. Alur, K. Etessami, and M. Yannakakis. Realizability and Verification of MSC Graphs. In *ICALP 2001*, LNCS 2076, pp. 797-808.
3. R. Alur, Th. A. Henzinger, and O. Kupferman. Alternating-time Temporal Logic. JACM 49(5):672-713 (2002).
4. R. Alur, K. McMillan, and D. Peled. Deciding Global Partial-Order Properties. In *ICALP 1998*, LNCS 1443, pp. 41-52.
5. R. Alur, D. Peled, and W. Penczek. Model-Checking of Causality Properties. In *LICS 1995*, pp. 90-100.
6. K. M. Chandy, L. Lamport. Distributed Snapshots: Determining the Global State of Distributed Systems. ACM Transactions on Computer Systems 3:63-75 (1985).
7. V. Diekert and P. Gastin. Local Temporal Logic is Expressively Complete for Cograph Dependence Alphabets. In *LPAR 2001*, LNAI 2250, pp. 55-69.
8. V. Diekert and P. Gastin. Pure Future Local Temporal Logics are Expressively Complete for Mazurkiewicz Traces. In *LATIN 2004*, LNCS 2976, pp. 232-241.
9. V. Diekert and G. Rozenberg. *The Book of Traces*. World Scientific, Singapore, 1995.
10. E. A. Emerson and C. S. Jutla. The complexity of Tree Automata and Logics of Programs. In *FOCS 1988*.
11. V.K. Garg, B. Waldecker. Detecting Weak Unstable Predicates in Distributed Programs. IEEE Transactions on Parallel and Distributed Systems, 5(3):299-307 (1994).
12. P. Gastin and D. Kuske. Satisfiability and Model-Checking for MSO-definable Temporal Logics are in PSPACE. In *CONCUR 2003*, LNCS 2761, pp. 222-236.
13. P. Gastin and M. Mukund. An Elementary Expressively Complete Temporal Logic for Mazurkiewicz Traces. In *ICALP 2002*, LNCS 2380, pp. 938-949.
14. R. Gerth, D. Peled, M. Vardi, and P. Wolper. Simple on-the-fly Automatic Verification of Linear Temporal Logic. In *PSTV 1995*, pp. 3-18.
15. B. Genest and A. Muscholl. Pattern Matching and Membership for Hierarchical Message Sequence Charts. In *LATIN 2002*, LNCS 2286, pp. 326-340.
16. D. Peled and A. Pnueli. Proving Partial Order Liveness Properties. In *ICALP 1990*, pp. 553-571.
17. D. Kuske. Infinite Series-parallel Pomsets: Logic and Languages. In *ICALP 2000*, LNCS 1853, pp. 648-662.
18. A. Mazurkiewicz. Trace semantics. In *Advances in Petri Nets 1986*, LNCS 255, pp. 279-324, 1987.
19. N. Markey and Ph. Schnoebelen. Model-checking a Path. In *Concur 2003*, LNCS 2761, pp. 251-265.
20. D. Peled. Specification and Verification of Message Sequence Charts. In *FORTE/PSTV 2000*, pp.139-154.
21. D. Peled, A. Pnueli. Proving Partial Order Properties. Theoretical Computer Science, 126:143-182 (1994).
22. W. Plandowski and W. Rytter. Complexity of Language Recognition Problems for Compressed Words. Jewels are Forever, Springer, pp. 262-272, 1999.
23. S. Stoller and Y.A. Liu. Efficient Symbolic Detection of Global Properties in Distributed Systems. In *CAV 1998*, LNCS 1427, pp. 357-368.

24. P.S. Thiagarajan and I. Walukiewicz. An Expressively Complete Linear Time Temporal Logic for Mazurkiewicz Traces. Information and Computation 179(2):230-249 (2002)
25. M.Y. Vardi and P. Wolper. Reasoning About Infinite Computations. Information and Computation, 115:1-37 (1994).
26. I. Walukiewicz. Difficult Configurations – On the Complexity of LTrL. In *ICALP 1998*, LNCS 1443, pp. 140-151.

Time-Efficient Model Checking with Magnetic Disk

Tonglaga Bao and Michael Jones

Dept. of Computer Science, Brigham Young U., Provo, Utah, USA
{tonga, jones}@cs.byu.edu

Abstract. Explicit model checking with magnetic disk is prohibitively slow if file input/output (IO) is not carefully managed. We give an empirical analysis of the two published algorithms for model checking with magnetic disk and show that both algorithms minimize file IO time but are dominated by delayed duplicate detection time (which is required to avoid regenerating parts of the transition graph). We present and analyze a more *time*-efficient algorithm for model checking with magnetic disk that requires more file IO time, but less delayed duplicate detection time and less total execution time. The new algorithm is a variant of parallel partitioned hash table algorithms and uses a time-efficient chained hash table implementation.

Model checking with magnetic disk can significantly increase the space available for storing visited states. In explicit model checking, visited states are stored to avoid generating duplicate states and to aid in termination detection. In this paper, we analyze the performance of the two published model checking algorithms for use with magnetic disk and find that, while file IO is an overhead in algorithms that use disk, delayed duplicate detection is the single largest overhead. We propose a new algorithm for explicit model checking with magnetic disk that requires more file IO time but reduces duplicate detection time and total execution time. The new algorithm solves large model checking problems in less time than other disk-based algorithms and solves small problems in 15% to 27% of the time required by the RAM-only algorithm.

Delayed duplicate detection is an extra processing step added to search algorithms that use magnetic disk to store visited states. The delayed duplicate detection step compares recently generated states with a set of visited states. The purpose of this comparison is to determine if the recently generated states are duplicates of visited states or not. The set of already visited states is called the *visited candidate set* and the set of new states is called the *duplicate candidate set*. Each state in the duplicate candidate set may have a different visited candidate set. During delayed duplicate detection, each state in the duplicate candidate set is compared with the states in its visited candidate set. The cost of delayed duplicate detection is a multiple of the product of the size of the visited candidate set and the average size of the delayed candidate sets. Reducing the size of either candidate set reduces the cost of delayed duplicate detection.

N. Halbwachs and L. Zuck (Eds.): TACAS 2005, LNCS 3440, pp. 526–540, 2005.

Korf [5] and Zhou [13] give a more thorough discussion of the role of delayed and immediate duplicate detection in search using magnetic disk in the context of artificial intelligence. Zhou's algorithm eliminates the delayed duplicate detection step for search problems that satisfy a strict locality requirement. The locality requirement is that all successors for a group of states to fall within a subset of the entire state space. The resulting search algorithm is as fast as RAM-only search for some problems and actually faster than the RAM-only algorithm for other problems (due to cache effects). Unfortunately, transition graphs often encountered in model checking do not satisfy the strict locality requirement. However, a similar focus on delayed duplicate detection in explicit model checking can yield similar positive results.

Published algorithms for explicit model checking with magnetic disk have focused on minimizing file IO time. File IO time is the time spent reading states from and writing states to magnetic disk. While these algorithms have successfully minimized file IO time, delayed duplicate detection time for these algorithms is actually much greater than file IO time. We propose two methods for reducing delayed duplicate detection time: a partitioned hash table search algorithm and a chained hash table data structure. Both methods require more space and less time than algorithms and data structures in the published methods for model checking with magnetic disk. However, such a trade off is well suited for model checking with large, but relatively slow, magnetic disks.

Stern and Dill published the first results for an explicit state enumeration algorithm for model checking with magnetic disk [11]. The Stern and Dill algorithm is inspired by an Roscoe's earlier algorithm for model checking CSP using magnetic disk [10]. The Stern and Dill algorithm, which we will refer to as the MONO algorithm, stores the visited candidate set in a large monolithic hash table on disk and keeps a smaller table of duplicate candidates in RAM. This algorithm was originally implemented using an open-address hash table for the delayed candidate set. In this implementation of this algorithm, the entire table on disk is the visited candidate set for each duplicate candidate state in RAM. The Roscoe algorithm also stores visited states on disk and delays duplicate detection, but the algorithm performs duplicate detection by sorting then merging duplicate and visited candidate sets (rather than performing a pairwise comparison as in MONO). Stern and Dill point out [11] that the sort and merge step is, perhaps, unduly complicated because it requires sorting a list that will not fit in RAM. The cost of delayed duplicate detection in the MONO algorithm grows quickly with the size of the visited candidate set because detecting duplicates requires searching the entire visited candidate set for each duplicate candidate.

Della Penna et al. published an algorithm for model checking with magnetic disk that is a modification of the MONO algorithm [7]. This algorithm, which we will refer to as the LOCAL algorithm, exploits transition locality by reading only the most recently written states from disk during delayed duplicate detection. The motivation for the design of this algorithm is to improve efficiency by reducing file IO. The algorithm is indeed faster than the MONO algorithm. Our empirical analysis of both algorithms shows that exploiting locality in this manner actually increases file IO time while greatly decreasing delayed duplicate detection time. Delayed duplicate detection time in the LOCAL algorithm is decreased because the visited candidate set is reduced to just the most recently written states rather than all visited states (as in the MONO algorithm). File IO is increased because some duplicates are not detected and their successors, which are also duplicates, are repeatedly transferred to and from disk. The LOCAL algorithm occasionally uses all visited states in duplicate detection to reduce the number and impact of missed duplicates.

In this paper, we reduce delayed duplicate detection time in a new model checking algorithm, called the PART algorithm, by reducing the visited candidate set with a partitioned hash table and reducing the duplicate candidate set with a chained hash table. While use of a chained hash table is perhaps the least interesting aspect of the new algorithm, it is responsible for the majority of the performance improvement. We reimplement the MONO and LOCAL algorithms using a chained hash table and compare the performance of both the MONO and LOCAL algorithms using either implementation. This allows us to focus on the algorithms rather than hash table implementations. As expected, both algorithms are faster when implemented with a chained hash table. However, the MONO algorithm becomes faster than the LOCAL algorithm when both are implemented with a chained hash table.

The second feature of the PART algorithm is the use of a partitioned hash table. The partitioned hash table is composed of n individual tables, each of which store a fraction of the visited states. A secondary hash function is used to divide states into partitions. The partitioned hash table improves delayed duplicate detection by reducing the visited candidate set. The partitioned hash table does increase file IO requirements because states must be read from and written to disk more frequently than the other algorithms.

Unlike switching to a chained hash table, switching to a partitioned hash table requires changing the state exploration algorithm. The most significant impact is that the usual double depth first search (DFS) used in linear temporal logic (LTL) model checking will miss property violations if naively implemented on a partitioned hash table. The state generation algorithm used in the PART algorithm is based on partitioned hash table algorithms used in parallel model checking and is not designed to detect violations of LTL properties. LTL model checking algorithms for partitioned hash tables require a serialization step to properly order the second DFS. This is costly for parallel algorithms, but should have little impact on the PART algorithm which is an inherently serial algorithm. The investigation of LTL model checking with magnetic disk is left for future work.

In the next section, we profile the MONO and LOCAL algorithms to show that delayed duplicate detection, not file IO, is the dominant overhead in both algorithms. Section 2 presents and discusses the PART algorithm. Section 3 contains an analytical comparison of the PART algorithm to the RAM-only, MONO and LOCAL algorithms. We give experimental results in section 4 and offer conclusions and future work in section 5.

1 Profiling Existing Uses of Disk

The original algorithm for model checking with magnetic disk was proposed by Stern and Dill [12]. Stern's algorithm, MONO, strives to minimize file IO time. Simply storing visited states on disk and performing immediate duplicate detection requires a disk access for every state generated. This creates a series of small disk accesses with poor locality which defeats caching and buffering techniques used to minimize average latency. The MONO algorithm minimizes file IO time by delaying duplicate state detection and writing each visited state to disk exactly once. The MONO algorithm maintains two sets of visited states[1] and a queue of states. One set stores the signatures of expanded states on magnetic disk and the other stores the signatures of expanded sets in RAM. The search is conducted breadth-first.

Delayed duplicate detection occurs when either a level of breadth-first search is finished or the table in memory becomes full. Delayed duplicate detection sequentially checks whether or not every state in the table on disk is contained in the table in RAM. If a state in the table in RAM is also in the table on magnetic disk, then that state in table is deleted from RAM. After the duplicate states are deleted, the remaining newly visited states are appended to the visited states on disk. The search then continues until either the disk becomes full or the queue becomes empty.

The more recent LOCAL algorithm proposed by Della Penna et al. improves on the execution time of Stern's algorithm by exploiting transition locality [7]. The LOCAL algorithm divides the table of states on disk into blocks. Rather than loading and comparing every state in the disk table during delayed duplicate detection, the LOCAL algorithm loads and compares states in only the most recently stored blocks. To avoid extensive duplication of previous work, older blocks are occasionally loaded for comparison.

Table 1. Total verification time, in seconds, for five verification problems. Both algorithms are implemented with an open-address hash table

Algorithm	atomix	mcslock1	newlist6	dense	atomix2
MONO	19654.7	19755.2	6346.2	15434.8	32404.2
LOCAL	5240.0	10645.0	3337.0	4039.0	11039.0

We have reimplemented and profiled the MONO and LOCAL algorithms in Hopper [4]. Both algorithms were profiled on a collection of five model checking problems. We measured wall clock time for disk access, performing delayed duplicate detection, inserting states into the table in RAM, generating successor states and the total from start to finish. Wall clock time, which is the amount of time that passes for "a clock on the wall" during program execution, is reported

---

[1] They are actually hash signatures created using hash compaction, but the difference is not relevant.

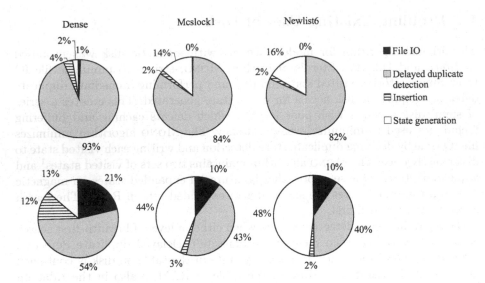

Fig. 1. Distribution of time between file IO, delayed duplicate detection, inserting into the RAM hash table and state generation in the MONO and LOCAL algorithm given 5% of the total RAM needed to complete each problem. Results for the MONO algorithm are on the top row and results for the LOCAL algorithm are on the bottom row

because it includes the time that a process is idle while waiting for file IO. All experiments were completed on an otherwise idle server with an Intel Pentium 4, 2.4 Ghz processor, 2 GB of RAM and a 42 GB SCSI hard drive.

Table 1 gives the total verification time for five problems and figure 1 shows the distribution of time between file IO, delayed duplicate detection, insertion and state generation for three of the five problems. The remaining two are similar, but ommited for brevity. See [1] for the full results of these and all other experiments in this paper. The LOCAL algorithm completes all problems in one-half to one-fourth of the time as the MONO algorithm. These results are comparable to the results in the original paper describing the LOCAL algorithm. In our profiling, the LOCAL algorithm is faster due to a reduction in the delayed duplicate detection time, not reduced file IO time.

2   A New Algorithm Based on Hash Table Partitioning

The analysis of MONO and LOCAL disk-based algorithm in the last section suggest that the performance of model checking algorithms that use magnetic disk can be improved by reducing state generation and delayed duplicate detection time, rather than file IO or even hash table insertion time. In this paper, we focus on improving delayed duplicate detection. State generation is a significant factor, but generic model checker implementation details, like how the formal description of the transition system is translated into an executable format, play a critical role in state generation time and are not generally applicable to different implementations of executable translations of formal protocol descriptions. We propose the PART algorithm to reduce delayed duplicate detection time in model checking with magnetic disk by

1. Using partitioned hash tables to reduce the cost of delayed duplicate detection. Partitioned hash tables have been used in distributed model checking [11] for some time. Rather than store each partition on a separate computing node, we store all but one of the partitions on disk and the remaining partition in RAM. Partitioning the hash table reduces the size of the set of states which must be searched during delayed duplicate detection.
2. Using a chained hash table rather than an open-address hash table. Previously, the hash table was implemented using an open-address table with double hashing, presumably to avoid the overhead of storing pointers and swapping them between disk and memory. Instead, we use a chained hash table which further reduces the size of the candidate set for delayed duplicate detection by requiring a state to be in a particular bucket or chain rather than allowing a state to be stored anywhere in the table. Finally, we use separate hash functions to partition and store states. This is a method, common to other parallel search problem domains, which further reduces penalties associated with increasing hash loads.

The pseudocode for the PART algorithm is given in figure 2. The algorithm uses a Partition function to map every state to a unique memory queue. There is the same number of disk files and memory queues. Memory queues store both unexplored and explored states; disk queues store states that overflow from the memory queues. The disk files store the explored candidate sets.

The search begins when the Search function generates start states and stores the start states in their corresponding queues. If a memory queue becomes full, then that queue is written to disk queue and memory queue is cleared (lines 4-6). In the pseudocode, q_i^m indicates the memory queue belongs to partition i and q_i^d indicates the disk queue belongs to partition i. The Search function then selects the queue, i , with the most states as the active queue and calls the Select function (lines 7-8).

The Select function loads the disk file that corresponds to the active queue into memory (line 12). Next, the function dequeues states from the active queue. If the newly dequeued states are not already in the table of visited states, then the states are stored in memory and every successor is generated (line 13-14). When the active queue in memory becomes empty, the corresponding disk queue, if it exists, is loaded into memory (line 15). After both the memory queue and the disk queue are empty, the table of expanded states is stored back to disk (line 17). The algorithm then chooses the next longest queue (line 18), loads the corresponding table and continues exploration. If all the queues are empty, the algorithm terminates (line 19).

The Explore function checks to see if the successors of the states in the active queue belong to the active queue. If they do, and they are not present in the current table in memory, then they are added to the current active queue. If they

```
1   var
2      M: RAM hash table; D[n]: files; Qm[n]: FIFO queues; Qd[n]: disk queues;
3   Search()
4      for every start state s0 do
5         i := Partition(s0); insert s0 into q_i^m;
6         if Full(q_i^m) then store q_i^m in q_i^d; q_i^m := ∅;
7         i := max_{i∈n}(|q_i^m + q_i^d|);
8         Select(i);
9   Select(i: int)
10     while i ≥ 0 do
11        while q_i^m ≠ ∅ do
12           load D[i] into M;
13           s = dequeue(q_i^m);
14           if s is not in M then insert s in M; Explore (i, s);
15           if q_i^d ≠ ∅ then load q_i^d to q_i^m;
16        while q_i^m ≠ ∅;
17        store M in D[i].
18        i := max_{i∈n}(|q_i^m + q_i^d|);
19        if |q_i^m + q_i^d| = 0 then i = −1;
20  Explore(i: int, s: state)
21     for all s' ∈ successors(s) do
22        i':= Partition(s');
23        if i' = i and s' is not in M then insert s' in q_i^m; else insert s' in q_{i'}^m;
24        if Full(q_{i'}^m) then store q_{i'}^m in q_{i'}^d; q_{i'}^m := ∅;
```

Fig. 2. The PART algorithm for model checking with magnetic disk

do not belong to the current queue, then they are stored to their corresponding queues (line 23). This allows duplicate and expanded states to be stored in the work queues. If any of the queues are full, then they are written to disk (line-24).

3   Comparative Analysis

First we compare the computation time of new algorithm with the usual RAM-only model checking algorithm. Then we compare the new algorithm with the MONO and LOCAL algorithms for model checking with magnetic disk. The analysis clarifies sources and costs of overheads associated with the PART algorithm.

3.1   Comparison with the RAM-Only Algorithm

In the results presented later, the new algorithm for model checking with magnetic disk requires up to 27% more computational time than the RAM-only algorithm–for large models, when only 5% of RAM memory required by the RAM-only algorithm is used.

Verification time in the RAM-only algorithm is composed of the following parts:

$$Total_{RAM} = Insertion_{RAM} + StateGeneration$$

Where $Insertion_{RAM}$ is the time spent on inserting newly generated states into memory and $StateGeneration$ is the time spent on the generation of successor states.

For the PART algorithm verification time consists of:

$$Total_{PART} = Insertion_{PART} + StateGeneration +$$
$$IO_{PART} + Computation + EnqueueDequeue$$

Where $Insertion_{PART}$ is the time spent on inserting states into memory, IO_{PART} is the time spent reading the states from disk to memory and writing the states from memory to disk, $Computation$ is the time spent on computing each state's corresponding partition and $EnqueueDequeue$ is the time overhead related to storing states in the queues.

For the PART algorithm, $Insertion_{PART}$ indicates delayed duplicate detection because the algorithm detects duplicates by attempting to insert them into the table of visited states. This value is similar to $Insertion_{RAM}$ since the number of reachable states, including duplicates, generated by both algorithms are the same. The new overhead introduced by PART algorithm is then:

$$IO_{PART} + Computation + EnqueueDequeue$$

The comparative performance of the PART algorithm can be improved by decreasing any of these values. The performance of the PART algorithm improves as the following conditions are met.

A small state vector, v, is used to minimize file IO time. Hash compaction reduces the size of the state vector which reduces the memory requirements for verification and also reduces the file IO overhead, IO_{PART} (the results in section 4 are generated using hash compaction).

The transition graph is partitioned so that states and their successors are often in the same partition. This reduces the number of duplicate states that are stored in the queues and hence reduces $EnqueueDequeue$ time. We do not address the problem of partitioning in this paper, but the partitioning scheme proposed by Rangarajan and others for parallel partitioned model checking [8] can be applied here.

The algorithms are applied to transition graphs with low average in-degree because this reduces the $EnqueueDequeue$ time associated with partitioning states and storing several copies of duplicate states for delayed duplication detection. This is a reasonable assumption in certain situations. More specifically, models of machine code tend to have low average in-degree while models of scheduling algorithms tend to have high average in-degree. Machine code models have low in-degree because very few instructions are the targets of multiple different branches. Scheduling algorithms tend to have higher in-degree because there are typically many different computational paths that lead to entry into a process–especially if non-determinism is used to obtain a control abstraction.

Pelánek's study of structural properties of state spaces concludes that industrial problems tend to have low average in-degree [6]. This suggests that algorithms that perform well on models with low average in-degree can be expected to perform well on most industrial models. In the study, Pelánek takes industrial models to be the non-trivial models distributed with the SPIN, Murphi, CADP and μCRL model checkers. The *clustering coefficient* used in Pelánek's study measures how many edges in a k-vertex neighborhood remain in that neighborhood. High clustering coefficients correspond to high in-degrees.[2] Pelánek concludes that the sampled industrial models have low clustering coefficients while "toy" examples tend to have high clustering coefficients. The dense problem in section 4 is a toy problem with a high clustering coefficient of nearly 7 and the PART algorithm performs poorly on this problem compared to the RAM-only algorithm.

3.2   Comparison with the Mono and Local Algorithms

The following analysis reveals why PART is usually faster. MONO must read each state from disk every time the memory table becomes full. When RAM is a small fraction of the total space needed, the memory table becomes full more often and thus MONO performs more reads.

The total time required by the MONO algorithm is

$$Total_{\text{MONO}} = Insertion_{\text{MONO}} + StateGeneration +$$
$$IO_{\text{MONO}} + DDD_{\text{MONO}}$$

where $StateGeneration$ measures time spent generating states. $Insertion_{\text{MONO}}$ measures the time spent on inserting newly generated states into memory. IO_{MONO} is the disk IO time and DDD_{MONO} is delayed duplicate detection time spent on comparing states in disk with states in memory. The value of IO_{MONO} is less than IO_{PART}, but DDD_{MONO} is significantly greater than $Insertion_{\text{PART}}$.

The comparison time for the MONO algorithm depends on the implementation of the hash table used in memory. The MONO algorithm was originally implemented with an open address hash table in memory. The double hash implementation of an open address table is slower on average than a chained hash table because it requires more comparison time than a chained hash table. An open address hash table stores states directly in the table. A chained hash table is essentially a table of pointers to chains of states. The double hash implementation of an open address hash table uses a sequence of combinations of two hash values to probe the table for a given state. While the performance trade-offs between chained and open-address implementations are well-understood (see [2] for a thourough discussion), they are of interest in this work because their use in the MONO algorithm amplifies the differences. We make the relevant differences more precise with the following equations.

Assume there are K_i states on disk when the passed state file is read the ith time and assume that the disk file is read a total of t times during the entire verification process. The total number of states read from disk is $K = \sum_{i=1}^{t} K_i$.

---

[2] However, clustering coefficients include only edges from "local" nodes in the neighborhood; edges from outside the neighborhood are not counted and will only increase the in-degree.

Assume the table of states stored in memory contains M bytes. For the open-address implementation, MONO-open, the average comparisons required to do duplicate detection for a state on disk is $M/(2|v|)$ because the state may be anywhere in the table. Duplicate detection occurs for every state read from disk and K states are read from disk so:

$$DDD_{\text{MONO}-open} = \frac{CKM}{2|v|}$$

where C is the time required to compute the next hash value and compare two states. Note that K is often quite large and the product KM in $DDD_{\text{MONO}-open}$ is significant.

However, if the MONO algorithm is implemented with a chained hash table then DDD_{MONO} is reduced because duplicate candidates are confined to a particular chain rather than the entire hash table. This means that the K term is multiplied by the average chain length, $\bar{C}$, instead of the entire table size:

$$DDD_{\text{MONO}-Chained} = \frac{CK\bar{C}}{2|v|}.$$

The product of $K\bar{C}$ is much smaller than KM as K becomes large.

Although an open-address hash table requires less memory (one fewer pointer per state stored) than a chained hash table, the space savings is offset by the increase in delayed duplicate detection overhead. This design trade-off is contradictory given that the fundamental trade-off in model checking with magnetic disk is to *increase* space at the expense of *increasing* computation time.

Returning to the comparison of the PART and MONO algorithms, we will assume that the MONO algorithm is implemented with a chained hash table. To make the PART algorithm faster than the MONO algorithm, we only need to make sure that the sum of IO_{PART}, $Computation$, and $EnqueueDequeue$ is less than or equal to the sum of IO_{MONO} and DDD_{MONO}. We ignore hash table insertion time because it is negligible. This is often the case because DDD_{MONO} is often much greater than any other overhead in the PART algorithm.

Similar analysis applies to the LOCAL algorithm; the only difference is that each K_i value is smaller because the algorithm considers only part of the disk table. However, the sum of the K_i terms may be bigger due to duplicate states.

When the RAM table is smaller, the PART algorithm becomes more efficient when compared with the MONO and LOCAL algorithms. For the MONO and LOCAL algorithms, the RAM table is full more often as RAM decreases and more invocations of the delayed duplicate detection process are required. Each of the additional delayed duplicate detection checks require traversing the set of all visited candidate states. For the PART algorithm, the number of partitions increases as RAM decreases and there are more swaps between disk file and memory. Since file IO time is significantly smaller than delayed duplicate detection time, the PART algorithm is comparatively more efficient with less RAM.

4   Experimental Results

This section presents the experimental results obtained by running the RAM-only, MONO, LOCAL and PART algorithms on several verification problems. We give results for two kinds of models: those that can be verified in less than 2GB of RAM and those that can not. We use the smaller models to test all algorithms and use the bigger models to test only the algorithms that use magnetic disk. The RAM-only algorithm can not complete the larger models because 32-bit UNIX processes can address at most 2GB of memory. The verification problems used are atomix, mcslock1, newlist6, dense, atomix2, 6-peterson and mcslock2. Each of the models can be obtained at [3].

Most of the following results are reported using a chained rather than an open-address hash table. Executing Stern's MONO algorithm and Della Penna's LOCAL algorithm with chained, rather than open-address, tables increases the space requirements for both, but reduces their execution time.

4.1   Small Models

In this section, we report results for problems that require less than 2 GB of memory to store visited states. The pie charts in figure 3 demonstrate the reduction in delayed duplicate detection time when using a chained hash table in the MONO and PART algorithms. Table 2 gives results for five models using all algorithms, including the RAM-only algorithm. Figure 4 gives the slowdown of each algorithm for model checking with magnetic disk relative to the RAM-only algorithm as the amount of allowed RAM varies on the same five models.

Figure 3 gives the distribution of time in various parts of the algorithm for MONO and PART implemented with chained hash tables. Compared with the pie graph in figure 1, the MONO algorithm using a chained hash table significantly decreases delayed duplicate detection time to 30% and 17% on the Mcslock1 and Newlist6 problems. Duplicate detection time continues to dominate in the Dense problem. File IO and insertion take between 1% and 4% and the percentage of state generation is increased to 65% and 77% for to Mcslock1 and Newlist6 problems due to the decrease in delayed duplicate detection time.

For the PART algorithm, delayed duplicate detection time is reflected in insertion time, which is comparable to insertion time for the other algorithms. The largest overhead introduced by the new algorithm is the enqueue/dequeue overhead which ranges from 6% to 53%. Duplicate states are detected before enqueueing them into the queues for the other three algorithms. However, states are all enqueued before doing duplicate detection in the PART algorithm. Since the number of duplicate states is usually much more than the number of unique states (particularly for the Dense problem), enqueue/dequeue takes a significant amount of time. The state generation section of the PART algorithm takes a greater percentage of total time, between 21% and 88%. This indicates an overall speed increase of PART algorithm since the time required for state generation is similar for both algorithms. The partitioning category measures the extra time

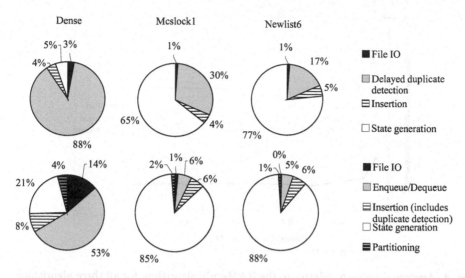

Fig. 3. Distribution of time between various parts of the MONO and PART algorithm given 5% of the total RAM needed to complete each problem. The MONO algorithm is on the top row and the PART algorithm is on the bottom row. Both algorithms are implemented with a chained hash table

required to partition states into hash tables. This new overhead accounts for only 1% to 4% of the total execution time.

Table 2 shows total verification time for all algorithms on five models. Included are the three models shown in figures 1 and 3. All algorithms except the RAM-only algorithm are allowed 5% of the total RAM necessary to complete the verification. The table shows a decrease in execution time for the PART algorithm compared to each of the the other disk based algorithms. Interestingly, the MONO algorithm benefits from chained hashing more than the LOCAL algorithm.

Figure 4 shows the average slowdown of the MONO, LOCAL and PART algorithms compared with the RAM-only algorithm. The average slowdown is

Table 2. Total verification times, in seconds, for five verification problems for several algorithm and hash table implementation combinations. The algorithms that use magnetic disk are given 5% of the total required RAM

Algorithm (hash table)	atomix	mcslock1	newlist6	dense	atomix2
RAM-only (chained)	281.2	2570.0	1031.6	322.9	379.8
PART(chained)	308.6	2713.1	1043.0	2611.1	545.8
MONO(chained)	488.4	3798.8	1270.8	5444.5	872.8
LOCAL(chained)	2599.3	6616.0	2070.4	3336.0	6081.0
LOCAL(open-address)	5240.0	10645.0	3337.0	4039.0	11039.0
MONO(open-address)	19654.7	19755.2	6346.2	15434.8	32404.2

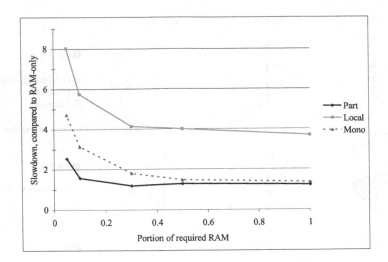

Fig. 4. Average slowdown, relative to the RAM-only algorithm, for all three algorithms for different portions of required RAM and averaged over five problems. Each algorithm is implemented with a chained hash table. A slowdown of x indicates that an algorithm is x times slower than the RAM-only algorithm

computed by dividing the running time of the algorithm by the running time of the RAM-only algorithm, and taking the average over the five problems in table 2. Given the same amount of memory as the RAM-only algorithm, the Mono and Part algorithms have similar slowdowns but Local is the slowest. As the amount of available memory decreases (moving to the left on the x-axis in the figure), each algorithm experiences greater slowdown. The Part algorithm experiences the least slowdown and has a slowdown of 2.8 when given 1/20th of the memory used by the RAM-only algorithm.

4.2 Big Models

Results for verification problems that can not be verified by the RAM-only algorithm are particularly interesting for disk based algorithms. In this section, we report results for two problems that require 5 GB and 8 GB of space to store visited states. The peak storage space during verification grows to 31 GB due to large queues of states waiting to be expanded. We verified these two models using the Mono, Local and Part algorithms. Hash compaction is used and 3% of space required to store visited states is allocated to each algorithm in RAM.

Table 3 shows the results. The Part algorithm is 2.0 and 2.7 times faster than the Mono algorithm and 5.1 and 3.3 times faster than the Local algorithm. Because the Local algorithm may miss duplicates and regenerate portions of the state space, the Local algorithm actually stores 999 M visited states for the mcslock2 model.

Table 3. Number of reachable states and total verification time, in seconds, for two large models. Each algorithm is allowed approximately 3% of the RAM required to store all reachable states

Models	States	MONO	LOCAL	PART
6-peterson	382,513,749	31,890.0	83,207.8	16,218.7
mcslock2	666,254,155	188,129.5	228,271.0	69,726.9

The ldash6 model is even larger than any of the "big" models in table 3. None of the algorithms are able to generate all of the states in this model using 42 GB of disk. The incomplete results reveal some drawbacks of the PART algorithm. The MONO algorithm requires 14992 seconds to generate 6 million states of ldash6. The PART algorithm requires 22788 seconds to generate the same number of states. Although it in not clear which algorithm would finish first,[3] it is clear that MONO performs more efficiently in the first 6 million states. This is due to the 1020 byte state vector, which is larger the state vectors of all other models reported in this paper, used in the ldash6 model. Since PART algorithm allows duplicate states to be stored in queues and queues have to store the actual state, instead of just the hash compacted state, the disk read/write overhead for disk queues becomes worse in proportion with the state vector size.

5   Conclusion

Reducing delayed duplicate detection time, even at the expense of increasing file IO time, reduces the total execution time of model checking algorithms that use magnetic disk. Delayed duplicate detection time can be reduced by partitioning the table of visited states and by storing visited states in a chained, rather than an open-address, hash table. The resulting model checking algorithm is faster than other published algorithms for model checking with magnetic disk, even when the other algorithms are reimplemented with the faster chained hash table. The performance of the new algorithm degrades more slowly than that of other algorithms as the amount of available RAM decreases.

In the new partitioned hash table algorithm, duplicate states are stored in queues for delayed duplicate detection. While this incurs the same amount of duplicate detection work as required by a RAM-only algorithm, enqueueing and dequeueing duplicate states becomes the dominant overhead. Storing more than one partition in memory at a time may reduce the enqueue and dequeue overhead by allowing immediate duplicate detection between partitions. Ideally, one could store exactly the partitions that would allow the immediate detection of all duplicates, as in [13]. However, an approximation based on prior locality patterns may provide some improvement.

---

[3] Because the state generation rates vary with hash and disk loads. The state generation rate of the new algorithm also depends on how often partitions are sswapped.

In this paper, we focus on explicit model checking with magnetic disk. Ranjan et al. give an efficient algorithm for symbolic model checking with magnetic disk [9]. This algorithm constructs binary decision diagrams using an iterative breadth-first technique that localizes memory accesses. The key problem in symbolic model checking with magnetic disk is determining child-node variable indices rather than delayed duplicate detection, as addressed here.

References

1. T. Bao. Emperical comparison of algorithms for model checking with magnetic disk. Technical Report VV-0402, Dept. of Computer Science, Brigham Young U., 2004.
2. T. H. Cormen, C. E. Leiserson, and R. L. Rivest. *Introduction to Algorithms*, chapter 11. McGraw-Hill, 1999.
3. Explicit model checking benchmarks. Available at vv.cs.byu.edu/emc, 2004.
4. M. D. Jones and E. Mercer. Explicit state model checking with Hopper. In *International SPIN Workshop on Software Model Checking (SPIN'04)*, number 2989 in LNCS, pages 146–150, Barcelona, Spain, March 2004. Springer.
5. R. E. Korf. Delayed duplicate detection: Extended abstract. In Georg Gottlob and Toby Walsh, editors, *Proceedings of the Eighteenth International Joint Conference on Artificial Intelligence (IJCAI-03), Acapulco, Mexico*. Morgan Kaufmann, 2003.
6. R. Pelanek. Typical structural properties of state spaces. In *International SPIN Workshop on Software Model Checking (SPIN'04)*, number 2989 in LNCS, pages 5–23, Barcelona, Spain, March 2004. Springer.
7. G. Della Penna, B. Intrigila, E. Tronci, and M. Venturini Zilli. Exploiting transition locality in the disk based Murϕ verifier. In M. Aagaard and J. O'Leary, editors, *Formal Methods in Computer Aided Design*, volume 2517 of *LNCS*, pages 202–219. Springer-Verlag, 2002.
8. M. Rangarajan, S. Dajani-Brown, K. Schloegel, and D. Cofer. Analysis of distributed spin applied to industrial-scale models. In S. Graf and L. Mounier, editors, *11th International SPIN Workshop on Model Checking of Software (SPIN'04)*, volume LNCS 2989 of *Lecture Notes in Computer Science*, 2004.
9. R. K. Ranjan, J. V. Sanghavi, R. K. Brayton, and A. Sangiovanni-Vincentelli. High performance BDD package by exploiting memory hierarchy. In *33rd Annual Conference on Design Automation (DAC'96)*, pages 635–641. ACM Press, June 1996.
10. A. W. Roscoe. Model-checking CSP. In *A Classical Mind: Essays in Honor of C. A. R. Hoare*, pages 353 – 378. Prentic-Hall, 1994.
11. Ulrich Stern and David L. Dill. Parallelizing the Murϕ verifier. In Orna Grumburg, editor, *Computer-Aided Verification, CAV '97*, volume 1254 of *Lecture Notes in Computer Science*, pages 256–267, Haifa, Israel, June 1997. Springer-Verlag.
12. Ulrich Stern and David L. Dill. Using magnetic disk instead of main memory in the Murϕ verifier. In Alan J. Hu and Moshe Y. Vardi, editors, *Computer-Aided Verification, CAV '98*, volume 1427 of *Lecture Notes in Computer Science*, pages 172–183, Vancouver, BC, Canada, June/July 1998. Springer-Verlag.
13. R. Zhou and E. Hansen. Structured duplicate detection in external-memory graph search. In D. L. McGuinness and G. Ferguson, editors, *Nineteenth National Conference on Artificial Intelligence (AAAI-04)*, pages 677–682, San Jose, California, July 2004. AAAI Press / MIT Press.

jMoped: A Java Bytecode Checker Based on Moped[*]

Dejvuth Suwimonteerabuth, Stefan Schwoon, and Javier Esparza

Institut für Formale Methoden der Informatik, Universität Stuttgart
{suwimodh, schwoosn, esparza}@informatik.uni-stuttgart.de

Abstract. We present a tool for finding errors in Java programs that translates Java bytecodes into symbolic pushdown systems, which are then checked by the Moped tool [1].

1 Introduction

We present jMoped, a checker for (a large class of) Java programs. jMoped consists of a translator that transforms Java bytecode into a *symbolic pushdown system* (SPDS), which is then checked by the Moped tool [1]. The translator, described in more detail in [2], supports a wide range of Java programming features including arithmetic operations, control statements, method calls, recursion, arrays, object manipulations, inheritance, and exception handling. On the other hand, its current implementation does not support float, double, or string variables, dynamic arrays, non-static global arrays, dynamic method binding, calling a method of an interface, implicit exceptions, and multi-threading. Moreover, every instance of a class must be initialized with a separate **new** statement.

The functionality of jMoped is very simple. The user writes a Java class satisfying the constraints above (like the one on the left of Figure 1), and adds either a method **error()**, which is executed if some invariant is violated, or a method **ok()** signaling termination. For instance, in order to check if the variable x may become zero at a certain program point, the user adds a line if x = 0 then error(). In the example of Figure 1, calling "jmoped -e -n LinkedList", where n is a number whose precise meaning is explained later, we obtain the answer that no execution of error() was found. However, if one changes the call in contains to return isExist(header.next, x); and runs the check again, jMoped reports that error() is executed. Calling "jmoped -t -n LinkedList" we obtain that no non-terminating execution was detected. Witness paths can also be printed in order to help finding bugs.

The main advantage of jMoped's translator is that SPDSs, its target language, closely matches Java bytecodes. In particular, invoke and return instructions are directly translated into push/pop SPDS rules. No inlining of bytecodes (which may yield an exponential blowup in size) and no artificial bound on the

---

[*] This work is supported by the EPSRC Grant GR/93346 "An Automata-theoretic Approach to Software Model Checking" and by the DFG project "Algorithms for Software Model Checking".

maximal depth of the stack of method calls are required. The only restrictions are on the data side: Moped requires a bound on the range of variables, and on the maximal number of objects that can be generated.

2   The Translation

We recall that a Java program is compiled into a class file containing bytecodes, the machine language of the Java Virtual Machine (JVM). Bytecodes of the form invokestatic <name> or invokevirtual <name> invoke the method <name>.

A pushdown system consists of a set of *control states*, a *stack alphabet*, and a number of *rules*, which correspond to the well-known transition rules of pushdown automata. An SPDS is a pushdown system together with two sets of *global* and *local* variables over a finite domain. Loosely speaking, there is one single copy of a global variable, but each stack symbol owns a copy of each local variable. The rules of an SPDS are best explained by means of an example. The rule

$$q1 \; \texttt{<f1>} \; \texttt{-->} \; q2 \; \texttt{<f2 \; f3>} \; (x > 3 \; \& \; y' = x'' + 1)$$

where x and y are local variables, is read as follows: If the current control state is q1, the topmost stack symbol is f1, and the value of the copy of x owned by f1 is greater than 3, then move to control state q2, replace f1 by f2 f3 on the stack, and set the copy of y owned by f2 to 1 plus the value of the copy of x owned by f3. The stack is useful whenever the front end is a procedural language. The local variables owned by a stack symbol correspond to the local variables of a procedure or method. A procedure call and a return are modeled by a push and a pop, respectively.

Our translator first fetches the bytecodes of the methods in the class, and of the methods from other classes called by them. Then, each bytecode instruction is directly mapped into one or more SPDS rules. The JVM uses two stacks: a local stack for each method, whose maximal size is determined at compile time, and the stack of method calls. The local stacks are modeled with *stack variables* called $(sv0, \ldots, svk\text{-}1)$, where k is the maximum stack depth (usually a low number) obtained from the Java compiler. sv0 represents the top of the stack. A push of number 1 to the local stack is modeled by a rule of the form

$$q \; \texttt{<f1>} \; \texttt{-->} \; q \; \texttt{<f2>} \; ((sv0'=1) \; \& \; (sv1'=sv0) \; \& \; (sv2'=sv1) \; \& \; \ldots)$$

Figure 1 shows fragments of a Java program and some corresponding bytecodes. Method contains checks if the list contains a given value. It calls the recursive method isExist. The methods insert and error (both omitted) add a node to the list and handle errors, respectively.

The translator produces a set of SPDS variables and a set of rules. Roughly speaking, the SPDS variables are the stack variables mentioned above, local SPDS variables matching the variables of a method, plus SPDS variables used to store the values of object fields. The translator assigns an *id* to each object reference created by a new bytecode. For every object field, an array of global SPDS variables is created with *ids* as array indices. In our example, the bytecode of the main method creates four references (one for the list 1 and three for nodes). The translator assigns *ids* 1 to 4, and creates three arrays: header[1,1], value[2,4], next[2,4]. The numbers in brackets indicate the array bounds.

We can now explain the meaning of the -*n* option when calling jMoped: it specifies the number of bits assigned by Moped to each variable, and so its range.

Figure 2 shows some SPDS rules produced by the translator. Notice that the JVM assigns to each method a set of variables indexed by 0,1,2,.... The translator creates the corresponding SPDS variables var0, var1, etc. The first line of the figure corresponds to bytecode 0: and pushes the value of var1 onto the local stack. The translation of 1: and 16: should be self-explanatory. The translation of 25: uses a variable ret to store the result of the method call. The translation of 46: in method main uses a push to model the method invocation and shows how the return value is evaluated.

```
public class ListNode {              isExist(ListNode, int):
  int value;                           0: aload_1
  ListNode next;                       1: ifnonnull +5
  public ListNode(int x)               4: iconst_0
  { value = x; next = null; }          5: ireturn
}                                      6: aload_1
                                       7: getfield <value>
public class LinkedList {             10: iload_2
  private ListNode header;            11: if_cmpne +5
  public LinkedList()                 14: iconst_1
  { header = null; }                  15: ireturn
  ...                                 16: aload_0
  public boolean contains(int x)      17: aload_1
  { return isExist(header, x); }      18: getfield <next>
  boolean isExist(ListNode n, int x) {21: iload_2
  if (n == null) return false;        22: invokevirtual <isExist>
  if (n.value == x) return true;      25: ireturn
  else return isExist(n.next, x);     main(String[]):
}                                      0: new <LinkedList>
  ...                                  3: dup
  public static void main(String[] args) {  4: invokespecial <init>
  LinkedList l = new LinkedList();     7: astore_1
  l.insert(new ListNode(1));           ...
  l.insert(new ListNode(2));          44: aload_1
  l.insert(new ListNode(3));          45: iconst_1
  if (!l.contains(1))                 46: invokevirtual <contains>
  error();                            49: ifne +6
}                                     52: invokestatic <error>
}                                     55: return
```

Fig. 1. Java code (left) and some of its bytecodes (right)

```
Some transition rules of isExist(ListNode, int):
  q <f0> --> q <f1>          ((sv0'=var1) & (sv1'=sv0) & (sv2'=sv1) & ...)
  q <f1> --> q <f6>          ((sv0!=0) & (sv0'=sv1) & (sv1'=sv2) & ...)
  q <f16> --> q <f17>        ((sv0'=var0) & (sv1'=sv0) & (sv2'=sv1) & ...)
  q <f25> --> q <>           ((ret'=sv0) & ...)
Some transition rules of main(String[]):
  q <m46> --> q <c0 m49a> ((var1'=sv0) & (var0'=sv1) & (sv0''=sv2) & ...)
  q <m49a> --> q <m49>    ((sv0'=ret) & (sv1'=sv0) & (sv2'=sv1) & ...)
```

Fig. 2. Part of the translation of the code of Figure 1

3   jMoped and Alloy

We compare our approach to the one of Vaziri and Jackson [3] using the Alloy system. There, Java code is translated into a SAT formula. This requires bounds not only on the range of variables and the number of generated objects, but also on the maximum depth of the call stack and on the number of times a loop can be executed. Moreover, method calls are dealt with by inlining. Our approach removes the last two bounds while staying within a decidable problem [4].

The bounds on the range of variables mean that both tools check the presence or absence of errors *within these bounds*. So, in fact, they are carrying out a sort of extended symbolic testing, in which many different test cases (often billions) are checked in one single symbolic computation, and in which non-termination can be explicitly detected.

We have considered the faulty insertion algorithm in red-black trees used in [3], and invariant properties. In [3] the property is written in Alloy, while we added an `error()` method that is executed when the invariant is violated. Vaziri and Jackson report being able to automatically find the bug when the number of nodes and the number of iterations of a loop are both limited to five in 18 seconds. In our case it took 10 seconds in a standard PC. While the two numbers are not directly comparable, because different machines were used, they indicate that our approach, while providing a more direct match to the structure of imperative languages, does not necessarily lose efficiency.

4   Conclusion and Future Work

We have described jMoped, a tool that allows to check invariant properties and termination of Java code by translating Java bytecodes into pushdown systems and then applying the Moped tool. The tool covers a large fragment of Java programs. Our ultimate goal (from which we are still far away) is to develop a checking tool for Java programs with a very simple interface that could be used routinely, even by people without a background on verification.

References

1. Schwoon, S.: Model-Checking Pushdown Systems. PhD thesis, TU Munich (2002)
2. Suwimonteerabuth, D.: Verifying Java bytecode with the Moped model checker. Master's thesis, University of Stuttgart (2004)
3. Vaziri, M., Jackson, D.: Checking properties of heap-manipulating procedures with a contraint solver. In: TACAS'03. LNCS 2619, Springer (2003) 505–520
4. Esparza, J., Schwoon, S.: A BDD-based model checker for recursive programs. In: Proc. CAV'01. LNCS 2102, Springer (2001) 324–336

Java-MOP: A Monitoring Oriented Programming Environment for Java

Feng Chen and Grigore Roşu

Department of Computer Science,
University of Illinois at Urbana - Champaign, USA
{fengchen, grosu}@uiuc.edu

Abstract. A Java-based tool-supported software development and analysis framework is presented, where monitoring is a foundational principle. Expressive requirements specification formalisms can be included into the framework via logic plug-ins, allowing one to refer not only to the current state, but also to both past and future states.

1 Introduction

This paper presents a monitoring oriented programming (MOP) software development and analysis environment for Java, named JAVA-MOP. Based on the belief that specification and implementation should *together* form a system and interact with each other by design, we proposed the MOP framework [2], aiming at increasing the quality of software through monitoring of formal specifications against running programs.

There are several software development approaches in the literature based on the very basic idea of monitoring. *Design by Contract* (DBC) [10] related approaches, e.g., JASS [3] and JML [8], allows specifications to be associated with classes as assertions and invariants, which are compiled into runtime checks. Runtime verification (RV) [5] is an expanding area dedicated to provide more rigor in testing, essentially as a complementary approach to model checking software systems. There are several RV systems, including JAVA-MAC [7], TEMPORAL ROVER and its follower DB ROVER [4], JPAX [6] and its followers EAGLE [1] and JMPAX [12].

What distinguishes the MOP from these approaches is its ability to be extended with new logics and to support self-recovery at violation. Practice has shown that there is no "silver bullet" logic to formally express any requirements. Some can be best expressed using a certain logical formalism, for example temporal logics, while others can be best expressed using other logics, like that of JML, or domain-specific logics. On the other hand, programming languages are intended to be universal. For these reasons, MOP provides the capability of adding logics on top of a target programming language via logic plugins.

Monitoring can also provide a strong foundation for increasing the quality, robustness, and confidence in the correctness of complex software systems. The Simplex [13] architecture shows an example to smoothly upgrade control sys-

N. Halbwachs and L. Zuck (Eds.): TACAS 2005, LNCS 3440, pp. 546–550, 2005.

tems based on monitoring. Therefore, MOP supports the user to define violation and/or validation handlers along with specifications, which can be highly complicated recovery actions. These handlers will be automatically triggered at runtime when the specification is violated or validated, in order to recover the program from unsafe states.

2 Overview of JAVA-MOP

JAVA-MOP is a development tool for Java, supporing the MOP paradigm. It provides both GUI and command-line interfaces for editing and processing specifications. Algorithms to synthesize optimized monitoring code for different logics have been implemented in order to incorporate useful specification languages into JAVA-MOP. Moreover, users are able to easily incorporate new formalisms which can be used later in specifications via logic plugins. JAVA-MOP does not only aim at specifying and monitoring system behaviors, but also gives users the ability to recover from errors at runtime. Here we only briefly present major features of JAVA-MOP. Interested readers can refer to our website [11] for the distribution package and related documents.

Extensible Architecture. JAVA-MOP follows a distributed architecture in design as shown in figure 1. This design facilitates extending the framework with logic formalisms added to the system as new components, which we simply call *logic plug-ins*. These components are usually comprised of two modules, namely a *logic engine* and a *language shell*. For example, the logic engine for ERE and the Java shell for ERE form the logic plugin for extended regular expressions. Logic engines translate formulae into efficient monitors, presented in some abstract representation (pseudocode). Then language shells transform abstract monitors into code for a specific language, e.g., Java. The output interface of the logic pluign is standarized. This way, if a new logical formalism is needed to specify the requirement of a certain application, then one can develop a synthesis algorithm for the specific logic, wrap the algorithm as a logic plugin for Java, and add the plugin into the JAVA-MOP. For some simple specification languages, or for programming-language-specific formalisms, such as Jass, the logic engine is unnecessary and the language shell only is sufficient to generate the monitor.

The client part contains the Java annotation processors, which integrate the monitoring code generated by the server into the system, according to configuration attributes of the monitor. In addition, the client part is also in charge of instrumenting the code to generate events to be monitored. Currently, JAVA-MOP is using ASPECTJ as the instrumentation mechanism. ASPECTJ aspects are produced for specifications to be monitored. ASPECTJ, however, also imposes some limitation in our implementation. The integration made by ASPECTJ is static while the monitoring is dynamic. This brings difficulties and inefficiencies when monitoring dynamic entities. For example, for a class invariant, one may need to monitor every update of `anObject.aField` instead of `afield` of any object whose class is the same as `anObject`.

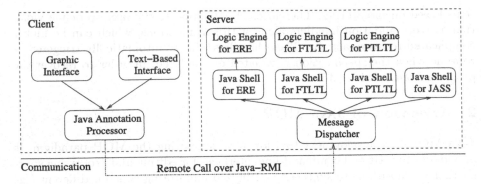

Fig. 1. The Architecture of JAVA-MOP

Monitor Synthesis. Every logic plugin essentially encodes an algorithm to synthesize monitoring code for a specific formalism. We have devised monitor synthesis algorithms for future time and past time temporal logics, as well as for extended regular expressions, JASS, and JML.

- *JML and Jass.* These DBC-based approaches follow the idea of including specifications into the code and then pre-compiling them into runtime checks. So we are able to smoothly include them in JAVA-MOP. The original syntax of JML and JASS annotations has been slightly modified, to fit the uniform, logic-independent syntactic conventions in JAVA-MOP.
- *Temporal Logics.* Temporal logics have proved to be indispensable and expressive formalisms in the field of formal specification and verification of systems [9]. Since MOP can be regarded at some extent as a complementary, but still related, approach to formal verification, we provide logic plug-ins to support past and future time variants of temporal logics.
- *Extended Regular Expression.* Regular expressions provide an elegant and powerful specification language for monitoring requirements, because an execution trace of a program is in fact a string of states. Extended regular expressions (ERE) add complementation to regular expressions, which gives one the power to express patterns on traces non-elementarily more compactly. A logic plugin for ERE has been incorporated into JAVA-MOP.

Steering Behaviors of Monitors. Besides adding more rigor to testing, MOP is especially intended to be a monitoring tool to assure correctness during program execution. To support runtime recovery, MOP provides a the capability to steer the execution of the program when requirements are violated or validated.

Users can provide handlers for the violation or validation of monitored properties. These handlers can not only report errors or throw exceptions, but also execute complicated actions, e.g., resetting states or rebooting the system. Therefore, critical monitors can be automatically integrated into the final system to correct the system at runtime.

MOP monitors can have different running scope. It can be a class invariant, which is checked at every change of the class state. Or it can be a interface constraint, which is checked when a client invokes the interface of the class. JAVA-MOP also supports method pre-/post- conditions and checkpoint assertions. Besides, users can also choose if the system needs to wait for the checking result or not. The keywords *synchronized* and *asynchronized* are used for this purpose. The motivation behind asynchronous monitors is that some properties are not critical and the system does not have to react to the violation. In such cases, asynchronous mode can avoid unnecessary waiting and reduce the runtime overhead. Besides, some logics, e.g., context-free languages, may require the generated monitor to wait until the next events to proceed.

3 Conclusion

This paper presents a development and analysis environment for Java, which supports the MOP paradigm. Monitors will be generated from formal specifications and then used to verify the execution of the system. Users can define self-recovery actions for the violation of specifications. More logic plugins for useful specification languages will be added into JAVA-MOP in order to support different domain requirements.

References

1. H. Barringer, A. Goldberg, K. Havelund, and K. Sen. Program monitoring with ltl in eagle. In *Workshop on Parallel and Distributed Systems: Testing and Debugging (PADTAD'04) (Satellite workshop of IPDPS'04)*, Santa Fe, New Mexico, USA, April 2004. IEEE digital library.
2. F. Chen, M. D'Amorim, and G. Roşu. A formal monitoring-based framework for software development and analysis. In *Proceedings of the 6th International Conference on Formal Engineering Methods (ICFEM'04)*, volume to appear of *Lecture Notes in Computer Science*. Springer-Verlag, 2004.
3. M. M. Detlef Bartetzko, Clemens Fischer and H. Wehrheim. Jass - java with assertions. In *Electronic Notes in Theoretical Computer Science*, volume 55. Elsevier Science Publishers, 2001.
4. D. Drusinsky. Monitoring Temporal Rules Combined with Time Series. In *Proc. of CAV'03: Computer Aided Verification*, volume 2725 of *Lecture Notes in Computer Science*, pages 114–118, Boulder, Colorado, USA, 2003. Springer-Verlag.
5. K. Havelund and G. Roşu. *Workshops on Runtime Verification (RV'01, RV'02, RV'04)*, volume 55, 70(4), to appear of *ENTCS*. Elsevier, 2001, 2002, 2004.
6. K. Havelund and G. Roşu. An overview of the runtime verification tool Java PathExplorer. *Formal Methods in System Design*, 24(2):189–215, 2004.
7. M. Kim, S. Kannan, I. Lee, and O. Sokolsky. Java-MaC: a Run-time Assurance Tool for Java. In *Proceedings of Runtime Verification (RV'01)*, volume 55 of *Electronic Notes in Theoretical Computer Science*. Elsevier Science, 2001.
8. G. T. Leavens, K. R. M. Leino, E. Poll, C. Ruby, and B. Jacobs. JML: notations and tools supporting detailed design in Java. In *OOPSLA 2000 Companion*, pages 105–106, 2000.

9. Z. Manna and A. Pnueli. *Temporal Verification of Reactive Systems: Safety.* Springer, New York, 1995.
10. B. Meyer. *Object-Oriented Software Construction, 2nd edition.* Prentice Hall, Upper Saddle River, New Jersey, 2000.
11. Mop website. http://fsl.cs.uiuc.edu/mop.
12. K. Sen, G. Roşu, and G. Agha. Runtime safety analysis of multithreaded programs. In *Proceedings of 4th joint* European Software Engineering Conference *and* ACM SIGSOFT Symposium on the Foundations of Software Engineering, (ESEC/FSE'03). ACM, 2003.
13. L. Sha, R. Rajkumar, and M. Gagliardi. The simplex architecture: An approach to build evolving industrial co mputing systems. In *Proceedings of The ISSAT Conference on Reliability*, 1994.

JML-Testing-Tools: A Symbolic Animator for JML Specifications Using CLP

Fabrice Bouquet, Frédéric Dadeau, Bruno Legeard, and Mark Utting

Laboratoire d'Informatique (LIFC),
Université de Franche-Comté, CNRS - INRIA,
16, route de Gray - 25030 Besançon cedex, France
{bouquet, dadeau, legeard, utting}@lifc.univ-fcomte.fr

Abstract. This paper describes a tool for symbolically animating JML specifications using Constraint Logic Programming. A customized solver handles constraints that represent the value of instance fields. We have extended a model-based approach to be able to handle object-oriented specifications. Our tool is also able to check properties during the simulation and exhibit counter-examples for false properties. Therefore, it can be used both for semi-automated verification and for validation purposes.

Keywords: Java Modeling Language, model-based, object-oriented, symbolic animation.

1 Motivations

Building formal models of systems is a valuable technique for improving the design of software, and analyzing safety and functionality, particularly when there is good tool support for the formal method. A variety of different modeling languages are used for building the formal models. The Java Modeling Language (JML) [LBR98, LBR99], is an object-oriented modeling language based on Java and designed to be used as well by developers as by modeling engineers.

The use of formal models makes it possible to check the coherence of the specification (*verification*) and also to check the conformance of the specification with the initial requirements (*validation*). Good tool support for these verification and validation processes is always appreciated by users of the modeling language. A key technique for validation is *animation* of the model. This is a semi-automated process, which simulates the execution of the specification, allowing the author to check that his specification has the desired behavior.

This paper describes a tool, called JML-Testing-Tools, which is able to symbolically execute a JML specification. It also allows users to specify constrained values as input for the method parameters, which is more general than entering specific values. We use a novel constraint solver to handle the constrained values of the resulting state variables. Moreover, our tool is able to check properties on-the-fly and to display counter examples for properties that fail. Thus, this tool may also be used for verification purposes. This technology has already

N. Halbwachs and L. Zuck (Eds.): TACAS 2005, LNCS 3440, pp. 551–556, 2005.

been applied to the animation of B [Abr96], Z [Spi92] or Statechart [Har87] specifications within the BZ-Testing-Tools environment [ABC⁺02].

2   Illustrating JML with an Example

JML is used to specify the behavior of Java modules. It is presented as annotations embedded within the Java code, starting with a comment-like syntax so that they do not interfere with usual Java tools, but specialized JML tools may take care of them.

The example in figure 1 presents a simplified electronic purse specification that illustrates the possibilities of JML. This class contains a field named `balance` which represents the amount of money stored in the purse, and a static field named `max` which designates the maximal amount that the purse may contain.

This specification illustrates the main clauses of JML, such as the class invariant (`invariant`), specifying that the balance should always be greater or equal to zero, or history constraints (`constraint`) specifying that the maximal balance, `max`, should never be modified. Notice the presence of the \old(x) operator in the before-after predicates, which expresses that the expression x has to be considered at its before value.

Each method specification clause is described by a keyword indicating its kind (e.g. `requires` for preconditions, `ensures` for normal postcondition, `signals` for exceptional postcondition, etc.), followed by a first-order logic predicate or an explicit keyword (e.g. \nothing, \not_specified, etc.). The `assignable` clause in the method specifications is used to list the fields which may be modified by the execution of the method. The `signals` clause is used to describe the postcondition the method establishes when the considered method throws an exception of the given type. In our example, the exception `NoCreditException` is raised when the amount to withdraw is greater than the value of the balance.

```
class Purse {

    //@ invariant balance >= 0;
    short balance;
    //@ constraint max == \old(max);
    static short max = 32767;

    /*@ behavior
      @    requires a > 0;
      @    assignable balance;
      @    ensures balance == \old(balance) - a;
      @    signals (NoCreditException e)
      @         balance == \old(balance) &&
      @         a > \old(balance);
      @*/
    public void withdraw(short a)
               throws NoCreditException {...}

    /*@ normal_behavior
      @    requires b > 0 && b <= max;
      @    assignable balance;
      @    ensures getBalance() == b;
      @*/
    public Purse(short b) {...}

    /*@ normal_behavior
      @    assignable \nothing;
      @    ensures \result == balance;
      @*/
    public /*@ pure @*/ short getBalance() {...}

}
```

Fig. 1. The JML specification of the Purse example

JML also introduces new kind of method declaration modifiers, including the notion of *purity*, meaning that a method specified as `pure` does not change the value of any field of the considered class. In our example, method `getBalance()` is described to observe the value of the field `balance`. Method specifications may contain method calls, if and only if these methods are described as *pure*, in order to avoid side-effects.

3 Description of JML-Testing-Tools

JML-Testing-Tools – JML-TT – is a recently developed JML specification animator. It relies on a model-based approach, meaning that we only consider the method specifications to simulate the activation of the behaviors of the system, and we do not execute the Java code itself.

This is an extension of the BZ-Testing-Tools technology, a framework for animation and automatic test generation from B, Z or Statechart specifications, extended for handling object concepts. At the present time, only the animation part has been studied and implemented.

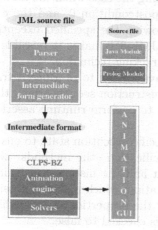

JML-TT takes as an input a JML annotated file of a Java class. The tool parses, type-checks and gathers all the referenced and needed classes which are then translated it to an intermediate format file, from which animation is realized. The animation relies on an original constraint solver named CLPS-BZ which handles constraints on the values of state variables, and method input parameters. Indeed, JML-TT makes it possible to constrain the value of an input to execute a method on an instance. Moreover, JML-TT is able to assign to the state variables a value satisfying the constraints store, by valuation of a constrained environment.

4 Animating a JML Specification

JML-Testing-Tools uses the JML annotations describing the specification of the Java module, i.e., class or interface, to symbolically execute it.

The CLPS-BZ animation engine manages an execution environment, which represents the classes, instances, fields and their corresponding values. Animating consists in identifying the predicates representing the different behaviors of a considered method, and interpreting them so that a new execution state is reached. Therefore, the methods are described using before-after predicates whose semantics is close to JML.

During the animation, the user is free to choose which objects he wants to create and which methods he wants to invoke on the created objects. The user is also asked to input the value of method parameters, which may also be left constrained. This latter creates a constrained variable to represent the value of the parameter, depending on its type and the constraints described in the JML method annotations. New constrained variable may appear to represent instance fields values, if they are related to the constrained parameter. A labeling can be performed at any time to get all the possible values for all the newly introduced constrained variables.

The invocation of a method may create choice-points identifying behaviors in the specification. For example, the following JML-annotated method:

```
/*@ behavior
  @    requires P;
  @    assignable A;
  @    ensures Q;
  @    signals (Exception) S;
  @*/
TypeReturn methodName(TypeParam1 param1, ...) { ... }
```

will induce two behaviors: $P \wedge Q$ and $P \wedge S$, describing the case when the method terminates normally and establishes the normal postcondition Q, and the case when the method terminates abnormally by throwing the specified exception and establishes the exceptional postcondition S. JML-TT makes it possible to execute each one of them by using a simple backtracking technique.

Each step of the animation is expressed in Java syntax to produce a trace of the symbolic execution performed. This Java instruction sequence may then be exported to a Java test case file and compiled to perform runtime assertion checking as described in [CL02].

Finally, properties can be checked within a specific execution state to ensure the conformance of the dynamic part of the specification –the methods– with the static properties of the system –the invariant and the history constraints. Properties are checked using the principle of refutation, which makes it possible to check either the validity or the satisfiability of the properties and to exhibit a reachable counter-example, when the property is checked to false.

5   Features of JML-Testing-Tools

JML-Testing-Tools has the following features:

- Animation of a JML specification in an environment also displaying all the referenced classes;
- Execution of the methods by activating their behaviors with precondition checking;
- Possibility to leave input values of method parameters unspecified, to create constrained states;
- Valuation of the constrained state to assign all their possible values to the constrained variables, with the possibility to take into account the invariant and/or the history constraints;

- Properties checking (invariant, history constraints) within an execution state, and exhibition of counter-examples for unchecked properties;
- Exportation of the user-defined execution sequence to a Java test case file, that can be checked by a runtime assertion checker;
- Good coverage of JML specifications clauses: class invariant, history constraints, preconditions (requires), postcondition (ensures, signals), delaying (when), divergence (diverges);
- Undo and redo features;
- Possibility to save and open animations.

All these features are realized by the user through a user-friendly Graphical User Interface described hereafter.

6 Description of the GUI

The Graphical User Interface displayed by the tool is presented in figure 2.

The left area (1) displays the state informations: the instances that have been created, the value of their fields, etc. From this area, the user can execute the class methods on the instances, or several specific actions on public fields such as directly assigning a value. The top-right area (2) displays the Java code corresponding to the execution sequence that is being created. The middle-right area (3) recalls information on the selected instance and on the corresponding class. The bottom-right area (4) is used to present the result of properties checking, such as invariant or history constraints. If a property evaluates to false, it is

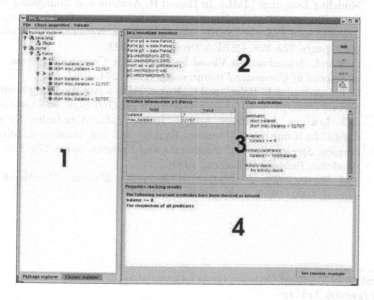

Fig. 2. The JML-Testing-Tools animator main frame

displayed and a counter-example exhibits the state of the system that presents an error. The menu is used to run the verification of properties or the valuation of a constrained environment.

7   General Information

The JML-Testing-Tools has been developed at the Computer Science Laboratory of the University of Franche-Comté CNRS INRIA (France), in the Constraint group led by Professor Bruno Legeard, in partnership with the GECCOO[1] and INRIA CASSIS[2] projects.

JML-Testing-Tools is available for download at the following address:

http://lifc.univ-fcomte.fr/~jmltt/

References

[ABC+02]   F. Ambert, F. Bouquet, S. Chemin, S. Guenaud, B. Legeard, F. Peureux, N. Vacelet, and M. Utting. BZ-TT: A Tool-Set for Test Generation from Z and B using Constraint Logic Programming. In Robert Hierons and Thierry Jerron, editors, *Formal Approaches to Testing of Software, FATES 2002 workshop of CONCUR'02*, pages 105–120. INRIA Report, August 2002.

[Abr96]   J.-R. Abrial. *The B-book: assigning programs to meanings.* Cambridge University Press, 1996.

[CL02]   Y. Cheon and G.T. Leavens. A runtime assertion checker for the Java Modeling Language (JML). In Hamid R. Arabnia and Youngsong Mun, editors, *Proceedings of the International Conference on Software Engineering Research and Practice (SERP '02), Las Vegas, Nevada, USA, June 24-27, 2002*, pages 322–328. CSREA Press, June 2002.

[Har87]   D. Harel. Statecharts: a Visual Formalism for Complex Systems. *Journal of Science of Computer Programming*, 8:231–274, 1987.

[LBR98]   G.T. Leavens, A.L. Baker, and C. Ruby. JML: a java modeling language. In *Formal Underpinnings of Java Workshop (at OOPSLA '98)*, October 1998.

[LBR99]   G.T. Leavens, A.L. Baker, and C. Ruby. JML: A notation for detailed design. In Haim Kilov, Bernhard Rumpe, and Ian Simmonds, editors, *Behavioral Specifications of Businesses and Systems*, pages 175–188. Kluwer Academic Publishers, Boston, 1999.

[Spi92]   J.M. Spivey. *The Z notation: A Reference Manual.* Prentice-Hall, 2nd edition, 1992. ISBN 0 13 978529 9.

---

[1] GEneration of Certified Code for Object-Oriented applications
http://geccoo.lri.fr
[2] Combining ApproacheS for the Security of Infinite state Systems
http://www.loria.fr/equipes/cassis/

jETI: A Tool for Remote Tool Integration

Tiziana Margaria[1], Ralf Nagel[2], and Bernhard Steffen[2]

[1] Service Engineering for Distributed Systems,
Institute for Informatics, University of Göttingen, Germany
margaria@cs.uni-goettingen.de
[2] Chair of Programming Systems, University of Dortmund, Germany
Ralf.Nagel@udo.edu, steffen@cs.uni-dortmund.de

Abstract. We present jETI, a redesign of the Electronic Tools Integration platform (ETI), that addresses the major issues and concerns accumulated over seven years of experience with tool providers, tool users and students. Most important was here the reduction of the effort for integrating and updating tools. jETI combines Eclipse with Web Services functionality in order to provide (1) lightweight remote component (tool) integration, (2) distributed component (tool) libraries, (3) a graphical coordination environment, and (4) a distributed execution environment. These features will be illustrated in the course of building and executing remote heterogeneous tool sequences.

1 Motivation

The Electronic Tool Integration platform (ETI) [10] is an online platform specifically designed to support the distributed use of and experimentation with tools over the internet. Born in 1996 and online since early 1997, it offered a unique service to tool providers and users: its solution for the remote execution of tools and the internet-based administration of user-specific home areas on the ETI server was well ahead of the technology of those times. Since then, users can

- *retrieve information* about the tools,
- *execute tools* in *stand-alone mode*, or
- *combine functionalities of different tools* to obtain sequential programs called *coordination sequences* and run them in *tool-coordination mode*.

In particular, ETI is unique in allowing users to combine functionalities of tools of different application domains to solve problems a single tool never would be able to tackle.

Obviously, the richness of the *tool repository* plays a crucial role in the success of ETI: the benefit gained from our experimentation and coordination facilities grows with the amount and variety of integrated software-tools. The success of the ETI concept is thus highly sensitive to the process and costs of *tool integration* and *tool maintenance*.

In this paper we show how, taking advantage of newer technologies that internally base on Web Services and Java technology, we can

N. Halbwachs and L. Zuck (Eds.): TACAS 2005, LNCS 3440, pp. 557–562, 2005.
© Springer-Verlag Berlin Heidelberg 2005

1. considerably simplify the integration process, and at the same time
2. flexibilize the distribution, version management and use of integrated tools,
3. broaden the scope of potential user profiles and roles, by seamlessly integrating ETI's coordination and synthesis features (cf. [8]) with a standard Java development environment, and
4. solve the scalability problem connected with tool maintenance and evolution.

The background and a first attempt to the new distributed way of tool integration for ETI have been described in [3]. Our current version of ETI, jETI,

- exploits Web Services technology [14, 13, 11] to further simplify the remote tool integration and execution,
- supports cross platform execution of the coordination models based on the quasi standard set by Java, and it naturally
- flexibilizes the original coordination level by seamlessly integrating the Eclipse development framework [2].

A more detailed description of jETI can be found in [4].

In the following, Section 2 sketches ETI's philosophy of remote tool integration, before we describe ETI's enhanced, formal methods-based coordination facility in Section 3, and ETI's framework view in Section 4. Our conclusions and directions are given in Section 5.

2   jETI as an Integration Tool

jETI's integration philosophy addresses the major obstacle for a wider adoption, as identified during seven years of experience with tool providers, tool users and students: the difficulty to provide the latest versions of the state-of-the-art tools. The tool integration process required on dedicated ETI servers was too complicated for both the tool providers and the ETI team, making it impossible to keep pace with the development of new versions and a wealth of new tools. jETI's new remote integration philosophy overcomes this problems, because it replaces the requirement of 'physical' tool integration by a very simple registration and publishing. This allows the provision of tool functionalities in a matter of minutes: fast enough to be fully demonstrated during our presentation. Moreover, whenever the portion of a tool's API which is relevant for a new version of a functionality remains unchanged, version updating is fully automatic!

Based on the Web Services functionality, the realization of this registration/publishing based integration philosophy required the implementation of four components, as illustrated in Figure 1:

1. a **HTML Tool Configurator**, which allows tool providers to register a new tool functionality just by filling our a simple template form,
2. the **jABC Component Server**, which (a) automatically generates appropriate Java classes from these specifications and (b) organizes all the registered tool functionalities, including the corresponding version control,

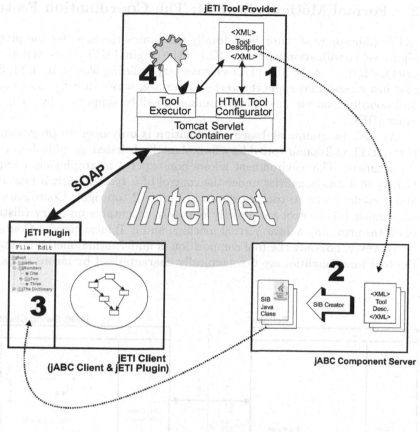

Fig. 1. The jETI Tool Integration Workflow

3. the **jETI client**, which automatically loads the relevant Java classes from the jABC Component Server and provides a flexible Java development environment for coordinating the so obtained tool functionalities. Depending on their goals and skill profile, users may just use our graphical coordination editor (as in Sect. 3) to experiment with the tools, or they may use the full development support of Eclipse to really embed remote functionalities into normal Java programs. Of course, this choice heavily influences the size of the required jETI-Client: only the first option is open to our envisaged 'pure HTML' solution.

4. a **Tool Executor**, which is able to steer the execution of the specified tools at the tool providers' site.

This approach enables *experts* to develop complex tools in Java on the basis of a library of remotely accessible tool functionalities, as well as *newcomers* to use jETI's formal methods-based, graphical coordination environment to safely combine adequate tool functionalities into heterogeneous tools.

3   Formal Methods in jETI: The Coordination Feature

jETI's philosophy of 'pure Java' totally eliminates the need for the proprietary high-level coordination language (HL) of the original ETI [8], as well as the proprietary format of the SIBs, ETI's elementary building blocks. In jETI, SIBs are now just classes that support a certain interface, which directly allows arbitrary tool coordination via Java programming, possibly supported by Eclipse [2] or other IDEs.

As Java programming-based coordination is only open to programming experts, jETI additionally provides a formal methods based, graphical coordination environment. This environment allows non-experts to graphically compose arbitrary tool functionalities under the control of a *type checker*, a *model checker* and a *model synthesis* tool, as shown in Figure 2 top right. Coordination models passing this control are directly remotely executable on every (distributed) platform providing a Java Virtual machine and a Tomcat Servlet Container.

However, not only the tool composition is under formal methods control. All the tool functionalities are taxonomically characterized by means of *ontologies*,

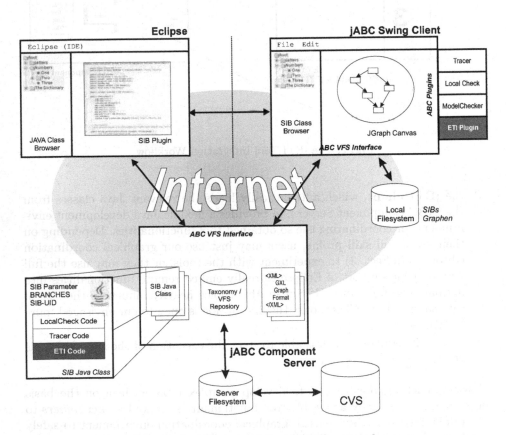

Fig. 2. Architecture of the jABC Framework

similar to the techniques adopted for the Semantic Web [1]. ETI supports a global classification, but users may also introduce their private classification scheme, which helps them to quickly identify the tools relevant for certain applications. In fact, the requirement for this organizational support of tool functionalities was a result of a common project with the CMU, aiming at introducing a larger variety of formal verification tools in the undergraduate curricula.

4   jETI: The Architecture

jETI can be seen as a tool that enhances other tools and frameworks by the integration, organization and execution of remote functionalities. E.g., the setup described above is based on jABC (cf. Figure 2), which is itself a framework for enhancing Java development environments (like Eclipse) with a graphical coordination level and dedicated control via formal methods. The charme of this architecture is that complex environment functionality can be added just via the plugin concept: this allows users to combine/exchange functionality in a transparent way, without touching the code of the kernel system. In our case, jABC can itself be seen as an Eclipse plugin, which, in addition to the ETI plugin, offers plugins for model checking, local checking, and a tracer. Dually, Eclipse can also be seen as an jABC plugin, enhancing the power of the jABC as a development environment. In particular, users may handily exchange Eclipse with their favorite Java development environment (or they may use jETI/jABC in a stand-alone fashion), and our game-based model checker [5] with their tool of trust, without having to touch anything of the jABC and jETI implementation.

5   Conclusions and Future Work

We have presented jETI, a tool for remote tool integration, which overcomes the bottlenecks of the ETI platform observed over the past seven years. Based on our remote tool integration and execution philosophy, jETI drastically lowers the entrance hurdle for tool providers and allows upgrading of tools essentially for free. In combination with the change to a 'pure Java' approach, jETI has the unique potential to become a standard for enhancing Java development environments with remote component execution, high level coordination, and formal methods-based control. We are planning to make jETI available as open source for this purpose in the near future.

Our current implementation must still be sees as a prototype, a status, which we want to overcome by the end of 2005, which, besides others, requires a redevelopment of the graphical user interface in particular for supporting the Semantic Web and the synthesis functionality. We plan to start the β-testing phase for a version hosted by us in Spring 2005, followed by a first system delivery to partners half a year later.

References

1. Tim Berners-Lee, James Hendler, Ora Lassila: *The Semantic Web* Scientific American, May 2001.
2. Eclipse Foundation: http://www.eclipse.org/
3. T. Margaria: *Web Services-Based Tool-Integration in the ETI Platform*, SoSyM, Int. Journal on Software and System Modelling, to appear, Springer Verlag (Springer Online First DOI: 10.1007/s10270-004-0072-z).
4. T. Margaria, R. Nagel, B. Steffen: *Remote Integration and Coordination of Verification Tools in JETI*, Proc. of ECBS 2005, 12th Annual IEEE Int. Conf. and Workshop on the Engineering of Computer Based Systems, 4-7 April 2005, Washington DC (USA), IEEE Press.
5. Markus Müller-Olm, Haiseung Yoo: *MetaGame: An Animation Tool for Model-Checking Games*, Proc. TACAS 2004, LNCS 2988, pp.163-167.
6. B. Steffen: *"Characteristic Formulae,"* Proc. ICALP'89, Stresa (I), July 1989, LNCS 372, Springer Verlag, 1989.
7. B. Steffen, A. Ingolfsdottir: *"Characteristic Formulae for Finite State Processes,"* Information and Computation, Vol. 110, No. 1, 1994.
8. B. Steffen, T. Margaria, V. Braun: *The Electronic Tool Integration platform: concepts and design*, [10], pp. 9-30.
9. B. Steffen, T. Margaria, A. Claßen: *Heterogeneous Analysis and Verification for Distributed Systems*, "SOFTWARE: Concepts and Tools" Vol. 17, N.1, pp. 13-25, March 1996, Springer Verlag.
10. *Special section on the Electronic Tool Integration Platform*, Int. Journal on Software Tools for Technology Transfer, Vol. 1, Springer Verlag, November 1997
11. SUN Microsystems. Java WebService Developer Pack *http://java.sun.com/ webservices/*
12. Tomcat homepage: http://jakarta.apache.org/tomcat/
13. WebServices.Org - homepage of the WebServices and SOA communities: http://www.webservices.org/
14. W3C. SOAP *http://www.w3.org/TR/SOAP/*
15. Web Service Choreography Interface (WSCI) 1.0, W3C Note, 8 August 2002, *http://www.w3.org/TR/2002/NOTE-wsci-20020808*.

FocusCheck: A Tool for Model Checking and Debugging Sequential C Programs

Curtis W. Keller[1], Diptikalyan Saha[2], Samik Basu[1], and Scott A. Smolka[2]

[1] Department of Computer Science, Iowa State University, Ames
{cwkeller, sbasu}@cs.iastate.edu
[2] Department of Computer Science, State University of New York, Stony Brook
{dsaha, sas}@cs.sunysb.edu

Abstract. We present the FocusCheck model-checking tool for the verification and easy debugging of assertion violations in sequential C programs. The main functionalities of the tool are the ability to: (a) identify all minimum-recursion, loop-free counter-examples in a C program using on-the-fly abstraction techniques; (b) extract focus-statement sequences (FSSs) from counter-examples, where a focus statement is one whose execution directly or indirectly causes the violation underlying a counter-example; (c) detect and discard infeasible counter-examples via feasibility analysis of the corresponding FSSs; and (d) isolate program segments that are most likely to harbor the erroneous statements causing the counter-examples. FocusCheck is equipped with a smart graphical user interface that provides various views of counter-examples in terms of their FSSs, thereby enhancing usability and readability of model-checking results.

1 Introduction

Software model checking typically follows a three-step, iterative process of abstraction, verification, and refinement [4, 1, 7]. First, given a program P, a finite-state abstract version P' of P is generated. Then, P' is verified with respect to the given property and a counter-example (sequence of program statements) is generated should a violation occur. Finally, constraint solvers and/or theorem provers are used to check whether the counter-example is feasible in the concrete program P; if not, the abstract program P' is refined. The three steps are iterated until a feasible counter-example is identified or the property is satisfied.

Counter-example feasibility analysis requires the user to understand the root-cause of the counter-example, and subsequently isolate and debug the error in the program. The presence of complex data and control structures in the program can make such analysis an extremely tedious and time-consuming process.

To render counter-example analysis more tractable, we present the FocusCheck model checker and debugger. FocusCheck takes C programs as input; using a model checker written in XSB Prolog [8] for push-down systems, it identifies in one pass *all* counter-examples (if any) in the program under investigation.

N. Halbwachs and L. Zuck (Eds.): TACAS 2005, LNCS 3440, pp. 563–569, 2005.

Generated counter-examples are analyzed to identify slices in the form of *focus-statement sequences* (FSSs): it is the execution of the program statements in the FSSs, and nothing else, that leads to the violation of property [3]. Feasible FSSs are ranked such that those of higher rank are likely to be easier to understand and debug than those of lower rank. Constraints on data variables in each FSS are determined to allow the tool to zoom in on specific program segments that are most likely to harbor the erroneous statements in the program.

2   Tool Description

In this section, we describe the main components of the FocusCheck model checker and counter-example analyzer. Figure 1 presents the architecture of the tool.

Translating C-programs to Push-down Models. The translator uses the CIL toolset [5] to transform C programs into XSB Prolog, from which push-down system transitions of the form S → S' are generated. Here S is the statement at the top of stack which, when executed, is replaced by S'. Push-down systems are a natural choice for accurately representing the control behavior of sequential programs as they capture the exact call-return patterns such programs exhibit.

Model Checker. The core of the model checker, written in XSB Prolog, is a reachability analyzer for push-down transition systems; this in turn is tightly integrated with a slicer. A model of a program can exhibit infinite-state behavior due to the presence of infinite-domain variables. A typical solution to such a problem is to perform forward reachability from the initial state by leaving the evaluation of infinite-domain variables un-interpreted. Once an error trace is

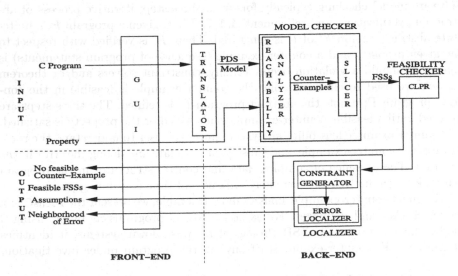

Fig. 1. Architecture of the FocusCheck tool

```
1: ... if ( x > 100 ) {          (a) uninterpreted variables: x, y
2:       if ( y < 50 ) {         (b) counter-examples:
3:         bigProcedure1();            [1,2,3,...,4], [1,2,6,...,7]
4:         i = 10; }             (c) FSSs: [1,2,4], [1,2,7]
5:       } else {                (d) assumptions:
6:         bigProcedure2();           [x>100, y<50],[x>100,y>=50]
7:         i = 10; } } ...       (e) localized lines: 2, 4, 7
```

Fig. 2. Example code-snippet illustrating main tool features

obtained, backward reachability analysis from the error state to the start state identifies all the un-interpreted variable operations and employs a constraint solver or theorem prover to check whether these operations in the error trace are feasible. In short, feasibility of an error trace is decided by the feasibility of operations on infinite-domain variables within the trace.

Note that leaving variable operations un-interpreted during forward analysis may lead to an infinite number of search paths in the program due to the presence of infinite-domain recursion control and loop control parameters. Our technique addresses this issue by detecting loop-free counter-examples with minimal recursion [2] which amounts to summarizing the *effect* of procedures and discards all unfoldings of recursion that do not alter the effect. By effect of a procedure, we mean the valuations of finite-domain variables present in its scope.

Slicing is performed on the counter-example itself using the variables present in the last statement of the counter-example sequence as the slicing criteria. The aim is to detect all the statements in the counter-example that directly or indirectly effect the assertion violation underlying the counter-example; i.e. the FSS of the counter-example.

Constraint-solver: CLP(R). The operations contained in an FSS are checked for feasibility using CLP(R), XSB's built-in constraint solver. We show in [3] that the feasibility of an FSS implies the existence of a feasible counter-example. An important aspect of FocusCheck is that all feasible counter-examples are detected (using the backtracking capabilities of XSB) in one cycle; as such, the typical abstraction-refinement iteration is avoided.

Localizer. In the presence of uninitialized or input variables in an FSS, feasibility analysis enforces certain constraints on these variables. We refer to these constraints as *assumptions*, and generate them by the constraint generator module. One of FocusCheck's distinguishing features is its ability to localize errors to specific program regions using assumptions [3]. This region is called a *neighborhood of error statements* (NEST). The technique relies on the presence of multiple feasible FSSs owing to branching behavior of the program.

Illustrative Example. The program of Figure 2 illustrates the main features of the FocusCheck tool. Assume that the property of interest is violated if i=10. The variables left uninterpreted are x and y and, as such, all possible conditional branches are explored. The line numbers of the counter-examples generated by

FocusCheck are shown in item (b). The "..." after Lines 3 and 6 represent respectively the line numbers of procedures bigProcedure1() and bigProcedure2(), which are present in the counter-examples. Since these procedures do not effect the valuation of i (=10), their line numbers do not appear in the corresponding FSSs given in item (c). The feasibility of the FSSs requires constraints over the uninterpreted variables and these are given in item (d). Finally, in item (e), Lines 2, 4, and 7 are classified as a NEST as both branches of the conditional block starting at Line 2 lead to the violation of the property.

Graphical User Interface. One of the major challenges in designing a debugger is to present the user with just enough information about counter-examples so that corrective measures can be taken. With this in mind, FocusCheck performs counter-example analysis in order to extract the relevant information from counter-examples, which it presents to the user via an intuitive GUI.

As discussed above, counter-examples are analyzed and sliced to generate focus-statement sequences (FSSs), while constraints (assumptions) over uninitialized/input variables are identified using a constraint solver. Given a program and its property, FocusCheck generates all possible feasible FSSs and their associated assumption sets. FSSs are ranked so that the user can examine conceptually easier-to-understand FSSs before the more difficult ones. Consequently, the GUI presents FSSs using a tabbed panel, where the number of tabs is equal to the total number of FSSs identified by FocusCheck. Moreover, a lower-numbered tab holds the information of a higher-rank FSS. This enables the user to concentrate on one FSS without having to look at any other FSS.

An FSS is represented in terms of line numbers and each line number is mapped to the program statement at that line number in the source code. Information associated with an FSS, e.g. the assumptions on uninitialized/input variables or the localized block of the program, can be also viewed by the user. Assumptions are shown in a separate pop-up window, while the localization information is presented by coloring the corresponding line numbers red.

If the user decides to examine multiple FSSs at a time, she can highlight the lines of the current FSS and move over to another FSS using the FSS tabs. For easy viewing, each FSS is color-coded so that the highlights for one FSS are distinct from another. The lines that are common to multiple FSSs are highlighted in grey. Furthermore, the user can consult the localization caused by different FSSs and their corresponding assumptions and analyze multiple FSSs at the same time.

Tool Demonstration. A number of examples are given in the test suite of the tool. In the following, we present one of the examples that illustrates the salient features of our tool. The program *merge.c* sorts five integers a1, a2, a3, a4, and a5, in only five comparisons given the partial order a1>a2, a3>a4, a1>a3. The output of the program is a sorted list of output variables o1, o2, o3, o4, o5 in descending order. The program is based on the algorithm for finding the median of a list of numbers in linear time.

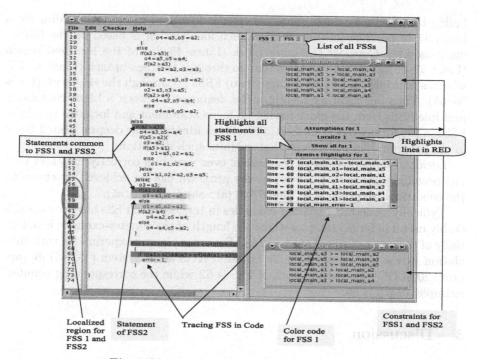

Fig. 3. Viewing counter-examples for merge.c

We injected an error into the program by replacing the conditional expression at Line 57, a1 > a5, with a1 < a5. Verification of the modified program with respect to the assertional property that all output elements should be sorted, produces two FSSs, the panels for which are labeled FSS1 and FSS2 in Figure 3. The figure contains a screenshot of the FocusCheck GUI, with the program source code viewer on the left, and various information pertaining to the currently selected FSS (FSS1) on the right. In particular, the statements of FSS1 can be seen in the scrollable text box, each of which is tagged by the corresponding source-code line number. The color-coding scheme for FSSs deployed by the GUI enables one to observe that the two FSSs differ in the if-then-else block of Lines 57–60. Noticing this difference, it can be inferred that both branches of the if-block at Lines 57–60 may be responsible for the assertion violation. Next we see the difference between constraints[1] associated with the FSSs are a1 < a5 and a1 >= a5. A quick inspection of the FSSs shows that the conditional expression at Line 57 is responsible for generation of these constraints.

Furthermore, localization indicates that Lines 57 and 58 of FSS1 and Lines 57 and 60 of FSS2 constitute a neighborhood of error statements (NEST). Com-

---

[1] Variables in constraints are shown by pre-pending information about the scope in which they are active. For example, a local variable var in procedure func is denoted local_func_var while a global variable x is denoted global_x.

bining the results for both FSSs, the error is localized to block extending from Lines 57 to 60. The intuition behind such localization is based on the following reasoning. Consider the outer block (Lines 45–65) of the localized region (Lines 57–60). There are no FSSs that go through the then-branch (Lines 46–54) whereas multiple (in this case exactly two) FSSs go through the else-block (Lines 56–65). Thus our localizer identifies the *deviation* between a block containing multiple FSSs from the block having no focus statement and localizes to all the FSSs in the former block. In short, FocusCheck identifies the deepest nested block in the program-block hierarchy that exhibits such deviations.

Localization coupled with constraints over variables correctly indicates that one possible remedy to the error in the program can be achieved by changing the conditional expression at Line 57 to (a1>a5) from (a1<a5).

Typically, generating counter-examples in terms of the FSSs has been considerably useful in large examples where the length of the counter-example is potentially of the order of size of the program. For example, our experiments with Resolution Advisory module of Traffic Collision Avoidance System (TCAS) [6] (approx. 200 LOC) show that length of FSS is 52 while the corresponding counter-example length is 89.

3   Discussion

FocusCheck provides a number of facilities aimed at allowing the user to understand and debug errors efficiently. The model checker is developed in a highly modular fashion with simple interfaces and disintegrates the domain-specific analysis (such as translators and constraint solvers) from the model checker's core. As such, components can be further enhanced and extended independently. This permits, for example, translators for procedural languages other than C to be plugged into the tool; or for the reachability analyzer to be coupled with guided-search or summarization techniques without effecting other modules. The FocusCheck tool is available from http://www.cs.iastate.edu/~sbasu/focuscheck along with its documentation and download instructions.

References

1. T. Ball, A. Podelski, and S.K. Rajamani. Relative completeness of abstraction refinement for software model checking. In *Proceedings of TACAS*, 2002.
2. S. Basu, D. Saha, Y-J. Lin, and S. A. Smolka. Generation of all counter-examples for push-down systems. In *Proceedings of FORTE*, 2003.
3. S. Basu, D. Saha, and S. A. Smolka. Counter-example analysis for Cimple debugging. In *Proceedings of FORTE*, 2004.
4. T. A. Henzinger, R. Jhala, R. Majumdar, and G. Sutre. Lazy abstraction. In *Proceedings of POPL*, 2002.
5. G. C. Necula, S. McPeak, S. P. Rahul, and W. Weimer. CIL: Intermediate language and tools for analysis and transformation of C programs.
6. RTCA. Minimum operational performance standards for traffic alert and collision avoidance system (TCAS) airborne equipment consolidated edition, 1990.

7. H. Saidi. Model checking guided predicate abstraction and analysis. In *Proceedings of SAS*, 2000.
8. XSB. The XSB logic programming system. http://xsb.sourceforge.net.

SATABS: SAT-Based Predicate Abstraction
for ANSI-C*

Edmund Clarke[1], Daniel Kroening[2], Natasha Sharygina[1,3], and Karen Yorav[4]

[1] Carnegie Mellon University, School of Computer Science
[2] ETH Zuerich, Switzerland
[3] Carnegie Mellon University, Software Engineering Institute
[4] IBM, Haifa, Israel

Abstract. This paper presents a model checking tool, SATABS, that implements a predicate abstraction refinement loop. Existing software verification tools such as SLAM, BLAST, or MAGIC use decision procedures for abstraction and simulation that are limited to integers. SATABS overcomes these limitations by using a SAT-solver. This allows the model checker to handle the semantics of the ANSI-C standard accurately. This includes a sound treatment of bit-vector overflow, and of the ANSI-C pointer arithmetic constructs.

1 Introduction

In the hardware domain, Model Checking [1] has become a well-established formal verification technique. In contrast to that, the software industry mostly relies on non-exhaustive techniques such as testing.

There are two issues that prohibit a wide-spread use of model checking tools for commercial software. First of all, most model checking tools do not scale gracefully when applied to software of substantial size. Thus, much of the research on model checking has focused on improving scalability. The second issue is that most model checking tools that are available use input languages that are not used for programming. The software system has to be translated into the input language of the model checker.

SATABS, the tool presented in this paper, is geared towards application by software engineers. ANSI-C is one of the most popular programming languages,

* This research was sponsored by the National Science Foundation (NSF) under grant no. CCR-9803774, the Office of Naval Research (ONR), the Naval Research Laboratory (NRL) under contract no. N00014-01-1-0796, and by the Defense Advanced Research Projects Agency, and the Army Research Office (ARO) under contract no. DAAD19-01-1-0485, and the General Motors Collaborative Research Lab at CMU and was conducted as part of the PACC project at the CMU Software Engineering Institute (SEI). The views and conclusions contained in this document are those of the author and should not be interpreted as representing the official policies, either expressed or implied, of SRC, NSF, ONR, NRL, DOD, ARO, or the U.S. government.

N. Halbwachs and L. Zuck (Eds.): TACAS 2005, LNCS 3440, pp. 570–574, 2005.

in particular for safety critical embedded software. Thus, the tool was designed to take ANSI-C programs as input. In SATABS, a special emphasis was made on supporting a rich subset of the ANSI-C language. The bit-vector semantics is modeled accurately, and thus the tool is able to detect errors that are related to bit-level operators and arithmetic overflow.

In order to address the scalability problem, SATABS automatically computes an abstraction of the program given as input. Abstraction is one principal method in state space reduction of software systems. *Predicate abstraction* [2, 3] is one of the most popular and widely applied methods. It abstracts data by only keeping track of certain predicates. Each predicate is represented by a Boolean variable in the abstract model, while the original variables are eliminated. The abstract program is created using *Existential Abstraction* [4], which is a conservative abstraction for reachability properties. If the property holds on the abstract model, it also holds on the original program.

The drawback of the conservative abstraction is that when model checking of the abstract program fails, it may produce a counterexample that does not correspond to a concrete counterexample. This is called a *spurious counterexample*. When a spurious counterexample is encountered, *refinement* is performed by adjusting the set of predicates in a way that eliminates this counterexample. This is automated by *Counterexample Guided Abstraction Refinement* [5, 6, 7].

Related Work. Counterexample guided abstraction refinement for ANSI-C programs was promoted by the success of the SLAM project at Microsoft [6]. Thus, there are already a number of other implementations, such as MAGIC [8], ComFoRT [9] and BLAST [10]. All these projects have support for concurrent software. Both SLAM and BLAST now implement forms of lazy abstraction.

The feature that distinguishes SATABS from these existing tools is the tight integration of a SAT solver into the abstraction, simulation, and refinement steps of the abstraction refinement loop. This allows precise encodings of the semantics of the ANSI-C language, including pointer-arithmetic and bit-vector overflow. In contrast to that, all the tools mentioned above rely on external theorem provers to reason about the programming language constructs. Initially, SLAM, BLAST, MAGIC, and ComFoRT used the theorem prover SIMPLIFY [11], which supports linear arithmetic on real numbers only. The remaining operators are approximated by means of uninterpreted functions. The SLAM project replaced SIMPLIFY by ZAPATO [12], which provides better performance, but no support for bit-vectors.

The use of propositional logic and a SAT solver to reason about ANSI-C language constructs is already found in CBMC [13], a Bounded Model Checker for ANSI-C programs. There is a prototype of SLAM, which has been integrated with parts of CBMC to reason about bit-vector constructs [14]. This version has found a previously unknown bug in Windows.

In [15], Lahiri, Bryant, and Cook use the SAT-based quantification engine implemented in SATABS in order to compute abstractions of C programs. However, the algorithm uses unbounded integer semantics for the program variables, and does not support bit-vector operators. An integration into a full abstraction refinement loop is not reported.

In order to make SATABS applicable to a wide range of low-level programs, SATABS supports most constructs found in the ANSI-C language. In particular, it has support for arrays (with possibly unbounded size), and unions. None of the tools cited above provides these features. SATABS is integrated into the graphical user interface (GUI) of CBMC. The user interface allows the user to step through counterexample traces generated by SATABS as if using a debugger. The GUI is described in more detail in [13].

2   Using SAT for Predicate Abstraction and Refinement

This section provides a short overview of the algorithm implemented by SA-TABS. For more information on the algorithm in the case of sequential code, we refer the reader to [16]. The algorithm is extended to concurrent programs with asynchronous interleaving semantics in [17].

SATABS uses SAT-based Boolean quantification in order to compute the abstract model. Let S denote the set of concrete states, R the concrete transition relation, and $\alpha(x)$ with $x \in S$ the abstraction function. The abstract model can make a transition from an abstract state $\hat{x}$ to $\hat{x}'$ iff there is a transition from x to x' in the concrete model and x is abstracted to $\hat{x}$ and x' is abstracted to $\hat{x}'$. Formally, the abstract transition relation is denoted by $\hat{R}$.

$$\hat{R} := \{(\hat{x}, \hat{x}') \mid \exists x, x' \in S : R(x, x') \wedge \alpha(x) = \hat{x} \wedge \alpha(x') = \hat{x}'\}$$

This formula is transformed into CNF by replacing the bit-vector arithmetic operators by arithmetic circuits. Due to the quantification over the abstract states this corresponds to an all-SAT instance. For efficiency, SATABS overapproximates $\hat{R}$ by partitioning the predicates into clusters [18].

The abstract model is passed to a model checker. SATABS support a variety of model checkers, e.g., MOPED, SPIN, NuSMV, and a QBF-based symbolic simulator. If the model checker returns a counterexample, it has to be simulated on the original code to check if it is spurious.

Given an abstract error trace, SATABS first checks if it contains any spurious transitions. These spurious transitions are caused by the partitioning done during the computation of the abstraction. SATABS forms a SAT instance for each transition in the error trace. If it is found to be unsatisfiable, the transition is spurious. As described in [18], the tool uses the unsatisfiable core of the instance for efficient refinement.

The absence of individual spurious transitions does not guarantee that the error trace is real. Thus, SATABS forms another SAT instance. It corresponds to Bounded Model Checking on the original program following the control flow given by the abstract error trace. If satisfiable, SATABS builds an error trace from the satisfying assignment, which shows the path to the error. If unsatisfiable, the abstract model is refined by adding predicates using weakest preconditions.

SATABS was applied to system-level descriptions given in SpecC, a concurrent variant of ANSI-C [17]. Also, in [19], SATABS was used for equivalence checking: SATABS verified weak bi-simulation of an ANSI-C program and a circuit given in Verilog.

3   Conclusion

This paper presents an implementation of previously presented techniques for verifying ANSI-C programs. The contribution of SATABS is its emphasis on precise encodings of the programming language constructs. The tool supports one of the most popular programming languages, ANSI-C. In contrast to other tools, it supports language features such as bit-vector operators, arrays, and unions. It comes with a graphical user interface that resembles a debugger. The distinguishing feature of SATABS is the tight integration with a SAT solver.

References

1. Clarke, E., Grumberg, O., Peled, D.: Model Checking. MIT Press (1999)
2. Graf, S., Saïdi, H.: Construction of abstract state graphs with PVS. In: CAV. Volume 1254 of LNCS., Springer (1997) 72–83
3. Colón, M., Uribe, T.: Generating finite-state abstractions of reactive systems using decision procedures. In: CAV. Volume 1427 of LNCS., Springer (1998) 293–304
4. Clarke, E., Grumberg, O., Long, D.: Model checking and abstraction. In: Principles of Programming Languages. (1992)
5. Kurshan, R.: Computer-Aided Verification of Coordinating Processes. Princeton University Press, Princeton (1995)
6. Ball, T., Rajamani, S.: Boolean programs: A model and process for software analysis. Technical Report 2000-14, Microsoft Research (2000)
7. Clarke, E.M., Grumberg, O., Jha, S., Lu, Y., Veith, H.: Counterexample-guided abstraction refinement. In: CAV. (2000) 154–169
8. Chaki, S., Clarke, E., Groce, A., Jha, S., Veith, H.: Modular verification of software components in C. In: ICSE. (2003) 385–395
9. Ivers, J., Sharygina, N.: Overview of ComFoRT: A Model Checking Reasoning Framework. Technical Report CMU/SEI-2004-TN-018, CMU SEI (2004)
10. Henzinger, T.A., Jhala, R., Majumdar, R., Sutre, G.: Lazy abstraction. In: POPL 02: Symposium on Principles of Programming Languages, ACM Press (2002) 58–70
11. Detlefs, D., Nelson, G., Saxe, J.B.: Simplify: A theorem prover for program checking. Technical Report HPL-2003-148, HP Labs (2003)
12. Ball, T., Cook, B., Lahiri, S.K., Zhang, L.: Zapato: Automatic theorem proving for predicate abstraction refinement. In: CAV. (2004)
13. Clarke, E., Kroening, D., Lerda, F.: A tool for checking ANSI-C programs. In: TACAS. Volume 2988 of LNCS., Springer (2004) 168–176
14. Cook, B., Kroening, D., Sharygina, N.: Cogent: Accurate Theorem Proving for Program Analysis. Technical Report 464, ETH Zurich, Computer Science (2004)
15. Lahiri, S.K., Bryant, R.E., Cook, B.: A symbolic approach to predicate abstraction. In: CAV. (2003) 141–153

16. Clarke, E., Kroening, D., Sharygina, N., Yorav, K.: Predicate abstraction of ANSI–C programs using SAT. Formal Methods in System Design **25** (2004) 105–127
17. Jain, H., Clarke, E., Kroening, D.: Verification of SpecC and Verilog using predicate abstraction. In: Proceedings of MEMOCODE 2004, IEEE (2004) 7–16
18. Clarke, E., Jain, H., Kroening, D.: Predicate Abstraction and Refinement Techniques for Verifying Verilog. Technical Report CMU-CS-04-139 (2004)
19. Kroening, D., Clarke, E.: Checking consistency of C and Verilog using predicate abstraction and induction. In: Proceedings of ICCAD, IEEE (2004) 66–72

DiVer: SAT-Based Model Checking Platform for Verifying Large Scale Systems

Malay K Ganai, Aarti Gupta, and Pranav Ashar

NEC Laboratories America, Princeton, NJ USA 08540
{malay, agupta, ashar}@nec-labs.com

Abstract. We present a SAT-based model checking platform (*DiVer*) based on robust and scalable algorithms that are tightly integrated for verifying large scale industry designs. *DiVer* houses various SAT-based engines each targeting capacity and performance issues inherent in verifying large designs. The engines with their respective roles are as follows: Bounded Model Checking (BMC) and Distributed BMC over a network of workstations for falsification, Proof-based Iterative Abstraction (PBIA) for model reduction, SAT-based Unbounded Model Checking and Induction for proofs, Efficient Memory Modeling (EMM) and its combination with PBIA in BMC for verifying embedded memory systems with multiple memories (with multiple ports and arbitrary initial state). Using several industrial case studies, we describe the interplay of these engines highlighting their contribution at each step of verification. *DiVer* has matured over 3 years and is being used extensively in several industry settings. Due to an efficient and flexible infrastructure, it provides a very productive verification environment for research and development.

1 Introduction

Verifying modern designs requires robust and scalable approaches in order to meet more-demanding time-to-market requirements. Compared to symbolic model checking [1, 2] based on Binary Decision Diagrams [3], SAT-based model checking techniques [4-17] have been able to scale and perform well due to the many recent advances in DPLL-style SAT solvers [18-20]. We present a SAT-based model checking platform (*DiVer*) based on robust and scalable algorithms [5-7, 11-17, 20, 21] that are tightly integrated for verifying large scale industry designs. We present a brief overview of *DiVer* with its engines each targeting capacity and performance issues inherent in verifying large designs. Using several industrial case studies, we describe the interplay of these engines highlighting their contribution at each step of verification.

2 Tool Overview

DiVer uses an efficient circuit representation with on-the-fly simplification algorithms [18, 21], and an incremental hybrid SAT solver [20] that combines the strengths of circuit-based and CNF-based solvers seamlessly. *DiVer* houses the following

N. Halbwachs and L. Zuck (Eds.): TACAS 2005, LNCS 3440, pp. 575–580, 2005.

SAT-based engines, each geared towards verifying large systems: bounded model checking (BMC) [7] and distributed BMC (d-BMC) over a network of workstations (NOW) [12] for falsification, proof-based iterative abstraction (PBIA) for model reduction [13], SAT-based unbounded model checking (UMC) [15] and induction for proofs [5, 11], Efficient Memory Modeling (EMM) [14] and its combination with PBIA in BMC for verifying embedded memory systems with multiple memories (with multiple ports and arbitrary initial state) and to discover irrelevant memories and ports for proving property correctness [17].

DiVer has matured over 3 years and is being used extensively by the designers in our company. Because of an efficient and flexible infrastructure, it provides a very productive environment for research and development. In this paper we provide useful pointers to the various research efforts, and describe how they fit well together. We present the tool as a "wheel of verification engines" in Figure 1(a). We show the interplay of these engines in verification flows for designs with and without embedded memory in Figures 1(b-c). In the following, we briefly describe various engines:

Internal Representation and Hybrid SAT Solver: The verification model is represented efficiently as a circuit graph with 2-input OR/INVERTER gates, using an on-the-fly multi-level functional hashing algorithm [18, 21] that detects and removes structural and local redundancies. We use this graph to represent the transition relation, unrolled time frames, and the set of enumerated states. For Boolean reasoning, we combine [20] the strengths of circuit-based [18] and CNF-based SAT solvers [19] with incremental SAT solving capabilities [7]. The solver uses deduction and diagnostics engines efficiently on the hybrid Boolean representation, i.e., circuit graph and CNF. The decision engine also benefits from both circuit and CNF based heuristics.

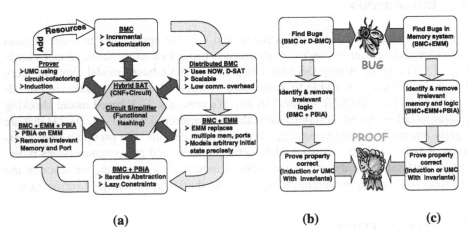

(a)   **(b)**   **(c)**

Fig. 1. *DiVer* Overview (a), Verification without (b) / with (c) embedded memory

BMC: Our SAT-based BMC engine uses the simplified circuit graph to represent unrolled time frames and the hybrid SAT solver to falsify the given the property. For commonly occurring properties, we use *customized translations* of LTL properties that involve partitioning the problem and using incremental model checking [7].

d-BMC: Our d-BMC engine over a network of workstations [12] overcomes the memory limitation of a single server to provide a scalable approach for carrying out deeper search on memory-intensive designs. We achieve a) *scalability* by not keeping the entire problem data on a single processor, and b) *low communication overhead* by making each process cognizant of the partition topology while communicating; thereby, reducing the process's receiving buffer with unwanted information.

BMC+EMM: Our EMM approach [14, 17] augments BMC to handle embedded memory systems (with multiple read, write ports) without explicitly modeling each memory bit, by capturing the memory data forwarding semantics efficiently using exclusivity constraints. An arbitrary initial state of the memory is modeled precisely using constraints on the new symbolic variables introduced [17].

BMC+PBIA: Our PBIA technique [13] generates a *property-preserving* abstract model (up to a certain depth) by a) obtaining a set of latch reasons (LR) involved in the unsatisfiability proof of a SAT problem in BMC, and b) by abstracting away all latches *not in this set* as pseudo-primary inputs. We further reduce the model size by using the abstraction *iteratively* and using *lazy constraints* [16].

BMC+EMM+PBIA: We combine the EMM and PBIA techniques [17] to identify fewer memory modules and ports that need to be modeled; thereby reducing the model size, and verification problem complexity. If no latch corresponding to the control logic for a memory module or port is in the LR set (obtained by PBIA), we do not add the EMM constraints for that memory module or port during BMC.

UMC: Our UMC approach [15] improves the SAT-based blocking clause approach [8] by several orders of magnitude, by using *circuit-based cofactoring* to capture a larger set of new states per enumeration, and representing them efficiently using a simplified circuit graph. The method is combined with inductive invariants, e.g., reachability constraints [11] for faster fixed-point computations.

3   Selected Case Studies

Using selected case studies from the industry, we demonstrate the role of various engines at each step of the verification. Note that without the interplay of the engines we could not have verified any of these designs. The first two case studies use the verification flow shown in Figure 1(b) and the next two use that shown in Figure 1(c). All experiments were performed on a server with 2.8 GHz Xeon processors with 4GB running Red Hat Linux 7.2.

Industry Design I: The design has 13K flip-flops (FFs), ~0.5M gates in the cone of influence of a safety property. Using BMC, we showed there was no witness up to depth 120 (in 1643s) before we run out of memory. Using d-BMC, we showed no witness up to depth 323 (in 8643s) using 5 workstations (configured as 1 Master and 4 Clients and connected with 1Gps Ethernet LAN), with a communication overhead of 30% and scalability factor of 0.1 (i.e, potentially we could do a 10 times deeper analysis than that on the single server.) We hypothesized that the property is correct. We used the PBIA engine to obtain an abstract model with 71 FFs and ~1K gates in 6 iterations taking ~1200s. With UMC, we proved the property correct taking ~2400s.

Industry Design II: The design with environmental constraints has 3.3K FFs and ~28K gates for a safety property. Using BMC, we showed there was no witness up to depth 113 (in ~3hr, 720MB). Again, we hypothesized the correctness of the property. We used PBIA to obtain an abstract model A1 with 163 FFs and ~2K gates in 4 iterations taking 9000s. Without the environmental constraints, the abstract model A2 has only 66 FFs and ~1K gates. We computed a reachability invariant [11] on the A2 model (in ~4s) and used this with UMC on the A1 model to obtain a proof in ~60s.

Industry Design III: The design has 756 FFs (excluding the memory registers), and ~15K gates. It has two memory modules, both having address width, AW = 10 and data width, DW = 8. Each module has 1 write and 1 read port, with the memory state initialized to 0. There are 216 reachability properties. Using BMC+EMM, we found witnesses for 206 of the 216 properties, taking ~400s and 50Mb. The maximum depth over all witnesses was 51. Using explicit modeling, we required 20540s (~6hrs) and 912Mb to find witnesses for all 206 properties. By using induction with BMC+EMM, we proved the remaining 10 properties in <1s (25 s for explicit modeling).

Quicksort: The implementation has two memory modules: an un-initialized array with AW=10, DW=32, 1 read and 1 write port and an un-initialized stack (for recursive function calls) with AW=10, DW=24, 1 read and 1 write port. The design has 167 FFs (excluding memory registers), and ~9K gates for array size 5. The property states that after return from a recursive call, the program counter should go to a recursive call on the right partition or return to the parent on the recursion stack. Using BMC+EMM+PBIA, we reduced the model to 91 FFs and ~3K gates, and also identified the array module as irrelevant for this property. On this reduced model we proved correctness using forward induction (proof diameter = 59) in 2.3Ks, 116MB. (Without the abstraction, the induction proof in BMC+EMM takes ~5Ks, 400MB. For explicit model, however, we could obtain neither a proof nor an abstract model in 3 hours).

References

[1] E. M. Clarke, O. Grumberg, and D. Peled, *Model Checking*: MIT Press, 1999.
[2] K. L. McMillan, Symbolic Model Checking: An Approach to the State Explosion Problem: Kluwer Academic Publishers, 1993.
[3] R. E. Bryant, "Graph-based algorithms for Boolean function manipulation," *IEEE Transactions on Computers*, vol. C-35(8), pp. 677-691, 1986.
[4] A. Biere, A. Cimatti, E. M. Clarke, M. Fujita, and Y. Zhu, "Symbolic model checking using SAT procedures instead of BDDs," in *Proceedings of DAC*, 1999.
[5] M. Sheeran, S. Singh, and G. Stalmarck, "Checking Safety Properties using Induction and a SAT Solver," in *Proceedings of FMCAD*, 2000.
[6] M. Ganai and A. Aziz, "Improved SAT-based Bounded Reachability Analysis," in *Proceedings of VLSI Design Conference*, 2002.

[7] M. Ganai, L. Zhang, A. Gupta, P. Ashar, and Z. Yang, "Efficient Approaches for Bounded Model Checking," *US Patent Application 2003-0225552*, Filed on May 30, 2002.

[8] K. McMillan, "Applying SAT methods in Unbounded Symbolic Model Checking," in *Computer-Aided Verification*, 2002.

[9] K. McMillan and N. Amla, "Automatic Abstraction without Counterexamples," in *Proceedings of TACAS*, 2003.

[10] K. McMillan, "Interpolation and SAT-based Model Checking," in *Proceedings of CAV*, 2003.

[11] A. Gupta, M. Ganai, C. Wang, Z. Yang, and P. Ashar, "Abstraction and Bdds Complement SAT-Based BMC in DiVer," in *Proceedings of CAV*, 2003.

[12] M. Ganai, A. Gupta, and P. Ashar, "Distributed SAT and Distributed Bounded Model Checking," in *Proceedings of CHARME*, 2003.

[13] A. Gupta, M. Ganai, P. Ashar, and Z. Yang, "Iterative Abstraction using SAT-based BMC with Proof Analysis," in *Proceedings of ICCAD*, 2003.

[14] M. Ganai, A. Gupta, and P. Ashar, "Efficient Modeling of Embedded Memories in Bounded Model Checking," in *Proceedings of CAV*, 2004.

[15] M. Ganai, A. Gupta, and P. Ashar, "Efficient SAT-based Unbounded Model Checking Using Circuit Cofactoring," in *Proceedings of ICCAD*, 2004.

[16] A. Gupta, M. Ganai, and P. Ashar, "Lazy Constraints and SAT Heuristics for Proof-based Abstraction," in *Proceedings of VLSI Design*, 2005.

[17] M. Ganai, A. Gupta, and P. Ashar, "Verification of Embedded Memory Systems using Efficient Memory Modeling," in *Proceedings of DATE, 2005*.

[18] A. Kuehlmann, M. Ganai, and V. Paruthi, "Circuit-based Boolean Reasoning," in *Proceedings of DAC*, 2001.

[19] M. Moskewicz, C. Madigan, Y. Zhao, L. Zhang, and S. Malik, "Chaff: Engineering an Efficient SAT Solver," in *Proceedings of DAC*, 2001.

[20] M. Ganai, L. Zhang, P. Ashar, and A. Gupta, "Combining Strengths of Circuit-based and CNF-based Algorithms for a High Performance SAT Solver," in *Proceedings of DAC*, 2002.

[21] M. Ganai and A. Kuehlmann, "On-the-fly Compression of Logical Circuits," in *Proceedings of IWLS*, 2000.

Appendix

DiVer is the core of the verification system as shown in the Figure 2. The tool has the ability to handle several industry design features including multiple clocks, phase, and gated clocks with arbitrary frequency ratios, embedded memories with multiple read and write ports, environmental and fairness constraints. Current input spec is LTL, but support for other specification like PSL is on the way. *DiVer* is used extensively by the designers within the company who are not verification experts. We have often received feedbacks that tool has been able to discover hard to detect bugs that simulations could not have found, or could have found at very high cost in terms of resources. As of now, the tool is not available for free download.

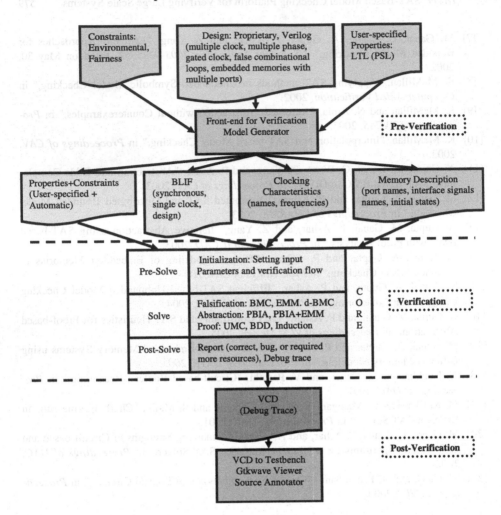

Fig. 2. Overview of Verification System

BISIMULATOR: A Modular Tool for On-the-Fly Equivalence Checking

Damien Bergamini, Nicolas Descoubes,
Christophe Joubert, and Radu Mateescu

INRIA Rhône-Alpes/VASY, 655, av. de l'Europe, 38330 Montbonnot St Martin, France
{Damien.Bergamini, Nicolas.Descoubes,
Christophe.Joubert, Radu.Mateescu}@inria.fr

1   Introduction

The equivalence checking problem consists in verifying that a system (e.g., a *protocol*) matches its abstract specification (e.g., a *service*) by comparing their Labeled Transition Systems (LTSs) modulo a given equivalence relation. Two approaches are traditionally used to perform equivalence checking: *global* verification requires to construct the two LTSs before comparison, whereas *local* (or *on-the-fly*) verification allows to explore them incrementally during comparison. The latter approach is able to detect errors even in prohibitively large systems, and therefore reveals more effective in combating state explosion.

Existing on-the-fly equivalence checking algorithms (see [2] for a survey) explore the synchronous product of the two LTSs in a forward manner, until either a wrong execution pattern (counterexample) is encountered, or the product is entirely explored (the LTSs are equivalent). Despite their usefulness, only a few implementations of these algorithms are available, most of them being targeted to specific input languages and/or equivalence relations. This is the case for ALDÉBARAN [4], whose efficient on-the-fly algorithms [3] only handle networks of communicating automata, being difficult to adapt to other description languages, such as process algebras. In this context, a more generic technology is desirable in order to reduce the development effort, handle new equivalence relations easily, and achieve a maximal reuse of existing algorithms.

In this paper, we present BISIMULATOR, an efficient on-the-fly equivalence checker with a highly modular architecture, developed within the CADP verification toolbox [6]. The front-end of the tool encodes five widely-used equivalence relations in terms of Boolean Equation Systems (BESs) by using the OPEN/CÆSAR [5] and BCG environments of CADP, which provide powerful LTS exploration primitives. This makes BISIMULATOR language-independent, the tool being directly available for any description language equipped with a compiler able to produce LTSs compliant with the OPEN/CÆSAR interface. The back-end of the tool carries out the verification by means of the generic CÆSAR_SOLVE [9] library of CADP, dedicated to (both sequential and distributed) on-the-fly BES resolution and diagnostic generation. This architecture clearly separates the implementation of equivalence relations and the verification engine, which can therefore be extended and optimized independently.

N. Halbwachs and L. Zuck (Eds.): TACAS 2005, LNCS 3440, pp. 581–585, 2005.
© Springer-Verlag Berlin Heidelberg 2005

2   Tool Architecture

BISIMULATOR (see below) takes as inputs two LTSs $\langle Q_i, A_i, T_i, q_{0i} \rangle$ ($i \in \{1, 2\}$), where Q_i are the sets of states, A_i the sets of actions, $T_i \subseteq Q_i \times A_i \times Q_i$ the transition relations, and $q_{0i} \in Q_i$ the initial states. The first LTS is represented implicitly (by its successor function) as an OPEN/CÆSAR program obtained by translating a system description, and the second one is represented explicitly (by its list of transitions) as a BCG file[1]. BISIMULATOR (12,000 lines of C code) consists of several modules, each one containing the BES translation and the diagnostic generation for a particular equivalence relation (strong, branching, observational, $\tau^*.a$, safety). BESs are derived directly from the definitions of equivalence relations; for instance, strong equivalence is translated into the greatest fixed point BES $\{X_{p,q} \stackrel{\nu}{=} \bigwedge_{p \stackrel{a}{\to} p'} \bigvee_{q \stackrel{a}{\to} q'} X_{p',q'} \wedge \bigwedge_{q \stackrel{a}{\to} q'} \bigvee_{p \stackrel{a}{\to} p'} X_{p',q'}\}$, where each variable $X_{p,q}$ is true iff the states $p \in Q_1$ and $q \in Q_2$ are strongly equivalent.

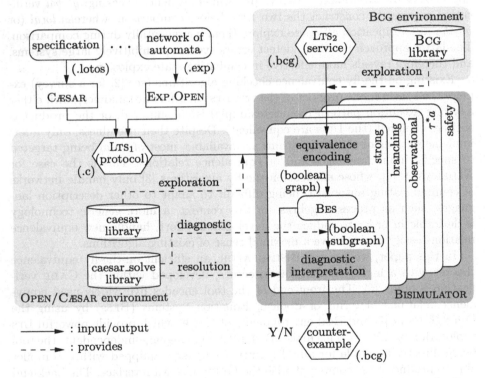

BESs are handled internally by the CÆSAR_SOLVE library as *boolean graphs* [1], which give an intuitive view of the dependencies between variables and facilitate the development of resolution algorithms. Boolean graphs are represented implicitly by their successor function, in the same way as LTSs

---

[1] This asymmetry, due to the current architecture of OPEN/CÆSAR, which does not allow to explore several LTSs on-the-fly, is likely to disappear in a future version.

in OPEN/CÆSAR. The library offers several on-the-fly resolution algorithms, based on different search strategies of boolean graphs: breadth-first, which produces small-depth diagnostics, and depth-first, with memory-efficient variants for acyclic or disjunctive/conjunctive boolean graphs (these kinds of graphs are obtained, e.g., by encoding comparison modulo strong equivalence when one LTS is acyclic or deterministic, respectively) [9]. Diagnostics are provided by the library as boolean subgraphs, which are subsequently converted by BISIMULATOR into counterexamples (directed acyclic graphs containing transition sequences that can be executed simultaneously in the two LTSs and lead to non equivalent states) represented as BCG files.

Recently, CÆSAR_SOLVE has been extended with a distributed on-the-fly resolution algorithm [8] running on several machines connected by a network. This allowed to immediately obtain a distributed version of BISIMULATOR, which scales up smoothly to larger systems.

3   Performance Measures

We give below some experimental data obtained using various LTSs taken from the CADP demo examples and from the VLTS benchmark suite [10].

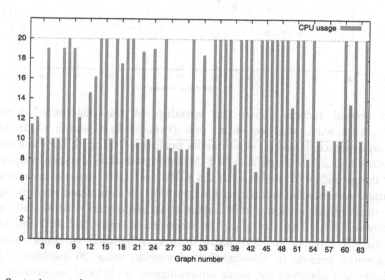

The first picture shows a comparison between BISIMULATOR and ALDÉBARAN (on-the-fly algorithms) for strong equivalence, based on experiments performed using 64 LTSs ranging from 3 Kstates and 6 Ktransitions to 3.8 Mstates and 11 Mtransitions, on a PC with 2.2 GHz and 1 Gbyte of memory. Each experiment consisted in checking that an LTS is equivalent with its minimized version modulo strong equivalence, which is a worst-case situation for on-the-fly algorithms, since both LTSs must be explored entirely. Each vertical line on the picture denotes a mark (between 0 and 20) comparing the speed of the tools on a given experiment. The mark is computed as follows: 20 if BISIMULATOR succeeds and ALDÉBARAN fails; 19 if BISIMULATOR is more than 5 times faster; 10..19 if BISIMULATOR is from 1 to 5 times faster; 10 if both tools are equally fast or they fail; 0..10 in a strictly symmetric way when BISIMULATOR is slower or fails. On 31 experiments out of 64, ALDÉBARAN fails because of memory shortage or too long computation, whereas BISIMULATOR only fails (together with ALDÉBARAN) on 4 experiments. On the remaining 33 experiments, the average time/memory are 11.8 sec./32.5 Mbytes for BISIMULATOR, and 20.5 sec./99 Mbytes for ALDÉBARAN.

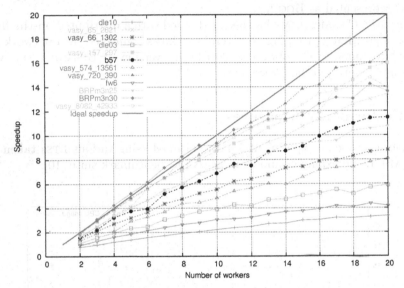

The second picture shows the speedup of the distributed version of BISIMULATOR w.r.t. the sequential one (breadth-first search algorithm) for strong equivalence, based on experiments performed using 12 LTSs ranging from 65 Kstates and 2.6 Mtransitions to 8 Mstates and 42.9 Mtransitions, on a PC cluster composed of 20 nodes with 2.4 GHz and 1.5 Gbytes of memory. Each experiment consisted in comparing an LTS with its minimized version. Speedup ranges uniformly from low – still better than sequential – to almost optimal, and increases with LTS size (e.g., the experiment vasy_157_297, involving an LTS with 157 Kstates and 297 Ktransitions, is handled 16 times faster than the sequential version by the distributed version using 20 machines). Similar behaviours are observed for weak equivalences; additional experimental data showing low memory overhead and good scalability of distributed BISIMULATOR is available in [8].

4   Conclusion and Future Work

The development of an on-the-fly equivalence checker "from scratch" is a complex and costly task. The modular architecture adopted for BISIMULATOR aims at making this process easier, by using the well-established verification framework of BESs, together with the generic libraries for LTS exploration and BES resolution provided by CADP. This tool architecture reduces the effort of implementing a new equivalence relation to its strict minimum: encoding the mathematical definition of the equivalence as a BES, and interpreting the counterexamples. Another advantage of our approach over previous dedicated on-the-fly equivalence checking algorithms [3] is that particular cases suitable for optimization can be handled more elegantly and precisely using the BES representation. For instance, in BISIMULATOR the encodings of equivalence relations exploit the determinism w.r.t. a given action and the absence of τ-transitions locally (i.e., on each state encountered during verification) to reduce the size of boolean equations, whereas in [3] the condition for applying the optimized algorithm handling the "deterministic case" is global (i.e., it involves all states of one LTS).

We plan to continue our work by extending BISIMULATOR with other equivalence relations (e.g., trace equivalence and its weak variant, Markovian bisimulation [7], etc.) and by studying new strategies for (sequential and distributed) on-the-fly BES resolution.

References

1. H. R. Andersen. Model Checking and Boolean Graphs. *Theoretical Computer Science*, 126(1):3–30, April 1994.
2. R. Cleaveland and O. Sokolsky. *Equivalence and Preorder Checking for Finite-State Systems*. In J. A. Bergstra, A. Ponse, and S. A. Smolka (eds.), *Handbook of Process Algebra*, chapter 6, pages 391–424. North-Holland, 2001.
3. J-C. Fernandez and L. Mounier. Verifying Bisimulations "On the Fly". In J. Quemada, J. Manas, and E. Vázquez (eds.), *Proc. of FORTE'90 (Madrid, Spain)*. North-Holland, November 1990.
4. J-C. Fernandez and L. Mounier. A Tool Set for Deciding Behavioral Equivalences. In *Proc. of CONCUR'91 (Amsterdam, The Netherlands)*, August 1991.
5. H. Garavel. OPEN/CÆSAR: An Open Software Architecture for Verification, Simulation, and Testing. In B. Steffen (ed.), *Proc. of TACAS'98 (Lisbon, Portugal)*, LNCS vol. 1384, pp. 68–84. Springer Verlag, March 1998. Full version available as INRIA Research Report RR-3352.
6. H. Garavel, F. Lang, and R. Mateescu. An Overview of CADP 2001. *EASST Newsletter* 4:13–24, August 2002. Also available as INRIA Report RT-0254.
7. H. Hermanns and M. Siegle. Bisimulation Algorithms for Stochastic Process Algebras and their BDD-based Implementation. In J-P. Katoen (ed.), *Proc. of ARTS'99 (Bamberg, Germany)*, LNCS vol. 1601, pp. 244–265. Springer Verlag, May 1999.
8. C. Joubert and R. Mateescu. Distributed On-the-Fly Equivalence Checking. In L. Brim and M. Leucker (eds.), *Proc. of PDMC'04 (London, United Kingdom)*, ENTCS, September 2004. To appear.
9. R. Mateescu. A Generic On-the-Fly Solver for Alternation-Free Boolean Equation Systems. In H. Garavel and J. Hatcliff (eds.), *Proc. of TACAS'2003 (Warsaw, Poland)*, LNCS vol. 2619, pp. 81–96. Springer Verlag, April 2003. Full version available as INRIA Research Report RR-4711.
10. http://www.inrialpes.fr/vasy/cadp/resources/benchmark_bcg.html

Author Index

Lecture Notes in Computer Science

For information about Vols. 1–3335

please contact your bookseller or Springer

Vol. 3452: F. Baader, A. Voronkov (Eds.), Logic for Programming, Artificial Intelligence, and Reasoning. XI, 562 pages. 2005. (Subseries LNAI).

Vol. 3448: G.R. Raidl, J. Gottlieb (Eds.), Evolutionary Computation in Combinatorial Optimization. XI, 271 pages. 2005.

Vol. 3441: V. Sassone (Ed.), Foundations of Software Science and Computational Structures. XVIII, 521 pages. 2005.

Vol. 3440: N. Halbwachs, L.D. Zuck (Eds.), Tools and Algorithms for the Construction and Analysis of Systems. XVII, 588 pages. 2005.

Vol. 3436: B. Bouyssounouse, J. Sifakis (Eds.), Embedded Systems Design. XV, 492 pages. 2005.

Vol. 3433: S. Bhalla (Ed.), Databases in Networked Information Systems. VII, 319 pages. 2005.

Vol. 3432: M. Beigl, P. Lukowicz (Eds.), Systems Aspects in Organic and Pervasive Computing - ARCS 2005. X, 265 pages. 2005.

Vol. 3427: G. Kotsis, O. Spaniol, Wireless Systems and Mobility in Next Generation Internet. VIII, 249 pages. 2005.

Vol. 3423: J.L. Fiadeiro, P.D. Mosses, F. Orejas (Eds.), Recent Trends in Algebraic Development Techniques. VIII, 271 pages. 2005.

Vol. 3422: R.T. Mittermeir (Ed.), From Computer Literacy to Informatics Fundamentals. X, 203 pages. 2005.

Vol. 3419: B. Faltings, A. Petcu, F. Fages, F. Rossi (Eds.), Constraint Satisfaction and Constraint Logic Programming. X, 217 pages. 2005. (Subseries LNAI).

Vol. 3418: U. Brandes, T. Erlebach (Eds.), Network Analysis. XII, 471 pages. 2005.

Vol. 3416: M. Böhlen, J. Gamper, W. Polasek, M.A. Wimmer (Eds.), E-Government: Towards Electronic Democracy. XIII, 311 pages. 2005. (Subseries LNAI).

Vol. 3415: P. Davidsson, B. Logan, K. Takadama (Eds.), Multi-Agent and Multi-Agent-Based Simulation. X, 265 pages. 2005. (Subseries LNAI).

Vol. 3414: M. Morari, L. Thiele (Eds.), Hybrid Systems: Computation and Control. XII, 684 pages. 2005.

Vol. 3412: X. Franch, D. Port (Eds.), COTS-Based Software Systems. XVI, 312 pages. 2005.

Vol. 3411: S.H. Myaeng, M. Zhou, K.-F. Wong, H.-J. Zhang (Eds.), Information Retrieval Technology. XIII, 337 pages. 2005.

Vol. 3410: C.A. Coello Coello, A. Hernández Aguirre, E. Zitzler (Eds.), Evolutionary Multi-Criterion Optimization. XVI, 912 pages. 2005.

Vol. 3409: N. Guelfi, G. Reggio, A. Romanovsky (Eds.), Scientific Engineering of Distributed Java Applications. X, 127 pages. 2005.

Vol. 3408: D.E. Losada, J.M. Fernández-Luna (Eds.), Advances in Information Retrieval. XVII, 572 pages. 2005.

Vol. 3407: Z. Liu, K. Araki (Eds.), Theoretical Aspects of Computing - ICTAC 2004. XIV, 562 pages. 2005.

Vol. 3406: A. Gelbukh (Ed.), Computational Linguistics and Intelligent Text Processing. XVII, 829 pages. 2005.

Vol. 3404: V. Diekert, B. Durand (Eds.), STACS 2005. XVI, 706 pages. 2005.

Vol. 3403: B. Ganter, R. Godin (Eds.), Formal Concept Analysis. XI, 419 pages. 2005. (Subseries LNAI).

Vol. 3401: Z. Li, L.G. Vulkov, J. Waśniewski (Eds.), Numerical Analysis and Its Applications. XIII, 630 pages. 2005.

Vol. 3398: D.-K. Baik (Ed.), Systems Modeling and Simulation: Theory and Applications. XIV, 733 pages. 2005. (Subseries LNAI).

Vol. 3397: T.G. Kim (Ed.), Artificial Intelligence and Simulation. XV, 711 pages. 2005. (Subseries LNAI).

Vol. 3396: R.M. van Eijk, M.-P. Huget, F. Dignum (Eds.), Agent Communication. X, 261 pages. 2005. (Subseries LNAI).

Vol. 3395: J. Grabowski, B. Nielsen (Eds.), Formal Approaches to Software Testing. X, 225 pages. 2005.

Vol. 3394: D. Kudenko, D. Kazakov, E. Alonso (Eds.), Adaptive Agents and Multi-Agent Systems III. VIII, 313 pages. 2005. (Subseries LNAI).

Vol. 3393: H.-J. Kreowski, U. Montanari, F. Orejas, G. Rozenberg, G. Taentzer (Eds.), Formal Methods in Software and Systems Modeling. XXVII, 413 pages. 2005.

Vol. 3391: C. Kim (Ed.), Information Networking. XVII, 936 pages. 2005.

Vol. 3390: R. Choren, A. Garcia, C. Lucena, A. Romanovsky (Eds.), Software Engineering for Multi-Agent Systems III. XII, 291 pages. 2005.

Vol. 3389: P. Van Roy (Ed.), Multiparadigm Programming in Mozart/OZ. XV, 329 pages. 2005.

Vol. 3388: J. Lagergren (Ed.), Comparative Genomics. VII, 133 pages. 2005. (Subseries LNBI).

Vol. 3387: J. Cardoso, A. Sheth (Eds.), Semantic Web Services and Web Process Composition. VIII, 147 pages. 2005.

Vol. 3386: S. Vaudenay (Ed.), Public Key Cryptography - PKC 2005. IX, 436 pages. 2005.

Vol. 3385: R. Cousot (Ed.), Verification, Model Checking, and Abstract Interpretation. XII, 483 pages. 2005.

Vol. 3383: J. Pach (Ed.), Graph Drawing. XII, 536 pages. 2005.

Vol. 3382: J. Odell, P. Giorgini, J.P. Müller (Eds.), Agent-Oriented Software Engineering V. X, 239 pages. 2005.

Vol. 3381: P. Vojtáš, M. Bieliková, B. Charron-Bost, O. Sýkora (Eds.), SOFSEM 2005: Theory and Practice of Computer Science. XV, 448 pages. 2005.

Vol. 3379: M. Hemmje, C. Niederee, T. Risse (Eds.), From Integrated Publication and Information Systems to Information and Knowledge Environments. XXIV, 321 pages. 2005.

Vol. 3378: J. Kilian (Ed.), Theory of Cryptography. XII, 621 pages. 2005.

Vol. 3377: B. Goethals, A. Siebes (Eds.), Knowledge Discovery in Inductive Databases. VII, 190 pages. 2005.

Vol. 3376: A. Menezes (Ed.), Topics in Cryptology – CT-RSA 2005. X, 385 pages. 2005.

Vol. 3375: M.A. Marsan, G. Bianchi, M. Listanti, M. Meo (Eds.), Quality of Service in Multiservice IP Networks. XIII, 656 pages. 2005.

Vol. 3374: D. Weyns, H.V.D. Parunak, F. Michel (Eds.), Environments for Multi-Agent Systems. X, 279 pages. 2005. (Subseries LNAI).

Vol. 3372: C. Bussler, V. Tannen, I. Fundulaki (Eds.), Semantic Web and Databases. X, 227 pages. 2005.

Vol. 3371: M.W. Barley, N. Kasabov (Eds.), Intelligent Agents and Multi-Agent Systems. X, 329 pages. 2005. (Subseries LNAI).

Vol. 3370: A. Konagaya, K. Satou (Eds.), Grid Computing in Life Science. X, 188 pages. 2005. (Subseries LNBI).

Vol. 3369: V.R. Benjamins, P. Casanovas, J. Breuker, A. Gangemi (Eds.), Law and the Semantic Web. XII, 249 pages. 2005. (Subseries LNAI).

Vol. 3368: L. Paletta, J.K. Tsotsos, E. Rome, G.W. Humphreys (Eds.), Attention and Performance in Computational Vision. VIII, 231 pages. 2005.

Vol. 3367: W.S. Ng, B.C. Ooi, A. Ouksel, C. Sartori (Eds.), Databases, Information Systems, and Peer-to-Peer Computing. X, 231 pages. 2005.

Vol. 3366: I. Rahwan, P. Moraitis, C. Reed (Eds.), Argumentation in Multi-Agent Systems. XII, 263 pages. 2005. (Subseries LNAI).

Vol. 3365: G. Mauri, G. Păun, M.J. Pérez-Jiménez, G. Rozenberg, A. Salomaa (Eds.), Membrane Computing. IX, 415 pages. 2005.

Vol. 3363: T. Eiter, L. Libkin (Eds.), Database Theory - ICDT 2005. XI, 413 pages. 2004.

Vol. 3362: G. Barthe, L. Burdy, M. Huisman, J.-L. Lanet, T. Muntean (Eds.), Construction and Analysis of Safe, Secure, and Interoperable Smart Devices. IX, 257 pages. 2005.

Vol. 3361: S. Bengio, H. Bourlard (Eds.), Machine Learning for Multimodal Interaction. XII, 362 pages. 2005.

Vol. 3360: S. Spaccapietra, E. Bertino, S. Jajodia, R. King, D. McLeod, M.E. Orlowska, L. Strous (Eds.), Journal on Data Semantics II. XI, 223 pages. 2005.

Vol. 3359: G. Grieser, Y. Tanaka (Eds.), Intuitive Human Interfaces for Organizing and Accessing Intellectual Assets. XIV, 257 pages. 2005. (Subseries LNAI).

Vol. 3358: J. Cao, L.T. Yang, M. Guo, F. Lau (Eds.), Parallel and Distributed Processing and Applications. XXIV, 1058 pages. 2004.

Vol. 3357: H. Handschuh, M.A. Hasan (Eds.), Selected Areas in Cryptography. XI, 354 pages. 2004.

Vol. 3356: G. Das, V.P. Gulati (Eds.), Intelligent Information Technology. XII, 428 pages. 2004.

Vol. 3355: R. Murray-Smith, R. Shorten (Eds.), Switching and Learning in Feedback Systems. X, 343 pages. 2005.

Vol. 3354: M. Margenstern (Ed.), Machines, Computations, and Universality. VIII, 329 pages. 2005.

Vol. 3353: J. Hromkovič, M. Nagl, B. Westfechtel (Eds.), Graph-Theoretic Concepts in Computer Science. XI, 404 pages. 2004.

Vol. 3352: C. Blundo, S. Cimato (Eds.), Security in Communication Networks. XI, 381 pages. 2005.

Vol. 3351: G. Persiano, R. Solis-Oba (Eds.), Approximation and Online Algorithms. VIII, 295 pages. 2005.

Vol. 3350: M. Hermenegildo, D. Cabeza (Eds.), Practical Aspects of Declarative Languages. VIII, 269 pages. 2005.

Vol. 3349: B.M. Chapman (Ed.), Shared Memory Parallel Programming with Open MP. X, 149 pages. 2005.

Vol. 3348: A. Canteaut, K. Viswanathan (Eds.), Progress in Cryptology - INDOCRYPT 2004. XIV, 431 pages. 2004.

Vol. 3347: R.K. Ghosh, H. Mohanty (Eds.), Distributed Computing and Internet Technology. XX, 472 pages. 2004.

Vol. 3346: R.H. Bordini, M. Dastani, J. Dix, A.E.F. Seghrouchni (Eds.), Programming Multi-Agent Systems. XIV, 249 pages. 2005. (Subseries LNAI).

Vol. 3345: Y. Cai (Ed.), Ambient Intelligence for Scientific Discovery. XII, 311 pages. 2005. (Subseries LNAI).

Vol. 3344: J. Malenfant, B.M. Østvold (Eds.), Object-Oriented Technology. ECOOP 2004 Workshop Reader. VIII, 215 pages. 2005.

Vol. 3343: C. Freksa, M. Knauff, B. Krieg-Brückner, B. Nebel, T. Barkowsky (Eds.), Spatial Cognition IV. Reasoning, Action, and Interaction. XIII, 519 pages. 2005. (Subseries LNAI).

Vol. 3342: E. Şahin, W.M. Spears (Eds.), Swarm Robotics. IX, 175 pages. 2005.

Vol. 3341: R. Fleischer, G. Trippen (Eds.), Algorithms and Computation. XVII, 935 pages. 2004.

Vol. 3340: C.S. Calude, E. Calude, M.J. Dinneen (Eds.), Developments in Language Theory. XI, 431 pages. 2004.

Vol. 3339: G.I. Webb, X. Yu (Eds.), AI 2004: Advances in Artificial Intelligence. XXII, 1272 pages. 2004. (Subseries LNAI).

Vol. 3338: S.Z. Li, J. Lai, T. Tan, G. Feng, Y. Wang (Eds.), Advances in Biometric Person Authentication. XVIII, 699 pages. 2004.

Vol. 3337: J.M. Barreiro, F. Martin-Sanchez, V. Maojo, F. Sanz (Eds.), Biological and Medical Data Analysis. XI, 508 pages. 2004.

Vol. 3336: D. Karagiannis, U. Reimer (Eds.), Practical Aspects of Knowledge Management. X, 523 pages. 2004. (Subseries LNAI).